Alteryx Designer Cookbook

Over 60 recipes to transform your data into insights and take your productivity to a new level

Alberto Guisande

BIRMINGHAM—MUMBAI

Alteryx Designer Cookbook

Group Product Manager: Reshma Raman

Publishing Product Manager: Apeksha Shetty

Content Development Editor: Joseph Sunil

Technical Editor: Devanshi Ayare

Copy Editor: Safis Editing

Project Coordinator: Farheen Fathima

Proofreader: Safis Editing

Indexer: Manju Arasan

Production Designer: Alishon Mendonca

Marketing Coordinator: Vinishka Kalra

First published: October 2023

Production reference: 1231023

Published by Packt Publishing Ltd.

Grosvenor House

11 St Paul's Square

Birmingham

B3 1R.

ISBN 978-1-80461-508-9

www.packtpub.com

To Mariana, my beloved wife, Agustina and Martín, the best daughter and son you can aspire to have. Thank you for being the reason that I open my eyes every morning and for making me better every day.

To my parents, for setting the foundations for who I am now.

To my fellow Alteryx ACEs, a second family I found in life.

To Roberto, the best business partner (cum friend) you can find, thank you for being so patient with me over the years.

Contributors

About the author

Alberto Guisande has been an Alteryx ACE since 2015 and is currently a C.A.O. at Decision Science, a company dedicated to providing data science consulting services to its clients. He has held top management positions in banking and consulting companies and General Management in logistics and Supply Chain.

With over 15 years of experience in the field of data science, he has helped numerous companies define and adopt an analytical culture, based on the exploitation of their data. He has created centers of excellence in numerous companies in America and serves as Chief Data Officer (CDO) in several of his clients.

He is certified in Alteryx Core, Alteryx Advanced, Alteryx Server, Tableau, and Vertica among others. In 2021, he was appointed as Veritone Ambassador by Veritone, an AI & ML leader company.

He is an international instructor in the Data Science for Business and Big Data for Business courses at the Instituto Tecnológico de Monterrey, having also collaborated in the creation of their pensums. He also continuously participates as a speaker at specialized data science conferences and exhibitions.

He serves as a mentor in the *Predictive Analytics for Business Nanodegree Program* at Udacity.com

Having Alteryx in my toolbox is the best thing that ever happened to me as a data professional – Alberto Guisande

I want to thank all the people who dedicated time to help with this book, especially the team from Packt (Apeksha, Kirti, and Joseph), and my family for being so patient while I worked on it.

About the reviewers

Thales Donizeti Silva, an engineer with advanced degrees in Business Analytics and AI, has over 8 years of experience in Business Intelligence. Based in Sao Paulo, Brazil, he's a Senior Analytics Engineering Consultant at phData and has led multiple Alteryx projects in the United States over the last 4 years. Thales is an Alteryx ACE and holds the Alteryx Designer Expert certification. Beyond his professional roles, Thales leads the Brazilian Alteryx User Group, owns the website "Alteryx Para Todos", runs the YouTube channel "Alteryx Simplifica", and mentors in the "Adote um Júnior" volunteer project. He's a Top Community Contributor with over 500 solutions in the Alteryx Community and has presented in 2 Alteryx Conferences.

Jean-Baptiste has been an Alteryx fan since he first tried it, loving the logic of the tool and working the same way the tool does. Since then, he has skilled up completing weekly challenges, writing blogs, passing certifications, and so on. He then became an Alteryx ACE in 2022, won the European Alteryx Grand Prix in Amsterdam, and passed the Expert Certification all in the same year. He always tries to give back to the community by helping others and building challenges for others to solve.

Marcus Montenegro is a certified expert in Alteryx, Matillion, and KNIME with years of experience in analytics engineering projects. He co-founded the first Matillion user group, is one of the Alteryx user group leaders in Brazil, and is one of the few Alteryx ACEs around the world. At phData, Marcus leads a team of consultants, assisting them in growing, delivering services, and pursuing business and professional objectives.

Due to his passion for teaching and assisting others, Marcus created his own YouTube channel to teach Alteryx to the Brazilian community for free.

Marcus has worked with clients to integrate multiple systems into Alteryx implementations and has taught new specialists for every company he has worked for.

Table of Contents

2

Working with Databases

3

Preparing Data

4

Transforming Data   121

5

Data Parsing   163

6

Grouping Data   185

7

Blending and Merging Datasets   221

8

Aggregating Data   269

9

Dynamic Operations   291

10

Macros and Apps   327

11

Downloads, APIs, and Web Services   439

14

Outputting Data — 623

Preface

Alteryx allows you to create repetitive data manipulation and analytic workflows with a simple, easy-to-use, code-free/code-friendly UI and performs very fast executing those workflows, offering multiple ways to achieve the same results.

This book is the result of compiling Alteryx users' frequent day-to-day use cases/situations they deal with and a comprehensive guide for leveraging your skills in Alteryx and finding the best way to perform these operations.

Through the chapters, this book's recipes will take you through an analyst's complete journey, covering all aspects of the data life cycle, from reading it, no matter what source you do it from, to obtaining reports/reports, and passing through the adjustment operations necessary for analysis. You'll learn how to read numerous and disparate files and databases and handle huge amounts of data. You'll then perform operations and transformations to your data to suit your needs. Also, you'll learn how to group data in different ways and criteria and blend different types of data sources. You'll understand how to pivot and un-pivot your data for easy manipulation and perform aggregations and calculations on your data. You will also learn how to encapsulate reusable logic into components (Macros), connect and download data from APIs and save your data or create reports in various formats.

By the end of this book, you will notice how your use of Alteryx Designer has improved and how you have discovered how to best perform tasks within it.

Who this book is for

This book is intended for any professional data user (from business intelligence professionals, data analysts, Citizen Data Scientists to Data Scientists) with a basic knowledge of Alteryx Designer, who wants to leverage its usage.

In summary, anyone who wants to:

- *Learn how to tackle analytics operations like a master*
- *Improve their data manipulation skills*
- *Save a lot of time and effort to get your data-driven insights*
- *Use best practices to get better with Alteryx Designer*

What this book covers

Chapter 1, Inputting Data from Files, will show you how Alteryx Designer makes connecting to any type of file very easy. Every format has its own requirements and oddities. You will get to know the best way to unleash the whole reading and writing capabilities of the Designer.

We'll show you recipes to handle and improve the way you connect and consume different file formats.

Chapter 2, Working with Databases, will explore some recipes to improve reading and writing from databases. As it does with files, Alteryx Designer allows you to connect with a vast amount of databases.

Chapter 3, Preparing Data, will guide you to help shape messy data into a workable dataset.

Chapter 4, Transforming Data, will explore various data transformations such as extracting/parsing fields, breaking one column into many, transposing, or converting data types, which are very common and widely needed operations when you work with data.

Chapter 5, Parsing Data, will show you how to extract or interpret what's inside a field value or making an unreadable field readable.

Chapter 6, Grouping Data, will show you how classifying your data into groups is very important when you work in real life use cases.

Chapter 7, Blending and Merging Datasets, will teach you how to convert the data into information and enrich it with various techniques like relating, joining, or unioning datasets.

Chapter 8, Aggregating Data, will showcase recipes to summarize and sort data. You will also get your first brush with visualizations.

Chapter 9, Dynamic Operations, will allow you to take advantage of the dynamic toolset that Alteryx Designer offers. These will allow you to handle the data dynamically.

Chapter 10, Macros and Apps, will show how to reuse repetitive pieces of logic, build applications with user input, to make Alteryx workflows even more dynamic and simpler to maintain.

Chapter 11, Downloads, APIs, and Web Services, will explore how to make use of the cloud and web services to get data from various sources.

Chapter 12, Developer Tools, showcases varioous external tools to solve some challenges that data presents. Alteryx offers a lot of options to incorporate source code, use existing programs, or execute external scripts to accomplish these tasks.

Chapter 13, Reporting with Alteryx, will show you how to properly communicate your data. These recipes will guide you in converting your information into business insights.

Chapter 14, Outputting Data, is our last step in this journey. Saving the resulting data from our workflows for later use is crucial to every analyst in every Company. These recipes will guide you into effective saving of your resulting data.

To get the most out of this book

You'll need to install Alteryx Designer on your computer (at the time of writing this book, the latest version was 22.4, and 23.1 was in beta).

For some recipes, access to a database engine will be necessary.

Software/Hardware covered in the book	OS Requirements
Alteryx Designer	Windows, Mac OS X (can be used with the help of Parallels or similar mechanisms to run Windows applications within Mac OS)

If you don't have an Alteryx License, you can get a free trial from here: `https://bit.ly/ayx_trial_Cookbook`

Or by scanning the following QR Code:

The test sets available for download contain the whole finished workflow/s. I strongly recommend using them to compare with the ones you create in the book.

Download the example code files

You can download the example code files for this book from GitHub at `https://github.com/PacktPublishing/Alteryx-Designer-Cookbook`. In case there's an update to the code, it will be updated on the existing GitHub repository.

We also have other code bundles from our rich catalog of books and videos available at `https://github.com/PacktPublishing/`. Check them out!

Conventions used

There are a number of text conventions used throughout this book.

`Code in text`: Indicates code words in text, database table names, folder names, filenames, file extensions, pathnames, dummy URLs, user input, and Twitter handles. Here is an example: " Drop an Input Data tool onto the canvas and point it to `..\DATA\Customers_by_City\ARVADA.csv`."

A block of code is set as follows:

```
IF CONTAINS([Name],[TY])
THEN "TY"
ELSEIF CONTAINS([Name],ToString(ToNumber([TY])-1))
THEN "LY"
ELSE ""
ENDIF
```

When we wish to draw your attention to a particular part of a code block, the relevant lines or items are set in bold:

```
!IsEmpty([Description])
```

Bold: Indicates a new term, an important word, or words that you see onscreen. For example, words in menus or dialog boxes appear in the text like this. Here is an example: "Add another **Dynamic Select** tool following the **Dynamic Rename** tool."

> **Tips or important notes**
> Appear like this.

Sections

In this book, you will find several headings that appear frequently (*Getting ready, How to do it..., How it works..., There's more...,* and *See also*).

To give clear instructions on how to complete a recipe, use these sections as follows:

Getting ready

This section tells you what to expect in the recipe and describes how to set up any software or any preliminary settings required for the recipe.

How to do it...

This section contains the steps required to follow the recipe.

How it works...

This section usually consists of a detailed explanation of what happened in the previous section.

There's more...

This section consists of additional information about the recipe in order to make you more knowledgeable about the recipe.

See also

This section provides helpful links to other useful information for the recipe.

Get in touch

Feedback from our readers is always welcome.

General feedback: If you have questions about any aspect of this book, mention the book title in the subject of your message and email us at customercare@packtpub.com.

Errata: Although we have taken every care to ensure the accuracy of our content, mistakes do happen. If you have found a mistake in this book, we would be grateful if you would report this to us. Please visit www.packtpub.com/support/errata, selecting your book, clicking on the Errata Submission Form link, and entering the details.

Piracy: If you come across any illegal copies of our works in any form on the Internet, we would be grateful if you would provide us with the location address or website name. Please contact us at copyright@packt.com with a link to the material.

If you are interested in becoming an author: If there is a topic that you have expertise in and you are interested in either writing or contributing to a book, please visit authors.packtpub.com.

Reviews

Please leave a review. Once you have read and used this book, why not leave a review on the site that you purchased it from? Potential readers can then see and use your unbiased opinion to make purchase decisions, we at Packt can understand what you think about our products, and our authors can see your feedback on their book. Thank you!

For more information about Packt, please visit packtpub.com.

Share Your Thoughts

Once you've read *Alteryx Designer Cookbook*, we'd love to hear your thoughts! Scan the QR code below to go straight to the Amazon review page for this book and share your feedback.

https://packt.link/r/1-804-61508-0

Your review is important to us and the tech community and will help us make sure we're delivering excellent quality content.

Download a free PDF copy of this book

Thanks for purchasing this book!

Do you like to read on the go but are unable to carry your print books everywhere?

Is your eBook purchase not compatible with the device of your choice?

Don't worry, now with every Packt book you get a DRM-free PDF version of that book at no cost.

Read anywhere, any place, on any device. Search, copy, and paste code from your favorite technical books directly into your application.

The perks don't stop there, you can get exclusive access to discounts, newsletters, and great free content in your inbox daily

Follow these simple steps to get the benefits:

1. Scan the QR code or visit the link below

https://packt.link/free-ebook/9781804615089

2. Submit your proof of purchase

3. That's it! We'll send your free PDF and other benefits to your email directly

1

Inputting Data from Files

As data workers, no matter how mature and evolved your actual working environment is, you'll have to deal with a good number of files and different formats, even when they refer to the same kind of data.

Through the years, I've seen a lot of analysts struggling with the same problems, such as vendor files that are not consistent, structure changes through versions of the same file, and so on.

In this chapter, we'll start defining recipes for those common situations you'll encounter when reading files using Alteryx Designer.

We'll read multiple Excel files from a single directory, multiple worksheets from an Excel file, and multiple Excel files having different structures between worksheets. Specifically, we'll look at the following recipes:

- Reading a worksheet from multiple Excel files all at once

- Reading all worksheets from an Excel file all at once—same schema

- Different schema Excel worksheets all at once

- Saving and preserving Excel sheet formats

- Accessing and determining which files are to be processed from a file repository

- Handling formats when reading text files

Technical requirements

To begin practicing and reproducing these recipes by yourself, you need to have Alteryx Designer installed on your computer. If you have no access to it, you can download a 1-month trial here: `https://bit.ly/ayx_trial_Cookbook`.

To follow along with the recipes included in this chapter, you can download the `ch1` folder from GitHub here:

`https://github.com/PacktPublishing/Alteryx-Designer-Cookbook/tree/main/ch1`

> **Important note**
>
> If you decided to apply these recipes to your own data, please read carefully the *Getting ready* section of each one, to be sure that your data fits the use case.

Reading a worksheet from multiple Excel files all at once

This is one of the most common situations you'll find when working with files. Maybe it's sales data, purchase orders, or any type of data—at the end, you'll have a bunch of Excel files in a folder or subfolders and you'll need to read, consolidate, and analyze them.

This recipe will help you with the case where those files are in the same folder (including its subfolders) and the files have the same structure (columns).

Even though the recipe was crafted using Excel files (because they present an extra complication, including different worksheets within), it can be adjusted and will work with any file format you need to deal with.

Getting ready

If you want to try this recipe before applying it to your own data, we have a test set here: https://github.com/PacktPublishing/Alteryx-Designer-Cookbook/tree/main/ch1/Recipe1. You'll find a ZIP file with a directory structure and files within it. We provided one file per year of sales data from 2018 to 2022, called MonthlySales_XXXX.xlsx (XXXX meaning the year of sales contained within that specific file), monthly summarized (1 month of each year per row), stored in a worksheet called MonthlySales.

If you're planning to follow this recipe with your own data, make sure your files are within the same folder (and/or subfolders within a unique parent folder) and all the worksheets you want to input have the same name:

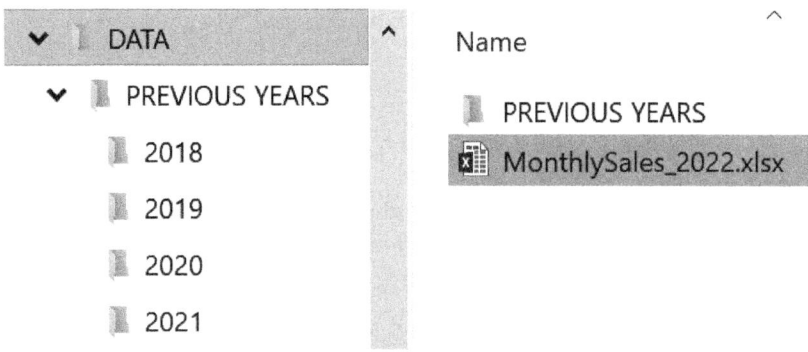

Figure 1.1: Folder hierarchy

The directory structure should look like this:

```
Data Root Folder
        Files within the root Folder
        Data Sub Folder 1
                Files within Sub Folder 1
        Data Sub Folder 2
                Files within Sub Folder 2
```

How to do it...

We'll get started with the following steps:

1. Drag an **Input Data** tool (from the **In/Out** category) and drop it onto the canvas.

2. Point your input to one of the files you want to read (preferably on the topmost folder) and select it:

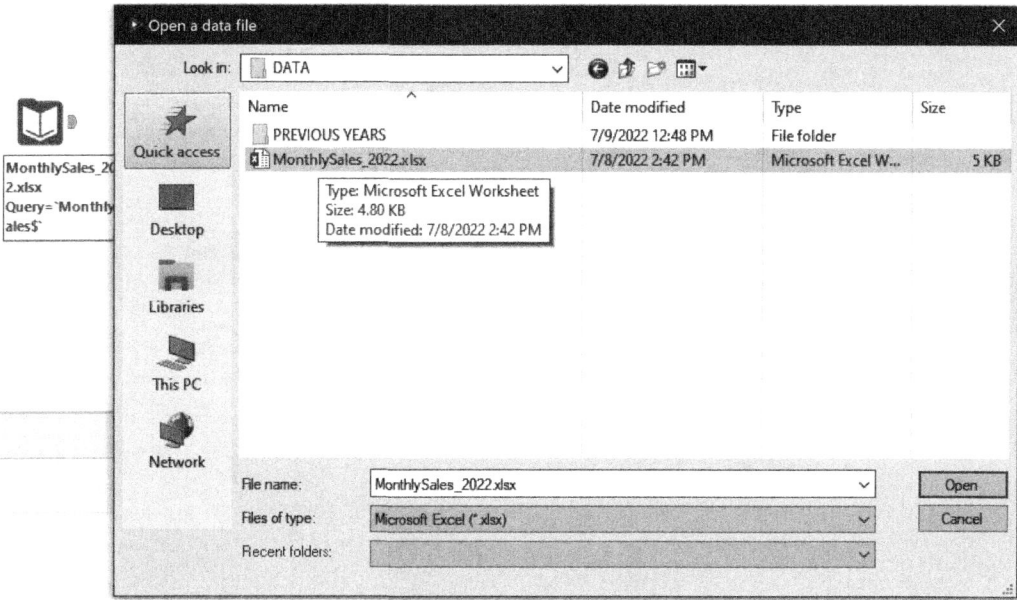

Figure 1.2: Selecting a file

Since we are selecting an Excel file, Alteryx Designer will ask you to select a worksheet within the selected file, so we do that (remember that for this recipe, all worksheets you need to read must have the same name and—of course— structure):

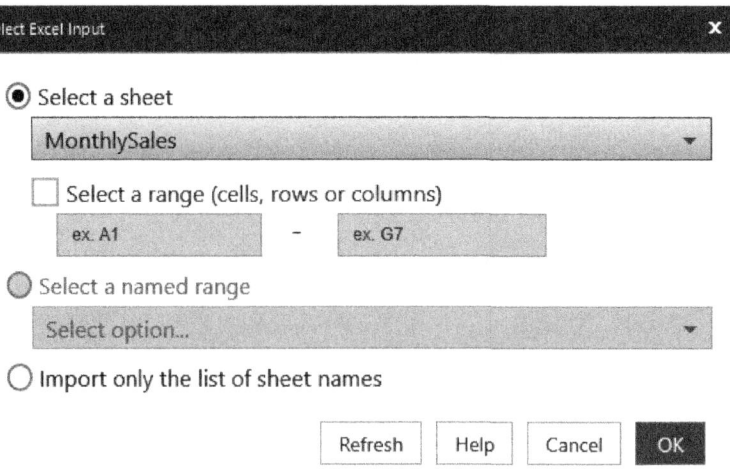

Figure 1.3: Selecting a worksheet

You'll get your **Input Data** tool configuration pointing to this file and with the default configurations:

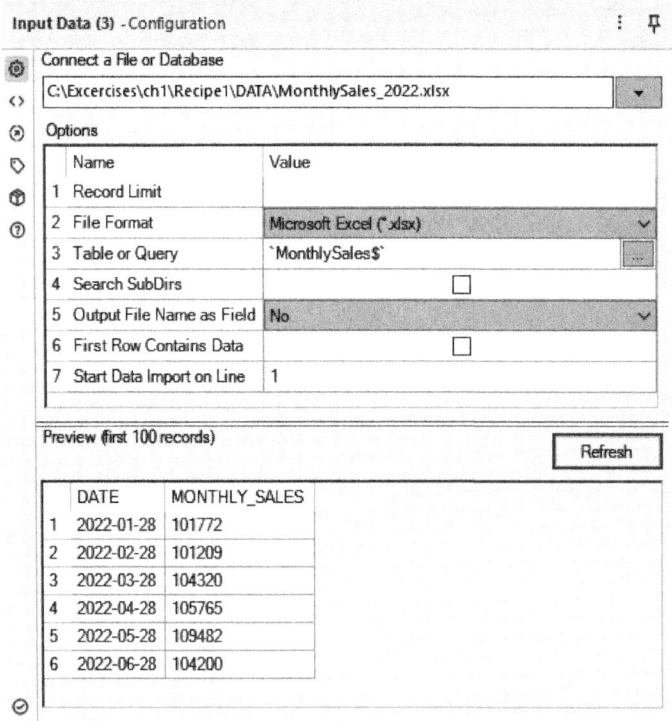

Figure 1.4: Input Data configurations

Now is when we start to exploit Alteryx Designer's configuration options to fulfill our needs.

3. Option *4* in the **Configuration** panel reads **Search SubDirs**. If we enable it, Alteryx will not only search for the file/s pointed to in the file selection, but also will be looking through all the subfolders beneath the actual folder:

Figure 1.5: Enabling SubDirs

So far, Alteryx will be looking for the `MonthlySales_2022.xlsx` file in the `\DATA` subfolder and *all* of its subfolders.

4. Replace the `2022` part of the filename with a `*` sign, like this:

Figure 1.6: Replacing part of the filename

And with that little change, you'll be telling Alteryx Designer to read the `MonthlySales` worksheet from *all* files within the `\DATA` folder and its subfolders that start with `MonthlySales_` and have *anything* in their names before the extension (`.xlsx`).

Give it a try, and you'll see that the contents of **Sales** for all years are now read by Alteryx.

How it works...

Alteryx Designer allows you to use wildcard characters (`*` and `?`) that give you the option of replacing a specific character or a sequence of them.

Use `*` when you need to replace any string, no matter its length.

Use `?` when you need to replace a character in the indicated position.

For instance, `MonthlySales_*.xlsx` will tell Alteryx Designer to read all files having `MonthlySales_` in the filename, followed by *any* character or characters (`MonthlySales_1234.xlsx`, `MonthlySales_1.xlsx`, and so on), and that end with a `.xlsx` extension.

When using `?`, it'll replace one character per `?` used, in the exact position where it is. For instance, `MonthlySales?2018.xlsx` will read `MonthlySales_2018.xlsx`, `MonthlySales-2018.xlsx`, `MonthlySalesX2018.xlsx`, and so on, but `MonthlySales%%2018.xlsx` won't (because there are two characters between `MonthlySales` and `2018`).

So, for example, this configuration will allow you to read all CSV files contained in `C:\DATASETS\DATA\` that start with `CityBike`:

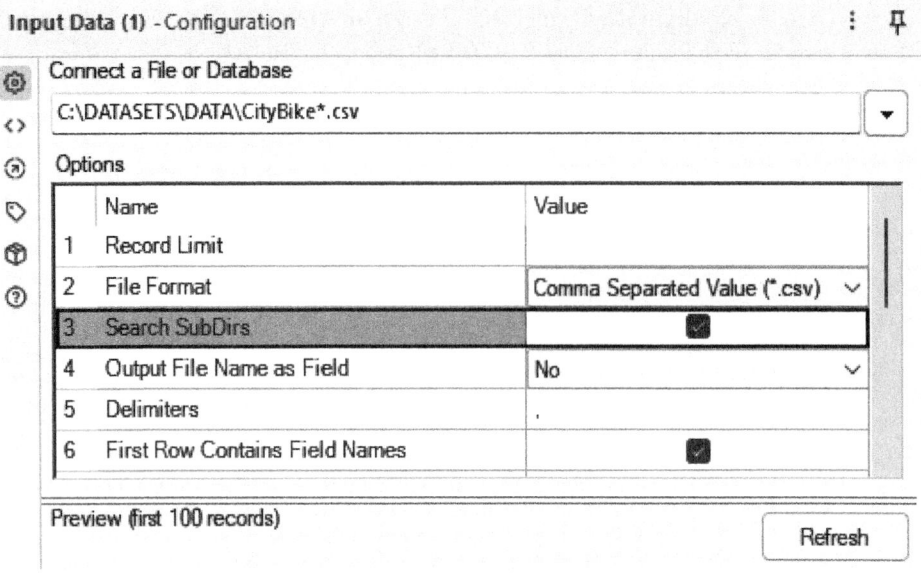

Figure 1.7: Reading multiple CSVs at once

There's more...

If you want to keep track of where every record comes from, you can use the **Output File Name as Field** option in the **Configuration** pane. This will create an additional column in your dataset, with the filename from where that record was read:

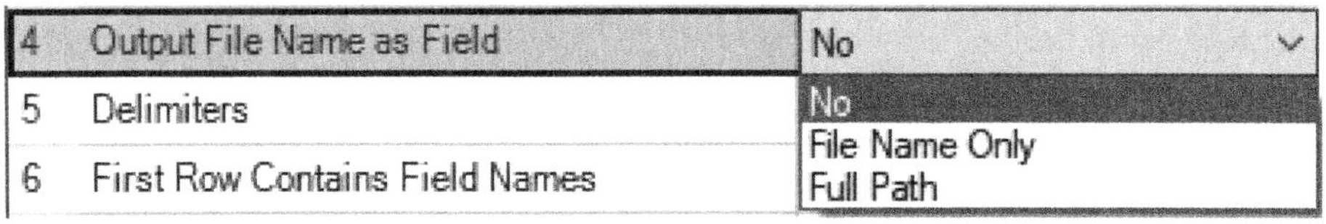

Figure 1.8: Getting a record's source file

Also, within Alteryx Designer, you can refer to a file location using the "dots convention," where a single dot (.) specifies the current workflow directory and two dots (. .) refers to a parent folder from the actual workflow location.

Have a look at the following examples:

- .\mydata.csv → Refers to a mydata.csv file located in the *same* folder as the actual workflow

- ..\DATA\mydata.csv → Refers to a mydata.csv file located in a folder called DATA, at the same hierarchy level as the folder containing the actual workflow

Reading all worksheets from an Excel file at once – same schema

Another common situation is to have all your data spread across multiple worksheets. So, we need to read them all and put them together:

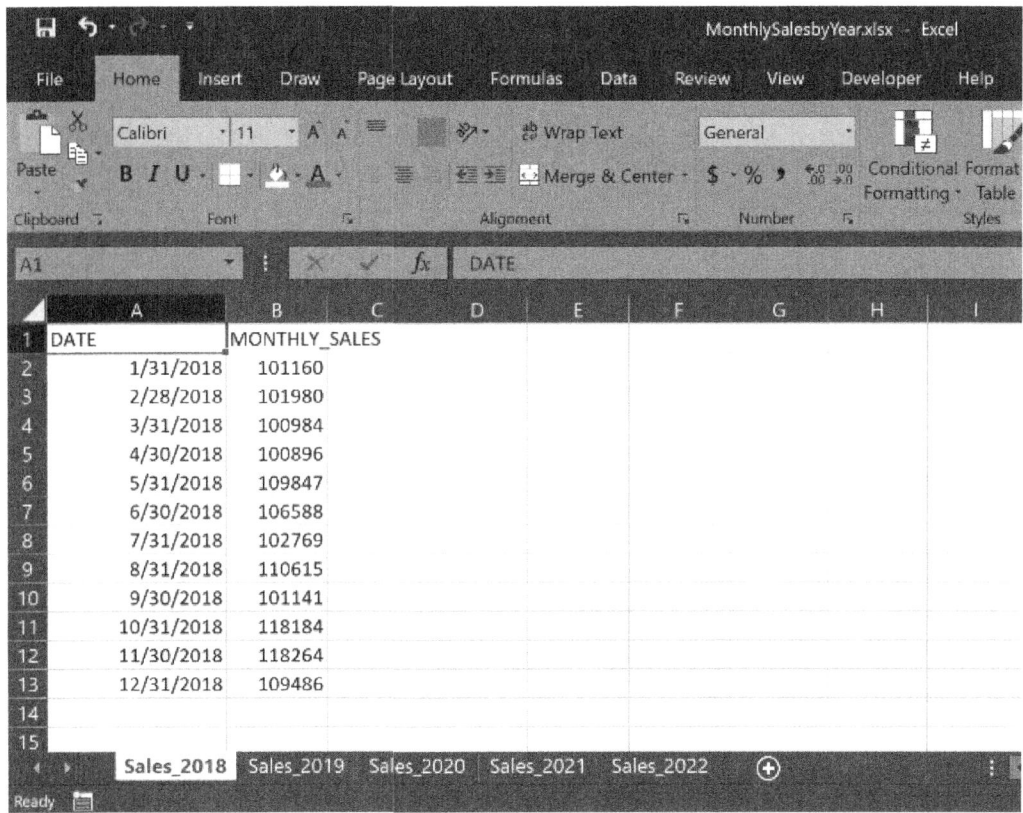

Figure 1.9: Our data file worksheets

As always, we'll make it simple for you, since Alteryx Designer allows us to.

Getting ready

If you want to follow along with this recipe, please download our test set here:

https://github.com/PacktPublishing/Alteryx-Designer-Cookbook/tree/main/ch1/Recipe2

Here, you'll find an Excel file with yearly data spread across multiple worksheets, and by applying this recipe, we'll be reading them all at once.

If you want to try this recipe with your data, make sure of the following:

- All your worksheets have the same schema (field/column names and data types).

- You have a list of worksheets to import (we'll get this directly when first accessing the file using a helpful option Alteryx has).

- You have a file with the schema to be used as a template. This file should be always available to the workflow, and won't be imported if it's not within the files-to-import list. If your file meets the first requirement, you can use the same file as the template.

How to do it...

Use the following steps:

1. Drop an **Input Data** tool onto the canvas, and point it to the Excel file you need to read:

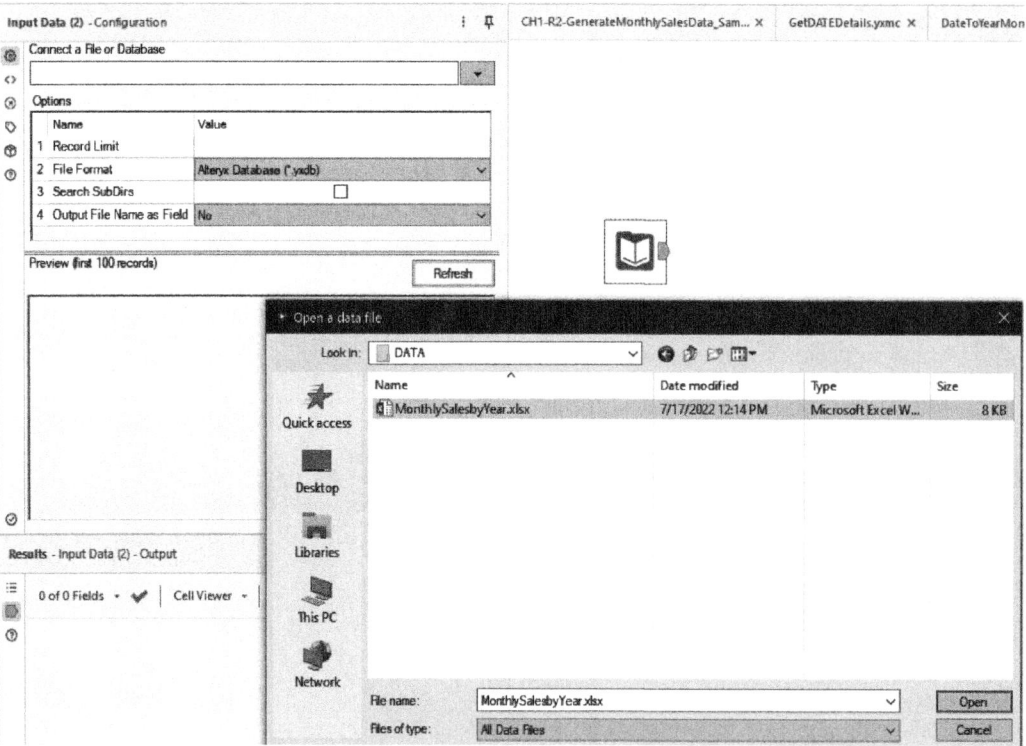

Figure 1.10: Selecting a file to read

Alteryx will prompt you for which of the worksheets you want to read.

2. Select the **Import only the list of sheet names** option:

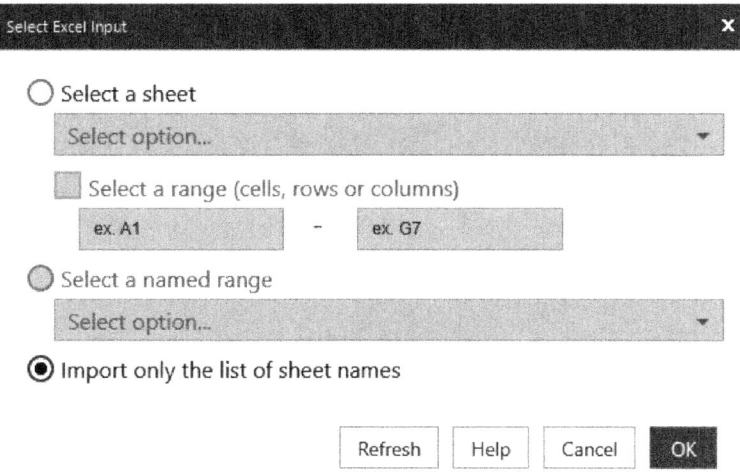

Figure 1.11: Selecting a list of sheet names

The selection will produce a list of sheets within the selected file, like this one:

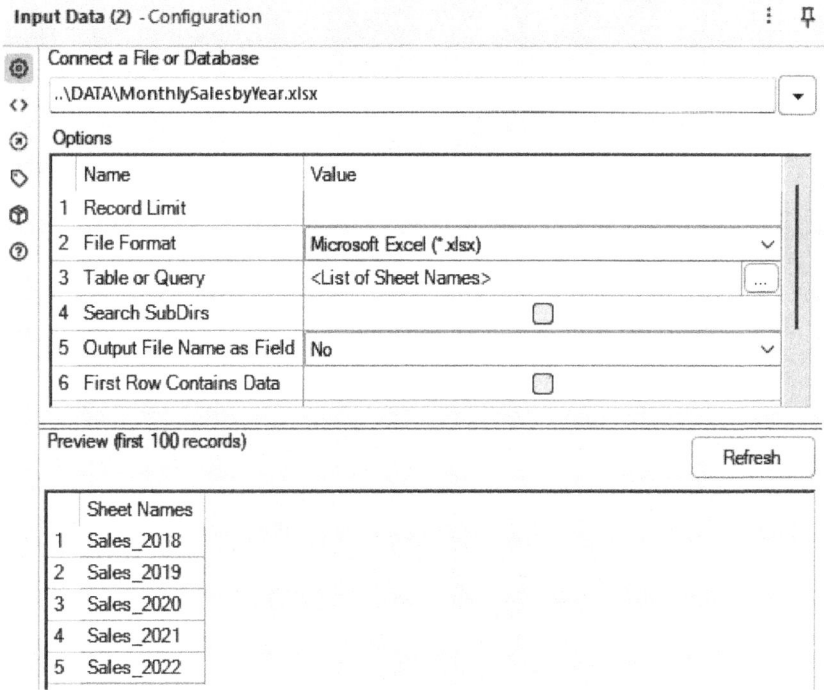

Figure 1.12: Results after reading the file

It's important to note that at this point, we still don't have the actual contents of those sheets, only their names.

3. To read the contents, we need the help of the **Dynamic Input** tool, so we drop one onto the canvas (from the **Developer** category).

4. Click on **Edit…** in the **Input Data Source Template** section, and you'll notice that the screen that pops up is the same as the **Input Data** tool one.

5. Point **Input Data Source Template** to your actual Excel file (or one that has the same schema as the one you need to read), and since we're reading an Excel file, Alteryx Designer will ask for the sheet we want to connect to.

6. Select one of the sheets and hit **OK**:

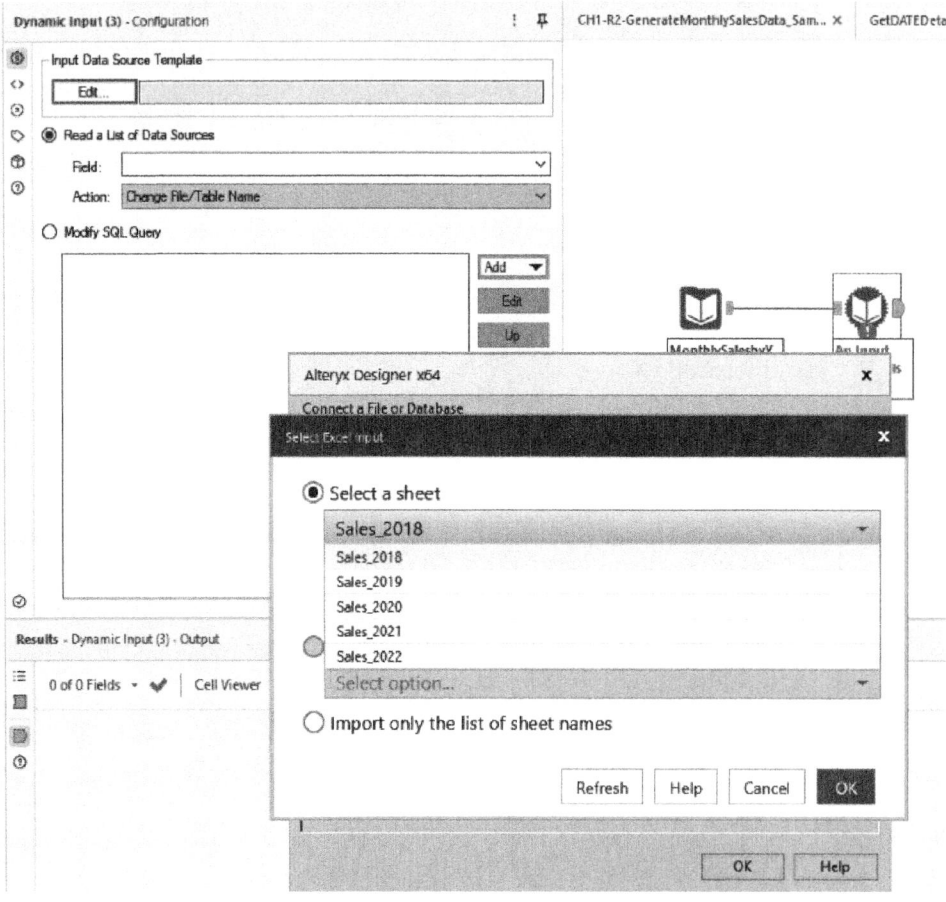

Figure 1.13: Selecting one of the sheets to use as a template

7. Hit **OK** again, and your template will be ready to be used as the sheet's schema for the upcoming data.

Now, we need to tell the **Dynamic Input** tool how we expect it to behave.

So, for the **Read a List of Data Sources** option, we are going to use the contents of the [**Sheet Names**] field, and for the **Action** field, we'll select **Change File/Table Name**:

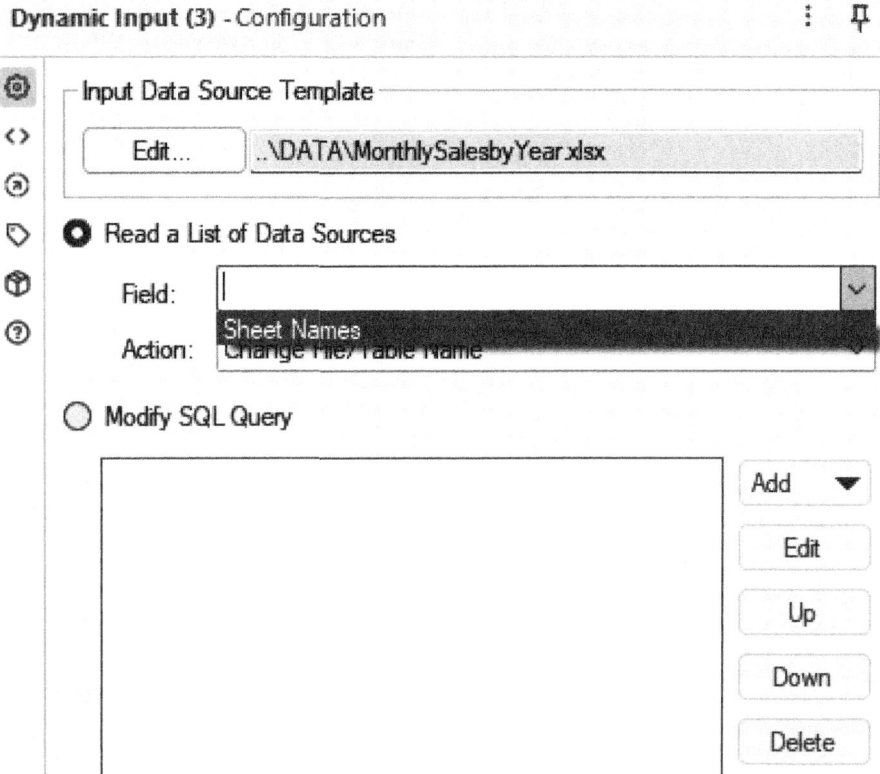

Figure 1.14: Setting data sources/tables/sheet names

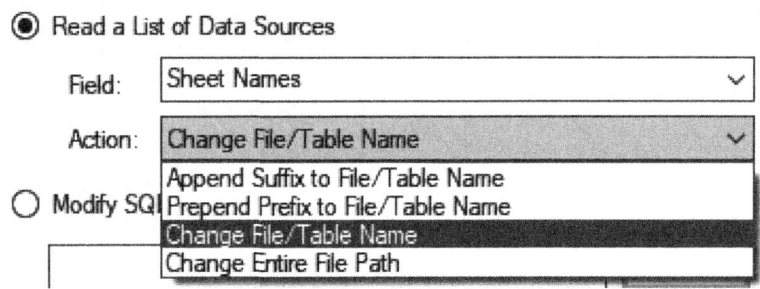

Figure 1.15: Setting the action to perform, based on field values

If you run your workflow, you'll see how the contents of each worksheet are read by Alteryx and stacked together:

Record	DATE	MONTHLY_SALES
1	2018-01-31	101160
2	2018-02-28	101980
3	2018-03-31	100984
4	2018-04-30	100896
5	2018-05-31	109847
6	2018-06-30	106588
7	2018-07-31	102769
8	2018-08-31	110615
9	2018-09-30	101141
10	2018-10-31	118184
11	2018-11-30	118264
12	2018-12-31	109486
13	2019-01-31	101392
14	2019-02-28	102598
15	2019-03-31	103917
16	2019-04-30	107903
17	2019-05-31	106878
18	2019-06-30	101129
19	2019-07-31	101303
20	2019-08-31	103120
21	2019-09-30	114326
22	2019-10-31	114694
23	2019-11-30	105269
24	2019-12-31	121199
25	2020-01-31	100890
26	2020-02-29	103188
27	2020-03-31	105749
28	2020-04-30	105527
29	2020-05-31	108294
30	2020-06-30	101437
31	2020-07-31	102582
32	2020-08-31	112994
33	2020-09-30	117632
34	2020-10-31	104457
35	2020-11-30	103061
36	2020-12-31	113724

Figure 1.16: Workflow results

How it works...

As its name suggests, the **Dynamic Input** tool performs several dynamic reading operations based on the configuration we set up.

In this particular case, we instructed the tool to read a list of worksheets (or tables) based on what's been gathered by the **Input Data** tool (the sheet names within our file), stating that the expected scheme or structure for those sheets *must* match the one we used as a template.

So, our first input record is `Sales_2018` (the name of the first sheet name), so Alteryx Designer compares its schema against the one we indicated. If it matches, Alteryx reads the data within it; if not, it throws an error. In both cases, Alteryx moves to the next record and performs the same tasks until we reach the end of the file.

There's more...

Sometimes we need to keep track of where every record comes from. Alteryx Designer allows us to do that very easily.

Just select the **Output File Name as Field** option, and Alteryx will add a new field to your data, containing—depending on which option you selected—either **File Name Only** or **Full Path** (the entire absolute path to the file) information:

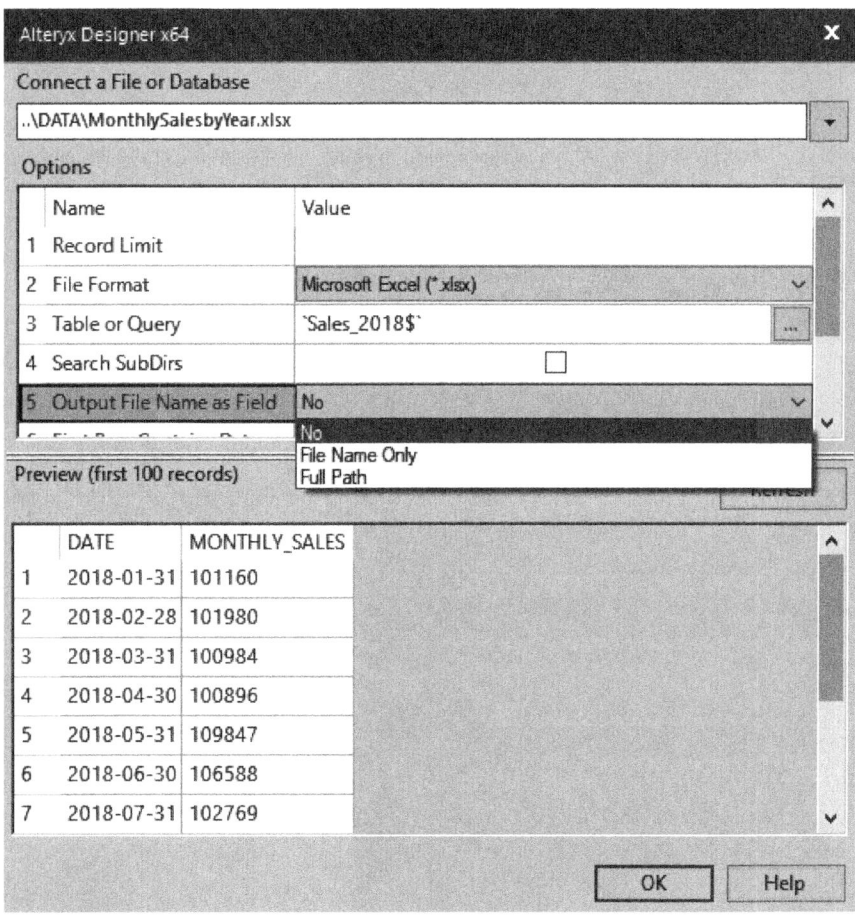

Figure 1.17: Output File Name as Field option

Different schema Excel worksheets all at once

The most complicated situation is when we need to consolidate Excel files that have different schemas.

As we saw in *recipe #2*, if the schema of the worksheets is not the same, we get a warning from Alteryx Designer, and the contents of that worksheet are not read:

Results - Workflow - Messages

≡	All	① 0 Errors	① 0 Conv Errors	⚠ 1 Warnings	☐ 1 Messages	🖹 6 Files

⊘	☐ Designer x64	Started running C:\Exercises\ch1\Recipe2\WORKFLOW\Force Error\CH01-R02-ReadMultipleSheets_Force Error.yxmd at 02/06/2023 16:56:06
	☐ Input Data (2)	5 records were read from "C:\Exercises\ch1\Recipe2\WORKFLOW\Force Error\DATA\MonthlySalesbyYear.xlsx" (<List of Sheet Names>)
	☐ Dynamic Input (3)	12 records were read from "C:\Exercises\ch1\Recipe2\WORKFLOW\Force Error\DATA\MonthlySalesbyYear.xlsx" (Sales_2018)
	☐ Dynamic Input (3)	12 records were read from "C:\Exercises\ch1\Recipe2\WORKFLOW\Force Error\DATA\MonthlySalesbyYear.xlsx" (Sales_2019)
	☐ Dynamic Input (3)	12 records were read from "C:\Exercises\ch1\Recipe2\WORKFLOW\Force Error\DATA\MonthlySalesbyYear.xlsx" (Sales_2020)
	⚠ Dynamic Input (3)	The file ".\DATA\MonthlySalesbyYear.xlsx||Sales_2021" has a different number of fields than the 1st file in the set and will be skipped
	☐ Dynamic Input (3)	2 records were read from "C:\Exercises\ch1\Recipe2\WORKFLOW\Force Error\DATA\MonthlySalesbyYear.xlsx" (Sales_2022)
	☐ Dynamic Input (3)	43 records were read from 5 files/queries
	🖹 Browse (4)	43 records
	⚠ Designer x64	Finished running CH01-R02-ReadMultipleSheets_Force Error.yxmd in 0.3 seconds with 1 warning

Figure 1.18: Warning for unmatching schema

In this recipe, we'll create a batch macro to read each worksheet within an Excel file, even when they have a different schema.

Getting ready

We prepared a test set for you to follow along with this recipe, available at https://github.com/PacktPublishing/Alteryx-Designer-Cookbook/tree/main/ch1/Recipe3.

If you decided to use your data to try this recipe, make sure that your files have different schemas (with some fields in common so that you can see the effects of different configurations).

Make sure that under the **Options→User Settings→Edit User Settings→Macros** tab, you have at least one directory/folder set up as a macro repository (this makes it easier for Alteryx Designer to find your macros). As you can see, there can be several repositories configured, but one of them will be the default one:

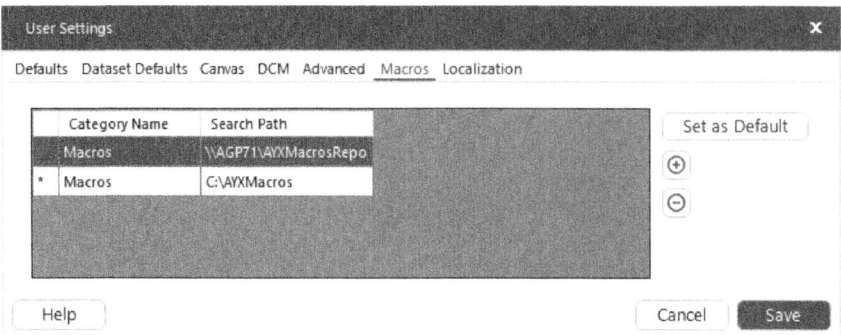

Figure 1.19: Default macro repositories

How to do it...

1. Let's start by creating a new workflow.

2. Drop an **Input Data** tool onto your canvas and point it to the file you want to read:

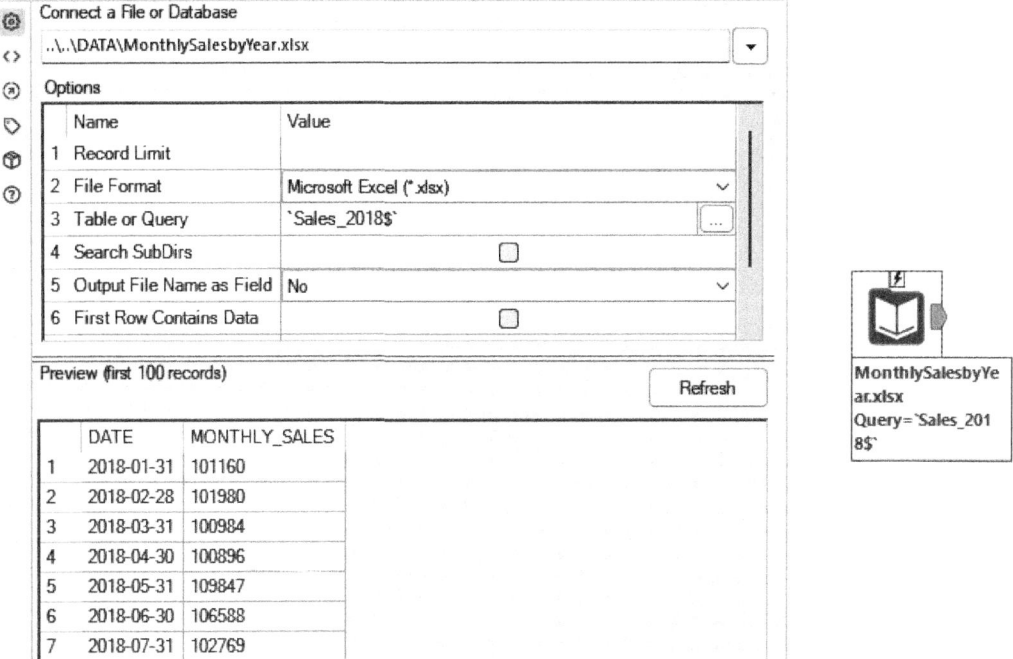

Figure 1.20: Input Data tool configuration

3. From the **Interface** category, drop a **Control Parameter** tool onto the canvas and change its label to something meaningful (this is going to be your tool's input anchor):

Figure 1.21: Control Parameter tool in the canvas

4. Once you have both tools, click and drag from the black Q connector of the **Control Parameter** tool and connect it to the lightning icon on top of the **Input Data** tool. You'll notice that Alteryx Designer inserts an **Action** tool in the middle.

5. Click on the **Action** tool to configure it, and select **Update Input Data Tool** from the **Select an action type:** dropdown, making sure that the **Required** option is selected:

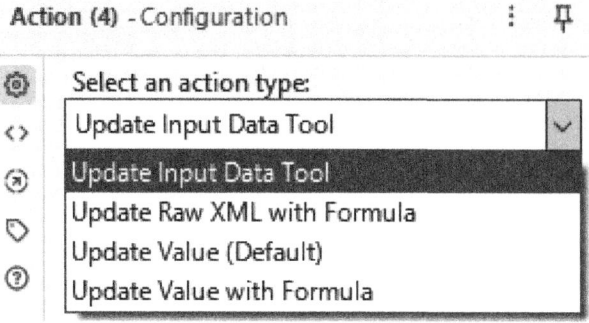

Figure 1.22: Updating the action type

6. From the **Interface** category, drop a **Macro Output** tool and connect it to the **Input Data** tool output anchor (this is going to be the output anchor of your tool):

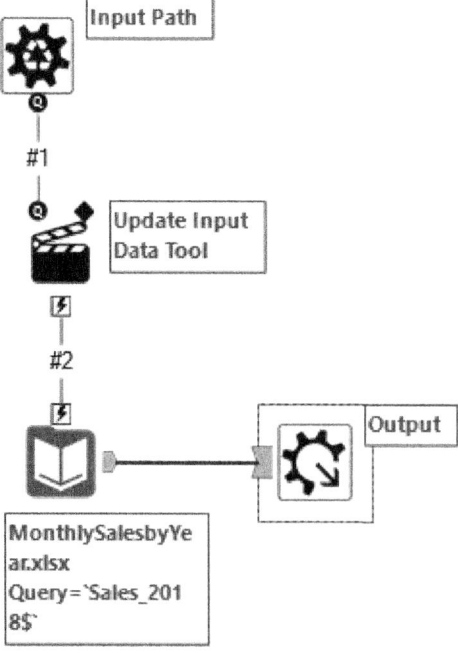

Figure 1.23: Completed macro

7. Open **Interface Designer** (from the **View** menu or by pressing *Ctrl + Alt + D*):

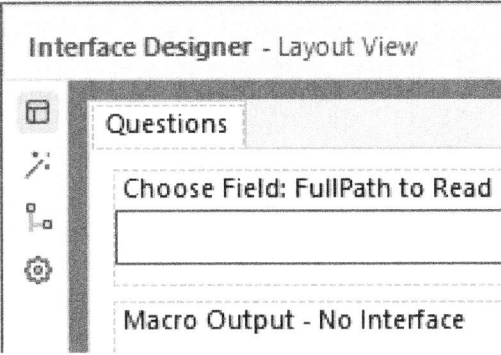

Figure 1.24: Interface Designer

8. Click on the gear icon at the left of the pop-up window so that you can access the output options:

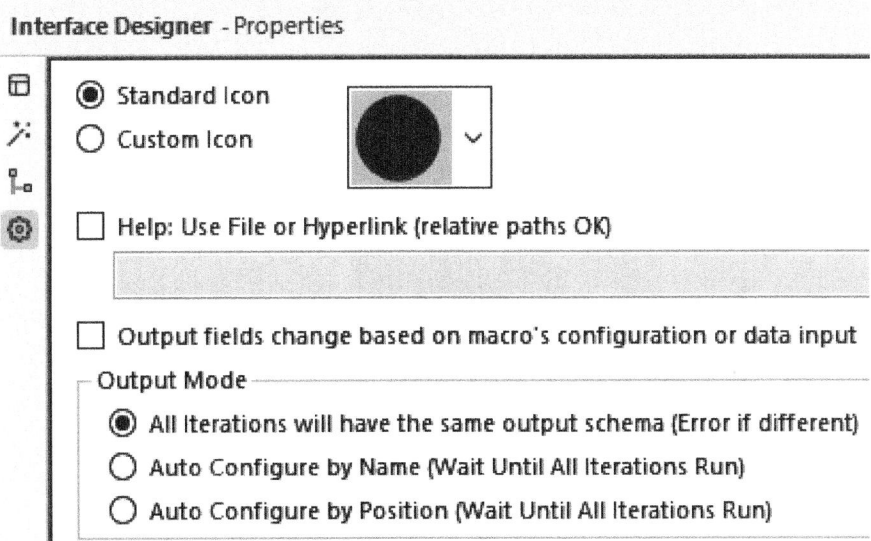

Figure 1.25: Macro output options

9. Make sure that **Output fields change based on macro's configuration or data input** is checked, and select **Auto Configure by Name (Wait Until All Iterations Run)** from the **Output Mode** option:

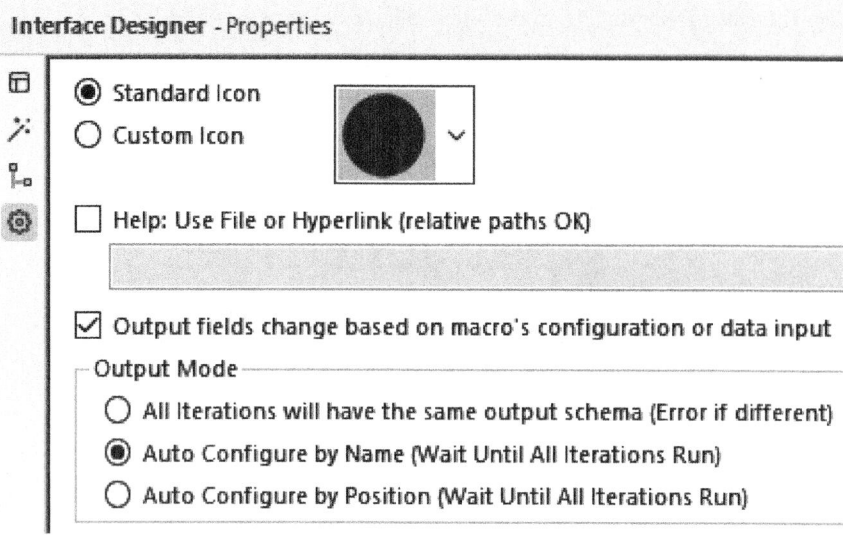

Figure 1.26: Macro output options configured

10. Now, save the workflow.

    If you pay attention, Alteryx Designer will present you the **Save** dialog, pointing to the same folder you have configured as the default macro repository, and the extension of the file to be saved is .yxmc ("yx" for Alteryx; "mc" for macro).

11. Name your macro BatchReadWorksheets.yxmc and save it. Close your workflow.

12. Now, create a new workflow and right-click on the canvas.

13. Go to **Insert**, and you'll notice a **Macro…** option way down on the menu:

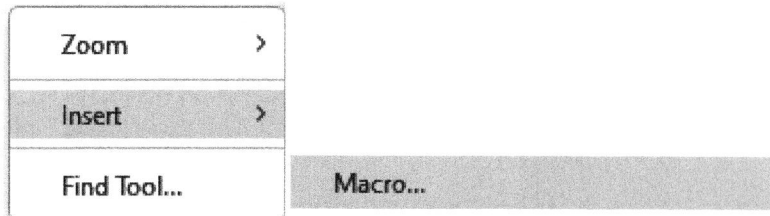

Figure 1.27: Inserting a macro into a new workflow

14. Click on **Macro…**, and Alteryx will present you with a **File Open** dialog. Navigate to your macro repository and select the BatchReadWorksheets.yxmc file.

    You'll see that Alteryx Designer inserted a "tool" in the canvas with one input and one output anchor:

Figure 1.28: Batch macro waiting for data to be connected

15. Now, drop a **Directory** tool from the **In/Out** category onto the canvas and connect its output to our tool's parameter input anchor (marked with ¿).

16. Point the **Directory** tool to the directory where your Excel files are:

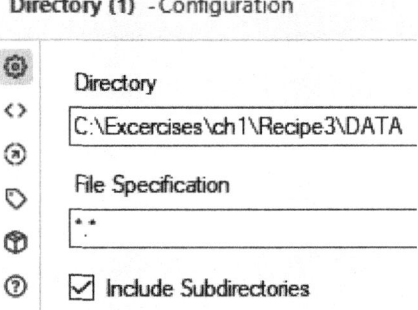

Figure 1.29: Directory tool pointing to the folder

17. Now, click again on our macro, and select the [FullPath] field from the **Choose Field: FullPath to Read** option:

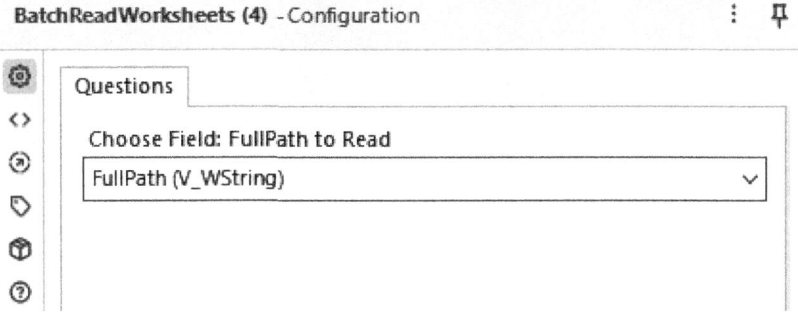

Figure 1.30: Selecting a field to use as the path to read files

18. Drop a **Browse** tool following the macro and run the workflow.

You'll see that all records from the Excel files are there, but the structures are not quite complete.

Notice that there'll be columns with a lot of `Null` values. This happens because some of the worksheets don't have that particular column, so Alteryx Designer fills them with `Null` values.

Saving and preserving Excel sheet formats

When working with Excel files, we often have to report using existing templates that have already been formatted, and we need to respect those formats.

Alteryx allows you to preserve the existing formatting, and we'll go through the process of getting this done within Alteryx Designer.

Getting ready

To follow along with this recipe, you can download our test set from here:

`https://github.com/PacktPublishing/Alteryx-Designer-Cookbook/tree/main/ch1/Recipe4`

If you decide to try it with your data, make sure you define ranges on which the data must be saved.

To make this recipe work, we need to have a range defined within the Excel file.

Our sample set contains a pre-formatted Excel worksheet, with explicit and conditional formats:

Figure 1.31: Excel template

How to do it...

We are going to tackle this recipe in two phases:

- Grabbing the template

- Writing to the template

1. We'll start reading our data source, so drop an **Input Data** tool onto the canvas and point it to MonthlySales_*.xlsx (you can revisit *recipe #1* to see how this works):

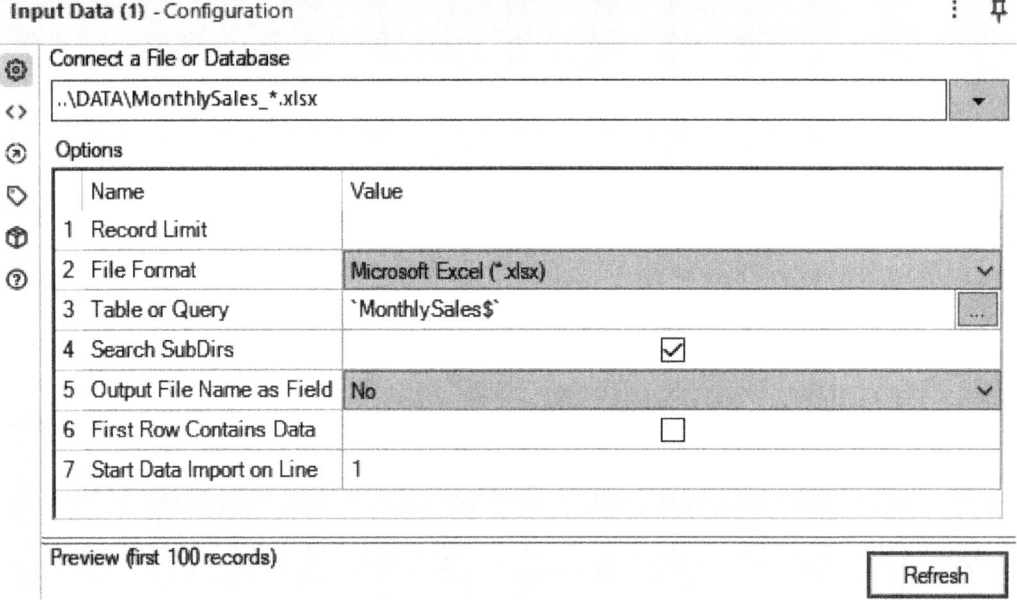

Figure 1.32: Reading the data source

This'll be the data we'll process and later save in our report template file.

2. Drop a **Block Until Done** tool (from the **Developer** category) following the **Input Data** tool.

To be able to save data into the template, we need to make a copy of the actual template in the final location where we want our output. We're going to use \OUTPUT as the location.

Also, we need to save our workflow first, for which Alteryx Designer provides a very handy variable ([Engine.WorkflowDirectory]) that stores the value to where our workflow is stored; otherwise, it'll point to a temp directory and we'll lose our relative references to the working files.

3. Drop a **Sample** tool onto the canvas and configure it to keep only the first record (**First N rows** selected and **N = 1**):

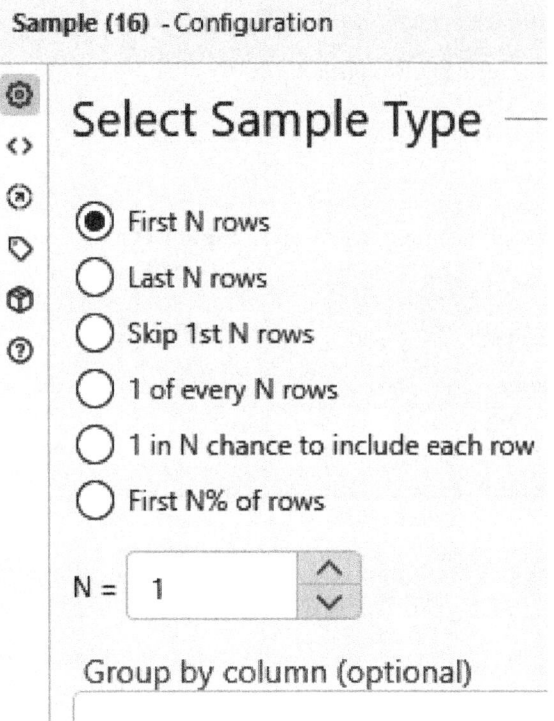

Figure 1.33: Configuring the Sample tool

4.   Drop a **Formula** tool and connect it to the output anchor labeled 1 in the **Block Until Done** tool.

Create a new column called `Copy_Command` and use this formula as its expression:

```
'copy "' + [Engine.WorkflowDirectory] +'..\TEMPLATE\
ReportingTemplate.xlsx" "' + [Engine.WorkflowDirectory]+
'..\OUTPUT\"'
```

As stated earlier, `[Engine.WorkflowDirectory]` refers to the folder where the workflow is stored (and runs from). So, no matter where we put it or copy it, it'll keep the relative references (such as `..\DATA`, for example).

Since our data contains more columns than needed, we'll drop a **Select** tool onto the canvas, to only keep the `[Copy_command]` field:

Select (17) - Configuration

	Field	Type		S
☐	DATE	Date	▾	1(
☐	MONTHLY_SALES	Double	▾	8
☑	Copy_command	V_WString	▾	1(
☐	*Unknown	Unknown	▾	0

Figure 1.34: Keeping only the [Copy_command] data field

To finish this step, we need to tell Alteryx Designer to execute the OS command contained within the [Copy_command] field, so for that, we need a **Run Command** tool (it's in the **Developer** category).

5. Drop it and configure it as in the following screenshot, making sure that you use %temp%\Copy. bat as the **Write Source** value and the same value for the **Run External Program** command:

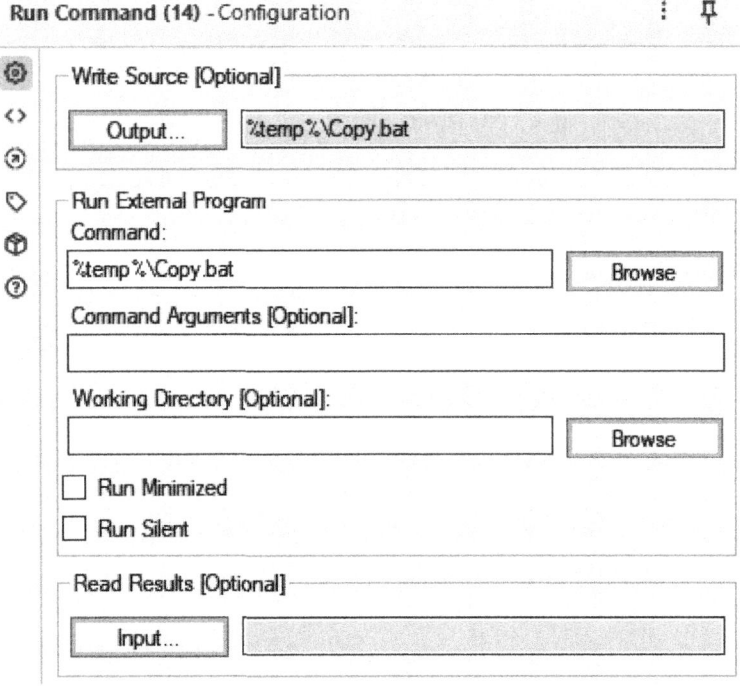

Figure 1.35: Run Command tool configuration

So far, if we run this workflow, we'll see that the original template located in the \TEMPLATES folder was copied to the \OUTPUT folder.

From now on, we can use it to write data within.

We can see we have three sections in the template to "fill" (Monthly Sales, starting at A11; Annual Sales, starting at F11; and there is another one— B3, where we are going to insert the date of the report's issue). You can see that we named those ranges too in the template: MONTHLY_SALES, YEARLY_SALES, and REPORT_DATE.

Additionally, the template has some conditional formatting rules configured, and a chart inserted to show the monthly sales in a line chart.

6.   To fill the monthly sales section of the report, we only need to write the contents of our incoming data, so for that, drop a **Sort** tool and connect it to the output anchor of the **Block Until Done** tool, labeled 2. Sort the data by date in ascending order, and following that, drop an **Output Data** tool onto the canvas.

7.   Point the **Write to File or Database** value to where the template was copied (in our case, it's the OUTPUT folder located one level up (..\) to where our workflow is in the hierarchy), and select the ReportingTemplate.xlsx file.

8.   Make sure that options 5 and 6 (**Skip Field Names** and **Preserve Formatting on Overwrite (Range Required)**) are checked:

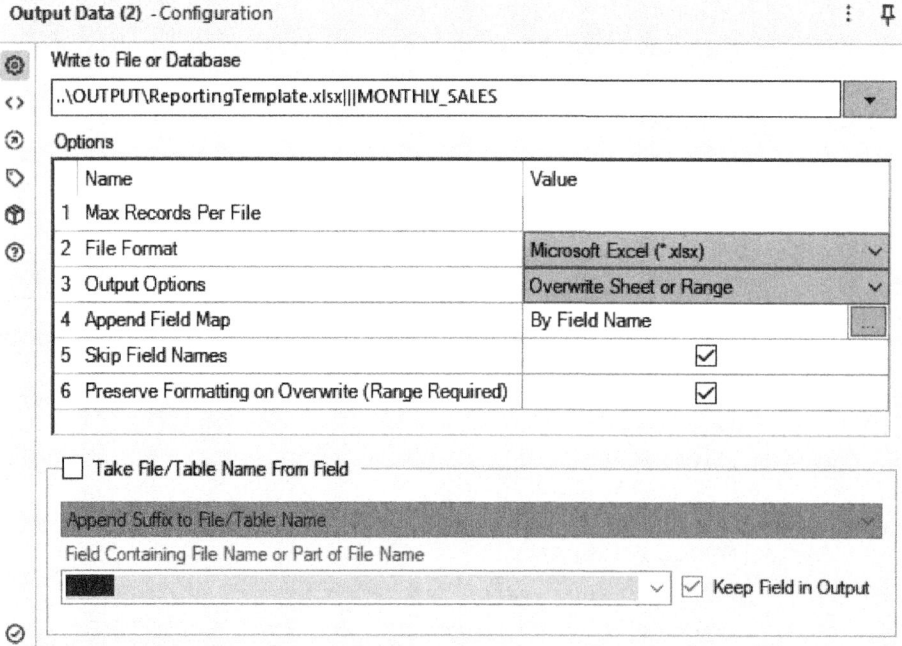

Figure 1.36: Configuring the Output Data tool

When Alteryx asks to specify a sheet, we have two options:

- Use the named range as the *sheet name* if we have one:

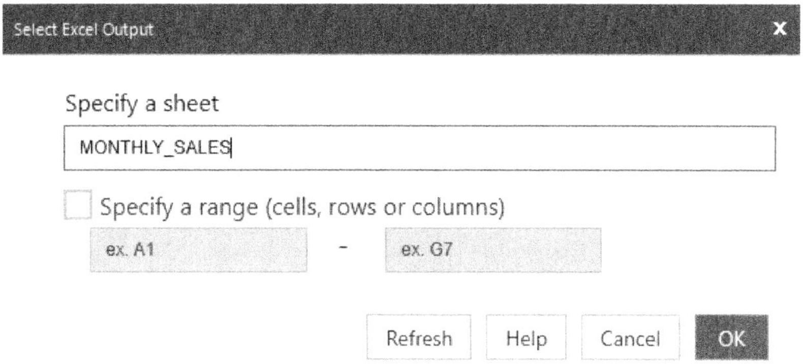

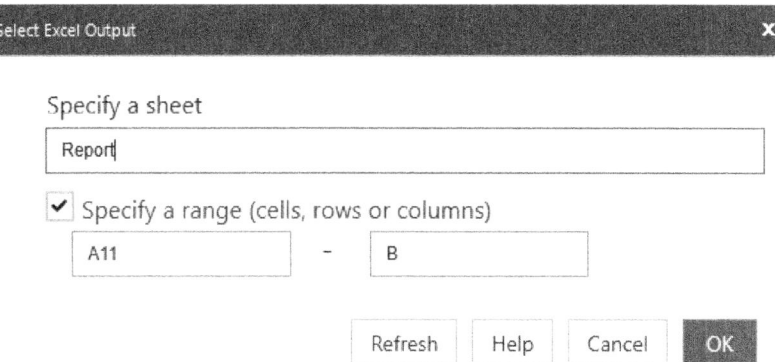

Figure 1.37: Specifying a named range to write data to

- Specify a range within the worksheet to save our data (notice that we define A11:B as the range because we know we'll be starting at A11, but we don't know where we'll be ending at B):

Figure 1.38: Specifying a range within a worksheet to write data to

For yearly sales, we need to perform an extra step, which consists of summarizing sales values per year.

9. To be able to do this with the actual data we have, we need to extract the [Year] value from the actual [DATE] field. This can be easily done by dropping a **Formula** tool onto the canvas. Connect this **Formula** tool to the output anchor 3 of the existing **Block Until Done** tool.

10. Add a new column on the **Formula** tool named [YEAR] and use this expression to extract the year from the [DATE] field:

```
DateTimeFormat([DATE],"%Y")
```

Now that we have the [YEAR] value of each record, we need a **Summarize** tool to perform the corresponding aggregations.

11. Drop a **Summarize** tool from the **Transform** category and configure it, like this:

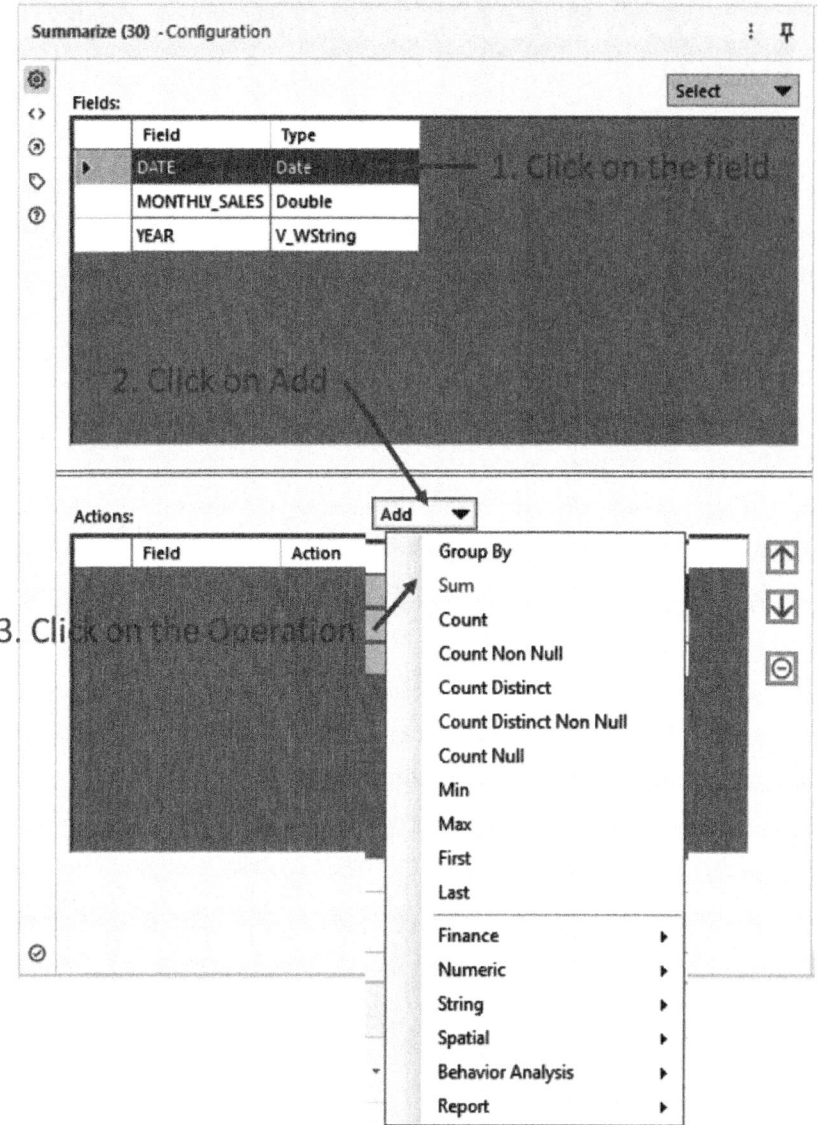

Figure 1.39: Summarizing tool configuration process

> **Note**
>
> To configure the **Summarize** tool, first, select a field from the top box, then click on **Add**, and from the dropdown, select the operation you want to apply to that particular field.

So, this configuration will give us the total sum of [MONTHLY_SALES] and the maximum (MAX) value of [DATE] per [YEAR]:

YEAR	Max_DATE	Sum_MONTHLY_SALES
2018	2018-12-31	1191798
2019	2019-12-31	1276087
2020	2020-12-31	1279636
2021	2021-12-31	1287053
2022	2022-07-31	711990

Figure 1.40: Summarized sales per year

12. Now, to save the data, drop another **Output Data** tool and configure it.

13. Select ReportingTemplate.xlsx from the OUTPUT directory, and use the YEARLY_SALES named range to write the data. Again, make sure that options 5 and 6 (**Skip Field Names** and **Preserve Formatting on Overwrite (Range Required)**) are selected; otherwise, you'll not only overwrite existing data but you'll be removing the existing formats:

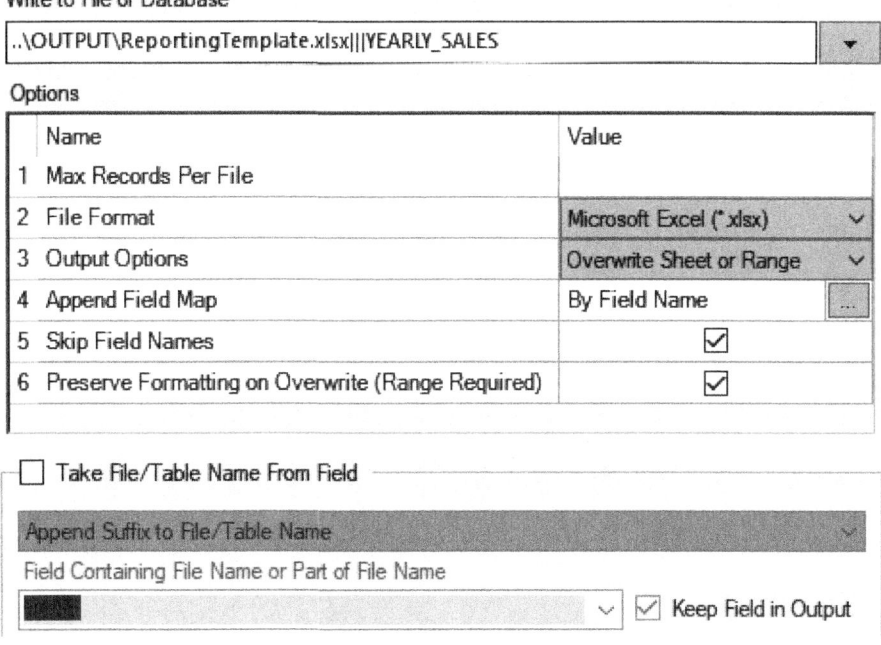

Figure 1.41: Writing yearly sales to the template

To finish, we'll add the date on which the report was issued.

14. To do so, we need a **Formula** tool that creates that value for us. Drop one, connect it to the **Select** output we added in the previous step (the same anchor the **Output Data** tool connects to), and create a new column called [REPORT_DATE] with this expression:

```
DateTimeStart()
```

15. Add a **Select** tool following the **Formula** tool, and just keep the [REPORT_DATE] field and a **Sample** tool to get the first row (**First N rows, N = 1**).

16. Finally, add a new **Block Until Done** tool and then drop an **Output Data** tool, and again select our ..\OUTPUT\ReportingTemplate.xlsx file. In this case, select the REPORT_DATE named range and make sure the **Skip Field Names** and **Preserve Formatting on Overwrite (Range Required)** options are both checked:

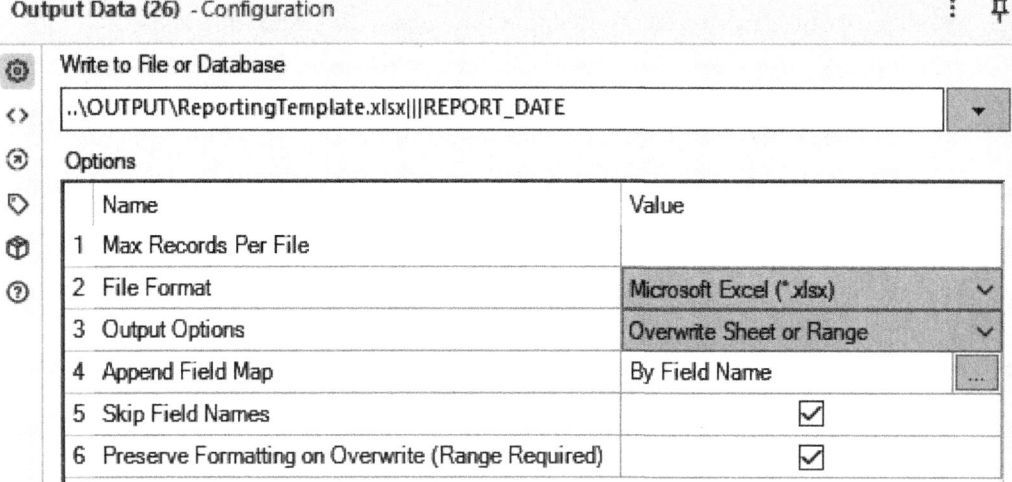

Figure 1.42: Writing the report-issuing date to a named range

Your workflow should look very close to this:

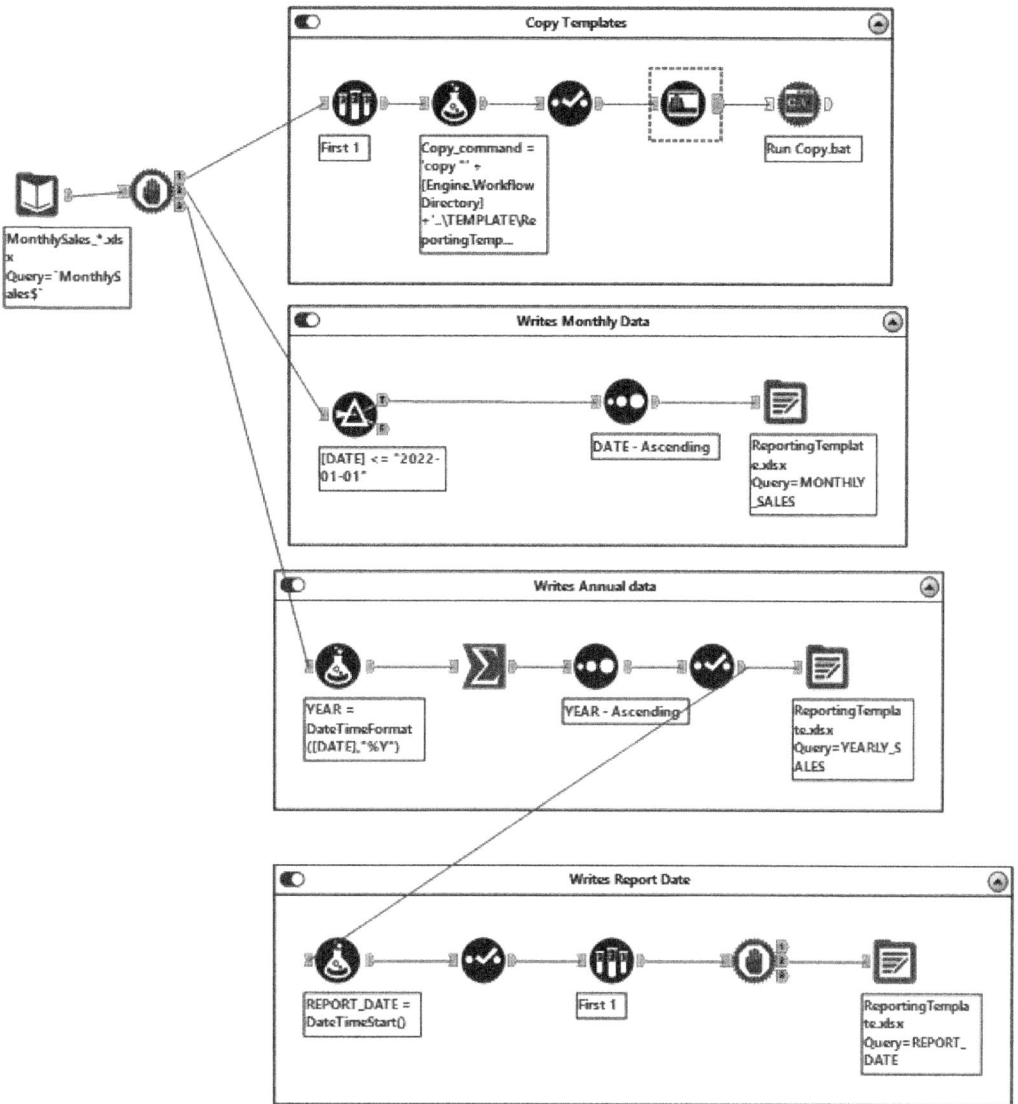

Figure 1.43: Overview of the finished workflow

If you run the workflow and open \OUTPUT\ReportTemplate.xlsx, it'll look like this:

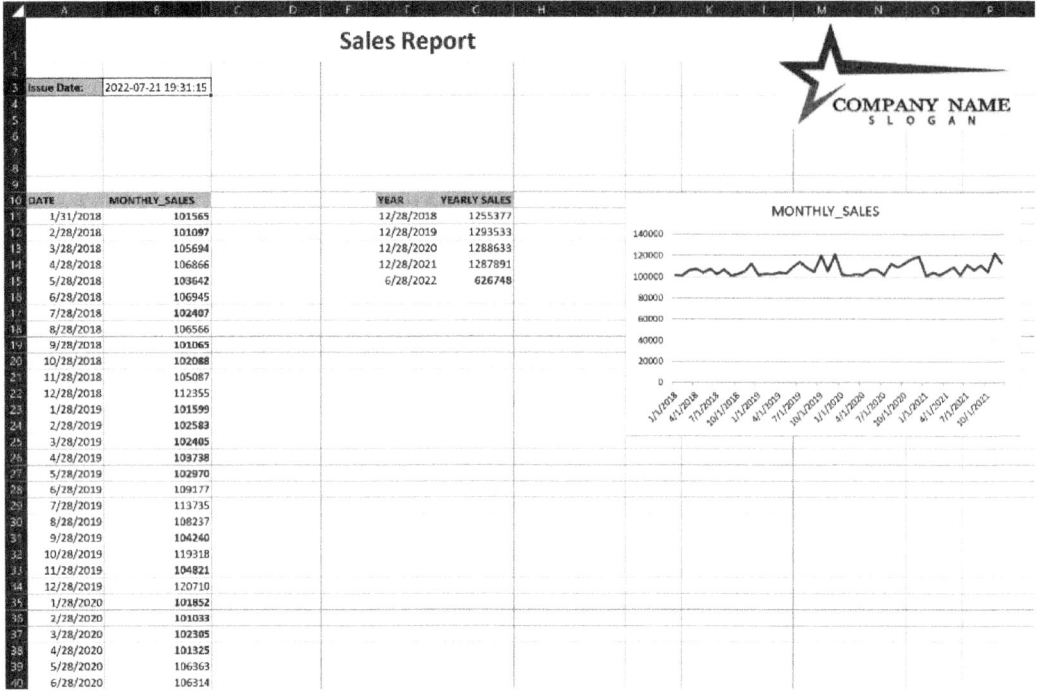

Figure 1.44: Final results (ranges and chart updated)

How it works...

Let's start explaining the **Block Until Done** tool, firstly according to Alteryx's documentation (https://help.alteryx.com/20221/designer/block-until-done-tool):

> *"Use Block Until Done to stop datasets from moving downstream until the last record in the set has been processed by all previous tools. In addition, this tool ensures that only a single output stream at a time receives the completed dataset. Subsequent streams are blocked until all the dataset records are pushed through the 1st stream."*

As you will have realized by now, this tool is essential for performing multiple write operations within the same file from the same workflow, serializing the operations connected to it.

The order in which we connected the tools to the **Block Until Done** tool is important too because they determine the order in which those operations will be executed.

Thanks to the **Run Command** tool, we can execute external commands such as the one we created to copy files.

It is a very powerful tool to interact with our environment, including the OS, or custom applications we can integrate into Alteryx:

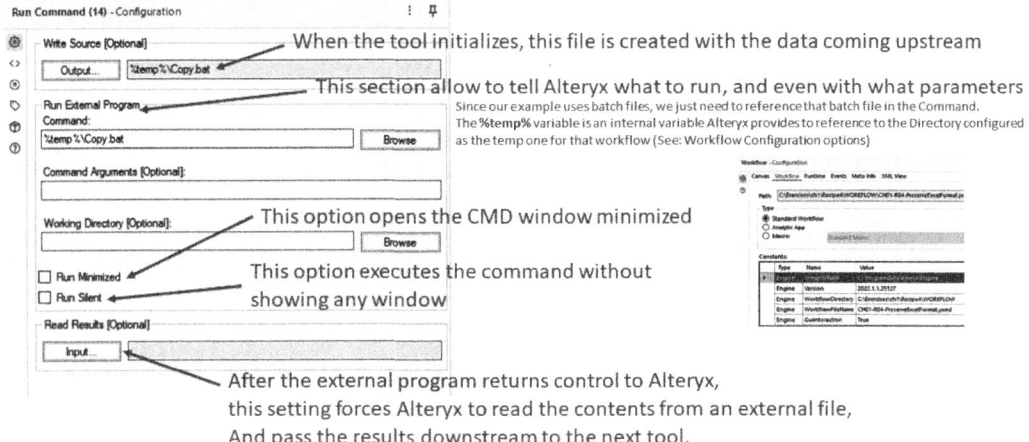

Figure 1.45: The "anatomy" of the Run Command tool

See also (follow-up steps)

You can learn more about the **Block Until Done** tool here:

https://help.alteryx.com/current/designer/block-until-done-tool

And you can find out more about the **Run Command** tool here:

https://help.alteryx.com/current/designer/run-command-tool

Accessing and determining which files are to be processed from a file repository

Sometimes, data is put in shared folders across the company's network, and we have no control over when and how that data is updated. We have some users updating files within a shared folder, and we need to keep the last updated one from a set of various versions of the same file.

This recipe will help you determine the newest files to be processed from within a folder.

Getting ready

To follow along with this recipe, use the ch1\r5 files from GitHub:

https://github.com/PacktPublishing/Alteryx-Designer-Cookbook/tree/main/ch1/Recipe5

If you decided to use your data to follow up on this recipe, the only thing you need to make sure of is that all your files are in one directory (and/or subdirectories).

How to do it...

1. Place a **Directory** tool onto the canvas and point it to where your data is (in our example set, it's on ..\DATA\).

    Select *.xlsx as the **File Specification** value and make sure **Include subdirectories** is checked:

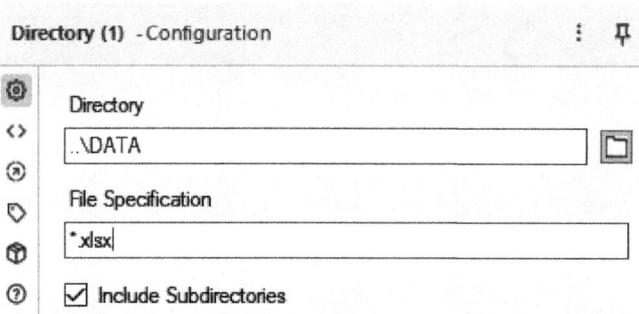

Figure 1.46: Directory tool configuration

2. Run your workflow and focus on the **Results** panel of Alteryx Designer:

Figure 1.47: Workflow results

You'll see important information about the files within the selected directory, such as the following:

- [FullPath]—Absolute path to the file

- [Directory]—Absolute path to the directory containing the file

- [FileName]—Name and extension of the file

- [ShortFileName]—For backward compatibility, shows the 8.3 filename format (mostly, you won't use this)

- [CreationTime]—Datetime of file creation (registered by the OS)

- [LastAccessTime]—Last time the file was accessed

- [LastWriteTime]—Last time the file was written within

- [Size]—Size in bytes

Along with these values, you'll see additional ones, depending on which attributes the OS has on each file:

AttributeArchive	AttributeCompressed	AttributeEncrypted	AttributeHidden	AttributeNormal	AttributeOffline	AttributeReadonly	AttributeReparsePoint	AttributeSparseFile	AttributeSystem	AttributeTemporary
True	False	False	False	False	False	False	False	False	False	False
True	False	False	False	False	False	False	False	False	False	False
True	False	False	False	False	False	False	False	False	False	False
True	False	False	False	False	False	False	False	False	False	False
True	False	False	False	False	False	False	False	False	False	False

Figure 1.48: Additional workflow results

We can use all these values to create conditions to read files.

For example:

- Getting the last modified file

3. After the **Directory** tool, drop a **Sort** tool and sort by [LastWriteTime] in descending order.

4. Drop a **Sample** tool, select **First N rows**, and set **N = 1**.

If our files contain worksheets with the same name, we can apply *recipe #2* (we'll follow this path here) to read the selected file's content, using the [FullPath] data instead of [List of Sheet Names]. If not, we can reshape *recipe #3* to read the selected file content (which will be explained in the *There's more...* section of this recipe).

To do so, we need to add a **Formula** tool to tell Alteryx which worksheet we'll be reading from the instructed file/s.

5. Add the **Formula** tool and create a new column called ToRead, with this expression:

```
[FullPath] + "|||MonthlySales"
```

This will add the worksheet name (MonthlySales) to be read from the selected files (the | | | separator is how Alteryx Designer recognizes tables/worksheets within databases/files).

6. Now, drop a **Dynamic Input** tool following the **Formula** tool:

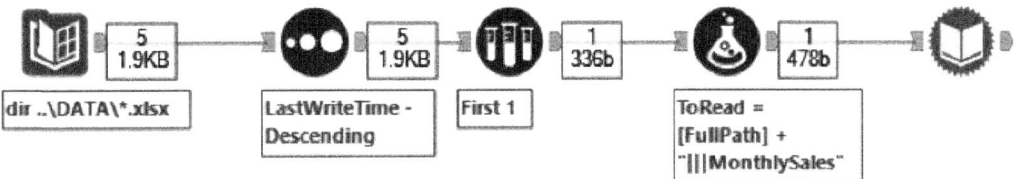

Figure 1.49: Our workflow so far

7. Change the **Dynamic Input** tool configuration. Using the recently generated [ToRead] field, we are telling the tool to carry out the following action: **Change Entire File Path** (this is where we'll change the *recipe #2* configuration):

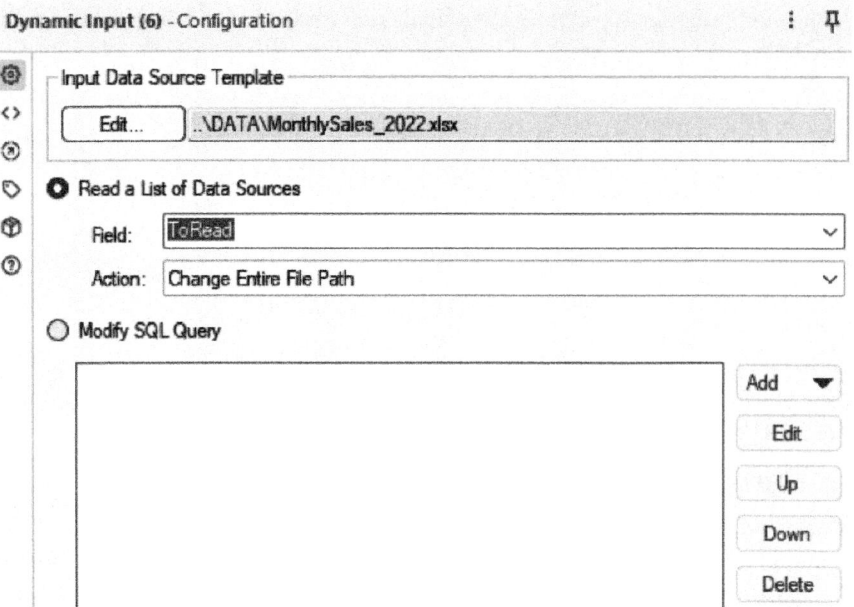

Figure 1.50: Dynamic Input tool configuration

Running the workflow will give us the contents of the last modified file within a folder:

Results - Browse (8) - Input

2 of 2 Fields ▾ ✔ | Cell Viewer ▾ 7 records displayed, 1,251 bytes | ↑ ↓ |

Record	DATE	MONTHLY_SALES
1	2022-01-31	100,879
2	2022-02-28	101,011
3	2022-03-31	101,741
4	2022-04-30	102,031
5	2022-05-31	100,959
6	2022-06-30	100,273
7	2022-07-31	105,096

Figure 1.51: Dynamic Input tool configuration

How it works...

The **Directory** tool allows you to target a specific directory/folder (and its subfolders if wanted), select a file pattern, and return a list of files from that folder with their attributes, allowing us to make decisions about which files to keep and what to discard in our workflow.

Once we got the file list from the desired location, we sorted the files by one of their attributes (`LastWriteTime`) in descending order, so the newest file will be always the first in our list, and having the **Sample** tool configured to get the first (**N** = 1) record, we are completely certain that always gets the last modified one.

> **Note**
>
> We can make endless decisions here, using **Filter** tools to select files based on any criteria we need to apply to finally read the ones we need, so feel free to take this recipe and adjust it to get the content you need from a bunch of files sitting in a folder.

We made this recipe using Excel files because this format presents us with an additional challenge since they may contain several worksheets (or tables) within each file, and we need to tell Alteryx Designer which ones we need to read. That's why we need to add a **Formula** tool before reading the actual contents of the files, adding the | | | notation to the [FilePath] value and building the entire path, not only to the file but to the worksheet within it.

From there, we can now leverage the **Dynamic Input** tool with another of its powerful methods, **Change Entire File Path**, based on the results of the [ToRead] field we created in the **Formula** tool.

There's more...

As stated before, if you combine this recipe with *recipe #3*, you can have a more dynamic way to read files, since you won't be depending on the worksheets having the same name (you'll be picking them up from the <List of Sheet Names> option Alteryx gives you).

Also, you can keep track of the files already processed simply by appending the [FullPath] field of the processed file/s and the date you processed those files to some kind of custom log (maybe another Excel file).

This method is very useful to avoid reprocessing files that have already been processed (before reading the contents, just join your **Directory** tool data stream with your custom log and only process the unjoined records coming from the **Directory** tool) and will save you a lot of time:

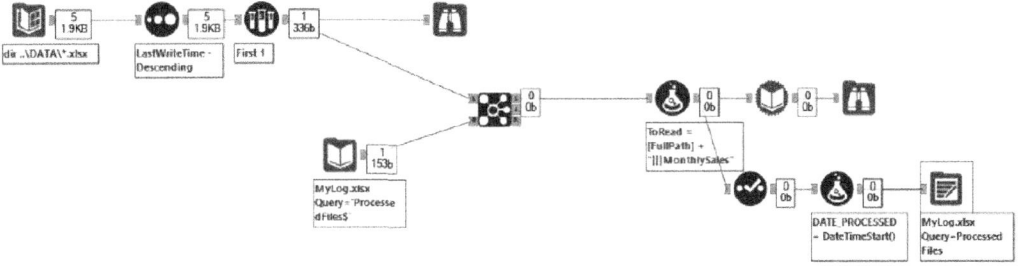

Figure 1.52: Joining input with a log of processed files

Handling formats when reading text files

Lots of applications provide data in a flat, fixed-width format. Even when Alteryx doesn't have a `.txt` format reader, it allows us to extract data from this type of file, by offering a parsing functionality (similar to what Excel has to determine columns and field types).

Every time we need to access this type of file, we need to know how and where is data organized, and most of the time, these files come with a "data dictionary" telling us the internal structure of the files.

In this recipe, we'll guide you to build an automated fixed-length file parser, leveraging some of Alteryx Designer's functionalities.

Getting ready

We got you covered to try this recipe with a sample set here:

https://github.com/PacktPublishing/Alteryx-Designer-Cookbook/tree/main/ch1/Recipe6

This sample data has a dictionary, indicating to us the name, type, size, and scale of each field within it. You can find the data dictionary in a file called `FileStructure.xlsx` inside the DATA DEFINITION folder of the test set:

Name	Type	Size	Scale
TRIPDURATION	Int32	4	
STARTTIME	DateTime	19	
STOPTIME	DateTime	19	
START_STATION_ID	V_String	4	
START_STATION_NAME	V_String	33	
START_STATION_LATITUDE	FixedDecimal	13	9
START_STATION_LONGITUDE	FixedDecimal	13	9
STATION_ID	Int32	4	
END_STATION_NAME	V_String	33	
END_STATION_LATITUDE	FixedDecimal	13	9
END_STATION_LONGITUDE	FixedDecimal	13	9
BIKE_ID	V_String	5	
MEMBERSHIP_TYPE	V_String	1	
USERTYPE	V_String	10	
BIRTH_YEAR	V_String	4	
GENDER	Byte	1	

Table 1: FileStructure.xlsx content

If you'll be following along with your data, please make sure that you have a fixed text file and the field definitions for that file (field names, data types, and lengths).

How to do it...

1. Start by dropping a **Text Input** tool onto the canvas and create a field named XML, with the following content:

    ```
    <flatfile version="1">
       <file eoltype="crlf" allowShortLines="t"
    allowLongLines="f" trimWhiteSpace="t" />
       <fields>
    ```

2. Drop another **Text Input** tool, and create a field also called XML, with the following content:

    ```
       </fields>
    </flatfile>
    ```

3. Drop an **Input Data** tool into your canvas, point it to the ..\DATA DEFINITION\ FileStructure.xlsx file, and select the Sheet1 worksheet from it:

Figure 1.53: Input data

4. Now, add a **Formula** tool to the **Input Data** tool output anchor and create a new column, also named XML, with the following expression:

```
'     <field name="'+[Name]+'" type="'+ [Type] +'"
length="'+ ToString([Size])+
IIF([Type]="FixedDecimal",'"
scale="'+ToString([Scale]),'')
+'" />'
```

5. Use a **Select** tool following the **Formula** tool to only select the XML field (be sure to uncheck the *Unknown field too).

6. Drop a **Union** tool and connect the output anchors of the tools in this order:

   - First text input—Its connection will be labeled *#1*

   - Select tool—Will become connection *#2*

   - Second text input—Connection *#3*

   At this point, youll have something similar to this:

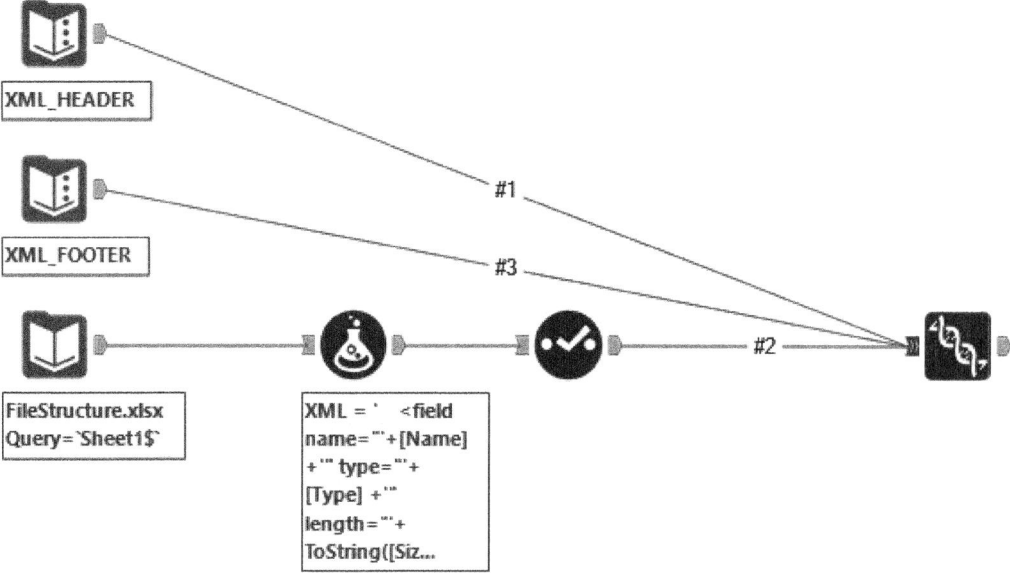

Figure 1.54: Connections to the Union tool

7. Now, click on the **Union** tool, make sure the method (on the top dropdown) is set to **Auto Config by Name**, which is the default setting, and check **Set a Specific Output Order** at the bottom of the configuration panel to set the order:

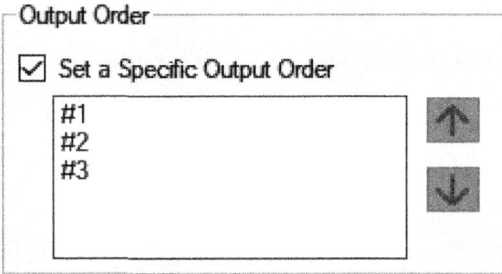

Figure 1.55: Setting the specific output order of records in the Union tool

8. To finish, we need to save the resulting XML file onto the DATA folder for later use, so we need to drop an **Output Data** tool following the **Union** tool and configure it, as in the following screenshot:

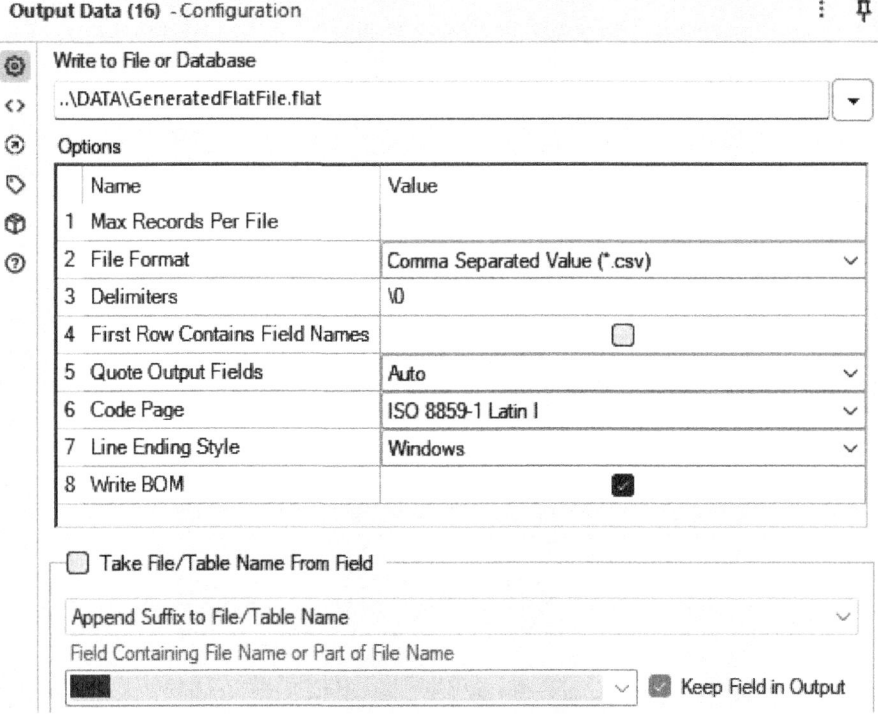

Figure 1.56: Saving the XML file (.flat)

Notice the \0 delimiter in option *3* and the unchecked box for **First Row Contains Field Names** (option *4*).

If you browse to your \DATA folder, you'll see the GeneratedFlatFile.flat file there.

9. Open it with the text editor of your choice, and you'll see this content:

```
<flatfile version="1">
  <file eoltype="crlf" allowShortLines="t" allowLongLines="f" trimWhiteSpace="t" />
  <fields>
    <field name="TRIPDURATION" type="Int32" length="4" />
    <field name="STARTTIME" type="DateTime" length="19" />
    <field name="STOPTIME" type="DateTime" length="19" />
    <field name="START_STATION_ID" type="V_String" length="4" />
    <field name="START_STATION_NAME" type="V_String" length="33" />
    <field name="START_STATION_LATITUDE" type="FixedDecimal" length="13" scale="9" />
    <field name="START_STATION_LONGITUDE" type="FixedDecimal" length="13" scale="9" />
    <field name="STATION_ID" type="Int32" length="4" />
    <field name="END_STATION_NAME" type="V_String" length="33" />
    <field name="END_STATION_LATITUDE" type="FixedDecimal" length="13" scale="9" />
    <field name="END_STATION_LONGITUDE" type="FixedDecimal" length="13" scale="9" />
    <field name="BIKE_ID" type="V_String" length="5" />
    <field name="MEMBERSHIP_TYPE" type="V_String" length="1" />
    <field name="USERTYPE" type="V_String" length="10" />
    <field name="BIRTH_YEAR" type="V_String" length="4" />
    <field name="GENDER" type="Byte" length="1" />
  </fields>
</flatfile>
```

Figure 1.57: Generated flat file contents

This ends the preparation step for this recipe, so from now on, we are going to use this `.flat` file as the template to read data files.

10. Create a new workflow and drop a **Data Input** tool, pointing to the `..\DATA\BikeRides.txt` file.

Since Alteryx doesn't recognize `.txt` as a known format, it'll prompt you for how this file must be treated:

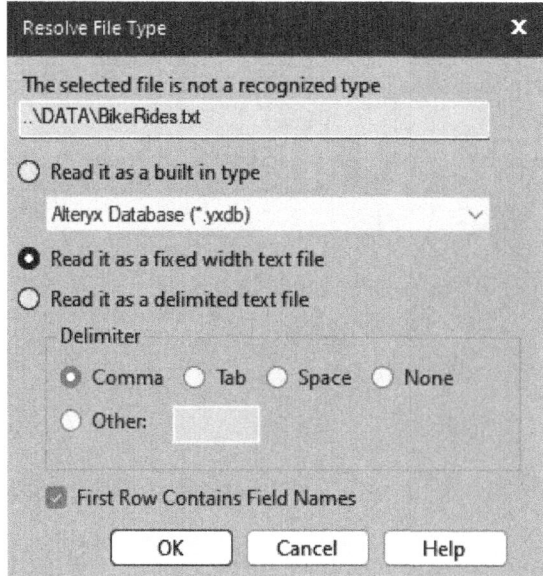

Figure 1.58: Reading an unknown format for Alteryx

11. Select **Read it as a fixed width text file** and click **OK**. A new window will pop up with three main sections:

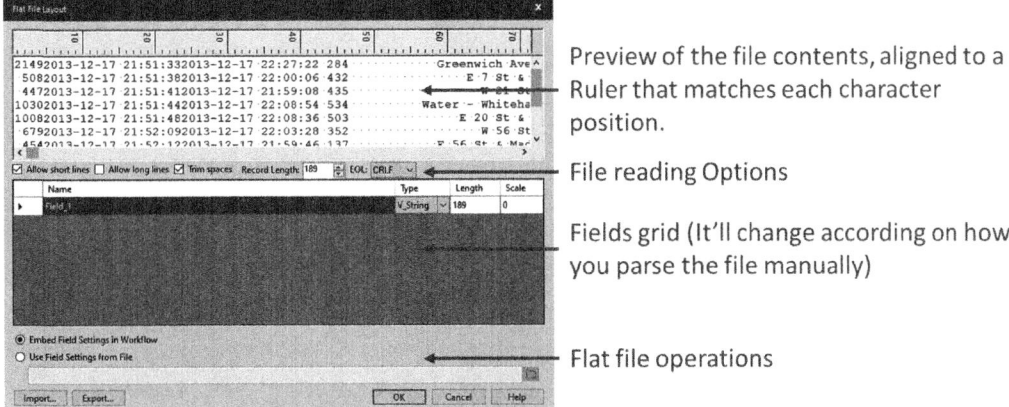

Preview of the file contents, aligned to a Ruler that matches each character position.

File reading Options

Fields grid (It'll change according on how you parse the file manually)

Flat file operations

Figure 1.59: Fixed-width file parsing utility

We can parse the file manually here, but we'll be using our generated template.

12. For this, click on **Use Field Settings from File** and the textbox will activate.

13. Click in the folder to browse to the `\DATA\GeneratedFlatFile.flat` file and select it.

You'll see your file completely parsed, and with the right field types and sizes:

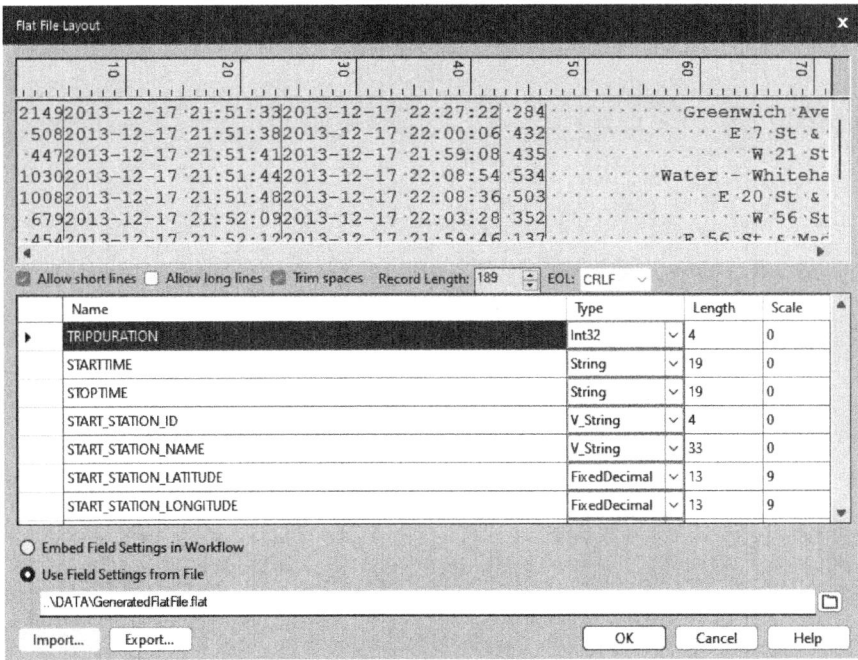

Figure 1.60: Red lines determine where a field ends and the next one starts

> **Note**
>
> Note that for the DateTime fields, Alteryx Designer automatically read them as strings (DateTimes are not allowed in this process, so we'll need to take care of them later on).

14. Hit **OK** and run the workflow. You'll see how your fixed text file is now completely parsed.

How it works...

Fixed-width text files are common in legacy systems, and since they do not have any indicator of what starts where, we need a file definition for each file.

Alteryx has a functionality that allows you to manually parse a text file (similar to what Excel allows you to do), but it can be time-consuming when you need to manually parse a file, and since most files need/have a field definition dictionary, we can automate this process by creating a helper workflow that'll generate it for us.

Every red line you put on the ruler to determine where each field ends and the next one starts, plus the ability to select its data type and size and scale, generates a `<field name=` line/record with attributes that are later saved to the XML file, wrapped around a `<flatfile...` definition and a `<file...` line registering special attributes for that particular template, for reusability.

2
Working with Databases

Accessing databases from Alteryx is very simple and fast. And the methods we use for files can apply to databases as well.

But databases have more peculiarities, many of which we, as analysts, cannot change (such as response speed, availability, and design).

Also, we'll be addressing the basics of **Data Connection Manager** (**DCM**), a very useful and powerful feature introduced by Alteryx in version 2021.4, but highly improved in version 2022.1.

DCM is a secure, centralized, single-source administration, storage, and connection-sharing capability for database and cloud interoperability, offering enhanced security improvements (credentials linked to data sources and resolved at runtime).

If you are an administrator within your company, you have probably already identified the huge benefits DCM brings to your job. If you're not, you'll realize how easy it is to administer your credentials and connections using DCM once you start using it.

Another powerful feature of Alteryx Designer is the **In-Database** (**In-DB**) tools. These tools allow us to perform blending and analysis against large sets of data without moving the data out of the database, providing performance improvements over the traditional methods, since everything is executed within our **Database Management System** (**DBMS**) and no traffic along the network is required (very low to no latency).

In this chapter, we'll be looking at some recipes to improve how we work with databases:

- Scanning databases dynamically (cursor behavior, but more efficient)
- Using Alteryx Calgary Databases
- Creating credentials in DCM
- Creating connections in DCM
- Getting information from your In-DB connections/queries

Technical requirements

We created a portable database (using SQLite) as a test set for these recipes, but if you want to try them with your own data, you'll need to have your connection information and access credentials at hand.

For the Calgary recipe, make sure you have enough free disk space (~2GB) on your computer.

> **Important note**
> Even when it's not required for the recipes, access to Alteryx Server will be needed in case you want to synchronize DCM against your existing enterprise credentials.

Cursor behavior, but more efficient

When working with databases, we call **cursor** to the process where, for each record of a given table, you need to sequentially scan/read all the records from a second table, in search of a condition.

This process is very useful for some use cases, but it might cause a huge overhead for the database management system and the network. For example, a cell phone provider company has all the data about each call – each IMEI for a period of time – and the marketing department is trying to predict the effects of a certain campaign on some customers.

If we analyze the amount of data produced by each call per phone, it'll be huge and it'll take us a lot of time. So, in this case, we probably will extract from the database the data associated with those customers targeted by the campaign first, then analyze it.

For that, we'll have a first input consisting of the conditions the targeted audience must fulfill, and we use that input data to scan and retrieve each record from the transactional data source (calls in this case) associated with the selected ones.

In this recipe, we'll learn how to perform a "cursor-like" reading of tables (for each record in one table, read all the records in a second table), using the **Dynamic Input** tool, avoiding the overhead, and not capturing the database's server resources.

Getting ready

For this example, we put together a portable database in SQLite that you can download from here:

```
https://github.com/PacktPublishing/Alteryx-Designer-Cookbook/
tree/main/ch2/Recipe1
```

This set contains a database with three tables:

- DOCUMENTS: Containing all the information about a company's billing (~254K records)

- ARTICLES: Containing a description of each ARTICLE_ID available for the company

- CUSTOMERS: FIRST, LAST, and EMAIL for each customer

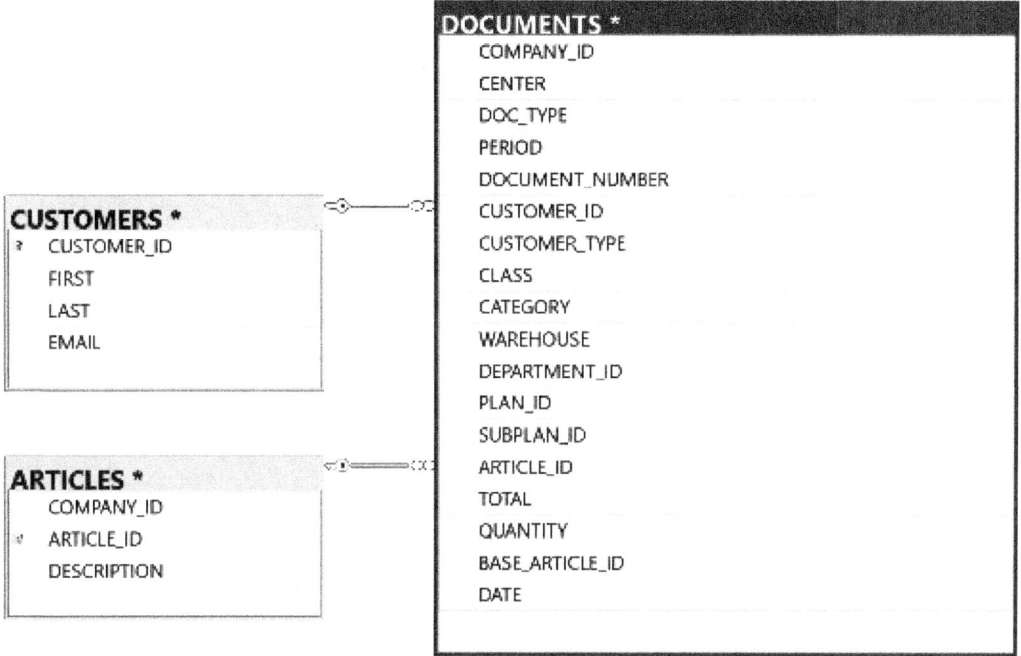

Figure 2.1: Database structure

The use case will be as follows: we, as a hardware store, need to gather the data corresponding to our top 10 CUSTOMERS from last year and get the top 10 ARTICLES each one bought.

We have DOCUMENTS (billing data) in one table, ARTICLES in another, and CUSTOMERS in a third one.

And our top 10 CUSTOMERS from last year come in an Excel File (DATA\Top10CUSTOMERS2021.xlsx).

How to do it...

We will do so using the following steps:

1. On a new workflow, drop an **Input Data** tool and point it to DATA\Top10CUSTOMERS2021.xlsx.

2. Select the 2021Top10 worksheet in **Select Excel Input** and click **OK**.

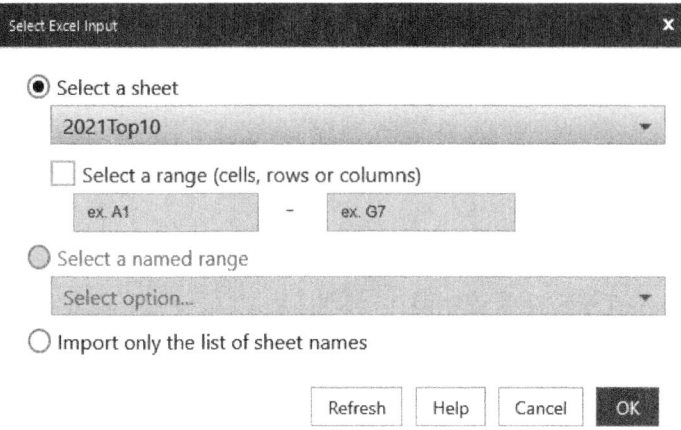

Figure 2.2: Select Excel Input

3. Drop a **Dynamic Input** tool (from the **Developer** category) and configure it as follows:

4. Click on **Edit...** for the **Input Data Source Template** option.

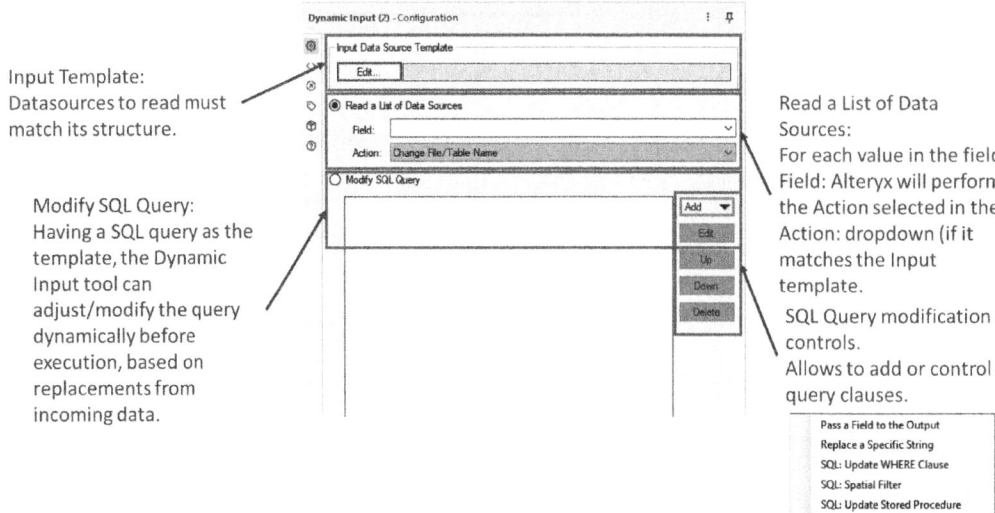

Figure 2.3: Dynamic Input tool configuration options

The **Connect a File or Database** screen will pop up.

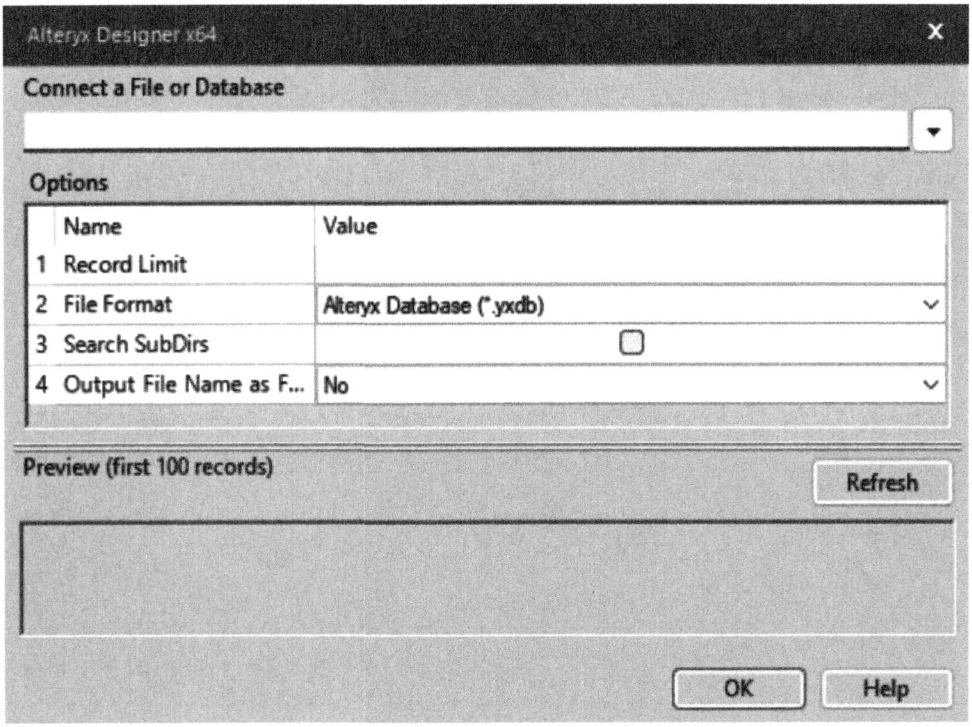

Figure 2.4: Dynamic Input template configuration

5. For the **Connect a File or Database** option, point it to the SQLite file. When prompted with
    Choose Table or Specify Query, click on the **SQL Editor** tab at the top of the window and
    write this SQL sentence:

    ```
    SELECT * FROM DOCUMENTS WHERE CUSTOMER_ID=1234 AND
    PERIOD=2022
    ```

    This can be seen here:

    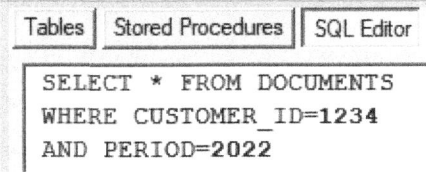

Figure 2.5: Dynamic Input template query

As you may notice, there is no CUSTOMER_ID=1234 in the database, but here is where Alteryx Designer will operate its magic.

Once Alteryx validates the query, your template will look like this:

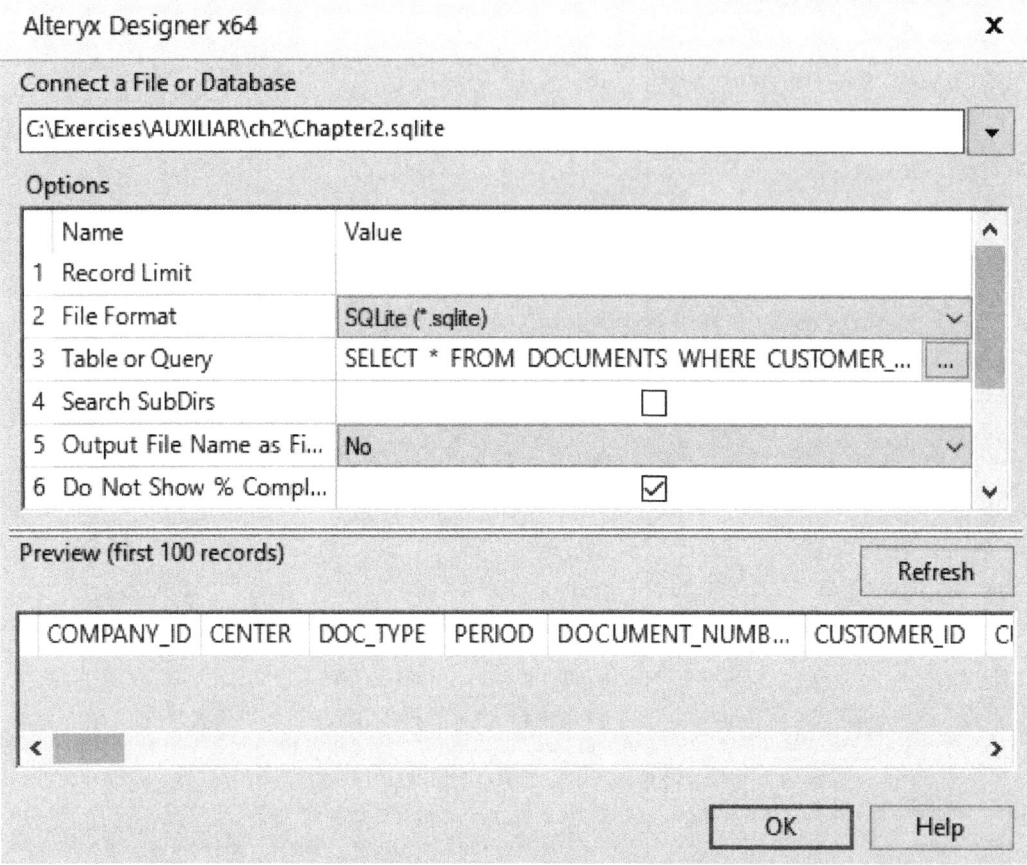

Figure 2.6: Template panel after the configuration

Now, we need to configure the action we want the tool to perform.

6. Select **Modify SQL Query**, and click **Add** on the right of the configuration panel. You'll be presented with five options. Select **SQL: Update WHERE Clause**:

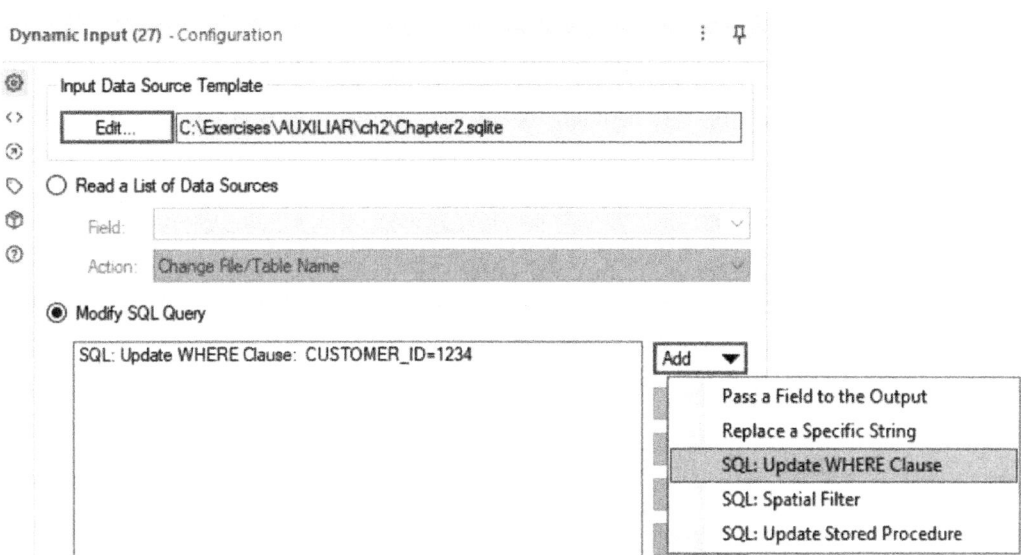

Figure 2.7: Modify SQL Query options

A new screen will be shown with pre-populated fields:

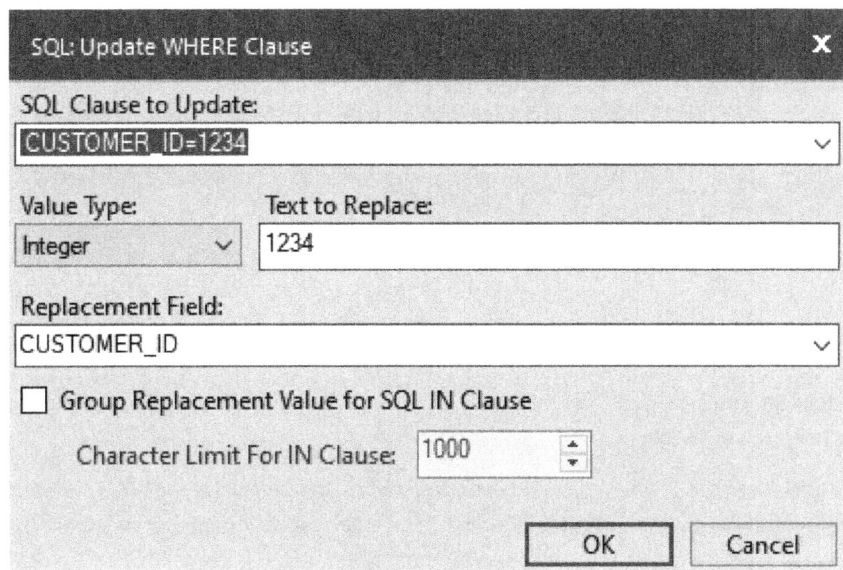

Figure 2.8: Configuring the Dynamic Input tool

7.   Make sure CUSTOMER_ID=1234 is selected for **SQL Clause to Update**, **Value Type** is set to **Integer**, **Text to Replace** is 1234 and **Replacement Field** shows **CUSTOMER_ID** and click **OK**.

If you run the workflow, you'll get all records for 2022 corresponding only to the customer IDs contained in the control file (top 10 buyers from the previous year). From here, you can start the process of getting the top 10 articles bought by each customer, but that will be part of another recipe.

How it works...

When configuring the **Dynamic Input** tool to any of the **Modify SQL Query** options, Alteryx Designer will read all the conditions within the query and will replace the parts you indicated within your selections. In this case, since **SQL: Update WHERE Clause** was selected, Alteryx will modify only the part corresponding to the WHERE CUSTOMER_ID = 1234 part.

For the second part of the clause (PERIOD=2022), since we didn't select any modifier for it, it'll remain untouched.

The amazing part is that Alteryx Designer will execute one straight query per record coming from the **Input Data** tool, so, instead of having a cursor scanning the database per record in the input file (a single process from start to finish), there'll be N individual queries running one after the other, causing the release of resources in the DBMS after each query.

Input Data (25)	10 records were read from "C:\Exercises\ch2\Recipe\DATA\Top10CUSTOMERS2021.xlsx" [2021Top10$]
Browse (26)	10 records
Dynamic Input (27)	171 records were read from "C:\Exercises\AUXILIAR\ch2\Chapter2.sqlite" (SELECT * FROM DOCUMENTS WHERE CUSTOMER_ID=74235 AND PERIOD=2022)
Dynamic Input (27)	168 records were read from "C:\Exercises\AUXILIAR\ch2\Chapter2.sqlite" (SELECT * FROM DOCUMENTS WHERE CUSTOMER_ID=75787 AND PERIOD=2022)
Dynamic Input (27)	115 records were read from "C:\Exercises\AUXILIAR\ch2\Chapter2.sqlite" (SELECT * FROM DOCUMENTS WHERE CUSTOMER_ID=75969 AND PERIOD=2022)
Dynamic Input (27)	147 records were read from "C:\Exercises\AUXILIAR\ch2\Chapter2.sqlite" (SELECT * FROM DOCUMENTS WHERE CUSTOMER_ID=96938 AND PERIOD=2022)
Dynamic Input (27)	97 records were read from "C:\Exercises\AUXILIAR\ch2\Chapter2.sqlite" (SELECT * FROM DOCUMENTS WHERE CUSTOMER_ID=110249 AND PERIOD=2022)
Dynamic Input (27)	12783 records were read from "C:\Exercises\AUXILIAR\ch2\Chapter2.sqlite" (SELECT * FROM DOCUMENTS WHERE CUSTOMER_ID=110522 AND PERIOD=2022)
Dynamic Input (27)	131 records were read from "C:\Exercises\AUXILIAR\ch2\Chapter2.sqlite" (SELECT * FROM DOCUMENTS WHERE CUSTOMER_ID=111029 AND PERIOD=2022)
Dynamic Input (27)	114 records were read from "C:\Exercises\AUXILIAR\ch2\Chapter2.sqlite" (SELECT * FROM DOCUMENTS WHERE CUSTOMER_ID=113001 AND PERIOD=2022)
Dynamic Input (27)	21 records were read from "C:\Exercises\AUXILIAR\ch2\Chapter2.sqlite" (SELECT * FROM DOCUMENTS WHERE CUSTOMER_ID=113045 AND PERIOD=2022)
Dynamic Input (27)	35 records were read from "C:\Exercises\AUXILIAR\ch2\Chapter2.sqlite" (SELECT * FROM DOCUMENTS WHERE CUSTOMER_ID=114959 AND PERIOD=2022)
Dynamic Input (27)	13782 records were read from 10 files/queries
Browse (28)	13,782 records

Figure 2.9: Multiple queries executed from just one tool

There's more...

Of course, you can combine multiple WHERE statements, and replace the part you need with incoming data every time you have to.

But, if you look at *Figure 2.7*, you have other options to make your database queries dynamic, such as replacing strings in queries, which can be very helpful for executing queries along different tables:

```
SELECT * FROM "TABLE" WHERE XXXX
```

You can set up a rule to indicate the tables you want to query, and in the WHERE clause, the conditions to query those tables, and all can be dynamic.

Working with Calgary databases

According to Alteryx's definition:

Calgary is a list count data retrieval engine designed to perform analyses on large scale databases containing millions of records. Calgary utilizes indexing methodology to quickly retrieve records. A database index is a data structure that improves the speed of data retrieval operations on a database table. Indexes can be created using one or more columns of a database table, providing the basis for both rapid random look ups and efficient access of ordered records.

Besides the actual definition, we can see Calgary as a proprietary file format, with the ability to handle huge amounts of data (~2B records) and to index the contents, so searches are extremely fast because there's no need to read all the records before filtering them.

Alteryx provides a tool category for Calgary containing a set of five native tools:

- **Calgary Input**: We'll use this tool to query Calgary databases
- **Calgary Join**: It'll allow us to take an input file and perform join queries against a Calgary database
- **Calgary Cross Count**: Performs aggregations across multiple Calgary databases and returns a count per record
- **Calgary Cross Count Append**: This will allow you to take an input file and append counts to records that join a Calgary database when those records match your criteria
- **Calgary Loader**: This is the tool we'll use to create/load data into a Calgary file (.cydb)

We'll be focusing on the Loader, Input, and Join tools throughout this recipe since they're the most used tools in this category.

Getting ready

We built a test set for this recipe you can download from here:

```
https://github.com/PacktPublishing/Alteryx-Designer-Cookbook/
tree/main/ch2/Recipe2
```

If you're planning to follow along with your own data, make sure you have a decent number of records in your dataset (millions).

In both cases, make sure that you have at least 2 GB of available disk space on your computer.

How to do it...

There are two phases in this recipe:

1. Creating/loading our data into a Calgary database
2. Consuming the loaded data

To create/load the data, we will use the following steps:

1. Drop an **Input Data** tool on the canvas and point it to the `CitiBike_2013.zip` file.
2. Immediately, you'll be prompted to select which file/s to read from the ZIP file and the type of the files. In our example, there's just one, so select it and make sure that **Select file type to extract** is set to **Comma Separated Value (*.csv)** and click **Open**.

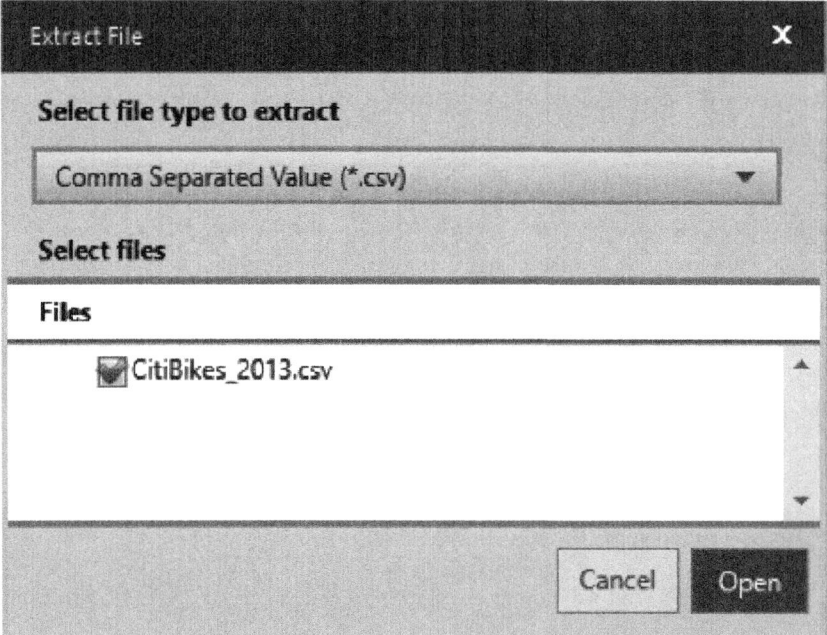

Figure 2.10: Read a file from a ZIP file

3. Go to the **Input Data** tool configuration panel and make sure you change option **9**, **Delimiters**, from a comma (,) to a pipe (|).

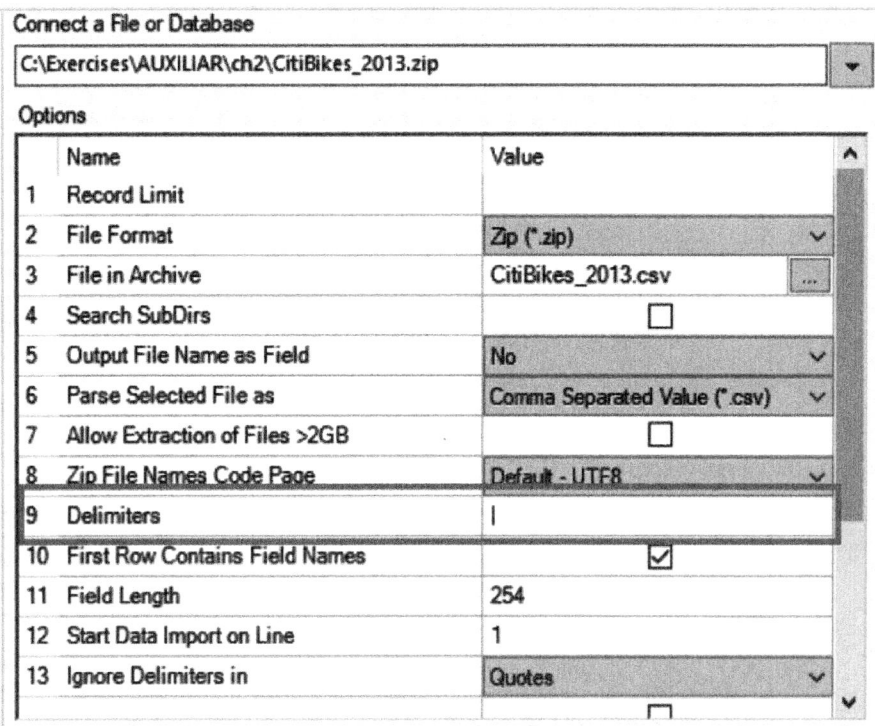

Figure 2.11: Input Data configuration panel – Delimiter option

4. Click the **Refresh** button and your **Preview** data will change from the following:

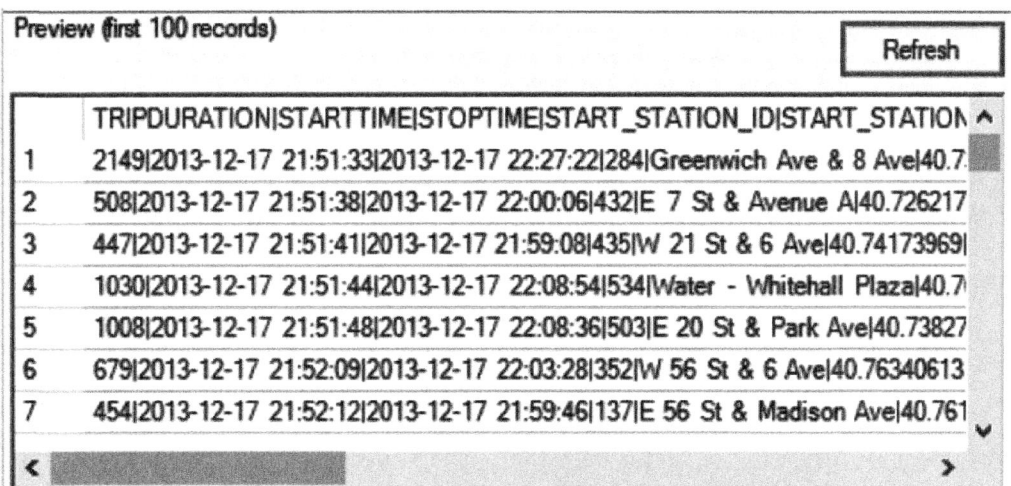

Figure 2.12: Contents with the wrong delimiter

It will change to this:

	TRIPDURATION	STARTTIME	STOPTIME	START_STATION_
1	2149	2013-12-17 21:51:33	2013-12-17 22:27:22	284
2	508	2013-12-17 21:51:38	2013-12-17 22:00:06	432
3	447	2013-12-17 21:51:41	2013-12-17 21:59:08	435
4	1030	2013-12-17 21:51:44	2013-12-17 22:08:54	534
5	1008	2013-12-17 21:51:48	2013-12-17 22:08:36	503
6	679	2013-12-17 21:52:09	2013-12-17 22:03:28	352
7	454	2013-12-17 21:52:12	2013-12-17 21:59:46	137

Figure 2.13: After selecting the right delimiter for our file

5. Add a **Select** tool to the canvas, and from the **Options** menu, click **Save/Load** and **Load Fields Names & Types**.

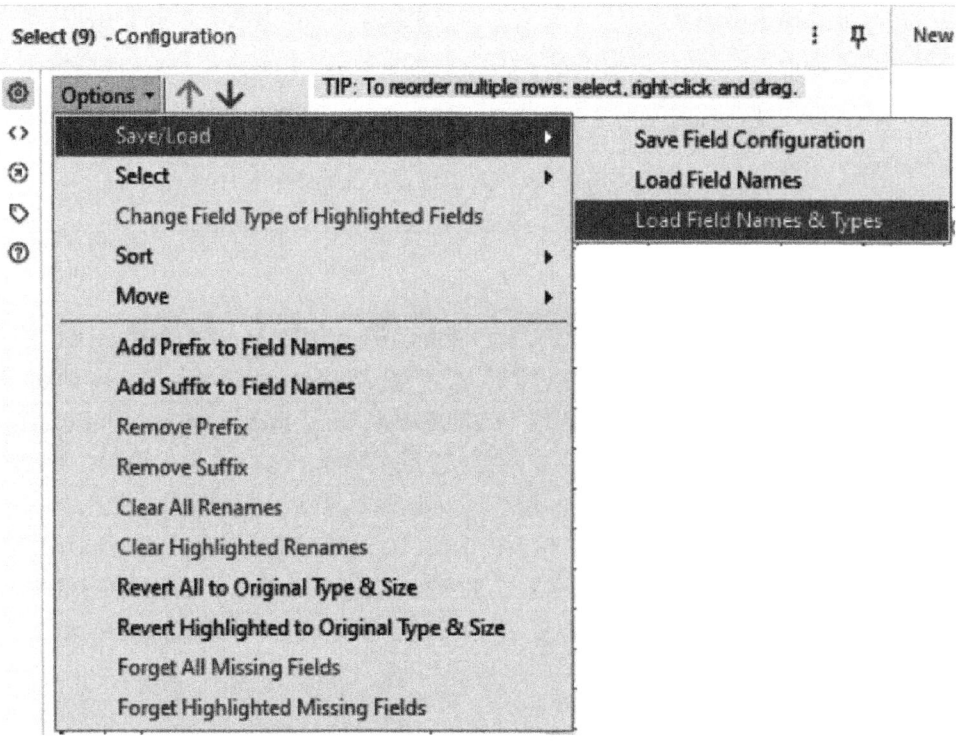

Figure 2.14: Shaping the data types based on saved configurations

6. Point to where you saved the recipe test set FIELD_TYPES\CitibikesFieldConfigura-
    tion.yxft and your **Select** tool will be populated with the field definitions saved in that file.

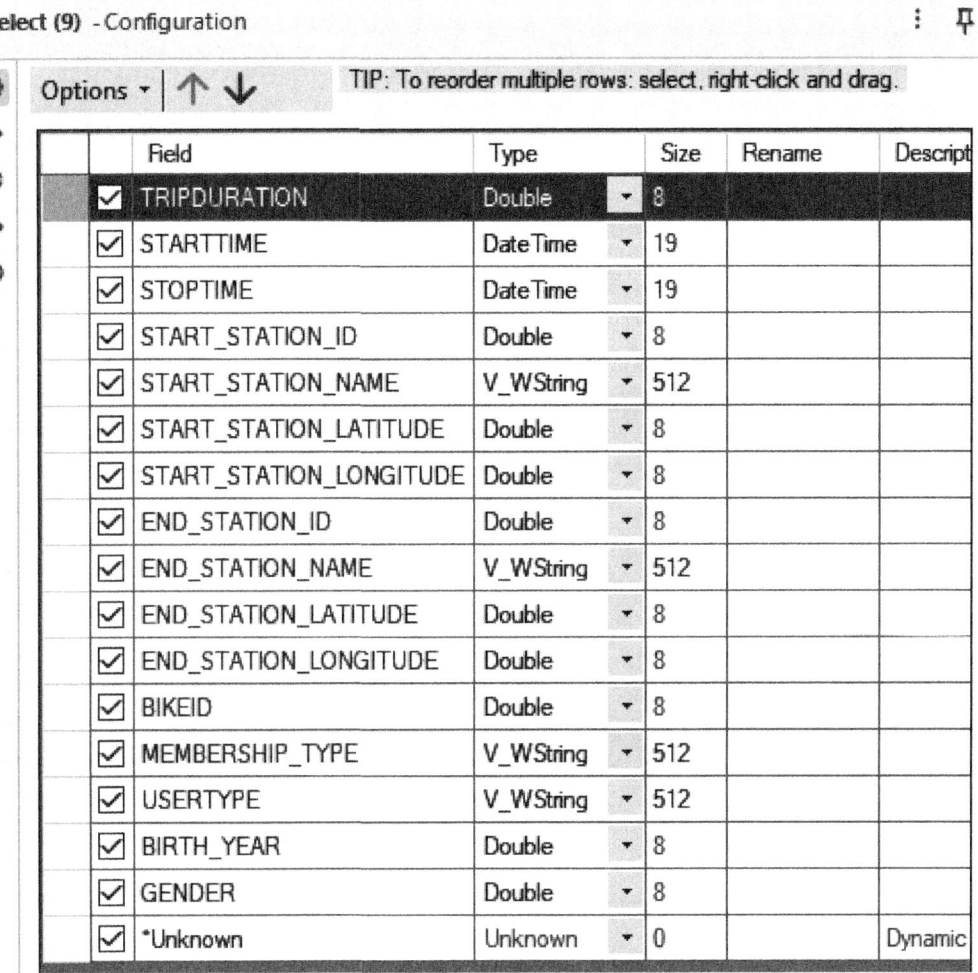

Figure 2.15: Resulting shape of our data

7. Now, drop a **Calgary Loader** tool from the Calgary category.

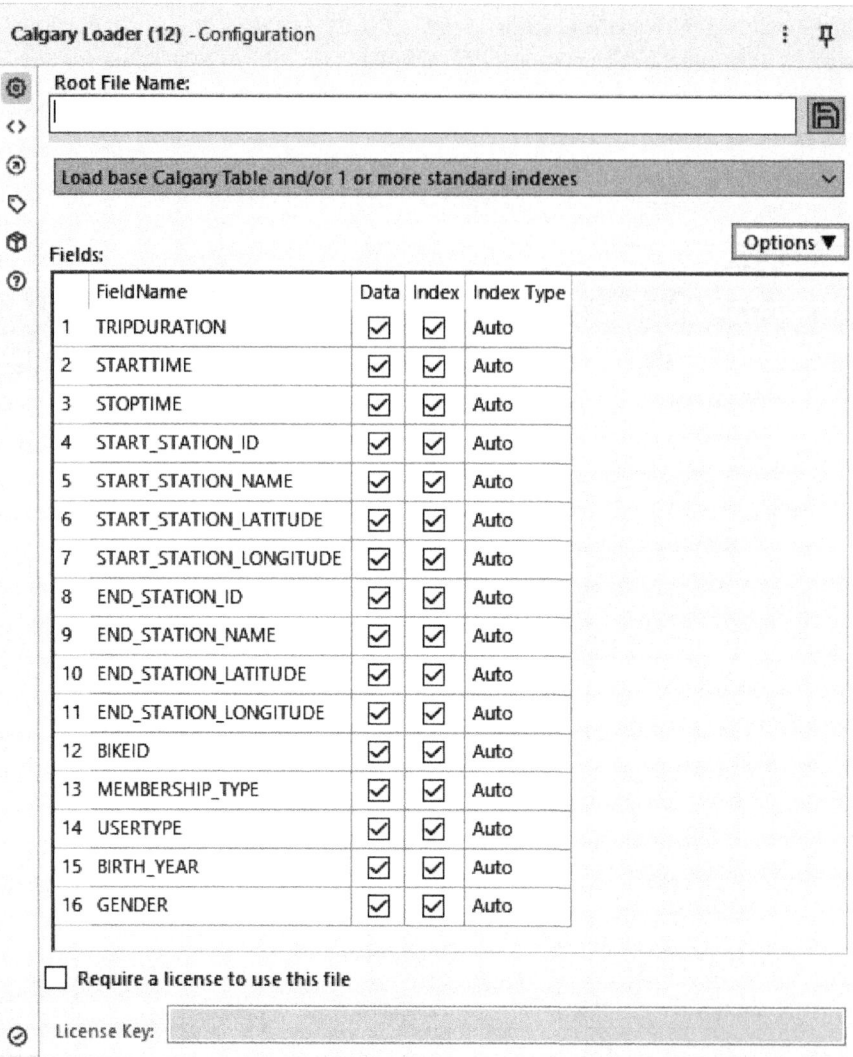

Figure 2.16: Calgary Loader configuration panel

8. Point **Root File Name** to the folder you want to save your files in and give the file a name. As a best practice, consider using a single folder per Calgary set of files.

At this point, we can select which fields to keep (save) in the Calgary file and which ones we'll be using to index. For this recipe, we'll be indexing all fields, with the Auto index type.

Run the workflow and you'll see that the file is being created and the data is being indexed. While loading and indexing, Alteryx analyzes the contents of our data (the first million records), selecting the best type of index based on the values contained within it.

Results - Workflow - Messages

≡	All	ⓘ 0 Errors ⓘ 0 Conv Errors ⚠ 0 Warnings ▭ 34 Messages 🖫 2 Files
⑦	▭ **Designer x64**	**Started running C:\Exercises\AUXILIAR\ch2\LoadFromZip.yxmd at 08/05/2022 10:00:58**
	▭ Calgary Loader (10)	BIKEID: Autoselected to high selectivity.
	▭ Input Data (11)	5614888 records were read from "C:\Exercises\AUXILIAR\ch2\CitiBikes_2013.zip" (CitiBikes_2013.csv)
	▭ Calgary Loader (10)	BIKEID: 6533 unique values; average of 859.5 records per value.
	▭ Calgary Loader (10)	BIRTH_YEAR: Autoselected to low selectivity.
	▭ Calgary Loader (10)	BIRTH_YEAR: 84 unique values; average of 66843.9 records per value.
	▭ Calgary Loader (10)	END_STATION_ID: Autoselected to high selectivity.
	▭ Calgary Loader (10)	END_STATION_LATITUDE: Autoselected to high selectivity.
	▭ Calgary Loader (10)	END_STATION_ID: 339 unique values; average of 16563.1 records per value.
	▭ Calgary Loader (10)	END_STATION_LATITUDE: 368 unique values; average of 15257.8 records per value.
	▭ Calgary Loader (10)	END_STATION_LONGITUDE: Autoselected to high selectivity.
	▭ Calgary Loader (10)	END_STATION_NAME: Autoselected to high selectivity.
	▭ Calgary Loader (10)	END_STATION_LONGITUDE: 368 unique values; average of 15257.8 records per value.
	▭ Calgary Loader (10)	END_STATION_NAME: 368 unique values; average of 15257.8 records per value.
	▭ Calgary Loader (10)	GENDER: Autoselected to low selectivity.
	▭ Calgary Loader (10)	GENDER: 3 unique values; average of 1871629.3 records per value.
	▭ Calgary Loader (10)	MEMBERSHIP_TYPE: Autoselected to high selectivity.
	▭ Calgary Loader (10)	MEMBERSHIP_TYPE: 1 unique values; average of 5614888.0 records per value.
	▭ Calgary Loader (10)	START_STATION_ID: Autoselected to high selectivity.
	▭ Calgary Loader (10)	START_STATION_LATITUDE: Autoselected to high selectivity.
	▭ Calgary Loader (10)	START_STATION_ID: 338 unique values; average of 16612.1 records per value.
	▭ Calgary Loader (10)	START_STATION_LATITUDE: 367 unique values; average of 15299.4 records per value.
	▭ Calgary Loader (10)	START_STATION_LONGITUDE: Autoselected to high selectivity.
	▭ Calgary Loader (10)	START_STATION_NAME: Autoselected to high selectivity.
	▭ Calgary Loader (10)	START_STATION_LONGITUDE: 367 unique values; average of 15299.4 records per value.
	▭ Calgary Loader (10)	START_STATION_NAME: 367 unique values; average of 15299.4 records per value.
	▭ Calgary Loader (10)	STARTTIME: Autoselected to high selectivity.
	▭ Calgary Loader (10)	STOPTIME: Autoselected to high selectivity.
	▭ Calgary Loader (10)	STARTTIME: 4364797 unique values; average of 1.3 records per value.
	▭ Calgary Loader (10)	STOPTIME: 4378397 unique values; average of 1.3 records per value.
	▭ Calgary Loader (10)	TRIPDURATION: Autoselected to high selectivity.
	▭ Calgary Loader (10)	TRIPDURATION: 20776 unique values; average of 270.3 records per value.
	▭ Calgary Loader (10)	USERTYPE: Autoselected to low selectivity.
	▭ Calgary Loader (10)	USERTYPE: 2 unique values; average of 2807444.0 records per value.
	🖫 Calgary Loader (10)	5614888 records were written to C:\Exercises\AUXILIAR\ch2\CALGARY\DB\CitiBike.cydb
	▭ Calgary Loader (10)	Index verification started for: "C:\Exercises\AUXILIAR\ch2\CALGARY\DB\CitiBike.cydb"
	▭ Calgary Loader (10)	Index verification complete, elapsed time: 2.7s
	▭ **Designer x64**	**Finished running LoadFromZip.yxmd in 1:46 minutes**

Figure 2.17: Results of running the workflow

By now, we'll have the files (one `.cydb` and one `.cyidx` per indexed field, plus `SelectedName_Indexes.xml` containing the index values).

Now, onto making fast queries to our Calgary database. For querying Calgary, Alteryx offers two methods:

- **Static**: Using the **Calgary Input** tool, you can define your query within the tool configuration panel

- **Dynamic**: Based on a data stream, you can query your Calgary database dynamically using conditions

We can build a static query as follows:

We'll be extracting all trips made by people that are 50 years old or more. Since the data is from 2013, we'll be querying the dataset for those records with BIRTH_YEAR <= 1963:

1. Drop a **Calgary Input** tool onto the canvas.

2. Point the **Calgary Data File** option to the Citibike.cydb file we just created.

    Once you point to the file, the tool's configuration panel will show you the options for building the query:

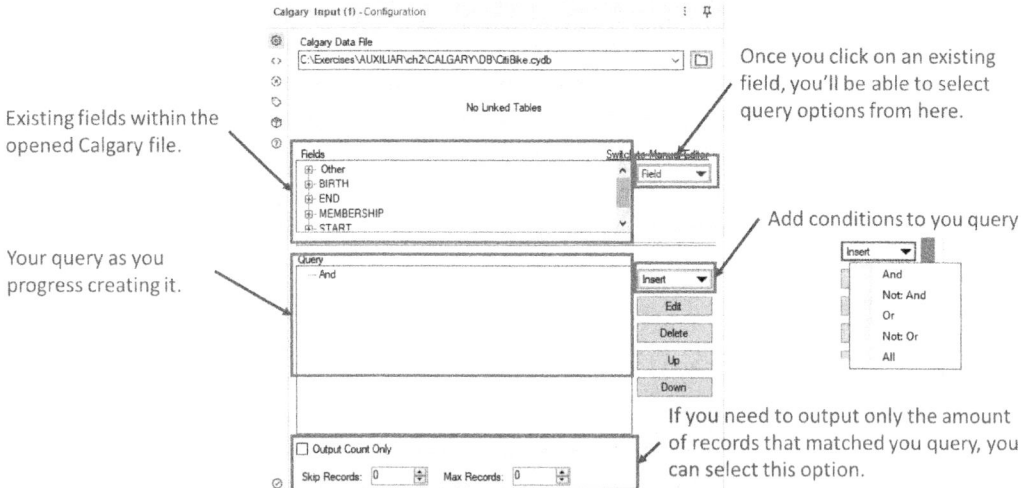

Figure 2.18: Calgary Input configuration

3. From the BIRTH group, double-click on the YEAR field. Alteryx will pop up a new window – **Edit Query Item**.

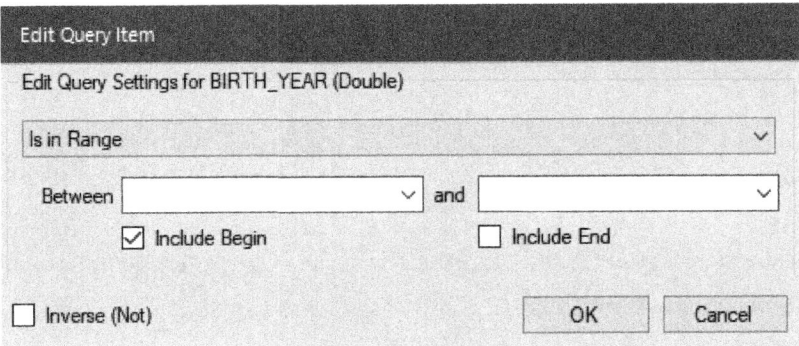

Figure 2.19: Setting the query item

4. We need to get a range starting at any value, but only up to 1963. So, uncheck **Include Begin**, check **Include End**, and enter 1963 for the end value.

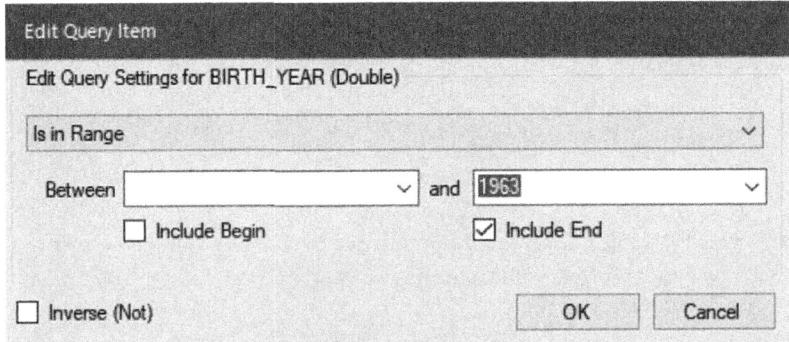

Figure 2.20: Using only range end

5. Click **OK**.

Your actual query clause will be added to the **Query** section of the configuration panel.

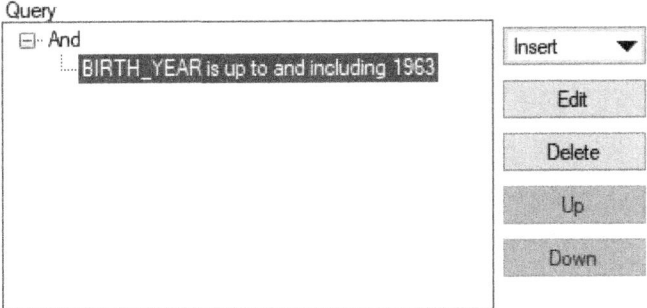

Figure 2.21: Query clause in the configuration panel

6. Drop a **Browse** tool following the **Calgary Input** tool and run the workflow. You'll be able to see all data regarding trips made by people 50 years or older.

We will now dynamically query a Calgary database:

We are going to query the Calgary database for the same results but using a different approach. We'll be getting some input from a data stream and using those values to query/join against the Calgary database:

1. In this case, we are going to use the age limit as an input, so drop a **Text Input** tool onto the canvas.

2. Create a column called AGE_LIMIT and add a record with 50 as the value.

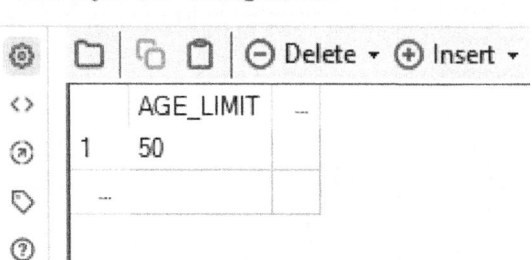

Figure 2.22: Incoming data

Since the input data we have is the minimum age to consider (remember, we are going to get rides done by people 50 years old or more), we need to transform it, so we can query our data based on BIRTH_YEAR.

3. Connect a **Formula** tool to the **Text Input** output anchor, and create a new field called MAX_BORN with the following expression to determine which year is the maximum to query (remember that data is from 2013):

```
2013-[AGE_LIMIT]
```

4. Add a second column called MIN_BORN with the value 1000 (to ensure all data that represents any year before 1963 is considered).

Your **Formula** tool must look like this:

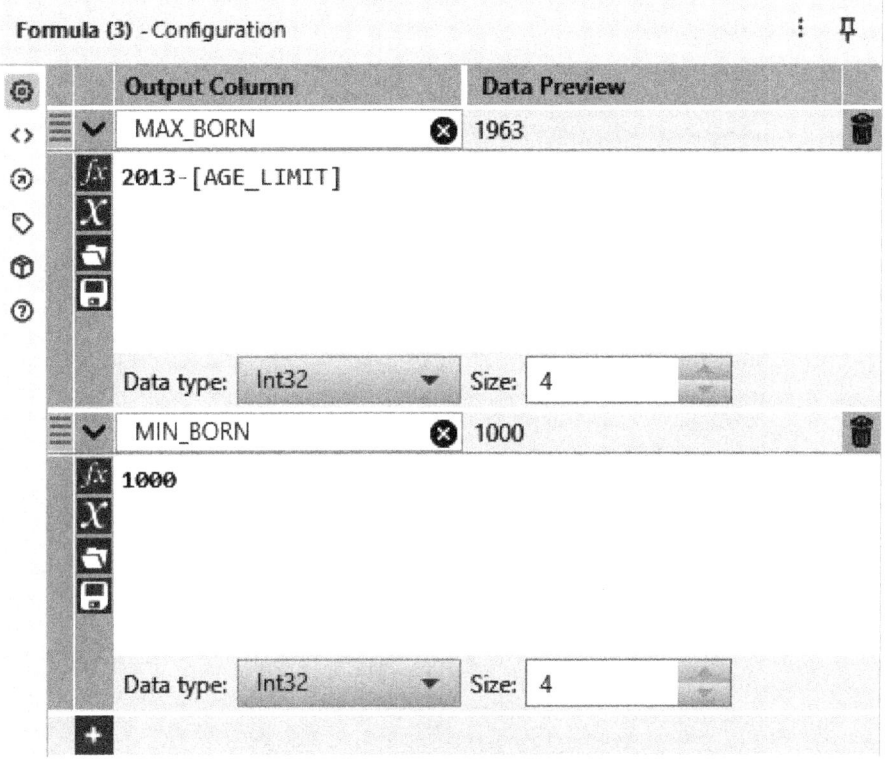

Figure 2.23: Formula to determine the range

At this point, we have already defined our year range to query (from 1000 to 1963):

Record	AGE_LIMIT	MAX_BORN	MIN_BORN
1	50	1963	1000

Figure 2.24: Input data enriched

5.   Connect a **Calgary Join** tool to the **Text Input** tool and point **Calgary Data File** to CitiBike. cydb.

6.   Select **Join Query Results to Each Input Record** for the **Action** option.

7.   Click on the MIN_BORN input field and select **BIRTH_YEAR** for **Index Field**, **Range - >=Begin AND <=End** for **Query Type**, and MAX_BORN for **End of Range**, as in the screenshot here:

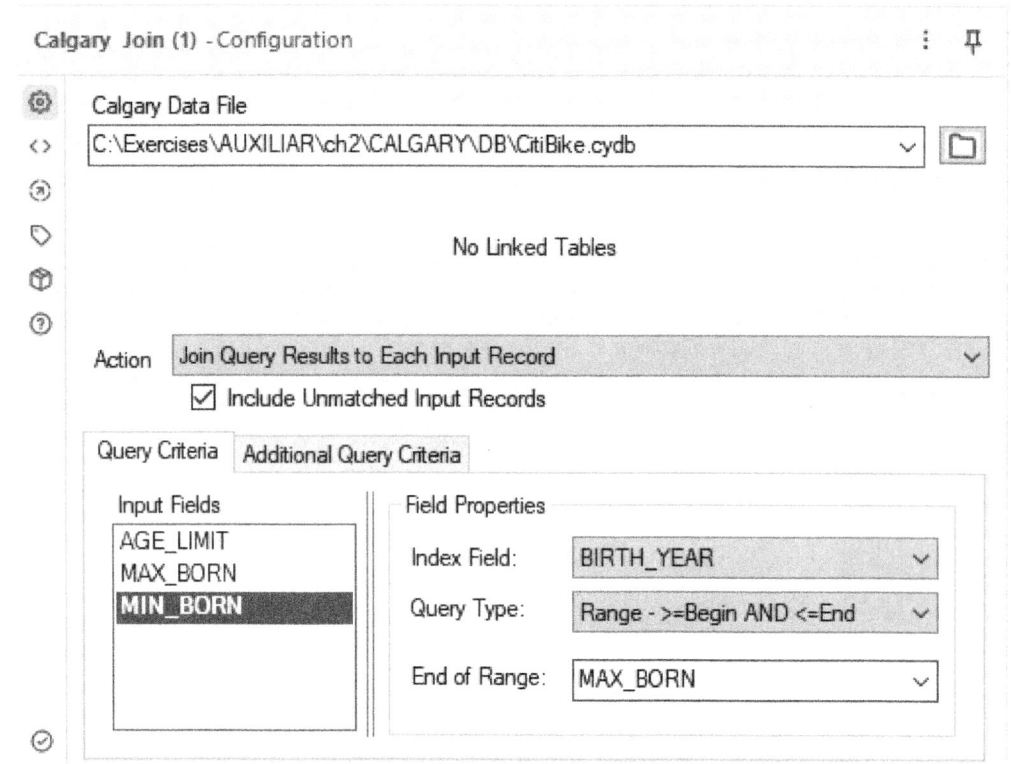

Figure 2.25: Calgary Join configured

If you run the workflow, you'll see that you'll get the same records as we got using the static query with the **Calgary Input** tool.

How it works...

Calgary is a proprietary format developed by Alteryx that provides very high compression and very fast reading performance and indexing, making it ideal to work with huge amounts of data for lookups.

We recommend always enriching your data as much as you can before creating a Calgary file (very similar to what you'll do when you create a multidimensional cube). For example, given the use case we used in this recipe, we'll probably add the age of each person in the Calgary database when creating it, so we can use the **Calgary Join** tool directly on the AGE input.

The **Calgary Input** tool is very straightforward, allowing you to build queries in a simple way and retrieve the results very fast.

The **Calgary Join** tool is more complex and provides lots of options to query the data based on incoming/existing data streams, multiple indices, and several actions.

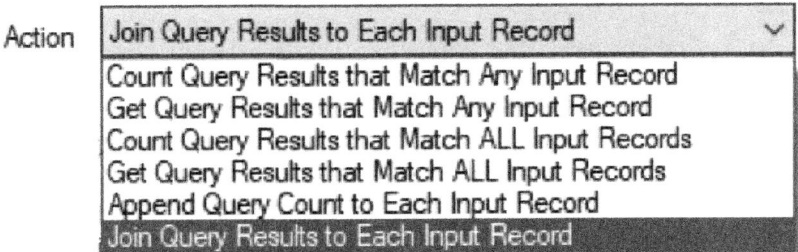

Figure 2.26: Calgary Join actions

> **Important note**
> You can't append records to a Calgary database, you need to re-create it.

There's more...

As you already may have noticed, the **Calgary Input** tool organizes the fields based on their names, so for example, for all the fields starting with START_ or END_, it created a group that has all the fields starting with START_ or END_ in it (such as START_STATION_ID or START_STATION_NAME).

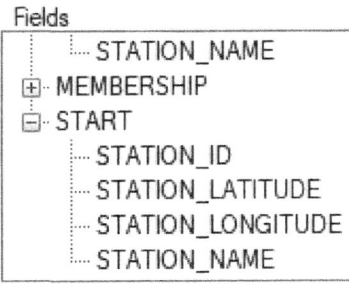

Figure 2.27: Fields grouped by prefix

It is good practice to add a prefix to your fields to have them organized.

Since Alteryx looks at the first million records to select the index type when set to **Auto**, it might select the incorrect type for your dataset. It's a good practice to analyze your data first and determine the selectivity of each index, based on the number of different values each data field might have. This can be easily achieved using a **Summarize** tool configured to perform a **Count Distinct** action on each field to be indexed.

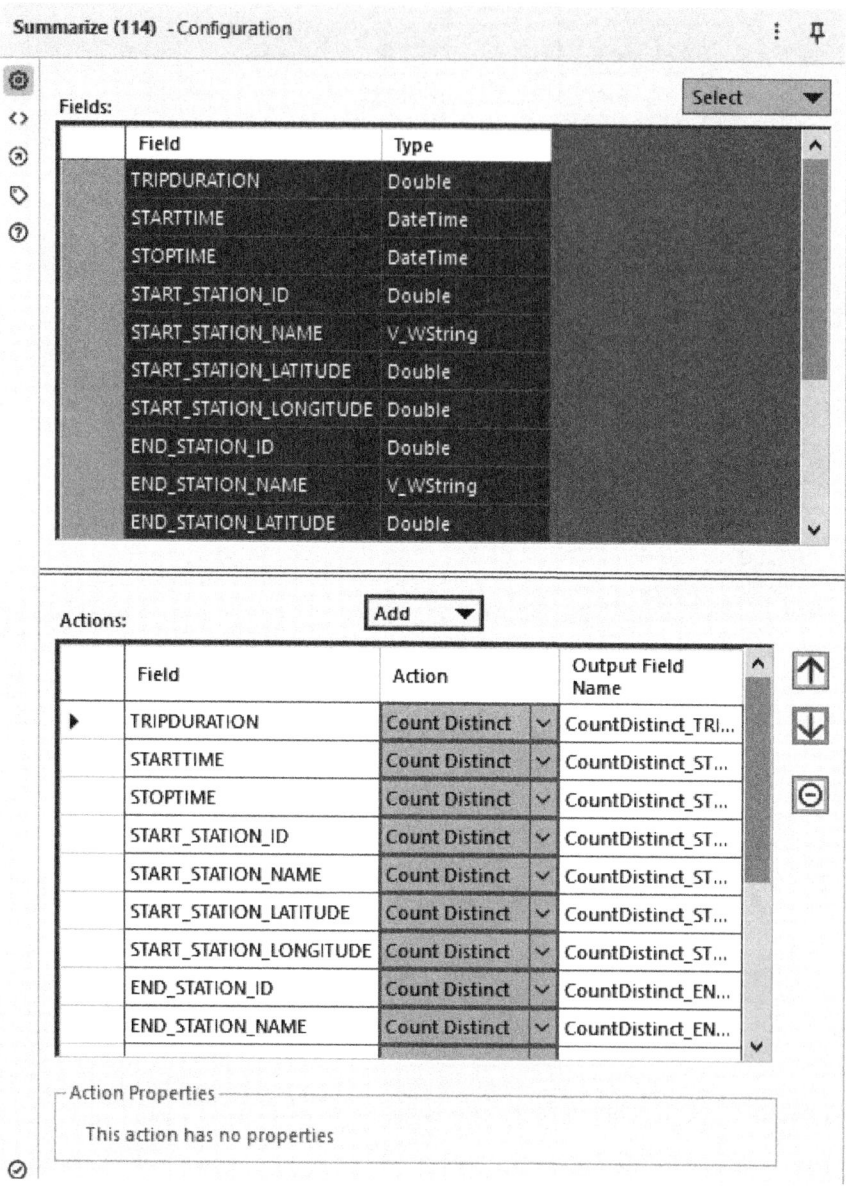

Figure 2.28: Count Distinct on each field to Index

The rules of thumb for this selection are as follows:

- If your field has many possible values (more than 550), use **High Selectivity** (for example, BIKE_ID)

- If your field has fewer unique values (less than 550), use **Low Selectivity** (for example, GENDER)

Doing this will also reduce the time Alteryx Designer needs to analyze your data (1 million records per index) and create the indices.

Finally, another good practice, that'll make your work easier is adding flags or identifiers to the data before loading a Calgary database, such as a CURRENT_PERIOD field to easily query all records corresponding to the current period, or a SAME_PERIOD_LAST_YEAR field to get all the records corresponding to a particular period, but from last year.

You can also read Calgary files with a regular **Input Data** tool, but can't take advantage of the indices (so the Calgary files will behave like a .yxdb file).

DCM – setting up credentials

As we saw in this chapter introduction, DCM allows you to administer credentials and passwords in a single-source, centralized way, so it solves some pain points, for example, multiple credential inputs, credentials being unsafely shared, loss of connection to data sources upon workflow sharing, among others.

Before getting into the matter, we need to identify three types of objects/concepts within DCM:

- **Credentials**: Authentication mechanism for the specific technology
- **Data Sources**: All accessible technologies supported by Alteryx
- **Connections**: The combination of a data source and the credentials used to validate within

Also, if you have Alteryx Server, you can synchronize and share your connections against it. If you don't, credentials, data sources, and connections created with DCM will remain local.

Getting ready

To follow this recipe, you must enable DCM on Alteryx Designer. To do so, go to **Options** → **User Settings** → **Edit User Settings** and from the **DCM** tab click on **Enable DCM**.

If the **Enable DCM** option appears disabled to you, click first on **Override DCM System Settings**, and it will enable it.

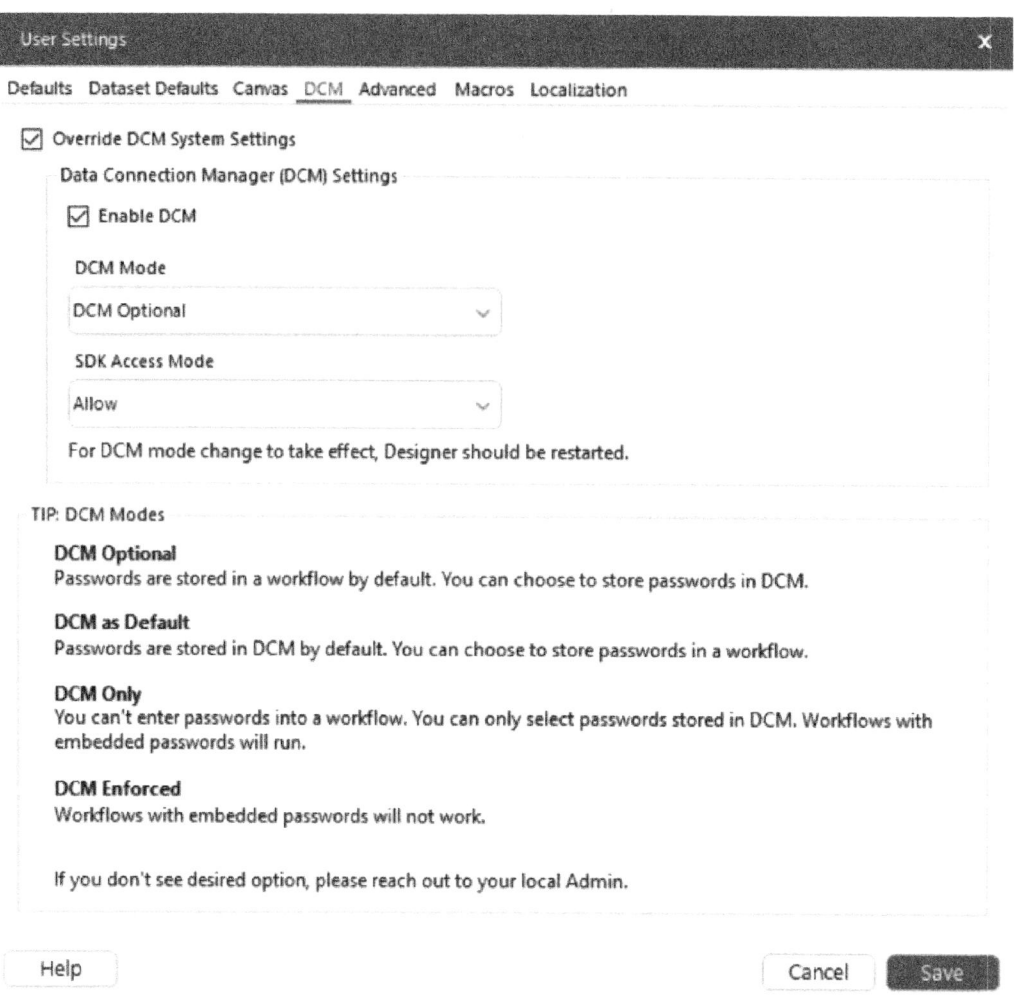

Figure 2.29: DCM options in User Settings

Make sure **DCM Optional** is the selected value for **DCM Mode** and **SDK Access Mode** is set to **Allow**.

Restart Alteryx Designer and you'll be ready to work with DCM.

How to do it...

We will get started using the following steps:

1.   Go to **File → Manage Connections**.

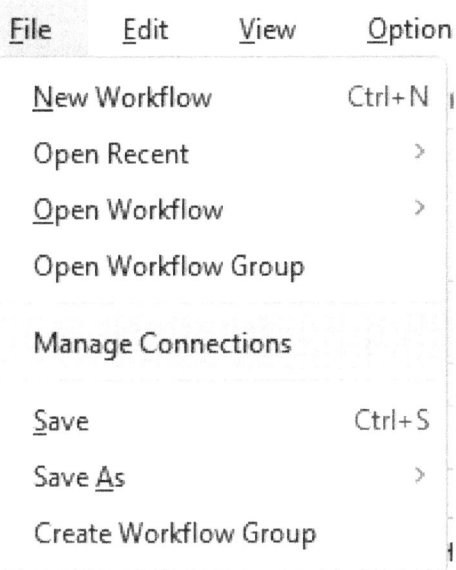

Figure 2.30: Manage Connections menu

A new window is displayed (yours might be blank):

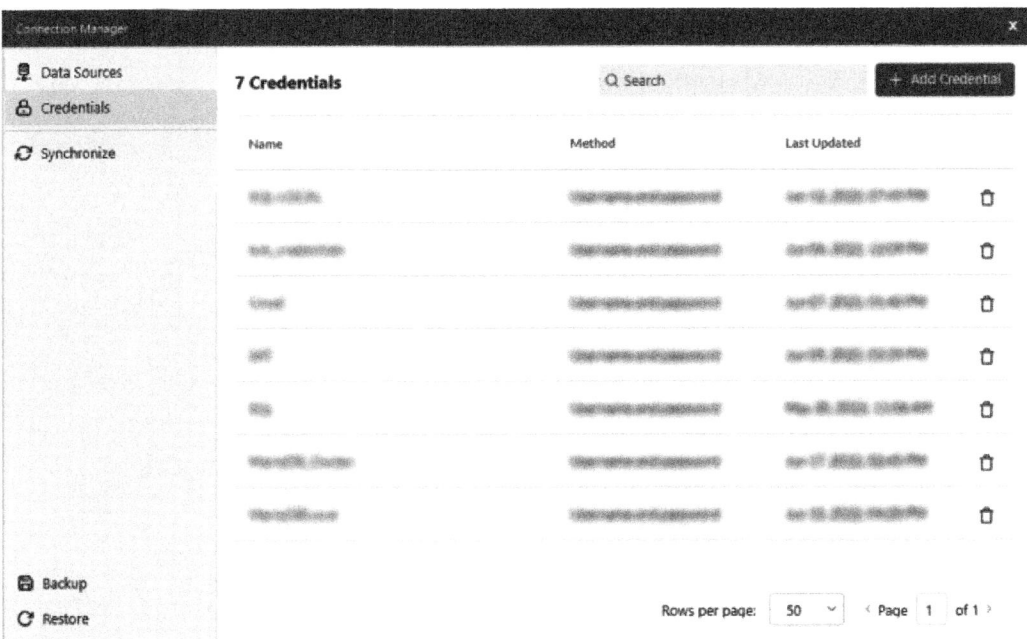

Figure 2.31: DCM main window

2. Click on + **Add Credential** at the top right of the window and Alteryx will ask you to enter values for **Credential Name** and **Method**.

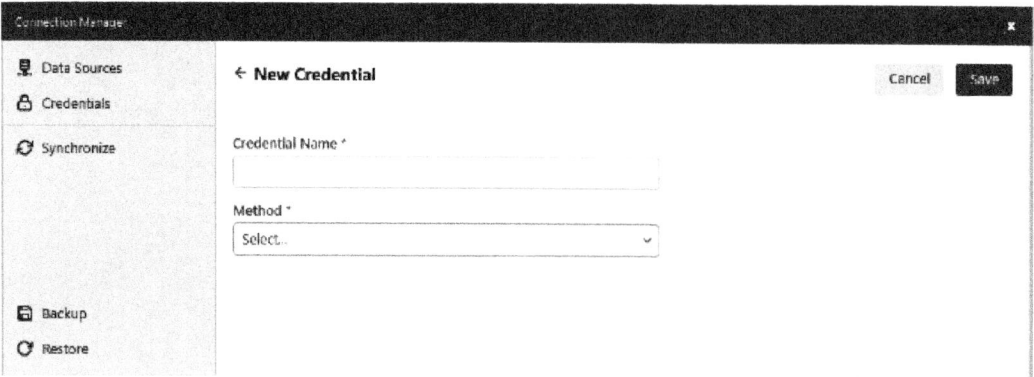

Figure 2.32: DCM main window

3. Enter a meaningful name for your credential, such as SQL SERVER System Administrator, and select from the dropdown for **Method**. In this case, we'll be using **Username and password**.

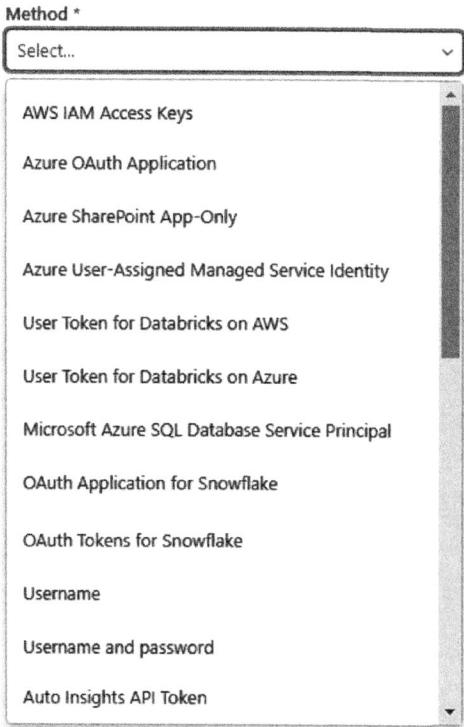

Figure 2.33: Credential Method options

4. Once you make a selection for **Method**, Alteryx will show you the **Username** and **Password** input fields, so fill them in with your credentials.

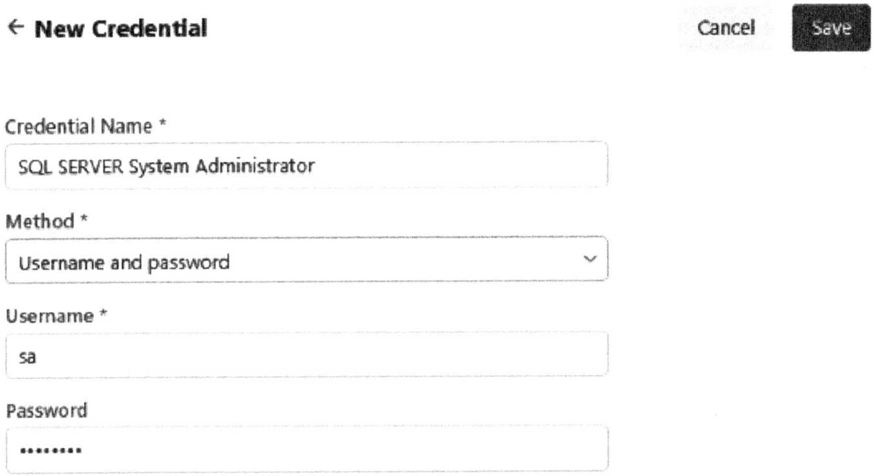

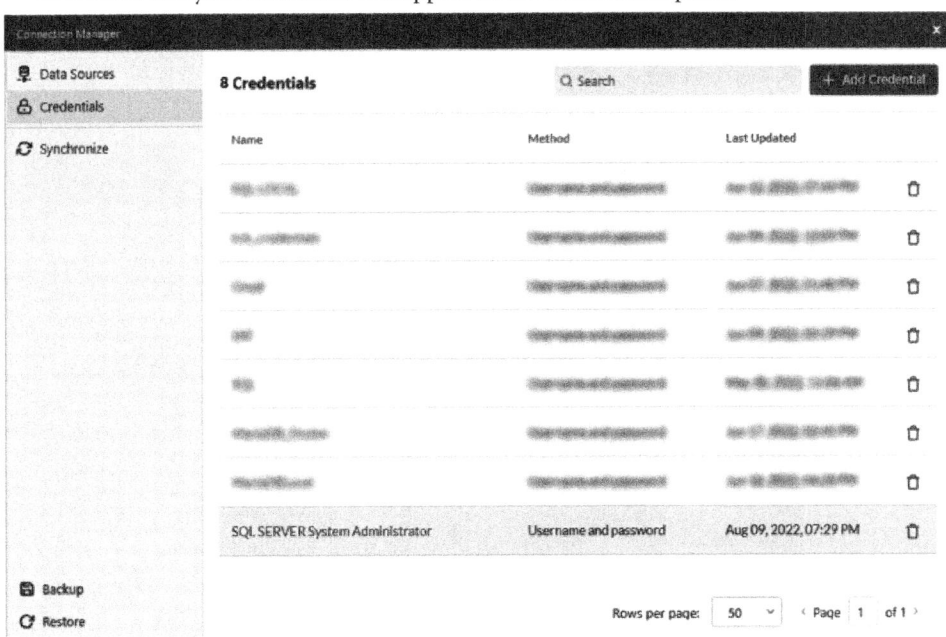

Figure 2.34: Credential Method options

Click **Save** and your credential will appear in the **Credentials** panel.

Figure 2.35: New credential added

Thus, we have learned how to set up credentials using DCM.

How it works...

DCM saves the credential information provided as a credential object, encrypted as a secure object, and makes it available to be reused when you need it.

This actually improves the way that credentials are managed, since using DCM changes how that information is saved (if DCM is disabled, credentials are embedded within the workflow).

DCM – setting up a connection

To be able to connect to data using credentials, DCM needs you to create a connection. A connection object is a combination of a data source and a set of credentials.

In this recipe, we'll be creating a new connection using DCM capabilities.

Getting ready

We'll prepare to do this using the following steps:

1. If you've already enabled DCM on Alteryx Designer you can skip this next step, otherwise, you need to do it to make DCM available for you. To do so, go to **Options** → **User Settings** → **Edit User Settings** and from the **DCM** tab click on **Enable DCM**.

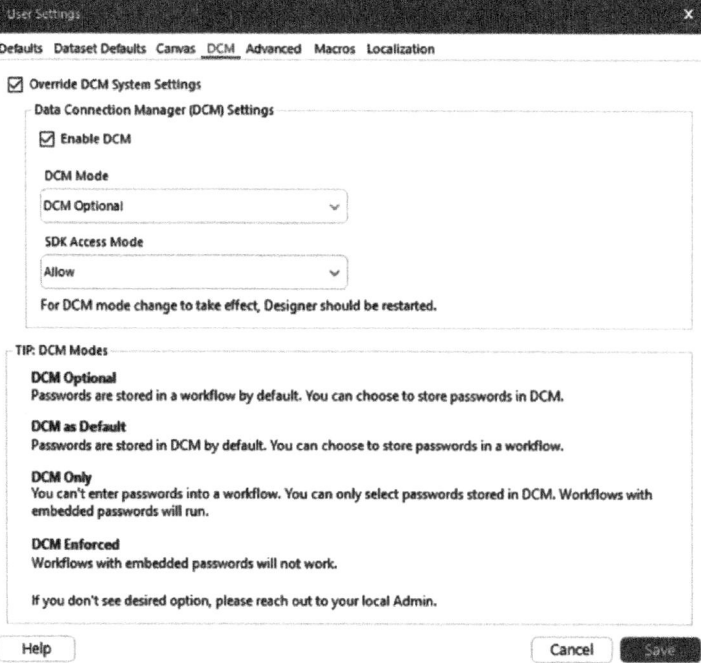

Figure 2.36: DCM options in User Settings

2. Make sure **DCM Optional** is the selected value for **DCM Mode** and **SDK Access Mode** is set to **Allow**.

3. Restart Alteryx Designer and you'll be ready to work with DCM.

If you have access to Alteryx Server, you'll be able to synchronize your local and remote connections with it.

Also, make sure you have access to at least one database from any of the technologies supported by Alteryx.

> **Important note**
> This synchronization process is manual and can only be triggered from Alteryx Designer.

How to do it...

We'll set up the actual connection using the following steps:

1. Go to **File** → **Manage Connections**.

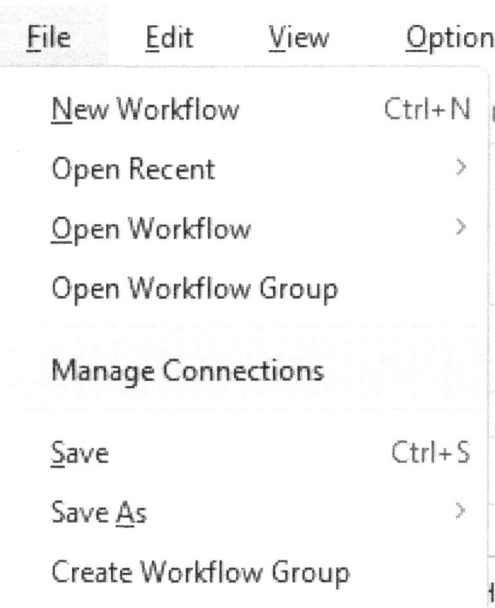

Figure 2.37: Manage Connections menu

A new window is displayed (yours might be blank).

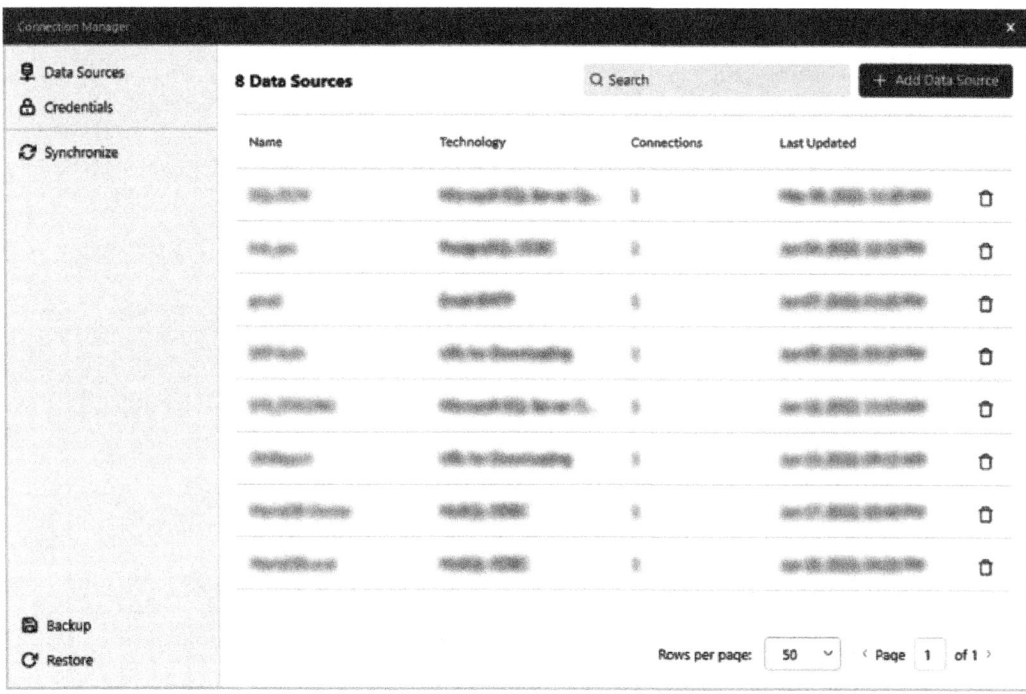

Figure 2.38: DCM main window

2. Click on **Add Data Source** at the top right of the new window, so the **Select Technology** option shows up.

3. From the dropdown, select the type of technology you will be connecting to (see the complete list of tools and technologies supported by DCM here: `https://help.alteryx.com/current/designer/dcm-designer`):

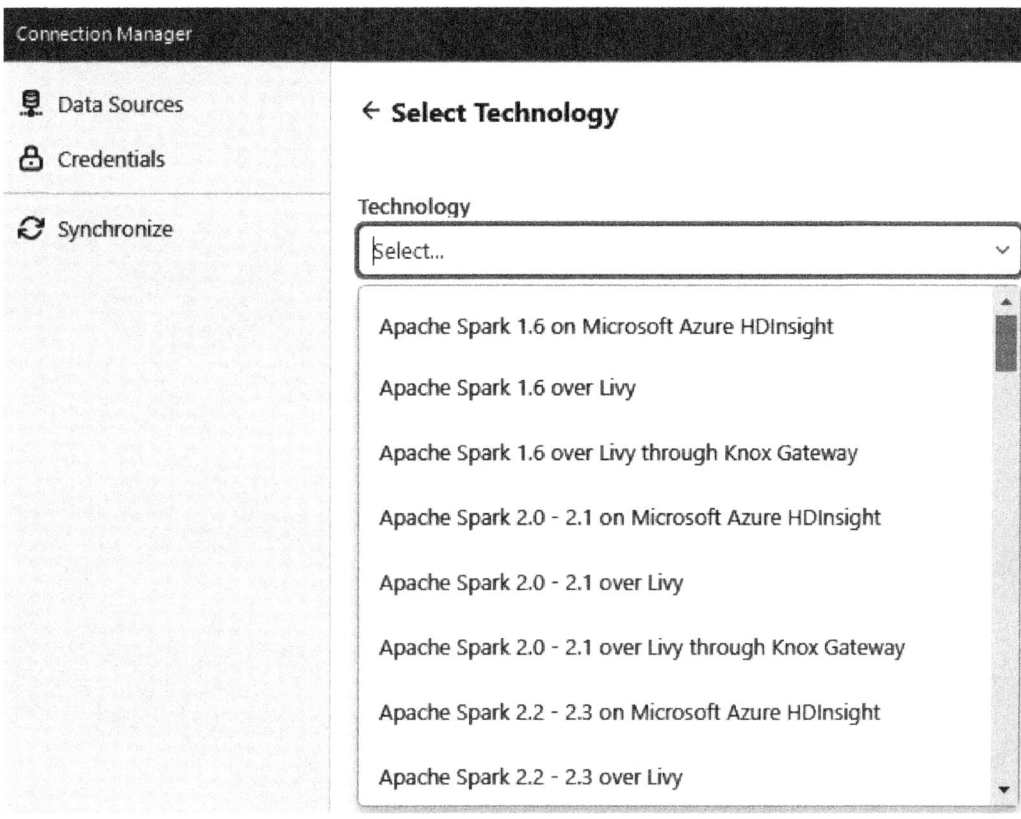

Figure 2.39: Technology selection for new connections

For this recipe, we'll be using **Microsoft SQL Server Quick Connect**, but feel free to select the technology you want. The steps will be the same – what will change is the data you need to enter to connect to that technology.

4.   Enter your connection's specifics and click **Save**.

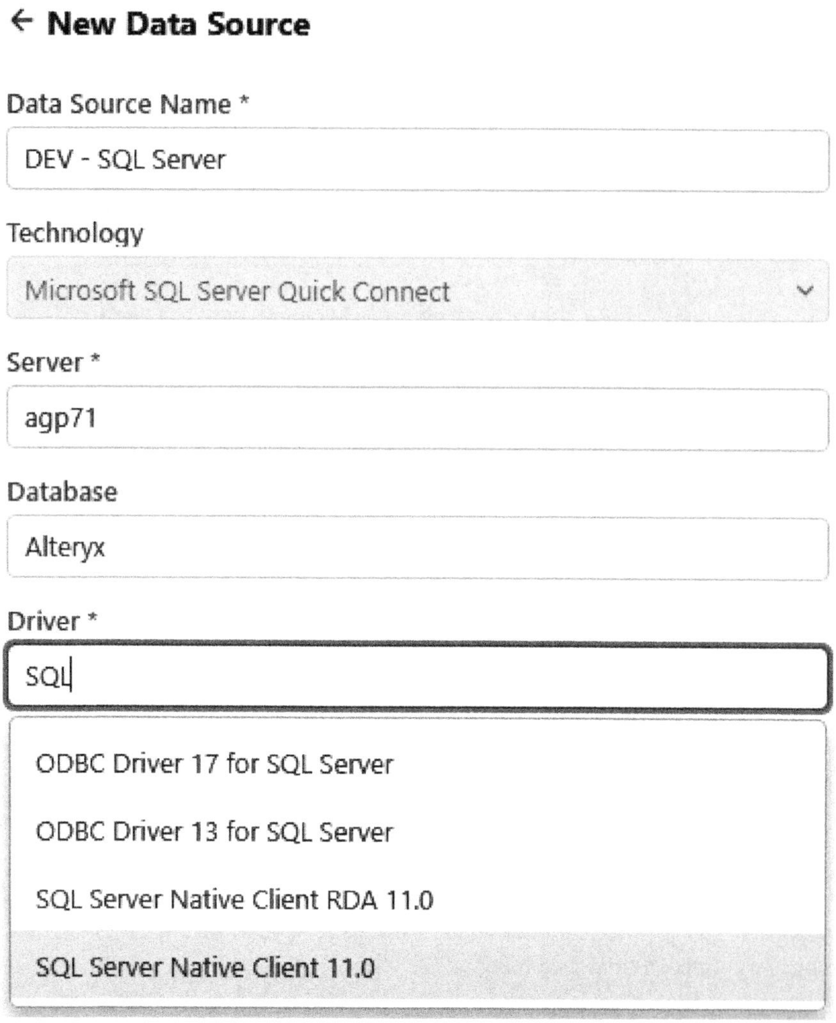

← **New Data Source**

Data Source Name *

DEV - SQL Server

Technology

Microsoft SQL Server Quick Connect   ⌄

Server *

agp71

Database

Alteryx

Driver *

SQL|

ODBC Driver 17 for SQL Server

ODBC Driver 13 for SQL Server

SQL Server Native Client RDA 11.0

SQL Server Native Client 11.0

Figure 2.40: Setting up a SQL Server connection

5.   Now, we need to link the credentials with the data source object to create a connection.

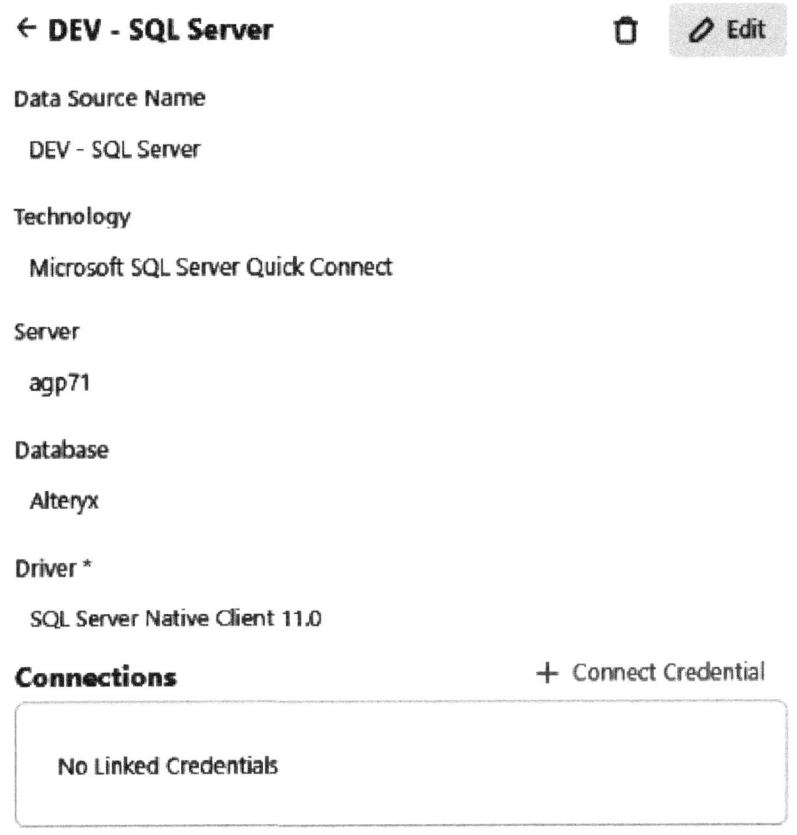

Figure 2.41: Linking credentials to a connection

6. Click on + **Connect Credential** and the panel will change, so you can select the type of credentials (Authentication Method) you'll be using for this connection.

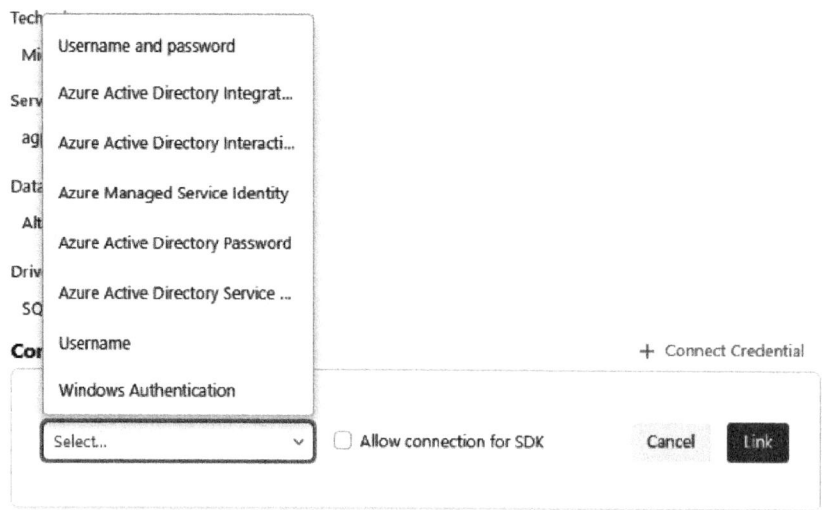

Figure 2.42: Selecting Authentication Method for linked credentials

Depending on your selection, Alteryx will filter and show all credentials of the selected type for you to choose.

Select **Username and password** and you'll see that a new field was added to the panel, with a dropdown to select from all existing username and password credentials.

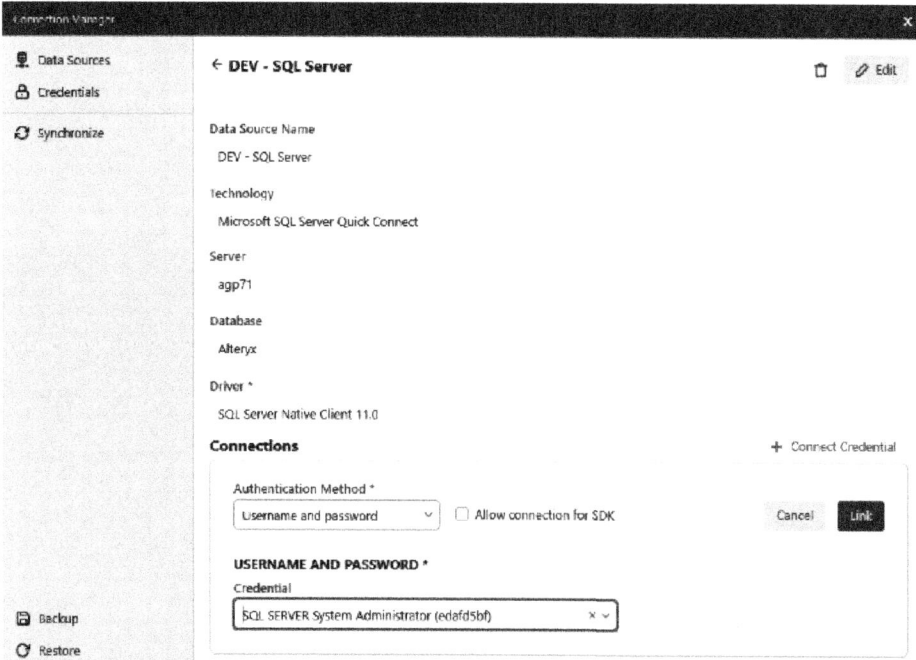

Figure 2.43: Selecting the credentials

7. Select the one we created in recipe #3 (SQL SERVER System Administrator) and click on the **Link** button.

 Username and password
SQL SERVER System Administrator | Username and password

Figure 2.44: Linked credential

Now we have our connection ready to be used.

How it works...

DCM allows us to create credentials and data sources. Those objects can be individually administrated in a centralized secure space. The combination of a data source and a set of credentials gives us a connection object that we can use in our workflows without caring about logins and server names.

> **Important note:**
> If you use DCM, every change you make to a connection will be picked up by your workflows. So, for example, you need to change your password once (in DCM's Connection Manager) and all workflows using that credential will get updated.

There's more...

If you see the underlying XML within the workflow for your connections, you'll notice the difference in how they're stored and managed by Alteryx Designer.

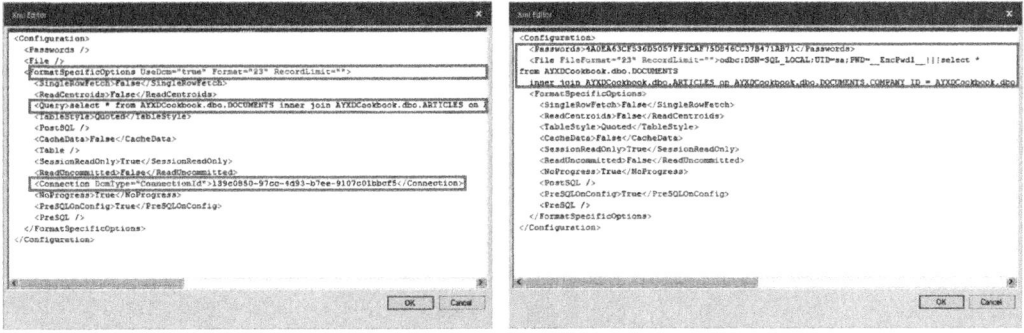

Figure 2.45: Using DCM and without using DCM

See the complete list of tools and technologies supported by DCM here: https://help.alteryx.com/current/designer/dcm-designer

Getting information from your In-DB connection/query

When working with In-Database tools in Alteryx, and probably using the **Visual Query Builder**, queries are built from within the tools by Alteryx and sometimes we'll need to take those queries and have somebody optimize them for us or test them outside Alteryx.

The **Dynamic Output** tool allows us to get a lot of information about what and how Alteryx queries our databases.

Throughout this recipe, we'll be exploring how to get that information and how we can make use of it.

Getting ready

To practice this recipe, we created a test set that you can download from here:

```
https://github.com/PacktPublishing/Alteryx-Designer-Cookbook/
tree/main/ch2/Recipe5
```

Before starting with the recipe, just make sure that you install the SQLite ODBC driver (in the \
SQLITE-ODBC folder). If you are on 32-bit Windows, use `sqliteodbc.exe` and if you are on
64-bit Windows, use `sqliteodbc_W64.exe` for the installation:

1. Once installed, go to the ODBC data sources corresponding to the actual version of your OS
    (32- or 64-bit).

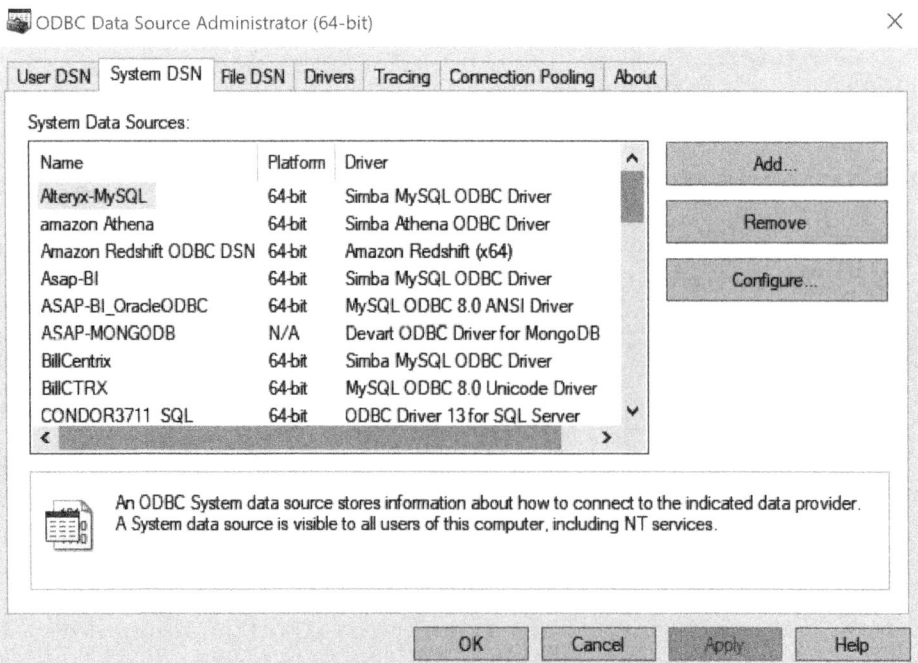

Figure 2.46: ODBC Data Source Administrator

2.   In the **System DSN** tab, click on **Add…**.

3.   Navigate to **SQLite3 ODBC Driver**, select it, and click **Finish**.

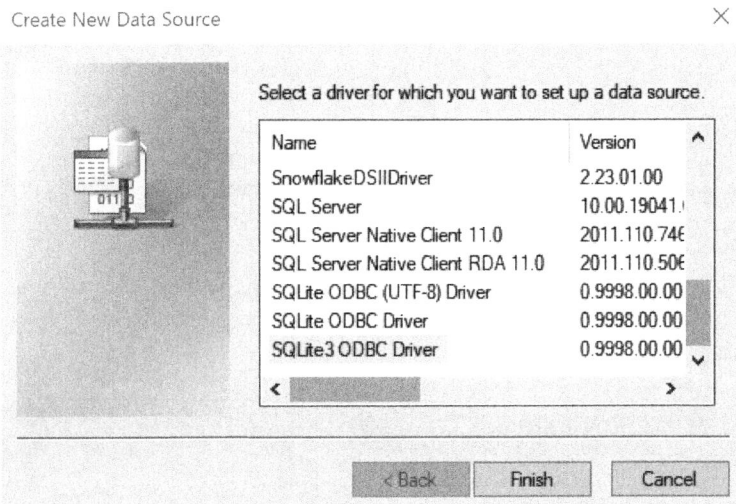

Figure 2.47: Selecting a driver for the data source

4.   On the new screen, give your connection a name.

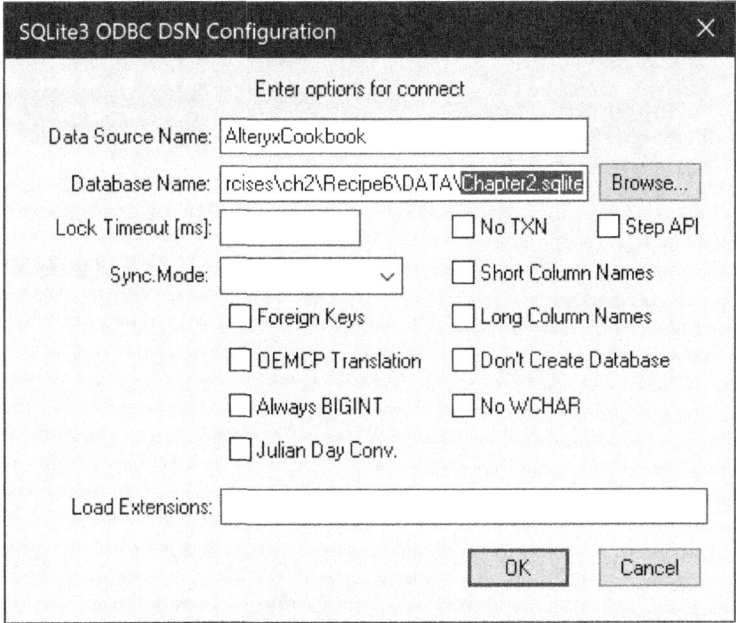

Figure 2.48: SQLite3 driver configuration

5. Click on the **Browse...** button and select where you saved the provided SQLite database (it should be in \DATA\Chapter2.sqlite).

For this recipe, we'll not be touching any other settings of the driver.

If you plan to use your own data, you'll only need to have access to a database you can query.

How to do it...

We are going to get the total billed amounts per customer. For this, we have three tables: DOCUMENTS, ARTICLES, and CUSTOMERS.

The DOCUMENTS table has all the information about the billing (including the amount in the TOTAL field) but has no details about customers or articles (just an ID). So we need to join the tables to get those details.

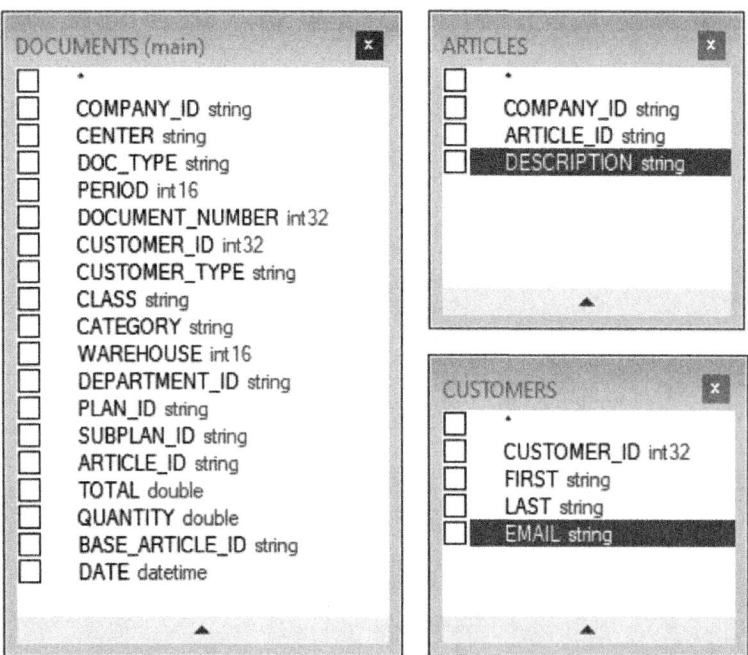

Figure 2.49: Structures of the tables

To be able to do so, we first need to connect to the database. We'll be using In-DB connections to do it.

1. Grab a **Connect In-DB** tool from the **In-Database** category and drop it onto the canvas.

2. From the tool configuration panel, click on **Manage Connections** to create an Alteryx In-DB connection.

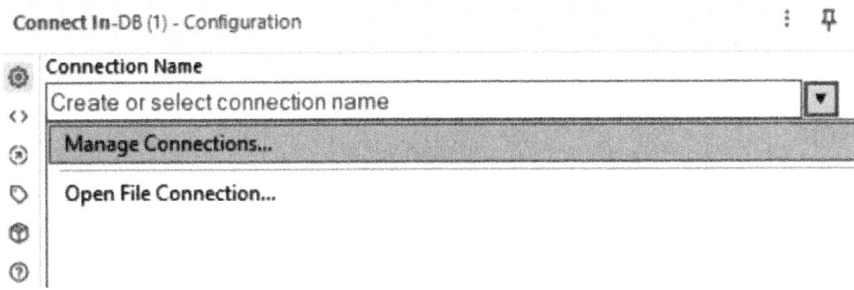

Figure 2.50: In-DB connection

The **Manage In-DB Connections** screen will pop up, allowing you to start configuring the new connection.

3. From the **Data Source** dropdown, select **Generic ODBC** (we'll be pointing it to the ODBC data source we created earlier).

4. For the **Connection Type** dropdown, leave it at **User** and click the **New** button for **Connections**. This will enable the **Connection Name** field, so give the connection a name (we used SQLITE as you can see in the following figure).

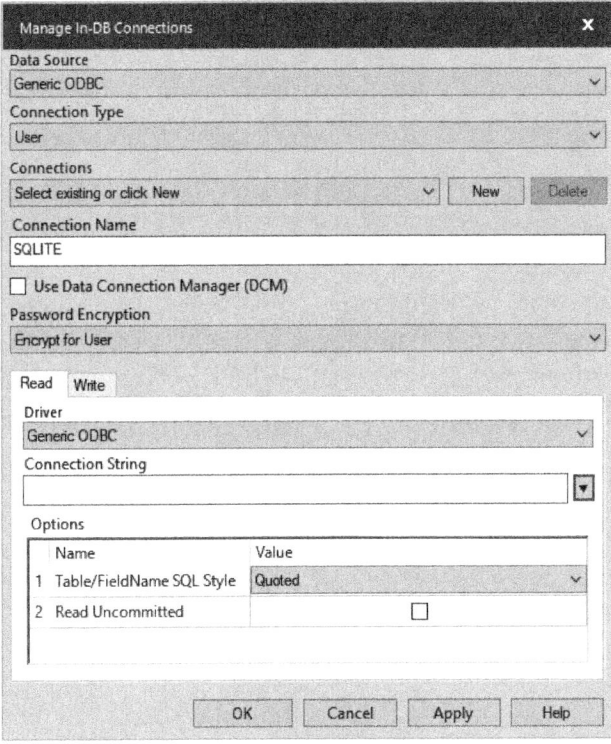

Figure 2.51: In-DB connection

5. Now, on **Connection String**, click on the down-pointing arrow and select **New database connection**….

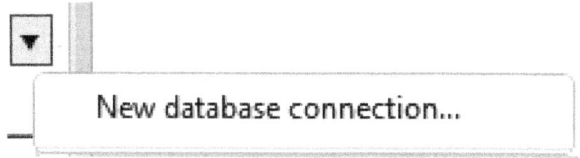

Figure 2.52: New database connection…

6. This will make the **ODBC Connection** screen pop up. From here, select the **AlteryxCookbook** connection (the one we created in the *Getting ready* part of this recipe) and click **OK**.

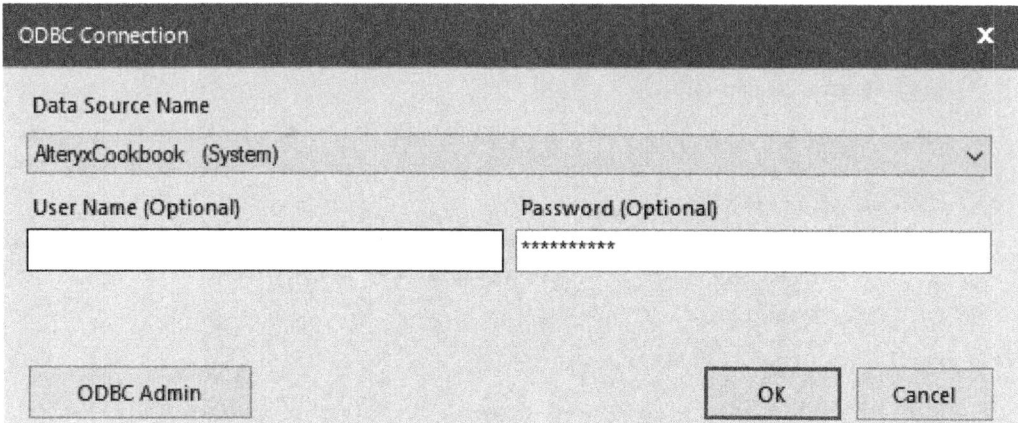

Figure 2.53: Selecting which ODBC data source to use for the current connection

7. Click **OK** on the **Manage In-DB Connections** window, and the **Choose Table or Specify Query** window will pop up showing existing tables within the actual connection (by default, it'll open in the **Tables** tab).

8. Click on the **Visual Query Builder** tab so you can start building a query using drag and drop.

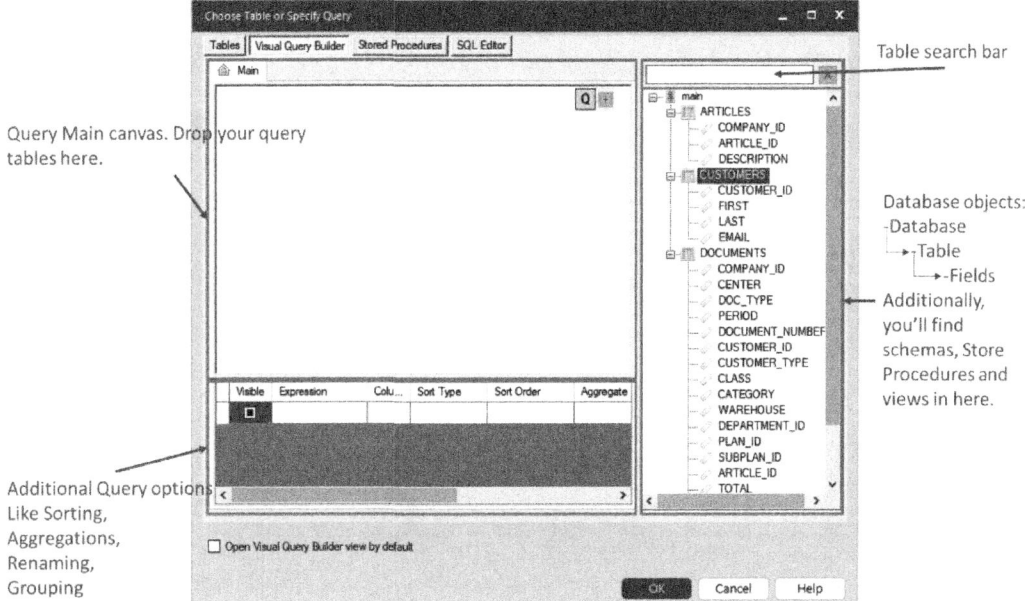

Figure 2.54: Visual Query Builder

9. Drag the DOCUMENTS table and drop it into the **Main** canvas.

10. Repeat the operation for the ARTICLES and CUSTOMERS tables.

    Now, we have the three tables available, and we'll create the relations between them.

11. From the DOCUMENTS table, drag the COMPANY_ID field and drop it over the ARTICLES table's COMPANY_ID field.

    Repeat the procedure, linking the following:

    • DOCUMENT.ARTICLE_ID with ARTICLES.ARTICLE_ID

    • DOCUMENTS.CUSTOMER_ID with CUSTOMERS.CUSTOMER_ID

12. Now click on the first checkbox in the DOCUMENTS table to select all fields from it (*), and select ARTICLES.DESCRIPTION, CUSTOMERS.FIRST, CUSTOMERS.LAST, and CUSTOMERS.EMAIL, checking the checkbox of each of these fields.

    Your query should look like this:

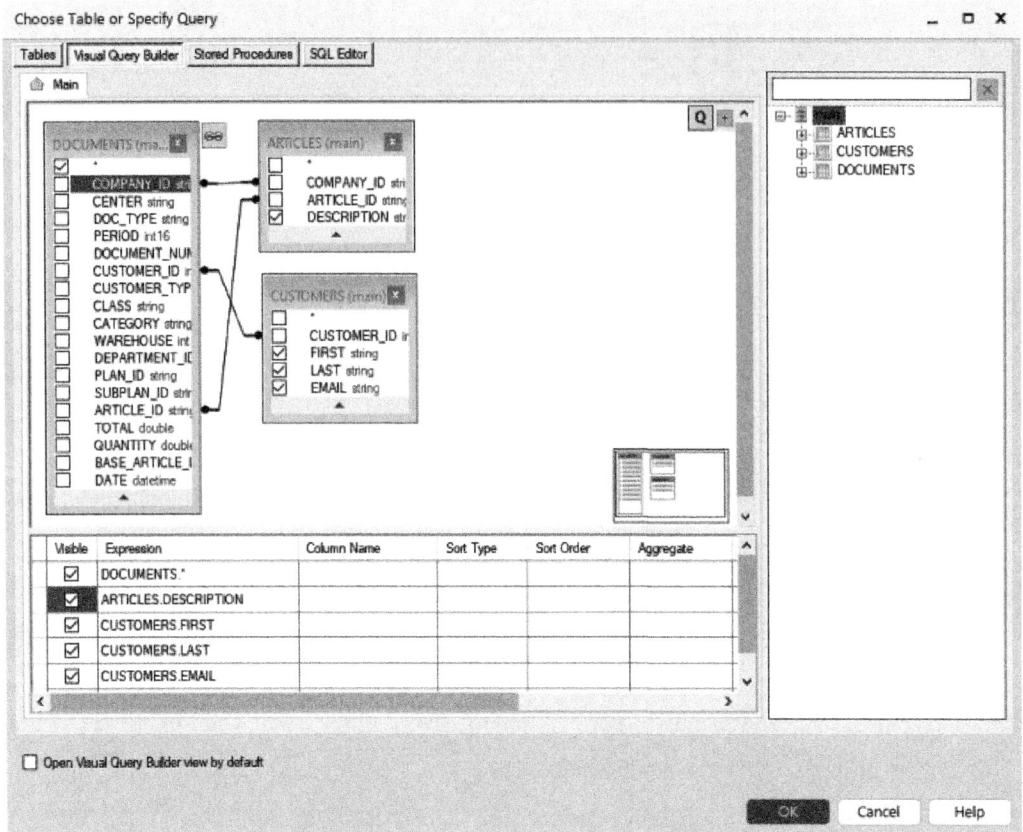

Figure 2.55: Completed query in Visual Query Builder

13. Click **OK** and you'll return to the Alteryx Designer canvas.

Now the tool is ready to execute the query. If you run the workflow, you'll notice that it returns all records after joining the tables.

Now, to get the total amounts per customer, we need to summarize, grouping by CUSTOMER_ID, and get FIRST, LAST, EMAIL, and sum on TOTAL.

14. Drop a **Summarize In-DB** tool onto the canvas, and configure it as shown in the following figure, so the tool's configuration panel looks like this:

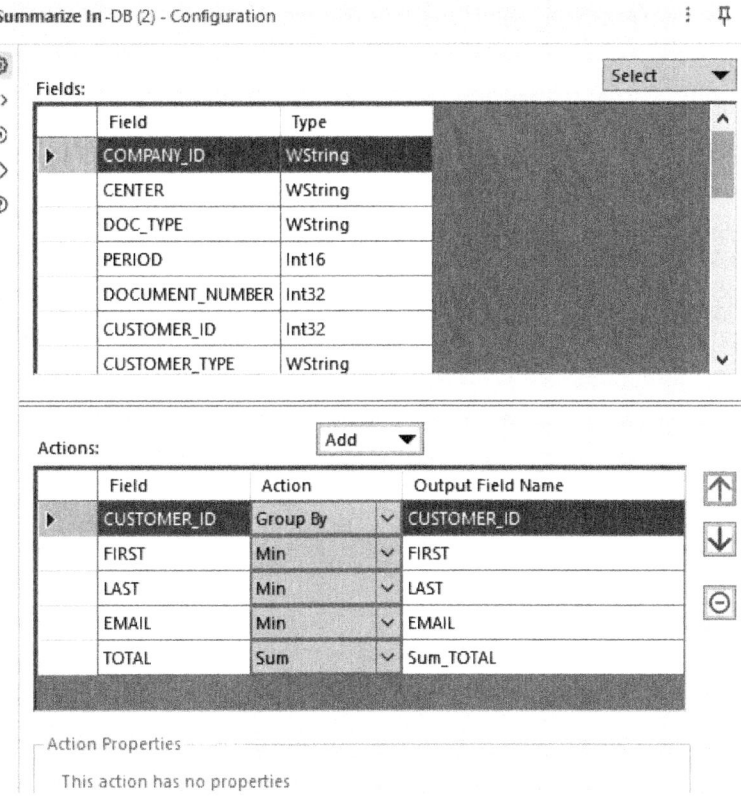

Figure 2.56: Summarize In-DB

Now, if we run the workflow, we'll get the total amount per customer.

	CUSTOMER_ID	FIRST	LAST	EMAIL	Sum_TOTAL
1	70123	Reese	Oconnor	egestas.Duis.ac@pharetrafeliseget.ca	6493502.0
2	70398	Deanna	Campbell	nulla.Donec.non@diam.co.uk	19728712.0
3	70723	Daquan	Montgomery	ac.mattis@semper.com	3372033.0
4	71143	Dean	Mullins	pede.ac.urna@non.edu	4751630.0
5	71448	Evan	Mcclain	et.netus.et@acorci.com	25581470.0
6	71649	Joel	Fox	libero.at.auctor@convalliscorvallisdolor.org	588300.0
7	72083	Ross	English	mattis@dolor.net	2430550.0
8	72327	Belle	Harvey	enim.consequat.purus@variusorci.ca	20281356.0
9	72623	Xena	Jacobson	urna.Vivamus@etmagnisdis.ca	1750000.0
10	73104	Quemby	Gonzales	nibh@nibh.co.uk	1214700.0
11	73421	Scarlett	Chang	dolor.sit.amet@Sed.org	108200.0
12	73451	Leslie	Franks	egestas.blandit@ProinultricesDuis.ca	385500.0

Figure 2.57: Workflow results

At this point, we need to see how Alteryx resolves the queries we created in its drag-and-drop interface, and we can extract that information using a **Dynamic Output In-DB** tool.

15. So, connect a **Dynamic Output In-DB** tool to the output anchor of the **Summarize In-DB** tool, and a regular **Browse** tool to the output anchor of the **Dynamic Output In-DB** tool.

At this point, your workflow should look like the following figure:

Figure 2.58: Our workflow

16. Click on the **Dynamic Output In-DB** tool and select all output fields, except for **Input Connection String** and **Output Connection String**.

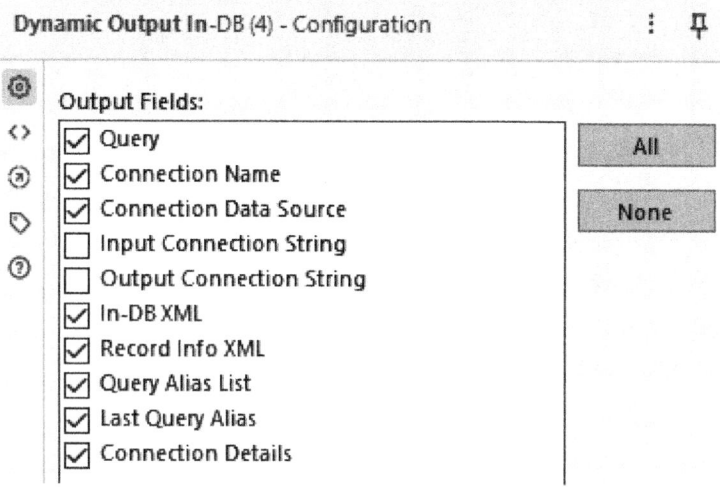

Figure 2.59: Dynamic Output In-DB output fields

17. Run the workflow and review the resulting fields.

Query	Connection Name	Connection Data Source
WITH "Tool1_fc91" AS (select DOCUMENTS.*,	SQLITE	Unknown

In-DB XML	Record Info XML
< LockIn DbType="SQL">	< RecordInfo LockIn="True" >

Query Alias List	Last Query Alias	Connection Details
Tool1_fc91=(select DOCUMENTS.*,	Tool2_342e	<ConnectionDetails></ConnectionDetails>

Figure 2.60: Results for Dynamic Output In-DB

The following fields can be found here:

- **Query**: This is the complete query generated up to this point in the workflow.

- **Connection Name**: The name of the Alteryx connection you're using (comes from the name you gave it when you created it).

- **Connection Data Source**: This is the database type. Note that since we used a generic ODBC type of connection, that value is not available to Alteryx – that's why we get **Unknown** here.

- **In-DB XML**: The Alteryx XML representation of the query.

- **Record Info XML**: The XML representation of the query fields.

- **Query Alias List**: This contains each segment of the query and the ID Alteryx gave to them.

- **Last Query Alias**: The last alias from the list.

From the **Query** field, you have access to the SQL query created by Alteryx Designer – in our case, the following:

```
WITH "Tool1_fc91" AS (select DOCUMENTS.*,
    ARTICLES.DESCRIPTION,
    CUSTOMERS.FIRST,
    CUSTOMERS.LAST,
    CUSTOMERS.EMAIL
from DOCUMENTS
    inner join ARTICLES on DOCUMENTS.COMPANY_ID =
ARTICLES.COMPANY_ID and DOCUMENTS.ARTICLE_ID = ARTICLES.
ARTICLE_ID
    inner join CUSTOMERS on DOCUMENTS.CUSTOMER_ID =
CUSTOMERS.CUSTOMER_ID) SELECT "CUSTOMER_ID", MIN("FIRST")
AS "FIRST", MIN("LAST") AS "LAST", MIN("EMAIL") AS
"EMAIL", SUM("TOTAL") AS "Sum_TOTAL" FROM "Tool1_fc91"
GROUP BY "CUSTOMER_ID"
```

Where `"Tool1_fc91"` is a unique ID Alteryx assigns to each tool to further reference part of the complete query (subquery).

From the **Query Alias List** field, we can access the different sub-queries created to that point within the workflow.

At this point, we can save or copy that information to analyze and further optimize our queries.

How it works...

Creating queries in a visual interface is easier than writing code, and not all of us are able to do SQL scripting. The Visual Query Designer gives us the ability to create complex queries without any programming knowledge, but sometimes we'll need assistance in optimizing those queries.

The Dynamic Output In-DB tool provides us with ease of access to the generated queries that Alteryx executes against our database management systems, by registering and extracting that information for us.

There's more...

You'll notice Alteryx added a black connector between both fields. If you double-click on it, the **Link Properties** screen will appear, allowing you to configure the link.

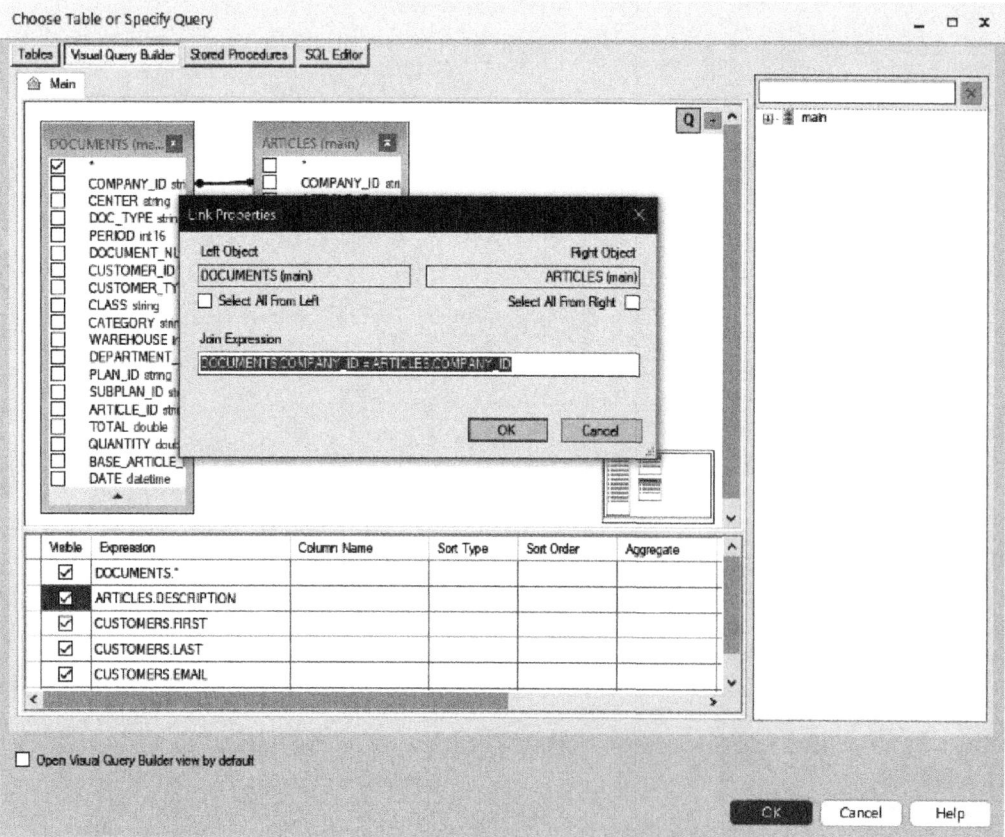

Figure 2.61: Configuring the relationships

See also (follow-up steps)

The **Connection Name** field and the **Query** or **Query Alias List** fields extracted from the **Dynamic Output In-DB** tool can be used to generate dynamic and/or batch queries using a **Dynamic Input In-DB** tool connected to a data stream.

> **Important note:**
> The Dynamic Input In-DB tool only supports one input record, so if you have several queries to run, maybe it's a good idea to create a macro.

3
Preparing Data

Being able to prep data fast and accurately will take us on a successful data analysis journey. And considering that the decisions made by business units are as good as the data that supports them, this phase is crucial to providing useful and complete insights to business leaders.

Looking at data preparation as the preprocessing phase of analytics, where we clean, validate, and enrich our raw data, is essential to driving better insights for decision-making and makes us trustworthy analysts.

This tends to be a very demanding and under-appreciated process, and most analysts spend much of their time performing these tasks. This chapter will help you prepare your data into a workable dataset with simple, automatable, and powerful methods.

We'll be exploring the following topics:

- Saving field configurations with the Select tool
- Working with ranges
- Applying data transformations to more than one field at a time (Multi-Field Formula)
- Using the previous/next N records' data in the current record operation (Multi-Row Formula)

Technical requirements

There are no special requirements for this chapter, other than having Alteryx Designer on your computer.

Saving field configurations with the Select tool

Working with several data sources, such as XML, CSV, or plain TXT forces us to continually adjust data types since they only return strings. Also, renaming fields to make them easier to understand can be a repetitive task we face when building our Alteryx workflows.

In this recipe, we'll be following a very effective method of getting the optimal data type and size for our fields, using the **Auto Field** tool once, and saving its result for later reuse, avoiding having to execute it every time we run the workflow, making us save a lot of runtime.

Getting ready

We've prepared a test set for you to follow along with this recipe that you can download here:

```
https://github.com/PacktPublishing/Alteryx-Designer-Cookbook/
tree/main/ch3/Recipe1
```

If you want to follow along with your own data, make sure you use one of the mentioned data source formats (CSV, XML, or TXT).

How to do it...

Let's get started using the following steps:

1. On a new workflow, drop the **Input Data** tool onto the canvas and point it to ..\DATA\ Citibikes_2013.csv.

2. From the **Preparation** category, drop the **Auto Field** tool and connect it to the **Input Data** tool.

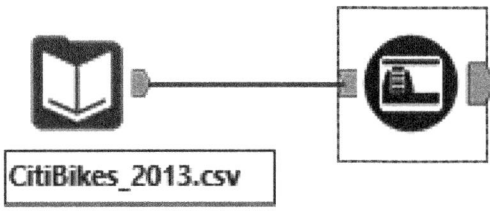

CitiBikes_2013.csv

Figure 3.1: Connecting the Auto Field tool

3. Drop the **Select** tool after the **Auto Field** tool.

4. Click on the **Auto Field** tool and uncheck the **Dynamic or Unknown Fields** option at the bottom of the fields list.

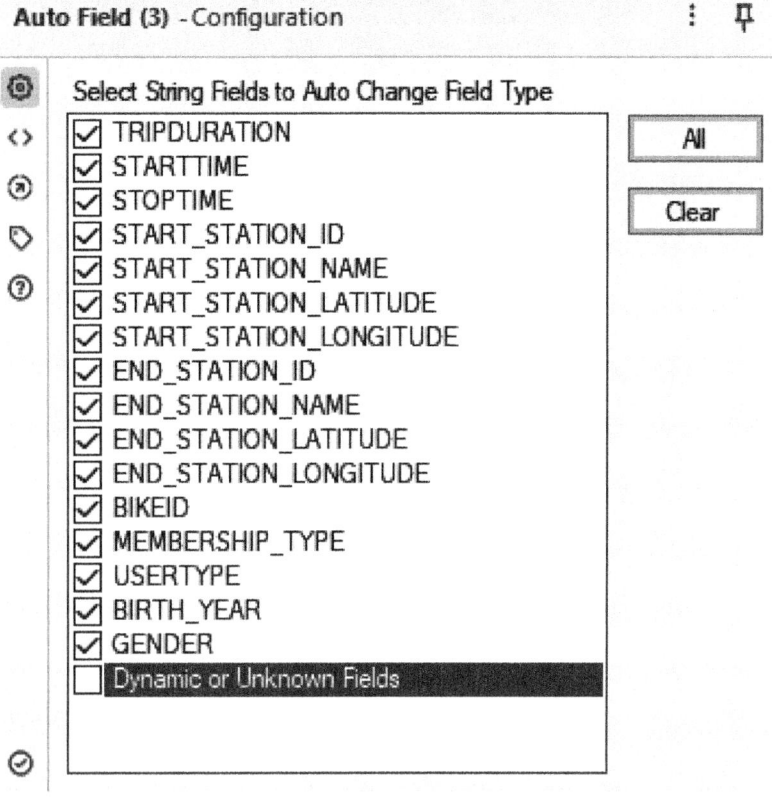

Figure 3.2: Auto Field tool configuration

5. Run your workflow.

6. Click on the **Select** tool once the workflow finishes running. You'll notice that Alteryx selected the best data type and size to fit your current data.

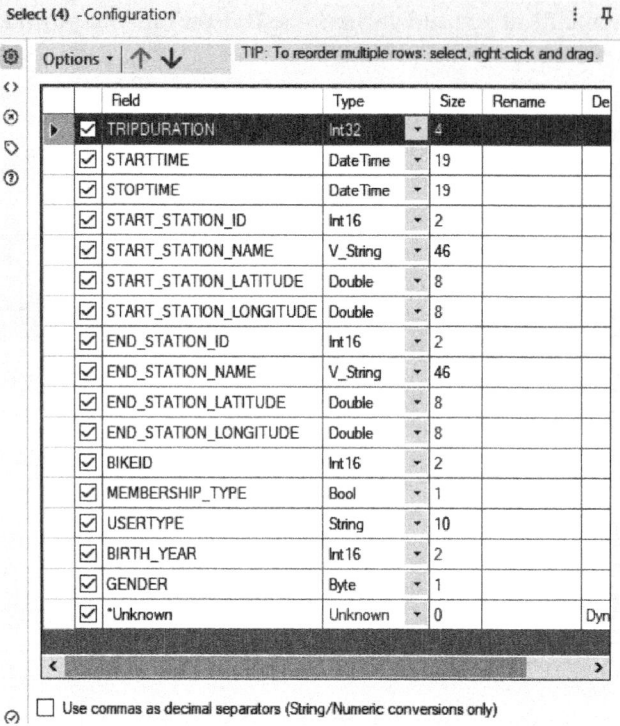

Figure 3.3: Select tool after running Auto Field

7.   From the **Options** menu (top left), go to **Save/Load → Save Field Configuration**:

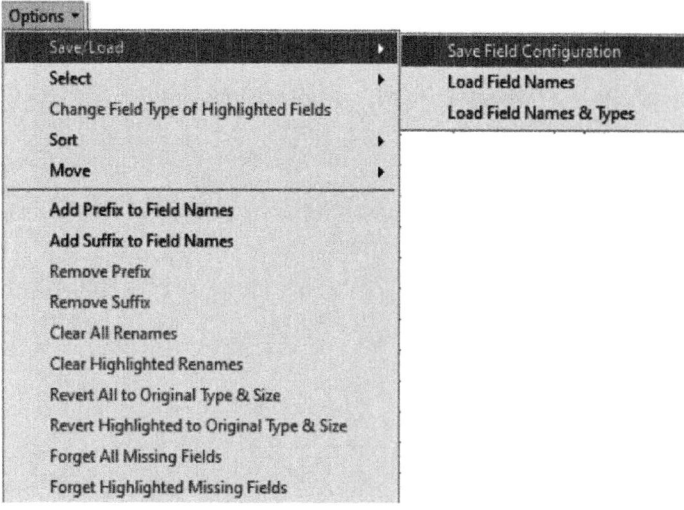

Figure 3.4: Saving the field configurations

8. Alteryx will prompt for where you want to save the **.YXFT** file (YX for Alteryx, FT for Field Types). Browse to the folder where your `Citibikes_2013.csv` file is stored, give the file a name (I like to use the same name as the data source for order and ease of use, but you can use the name you want), and hit **Save**. (You can use any folder, but it's a good practice to save the `.yxft` file in the same folder as your data.)

Use the new field settings:

I.   Create a new workflow.

II.   Drop the **Input Data** tool onto the canvas and point it to `\DATA\Citibikes_2013.csv`.

III. Connect the **Select** tool to the output anchor of the **Input Data** tool.

IV.   From the **Options** menu, go to **Save/Load → Load Field Names & Types**

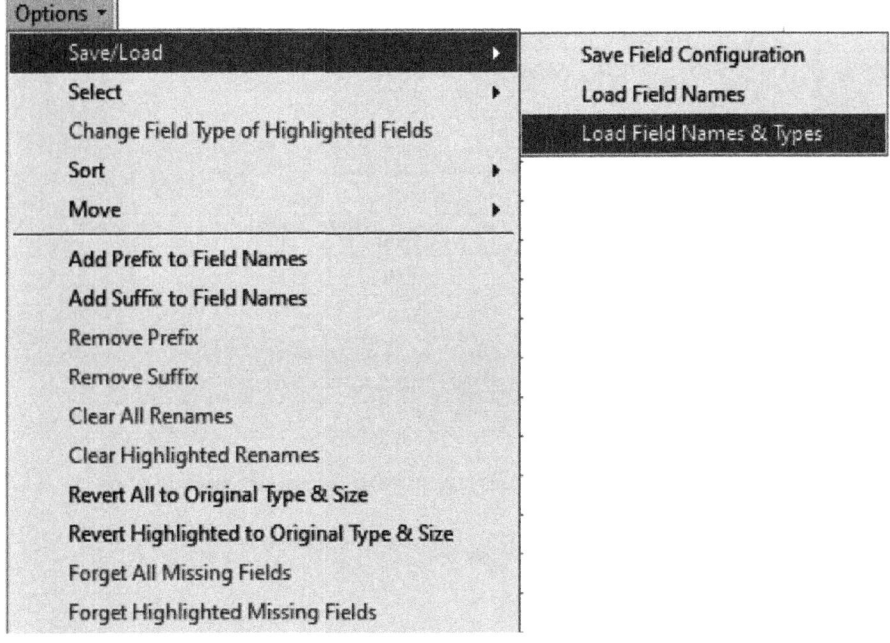

Figure 3.5: Loading/applying the field configurations

9. Navigate to the `.yxft` file you just saved, select it, and hit **Open**.

You'll see that Alteryx applied the settings generated, so now you have the optimal data types and sizes for your data:

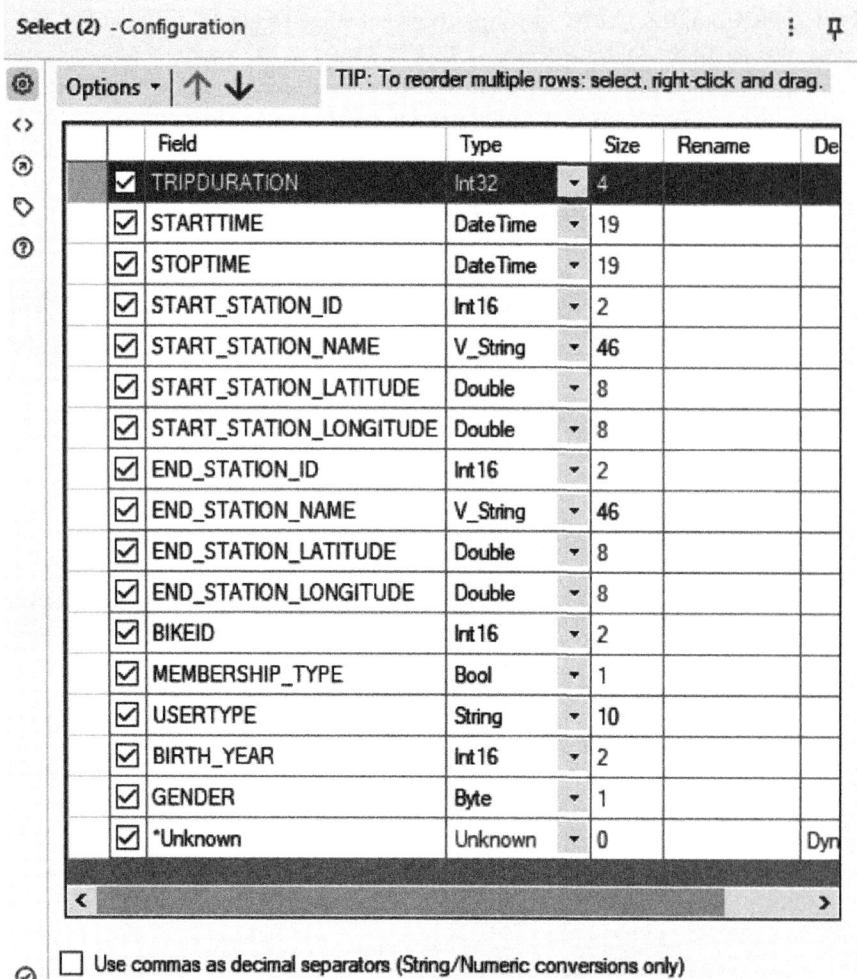

Figure 3.6: Field configurations applied

How it works...

The **Auto Field** tool analyzes *all* the records from a data source and sets the field type and size to the smallest possible ones that can contain the actual data, based on the file contents. To perform this task, every time you run the workflow, the tool reads the whole file and selects the best types and sizes, so it adds some extra processing time to the workflow.

Applying this recipe will save you a lot of running time since you only need to generate the .YXFT file once (or every time your file changes), and reuse it, instead of applying **Auto Field** to every run.

Working with ranges

Ranges are a very common method for reducing and organizing data when you have a certain value for a group determined by some STARTING and ENDING attributes. For example, zip code ranges and cities, purchase amounts, customer categories, and so on.

In this recipe, we'll go through the process of classifying people by their ages using an age range dictionary with categories.

So basically, we have the following:

USERTYPE	BIRTH_YEAR	GENDER	BIRTH_MONTH	BIRTH_DAY	BIRTHDAY_STR	BIRTHDAY	AGE
Subscriber	1979	1	4	30	1979-04-30	1979-04-30	43
Subscriber	1978	2	9	08	1978-09-08	1978-09-08	43
Subscriber	1979	1	7	13	1979-07-13	1979-07-13	43
Subscriber	1979	2	7	04	1979-07-04	1979-07-04	43
Subscriber	1979	1	6	08	1979-06-08	1979-06-08	43
Subscriber	1979	1	5	05	1979-05-05	1979-05-05	43
Subscriber	1978	1	9	19	1978-09-19	1978-09-19	43
Subscriber	1978	1	9	18	1978-09-18	1978-09-18	43
Subscriber	1979	2	3	02	1979-03-02	1979-03-02	43
Subscriber	1979	1	2	19	1979-02-19	1979-02-19	43

Figure 3.7: Dataset that'll be enriched

And our question is, how do we join that table with this?

CATEGORY	MIN	MAX
Child	0	12
Adolescent	13	18
Adult	19	59
Senior Adult	60	130

Figure 3.8: A custom dictionary that contains CATEGORY descriptions by ranges

Getting ready

For this recipe, we prepared a test set, including some range-based dictionaries and a dataset to join. You can download it here:

https://github.com/PacktPublishing/Alteryx-Designer-Cookbook/tree/main/ch3/Recipe2

If you decide to test with your own data, make sure your custom dictionaries have the **MIN** and **MAX** values for a range, and all the values within each range correspond to a single description.

How to do it...

We'll work with ranges in our data, using the following steps:

1. On a new workflow, drop the **Input Data** tool and point it to CityBike_extract.yxdb.

2. Drop another instance of the **Input Data** tool and point it to Ranges.xlsx, and the CATEGORIES by AGE worksheet.

3. Add the **Generate Rows** tool to the last **Input Data** tool instance and select **Create New Field**:

    I.   Name the new field Range_Age and select **Int32** for **Type**.

    II.   For **Initialization Expression**, write [MIN].

    III. For **Condition Expression**, use Range_Age <= [MAX].

    IV.   And for **Loop Expression (Usually Increment)**, use Range_Age + 1.

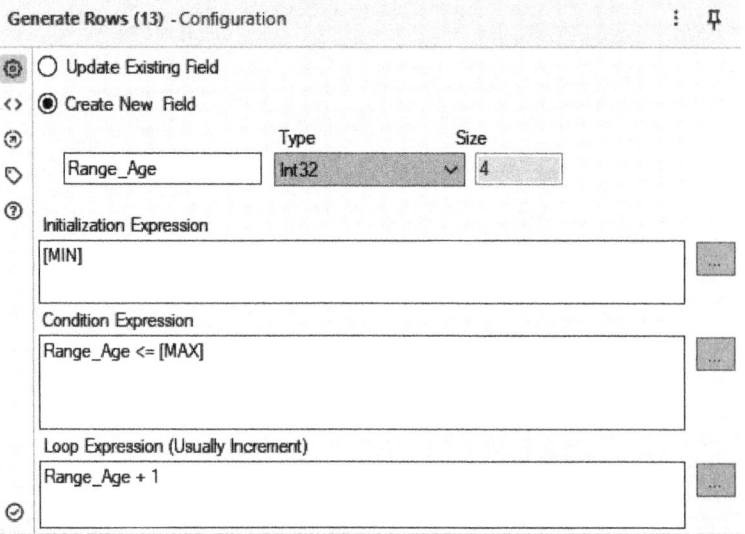

Figure 3.9: Generate Rows configuration

4. Run the workflow.

    You'll notice Alteryx created each data point for the age contained within the MIN-MAX range, so now, we have a field we can use to join (the one we just created with the **Generate Rows** tool: [Range_Age]).

5. So, drop the **Join** tool onto the canvas:

    I.   For the **LEFT** input anchor, connect the first instance of the **Input Data** tool's output anchor.

    II.   For the **RIGHT** input anchor, connect the **Generate Rows** output anchor.

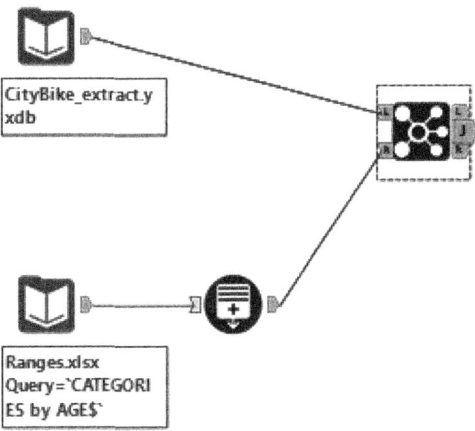

Figure 3.10: Join tool connections

III.   Select AGE as the **Left** input and Range_Age for the **Right** input to join.

IV.   Deselect the MIN, MAX, and Range_Age fields of the **Right** input (just keep the CATEGORY field).

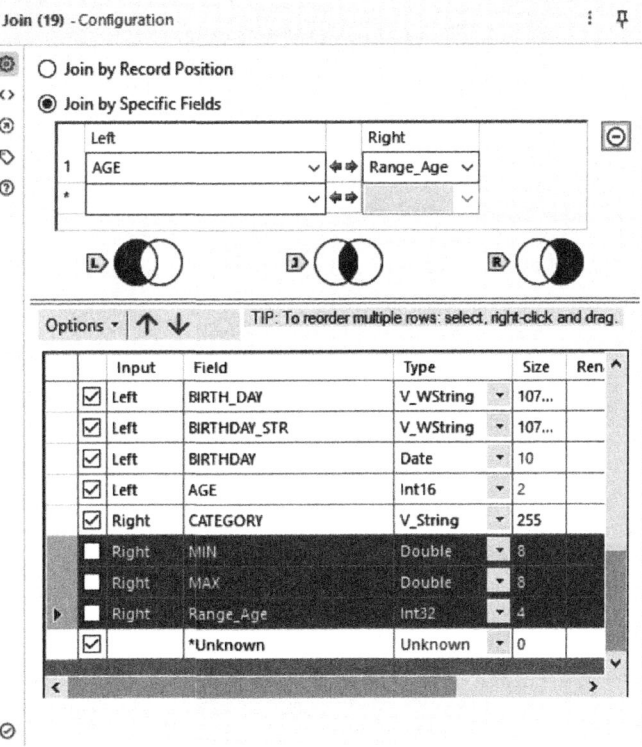

Figure 3.11: Join tool configuration

6. Run the workflow:

You'll notice that CATEGORY corresponds to AGE for every record.

AGE	CATEGORY
34	Adult
62	Senior Adult
34	Adult
34	Adult
62	Senior Adult
62	Senior Adult
43	Adult
62	Senior Adult
34	Adult
43	Adult

Figure 3.12: Joined data result

How it works...

In our example, we had to join every record with values that were grouped in a range by AGE. Since we can't do that without generating each value for the range, we used the **Generate Rows** tool.

The **Generate Rows** tool allows us to create individual values for a range specified by its limits, like in our recipe, the age range.

Starting at the value indicated by **Initialization Expression** (its first value will be the minimum age in the range), Alteryx will apply **Loop Expression** (adding 1 to the actual value), record by record, WHILE **Condition Expression** (us reaching the maximum age for that category) remains TRUE.

Choose the behavior of the tool, if it'll Update an existing field or creates a new one for us.

Since we chose to create a New field Alteryx ask for it's Name, Type and Size. For updating an existing field, we'll find a drop down menu with fields present in the current dataset.

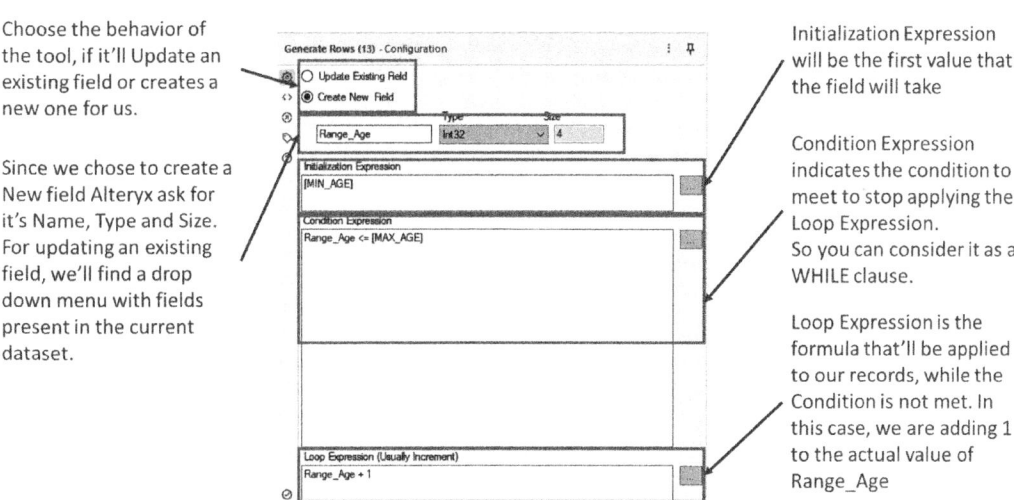

Initialization Expression will be the first value that the field will take

Condition Expression indicates the condition to meet to stop applying the Loop Expression. So you can consider it as a WHILE clause.

Loop Expression is the formula that'll be applied to our records, while the Condition is not met. In this case, we are adding 1 to the actual value of Range_Age

Figure 3.13: Anatomy of Generate Rows

There's more…

Since **Loop Expression** is a formula, you can create whatever you may need in it. Such as this, for example:

```
IF <Some Condition> THEN <Increment> ELSE <DECREMENT> ENDIF
```

Or, any combination of logic you may need.

Applying data transformations to more than one field at a time

Being able to apply transformations to several fields at a time is a huge advantage Alteryx provides to us as analysts. From updating all months' data to correcting or replacing strings in one go is a real improvement in the amount of time needed to adjust our data.

In this recipe, we'll go through the process of updating several fields all at once.

Getting ready

For this recipe, we created a test set for you to follow. You can download it here:

https://github.com/PacktPublishing/Alteryx-Designer-Cookbook/tree/main/ch3/Recipe3.

If you decide to test it with your own data, make sure your dataset contains several fields that you need to apply a single function to (such as capitalization, or applying a formula to them).

How to do it...

We'll transform our data as follows:

1. Create a new workflow and drop the **Input Data** tool.

2. Point the **Input Data** tool to `DATA\ARTICLES.yxdb`.

    You'll see that our data source has multiple columns, one per month, and the unit price for each `ARTICLE_ID` for that month.

ARTICLE_ID	January	February	March	April	May	June	July	August	September	October	November	December
001-1/2	0.011	0.011	0.011	0.011	0.011	0.011	0.011	0.011	0.011	0.011	0.011	0.011
001-1/4	0.001	0.001	0.001	0.001	0.001	0.001	0.001	0.001	0.001	0.001	0.001	0.001
001-3/8	0.004	0.004	0.004	0.004	0.004	0.004	0.004	0.004	0.004	0.004	0.004	0.004
001-5/16	0.01	0.01	0.01	0.01	0.01	0.01	0.01	0.01	0.01	0.01	0.01	0.01

Figure 3.14: Unit prices for each article per month

3. Now add the Multi-Field Formula tool to the workflow:

    I. Select all numeric fields.

    II. Uncheck the **Copy Output Fields and Add** option.

    III. Use this code for **Expression**:

```
IF [_CurrentFieldName_] IN ("January","February","March")
THEN [_CurrentField_]*1.01
ELSE [_CurrentField_]*1.05
ENDIF
```

This formula will cause a 1% increment for January to March and a 5% increase for the other months.

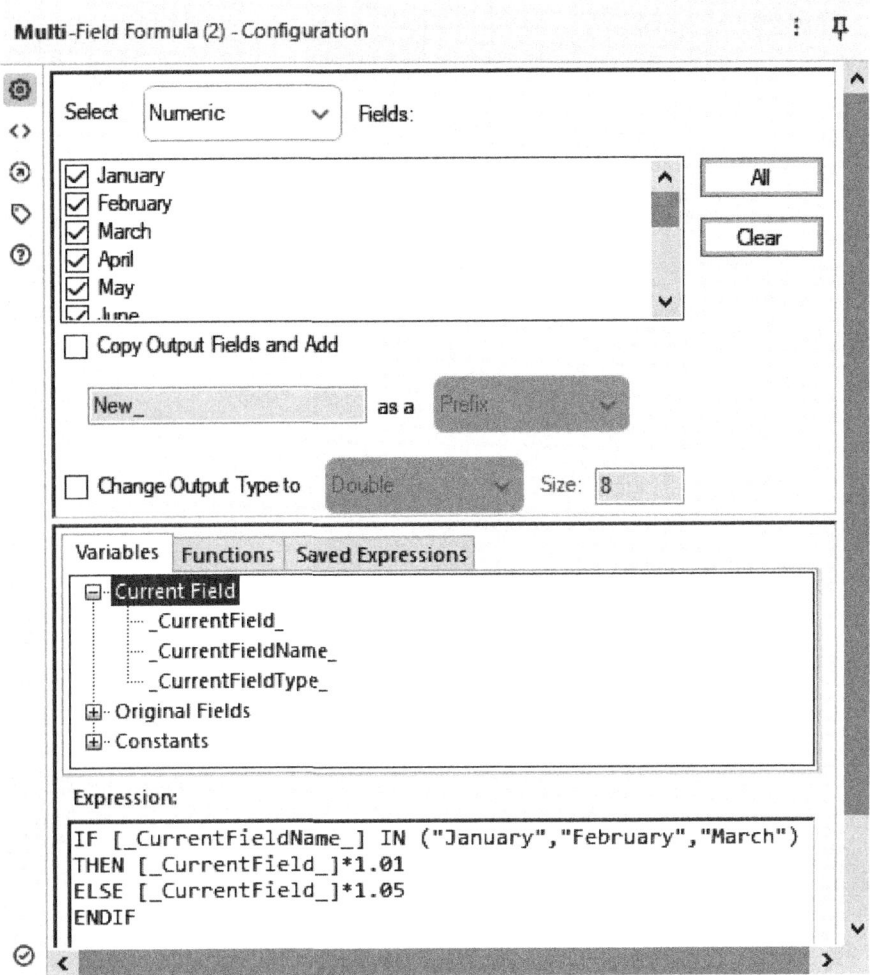

Figure 3.15: Multi-Field Formula tool configuration

4. Run the workflow and you'll find that the formula was applied to the fields, so the prices were updated all at once, 1% for January to March and 5% for the rest.

ARTICLE_ID	January	February	March	April	May	June	July	August	September	October	November	December
001-1/2	0.01111	0.01111	0.01111	0.01155	0.01155	0.01155	0.01155	0.01155	0.01155	0.01155	0.01155	0.01155
001-1/4	0.00101	0.00101	0.00101	0.00105	0.00105	0.00105	0.00105	0.00105	0.00105	0.00105	0.00105	0.00105
001-3/8	0.00404	0.00404	0.00404	0.0042	0.0042	0.0042	0.0042	0.0042	0.0042	0.0042	0.0042	0.0042
001-5/16	0.0101	0.0101	0.0101	0.0105	0.0105	0.0105	0.0105	0.0105	0.0105	0.0105	0.0105	0.0105

Figure 3.16: Results after applying the Multi-Field Formula

How it works...

The **Multi-Field Formula** tool allows you to apply the results of an expression to a set of fields. These fields are selected in the top part of the tool's configuration panel.

It iterates record by record and selected field by selected field to apply the formula.

It also provides a set of three new variables, internal to the tool:

- **_CurrentField_**: This references the **VALUE** of the current iteration between records and fields. So in the first iteration, it'll reference selected field #1 – record #1, selected field #2 – record #1, and so on, as in this list:

```
Record #1:
    Selected Field #1 value
    Selected Field #2 value
    Selected Field #N value
Record #2:
    Selected Field #1 value
    Selected Field #2 value
    Selected Field #N value
Record #N:
    Selected Field #1 value
    Selected Field #2 value
    Selected Field #N value
```

In our example, we used it to alter the value of each field by a given ratio:

```
IF [_CurrentFieldName_] IN ("January","February","March")
THEN [_CurrentField_]*1.01
ELSE [_CurrentField_]*1.05
ENDIF
```

- **_CurrentFieldName_**: This is the name of the current field at the current iteration. In our example, we used it to identify `"January"`, `"February"`, and `"March"` to apply a different coefficient to them in the `IF` statement of our expression:

```
IF [_CurrentFieldName_] IN ("January","February","March")
THEN [_CurrentField_]*1.01
ELSE [_CurrentField_]*1.05
ENDIF
```

- **_CurrentFieldType_**: The field type of the current field.

There's more...

In this recipe, we deselected the **Copy Output Fields and Add** option, but if we keep it enabled, we can create a copy of the original data, and apply the results to the newly created fields.

To test this, let's say that we need to calculate the percentage that each month's sales represent over yearly sales for each `ARTICLE_ID`:

1. Create a new workflow and point it to `..\DATA\ARTICLE_Sales.yxdb`. This dataset contains the monthly and yearly total sales for articles.

2. Drop the **Multi-Field Formula** tool into the workflow and configure it as follows:

   I.   Select all numeric fields and uncheck/deselect **YEARLY_SALES**.

   II. Leave the **Copy Output Fields and Add** option checked.

   III. Use `_%_Over_Total` andset as a to Suffix, so your fields will be named `[Name of the Selected Field]_%_Over_Total`.

Check the **Change Output Type to Fixed Decimal** option and type 5.2 as the size (5 is the total length of the number and .2 is how many of those 5 positions will be reserved for decimals, so a 5.2 fixed decimal will be XXX.XX).

Use this for the expression:

```
([_CurrentField_] / [YEARLY_SALES])*100
```

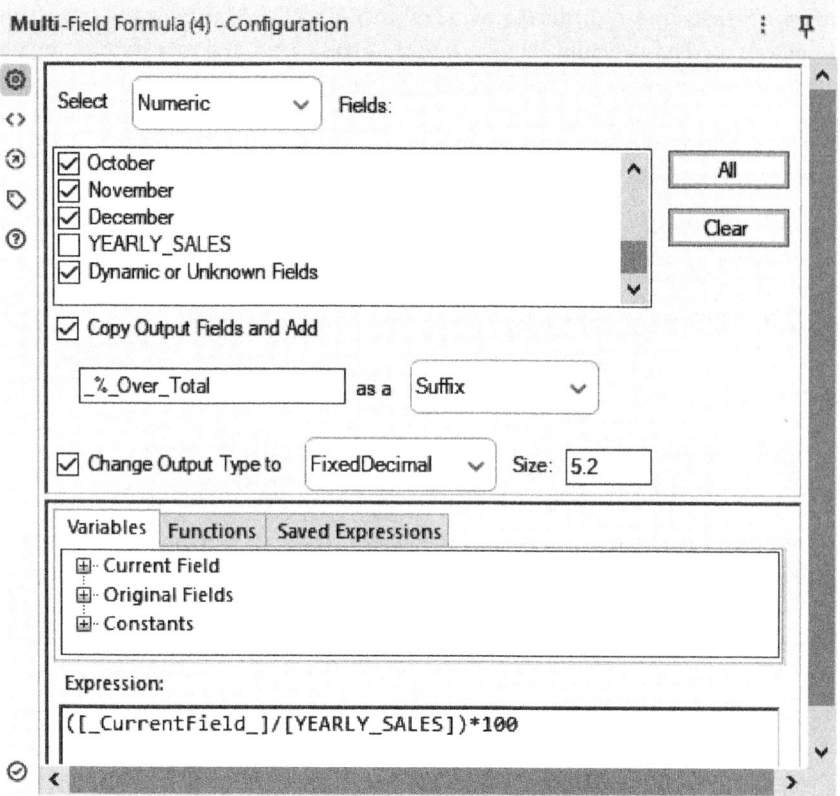

Figure 3.17: Multi-Field Formula tool configuration

1. Run the workflow and check the results.

ARTICLE_ID	January	February	March	April	May	June	July	August	September	October	November	December	YEARLY_SALES	January_%_Over_Total	February_%_Over_Total	March_%_Over_Total
001-1/2	2161670	6176200	9264300	5558580	4632150	6793820	6176200	4323340	5249770	4632150	3705720	1852860	60526760	3.57	10.20	15.31
001-1/4	5386250	7818750	8687500	9208750	7297500	8861250	11120000	7645000	9382500	8687500	8513750	7818750	100427500	5.36	7.79	8.65
001-3/8	7139800	3939200	8124600	4677800	2954400	4677800	5908800	5170200	5908800	6155000	5662600	7139800	67458800	10.58	5.84	12.04
001-5/16	3133100	1649000	1484100	824500	824500	2308600	2308600	2143700	2308600	3133100	3133100	1649000	24899900	12.58	6.62	5.96

Figure 3.18: Results of the actual workflow

You'll see the original dataset's fields, plus one new one created for each selected field, corresponding to the % of each product, each month over YEARLY_SALES.

For instance, for ARTICLE_ID=001-1/2, January is 2161670/60526760=3.57%, February is 6176200/60526760=10.20%, and so on.

Using the previous/next N records' data in the current record operation

We all know Alteryx performs its processing one record at a time, but there are some situations where we need to compare an actual value against previous (or next) values of the same field.

The **Multi-Row Formula** tool allows us to bring more records to the actual calculation, so Alteryx Designer can use previous or next values from the same field in the current data operation.

In this recipe, we'll be using the **Multi-Row Formula** tool to fill a series of data, such as the data we get from reading Excel files with merged cells.

Let's say we have a file that we would see in Excel such as this one:

	A	B	C	D	E
1	City	Zip	Customer Segment	Store Number	Sales
2	ARVADA	80002	Consumer	103	80
3				106	427
4				107	4,947
5				108	13,869
6			Corporate	103	260
7				106	4,610
8				107	9,056
9				108	13,189
10			Home Office	103	983
11				107	3,089
12				108	31
13			Small Business	103	1,031
14				107	776
15				108	78,317
16				109	1,742
17		80003	Consumer	100	7,308
18				103	10,005
19				106	289
20				107	1,464
21				108	6,553
22			Corporate	100	19,076
23				103	101,658
24				106	890
25				107	1,268
26				108	2,769
27				109	20,107
28			Home Office	100	340
29				103	11,890
30				106	1,580
31				107	5,614
32				108	676
33				109	13,064
34			Small Business	100	7,190
35				103	23,800
36				106	4,019
37				107	2,121

Figure 3.19: Excel file with merged cells

This is read this way by Alteryx:

Record	City	Zip	Customer Segment	Store Number	Sales
1	ARVADA	80002	Consumer	103	80.36
2	[Null]	[Null]	[Null]	106	426.51
3	[Null]	[Null]	[Null]	107	4946.94
4	[Null]	[Null]	[Null]	108	13868.9
5	[Null]	[Null]	Corporate	103	260.48
6	[Null]	[Null]	[Null]	106	4610.22
7	[Null]	[Null]	[Null]	107	9056.44
8	[Null]	[Null]	[Null]	108	13188.78
9	[Null]	[Null]	Home Office	103	983.06
10	[Null]	[Null]	[Null]	107	3088.84
11	[Null]	[Null]	[Null]	108	30.87
12	[Null]	[Null]	Small Business	103	1030.85
13	[Null]	[Null]	[Null]	107	776.13
14	[Null]	[Null]	[Null]	108	78317.24
15	[Null]	[Null]	[Null]	109	1742.33

Figure 3.20: Alteryx result of reading the previous file

We need to complete the values for `City`, `Zip`, and `Customer Segment` to make this dataset "workable."

Getting ready

We created a test set for this recipe that you can download from here:

https://github.com/PacktPublishing/Alteryx-Designer-Cookbook/tree/main/ch3/Recipe4

How to do it...

We'll get started using the following steps:

1. On a new workflow, drop the **Input Data** tool, point it to DATA\StartingData.xlsx, and select the Sheet1 worksheet.

2. Drop the **Multi-Row Formula** tool onto the canvas.

3. Select **Update Existing Field** and **City** from the field drop-down.

4. Leave **Num Rows** as 1 and **Values for Rows that don't Exist** as 0 or Empty (default values).

5. Use this formula for the expression:

```
IF IsNull([City])
THEN [Row-1:City]
ELSE [City]
ENDIF
```

The configuration window should look similar to this:

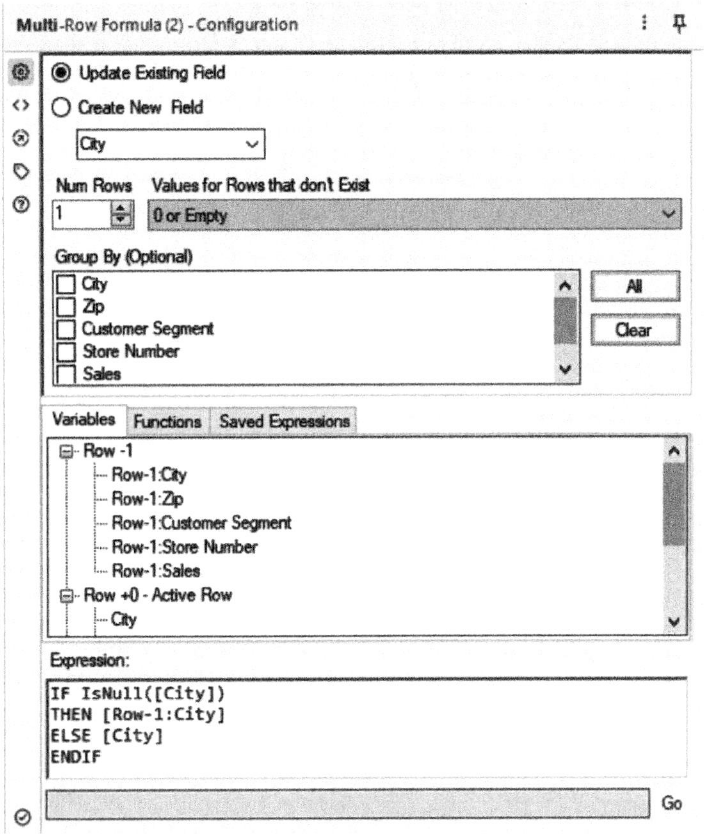

Figure 3.21: Multi-Row Formula configuration for [City]

6. Run the workflow and check the results. You'll see that the City field has been completed.

Record	City	Zip	Customer Segment	Store Number	Sales
1	ARVADA	80002	Consumer	103	80.36
2	ARVADA	[Null]	[Null]	106	426.51
3	ARVADA	[Null]	[Null]	107	4946.94
4	ARVADA	[Null]	[Null]	108	13868.9
5	ARVADA	[Null]	Corporate	103	260.48
6	ARVADA	[Null]	[Null]	106	4610.22
7	ARVADA	[Null]	[Null]	107	9056.44
8	ARVADA	[Null]	[Null]	108	13188.78
9	ARVADA	[Null]	Home Office	103	983.06

Figure 3.22: Results after the Multi-Row Formula expression for [City] was applied

7. Now, select the existing **Multi-Row Formula** tool instance, copy it, paste it onto the canvas, and connect its input anchor to the previous **Multi-Row Formula** tool instance's output anchor.

8. In the second **Multi-Row Formula** tool instance, select **Zip** from the dropdown.

9. Replace every appearance of the word `City` in the expression with the word `Zip`.

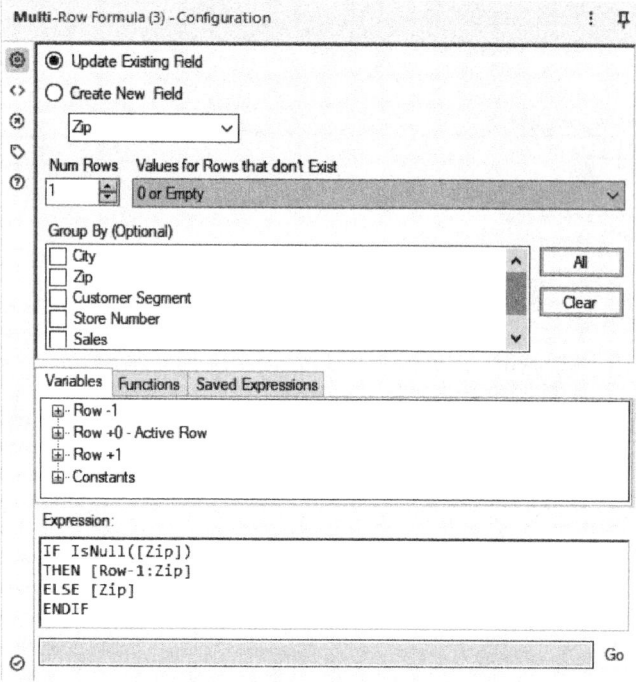

Figure 3.23: Multi-Row Formula configuration for [Zip]

10. Run the workflow. Now we have filled the `City` and `Zip` data from the dataset.

Record	City	Zip	Customer Segment	Store Number	Sales
1	ARVADA	80002	Consumer	103	80.36
2	ARVADA	80002	[Null]	106	426.51
3	ARVADA	80002	[Null]	107	4946.94
4	ARVADA	80002	[Null]	108	13868.9
5	ARVADA	80002	Corporate	103	260.48
6	ARVADA	80002	[Null]	106	4610.22
7	ARVADA	80002	[Null]	107	9056.44
8	ARVADA	80002	[Null]	108	13188.78
9	ARVADA	80002	Home Office	103	983.06

Figure 3.24: Results after the Multi-Row Formula expression for [Zip] was applied

11. Repeat these steps one more time and now use `Customer Segment` as the field to update the replacement text.

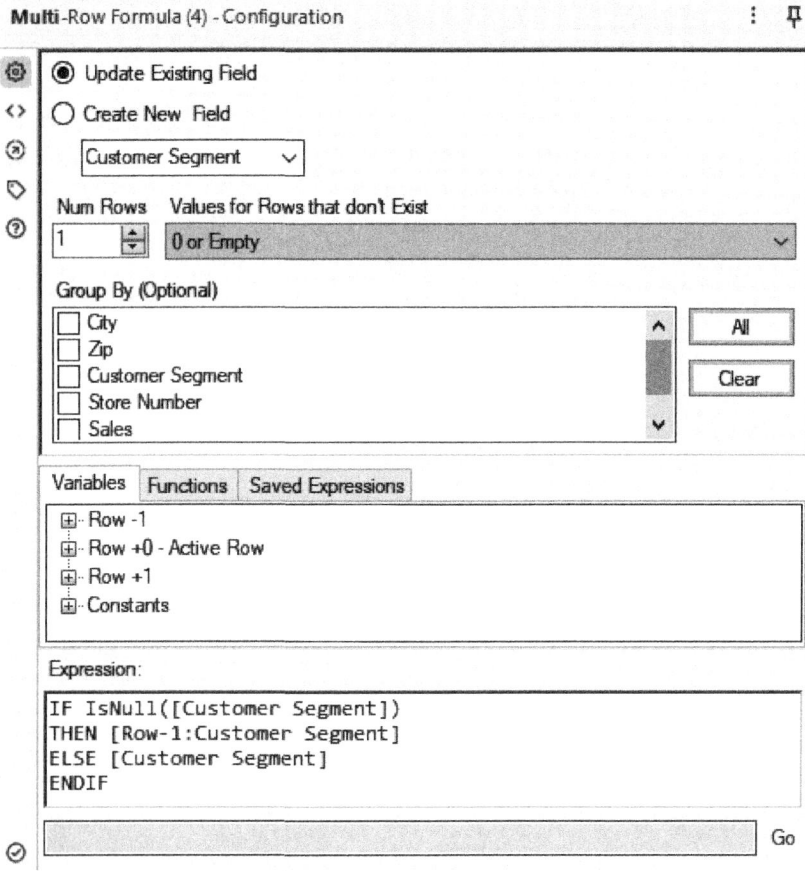

Figure 3.25: Multi-Row Formula configuration for [Customer Segment]

Your workflow should look like this:

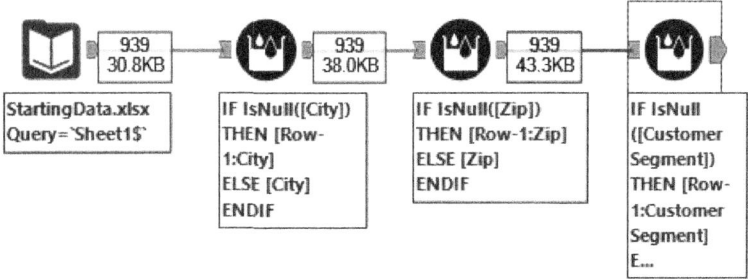

Figure 3.26: Workflow overview

12. Run the workflow and you'll see that Alteryx filled each field with the corresponding values.

Record	City	Zip	Customer Segment	Store Number	Sales
1	ARVADA	80002	Consumer	103	80.36
2	ARVADA	80002	Consumer	106	426.51
3	ARVADA	80002	Consumer	107	4946.94
4	ARVADA	80002	Consumer	108	13868.9
5	ARVADA	80002	Corporate	103	260.48
6	ARVADA	80002	Corporate	106	4610.22
7	ARVADA	80002	Corporate	107	9056.44
8	ARVADA	80002	Corporate	108	13188.78
9	ARVADA	80002	Home Office	103	983.06

Figure 3.27: Results after all Multi-Row Formula expressions were applied

How it works...

By now, we know that Alteryx processes our datasets record by record, but with this functionality, we can use previous and next records and use them in processing the actual record.

The complete set of options that the Multi-Row Formula tool offers are as follows:

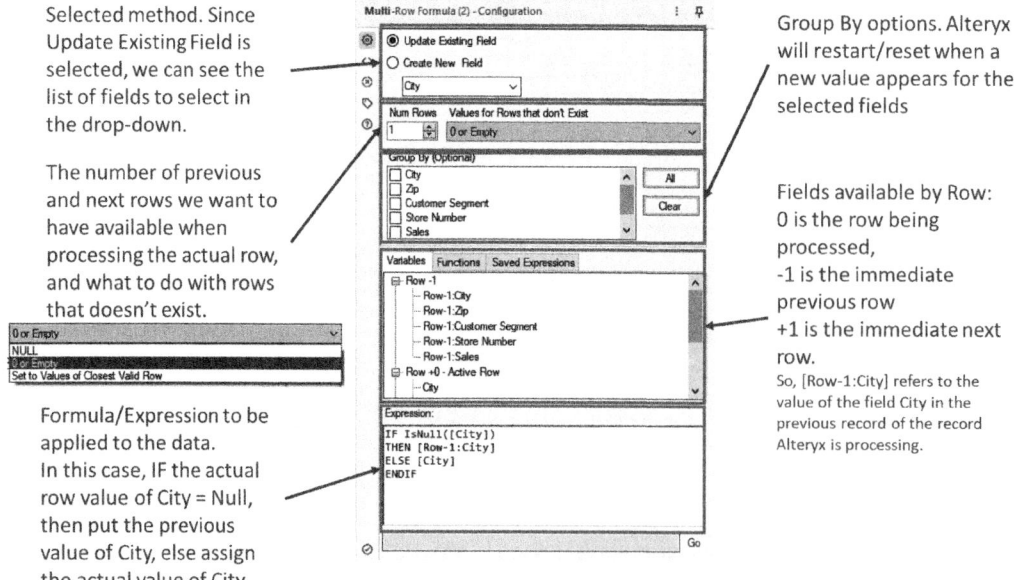

Selected method. Since Update Existing Field is selected, we can see the list of fields to select in the drop-down.

The number of previous and next rows we want to have available when processing the actual row, and what to do with rows that doesn't exist.

Formula/Expression to be applied to the data.
In this case, IF the actual row value of City = Null, then put the previous value of City, else assign the actual value of City.

Group By options. Alteryx will restart/reset when a new value appears for the selected fields

Fields available by Row:
0 is the row being processed,
-1 is the immediate previous row
+1 is the immediate next row.
So, [Row-1:City] refers to the value of the field City in the previous record of the record Alteryx is processing.

Figure 3.28: Options for the Multi-Row Formula

As you might have already discovered, the results of a multi-row formula depend on how the data is sorted when it enters the tool, so it is very important to check the sorting before configuring the **Multi-Row Formula** tool:

- **Row + 0**: This is the actual record that is being processed by Alteryx Designer
- **Row - 1**: This is the immediate *previous* record on the actual sort from the record being processed
- **Row + 1**: This is the immediate *next* record on the actual sort from the record being processed

There's more...

Grouping options within the **Multi-Row Formula** tool allows us to perform operations on a set of data, resetting every group change.

Let's say we want to get a running sum of sales per city:

1. Drop a new **Multi-Row Formula** tool instance onto the canvas and connect its input anchor to the output anchor of the last tool on the canvas.

2. Select **Create New Field**, name the new field Running_Sum, and make it of the type **Double**.

3. Select **City** in the **Group By (Optional)** section of the tool configuration and use this formula for **Expression**:

   ```
   [Row-1:Running_Sum]+[Sales]
   ```

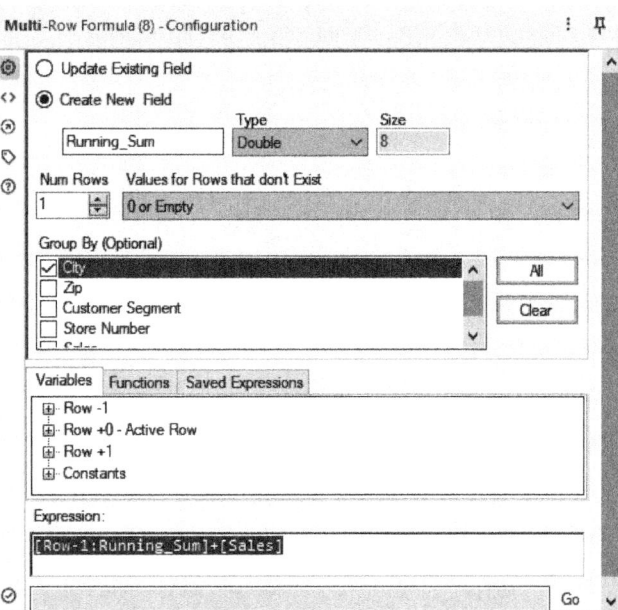

Figure 3.29: Grouping options for the Multi-Row Formula tool

4.   Run the workflow.

You'll notice that each record has the running sum, and when `City` changes, `Running_Sum` restarts.

Record	City	Zip	Customer Segment	Store Number	Sales	Running_Sum
1	ARVADA	80002	Consumer	103	80.36	80.36
2	ARVADA	80002	Consumer	106	426.51	506.87
3	ARVADA	80002	Consumer	107	4946.94	5453.81
4	ARVADA	80002	Consumer	108	13868.9	19322.71
5	ARVADA	80002	Corporate	103	260.48	19583.19
6	ARVADA	80002	Corporate	106	4610.22	24193.41
7	ARVADA	80002	Corporate	107	9056.44	33249.85
8	ARVADA	80002	Corporate	108	13188.78	46438.63
9	ARVADA	80002	Home Office	103	983.06	47421.69
10	ARVADA	80002	Home Office	107	3088.84	50510.53
11	ARVADA	80002	Home Office	108	30.87	50541.4
12	ARVADA	80002	Small Business	103	1030.85	51572.25
13	ARVADA	80002	Small Business	107	776.13	52348.38
14	ARVADA	80002	Small Business	108	78317.24	130665.62
15	ARVADA	80002	Small Business	109	1742.33	132407.95
16	ARVADA	80003	Consumer	100	7308.44	139716.39
17	ARVADA	80003	Consumer	103	10004.92	149721.31
18	ARVADA	80003	Consumer	106	289	150010.31
19	ARVADA	80003	Consumer	107	1463.82	151474.13

Figure 3.30: Grouping calculations with Multi-Row Formula

The following screenshot showcases the change in the formula:

Record	City	Zip	Customer Segment	Store Number	Sales	Running_Sum
73	ARVADA	80007	Consumer	108	11.71	845771.54
74	ARVADA	80007	Corporate	103	4953.14	850724.68
75	ARVADA	80007	Corporate	108	943.21	851667.89
76	ARVADA	80007	Home Office	106	12071.02	863738.91
77	ARVADA	80007	Home Office	109	10033.45	873772.36
78	ARVADA	80007	Small Business	107	0	873772.36
79	ARVADA	80007	Small Business	108	268.16	874040.52
80	AURORA	80010	Consumer	100	11033.69	11033.69
81	AURORA	80010	Consumer	105	15289.28	26322.97
82	AURORA	80010	Corporate	100	880.61	27203.58
83	AURORA	80010	Corporate	104	4810.3	32013.88
84	AURORA	80010	Corporate	105	10719.27	42733.15
85	AURORA	80010	Home Office	100	6919.94	49653.09
86	AURORA	80010	Home Office	104	827.88	50480.97
87	AURORA	80010	Home Office	105	45887.97	96368.94
88	AURORA	80010	Small Business	100	8265.27	104634.21
89	AURORA	80010	Small Business	104	1266.97	105901.18
90	AURORA	80010	Small Business	105	7261.9	113163.08
91	AURORA	80011	Consumer	100	5294.77	118457.85
92	AURORA	80011	Consumer	105	64777.75	183235.6
93	AURORA	80011	Corporate	100	14646.78	197882.38
94	AURORA	80011	Corporate	104	135.42	198017.8
95	AURORA	80011	Corporate	105	23415.54	221433.34
96	AURORA	80011	Home Office	100	4056.61	225489.95
97	AURORA	80011	Home Office	105	26002.45	251492.4
98	AURORA	80011	Small Business	100	47609.42	299101.82
99	AURORA	80011	Small Business	105	4233.63	303335.45

Figure 3.31: Grouping on value changes, so multi-row formula restarts

5. Now, select **City, Zip, and Customer Segment** as the **Group By** options, and the results will be more obvious:

Record	City	Zip	Customer Segment	Store Number	Sales	Running_Sum
1	ARVADA	80002	Consumer	103	80.36	80.36
2	ARVADA	80002	Consumer	106	426.51	506.87
3	ARVADA	80002	Consumer	107	4946.94	5453.81
4	ARVADA	80002	Consumer	108	13868.9	19322.71
5	ARVADA	80002	Corporate	103	260.48	260.48
6	ARVADA	80002	Corporate	106	4610.22	4870.7
7	ARVADA	80002	Corporate	107	9056.44	13927.14
8	ARVADA	80002	Corporate	108	13188.78	27115.92
9	ARVADA	80002	Home Office	103	983.06	983.06
10	ARVADA	80002	Home Office	107	3088.84	4071.9
11	ARVADA	80002	Home Office	108	30.87	4102.77
12	ARVADA	80002	Small Business	103	1030.85	1030.85
13	ARVADA	80002	Small Business	107	776.13	1806.98
14	ARVADA	80002	Small Business	108	78317.24	80124.22
15	ARVADA	80002	Small Business	109	1742.33	81866.55
16	ARVADA	80003	Consumer	100	7308.44	7308.44
17	ARVADA	80003	Consumer	103	10004.92	17313.36
18	ARVADA	80003	Consumer	106	289	17602.36
19	ARVADA	80003	Consumer	107	1463.82	19066.18

Figure 3.32: For each change in the grouping values, the sum restarts

Finally, let's take into consideration that the sort order affects the position of rows (mainly considering how to take advantage of it to perform operations). So, let's go back to *Recipe 1* in *Chapter 1*.

We are reading a set of monthly sales information from several Excel files that might be unordered.

Record	DATE	MONTHLY_SALES
1	2022-01-31	100879
2	2022-02-28	101011
3	2022-03-31	101741
4	2022-04-30	102031
5	2022-05-31	100959
6	2022-06-30	100273
7	2022-07-31	105096
8	2018-02-28	101797
9	2018-03-31	102037
10	2018-04-30	100496
11	2018-05-31	102766
12	2018-06-30	111729
13	2018-07-31	100662
14	2018-08-31	114785
15	2018-09-30	116741
16	2018-10-31	112455
17	2018-11-30	107488
18	2018-12-31	120842
19	2019-01-31	100546

Figure 3.33: Monthly data read from several Excel files

6. Drop the **Sort** tool onto the canvas and select **DATE** in **Ascending** order.

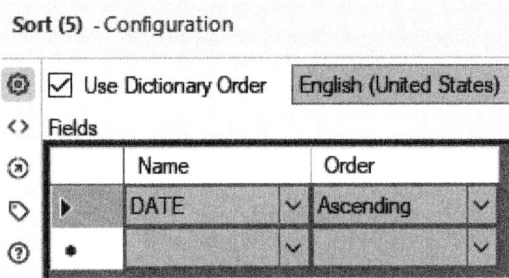

Figure 3.34: Sorting by DATE in Ascending order

Now that the data is sorted chronologically, we can think about performing calculations based on the actual order.

7. Drop the **Multi-Row Formula** tool and create a new field named `Monthly_Variance` of type **Double**.

8. Use the following formula for the expression:

```
[MONTHLY_SALES] - [Row-1:MONTHLY_SALES]
```

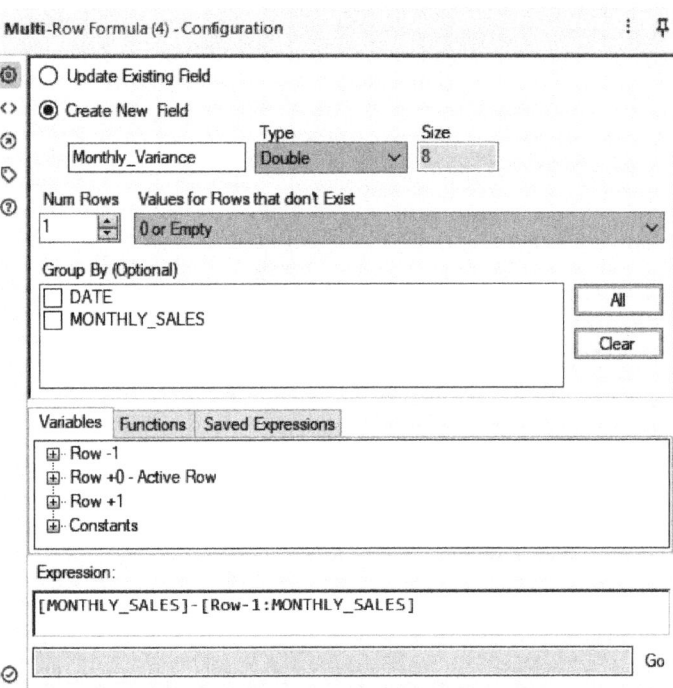

Figure 3.35: Calculating the difference between monthly sales

9. Run the workflow.

There is something "odd" within the results. Since there is no record -1 when Alteryx Designer is processing the first record, the difference is calculated against 0, Empty, or Null, so the difference is the same value as MONTHLY_SALES.

Record	DATE	MONTHLY_SALES	Monthly_Variance
1	2018-02-28	101797	101797
2	2018-03-31	102037	240
3	2018-04-30	100496	-1541
4	2018-05-31	102766	2270
5	2018-06-30	111729	8963

Figure 3.36: The first record has no Record 1

This situation may affect calculations, for example, if we need the month over month % VARIATION (it'll generate a **Divide by 0** error). There's a neat trick to fix this situation though:

10. Insert the **RecordID** tool between the **Sort** tool and the **Multi-Row Formula** tool, and change the expression of the **Multi-Row Formula** tool to the following:

```
IF [RecordID]=1
THEN 100
ELSE Round((([MONTHLY_SALES]/[Row-1:MONTHLY_SALES])-
1)*100,0.01)
ENDIF
```

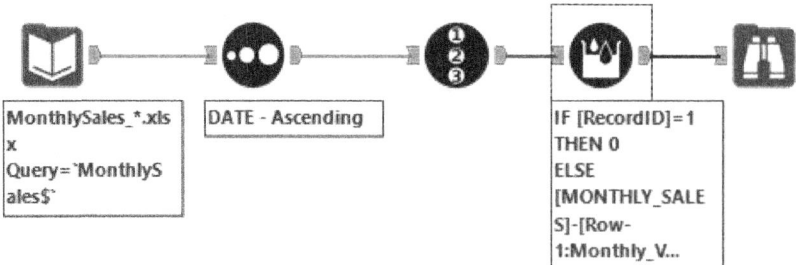

Figure 3.37: The workflow after inserting the RecordID tool

Checking the results, now we see the first record has a value of 100 (coming from the THEN clause in the expression), and the other records show the % difference against the previous period (from the ELSE clause).

Record	RecordID	DATE	MONTHLY_SALES	Monthly_Variance
4 of 4 Fields		2018-02-28	101797	100
2	2	2018-03-31	102037	0.24
3	3	2018-04-30	100496	-1.51
4	4	2018-05-31	102766	2.26
5	5	2018-06-30	111729	8.72
6	6	2018-07-31	100662	-9.91
7	7	2018-08-31	114785	14.03
8	8	2018-09-30	116741	1.7
9	9	2018-10-31	112455	-3.67
10	10	2018-11-30	107488	-4.42
11	11	2018-12-31	120842	12.42

Figure 3.38: Results after avoiding the divide by 0 error

4

Transforming Data

No matter how you start working with your data, it'll need to be transformed. Extracting/parsing fields, breaking one column into many, transposing, and arranging data are very common and necessary operations when working with data.

In this chapter, we'll see some useful methods to accomplish highly demanding tasks at ease so that your data is made ready for analysis.

Our main focus will be transposing (pivoting) and arranging data. Alteryx is very powerful and fast at performing these operations, which are crucial to correctly shape our datasets. We'll be providing recipes for the following tasks:

- Pivoting (and un-pivoting) your data
- Fixing field names after a Cross Tab operation
- Laying out data in columns
- Arranging data

Pivoting (and un-pivoting) your data

In *Applying data transformations to more than one field at a time* (the third recipe in *Chapter 3*), we worked with a file that had all the monthly sales data in columns, and we performed a series of transformations to all of the columns simultaneously with the **Multi-Field Formula** tool.

Now, we will apply different kinds of transformations to a very similar file, to see what is possible. We'll transpose columns to rows and back (Cross Tab) so that we can shape our data to perform complex calculations in a very simple way.

Also, this kind of pivoting is beneficial when working with BI/visualization products because we need to reshape the data from columns to rows (pivoting), so this recipe will apply to those cases too.

Getting ready

We prepared another test set for this recipe that you can download from here: `https://github.com/PacktPublishing/Alteryx-Designer-Cookbook/tree/main/ch4/Recipe1`.

The sample set contains CASH SALES, CASH AMOUNT, CREDIT SALES, CREDIT AMOUNT, TOTAL SALES, and TOTAL AMOUNT data for a category of products by year (2016–2022) and month (1–12).

Category	Year	Month	CASH_SALES	CASH_AMOUNT	CREDIT_SALES	CREDIT_AMOUNT	TOTAL_SALES	TOTAL_AMOUNT
100	2016	1	56	319316	162	859632	218	1178948
100	2016	2	44	248806	156	818168	200	1066974
100	2016	3	52	285730	220	1114028	272	1399758
100	2016	4	42	235730	136	760452	178	996182
100	2016	5	60	333908	140	783250	200	1117158
100	2016	6	70	371568	188	984888	258	1356456
100	2016	7	68	343940	202	1014486	270	1358426
100	2016	8	48	236706	212	933436	260	1170142

Figure 4.1: The raw data for this recipe

We are going to calculate a three-month rolling average for each of the fields.

If you decide to try this with your data, note that at some point you'll need to "rotate" rows to columns or columns to rows in your dataset.

How to do it...

We will get started by following the following steps:

1. On a new workflow, drop an **Input Data** tool onto the canvas, point it to \DATA\RawData. xlsx, and use the RawData worksheet as input.

2. From the **Preparation** category, add a **RecordID** tool after the **Input Data** tool, and leave it with the default configuration.

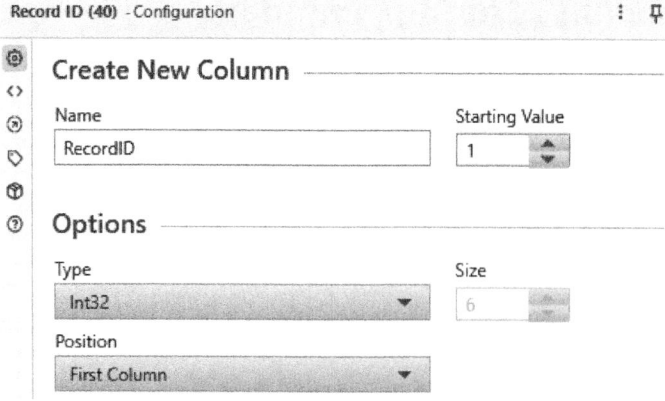

Figure 4.2: The RecordID tool default configuration

3. From the **Transform** category, add a **Transpose** tool to the canvas, connected to the **RecordID** output anchor.

4. Select **RecordID** and **Category** as **Key Columns**.

5. Select **CASH_SALES, CASH_AMOUNT, CREDIT_SALES, CREDIT_AMOUNT, TOTAL_SALES**, and **TOTAL_AMOUNT** as **Data Columns**.

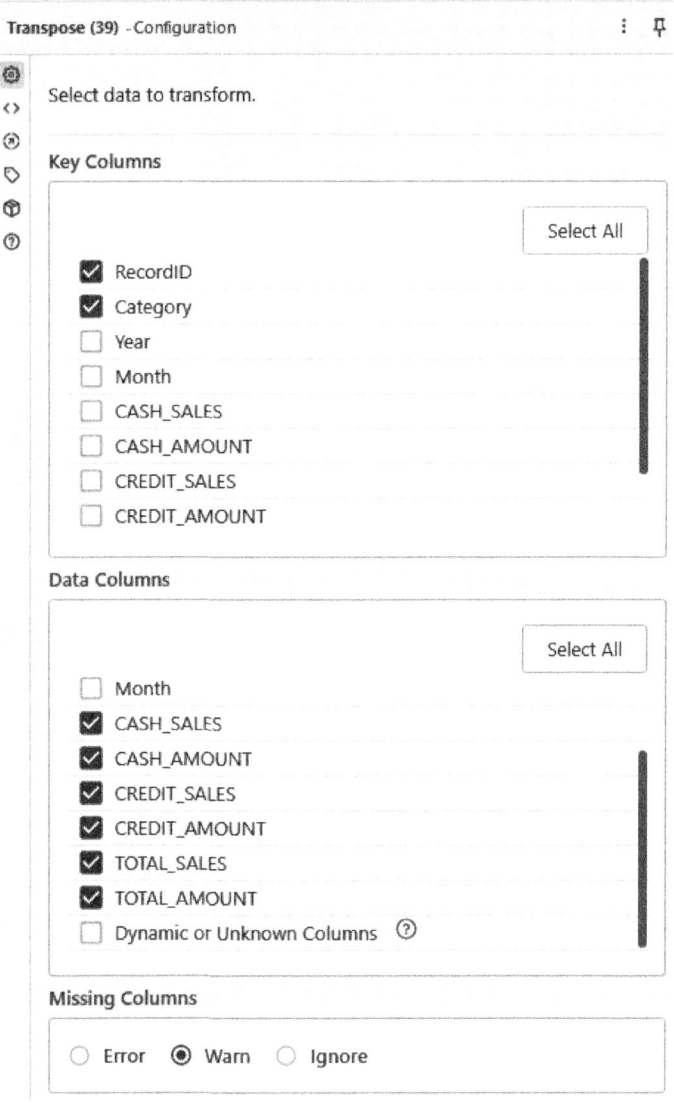

Figure 4.3: The Transpose tool configuration

6. Run the workflow.

Note how the **Transpose** tool takes the data columns and their values and converts them into rows (Name and Value).

RecordID	Category	Name	Value
1	100	CASH_SALES	56
1	100	CASH_AMOUNT	319316
1	100	CREDIT_SALES	162
1	100	CREDIT_AMOUNT	859632
1	100	TOTAL_SALES	218
1	100	TOTAL_AMOUNT	1178948
2	100	CASH_SALES	44
2	100	CASH_AMOUNT	248806
2	100	CREDIT_SALES	156
2	100	CREDIT_AMOUNT	818168
2	100	TOTAL_SALES	200
2	100	TOTAL_AMOUNT	1066974
3	100	CASH_SALES	52
3	100	CASH_AMOUNT	285730

Figure 4.4: The transposed data

Now that we have our data transposed, we can apply a **Multi-Row Formula** tool to create the rolling forecast for our categories.

7. Drop a **Multi-Row Formula** and connect it to the output anchor of the **Transpose** tool.

8. For the method, select **Create New Field**.

9. Name your new field Rolling_AVG_3 and make it the **Double** type.

10. For **Num Rows**, select **2**, and for **Values for Rows that don't Exist**, select **Set to Values of Closest Valid Row**.

11. In the **Group By** box, select **Category** and **Name** to group the rows.

12. For **Expression**, use this formula:

```
Average([Row-2:Value], [Row-1:Value], [Value])
```

Then, your tool configuration should look like this:

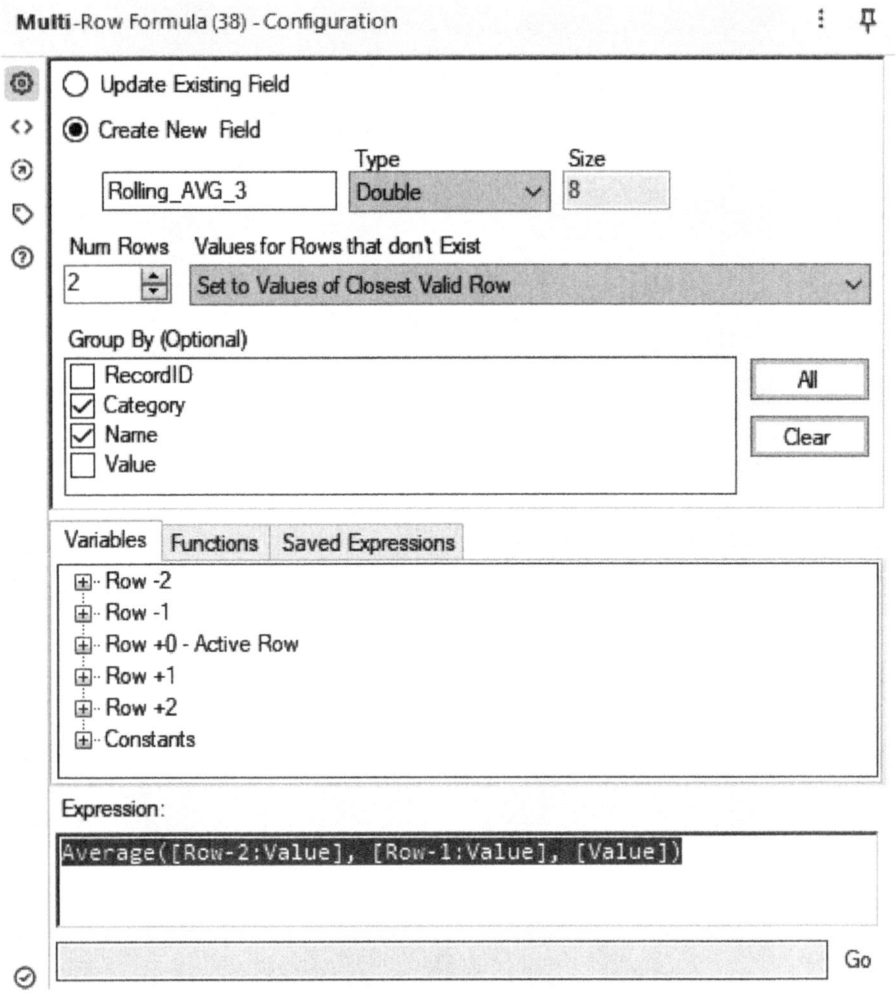

Figure 4.5: The Multi-Row Formula tool configuration

13. From the **Transform** category, add a **Cross Tab** tool next to the **Multi-Row Formula** tool.

14. Select **RecordID** as the **Group data by these values** option.

15. Select **Name** from the **Change Column Headers** dropdown.

16. Select **Rolling_AVG_3** as the **Values for New Columns** dropdown.

17. Click on **First** under **Method for Aggregating Values**.

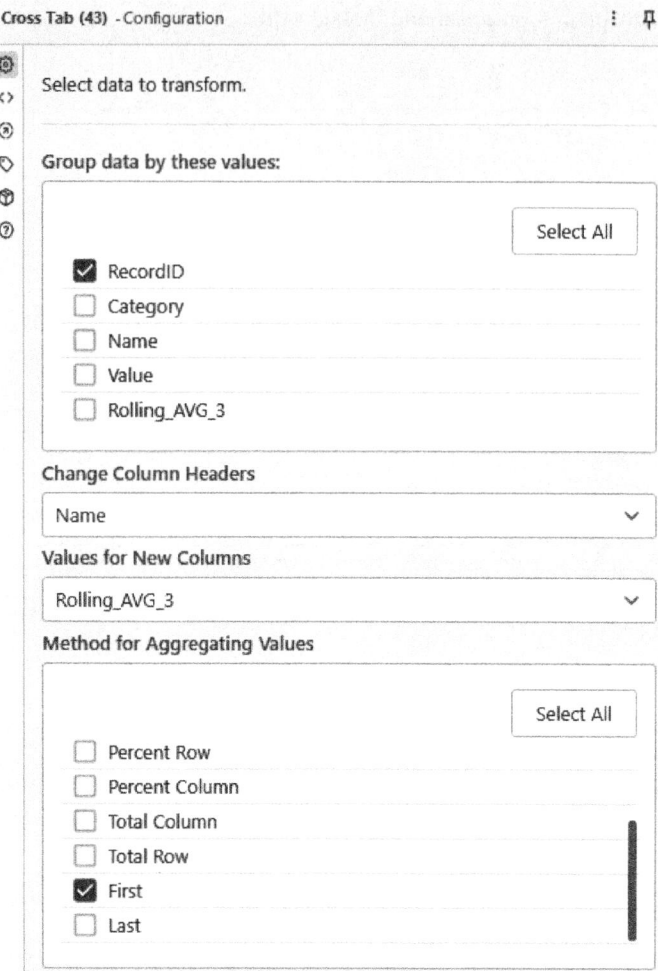

Figure 4.6: The Cross Tab tool configuration

18. Run the workflow.

    Note that the data returns to its original columnar shape, and for each `RecordID`, we have the original columns' names, but for the values, we now have the results of calculating a three-month rolling average.

    Since this is the rolling average and not the actual values, we will identify these fields correctly (that is, rename them so that we know they refer to the average and not to the original values).

19. Add a **Select** tool to the canvas.

20. Select the `CASH_AMOUNT`, `CASH_SALES`, `CREDIT_AMOUNT`, `CREDIT_SALES`, `TOTAL_AMOUNT`, and `TOTAL_SALES` fields.

21. Click **Options** and then **Add Prefix to Field Names**.

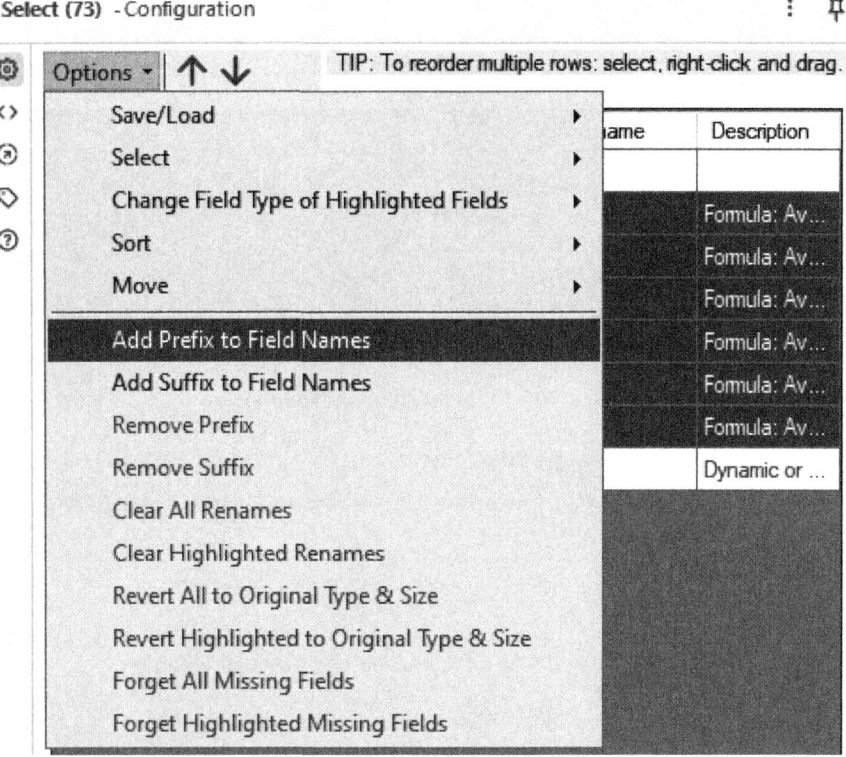

Figure 4.7: Renaming the updated fields

22. Make sure the **Only Add Prefix to Highlighted Fields** option is clicked in the pop-up window.

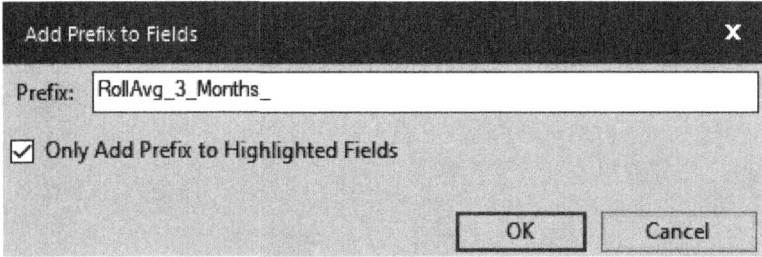

Figure 4.8: The Add Prefix to Fields option

Hit **OK**.

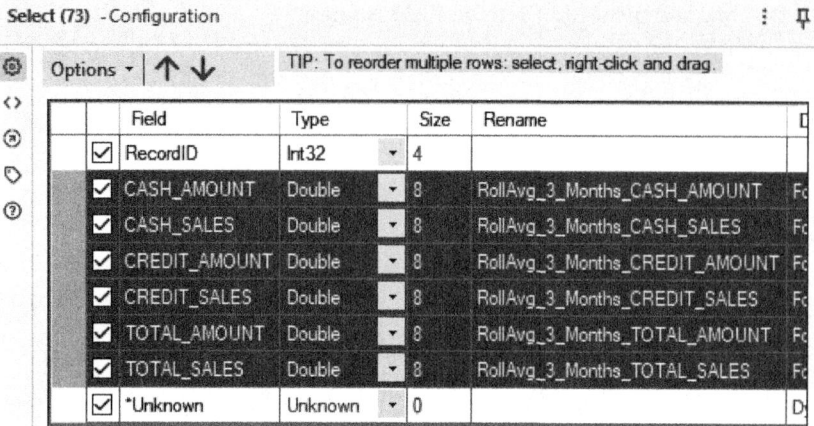

Figure 4.9: The Select tool configuration

You now have correctly identified the columns.

RecordID	RollAvg_3_Months_CASH_AMOUNT	RollAvg_3_Months_CASH_SALES	RollAvg_3_Months_CREDIT_AMOUNT	RollAvg_3_Months_CREDIT_SALES	RollAvg_3_Months_TOTAL_AMOUNT	RollAvg_3_Months_TOTAL_SALES
1	319316	56	859632	162	1178948	218
2	295812.666667	52	845810.666667	160	1141623.333333	212
3	284617.333333	50.666667	930609.333333	179.333333	1215226.666667	230
4	256755.333333	46	897549.333333	170.666667	1154304.666667	216.666667
5	285122.666667	51.333333	885910	165.333333	1171032.666667	216.666667
6	313735.333333	57.333333	842863.333333	154.666667	1156598.666667	212
7	349805.333333	66	927541.333333	176.666667	1277346.666667	242.666667
8	317404.666667	62	977603.333333	200.666667	1295008	262.666667
9	322350.666667	63.333333	1145880	247.333333	1468230.666667	310.666667

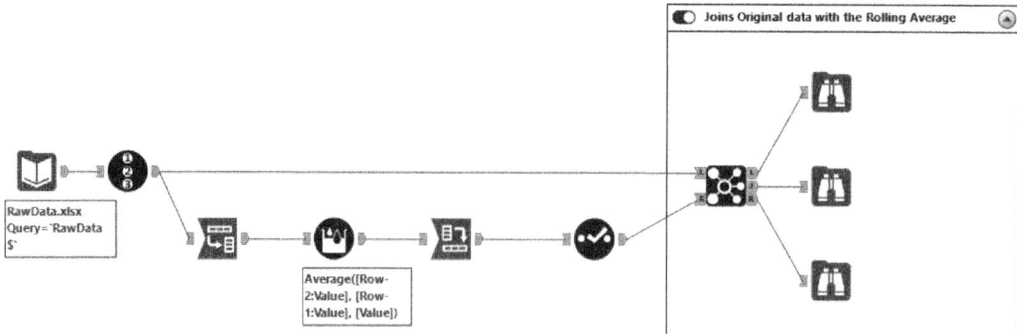

Figure 4.10: The results after renaming the updated columns

Now, we will join the original data to the rolling average we calculated.

23. From the **Join** category, drop a **Join** tool onto the canvas, and connect the output anchor of the **RecordID** tool (our original raw data and the **RecordID**), and to the **L** input anchor of the **Join** tool.
24. Connect the **Select** tool output anchor to the **Join** tool's **R** input anchor.

Figure 4.11: An overview of the workflow

25. Click on the **Join** tool to configure it.

26. Select **RecordID** from the **Left** input dropdown, and make sure **RecordID** appears in the **Right** dropdown as well.

27. Deselect **RecordID** from the **Right** input option (or click on the **Options** menu and click on **Deselect Duplicate fields**).

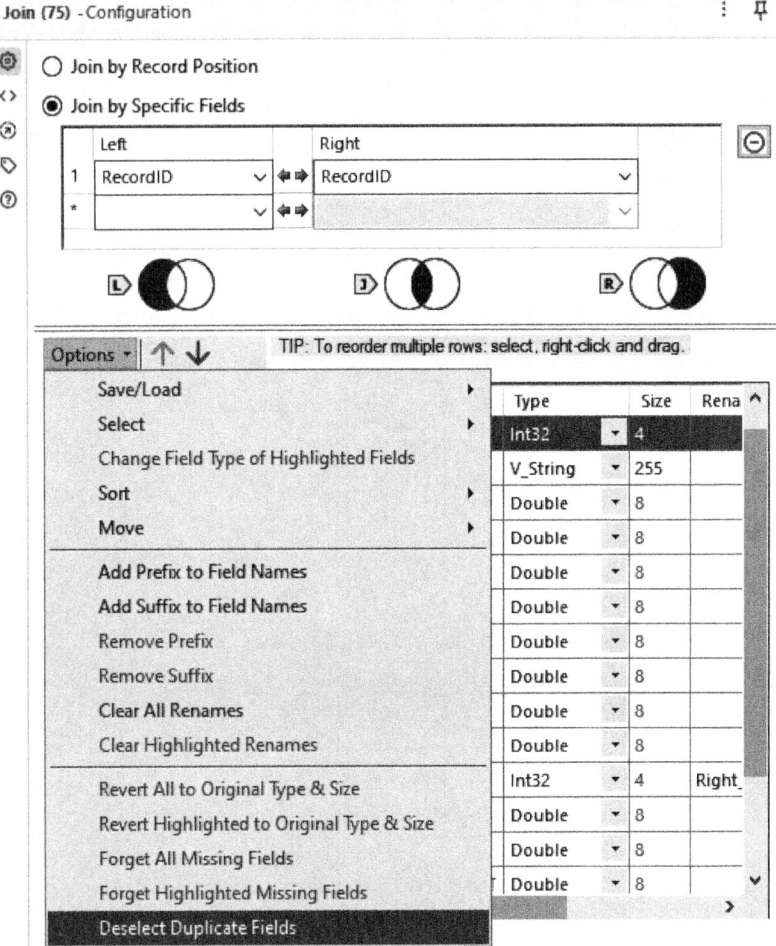

Figure 4.12: The Join tool configuration

Run the workflow and note the results.

How it works...

Alteryx Designer offers two tools to pivot a dataset, **Transpose** and **Cross Tab**, each one with its own way of working.

Transpose allows you to transform columns into rows:

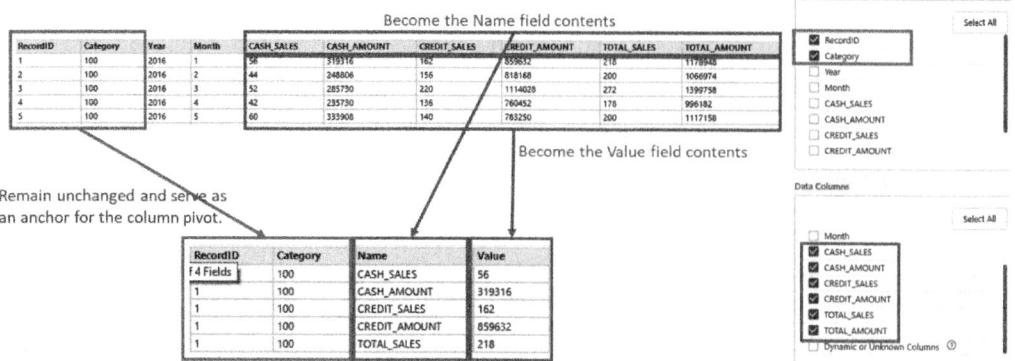

Figure 4.13: The Transpose tool configuration and operation

Cross Tab converts rows to columns:

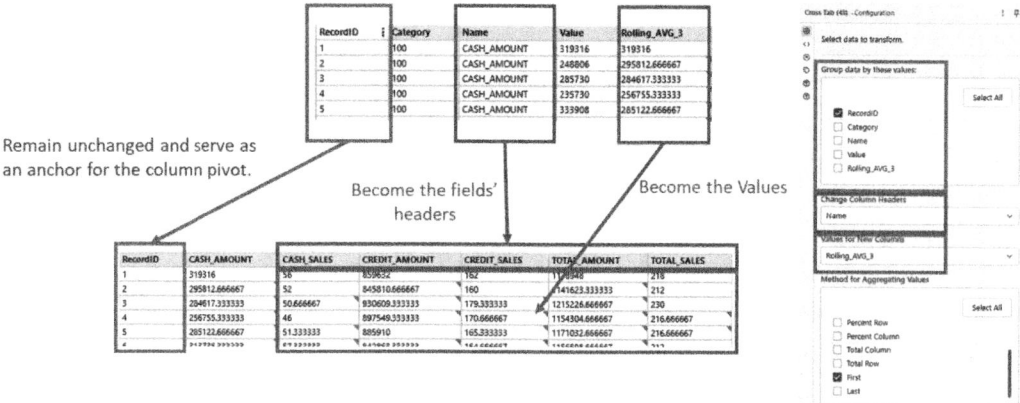

Figure 4.14: The Cross Tab tool configuration and operation

The easiest way to figure out which tool to use is by looking at their icon:

- The **Transpose** tool icon shows columns converted to rows.

Figure 4.15: The Transpose tool icon showing the columns to row pivot

- The **Cross Tab** tool icon shows rows being converted to columns.

Figure 4.16: The Cross Tab tool icon showing the rows to columns pivot

Once you have selected the right tool for the conversion you need, just figure out which fields will be used as keys (the one that'll define the pivot action and remain untouched), select the operation to aggregate values, and Alteryx will give you the results (for the **Cross Tab** tool, you also need to figure out which field will be used for the header's names and where you'll be taking the values from).

Fixing your field names after a Cross Tab operation

In the previous recipe, we didn't see this behavior, but we modified the use case slightly to learn how to fix it.

When we use the **Cross Tab** tool to use the values of a field as field names, Alteryx replaces special characters with underscores, as we can see in the following example:

Category	Year	Month	CASH_SALES	CASH_AMOUNT	CREDIT_SALES	CREDIT_
50 & less	2018	10	48	175172	192	719904
50 & less	2018	11	38	141830	166	636946
50 & less	2018	12	38	137866	258	933326
50 & less	2019	1	32	108380	244	814170

Year	Month	7_50	50___less	100	150	200	250
2016	1	900976	542990	1178948	2305464	1841288	2667756
2016	2	819070	401492	1066974	1958844	1413356	2474360
2016	3	986382	836282	1399758	2500008	1639288	2360076
2016	4	854750	943228	996182	1673838	1410388	1885504
2016	5	626504	622694	1117158	2009836	1249870	1984324
2016	6	835022	718588	1356456	1905384	1723896	2117530

Figure 4.17: Characters replaced by the Cross Tab tool

In this recipe, we'll learn how to fix this behavior and restore the values to their original state.

Getting ready

We will use the data from the previous recipe. If you need to download it, you can find it here: https://github.com/PacktPublishing/Alteryx-Designer-Cookbook/tree/main/ch4/Recipe2.

However, if you decide to practice on your data, make sure that you take the **Cross Tab** field names from a field that contains whitespace and/or special characters within its values.

How to do it...

1. On a new workflow, add an **Input Data** tool, point it to \DATA\RawData.xlsx, and select the RawData worksheet.

2. Connect a **Cross Tab** tool and configure it like this:

    - **Group data by these values**: Select **Year** and **Month**

    - **Change column Headers**: **Category**

    - **Values for New Columns**: Take the values from the TOTAL_AMOUNT field

    - **Method for Aggregating Values**: Select **Sum**

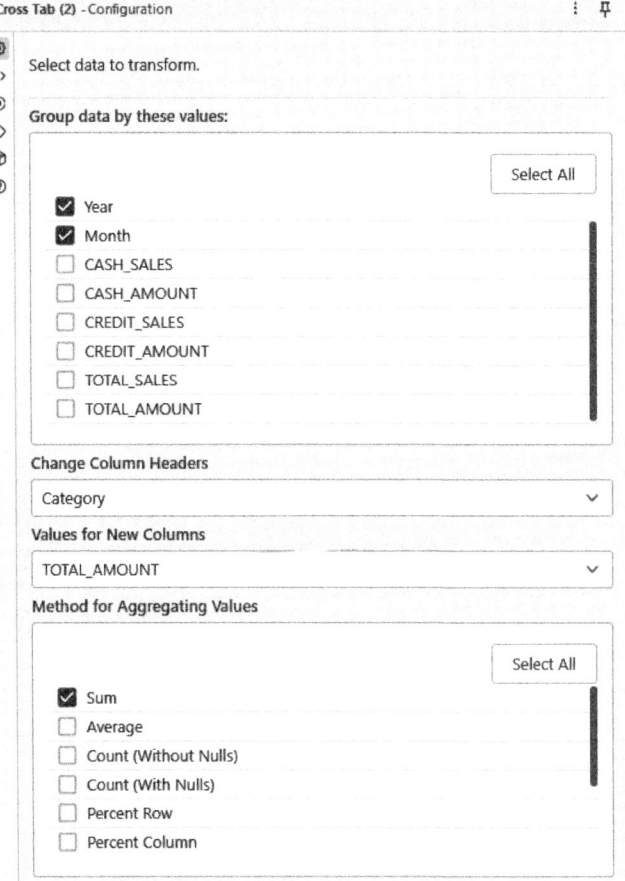

Figure 4.18: Cross Tab tool configuration

3. Run the workflow:

You'll see that the dataset now has the values from the Category field as column/field headers, but the values were changed. Where originally there was whitespace, punctuation, or a special character, there is now an underscore.

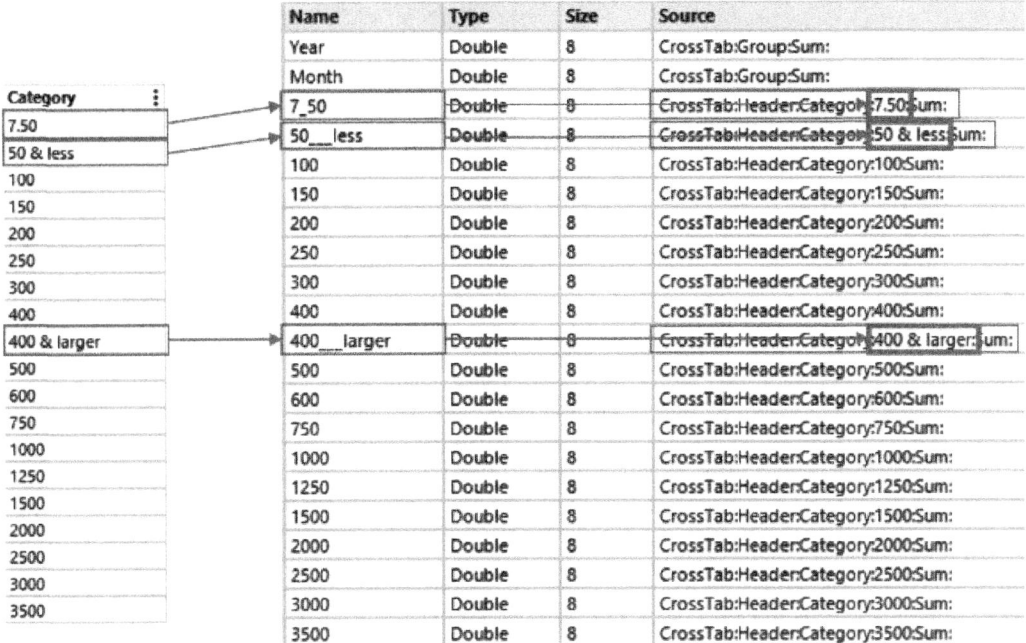

Figure 4.19: Metadata after a Cross Tab tool operation

Fortunately for us, Alteryx Designer kept the original values in the Source metadata value for each field, so we can fix this easily.

To access the dataset's metadata, we will use a **Field Info** tool (from the **Developer** category).

4. Add a **Field Info** tool, and connect its input anchor to the output anchor of the **Cross Tab** tool. The **Field Info** tool has no configuration.

5. Connect a **Text To Columns** tool to the **Field Info** tool.

6. Select the **Source** column as the **Column to Split** and : as the **Delimiter**.

7. Make sure **Split to Columns** is the current selection, and set the **Number of columns** to **5**.

8. Make sure **Leave extra in last column** is the option for **Extra characters**, and use Source as **Output root name**.

Leave all the other options unchecked.

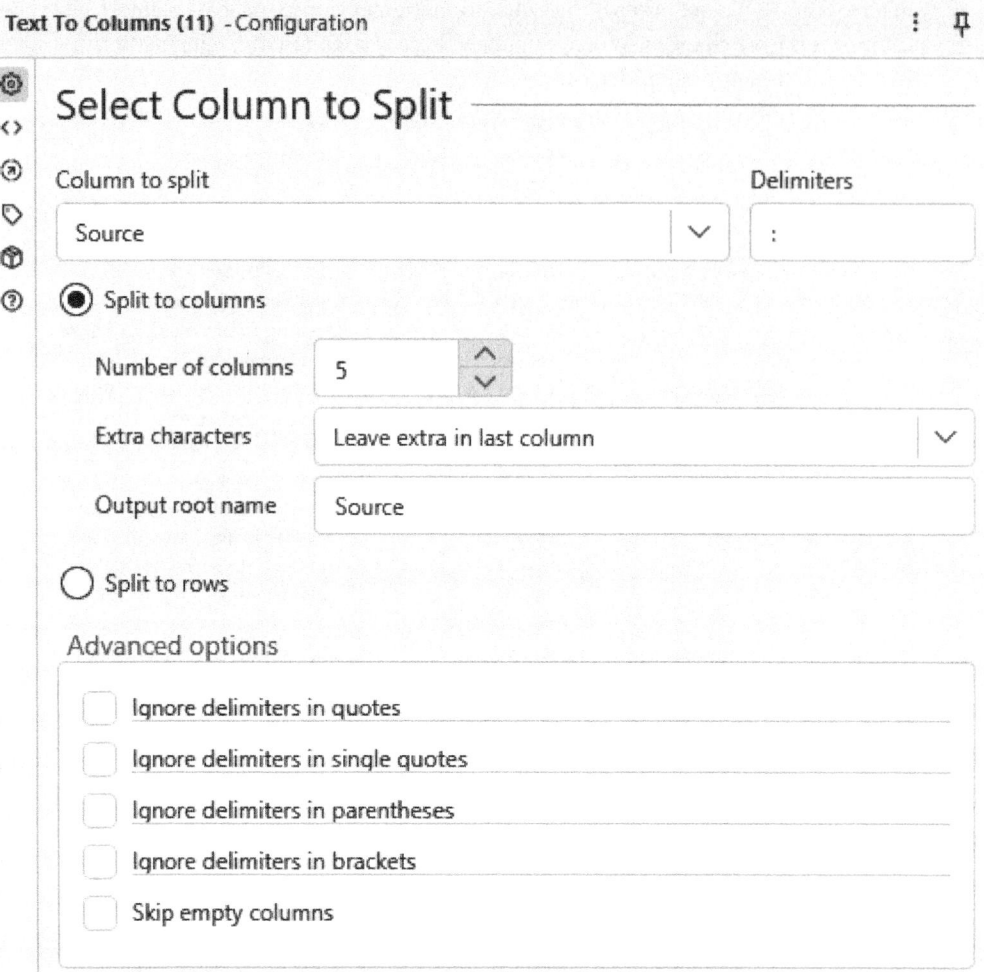

Figure 4.20: The Text To Columns tool configuration

9. Add a **Select** tool to the workflow, and select only the Name field and the Source4 name.

10. In the **Rename** column for the Source4 field, type OriginalName as the new name for the field.

Select (13) - Configuration   ⋮ 📌

⚙ Options ▾ | ↑ ↓   TIP: To reorder multiple rows: select, right-click and drag.

	Field	Type		Size	Rename	Description
☑	Name	V_String	▾	12		
☐	Type	String	▾	6		
☐	Size	Int32	▾	4		
☐	Scale	Int32	▾	4		
☐	Source	V_WString	▾	42		
☐	Description	V_WString	▾	1		
☐	Source1	V_WString	▾	42		TextToColumns: Parsed from ...
☐	Source2	V_WString	▾	42		TextToColumns: Parsed from ...
☐	Source3	V_WString	▾	42		TextToColumns: Parsed from ...
☑	Source4	V_WString	▾	42	OriginalName	TextToColumns: Parsed from ...
☐	Source5	V_WString	▾	42		TextToColumns: Parsed from ...
☑	*Unknown	Unknown	▾	0		Dynamic or Unknown Fields

☐ Use commas as decimal separators (String/Numeric conversions only)

Figure 4.21: The Select tool configuration

11. Now, add a **Filter** tool and use the **Basic filter** option. Select `OriginalName` for the field and `Is not null` for the expression.

12. Run your workflow, and note that you now have two columns – the `Name` column, which contains the auto-renamed fields from the **Cross Tab** tool, and `OriginalName`, which contains the values we extracted from the dataset's metadata.

    We will use this dataset as a custom dictionary to tell Alteryx how we will rename the columns.

13. Drop a **Dynamic Rename** tool onto the canvas, and make sure you connect the **Cross Tab** output anchor to the **L** input anchor of the **Dynamic Rename** tool and the **T** output from the **Filter** tool to the **R** input anchor of the **Dynamic Rename** tool, so your workflow should look like this:

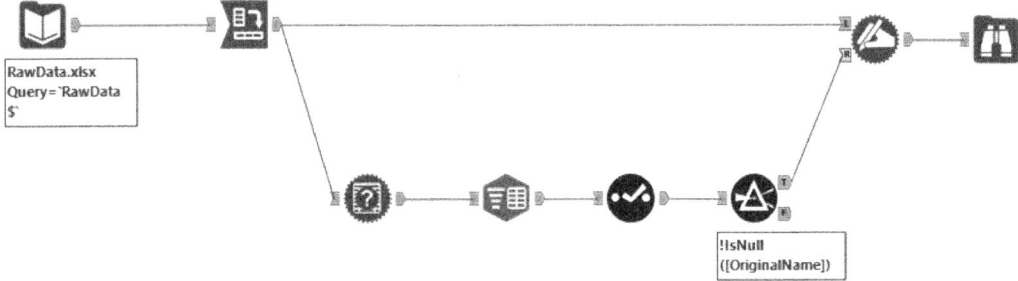

Figure 4.22: A workflow overview

14. Run the workflow, and your fields/columns should be renamed correctly now.

Year	Month	7.50	50 & less	100	150	200	250	300	400	400 & larger
2016	1	900976	542990	1178948	2305464	1841288	2667756	2541816	1809978	2267380
2016	2	819070	401492	1066974	1958844	1413356	2474360	2413114	1749486	2257158
2016	3	986382	836282	1399758	2500008	1639288	2360076	3250028	1959182	2422034

Figure 4.23: The results after applying this recipe

How it works...

For some reason, the **Cross Tab** tool needs to replace whitespace and special characters from the values it uses for the columns when they are present. Since we can use any field as a column header, we'll probably encounter this situation quite often.

The **Field Info** tool returns the dataset metadata as a data source, so we can access it anytime – in this case, to extract the original value of the column we will use as we did with the headers.

With the **Text To Columns** tool, we will split the value of the source column, one value per : appearance. So, setting the number of columns to **5** allows us to get the first four columns and a fifth that holds everything that remains on the field value (because we told the tool to leave extra characters in the last column in its configuration).

Using Source as the output root name will produce a sequence of fields named Source1, Source2, and SourceN (where N = the number of columns we selected).

So, let's take the following value (: = the separator has been discarded):

```
CrossTab:Header:Category:50 & less:Sum:
```

This will produce the following:

- One column with the name Source1 and the CrossTab value
- A second column with the name Source2 and the Header value
- A third column called Source3 with the Category value
- A fourth column called Source4 with the 50 & less value
- A fifth column named Source5 with all the remaining characters after the separator (Sum:)

Then, the **Select** and **Filter** tools complete the tidying up, so we get a very simple custom dictionary that we can use to rename the fields.

Name	OriginalName
7_50	7.50
50___less	50 & less
100	100
150	150
200	200
250	250
300	300
400	400
400___larger	400 & larger
500	500
600	600
750	750
1000	1000
1250	1250
1500	1500
2000	2000
2500	2500
3000	3000
3500	3500

Figure 4.24: A custom dictionary created

For this, we will use the **Dynamic Rename** tool. One of its modes to rename fields is **Take Field Names from Right Input Rows**, and this only needs an input dataset that has, at least, the actual name of the field and how we want to call it, which is exactly what we did in the previous steps.

So, we select the actual name of the field in **Old Field Name from Column** and how we want to call it in **New Field Name from Column**.

Alteryx Designer will check for the actual name in our dictionary (in the **Name** column) and, when it finds a match, rename the field with the values from the column we select (with the value from the **OriginalName** field).

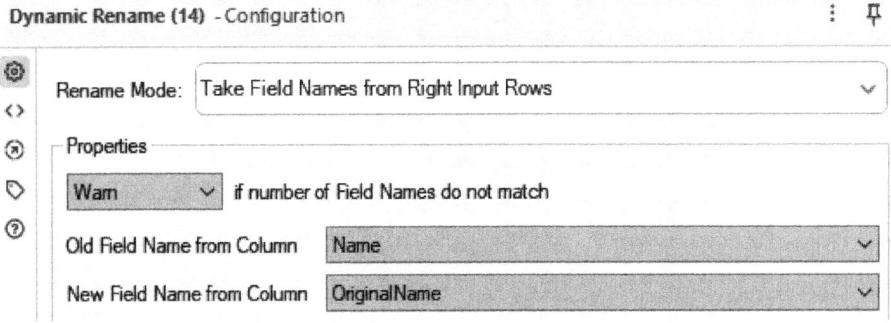

Figure 4.25: The Dynamic Rename tool configuration

Laying out your data in columns

Sometimes, we need to arrange our data in columns, for presentation or other purposes. As we'll see in this recipe, doing so is very easy with Alteryx Designer.

We will work with a US Presidents dataset and lay out the output in columns so that we can show it properly.

Getting ready

We created a dataset containing the data, plus a folder with the pictures of each president, and we'll distribute them in columns throughout this recipe. You can download the whole set from here: https://github.com/PacktPublishing/Alteryx-Designer-Cookbook/tree/main/ch4/Recipe3.

Also, we included an additional use case that can be solved with a little modification of this recipe in the ADDITIONAL USE CASE folder.

How to do it...

1. Drop an **Input Data** tool onto the canvas and point it to \DATA\US_Presidents.CSV.

#	Name	File
16	Abraham Lincoln	..\PICS\100px-Al16.jpg
7	Andrew Jackson	..\PICS\100px-Andrew_jackson_head.gif
17	Andrew Johnson	..\PICS\100px-Aj17.gif

Figure 4.26: Contents of US_Presidents.CSV

You'll see that you have the number (#), the name of the president, and a File field, with a relative path to the president's picture.

2. Add a **Sort** tool, and select # for **Name** and **Ascending** for **Order**.

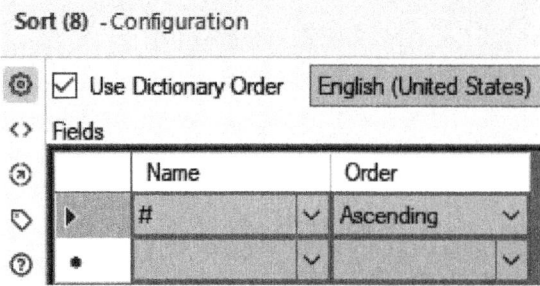

Figure 4.27: The Sort tool configuration

3.   Drop an **Image** tool from the **Reporting** category.

4.   Make sure **Retrieve Image From Disk At Runtime** is the option selected (it should be the default option).

5.   From the **Filename:** dropdown, use any string (we'll replace it entirely with the next configuration).

6.   Click and enable **Modify filename for each record**.

7.   From the **Modify Filename By:** dropdown, select **Replacing Entire Path With Field**.

8.   Select **File** from the **Using This Field:** dropdown.

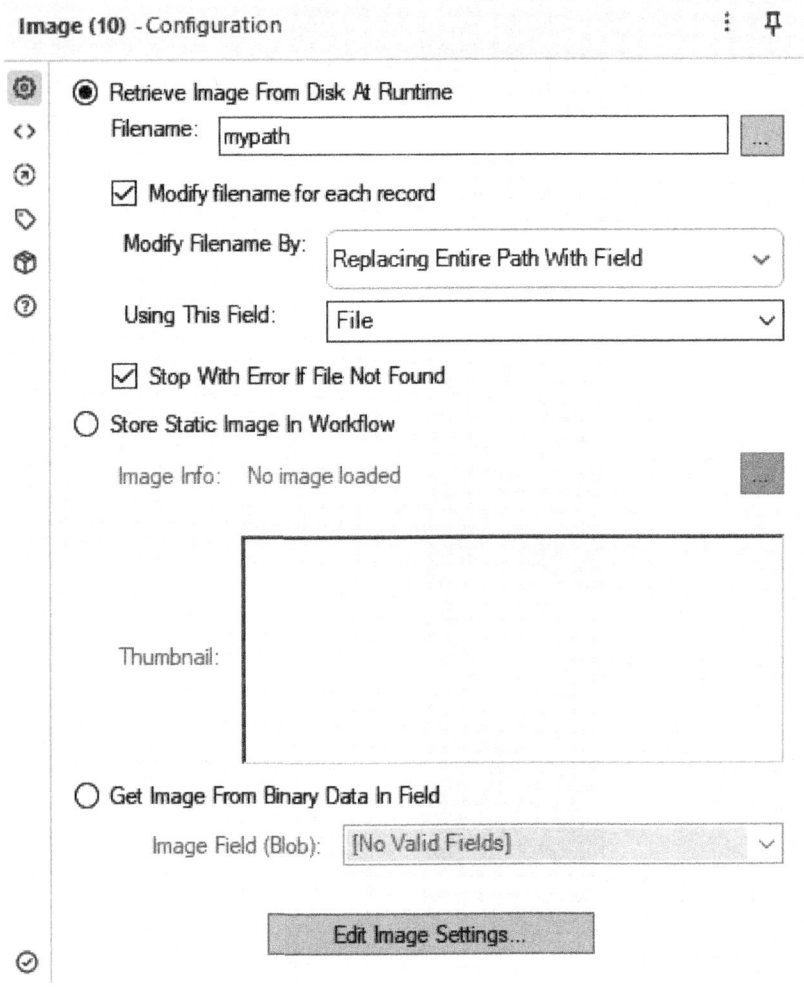

Figure 4.28: The Image tool configuration

9.   Add a **Browse** tool to the **Image** tool and run the workflow.

You'll see that Alteryx presents a list of the president's images sorted by #.

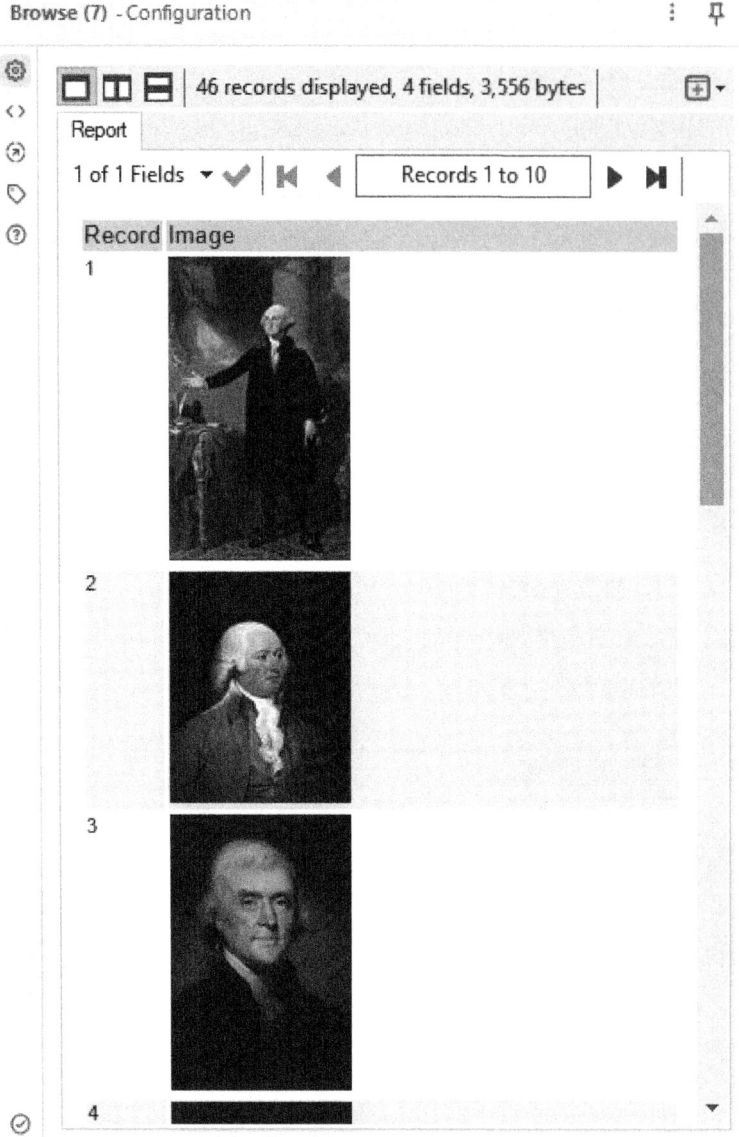

Figure 4.29: The Browse tool results (before making columns)

10. Add a **Make Columns** tool from the **Laboratory** category, and select **4** as the number of columns.

11. Leave **Arrange Horizontally** selected (which is the default).

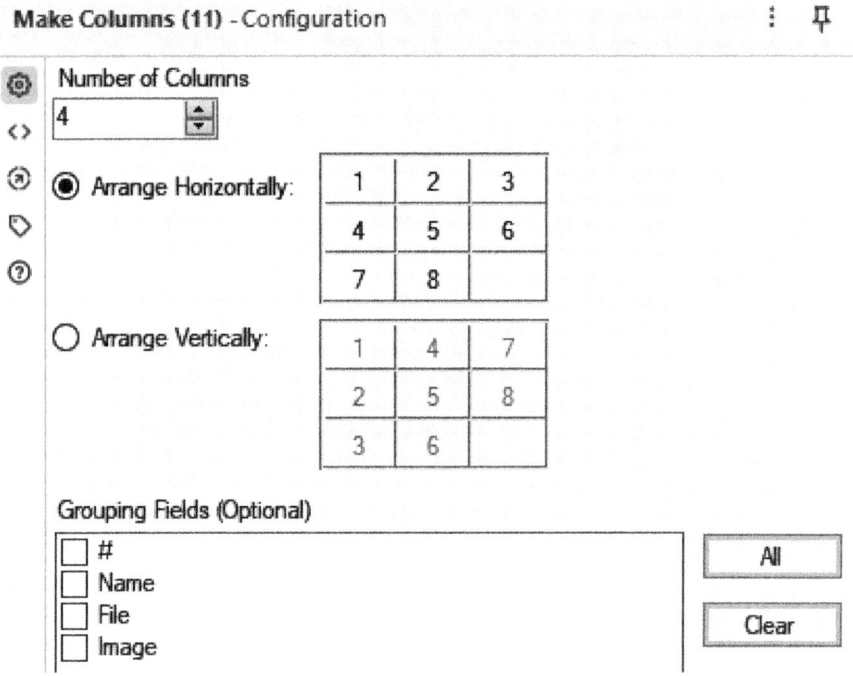

Figure 4.30: The Make Columns tool configuration

12. Add another **Browse** tool to the canvas, connected to the output anchor of the **Make Column** tool.

13. Run the workflow.

Now, you'll be presented with the president's pictures distributed in four columns (as selected).

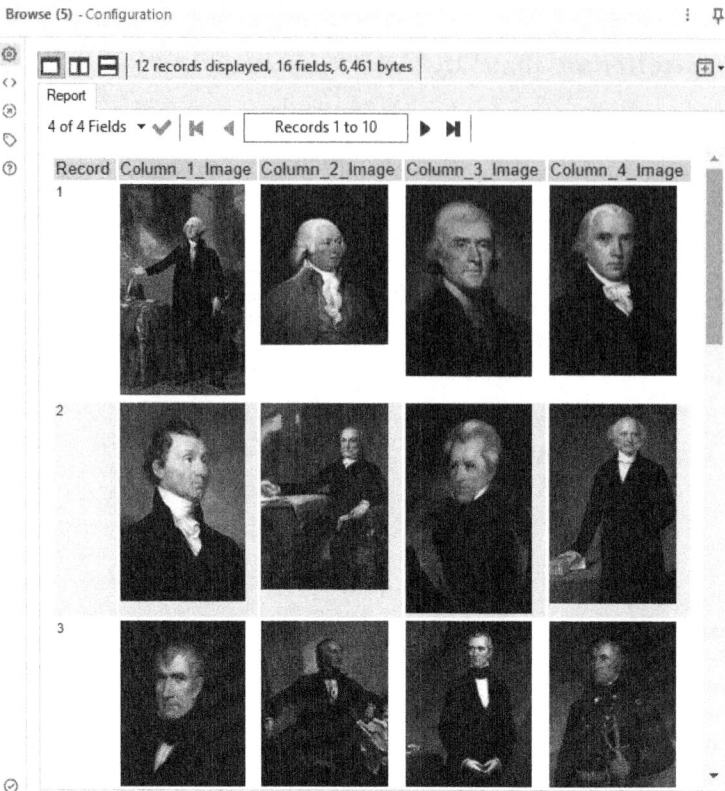

Figure 4.31: The Browse tool results (after making columns)

And the dataset will also be distributed horizontally into four columns, with the `Column_<number of column>_` prefix added to the field name.

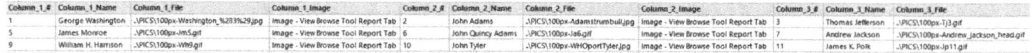

Figure 4.32: The dataset arranged into columns

How it works...

The **Image** tool allows us to pick an image from different sources – in this case, we picked it from the hard drive, based on a relative path (`..\PICS\etc`...). We'll explore more options using this tool in *Chapter 13*.

The **Make Columns** tool distributes all the fields in several columns (indicated by us in the **Number of Columns** option), horizontally or vertically. It also renames each one, depending on the column it falls on, by adding a prefix that will help us identify the original field.

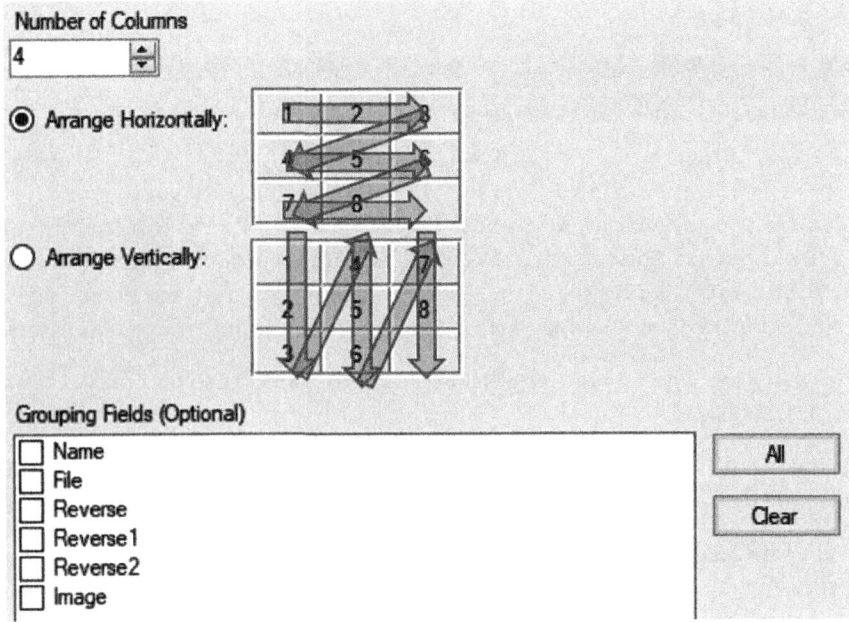

Figure 4.33: The Make Columns tool distribution of columns

There's more...

Excel data from users tends to arrive in a variety of shapes and sizes and is mostly configured for easy human readability and interpretation.

With only a few, this recipe can also help us convert this data:

Customers	Plans		
ID	Plan	Start Date	Annual Increment
Name	Fee	End Date	Years
Marital Status			
Education			
1			
John Smith	Basic	12/1/2021	0.08
Single	30	12/1/2022	1
some College			
2			
Mary Stuart	Premium		
Married	55.4	5/1/2020	0.09
College Degree		4/30/2025	3

Figure 4.34: A complex distribution of Excel data

We can convert it into this:

ID	Name	Marital Status	Education	Plan	Fee	Start Date	End Date	Annual Increment	Years
1	John Smith	Single	some College	Basic	30	2021-12-01	2022-12-01	0.08	1
2	Mary Stuart	Married	College Degree	Premium	55.4	2020-05-01	2025-04-30	0.09	3

Figure 4.35: The tabular results

Just read the data and analyze each field. You'll see that Customers has four headers (ID, Name, Marital Status, and Education). After that, you'll find the data corresponding to each field (1 for ID, John Smith for Name, Single for Marital Status, and Some College for Education). At first glance, we can guess that we'll need four columns to solve this part of the data.

We'll fix this part using a **Select** tool to isolate the Customers field and four **Make Columns** tools distributed horizontally.

Repeat the same on each field (bearing in mind that each one has its own number of columns, depending on the amount of data present) and repeat the operation.

Finally, use a **Join Multiple** tool, joining by record position, and the resulting data will be in a tabular shape.

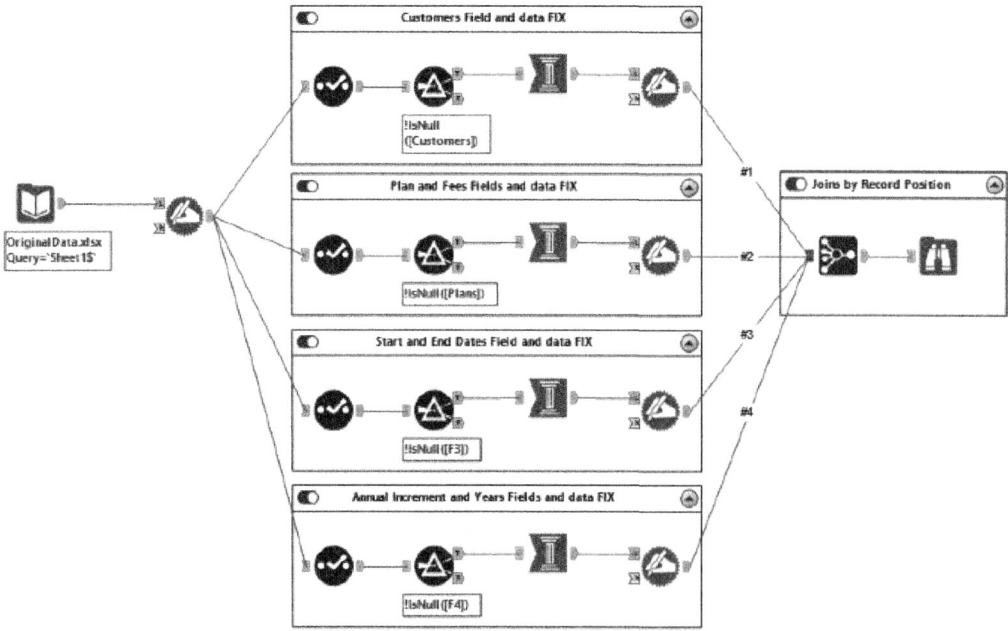

Figure 4.36: A workflow overview

You can find this complete use case in the same folder as this recipe, in the \ADDITIONAL USE CASE folder.

Arranging data

In the previous recipes, we've manipulated our datasets but in a relatively ordered way. Alteryx Designer also allows us to arrange datasets manually in the way we want, creating columns and rows based on a dataset's contents.

So, for example, let's take the tabular data from the previous recipe's additional use case:

ID	Name	Marital Status	Education	Plan	Fee	Start Date	End Date	Annual Increment	Years
1	John Smith	Single	some College	Basic	30	2021-12-01	2022-12-01	0.08	1
2	Mary Stuart	Married	College Degree	Premium	55.4	2020-05-01	2025-05-01	0.09	5
3	Giacomo K. Stafford	Single	Some College	Plus	40	2023-06-18	2025-06-18	0.035	2
4	Odysseus Hester	Single	High School	Basic	30	2022-10-27	2023-10-27	0.03	1
5	Abra R. Hammond	Single	Bachelor's degree	Basic	30	2023-05-29	2031-05-29	0.03	8
6	Indira N. Bradley	Married	High School	Premium	55.4	2023-05-30	2027-05-30	0.04	4
7	Tobias G. Casey	Common-Law	Some College	Basic	30	2022-03-03	2024-03-03	0.03	2
8	Jarrod S. Cameron	Married	Master/Post-Degree	Basic	30	2023-02-28	2031-02-28	0.03	8
9	Piper Lara	Married	High School	Basic	30	2022-04-20	2031-04-20	0.03	9

Figure 4.37: Incoming tabular data

We want to group several pieces of data into columns and rows, so we can present the data in this way (arranged very similarly to the original file):

	A	B	C	D
1	ID	Plan	Start Date	Annual Increment
2	Name	Fee	End Date	Years
3	Marital Status			
4	Education			
5	1	Basic	2021-12-01	0.08
6	John Smith	30	2022-12-01	1.00
7	Single			
8	some College			
9	2	Premium	2020-05-01	0.09
10	Mary Stuart	55.4	2025-05-01	5.00
11	Married			
12	College Degree			
13	3	Plus	2023-06-18	0.04
14	Giacomo K. Stafford	40	2025-06-18	2.00
15	Single			
16	Some College			
17	4	Basic	2022-10-27	0.03
18	Odysseus Hester	30	2023-10-27	1.00
19	Single			
20	High School			
21	5	Basic	2023-05-29	0.03
22	Abra R. Hammond	30	2031-05-29	8.00
23	Single			
24	Bachelor's degree			
25	6	Premium	2023-05-30	0.04
26	Indira N. Bradley	55.4	2027-05-30	4.00
27	Married			
28	High School			
29	7	Basic	2022-03-03	0.03
30	Tobias G. Casey	30	2024-03-03	2.00
31	Common-Law			
32	Some College			
33	8	Basic	2023-02-28	0.03
34	Jarrod S. Cameron	30	2031-02-28	8.00
35	Married			
36	Master/Post-Degree			
37	9	Basic	2022-04-20	0.03

Figure 4.38: Outputting the formatted data

We'll focus on data arrangement and not so much on the reporting tools, since we're going to explore reporting tools in *Chapter 13*.

Getting ready

You can download all the data and workflows from here: `https://github.com/PacktPublishing/Alteryx-Designer-Cookbook/tree/main/ch4/Recipe4`.

If you decide to try this recipe with your data, design an output that involves arranging rows and/or columns so that you can see how this recipe works.

How to do it...

1. On a new workflow, drop an **Input Data** tool onto the canvas.

2. Point it to `..\DATA\PlansData.xlsx` and the `PlansDetails` worksheet.

3. Now, add an **Arrange** tool (from the **Transform** category).

4. Select **ID** as **Key Field**.

5. From the **Column** dropdown, click **Add**. A new window will pop up.

6. For **Column Header**, type `Customers`.

7. For the **Fill in Description Column** dropdown, select **Add New Description**.

8. For the **Description Mode** drop-down, select **Take from Field Names**.

9. For **Description Header,** type `Customers Headers.`

10. In the **Fields** selection box, click on **ID**, **Name**, **Marital Status**, and **Education**.

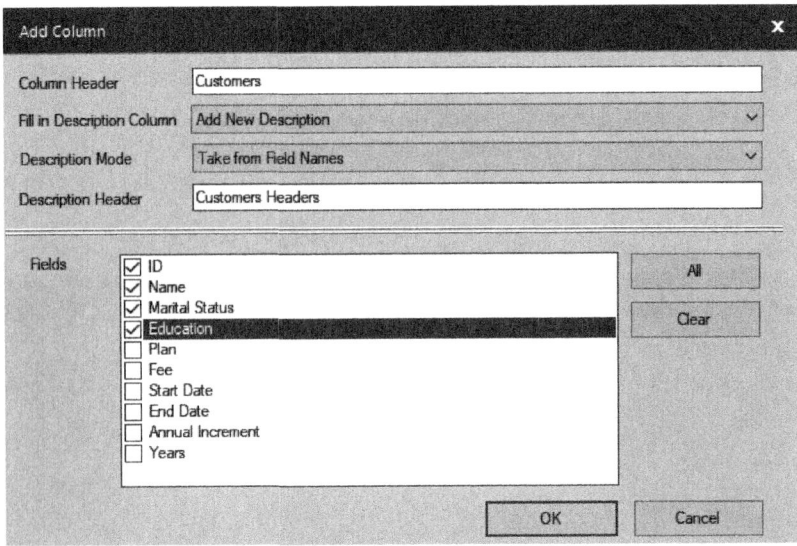

Figure 4.39: Adding columns in the Arrange tool

11. Hit **OK**, and you'll see that Alteryx has added two columns – `Customers Headers` and `Customers`.

The first column contains the field names selected, and the second will be filled with the selected field name's values.

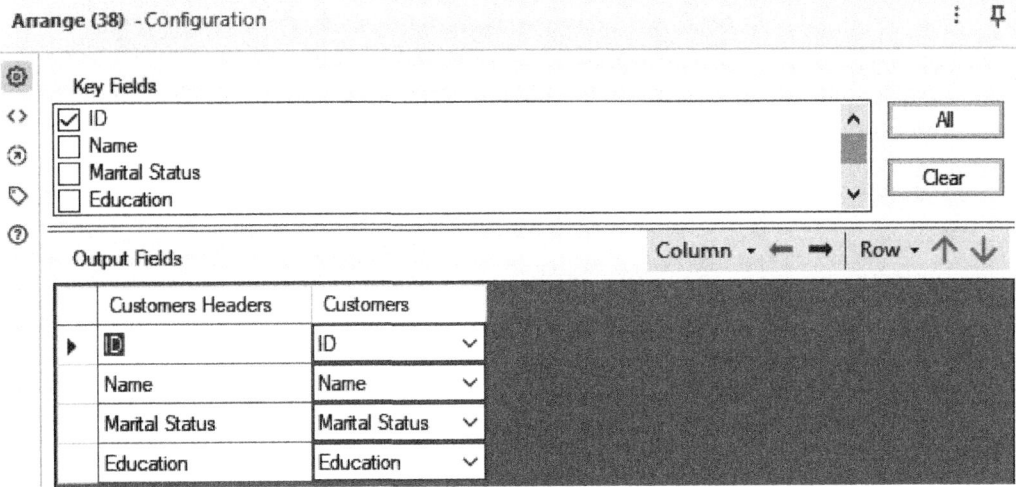

Figure 4.40: The Arrange tool configuration

So, we will now add the remaining columns.

12. Click on **Columns** and then **Add**.

13. Type `Plan` in the **Column Header** input.

14. Select **Add New Description** for **Fill in Description Column**.

15. Select **Take from Field names**.

16. Type `Plan Headers` for **Description Header**.

17. Select **Plan** and **Fee** from the **Fields** selection box.

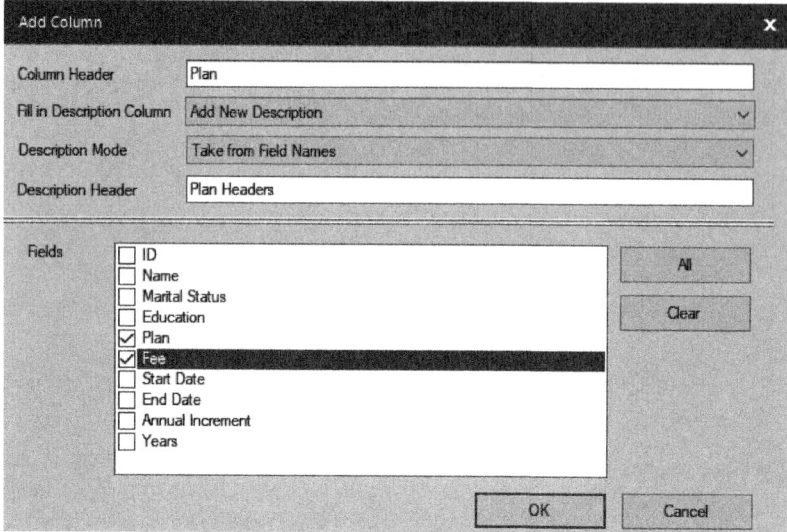

Figure 4.41: Adding the Plan and Fee columns

18. Hit **OK**, and another two columns will be added to your **Output Fields** section (`Plan Headers` and `Plan`).

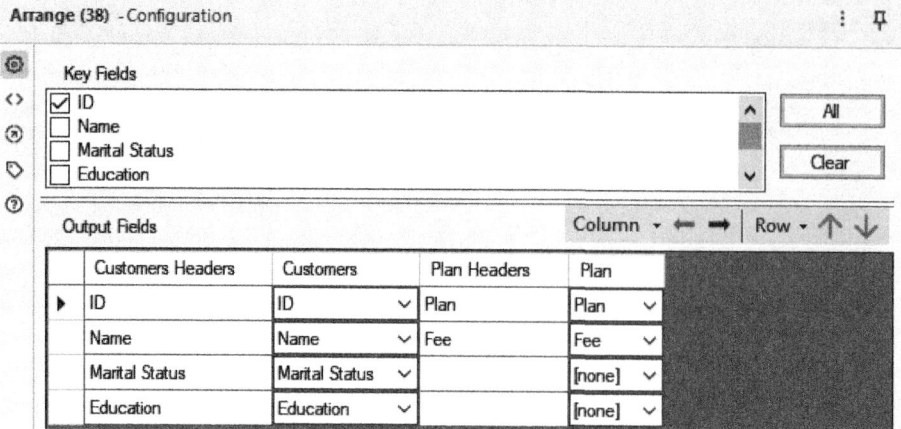

Figure 4.42: The Plan and Fee columns added

19. Repeat the last procedure for the remaining two groups of two fields each.

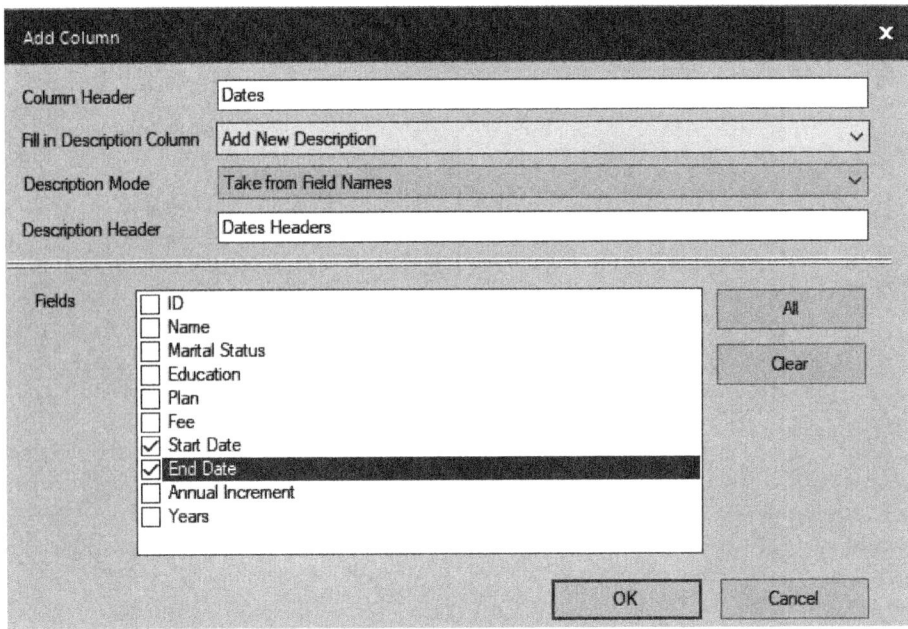

Figure 4.43: Adding the date columns

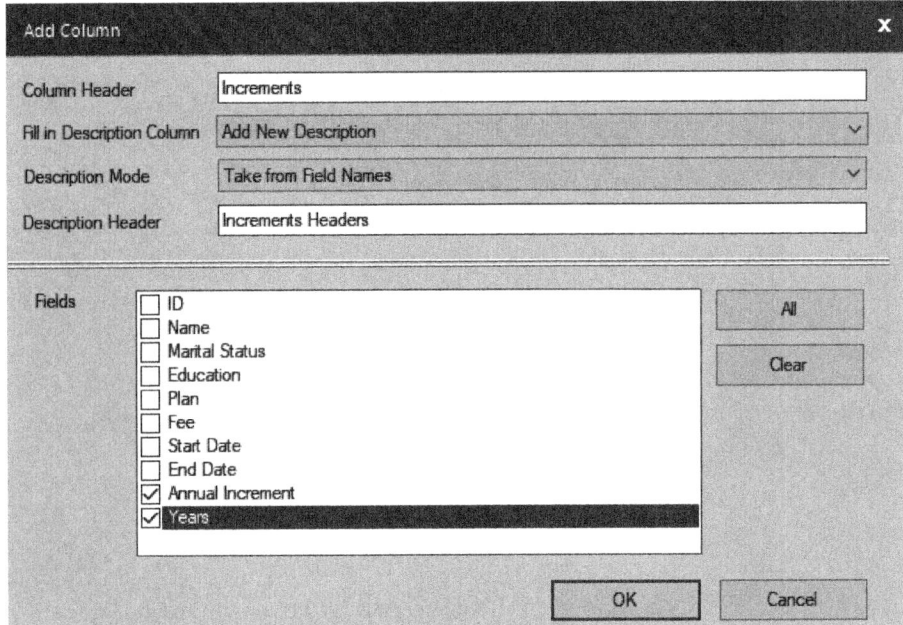

Figure 4.44: Adding Annual Increment and Years columns

Once you've finished, you'll see that the **Output Fields** section looks like this:

Arrange (3) - Configuration								

Key Fields

☑ ID
☐ Name
☐ Marital Status
☐ Education

All

Clear

Output Fields

Column ▾ ← → Row ▾ ↑ ↓

Customers Headers	Customers	Plan Headers	Plan	Dates Headers	Dates	Increments Headers	Increments
ID	ID	Plan	Plan	Start Date	Start Date	Annual Increment	Annual Incre...
Name	Name	Fee	Fee	End Date	End Date	Years	Years
Marital Status	Marital Status		[none]		[none]		[none]
Education	Education		[none]		[none]		[none]

Figure 4.45: The Arrange tool interface with all columns and descriptions added

20. Run the workflow.

You'll see that Alteryx arranged the data as instructed, having the descriptions (**Headers**) and the values following it for each group of columns we created.

ID	Customers Headers	Customers	Plan Headers	Plan	Dates Headers	Dates	Increments Headers	Increments
1	ID	1	Plan	Basic	Start Date	2021-12-01	Annual Increment	0.08
1	Name	John Smith	Fee	30	End Date	2022-12-01	Years	1
1	Marital Status	Single		[Null]		[Null]		[Null]
1	Education	some College		[Null]		[Null]		[Null]
2	ID	2	Plan	Premium	Start Date	2020-05-01	Annual Increment	0.09
2	Name	Mary Stuart	Fee	55.4	End Date	2025-05-01	Years	5
2	Marital Status	Married		[Null]		[Null]		[Null]
2	Education	College Degree		[Null]		[Null]		[Null]
3	ID	3	Plan	Plus	Start Date	2023-06-18	Annual Increment	0.035
3	Name	Giacomo K. Stafford	Fee	40	End Date	2025-06-18	Years	2

Figure 4.46: The Arrange tool's resulting data

How it works...

The **Arrange** tool allows us to manually select what we want to show and how, offering us the option to describe the contents of the value in a different column, which it calls **Description**, and auto-populates it according to our selection – in this case, the field names (we can manually change the descriptions, re-utilize them, or use [None]).

It also provides options to manually rearrange the columns or rows, so we can change how they appear. Just select the column or row you need to move and click on the corresponding arrows.

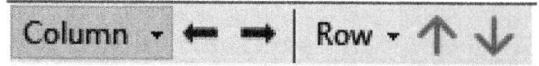

Figure 4.47: Repositioning the Column and Row options

There's more...

We focused this recipe on the **Arrange** tool, but if we combine this one with the previous recipe, we can generate the output shown in *Figure 4.46*.

To accomplish the results shown in that figure, follow these steps:

1. Connect a **Select** tool to the **Arrange** output anchor, and only select the Customers Headers field.

Select (8) - Configuration

Options ▾ | ↑ ↓   TIP: To reorder multiple rows: select, right-click and drag.

	Field	Type		Size	Rename	Description
▶ ☐	ID	Double	▾	8		
☑	Customers Headers	String	▾	14		
☐	Customers	V_String	▾	255		
☐	Plan Headers	String	▾	4		
☐	Plan	V_String	▾	255		
☐	Dates Headers	String	▾	10		
☐	Dates	Date	▾	10		
☐	Increments Headers	String	▾	16		
☐	Increments	Double	▾	8		
☐	*Unknown	Unknown	▾	0		Dynamic or Unknown Fields

Figure 4.48: Selecting Customers Headers only

2. Drop a **Sample** tool, leave the **First N rows** option selected (as default), and set **N** as **4** (since our **Customers** section has four values in it).

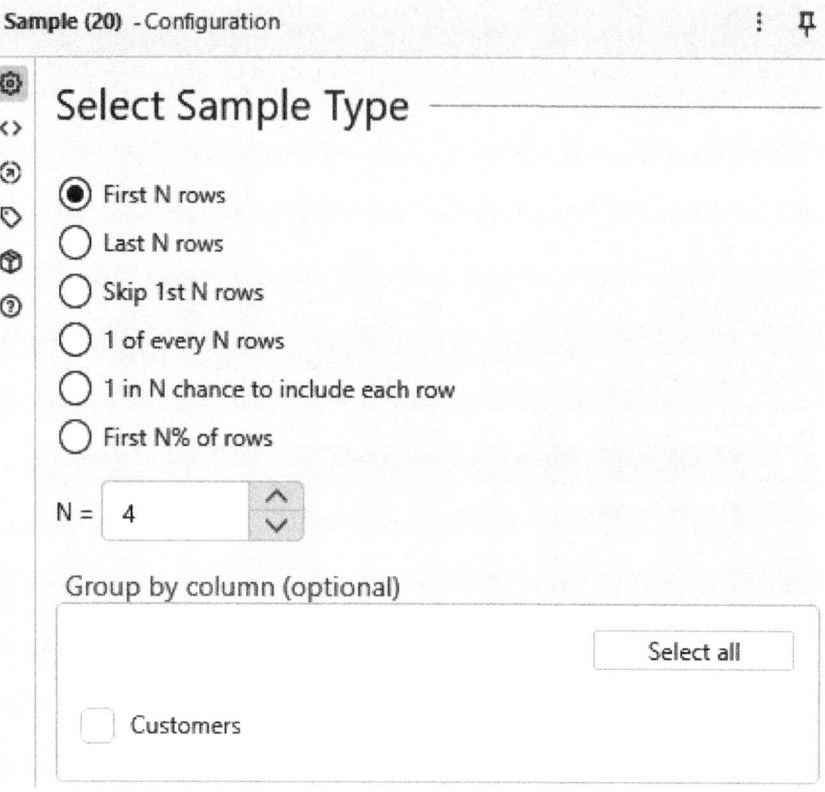

Figure 4.49: The Sample tool configuration

3. Connect another four **Select** tools to the output anchor of the **Arrange** tool, and configure them as follows:

    - Select only `Plan Headers` in the first one

    - Select only `Dates Headers` in the second one

    - Select only `Increment Headers` in the third one

    - Select all the fields, except the ones that contain `Headers` in their names

4. Drop a **Sample** tool after each **Select** tool, except the last one (the one without fields containing `Headers` in their names).

5. Each **Sample** tool must be configured to **First N rows** and **N** set to **2** (because each group of fields contains two values).

6. Add a **Join Multiple** tool, and connect all the **Sample** tools to it. Set the **Join Mode** to **Join by Record Position**.

At this point, your workflow should look like this:

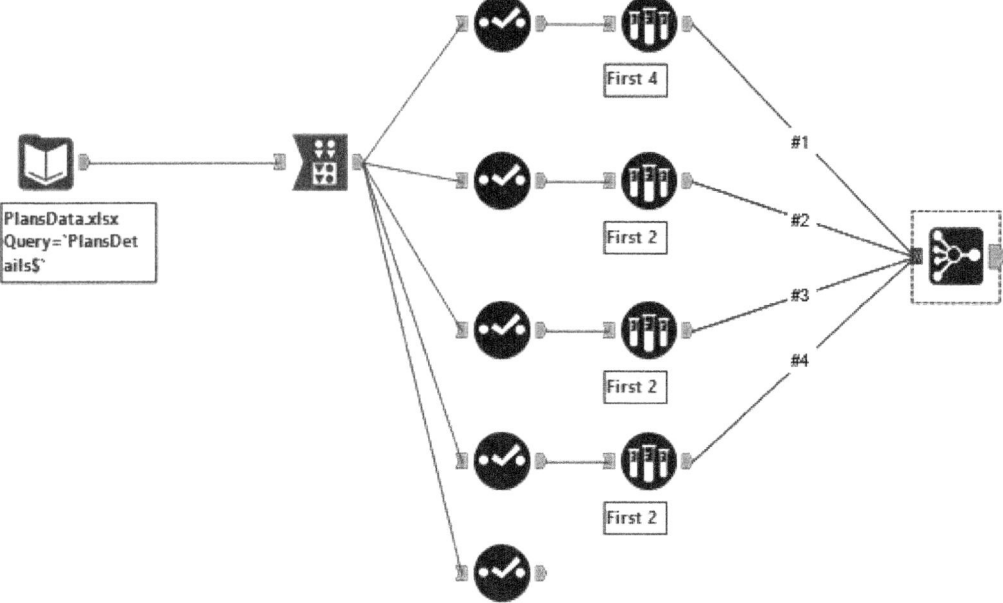

Figure 4.50: A workflow overview

If you run the workflow, you'll see that from the **Join Multiple** output anchor, we will get the headers that will be the first row of your results (at the top of the data).

Customers Headers	Plan Headers	Dates Headers	Increments Headers
ID	Plan	Start Date	Annual Increment
Name	Fee	End Date	Years
Marital Status	[Null]	[Null]	[Null]
Education	[Null]	[Null]	[Null]

Figure 4.51: The resulting headers

And from the output anchor of the **Select** tool at the bottom of the workflow, we get the actual data:

ID	Customers	Plan	Dates	Increments
1	1	Basic	2021-12-01	0.08
1	John Smith	30	2022-12-01	1
1	Single	[Null]	[Null]	[Null]
1	some College	[Null]	[Null]	[Null]
2	2	Premium	2020-05-01	0.09
2	Mary Stuart	55.4	2025-05-01	5
2	Married	[Null]	[Null]	[Null]
2	College Degree	[Null]	[Null]	[Null]
3	3	Plus	2023-06-18	0.035
3	Giacomo K. Stafford	40	2025-06-18	2

Figure 4.52: The resulting data

At this point, we can just unite both datasets and get our results, but we need to format the datasets first.

7. Add a **Table** tool (from the **Reporting** category) and connect it to the **Join Multiple** tool.

8. Make sure that **Basic** is selected for **Table Mode**, no fields are selected in the **Group By** selection box, deselect **Show Column Headings**, and the four fields containing our Headers are selected and **Dynamic or Unknown Fields** is deselected.

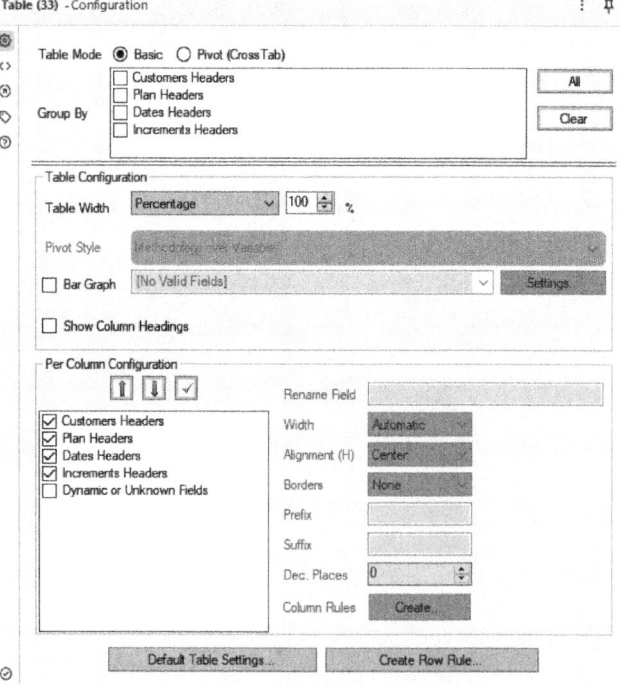

Figure 4.53: The header's Table tool configuration

9. Click on **Default Table Settings…** at the bottom of the configuration panel, and a new window will pop up.

    From the **Data** tab, we did the following:

    - We selected **Calibri** as the font (Alteryx Designer's default is Arial, but Excel's is Calibri)

    - We increased the font size to **14** and selected an orange tone for the text color.

    - **Background** and **Alternate Color** are both White and **Rows Per Group** = **1**.

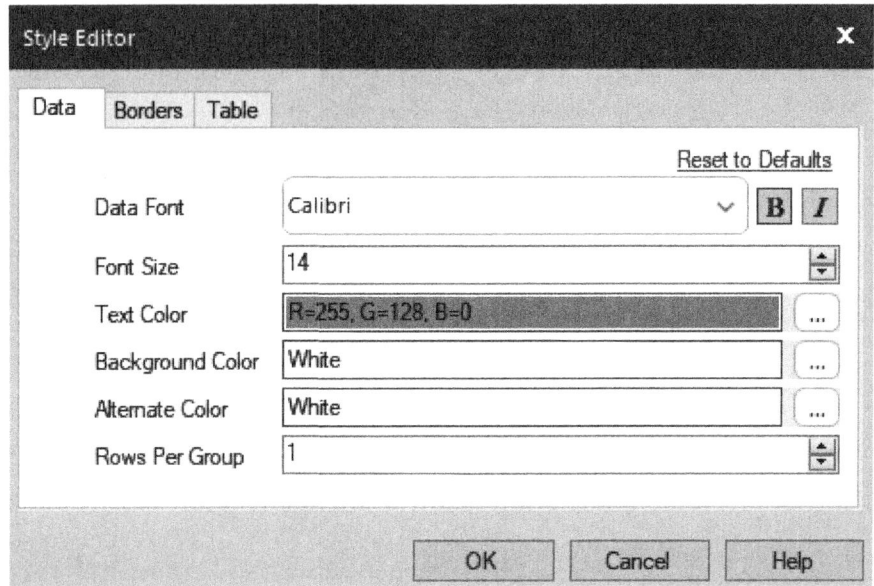

Figure 4.54: The header's table Style Editor

    Leave the **Borders** and **Table** tabs as default.

10. Hit **OK**.

11. Now, add a new **Table** tool, and connect it to the **Select** tool output anchor at the bottom of the workflow.

    Make sure **Basic** is selected under **Table Mode**, select **ID** in the **Group By** selection box, deselect **Show Column Headers**, and deselect **ID** and **Dynamic or Unknown Fields**.

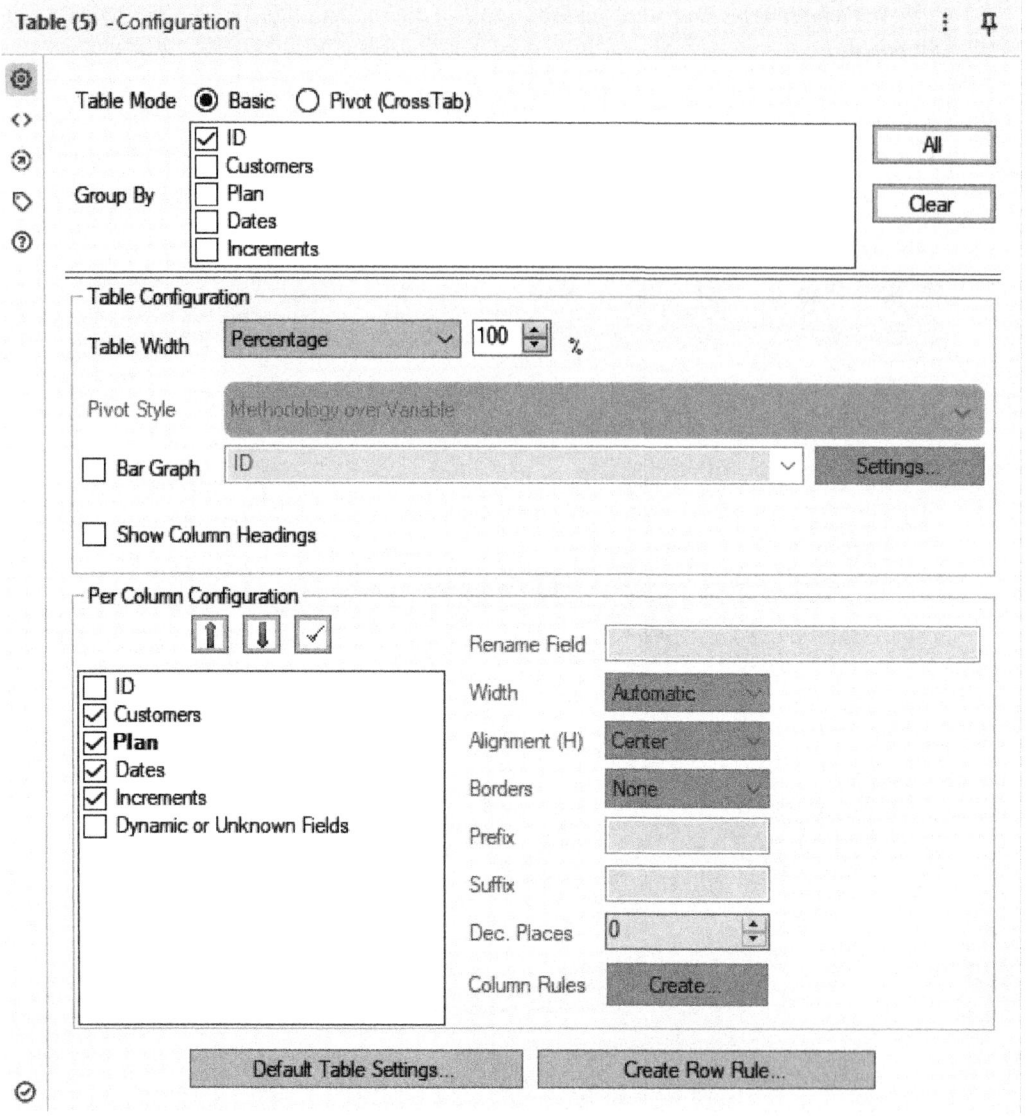

Figure 4.55: The data's Table tool configuration

As you can see in *Figure 4.55*, the **Plan** field is in bold, which means there are some rules affecting that field. In this case, we defined three column rules so that we can show the **Plan** name in different shades of blue.

12. To create these rules, click on **Plan** and then **Create…**, next to **Column Rules**.

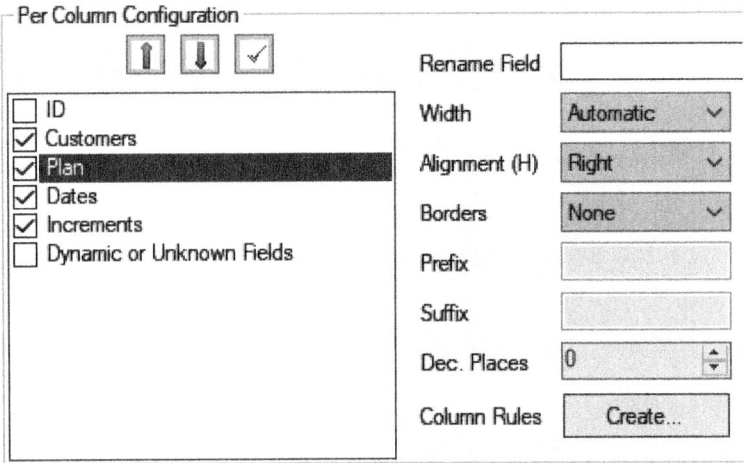

Figure 4.56: Creating the column rules

A new window will appear.

13. Replace the suggested **Plan Rule 1** text under **Rule Name** with `Basic Plan`.

14. In the **Apply** section, click on **Formula** and use this one:

    ```
    [Plan]="Basic"
    ```

15. Click on **Text Color**; the **Color** selection pallet will appear, where you can select a light blue shade for this rule (we've used `155` for red, `205` for green, and `255` for blue).

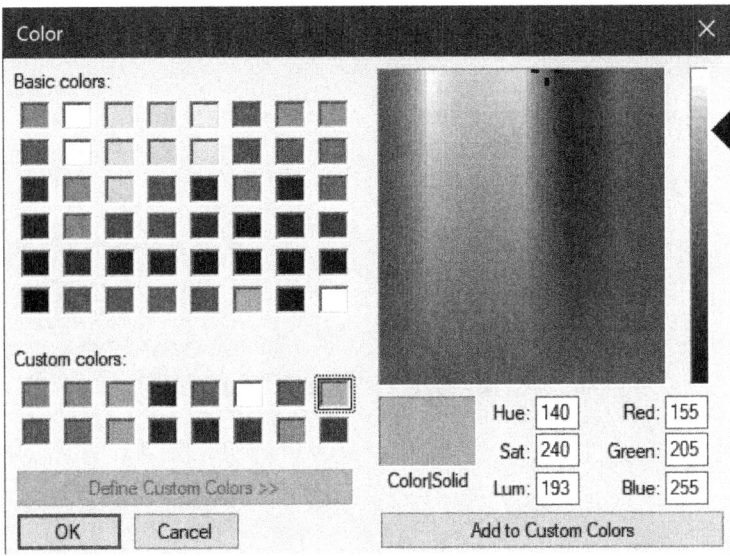

Figure 4.57: The Color selection

16. Hit **OK**.

17. On the **Column Styling Rules - Plan** popup, click on the **New** button.

18. Name the new rule `Plus Plan` and, again, select **Formula**, using this one for it:

    ```
    [Plan]="Plus"
    ```

19. Click on **Text Color** and select a darker shade of blue (we've used `102` for red, `179` for green, and `255` for blue for this one).

20. Finally, create a new rule; this time, name it `Premium Plan` and, again, select **Formula**, using this one:

    ```
    [Plan]="Premium"
    ```

21. Select **Text Color** and a darker shade of blue (we've used `0` for red, `117` for green, and `234` for blue).

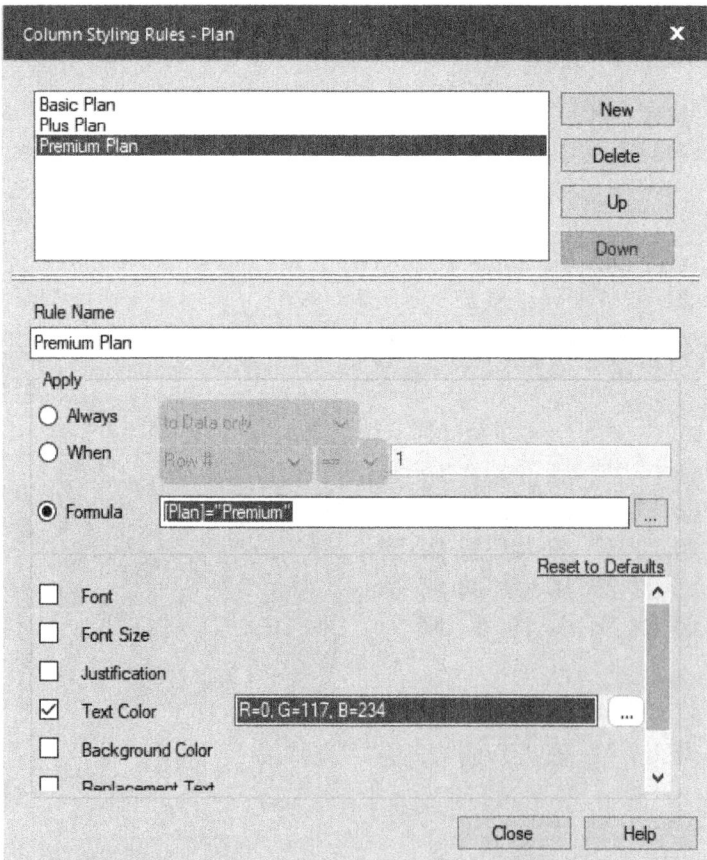

Figure 4.58: The column rules defined

22. Click on **Close**, and your `Plan` field should be in bold letters.

23. Finally, click on the **Default Table Settings...** at the bottom of the configuration panel and a new window will pop up.

    From the **Data** tab, we do the following:

    - Again, we select **Calibri** as the font, but this time, its size is **11**

    - **Background** and **Alternate Color** are both `White`, and **Rows Per Group** = **1**

    - All other options remain as default

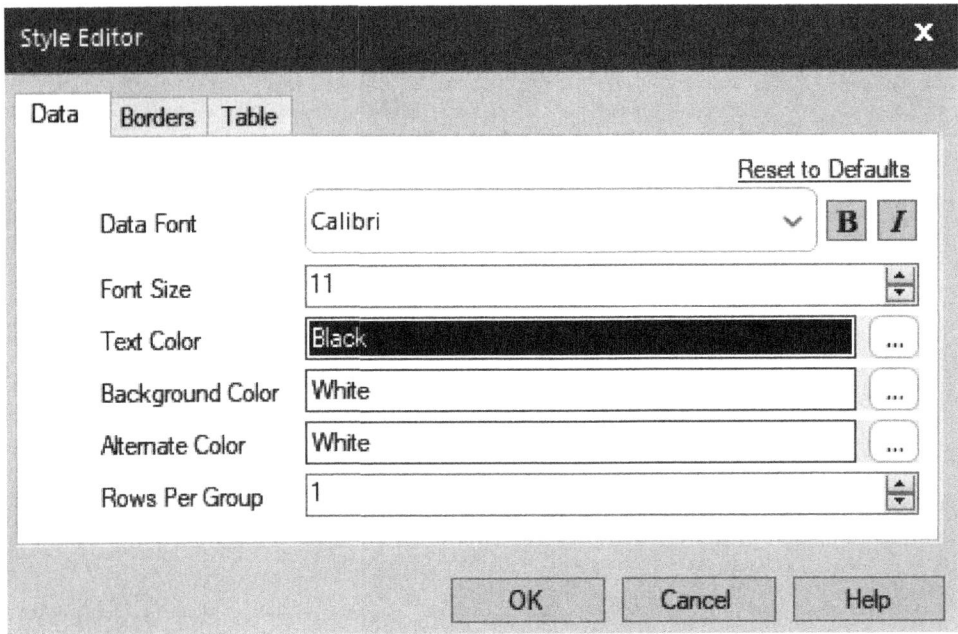

Figure 4.59: The data table Style Editor options

To finish the formatted output, we need to unite both tables and add a **Render** tool (from the **Reporting** category).

24. Add a **Select** tool and connect it to the data table **Table**. Deselect the ID field.

25. Add a **Union** tool and connect both the header's **Table** tool and the **Select** tool output anchors to it.

26. Make sure **Auto Config by Name** (the default) is selected, and click on **Set a specific Output Order**, ensuring that the one on top is the header's and the second one comes from the **Select** tool.

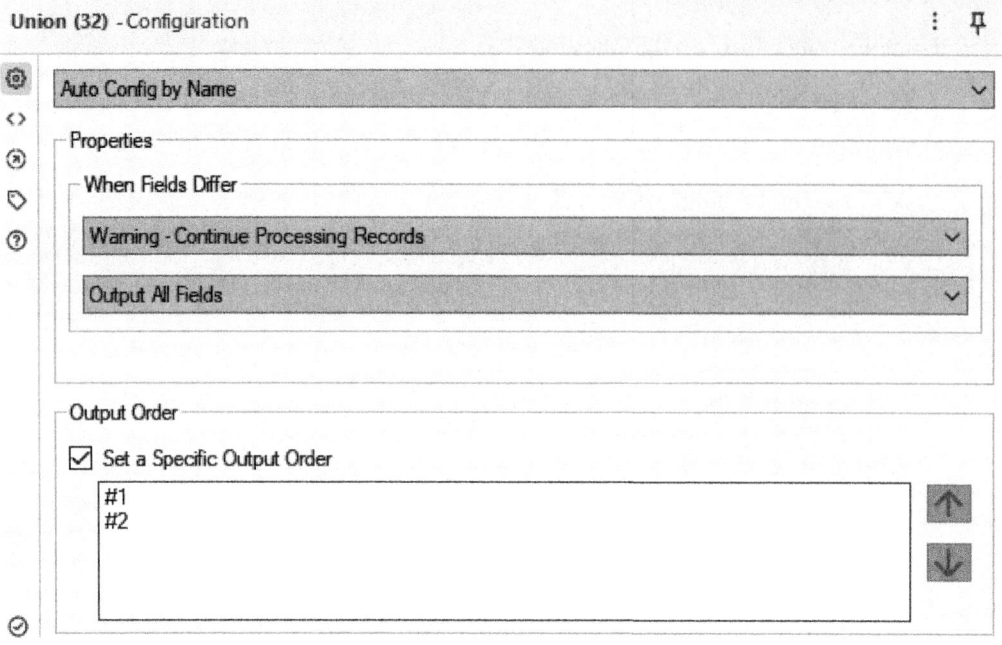

Figure 4.60: The Union tool configuration

27. Connect a **Render** tool to the **Union** tool output anchor.

28. Select **Choose a Specific Output File** for **Output Mode:**, point the output to the . . \OUTPUT folder within the recipe folder, and select the Excel file (if you want just to check the results, you can select **Temporary Excel format** instead of **Choose a Specific Output File**).

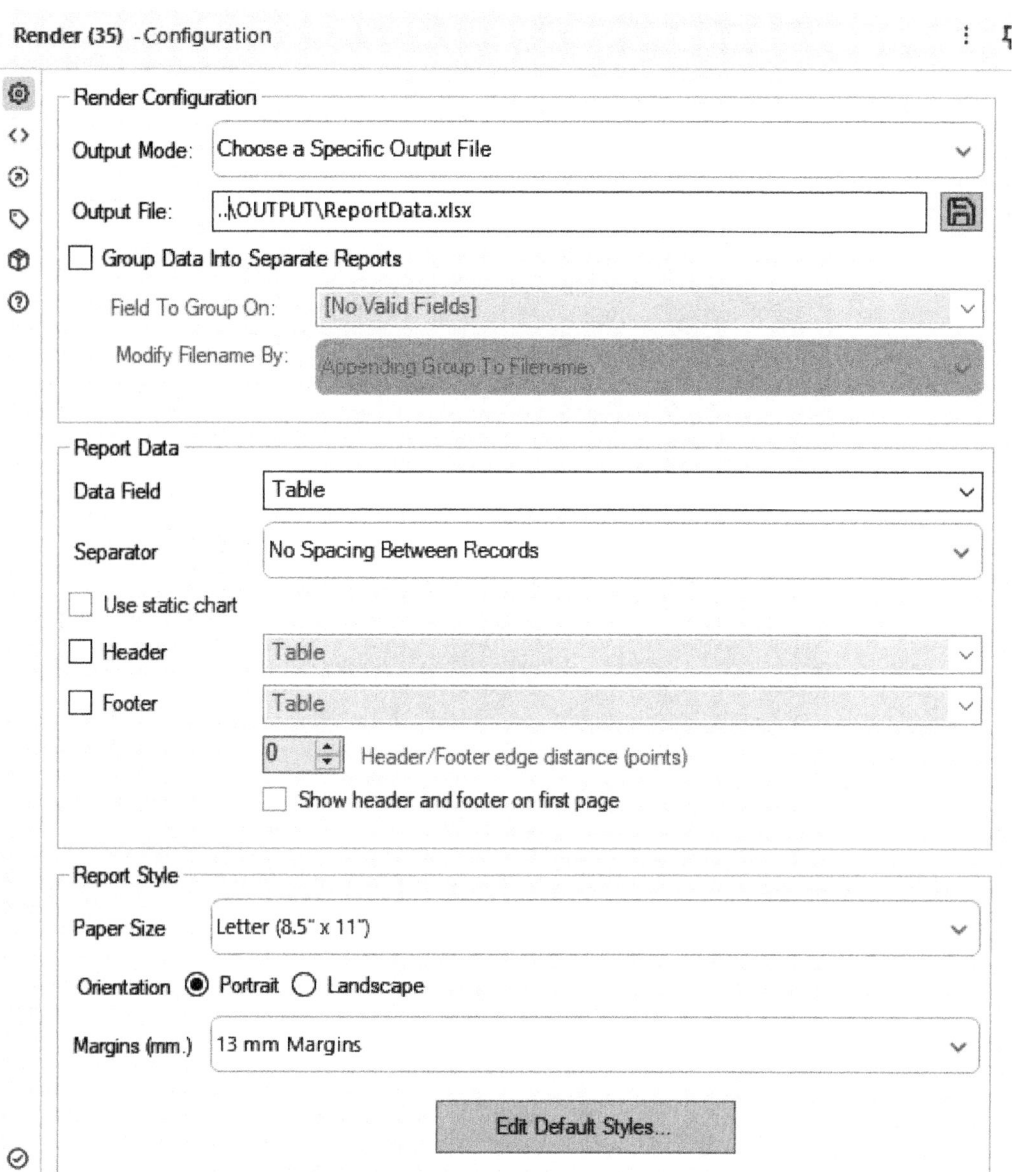

Figure 4.61: The Render tool configuration

At this point, your workflow should look like this:

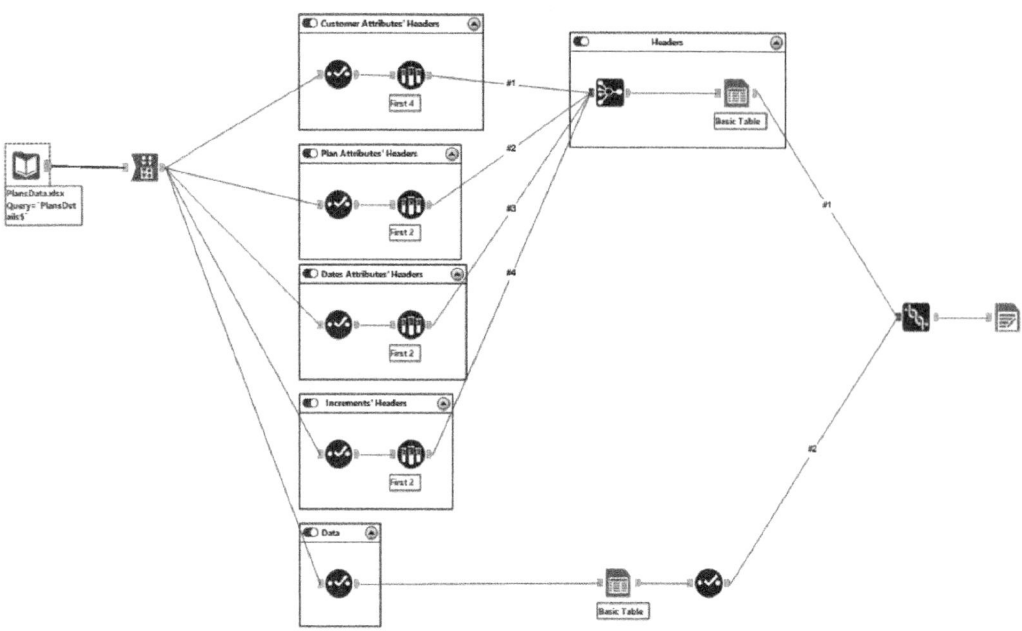

Figure 4.62: A final workflow overview

Run the workflow and open the resulting file. You'll see how Alteryx Designer saved your results.

5

Data Parsing

Data parsing is vital when preparing data for analysis. Converting data from one format (or no format) and being able to identify and extract data pieces from a field is a crucial procedure for making semi-unusable data useful.

In this chapter, we'll present recipes to parse/extract data that may look unusable or too complicated to interpret at first. These are the recipes we will cover:

- Preparing a free text field for analysis/patterns findings

- Identifying and classifying free text

- Extracting the last part of a delimited field

- Using ReGex or not

Technical requirements

For this chapter, we don't need any extra preparation besides having Alteryx Designer installed on our computers.

Preparing, identifying, and classifying free text

Working with free text fields can be daunting. Parsing and understanding what these fields contain is a very difficult task and requires specialized tools to analyze them in detail.

We often use AI and ML models to do this, but in this recipe, we'll explore a very easy yet powerful approach to parsing and classifying free text data.

Getting ready

For this recipe, you can download a test set from here: `https://github.com/PacktPublishing/Alteryx-Designer-Cookbook/tree/main/ch5/Recipe1`.

If you decide to try it with your own data, make sure you have at least a free text field and a dictionary of words to identify within that field.

We are going to read a series of free text transcriptions from customer service, and we want to classify them based on some keywords mentioned within those messages. We'll assign a category based on a dictionary provided by the business unit, where a keyword corresponds to a category.

How to do it...

In a new workflow, drop an **Input Data** tool, point it to `\DATA\CustomerServiceTexts.xlsx`, and select the `Sheet1` worksheet as the data source:.

1. Connect a **RecordID** tool to the **Input Data** tool. Leave the default settings.

2. Drop a **Data Cleansing** tool (from the **Preparation** category) and check **Remove null rows** and **Remove null columns**. In the **Remove Unwanted Characters** section, select **Leading and Trailing Whitespace** and **Punctuation** for the text field.

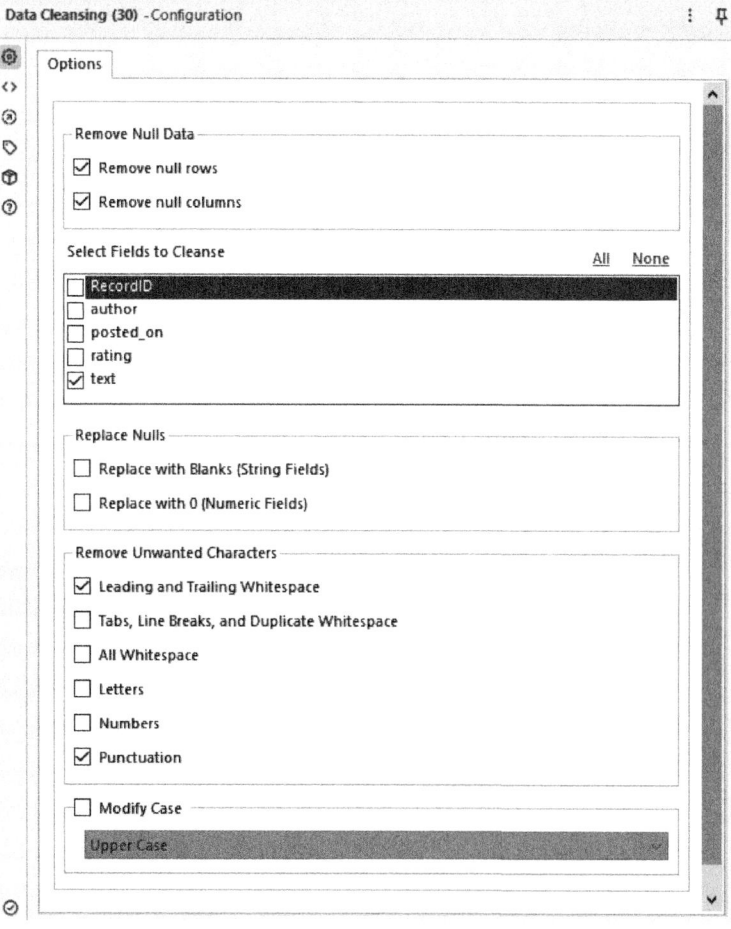

Figure 5.1: Data Cleansing tool configuration

3. Following the **Data Cleansing** tool, connect the **Text To Columns** tool (from the **Parse** category) and select **text** in **Column to split**, enter \s (whitespace) in **Delimiters**, and select **Split to rows** as the method for splitting.

Text To Columns (12) - Configuration

Select Column to Split

Column to split

text

Delimiters

\s

○ Split to columns

● Split to rows

Advanced options

☐ Ignore delimiters in quotes

☐ Ignore delimiters in single quotes

☐ Ignore delimiters in parentheses

☐ Ignore delimiters in brackets

☐ Skip empty columns

Figure 5.2: Text To Columns tool configuration

4. Run the workflow and you'll see that Alteryx Designer has created ~20K records and transformed the **text** field so it contains just one word per record.

RecordID	author	posted_on	rating	text
1	Alantae of Chesterfeild, MI	Nov. 22, 2021	1	I
1	Alantae of Chesterfeild, MI	Nov. 22, 2021	1	used
1	Alantae of Chesterfeild, MI	Nov. 22, 2021	1	to
1	Alantae of Chesterfeild, MI	Nov. 22, 2021	1	love
1	Alantae of Chesterfeild, MI	Nov. 22, 2021	1	XXXXXX
1	Alantae of Chesterfeild, MI	Nov. 22, 2021	1	Until
1	Alantae of Chesterfeild, MI	Nov. 22, 2021	1	all
1	Alantae of Chesterfeild, MI	Nov. 22, 2021	1	these

Figure 5.3: Results after splitting into rows

Now that we have individual words per row, we can start classifying them.

5. Add a new **Input Data** tool to the canvas and point it to the custom dictionary (in our case, \ DATA\SearchDictionary.xlsx and Sheet1 for the worksheet).

You'll see that there is a list of words provided by the business unit (the **Look_For** field) and the classification for each one (the **Category** field).

Look_For	Category
crash	Internet
crashed	Internet
internet	Internet
online	Internet
customer	Customer Service
service	Customer Service
billing	Contract
contract	Contract

Figure 5.4: Custom lookup dictionary

6. Drop a **Find Replace** tool (from the **Join** category) to the canvas and connect the **Text To Columns** output anchor to the **F** input anchor and the **Custom Dictionary Input Data** tool output anchor to the **R** input anchor.

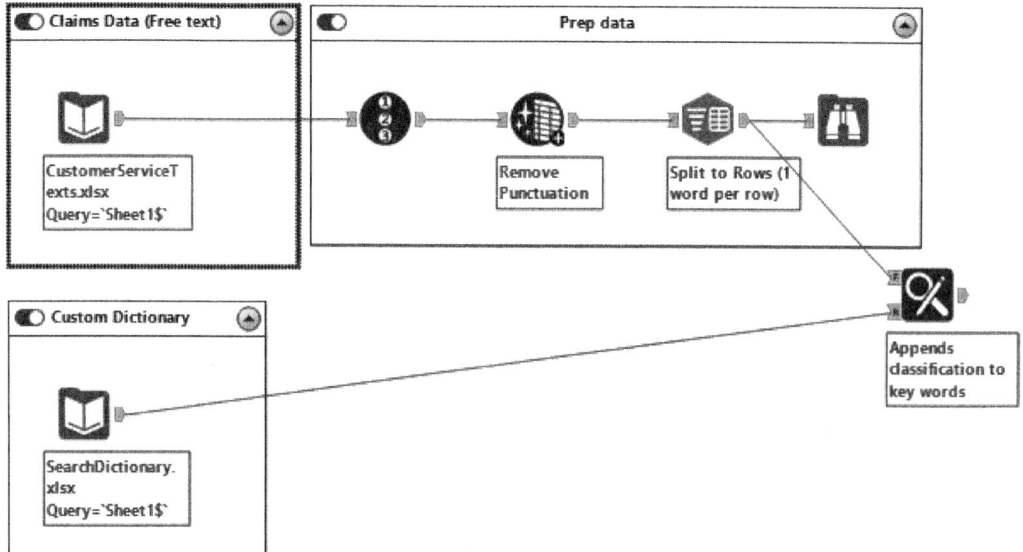

Figure 5.5: Workflow overview so far

7. Now, configure the **Find Replace** tool like this:

    • Make sure **Any Part of Field** is the selected method

    • Select **text** for the **Find Within Field** option

- Select **Look_For** for the **Find Value** option

- Select **Case Insensitive Find**

- Click on **Append Field(s) to Record** as the **Replace** method and select the **Category** field:

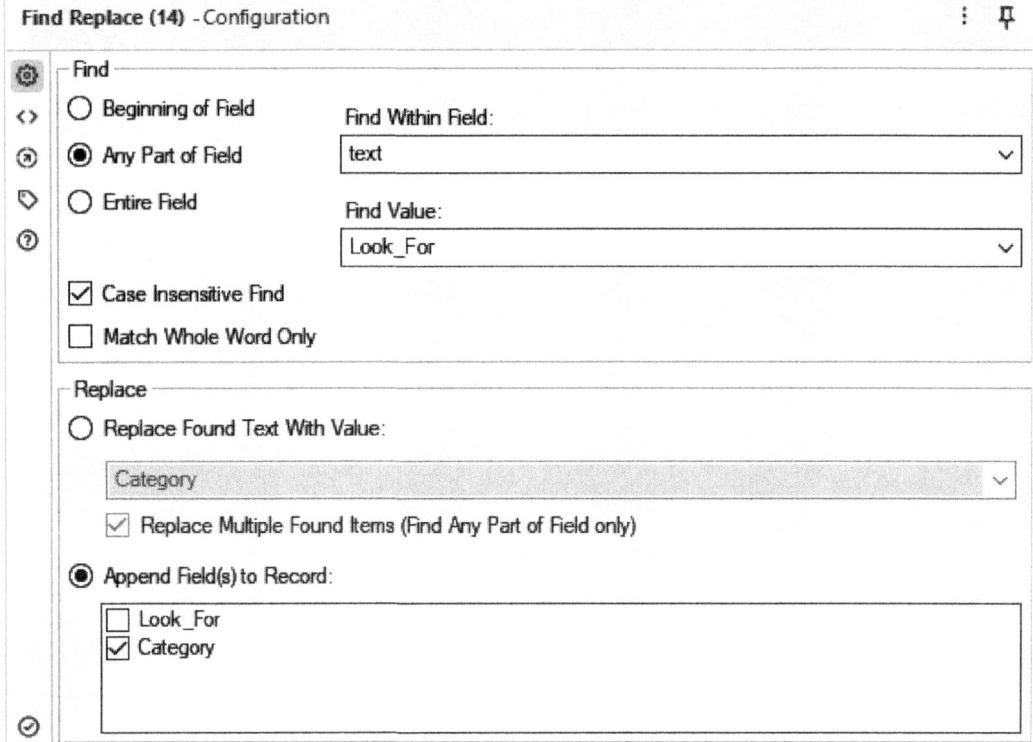

Figure 5.6: Find Replace tool configuration

If you run the workflow now, you'll notice that each record now has its **Category** added.

RecordID	author	posted_on	rating	text	Category
3	Sarah of Rancho Cordova, CA	Nov. 17, 2021	1	ALL	[Null]
3	Sarah of Rancho Cordova, CA	Nov. 17, 2021	1	ISSUES	[Null]
3	Sarah of Rancho Cordova, CA	Nov. 17, 2021	1		[Null]
3	Sarah of Rancho Cordova, CA	Nov. 17, 2021	1	billing	Contract
3	Sarah of Rancho Cordova, CA	Nov. 17, 2021	1	connectionserv...	Customer Ser...
3	Sarah of Rancho Cordova, CA	Nov. 17, 2021	1	adding	[Null]
3	Sarah of Rancho Cordova, CA	Nov. 17, 2021	1	or	[Null]
3	Sarah of Rancho Cordova, CA	Nov. 17, 2021	1	removing	[Null]
3	Sarah of Rancho Cordova, CA	Nov. 17, 2021	1	service	Customer Ser...

Figure 5.7: Results after Find Replace

At this point, we have the free text classified according to the dictionary that the business unit provided, and we can start making some aggregations to give it an idea of what is mentioned in the complaints.

We'll start with knowing what each customer complained about.

8.   Drop a **Filter** tool and connect it to the output anchor of the **Find Replace** tool.

9.   In the **Basic filter** option, select **Category** from the first dropdown and **Is not null** from the second.

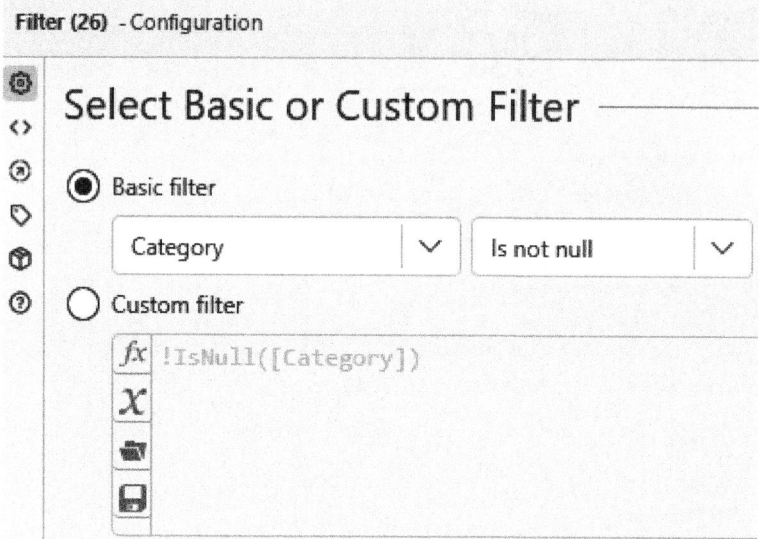

Figure 5.8: Filter tool configuration

10.   Connect a **Summarize** tool to the **T** output anchor of the **Filter** tool and configure it as follows:

   • Select **RecordID** from the **Fields** list, click on **Add**, and select **Group By**

   • Click the **author** field, click on **Add**, and select **First**

   • Select the **Category** field from the list, click on **Add**, and select **Group By**

   • With the **Category** field still selected in the **Fields** list, click on **Add** again, and select **Count** from the list of actions:

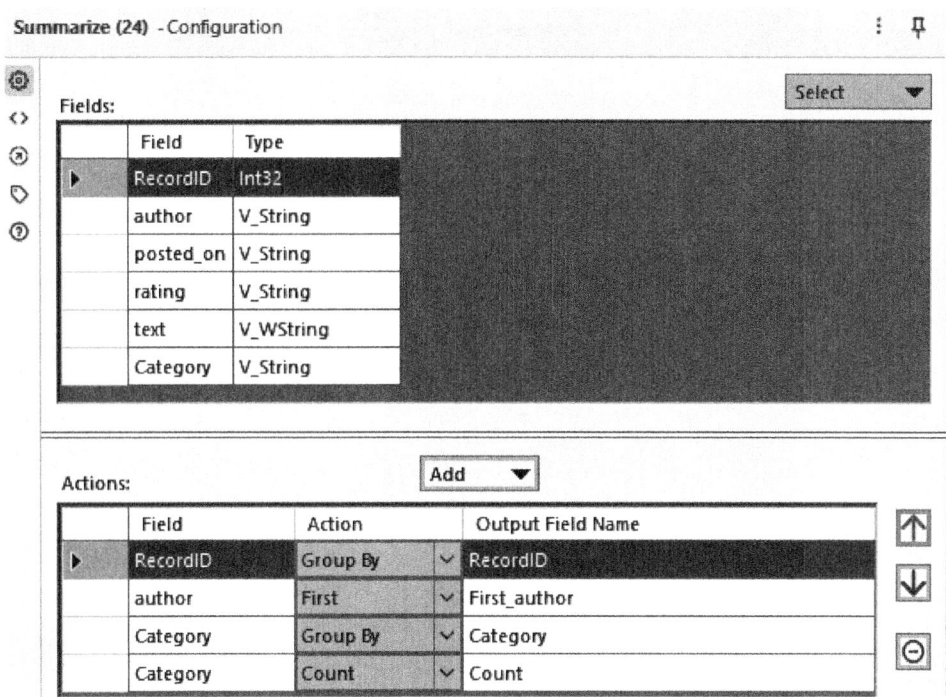

Figure 5.9: Summarize tool configuration

Run the workflow and you'll have all the mentions and the times that mention appears in the text per user.

RecordID	First_author	Category	Count
1	Alantae of Chesterfeild, MI	Cable	1
1	Alantae of Chesterfeild, MI	Internet	4
2	Vera of Philadelphia, PA	Customer Service	1
2	Vera of Philadelphia, PA	Internet	4
3	Sarah of Rancho Cordova, CA	Contract	3

Figure 5.10: Results after summarizing

To classify these into a more global aspect, we can get groups of mentions and how many times those combinations of mentions appear in our dataset.

11. To do it, just drop a **Unique** tool following the **Find Replace** tool (we want just one mention per category) and select **RecordID** and **Category** in **Column Names**.

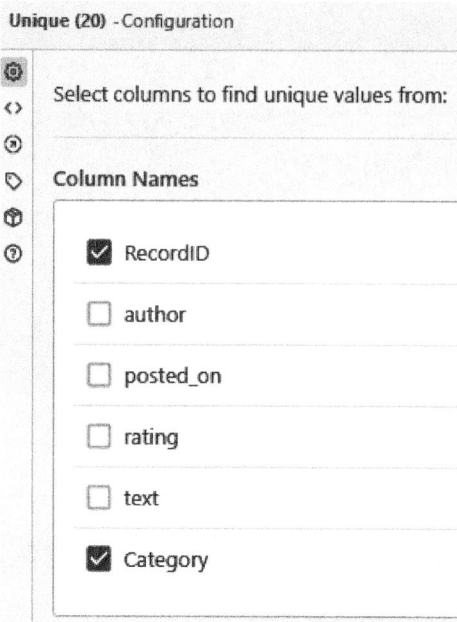

Figure 5.11: Unique tool configuration

12. Drop a **Summarize** tool and connect it to the **U** output of the **Unique** tool.

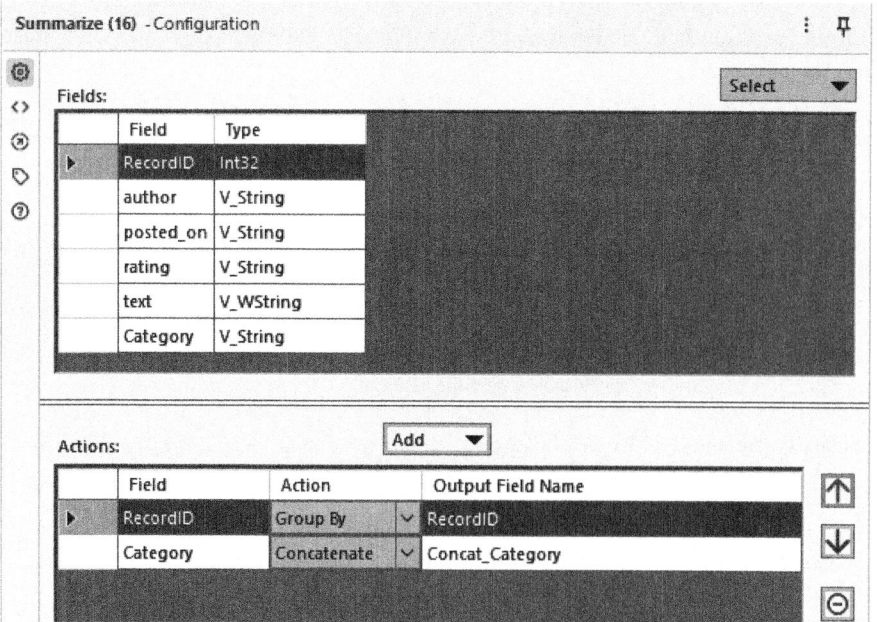

Figure 5.12: Summarize tool configuration

- Select **Group By** for **RecordID** and **Concatenate** for **Category**

RecordID	Concat_Category
1	Cable,Internet
2	Customer Service,Internet
3	Contract,Customer Service
4	Customer Service
5	Contract,Internet

Figure 5.13: Results after summarizing

This will tell us what categories are mentioned together for each customer.

13. Drop a new **Summarize** tool and connect it to the output anchor of the previous **Summarize** tool:

- Select **Group By** for **Concat_Category** and **Count** for **Concat_Category**:

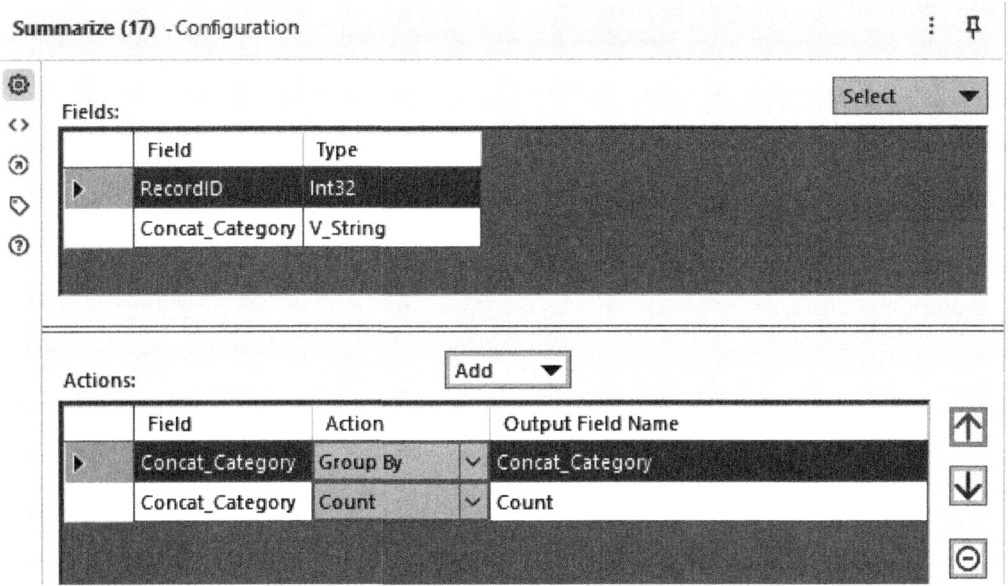

Figure 5.14: Summarize tool configuration

14. Drop a **Filter** tool and configure **Basic filter** by selecting **Concat_Category** and **Is not empty**.

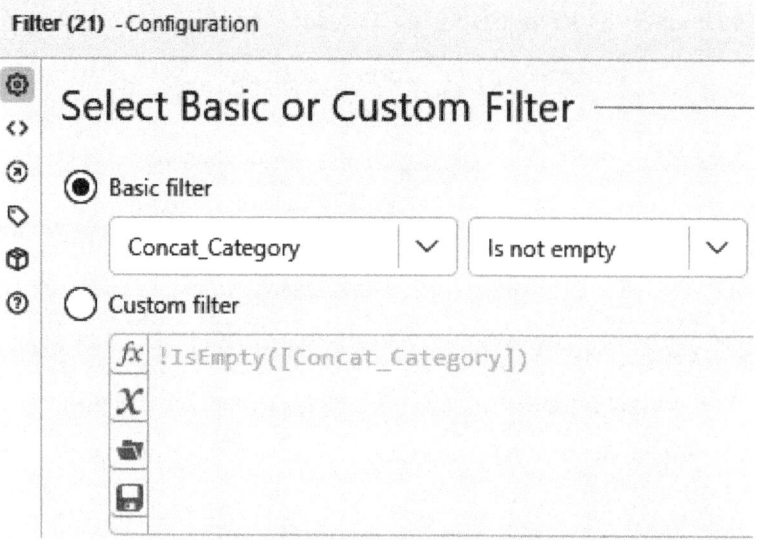

Figure 5.15: Filter tool configuration

After completing the previous configuration, your workflow will look like this:

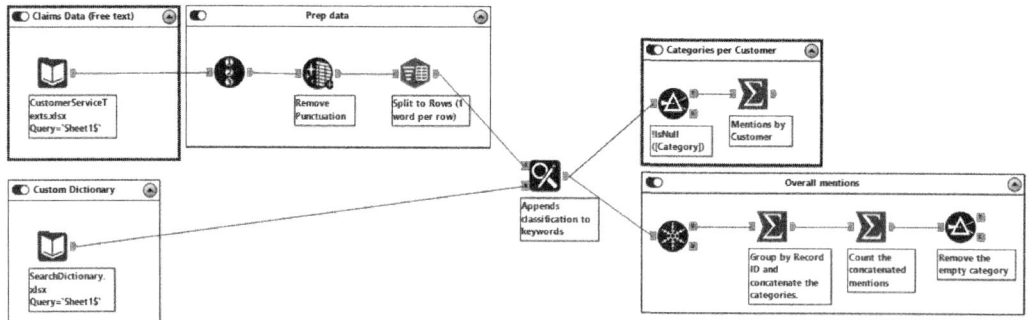

Figure 5.16: Final workflow overview

How it works...

We used a couple of tricks to process an input file that, at first, seems too complex to interpret due to its free text field, but the most powerful one is using the power of the **Text To Columns** tool (used as a **Text to Rows** in this case) to break that complex text into individual words that can be matched to a dictionary. The addition of **RecordID** allowed us to keep the reference to the original poster along the workflow.

Also, we used the **Find Replace** tool as a **Join** tool, and we'll see more of this in *Chapter 7*.

There's more...

In this example, each appearance of any of the search words will count as one, but if you noticed, we have a `rating` field for each customer, so we can define a weight for each customer's mention. Just use it as a multiplier or divider, accordingly to your rating scale.

Getting the last part of a delimited string

Sometimes, when working with delimited fields, we need to keep the last part of each, and the number of columns is unknown. One of the most frequent use cases is parsing a path/UNC/URL and getting the filename, which is at the end of the string.

This recipe is ideal for these use cases, where we have a delimited field but we don't know the number of columns, and we need the last one(s) – for example, the filename of a complete path.

Getting ready

We prepared a test here: `https://github.com/PacktPublishing/Alteryx-Designer-Cookbook/tree/main/ch5/Recipe2`.

We have a list of files, and we need to retrieve the filename and extension from them, but since they are distributed across different folders and subfolders, splitting the whole path by a delimiter (like we do with the **Text To Columns** tool) will require a lot of post-processing tasks.

How to do it...

We'll start by showing the regular procedure using the **Text To Columns** tool:

1. Drop an **Input Data** tool and point it to `\DATA\FileLocations.csv`.

2. Just for demonstration purposes, drop a **Text To Columns** tool and configure it like this:

   - Enter \ in **Delimiters.**

   - Make sure **Split to columns** is selected and set **Number of columns** to **7.**

   - Leave the default for **Extra characters** (**Leave extra in last column**):

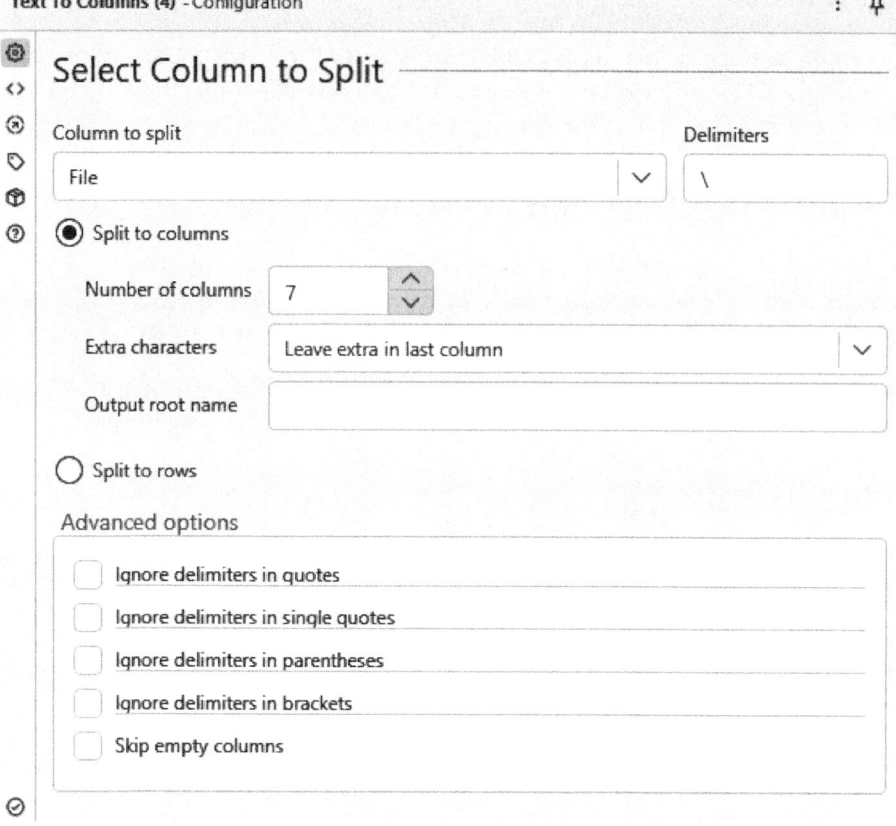

Figure 5.17: Text To Columns tool configuration

You'll see that the parsing is right, but working with the results is going to be a very hard task.

File	1	2	3	4	5	6	7
C:\DATASETS\Tabla_X.xlsx	C:	DATASETS	Tabla_X.xlsx	[Null]	[Null]	[Null]	[Null]
C:\DATASETS\test.flat	C:	DATASETS	test.flat	[Null]	[Null]	[Null]	[Null]
C:\DATASETS\tipo_documento.flat	C:	DATASETS	tipo_documento.flat	[Null]	[Null]	[Null]	[Null]
C:\DATASETS\tipo_documento.lst	C:	DATASETS	tipo_documento.lst	[Null]	[Null]	[Null]	[Null]
C:\DATASETS\DATA\202206-citbike-tripdata.csv.zip	C:	DATASETS	DATA	202206-citbike-tripdata.csv.zip	[Null]	[Null]	[Null]
C:\DATASETS\DATA\CityBike_2013.yxdb	C:	DATASETS	DATA	CityBike_2013.yxdb	[Null]	[Null]	[Null]
C:\DATASETS\DATA\CityBike_2014.yxdb	C:	DATASETS	DATA	CityBike_2014.yxdb	[Null]	[Null]	[Null]
C:\DATASETS\DATA\CityBike_2015.yxdb	C:	DATASETS	DATA	CityBike_2015.yxdb	[Null]	[Null]	[Null]
C:\DATASETS\DATA\CityBike_2016.yxdb	C:	DATASETS	DATA	CityBike_2016.yxdb	[Null]	[Null]	[Null]
C:\DATASETS\DATA\202206-citbike-tripdata.csv\2...	C:	DATASETS	DATA	202206-citbike-tripdata.csv	202206-ci...	[Null]	[Null]
C:\DATASETS\DATA\202206-citbike-tripdata.csv_...	C:	DATASETS	DATA	202206-citbike-tripdata.csv	__MACOSX	._202206-...	[Null]
C:\DATASETS\SUBFOLDER\ARTICULOS.yxdb	C:	DATASETS	SUBFOLDER	ARTICULOS.yxdb	[Null]	[Null]	[Null]
C:\DATASETS\SUBFOLDER\DOCUMENTOS.yxdb	C:	DATASETS	SUBFOLDER	DOCUMENTOS.yxdb	[Null]	[Null]	[Null]

Figure 5.18: Results after splitting into columns

So, we are going to make this very simple.

3. Cut the **Text To Columns** tool (keep it in your clipboard) and drop a **Formula** tool onto the canvas.

4. Paste the **Text To Columns** tool and connect it to the output anchor of the **Formula** tool.

5. Create a new field by clicking in the **Select Column** dropdown and then in + **Add Column** (you can perform this operation on the original **File** field, but we are creating a new one so you can see the progress of the operations).

6. Name the new field `Reverse_File` and use this expression:

    ```
    ReverseString([File])
    ```

7. Now, click on the **Text To Columns** tool and modify the original configuration as follows:

    - **Column to split**: `Reverse_File`

    - **Number of columns**: **2**

    - Leave all other settings on their defaults.

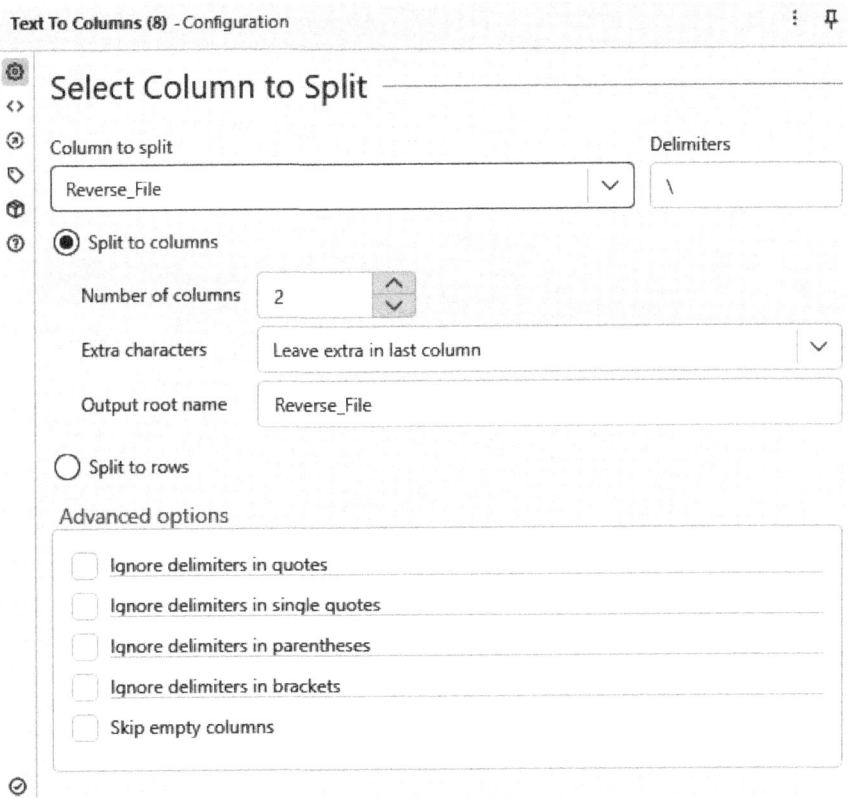

Figure 5.19: Text To Columns tool new configuration

8. Drop a new **Formula** tool and connect it to the output anchor of the **Text To Columns** tool.

9. Create a new field and name it `File_Name`.

Use this expression for the formula:

```
ReverseString([Reverse_File1])
```

10. Run the workflow.

You'll see that the **File_Name** field contains the last part (everything following the last delimiter, no matter how many are there) of the original **File** field.

File	Reverse_File	Reverse_File1	Reverse_File2	File_Name
C:\DATASETS\Tabla_X.xlsx	xslx.X_albaT\STESATAD\:C	xslx.X_albaT	STESATAD\:C	Tabla_X.xlsx
C:\DATASETS\test.flat	talf.tset\STESATAD\:C	talf.tset	STESATAD\:C	test.flat
C:\DATASETS\tipo_documento.flat	talf.otnemucod_opit\STESATAD\:C	talf.otnemucod_opit	STESATAD\:C	tipo_documento.flat
C:\DATASETS\tipo_documento.lst	tsl.otnemucod_opit\STESATAD\:C	tsl.otnemucod_opit	STESATAD\:C	tipo_documento.lst
C:\DATASETS\DATA\202206-citbike-tripdata.csv.zip	piz.vsc.atadpirt-ekibtic-602202\ATAD\STESATAD\:C	piz.vsc.atadpirt-ekibtic-602202	ATAD\STESATAD\:C	202206-citbike-tripdata.csv.zip
C:\DATASETS\DATA\CityBike_2013.yxdb	bdxy.3102_ekiBytiC\ATAD\STESATAD\:C	bdxy.3102_ekiBytiC	ATAD\STESATAD\:C	CityBike_2013.yxdb
C:\DATASETS\DATA\CityBike_2014.yxdb	bdxy.4102_ekiBytiC\ATAD\STESATAD\:C	bdxy.4102_ekiBytiC	ATAD\STESATAD\:C	CityBike_2014.yxdb
C:\DATASETS\DATA\CityBike_2015.yxdb	bdxy.5102_ekiBytiC\ATAD\STESATAD\:C	bdxy.5102_ekiBytiC	ATAD\STESATAD\:C	CityBike_2015.yxdb
C:\DATASETS\DATA\CityBike_2016.yxdb	bdxy.6102_ekiBytiC\ATAD\STESATAD\:C	bdxy.6102_ekiBytiC	ATAD\STESATAD\:C	CityBike_2016.yxdb
C:\DATASETS\DATA\202206-citbike-tripdata.csv\2...	vsc.atadpirt-ekibtic-602202\vsc.atadpirt-ekibtic-6...	vsc.atadpirt-ekibtic-602202	vsc.atadpirt-ekibtic-602...	202206-citbike-tripdata.csv
C:\DATASETS\DATA\202206-citbike-tripdata.csv_...	vsc.atadpirt-ekibtic-602202_.\XSOCAM__\vsc.ata...	vsc.atadpirt-ekibtic-602202_.	XSOCAM__\vsc.atadpirt-...	_202206-citbike-tripdata.csv
C:\DATASETS\SUBFOLDER\ARTICULOS.yxdb	bdxy.SOLUCITRA\REDLOFBUS\STESATAD\:C	bdxy.SOLUCITRA	REDLOFBUS\STESATAD\:C	ARTICULOS.yxdb
C:\DATASETS\SUBFOLDER\DOCUMENTOS.yxdb	bdxy.SOTNEMUCOD\REDLOFBUS\STESATAD\:C	bdxy.SOTNEMUCOD	REDLOFBUS\STESATAD\:C	DOCUMENTOS.yxdb

Figure 5.20: Results so far

So, this is what Alteryx did:

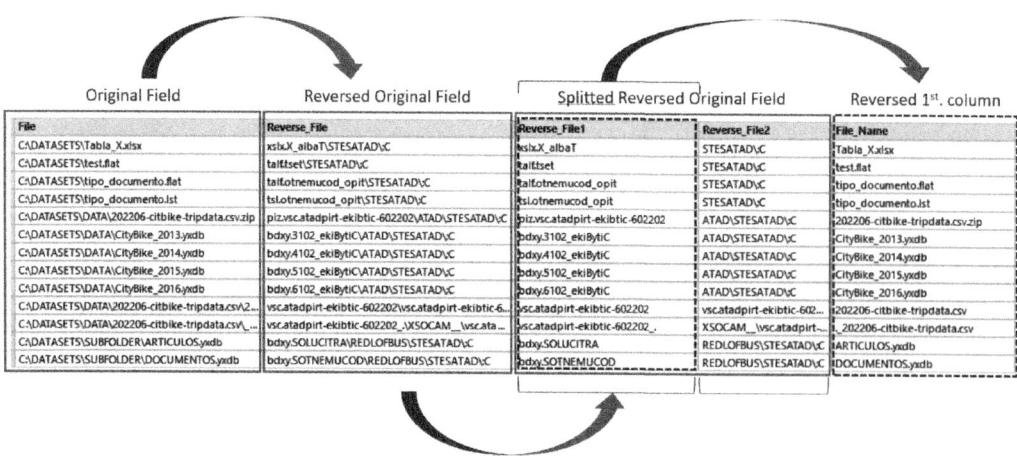

Figure 5.21: Reversing and splitting process

Of course, you can (maybe you must) use a **Select** tool to clean up the results. We left them here, just to show the progress of what we did.

How it works...

By being able to reverse the strings character by character, we can make sure that whatever is to the left of the first delimiter is the last part of the string, so we always split the reversed string into two columns and reverse the first one again to retrieve the correct results.

If we configure the **Text To Columns** to more than two columns, we can extract values up to the level we need. For example, let's say we are moving assets from one location to another, and we want to keep the original folder name where our files are located, so we can use **3** for the **Number of columns**, and we now need to reverse the first two results.

File	Reverse_File	Reverse_File1	Reverse_File2	Reverse_File3	File_Name	DIRECTORY
C:\DATASETS\Tabla_X.xlsx	xslxX_albaT\STESATAD\:C	xslxX_albaT	STESATAD	:C	Tabla_X.xlsx	DATASETS
C:\DATASETS\test.flat	talf.tset\\STESATAD\:C	talf.tset	STESATAD	:C	test.flat	DATASETS
C:\DATASETS\tipo_documento.flat	talf.otnemucod_opit\STESATAD\:C	talf.otnemucod_opit	STESATAD	:C	tipo_documento.flat	DATASETS
C:\DATASETS\tipo_documento.lst	tsl.otnemucod_opit\STESATAD\:C	tsl.otnemucod_opit	STESATAD	:C	tipo_documento.lst	DATASETS
C:\DATASETS\DATA\202206-citbike-tripdata.csv.zip	piz.vsc.atadpirt-ekibtic-602202\ATAD\STESATAD\:C	piz.vsc.atadpirt-ekibtic-602202	ATAD	STESATAD\:C	202206-citbike-tripdata.csv.zip	DATA
C:\DATASETS\DATA\CityBike_2013.yxdb	bdxy.3102_ekiBytiC\ATAD\STESATAD\:C	bdxy.3102_ekiBytiC	ATAD	STESATAD\:C	CityBike_2013.yxdb	DATA
C:\DATASETS\DATA\CityBike_2014.yxdb	bdxy.4102_ekiBytiC\ATAD\STESATAD\:C	bdxy.4102_ekiBytiC	ATAD	STESATAD\:C	CityBike_2014.yxdb	DATA
C:\DATASETS\DATA\CityBike_2015.yxdb	bdxy.5102_ekiBytiC\ATAD\STESATAD\:C	bdxy.5102_ekiBytiC	ATAD	STESATAD\:C	CityBike_2015.yxdb	DATA
C:\DATASETS\DATA\CityBike_2016.yxdb	bdxy.6102_ekiBytiC\ATAD\STESATAD\:C	bdxy.6102_ekiBytiC	ATAD	STESATAD\:C	CityBike_2016.yxdb	DATA
C:\DATASETS\DATA\202206-citbike-tripdata.csv\2...	vsc.atadpirt-ekibtic-602202\vsc.atadpirt-ekibtic-6...	vsc.atadpirt-ekibtic-602202	ATAD\STESATAD\:C	202206-citbike-tripdata.csv	202206-citbike-t...
C:\DATASETS\DATA\202206-citbike-tripdata.csv_...	vsc.atadpirt-ekibtic-602202_\XSOCAM__\vsc.ata...	vsc.atadpirt-ekibtic-602202_.	X:SOCAM__	vsc.atadpirt-ekibti...	_202206-citbike-tripdata.csv	_MACOSX
C:\DATASETS\SUBFOLDER\ARTICULOS.yxdb	bdxy.SOLUCITRA\REDLOFBUS\STESATAD\:C	bdxy.SOLUCITRA	REDLOFBUS	STESATAD\:C	ARTICULOS.yxdb	SUBFOLDER
C:\DATASETS\SUBFOLDER\DOCUMENTOS.yxdb	bdxy.SOTNEMUCOD\REDLOFBUS\STESATAD\:C	bdxy.SOTNEMUCOD	REDLOFBUS	STESATAD\:C	DOCUMENTOS.yxdb	SUBFOLDER

Figure 5.22: Splitting the last two pieces of a delimited string

Working with RegEx

We are not going to get into the details of **regular expressions** in this recipe; we are just going to mention concepts that will help you decide when (and when not) to use them.

Regular expressions refer to a set of characters on a particular notation, where each one can have a literal or special meaning (metacharacters); they can be used for pattern recognition within a text, and are very useful for parsing and matching strings in unstructured data. It's all about determining likenesses or differences between the notation and the real text.

There are many types of syntaxes, based on the processor used, so we are going to focus on the Perl one, which is the one that Alteryx uses (through the Boost library) and one of the most used in general.

One important thing to notice about regular expressions is that they focus on patterns, so if you don't have a pattern in your text, RegEx won't be the right method for parsing it.

Getting ready

We prepared several test sets for you to try, which you can download from here: `https://github. com/PacktPublishing/Alteryx-Designer-Cookbook/tree/main/ch5/Recipe3`.

We are going to work with a dataset of references taken from the bibliography section of a book, which follows the *IEEE Reference Guide* (you can access the complete reference guide here: `http:// ieeeauthorcenter.ieee.org/wp-content/uploads/IEEE-Reference-Guide.pdf`).

The data follows this definition (note that we are using \s to represent whitespace):

Field/Separator	Value	Example	RegEx that matches
Reference number	Number of the reference, from 1 to N	1	`^(\d+)`
:\s	A colon followed by a whitespace		`:\s`
Author(s)	List of authors in the last name, first initial format plus a "."	Smith, J., Doe, J.	`(.+)`
,\s"	A comma, whitespace, and opening double quotes		`\,\s\"`
Title of the Chapter	Title of the chapter	Chapter 1: Input Data from Files	`(.*)`
"\sin:\s	Closing double quotes for the chapter, whitespace, the "in:" literal, and a whitespace		`\"\sin:\s`
Title of the Book	Title of the book	Alteryx Designer Cookbook	`(.+)`
.\s	A period followed by a whitespace		`\.\s`
City	City of publication	Birmingham	`(.*)`
:\s	Colon and a whitespace		`:\s`
Publisher		Packt Publishing	`(.+)`
,\s	Comma followed by a whitespace		`\,\s`
Year		2023	`(\d{2,4})`
,\s(pp.\s	Comma, whitespace, open parenthesis, and the "pp." literal, plus a whitespace		`,\s\(pp.\s`
Page From		5	`(\d+)`
-	Literal		`\-`

Page To		10	(\d+)
).\s	Closing parenthesis, a period, followed by a whitespace		\)\.\s

This example will be presented as follows:

1: Smith, J., Doe, J., "Chapter 1: Input Data from Files" in: Alteryx Designer Cookbook. Birmingham: Packt Publishing, 2023, (pp. 5-10).

Reference
1: Baker, R., & Siemens, G., "Educational data mining and learning analytics" in: The Cambridge handbook of the learning sciences.Cambridge: Cambridge University Press, 2015, (pp. 253-274).
2: Berg, A., Scheffel, M., Drachsler, H., Ternier, S., & Specht, M., "Dutch cooking with xAPI recipes: The good, the bad, and the consistent" in: 2016 IEEE 16th international conference on advanced learning technologies.Austin: UNESCO, 2016, (pp. 35-42). h
3: Chatti, M. A., Dyckhoff, A. L., Schroeder, U., & Thüs, H., "A reference model for learning analytics" in: International Journal of Technology Enhanced Learning:, 2012, (pp.318-331).
4: Papamitsiou, Z. K., Terzis, V., & Economides, A. A., "Temporal learning analytics for computer based testing" in: Proceedings of the fourth international conference on learninganalytics and knowledge.Indianapolis: ACM, 2014, (pp. 31-35).
5: Sang, L, Mingchuan, Y., Han, L, Zixin, Z., Ruoyu, J., "" in: Big data, technology capability and construction project quality: across-level investigation: ECAM, 2021, (pp. 706-727).

Figure 5.23: Sample data

As a very brief reference for those who never used regular expressions before, these are basic things to know:

- \d = Represents any digit

- \D = Represents anything BUT a digit

- \w = Any alphanumeric character

- \W = Anything BUT an alphanumeric character

- ? = One character of any type

- . = Any character except a line break

When we need to specify a period character (or any character that needs to be evaluated as a literal), we need to escape that character. We escape a character by placing \ before the character. So \ . means a period character (literally), \ (means an open bracket, \ ? means a question mark, and so on.

Repetitions

What we showed previously refers to one and only one character in the pattern and, since RegEx is a positional parser, specifying \d will look for a digit and only one digit in that position.

Luckily, some metacharacters allow us to specify repetitions, such as the following:

- + indicates one or more of the preceding expression

- * indicates zero or more of the pattern appearances

- ? indicates zero or one appearance (may be there or not, conditional)

- { } indicates a range of possible repetitions:

  - \d{n} = Looks for n amount of digits

  - \d{,n} = Looks for a sequence of digits between zero and n in length

  - \d{n,} = Looks for a sequence of at least n digits in lengt

  - \d{n,m} = Looks for a sequence of digits between n and m in length

Reserved metacharacters

RegEx has some reserved characters that, by themselves have a particular meaning, and need to be escaped too when you need to include them literally in a search pattern:

- ^ = Indicates the beginning of the line, but also negates the expression when used within square brackets.

- $ = Indicates the end of the line.

- (= Opens a capturing group. Everything between non-escaped parenthesis is a parse group for the RegEx parser. So you can group multiple tokens that work together in these groups.

-) = Closes a capturing group.

- [= Starts an enumeration group or range. You can specify exactly what to look for between squared brackets, such as these examples:

  - [a-z] means any character in between a (ASCII code 97) and z (ASCII code 122)

  - [a-zA-Z] allows any character between a and z AND A and Z (ASCII codes from 97 through 122 and ASCII codes 65 to ASCII code 90)

  - [abc] will match only with a, b, or c characters

  - [^abc] means everything except a, b, or c characters

-] = the end of an enumeration group or range.

- | = An OR operator. It will match any token within the expression.

I'd recommend reading the whole recipe before laying hands on Alteryx Designer, especially if you are new to RegEx.

How to do it...

For those who never used regular expressions before, this may appear very complicated, but for this example, and since this is not a RegEx book, we are going to use expressions that will parse what we need. Even when they are not the ideal ones in terms of excellence, we'll use them for simplicity.

Besides, I want to show you alternative methods for some of them that will make your life easier and get the same results:

1. Drop an **Input Data** tool and point it to `\DATA\Bibliography.csv`.

    Our first task will be to examine the data and find patterns within it. This is simplified because, in this case, we have the definition of the dataset.

    So basically, we'll be translating the definition into a regular expression, in plain English, to get the following:

    -   `Reference number` = Starting at every line, parse all the digits before `:\s`

    -   `Author(s)` = Everything that is between the first semicolon and `,\s"` (comma followed by a whitespace and a double quote)

    -   `Title of the Chapter` = Everything that is between `,\s` and a closing double quote

    -   `Title of the Book` = Everything that follows the preceding closing double quotes and a literal `\sin:\s` string and is followed by `.\s` (period and a space)

    -   `City` = What follows the preceding `.\s` and `:\s` (colon)

    -   `Publisher` = Everything after the `City` end delimiter (`:\s`) and before a comma followed by a whitespace (`,\s`)

    -   `Year` = Four digits after the comma and whitespace, and before the `,\s` (`pp.\s` literal

    -   `Page From` = All digits after the `Year` ending and `-` (dash)

    -   `Page To` = All digits after the `Page From` ending metacharacter and a closing parenthesis, a period, and a whitespace (`\).\s`)

2. So, drop a **RegEx** tool onto the canvas, and in the **Regular Expression** field, paste this expression:

    ```
    ^(\d+):(.+)\"(.*)\"\sin:(.+)\.\s(.*):(.+),\s(\d{2,4}),\s\
    (pp.\s(\d+)-(\d+)\)
    ```

    In **Output Method**, select **Parse**, and rename **Output Columns** accordingly.

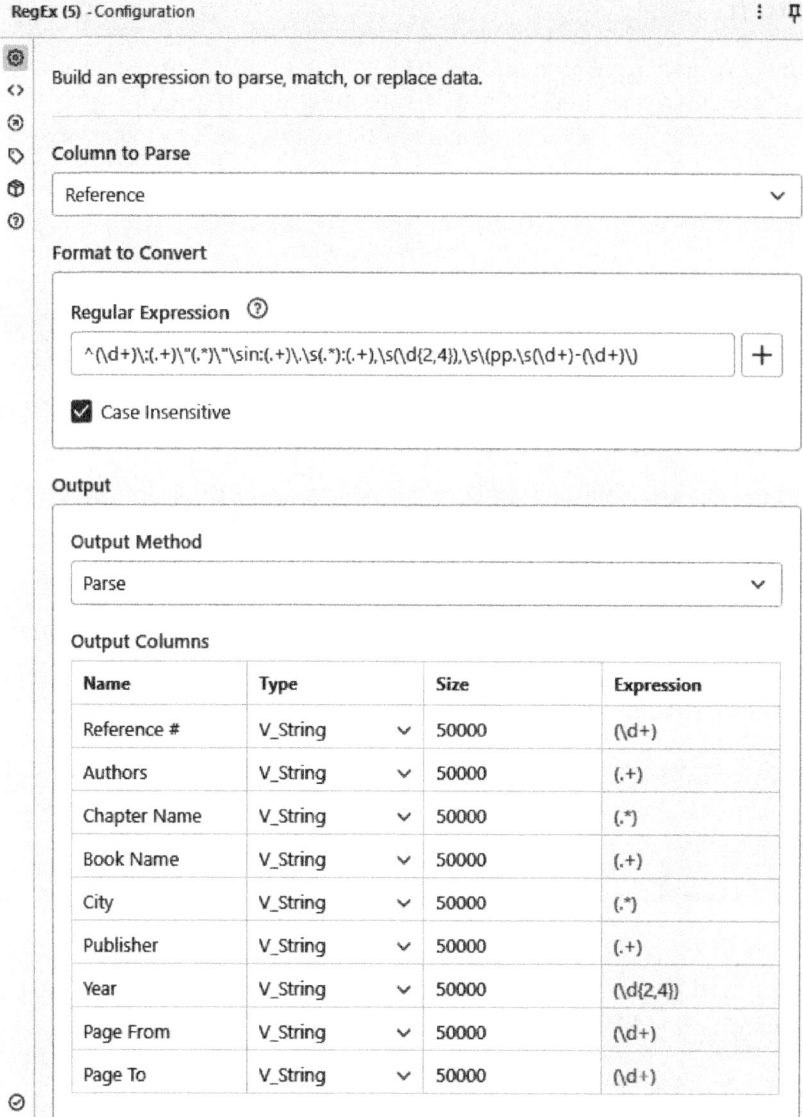

Figure 5.24: RegEx tool configuration

But if we run the workflow, even when we followed the patterns, we'll notice that this expression doesn't match record #3, so none of its fields are parsed.

Reference	Reference #	Authors	Chapter Name	Book Name	City	Publisher	Year	Page From	Page To
1: Baker, R., & Siemens, G., "Educational data mi...	1	Baker, R., & Siemens, G.,	Educational data mining and learning analytics	The Cambridge handbook of the learning sciences	Cambridge	Cambridge University Press	2015	253	274
2: Berg, A., Scheffel, M., Drachsler, H., Temter, S...	2	Berg, A., Scheffel, M., Drachsler, H., Temter, S., A...	Dutch cooking with xAPI recipes: The good, the b...	2016 IEEE 16th international conference on adva...	Austin	UNESCO	2016	35	42
3: Chatti, M. A., Dyckhoff, A. L., Schroeder, U., & T...	[Null]	[Null]	[Null]	[Null]	[Null]	[Null]	[Null]	[Null]	[Null]
4: Papamitsiou, Z. K., Terzis, V., & Economides, A...	4	Papamitsiou, Z. K., Terzis, V., & Economides, A.A.	Temporal learning analytics for computer based t...	Proceedings of the fourth international conferen...	Indianapolis	ACM	2014	31	35
5: Sang, L., Mingchuan, Y., Han, L, Zixin, Z, Ruoyu...	5	Sang, L., Mingchuan, Y, Han, L, Zixin, Z, Ruoyu, J,		Big data, technology capability and construction...		BCAM	2021	706	727

Figure 5.25: Unmatched record after RegEx parsing

This is caused by the `City` and `Publisher` fields not appearing in record #3, so for this to work, we need to add some modifications to the RegEx expression. We are going to tell the parser that `City` and `Publisher` are not mandatory within the parsing (they can be there or not), just by adding a ? metacharacter to the corresponding parsing groups.

3. Change the **Regular Expression** details in the **RegEx** tool to this:

```
^(\d+):\s(.+)\,\s\"(.*)\"\sin:\s(.+)\.\s(.*)?:(.*)?\,\s(\
d{2,4}),\s\(pp.\s(\d+)-(\d+)\)\.
```

4. Run the workflow.

    You'll notice that record #3 is still not being parsed. If you look at its contents, you'll see that there is a missing whitespace (\s) after the `,\s\(pp.\s` token, so we need to tell the parser again to fix this and make its appearance optional.

    Add a ? After `(pp.\s` so your expression is like this:

```
^(\d+):\s(.+)\,\s\"(.*)\"\sin:\s(.+)\.\s(.*)?:(.*)?\,\s(\
d{2,4}),\s\(pp.\s?(\d+)-(\d+)\)\.
```

Now, we have fixed our parsing expression and parsed all our data.

Some notes

Trying to parse everything at once is one of the biggest mistakes we make when starting with regular expressions. Since it is so powerful, we can try to tackle it all at once, ending in countless hours of debugging and trial and error. And when we are versed in RegEx, using it for everything is another of the common situations I have found over time.

So, for maintainability and readability, we always tend to focus on extracting the pieces of content needed, one at a time. In this case, we'll start with the reference number.

We can use a `(\d+):(.+)` expression to split the reference number and the rest of the data in the field, but actually, we have a better method: using a **Text To Columns** tool.

The same reasoning may apply to the `Page From` and `Page To` fields, but it's OK if you use RegEx to extract it from the original string `(\,\s\(pp.\s?(\d+\-\d+)\)\.)` and then split to two columns with another **Text To Columns** tool.

Important note

When working with dates, always use a **DateTime** tool or a **Formula** tool to convert the RegEx results into the Date/DateTime format. This will ensure you are not considering invalid dates as valid ones. Remember that RegEx only parses and returns strings.

For example, let's say that we have this dataset:

Text
First access was on 2022-01-29
First access was on 2022-02-28. But was reaccessed.
First access was on 2022-02-29
First access was on 2022-03-12

Figure 5.26: Using RegEx on dates

You can extract the date from the `Text` field with `(\d{4}\-\d{2}\-\d{2})`.

But there is a problem here: 2022 was not a leap year, so February 29th, 2022 is not a valid date. If we go through a **DateTime** tool with the extracted date, it'll return a **Null** value for this row:

Text	DateRegEx	DateTime_Out
First access was on 2022-01-29	2022-01-29	2022-01-29
First access was on 2022-02-28. But was reaccess...	2022-02-28	2022-02-28
First access was on 2022-02-29	2022-02-29	[Null]
First access was on 2022-03-12	2022-03-12	2022-03-12

Figure 5.27: Always use a DateTime tool after RegEx involving dates

See also

Perl Regular Expression Syntax (the Boost library used in Alteryx):

`https://www.boost.org/doc/libs/1_68_0/libs/regex/doc/html/boost_regex/syntax/perl_syntax.html`

Useful websites on regular expressions:

`https://regex101.com/`: A sandbox for trying your regular expressions, plus quick references, explanations of each token used, and more.

`https://regexr.com`: Similar to regex101.

`https://www.regular-expressions.info`: A complete quick start, reference, tutorial, tools, and examples reference site.

`https://www.autoregex.xyz/`: An AI model to tell in natural language what you need, and it'll suggest regular expressions that match. This one is still in development, so it's not 100% accurate all the time.

6

Grouping Data

Grouping data is one of the techniques we need to master as analysts. This is because grouping is not only a way to correctly classify and/or aggregate data to get insights, but is also sometimes an insight in itself (such as for customer classification).

We need to differentiate grouping from clustering, which involves using statistical models to determine groups. In this chapter, we'll focus on grouping data based on conditions so that we can reduce large datasets for analysis (such as individual transactions into total expenses).

We'll be using Alteryx's powerful tools to accomplish this easily and with different approaches. To do so, we will cover the following recipes:

- Grouping data
- Finding groups within groups
- Exploring the **Make Group** tool
- Binning numeric fields

Grouping data

Alteryx allows you to assign data to groups based on conditions very easily. It provides the **Tile** tool, one of the most underestimated tools in the palette, which is very powerful and fast when it comes to achieving non-statistical grouping.

In this recipe, we'll be assigning groups to our data based on several configurations that the **Tile** tool allows, such as the following:

- Equal Sum
- Equal Records
- Smart Tiling

We'll leave the Manual and Unique Values methods for the next recipe.

Getting ready

We have prepared a test set so that you can follow along with this recipe. You can download it from here: `https://github.com/PacktPublishing/Alteryx-Designer-Cookbook/tree/main/ch6/Recipe1`.

If you decide to complete this recipe with your data, just make sure you have a transactional dataset, with several transactions per customer, and a couple of measures that, when combined, determine grouping criteria (for example, visits to a store and spending, product quantity and cost, and so on).

In this recipe, we'll be calculating deciles per sale (10 categorical buckets based on `Sales` values) from a list of customers. I'll help you get this insight more traditionally, and make this simpler later.

We'll start with the following data, which consists of aggregated data (`Sales` and `Visits`) per `Customer_ID` (the OUTPUT worksheet of the `..\DATA\Cust_wTransactions.xls` file):

Customer_ID	Store Number	Customer Segment	First Name	Last Name	Address	City	State	Zip	Visits	Spend
10	100	Home Office	PAMELA	WRIGHT	2316 E 5TH AVE	DENVER	CO	80206	1	206.95
100	100	Consumer	MELISSA	RUFF	2753 S MILWAUKEE ST	DENVER	CO	80210	1	228.27
1000	104	Small Business	CONSTANTI	VLASSIS	16911 E HARVARD AVE	AURORA	CO	80013	1	432.44
1002	104	Home Office	AMY	LOCKEMER	3721 S PITKIN CT	AURORA	CO	80013	4	2101.11
1003	101	Home Office	DANELL	VALDEZ	2925 W COLLEGE AVE	DENVER	CO	80219	1	1404.09
1005	107	Small Business	JESSICA	RINEHART	4220 W 35TH AVE	DENVER	CO	80212	2	962.61
1006	104	Small Business	NANCY	CLARK	8785 CLOVERLEAF CIR	PARKER	CO	80134	4	552.53
1008	107	Home Office	ANDREA	BRUN	2080 FENTON ST	DENVER	CO	80214	1	25.37
1009	104	Corporate	DENISE	PENTICO	4125C S EVANSTON CIR	AURORA	CO	80014	2	7026.44

Figure 6.1: Preview of the dataset

The logical process will be to do the following:

1. In a new workflow, use the **Input Data** tool and point it to `..\DATA\Cust_wTransactions.xls`. Then, select the OUTPUT worksheet as the data source.

2. Connect a **Summarize** tool to it and add `Customer_ID` as **Group By**.

3. Select both the `Visits` and `Spend` fields and add them with the **Sum** aggregation method. This will summarize the actual data (just in case we have duplicates) to get TOTAL_VISITS and TOTAL_SPEND per `Customer_ID`:

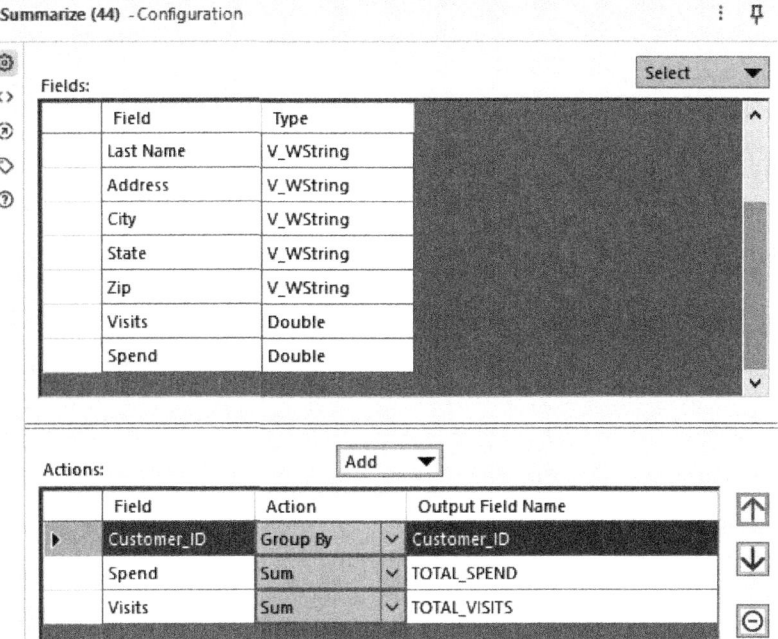

Figure 6.2: Configuring the Summarize tool

4. Run the workflow and see how TOTAL_SPEND and TOTAL_VISITS are summed up for each Customer_ID:

Customer_ID	TOTAL_SPEND	TOTAL_VISITS
10	206.95	1
100	228.27	1
1000	432.44	1
1002	2101.11	4
1003	1404.09	1
1005	962.61	2
1006	552.53	4
1008	25.37	1
1009	7026.44	2

Figure 6.3: The results so far

In a second stream, we'll be counting TOTAL_CUSTOMERS that exist within the dataset with another **Summarize** tool.

5. So, connect a new **Summarize** tool to the previous one's output anchor, select `Customer_ID` from the `Fields` section, then click **Add** and select **Count** as the aggregation method. For **Output Field Name**, use `TOTAL_CUSTOMERS` to replace the default name that Alteryx assigns (`Count`):

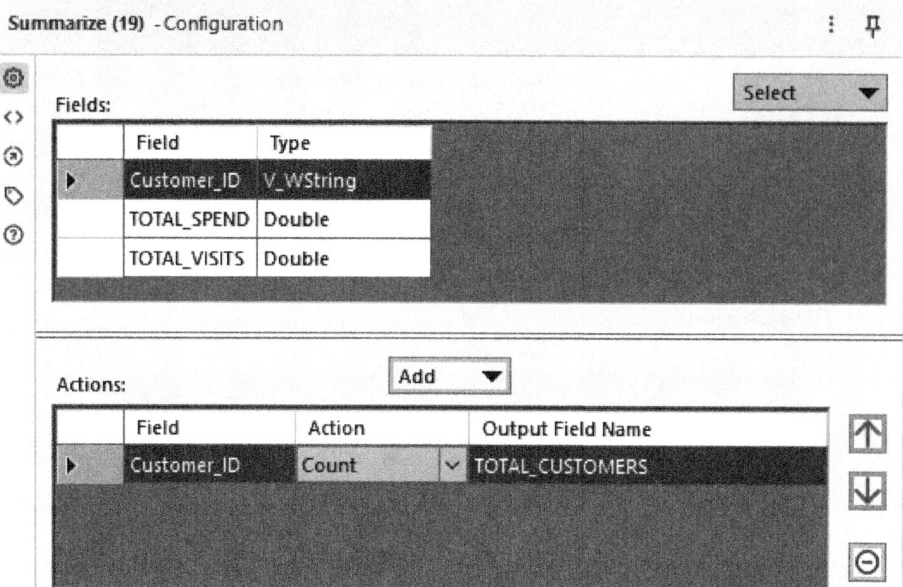

Figure 6.4: The second Summarize tool's configuration

So far, we have two data streams that contain important data, and we need to combine them. We'll be appending `TOTAL_CUSTOMERS` (coming from the second **Summarize** tool) to `TOTALS` per `Customer_ID` (coming from the first **Summarize** tool).

6. To do this, move the second **Summarize** tool a little bit down, add an **Append Fields** tool (from the **Join** category), and connect the first **Summarize** output to the T input and the **Summarize** tool's output for `TOTAL_CUSTOMERS` to the S input of the **Append Fields** tool.

Your workflow should look like this:

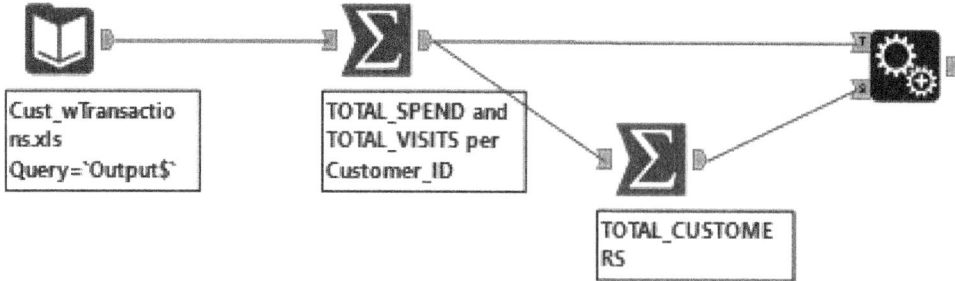

Figure 6.5: Our workflow so far

7. Run the workflow; your dataset should now include all the necessary fields:

Customer_ID	TOTAL_SPEND	TOTAL_VISITS	TOTAL_CUSTOMERS
10	206.95	1	2669
100	228.27	1	2669
1000	432.44	1	2669
1002	2101.11	4	2669
1003	1404.09	1	2669

Figure 6.6: The results after running the workflow

Our analysis requires that we start selecting records (customers) based on TOTAL_SPEND and assign them to a decile. Simply put, we must determine their position within the dataset so that we can group them based on it into 10% increments over the total.

To accomplish this, we need to sort them based on our quantifier (TOTAL_SPEND) in Descending order so that we get the top spenders first to assign them to the first decile and keep assigning them to further groups based on the spend.

8. Drop a **Sort** tool and connect it to the **Append Fields** output anchor. Select TOTAL_SPEND from the **Name** dropdown and Descending from the **Order** dropdown. Do the same for TOTAL_VISITS, but in this case, select Ascending for the sort order (this is optional, but I wanted to prioritize bigger spending on fewer visits):

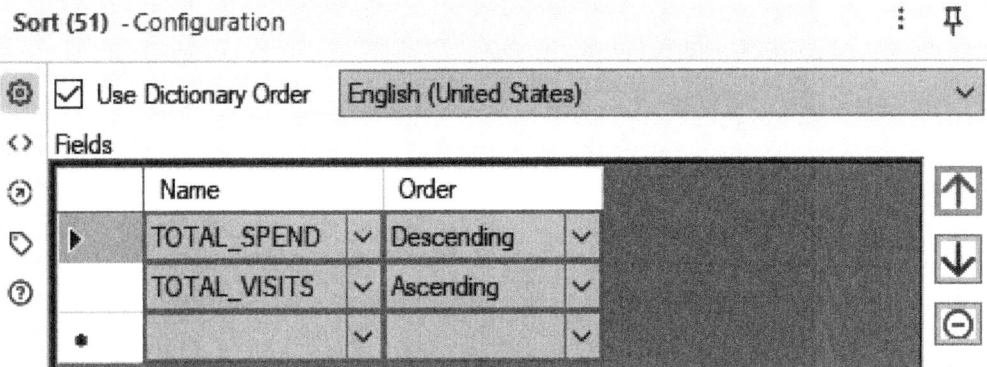

Figure 6.7: Configuring the Sort tool

After getting the sorted results, we must assign them a RecordID value (this will work as a ranking measure).

9. Drop a **RecordID** tool and connect it to the output anchor of the **Sort** tool. Leave the defaults as is:

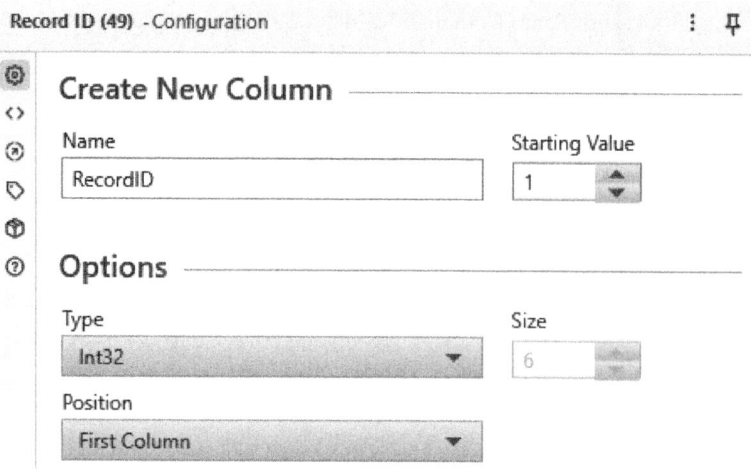

Figure 6.8: Configuring the RecordID tool

With that, our records have been identified based on the overall spend within the dataset, with RecordID set to 1 as the bigger spender, and so on until we get to the end of the record set so that we can start assigning the groups.

If we divide the RecordID value by the total amount of records, we can easily get the percentage position of that record within the whole dataset (a lower RecordID value represents a higher "rank" within the dataset).

10. Add a **Formula** tool, create a new column called Position_percent, set **Data type** to Double, and use the following expression:

    [RecordID] / [TOTAL_CUSTOMERS] This can be seen here:

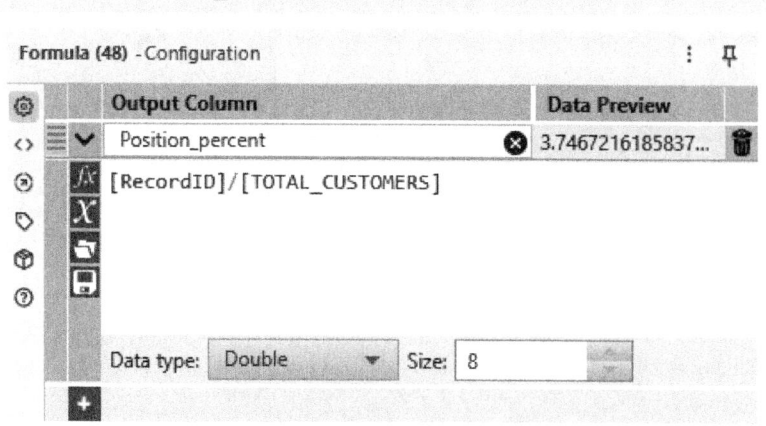

Figure 6.9: Configuring the Formula tool

With this record "ranked," we can start assigning them to our 10 groups (deciles).

The group will be assigned with Group #1 containing 10% of the top records in sales, Group #2 containing the following 10%, and so on.

To do this, we have to create a new variable that, based on the "position" of the actual record within the dataset, assigns it to a group.

11. Drop a new **Formula** tool (you can use the existing one, but for maintainability and ease of understanding, we will add a second one so that each formula has only one calculation), create a new column called `Decile`, set `Double` as **Data type**, and use the following code for the expression:

```
IF [Position_percent]>0 AND [Position_percent]<=.1
THEN 1
ELSEIF [Position_percent]>.1 AND [Position_percent]<=.2
THEN 2
ELSEIF [Position_percent]>.2 AND [Position_percent]<=.3
THEN 3
ELSEIF [Position_percent]>.3 AND [Position_percent]<=.4
THEN 4
ELSEIF [Position_percent]>.4 AND [Position_percent]<=.5
THEN 5
ELSEIF [Position_percent]>.5 AND [Position_percent]<=.6
THEN 6
ELSEIF [Position_percent]>.6 AND [Position_percent]<=.7
THEN 7
ELSEIF [Position_percent]>.7 AND [Position_percent]<=.8
THEN 8
ELSEIF [Position_percent]>.8 AND [Position_percent]<=.9
THEN 9
ELSEIF [Position_percent]>.9 AND [Position_percent]<=1
THEN 10
ELSE 0
ENDIF
```

So far, your workflow should look like this:

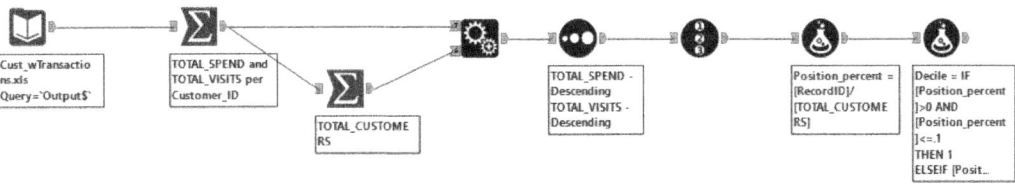

Figure 6.10: Final workflow overview

12. Run the workflow – you'll see that every `Customer_ID` was assigned to a `Decile` value based on its sales:

RecordID	Customer_ID	TOTAL_SPEND	TOTAL_VISITS	TOTAL_CUSTOMERS	Position_percent	Decile
263	1767	7201.73	3	2669	0.098539	1
264	2630	7189.7	9	2669	0.098913	1
265	862	7183.43	6	2669	0.099288	1
266	2048	7181.43	7	2669	0.099663	1
267	2671	7179.92	4	2669	0.100037	2
268	1400	7144.04	1	2669	0.100412	2
269	3083	7130.62	8	2669	0.100787	2
270	3218	7103.55	5	2669	0.101161	2
271	413	7099.12	1	2669	0.101536	2

Figure 6.11: Final results

Even though building this workflow solves the use case for us, we can simplify it a lot with the help of just one tool, the **Tile** tool, which is what this recipe is all about.

How to do it...

To get started, follow these steps:

1. In a new workflow, add an **Input Data** tool, point it to `..\DATA\Cust_wTransactions.xls`, and select the `OUTPUT` worksheet as the data source.

2. Drop a **Tile** tool (from the **Preparation** category) and connect it to the **Input Data** tool's output anchor.

3. From the **Tile Method** dropdown, select `Equal Records` and enter `10` for **Number of Tiles**.

4. Leave **Do not split tile on column** blank.

5. For **Sort Column**, select **Spend**.

6. Select **Sort Method** according to your data (in this case, we have a dataset in `English`, but it could be in a different language, so we can adjust the sorting method).

7. Leave **Group by Columns** blank (all deselected):

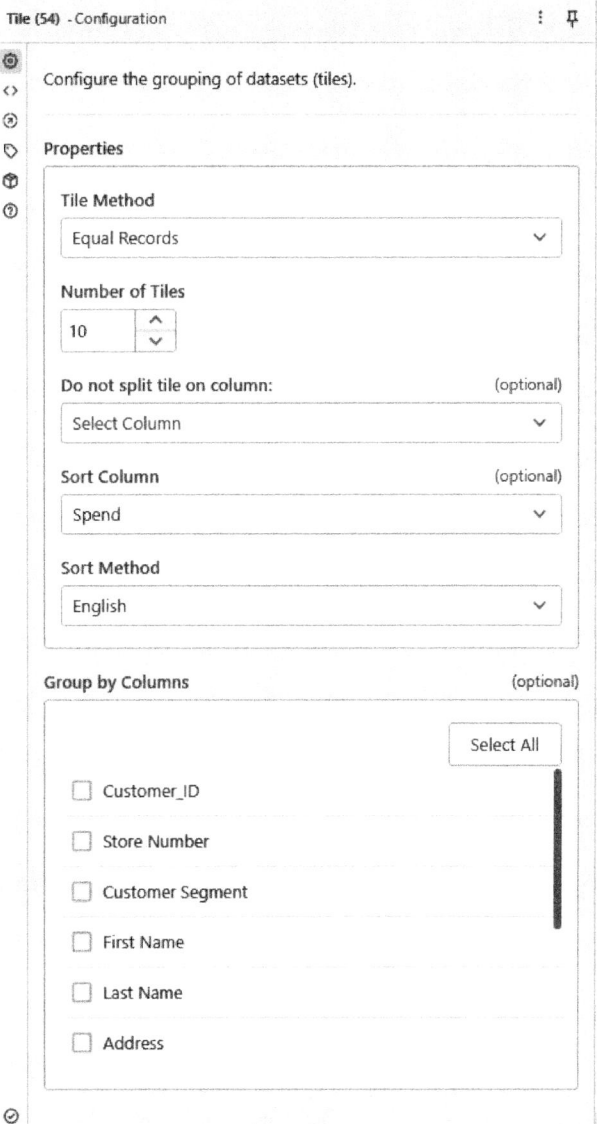

Figure 6.12: Configuring the Tile tool

8. Run the workflow.

    You'll see that Alteryx added two columns to your dataset: Tile_Num and Tile_SequenceNum:

    - Tile_Num is the decile assigned

    - Tile_SequenceNum is the position of the record within that specific group:

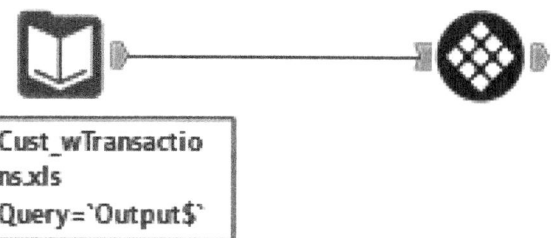

Figure 6.13: Workflow overview

Just one tool to solve the whole use case! Cool, right?

How it works...

The **Tile** tool groups data based on its configuration.

You can choose from several methods of tiling:

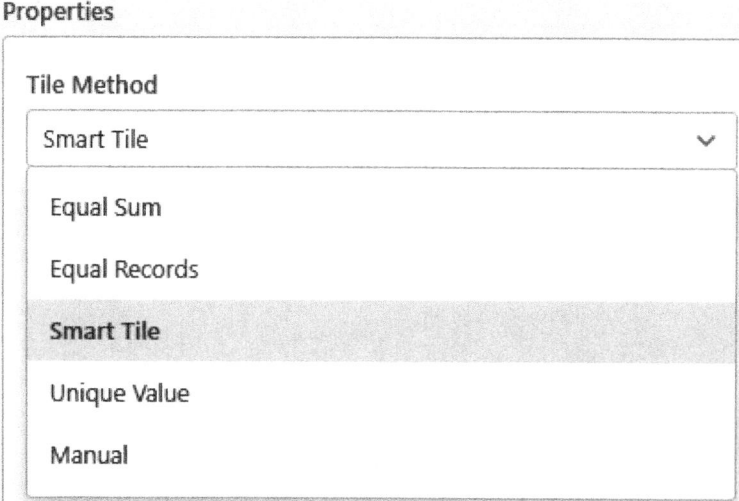

Figure 6.14: The available tiling methods

Let's take a closer look:

- **Equal Sum**: This method assigns tiles that cover a range of values where each tile has the same total as the **Sum** field. It is based on how incoming records are sorted.

- **Equal Records**: This method assigns a specified number of tiles so that each tile has the same amount of records. This highly depends on how the records are sorted.

- **Smart Tile**: Even when there is not a specific document explaining how this method works in detail, we know that it creates the tiles based on the standard deviation and the average of the selected field's values in the dataset, and assigns the tiles based on whether the record falls within the average range (`Tile=0`), above (`1`), or below (`-1`). The number of tiles will be determined by the dispersion of the values. (The higher the standard deviation is, the more dispersed the values are. In our example dataset, our standard deviation is ~7285.48, so we get seven smart tiles, ranging from -3 to 3.)

- **Unique Value**: This method assigns a tile to each value from the selected field/s.

- **Manual**: This method allows the user to determine, upon inputting the upper limit for each group, how the values are going to be assigned. There must be one value per line.

> **Important note**
> When you choose to **group by** any column/s, the tiles are calculated for each set of values within each group.

Finding groups within groups

In the previous recipe, we mentioned that we'll be leaving the **Tile** tool's `Unique values` and `Manual` methods for later. In this recipe, we are going to use them to easily solve some grouping challenges we may encounter, such as the big formula we used in the previous recipe to assign the groups.

The **Tile** tool will allow us to categorize records based on conditions in a really simple way.

Getting ready

For this recipe, we'll be using some assets from the previous recipe. You can download them here: `https://github.com/PacktPublishing/Alteryx-Designer-Cookbook/tree/main/ch6/Recipe2`.

How to do it...

Follow these steps:

1. Open the `GroupingData.yxmd` workflow (**File** | **Open Workflow** | **Browse** and point it to this recipe's folder – that is, the `WORKFLOW` subfolder:

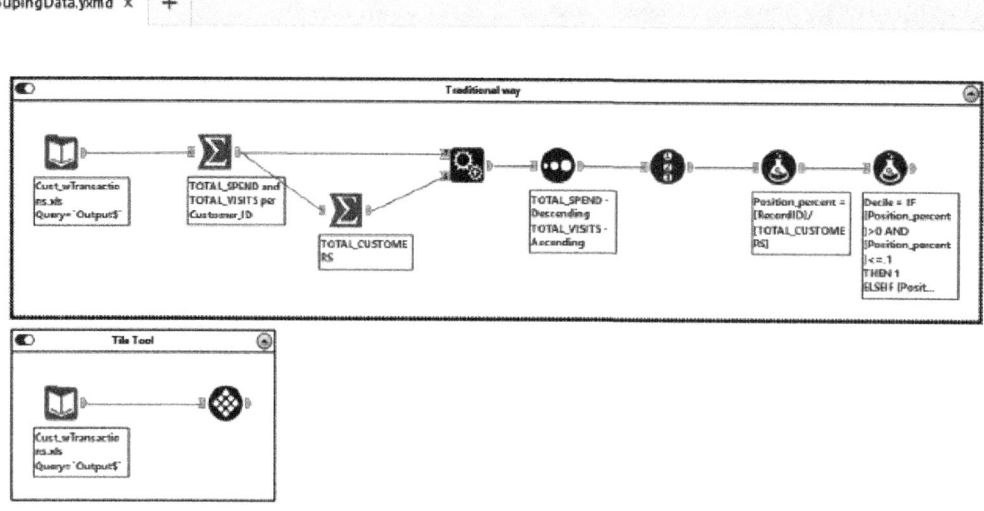

Figure 6.15: The GroupingData.yxmd workflow

2. Drop a **Tile** tool and connect it to the output of the **Formula** tool, which calculates `Position_` `percent` (the leftmost one).

    Configure the **Tile** tool as follows:

    - **Tile Method**: `Manual`

    - **The Numeric Column**: `Position_percent`

    - In the **Enter one or more tile cutoffs** section, paste the following list:

    ```
    .1
    .2
    .3
    .4
    .5
    .6
    .7
    .8
    .9
    1
    ```

    Make sure that each value is in its own row.

- Leave **Group by Columns** blank (everything should be deselected):

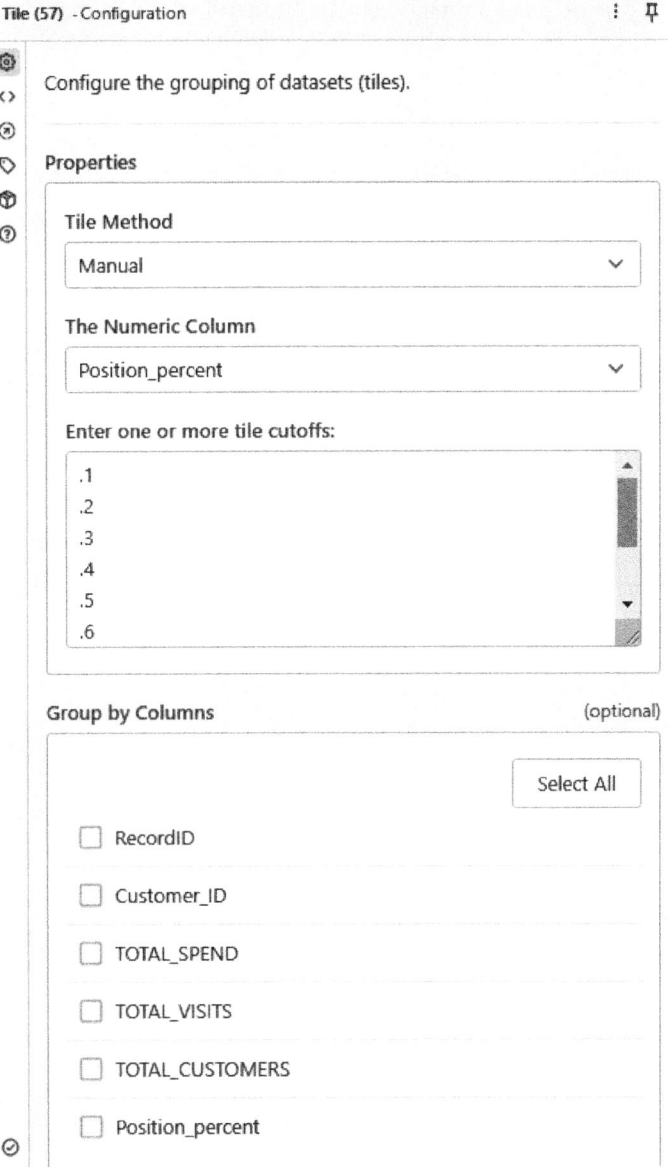

Figure 6.16: Configuring the Tile tool (manual tiling)

If you run the workflow, you'll see that the `Tile_Num` field that's assigned to each record is the same one we obtained from that very long formula in the previous recipe.

The only thing we need to do is rename the `Tile_Num` field to `Decile` using the **Select** tool.

This is a very simple, fast, clean, and effective method to classify our data.

How it works...

This method requires that we set the upper limit for each group that needs to be classified. In our example, we have a calculation that determines the percentage position of each record within the dataset (`Position_percent`). Using the decile limits (`.1` is the first 10% of the records, `.2` is the second 10%, and so on), Alteryx fits the values within the specified ranges automatically.

There's more...

As easy as it is to assign groups to records with the **Tile** tool, we can use it to assign group IDs based on several fields.

Let's say that we want to do the same grouping exercise, but now, we want to do it on a `Store Number` and `Customer Segment` basis (we want to calculate the sales deciles for each combination of `Store` and `Segment`). Let's take a look:

1. Drop a **Tile** tool and connect it to the **Input Data** tool.

2. Configure the **Tile** tool like this:

    -   **Tile Method**: `Unique Value`

    -   **Unique Column**: Select `Store Number` and `Customer Segment` (our new group calculation criteria)

    -   Leave **Group by Columns** blank (everything should be deselected):

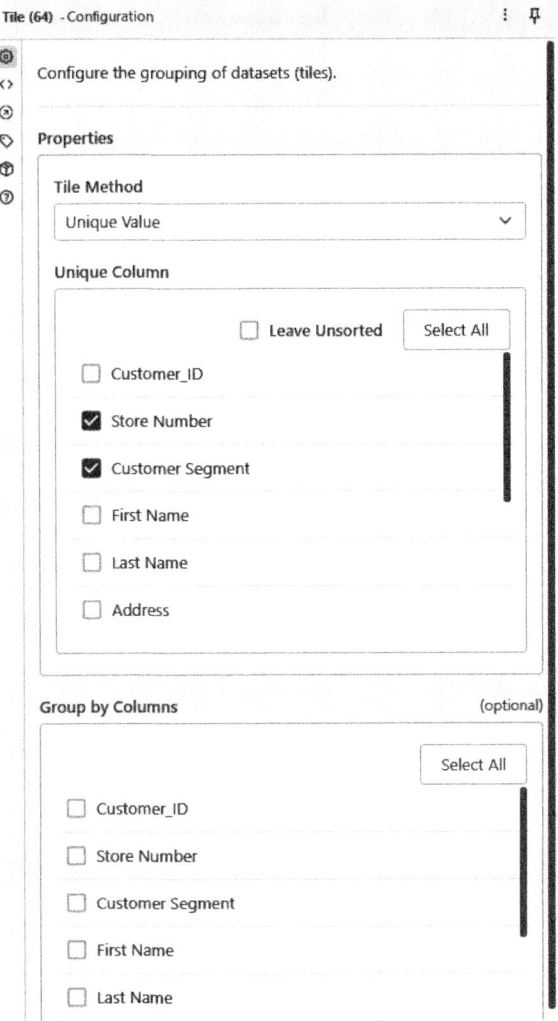

Figure 6.17: Configuring the Tile tool (unique values)

If you run the workflow, you'll see that for each combination of `Store Number` and `Customer Segment`, you got a `Tile_Num` value:

Customer_ID	Store Number	Customer Segment	First Name	Last Name	Address	City	State	Zip	Visits	Spend	Tile_Num
890	100	Consumer	VALERIE	SALLS	5676 W 71ST PL	ARVADA	CO	80003	7	4557.91	1
893	100	Consumer									1
956	100	Consumer	JEANIE	CONQUET	4710 E MISSISSIPPI AVE	DENVER	CO	80246	6	814.81	1
1092	100	Corporate	BONNIE	GILL	401 S LEYDEN ST	DENVER	CO	80224	2	351.41	2
1151	100	Corporate									2
1236	100	Corporate	DEBRA	MAXWELL	16576 E ARKANSAS AVE	AURORA	CO	80017	2	1415.27	2
1238	100	Corporate	ALEXANDRIA	HOLMES	9123 E MISSISSIPPI AVE	DENVER	CO	80247	8	6183.02	2

Figure 6.18: Each combination of selected unique columns gets their own Tile_Num value

With this classification, we are ready to get the deciles within each initial grouping.

3. Drop the **Select** tool to rename the tiles to `Grouping_Tile` and deselect `Tile_SequenceNum`. We are doing this for clarity and maintainability.

4. Add a new **Tile** tool and configure it as follows:

    - **Tile Method**: `Equal Records`

    - **Number of Tiles**: `10` (deciles)

    - **Do not split tile on column**: `Grouping_Tile` (this will ensure that we won't get different tiles for the same group of `Store Number` and `Segment`)

    - **Sort Column**: `Spend`

    - **Sort Method**: `English` (or the method that better fits your dataset)

    - **Group by Columns**: Leave everything deselected:

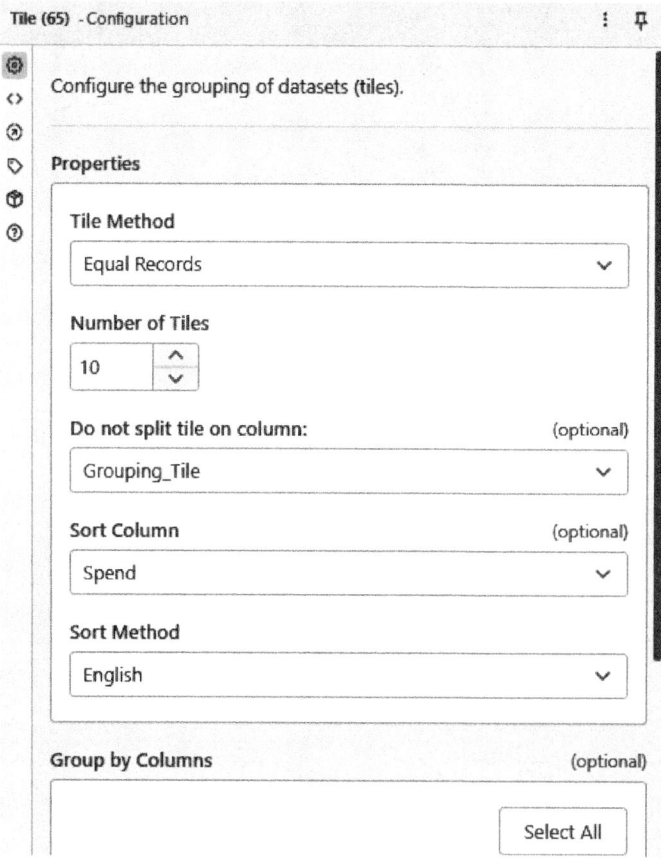

Figure 6.19: Configuring the Tile tool (Equal Records per Grouping_Tile)

Now, you have sales deciles per `Store` and `Segment`!

To get a better view of the generated groups, just add a **Sort** tool, and sort by `Grouping_Tile` and `Tile_Num` in ascending order:

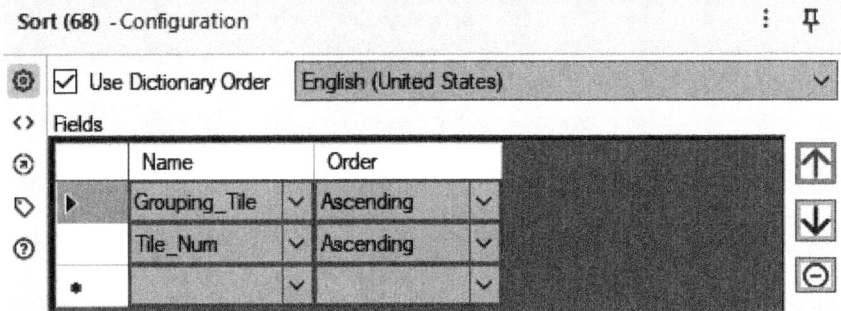

Figure 6.20: Configuring the Sort tool

Finally, if you want to get the top decile for each store and segment, just add a **Filter** tool and select `Tile_Num=1`:

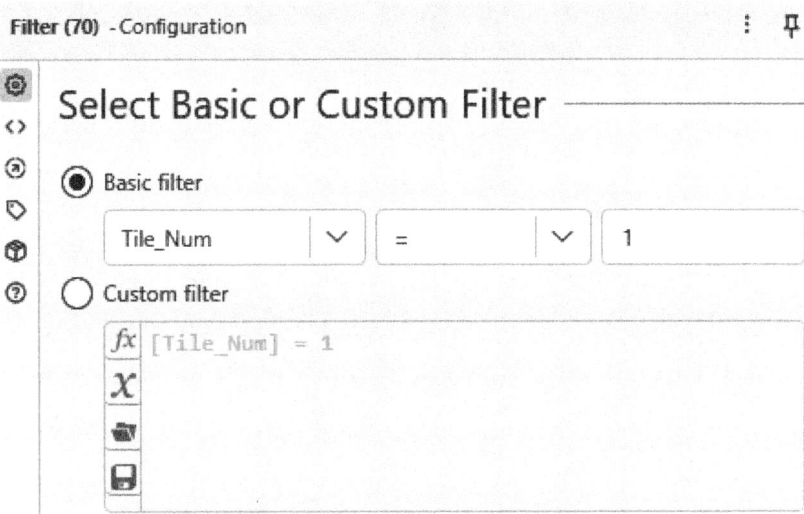

Figure 6.21: Configuring the Filter tool

Try the different grouping/configuration options – the possibilities are endless and very powerful!

Exploring the Make Group tool

Sometimes, groups within the data are not so obvious to the naked eye. This tends to happen when we analyze social media data, for example. Connections between group members may exist, but we can't "see" them.

Here is where the **Make Group** tool comes in – we can use it to discover groups via their members' transitive associations. For example, let's look at this tiny dataset:

	Person 1	Person 2
1	A	B
2	C	D
3	E	D

Figure 6.22: Simple example of related IDs

Here, we can see the following:

- A is related to B
- C is related to D
- E is related to D

The **Make Group** tool will solve hidden transitive relations for us. In this case, since C is related to D (Record 2), and D is related to E (Record 3), it'll mark them as part of the same group:

Record	Group	Key
1	A	A
2	A	B
3	C	C
4	C	D
5	C	E

Figure 6.23: The resulting groups

Something important to note is that the Group field's value (that is, the group's name) is taken arbitrarily by Alteryx from one of its members.

> **Important note**
> The key in the **Make Group** tool must be the same type and size.

Getting ready

We have a test dataset for you to follow along with this recipe. You can download it from here: https://github.com/PacktPublishing/Alteryx-Designer-Cookbook/tree/main/ch6/Recipe3.

If you decide to try this recipe with your data, just make sure you have individual relations between records, similar to what we used as an example here.

In this recipe, we'll be using two datasets:

- One that contains people that are related in some way (we called it PROJECT, but it could be anything, such as people that work together, friends, and so on):

	PROJECT	PERSON1	PERSON2	...
1	Project 1	User 1	User 2	
2	Project 1	User 1	User 3	
3	Project 1	User 1	User 4	
4	Project 1	User 2	User 5	
5	Project 2	User 10	User 15	
6	Project 2	User 10	User 11	
7	Project 2	User 11	User 12	
8	Project 2	User 11	User 14	
9	Project 3	User 1	User 24	

Figure 6.24: Relations dataset

- Another that contains interests in some categories that people expressed (maybe through a survey or a website registration process):

	PERSON	INTEREST1	INTEREST2	INTEREST3
1	User 1	Analytics	Data	Software
2	User 2	Software	Development	Security
3	User 3	Development	Hardware	Telecommunications
4	User 4	Analytics	Security	Data
5	User 5	Analytics	Data	Software
6	User 6	Software	Development	Security
7	User 7	Development	Hardware	Telecommunications
8	User 8	Analytics	Security	Data
9	User 9	Analytics	Data	Software
10	User 10	Software	Development	Security
11	User 11	Development	Hardware	Telecommunications
12	User 12	Analytics	Security	Data
13	User 13	Analytics	Data	Software
14	User 14	Software	Development	Security
15	User 15	Development	Hardware	Telecommunications
16	User 16	Analytics	Security	Data
17	User 17	Analytics	Data	Software
18	User 18	Software	Development	Security
19	User 19	Development	Hardware	Telecommunications
20	User 20	Analytics	Security	Data

Figure 6.25: Interests expressed by people

How can we determine what to communicate to a particular set of people? If we have a message, promotion, or strategy to communicate, how can we pick who to communicate it with?

How to do it...

Let's get started:

1. Let's start by dropping an **Input Data** tool onto the canvas. Point it to . . \DATA\MakeGroups. xlsx and select the PEOPLE worksheet.

2. Add a **Make Group** tool and select PERSON1 as **1st Key** and PERSON2 as **2nd Key**:

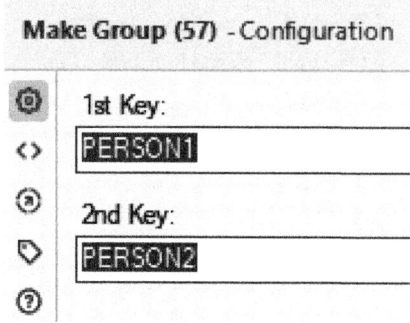

Figure 6.26: Configuring Make Group

3. Run the workflow and inspect the results:

Group	Key
User 1	User 1
User 1	User 2
User 1	User 24
User 1	User 3
User 1	User 4
User 1	User 5
User 10	User 10
User 10	User 11
User 10	User 12
User 10	User 14
User 10	User 15

Figure 6.27: Generated groups

Alteryx generated 11 records, with two fields: `Group` and `Key`:

- `Group` is the name of the group (and takes its value arbitrarily from a sorted list of all the members in the group). It is the Group ID.

- `Key` represents each of the members of a group.

Now, let's start giving these groups meaning.

4. Drop a new **Input Data** tool onto the canvas and point it so that it reads the same Excel file (`MakeGroups.xlsx`), but now, select the `INTERESTS` worksheet:

PERSON ⋮	INTEREST1	INTEREST2	INTEREST3
User 1	Analytics	Data	Software
User 2	Software	Development	Security
User 3	Development	Hardware	Telecommunications
User 4	Analytics	Security	Data
User 5	Analytics	Data	Software
User 6	Software	Development	Security
User 7	Development	Hardware	Telecommunications
User 8	Analytics	Security	Data
User 9	Analytics	Data	Software
User 10	Software	Development	Security
User 11	Development	Hardware	Telecommunications
User 12	Analytics	Security	Data
User 13	Analytics	Data	Software
User 14	Software	Development	Security

Figure 6.28: Contents of the INTERESTS data source

You'll notice that for each `PERSON`, we have a set of three interests.

5. Add a **Join** tool and connect the **Make Group** tool's output anchor to the L input. Then, add the **Input Data** tool that reads the `INTERESTS` worksheet output anchor to the R input so that your workflow looks like this:

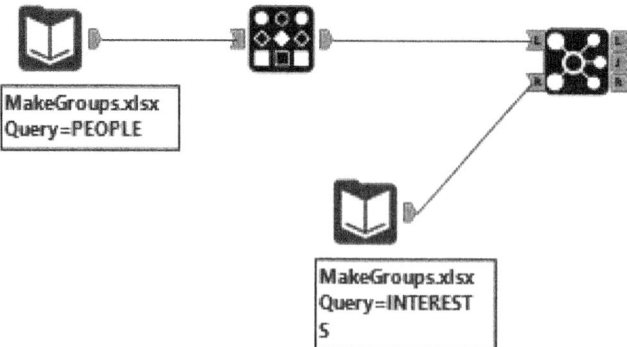

Figure 6.29: Workflow overview so far

6. Click on the **Join** tool and configure it as follows:

    - Make sure **Join by Specific Fields** is selected (it's the default).

    - For **Left**, select the Key field from the dropdown

    - For **Right**, select the PERSON field from the dropdown

    - Deselect PERSON from the embedded selection box (since it's the field we are joining in, it will have the same value as the other one – that is, Key):

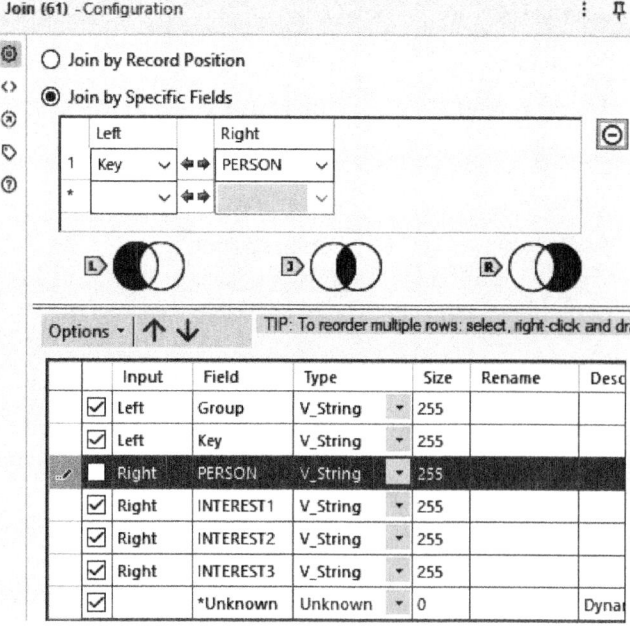

Figure 6.30: Configuring the Join tool

7. Run the workflow:

Group	Key	INTEREST1	INTEREST2	INTEREST3
User 1	User 1	Analytics	Data	Software
User 10	User 10	Software	Development	Security
User 10	User 11	Development	Hardware	Telecommunications
User 10	User 12	Analytics	Security	Data
User 10	User 14	Software	Development	Security
User 10	User 15	Development	Hardware	Telecommunications
User 1	User 2	Software	Development	Security
User 1	User 24	Analytics	Security	Data
User 1	User 3	Development	Hardware	Telecommunications
User 1	User 4	Analytics	Security	Data
User 1	User 5	Analytics	Data	Software

Figure 6.31: The results so far

With that, we have the interests of each member of each group, but it looks difficult to process it due to how we got it.

8. Add a **Transpose** tool and connect its input anchor to the J output anchor of the **Join** tool.

For the **Transpose** tool's configuration, do the following:

- Select Group and Key in the **Key Columns** section
- Make sure that Group and Key are deselected in the **Data Columns** sections and that INTEREST1, INTEREST2, and INTEREST3 are selected
- Leave **Missing Columns** set to Warn (default):

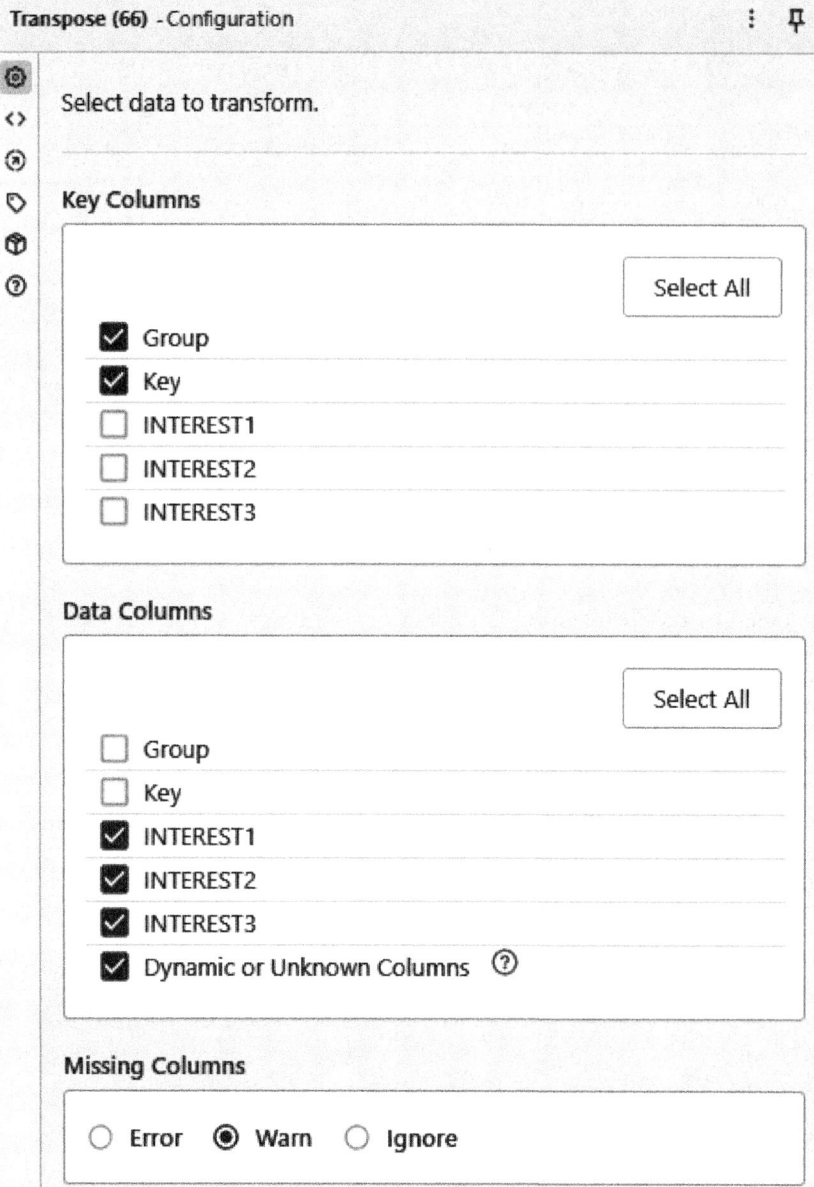

Figure 6.32: Configuring the Transpose tool

This tool will pivot the data, creating two columns:

- `Name`: This will contain the previous column's headers
- `Value`: This contains the values that correspond to `Name`:

Group	Key	Name	Value
User 1	User 1	INTEREST1	Analytics
User 1	User 1	INTEREST2	Data
User 1	User 1	INTEREST3	Software
User 10	User 10	INTEREST1	Software
User 10	User 10	INTEREST2	Development
User 10	User 10	INTEREST3	Security
User 10	User 11	INTEREST1	Development
User 10	User 11	INTEREST2	Hardware
User 10	User 11	INTEREST3	Telecommunications
User 10	User 12	INTEREST1	Analytics
User 10	User 12	INTEREST2	Security

Figure 6.33: The results after transposing the data

9. Add a **Summarize** tool and connect it to the **Transpose** tool.

10. For the summarization, select the **Group** field in the **Fields** panel, click **Add**, and select **Group By**.

11. Select the **Value** field, click **Add**, and select **Group By**.

12. With the **Value** field still selected, click **Add** again and select **Count** from the dropdown:

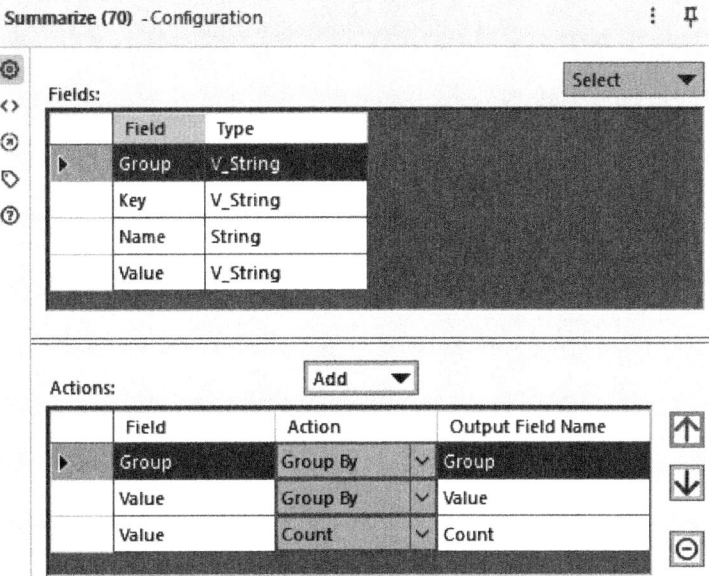

Figure 6.34: Configuring the Summarize tool

This will give us the complete list of interests by group and the number of users that expressed each interest:

Group	Value	Count
User 1	Analytics	4
User 1	Data	4
User 1	Development	2
User 1	Hardware	1
User 1	Security	3
User 1	Software	3
User 1	Telecommunications	1
User 10	Analytics	1
User 10	Data	1
User 10	Development	4
User 10	Hardware	2
User 10	Security	3
User 10	Software	2
User 10	Telecommunications	2

Figure 6.35: Summarized results

13. Connect a **Sort** tool and configure it so that it performs a sort on **Group Ascending** and **Count Descending**:

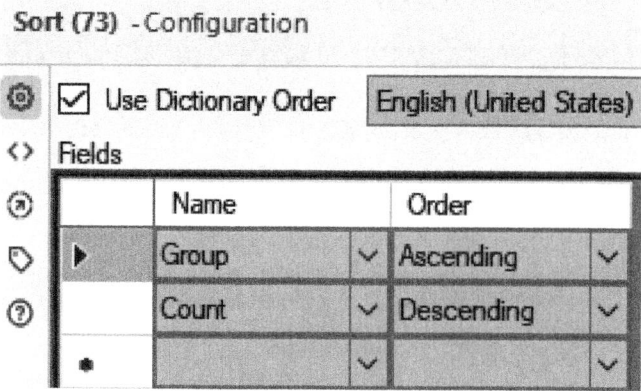

Figure 6.36: Configuring the Sort tool

With that, we have sorted the groups and interests of each group:

Group	Value	Count
User 1	Analytics	4
User 1	Data	4
User 1	Security	3
User 1	Software	3
User 1	Development	2
User 1	Hardware	1
User 1	Telecommunications	1
User 10	Development	4
User 10	Security	3
User 10	Hardware	2
User 10	Software	2
User 10	Telecommunications	2
User 10	Analytics	1
User 10	Data	1

Figure 6.37: The results after sorting

Now, let's look at what we can do if we want to extract the top two interests per group.

14. Add a **Sample** tool to the canvas and configure it. Select **First N Rows**, set **N** to 2, and make sure you check the **Group** field in the **Group by column** section:

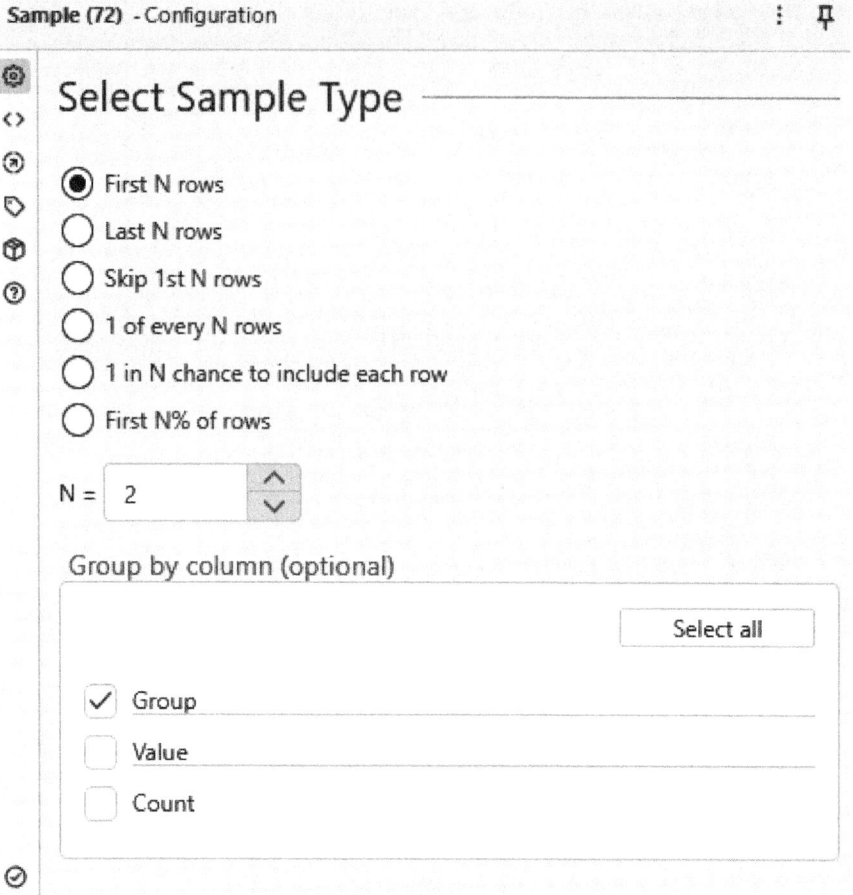

Figure 6.38: Sample tool configuration

This way, we know the top two interests per group:

Group	Value	Count
User 1	Analytics	4
User 1	Data	4
User 10	Development	4
User 10	Security	3

Figure 6.39: Final results (top two interests per group)

With that, we know that we can communicate `Analytics` and/or `Data` related messages, promotions, and so on to the members of the `User 1` group and `Development` and/or `Security` materials to the members of the `User 10` group:

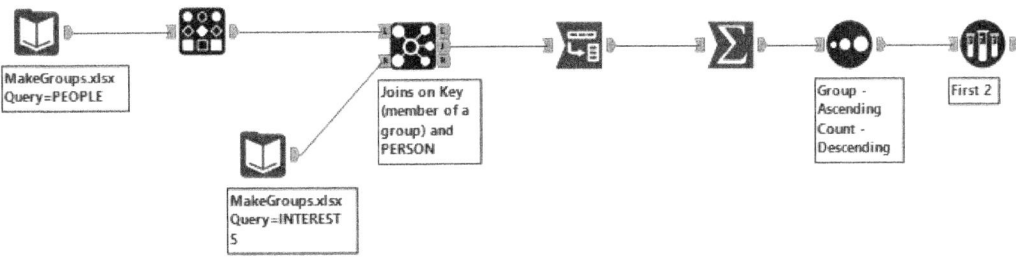

Figure 6.40: Overview of the finished workflow

How it works...

At first glance, **Make Group** may appear challenging and confusing, but when you understand how it works, you can automatically find relations that are not that obvious in your dataset.

Since the generated **Group** field uses one of the members as its value, don't get confused. See the **Group** field as the group name/identifier. The members of each group are in the **Key** field:

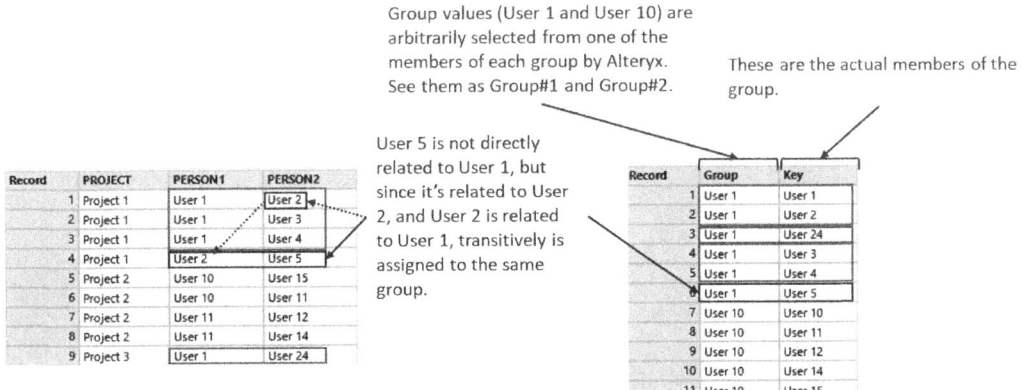

Figure 6.41: How the Make Group tool works

This tool is also very useful when you work with **Fuzzy Match** to pair similar values into groups.

Binning numeric fields

So far, we have been working with string-type fields, but what happens when we need to group data from numeric-type fields?

Alteryx has us covered. With the **Multi-Field Binning** tool, we can reproduce some of the **Tile** tool's functionalities on numeric fields.

In this recipe, we will be grouping data based on its numerical values, with the help of the **Multi-Field Binning** tool.

Getting ready

We have prepared a dataset for you to follow along with this recipe. You can download it here: `https://github.com/PacktPublishing/Alteryx-Designer-Cookbook/tree/main/ch6/Recipe4`.

If you decide to follow along with your data, just make sure you have some quantitative data that needs to be grouped (for example, sales amounts in *n* groups).

How to do it...

Follow these steps:

1. Drop an **Input Data** tool onto the canvas and point it to `..\DATA\DOCUMENTS.yxdb`:

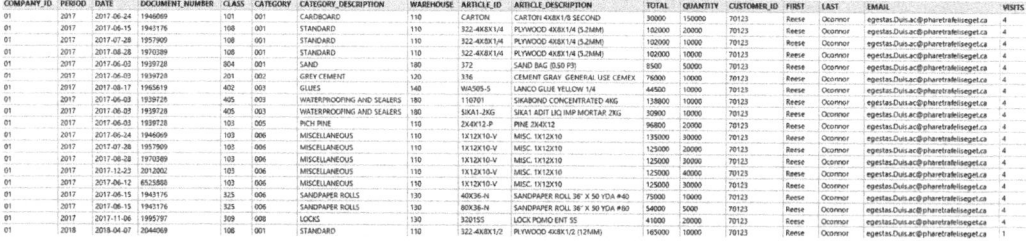

Figure 6.42: The dataset's contents

We can see that we have several numeric fields in our dataset:

Name	Type	Size
COMPANY_ID	String	2
PERIOD	Int16	2
DATE	Date	10
DOCUMENT_NUMBER	Int32	4
CLASS	String	3
CATEGORY	String	3
CATEGORY_DESCRIPTION	V_String	255
WAREHOUSE	Int16	2
ARTICLE_ID	V_String	15
ARTICLE_DESCRIPTION	V_String	35
TOTAL	Double	8
QUANTITY	Double	8
CUSTOMER_ID	Int32	4
FIRST	String	10
LAST	String	10
EMAIL	V_String	51
VISITS	Int16	2

Figure 6.43: Dataset metadata

If we try to group/tile the dataset by **PERIOD** (**PERIOD** contains the year of the bill), for example, we need to create a new field or convert it into a string.

2. Drop a **Multi-Field Binning** tool onto the canvas. You'll notice that all of the numeric type fields appear in the **Select Fields** panel.

3. Select **PERIOD** from the **Select fields for binning** section.

4. Click **Equal Intervals** and select 6 for **Number of Tiles**:

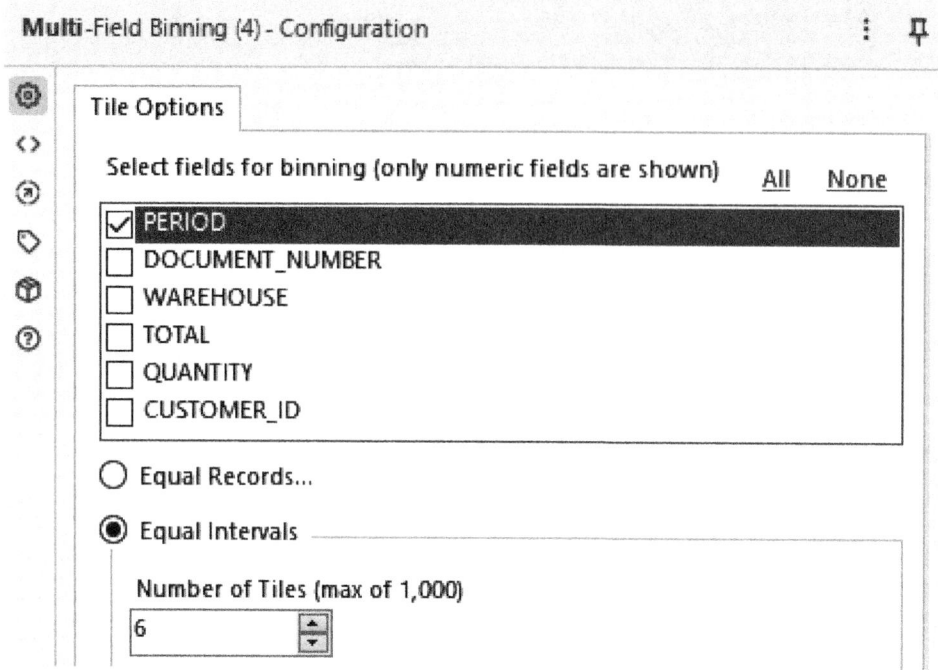

Figure 6.44: Configuring the Multi-Field Binning tool

5.   Run the workflow.

You'll see that each PERIOD was assigned within a bin (bin 1 is PERIOD=2017, bin 2 is PERIOD=2018, and so on) called PERIOD_Tile_Num (bin names follow the NAME-OF-THE-FIELD_Tile_Num rule).

We can also perform binning on multiple fields at the same time.

6.   Add a **Summarize** tool and connect it to the **Input Data** tool's output anchor.

In the **Summarize** tool's configuration panel, do the following:

I.   Select the **COMPANY_ID** field, click **Add**, and select **Group By**.

II.   Click the **DOCUMENT_NUMBER** field, click **Add**, and select **Count Distinct**.

III.   Click **TOTAL**, press and hold the *Ctrl* key, and click **QUANTITY** (both fields should be highlighted in blue). Click **Add** and select **Sum** from the dropdown.

IV.   Click **VISITS**, click **Add**, select **Numeric**, and then select **Average** from the dropdown (because our dataset comes with the visits per year for each record).

V.   Click **FIRST** and without releasing the mouse button, drag it so that **FIRST**, **LAST**, and **EMAIL** are highlighted in blue. Click **Add** and select **First** from the drop-down list.

Remove the prefixes that Alteryx added:

- `CountDistinct_` for **COMPANY_ID**

- `Sum_` for **TOTAL** and **QUANTITY**

- `Avg_` for **VISITS**

- `First_` for **FIRST**, **LAST**, and **EMAIL**

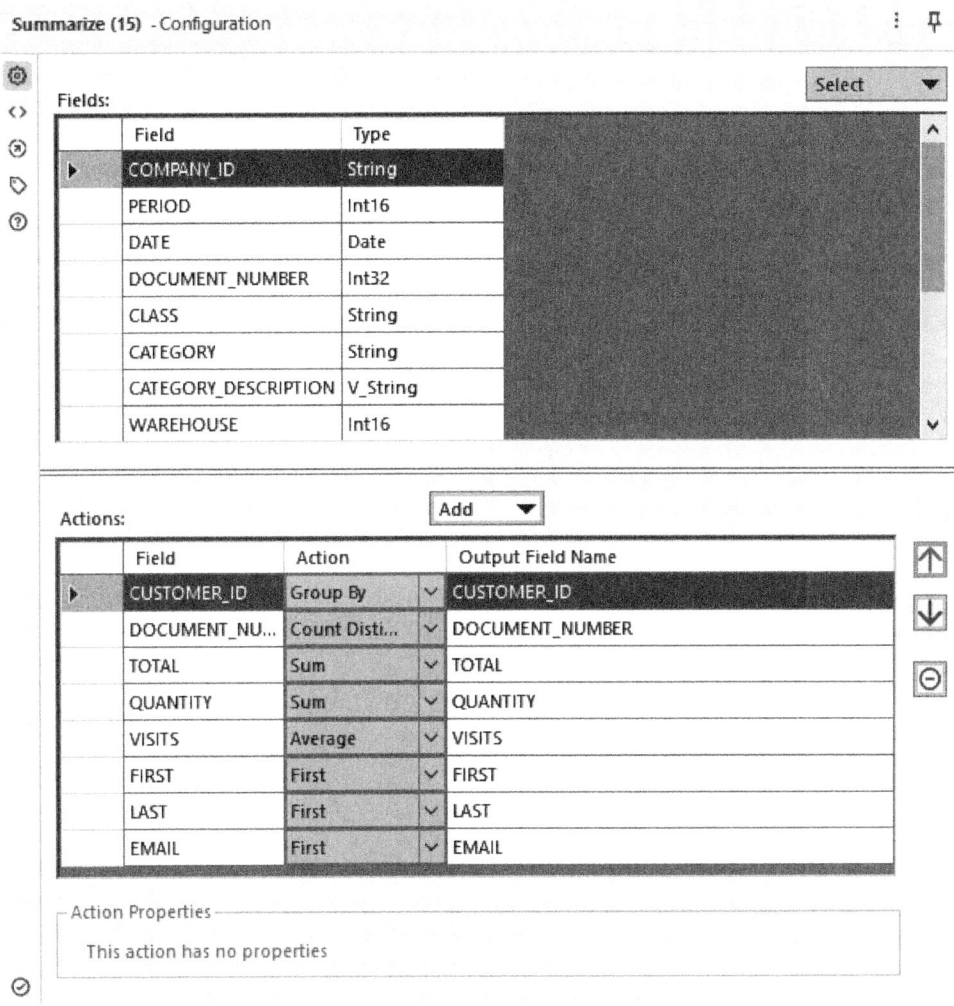

Figure 6.45: Configuring the Summarize tool

7. Drop a new **Multi-Field Binning** tool onto the canvas and connect it to the **Summarize** tool.

8. Select **TOTAL**, **QUANTITY**, and **VISITS** from the **Select fields for binning** section.

9. Click **Equal Intervals** and enter 10 in the **Number of Tiles** input:

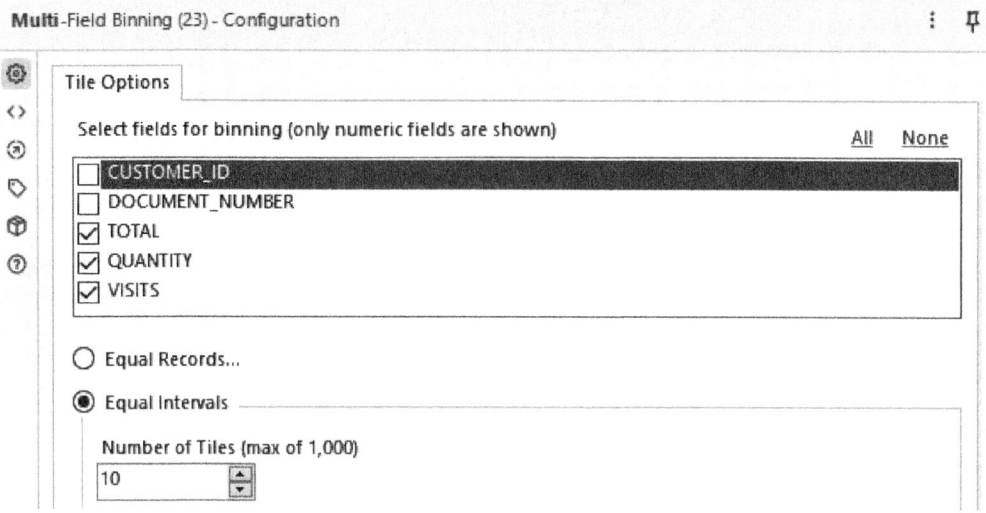

Figure 6.46: Configuring the Multi-Field Binning tool for multiple fields

10. Your workflow should look like this:

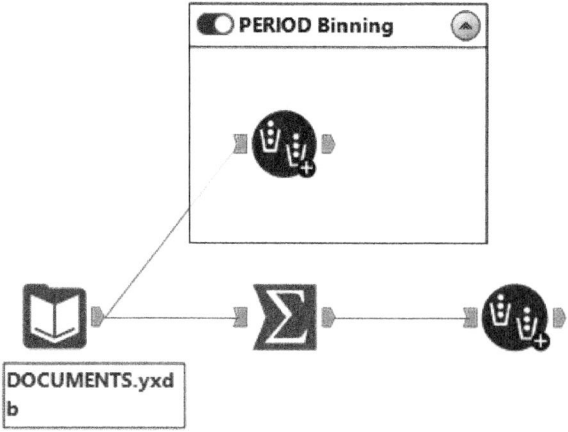

Figure 6.47: Workflow overview

11. Run the workflow – you'll see that a tile was assigned to each of the selected fields.

Now, we can classify customers based on how they belong to these tiles.

For example, if a customer has a combined score of 20 for TOTAL_Tile_Num and QUANTITY_Tile_Num (they belong to both upper tiles), we can say they're an excellent customer (high TOTAL and high QUANTITY). From here, we can create a scale.

We can add `VISITS_Tile_Num` to the equation, but for this case, the lower the tile, the better (the customer spends more in fewer visits).

From here, you can create your scale to classify customers, based on numeric bins.

How it works...

The **Multi-Field Binning** tool assigns tiles (or group numbers) to the records based on ascending sorted values within the dataset (the tool sorts them).

The options the tool provides, according to Alteryx's help, are as follows:

- **Equal Records**: Input records are divided into a specified number of bins. Each bin is assigned the same number of records. This is based solely on the record's position in the input file.

- **Equal Intervals**: The minimum and maximum values of the selected fields are determined. The range is split into equal-sized sub-ranges. Records are assigned to bins based on these ranges.

7
Blending and Merging Datasets

So, you've got some workable datasets, but they're all disconnected. We are going to convert the data into information and enrich it with these recipes, relating, joining, blending, or unioning datasets.

In this chapter, we'll be exploring different methods to merge data sources, based on common fields or values, conditions, or schemas.

This chapter will cover the **Join**, **Union**, and **Appending Fields** tools through these recipes:

- Join or Find Replace
- Stacking data sources with different structures
- Joining tips and tricks
- Appending fields to a data source

Technical requirements

Even when there are no technical requirements per se in this chapter, I'd like to make sure about the use cases we'll be tackling here, and some terminology related to them.

We are going to be using these concepts throughout this chapter:

- **Join**: Refers to an association between one or more data sources, based on one or more values from fields. We've used this functionality in previous recipes.

- **Union**: Refers to the operation where we stack multiple datasets (mostly with the same structure, even when they can have different ones) one on top of another.

- **Append Fields**: This is the operation where, for each record from one dataset, we add all the records from a second one. This is called **Cartesian Product** too.

- **Find Replace**: This is self-explanatory. We can find some value within a data source field and replace it with the values from another, but it is worth mentioning that Alteryx also allows us to append fields to a data source, based on the Find/Replace configuration. It might be a better choice than the Join tool, depending on the use case.

Join or Find Replace

Depending on our use case, a **Find Replace** tool can provide the same results as the **Join** tool, but in a more performant way.

Getting ready

We are going to use some data about a company's billing, which we need to relate to the customer's data and the article's descriptions. You can access this test set here: `https://github.com/PacktPublishing/Alteryx-Designer-Cookbook/tree/main/ch7/Recipe1`.

The `DOCUMENTS.yxdb` file contains the data related to the bills, including a `CUSTOMER_ID` field that can be used to relate this data to the customer's data within the `CUSTOMER.yxdb` file.

COMPANY_ID	DOC_TYPE	DOCUMENT_NUMBER	CUSTOMER_ID	ARTICLE_ID	TOTAL	QUANTITY	DATE
01	FA	0	107614	300137	62500	10000	2017-09-10
01	FA	0	107614	RC200-4	239500	20000	2017-09-10
01	FA	0	107614	69-26G-6	108000	10000	2017-09-10
01	FA	0	107614	106-2 1/2	600	120000	2017-09-10
01	FA	11	132269	FB992B	11000	20000	2017-09-10
01	FA	11	132269	260-1/2	6900	300000	2017-09-10
01	FA	11	132269	375-G	7500	1600000	2017-09-10
01	FA	12	149237	0064	66500	160000	2017-09-10
01	FA	12	149237	STUD	15900	300000	2017-09-10

Figure 7.1: The DOCUMENTS dataset

The `CUSTOMERS.yxdb` file contains attributes of each customer, identified by the `CUSTOMER_ID` field.

CUSTOMER_ID	FIRST	LAST	EMAIL
70123	Reese	Oconnor	egestas.Duis.ac@pharetrafeliseget.ca
70398	Deanna	Campbell	nulla.Donec.non@diam.co.uk
70723	Daquan	Montgomery	ac.mattis@semper.com
71143	Dean	Mullins	pede.ac.urna@non.edu
71448	Evan	Mcclain	et.netus.et@acorci.com
71649	Joel	Fox	libero.at.auctor@convallisconvallisdolor.org
72083	Ross	English	mattis@dolor.net
72327	Belle	Harvey	enim.consequat.purus@variusorci.ca
72623	Xena	Jacobson	urna.Vivamus@etmagnisdis.ca

Figure 7.2: The CUSTOMERS dataset

And the `ARTICLES.yxdb` file has the `DESCRIPTION` field for each article identified by a combination of two values: `COMPANY_ID` and `ARTICLE_ID`.

COMPANY_ID	ARTICLE_ID	DESCRIPTION
01	001-1/2	GALV FLAT WASHER 1/2
01	001-1/4	GALV FLAT WASHER 1/4
01	001-3/8	GALV FLAT WASHER 3/8
01	001-5/16	GALV FLAT WASHER 5/16
01	001-5/32	GALV FLAT WASHER 5/32 NO. 8
01	005-6/32X3	ELECT SCREW C/P 6/32X3
01	006-8/32X1 1/2	ELECT SCREWC/R 8/32X1 1/2
01	0064	GYPSUM BOARD 4X8X1/2
01	0096	COLORING POWDER BLACK

Figure 7.3: The ARTICLES dataset

So, we can associate the three files based on the corresponding fields and add the extra information to our dataset.

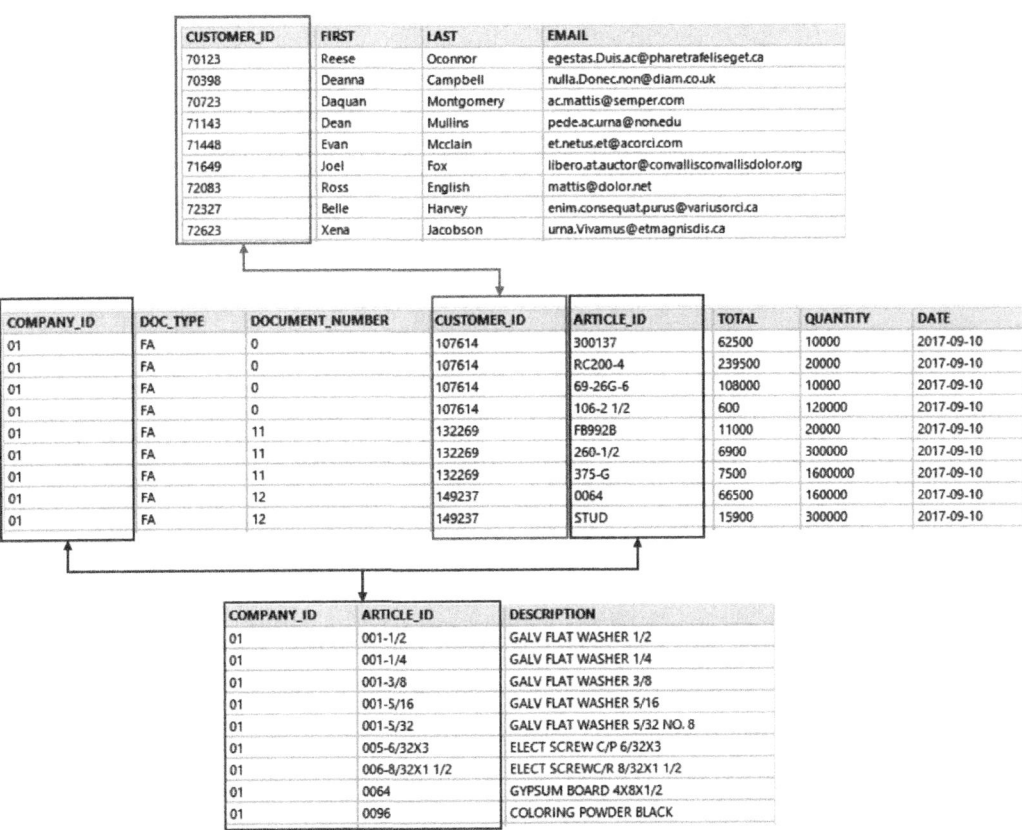

Figure 7.4: Existing relations within the three datasets

If you decide to work with your own data, just make sure the files or database tables have some common fields to join on.

How to do it...

We'll perform these operations using the following steps:

1. Drop an **Input Data** tool on a new workflow and point it to . . \DATA\DOCUMENTS.yxdb.

2. Add another **Input Data** tool and point it to . . \DATA\CUSTOMERS.yxdb.

3. Drop a **Join** tool and connect the DOCUMENTS output anchor to the L input anchor, and the CUSTOMERS output anchor to the R input.

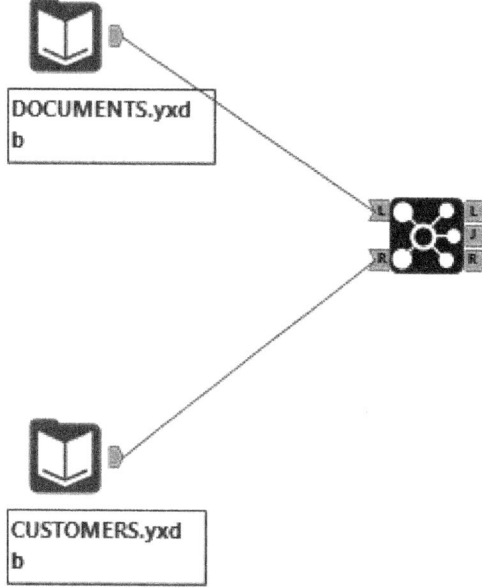

Figure 7.5: Joining two datasets

Now, onto the **Join** configuration.

4. Click on the **Join** tool and, in its configuration panel, do the following:

    • Make sure **Join by Specific Fields** is selected (it should be because it is the default setting).

    • Select CUSTOMER_ID from the **Left** dropdown.

    • Make sure CUSTOMER_ID is automatically populated in the **Right** dropdown (Alteryx does this when fields with the same name are present in the **Right** input). If not, select CUSTOMER_ID from the **Right** dropdown.

- You can choose to deselect the CUSTOMER_ID coming from the **Right** input (it'll be the same as the CUSTOMER_ID from the **Left** input, or you can click on the **Options** menu and then click on **Deselect Duplicate Fields**.

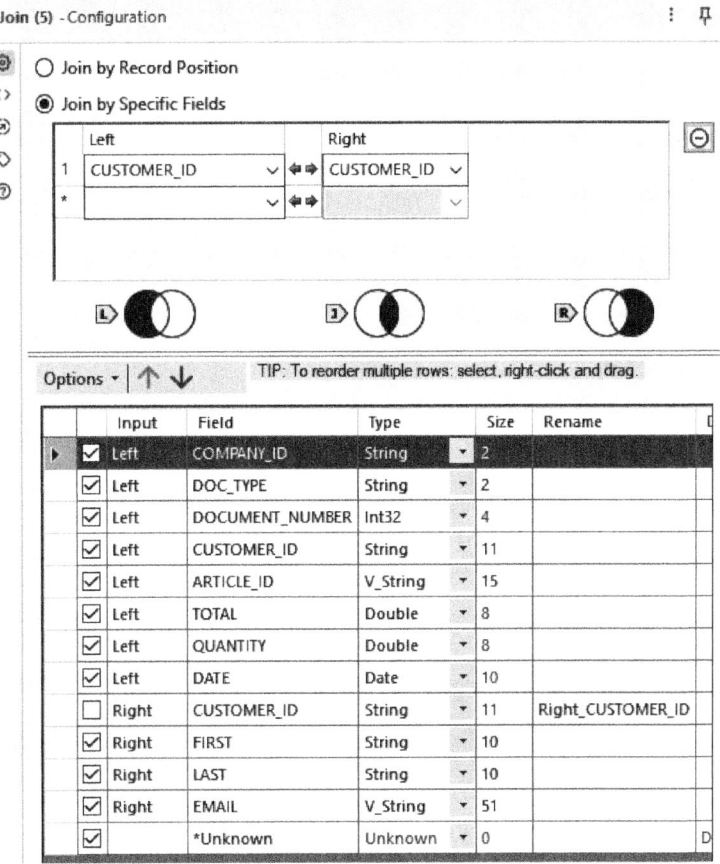

Figure 7.6: Join tool configuration

5. Run the workflow and you'll see that from the J output, all records that have a matching CUSTOMER_ID value coming from both inputs are shown:

COMPANY_ID	DOC_TYPE	DOCUMENT_NUMBER	CUSTOMER_ID	ARTICLE_ID	TOTAL	QUANTITY	DATE	FIRST	LAST	EMAIL
01	FA	1939728	70123	2X4X12-P	96800	20000	2017-06-03	Reese	Oconnor	egestas.Duis.ac@pharetrafeliseget.ca
01	FA	1939728	70123	372	8500	50000	2017-06-03	Reese	Oconnor	egestas.Duis.ac@pharetrafeliseget.ca
01	FA	1939728	70123	336	76000	10000	2017-06-03	Reese	Oconnor	egestas.Duis.ac@pharetrafeliseget.ca
01	FA	1939728	70123	SIKA1-2KG	30900	10000	2017-06-03	Reese	Oconnor	egestas.Duis.ac@pharetrafeliseget.ca
01	FA	1939728	70123	110701	138800	10000	2017-06-03	Reese	Oconnor	egestas.Duis.ac@pharetrafeliseget.ca
01	FA	1943176	70123	322-4X8X1/4	102000	20000	2017-06-15	Reese	Oconnor	egestas.Duis.ac@pharetrafeliseget.ca
01	FA	1943176	70123	80X36-N	54000	5000	2017-06-15	Reese	Oconnor	egestas.Duis.ac@pharetrafeliseget.ca
01	FA	1943176	70123	40X36-N	75000	10000	2017-06-15	Reese	Oconnor	egestas.Duis.ac@pharetrafeliseget.ca
01	FA	1946069	70123	CARTON	30000	150000	2017-06-24	Reese	Oconnor	egestas.Duis.ac@pharetrafeliseget.ca
01	FA	1946069	70123	1X12X10-V	135000	30000	2017-06-24	Reese	Oconnor	egestas.Duis.ac@pharetrafeliseget.ca

Figure 7.7: Resulting data after the join operation

Also, you can see that fields (only the selected ones) appear within your actual dataset.

So, we can say mission accomplished, right? Well, yes and no. Yes because we got the dataset as we needed, but no because we didn't solve it in the best possible way (we need this workflow to run as fast as it can and with as little resource consumption as possible).

So, we are going to try to get to the same point but in the best-performing way.

6.   Drop a **Find Replace** tool from the **Join** category onto the canvas.

7.   Connect the DOCUMENTS output anchor of the **Input Data** tool to the F input anchor and the CUSTOMERS output anchor to the R input anchor.

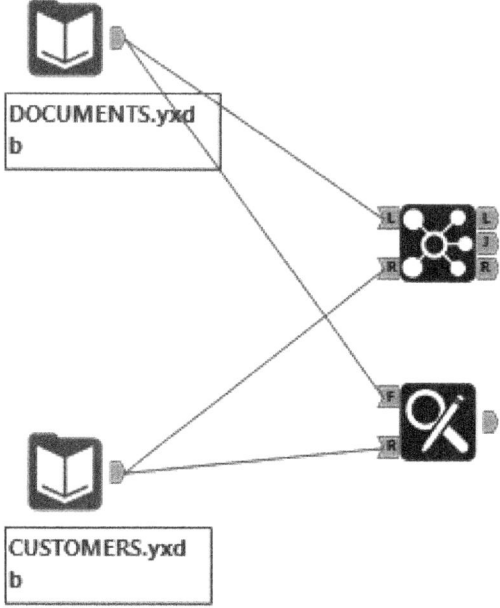

Figure 7.8: Adding a Find Replace tool

8.   Click on the **Find Replace** tool to access its configuration panel, and select the following:

- **Any Part of Field** as the **Find** method

- CUSTOMER_ID from the **Find Within Field** dropdown

- CUSTOMER_ID from the **Find Value** dropdown

- **Append Field(s) to Record** from the **Replace** section

- FIRST, LAST, and EMAIL from the list of fields

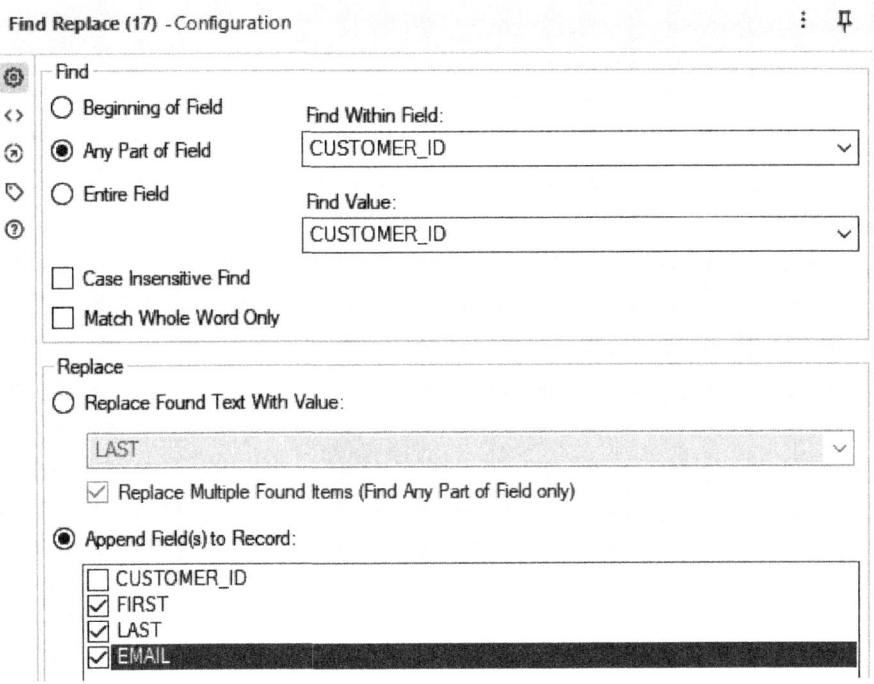

Figure 7.9: Find Replace tool configuration

If you run the workflow, you'll see that the results are the same (except for the **Join** tool sorting the records).

COMPANY_ID	DOC_TYPE	DOCUMENT_NUMBER	CUSTOMER_ID	ARTICLE_ID	TOTAL	QUANTITY	DATE	FIRST	LAST	EMAIL
01	FA	1939104	110522	3201SS	45000	20000	2017-06-01	Carson	Atkinson	tempus.eu.ligula@Crasvehicula.co.uk
01	FA	1939104	110522	1081-15X15	249500	10000	2017-06-01	Carson	Atkinson	tempus.eu.ligula@Crasvehicula.co.uk
01	FA	1939104	110522	737-1/2X3/8	38500	10000	2017-06-01	Carson	Atkinson	tempus.eu.ligula@Crasvehicula.co.uk
01	FA	1939104	110522	333P-1 1/2	16500	10000	2017-06-01	Carson	Atkinson	tempus.eu.ligula@Crasvehicula.co.uk
01	FA	1939106	100150	WA502-5	42500	10000	2017-06-01	Chester	Harrell	mauris.rhoncus@ornareelitelit.co.uk
01	FA	1939106	100150	80X36-N	54000	20000	2017-06-01	Chester	Harrell	mauris.rhoncus@ornareelitelit.co.uk
01	FA	1939106	100150	M4634716	21000	10000	2017-06-01	Chester	Harrell	mauris.rhoncus@ornareelitelit.co.uk
01	FA	1939106	100150	G3670041	35000	10000	2017-06-01	Chester	Harrell	mauris.rhoncus@ornareelitelit.co.uk

Figure 7.10: Resulting data after the find and replace operation

But how can we determine whether this is a better method?

First, we have string-type key fields (the **Find Replace** tool only works with string fields as you may notice when selecting fields from the dropdowns).

Then, we have a method to measure the performance of each tool within a workflow in Alteryx. To use it, we need to do the following.

9. Click on any open canvas area to access the workflow's properties.

10. Click on **Runtime**.

11. Click on **Enable Performance Profiling**.

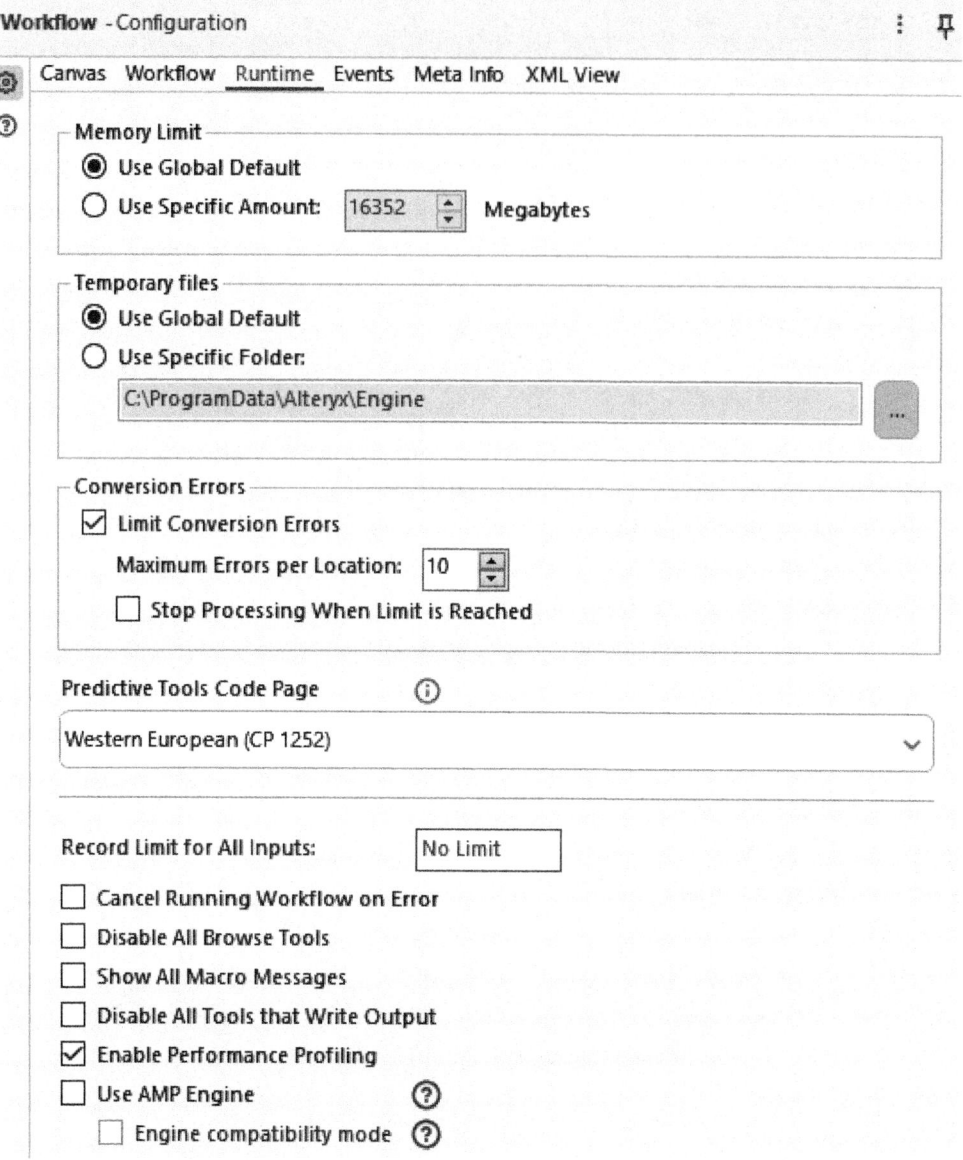

Figure 7.11: Enabling the Performance Profiling feature

12. Run the workflow again, and pay attention to the **Results** panel.

You'll notice some statistics added to the usual tool messages. These numbers represent the percentage of the total execution time for each tool.

Results - Workflow - Messages

All	⊙ 0 Errors ⊙ 0 Conv Errors ⚠ 0 Warnings ▭ 6 Messages ▭ 2 Files	
Designer x64	**Started running at 10/09/2022 17:39:03**	
Input Data (2)	200 records were read from "C:\Exercises\ch7\Recipe1\DATA\CUSTOMERS.yxdb"	
Input Data (1)	235031 records were read from "C:\Exercises\ch7\Recipe1\DATA\DOCUMENTS.yxdb"	
Join (5)	235031 records were joined with 0 un-joined left records and 24 un-joined right records	
Find Replace (17)	235031 records were found and 0 records were not found.	
Join (5)	Profile Time: 201.79ms, 69.41% ◄━━━━	
Find Replace (17)	Profile Time: 45.19ms, 15.54% ◄━━━━	
Input Data (1)	Profile Time: 41.86ms, 14.40%	
Input Data (2)	Profile Time: 1.88ms, 0.65%	
Designer x64	**Finished running in 0.5 seconds**	

Figure 7.12: Results panel with Performance Profiling output

You can see that the **Join** tool took 69.41% of the total workflow execution time to run, while the **Find Replace** tool only needed 15.54% to complete the task (~4.4 times less than the **Join** tool).

Now, let's focus on the ARTICLES table.

13. Drop an **Input Data** tool on the canvas and point it to ..\DATA\ARTICLES.yxdb.

It has two fields that need to match to associate it with our main data stream: COMPANY_ID and ARTICLE_ID.

14. Run the workflow to populate the metadata for the new data source.

As you can see in the metadata, COMPANY_ID is of the numeric type, so we already know that the **Find Replace** tool won't allow us to use it as is.

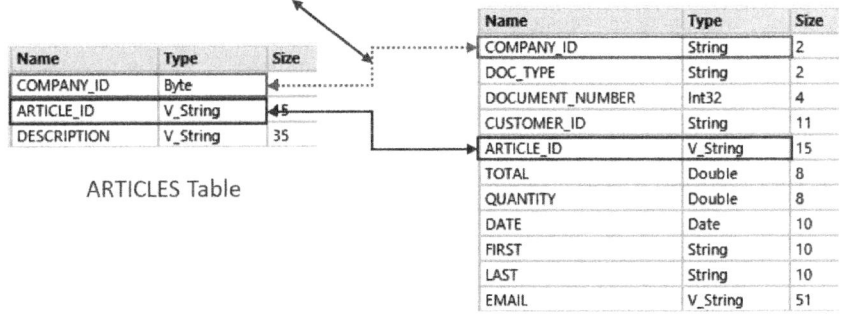

Figure 7.13: Keys to join the ARTICLES dataset won't work due to data type conflict

We have two ways of doing this blending – use a **Join** tool or make some changes in the dataset to prepare it for the **Find Replace** tool:

- For the **Join** method: Since string types only join to other string types, we need to convert our numeric field/s to string:

  - Drop a **Select** tool and connect it to the output anchor of the existing **Find Replace** tool (this is our main data stream).

  - Click on **Type** for the COMPANY_ID field, and change it to Byte.

  - Drop a new **Join** tool and connect the output from the **Select** tool to the L input and the output of the **Input Data** tool that reads ARTICLES.yxdb to the R input.

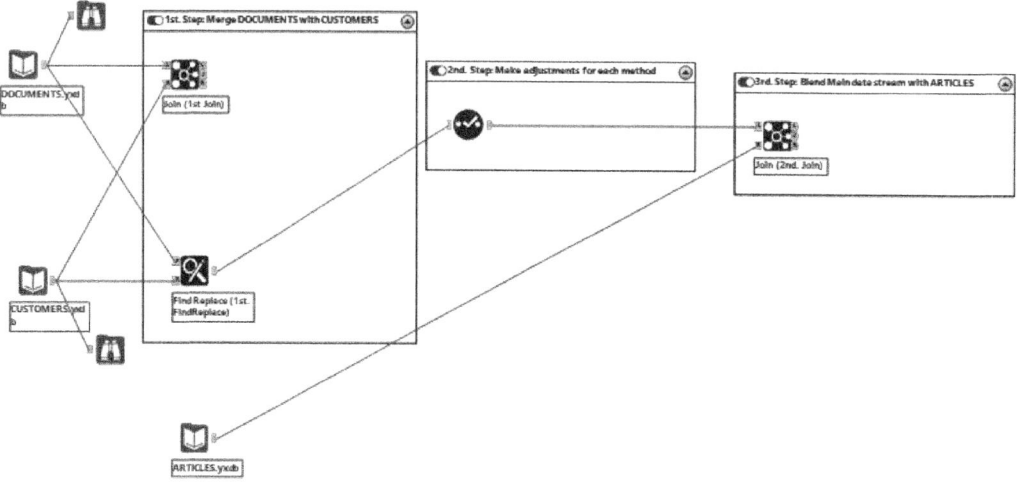

Figure 7.14: Workflow so far

- For the **Find Replace** method: We need to have one string field on each data stream to match using the **Find Replace** tool, and that's why we are going to create them. But our blending key has two fields, so we need to have this newly created field considering both. If you're familiar with working with Excel, you've probably done this many times. We'll create a Key field for each data stream to concatenate both values and perform the **Find Replace** operation:

  - Drop a **Formula** tool onto the canvas, connect it to the existing **Find Replace** tool output, and create a new field. Name it ARTICLES_KEY and use this expression:

```
ToString([COMPANY_ID])+"-"+[ARTICLE_ID]
```

  - Copy the **Formula** tool (click on it in the canvas, copy and paste or *Ctrl + C* then *Ctrl + V*) and connect this new instance of the tool to the ARTICLES output of the **Input Data** tool.

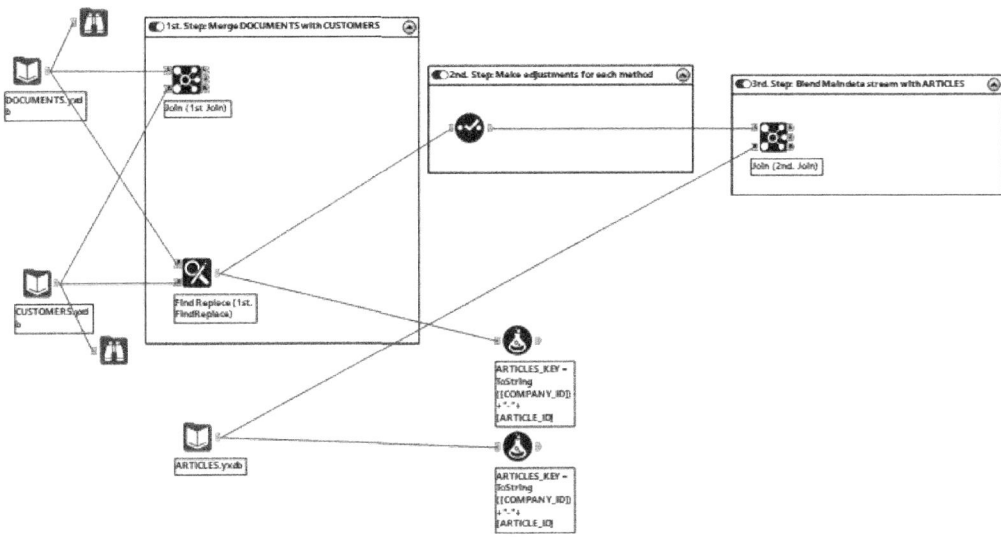

Figure 7.15: Workflow so far

- Now, drop a new **Find Replace** tool, and connect each **Formula** tool output to the closest input (the one on the top to the F input and the one at the bottom to the R input).

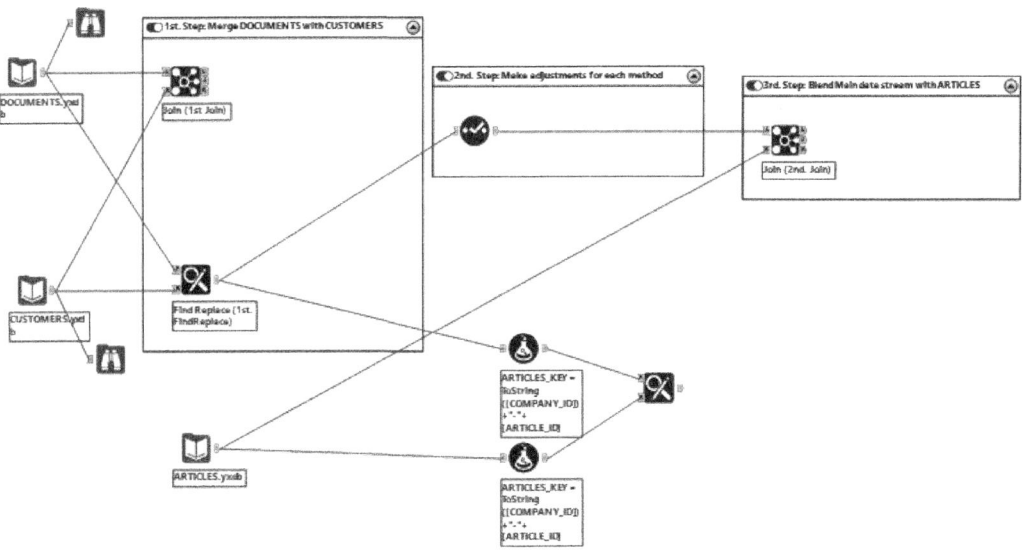

Figure 7.16: Final workflow (delete Join tools after finishing the recipe)

To easily identify the tools, we are going to make some internal renaming.

15. Click on the first **Join** tool, then press *F2* (or click on the little gray tag icon in the configuration panel).

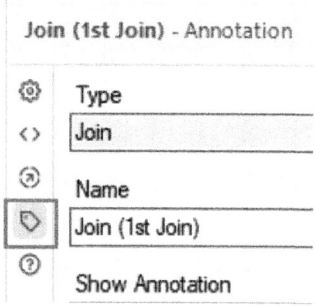

Figure 7.17: Renaming a tool

16. Name this tool Join (1st Join) in the **Name** text input.

17. Click on the first **Find Replace** tool and do the same; this time, enter Find Replace (1st. FindReplace) in the **Name** textbox.

18. Repeat this operation with the second **Join** tool (name it Join (2nd. Join)) and the second **Find Replace** tool (name it Find Replace (2nd. FindReplace)).

19. Run the workflow and look at the **Results** messages:

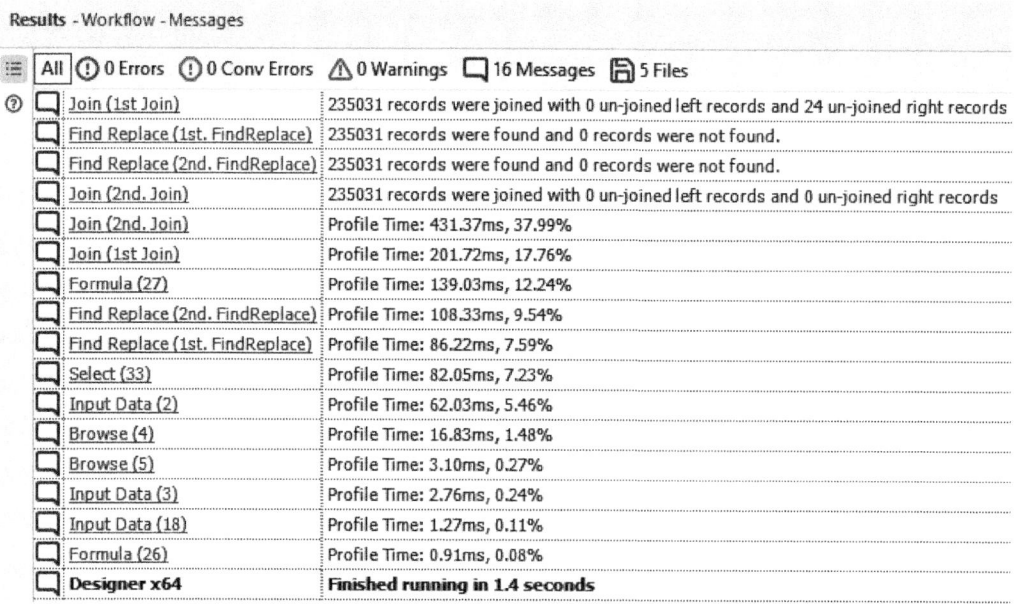

Figure 7.18: Final results messages with Performance Profiling enabled

The math we need to do here is as follows:

- For the **Join** method: We added a **Select** tool (`Select (33)`) and the join operation.

`Join (2nd. Join)` took 37.99% and `Select (33)` took 7.23%. All this adds up to 45.22% of the total time.

- For the **Find Replace** method: We added two **Formula** tools to allow this method to work.

`Formula (27)` took 12.24%, `Formula (26)` took .08%, and `Find Replace (2nd. FindReplace)` took 9.54%. This adds up to 21.86% of the total time – almost half of the previous method.

> **Important note**
>
> After finishing this recipe, remember to delete the **Join** tools and the **Select** tool we used for this method, or wrap them within a **Tool** container and disable it.

Unioning data sources with different structures

It is a very common situation to find that we need to stack up a series of data sources, either because we have the data scattered in several files, we receive different files from different vendors, or we need to blend actual data with historic ones. No matter which use case is yours, we'll find a very simple way to do it within Alteryx.

Getting ready

We have a whole test set ready for you to try this recipe here: `https://github.com/PacktPublishing/Alteryx-Designer-Cookbook/tree/main/ch7/Recipe2`.

If you want to go with your own data, just use some that has at least a couple of fields that are the same type of information (it may be a field that represents sales amounts but with different names and/or orders within your files/tables).

In both cases, we'll make these different structure files make sense with this recipe.

In the test dataset, we have a list of customers from different countries/regions. The headers and the column order are different, and we need to build a master customer file, so we need to add up all the customers within a file, making sense of each column/field.

CLIENTE_ID	NOMBRE	APELLIDO	CORREO_ELECTRONICO	DIRECCION ✕
E0549640-F5A0-C6C4-5217-F6D43DABD442	Jemima	Weeks	Sed.diam.lorem@imperdieteratnonummy.edu	Ap #867-353 Malesuada Avenue
180E818B-6BFE-E08D-855B-09029731C883	Hyacinth	Manning	erat.vitae@iaculis.org	P.O. Box 290, 2803 Cras Avenue
A947FD6D-72A0-6056-EA75-160A927CD0D7	Chester	Livingston	non@sitamet.co.uk	661-2052 Consectetuer St.

Argentina (row label at left)

KUNDEN_ID	EMAIL	NACHNAME	NAME
63BE7CB7-EABC-E568-632C-2BCBA3A7BD11	Quisque.fringilla.euismod@ipsumacmi.com	Lowery	Kieran
3999F9B4-208E-43F8-6494-07911A5754E0	nisl.sem@nislelementum.ca	Sanders	Madaline
22948A24-57DC-9D18-8EAD-38861EA4B197	nec@Aliquamvulputateullamcorper.com	Beasley	Kai

Germany (row label at left)

CLIENTE_ID	NOME	SOBRENOME	CORREIO_ELETRÔNICO	VENDAS_2021 ✕	VENDAS_2022 ✕
01DCCF3E-8417-6738-220C-AADA690ED85B	Robert	Conner	congue@odio.ca	156194	200262
677C2BE3-4A7C-76AF-5F79-00BB2256B320	Eagan	Moran	inaliquet@Suspendissetristiqueneque.org	215160	27547
84655F35-B5F2-A92F-3FC3-DEC826068E2A	Tobias	Nicholson	In@Aliquam.org	316028	10834

Brazil (row label at left)

Figure 7.19: Datasets and matching fields by color

If we try to union these datasets with Alteryx's **Union** tool's default settings (**Auto Config by Name**), we won't be able to accomplish this task properly, and we'll get this kind of result:

Figure 7.20: Union results based on different field names

Since only CLIENTE_ID has the same name in more than one file (in our case, for the Argentina and Brazil data sources), we get them stacked correctly. The other fields are also stacked up but, because they have different names, for the files not having any of those particular fields, Alteryx Designer fills their values with Null.

How can we fix and properly align the columns, without changing their names? On to the recipe.

How to do it...

We already saw how to read different files with different structures all at once in *Chapter 1*, and because we are focusing on stacking up the data contents, we'll be reading them one by one (but feel free to use recipes from *Chapter 1* if you like):

1. Drop an **Input Data** tool onto the canvas and point it to ..\DATA\Argentina\data-Oct-11-2022 (ARG).csv.

2. Select **File Name Only** for **Output Field Name as Field** and for **Delimiters**, select | (pipe).

Input Data (1) - Configuration   ⋮ 📌

Connect a File or Database

..\DATA\Argentina\data-Oct-11-2022 (ARG).csv   ▼

Options

	Name	Value
1	Record Limit	
2	File Format	Comma Separated Value (*.csv) ⌄
3	Search SubDirs	☐
4	Output File Name as Field	File Name Only ⌄
5	Delimiters	|
6	First Row Contains Field Names	☑
7	Field Length	254
8	Start Data Import on Line	1
9	Ignore Delimiters in	Quotes ⌄
10	Treat Read Errors as Warnings	☐
11	Code Page	ISO 8859-1 Latin I ⌄
12	Allow Shared Write Access	☐
13	AMP Only: Allow Newlines in Quoted Fields	☐
14	AMP Only: Force Single-threaded Reading	☐

Preview (first 100 records)   Refresh

	CLIENTE_ID	NOMBRE	APELLIDO	CORREO_ELECTRONICO
1	E0549640-F5A0-C6C4-5217-F6D43DABD442	Jemima	Weeks	Sed.diam.lorem@imperdieterati
2	180E81BB-6BFE-E08D-855B-09029731C883	Hyacinth	Manning	erat.vitae@iaculis.org
3	A947FD6D-72A0-6056-EA75-160A927CD0D7	Chester	Livingston	non@sitamet.co.uk
4	2D44743B-58AB-95F7-7B29-BAB9ECAA3B5C	Brendan	Parsons	nec@facilisisloremtristique.ca
5	5708756E-0B51-DCC9-FC0F-DBA8C4E53559	Lara	Hurley	Duis@Aenean.net
6	24C215D7-274E-DC82-E2AE-5EC4D2B07955	Willow	Thomas	risus@Donecsollicitudinadinio

Figure 7.21: Input Data configuration for Argentina's dataset

3. Drop another **Input Data** tool and point it to `..\DATA\Brazil\dataOct-11-2022 (BRA).xlsx` and select the `Outubro` worksheet as the data source.

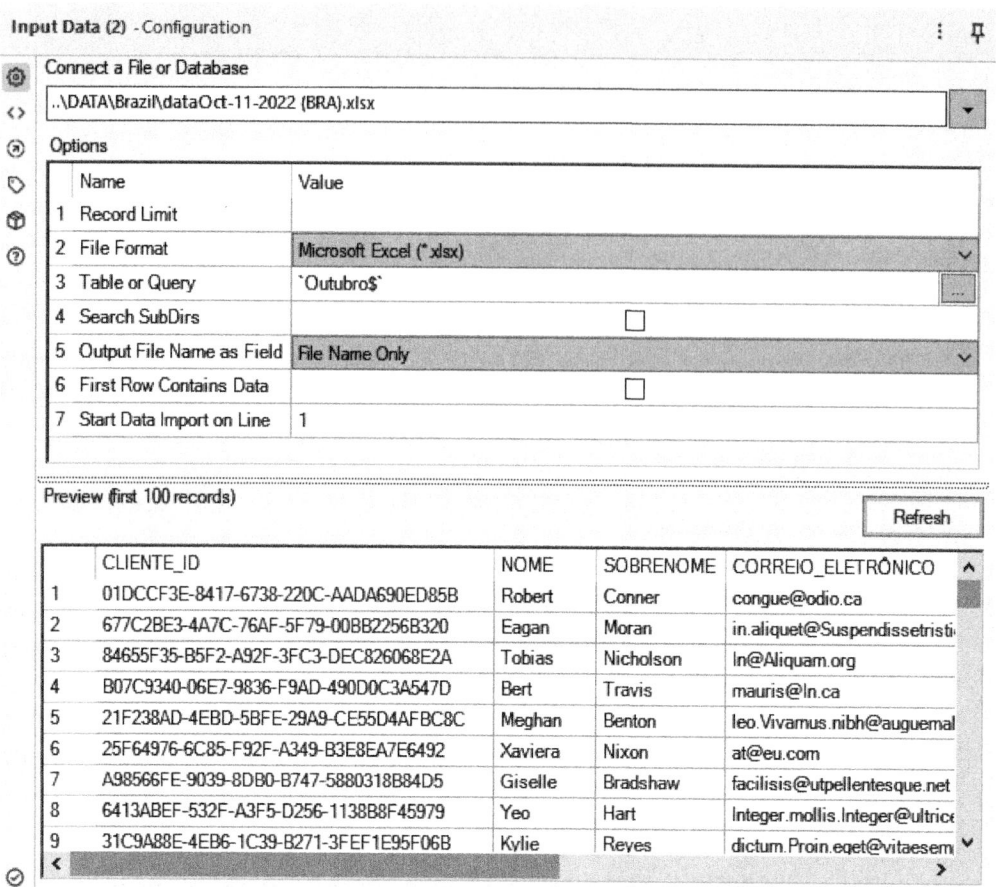

Figure 7.22: Input Data configuration for Brazil's dataset

4. Drop a third **Input Data** tool and point it to `..\DATA\Germany\Kunden2022 (DEU).csv`.

5.   Select **File Name Only** for **Output Field Name as Field**.

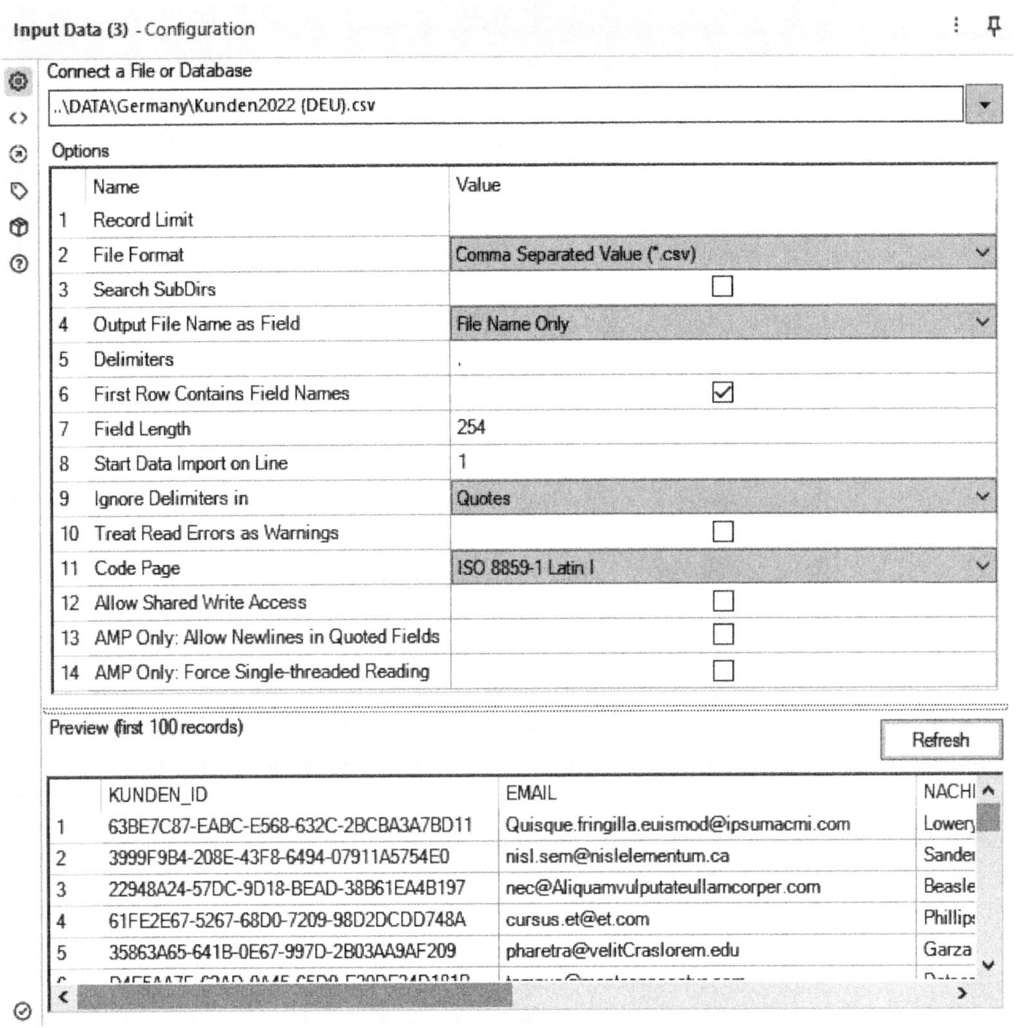

Figure 7.23: Input Data configuration for Germany's dataset

6.   Drop a **Union** tool (from the **Join** category) and connect the three **Input Data** tools to their input anchor.

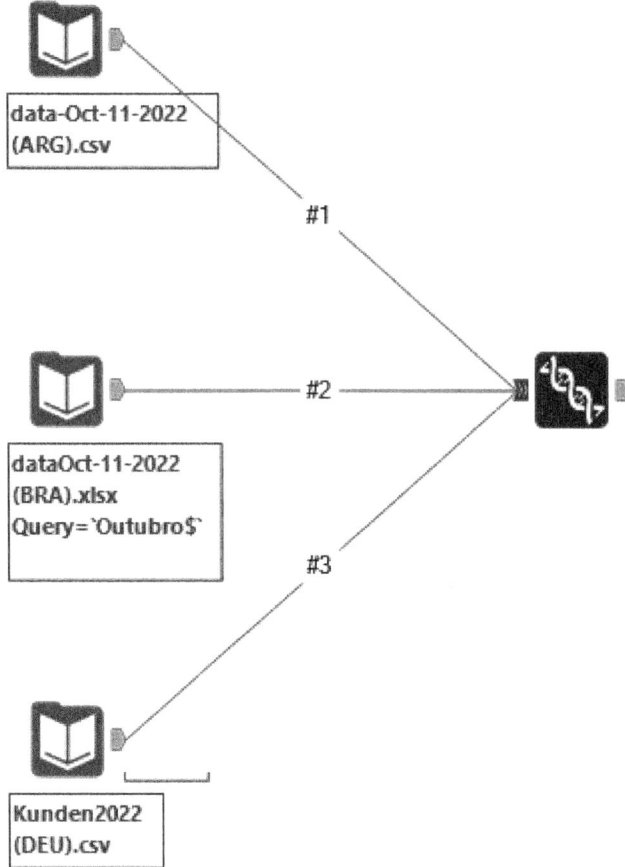

Figure 7.24: Workflow so far

7.   Click on the **Union** tool to access its configuration.

As you can see, the default for the tool is to match the field names and stack them accordingly. When one or many fields are not present in any of the data streams entering the tool, Alteryx fills their values with Null.

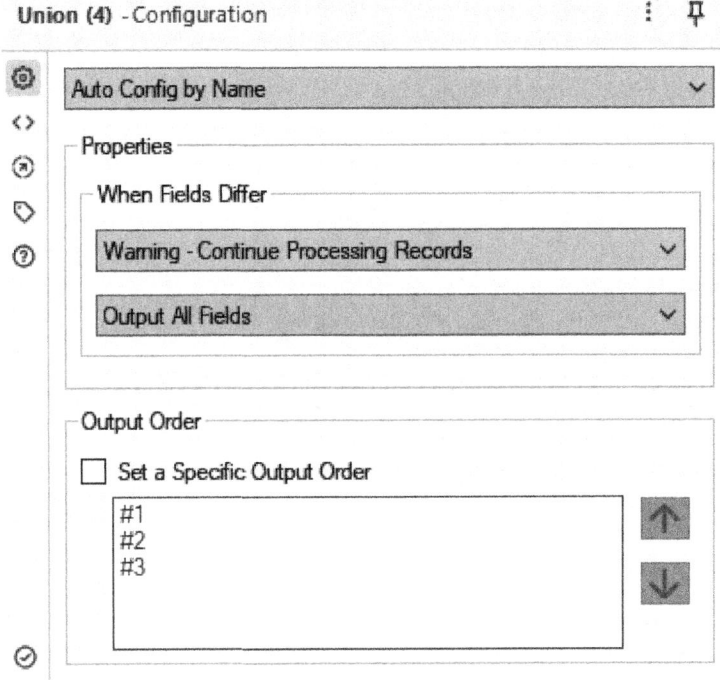

Figure 7.25: Union toll configuration

Run the workflow and you'll see the results – a dataset containing all the fields and only the ones that are repeated in more than one data stream are aligned and correct (such as `FileName` for the three data sources, or `CLIENTE_ID` for the Argentina and Brazil ones).

CLIENTE_ID	NOMBRE	APELLIDO	CORREO_ELECTRONICO	DIRECCION	NOME	SOBRENOME	CORREIO_ELETRÔNICO	VENDAS_2021	VENDAS_2022	KUNDEN_ID	EMAIL
[Null]	[Null]	[Null]	[Null]	[Null]	[Null]	[Null]	[Null]	[Null]	[Null]	638E7C87-EABC-E568-632C-28CBA3A78D11	Quisque.fringilla.euismod@
[Null]	[Null]	[Null]	[Null]	[Null]	[Null]	[Null]	[Null]	[Null]	[Null]	3999F984-208E-4398-9494-07911A5754E0	nisl.sem@malelementum.c
[Null]	[Null]	[Null]	[Null]	[Null]	[Null]	[Null]	[Null]	[Null]	[Null]	22948A24-57DC-9D18-8EAD-38861EA4B197	nec@Aliquam.vulputate.ulla
E0549640-F5A0-C6C4-5217-F6D43DA8D442	Jerusha	Weeks	Sed.diam.lorem@imperdieteratncnummy.edu	Ap #867-353 Malesuada Avenue	[Null]	[Null]	[Null]	[Null]	[Null]	[Null]	[Null]
18281B8-68FE-E06D-8588-09029771CD83	Hyacinth	Manning	erat.vitae@aculis.org	P.O. Box 290, 2801 Cras Avenue	[Null]	[Null]	[Null]	[Null]	[Null]	[Null]	[Null]
A9417D60-72A0-6056-EA75-160AB27CD0D7	Chester	Livingston	non@tillamet.co.uk	661-2052 Consectetuer St.	[Null]	[Null]	[Null]	[Null]	[Null]	[Null]	[Null]
01DCCF5E-8417-6738-220C-AADA690ED458	[Null]	[Null]	[Null]	[Null]	Robert	Conner	congur@odio.ca	156194	202262	[Null]	[Null]
677C28E1-4A7C-76AF-5F79-008N22566B320	[Null]	[Null]	[Null]	[Null]	Eagan	Mcran	maliquet@Suspendisseristiquenequat.org	215160	27547	[Null]	[Null]
84655F35-B5F2-A92F-3FC3-0EC82606BE2A	[Null]	[Null]	[Null]	[Null]	Tobias	Nicholson	In@Aliquam.org	314026	10854	[Null]	[Null]

Figure 7.26: Unioning with Auto Config by Name

Back to the **Union** tool configuration, we have three options for field matching:

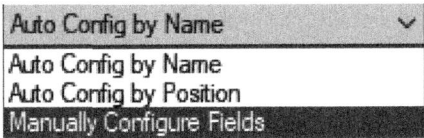

Figure 7.27: Union field alignment options

8. Select **Manually Configure Fields**, and you'll see how the panel changes to a grid. Also, at this point, you may want to expand the configuration panel, so you have a better working area.

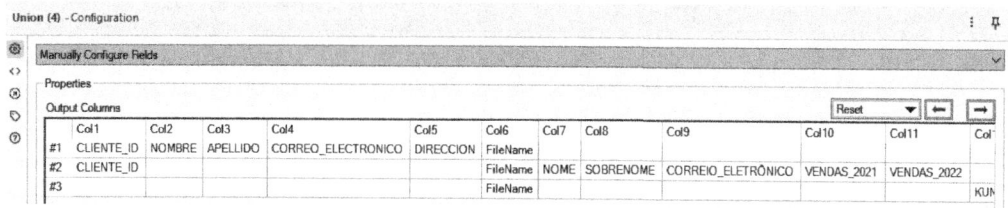

Figure 7.28: Starting to manually match fields/columns

9. Click on row #2, Col7 over NOME, and drag until you find VENDAS_2022.

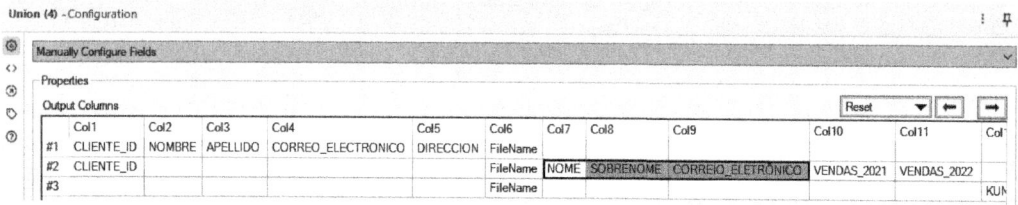

Figure 7.29: Aligning multiple columns

10. With these three fields selected, click five times on the left pointing arrow you have just above the grid (until NOME is right below NOMBRE).

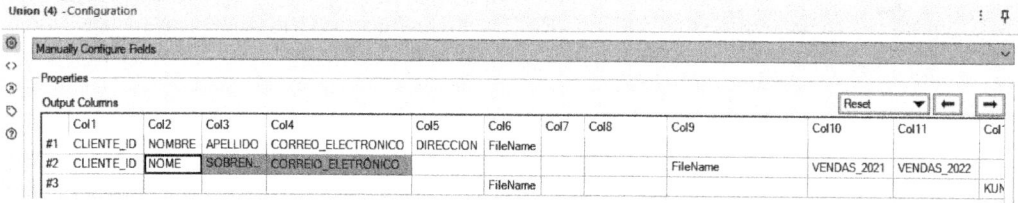

Figure 7.30: Multiple columns aligned

You can see the fields moved to the left, and they're aligned with the fields of row #1.

11. Now click on FileName, and with FileName selected, click three times on the left pointing arrow so all FileName fields are aligned.

12. Now, scroll to the right and select KUNDEN_ID, EMAIL, NACHNAME, and NAME and click 11 times on the left arrow, until you match KUNDEN_ID with CLIENTE_ID (in Col1).

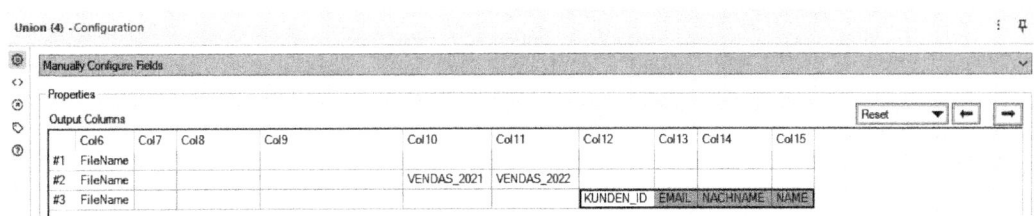

Figure 7.31: Alignment of the German dataset columns

Again, since we moved the blank field names to fit the ones we selected, `FileName` was moved.

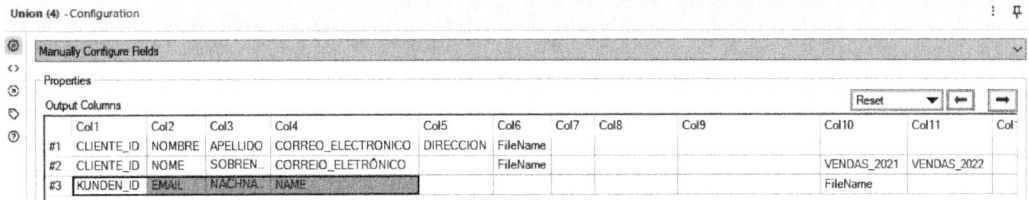

Figure 7.32: Fixing FileName misalignment

13. Click on `FileName` on row #3 and click the arrow until it aligns with the other `FileName` fields.

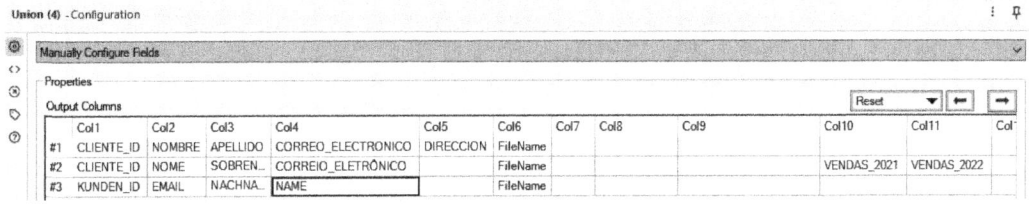

Figure 7.33: Filename aligned

14. Now, click on `NAME` on row #3, and click the right-pointing arrow until it is aligned with `NOMBRE` and `NOME (Col2)`.

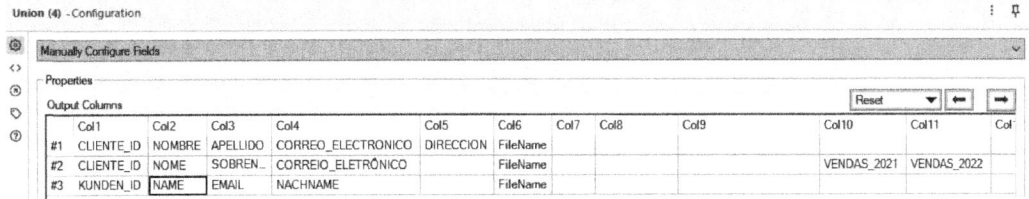

Figure 7.34: Aligning the name fields

15. Do the same for `EMAIL` (aligning it with `CORREO_ELECTRONICO` and `CORREIO_ELETRÔNICO`).

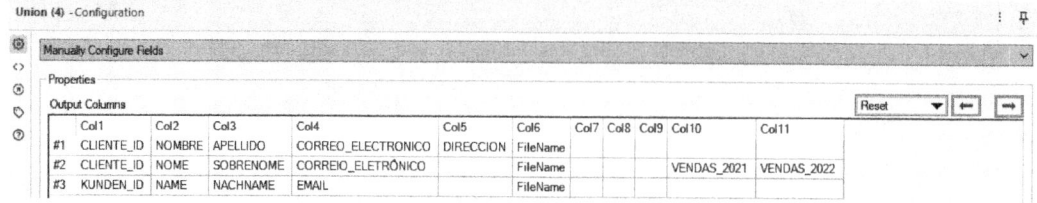

Figure 7.35: Aligning the emails

Finally, we need to deal with the gaps we left within the fields matching definitions.

16. Select the three rows for `Col5` and move them to the right (one click to the right-pointing arrow is enough).

17. Click on `Col7`, row #1, and drag until you reach `Col9`, row #3. Move them to the right of `Col11` (two clicks on the right arrow).

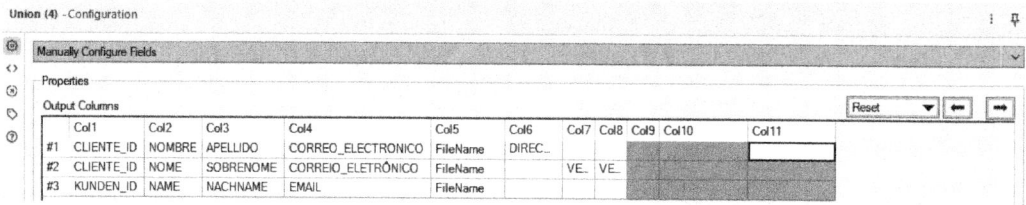

Figure 7.36: Moving unwanted fields to the far right

Run the workflow and you'll see that all fields are perfectly aligned and the different schema files are stacked in the right way.

CLIENTE_ID	NOMBRE	APELLIDO	CORREO_ELECTRONICO	FileName	DIRECCION	VENDAS_2021	VENDAS_2022
63BE7C87-EABC-E568-632C-2BCBA3A78D11	Kieran	Lowery	Quisque.fringilla.euismod@ipsumacmi.com	Kunden2022 (DEU)	[Null]	[Null]	[Null]
3999F9B4-208E-43F8-6494-07911A5754E0	Madaline	Sanders	nisl.sem@nislelementum.ca	Kunden2022 (DEU)	[Null]	[Null]	[Null]
22948A24-57DC-9D18-BEAD-38861EA4B197	Kai	Beasley	nec@Aliquamvulputateullamcorper.com	Kunden2022 (DEU)	[Null]	[Null]	[Null]
E0549640-F5A0-C6C4-5217-F6D43DABD442	Jemima	Weeks	Sed.diam.lorem@imperdieteratnonummy.edu	data-Oct-11-2022 (ARG)	Ap #867-353 Malesuada Avenue	[Null]	[Null]
180E818B-6BFE-E08D-855B-09029731C883	Hyacinth	Manning	erat.vitae@iaculis.org	data-Oct-11-2022 (ARG)	P.O. Box 290, 2803 Cras Avenue	[Null]	[Null]
A947FD6D-72A0-6056-EA75-160A927CD007	Chester	Livingston	non@sitamet.co.uk	data-Oct-11-2022 (ARG)	661-2052 Consectetuer St.	[Null]	[Null]
01DCCF3E-8417-6738-220C-AADA690ED858	Robert	Conner	congue@odio.ca	dataOct-11-2022 (BRA)	[Null]	156194	200262
677C2BE3-4A7C-76AF-5F79-008822568320	Eagan	Moran	in.aliquet@Suspendissetristiqueneque.org	dataOct-11-2022 (BRA)	[Null]	215160	27547
84655F35-B5F2-A92F-3FC3-DEC826068E2A	Tobias	Nicholson	In@Aliquam.org	dataOct-11-2022 (BRA)	[Null]	316028	10834

Figure 7.37: Results so far – all fields are perfectly aligned, but we still have unwanted fields

To finish this recipe, we can add a **Select** tool to clean up the final output, by deselecting the fields we don't want in the CUSTOMER'S MASTER FILE.

18. Drop a **Select** tool and connect it to the **Union** tool.

19. From the **Field** list, deselect `DIRECCION`, `VENDAS_2021`, and `VENDAS_2022` (we'll keep the `FileName` field so we know where each record comes from).

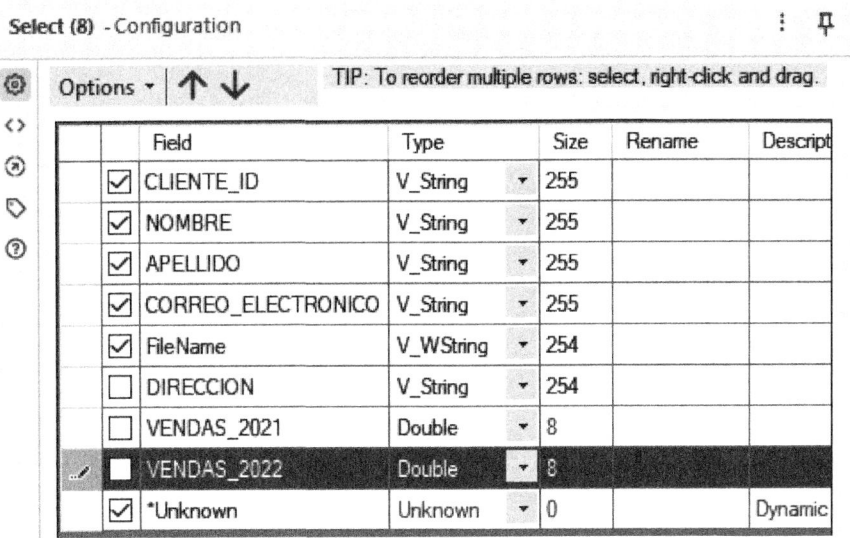

Figure 7.38: Getting rid of unwanted fields

And your final output must look like this:

CLIENTE_ID	NOMBRE	APELLIDO	CORREO_ELECTRONICO	FileName
63BE7C87-EABC-E568-632C-2BCBA3A7BD11	Kieran	Lowery	Quisque.fringilla.euismod@ipsumacmi.com	Kunden2022 (DEU)
3999F9B4-208E-43F8-6494-07911A5754E0	Madaline	Sanders	nisl.sem@nislelementum.ca	Kunden2022 (DEU)
22948A24-57DC-9D18-BEAD-38B61EA4B197	Kai	Beasley	nec@Aliquamvulputateullamcorper.com	Kunden2022 (DEU)
E0549640-F5A0-C6C4-5217-F6D43DABD442	Jemima	Weeks	Sed.diam.lorem@imperdieteratnonummy.edu	data-Oct-11-2022 (ARG)
180E81BB-6BFE-E08D-855B-09029731C883	Hyacinth	Manning	erat.vitae@iaculis.org	data-Oct-11-2022 (ARG)
A947FD6D-72A0-6056-EA75-160A927CD0D7	Chester	Livingston	non@sitamet.co.uk	data-Oct-11-2022 (ARG)
01DCCF3E-8417-6738-220C-AADA690ED85B	Robert	Conner	congue@odio.ca	dataOct-11-2022 (BRA)
677C2BE3-4A7C-76AF-5F79-00BB2256B320	Eagan	Moran	in.aliquet@Suspendissetristiqueneque.org	dataOct-11-2022 (BRA)
84655F35-B5F2-A92F-3FC3-DEC826068E2A	Tobias	Nicholson	In@Aliquam.org	dataOct-11-2022 (BRA)

Figure 7.39: Final results

How it works...

Alteryx gives us the advantage of automatically stacking fields based on their names or position. But as we saw in the test dataset, that's not always possible. Since Designer has a manual configuration option, we can use it to make disparate fields match to stack them up, without changing them.

Next are some additional notes on this method.

As you can see, the resulting field names are taken from the first connection name (being the names of connection #1, #2, and #3, which is the default for Alteryx).

But we can change them by clicking on the line that connects the **Input Data** tools to the **Union** tool.

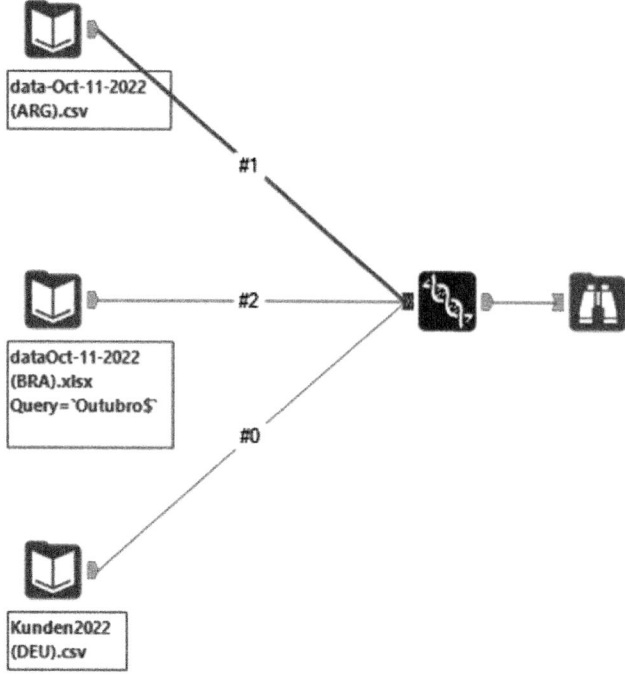

data-Oct-11-2022
(ARG).csv

#1

dataOct-11-2022
(BRA).xlsx
Query=`Outubro$`

#2

#0

Kunden2022
(DEU).csv

Figure 7.40: Workflow overview

We can access the **Connection** configuration:

Connection - Configuration				⋮ 📌

Name

#1

☐ **Wireless**

Fields

	Name	Type	Size	Source
1	CLIENTE_ID	V_String	254	File: C:\Exercises\ch7\Recipe2\DATA
2	NOMBRE	V_String	254	File: C:\Exercises\ch7\Recipe2\DATA
3	APELLIDO	V_String	254	File: C:\Exercises\ch7\Recipe2\DATA
4	CORREO_ELECTRONICO	V_String	254	File: C:\Exercises\ch7\Recipe2\DATA
5	DIRECCION	V_String	254	File: C:\Exercises\ch7\Recipe2\DATA
6	FileName	V_WString	254	File: FileName

Figure 7.41: Connection properties panel

And we can change their names, by changing the value in the **Name** text input:

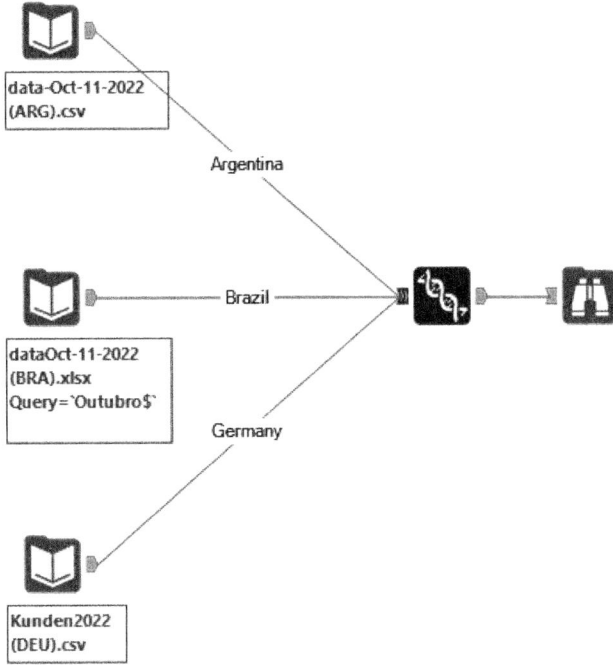

Figure 7.42: Connections renamed – view from the workflow

This will help us a lot to identify the connections within the tools.

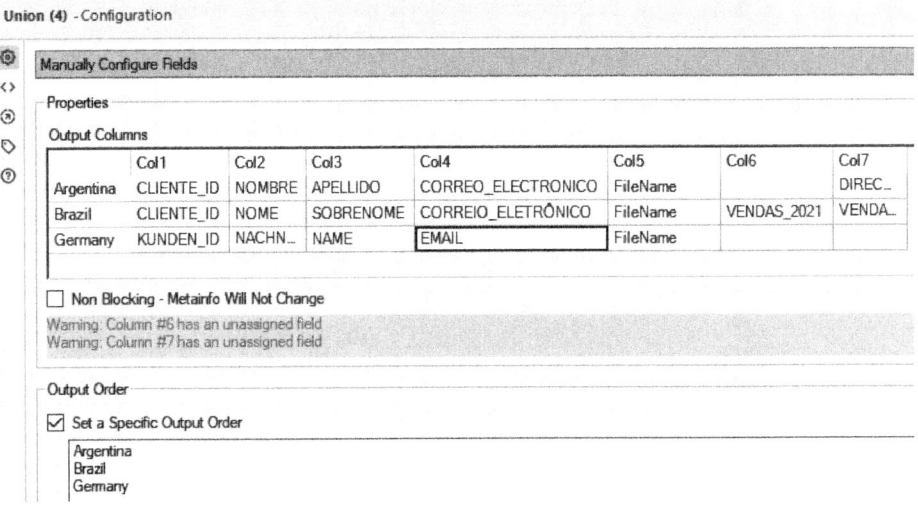

Figure 7.43: Connections renamed – view within the Union tool configuration panel

Also, if you notice at the bottom of the configuration panel, you can tell Alteryx Designer the order in which you want your dataset (but still it'll take the resulting field names from whatever incoming data stream is first in the grid).

Advanced joining (using conditions in your joins)

As we saw in a previous recipe, the Join operation can be performed with other tools too, not only with the **Join** tool. I'll use the *joining* word to describe the blending operation between datasets, not referring specifically to the **Join** tool.

But to perform a good Join operation, we must ensure a couple of things.

I've seen a lot of tutorials and articles that recommend using the **Unique** tool for cases where we need to use a lookup table to add additional fields to our dataset. This method is OK when we have the same attributes for the same keys occurring more than once in our lookup table/s. But what happens when we have duplicate occurrences and we need to apply a condition to determine which one to use?

For example, we have a billing dataset with the article code. We need to add the product description to our analysis, so we need to blend our original dataset with another one containing the article's description.

	A	B	C	D	E
1	BILL	BILL_DATE	ARTICLE	QUANTITY	AMOUNT
2	1	2/1/2022	A	1	100
3	2	2/1/2022	A	2	200
4	3	1/3/2022	B	2	100
5	4	1/2/2022	A	2	200
6	5	3/3/2022	C	1	25
7	6	3/22/2022	A	2	200

Figure 7.44: Billing dataset

When we receive it, let's call it the *articles master dataset*, we discover that it (as it should) contains different descriptions for a single article code, depending on the date. This dataset is telling us that Record #1 is only valid for the period between FIRST_SEEN and LAST_SEEN (a very common method used to manage dimension tables) while Record #3 is valid from FIRST_SEEN and today (because LAST_SEEN is null), so based on BILL_DATE, we need to select the proper DESCRIPTION from this table.

	A	B	C	D	E
1	RecordID	CODE	FIRST_SEEN	LAST_SEEN	DESCRIPTION
2	1	A	1/1/2022	1/2/2022	Description for A
3	2	B	1/2/2022	3/2/2022	Description for B
4	3	C	1/1/2022		Description for C
5	4	A	1/3/2022	2/2/2022	2nd. Description for A
6	5	A	2/3/2022		3rd. Description for A
7	6	B	3/3/2022		2nd. Description for B

Figure 7.45: Articles dataset

So, at this point, we have a situation. How can we solve the multiple changes that CODE presents over time?

If we go with the **Unique** method for CODE, we'll get these results:

BILL	BILL_DATE	ARTICLE	QUANTITY	AMOUNT	RecordID	CODE	FIRST_SEEN	LAST_SEEN	DESCRIPTION
1	2022-02-01	A	1	100	1	A	2022-01-01	2022-01-02	Description for A
2	2022-02-01	A	2	200	1	A	2022-01-01	2022-01-02	Description for A
4	2022-01-02	A	2	200	1	A	2022-01-01	2022-01-02	Description for A
6	2022-03-22	A	2	200	1	A	2022-01-01	2022-01-02	Description for A
3	2022-01-03	B	2	100	2	B	2022-01-02	2022-03-02	Description for B
5	2022-03-03	C	1	25	3	C	2022-01-01	[Null]	Description for C

Figure 7.46: Wrong results

This is wrong because bill #2 refers to article CODE as A, but it changed on LAST_UPDATE (1/3/2022), so we need to get that description (2nd. Description for A, and not the one we got). This happens because the **Unique** tool returns the first unique combination it finds for the selected fields within a dataset.

And if we include FIRST_SEEN as part of the **Unique** key, we'll be creating what's called a **Cartesian product** (for each of the records within the first dataset, we'll join all records from the second one that matches).

BILL	BILL_DATE	ARTICLE	QUANTITY	AMOUNT	RecordID	CODE	FIRST_SEEN	LAST_SEEN	DESCRIPTION
1	2022-02-01	A	1	100	1	A	2022-01-01	2022-01-02	Description for A
2	2022-02-01	A	2	200	1	A	2022-01-01	2022-01-02	Description for A
4	2022-01-02	A	2	200	1	A	2022-01-01	2022-01-02	Description for A
6	2022-03-22	A	2	200	1	A	2022-01-01	2022-01-02	Description for A
1	2022-02-01	A	1	100	4	A	2022-01-03	2022-02-02	2nd. Description for A
2	2022-02-01	A	2	200	4	A	2022-01-03	2022-02-02	2nd. Description for A
4	2022-01-02	A	2	200	4	A	2022-01-03	2022-02-02	2nd. Description for A
6	2022-03-22	A	2	200	4	A	2022-01-03	2022-02-02	2nd. Description for A
1	2022-02-01	A	1	100	5	A	2022-02-03	[Null]	3rd. Description for A
2	2022-02-01	A	2	200	5	A	2022-02-03	[Null]	3rd. Description for A
4	2022-01-02	A	2	200	5	A	2022-02-03	[Null]	3rd. Description for A
6	2022-03-22	A	2	200	5	A	2022-02-03	[Null]	3rd. Description for A
3	2022-01-03	B	2	100	2	B	2022-01-02	2022-03-02	Description for B
3	2022-01-03	B	2	100	6	B	2022-03-03	[Null]	2nd. Description for B
5	2022-03-03	C	1	25	3	C	2022-01-01	[Null]	Description for C

Figure 7.47: Cartesian results

As you can see, for article A, we got all combinations that have article A in our lookup table.

In this recipe, we'll be exploring a method to create effective and correct joins between datasets, and it's based on a very useful macro/tool created by Neal Ryan (@NeilR) and available in Alteryx's Gallery. The tool/macro is called **Advanced Join**, and you can download it for free here: https://community.alteryx.com/t5/Public-Community-Gallery/Advanced-Join/ta-p/882351.

It also has a very useful accompanying blog post in Alteryx's Community here: https://community.alteryx.com/t5/Engine-Works/Advanced-Join-Macro/ba-p/2355.

Getting ready

For this recipe, we prepared a test set for you, which can be downloaded here: `https://github.com/PacktPublishing/Alteryx-Designer-Cookbook/tree/main/ch7/Recipe3`.

If you decide to follow along with your own data, make sure that your lookup tables (the ones you'll be joining to the primary dataset) have at least one record repeated for the joining criteria you'll use.

In both cases, you need to download and install the **Advanced Join** macro from the URL mentioned previously.

Additionally, we'll check whether you already have a default location for your macros. You can revisit the *Getting ready* section in the third recipe in *Chapter 1* to see how:

1. When you access the URL, click on the **Download** button and select where to save the file. It'll be in a `.yxzp` (Alteryx package) format.

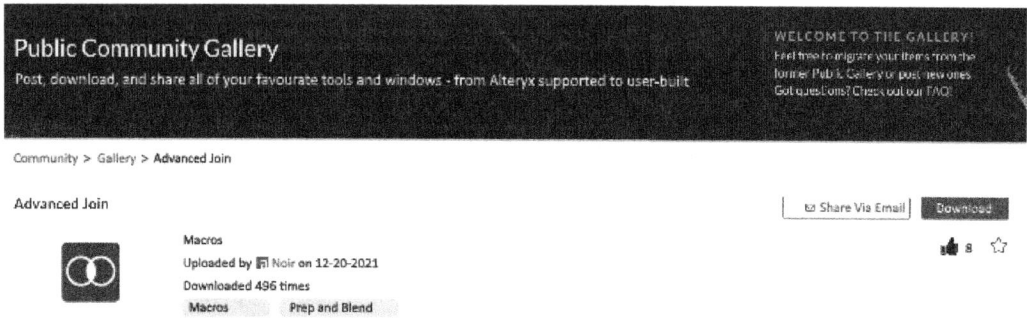

Figure 7.48: Advanced Join page on Alteryx Gallery

Once the download is complete, we need to install it.

2. Go to Alteryx Designer and click on **File → Open Workflow**.
3. Point to where you saved the downloaded file and select it.

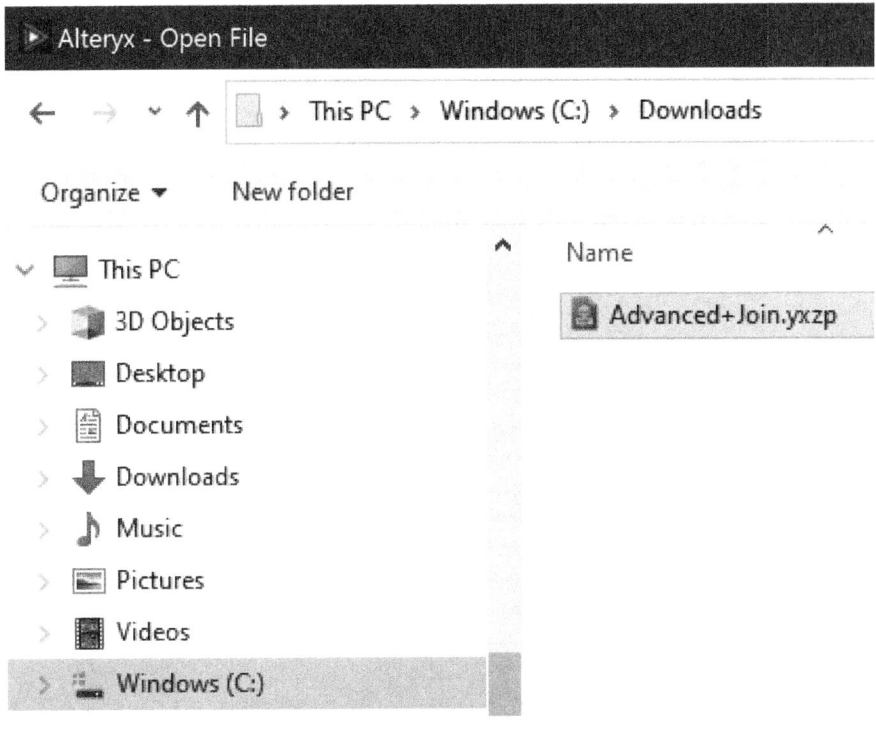

Figure 7.49: Selecting the downloaded package

Alteryx will ask you whether you want to import it.

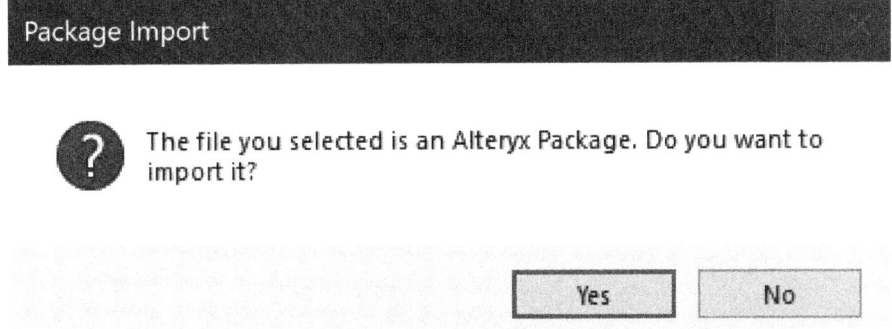

Figure 7.50: Importing package confirmation

4. Click on **Yes**, and a new window appears. This window asks where you want to save your macro.

    You can type the full path in **Destination Directory** or click the *save* icon to browse your hard drive.

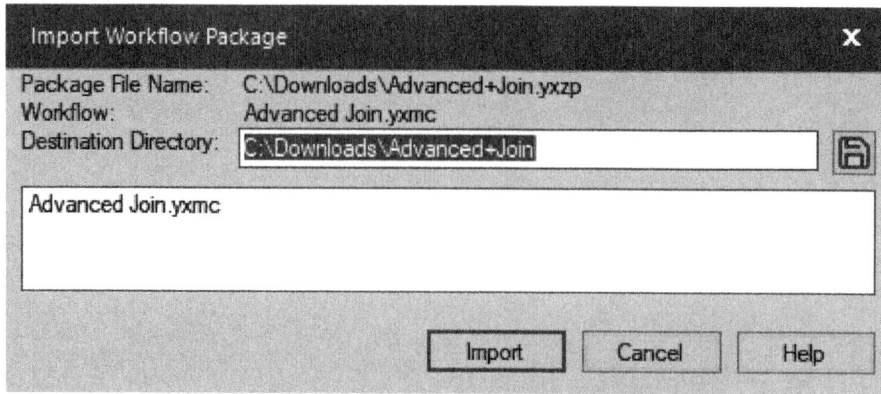

Figure 7.51: Importing workflow package

If you select the *save* icon, a new window appears asking you to browse to where you want the tool to be installed.

5. Point the folder to your macro's default location, click on the **Make New Folder** button at the bottom left of the actual window, and name the new folder `Advanced+Join`.

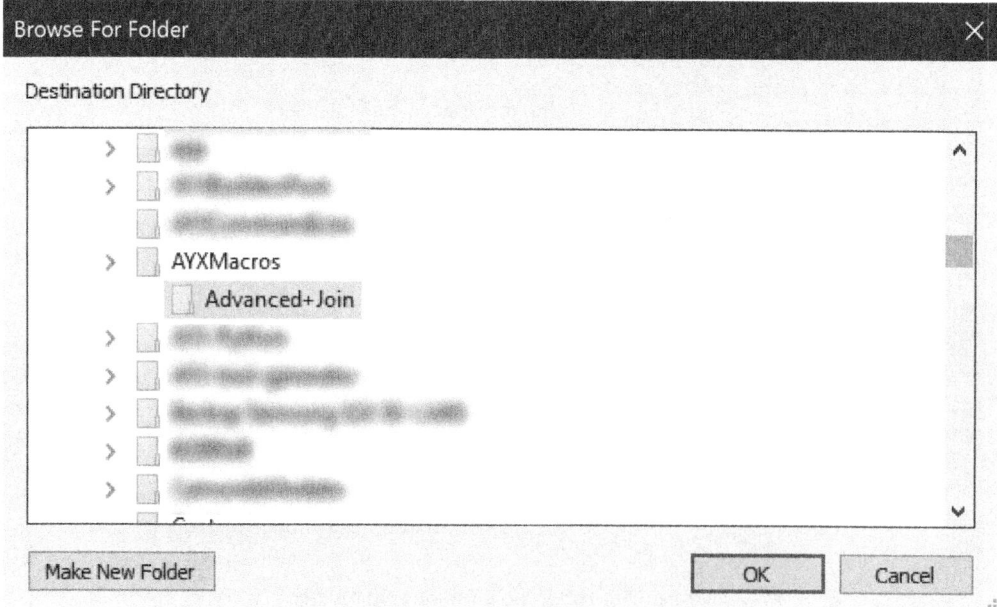

Figure 7.52: Selecting the default folder

6. Select the `Advanced+Join` folder we just created, and hit **OK**.

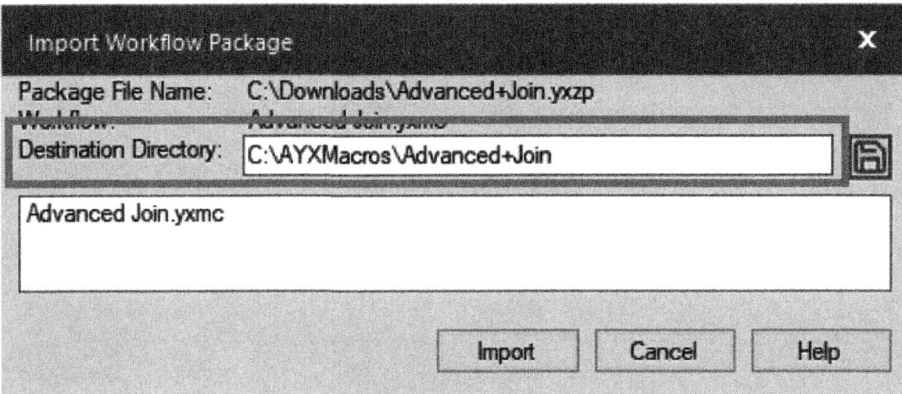

Figure 7.53: Ensuring the install destination

7. Make sure **Destination Directory** is updated to the new location, and click on **Import**.

Alteryx will inform you about the import progress and ask whether you want to import the workflow. If you click **Yes**, the macro will be opened as a workflow; otherwise, the popup window will close.

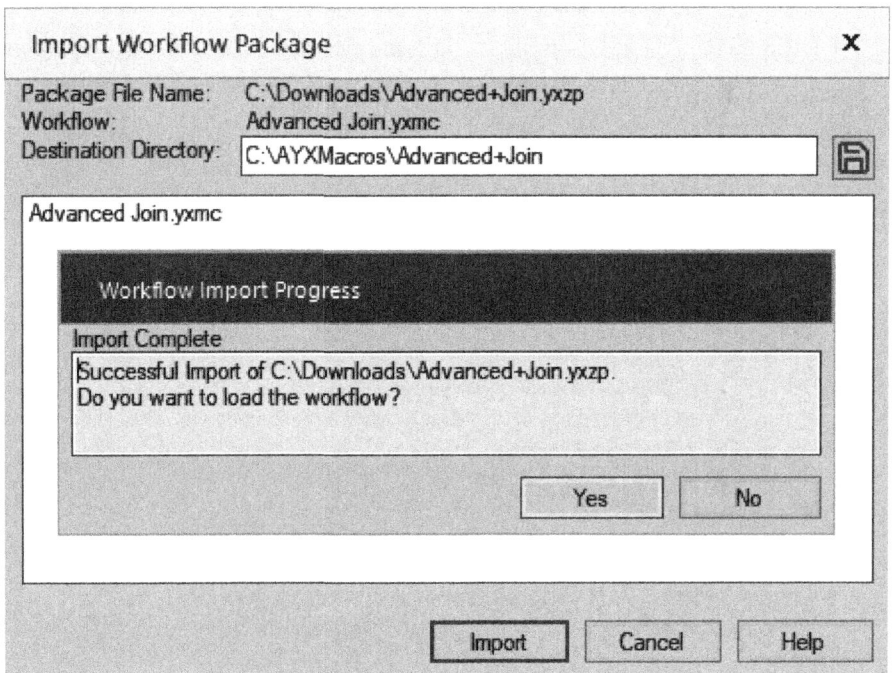

Figure 7.54: Importing the package

Now, you have the new tool installed. You can check for it by going to the **Join** tool category and seeing whether the **Advanced Join** tool is present there.

Figure 7.55: An installed tool in the ribbon

How to do it...

Back to our use case, since we need to join our two data sources based on a condition, we'll need this new tool in our arsenal:

1. Drop an **Input Data** tool onto the canvas, point it to `..\DATA\BILLS.xlsx`, and use `Sheet1` as the data source.

2. Drop another **Input Data** tool and point it to `..\DATA\ARTICLES.xlsx`, and select `Sheet1` as the data source.

3. Add a **Formula** tool to the **Input Data** tool that has `ARTICLES` as its data source.

4. In the **Formula** tool, select `LAST_SEEN` from the dropdown and enter this expression:

    ```
    IF IsNull([LAST_SEEN])
    THEN DateTimeStart()
    ELSE [LAST_SEEN]
    ENDIF
    ```

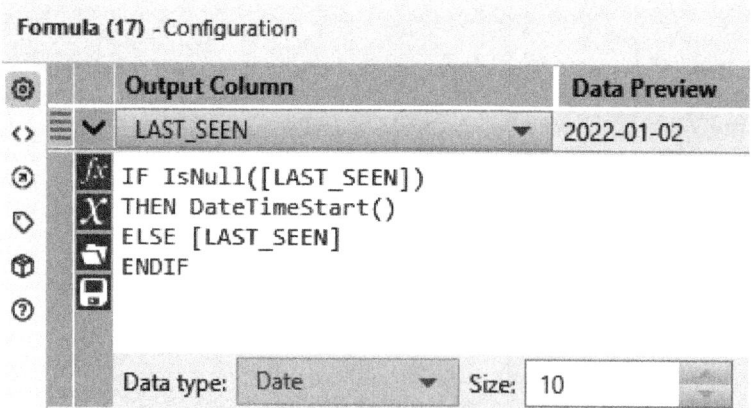

Figure 7.56: Formula tool configuration

5. Now drop an **Advanced Join** tool onto the canvas and connect it like this:

• The **Input Data** tool that uses `BILLS` as its data source output anchor to the A labeled input anchor of the **Advanced Join** tool

• The **Formula** tool output anchor to the **Advanced Join** input labeled B

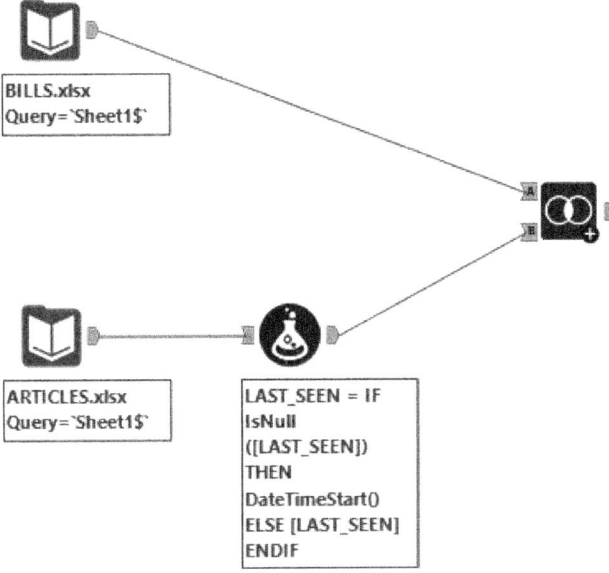

Figure 7.57: Workflow so far

6. Click on the **Advanced Join** tool to access its configuration panel.

7. Make sure **Conventional join** is selected for the method.

8. Select **ARTICLE** from the A join field dropdown.

9. Select **CODE** from the B join field dropdown.

10. Select **A and B (inner join)** from **Keep records that match join field** from the drop-down options.

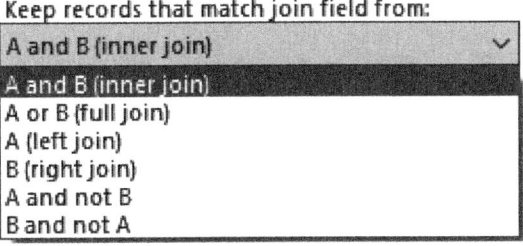

Figure 7.58: Advanced types of join

11. In the **Condition** field, use this expression:

```
BILL_DATE<=LAST_SEEN AND BILL_DATE>=FIRST_SEEN
```

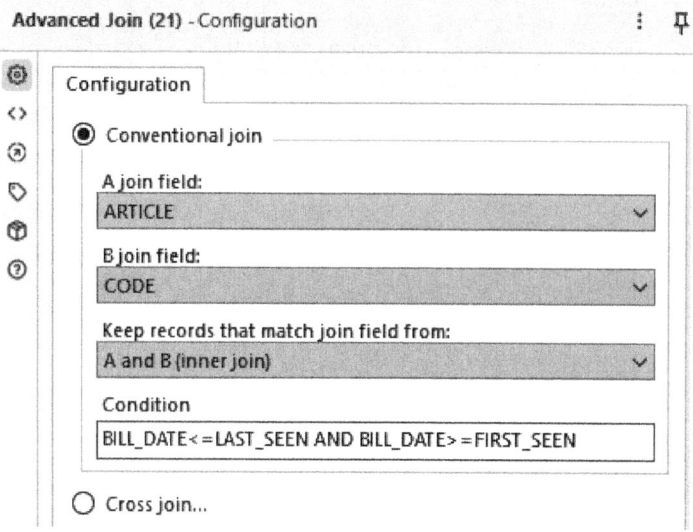

Figure 7.59: Advanced Join tool configuration

12. Add a **Sort** tool to the **Advanced Join** tool, just to get the records in the same order as the original input.

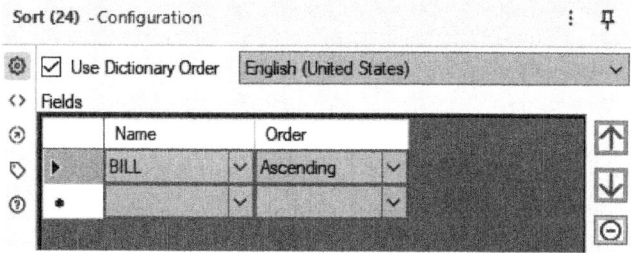

Figure 7.60: Sorting the results

Run the workflow and you'll see that **Advanced Join** solved the problem for us.

BILL	BILL_DATE	ARTICLE	QUANTITY	AMOUNT	RecordID	FIRST_SEEN	LAST_SEEN	DESCRIPTION
1	2022-02-01	A	1	100	4	2022-01-03	2022-02-02	2nd. Description for A
2	2022-02-01	A	2	200	4	2022-01-03	2022-02-02	2nd. Description for A
4	2022-01-02	A	2	200	1	2022-01-01	2022-01-02	Description for A
6	2022-03-22	A	2	200	5	2022-02-03	2022-10-17	3rd. Description for A
3	2022-01-03	B	2	100	2	2022-01-02	2022-03-02	Description for B
5	2022-03-03	C	1	25	3	2022-01-01	2022-10-17	Description for C

Figure 7.61: Final results

How it works...

The **Advanced Join** tool (or macro) helps us add conditions to our joins, avoiding all the work needed to define all possible values for the ranges, or separating our data to process it accordingly.

In our case, we used an expression (BILL_DATE<=LAST_SEEN AND BILL_DATE>=FIRST_SEEN) to tell the tool that we wanted to join on BILL_DATE within the range defined by FIRST_SEEN and LAST_SEEN.

BILL_DATE must be between FIRST_SEEN and LAST_SEEN to join

BILL	BILL_DATE	ARTICLE	QUANTITY	AMOUNT	RecordID	FIRST_SEEN	LAST_SEEN	DESCRIPTION
1	2022-02-01	A	1	100	4	2022-01-03	2022-02-02	2nd. Description for A
2	2022-02-01	A	2	200	4	2022-01-03	2022-02-02	2nd. Description for A
4	2022-01-02	A	2	200	1	2022-01-01	2022-01-02	Description for A
6	2022-03-22	A	2	200	5	2022-02-03	2022-10-17	3rd. Description for A
3	2022-01-03	B	2	100	2	2022-01-02	2022-03-02	Description for B
5	2022-03-03	C	1	25	3	2022-01-01	2022-10-17	Description for C

Figure 7.62: Joining results on date ranges

Appending fields to your data

Sometimes, we find that we need to get some calculations from our datasets (SUMs, Averages, Counts, or Distinct Counts), and later add them back to the source, or maybe have a very small dataset that we need to add to each record from our main data source (for example, the location of our distribution center to a dataset that contains different locations and we need to get the distance from one to the other). Appending fields is a very useful technique that will allow us to do this, and we'll be covering it in this recipe.

This is a cross-join operation where, for each record in the first dataset, all the records from the second dataset are added (generating what is called a **Cartesian Join**), and even when we think it is dangerous (and believe me, it is), if you understand well how to leverage it, you'll realize how useful and powerful this technique is.

> **Important note**
>
> Alteryx Designer has its fail-safe mechanism to avoid entering a machine-killing state with this operation, allowing, by default, 16 records and erroring if there are more.
>
> You can change this behavior, by selecting any of the options from the **Append Fields** tool configuration, but do it carefully.

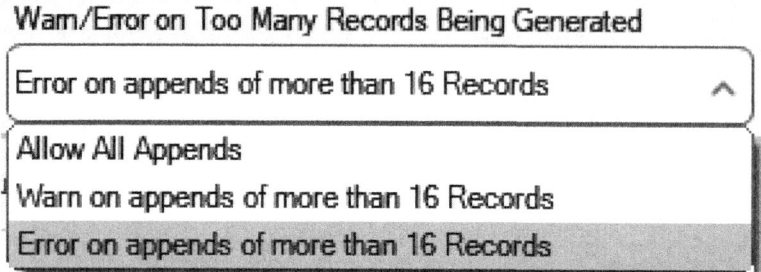

Figure 7.63: Append Fields fail-safe

Getting ready

As per each recipe, we prepared a test set to follow along, which you can download here: `https://github.com/PacktPublishing/Alteryx-Designer-Cookbook/tree/main/ch7/Recipe4`.

You can try this recipe with your own data – just make sure you have at least one numeric field at the lower level of granularity possible, so when it's summarized, it will represent the total for that particular measure (such as sales or inventory levels, for instance).

We'll be taking a dataset that shows one month of a company's sales, at the invoices line level, and calculate the participation percentage of each store in the total monthly sales, using just this dataset.

As we stated earlier, we'll be consuming a file that has data about the sales, on an invoice basis, for a company, for a determined period, among other useful information.

This dataset also contains the `Store Number` where each invoice was issued.

Based on only this data, we're asked to get the participation percentage of each store over the total sales of the company, and the participation percentage on invoices issued over the total in the given period.

Figure 7.64: Our dataset

As we can see in the data, each record represents a line of an invoice and provides several fields to focus on for our analysis:

- `Store Number`: This is the ID of the store where the invoice (`Order_ID`) was generated.

- `Order_ID`: This represents each invoice issued by the company. Since each record is a line within an invoice, we may find repeated values here.

- `Sales`: This is the subtotal amount of each particular invoice line. For invoices with only one product, this is the total too.

To get the participation percentage of each store over the total, we need to get the totals per store and then the overall total.

So, let's dive in.

How to do it...

We will get started by using the following steps:

1. Drop an **Input Data** tool onto the canvas, point it to `..\DATA\SALES.xlsx`, and select the `Oct-2022` worksheet as the data source.

    First, we need to get the total `Sales` amount and the number of unique invoices issued by each `Store Number`.

2. Drop a **Summarize** tool after the **Input Data** tool and configure it in this way:

    - Click on **Store Number** in the **Fields** panel.

    - Click on **Add**, and select **Group By**.

    - In the **Fields** section on the top, scroll down and click on **Sales**.

    - With **Sales** selected, click on **Add** and select **Sum**.

- Click on `Order_ID` on the top **Fields** panel.
- Click on **Add**, and then on **Count Distinct**.

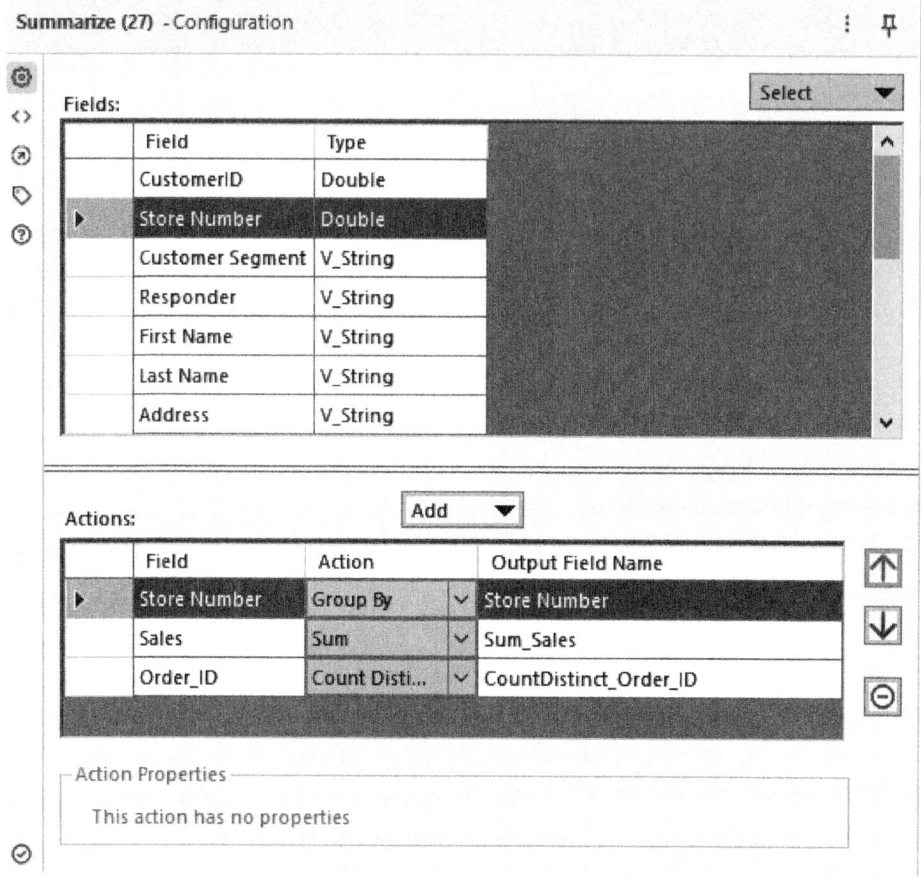

Figure 7.65: Summarize configuration

3. For a clearer dataset, click on the **Actions** panel, where `Sum_Sales` is, and rename it `Store_Sales`. Rename `CountDistinct_Order_ID` to `Quantity_Order_ID`.

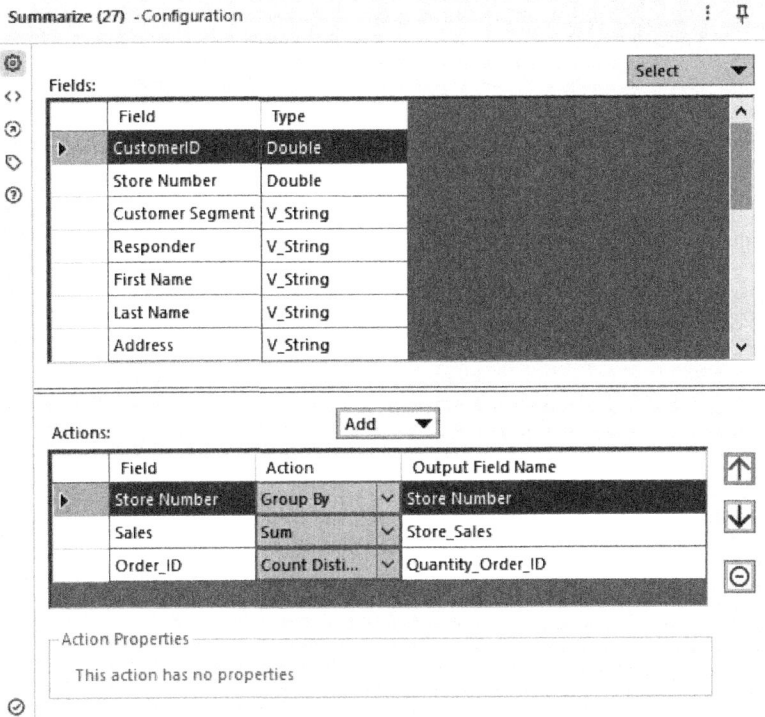

Figure 7.66: Summarize output fields renamed

You can read the **Actions** panel from the bottom up in this way: Give me the count of different (**Count Distinct**) values from the `Order_ID` field and the total (**Sum**) of the `Sales` field per (**Group By**) `Store Number`.

Run the workflow and you'll see the results.

Store Number	Store_Sales	Quantity_Order_ID
100	1324557.13	941
101	1163252.09	831
102	257316.63	252
103	865103.91	667
104	904958.08	793
105	1192592.36	957
106	936910.82	811
107	795420.18	709
108	619594.59	519
109	644612.52	497

Figure 7.67: Summarize results

So far, we have the sales and invoices per store. Now, we need to get the total for the whole dataset.

4. Add a new **Summarize** tool and connect it to the existing **Summarize** output anchor.

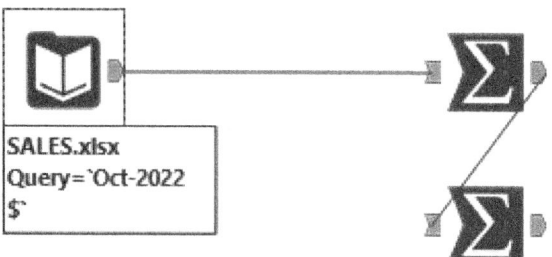

Figure 7.68: Workflow so far

5. Click on the newly added **Summarize** tool to access its configuration, and from the **Actions** pane, click on `Store_Sales` and drag until you have selected both `Store_Sales` and `Quantity_Order_ID`.

6. Click on **Add**, and select **Sum** as the aggregation.

7. Rename **Output Field Name** for each resulting field to `Total_Sales` and `Total_Order_ID`, so your second **Summarize** tool looks like this:

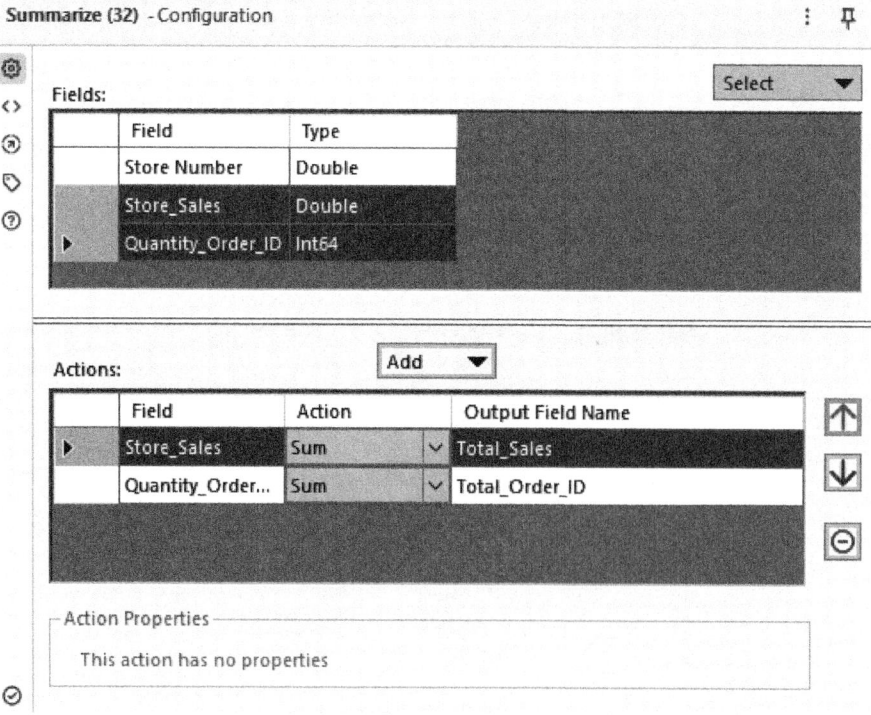

Figure 7.69: Summarize (second) configuration

Now, since there is no **Group By** clause, the operation will be performed on all records, so you can read this expression as follows: Total (**Sum**) of `Sales` and total (**Sum**) of `Order_IDs` for the entire dataset.

We built our information pieces, now it's time to put them together.

Let's start by having all the calculated values together to get the participation percentage for `Sales` and Invoice quantity.

8. Drop an **Append Fields** tool onto the canvas.

9. Connect the **Summarize** tool that has the grouping per store in it to the `T` input, and the other **Summarize** tool to the `S` input.

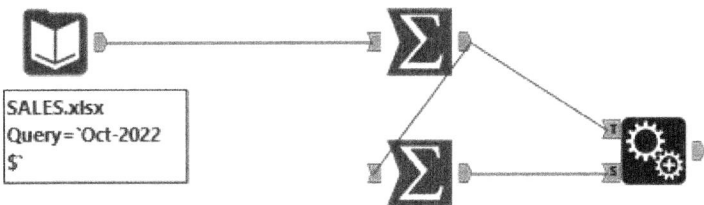

Figure 7.70: Workflow so far

Let's explore the results so far:

Store Number	Store_Sales	Quantity_Order_ID	Total_Sales	Total_Order_ID
100	1333007.012946	941	8771917.373566	6977
101	1172640.848829	831	8771917.373566	6977
102	259194.381766	252	8771917.373566	6977
103	869798.289414	667	8771917.373566	6977
104	914346.838829	793	8771917.373566	6977
105	1204797.746477	957	8771917.373566	6977
106	941605.199414	811	8771917.373566	6977
107	801053.435297	709	8771917.373566	6977
108	623350.093531	519	8771917.373566	6977

Figure 7.71: Results so far

1. Drop a **Formula** tool and connect it to the **Append Fields** output.

2. In the **Formula** tool, create a new column called `%_Of_Sales`, select its type as **Double**, and enter this as the expression:

```
[Store_Sales]/[Total_Sales]
```

Important note

I see a lot of people rounding percentage calculations to a desired number of decimals, for example, using this expression:

```
Round([Store_Sales]/[Total_Sales],0.01)
```

I recommend doing it only when we are going to present the final numbers (and only for presentation purposes). This is because Alteryx works with very high precision on the `Double` type and we might be losing accuracy by rounding them. See the *There's more* section to see what I mean and try it yourself.

3. Click on the blue background plus (+) icon at the bottom left to create a new formula within the same tool.

4. Select **Add Column**, name it `%_Of_Invoices`, and use this expression:

   ```
   [Quantity_Order_ID]/[Total_Order_ID]
   ```

Formula (39) - Configuration		⋮ 📌
Output Column		**Data Preview**
∨ %_Of_Sales	❌	0.151963015174167 🗑
fx [Store_Sales]/[Total_Sales]		
Data type: Double ▼ Size: 8		
≡ ∨ %_Of_Invoices	❌	0.134871721370216 🗑
fx [Quantity_Order_ID]/[Total_Order_ID]		
Data type: Double ▼ Size: 8		

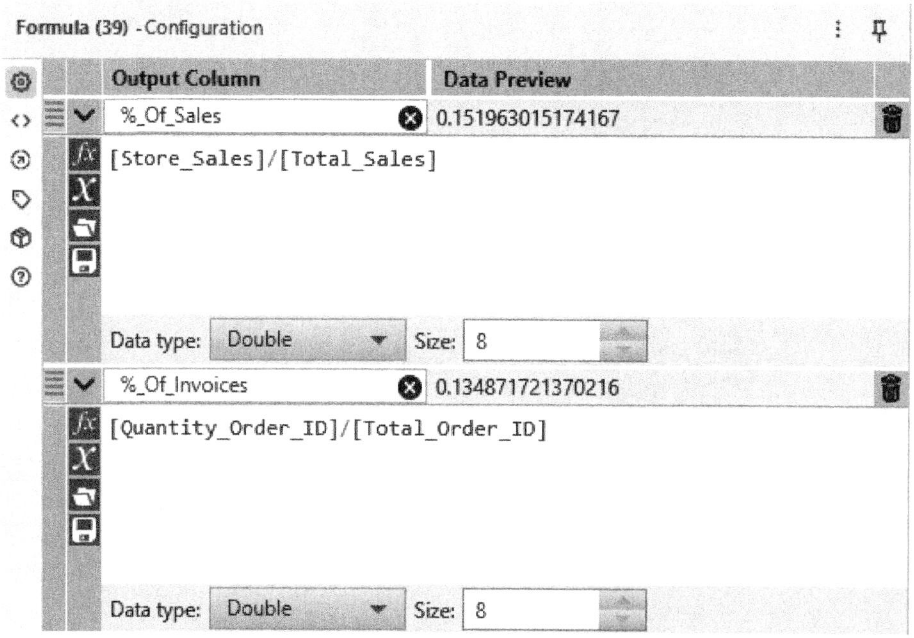

Figure 7.72: Formula tool configuration

Run the workflow and you'll see that, for each `Store Number`, we already have the percentage of sales and the percentage of issued invoices.

Store Number	Store_Sales	Quantity_Order_ID	Total_Sales	Total_Order_ID	%_Of_Sales	%_Of_Invoices
100	1333007.012946	941	8771917.373566	6977	0.151963	0.134872
101	1172640.848829	831	8771917.373566	6977	0.133681	0.119106
102	259194.381766	252	8771917.373566	6977	0.029548	0.036119
103	869798.289414	667	8771917.373566	6977	0.099157	0.0956
104	914346.838829	793	8771917.373566	6977	0.104236	0.113659
105	1204797.746477	957	8771917.373566	6977	0.137347	0.137165
106	941605.199414	811	8771917.373566	6977	0.107343	0.116239
107	801053.435297	709	8771917.373566	6977	0.09132	0.10162
108	623350.093531	519	8771917.373566	6977	0.071062	0.074387

Figure 7.73: Results including percentages

As a final step (this is optional but very useful in case we need this dataset as a data source for a visualization or reporting tool), we are going to append the percentage values to our original data source (SALES.XLSX).

5. Drop a **Join** tool and connect the **Formula** tool output anchor to its R input and the **Input Data** tool output anchor to its L input.

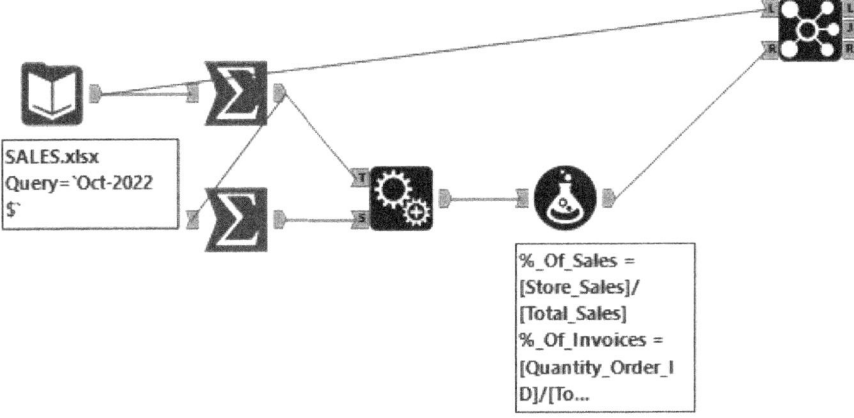

Figure 7.74: Workflow so far

6. Click on the **Join** tool to access its configuration panel.

7. Make sure **Join by Specific Fields** is selected.

8. Select **Store Number** from the **Left** field to join on, and the **Right** dropdown should auto-populate with **Store Number** (if it doesn't, make sure you didn't rename it somewhere before this step).

9. Deselect **Right Store Number** in the output field list (the one that was renamed to `Right_Store Number`). I decided to keep the other aggregations but feel free to keep only the ones you need.

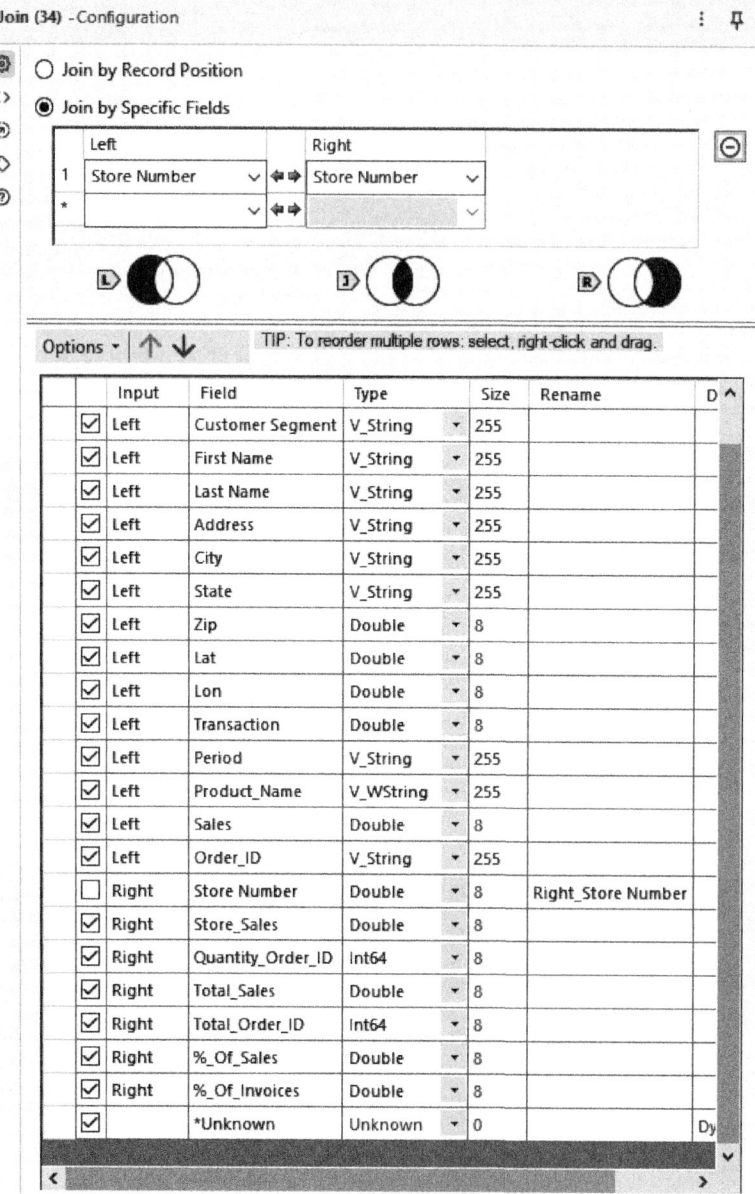

Figure 7.75: Join tool configuration

Run the workflow, and now the original dataset has all the fields and calculations correctly added.

CustomerID	Store Number	Customer Segment	First Name	Last Name	Address	City	State	Zip	Lat	Lon	Transaction
972	100	Corporate	LLSA	SIEDERS	850 NEWPO...	DENVER	CO	80220	39.729902	-104.909182	2531
972	100	Corporate	LLSA	SIEDERS	850 NEWPO...	DENVER	CO	80220	39.729902	-104.909182	2532
978	100	Corporate	KENDRA	RUSSELL	2240 CLAY ST	DENVER	CO	80211	39.750779	-105.020334	2541
997	100	Small Business	ILA	CRAMER	2984 E AMH...	DENVER	CO	80210	39.664561	-104.952418	2575
1003	101	Home Office	DANELL	VALDEZ	2925 W COL...	DENVER	CO	80219	39.668677	-105.024205	2583
1023	101	Small Business	DARCY	SOUZA	7867 S JERS...	ENGLEW...	CO	80112	39.573542	-104.920705	2633
1023	101	Small Business	DARCY	SOUZA	7867 S JERS...	ENGLEW...	CO	80112	39.573542	-104.920705	2634
1023	101	Small Business	DARCY	SOUZA	7867 S JERS...	ENGLEW...	CO	80112	39.573542	-104.920705	2635
1023	101	Small Business	DARCY	SOUZA	7867 S JERS...	ENGLEW...	CO	80112	39.573542	-104.920705	2636

Period	Product_Name	Sales	Order_ID	Store_Sales	Quantity_Order_ID	Total_Sales	Total_Order_ID	%_Of_Sales	%_Of_Invoices
Oct-2022	Canon BP1200DH 12-...	898	87267	1333007.012946	941	8771917.373566	6977	0.151963	0.134872
Oct-2022	#10 Self-Seal White En...	241.42	87268	1333007.012946	941	8771917.373566	6977	0.151963	0.134872
Oct-2022	Coloredge Poster Frame	165.04	87269	1333007.012946	941	8771917.373566	6977	0.151963	0.134872
Oct-2022	Fellowes Command Ce...	63.66	89431	1333007.012946	941	8771917.373566	6977	0.151963	0.134872
Oct-2022	Canon S750 Color Inkj...	1404.09	88435	1172640.848829	831	8771917.373566	6977	0.133681	0.119106
Oct-2022	Ibico Recycled Linen-St...	640.71	88633	1172640.848829	831	8771917.373566	6977	0.133681	0.119106
Oct-2022	Vinyl Sectional Post Bi...	659.6	88633	1172640.848829	831	8771917.373566	6977	0.133681	0.119106
Oct-2022	Wausau Papers Astrob...	30.63	88637	1172640.848829	831	8771917.373566	6977	0.133681	0.119106
Oct-2022	Staples Pen Style Liqui...	55.95	88638	1172640.848829	831	8771917.373566	6977	0.133681	0.119106

Figure 7.76: Final results

How it works...

The **Append Fields** tool allows us to add to each record of a dataset, all the records from another. This is a very powerful feature, but we need to keep an eye on our data because we can generate a Cartesian product between both datasets, resulting in the number of records from the first dataset multiplied by the number of records from the second.

For example, if we have 10 records in our first dataset and 10 records in our second dataset, we will generate a 100-record output:

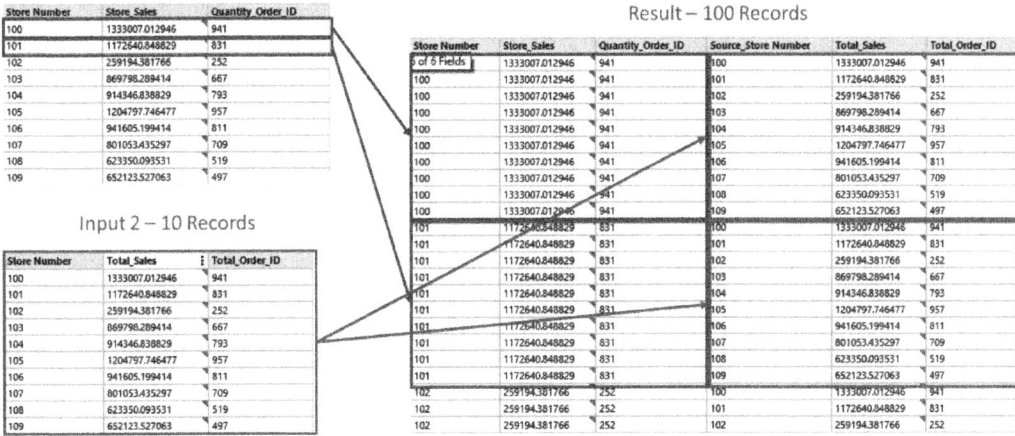

Figure 7.77: Representation of the Cartesian product results

There's more...

We mentioned earlier that it's not recommended to round the `Double` type values resulting from the percentage calculation we did; I'll show you why now.

Let's start with the workflow we already have:

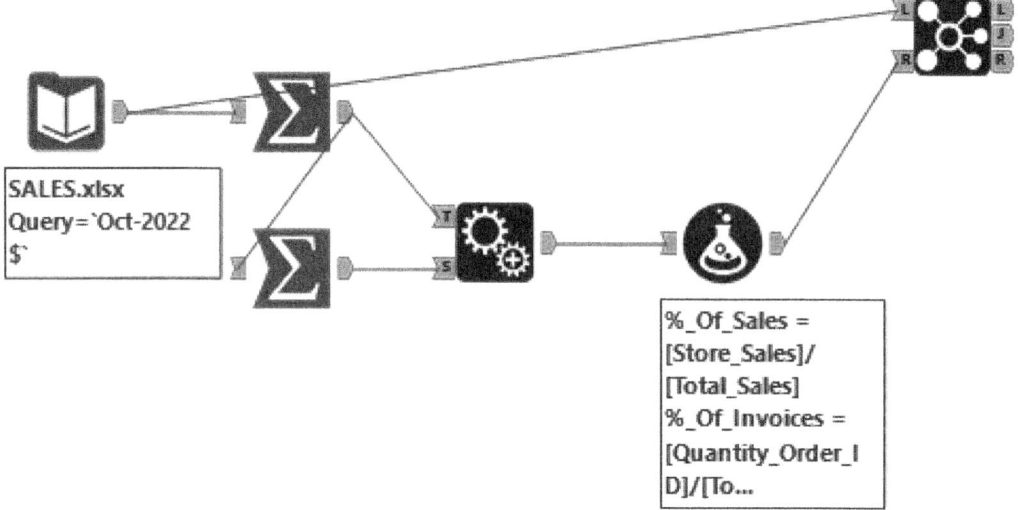

Figure 7.78: Workflow we built

1. Select the **Formula** tool, copy and paste it on the canvas, and connect the **Append Fields** output anchor to its input anchor.

2. Click on the **Formula** tool to access its configuration.

3. Change the expression for `%_Of_Sales` to `Round([Store_Sales]/[Total_Sales],0.001)`, to get the percentage calculation with a precision of three decimals.

4. Change the expression for `%_Of_Invoices` to `Round([Quantity_Order_ID]/[Total_Order_ID],0.01)` to get the value with two decimal positions.

5. Drop a **Summarize** tool and connect it to the newly added **Formula** tool.

6. Select `%_Of_Sales` and *Ctrl + click* on `%_Of_Invoices` so you get both selected.

7. Click on **Add** and select **Sum** from the menu.

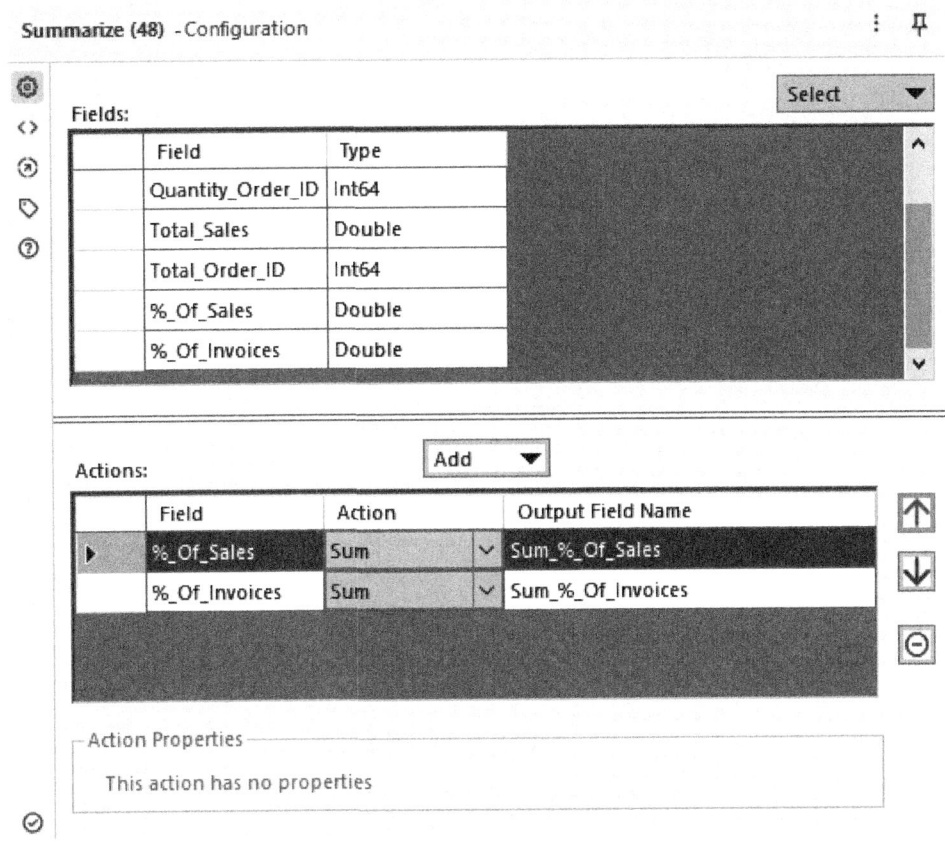

Figure 7.79: Summarizing the rounded results

Run the workflow and see the results.

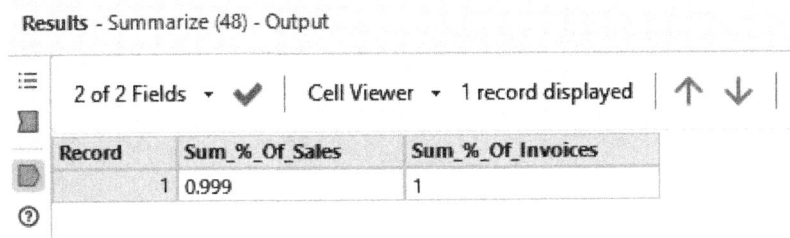

Figure 7.80: Results don't add up to 1

Due to the precision change caused by rounding the double type values, the total sum of `%_Of_Sales` is below 1 (or 100%). It's around the fifth decimal position, where our dataset doesn't show any loss (and this is for the current dataset – different ones might have different levels of decimals where they lose precision).

8

Aggregating Data

Taking granular datasets and having to aggregate data within them is a very common, recurring, and sometimes exhausting task. No matter whether we need to get the total sales per item over a given period or the number of flights between cities, it all involves aggregating data. But sometimes, it is not just aggregating data but also having to re-shape it.

In this chapter, we'll be going through some steps and recipes to accomplish these steps, in the best way possible. The recipes we will be covering are the following:

- Using **Cross Tab** to summarize values
- Preparing data for visualizations
- Grouping and summarizing your data
- Appending fields to data sources

Technical requirements

For this chapter, it is recommended, but not mandatory, to have a visualization tool such as Tableau or Power BI at hand. If you can't get them, you can use the **Interactive Visualization** tool from the **Reporting** tool category in Alteryx.

Using Cross Tab to summarize values

Let's face it, a big part of our analytics journey consists of summarizing data in one way or another, from aggregating detailed/transactional data into higher levels to getting percentages, distributions, and more.

Alteryx gives us a lot of ways to get our jobs done with some specific tools, and even with not-so-specific ones.

In this recipe, we'll be using the **Cross Tab** tool to create a series of aggregations on our data, just in one simple pass.

Getting ready

We have a test set for this recipe that you can download here: `https://github.com/PacktPublishing/Alteryx-Designer-Cookbook/tree/main/ch8/Recipe1`

This set contains a file received from a bank with credit card statements (this is part of a broader analytic model, but we'll be focusing on the aggregations done at a certain point). Since they are corporate cards, they are assigned to groups for easier administration:

STATEMENT#	GROUP	CC#	DATE	REFERENCE#	AMOUNT
638022486359540594	2	************6063	2022-10-24	229801083087	2.59
638022486359540594	2	************1392	2022-10-23	229620036557	415.81
638022486359540594	2	************1535	2022-10-23	229618087248	15.6
638022486359540594	2	************1535	2022-10-24	229718495944	26.75
638022486359540594	2	************0545	2022-10-23	229617478718	10.16
638022486359540594	2	************0545	2022-10-24	229701264097	21.35
638022486012678914	3	************9542	2022-10-23	229614018475	183.13
638022486012678914	3	************9542	2022-10-23	229614018476	30.17
638022486012678914	3	************9542	2022-10-23	229614022853	7.99

Figure 8.1: Credit card statements data preview

We need to get the total amount spent, the average, the number of charges, the percent of amount spent per group, and per date, adding totals for rows and columns. That's a lot of calculations with only one tool.

How to do it...

To accomplish what we need, just follow these simple steps:

1. Drop an **Input Data** tool onto the canvas and point it to `..\DATA\CCStatements.yxdb`.
2. Add a **Cross Tab** tool and configure it as follows:

    - From **Group data by these values**, select GROUP
    - From the **Change Column Headers** dropdown, select DATE
    - From the **Values for New Columns** dropdown, select AMOUNT
    - From the **Method for Aggregating Values** field, select the following:

      - Sum
      - Average
      - Count (Without Nulls)
      - Percent Row

- Percent Column
- Total Column
- Total Row

These selections can be seen in the following screenshot:

Figure 8.2: Cross Tab tool configuratio3

1. Run the workflow and you'll see all the calculations are there in the output:

GROUP	Sum_2022_10_18	Avg_2022_10_18	XRow_2022_10_18	XCol_2022_10_18	Count_2022_10_18	Sum_2022_10_19	Avg_2022_10_19	XRow_2022_10_19	XCol_2022_10_19	Count_2022_10_19
2	[Null]	[Null]	[Null]	[Null]	[Null]	450.9	37.575	3.462993	6.27039	12
3	[Null]	[Null]	[Null]	[Null]	[Null]	1685.46	48.156	7.07709	23.43866	35
4	[Null]	[Null]	[Null]	[Null]	[Null]	2567.25	73.35	12.26038	35.701174	35
5	[Null]	[Null]	[Null]	[Null]	[Null]	657.87	32.8935	4.87706	9.148595	20
6	69.9	69.9	0.278535	100	1	1829.46	67.757778	7.289972	25.44118	27
[Null]	69.9	69.9	0.07254	100	1	7190.94	55.743721	7.462555	100	129

Figure 8.3: Resulting data

How it works...

As we can see in the **Results** pane, the power of the **Cross Tab** tool is enormous. It pivots the data and offers several aggregation methods, including Sum, Average, Count (Without Nulls), Count (With Nulls), Percent Row, Percent Columns, First, Last, Total Row, and Total Column.

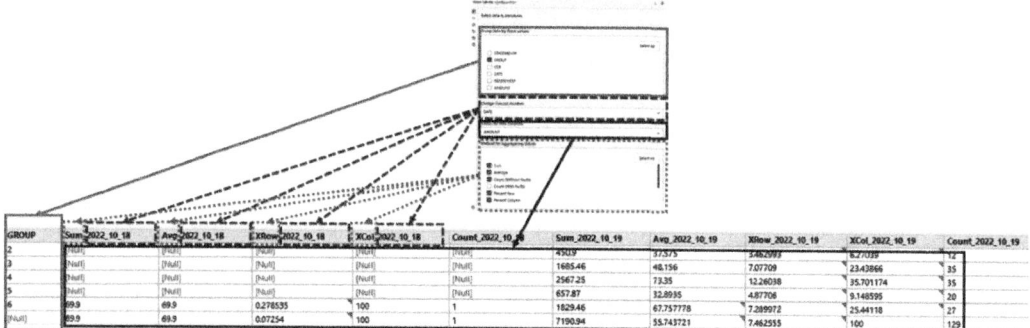

Figure 8.4: How the Cross Tab tool works

However, since we selected almost all of the possible aggregations within the tool, its output looks a bit messy.

Because we selected GROUP as the field to group by, each row represents the values for that specific group, plus an additional row that contains the Total Column values.

For each additional field, we get the following naming convention:

```
[AGG]_[Value_Of_Selected_Column_Headers]
```

We can break this down as follows:

- AGG (Aggregation abbreviation): Depending on the **Method for Aggregating Values** value you select, you get Sum for Sum, Avg for Average, XRow for Percent Row, XCol for Percent Column, Count for Count (Without Nulls), CountWithNulls for Count (With Nulls), First, and Last

- Value_Of_Selected_Column_Headers: For each value of the field you selected in **Change Column Header**, you'll get one field of each aggregation for its value

The data cells represent the result of performing the corresponding aggregation per selected group and header. Take the following example:

`Sum_2022_10_18` refers to the sum per GROUP for `Oct, 18th. 2022`

Preparing data for visualizations

Most visualization tools require that we provide a denormalized tabular data source to work properly and others require you to build a model. In *Chapter 4, Recipe 1, Pivoting and unpivoting your data*, we used the **Transpose** and **Cross Tab** tools to facilitate a series of operations that allowed us to prepare a tabular format to use in a visualization.

In this recipe, we'll be preparing a dataset to perfectly work with visualization tools.

Our file comes from a previous preparation process, and what we have so far is the following:

Product	Category	Suggested Age Range	Average Monthly Sales	January	February	March	April	May	June	July	August	September	October	November	December
Graphing Calculators	General	13+	84020.17	191017	434	70654	166571	99066	64423	72846	52744	16150	98130	42312	133095
Office Supplies	General	All ages	83319.17	156628	82183	125043	11205	130096	31214	199032	121453	61048	16063	18098	46061
Encyclopedias	Educational	All ages	79280.75	6299	119153	161717	145195	22305	38385	9183	157398	169816	30902	74336	17180
Building Blocks	Fun and Games	6-Mar	97381.33	8313	184270	186021	190255	8211	134736	154287	4735	71620	113519	20765	91844
Books about Dinosaurs	Fun and Games	All ages	106179.58	193667	76441	163244	116158	42346	166919	153584	72374	155810	44161	55709	33694
Viggo Mortenson DVDs	Fun and Games	13+	117805.5	181291	178860	144830	35341	136331	199431	42309	42458	184727	80648	54734	132706
Clothing	General	All ages	121212.5	6988	71830	69881	137635	168495	118806	199716	153901	145946	20584	190893	169075
Frisbee and Frisbee Accessories	Fun and Games	7+	92629.92	4940	105607	53949	72655	140850	68332	154956	158538	116732	153754	48668	34578
Legumes	General	All ages	116122.75	73467	154459	92995	68466	159429	130945	32238	140673	153088	73637	176341	137683
Microscopes	Educational	7+	602.83	206	324	825	633	487	168	235	154	1432	861	530	1279

Figure 8.5: Data input preview

This output format (mostly putting data partitions in columns) is a commonly used process to generate outputs, let's say for Excel.

But we are going to elevate this report a little bit, using a visualization tool, so we need to get it into a format that works well with these tools.

Getting ready

For this recipe, we prepared a test set that you can download from here: `https://github.com/PacktPublishing/Alteryx-Designer-Cookbook/tree/main/ch8/Recipe2`

If we try to use this dataset as is, we'll find that building a simple visualization on sales per month per product will take a lot of time (because we'll need to add one layer per month), as well as creating some problems with aggregating data, such as getting the total sales.

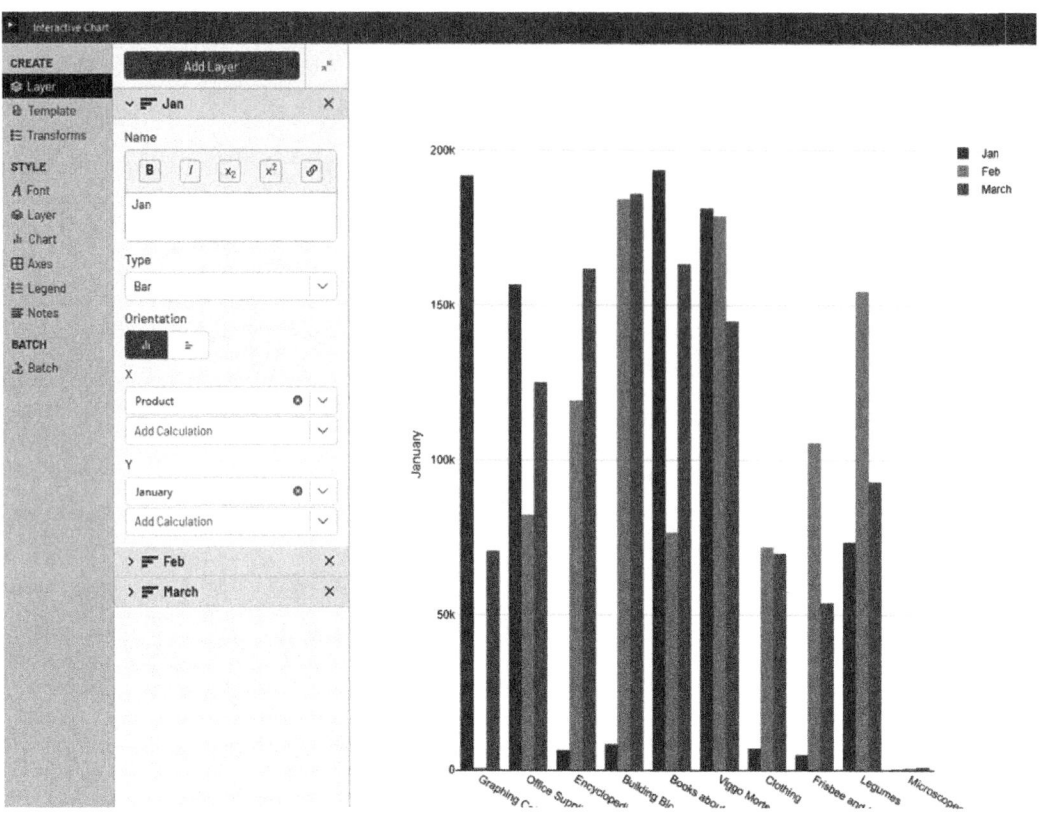

Figure 8.6: Visualization preview (one layer per column)

If you have no access to a visualization tool (such as Tableau or Power BI), don't worry; you can use Alteryx's **Interactive Visualization** tool (from the **Reporting** category) or download a trial version of the tool you want.

First, we need to understand what the data represents. If we look at our dataset (*Figure 8.6*), we can see that we have MONTHLY Sales and Average Monthly Sales over a year by Product, Category, and Suggested Age Range.

To build useful visualizations (and avoid further complications later), we need to arrange the data in a way that all dimensions and measures are correct.

With Alteryx, this is a simple step. Let's dive in.

How to do it...

As stated earlier, our dataset looks like the result of a more complex model, but we'll be focusing on obtaining a very good dataset for visualizations, so we'll be adding these extra steps to the process:

1. Drop an **Input Data** tool on your canvas and point it to `..\DATA\Viz.yxdb`.

2. Add a **Transpose** tool to the canvas. Select `Product`, `Category`, `Suggested Age Range`, and `Average Monthly Sales` as the key columns.

3. Make sure that all fields corresponding to the months are selected in the **Data Columns** section:

Figure 8.7: Transpose tool configuration

If you run the workflow, you'll see that at this point we'll have all month names under a **Name** field and the value for each month in the **Value** field, so we need to properly name these fields.

4.   Drop a **Select** tool, and rename the **Name** field to Month and **Value** to Sales:

	Field	Type	Size	Rename	Description
☑	Product	V_String ▾	31		
☑	Category	String ▾	13		
☑	Suggested Age Range	String ▾	8		
☑	Average Monthly Sales	Double ▾	8		
☑	Name	String ▾	9	Month	
☑	Value	Int32 ▾	4	Sales	
☑	*Unknown	Unknown ▾	0		Dynamic or

Select (4) - Configuration

⚙ Options ▾ | ↑ ↓   TIP: To reorder multiple rows: select, right-click and drag.

Figure 8.8: Select tool configuration

Our workflow should look like this by now:

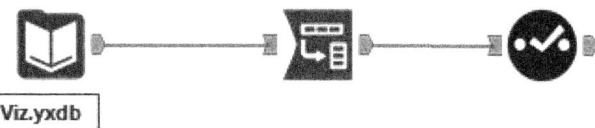

Viz.yxdb

Figure 8.9: Workflow so far

If you run the workflow now, you'll notice that we have all the data pivoted to reference a particular Sales amount per each of our dimensions.

Product	Category	Suggested Age Range	Average Monthly Sales	Month	Sales
Graphing Calculators	General	13+	84020.17	January	191817
Graphing Calculators	General	13+	84020.17	February	434
Graphing Calculators	General	13+	84020.17	March	70654
Graphing Calculators	General	13+	84020.17	April	166571
Graphing Calculators	General	13+	84020.17	May	99066
Graphing Calculators	General	13+	84020.17	June	64423
Graphing Calculators	General	13+	84020.17	July	72846
Graphing Calculators	General	13+	84020.17	August	52744
Graphing Calculators	General	13+	84020.17	September	16150
Graphing Calculators	General	13+	84020.17	October	98130

Figure 8.10: Results that'll allow us to build effective visualizations

Now, getting a visualization from this dataset will be easier since our months are in a single field. Any visualization program will allow us to aggregate its content.

How it works...

Having to present data in a visualization requires extra steps and sometimes, some re-shaping is involved as we saw in this recipe.

Visualizations present summarized data by dimensions (in this recipe, we have Sales by Product, Category, and Month). So, if we need to build a visualization, we can offer the user the ability to visualize annual sales by Category, and that requires that our dataset is properly shaped.

Let's try to build a visualization with both datasets to see the differences:

1. Drop a new **Interactive Chart** tool from the **Reporting** category and connect it to the **Input Data** tool output anchor.

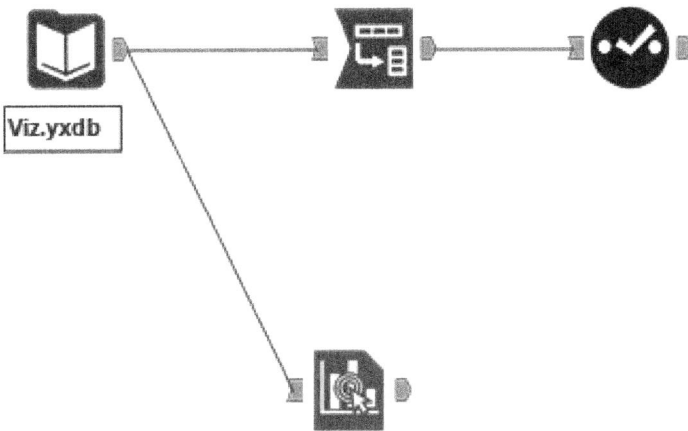

Figure 8.11: Connecting the Interactive Chart tool

2. Click on the **Configure Chart** button (if it's disabled, you may need to run your workflow, so the tool can get the metadata it needs).

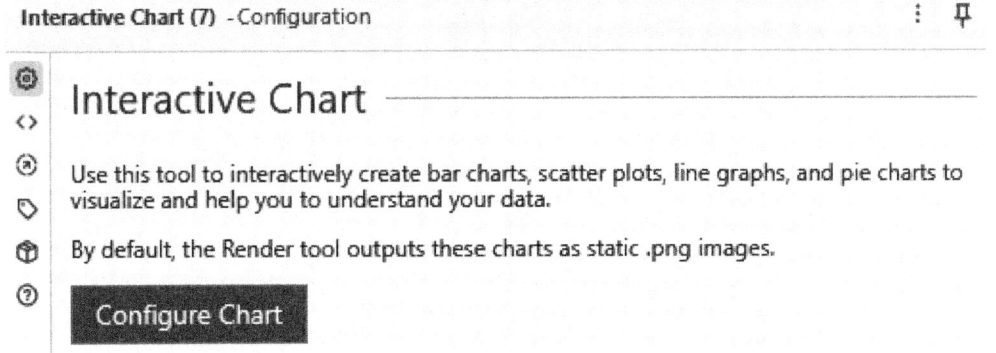

Figure 8.12: Interactive Chart configuration start point

Once you click it, a new window will pop up:

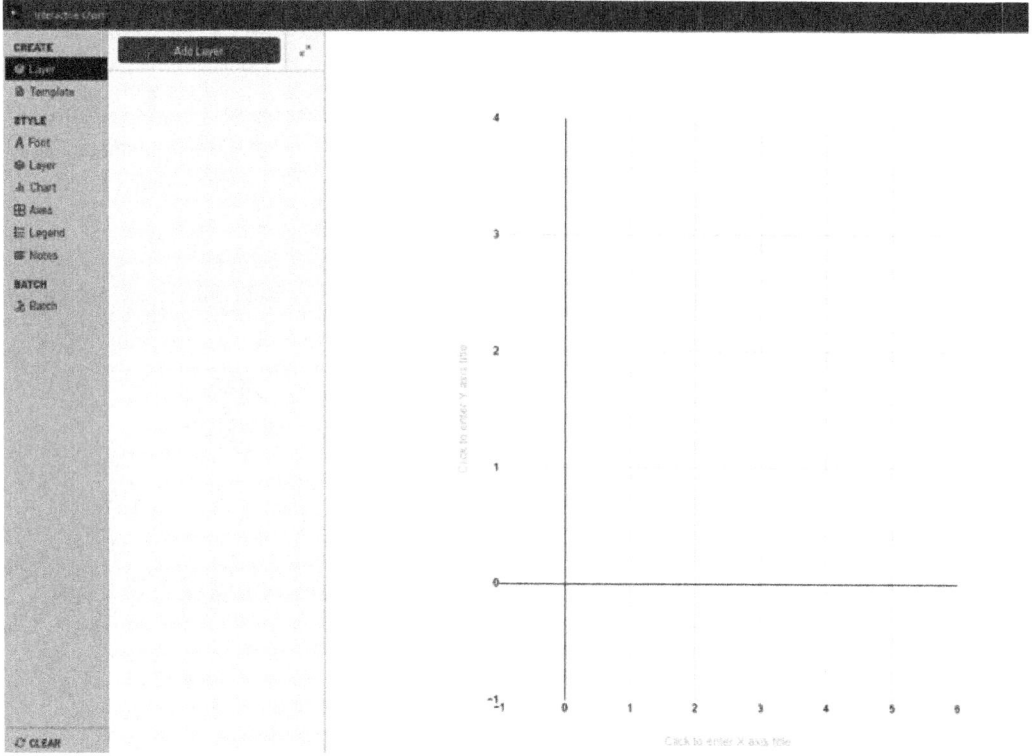

Figure 8.13: Interactive Chart main configuration window

3. Click on **Add Layer** to access the layer configuration.

4. In the **Name** section, enter Sales.

5. Select **Bar** from the **Type** drop-down menu.

6. Select **Product** as the **X** axis value.

7. Select **January** for the **Y** axis value.

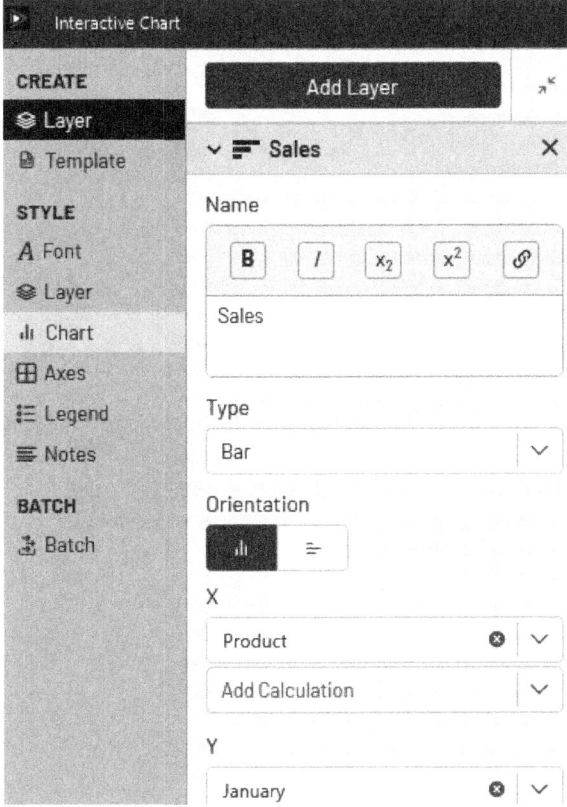

Figure 8.14: Adding a layer

As you can see, the dataset shape doesn't allow us to create a very useful visualization, forcing us to add a new layer per month, and forbidding us to, for example, represent the total sales for all months together.

8. Now, drop a new **Interactive Chart** tool onto the canvas, and this time, connect it to the existing **Select** tool output anchor, so your workflow looks like this:

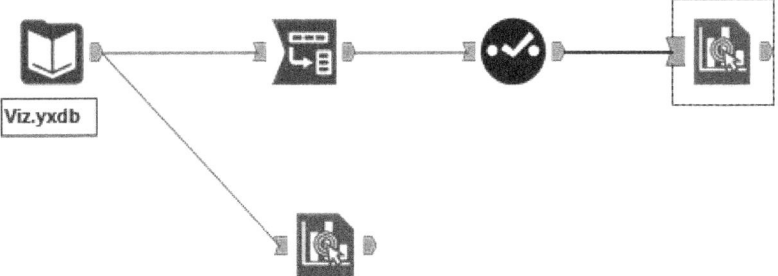

Figure 8.15: Workflow with both chart tools

9. Again, click on the **Configure Chart** button (run the workflow if it's disabled).

    You'll see the blank pop-up window again.

10. Click on the **Add Layer** button.

11. Use Sales for the **Name** field.

12. Select Bar for the **Type** field.

13. Select Product for the **X** axis field.

14. Select Sales for the **Y** axis field.

15. Select Sum for the aggregation (if you don't select it, you'll notice how Alteryx aggregates the values, separating them by a very thin line).

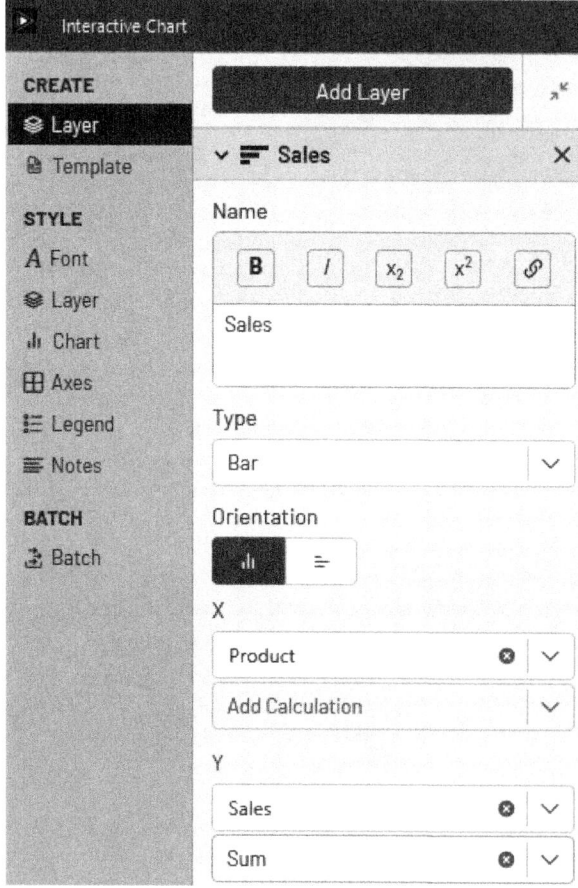

Figure 8.16: Configure the second chart

At this point, we have the total sales for each product.

This is not intended to teach you how to use the **Interactive Chart** tool, just to showcase why it is important to shape the datasets properly. If you want to dive deep into the **Interactive Chart** tool, Alteryx Help and Alteryx Community are great places to start. Also, you can build great dashboards using Tableau or Power BI if you shape your datasets correctly.

See also

As mentioned before, there are several useful resources within Alteryx Help here: `https://help.alteryx.com/20221/designer/interactive-chart-tool`

There are also useful resources in the **Interactive Lessons** section on Alteryx Community: `https://community.alteryx.com/t5/Interactive-Lessons/Creating-Interactive-Charts/ta-p/553701`

Grouping and summarizing your data

In this recipe, we'll be creating a **design pattern**, or a combination of tools, that will allow us to solve a very common format problem found in data preparation.

We have a dataset of registered flight delays (in minutes). The data has two records per registered flight. The first row is the delay registered at departure, and the second is the delay registered at arrival.

FLIGHT#	Carrier	OriginAirportID	Delay	city	state	name	DestAirportID
AIR-111	HA	12173	0	Honolulu	HI	Honolulu International	[Null]
AIR-111	HA	[Null]	-9	Portland	OR	Portland International	14057
AIR-222	HA	12173	10	Honolulu	HI	Honolulu International	[Null]
AIR-222	HA	[Null]	14	Portland	OR	Portland International	14057

Figure 8.17: Dataset preview

There are many ways of solving this situation (sampling alternating rows, filtering, and more), but we are going to do the easiest one, based on the **Multi-Row Formula** tool, a very powerful tool that Alteryx provides.

Getting ready

We prepared this test set for you to follow along with the recipe: `https://github.com/PacktPublishing/Alteryx-Designer-Cookbook/tree/main/ch8/Recipe3`

As you can see in the data preview, we again used a dataset that is the result of previous preparation tasks, and we face the challenge of extracting the total delay per flight, or the total delay registered between airports.

How to do it...

Even when the design pattern is simple, you'll see how powerful it can be, by following these steps:

1. Drop an **Input Data** tool onto the canvas and point it to `..\DATA\FlightDelays.yxdb`.

2. Add a **Tile** tool and configure it as follows:

   - For **Tile Method**, select **Unique Value**

   - For **Unique Column**, select FLIGHT#

   - Make sure nothing is selected in the **Group by Columns** section:

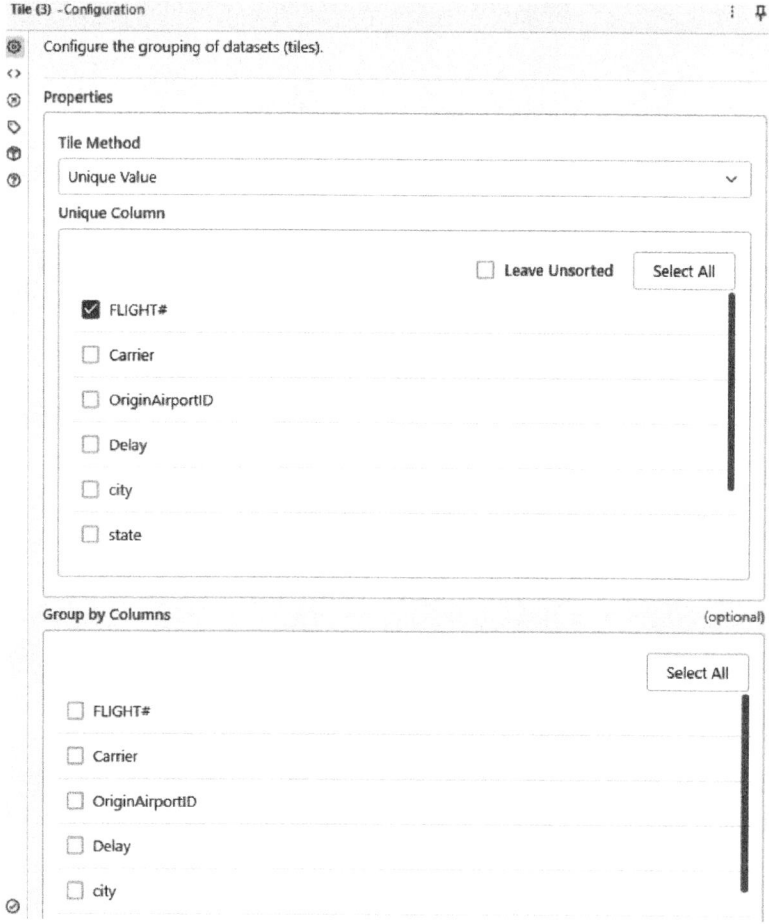

Figure 8.18: Tile tool configuration

Now we are going to identify the overall delay for the journey, taking the departure city and arrival city (which is in the next row).

3. Drop a **Multi-Row Formula** tool and do the following:

- Make sure **Create New Field** is selected

- Name the new field LEG_COMPLETE and select V_WString for **Type** and 100 for **Size**

- Select FLIGHT# in the **Group By** section

- Use this formula for the **Expression** section:

```
[city]+"-"+[Row+1:city]
```

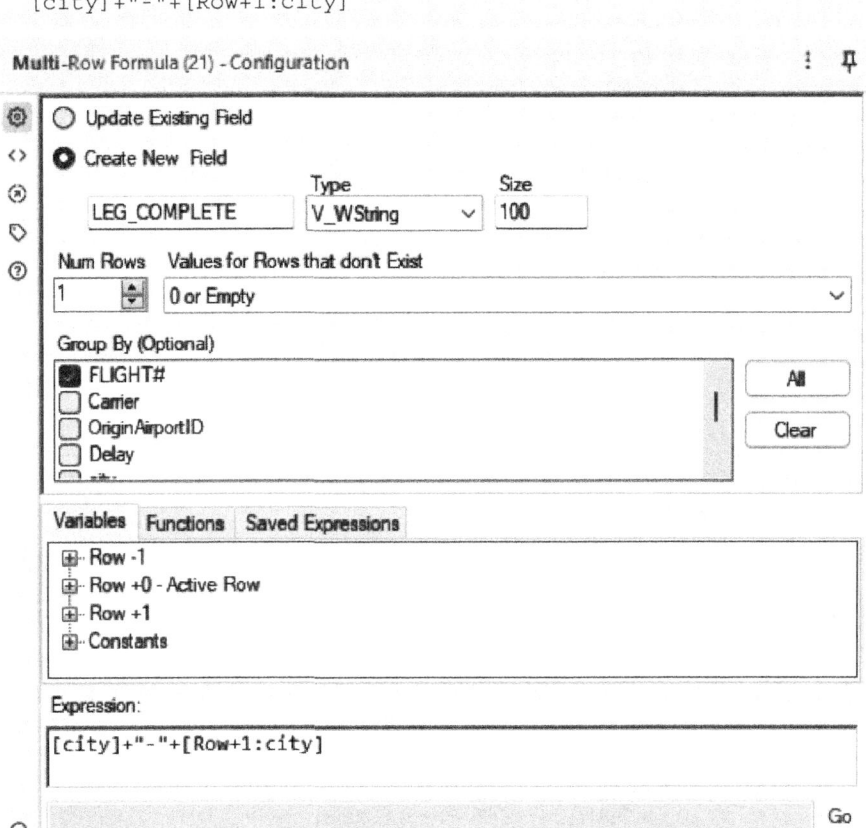

Figure 8.19: Multi-Row Formula tool configuration

4. Now, drop a **Cross Tab** tool onto the canvas and do the following:

- Make sure no fields are selected for the **Group data by these values** section

- Select LEG_COMPLETE from the **Change Column Headers** dropdown

- Select **Delay** for the **Values for New Columns** dropdown

- Select **Sum** for **Method for Aggregating Values**

Figure 8.20: Cross Tab tool configuration

5. Run the workflow and you'll have the total delay registered for each leg (departure – arrival city). As we can see, for example, the flight between Honolulu and Kahului registers negative delays, meaning that those flights arrived earlier than stated, while Honolulu to Las Vegas registers 1,111 minutes of delay.

Honolulu_	Honolulu_Kahului	Honolulu_Las_Vegas	Honolulu_Los_Angeles	Honolulu_New_York	Honolulu_Oakland
19330	-10846	1111	4076	348	523

Figure 8.21: Results

Appending fields to data sources

Building custom catalogs or dictionaries is something that we are forced to do sometimes for several reasons. In this recipe, we'll be taking three lists or attributes – T-shirt brands, sizes, and colors – to create all possible combinations between them to build our dictionary.

Alteryx offers a very simple way to do this with minimal effort and great power through the **Append Fields** tool, which, for those who are tech-savvy, forces a cross-join operation between datasets. For those who are not, a cross-join operation (or Cartesian product) is the process where for each record in one dataset you add all of the records from another dataset.

We used this method in *Chapter 7, Recipe 4, Appending data calculations*, to add summarized values to a dataset. Now, we'll be using it to build our T-shirts catalog.

Getting ready

We prepared a test set for you to try this recipe. Download it here: `https://github.com/PacktPublishing/Alteryx-Designer-Cookbook/tree/main/ch8/Recipe4`.

We are going to use a simple Excel sheet to demonstrate the power of this technique, but feel free to use it with any data you may have.

The provided Excel file contains three worksheets. Each one contains all possible values for each BRAND, SIZE, and COLOR, and as stated earlier, we'll be getting the resulting combination of all of them.

BRANDS ⋮	SIZES	COLORS
Brand1	XS	Black
Brand2	S	White
Brand3	M	Red
Brand4	L	Green
Brand5	XL	Pink
Brand6	XXL	Yellow
Brand7		

Figure 8.22: The three simple data sources to combine

Even if this process appears simple to you, it is a very powerful and useful one that you'll find yourself using on numerous occasions.

How to do it...

We need to start getting our data in. To do that, we'll need three **Input Data** tools on our canvas:

1. Drop an **Input Data** tool onto the canvas, point it to `..\DATA\t-shirts.xlsx`, and select the Brands worksheet as the data source.

2. Now, copy and paste the **Input Data** tool, and click on the ellipsis in option 3 – **Table or Query** – to open the **Select Excel Input** window.

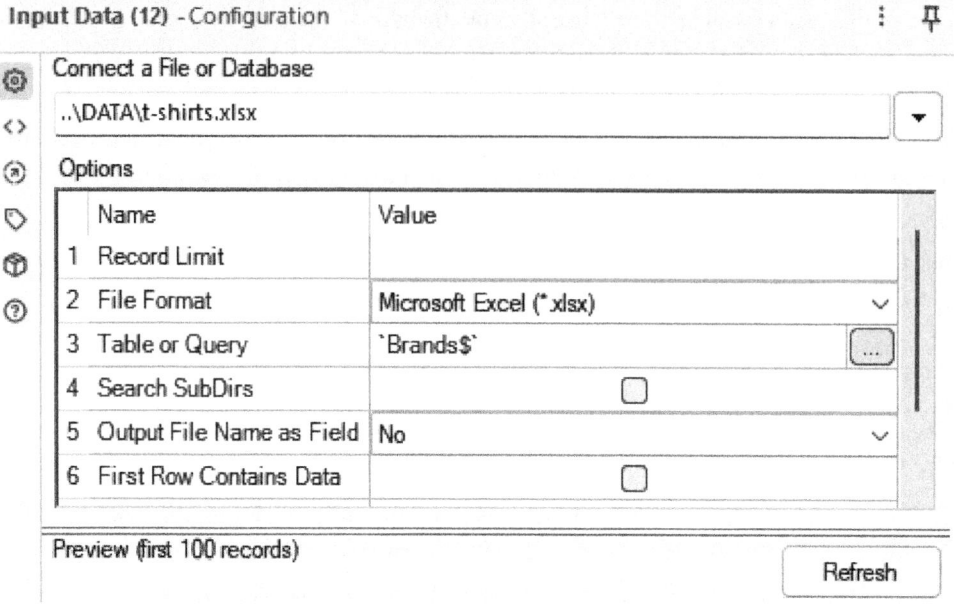

Figure 8.23: Table or Query selection in the Input Data tool configuration

3. Select the `Sizes` worksheet from the **Select a sheet** dropdown and hit **OK**.

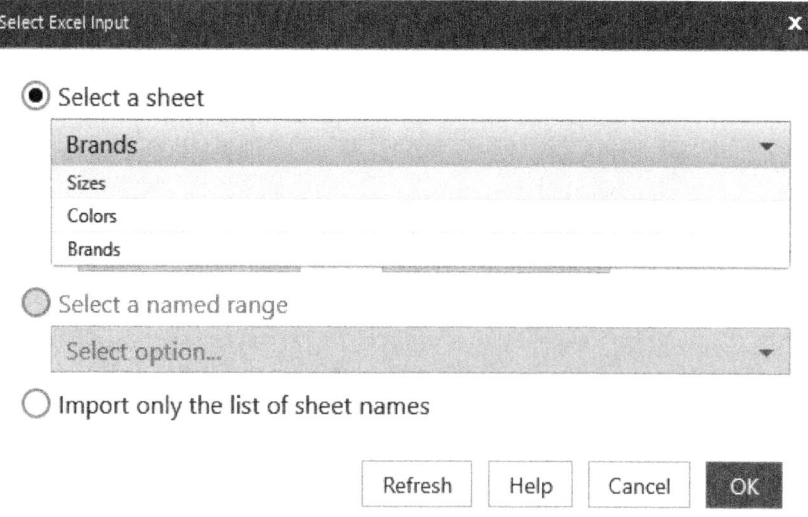

Figure 8.24: Select a sheet option

4. Paste again to get a third **Input Data** tool on the canvas.

5. For this last one, select the Colors worksheet as the source of data.

Your workflow should look like this so far:

Figure 8.25: Workflow so far

6. Drop an **Append Fields** tool and connect the first **Input Data** tool output anchor to the **T** input anchor of the **Append Fields** tool.

7. Connect the second **Input Data** tool output anchor to the **S** input of the **Append Fields** tool.

8. Copy and paste the **Append Fields** tool.

9. Connect the previous **Append Fields** tool output anchor to the **T** input anchor of the pasted **Append Fields** tool.

10. Finally, connect the remaining **Input Data** tool output anchor to the **S** input anchor on the second **Append Fields** tool.

The workflow should look like this:

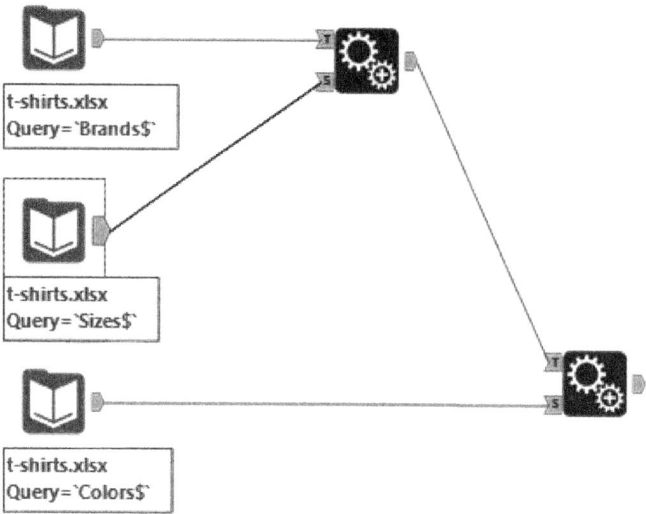

Figure 8.26: Finished workflow

Run the workflow and you'll see a resulting dataset, containing all the possible combinations between the three datasets.

BRANDS	SIZES	COLORS
Brand1	XS	Black
Brand1	XS	White
Brand1	XS	Red
Brand1	XS	Green
Brand1	XS	Pink
Brand1	XS	Yellow
Brand1	S	Black
Brand1	S	White
Brand1	S	Red
Brand1	S	Green
Brand1	S	Pink
Brand1	S	Yellow
Brand1	M	Black
Brand1	M	White
Brand1	M	Red
Brand1	M	Green
Brand1	M	Pink

Figure 8.27: Final results

How it works...

You can refer to the full explanation of how **Append Fields** works in *Chapter 7, Recipe 4, Appending fields to your data* from the same dataset.

What we did here was use the same capabilities to combine a series of data sources to create one source that contains all possible combinations between them.

There's more...

Even though we didn't need to configure anything in the **Append Fields** tool we used, there are several options in its configuration panel to be aware of.

The first section is exactly like the **Select** tool, where you can select to keep or remove fields from the data stream, change the data type or size, rename them, or add a description.

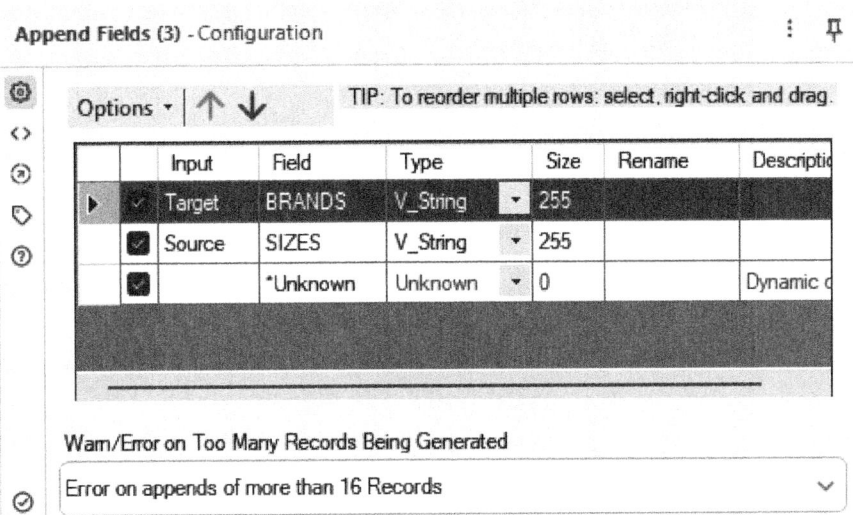

Figure 8.28: Append Fields configuration

Also, it's worth noticing that at the bottom there is the **Warn/Error on Too Many Records Being Generated** dropdown:

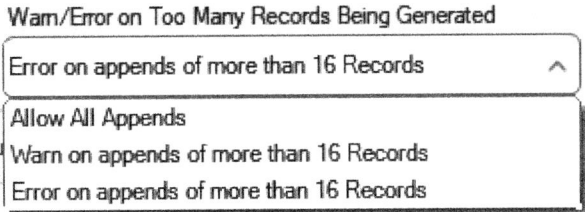

Figure 8.29: Fail-safe option in the Append Fields tool

Alteryx offers this mechanism to allow putting the computer in a machine-killing state due to the Cartesian product behavior. By default, it'll generate an error when more than 16 records are appended.

As you saw in this recipe, we started with three data sources:

- `Brands` = seven records
- `Sizes` = six records
- `Colors` = six records

The final result was a catalog of 252 records (7 * 6 * 6).

However, working with more complex data and multiple fields can cause a deadlock in your computer. To avoid this, I always recommend running your workflows with the default settings (**Error on appends of more than 16 records**), and if a deadlock happens, check your data.

Once you've checked your data, it's possible that changing the setting makes sense, or maybe you find that some previous cleanup/aggregation was needed.

9

Dynamic Operations

We saw the power of the Dynamic tools, or at least one of them, in *Chapter 1, Recipe 2 – Read a worksheet from multiple Excel files all at once – same schema different folders/subfolders*, in *Chapter 2, Recipe 5 – Access and determine which files to be processed from a file repository*, and in *Chapter 2, Recipe 1 – Cursor behavior*, but more efficiently when we used the **Dynamic Input** tool to read the contents of several inputs all at once and to create a more efficient cursor behavior over databases.

In this chapter, we'll explore several recipes using Dynamic tools to perform powerful dynamic operations over data.

These operations include the following:

- Renaming fields dynamically based on dictionaries, conditions, or even data in the same file
- Select fields based on their metadata
- Replace contents dynamically based on expressions/conditions
- Building complex formula expressions from within your data

Dynamically renaming fields

Dealing with field names is crucial in our data journey. From structure homologation to missing field names and everything in between, we need to know these techniques, and that's what we will tackle in this recipe.

At first, you may think of a **Select** tool to get this job done, but we will use a more dynamic process here.

Getting ready

We prepared a test set for you to follow along with this recipe. You can download it here: `https://github.com/PacktPublishing/Alteryx-Designer-Cookbook/tree/main/ch9/Recipe1`.

We'll be using the **Dynamic Rename** tool to fix some of the most common situations we'll find with headers, either due to lack of them, differences/errors in their naming, or to standardize structures between different data sources.

In our test set, we have several files we need to combine, starting with a list of customers by City (in CSV format without headers). Also, to help us get the correct header names, we grabbed the structure of last year's customer file (in Excel format) to dynamically name our fields. This customer data needs to be combined with transactional data coming from our **point of sale** (**PoS**) system (in CSV, too, without headers). Since we don't have the actual structure, we will use a custom dictionary to appropriately rename our fields.

How to do it...

We can get started with renaming the fields using the following steps:

1.   Drop an **Input Data** tool onto the canvas and point it to `..\DATA\Customers_by_City\ARVADA.csv`.

     You'll notice that, since the file doesn't have headers and Alteryx's default option for **First Row Contains Field Names** is checked when reading CSV files, you need to deselect it. Otherwise, your first record will become a header:

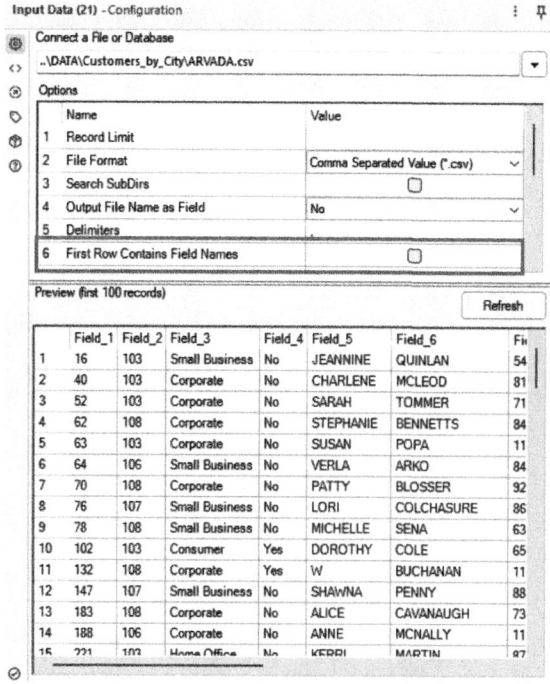

Figure 9.1: The Input Data tool configuration

2. Now, replace ARVADA in the file name with an asterisk (*). This will allow us to read all the CSV files from that directory at once:

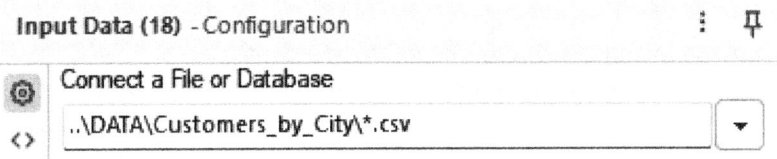

Figure 9.2: Replace the specific file with * to read all at once

3. Since we are reading multiple files at once, we do not have the chance to preview the input data, so run the workflow and see what we have so far:

Field_1	Field_2	Field_3	Field_4	Field_5	Field_6	Field_7	Field_8	Field_9	Field_10	Field_11	Field_12
16	103	Small Business	No	JEANNINE	QUINLAN	5400 SHERIDAN BLVD	ARVADA	CO	80002	39.7940857151194	-105.052900133329
40	103	Corporate	No	CHARLENE	MCLEOD	8192 W 81ST DR	ARVADA	CO	80005	39.8422976596147	-105.087932689214
52	103	Corporate	No	SARAH	TOMMER	7130 SIMMS ST	ARVADA	CO	80004	39.8250851862873	-105.12832044967
62	108	Corporate	No	STEPHANIE	BENNETTS	8463 CHASE ST	ARVADA	CO	80003	39.850665147918	-105.057174799326
63	103	Corporate	No	SUSAN	POPA	11921 W 76TH DR	ARVADA	CO	80005	39.8396684404781	-105.130708558465

Figure 9.3: Results after reading all files

The data is present, but unfortunately, headers are missing (Alteryx named them Field_1 through Field_N). We have to get them right, so we will use a previous customer's file as a source for those names.

4. Drop a new **Input Data** tool onto the canvas and point it to ..\DATA\CUSTOMERS_2021.xlsx and select the CUSTOMERS worksheet as the source for the data:

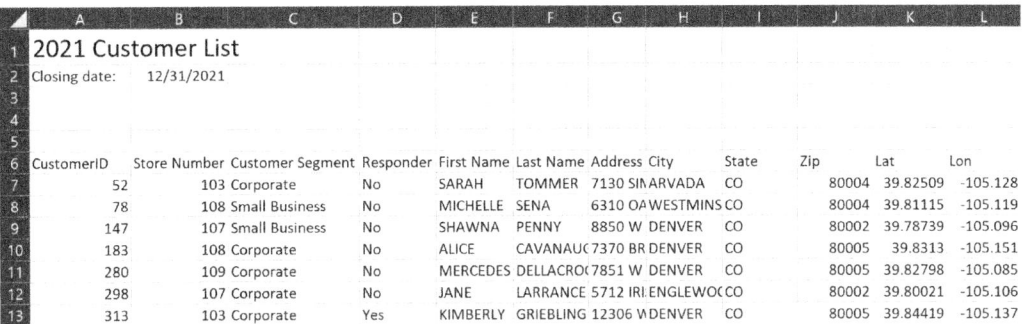

Figure 9.4: Customer list in Excel used to get the right headers

5. The Excel worksheet has a lot of pre-data headers we don't need, so we'll use a very useful combination of options from the **Input Data** tool: **Start Data Import on Line** (set the line where the field names are to 5) and **Record Limit** (set it to -1, which will only allow us to get the metadata from the actual data source):

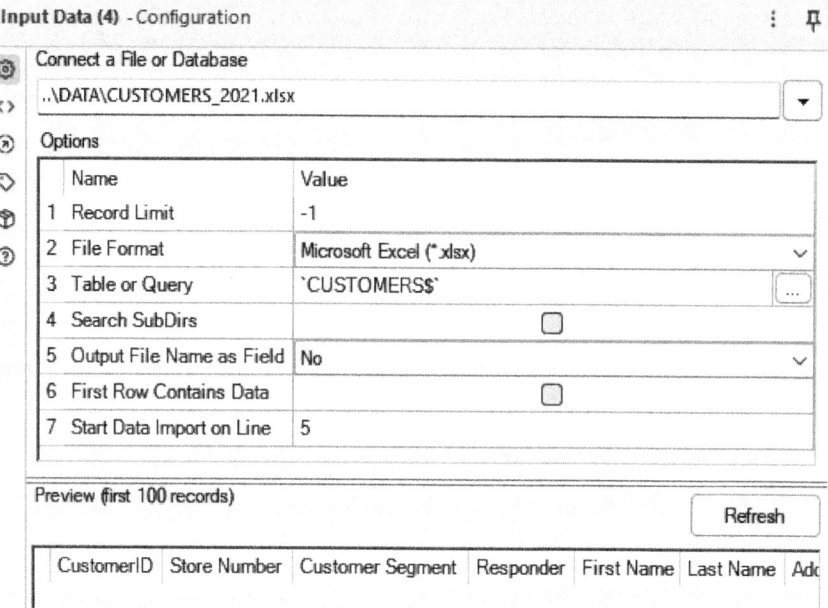

Figure 9.5: The Input Data tool configuration to extract only the metadata

6. Drop a **Dynamic Rename** tool (from the **Developer** category) and connect the **Input Data** tool that reads all the CSV files to the L input anchor and the other one to the R input anchor:

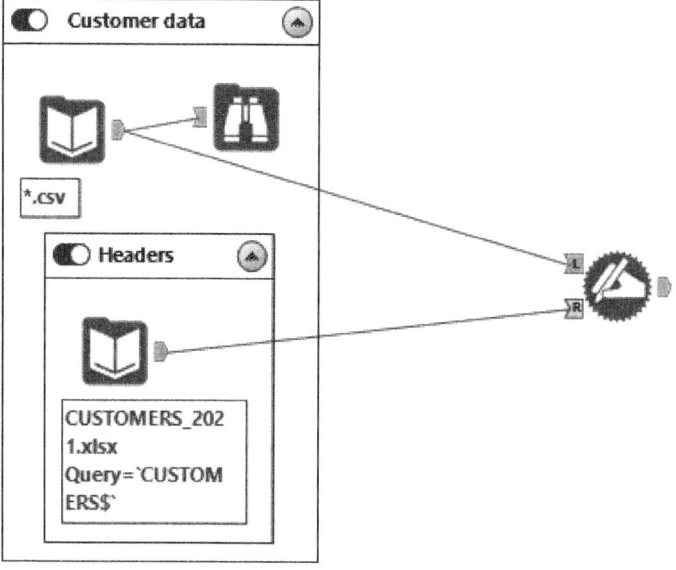

Figure 9.6: Workflow after adding the Dynamic Rename tool

7. Select **Take Field Names from Right Input Metadata** as the **Rename Mode**:

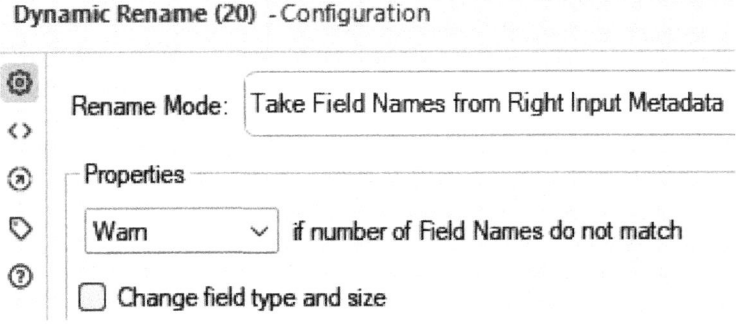

Figure 9.7: The Dynamic Rename tool configuration

If you run the workflow, you'll see that our customer data from the CSV files have the right headers:

CustomerID	Store Number	Customer Segment	Responder	First Name	Last Name	Address	City	State	Zip	Lat	Lon
16	103	Small Business	No	JEANNINE	QUINLAN	5400 SHERIDAN BLVD	ARVADA	CO	80002	39.7940857151194	-105.052900133329
40	103	Corporate	No	CHARLENE	MCLEOD	8192 W 81ST DR	ARVADA	CO	80005	39.8422976596147	-105.087932689214
52	103	Corporate	No	SARAH	TOMMER	7130 SIMMS ST	ARVADA	CO	80004	39.8250851862873	-105.12832044967
62	108	Corporate	No	STEPHANIE	BENNETTS	8463 CHASE ST	ARVADA	CO	80003	39.850665147918	-105.057117479326
63	103	Corporate	No	SUSAN	POPA	11921 W 76TH DR	ARVADA	CO	80005	39.8396684404781	-105.130708558465

Figure 9.8: Results after dynamic renaming

Now, we are going to incorporate our transactional data.

8. Drop a new **Input Data** tool onto the canvas and point it to `..\DATA\Pos_data.CSV`.

    Reviewing the **Preview** panel, you'll notice that the headers are the first record of the data.

9. Deselect **First Row Contains Field Names** and hit **Refresh** to let Alteryx rename the headers and read the data rows properly:

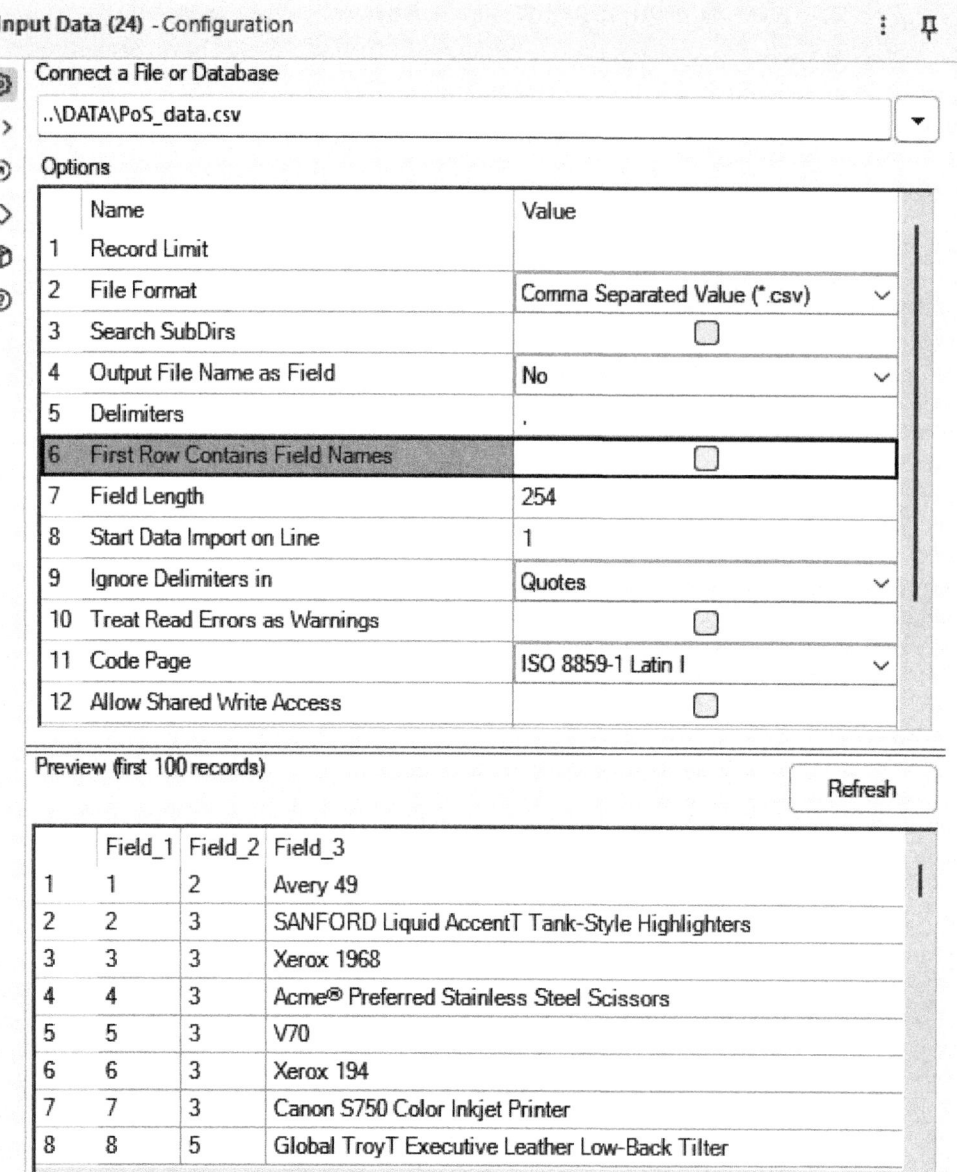

Figure 9.9: Transactional Input Data tool configuration

Again, we have missing headers.

10. Drop another **Input Data** tool onto the canvas and point it to `..\DATA_DICTIONARY\`
`PoSDataDictionary.xlsx` and select the `PoS data dictionary` worksheet as
the data source:

Input Data (10) - Configuration

Connect a File or Database

`..\DATA_DICTIONARY\PoSDataDictionary.xlsx`

Options

	Name	Value
1	Record Limit	
2	File Format	Microsoft Excel (*.xlsx)
3	Table or Query	`PoS data dictionary$`
4	Search SubDirs	☐
5	Output File Name as Field	No
6	First Row Contains Data	☐
7	Start Data Import on Line	1

Preview (first 100 records)   Refresh

	Field_Name
1	Transaction#
2	CustomerID
3	ProductName
4	Sales
5	OrderID

Figure 9.10: Transactional data headers dictionary

11. Drop another **Dynamic Rename** tool and connect `PoS_data` to the L input anchor and the
`PoSDictionary` to the R input anchor:

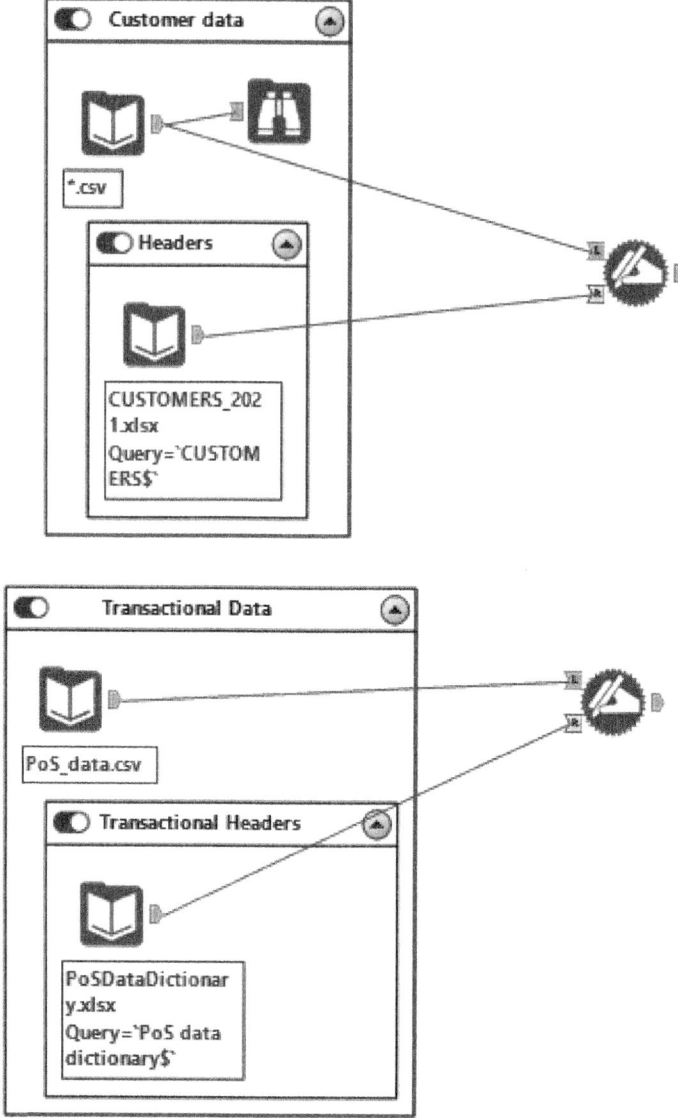

Figure 9.11: Workflow with the transactional data

12. Now, click on the **Dynamic Input** tool to configure it.

13. Select **Take Field Names from Right Input Rows** for **Rename Mode**.

14. Select -**Use positional rename**- from the **Old Field Name from Column** drop-down list.

15. Select **Field_Name** from the **New Field Name from Column** drop-down list:

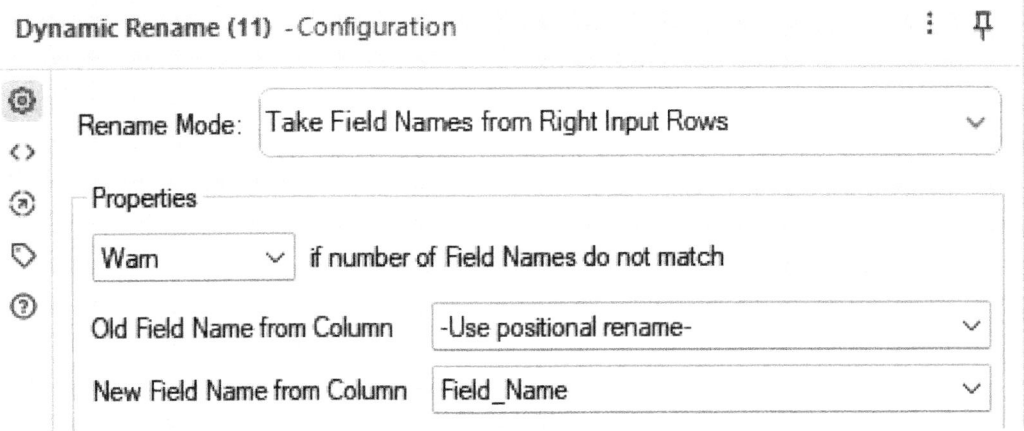

Figure 9.12: The Dynamic Rename tool configuration

Run the workflow and notice that Alteryx renamed the headers based on the dictionary we used:

Transaction#	CustomerID	ProductName	Sales	OrderID
2	3	SANFORD Liquid AccentT Tank-Style Highlighters	13.01	88522
3	3	Xerox 1968	49.92	88523
4	3	Acme® Preferred Stainless Steel Scissors	41.64	88523
5	3	V70	1446.67	88523
6	3	Xerox 194	2011.67	88524
7	3	Canon S750 Color Inkjet Printer	1451.37	88526

Figure 9.13: Results of the dynamic renaming process

From this point on we only need to join both datasets.

16. Drop a **Join** tool and connect the output anchor from the **Dynamic Rename** tool with the customer's data to the L input anchor and the other **Dynamic Rename** tool output anchor into the R input anchor:

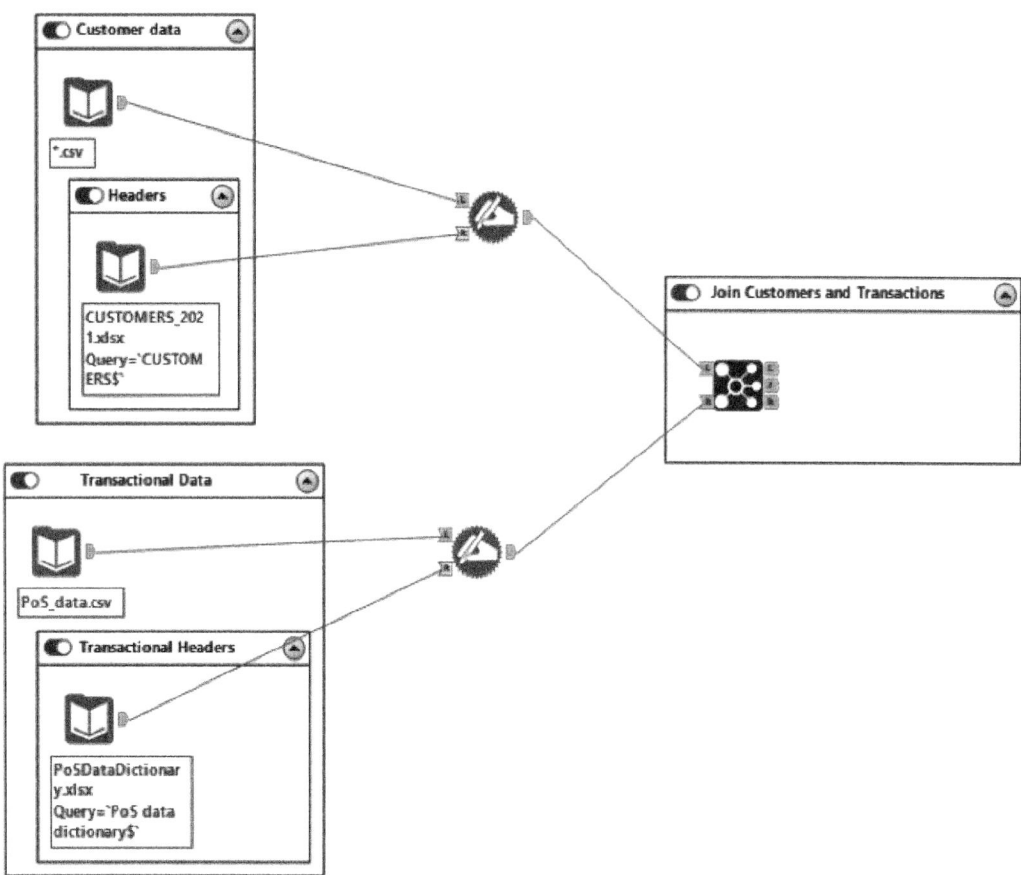

Figure 9.14: Adding a Join tool to the workflow

For the **Join** tool configuration, make sure **Join by Specific Fields** is selected and from the **Left** drop-down list, select CustomerID (Alteryx should populate the right drop-down list with CustomerID, but if it doesn't, select CustomerID from the **Right** drop-down option):

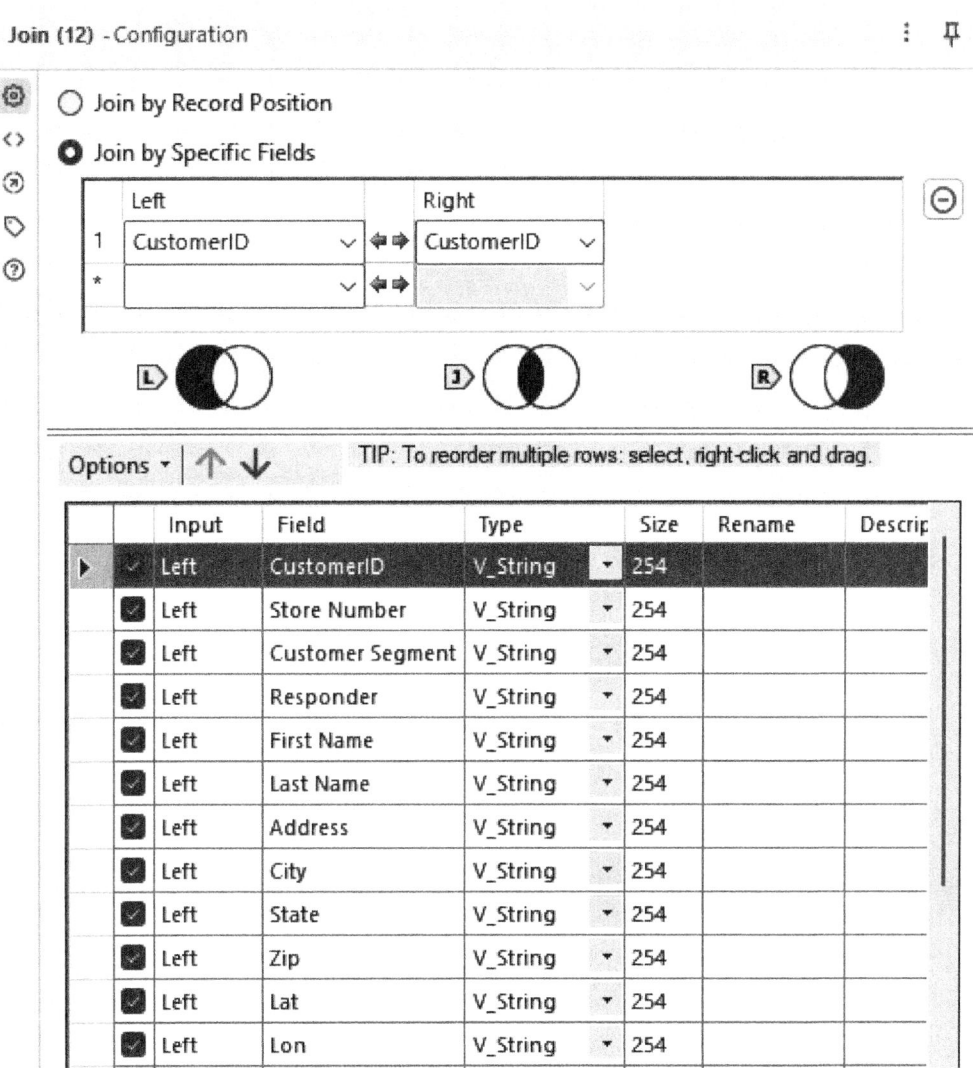

Figure 9.15: The Join tool configuration

Run the workflow, and you'll see that we have the expected results.

How it works...

The **Dynamic Rename** tool offers a wide variety of options to rename headers according to our needs:

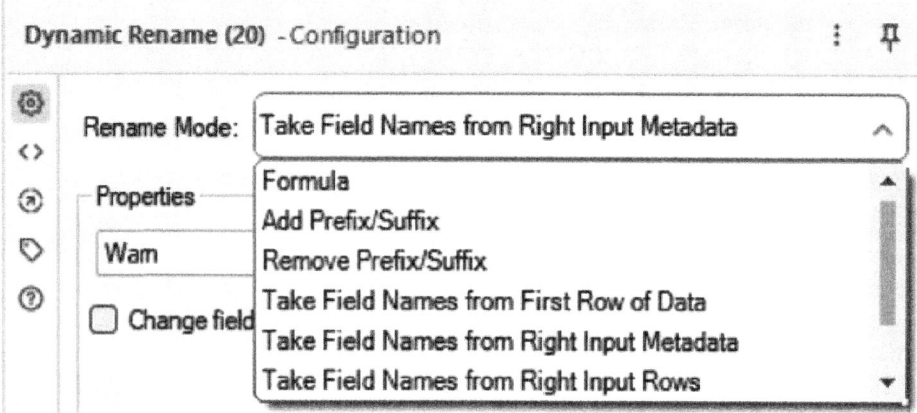

Figure 9.16: Dynamic Rename Mode options

We'll explore the options in depth in the following list:

- **Formula**: You can use all the functions and expressions available in Alteryx Designer to rename your headers.

  This method offers you a special variable called _CurrentField_ that refers to each of the selected fields.

  It will subsequently take the selected field's name from the list and refer to it. In this case, it'll take CustomerID as the first value, apply the expression (replacing whitespaces with underscores and converting the result to uppercase) to that field; then it'll take Store Number, apply the same expression, and so on until there are no more fields in the list:

Figure 9.17: Using a formula to rename fields

- **Add Prefix/Suffix**: This allows you to select to add the entered text as a prefix or suffix to the actual field name:

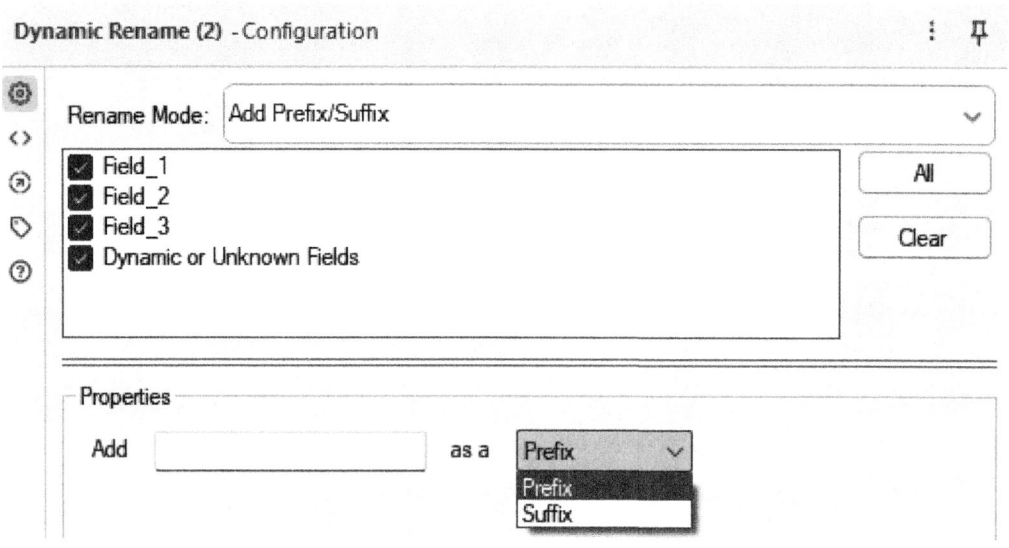

Figure 9.18: Adding prefixes or suffixes

- **Remove Prefix/Suffix**: Similar to the previous option, but instead of adding, it'll remove the prefix or suffix. It also offers the chance to select what'll happen when a field is not renamed:

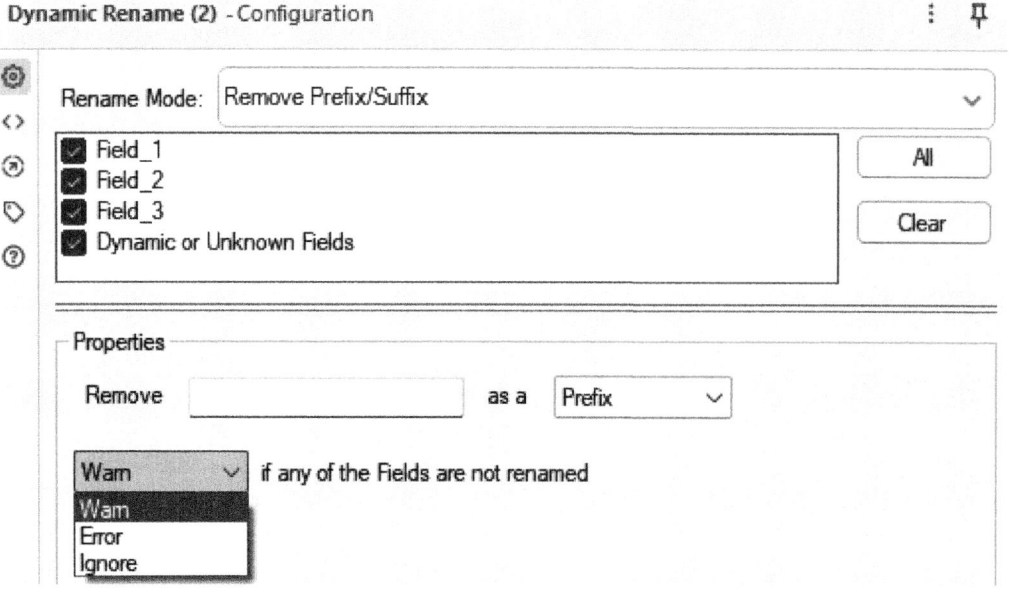

Figure 9.19: Removing prefixes or suffixes

- **Take Field Names from First Row of Data**: Will take the first row values and rename the fields with them:

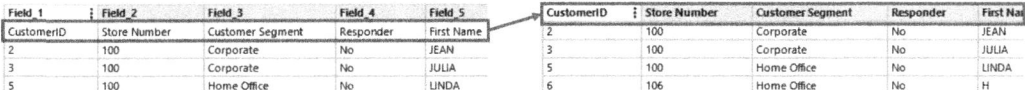

Figure 9.20: The Taking Field Names from the First Row option

> **Important note**
>
> Note that to use any of these four methods, you shouldn't have anything connected to the R input anchor of the **Dynamic Rename** tool, while the following four require a connection.

- **Take Field Names from Right Input Metadata**: This will take field names from the R input and rename headers from the L input positionally:

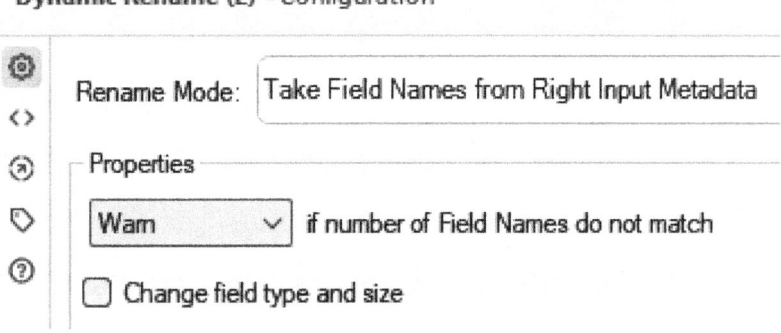

Figure 9.21: The taking headers from a second dataset metadata

A very powerful feature of this option is that it allows you to change **Type** and **Size** at the same time as it renames the field.

- **Take Field Names from Right Input Rows**: This option will allow us to use a dictionary to rename fields. This dictionary may be based on existing field names and their replacements or a direct rename based on row values from data input.

If -Use positional rename- is selected from the **Old Field Name from Column** drop-down list, the first row of the field selected in the **New Field Name from Column** drop-down list will be used as the name of the first field, the second-row value for the second column, and so on:

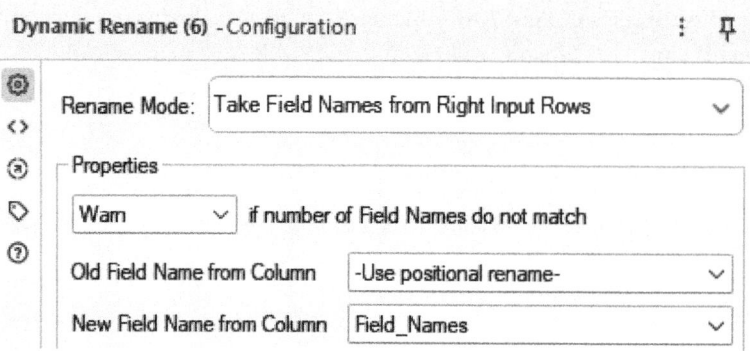

Figure 9.22: Renaming positionally from the second input rows

We can also use a custom dictionary, where we can have at least two columns, one with the actual name and the other with the desired new name:

	New_Name	Original_Name
1	CLIENT_ID	CustomerID
2	STOREID	Store Number
3	SEGMENT	Customer Segment
4	SURVEY_RESPONDER	Responder
5	FIRST_NAME	First Name
6	LAST_NAME	Last Name
7	ADDRESS	Address
8	CITY	City
9	STATE	State
10	ZIP	Zip
11	LATITUDE	Lat
12	LONGITUDE	Lon

Figure 9.23: Basic second input for renaming

Select the original name in the **Old Field Name from Column** option and the wanted output name in **New Field Name from Column**. Alteryx will search within the values of the selected column in **Old Field Name from Column**, and if it finds a match, it will return the value for the corresponding row from the field selected in the **New Field Name from Column** field. If no matches are found, the field name will remain the original:

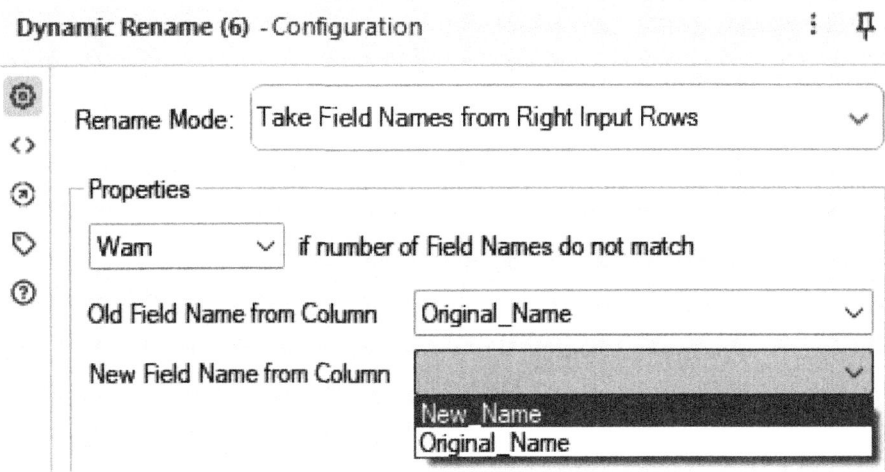

Figure 9.24: Renaming based on find and replace

- **Take Field Descriptions from Right Input Rows**: This allows you to dynamically add a description to any field from another. The procedure is similar to the previous one, except that it'll prompt you for field descriptions, not names:

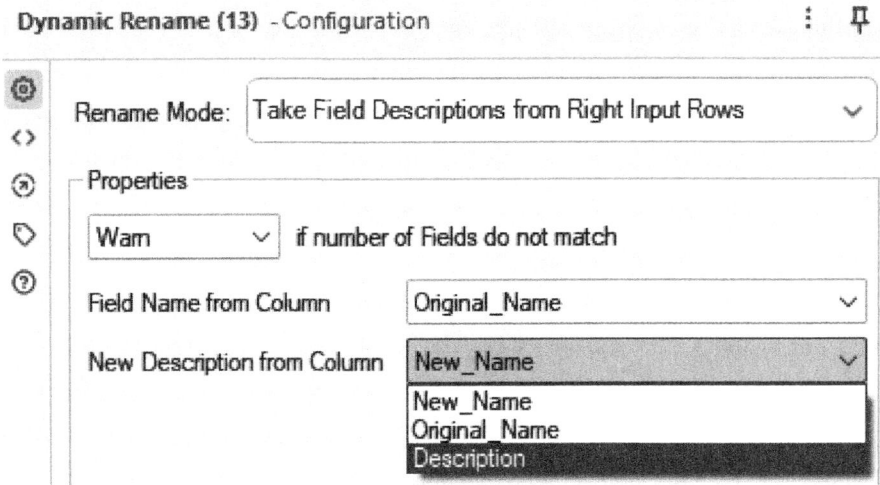

Figure 9.25: Renaming from the second input descriptions

- **Take Field Descriptions from Right Input Metadata**: This is similar to the previous one, except that it'll get the R input descriptions and add them to the L input data:

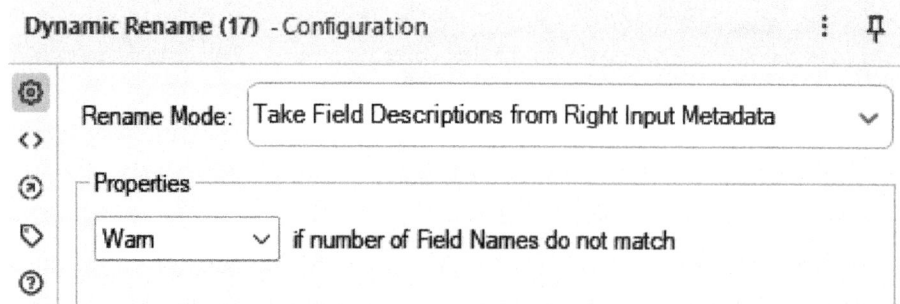

Figure 9.26: Taking the second input metadata for renaming

Dynamically selecting fields

Sometimes, we need to select (or deselect) fields based on conditions. These conditions could be their type or any other that can be set in an expression within Alteryx.

The **Dynamic Select** tool allows us to do exactly that, based on the field type, description, or formula, to dynamically select what fields to keep and which not to.

Getting ready

You can download a test set for this recipe here: `https://github.com/PacktPublishing/Alteryx-Designer-Cookbook/tree/main/ch9/Recipe2`.

We have a summarized dataset from a previous analysis that contains the sales and quantity sold per year per each of our company's articles. We will perform dynamic selects on columns based on several criteria:

COMPANY_ID	ARTICLE_ID	DESCRIPTION	2017_Sales	2018_Sales	2019_Sales	2020_Sales
01	001-1/2	GALV FLAT WASHER 1/2	84300	89800	49510	46500
01	001-1/4	GALV FLAT WASHER 1/4	38700	68300	36350	9800
01	001-3/8	GALV FLAT WASHER 3/8	32900	43200	70400	37700
01	001-5/16	GALV FLAT WASHER 5/16	65700	36500	12000	19700
01	001-5/32	GALV FLAT WASHER 5/32 NO. 8	500	[Null]	[Null]	[Null]
01	005-6/32X3	ELECT SCREW C/P 6/32X3	8400	11700	5200	5600
01	006-8/32X1 1/2	ELECT SCREWC/R 8/32X1 1/2	2400	5600	7200	2400
01	0064	GYPSUM BOARD 4X8X1/2	58390400	80497800	55010400	47992850
01	0096	COLORING POWDER BLACK	153500	139500	204500	117500

2021_Sales	2022_Sales	2017_Quantity	2018_Quantity	2019_Quantity	2020_Quantity	2021_Quantity	2022_Quantity
22500	16200	5080000	7280000	4740000	5700000	4680000	930000
15200	5400	20050000	88150000	32650000	7860000	11100000	2150000
52500	9500	8770000	14730000	5300000	22950000	8730000	1030000
25000	6000	6330000	2330000	930000	1760000	4950000	100000
[Null]	[Null]	300000	[Null]	[Null]	[Null]	[Null]	[Null]
1600	800	660000	3910000	1890000	1350000	200000	300000
1600	[Null]	130000	610000	620000	420000	110000	[Null]
52802610	23118000	98200000	147040000	107525000	73450000	85980000	34810000
115500	102000	240000	100000	380000	80000	60000	200000

Figure 9.27: The starting dataset

We will build a workflow that automatically selects the fields that correspond to the actual year plus the previous year.

How to do it...

We will get started using the following steps:

1. Drop an **Input Data** tool onto the canvas and point it to `..\DATA\ YearlySalesAndQuantities.xlsx` and select `Sheet1` as the data source.

    We are going to pay special attention to the metadata because we'll base our operations on it (using the **Metadata** button on the **Results** panel):

Name	Type	Size
COMPANY_ID	V_String	255
ARTICLE_ID	V_String	255
DESCRIPTION	V_String	255
2017_Sales	Double	8
2018_Sales	Double	8
2019_Sales	Double	8
2020_Sales	Double	8
2021_Sales	Double	8
2022_Sales	Double	8
2017_Quantity	Double	8
2018_Quantity	Double	8
2019_Quantity	Double	8
2020_Quantity	Double	8
2021_Quantity	Double	8
2022_Quantity	Double	8

Figure 9.28: The dataset's metadata

As we can see, we have three `V_String` fields that represent our dimensions (or the detail used for the calculated fields), meaning that all the yearly sales and quantities sold are computed by `COMPANY_ID`, `ARTICLE_ID`, and `DESCRIPTION`.

Our first task will then be to isolate the dimensions, so we can use them to describe the measures later:

1. Drop a **Dynamic Select** tool and connect it to the **Input Data** tool.

2. Make sure **Select Field Types** is selected in the drop-down list and select all of the `String` and `Date` types:

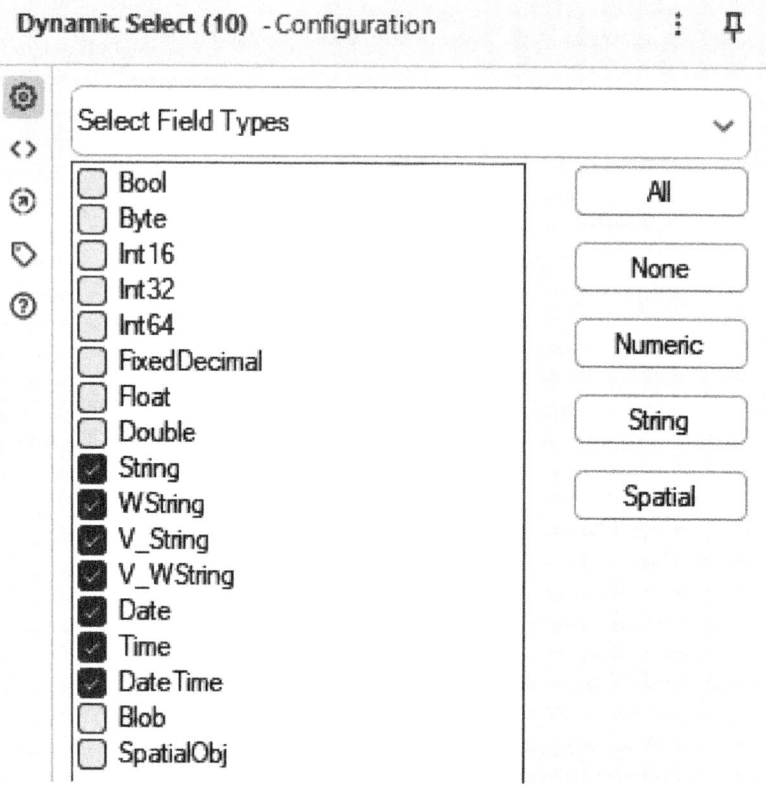

Figure 9.29: Selecting all string and date type fields dynamically

Now we'll determine which fields we will keep and which to discard.

3. Drop a **Field Info** tool onto the canvas and connect it to the output anchor of the **Input Data** tool.

4. Add a **Formula** tool following the **Field Info** tool, and create a column called `TY` with this expression:

```
DateTimeYear(DateTimeStart())
```

After configuring the **Formula** tool, your workflow will look like this:

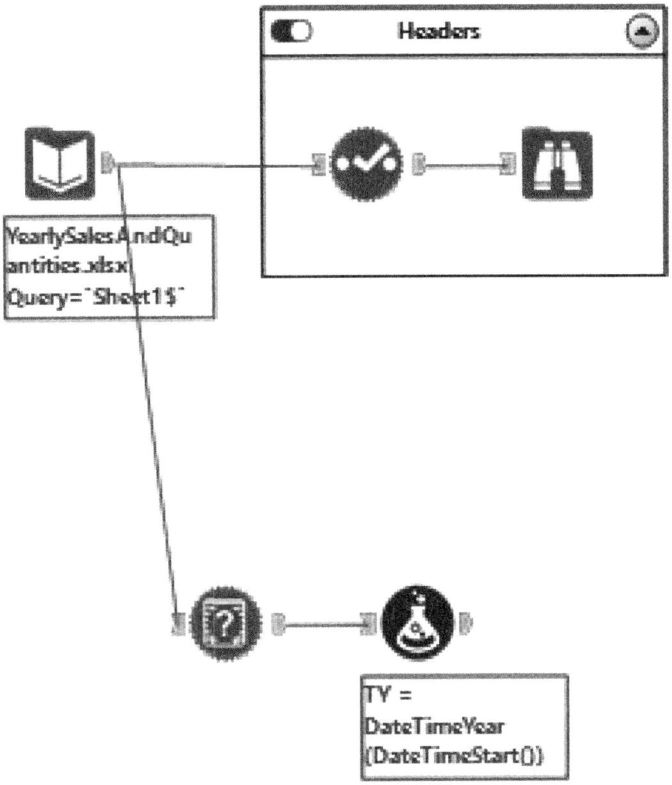

Figure 9.30: Workflow after adding the Formula tool

5. Add another **Formula** tool following the existing one (I like to do this for readability and maintainability, but if you prefer, you can add a new field within the existing **Formula** tool just by pressing the blue plus sign (➕).

6. Create a new column called `Selection` and use this expression:

```
IF CONTAINS([Name],[TY])
THEN "TY"
ELSEIF CONTAINS([Name],ToString(ToNumber([TY])-1))
THEN "LY"
ELSE ""
ENDIF
```

7. Add a **Dynamic Rename** tool to the canvas and connect the output anchor from the **Formula** tool to the R input and the output anchor from the **Input Data** tool to the L input:

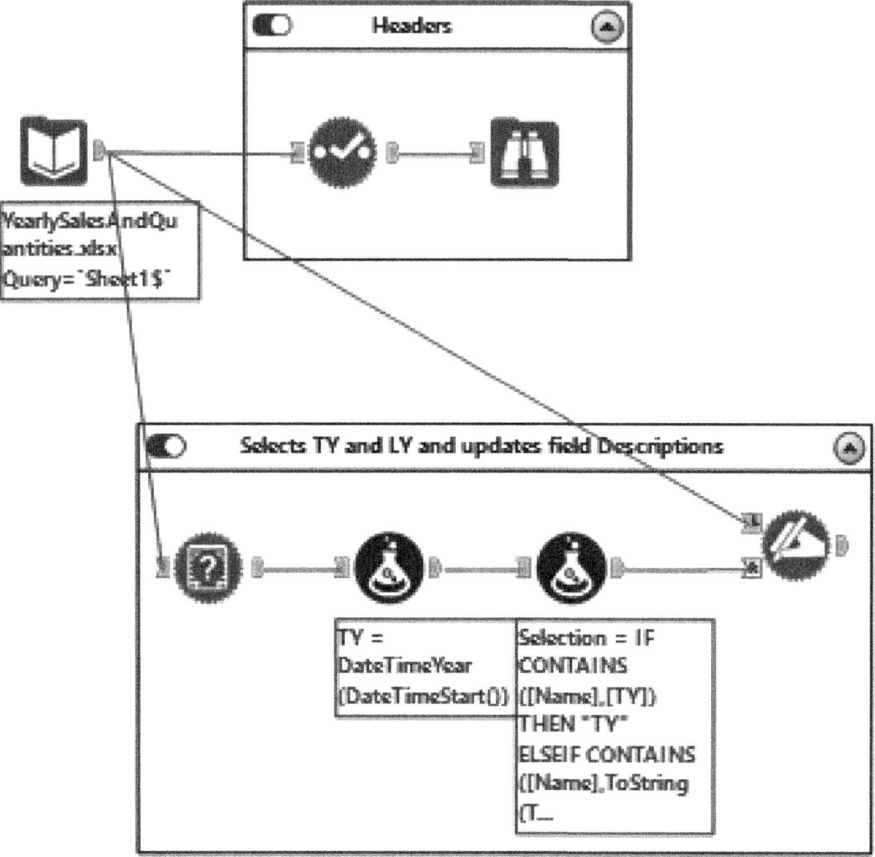

Figure 9.31: Workflow after adding the Dynamic Rename tool

8. Configure the **Dynamic Rename** tool to use Take Field Descriptions from the Right Input Rows.

9. From the **Field Name from Column** drop-down list, select Name.

10. From the **New Description from Column** drop-down list, select Selection:

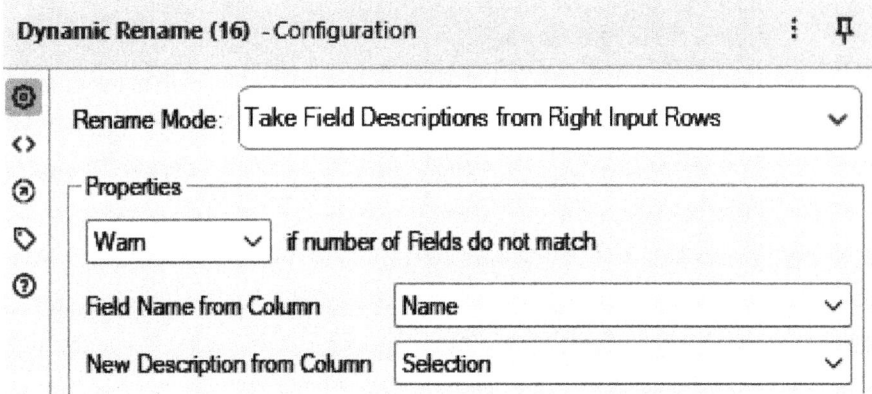

Figure 9.32: The Dynamic Rename tool configuration

11. Run the workflow and click on **Metadata** in the **Results** panel. As you can see, **Field Descriptions** were updated by the **Dynamic Rename** tool, and now we can identify the fields containing this year's and last year's data:

Results - Dynamic Rename (16) - Output

15 of 15 Fields ▾ ✔ | Cell Viewer ▾ | ↑ ↓ |

Record	Name	Type	Size	Source	Description
1	COMPANY_ID	V_String	255	File: C:\Exercises\AUXILIAR\ch9\YearlySalesAndQ...	
2	ARTICLE_ID	V_String	255	File: C:\Exercises\AUXILIAR\ch9\YearlySalesAndQ...	
3	DESCRIPTION	V_String	255	File: C:\Exercises\AUXILIAR\ch9\YearlySalesAndQ...	
4	2017_Sales	Double	8	File: C:\Exercises\AUXILIAR\ch9\YearlySalesAndQ...	
5	2018_Sales	Double	8	File: C:\Exercises\AUXILIAR\ch9\YearlySalesAndQ...	
6	2019_Sales	Double	8	File: C:\Exercises\AUXILIAR\ch9\YearlySalesAndQ...	
7	2020_Sales	Double	8	File: C:\Exercises\AUXILIAR\ch9\YearlySalesAndQ...	
8	2021_Sales	Double	8	File: C:\Exercises\AUXILIAR\ch9\YearlySalesAndQ...	LY
9	2022_Sales	Double	8	File: C:\Exercises\AUXILIAR\ch9\YearlySalesAndQ...	TY
10	2017_Quantity	Double	8	File: C:\Exercises\AUXILIAR\ch9\YearlySalesAndQ...	
11	2018_Quantity	Double	8	File: C:\Exercises\AUXILIAR\ch9\YearlySalesAndQ...	
12	2019_Quantity	Double	8	File: C:\Exercises\AUXILIAR\ch9\YearlySalesAndQ...	

Figure 9.33: Changed descriptions after dynamic renaming

12. Add another **Dynamic Select** tool following the **Dynamic Rename** tool.

13. From the top drop-down option (the method), select `Select via a Formula`.

14. Use this in the **Expression** box:

```
!IsEmpty([Description])
```

Your **Dynamic Select** tool should be like this:

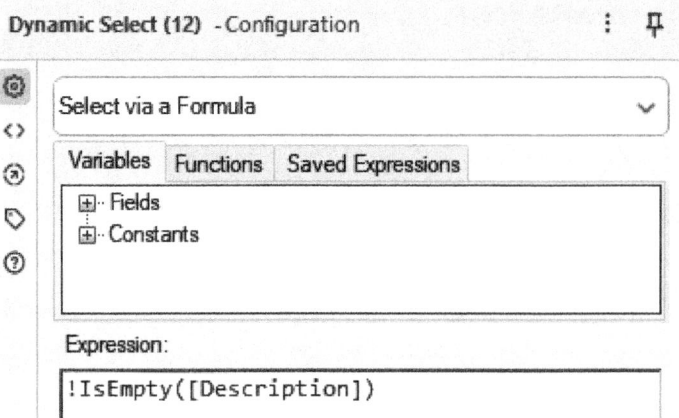

Figure 9.34: Dynamic Select configuration

We only need to get our headers and data together to finish the workflow:

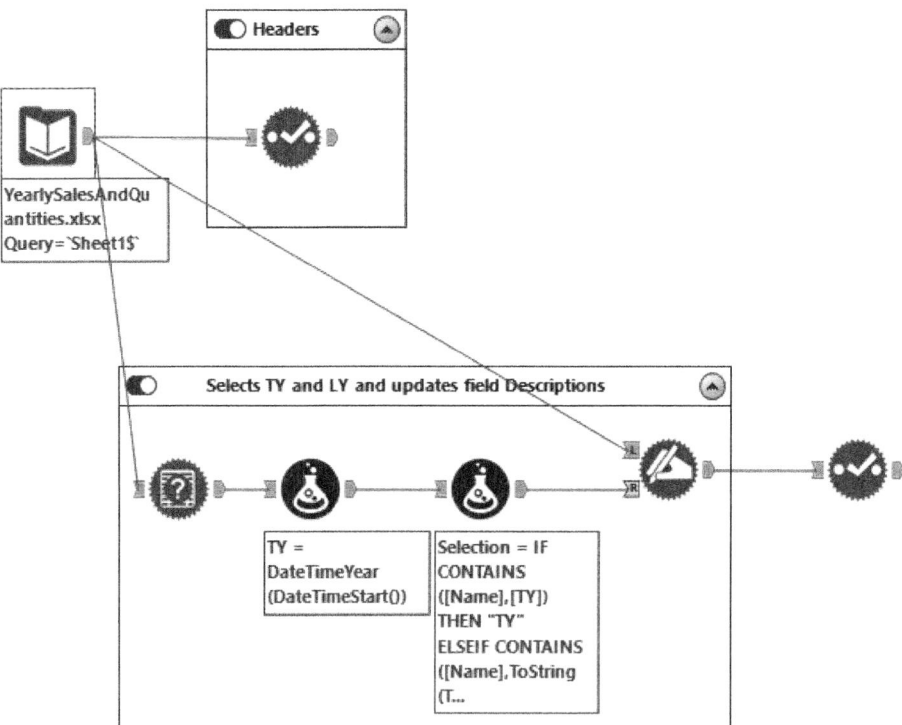

Figure 9.35: Adding the Dynamic Select tool to the workflow

15. Add a **Join** tool to the canvas and connect the output anchor from the first **Dynamic Select** tool we have to the L input and the second **Dynamic Select** to the R input:

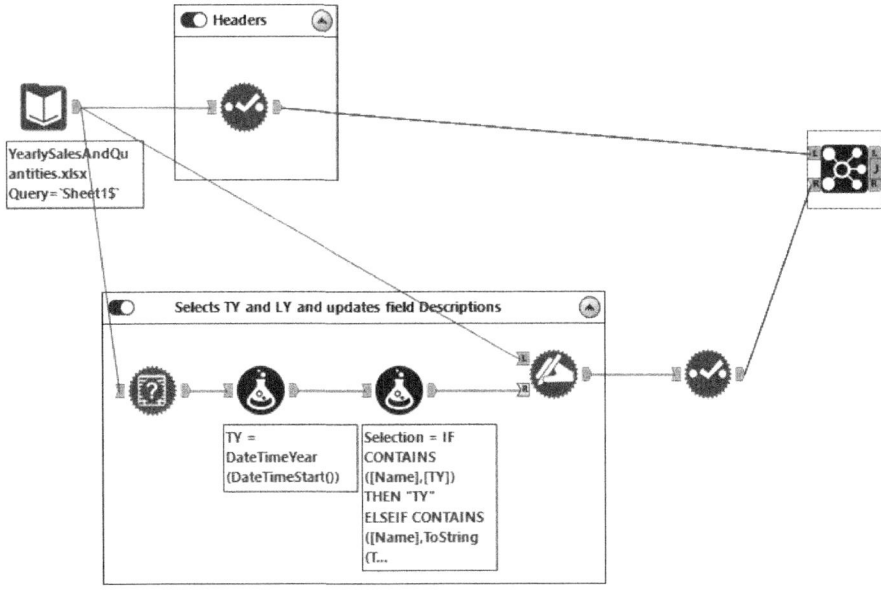

Figure 9.36: Final workflow

16. Configure the **Join** tool to **Join by Record Position**:

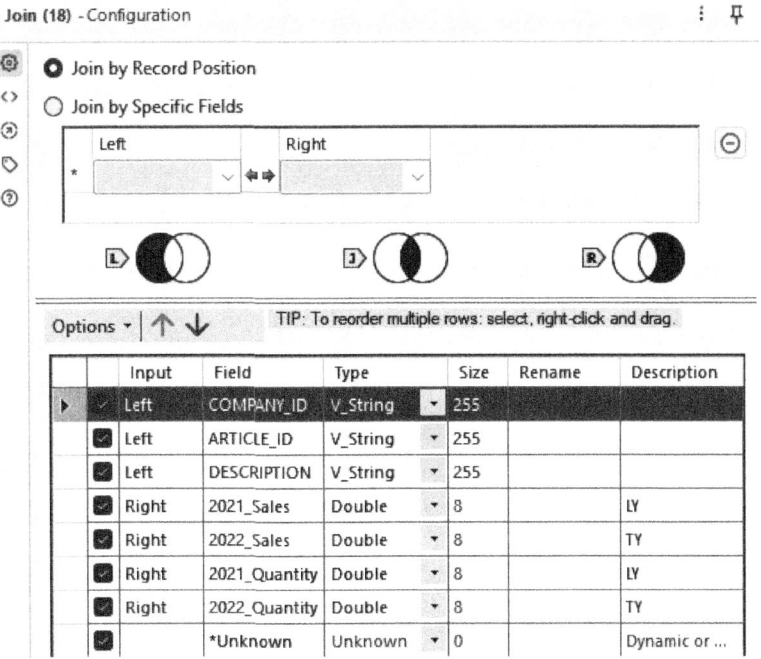

Figure 9.37: The Join by Record Position configuration

Run the workflow and see whether you get the desired fields:

COMPANY_ID	ARTICLE_ID	DESCRIPTION	2021_Sales	2022_Sales	2021_Quantity	2022_Quantity
01	001-1/2	GALV FLAT WASHER 1/2	22500	16200	4680000	930000
01	001-1/4	GALV FLAT WASHER 1/4	15200	5400	11100000	2150000
01	001-3/8	GALV FLAT WASHER 3/8	52500	9500	8730000	1030000
01	001-5/16	GALV FLAT WASHER 5/16	25000	6000	4950000	100000
01	001-5/32	GALV FLAT WASHER 5/32 NO. 8	[Null]	[Null]	[Null]	[Null]
01	005-6/32X3	ELECT SCREW C/P 6/32X3	1600	800	200000	300000
01	006-8/32X1 1/2	ELECT SCREWC/R 8/32X1 1/2	1600	[Null]	110000	[Null]
01	0064	GYPSUM BOARD 4X8X1/2	52802610	23118000	85980000	34810000

Figure 9.38: Final results

Dynamically replacing values

Being able to make dynamic replacements in the data based on formulas or conditions helps us to shape our data perfectly.

The **Dynamic Replace** tool is one underestimated tool within the Alteryx arsenal that allows us to create rules to replace values within a field or set of fields. In this recipe, we'll be using it to perform some powerful transformations in the data values.

Getting ready

We built a test set for you to try this recipe. Download it here: https://github.com/PacktPublishing/Alteryx-Designer-Cookbook/tree/main/ch9/Recipe3.

In this test set, we have some data coming from survey software that we need to standardize and shape.

The questions for this particular survey are as follows:

- Q1 – Are you a current customer?

- Q2 – The service I receive is what I expect…

- Q3 – Have you contacted customer services in the last three months?

- Q4 – My customer service experience was great…

- Q5 – Would you recommend our service to others?

We receive data in both Spanish and English for *Q1*, *Q3*, and *Q5*, while *Q2* and *Q4* are a Likert scale response, where the following options are available for selection:

- 1=Strongly disagree

- 2=Disagree

- 3=Neutral

- 4=Agree

- 5=Strongly agree

And this is how it looks in Excel:

Responder_ID	Start time	Completion time	Q1	Q2	Q3	Q4	Q5
13d8795e-6303-4141-ad7d-5640324004fe	3/30/2022 11:30	3/30/2022 11:32	Yes	3	Yes	2	Yes
48b19891-afa3-4739-80ee-244639775ef6	3/30/2022 11:30	3/30/2022 11:33	No	4	Yes	3	Yes
06f5e95b-7b09-4eb2-8630-a5d2032e7a05	3/30/2022 11:30	3/30/2022 11:33	Yes	5	Yes	1	No
f6f6f58e-d298-4945-b743-a822d208ca50	3/30/2022 11:30	3/30/2022 11:33	Yes	5	Yes	4	Yes
bf7d1799-0737-48b9-a913-fc62ef067927	3/30/2022 11:32	3/30/2022 11:33	Yes	5	Yes	5	Yes
c069d4b4-e24b-4130-a73e-5cf93243348e	3/30/2022 11:34	3/30/2022 11:36	Yes	4	Yes	2	Yes
1e879fa4-6a4a-44b1-b424-dfefd8c11473	3/30/2022 11:30	3/30/2022 11:36	Yes	4	Yes	4	Yes
39eafc60-35ce-4e7f-882e-0f2bcf59ec82	3/30/2022 11:32	3/30/2022 11:36	Yes	3	Yes	5	Yes
8bcb4b58-6041-4f6b-a894-02a95d7be20b	3/30/2022 11:35	3/30/2022 11:36	Yes	4	Yes	2	Yes
c3a86ccd-389c-4cfb-b7bc-d621f6988577	3/30/2022 11:34	3/30/2022 11:37	Yes	5	Yes	1	Yes
d3b2a6d7-f570-46aa-899b-6e4ddb73dae9	3/30/2022 11:36	3/30/2022 11:38	Yes	2	Yes	3	Yes
ff21c6b2-991d-4bde-b195-813fc089c4ec	3/30/2022 11:37	3/30/2022 11:38	Yes	5	Yes	4	Yes
a8cbe4c6-d514-42ca-affe-725e9cac59d3	3/30/2022 11:38	3/30/2022 11:39	Yes	4	Yes	5	Yes
90856422-edbe-4451-84fe-5069084846f1	3/30/2022 11:38	3/30/2022 11:39	No	3	Yes	1	Yes
6d4a4a02-7ab5-436d-bfc0-6d136dc44c94	3/30/2022 11:38	3/30/2022 11:39	Yes	5	Yes	5	Yes
c72b3bdc-95d1-4079-bfe1-1a7c78a09537	3/30/2022 11:39	3/30/2022 11:40	No	5	Yes	5	No
7c2c376f-860e-4e1b-b60c-1bacfc450917	3/30/2022 11:36	3/30/2022 11:43	No	3	Yes	2	Yes
530d36bf-e0d6-4edc-97c7-bc0aadbfcb67	3/30/2022 11:42	3/30/2022 11:44	Yes	4	Yes	4	Yes
309b7b9f-eae5-4ddc-a815-db86a0bccc05	3/30/2022 11:37	3/30/2022 11:50	No	5	Yes	5	Yes
ba6b5491-672d-40ee-9499-af722529926f	3/30/2022 14:43	3/30/2022 14:43	Yes	4	Yes	4	Yes

Figure 9.39: Data downloaded from the survey software

Where values 1 and 2 are considered Negative, 3 is considered Neutral, and 4 and 5 are considered Positive.

Since our survey system always exports the data in the same way, we'll try to create a standardized workflow to automate the data processing using external dictionaries and the benefits of the Dynamic tools.

How to do it...

We'll work on this using the following steps:

1. Drop an **Input Data** tool onto the canvas, and since we have one file for Spanish responses and one for English ones, point it to ..\DATA\SurveyData_*.xlsx (to read all of them at once) and select the Survey1 worksheet as the data source.

2. Select File Name Only from Output File Name as Field so we can get a new column called FileName with the filename where each record comes from:

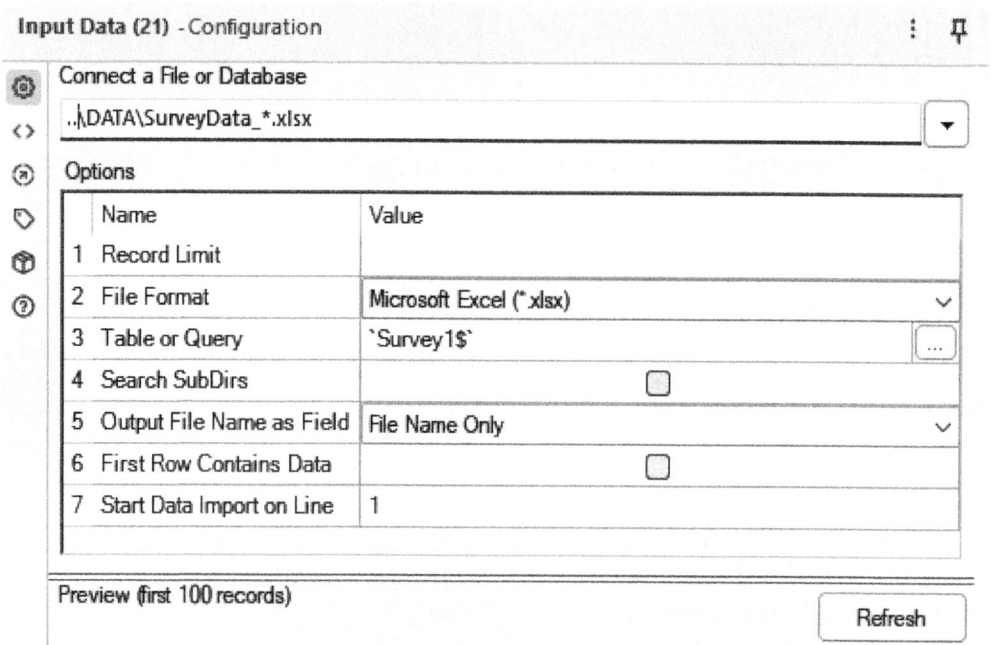

Figure 9.40: The Input Data tool configuration

Running the workflow will give you access to the loaded data:

Responder_ID	Start time	Completion time	Q1	Q2	Q3	Q4	Q5	FileName
7c2c376f-860e-4e1b-b60c-1bacfc450917	2022-03-30 11:36:31	2022-03-30 11:43:33	No	3	Yes	2	Yes	SurveyData_EN
530d36bf-e0d6-4edc-97c7-bc0aadbfcb67	2022-03-30 11:42:14	2022-03-30 11:44:05	Yes	4	Yes	4	Yes	SurveyData_EN
309b7b9f-eae5-4ddc-a815-db86a0bccc05	2022-03-30 11:37:22	2022-03-30 11:50:52	No	5	Yes	5	Yes	SurveyData_EN
ba6b5491-672d-40ee-9499-af722529926f	2022-03-30 14:43:54	2022-03-30 14:43:59	Yes	4	Yes	4	Yes	SurveyData_EN
405290da-60f0-4ef0-8beb-221a396eea7a	2022-03-30 11:30:24	2022-03-30 11:32:39	Sí	3	Sí	2	Sí	SurveyData_SP
153969db-3b4d-4bea-8c08-cae7e1e32ff4	2022-03-30 11:30:40	2022-03-30 11:33:10	No	4	Sí	3	Sí	SurveyData_SP
fd1f7e80-6109-4084-9f7c-73446ff97a22	2022-03-30 11:30:14	2022-03-30 11:33:48	Sí	5	Sí	1	No	SurveyData_SP
60ffadbd-3902-4284-91d6-8c2633839a5d	2022-03-30 11:30:36	2022-03-30 11:33:48	Sí	5	Sí	4	Sí	SurveyData_SP
f06e6f35-99b8-43e1-80da-86fd2139cd8c	2022-03-30 11:32:06	2022-03-30 11:33:48	Sí	5	Sí	5	Sí	SurveyData_SP
66db18c2-b485-449d-80ee-1535465c65ea	2022-03-30 11:34:11	2022-03-30 11:36:12	Sí	4	Sí	2	Sí	SurveyData_SP
db5c30b6-b708-47ac-86f6-ee4061396254	2022-03-30 11:30:26	2022-03-30 11:36:31	Sí	4	Sí	4	Sí	SurveyData_SP

Figure 9.41: Data read in Alteryx

To start working, and because we don't want to touch the original data (so we can use it as a reference to validate our logic), we will create a set of columns to replicate the actual values of Q2 and Q4 but in string format.

3. Drop a **Formula** tool onto the canvas, and create a new column call it Q2_Score with this expression:

```
ToString([Q2])
```

4. Create a new column within the same **Formula** tool, called Q4_SCORE, and use this expression:

```
ToString([Q4])
```

Also, we'll create two sets of three columns for the different language responses.

You can use the same **Formula** tool or drop another one (I like the latter since it simplifies debugging, documentation, and maintenance without adding much overhead in the processing of data):

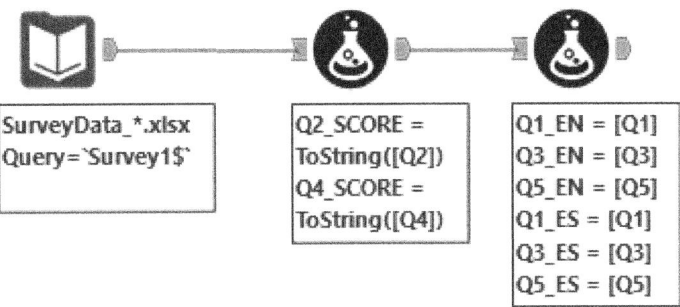

Figure 9.42: Workflow with the Formula tool

5. Create the following columns:

- Name= Q1_EN; Expression= [Q1]

- Name= Q2_EN; Expression= [Q2]

- Name= Q3_EN; Expression= [Q3]

- Name= Q1_ES; Expression= [Q1]

- Name= Q1_ES; Expression= [Q2]

- Name= Q1_ES; Expression= [Q3]

After adding the columns, your **Formula** tool should look like this:

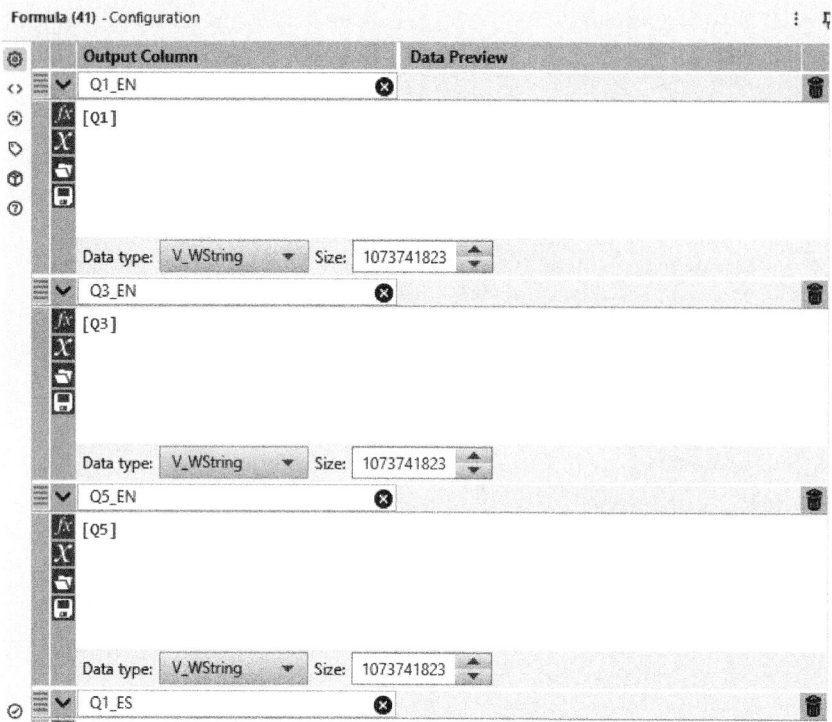

Figure 9.43: The Formula tool configurations

Our data should look like this with the new columns added:

Responder_ID	Start time	Completion time	Q1	Q2	Q3	Q4	Q5
13d8795e-6303-4141-ad7d-5640324004fe	2022-03-30 11:30:24	2022-03-30 11:32:39	Yes	3	Yes	2	Yes
48b19891-afa3-4739-80ee-244639775ef6	2022-03-30 11:30:40	2022-03-30 11:33:10	No	4	Yes	3	Yes
06f5e95b-7b09-4eb2-8630-a5d2032e7a05	2022-03-30 11:30:14	2022-03-30 11:33:48	Yes	5	Yes	1	No
f6f6f58e-d298-4945-b743-a822d206ca50	2022-03-30 11:30:36	2022-03-30 11:33:48	Yes	5	Yes	4	Yes
bf7d1799-0737-48b9-a913-fc62ef067927	2022-03-30 11:32:06	2022-03-30 11:33:48	Yes	5	Yes	5	Yes
c069d4b4-e24b-4130-a73e-5cf93243348e	2022-03-30 11:34:11	2022-03-30 11:36:12	Yes	4	Yes	2	Yes
1e879fa4-6a4a-44b1-b424-dfefd8c11473	2022-03-30 11:30:26	2022-03-30 11:36:31	Yes	4	Yes	4	Yes
39eafc60-35ce-4e7f-882e-0f2bcf59ec82	2022-03-30 11:32:34	2022-03-30 11:36:36	Yes	3	Yes	5	Yes
8bcb4b58-6041-4f6b-a894-02a95d7be20b	2022-03-30 11:35:26	2022-03-30 11:36:43	Yes	4	Yes	2	Yes
c3a86ccd-389c-4cfb-b7bc-d621f6988577	2022-03-30 11:34:51	2022-03-30 11:37:37	Yes	5	Yes	1	Yes

FileName	Q2_SCORE	Q4_SCORE	Q1_EN	Q3_EN	Q5_EN	Q1_ES	Q3_ES	Q5_ES
SurveyData_EN	3	2	Yes	Yes	Yes	Yes	Yes	Yes
SurveyData_EN	4	3	No	Yes	Yes	No	Yes	Yes
SurveyData_EN	5	1	Yes	Yes	No	Yes	Yes	No
SurveyData_EN	5	4	Yes	Yes	Yes	Yes	Yes	Yes
SurveyData_EN	5	5	Yes	Yes	Yes	Yes	Yes	Yes
SurveyData_EN	4	2	Yes	Yes	Yes	Yes	Yes	Yes
SurveyData_EN	4	4	Yes	Yes	Yes	Yes	Yes	Yes
SurveyData_EN	3	5	Yes	Yes	Yes	Yes	Yes	Yes
SurveyData_EN	4	2	Yes	Yes	Yes	Yes	Yes	Yes
SurveyData_EN	5	1	Yes	Yes	Yes	Yes	Yes	Yes

Figure 9.44: New columns added by the Formula tools

As you can see in the resulting data, we need to make some changes to finalize our dataset:

Q1_ES, Q3_ES, and Q5_ES need to be translated to Spanish (Yes will become Sí and No will remain No).

Q2_SCORE and Q4_SCORE will be translated like this:

- The 1 and 2 values will become Negative

- 3 will become Neutral

- The 4 and 5 values will become Positive

What is great about Alteryx is that it will be performing all this in just one step, with just one tool.

6. Drop a **Dynamic Replace** tool onto the canvas and connect the **Formula** tool output anchor to its D input.

7. Drop a new **Input Data** tool and point it to ..\DICTIONARY\Dictionaries.xlsx and select the RULES worksheet as the data source:

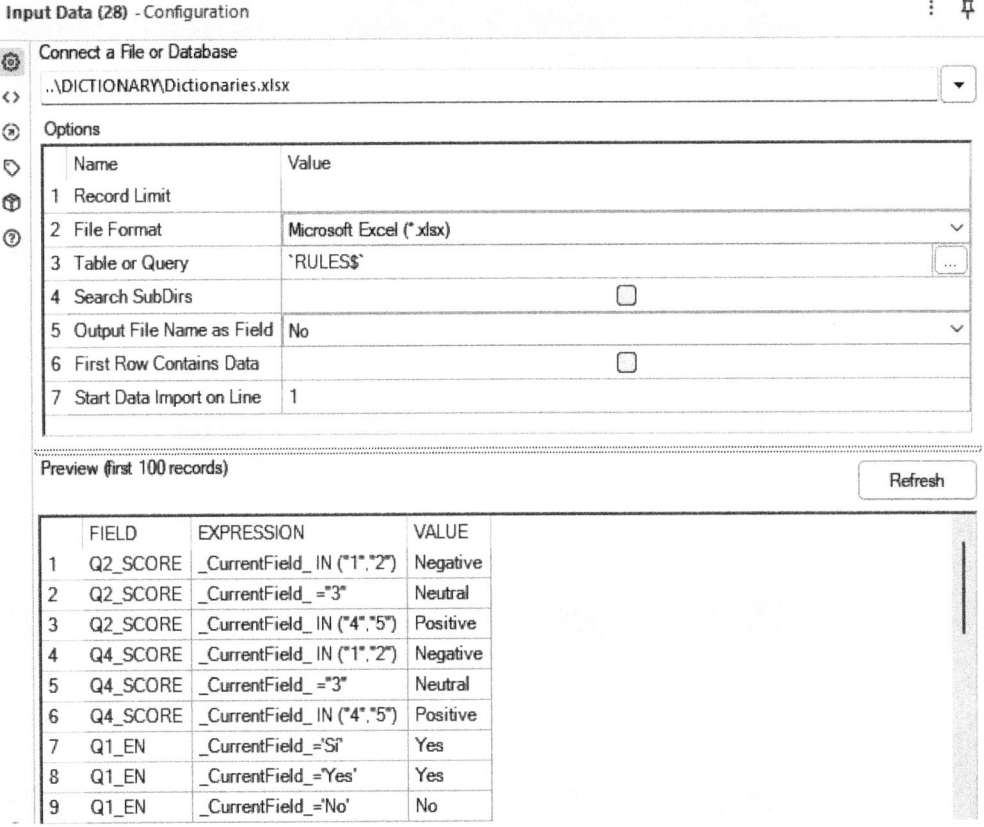

Figure 9.45: The RULES Input Data tool configuration

8.   Connect the **Input Data** tool output anchor to the R input of the **Dynamic Replace** tool.

If you view the **Preview** pane, you'll notice that this dictionary has three fields:

- FIELD: This refers to the field that'll be modified by **Dynamic Replace**.

- EXPRESSION: This is a Boolean expression that, if evaluated to True, will make Alteryx replace the value of FIELD with the contents of VALUE. If it evaluates to False, Alteryx will replace the value with Null.

- VALUE: This value will be used to replace the actual value of FIELD if EXPRESSION evaluates to True.

Important note

The VALUE field can also be an expression/formula in itself and will also be applied; just make sure you let the **Dynamic Replace** tool know it by clicking the **Values are Expressions/Formulas** checkbox.

Also, note that _CurrentField_ can be used to refer to the FIELD value in EXPRESSION, so maintaining/creating this kind of dictionary gets easier.

As an example, for record #1 in the dictionary, after Alteryx replaces _CurrentField_ in EXPRESSION with the value from FIELD, the EXPRESSION value will be [Q2_SCORE] IN ("1","2"), meaning that if it is True, the Q2_SCORE actual value will be replaced by Negative.

9.   Click on the **Dynamic Replace** tool to access its configuration panel, and configure it like this:

- From the **Field Name Field** drop-down list, select FIELD.

- From the **Boolean Expression Field** drop-down list, select EXPRESSION.

- From the **Output Value Field** drop-down list, select VALUE.

- Make sure that **Values are Expressions/Formulas** is unchecked:

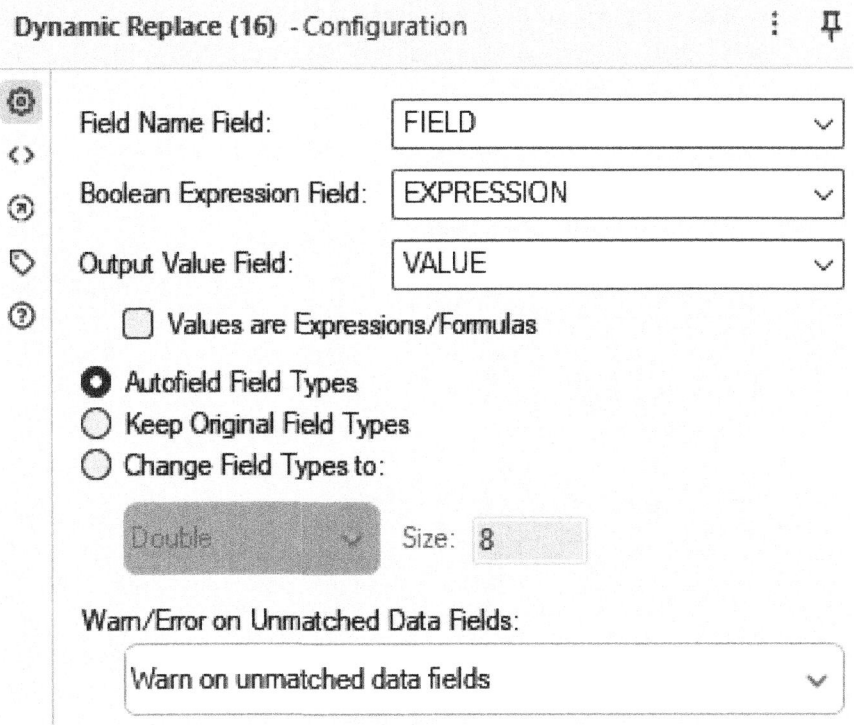

Figure 9.46: The Dynamic Replace tool configuration

Run the workflow, and you'll see that all replacements were done and the dataset is almost ready. So, we only need to rename the **Q** fields with the survey's actual questions.

10. To do this, drop another **Input Data** tool, point it to `..\DICTIONARY\Dictionaries.xlsx`, and this time, select the `QUESTIONS` worksheet:

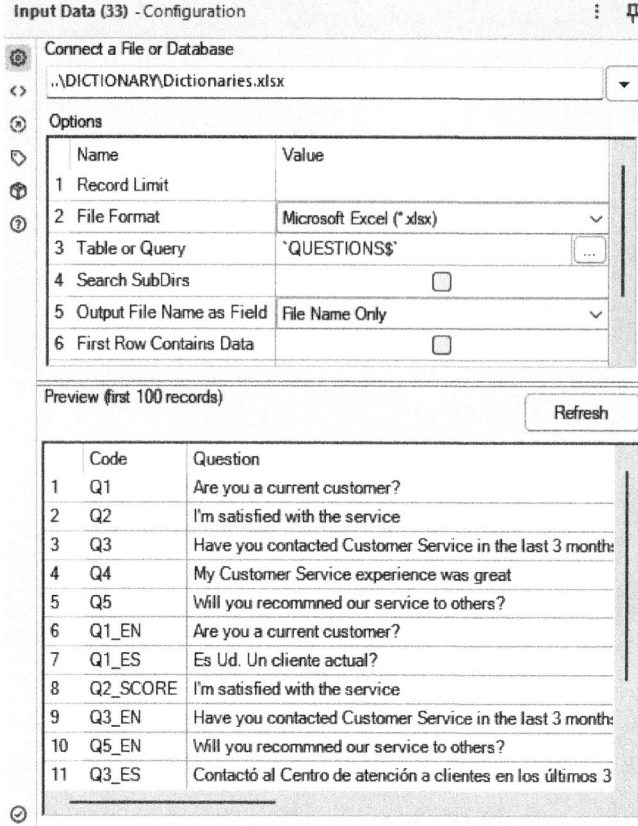

Figure 9.47: Field headers dictionary

11. Drop a **Dynamic Rename** tool onto the canvas and connect the O output from the **Dynamic Replace** tool to the L input, and the **Input Data** tool's output anchors to the R input:

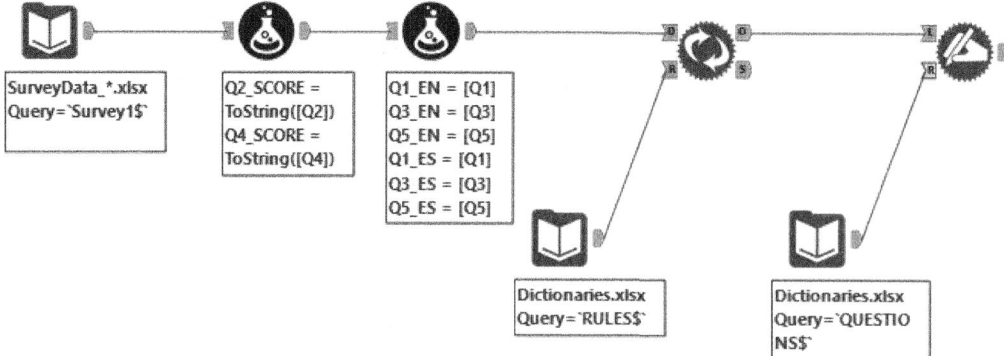

Figure 9.48: Workflow so far

12. Click on the **Dynamic Rename** tool to configure it:

- For **Rename Mode**, select **Take Field Names from Right Input Rows** from the drop-down list.

- Select **Code** from the **Old Field Name from Column** drop-down list.

- Select **Question** from the **New Field Name from Column** drop-down list:

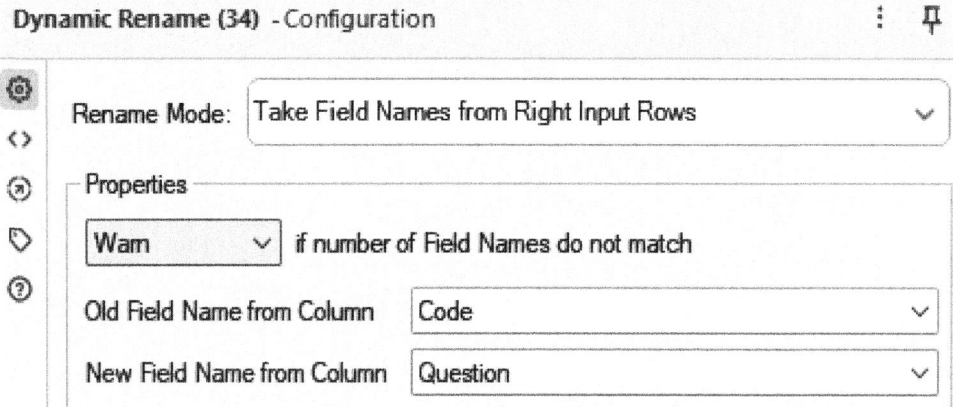

Figure 9.49: Dynamic Rename configuration

Run the workflow, and you'll see all data has been properly shaped in a couple of steps:

Figure 9.50: Final results after running the workflow

How it works...

The **Dynamic Replace** tool allows us to quickly replace data on a series of fields based on conditions. These conditions could be any Boolean expression (evaluates to True or False), and the replacement values could also be static values or expressions.

Allow me to remark on the following point since it's where I found that we all struggle at first when using this tool. The Boolean expressions used to evaluate whether a replacement must be done or not must consider all possibilities; otherwise, you'll get Null values.

For example, let's see within the provided dictionary of rules:

FIELD	EXPRESSION	VALUE
Q4_SCORE	_CurrentField_ ="3"	Neutral
Q4_SCORE	CurrentField_ IN ("4","5")	Positive
Q1_EN	_CurrentField_='Sí'	Yes
Q1_EN	_CurrentField_='Yes'	Yes
Q1_EN	_CurrentField_='No'	No
Q3_EN	_CurrentField_='Sí'	Yes
Q3_EN	_CurrentField_='Yes'	Yes
Q3_EN	_CurrentField_='No'	No
Q5_EN	_CurrentField_='Sí'	Yes
Q5_EN	CurrentField_='Yes'	Yes

Figure 9.51: Boolean expressions in a dictionary

In the highlighted records, you will notice that for FIELD=Q1_EN, we are evaluating Sí, and if it's true, replace it with Yes. But we also check for Yes and No and replace them with Yes and No respectively. If you don't do this in your dictionaries, you'll get Null values when Alteryx finds those values (or any other value) in the specified field.

10
Macros and Apps

So far, we have worked with straightforward workflows within Alteryx. In this chapter, we will explore recipes to take Alteryx functionalities to another level, creating and reusing pieces of logic.

Alteryx's help page defines a macro as follows:

"A macro is a workflow or group of tools built into a single tool that can be inserted into another workflow. Create a macro to save an analytic process you perform repeatedly. Use the macro within a workflow without having to recreate the analytic process each time."

There are four types of macros:

- **Standard macro**: This macro is designed to package a process into a workflow to be used as a tool.

- **Batch macro**: This macro runs multiple times in a workflow and creates an output after each run. The macro runs once for each record or a selected group of records in data. The macro requires at least one **control parameter** tool as an input.

- **Iterative macro**: This macro runs in the workflow the number of times set in the configuration, or continuously until a condition is met, re-feeding itself with the records that don't meet that condition.

- **Location optimizer macro**: This macro is an iterative macro that can be used in network analysis to identify the optimal location(s).

In summary, a macro is a workflow that allows dynamic data in, and via the **Interface** tools, it allows you to modify its behavior for each instance you use it.

Also, you can make your macros appear wherever you want in the toolbar, since they are presented as a tool once you save them.

Technical requirements

There are some useful tasks we can perform to work with macros and share them. The most important one is to define at least one macro repository within Alteryx Designer.

This repository will allow you to easily access and organize your saved macros. If you need to share your macros with your team, a shared location can be used to update the last version of each tool for the whole team.

To create a macro repository, you can revisit the *Getting ready* section of the third recipe in *Chapter 1*, *Different schema Excel worksheets all at once,* where we created one from scratch.

Distributing data connections

Sometimes, we need to distribute connections to data sources because we are the owners or administer them. This recipe will show you how you can transform a specific connection into a tool so that you can distribute it and users can consume its data, without revealing credentials and/or the data source.

Also, we'll explore a great feature that allows you to lock (we previously used to say *encrypt*) workflows so that no one (unless you specifically give permission to a user or users) can open and see its content.

Getting ready

As for every recipe, we have prepared a test set for you, which can be downloaded here: `https://github.com/PacktPublishing/Alteryx-Designer-Cookbook/tree/main/CH10/Recipe01`.

You'll need to have access to a shared directory (where all the input files will be stored).

If you don't know how to create one, you can learn how here: `https://support.microsoft.com/en-us/windows/file-sharing-over-a-network-in-windows-b58704b2-f53a-4b82-7bc1-80f9994725bf`.

We have ours saved at `\\AGP71\AYXServerRepo\DATA`, so every time you see this path, you must replace it with yours (`\\Machine_Name\Shared_Folder_Name`).

We'll start placing the files into the shared folder we created. Please copy the test set into the shared location you defined.

In this recipe, we'll create a tool that reads a chart of accounts, which is placed in a shared network folder, and we'll offer users the ability to select which groups of accounts they want to retrieve, using a **List Box** tool (from the **Interface** category), filled with the contents of the Group field read from the file.

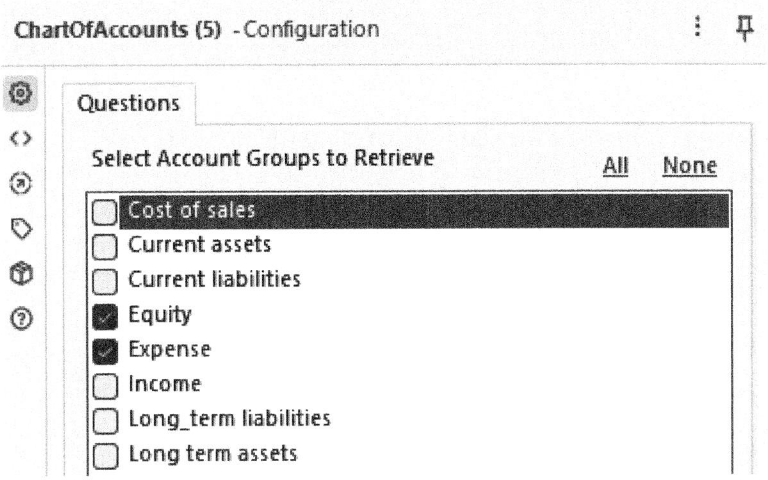

Figure 10.1: The UI of the tool we'll create

Once the user selects the account group (or groups), the tool will return only the accounts in that group (or groups).

All of this is accomplished without the user needing to know where the file is or how the process is handled.

How to do it...

We will divide this recipe into two parts. The first part will see us create the tool, followed by the workflow that uses it:

1. To build the macro, drop an **Input Data** tool onto the canvas and point it to ChartOfAccounts. xlsx within your shared folder (we'll use \\AGP71\AYXServerRepo\DATA for our data, so our complete path will be \\AGP71\AYXServerRepo\DATA\ChartOfAccounts. xlsx), and then select the Master worksheet as the data source.

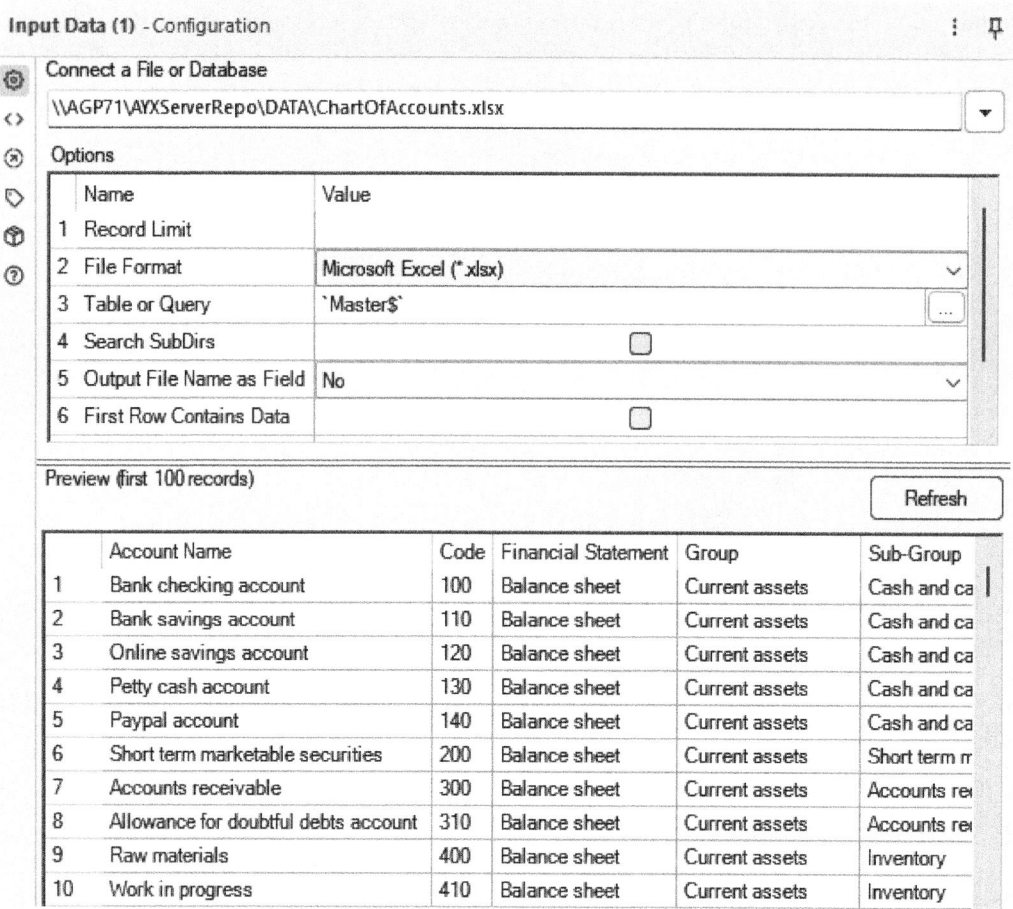

Figure 10.2: Connecting to the data

2. Now, drop a **Summarize** tool and click on the Group field.

3. Click on **Add** and select **Group By**. The Group field should be now placed in the **Actions** panel, with the **Group By** action selected.

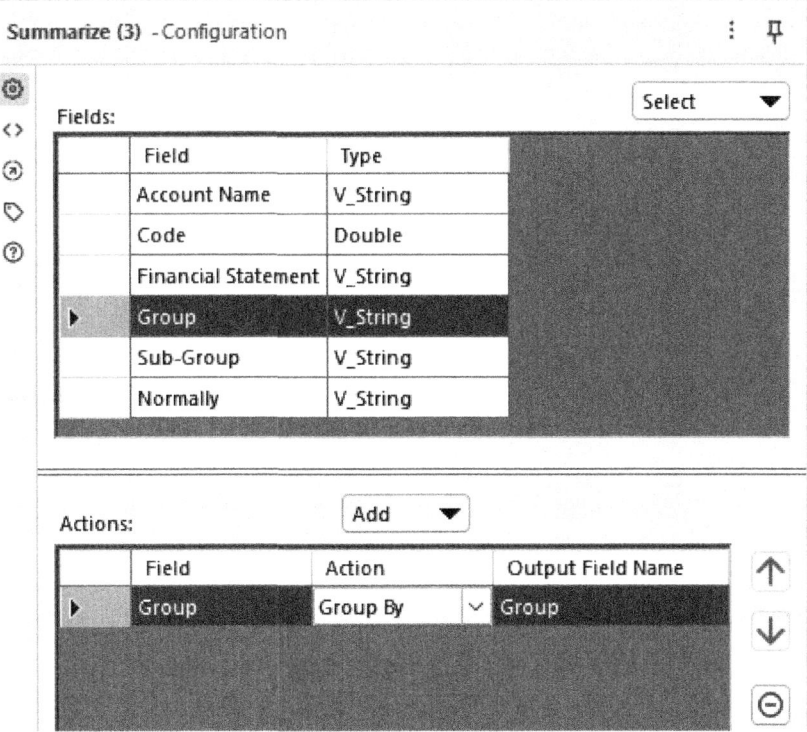

Figure 10.3: Summarization

4.   Add a **Record ID** tool after the **Summarize** tool and leave it with its default values.

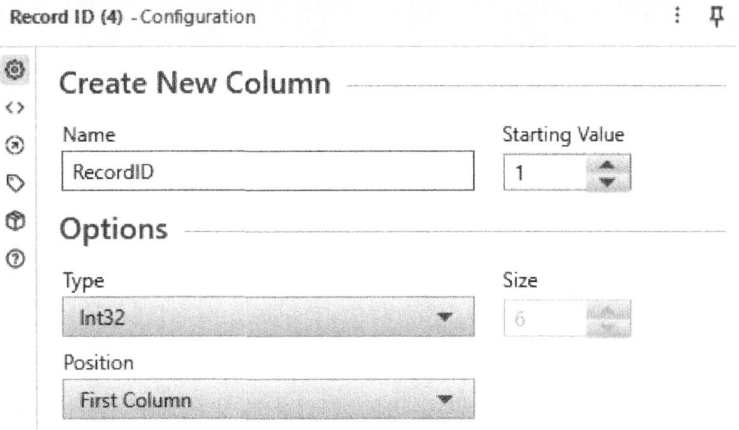

Figure 10.4: Adding Record ID

5.   Add a **Formula** tool and connect it to the **Record ID** output.

6. From the **Output Column** dropdown, select the `Group` field and use this expression in the formula:

```
Replace([Group], " ","__Replace__")
```

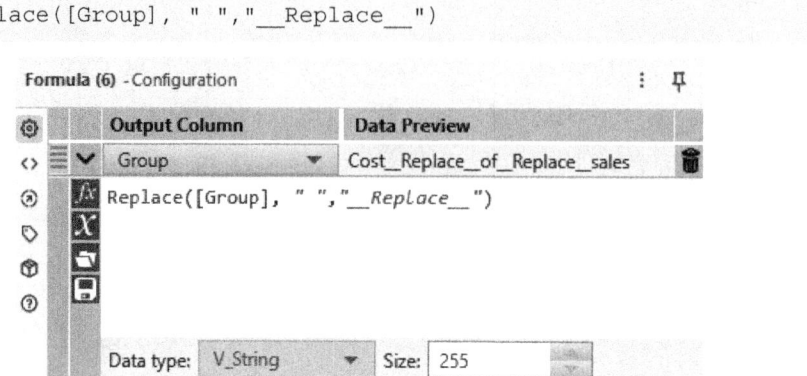

Figure 10.5: The Formula tool configuration

7. Now, add a **Cross Tab** tool and configure it as follows.

8. Make sure nothing is selected in the **Group data by these values** panel.

9. From the **Change Column Headers** dropdown, select **Group**.

10. From the **Values for New Columns** dropdown, select **RecordID**.

11. For **Method for Aggregating Values**, select **Sum**.

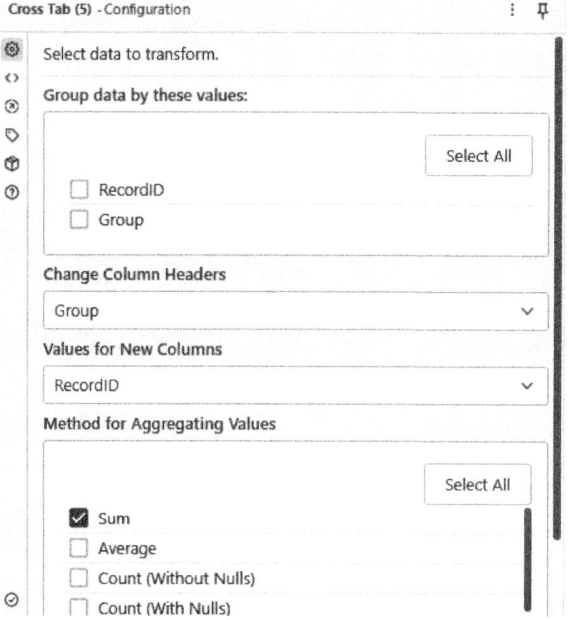

Figure 10.6: The Cross Tab tool configuration

12. Add a **Dynamic Rename** tool and connect its **L** input anchor to the **Cross Tab** tool output anchor.

13. From the **Rename Mode** dropdown, select **Formula**.

14. Select all the fields.

15. In the **Expression** box, use this formula:

```
Replace([_CurrentField_],"__Replace__"," ")
```

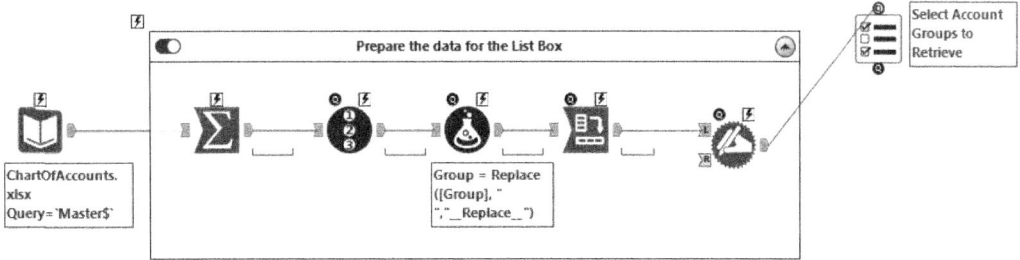

Figure 10.7: The Dynamic Rename tool configuration

16. Add a **List Box** tool to the canvas, and connect the output anchor from the **Dynamic Rename** tool to the circled **Q** on top of the tool.

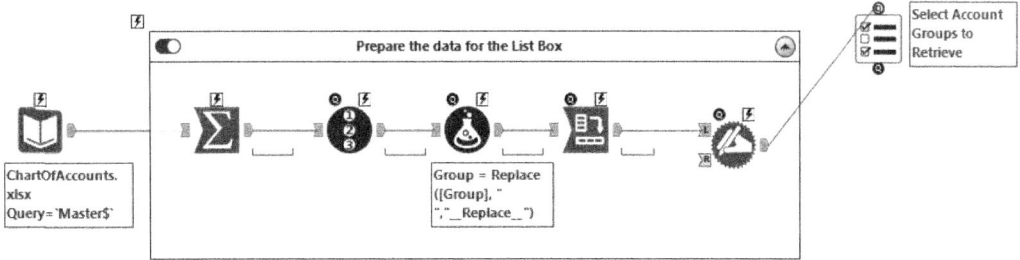

Figure 10.8: Adding the List Box tool to the workflow

17. Replace the default text in the **Enter the text or question to be displayed** box with `Select Account Groups to Retrieve`.

18. Click on **Generate Custom List** (**Select Tool Mode** is the default for Alteryx). This will enable the **Start Text, Separator,** and **End Text** fields. Leave them with their default values.

This will create a list, based on the user's selection, with the following structure:

`Start Text` | the first selected value | `Separator` | the second selected value | `Separator` | the *n* selected value | `End Text`

Since we already connected the **Q** input anchor on top to the **Dynamic Rename** output anchor, the **List Values** dropdown will be populated with **Fields from Connected Tool**, which you can't change.

19. Make sure that all field types are selected.

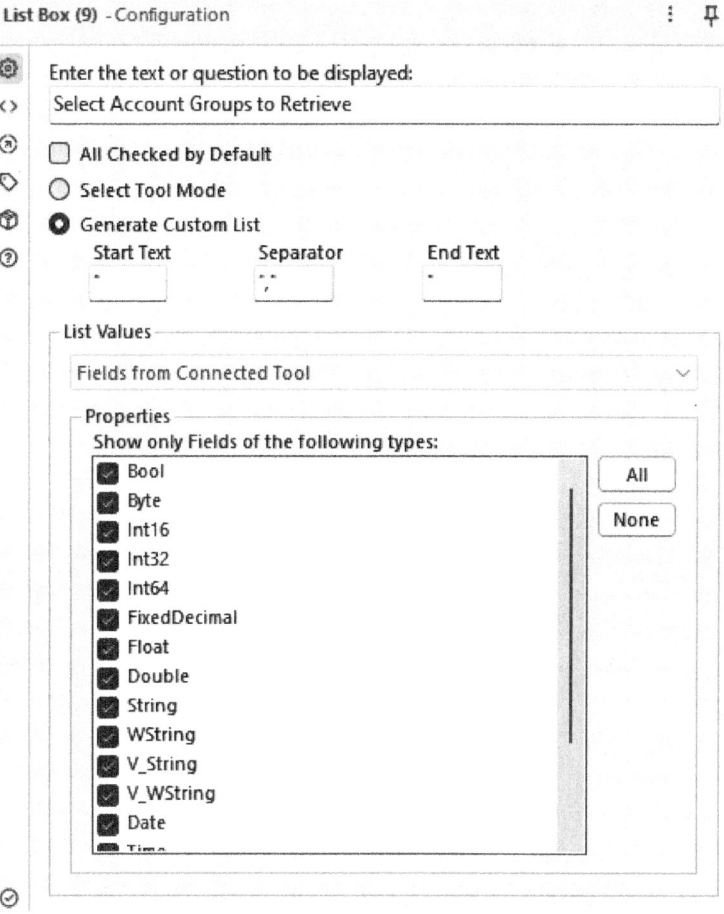

Figure 10.9: The List Box tool configuration

20. Now, add a **Filter** tool to the workflow, connecting its input anchor to the output anchor of the **Input Data** tool.

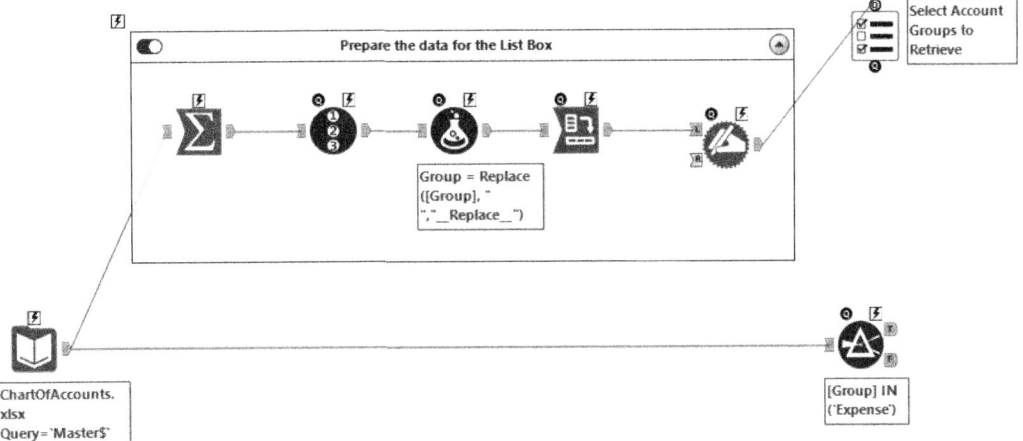

Figure 10.10: Adding the Filter tool to the workflow

21. Click on **Custom filter**, and use this expression for the filter:

```
[Group] IN ('Expense')
```

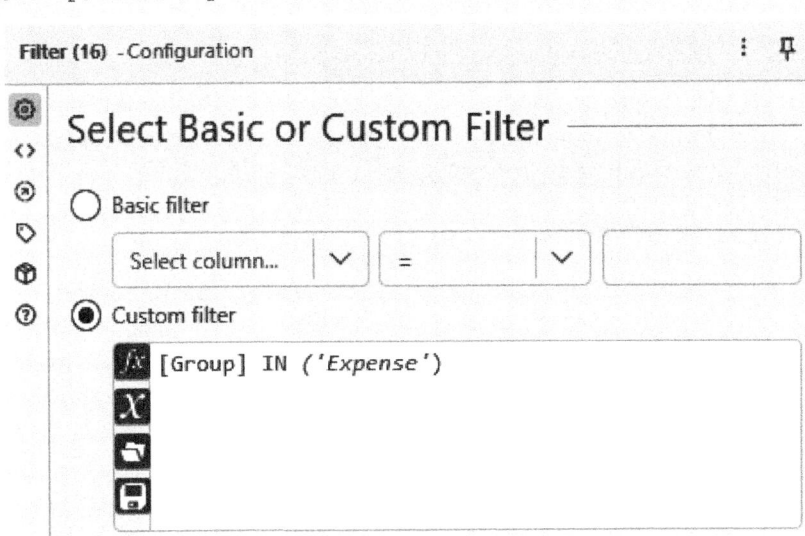

Figure 10.11: Formula tool configuration

Now, we tie everything up.

22. Click on the black **Q** icon at the bottom of the **List Box** tool, and drag a connection to the lightning icon on top of the **Filter** tool.

Note that Alteryx has added a new tool (an **Action** tool) between them. This tool will allow us to tell Alteryx Designer what to do with the user's input.

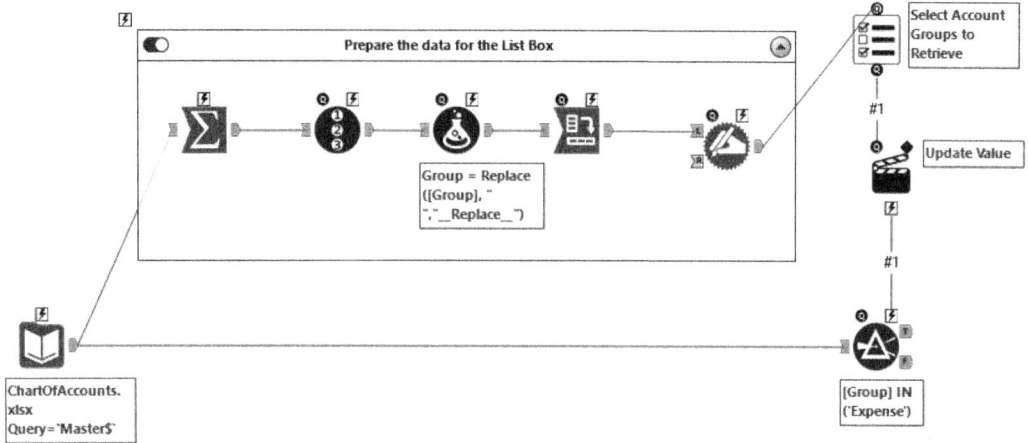

Figure 10.12: Connecting the tools in the workflow

23. Click on the **Action** tool to access its configuration.

24. Make sure **Update Value (Default)** is selected in the **Select an action type** dropdown.

25. Click on the **Expression - value** line until it's marked in blue.

26. Find the **Replace a specific string** option at the bottom of the **Configuration** panel and enable it. Alteryx will populate it with the whole filter expression, so delete everything but the **'Expense'** string (make sure not to remove the quotes).

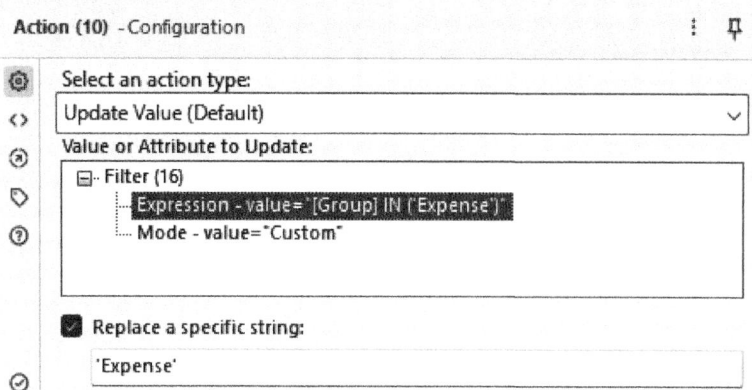

Figure 10.13: The Action tool configuration

27. Add a **Macro Output** tool, connected to the **T** output anchor of the **Filter** tool.

28. Change the output name to `Selected Accounts`, and enter A for **Anchor Abbreviation**.

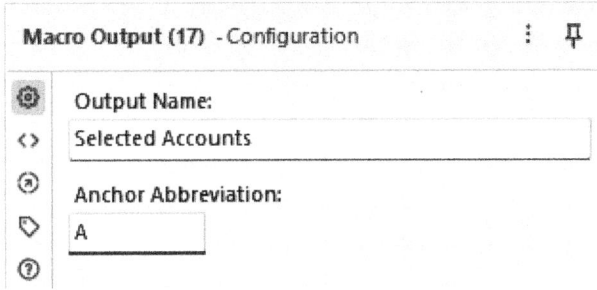

Figure 10.14: Naming the label and anchor abbreviation

The workflow should look like this.

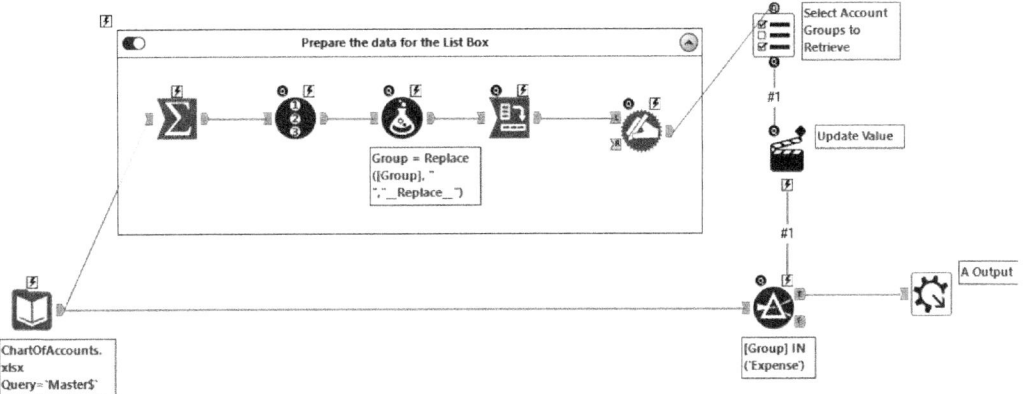

Figure 10.15: The workflow so far

To use this new tool within our workflows, we need to save it first. However, to share the workflow, we need to save the tool where a user will be able to access it.

We will create a new shared folder to place all shared macros/tools within it (if you have access to one within your network, you can use it:.

1. Create a new folder in your shared folder, called `AYXMacrosRepo` (in our case, it'll be `\\AGP71\AYXMacrosRepo`).

2. Save the workflow in the folder you just created, and name it `ChartOfAccounts` (note that Alteryx will use `.yxmc` for an Alteryx macro extension).

Also, you can revisit the *Getting ready* section in the third recipe of *Chapter 1, Different schema Excel worksheets all at once*; you'll see how to add this folder as a macro repository so that Alteryx can find these tool(s) automatically.

Now that we have saved the tool, we need to create a new workflow.

3. Click on **File | New Workflow** (or hit *Ctrl + N*).

4. Right-click on white space in the canvas, click on **Insert**, and scroll down until you find the **Macro** option.

5. If you kept the tool open after saving, you'll see it within the options; otherwise, hit **Browse...** and locate it in your shared folder.

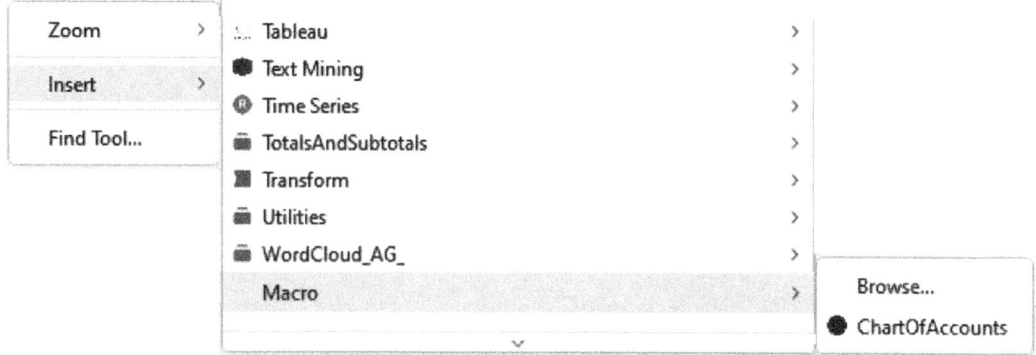

Figure 10.16: The macro Insert menu

Once you select the macro, you'll see it in the canvas along with its **Configuration** panel.

As you can see, the elements we configured in the macro are present/exposed to the user.

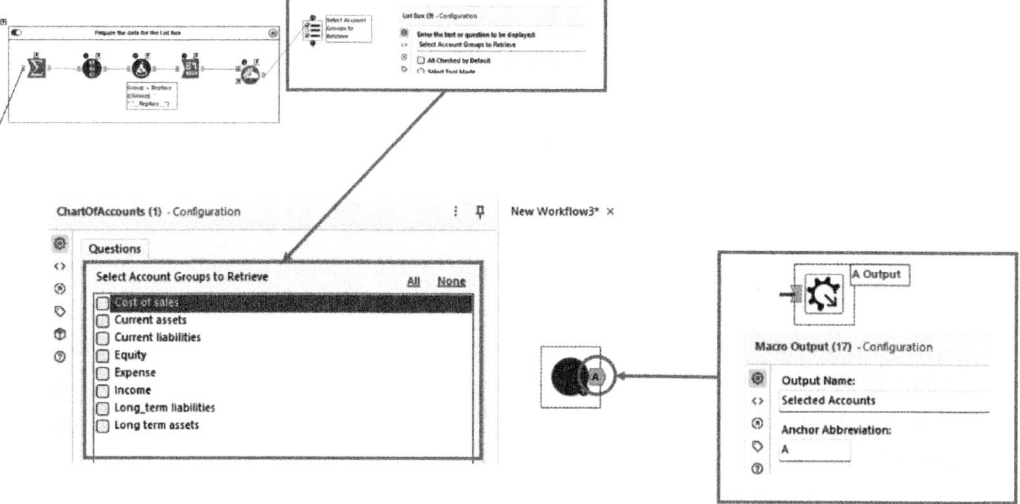

Figure 10.17: The macro elements presented to the user

6.   Select some values from the account groups exposed and run the workflow. You'll see that it only retrieves the ones you selected.

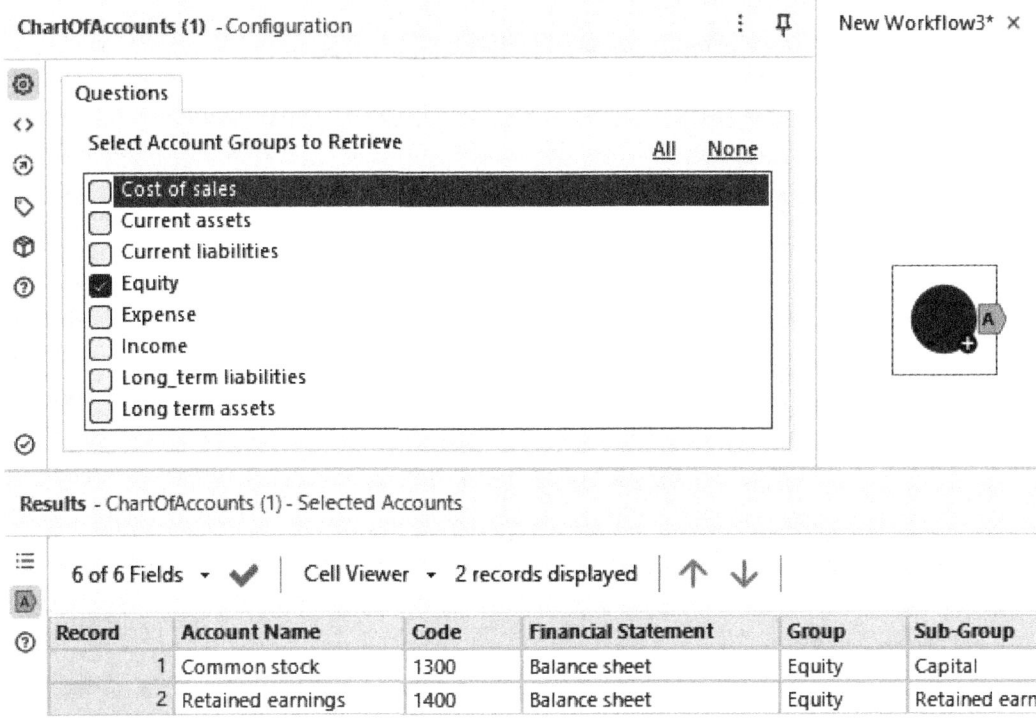

Figure 10.18: The final workflow (using the macro)

How it works...

A macro is an Alteryx workflow that is "packed" as a tool. We designed a workflow that filters the output based on account groups (within the macro, we instructed it to return only the **'Expenses'** group).

Using the **Interface** tools, we can modify the workflow behavior based on user input at runtime. The **Action** tool was configured to replace the **'Expenses'** group of accounts for whatever comes from the **List Box** tool, and since **List Box** is configured as **Generate Custom List**, it'll produce a list that can be evaluated within our expression and produce the desired output.

> **Important note**
> Ensure that users using the tool have access to the shared directory; otherwise, it won't show in their toolbars.

There's more...

As we can see in the finished tool, the icon doesn't help much to understand what type of tool we have. It is better to use a custom icon that better represents the tool's purpose, so we will change it. To do so, we will explore some of the **Interface Designer** capabilities in Alteryx Designer:

1. Activate the **Interface Designer** panel by hitting *Ctrl + Alt + D* or by going to the **View** menu and selecting **Interface Designer**.

    The **Interface Designer** panel will appear.

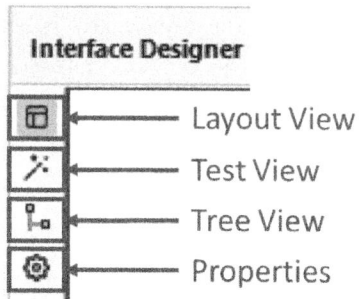

Figure 10.19: Interface Designer UI

It presents four icons on the left most part of the panel that allow access to all the available configurations:

*   **Layout View**: This shows the design version of the tool UI, with the option to add and rearrange controls.

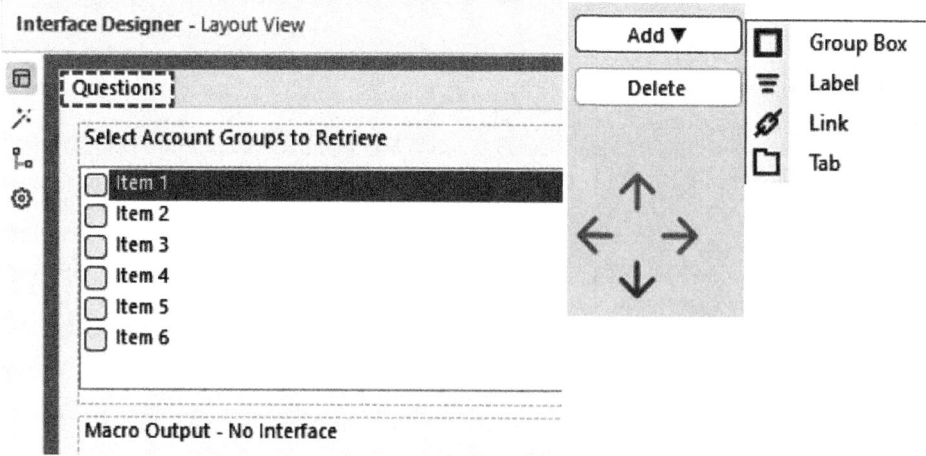

Figure 10.20: Layout View

- **Test View**: This presents the runtime version of the actual UI, along with some debugging options (such as viewing the XML that goes between tools).

One big functionality of this view is the ability to create a plain workflow, based on the actual selected values to debug macros/apps, by clicking the **Open Debug** button.

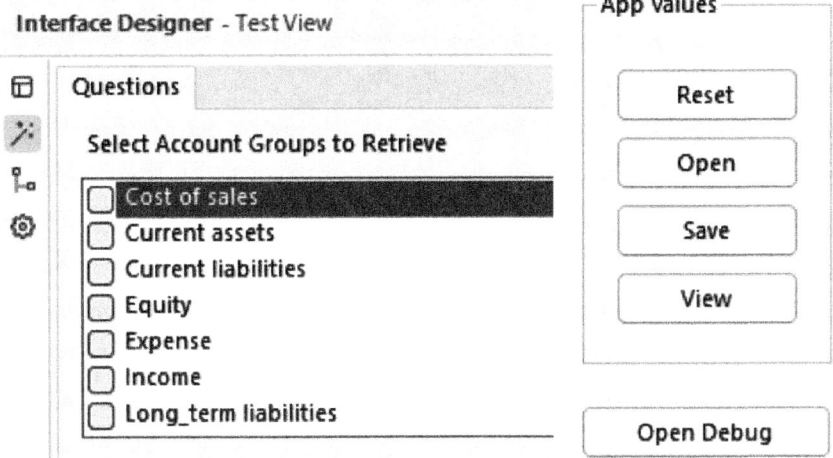

Figure 10.21: Test View

- **Tree View**: This provides a tree view (hierarchical relationship) representation of the questions and actions in the current workflow/macro/app, allowing the user to reorder the selected elements.

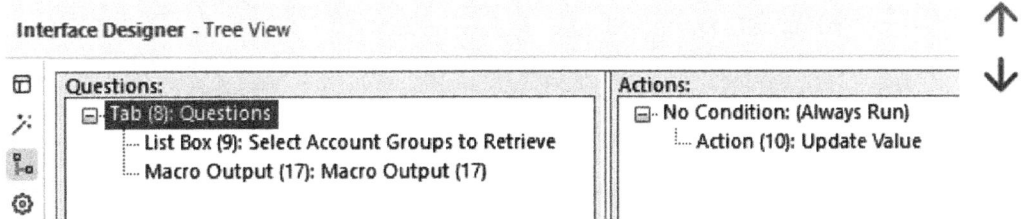

Figure 10.22: Tree View

- **Properties**: This allows a user to customize the macro behavior. This setting differs when accessed from a macro or app.

Also, here is where we'll find the feature to change the tool icon.

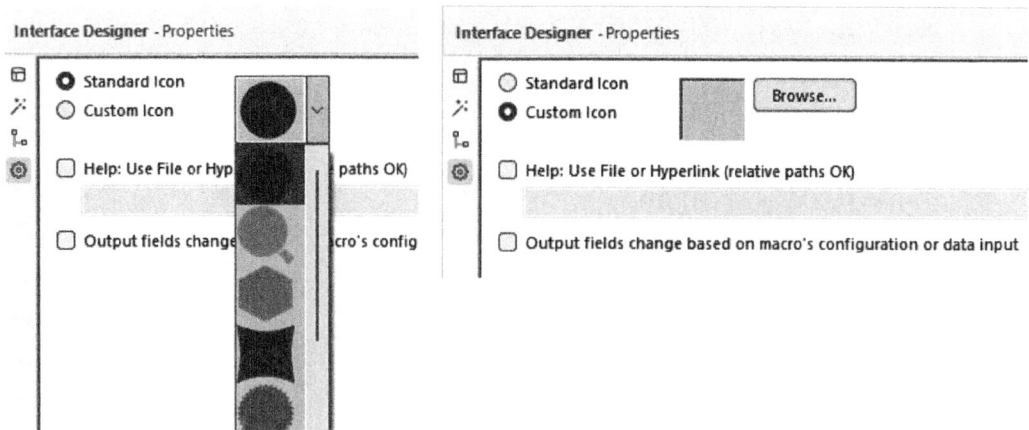

Figure 10.23: Properties

We can use some prepackaged icons from Alteryx or use our own.

2. Select **Custom Icon**, hit **Browse…**, and select the ChartOfAccounts.png file in the PICS subfolder, saved in the actual macro folder.

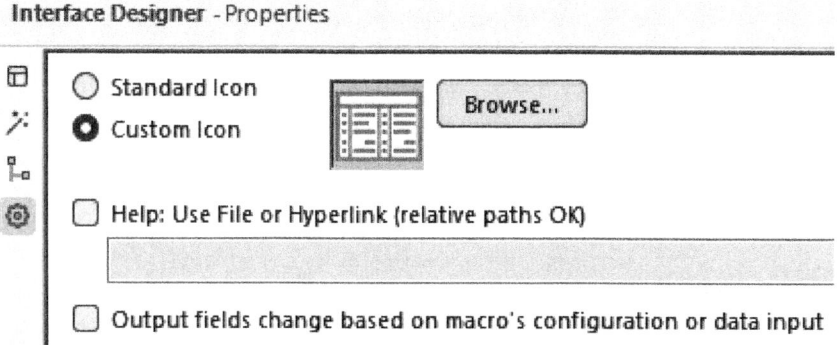

Figure 10.24: Change the macro icon (the Properties view)

3. Save the macro (hit *Ctrl + S*) and return to your workflow. Now, you'll see that the icon of the tool changed, and it uses the icon we chose.

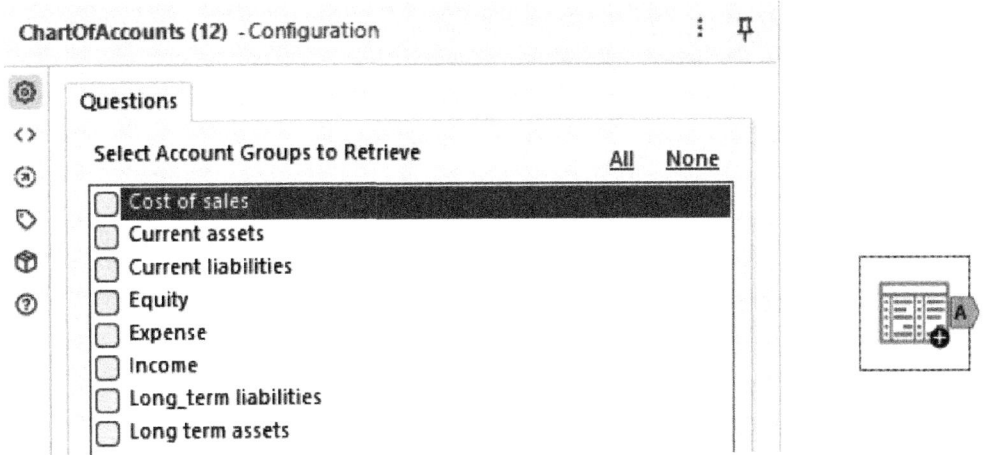

Figure 10.25: The macro updated with the new icon

Also, we can change where the new tool will appear in the user's toolbar by changing some values in its configuration.

4. To do so, with the macro workflow open, click on any white space in the canvas. This will bring up the workflow configuration options.

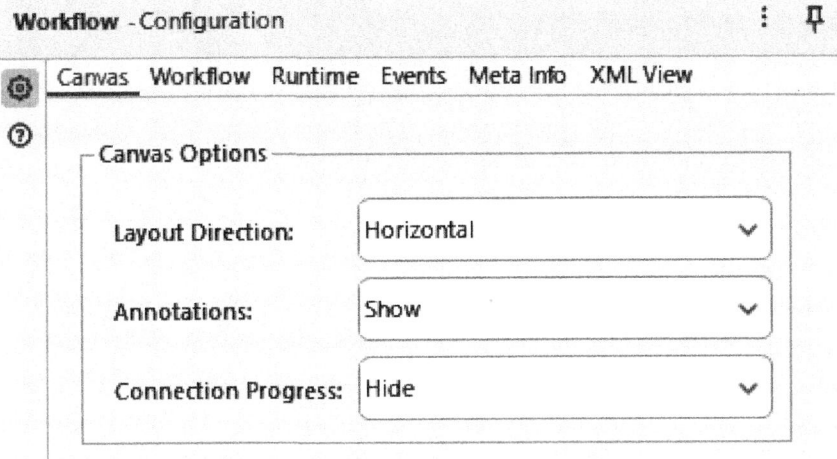

Figure 10.26: The workflow configuration options

5. On the panel, click on **Meta Info** to access the meta info of the tool.

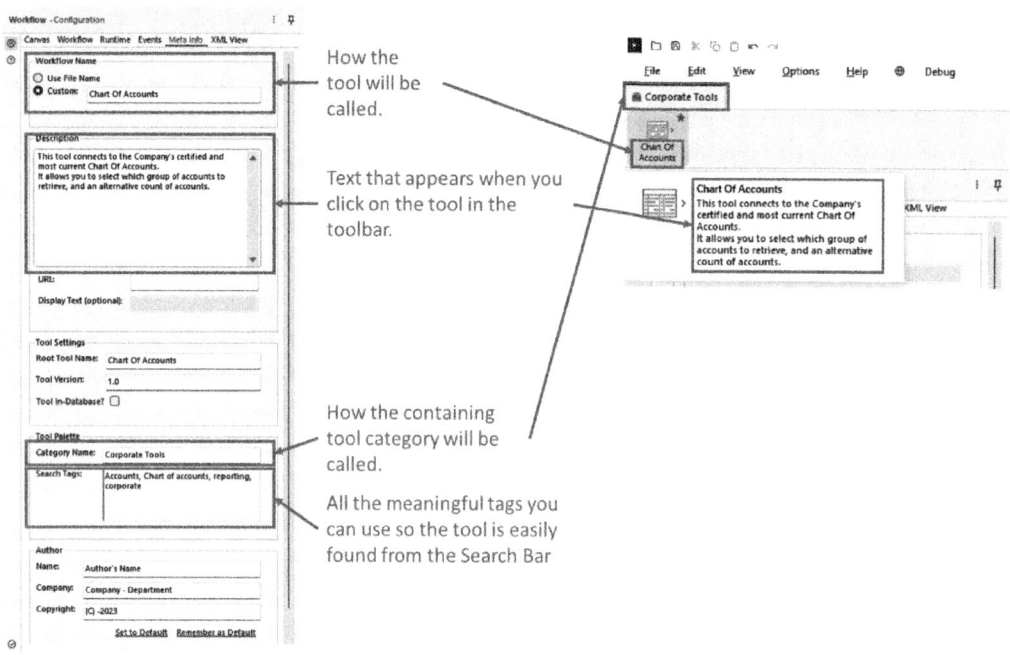

Figure 10.27: The Meta Info options

6.   Fill in the info for the tool and save the macro again.

You'll see that if you used a custom tool category name (a name that is not one of Alteryx's), it will be created and available in your toolbar (if you can't find it, close and restart Alteryx Designer), and you can find this new tool inside that category and via the search bar.

Using Detour in your data stream

When developing analytics solutions, we sometimes want to try alternative logic within the same workflow. We can do that by using the **Detour** tool to instruct our workflow to execute one datastream or an alternative one with a click. The **Detour** tool allows us to do exactly that, taking a right or left path depending on our decision.

With a simple user interface, this tool will take you left or right, avoiding the execution of the other, depending on one setting, but this is just a small part of what this tool can do. When used within a macro, it can enable or disable entire processes based on user selections.

Within this recipe, we will add a new feature to the macro we created in the first recipe of *Chapter 10*. This feature will be a checkbox that instructs our tool to return the number of accounts in each group if checked, not returning it if unchecked.

Just by adding an interface control, and with the help of the **Detour** tool, we will be able to execute and switch between one stream of logic and another.

Getting ready

As always, we have prepared the test set for you to follow along with this recipe; you can download it from here: `https://github.com/PacktPublishing/Alteryx-Designer-Cookbook/tree/main/CH10/Recipe02`.

Before getting into the recipe, let's see how the **Detour** tool works. For starters, it is a pair of tools, not just one. The **Detour** tool switches between left or right paths, and the **Detour End** tool brings the two data streams back to one. By adding an **Output Data** tool to each output connector of the **Detour** tool, it can be replaced.

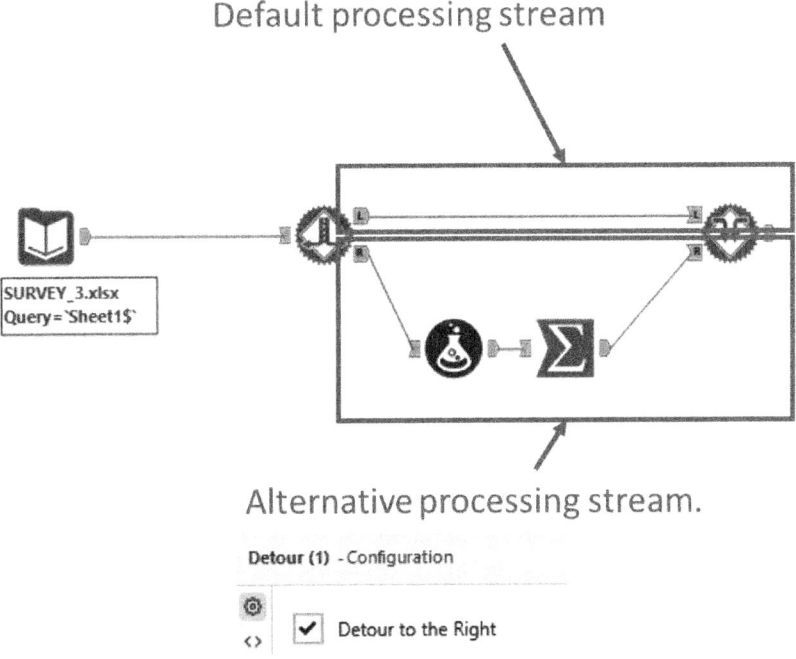

Figure 10.28: The Detour tool concept

How to do it...

Let's get started as follows:

1. Go to **File** | **Open Workflow** | **Browse** (or hit *Ctrl + O*), and open the workflow located in ..\ `MACROS\ChartOfAccounts.yxmc`. This is the tool we built in the first recipe of this chapter.

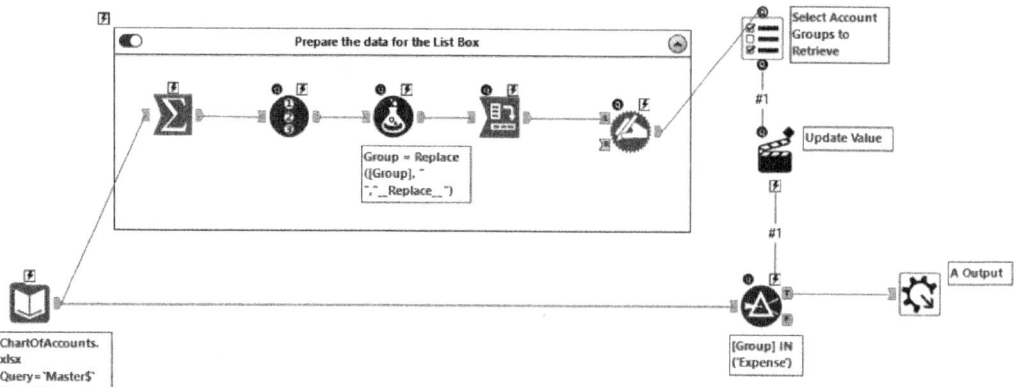

Figure 10.29: The macro from the previous recipe

2. Drop a **Check Box** tool (from the **Interface** category) onto the canvas, to the right of the existing **List Box** tool.

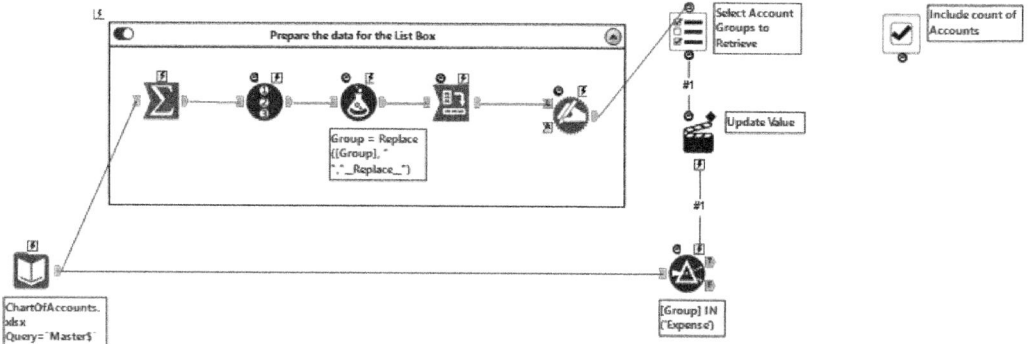

Figure 10.30: Adding a Check Box tool

3. Click on it to access its configuration, enter Include count of Accounts in the **Enter the text or question to be displayed** textbox, and click **Default Value** to select it.

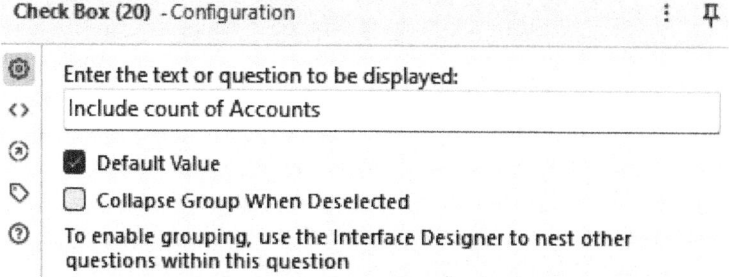

Figure 10.31: The Check Box configuration

4.   Now, drop a **Detour** tool onto the canvas and connect it to the **T** output anchor of the existing **Filter** tool.

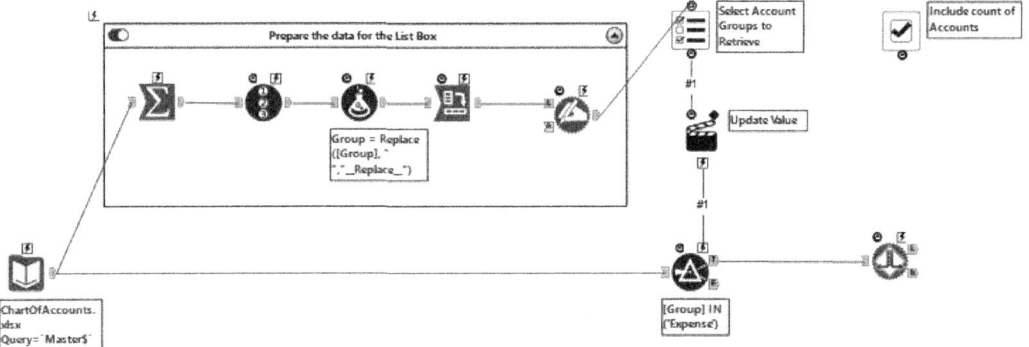

Figure 10.32: Adding the Detour tool to the macro

5.   Now, connect the **Q** output (the black background **Q** connector below the **Check Box** tool) to the lightning connector of the **Detour** tool. An **Action** tool will appear between both tools.

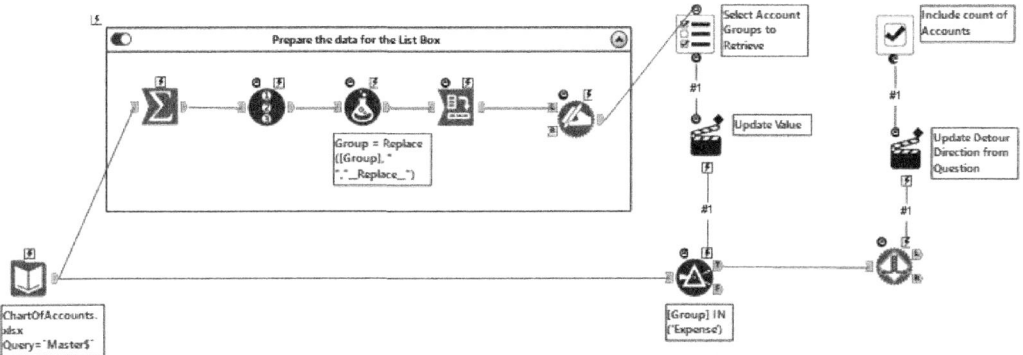

Figure 10.33: Connecting the Check Box tool to the Detour tool

6.   Click on the added **Action** tool, and make sure that **Update Detour Direction from Question** is the option in the **Select an action type** dropdown (it's the default option when connected to a **Detour** tool).

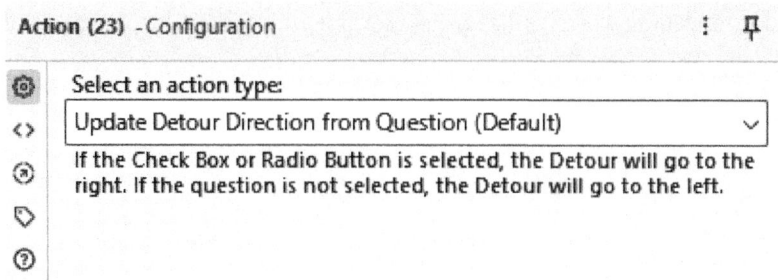

Figure 10.34: The Action tool configuration

So far, we have a tool that returns all the accounts within a data source, based on groups' selections. Now, we need to build the logic to count the number of accounts within each selected group.

7.   Add a **Summarize** tool following the **R** output from the **Detour** tool (that's the path Alteryx will use if the **Check Box** tool is selected).

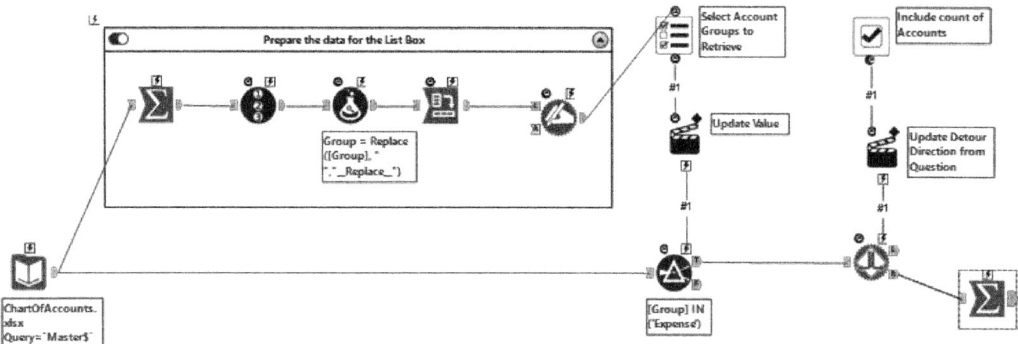

Figure 10.35: Detour right Summarize

8.   Click it to access its configuration.

9.   Click on Group, then **Add**, and select Group By.

10.   Click on **Code**, then **Add**, and click on **Count Distinct**.

11.   Rename **CountDistinct_Code to** Accounts, by changing the value Alteryx put in the **Output Field Name** row.

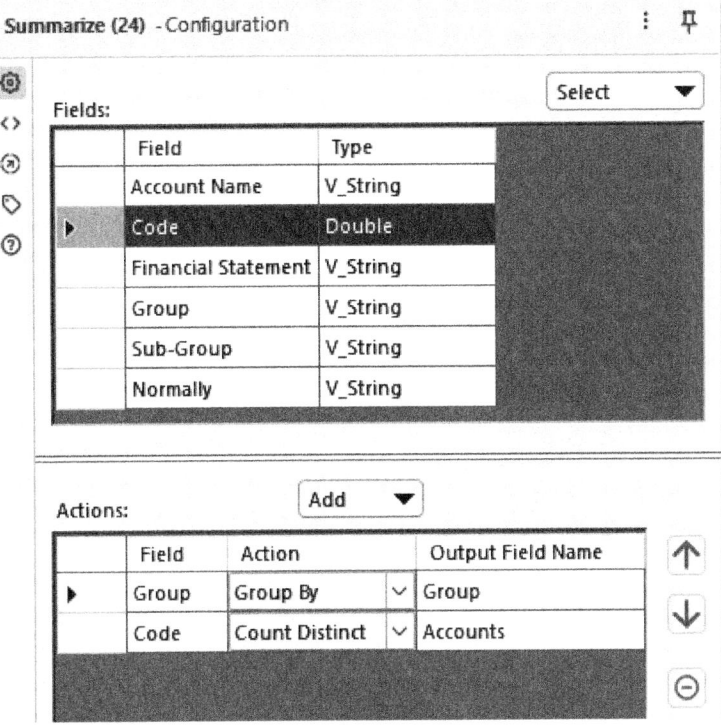

Figure 10.36: The Summarize tool configuration

This will produce the number of accounts within each group.

12. Add a **Join** tool, connecting the **T** output anchor from the **Filter** tool to the **L** input anchor and the **Summarize** tool output anchor to the **R** input.

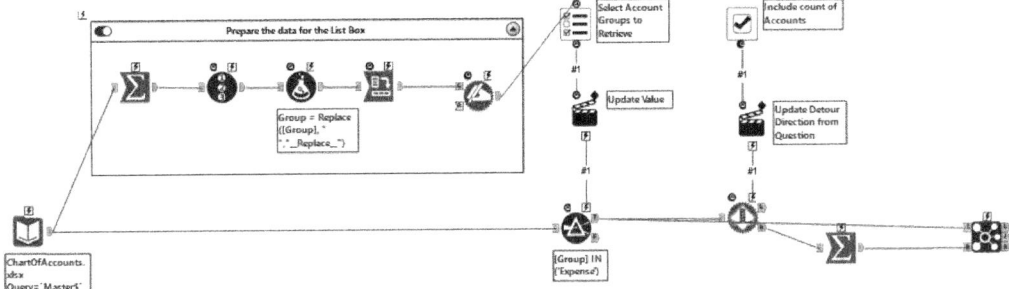

Figure 10.37: Adding the Join tool

13. Select **Group** from the **Left** dropdown, and make sure that Alteryx sets **Group** as the **Right** dropdown (if not, select **Group** as the **Right** joining field).

14. Remember to deselect the Group field from the **Right** input to avoid unnecessary fields.

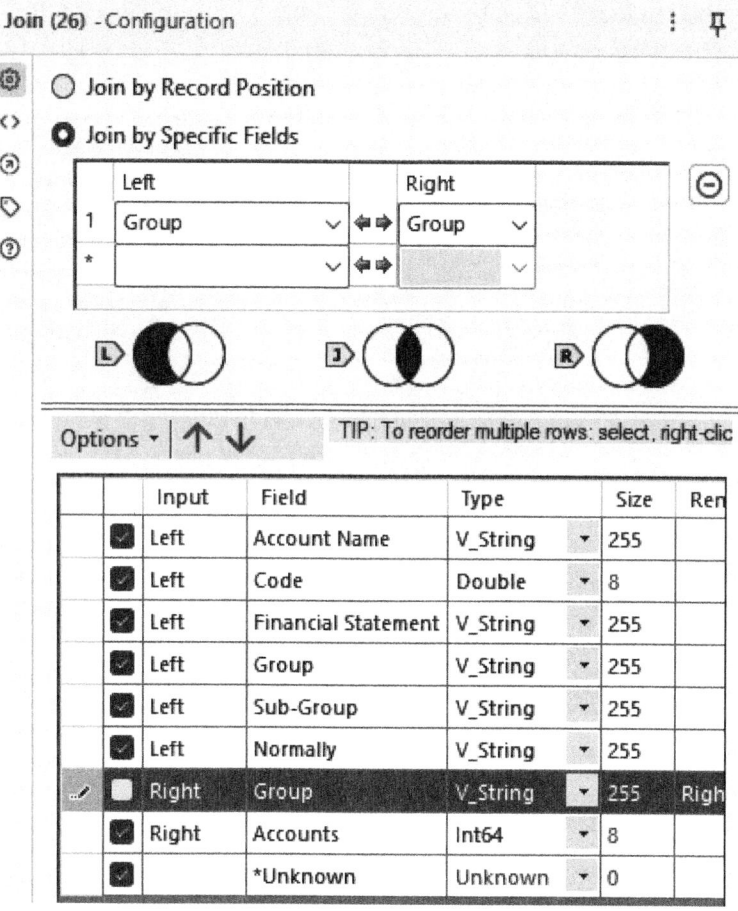

Figure 10.38: The Join tool configuration

15. To complete the **Detour** part of our "new" tool, drop a **Detour End** tool (this tool has no configuration) and connect the **J** output anchor of the **Join** tool to the **R** input and the **L** output from the **Detour** tool to the **L** input of the **Detour End** tool.

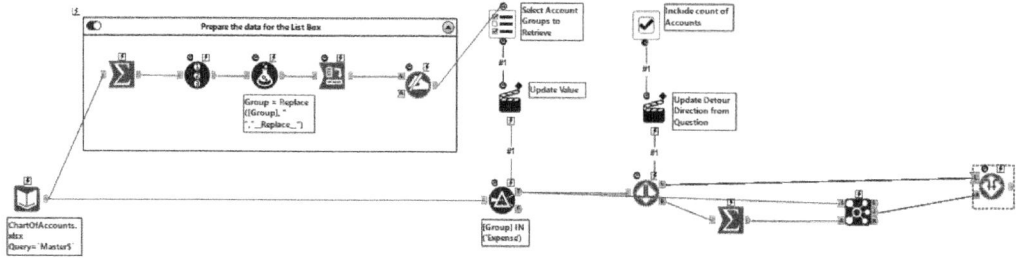

Figure 10.39: Completing the Detour tool (with a Detour End tool)

16. Finally, connect the output anchor of the **Detour End** tool to the **Macro Output** tool that was already in the workflow.

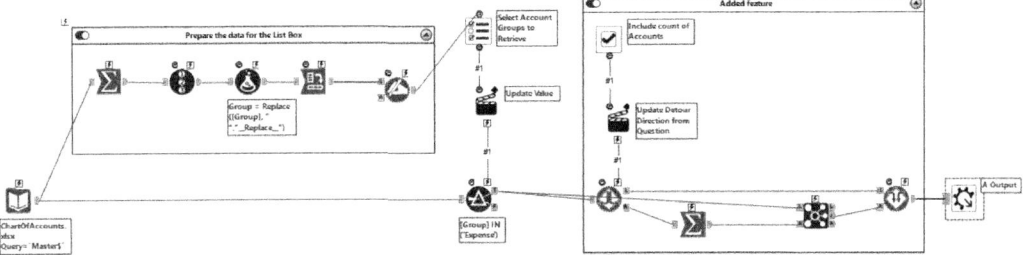

Figure 10.40: Setting the Macro Output tool

17. Save the new tool (verify that it's saved as .yxmc).

18. Create a new workflow (*Ctrl + N* or **File | New Workflow**).

19. If you kept the macro opened, right-click on any white space on the canvas where you want the new tool to be inserted.

20. Click on **Insert**.

21. Navigate to the bottom of the menu, then click on **Macro**, and select the macro you just saved.

    You'll have a workflow with one tool that allows you to retrieve accounts by selecting their Group, and you'll see the new feature selected (**Include count of Accounts**).

22. To test the tool, select a couple of Group fields, leave the new checkbox checked, and run the workflow.

    Note the Accounts field on the right of the resulting data. It contains the number of different accounts in that group.

Account Name	Code	Financial Statement	Group	Sub-Group	Normally	Accounts
Materials purchased	2200	Income Statement	Cost of sales	Cost of sales	Debit	9
Packaging	2210	Income Statement	Cost of sales	Cost of sales	Debit	9
Discounts taken	2220	Income Statement	Cost of sales	Cost of sales	Debit	9
Carriage	2230	Income Statement	Cost of sales	Cost of sales	Debit	9
Import duty	2240	Income Statement	Cost of sales	Cost of sales	Debit	9
Transport insurance	2250	Income Statement	Cost of sales	Cost of sales	Debit	9
Opening inventory	2260	Income Statement	Cost of sales	Cost of sales	Debit	9
Closing inventory	2270	Income Statement	Cost of sales	Cost of sales	Credit	9
Productive Labour	2280	Income Statement	Cost of sales	Cost of sales	Debit	9
Research and development	2300	Income Statement	Expense	Research and development	Debit	62
Sales commissions	2400	Income Statement	Expense	Sales and marketing	Debit	62
Sales promotion	2410	Income Statement	Expense	Sales and marketing	Debit	62
Advertising	2420	Income Statement	Expense	Sales and marketing	Debit	62
Gifts & samples	2430	Income Statement	Expense	Sales and marketing	Debit	62
Marketing expenses	2440	Income Statement	Expense	Sales and marketing	Debit	62

Figure 10.41: Results when selecting Include count of Accounts

23. Click on **Include count of Accounts** to deselect it, and run the workflow again. You'll see that the Accounts field is not present when we instruct our tool not to return it.

Account Name	Code	Financial Statement	Group	Sub-Group	Normally
Sales	2000	Income Statement	Income	Revenue	Credit
Discounts allowed	2100	Income Statement	Income	Revenue	Debit
Materials purchased	2200	Income Statement	Cost of sales	Cost of sales	Debit
Packaging	2210	Income Statement	Cost of sales	Cost of sales	Debit
Discounts taken	2220	Income Statement	Cost of sales	Cost of sales	Debit
Carriage	2230	Income Statement	Cost of sales	Cost of sales	Debit
Import duty	2240	Income Statement	Cost of sales	Cost of sales	Debit
Transport insurance	2250	Income Statement	Cost of sales	Cost of sales	Debit
Opening inventory	2260	Income Statement	Cost of sales	Cost of sales	Debit
Closing inventory	2270	Income Statement	Cost of sales	Cost of sales	Credit
Productive Labour	2280	Income Statement	Cost of sales	Cost of sales	Debit
Research and development	2300	Income Statement	Expense	Research and development	Debit
Sales commissions	2400	Income Statement	Expense	Sales and marketing	Debit
Sales promotion	2410	Income Statement	Expense	Sales and marketing	Debit
Advertising	2420	Income Statement	Expense	Sales and marketing	Debit

Figure 10.42: The Include count of Accounts deselected results

How it works...

The **Detour** tool provides a way to take an alternative path in our data stream. By default, it executes what follows the L output, but we can change that with a click, or by using it within a macro and swapping paths, based on user input and an **Action** tool.

In our example, we configured it to, by default, take the right path (with the checkbox selected when we used the **Default Value** option of the **Check Box** tool configuration). Unselecting **Include count of Accounts** will cause Alteryx to take the L path of the **Detour** tool, so no aggregations will be done.

Once any paths are taken and the logic executed, the **Detour End** tool will unify the data stream again, allowing us to continue the workflow (in our example, just outputting the results).

Another interesting way of using the **Detour** tool is by ending it, using an **Output Data** tool on each path instead of the **Detour End** tool.

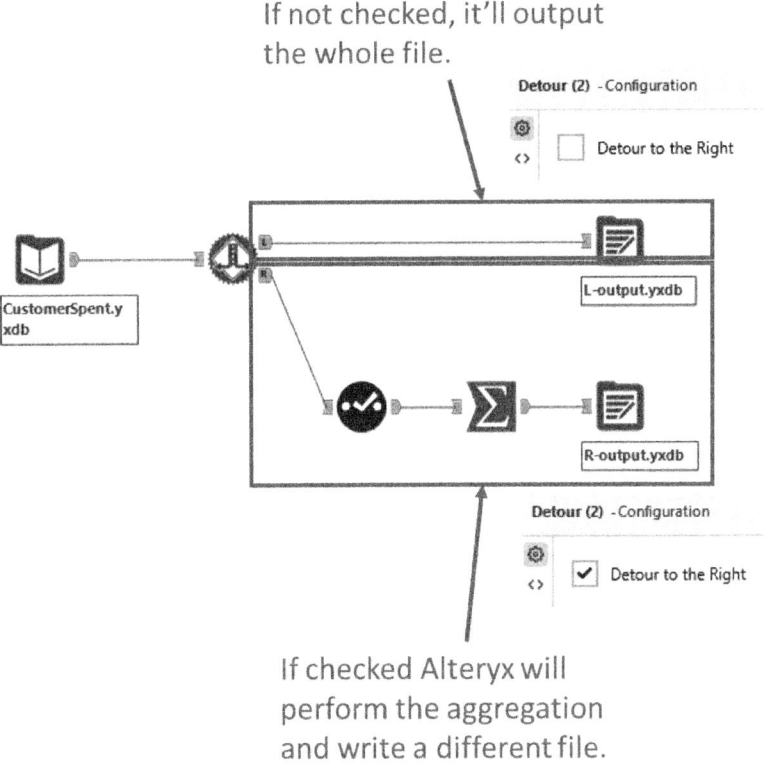

If not checked, it'll output the whole file.

If checked Alteryx will perform the aggregation and write a different file.

Figure 10.43: The Detour tool ending with the Output Data tools

Enabling/disabling tool containers

In the previous recipe, we saw how to deal with alternative/conditional executions with two alternatives. But what happens when we have more than two alternatives to execute or bypass?

The **Tool Container** tool not only gives us the ability to document and organize our workflows; it also allows us to enable or disable their content so that it can be executed (or not).

In this recipe, we'll build a reporting tool/macro that allows us to select, using a **List Box** tool, which reports it'll generate and which it won't.

Getting ready

We have you covered with a test set for this recipe that you can download here: https://github.com/PacktPublishing/Alteryx-Designer-Cookbook/tree/main/CH10/Recipe03.

We'll use a sales dataset that contains a series of attributes and the number of visits and spending per customer.

Customer_ID	Store Number	Customer Segment	First Name	Last Name	Address	City	State	Zip	Visits	Spend
10	100	Home Office	PAMELA	WRIGHT	2316 E 5TH AVE	DENVER	CO	80206	1	206.95
100	100	Consumer	MELISSA	RUFF	2753 S MILWAUKEE ST	DENVER	CO	80210	1	228.27
1000	104	Small Business	CONSTANTI	VLASSIS	16911 E HARVARD AVE	AURORA	CO	80013	1	432.44
1002	104	Home Office	AMY	LOCKEMER	3721 S PITKIN CT	AURORA	CO	80013	4	2101.11
1003	101	Home Office	DANELL	VALDEZ	2925 W COLLEGE AVE	DENVER	CO	80219	1	1404.09
1005	107	Small Business	JESSICA	RINEHART	4220 W 35TH AVE	DENVER	CO	80212	2	962.61
1006	104	Small Business	NANCY	CLARK	8785 CLOVERLEAF CIR	PARKER	CO	80134	4	552.53
1008	107	Home Office	ANDREA	BRUN	2080 FENTON ST	DENVER	CO	80214	1	25.37
1009	104	Corporate	DENISE	PENTICO	4125C S EVANSTON CIR	AURORA	CO	80014	2	7026.44

Figure 10.44: The dataset we'll use

Based on this data, we need to provide our users with a tool that generates a series of reports to management:

- **Total Sales per Store**

- **Total Sales per Store and Customer Segment**

- **Total Sales by Zip Code**, from highest to lowest

- **Top 5 Customers per Store by Spend**

- **Top Customers' average spend by visit**

However, these reports are not always required together, so we will add a feature that allows a user to select which ones we'll output on every run, bypassing the logic for the ones that are not selected.

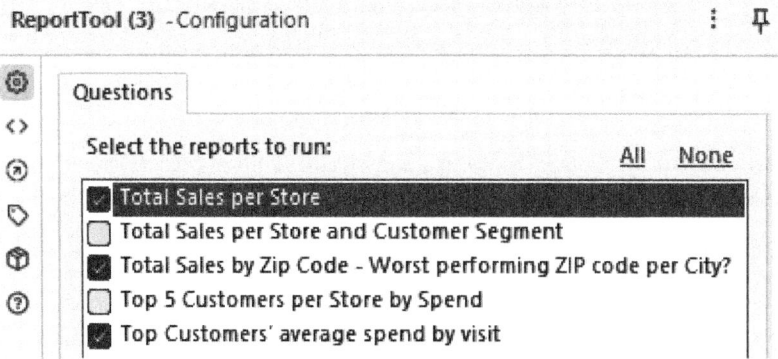

Figure 10.45: The UI for the tool we'll build

How to do it...

First, we will build the macro, and as we already know, a macro is nothing more than a workflow with some tweaks.

Also, we won't focus on the complexity of the reports (we will use very simple ones). Our focus will be on the selection of what to output or not from the tool:

1. Drop an **Input Data** tool onto the canvas and point it to `..\DATA\CustomerSpent.yxdb`.

2. To get the **Total Sales per Store** report, drop a **Summarize** tool connected to the **Input Data** tool.

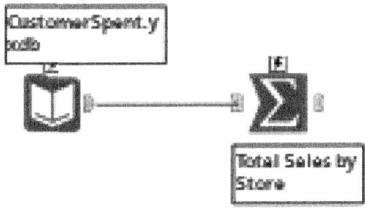

Figure 10.46: Adding a Summarize tool

3. Click on the **Summarize** tool to configure it.

4. Click on `Store Number` in the **Field** panel, then click on **Add**, and select **Group By**.

5. Once **Store Number Group By** is added to the **Actions** panel, click on `Spend`, then **Add**, and select **Sum** from the drop-down list.

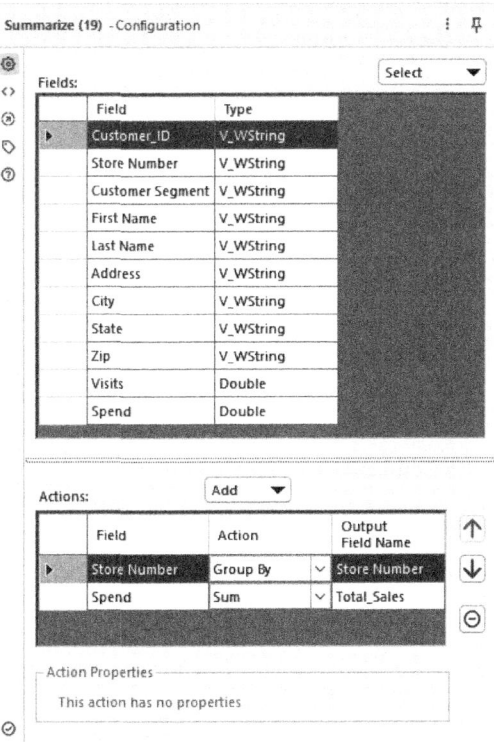

Figure 10.47: The Summarize tool configuration

This will give us the total spend by store.

Store Number	Total_Sales
100	1,324,557.13
101	1,163,252.09
102	257,316.63
103	865,103.91

Figure 10.48: The total spend by store

Best practice tip

With any tool selected, hitting *F2* will take you directly to the **Annotation** panel of that tool. Use this shortcut to immediately document/annotate the purpose of the tool.

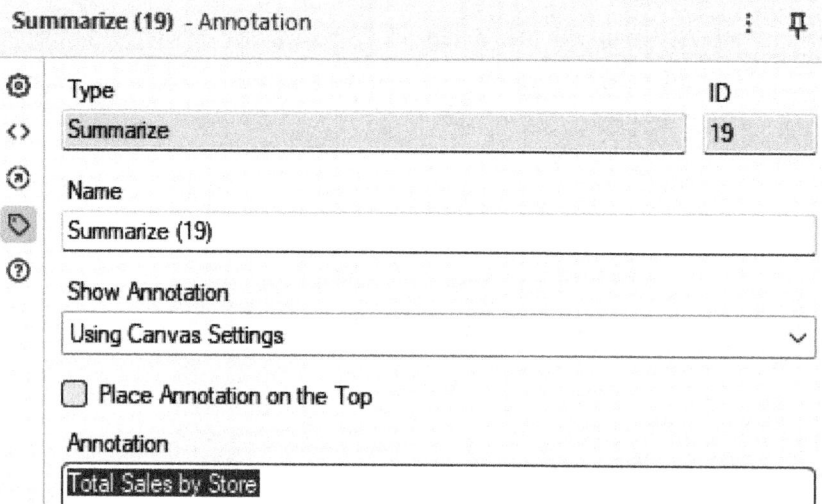

Figure 10.49: Using Annotation to identify tools

6. To get the **Total Sales per Store and Customer Segment** report, right-click on the **Summarize** tool and select **Copy** (or click it and hit *Ctrl + C*).

7. Select a place in the canvas where the new tool will be, and right-click and select **Paste** (or hit *Ctrl + V*).

8. Connect the **Input Data** tool output anchor to the pasted **Summarize** tool.

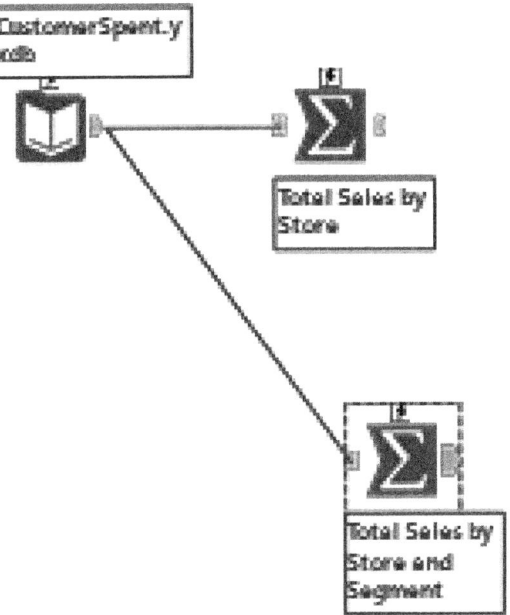

Figure 10.50: Adding the second Summarize tool

9. Click on the **Summarize** tool to configure it.

10. Select Customer Segment from the **Field** list, click on **Add**, and select **Group By** for **Action**. You'll see that it was added at the bottom of the aggregations. Even when this produces the right summarizations, I like to have the actions ordered in the way I expect the output to come. In this case, I want all the dimensions first (Store Number and Customer Segment) and the measures after (Sum_Spend).

11. Click on Customer Segment, and press the arrows on the right part of the **Configuration** panel until Customer Segment is right below Store Number.

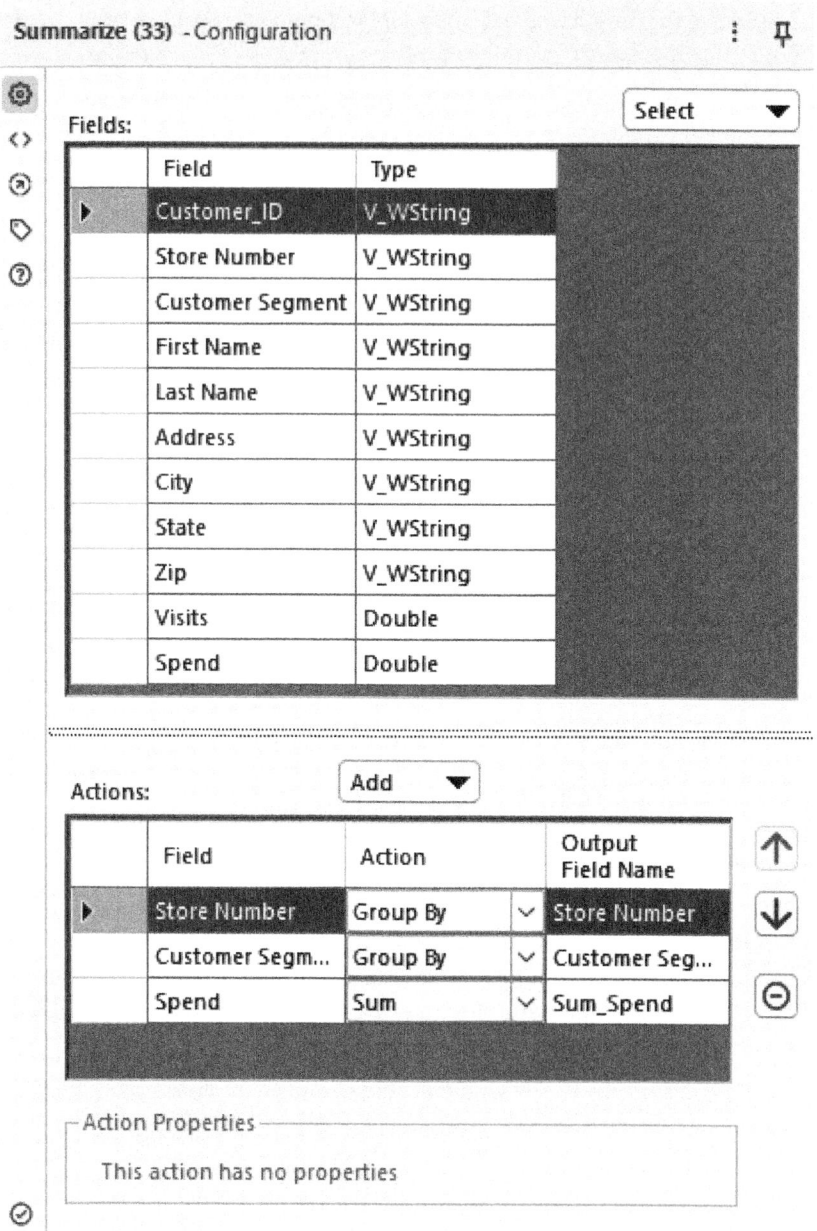

Figure 10.51: The Summarize tool configuration

And that is our second report, **Total Sales per Store and Customer Segment**.

Store Number	⋮	Customer Segment	Sum_Spend
100		Consumer	276,608.59
100		Corporate	467,350.62
100		Home Office	306,011.21
100		Small Business	274,586.71
101		Consumer	263,338.23
101		Corporate	390,355.57
101		Home Office	272,723.17

Figure 10.52: Total Sales by Store and Customer Segment

12. To get the **Total Sales by Zip Code** report, add a new **Summarize** tool and connect the **Input Data** tool output anchor to it.

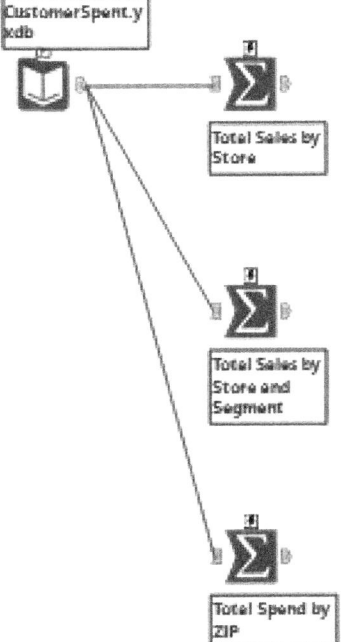

Figure 10.53: Adding a third Summarize tool

13. Click on the newly added tool to configure it.

14. Click on Zip, then **Add**, and select **Group By**.

15. Click on Spend, then **Add**, and select **Sum**.

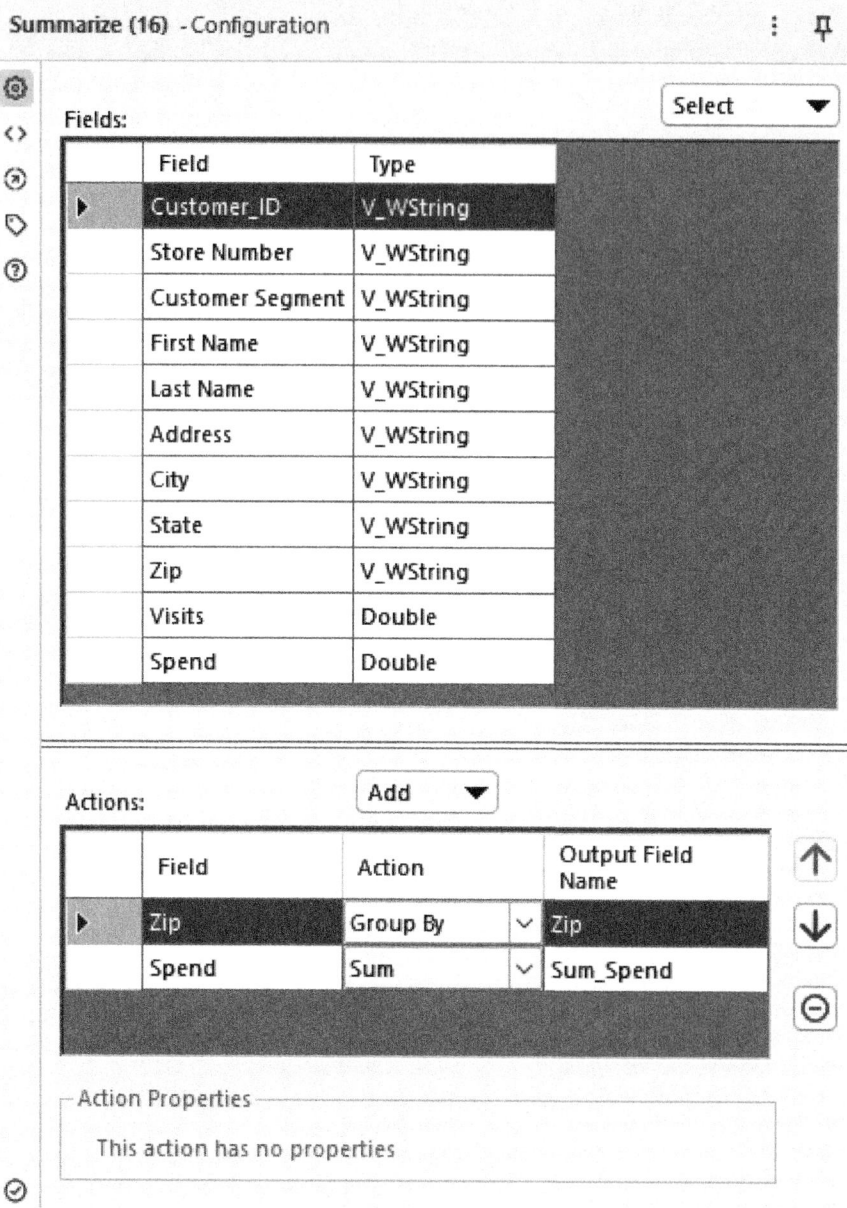

Figure 10.54: The Summarize tool configuration

This report requires that the zip codes with a bigger spend appear on top, so we need to sort them.

16. Add a **Sort** tool and connect it to the **Summarize** tool.

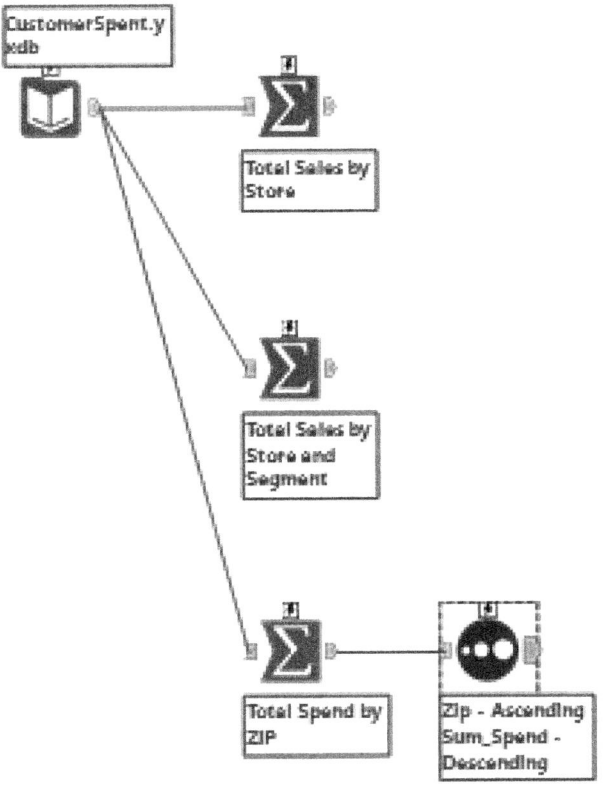

Figure 10.55: Adding a Sort tool

17. Click on it, and select **Sum_Spend** from the **Name** dropdown and **Descending** from the **Order** one.

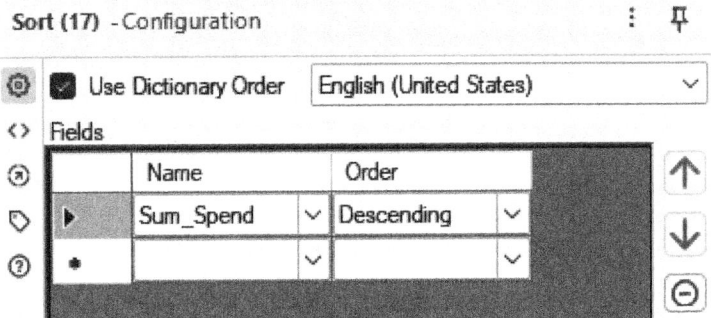

Figure 10.56: The Sort tool configuration

Here, we have the spend by zip code sorted from higher to lower.

Zip	Sum_Spend
80219	446,288.01
80013	410,222.68
80012	390,631.53
80247	323,115.98
80214	270,275.01
80014	267,607.23
80015	259,462.92

Figure 10.57: The spend by zip results sorted

18. To get the **Top 5 Customers per Store by Spend** report, add a **Summarize** tool and connect it to the **Input Data** tool output anchor.

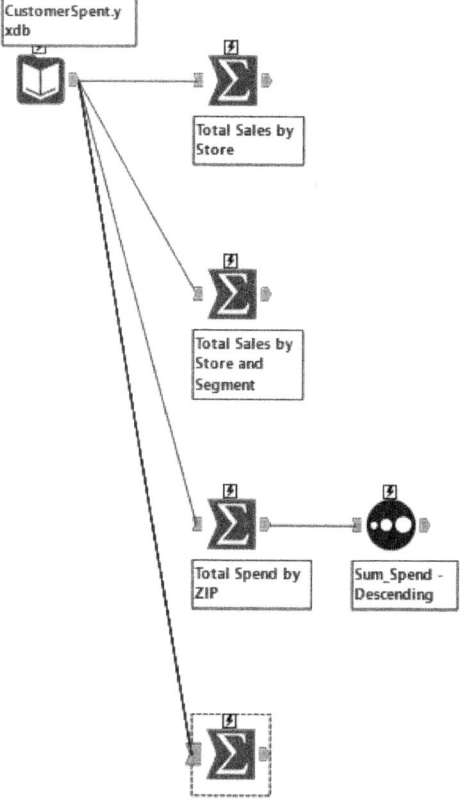

Figure 10.58: Adding the fourth Summarize tool

19. On the newly added **Summarize** tool, press *Ctrl* and select Customer_ID, Store Number, First Name, and Last Name.

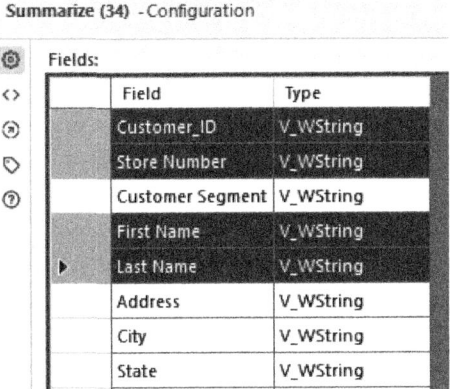

Figure 10.59: Pressing Ctrl and selecting multiple fields

20. Click on **Add** and select **Group By**.

21. Click on Spend in the **Field** panel, then **Add**, and then **Sum**.

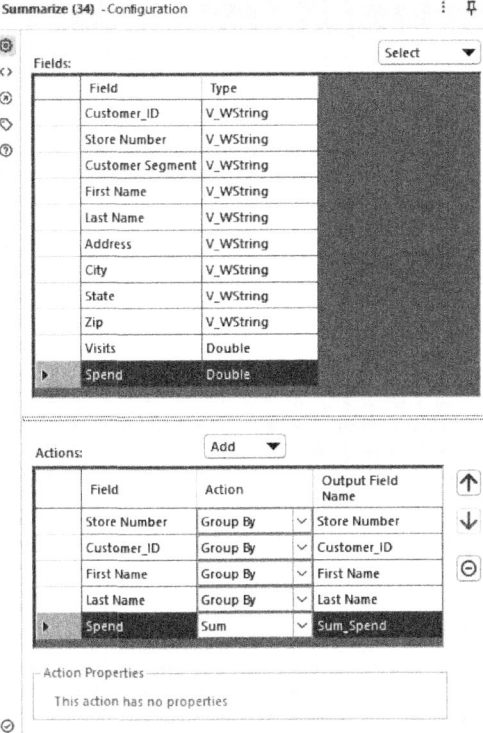

Figure 10.60: Configuring the Summarize tool

Now that we have the **Top 5 Customers per Store by Spend** report, we need to sort the records by spend.

22. Drop a **Sort** tool and connect it to the **Summarize** tool, as we did in the previous report.

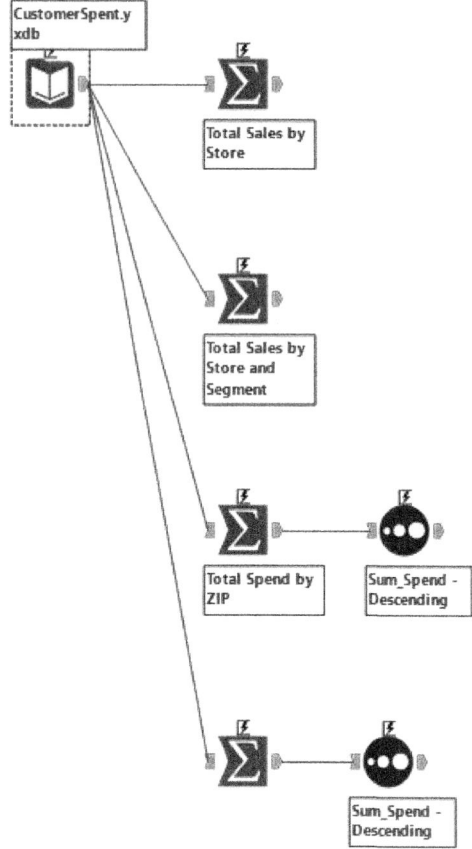

Figure 10.61: Adding the Sort tool

23. Select **Sum_Spend** from the **Name** dropdown and **Descending** from the **Order** one.

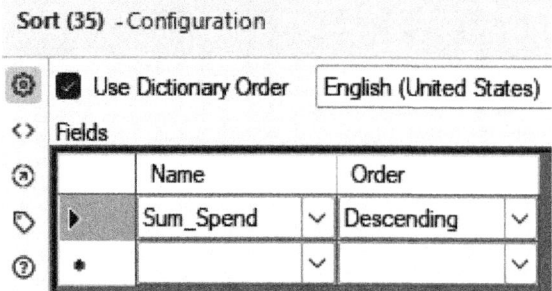

Figure 10.62: The Sort tool configuration

This will output all spending in descending order.

24. To get the **Top 5 Customers per Store by Spend** report, drop a **Sample** tool following the **Sort** tool.

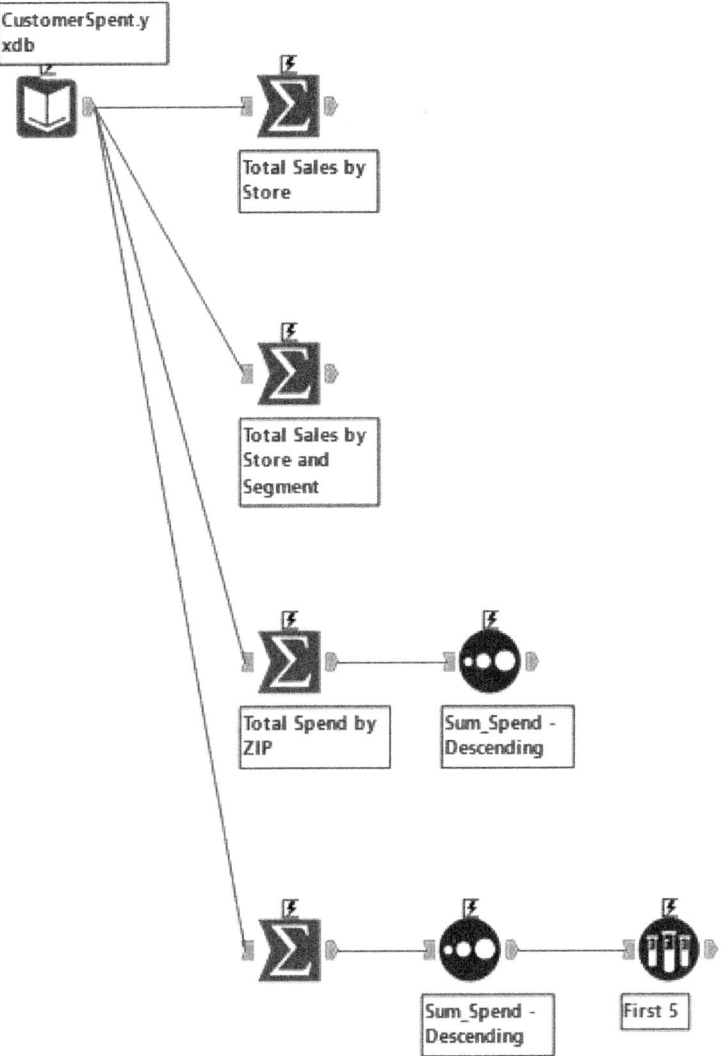

Figure 10.63: Adding a Sample tool

25. In the **Sample** tool configuration, select **First N rows** and change the **N** value to **5**.

26. Click **Store Number** in the **Group by column** panel.

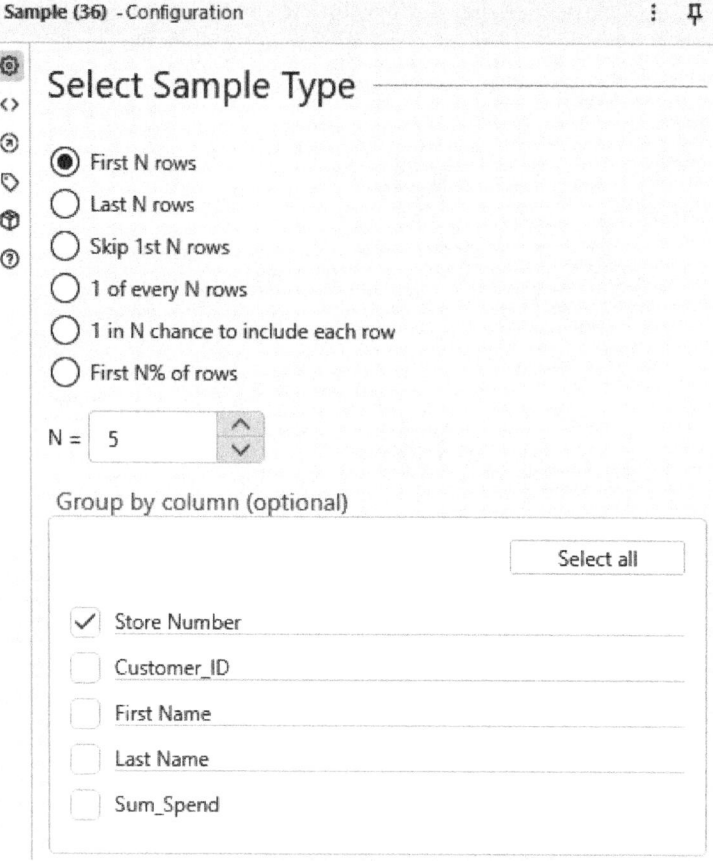

Figure 10.64: The Sample tool configuration

This will give us the first N records per store number (and since we sorted them first, the first N are the ones with the biggest spend in the dataset).

Store Number	Customer_ID	First Name	Last Name	Sum_Spend
100	2571	DENYSE	ALBERTUS	86,540.75
100	1999	MELISSA	LOPEZ	61,610.6
100	2867	DIANE	KING	61,298.98
100	2491	LESLEY	WEST	55,241.63
100	68	HEATHER	BLACK	54,091.64
101	308	PAMELA	WEBSTER	89,269.7

Figure 10.65: The top five spenders by store

27. To get the **Top Customers' average spend by visit** report, drop a new **Summarize** tool onto the canvas and connect its input to the **Input Data** tool.

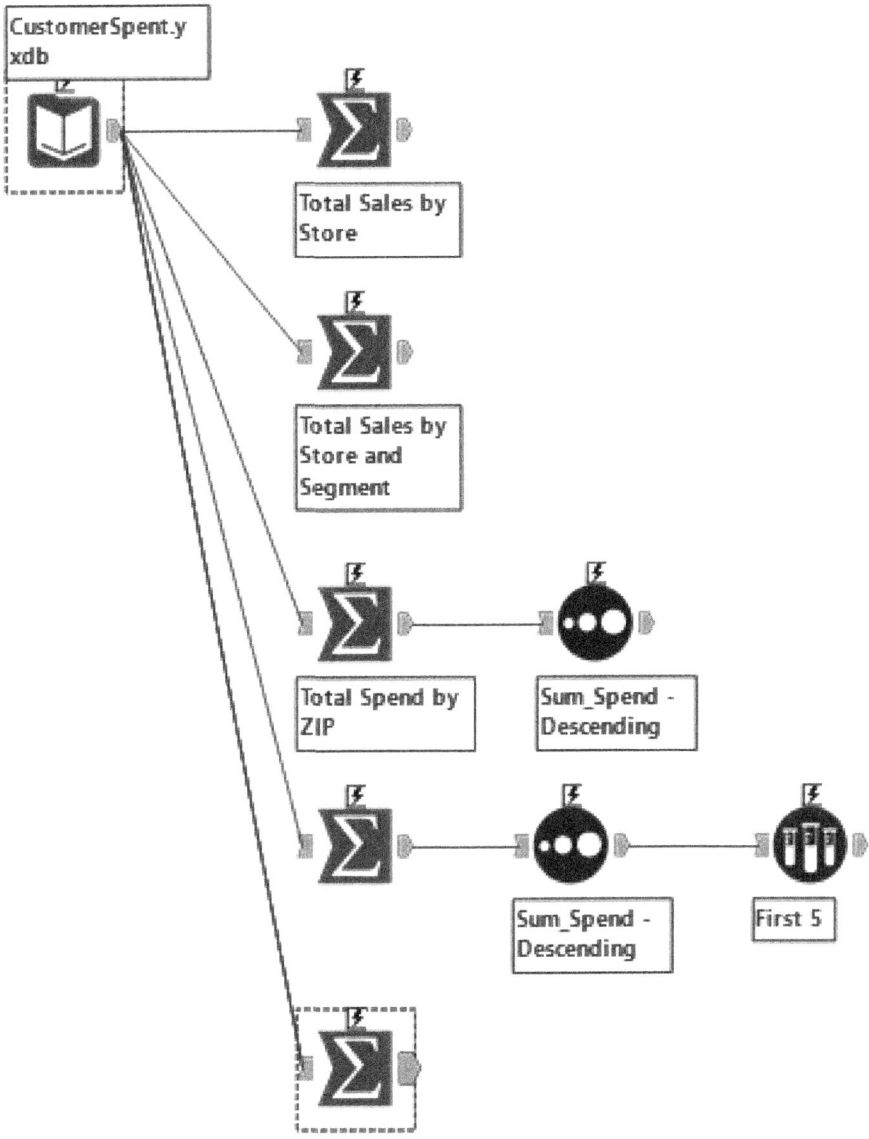

Figure 10.66: Adding the last Summarize tool

28. *Ctrl* + click Customer_ID, First Name, and Last Name, then click on **Add**, and select **Group By**.

29. *Ctrl* + click on Visits and Spend, click on **Add**, and select **Sum**.

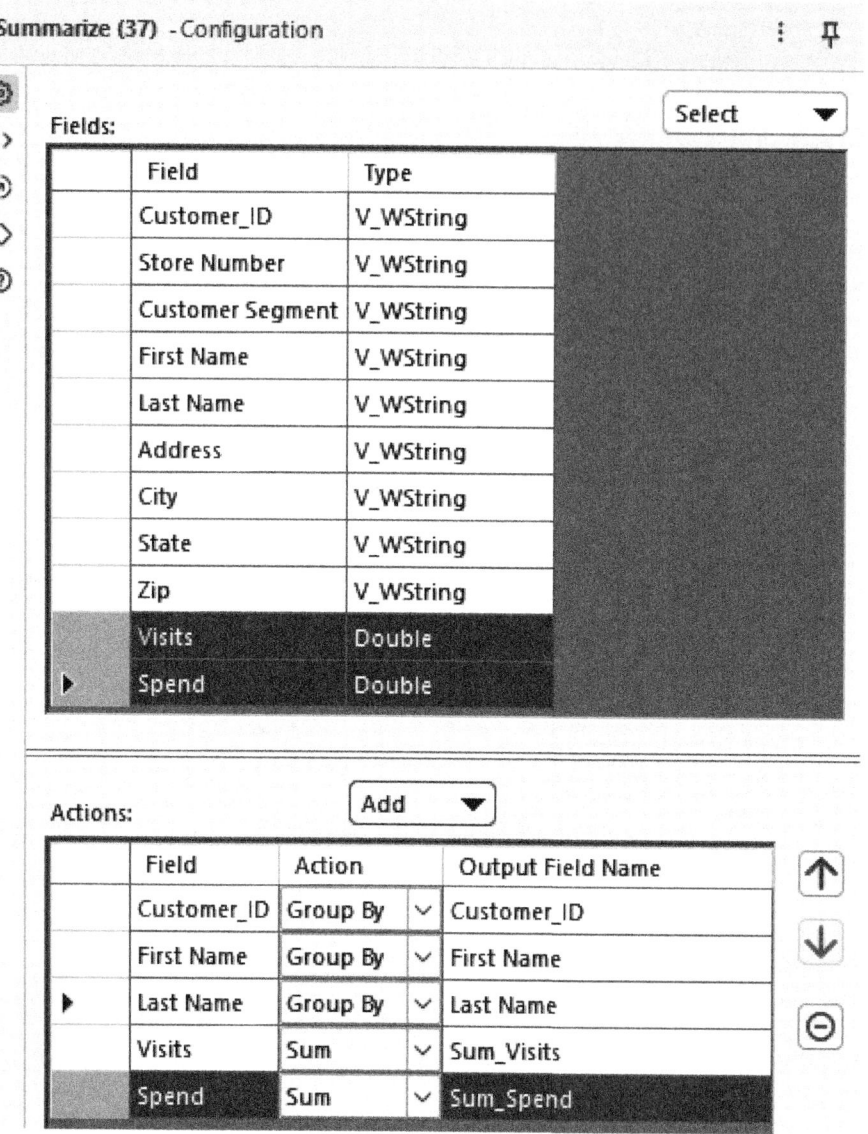

Figure 10.67: The Summarize tool configuration

30. Add a **Formula** tool after the **Summarize** tool.

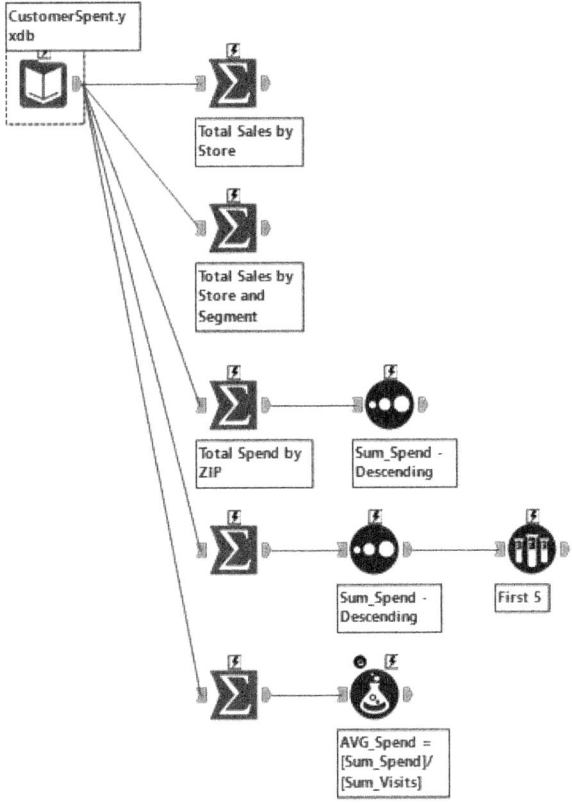

Figure 10.68: Adding a Formula tool

31. Create a new field called `Avg_Spend` and use this expression:

    ```
    [Sum_Spend]/[Sum_Visits]
    ```

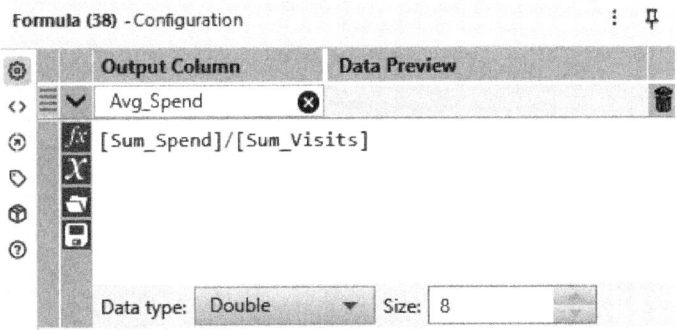

Figure 10.69: The Formula tool configuration

As we did in the previous report, we will sort the outgoing records, this time by **Avg_Spend**.

32. Drop a **Sort** tool next to the **Formula** tool.

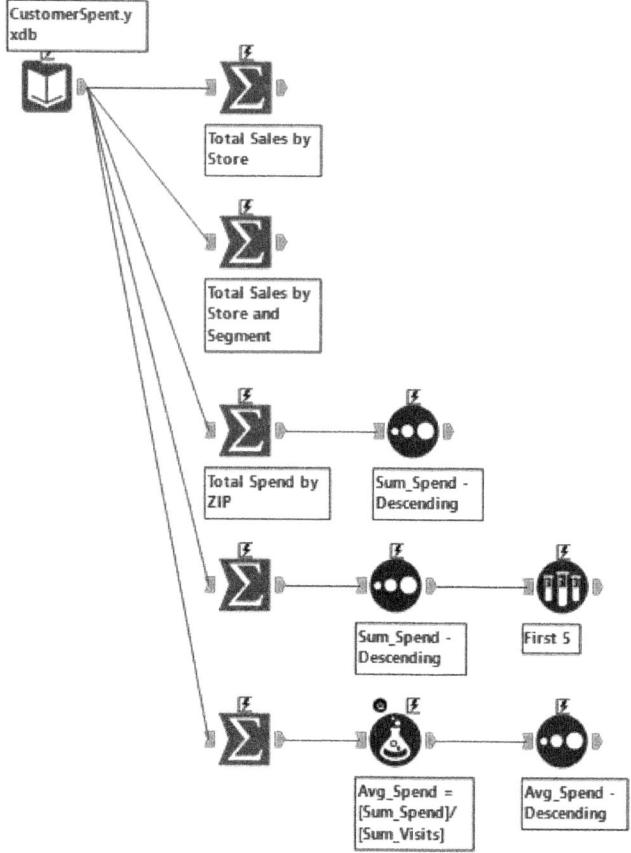

Figure 10.70: Adding a Sort tool

33. Select **Avg_Spend** from the **Field** dropdown and **Descending** from **Order**.

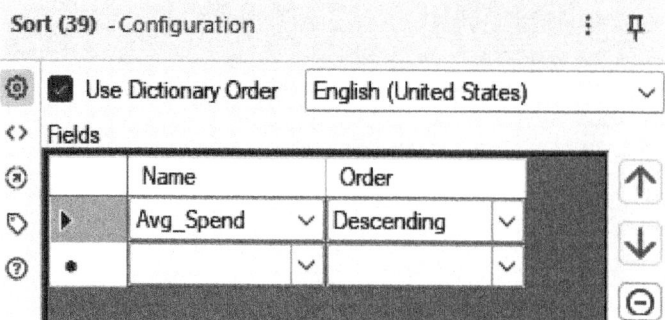

Figure 10.71: The Sort tool configuration

34. Drop a **Sample** tool next to the **Sort** tool.

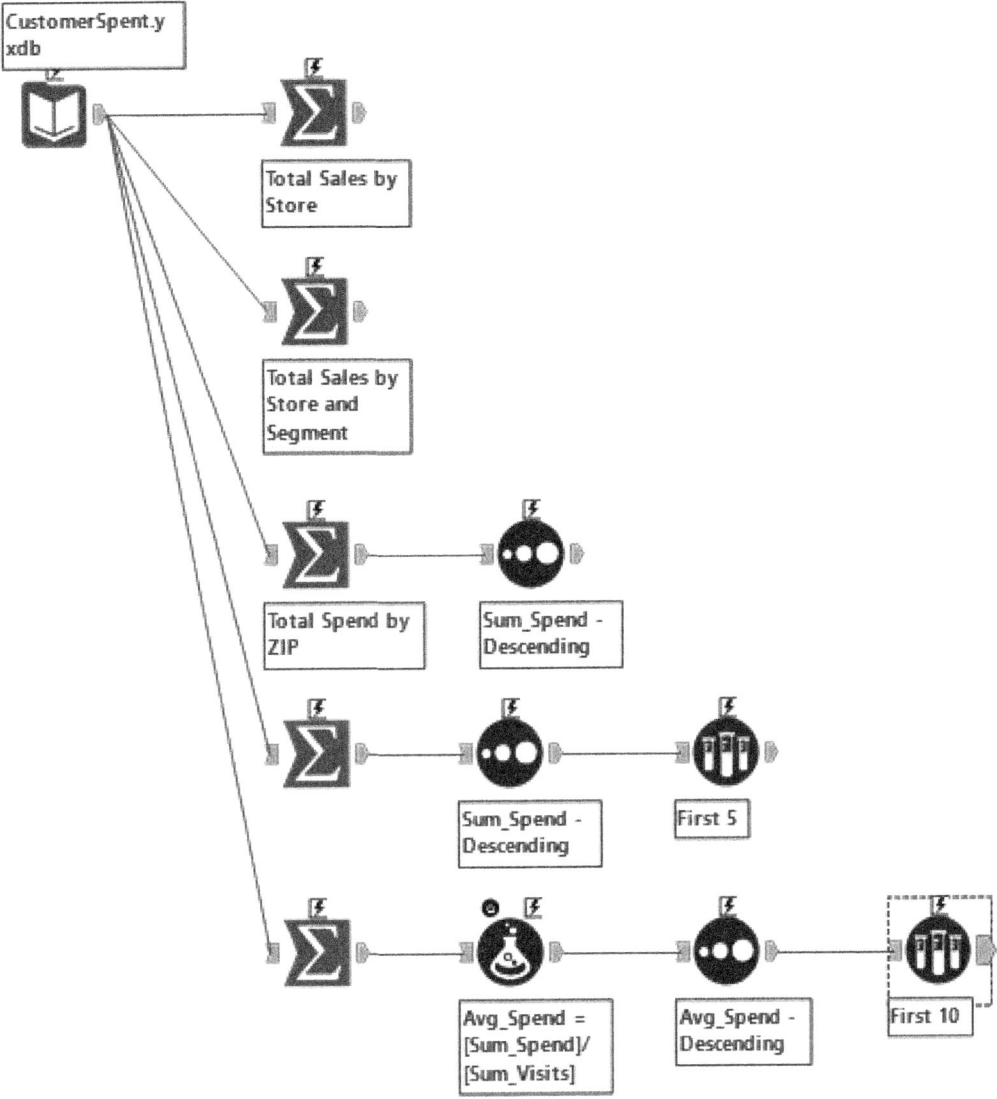

Figure 10.72: Adding a Sample tool

35. Select **First N rows** and modify the **N=** value to **10**. Make sure nothing is selected in the **Group by column** panel (we need the top 10 records overall).

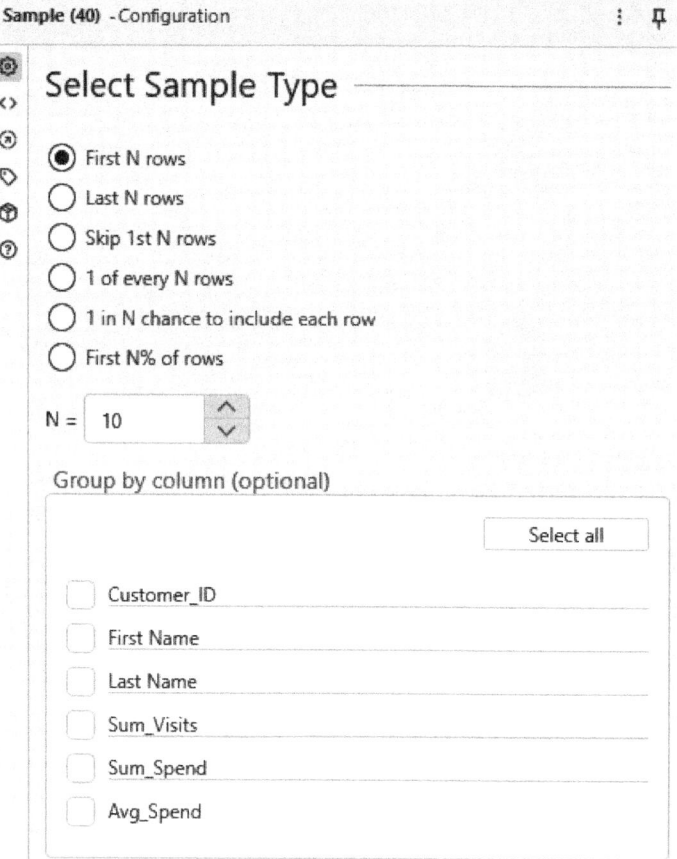

Figure 10.73: The Sample tool configuration

This will output the top 10 **Avg_Spend** values by customer visits.

Customer_ID	First Name	Last Name	Sum_Visits	Sum_Spend	Avg_Spend
794	DORIS	PURVIS	1	15,503.7	15,503.7
1610	MARIANN	IMMORDINO	1	12,163.61	12,163.61
35	VALERIE	GINSBURG	2	21,760.88	10,880.44
2507	TALLOY	HUNTZINGER	1	10,180.01	10,180.01
1166	BEATRIZ	CRUZ	1	10,020.48	10,020.48

Figure 10.74: The top 10 customers by average spend per visit

Now, we have the basic logic that our reporting needs. This workflow can be run every time a report is needed, and it'll produce all five reports for us.

However, this behavior is not optimal. We will use resources we don't need to run the entire workflow just to get one report. Also, we have five options with a lot of possible combinations, so the previous recipe won't be a good fit.

Therefore, we will make some changes to improve it. We will use **Tool Containers**, not only to organize our workflow but also to enable/disable the execution of the tool contained within them, based on the **Interface** tools. Also, during this process, we'll move our tools so that we can adjust the additional logic easily.

36. Right-click on the first **Summarize** tool and click on **Add To New Container**.

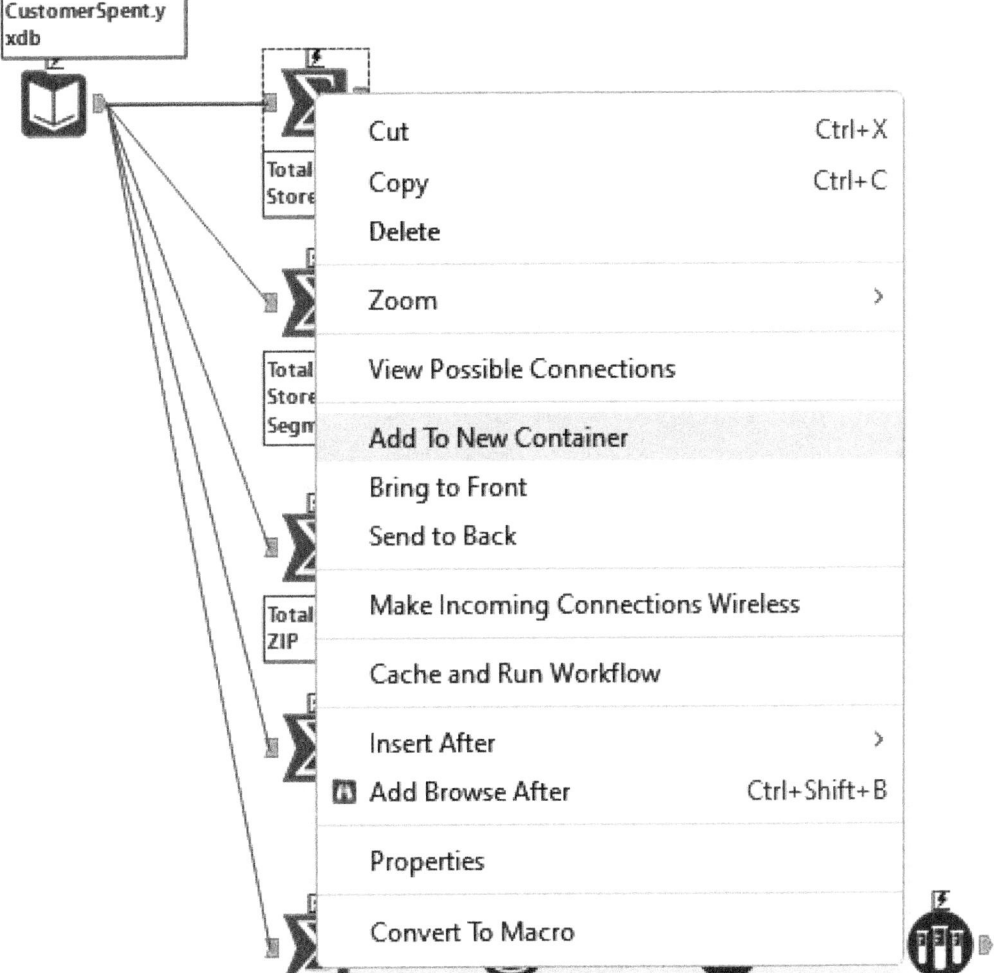

Figure 10.75: The Add To New Container option

Alteryx will create a **tool container** that contains the selected tools (in this case, just the **Summarize** tool).

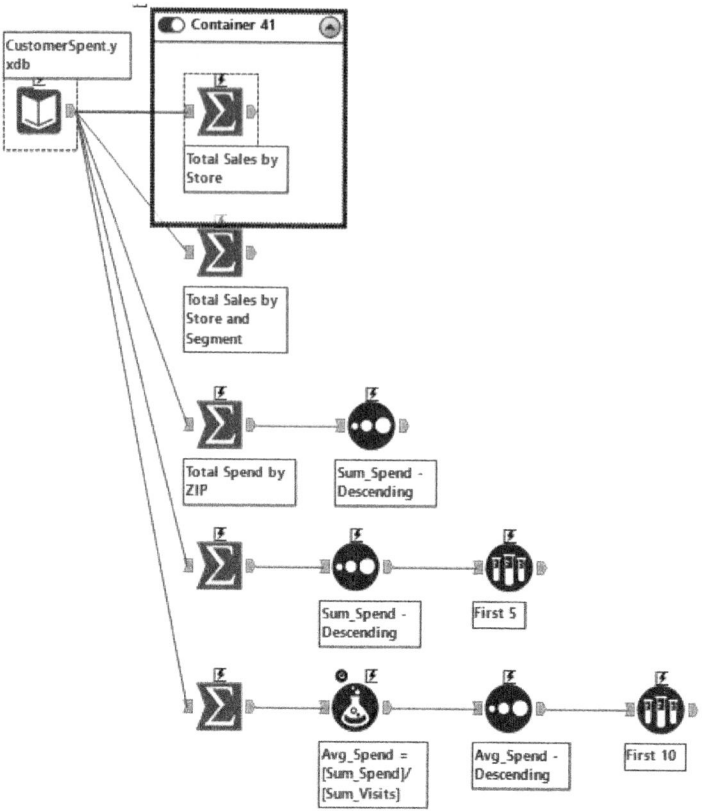

Figure 10.76: The Tool Container tool added to the workflow

Tool Containers has several configuration options:

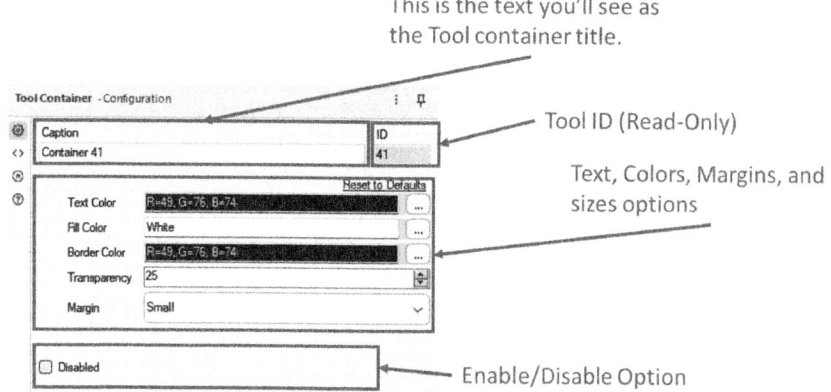

Figure 10.77: The Tool Container configuration options

Some of them are also present in the **Tool Container** tool itself and can be changed from the canvas.

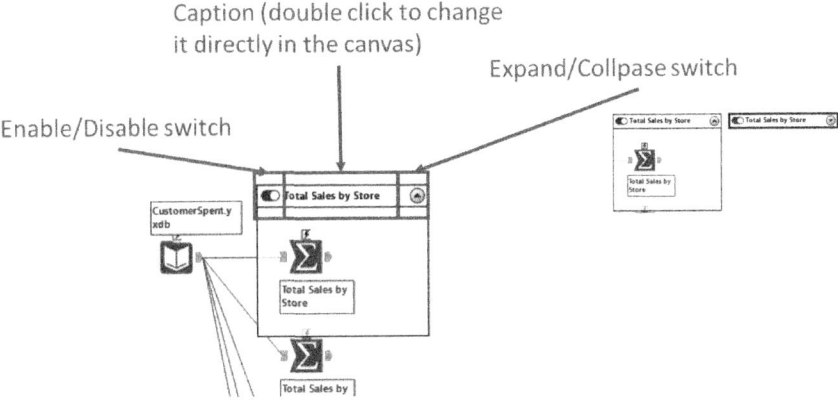

Figure 10.78: The Tool Container canvas options

We will change the caption to identify each report within its container.

37. Click on the **Caption** field in the **Configuration** panel (or double-click it on the tool) and change it to `Total Sales by Store`.

38. Now, right-click on the second **Summarize** tool and, again, select **Add To New Container**. You'll probably notice that the tools overlap.

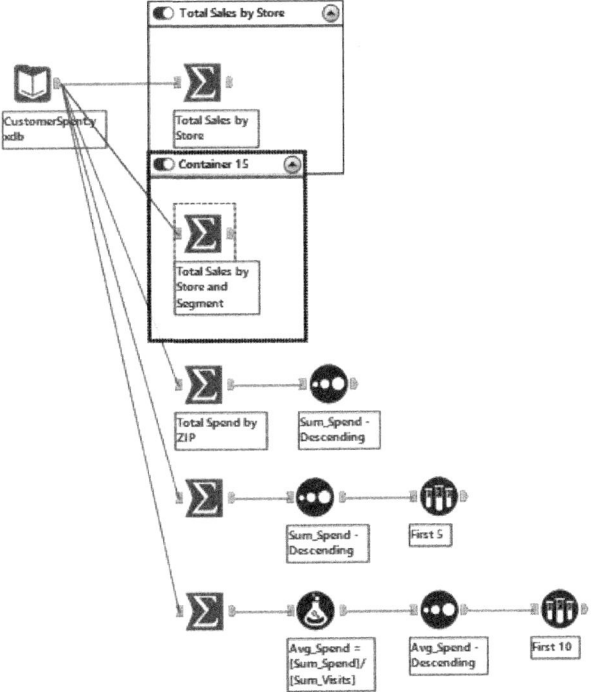

Figure 10.79: Adding a second Tool Container tool

You can move the **tool containers** around the canvas, and Alteryx will move all its contents with it.

39. So, grab the recently created **tool container** and move it to the right of the existing one.

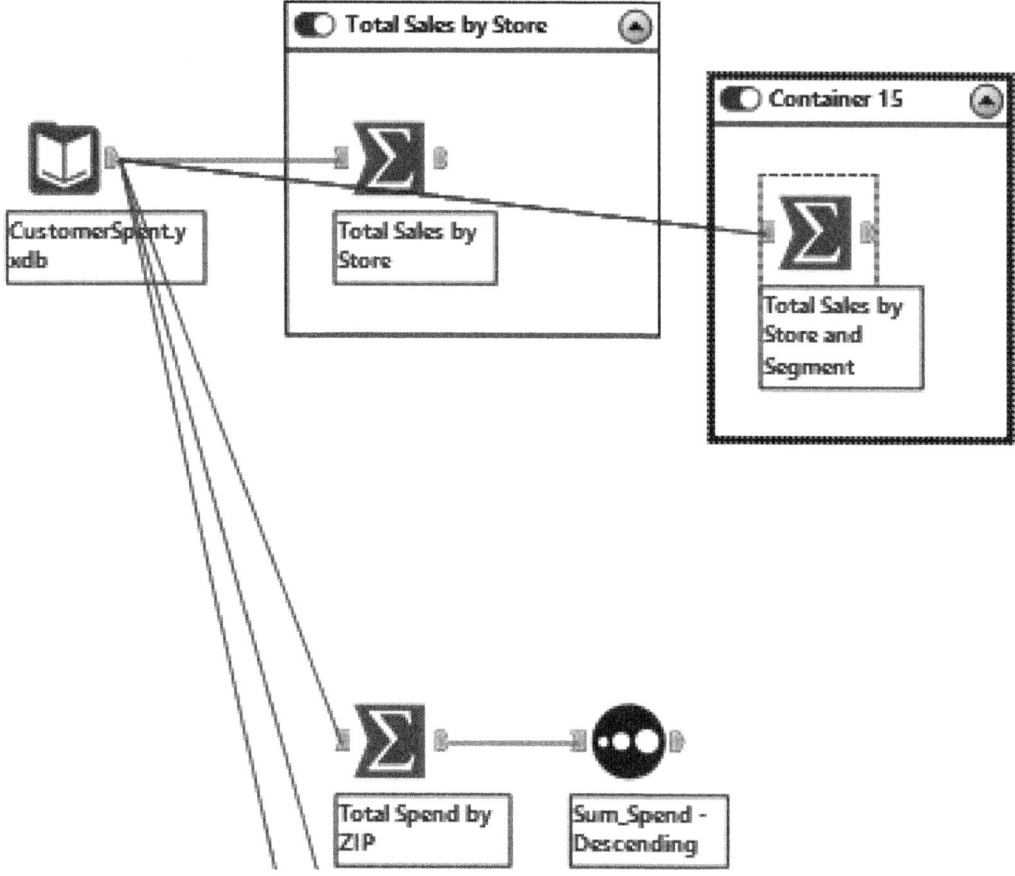

Figure 10.80: Fixing the overlap

40. Rename it Total Spend by Store and Segment.

41. Now, select the **Summarize** and **Sort** tools.

42. Right-click on any of the selected tools, and again, click on **Add To New Container**. You will see the new container wraps for both selected tools.

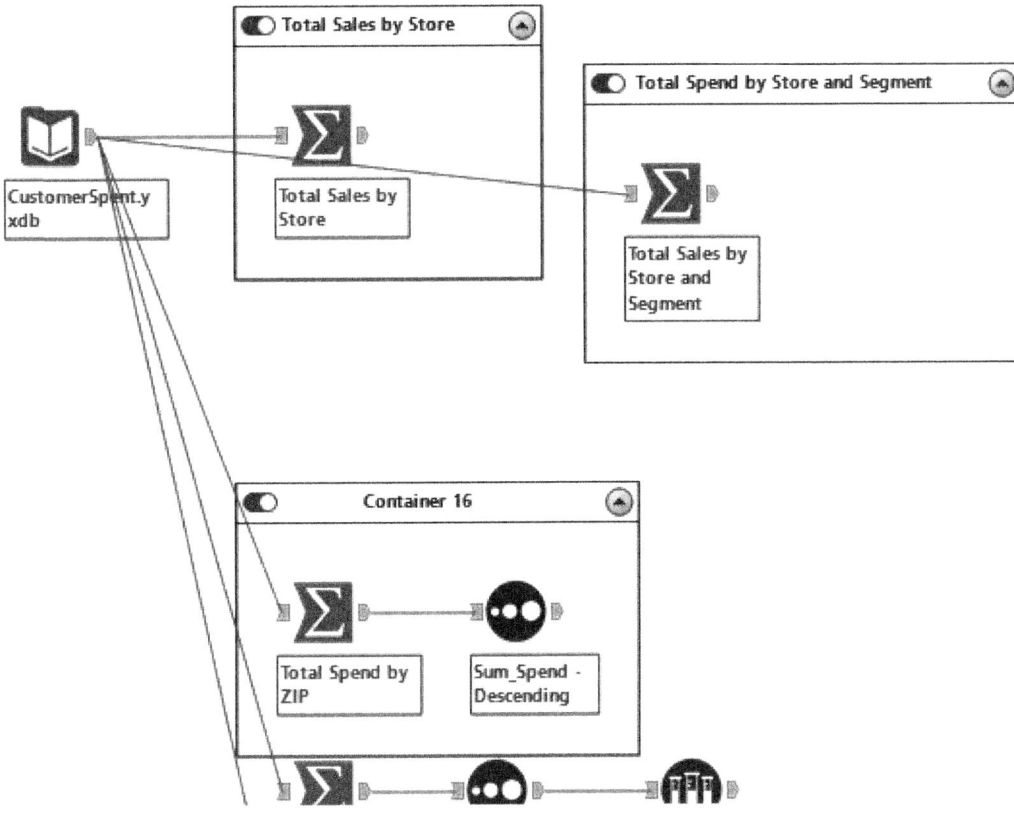

Figure 10.81: Adding more tool containers

43. Rename the container `Spend by Zip` and move it to the left of the **Total Spend by Store and Segment** container.

44. Repeat the task with the remaining sets of logic until you get every report inside a **tool container**.

    You may end up with something similar to this:

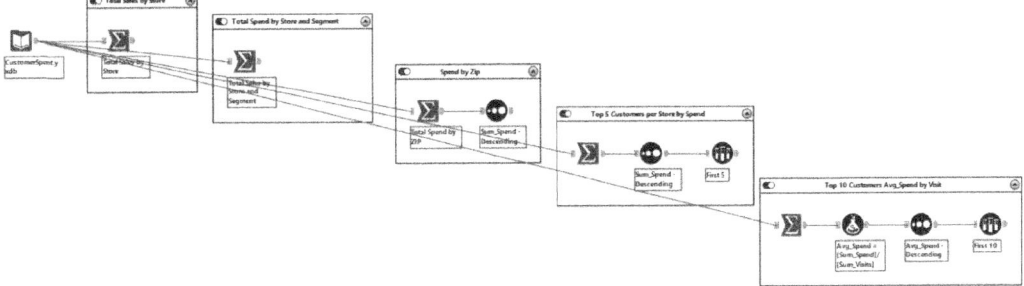

Figure 10.82: The workflow so far

Now, we need to start converting this plain workflow into a macro.

First, we will add the tools that will allow us to receive and output data.

Since our workflow already has an **Input Data** tool, we can right-click on it and select **Convert To Macro Input**. This will become the input anchor of the new tool.

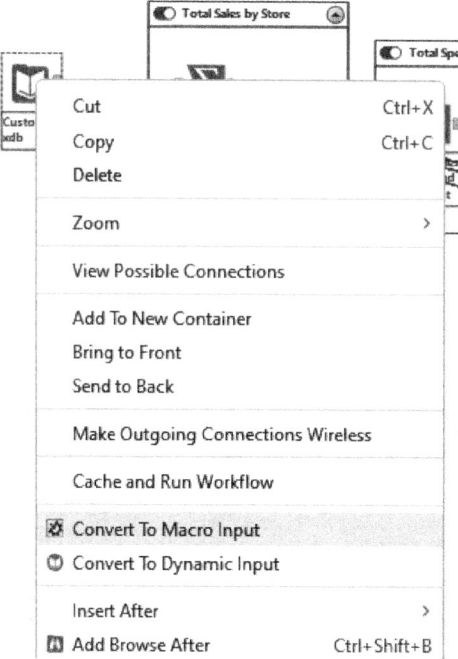

Figure 10.83: The Convert To Macro Input menu option

Once done, you'll see that the tool changed and lightning icons appeared on every tool. We will use them later to add the conditions and change their status.

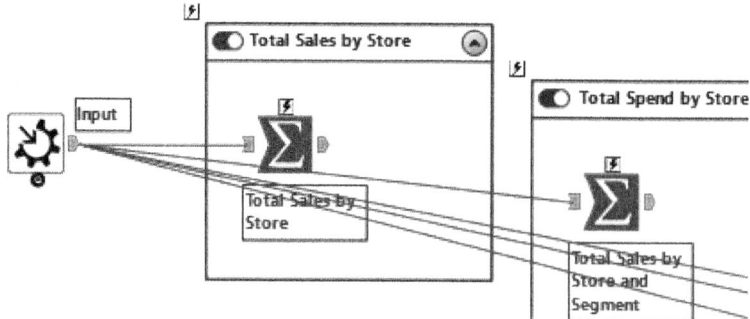

Figure 10.84: The macro controls appear

For each report, we'll create an output, using the **Macro Output** tools.

45. Drag a **Macro Output** tool (from the **Interface** category) and drop it below the first tool container (we will drop them outside the **Tool Container** tool because Alteryx doesn't allow us to disable a **Tool Container** tool that has **Interface** objects inside).

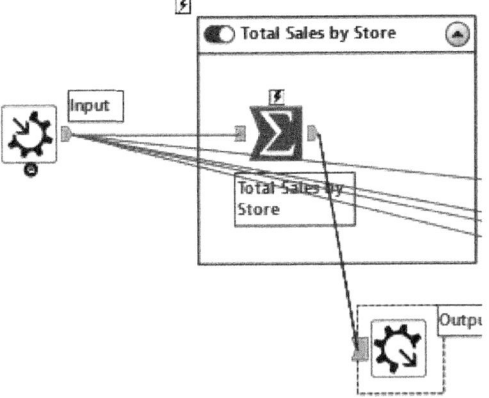

Figure 10.85: Adding a Macro Output tool

46. Repeat this procedure, adding one **Macro Output** tool to the last tool in each container, until you get something similar to this (don't hesitate to move tools and containers around until you feel OK with your tool layout):

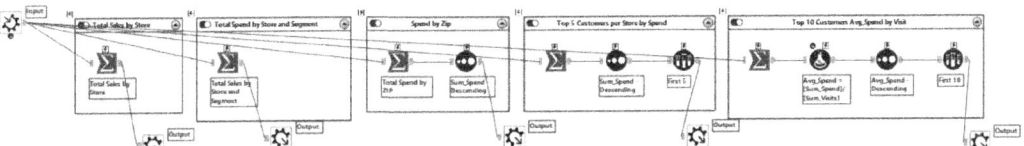

Figure 10.86: The workflow so far

Now, we will identify each output tool so that it'll become easy to identify the outputs generated.

47. Click on the **Macro Output** tool first from the left, and from its configuration, change **Output Name** to `Total Sales by Store` and **Anchor Abbreviation** to `1`.

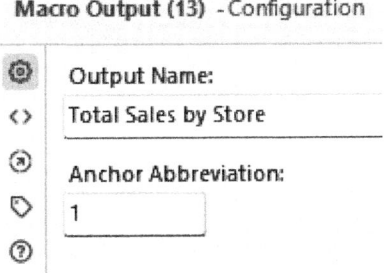

Figure 10.87: The label and anchor identification for the first Macro Output tool

48. Go to the second **Macro Output** tool and change **Output Name** to `Total Sales by Store and Customer Segment` and **Anchor Abbreviation** to 2.

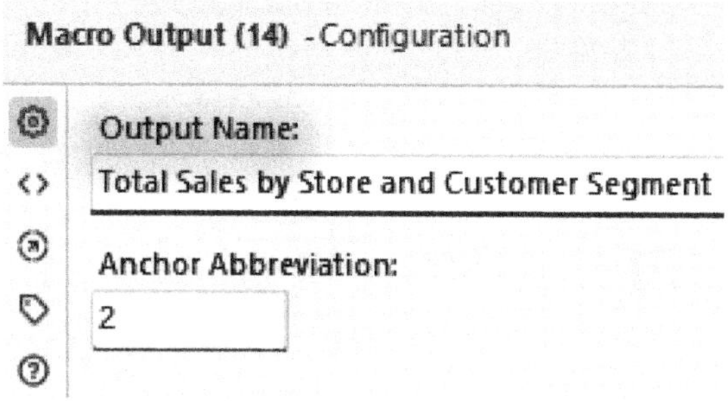

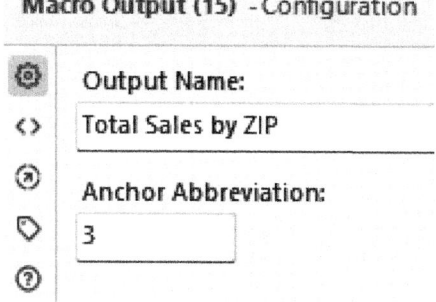

Figure 10.88: The label and anchor identification for the second Macro Output tool

49. The third one will be `Total Sales by ZIP` with 3 as **Anchor Abbreviation**.

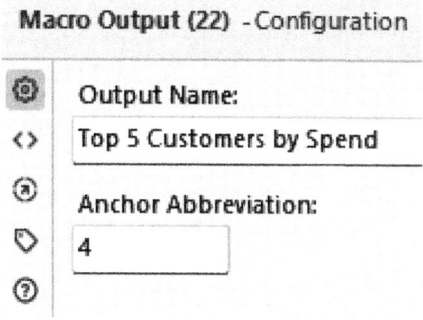

Figure 10.89: The label and anchor identification for the third Macro Output tool

50. The next one is `Top 5 Customers by Spend` and 4.

Figure 10.90: The label and anchor identification for the fourth Macro Output tool

51. And the last one is `Top 10 Customers by Avg. Spend by Visit` and 5.

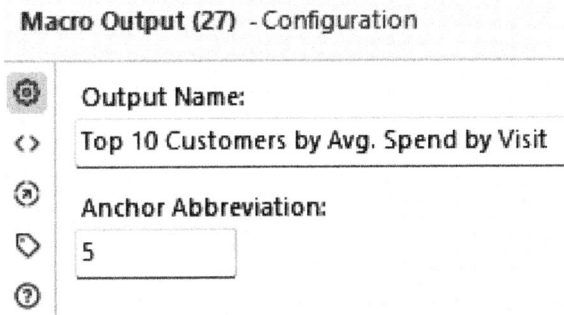

Figure 10.91: The label and anchor identification for the fifth Macro Output

Finally, let's move on to the interaction.

52. Add a **List Box** tool (from the **Interface** category). Place it on top of the existing tools and around the center of the workflow.

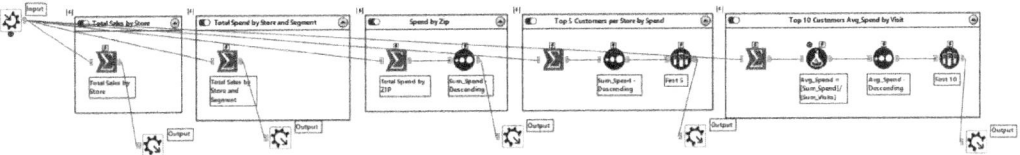

Figure 10.92: Adding the report selection (the List Box tool)

53. Click the **List Box** tool to configure it.

54. For **Enter the text or question to be displayed**, enter `Select the reports to run:`.

55. Select the **Select Tool Mode** radio button.

56. From the **List Values** dropdown, select **Manually set values** and enter the following text (make sure that there is one value per row):

```
Total Sales per Store:1
Total Sales per Store and Customer Segment:2
Total Sales by Zip Code:3
Top 5 Customers per Store by Spend:4
Top Customers' average spend by visit:5
```

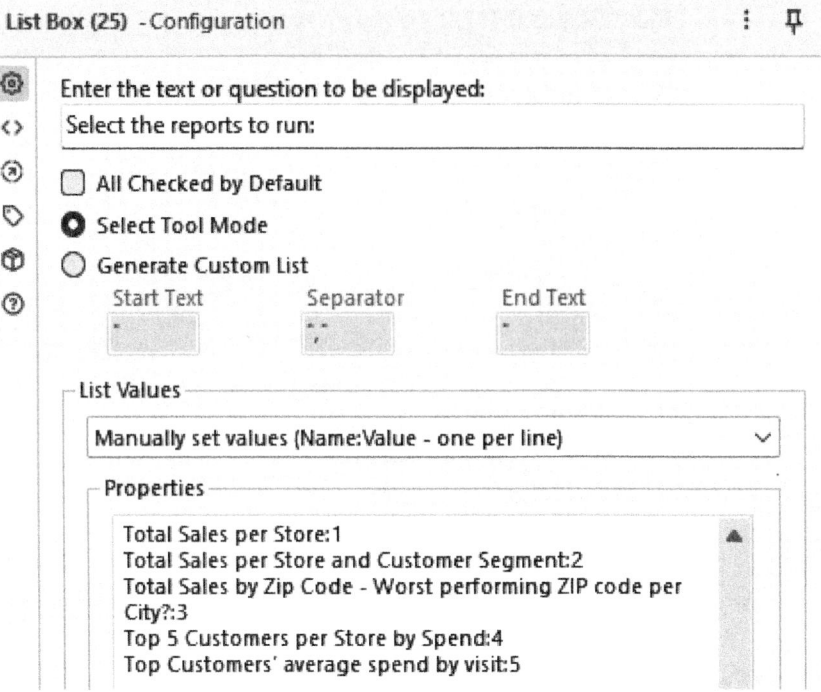

Figure 10.93: The List Box configuration

57. Click and drag from the black background **Q** anchor below the **List Box** tool to the lightning anchor of the first **Tool Container** tool, and note the **Action** tool inserted into the connection.

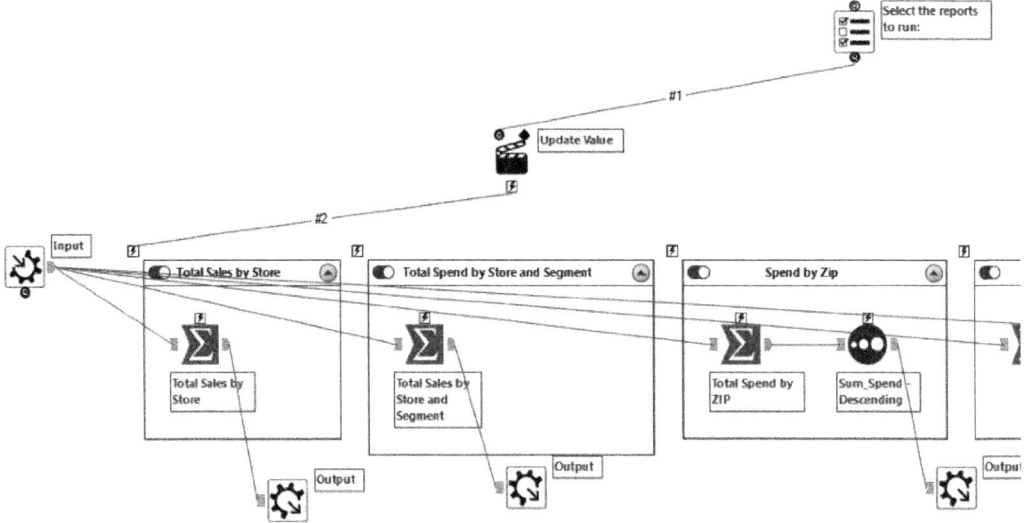

Figure 10.94: Connecting the List Box tool

58. Click on the **Action** tool to configure it.

Because the checked state of the checkbox items used by the **List Box** tool is `True` (if the item is selected) and `False` (if the item is deselected), we need to reverse them to match the status of the **Tool Container** tool (**Disabled** = `True` and **Enabled** = `False`).

59. From the **Select an action type** dropdown, select **Update Value with Formula**.

60. Click on the + button in front of **Disabled** to expand the options, and click on the `@value - value='False'` option. Make sure that it remains highlighted.

61. In the **Formula** expression, type the following:

```
IIF(Contains([#1],"1=True"),'False','True')
```

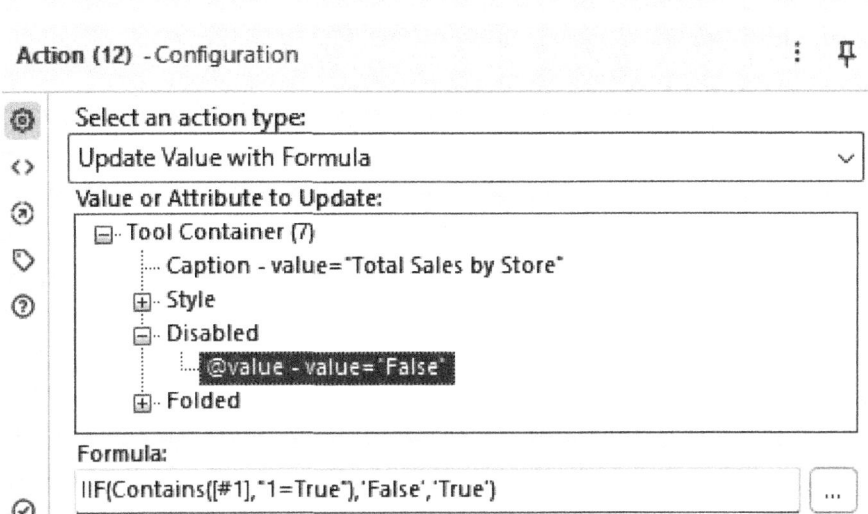

Figure 10.95: The Action tool configuration

We need to repeat this operation for each **Tool Container** tool on the canvas.

62. Connect the **Q** output of the **List Box** tool to the lightning icon of the second **Tool Container** tool (or you can copy and paste the **Action** tool from the one we already configured and then drag the corresponding connections).

No matter which method you use, you will end up with something similar to this:

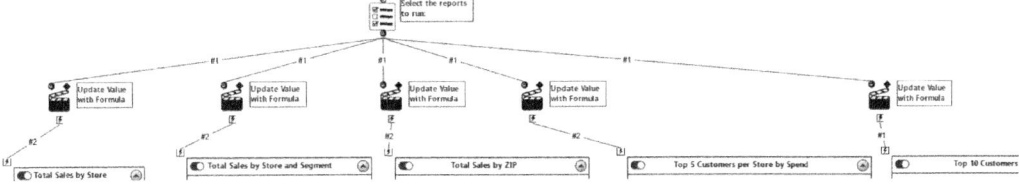

Figure 10.96: The report selection List Box tool connected to each Tool Container tool

Our first **Action** tool is already configured, but the others are not, even if we decided to copy and paste, because what was copied is the first tool's configuration, and it needs to be adjusted.

63. Click on the second **Action** tool from the left, and make sure that **Update Value with Formula** is the selected action type,

64. The expression for the formula is as follows:

```
IIF(Contains([#1],"2=True"),'False','True')
```

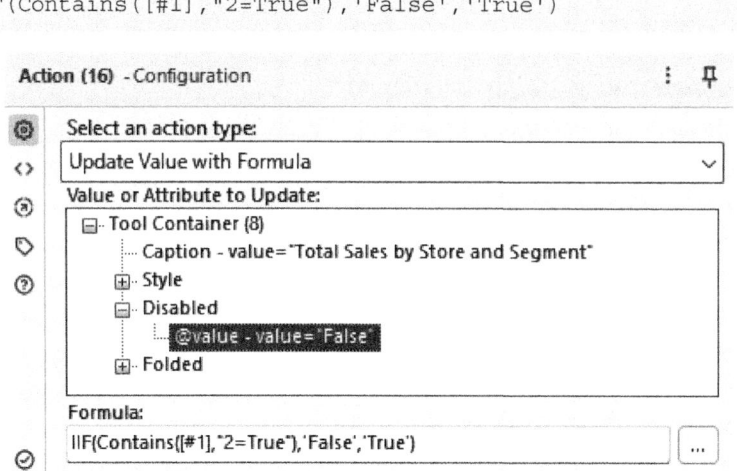

Figure 10.97: The second report Action tool configuration

65. Click on the third **Action** tool and repeat the configuration, this time using this expression for the formula:

```
IIF(Contains([#1],"3=True"),'False','True')
```

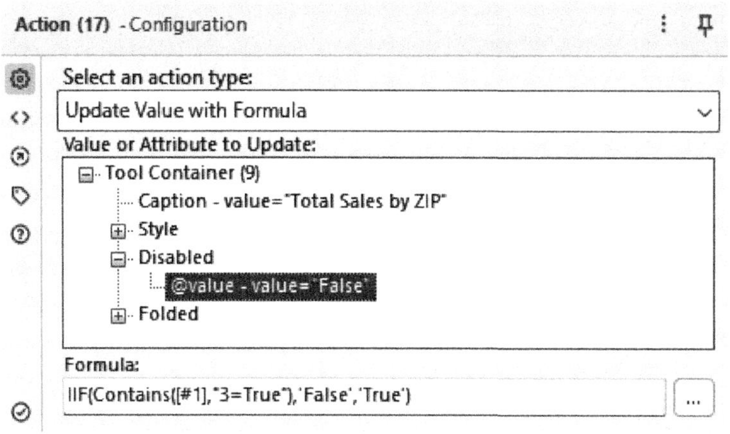

Figure 10.98: The third report Action tool configuration

66. For the fourth **Action** tool, use this expression:

```
IIF(Contains([#1],"4=True"),'False','True')
```

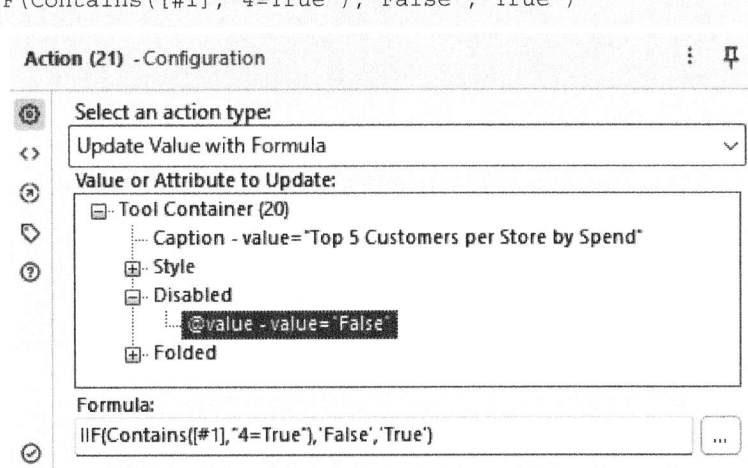

Figure 10.99: The fourth report Action tool configuration

67. And for the last one, use this:

```
IIF(Contains([#1],"5=True"),'False','True')
```

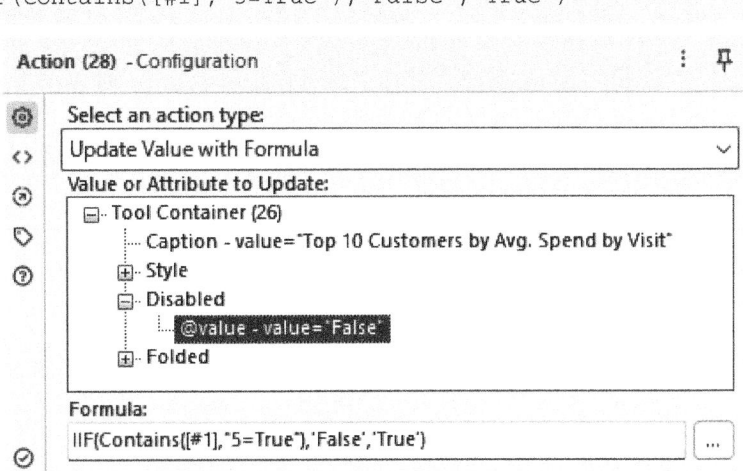

Figure 10.100: The fifth report Action tool configuration

Now, it's time to save our new tool, but before saving, click on any white space area of the canvas to access its configuration.

68. Click on **Workflow**, and make sure that **Type** is **Macro** and **Standard Macro** is selected in the dropdown.

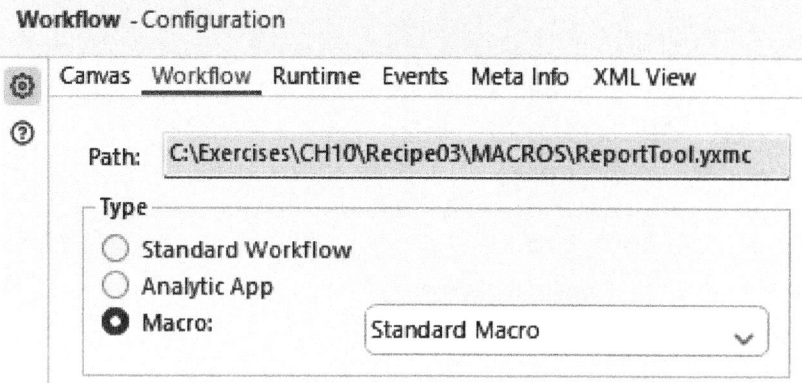

Figure 10.101: The Workflow Type configuration option

69. Hit *Ctrl + S* or go to **File | Save**. Alteryx will open the save dialog, with our default macro repository selected.

70. Name the tool ReportTool(.yxmc) and save it.

Now, we'll use it in a new workflow.

71. Hit *Ctrl + N* (or **File | New Workflow**).

72. On the blank canvas, right-click and then click on **Insert**.

73. Navigate to the very bottom of the menu and click on **Macro**.

74. If you didn't close the recently saved macro, it'll appear in the menu, so click it to insert it into the new workflow.

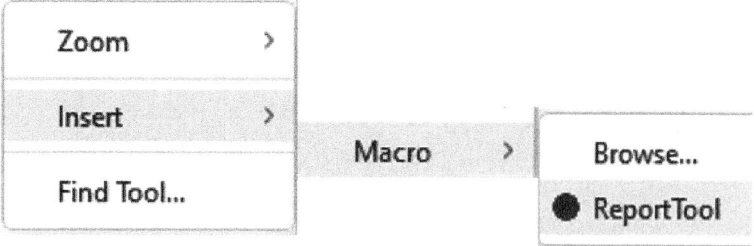

Figure 10.102: The Insert | Macro menu

When the tool is inserted, you'll see the options we configured for the **List Box** tool.

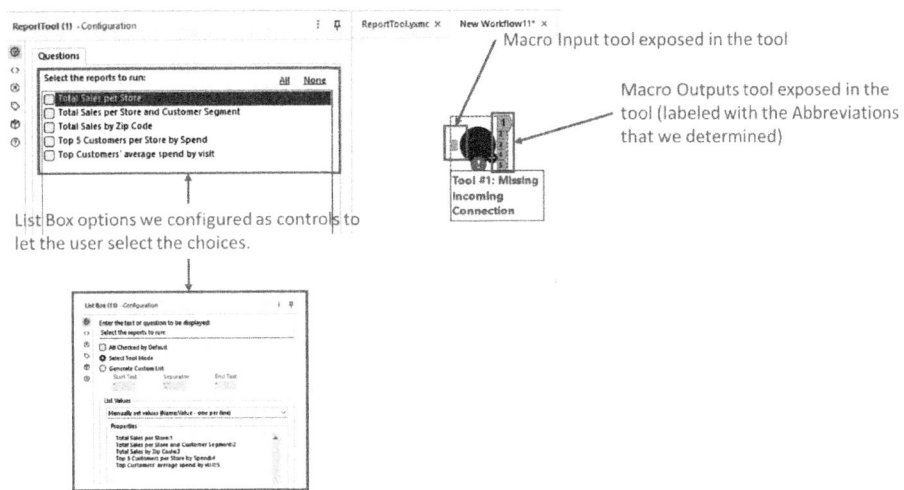

Figure 10.103: The tool inserted in a workflow

Now, we need to connect our data to the tool. Let's use the same file we used to build it.

75. Add an **Input Data** tool and point it to the `CustomerSpent.yxdb` file. Connect the output anchor of the **Input Data** tool to the input anchor of our tool.

76. Click on `ReportTool` (our macro) and hit *Ctrl + Shift + B* (or right-click it and select **Add All Browses**).

We should get something like this:

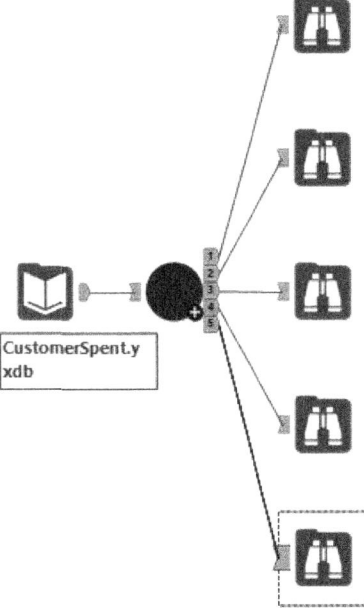

Figure 10.104: Adding a Browse tool to each output

77. Now, click on `ReportTool` again and select any of the available reports.

Run the workflow, and you'll see that only the selected ones were output (the ones that weren't selected didn't run at all).

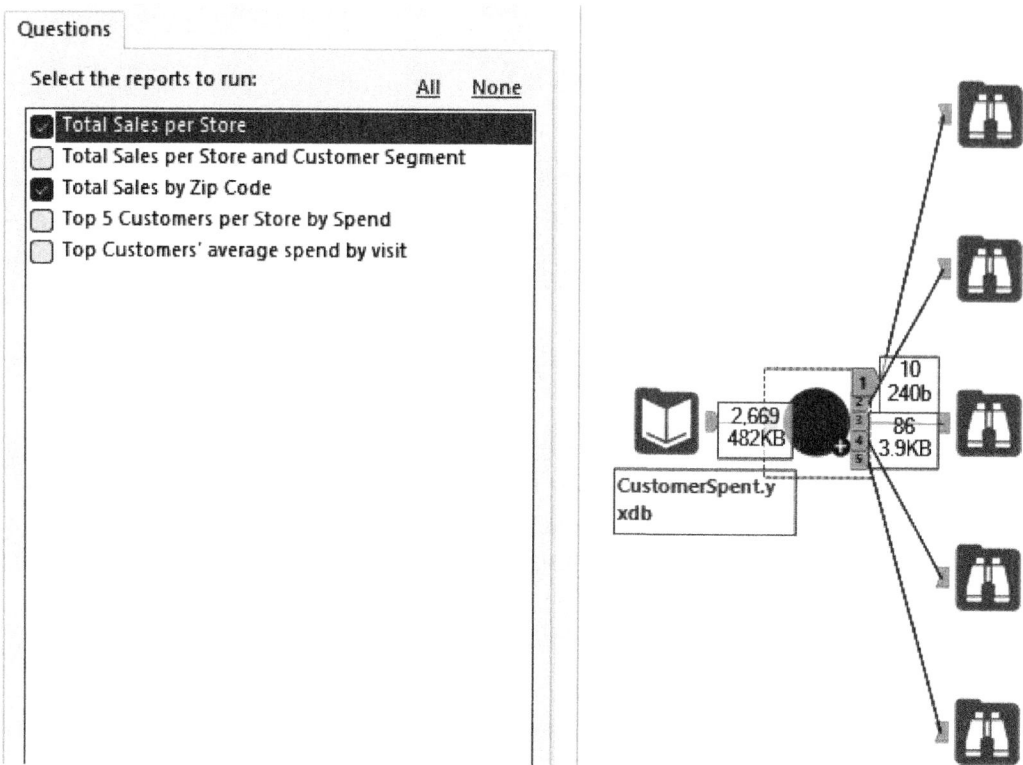

Figure 10.105: Running the selected reports

How it works...

As we know by now, the **Interface** tools provide features to modify the behavior of specific tools in a workflow, so you can create a macro or app. They gather user selections and allow us to configure some actions to take based on the user selections.

In this case, we had a full workflow built, and by adding some **Interface** tools, we were able to build a macro (a reusable component/tool) that will behave differently depending on a user's selections. We used a **List Box** tool to offer the user a friendly way of selecting options, and through the **Action** tool, we used the values captured from the user and modified the behavior of a tool container to enable or disable all the tools/logic contained in it.

The **Macro Input** tool allows us to plug any data source (this is relative, since the macro has specific actions based on the fields), and if the data source we connect to the tool doesn't have those fields present, it'll throw an error.

However, there is a nice feature that allows us to treat/map fields from the data source onto the tool.

From the **Macro Input** tool's **Configuration** panel, click **Show Field Map** to enable it and save the macro.

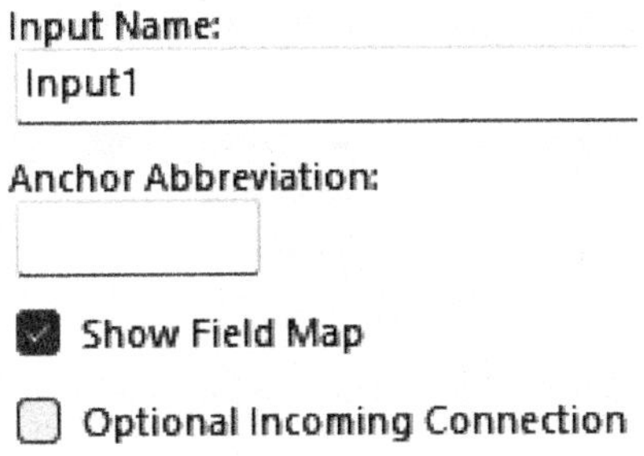

Input Name:

Input1

Anchor Abbreviation:

☑ Show Field Map

☐ Optional Incoming Connection

Figure 10.106: The Show Field Map option

You'll see that in the workflow where you use the macro, a message will appear, telling you that the macro has changed and Alteryx Designer refreshed it with the newest version.

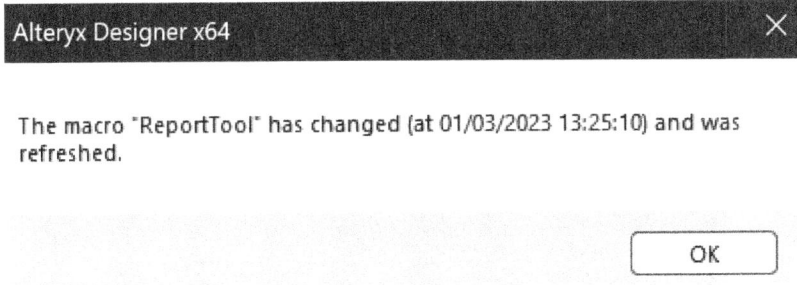

Figure 10.107: Alteryx detects changes in the macro and updates it

Also, note that Alteryx added all the expected fields with a dropdown, so you can map your input data to the expected fields within the tool. Alteryx Designer will automatically map all matching fields, but you'll need to manually map all those that didn't match by selecting the corresponding field from each dropdown.

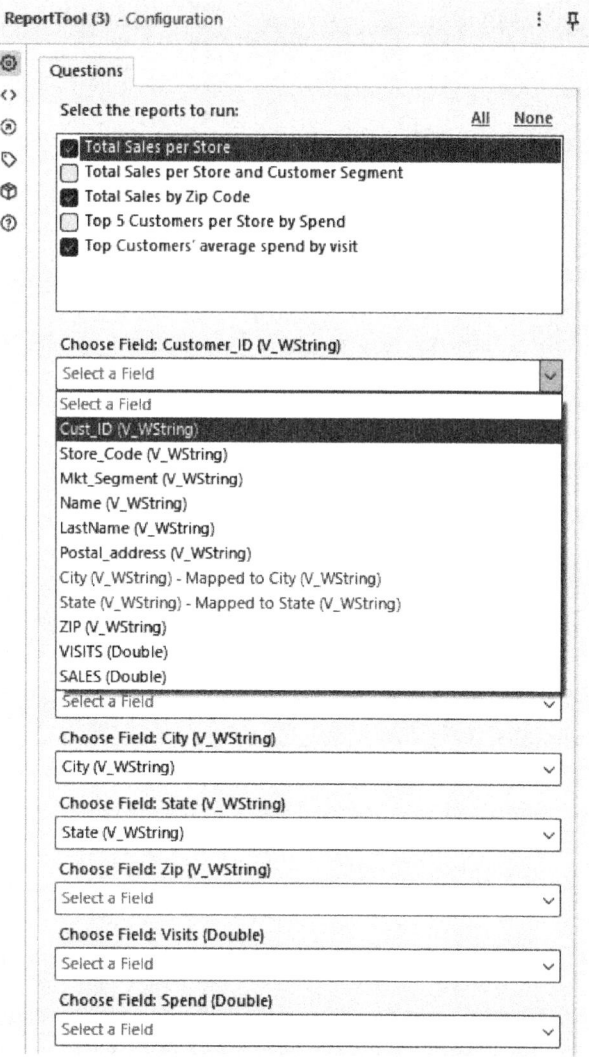

Figure 10.108: The field map exposed to the UI

> **Recommendation**
>
> For the **Macro Input** tool template input, just use the fields that you'll use in the tool.

There's more...

If we replace the **Macro Input** and **Macro Output** tools with the **Input Data** and **Output Data** tools, we can convert our macro into an Analytic App.

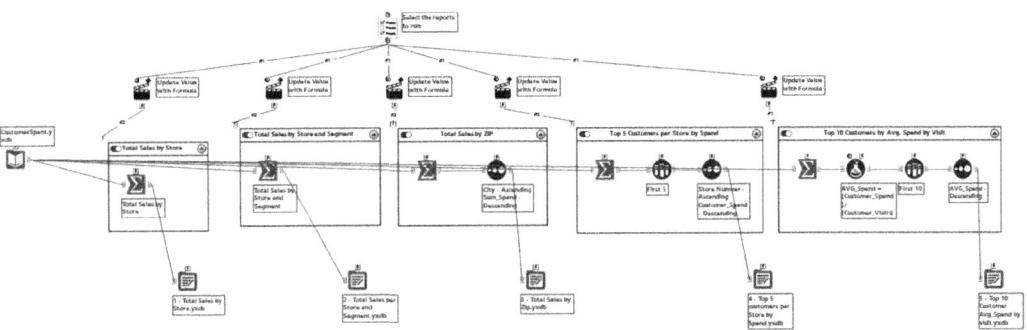

Figure 10.109: Converting a macro into an app

An Analytic App is simply a workflow with a user interface that takes the user input and produces a result.

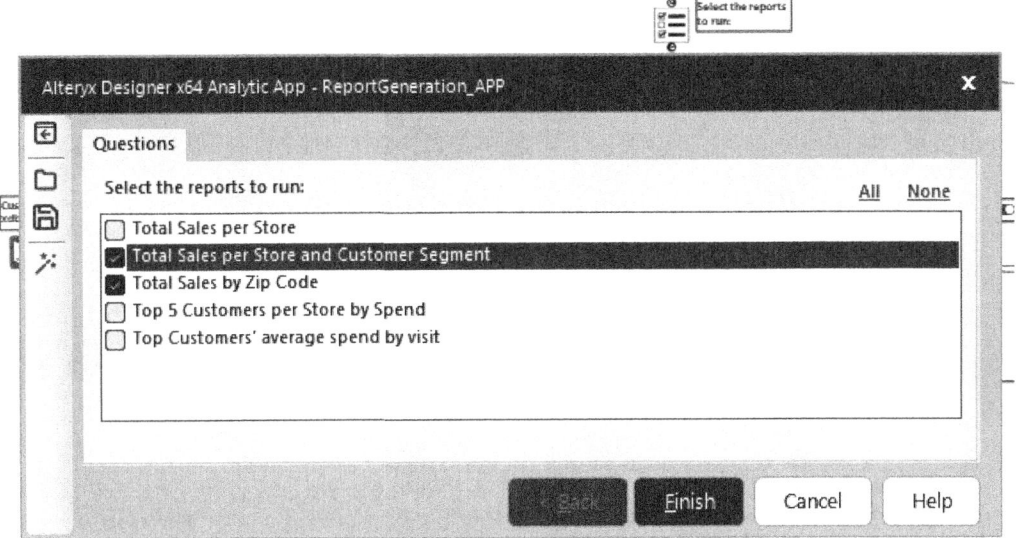

Figure 10.110: Running the app

You can execute an Analytic App using the magic wand icon to the left of the **Run** button (note that if you use the **Run** button or hit *Ctrl + R*, the workflow will run normally, without considering the **Interface** tools and their modifiers).

Figure 10.111: The magic wand to execute the app

If you don't see the wand icon, make sure that in the **Workflow** configuration tab, **Analytic App** is selected as the workflow type.

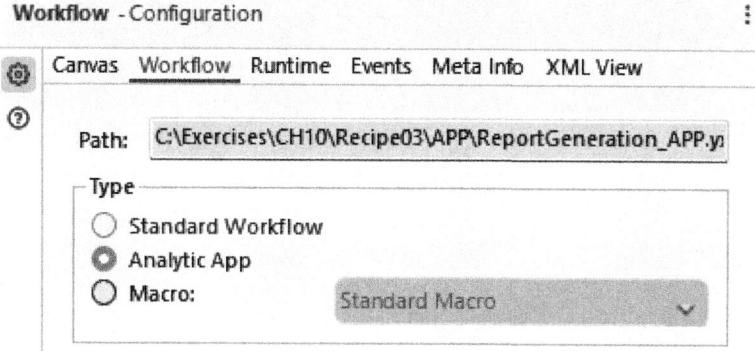

Figure 10.112: Workflow set to Analytic App

In the app interface, make your selections, and click on **Finish**.

You'll see a progress bar indicating that the app is running, and then, the **App Results** window will pop up, showing the outputs it generated, the option to show/hide the execution log, and the option to open the generated files from there.

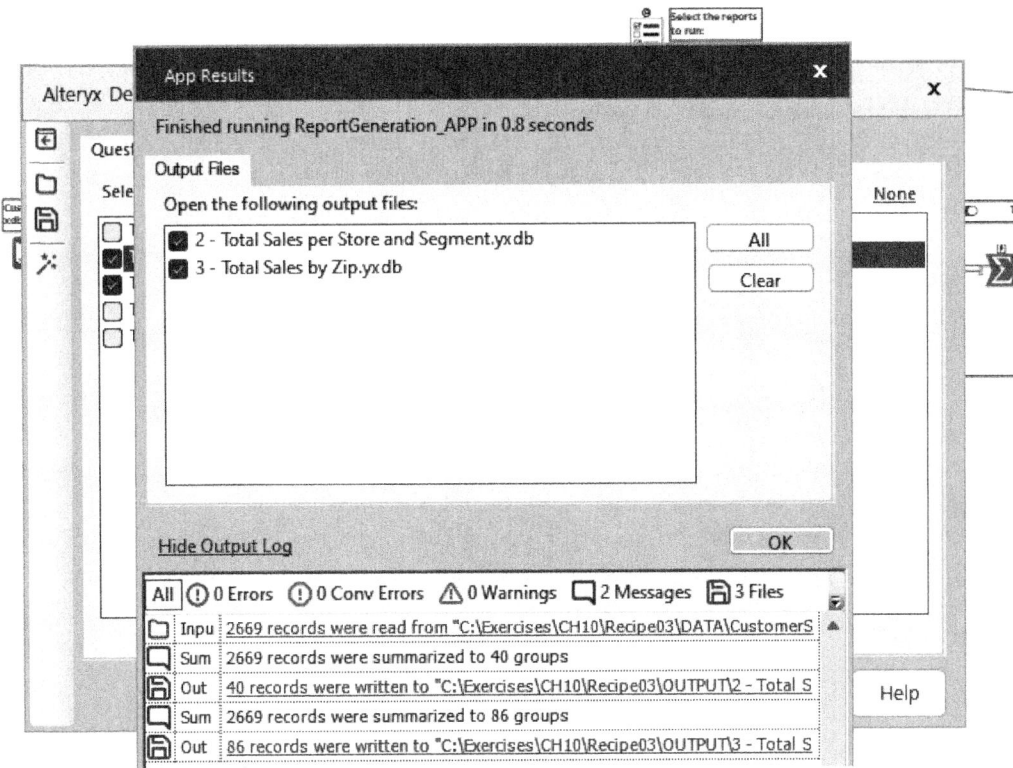

Figure 10.113: The Analytic App execution results

Analytic Apps can be uploaded to Alteryx Server to provide full functionalities to users via Alteryx Gallery.

Working with the underlying XML

So far, we have used **Action** tools and a formula to modify/replace existing values of a connected tool. Alteryx offers a more complex (and powerful) way to accomplish operations within macros and Analytic Apps that involves changing the XML that Alteryx uses to shape the workflows.

We'll use the same customer spend data we used in the previous recipe, but now, we'll create an Analytic App that uses the **Modify the underlying XML** feature, allowing the user to select which fields to use to calculate total visits and spending.

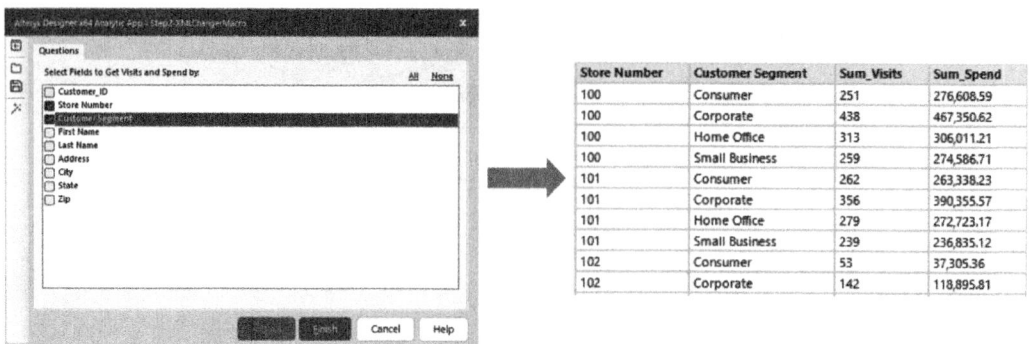

Figure 10.114: The tool we'll create

Because of how Alteryx works, we need to architect our app in a way that we can handle the requirements smartly, and since we need to build the new XML based on the input selected by the user dynamically, we need some mechanism that allows us to do that. A **Batch Macro** is a special type of macro that allows you to pass parameters for its execution, and that's why we will build one for this recipe.

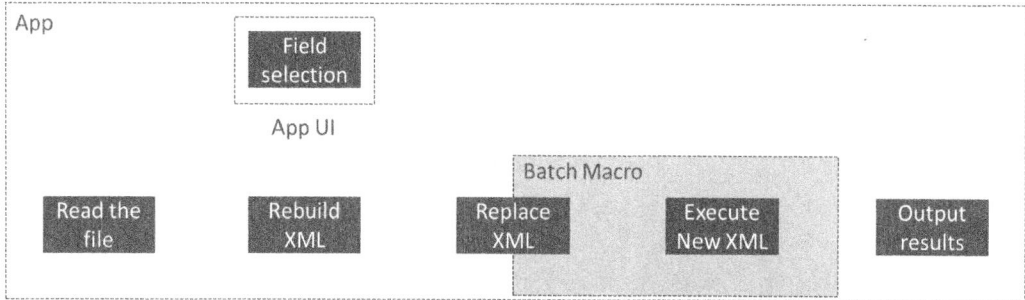

Figure 10.115: A design concept of how to build the Batch Macro

Sometimes, I like to start with a set of empty **tool containers** that represent the main logic I need to build.

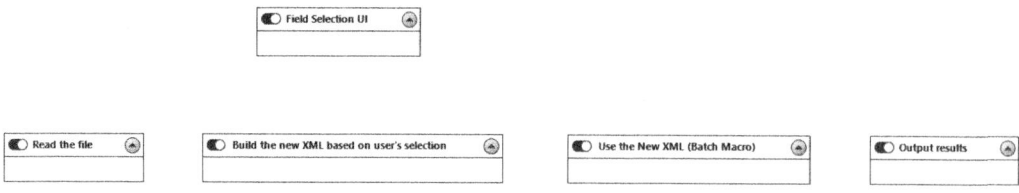

Figure 10.116: The Tool Container structure to be filled

Getting ready

We have prepared a test set for you to follow along with this recipe that can be downloaded from here: `https://github.com/PacktPublishing/Alteryx-Designer-Cookbook/tree/main/CH10/Recipe04`.

However, before starting, let's change a little configuration in Alteryx Designer. One useful setting (at least for this recipe) is the ability to show the XML for each tool in its **Configuration** panel (the workflow XML view is always accessible by clicking on any white space area of the canvas to navigate to the workflow configuration, and then clicking on the XML view):

1. To enable the tool's XML view, go to **Options | User Settings | Edit User Settings**, click on the **Advanced** tab, and check the **Display XML in Properties Window** option.

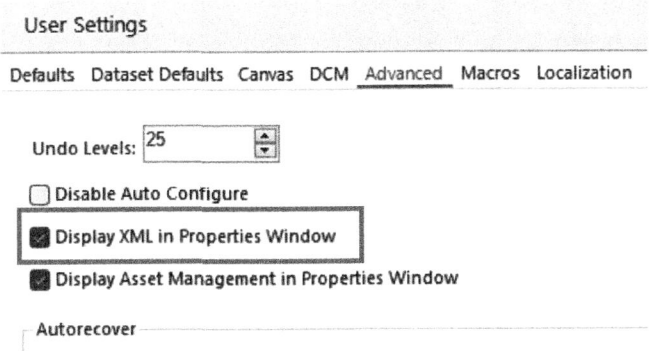

Figure 10.117: The Display XML in Properties Window option in User Settings

2. Click **Save**.

    Now, if you select a tool in the canvas, you'll see that the icons on the far-left side of the panel show a new one between the configuration (the gear icon) and the navigation (the circle with an arrow icon). This new icon allows you to access all the XML that corresponds to the selected tool. This XML manages all the settings and behaviors of the selected tool.

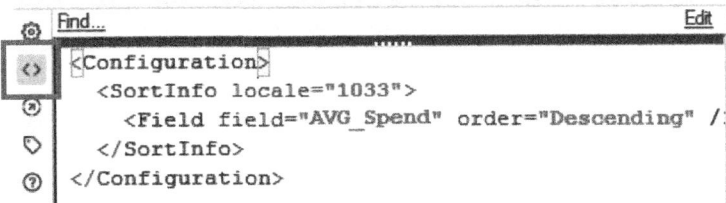

Figure 10.118: The XML icon in the Properties window

Now, you can see all the attributes of a tool, and throughout this recipe, you'll interact with it to make the tools behave as you want.

How to do it...

First, we need to start building the batch macro that will handle the final output and get the necessary XML structure to build in our app:

1. Let's start a new workflow and drop an **Input Data** tool and point it to ..\DATA\ CustomerSpent.yxdb.

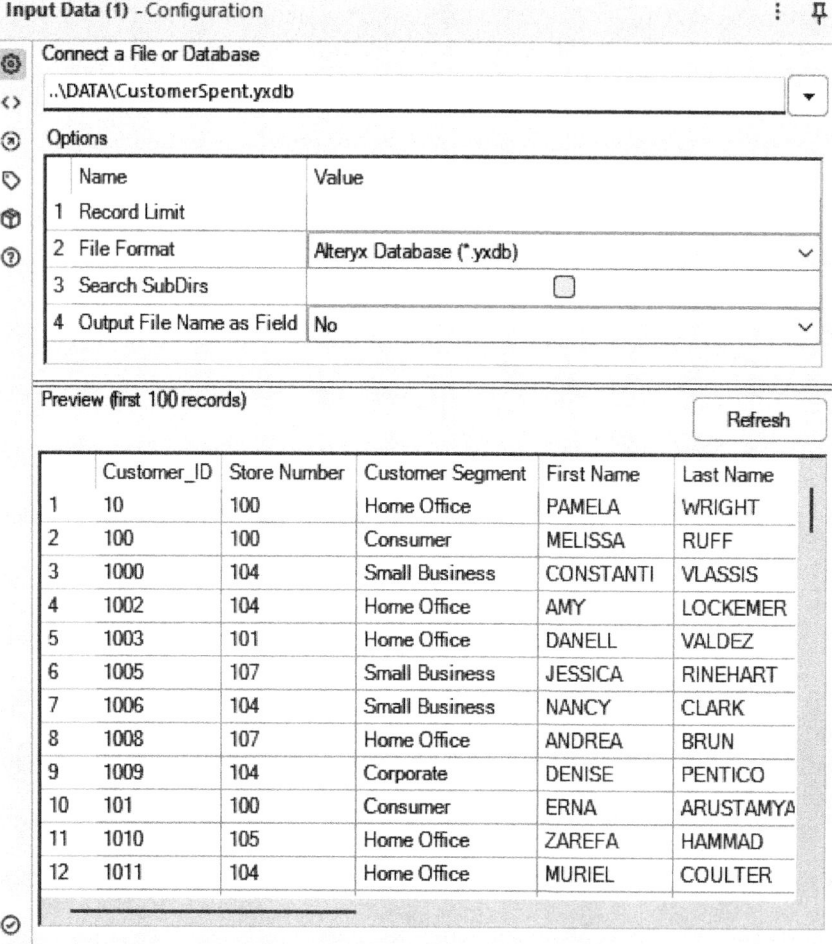

Figure 10.119: The Input Data configuration

2. Add a **Summarize** tool after the **Input Data** tool.

3. Click on Customer_ID, then **Add**, and select **Group By**.

4. Click on Visits, press *Ctrl*, and then click on Spend so that both fields are selected.

5.   Click on **Add** and select **Sum**.

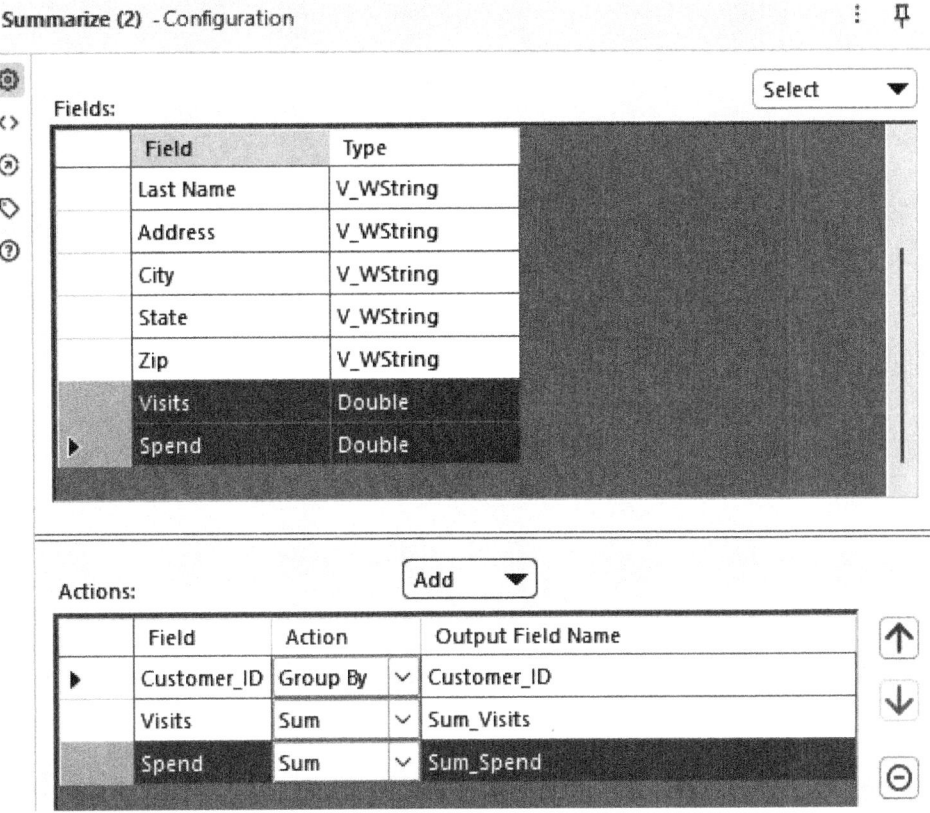

Figure 10.120: Summarize tool configuration

6.   Drop a **Browse** tool next to the **Summarize** tool.

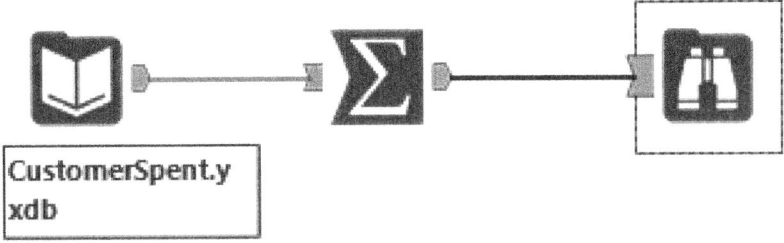

Figure 10.121: The workflow so far

Run the workflow and check that it works. You should be able to get the **Sum_Visits** and **Sum_Spend** values for a specific **Customer_ID**.

Record	Customer_ID	⋮ Sum_Visits	Sum_Spend
1	10	1	206.95
2	100	1	228.27
3	1000	1	432.44
4	1002	4	2,101.11
5	1003	1	1,404.09
6	1005	2	962.61
7	1006	4	552.53
8	1008	1	25.37

Figure 10.122: The results

7. Add a **Control Parameter** tool (from the **Interface** category) and place it above the **Summarize** tool, leaving some vertical space between them.

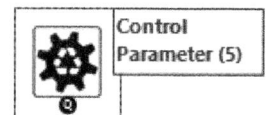

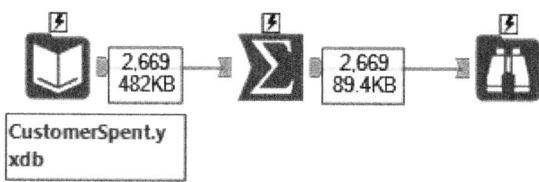

Figure 10.123: Adding the Control Parameter tool

8. Change the label for the **Control Parameter** tool to XML.

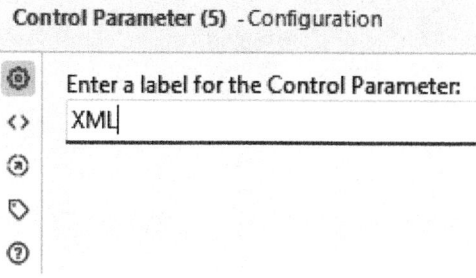

Figure 10.124: Setting a label for the parameter

9. Now, start dragging from the black **Q** below the **Control Parameter** tool, and connect it to the lightning connector on top of the **Summarize** tool.

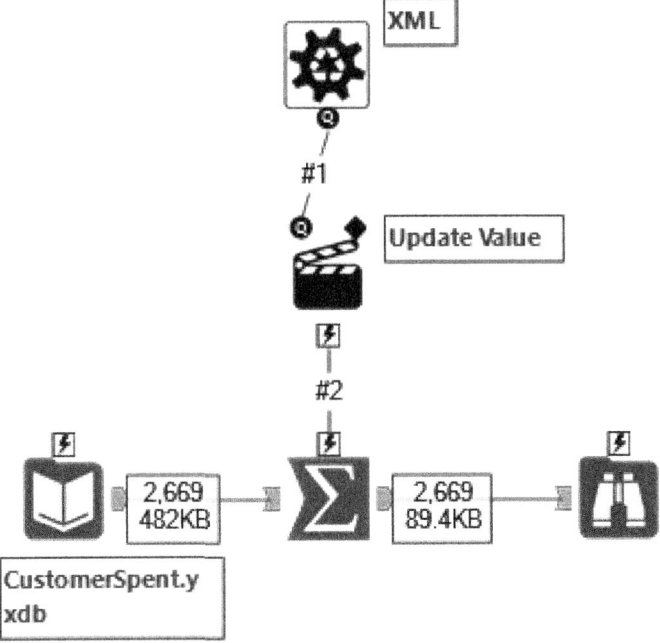

Figure 10.125: Connecting the Control Parameter tool to the Summarize tool

10. Click on the **Action** tool to configure it.

11. Select **Update Raw XML with Formula** from the **Select an action type** dropdown.

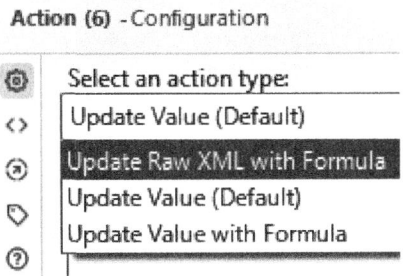

Figure 10.126: The Action tool action type selection

12. Expand the **SummarizeFields** option by clicking the + icon.

13. Click on **SummarizeField[@field='Customer_ID']**, and make sure that it remains highlighted.

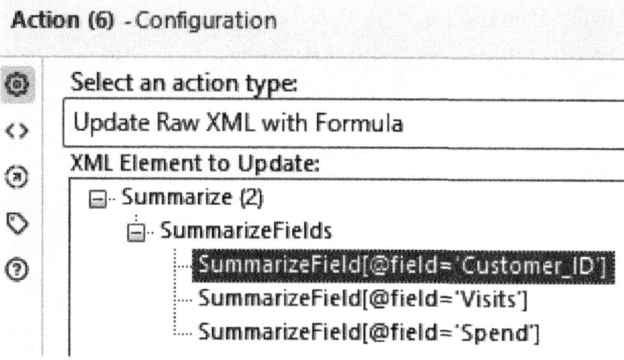

Figure 10.127: The Action tool configuration

14. Select **Update Outer Xml** at the bottom of the panel, and enter [#1] under **Formula to Generate New XML** (this will tell the tool to use whatever comes from the **Control Parameter** tool and replace the highlighted elements in the **Summarize** tool configuration).

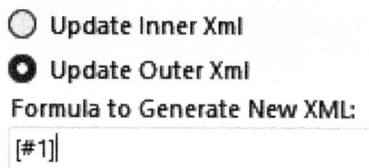

Figure 10.128: Selecting the Update Outer Xml option

15. Click on the **Summarize** tool to activate its configuration.

16. From the left icons, select the <> icon to view the tool's XML.

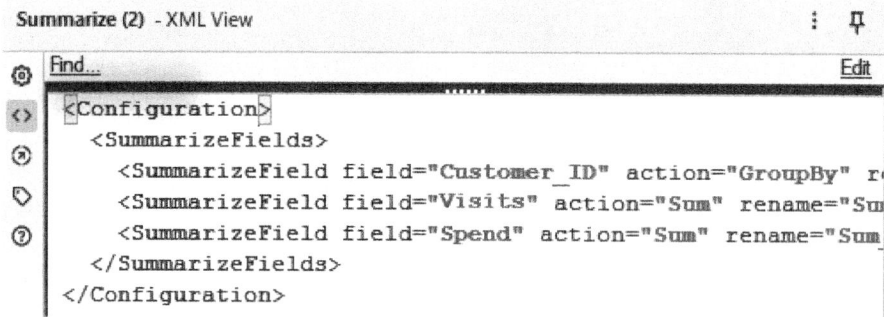

Figure 10.129: Exploring the Summarize tool's XML

17. Click on **Edit** to access the XML editor, and select the highlighted line (the one that contains the **GroupBy** action in it)

```
Xml Editor                                                              x

<Configuration>
  <SummarizeFields>
    <SummarizeField field="Customer_ID" action="GroupBy" rename="Customer_ID" />
    <SummarizeField field="Visits" action="Sum" rename="Sum_Visits" />
    <SummarizeField field="Spend" action="Sum" rename="Sum_Spend" />
  </SummarizeFields>
</Configuration>

                                                        OK        Cancel
```

Figure 10.130: The Alteryx XML editor

18. Hit *Ctrl + C* to copy the line, and close the XML editor.

19. Add a **Comment** tool (from the **Documentation** category), and paste the copied text in it to save it for later (this is the XML that we will replace in our app).

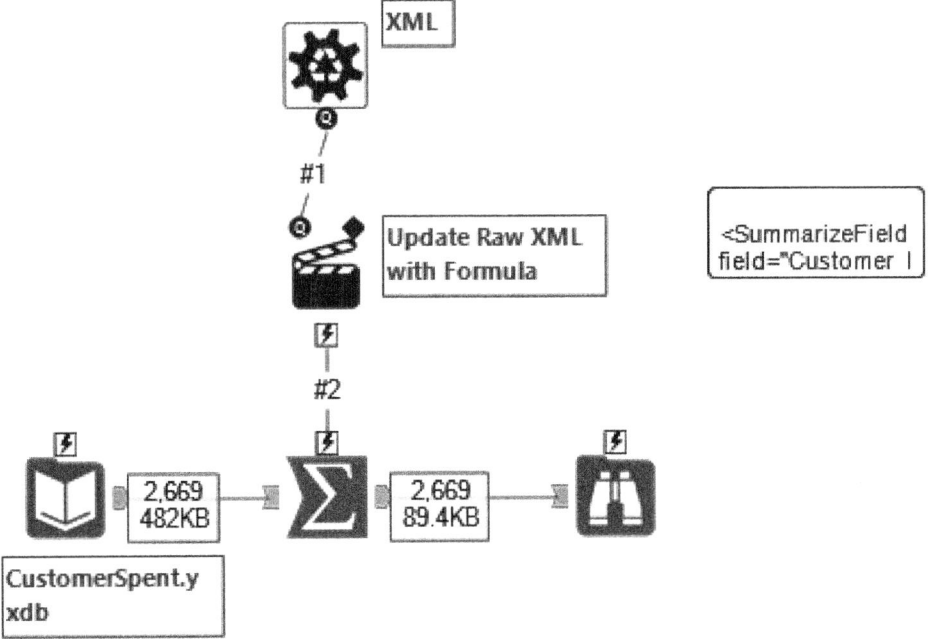

Figure 10.131: Using a Comment tool to save useful info (XML)

20. Right-click on the **Input Data** tool and select **Convert To Macro Input**.

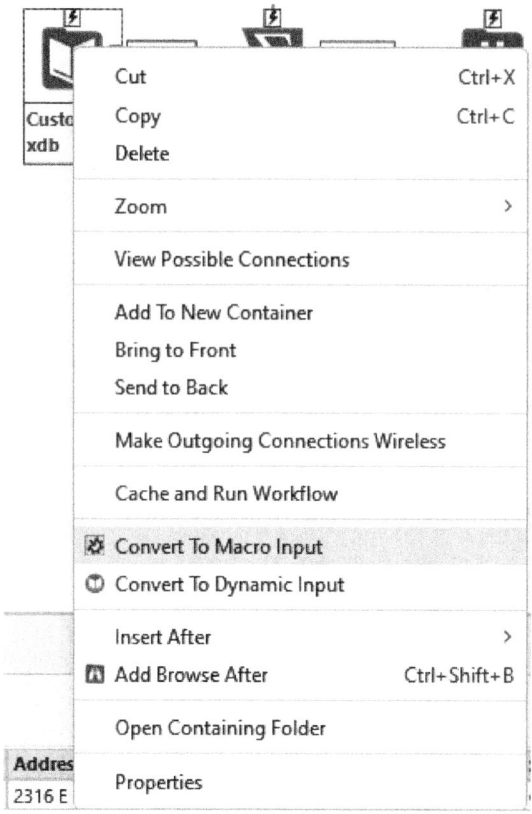

Figure 10.132: The Convert To Macro Input option

21. Right-click on the **Browse** tool and select **Convert To Macro Output**.

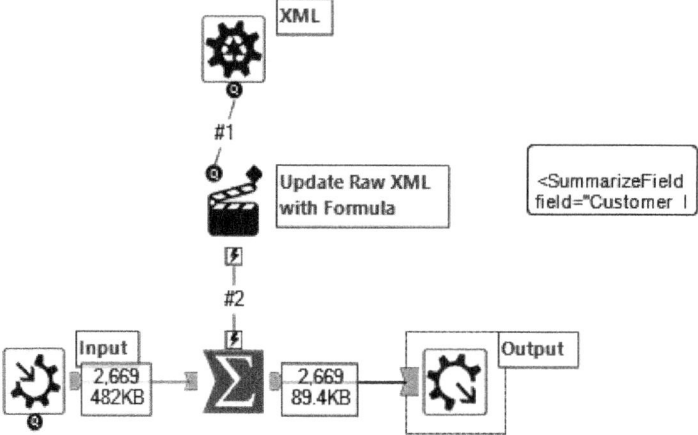

Figure 10.133: Converting the Browse tool into a Macro Output tool

22. Now that our Batch Macro is finished, we will save it as `BatchMacro_XML.yxmc` (if you plan to share it later, use a shared macro repository).

23. On a new workflow, let's start building an empty tool containers layout.

24. Click on the **Documentation** category and drop a **Tool Container** tool onto the canvas.

25. Double-click on its name and rename it `Read the file`.

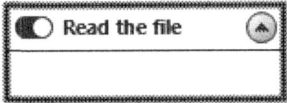

Figure 10.134: The empty container layout

26. Drop another **Tool Container** tool to the right of the existing one, and rename it `Build the new XML based on user's selection`.

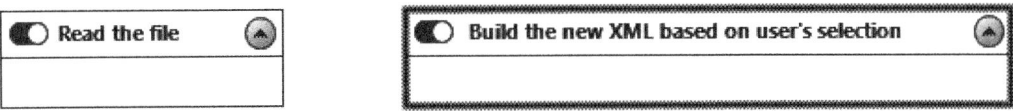

Figure 10.135: Adding containers to the layout

27. Add another one on top of the last added **Tool Container** tool, and rename it `Field Selection UI`.

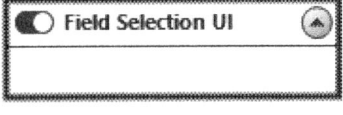

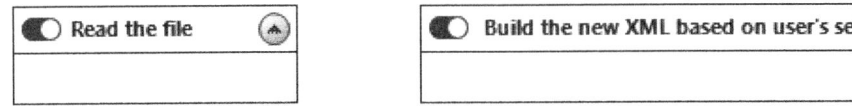

Figure 10.136: The selector will be in this container

28. Repeat adding containers and renaming them until you have the same structure as this one:

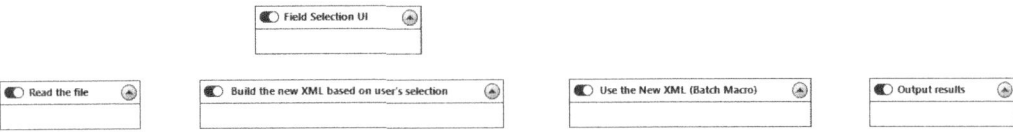

Figure 10.137: The final empty containers layout

We'll start by adding an **Input Data** tool to the **Read the file Tool Container** tool.

29. From the **In/Out** tool category, add an **Input Data** tool, and drop it inside the **Tool Container** tool when it turns light blue (which will ensure that the tool is placed within the container and not outside it).

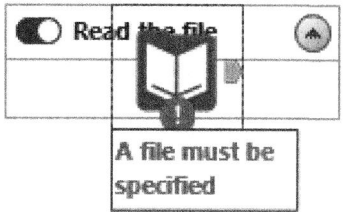

Figure 10.138: Dropping a tool inside a container

30. Point the **Input Data** tool to . . \DATA\CustomerSpent.yxdb.

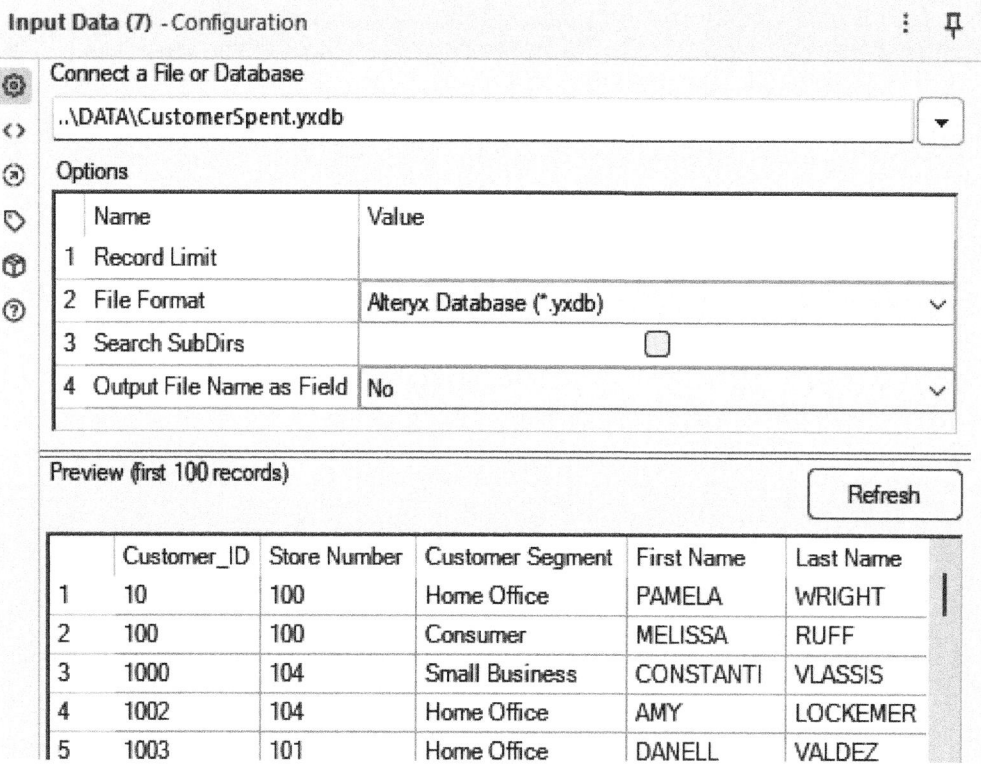

Figure 10.139: The Input Data tool configuration

31. From the **Developer** category (or by searching for Field Info in the search bar), drop a **Field Info** tool inside the container labeled **Build the new XML based on the user's selection**, and connect its input anchor to the **Input Data** tool output anchor.

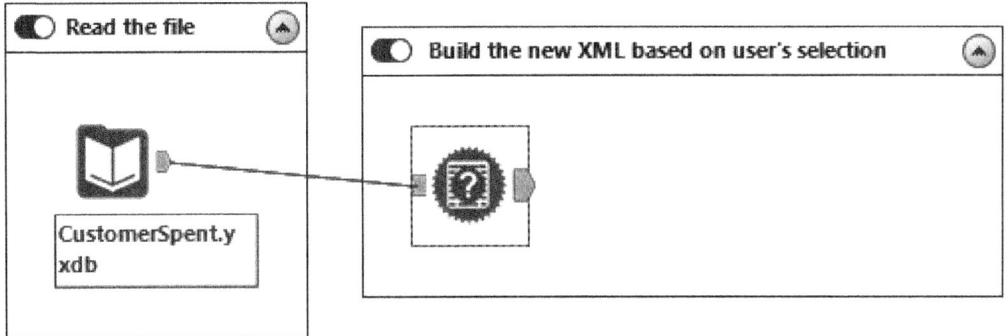

Figure 10.140: Adding a Field Info tool

32. Add a **Filter** tool to the same container after the **Field Info** tool.

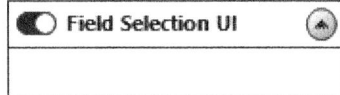

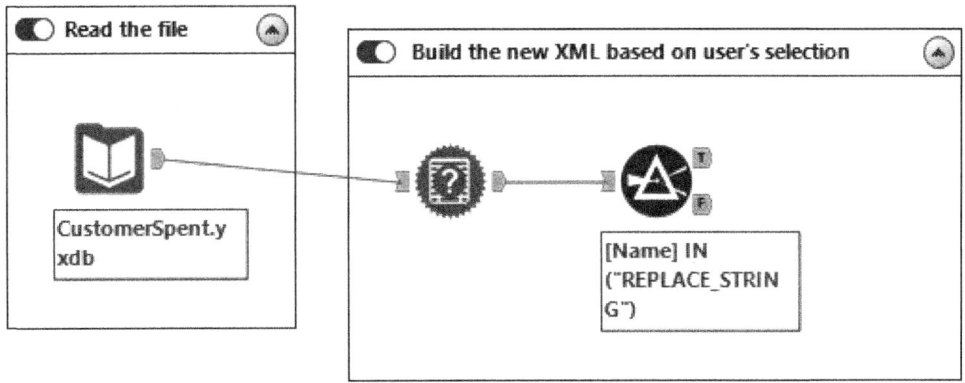

Figure 10.141: Adding a Filter Tool

33. Use this expression as a custom filter:

```
[Name] IN ("REPLACE_STRING")
```

34. Add a **Transpose** tool, and connect it to the **T** output anchor of the **Filter** tool.

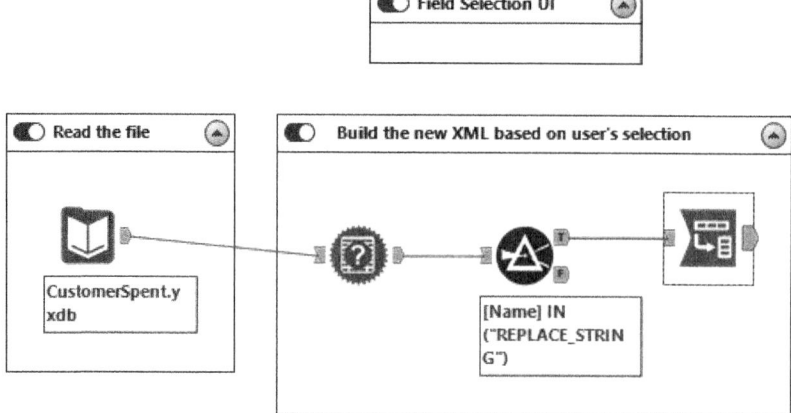

Figure 10.142: Adding a Transpose tool

35. Click on the **Deselect All** button in the **Data Columns** panel. Make sure that nothing is selected in the **Key Columns** panel.

36. Click on **Name** in the same panel so that we get only that field.

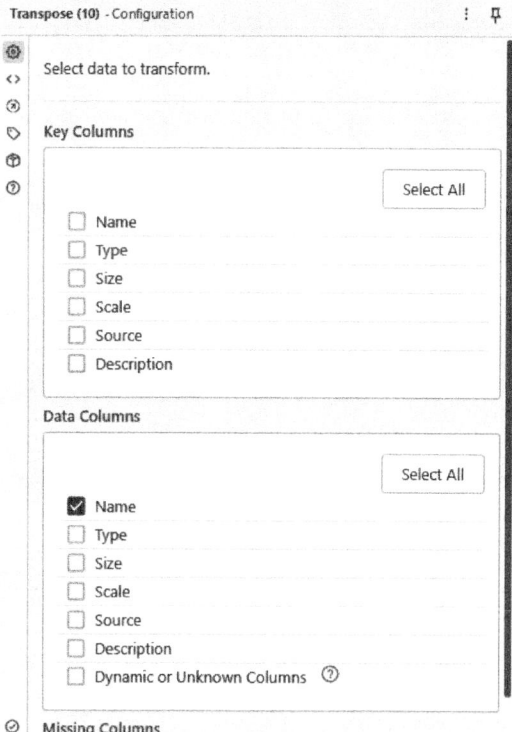

Figure 10.143: The Transpose tool configuration

This tool will output two columns, `Name` and `Value`. The former will contain the `Name` string as the value for all rows (because it's the only field selected), and `Value` will contain the selected field names.

Name	Value
Name	City
Name	State

Figure 10.144: The results after transposing the data

Now, we need to understand what is needed to move on with the current workflow.

37. Drop a **Formula** tool next to the **Transpose** tool (move the overlapping **Containers** tool if you need space to work).

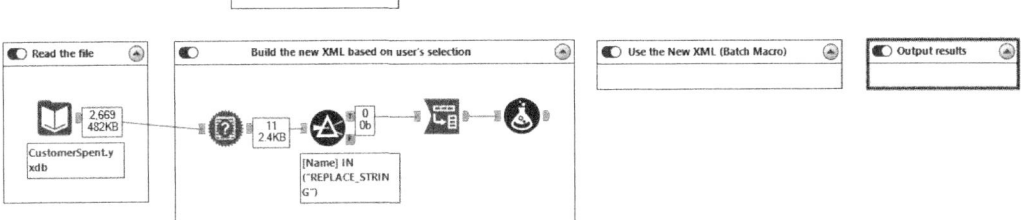

Figure 10.145: Adding a Formula tool

38. Select + **Add Column** from the dropdown and name the new field XML.

Now, we need to retrieve the XML we saved for later.

39. Switch to the tab where you have the batch macro we created, and copy the text from the **Comment** tool.

The text we saved is as follows:

```
<SummarizeField field="Customer_ID" action="GroupBy"
rename="Customer_ID" />
```

We need to replace the field and rename the attributes of the `SummarizeField` element with the ones we got from the user. Because we are generating a string field, values must be surrounded by quotes, and since there are double quotes already in the values, we'll use single quotes.

40. Wrap the expression in single quotes so that it reads as follows:

```
'<SummarizeField field="Customer_ID" action="GroupBy"
rename="Customer_ID" />'
```

41. Replace each appearance of `Customer_ID` with `'+[Value]+'` so that the expression ends up like this:

```
'      <SummarizeField field="'+ [Value] +'" action="GroupBy"
rename="'+ [Value] +'" />'
```

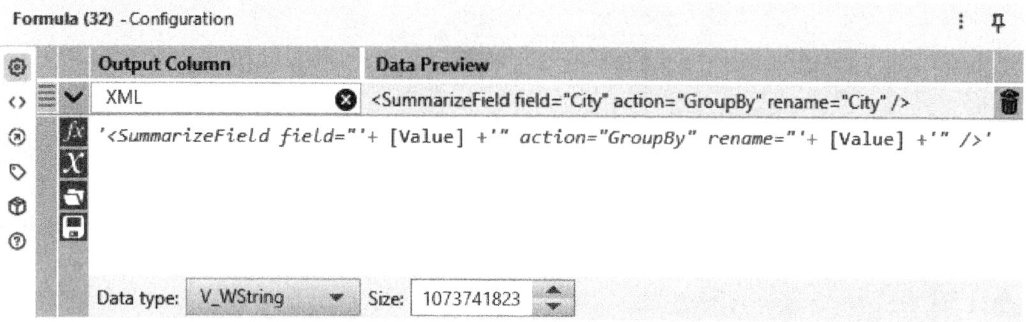

Figure 10.146: The Formula tool configuration

42. Add a **Select** tool after the **Formula** tool, and leave selected only the XML field (make sure to deselect the *Unknown field).

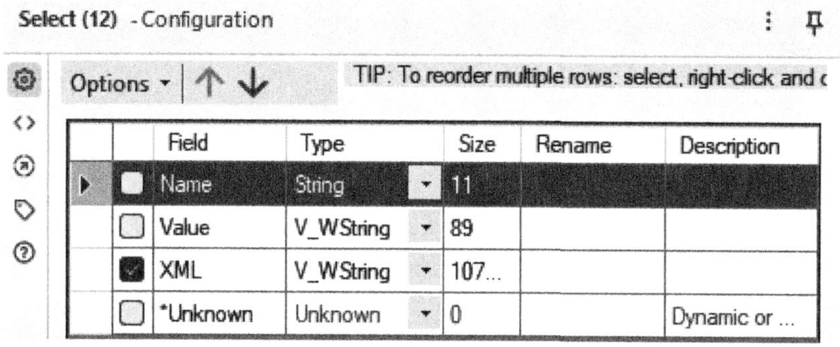

Figure 10.147: The Select tool configuration

At this point, for each selected field, we'll get a record with an XML, but what we need to do is consolidate all these records into just one, which will be the XML code that will be injected into our batch macro.

43. Drop a **Summarize** tool after the **Select** tool.

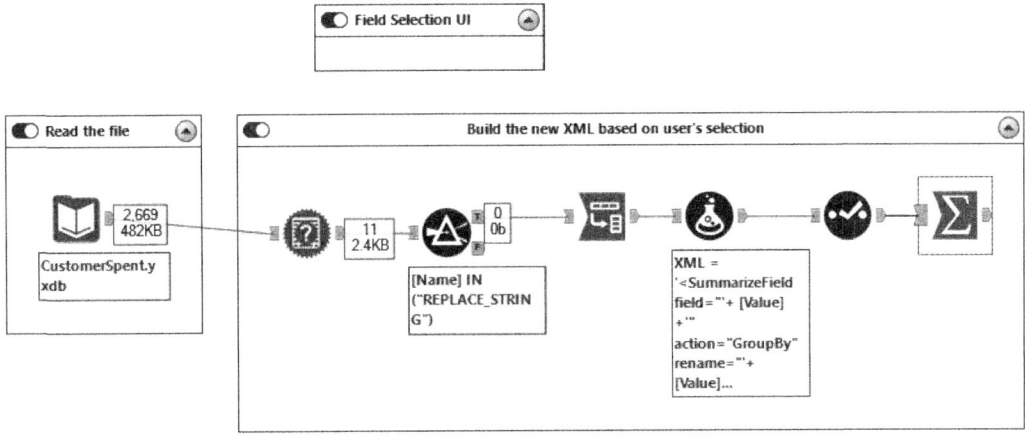

Figure 10.148: Adding a Summarize tool to the workflow

44. You have only one field (XML). Click on **Add**, and from the **String** menu, select **Concatenate**.

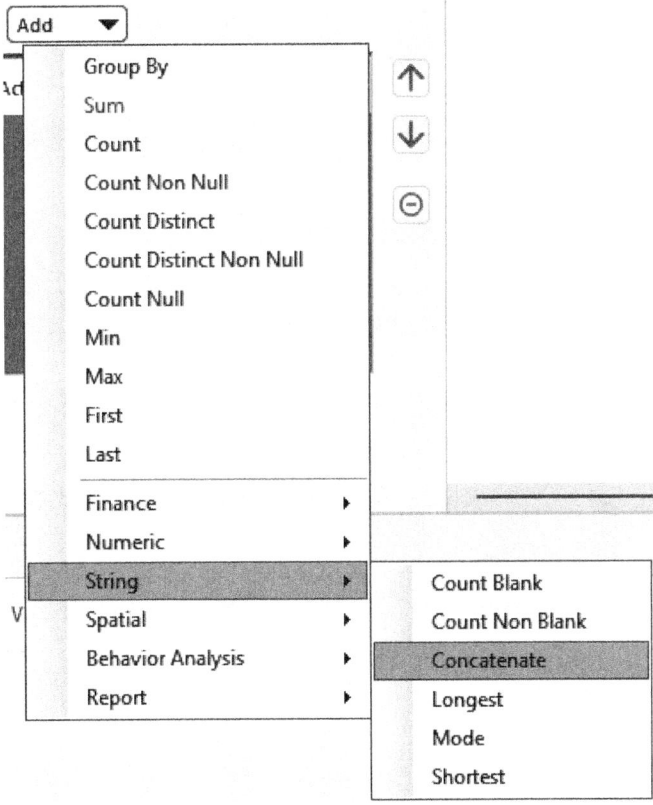

Figure 10.149: The Concatenate option under the String submenu

45. Make sure that the **Concatenate Properties** fields at the bottom of the panel are empty for **Start** and **End** and that there is a comma (,) for **Separator**.

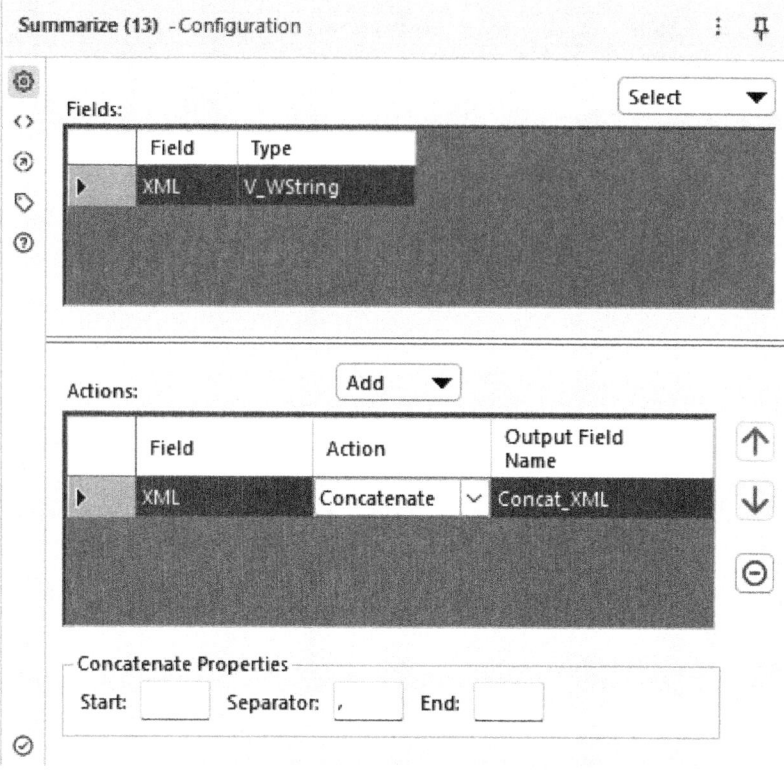

Figure 10.150: The Summarize tool configuration

46. Right-click on white space on the canvas, then click on **Insert**, and then **Macro**. Since the batch macro we created is still open, it can be easily selected.

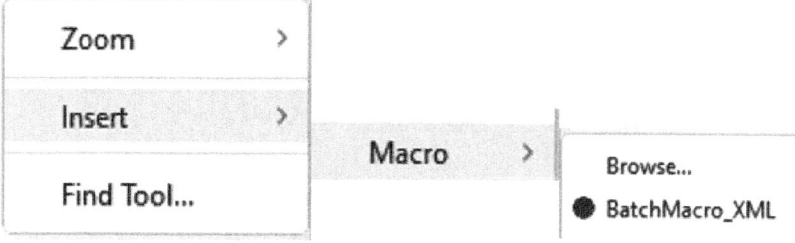

Figure 10.151: The Insert | Macro menu option

47. The macro was inserted where you clicked. Drag the macro and drop it inside the **Tool Container** tool labeled **Use the New XML (Batch Macro)** when it turns light blue.

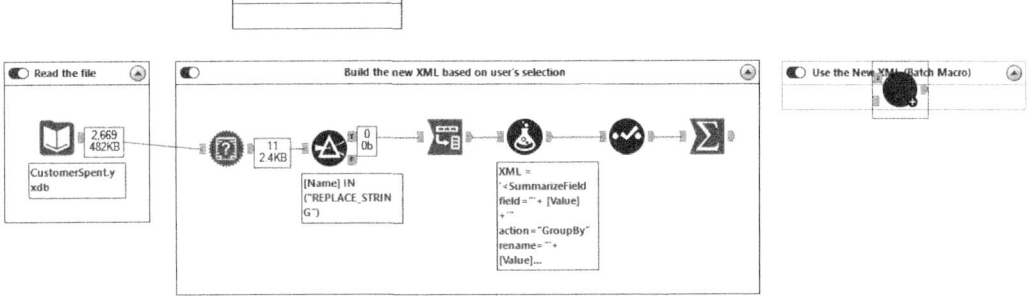

Figure 10.152: Inserting the macro into the workflow

The macro has two inputs:

- The one on top, with the question mark, is where we need to connect the parameters

- The other one (below) is where we'll connect the data that the macro will process

48. Connect the **Summarize** output to the question mark (¿) label input and the **Input Data** tool output anchor to the remaining input on the macro.

Once you connect them, you'll probably get an error message from Alteryx Designer.

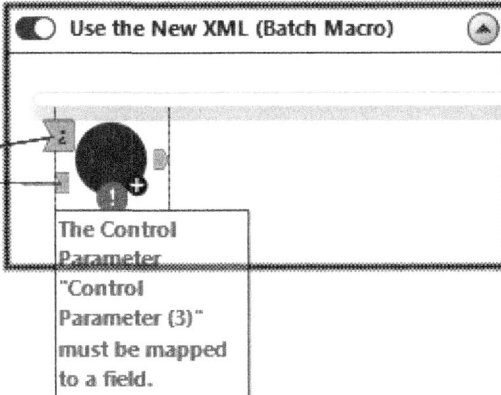

Figure 10.153: An error because the parameter has not been mapped yet

49. To fix this, click on the macro, and in the **Questions** tab, select the Concat_XML field to map it to the expected XML parameter.

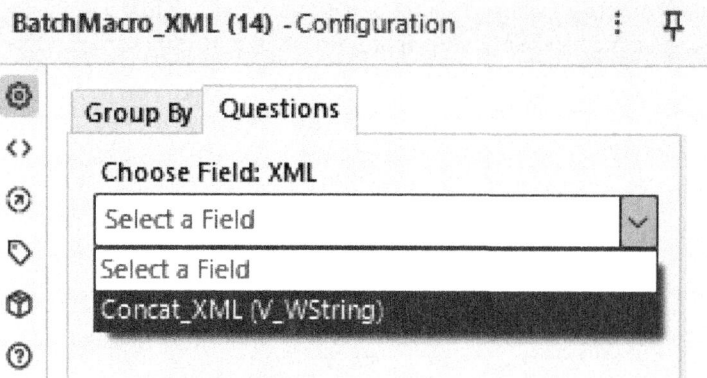

Figure 10.154: Mapping the parameter to a field

Once you do that and click on a white space area of the canvas, the message will disappear.

50. Drop a **Browse** tool inside the **Output results Tool Container** tool, and connect the output anchor of the macro to its input anchor.

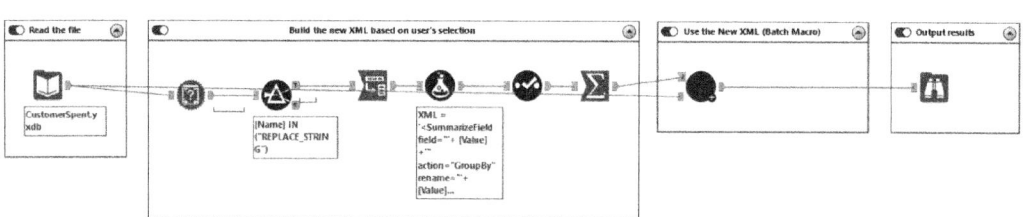

Figure 10.155: The workflow so far

51. Finally, we'll add the **Interface** tools to allow the user to select the incoming fields.

52. Drop a **List Box** tool from the **Interface** category inside the **Field Selection UI Tool Container** tool. Again, you will probably need to rearrange the containers to make some space.

53. You can hold *Ctrl* + click the containers to move them down, and Alteryx will move all the tools within them.

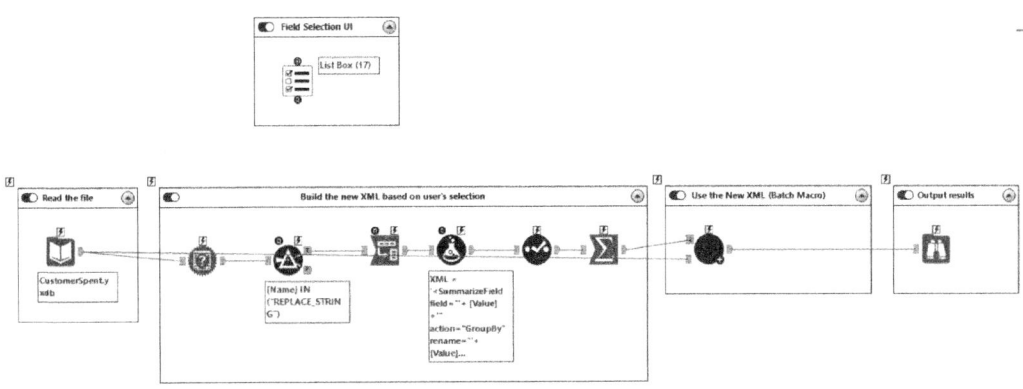

Figure 10.156: Adding the List Box tool

54. Start dragging from the **Input Data** tool output anchor, and connect it to the white-background **Q** icon on top of the **List Box** tool.

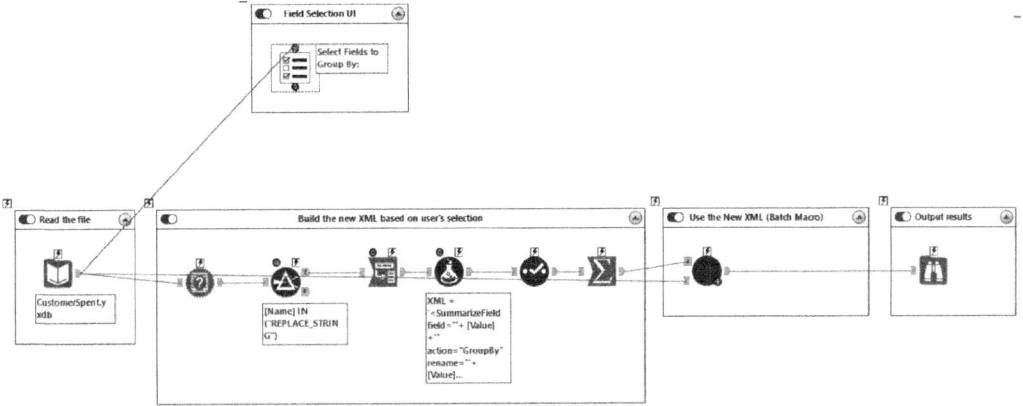

Figure 10.157: Connecting the input data to the List Box tool

55. Click on the **List Box** tool to access its configuration.

56. Type `Select Fields to Group By:` in the **Enter the text or question to be displayed** textbox.

57. Select **Generate Custom List**, and make sure that the **Start Text** and **End Text** values are double quotes (one on each) and **Separator** is `","`.

    Note that because we connected the **Input Data** tool to the tool, **Fields from Connected Tool** appears in the **List Values** dropdown, and you cannot change it (unless you remove the connector from the **Input Data** tool).

58. From the **Properties** list, we need only the string and date field types, so leave only those types selected (you can click on **None** to deselect all fields and then only enable the ones you need).

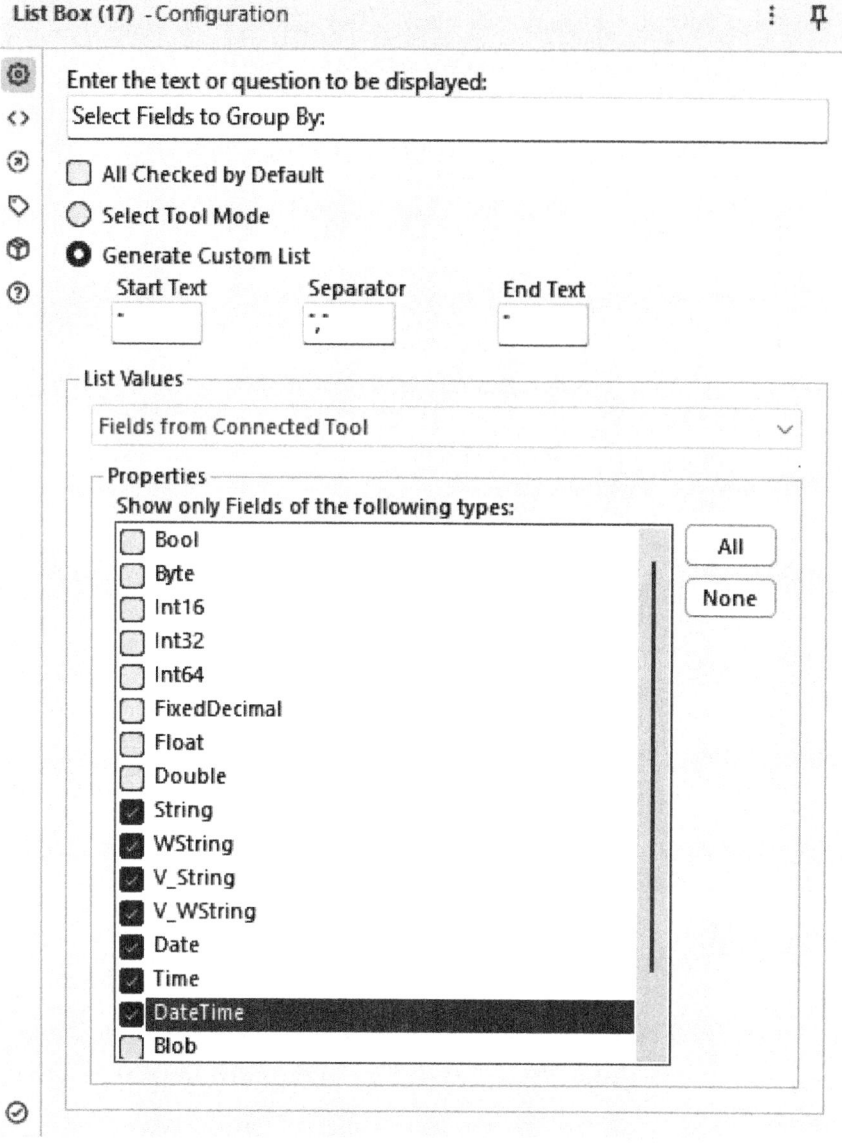

Figure 10.158: The List Box tool configuration

59. Drag from the black **Q** at the bottom of the **List Box** tool, and connect it to the lightning icon of the **Filter** tool. Then, an **Action** tool will appear. Move it inside the **Field Selection UI Tool Container** tool.

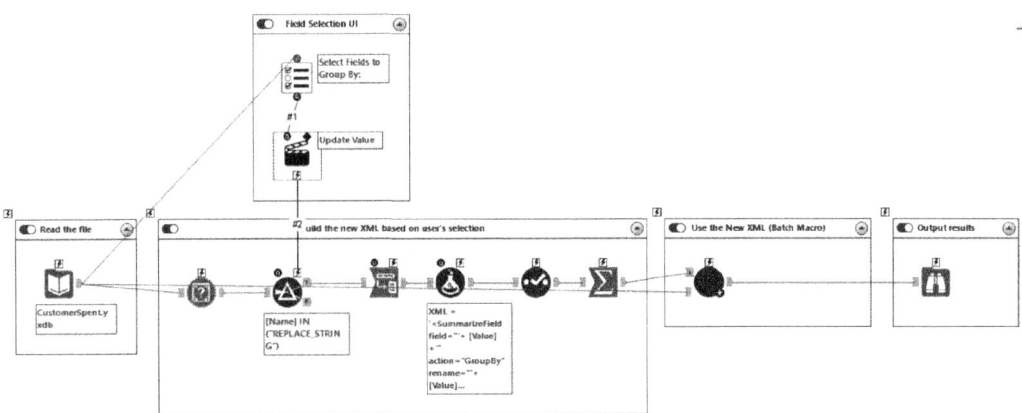

Figure 10.159: Connecting the List Box tool to the Filter tool

60. In the **Action** tool configuration, make sure **Update Value (Default)** is selected in the action type dropdown.

61. Click on **Expression - value="[Name] IN ("REPLACE_STRING")"** to highlight it.

62. At the bottom of the panel, click **Replace a specific string** and delete everything except "**REPLACE_STRING**" (the double quotes included).

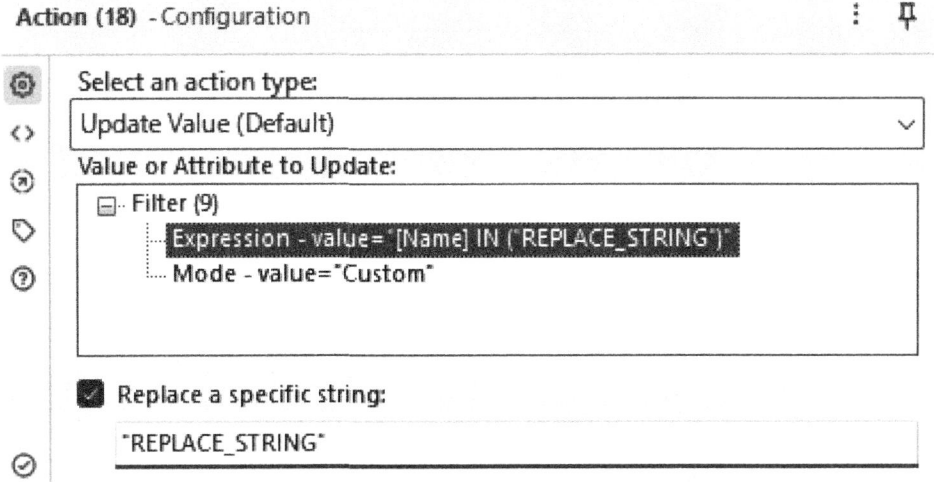

Figure 10.160: The Action tool configuration

Before testing the Analytic App, we need to make a few adjustments.

63. Activate the **Interface Designer** tool and click on the gear icon on the left.

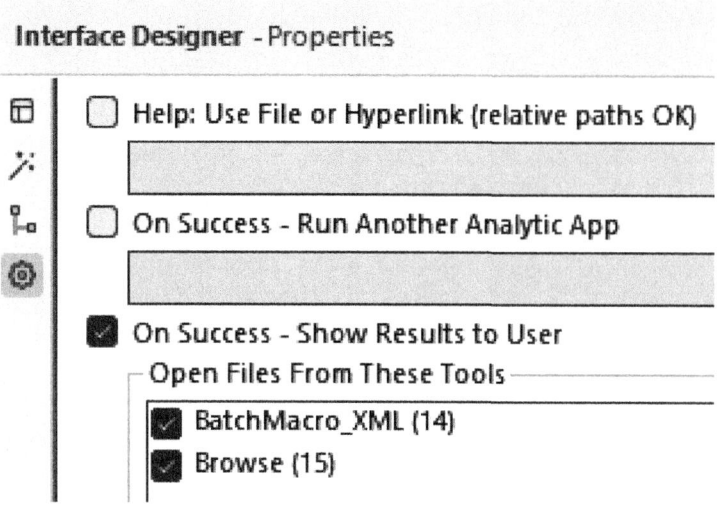

Figure 10.161: The Interface Designer tool configuration

64. Make sure you select the **Browse** tool (yours may have a different number between the parentheses, as shown in the preceding screenshot).

65. Run the app using the wand so that the UI is displayed

Figure 10.162: The magic wand to execute the apps

Alteryx will open the UI and wait for you to select some fields.

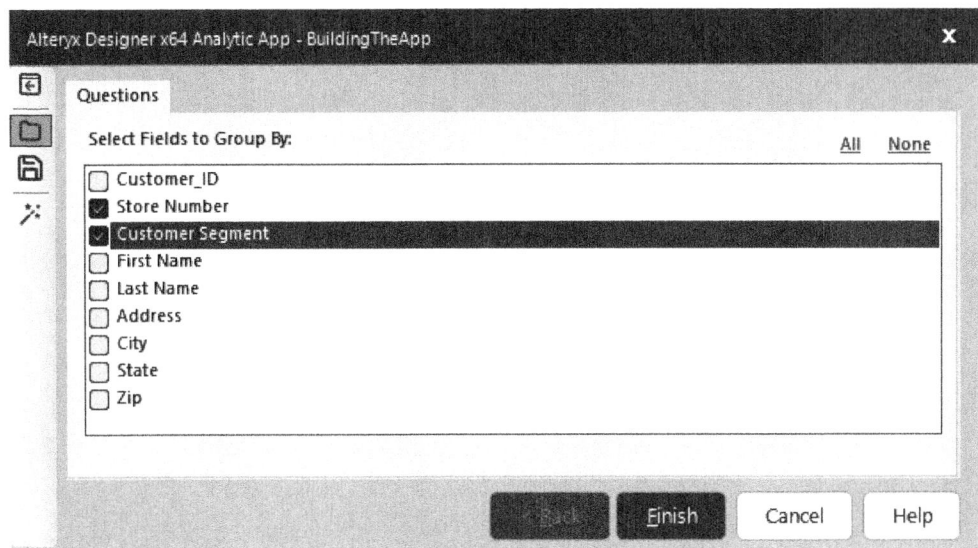

Figure 10.163: The app UI

66. Select any field (or fields) and click on **Finish**. A popup with a progress bar will appear while Alteryx runs the app.

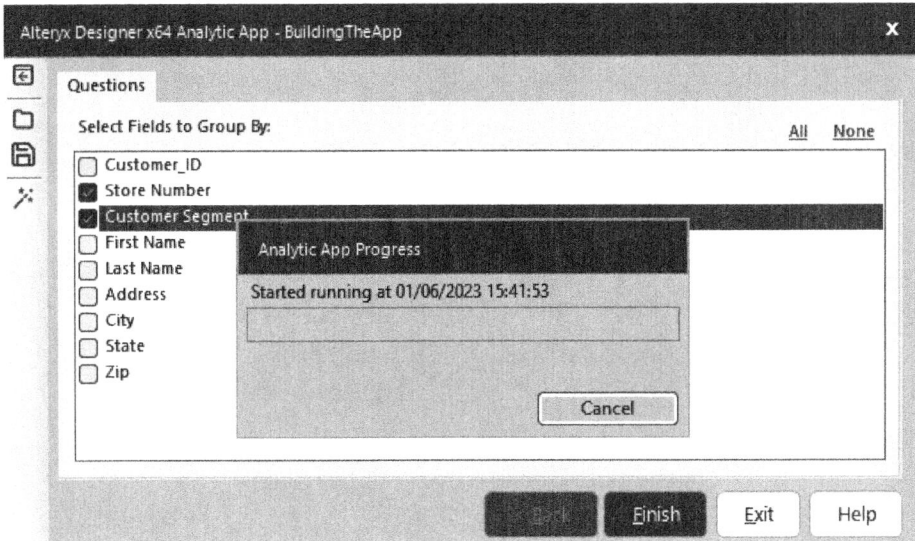

Figure 10.164: The app progress bar

When it finishes, the **App Results** windows will appear, showing the results from the **Browse** tool and the option to show/hide the output log.

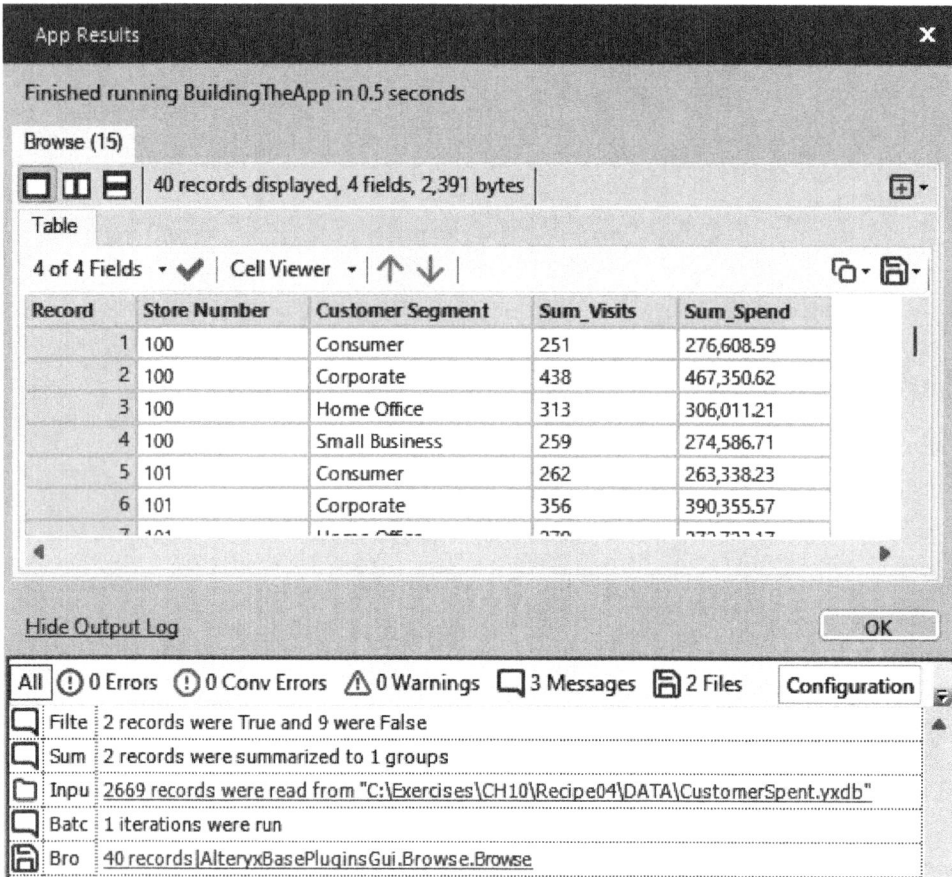

Figure 10.165: The app results after execution

This recipe outputs to a **Browse** tool. From here, you can add the outputs you need to save your summarized results wherever you need to.

Populating a list box with the fields of a File Browse tool selection

In the previous recipe, we created an Analytic App that allows users to select which fields they want to use to create summarizations.

In this recipe, we'll add a little more interactivity to the same app so that users can select the input file to create the summarizations.

The summarization fields will remain the same (`Visits` and `Spend`) and must be present in the file.

Getting ready

We have prepared a test set for you. It consists of the results of the previous recipe, and you can download it from here: https://github.com/PacktPublishing/Alteryx-Designer-Cookbook/tree/main/CH10/Recipe05. The test set is as follows:

- The resulting app from the fourth recipe:

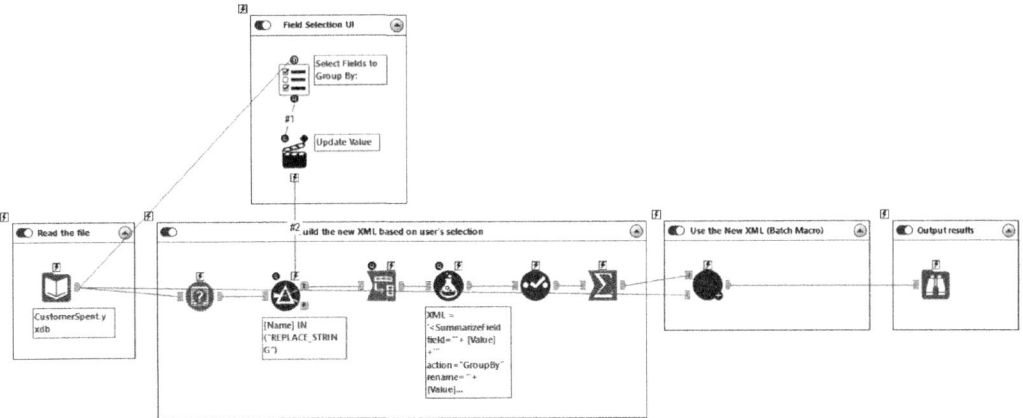

Figure 10.166: The starting point for this recipe

- The UI of the app:

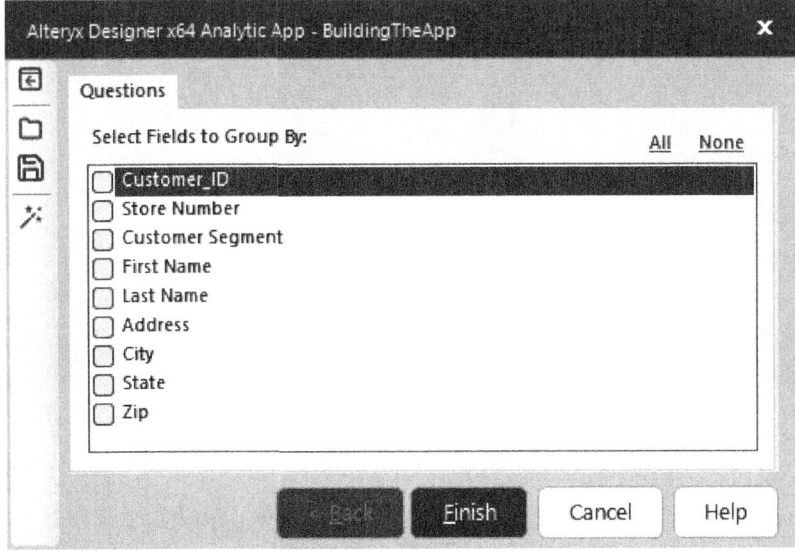

Figure 10.167: The UI for the starting point

We will add a feature to select what data source to read, presenting it to the user so that grouping fields can be selected.

How to do it...

Let's get started as follows:

1. Open the workflow from `..\WORKFLOWS\PreviousApp.yxwz`.

    We will make some modifications to the app to include the **File Browser** tool.

2. Drop a **File Browse** tool above the **Input Data** tool from the **Interface** category.

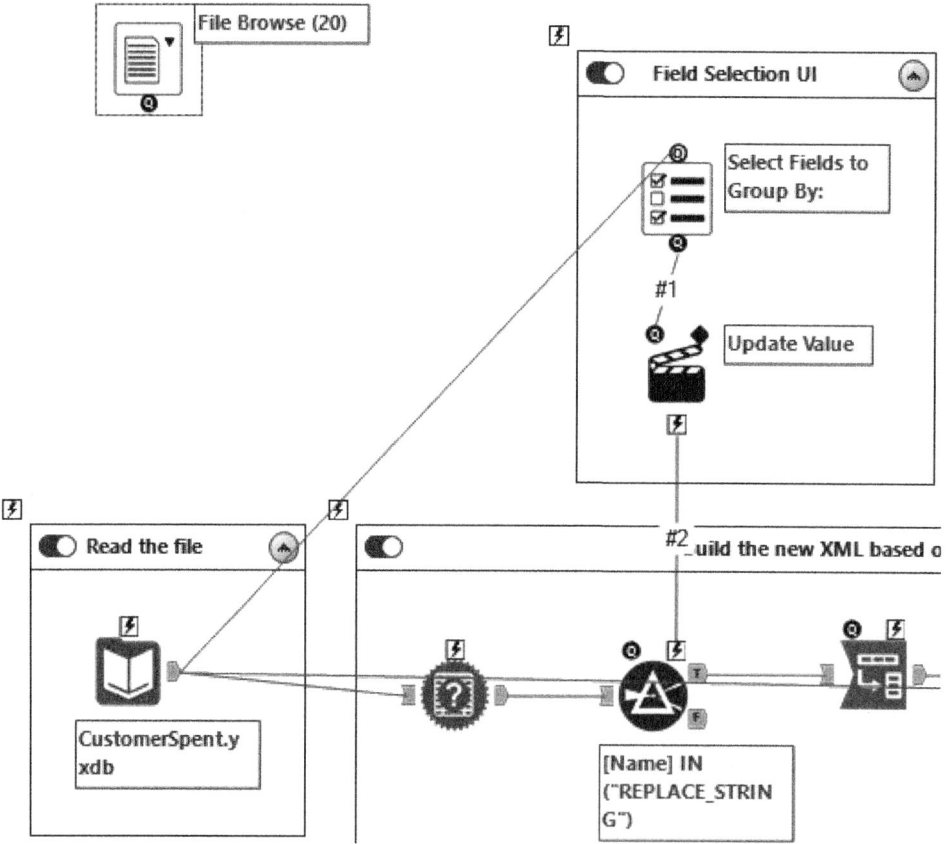

Figure 10.168: Adding a File Browse tool to the macro/app

3. Change the text/question so that it becomes more helpful (I used `Select Data Source to Connect To:`), and make sure that your tool configuration is set to **Standard Database File Formats**.

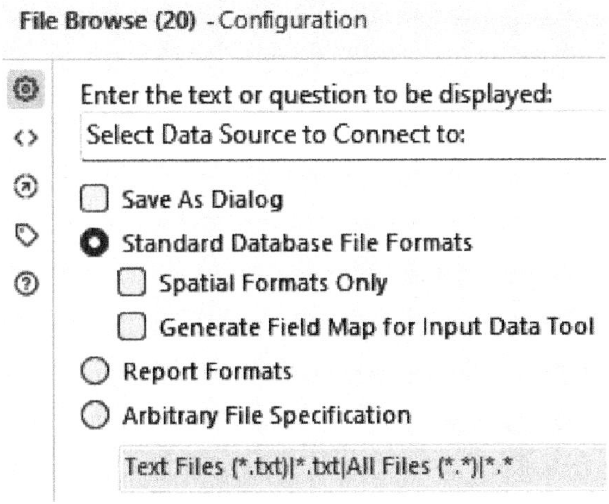

File Browse (20) - Configuration
Enter the text or question to be displayed:
Select Data Source to Connect to:
Save As Dialog
Standard Database File Formats
Spatial Formats Only
Generate Field Map for Input Data Tool
Report Formats
Arbitrary File Specification
Text Files (*.txt)|*.txt|All Files (*.*)|*.*

Figure 10.169: The File Browse tool configuration

4. Connect it to the **Input Data** tool (the black Q connector from the **File Browse** tool to the lightning connector on top of the **Input Data** tool) so that an **Action** tool is placed between both connected tools.

Select Data Source to Connect to:
#1
Update Input Data Tool
#2
Read the file
CustomerSpent.yxdb
Field Selecti
#1
#2
uild the
[Name] IN ("REPLACE_STRIN

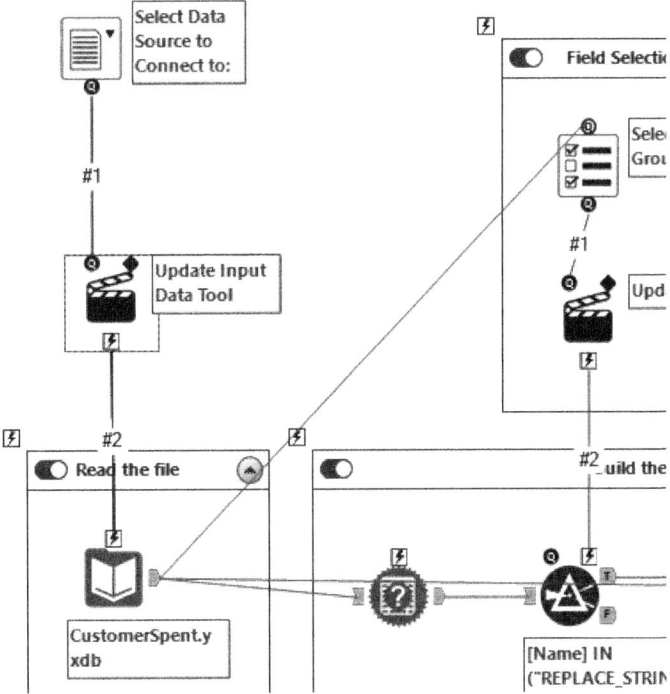

Figure 10.170: Connecting the File Browse tool to the Input Data tool

5.   Click on the **Action** tool, and make sure that **Update Input Data Tool (Default)** is selected in the **Select an action type** dropdown and **Required** is checked.

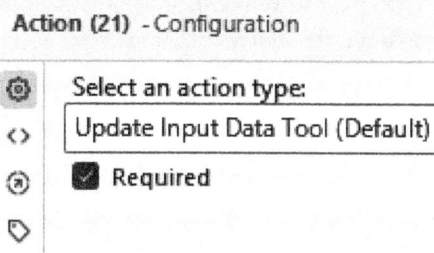

Figure 10.171: The Action tool configuration

If we run the app now, you'll notice two main things:

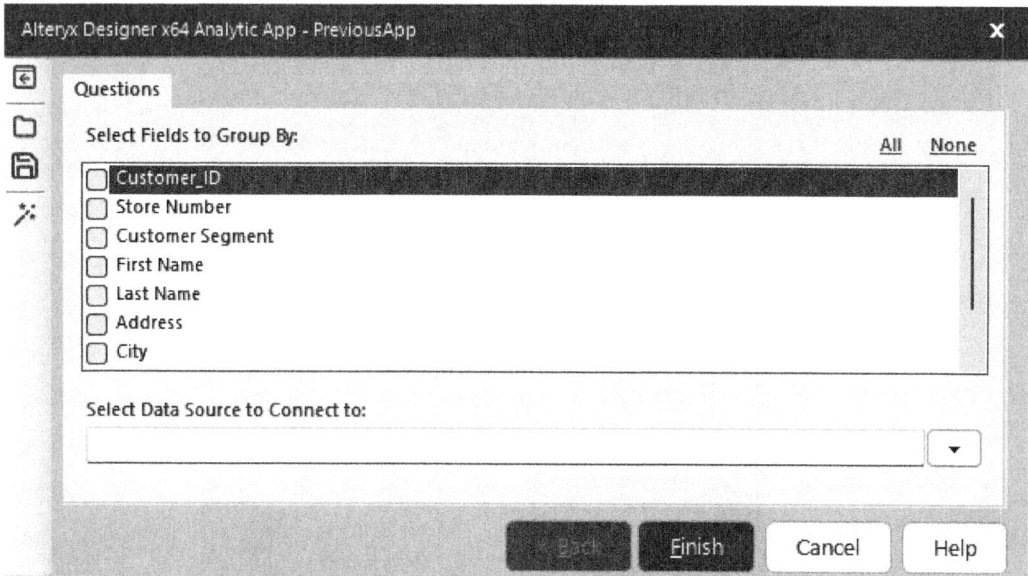

Figure 10.172: The new UI (with the File Browse tool added)

The data source selection option is located below the field selection list, and the options under **Select Fields to Group By** are the same and don't change based on the data source input.

We'll fix both things very quickly.

6.   Click on **Cancel** to close the app.

7.   Activate the **Interface Designer** tool (**View | Interface Designer** from the menu, or *Ctrl + Alt + D*).

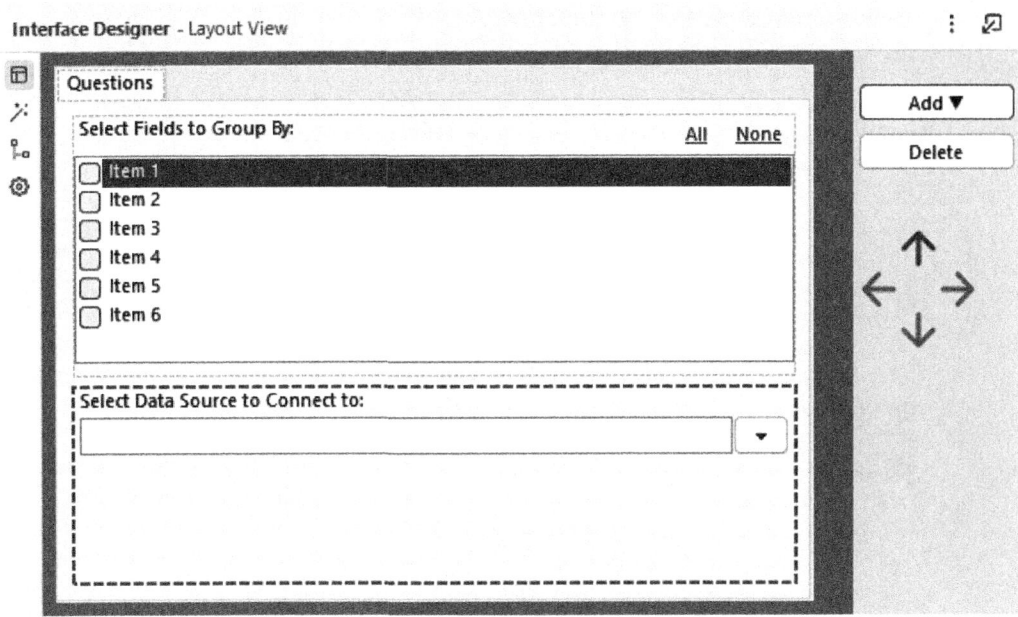

Figure 10.173: The Interface Designer tool to reorder items

8. Click the drop-down control corresponding to the **File Browse** tool, and use the arrows on the right to place it within the UI (in this case, it's just one place above).

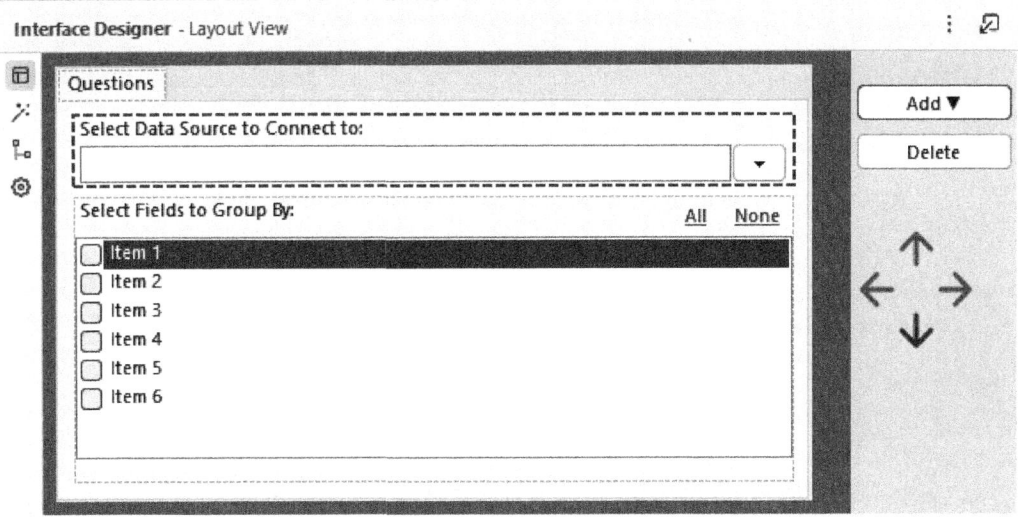

Figure 10.174: The UI elements reordered

To change the field list on the **Select Fields to Group By** panel, we need to change the source for the field list presented by the **Field Selection List Box** tool.

9. Click on the connection from the **Input Data** tool to the **List Box** tool and delete it (that is, the line that connects both tools).

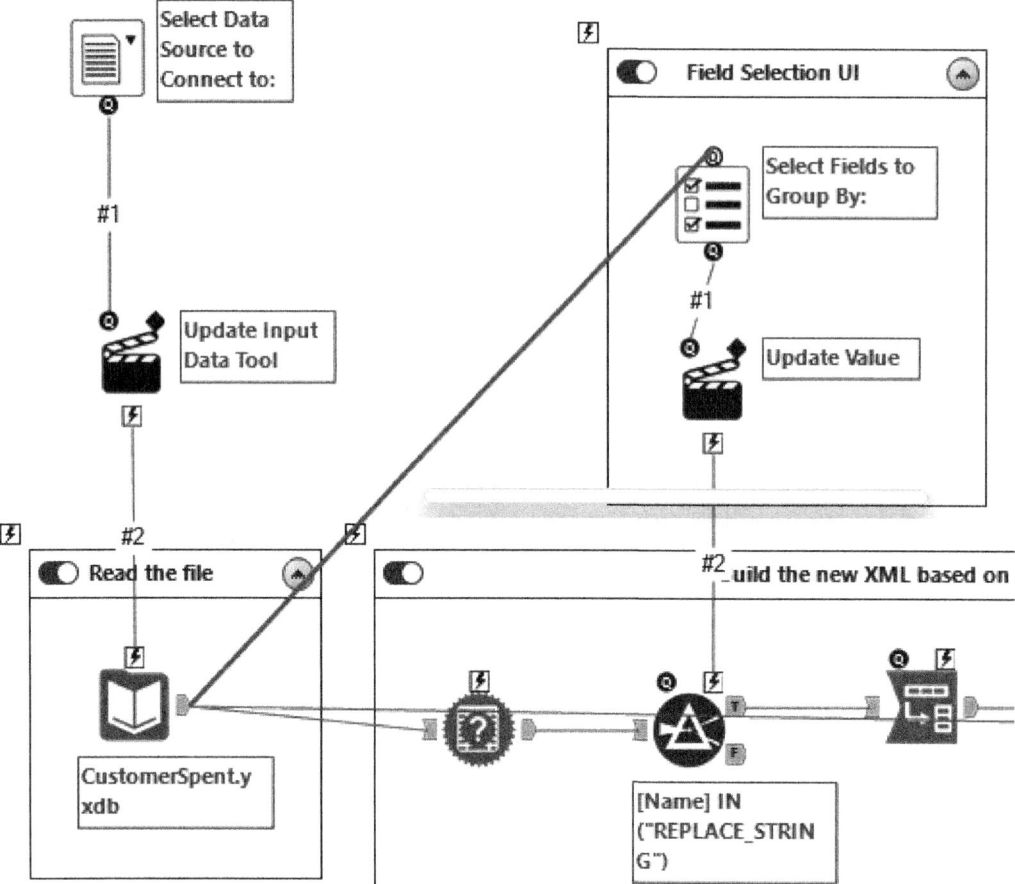

Figure 10.175: Fixing the field list for the List Box tool

10. Once the connection disappears, drag a new connection from the black **Q** connector of the **File Browse** tool and drop it in the white **Q** connector on top of the **List Box** tool.

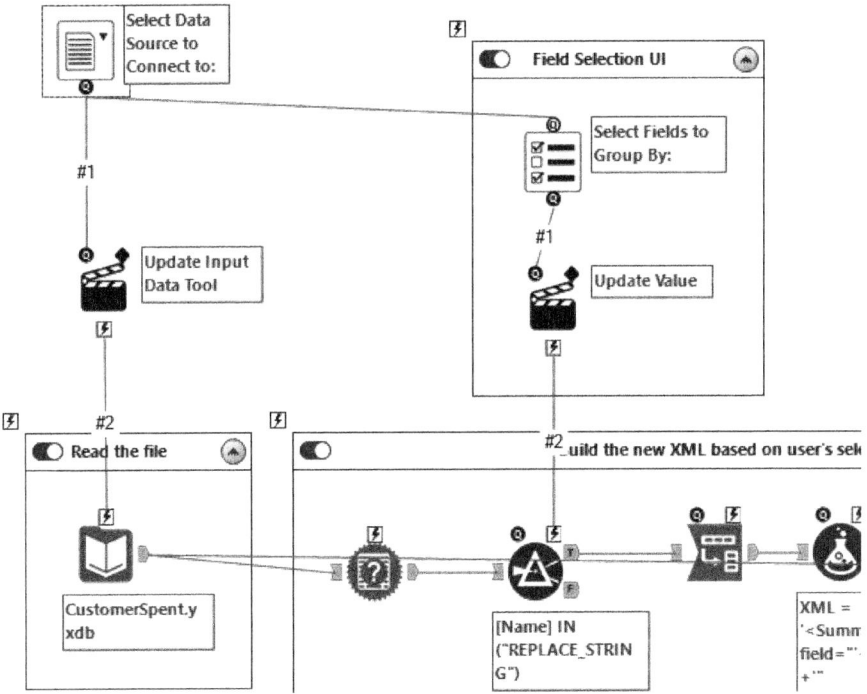

Figure 10.176: Setting the fields from the File Browse tool

11. Run the app.

   At this point, you may receive an error from Alteryx, stating **Fields can only be returned from data tools**. This is caused by the change in the underlying metadata.

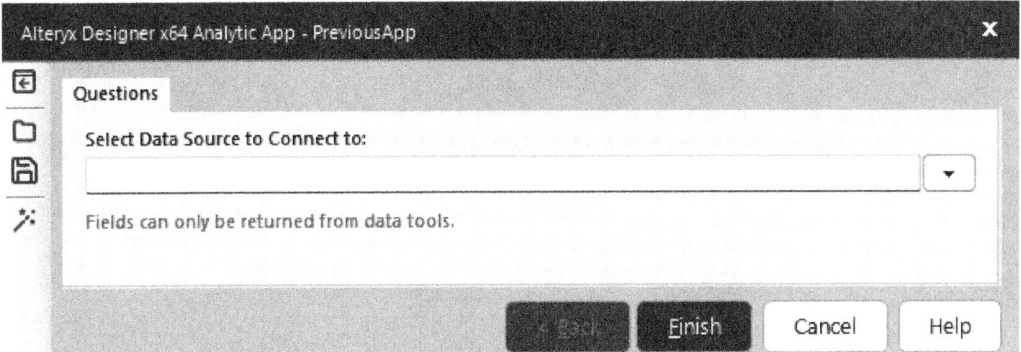

Figure 10.177: Metadata changes may cause an error message

To fix this, just close the app and run it again.

You'll see empty panels.

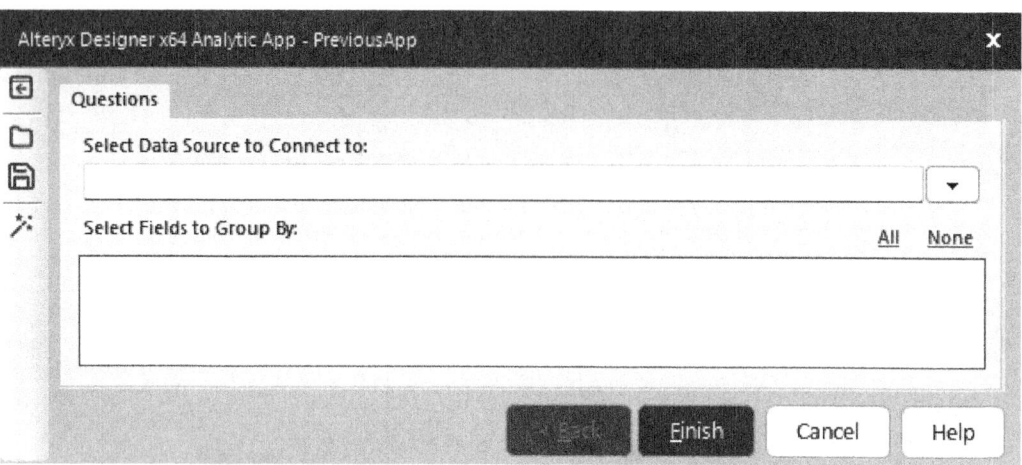

Figure 10.178: The fixed UI

12. Select a data source from the dropdown (in `..\DATA\CustomerSpent_2.yxdb`, you'll find a test file with different field names than the original) and you'll see how the field list populates with all the string and date fields from the selected source.

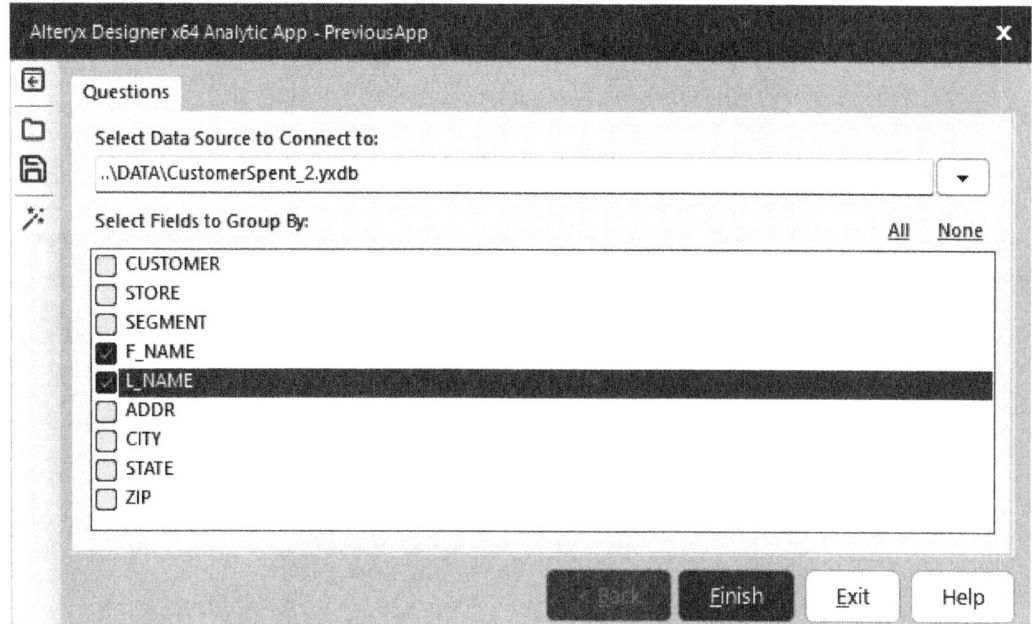

Figure 10.179: After selecting a data input source, the List Box tool auto-populates

13. Select some fields and click on **Finish**.

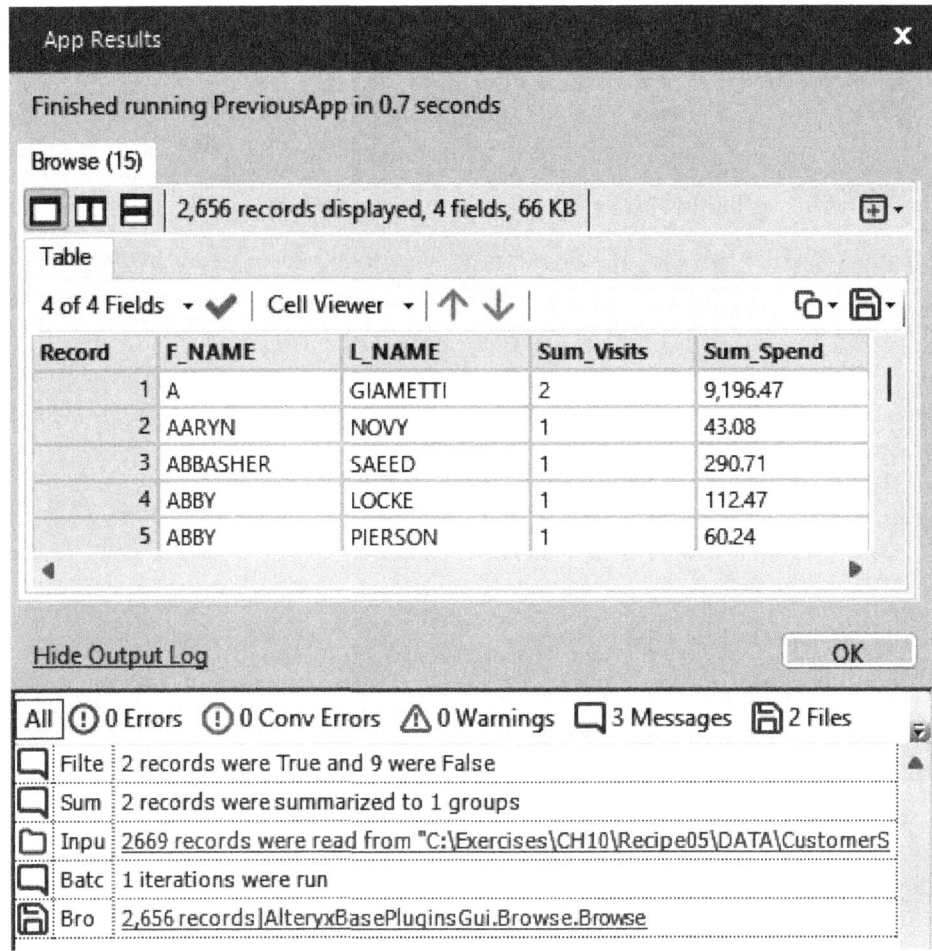

Figure 10.180: Executing the app

The app returned `Sum_Visits` and `Sum_Spend` grouped by the new fields.

Notifying yourself or others

Debugging and notifying users of what's going on with a workflow execution is a very important practice that we need to implement when developing Alteryx workflows/macros.

The **Message** tool allows us to do this, by providing a very flexible and powerful set of features to track and notify us of whatever we want at any point in a process. From a simple status message as a breakpoint and counting read records to evaluating a condition or a data integrity rule, we can use the **Message** tool to decide when to display a message, a warning, or an error (which will force the workflow to stop), or even decide to force the workflow to stop passing records downstream through the tool.

Getting ready

Download the test set for this recipe from here: `https://github.com/PacktPublishing/Alteryx-Designer-Cookbook/tree/main/CH10/Recipe06`.

We'll use the **Message** tool to let a user know when a process starts, provide a record counter, and let them know if there are any missing records after a join operation.

Knowing this can save you a lot of time re-processing files because you can evaluate and catch inconsistencies before waiting for the whole workflow to run and access some debugging information with a simple click.

This use case is very simple; we'll perform a join between two datasets, notify the record reading process when there are unjoined records, and provide a hyperlink to a debug file that contains those unjoined records for each dataset.

How to do it...

Let's get started as follows:

1. Add an **Input Data** tool and point it to `..\DATA\DOCUMENTS.yxdb`.
2. Add a second **Input Data** tool and point it to `..\DATA\CUSTOMERS.yxdb`.
3. Add a **Join** tool, and connect **DOCUMENTS** to the **L** input and **CUSTOMERS** to the **R** input.

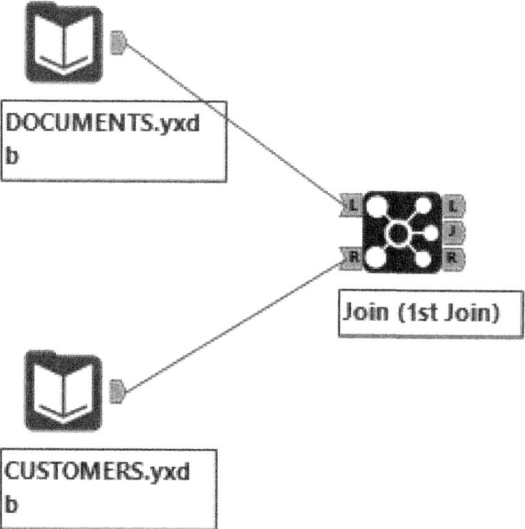

Figure 10.181: A basic starting point joining two sources

4. Click on the **Join** tool and configure it, selecting **CUSTOMER_ID** from the **Left** dropdown.

5. Deselect **CUSTOMER_ID** from the **Right** input (or click on **Options | Deselect Duplicate Fields**).

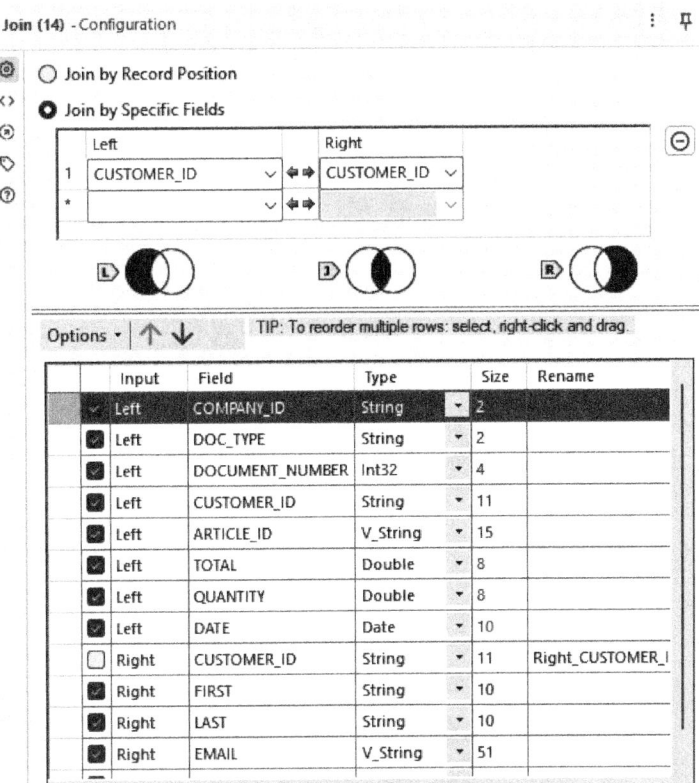

Figure 10.182: The Join tool configuration

6. Run the workflow and check the **Results** pane.

Alteryx provides information on the current execution, data inputs, and join operation results.

Figure 10.183: The Results pane

We'll add additional information to the user now.

7. Drag a **Message** tool, and drop it over the connection that goes from the **Input Data** tool to the **L** input anchor of the **Join** tool.

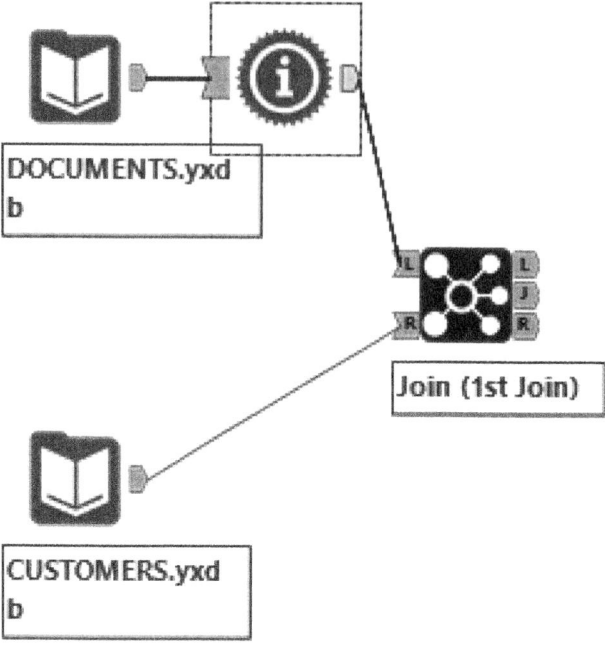

Figure 10.184: Adding a Message tool

For now, just as a preview, we'll add a very simple message to let the user know that the process started.

8. Click on the **Message** tool to access its configuration.

9. In the **When To Send Message** section, make sure **Before First Record** is selected (which is the default option).

10. For the **Message Type** and **Message Priority** dropdowns, we'll leave the default options for now (**Message** as the type and **Normal** as the priority).

11. For **Message Expression**, use this formula:

```
ToString(DateTimeNow()) + " - I started processing the DOCUMENTS
file."
```

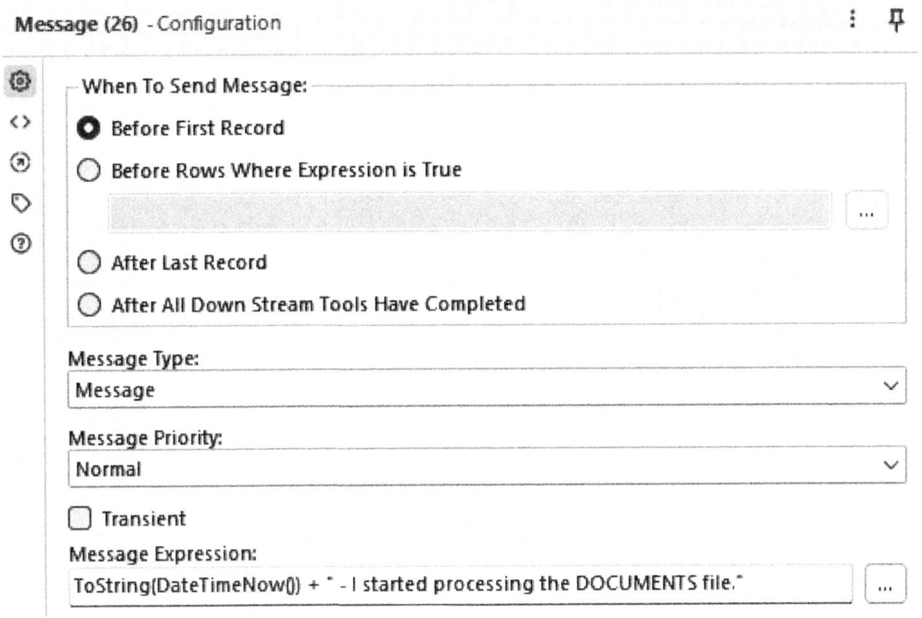

Figure 10.185: The Message tool configuration

Run the workflow and note the **Results** pane. The custom message is presented before everything else (because we selected **Before First Record** as the place to show it; you can try other options and see the point in the log where the message appears).

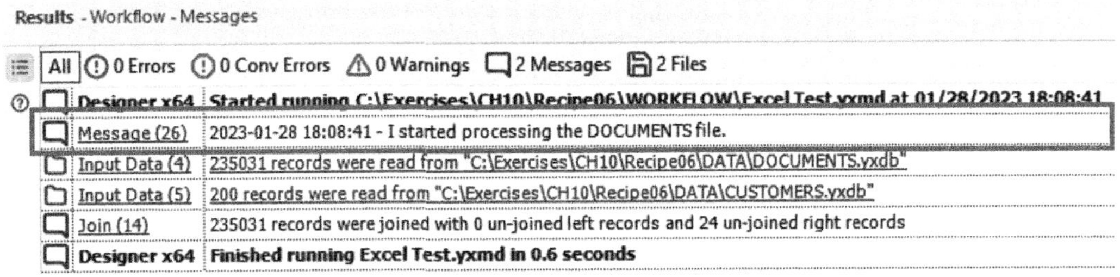

Figure 10.186: The Results pane with the custom message added

After trying this, you might think that this message is not helpful at all (at least in this context), and you are right, mostly because it repeats what Alteryx does by default – letting us know when the process starts (in the top line of the log).

12. Click on the **Message** tool in the canvas to access its configuration.

13. Click on **Before Rows Where Expression is True**, and use this expression in the enabled formula field:

```
Mod([_RecordNumber_],10000)=0
```

14. Leave the **Transient** option deselected (for now), and change the existing message expression to this one:

```
ToString([_RecordNumber_],0,1) + " Record Processed From
DOCUMENTS."
```

Message (26) - Configuration   ⋮   📌

—When To Send Message:—

○ Before First Record

● Before Rows Where Expression is True

Mod([_RecordNumber_],10000)=0   [...]

○ After Last Record

○ After All Down Stream Tools Have Completed

Message Type:

Message   ⌄

Message Priority:

Normal   ⌄

☐ Transient

Message Expression:

ToString([_RecordNumber_],0,1) + " Record Processed From DOCUMENTS."   [...]

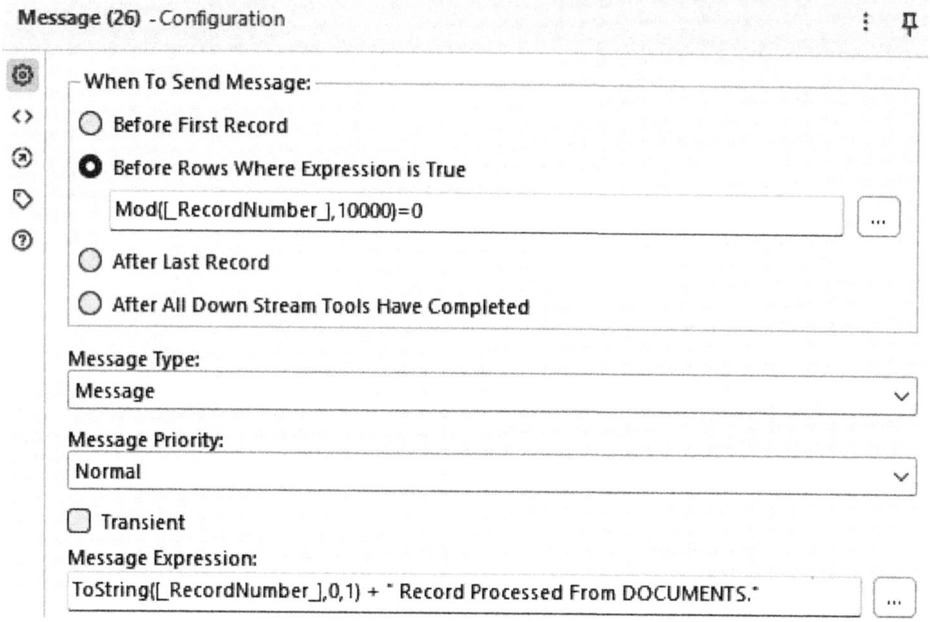

Figure 10.187: Changing the message to something more useful

Run the workflow again and check the **Results** panel. We got a message every 10,000 records read, consistent with the expression we used to show the message (if a read record number when divided by 10,000 is an exact number).

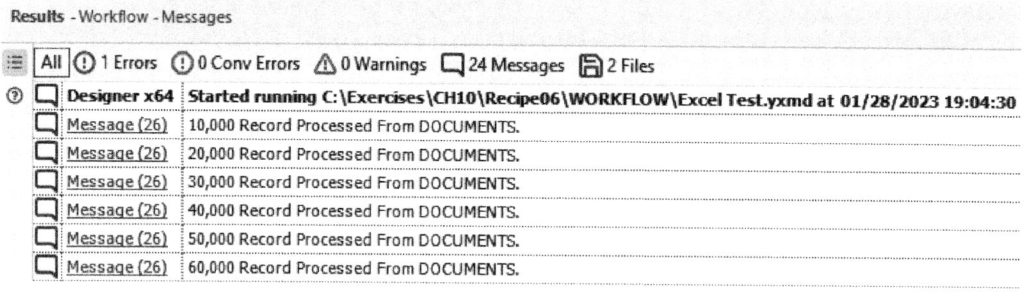

Results - Workflow - Messages

| All | ⓘ 1 Errors | ⓘ 0 Conv Errors | ⚠ 0 Warnings | ☐ 24 Messages | 🗎 2 Files |

Designer x64	Started running C:\Exercises\CH10\Recipe06\WORKFLOW\Excel Test.yxmd at 01/28/2023 19:04:30
Message (26)	10,000 Record Processed From DOCUMENTS.
Message (26)	20,000 Record Processed From DOCUMENTS.
Message (26)	30,000 Record Processed From DOCUMENTS.
Message (26)	40,000 Record Processed From DOCUMENTS.
Message (26)	50,000 Record Processed From DOCUMENTS.
Message (26)	60,000 Record Processed From DOCUMENTS.

Figure 10.188: A non-transient message display (every 10,000 records read)

Having the log show a line every 10,000 records may be useful for some cases, but Alteryx gives us another option, a **Transient** one, which allows us to replace the previous message with an updated one on the same line.

15. Click on the **Message** tool to access its configuration, and click on the **Transient** option.

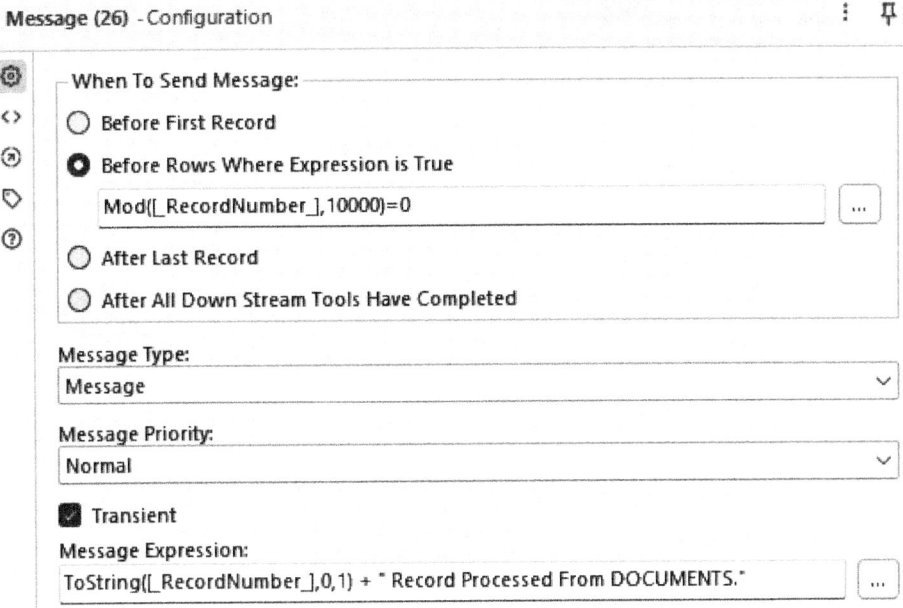

Figure 10.189: Changing the message to Transient

Run the workflow again, and note the **Results** pane while the workflow runs.

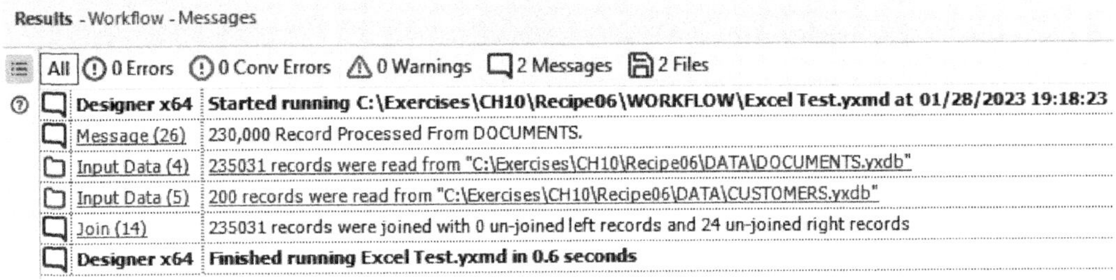

Figure 10.190: The Transient message updates on the same line

Now, we have just one line with the record count (if you have a fast enough computer and can't see the updates in the line, change 10,000 in the expression to a lower number and run the workflow again).

Also, we can track other operations easily, even providing a link to the results from the **Results** pane.

16. Drop an **Output Data** tool onto the canvas and connect it to the **R** output of the **Join** tool. We will output the unjoined customers here.

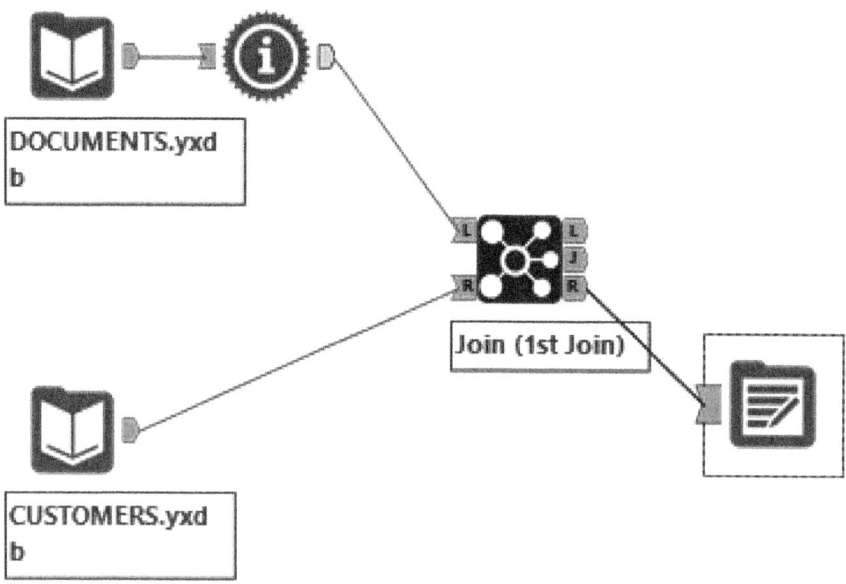

Figure 10.191: Adding an Output Data tool for rightmost unjoined records

17. Point the output file to `..\DATA\Debug.xlsx|||CUSTOMERS with no documents` and change **Output Options** to **Overwrite Sheet or Range**.

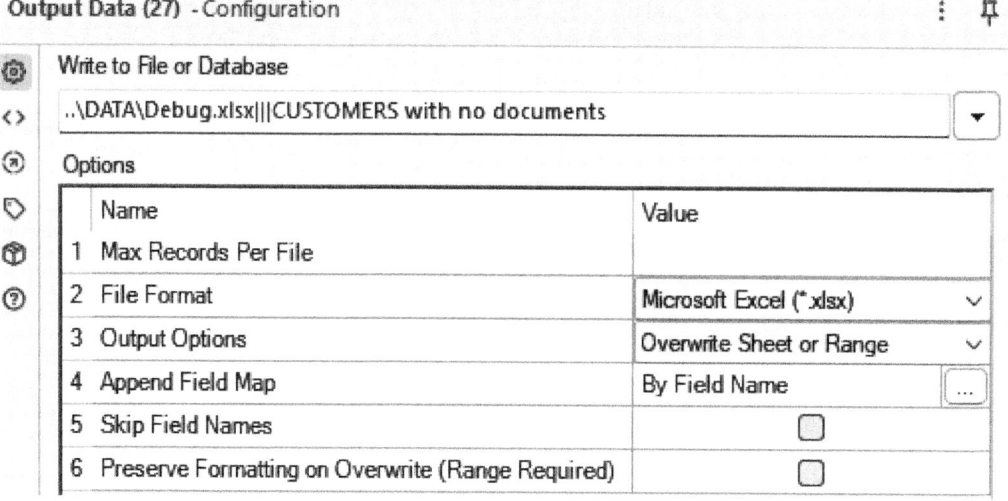

Figure 10.192: The Output Data tool configuration

18. From the **Transform** category, add a **Count Records** tool and connect it to the **R** output anchor of the **Join** tool.

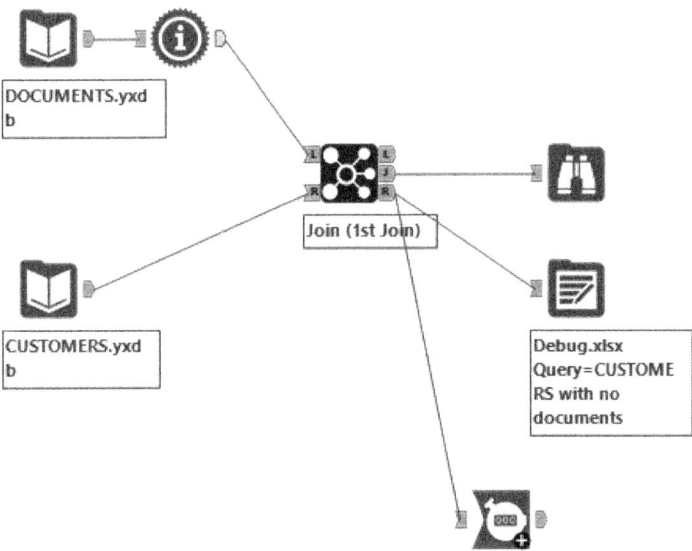

Figure 10.193: Adding a Count Records tool

19. Drop a new **Message** tool after the **Count Records** tool.

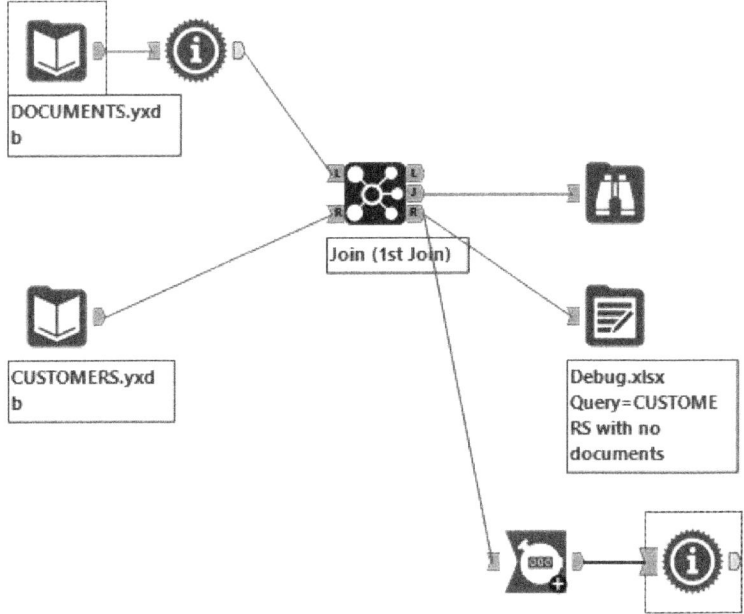

Figure 10.194: Adding another Message tool

20. Select **After All Down Stream Tools Have Completed** as the **When To Send Message** option.

21. From the **Message Type** dropdown, select **File Output V2 (Path|Description|ToolType)**.

22. Change **Message Priority** to **High**.

23. Under **Message Expression**, use the following formula:

```
[Engine.WorkflowDirectory] + "..\DEBUG\DEBUG.
xlsx|***********************Open CUSTOMERS without
documents|Debug"
```

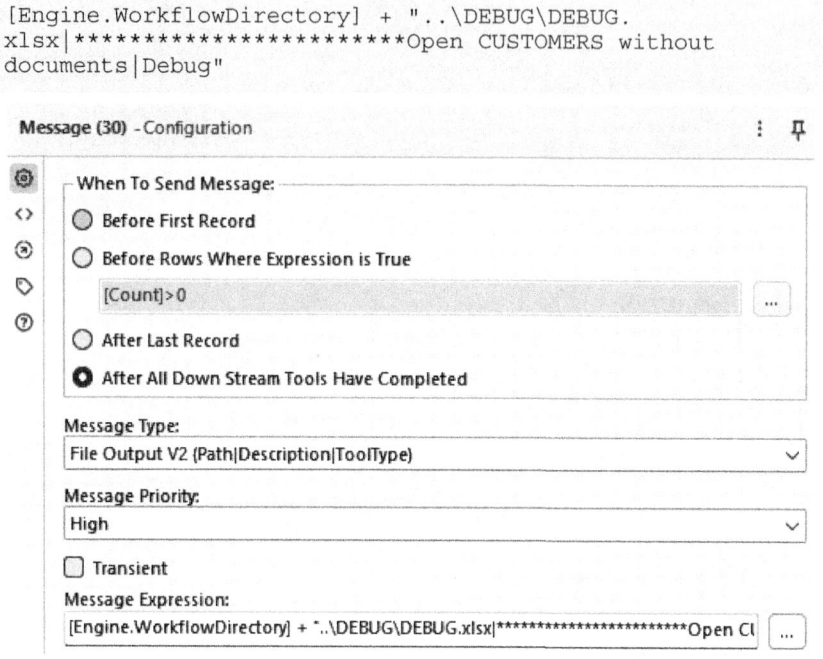

Figure 10.195: The Message tool configuration

Run the workflow, and you'll see in the **Results** pane that our message provides a link to the `Debug.xlsx` file that the same workflow created.

24. Click on the link, and you'll see that the file opens directly from the **Results** pane (we can also right-click on the link and open the containing folder for the file).

Results - Workflow - Messages

☰	All ① 0 Errors ① 0 Conv Errors ⚠ 0 Warnings 🗨 2 Messages 🖹 5 Files	
⑦ 🗨	**Designer x64**	**Started running C:\Exercises\CH10\Recipe06\WORKFLOW\Excel Test.yxmd at 01/29/2023 17:21:45**
🗨	Message (26)	230,000 Record Processed From DOCUMENTS.
🗀	Input Data (4)	235031 records were read from "C:\Exercises\CH10\Recipe06\DATA\DOCUMENTS.yxdb"
🗀	Input Data (5)	200 records were read from "C:\Exercises\CH10\Recipe06\DATA\CUSTOMERS.yxdb"
🗨	Join (14)	235031 records were joined with 0 un-joined left records and 24 un-joined right records
🖹	Output Data (27)	24 records were written to "C:\Exercises\CH10\Recipe06\DATA\Debug.xlsx" (CUSTOMERS with no documents)
🖹	Message (30)	***********************Open CUSTOMERS without documents
🖹	Browse (28)	235,031 records
🗨	**Designer x64**	**Finished running Excel Test.yxmd in 0.6 seconds**

Figure 10.196: The Message tool shows a link to a file

How it works...

The **Message** tool has the ability to display expression results in the **Results** pane. We showed our example on a simple workflow, but this recipe applies to macros and Analytic Apps as well.

Something important to mention is the appearance of the [_RecordNumber_] variable provided by Alteryx Designer, which takes the value of each record being read. This gives us total control over the number of records, as we saw in the message that updates every 10,000 records.

Also, we can handle several message types to alert a user about what's going on with the workflow execution. Select the one that better fits the condition being evaluated.

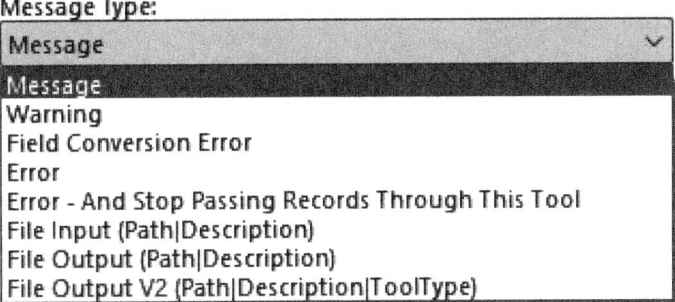

Figure 10.197: The Message Type options

> **Important note**
>
> Sometimes, when evaluating conditions, we want a workflow to stop processing records on that particular stream. In those cases, select the **Error - And Stop Passing Records Through This Tool** option, and if Alteryx finds an error, it'll stop record processing in that stream.

11
Downloads, APIs, and Web Services

Working with data doesn't only include handling in-house or cloud data sources. In today's world, the use of **application programming interfaces** (**APIs**) is becoming almost a necessity.

A lot of data lies in the cloud only accessible via API calls, and some of that data may be useful to us to enrich our local data sources or to acquire additional details about what is being analyzed, and sometimes even for fun.

Alteryx has a very powerful tool to access APIs—the **Download** tool, which allows us to connect to any URI, including an API, a web service (a type of API), and so on.

This chapter covers the following recipes:

- Managing APIs' **Extensible Markup Language** (**XML**) responses
- Parsing **JavaScript Object Notation** (**JSON**)
- Getting paged results from APIs (Iterative Macros)

But before starting to consume them, let's review some basic terminology involving APIs, as follows:

- **API**: A software component that enables two otherwise unrelated/disconnected applications to communicate with each other. Acting as messengers, APIs deliver one application's request to another and return a response in real time.
- **Web service**: A particular subset of APIs, based on how the API is implemented.
- **Representational State Transfer** (**REST**): A set of guidelines to build easy-to-use, lightweight web APIs. It uses HTTP as the only protocol to communicate.
- **RESTful API**: An API that follows REST guidelines.

- **Simple Object Access Protocol** (**SOAP**): A protocol for transmitting data across networks. It relies on XML to encode the data and is standardized by the **World Wide Web Consortium** (**W3C**). Unlike REST, SOAP can use different protocols to establish communication between applications.

- **Remote Procedure Call** (**RPC**): An invoking-process protocol. It executes code or scripts on a server. It uses either XML or JSON to encode message interchange.

- **Request**: The way you call an API (and start the communication process). There are several methods to call an API, as outlined next:

  - GET: To retrieve a resource

  - POST: To create a new resource

  - PUT: To edit or update an existing resource

  - DELETE: To delete a resource

  A request also refers to the message you encode (XML or JSON) to call the API.

- **Response**: The resulting encoded message for a request.

- **API key**: A mechanism to allow only authorized clients to initiate an API call.

- **Open Authorization** (**OAuth**): An open-access delegation standard designed specifically to work with HTTP.

- **Authorization token**: Object that encapsulates the security identity, issued by an authorization server to third-party clients.

Technical requirements

This chapter will require that you access the internet from your Alteryx Designer installation, so make sure you can. If you can't, we included the response file in each recipe's test sets.

Managing APIs' XML responses

XML uses tags to define elements within a document, similar to HTML. However, unlike HTML, XML allows for the creation of custom tags, which means that it can be used to represent a wide variety of data types.

For users who are not technologically advanced, dealing with API responses in XML can be frustrating.

Understanding the tree structure within an XML file and identifying its components requires some additional knowledge, something that not everyone is willing to acquire.

In this recipe, we are going to provide you with a way to eliminate that frustration and obtain optimal performance by parsing the responses of an API in XML.

Getting ready

We created a test set that you can download from here: `https://github.com/PacktPublishing/Alteryx-Designer-Cookbook`. In this example, we'll be connecting to a public API that provides data about clinical trials. The API is free and does not require us to register, but it does require that we read and accept its terms and conditions here: `https://clinicaltrials.gov/ct2/about-site/terms-conditions`.

From `https://clinicaltrials.gov/api/gui/home`, you can access the API documentation.

For this particular recipe, we'll be focusing on the *Full Studies* query URL provided here: `https://clinicaltrials.gov/api/gui/ref/api_urls#queryURLs`. This is what it looks like:

Name	Example Query URL	Description	Default Returned	Format
Full Studies (demo)	ClinicalTrials.gov/api/query /full_studies?expr=heart+attack	Returns all content for a small set of study records.	Returns one study record by default. Returns up to 100 study records per query when the minimum rank and maximum rank parameters are set.	Returns in tree format when the format parameter is set (fmt=tree).

Figure 11.1: API details

As you can see in the example query URL, the request has a fixed part, `ClinicalTrials.gov/api/query/full_studies`, and a set of query parameters separated by ? (in this case, `expr=heart+attack`).

You can see all the parameters that the API accepts here: `https://clinicaltrials.gov/api/gui/ref/api_urls#urlParams`

Any of the listed parameters can be used in the query, appending them with an & symbol.

So, according to the documentation, if we wanted to generate a specific query, we should use this endpoint: `https://ClinicalTrials.gov/api/query/full_studies?`

And we can add as many parameters as we need to refine it, separating them with &.

Here's an example: `https://clinicaltrials.gov/api/query/study_fields?expr=heart+attack&fields=NCTId,Condition,BriefTitle&fmt=xml`

This will query the API to return an XML response (`fmt=xml`) with the contents of the `FNCTId`, `Condition`, and `BriefTitle` fields (`fields=NCTId,Condition,BriefTitle`) for all heart attack studies (`expr=heart+attack`).

Note that the space character was replaced by a + symbol, according to the documentation. Also, if you need to add a & symbol in your query, replace it with %26:

```
1   <FullStudiesResponse>
2     <APIVrs>1.01.05</APIVrs>
3     <DataVrs>2023:06:02 00:55:53.069</DataVrs>
4     <Expression>heart+attack</Expression>
5     <NStudiesAvail>454305</NStudiesAvail>
6     <NStudiesFound>1990</NStudiesFound>
7     <MinRank>1</MinRank>
8     <MaxRank>1</MaxRank>
9     <NStudiesReturned>1</NStudiesReturned>
10    <FullStudyList>
11      <FullStudy Rank="1">
12        <Struct Name="Study">
13          <Struct Name="ProtocolSection">
14            <Struct Name="IdentificationModule">
15              <Field Name="NCTId">NCT00929994</Field>
16              <Struct Name="OrgStudyIdInfo">
17                <Field Name="OrgStudyId">Brooks - 001</Field>
18              </Struct>
19              <Struct Name="Organization">
20                <Field Name="OrgFullName">Toronto Rehabilitation Institute</Field>
21                <Field Name="OrgClass">OTHER</Field>
22              </Struct>
23              <Field Name="BriefTitle">Effects of Cardiac Rehabilitation for Individuals With Transient Ischemic
              Attack</Field>
24              <Field Name="OfficialTitle">Effects of Cardiac Rehabilitation for Individuals With Transient
              Ischemic Attack</Field>
25            </Struct>
26            <Struct Name="StatusModule">
27              <Field Name="StatusVerifiedDate">April 2019</Field>
28              <Field Name="OverallStatus">Completed</Field>
29              <Struct Name="ExpandedAccessInfo">
30                <Field Name="HasExpandedAccess">No</Field>
31              </Struct>
32              <Struct Name="StartDateStruct">
33                <Field Name="StartDate">March 2010</Field>
34              </Struct>
35              <Struct Name="PrimaryCompletionDateStruct">
36                <Field Name="PrimaryCompletionDate">November 2014</Field>
37                <Field Name="PrimaryCompletionDateType">Actual</Field>
38              </Struct>
39              <Struct Name="CompletionDateStruct">
40                <Field Name="CompletionDate">November 2014</Field>
41                <Field Name="CompletionDateType">Actual</Field>
42              </Struct>
43              <Field Name="StudyFirstSubmitDate">June 29, 2009</Field>
44              <Field Name="StudyFirstSubmitQCDate">June 29, 2009</Field>
45              <Struct Name="StudyFirstPostDateStruct">
46                <Field Name="StudyFirstPostDate">June 30, 2009</Field>
47                <Field Name="StudyFirstPostDateType">Estimate</Field>
48              </Struct>
```

Figure 11.2: XML returned by the API

First, we need to understand the structure, elements, and levels of the data within the received response to start parsing the data.

To help with this task, you can use any text editor, but it's very helpful to use one that handles the XML structure. As a recommendation, **Notepad**++ has a plugin called **Npp XML TreeView** that allows you to navigate the XML data from the hierarchical structure of the file:

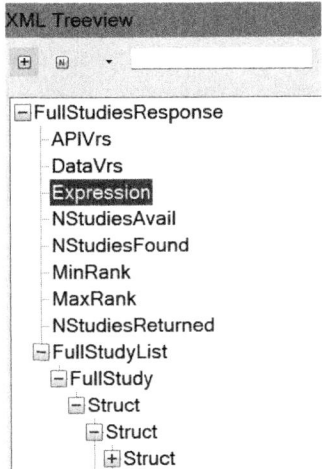

Figure 11.3: Exploring XML with XML Treeview

Also, **Notepad++**'s **XML Tools** plugin provides a wide range of XML operations to facilitate your work:

Figure 11.4: XML Tools options

Another useful tool I use is **MindFusion XML Viewer**, which is free for non-commercial use and can be downloaded from `https://www.mindfusion.eu/downloads.html`:

```
MindFusion XML Viewer (Free for non-commercial use)

  File   Edit   Tools   View   Help

 Study_Fields.xml

    1  <FullStudiesResponse>
    2    <APIVrs>
            1.01.05
    3    <DataVrs>
            2023:06:02 00:55:53.069
    4    <Expression>
            heart+attack
    5    <NStudiesAvail>
            454305
    6    <NStudiesFound>
            1990
    7    <MinRank>
            1
    8    <MaxRank>
            1
    9    <NStudiesReturned>
            1
   10    <FullStudyList>
   11      <FullStudy Rank="1">
   12        <Struct Name="Study">
   13          <Struct Name="ProtocolSection">
  222          <Struct Name="ResultsSection">
  763          <Struct Name="DerivedSection">
  764            <Struct Name="MiscInfoModule">
  767            <Struct Name="ConditionBrowseModule">
```

Figure 11.5: Viewing XML with MindFusion XML Viewer

No matter which tool you use, the content of the response object is what we need to analyze:

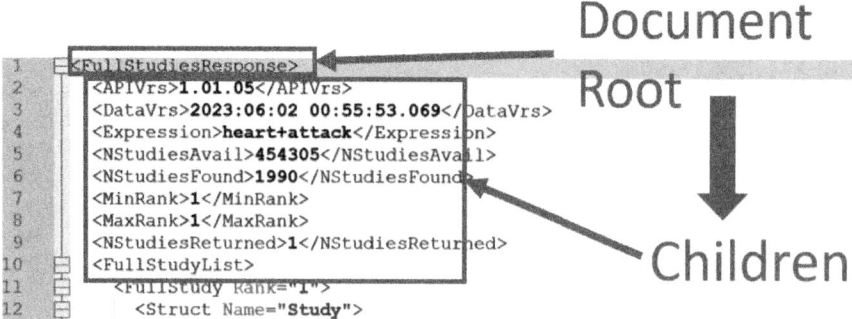

Figure 11.6: XML structure

As you can see, there is a document root element (`<FullStudiesResponse>`) with a series of child elements.

Also, we found that there is one element, `<FullStudyList>`, that also has child elements, and within its child elements, there are new child elements too, and so on up to seven levels deep:

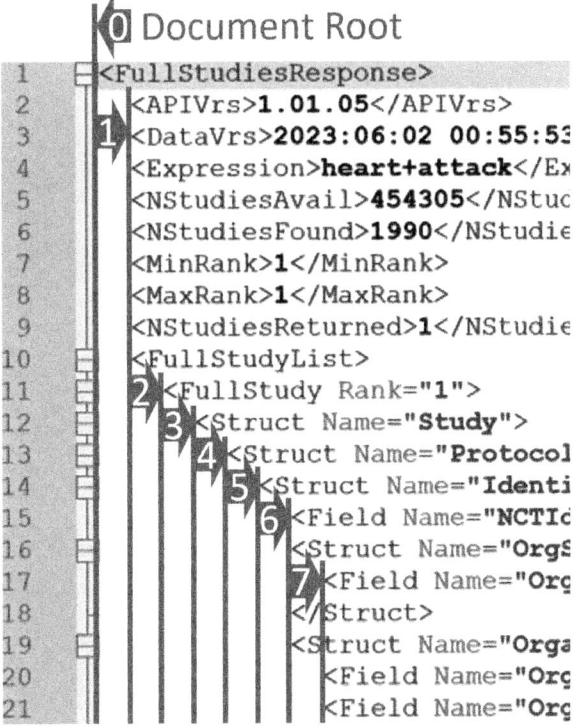

Figure 11.7: Tag hierarchy within an XML file

The important thing here is to identify where the data we need to extract is.

Navigating the entire file, we see that the data we need, despite being within a hierarchy determined by `<Struct>` elements, comes from `<Field>` elements.

So, if we focus on extracting the values from `<Field>` elements, we should get what we need.

How to do it...

Now that we have the theory right and we are clear about what we need to accomplish, let's do it in Alteryx:

1. Drop a **Text Input** tool onto the canvas. Create a column called `url` and use this text in the first row:

```
https://clinicaltrials.gov/api/query/full_studies?expr=heart+at-
tack&fields=NCTId,Condition,BriefTitle&fmt=xml
```

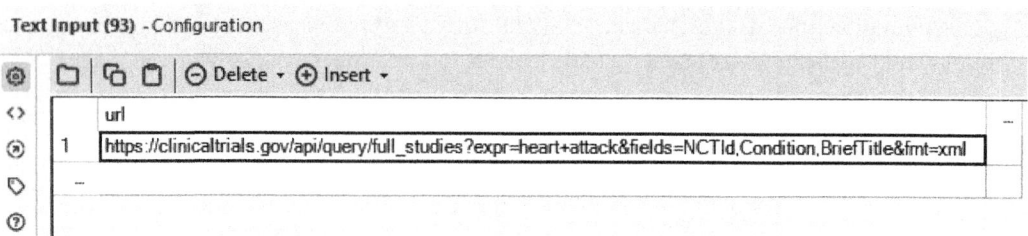

Figure 11.8: Text Input configuration

2. Drop a **Download** tool from the **Developer** category:

Figure 11.9: Adding a Download tool

3. From the **Download** tool configuration panel, select `url` for the **Field** option, and make sure **Encode URL Text** is checked.

4. Make sure **String** is selected from the **Output** section, and **Data Encoded As** is set as **Unicode UTF-8** (those are Alteryx's default options):

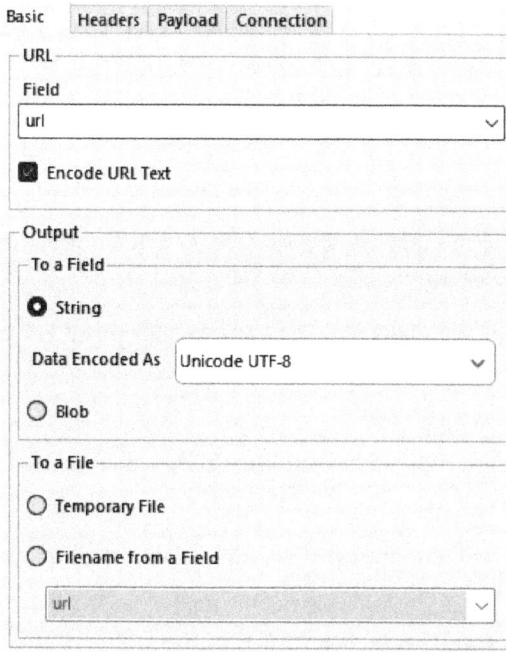

Figure 11.10: Download tool basic configuration

This will execute the request to the URL, grab the response, and store it in a string-type field called `DownloadData`. It'll also save the response headers in a field called `DownloadHeaders`:

url	DownloadData	DownloadHeaders
1 https://clinicaltrials.gov/api/query/full_studies?ex...	\<FullStudiesResponse>	HTTP/1.1 200 OK

Figure 11.11: Results after using the Download tool

5. Add an **XML Parse** tool to your workflow:

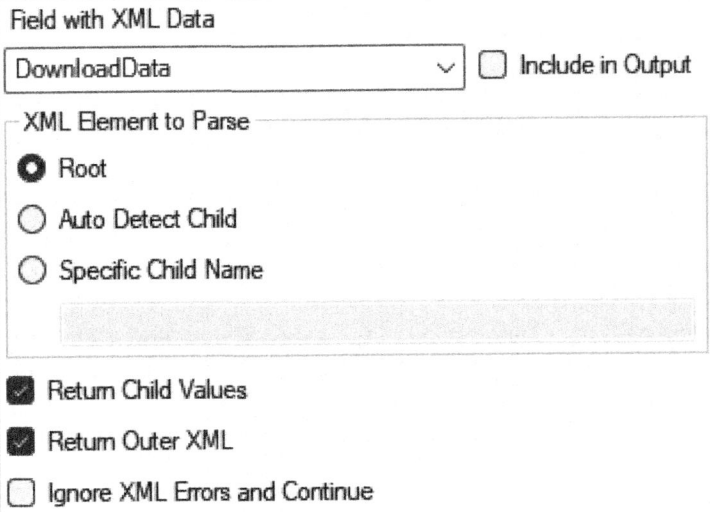

Figure 11.12: Adding an XML Parse tool

6. Configure the tool like this:

   - For the **Field with XML Data** option, select **DownloadData** from the dropdown and uncheck the **Include in Output** checkbox so that you stop carrying it downstream on the workflow

   - For the **XML Element to Parse** option, click on **Root**

   - Enable the **Return Child Values** and **Return Outer XML** options:

Field with XML Data

DownloadData ⌄   ☐ Include in Output

XML Element to Parse
  ● Root
  ○ Auto Detect Child
  ○ Specific Child Name

☑ Return Child Values
☑ Return Outer XML
☐ Ignore XML Errors and Continue

Figure 11.13: XML Parse configuration

7. Run the workflow and check the results. You'll notice a lot of fields created by Alteryx:

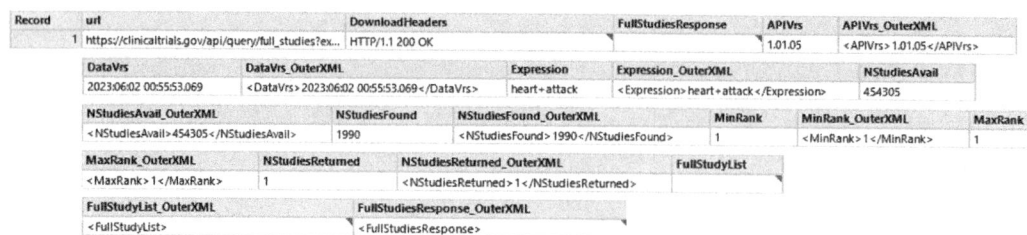

Figure 11.14: Parsed results

As we review the resulting data, we'll see that we got the first child level from the actual root element, and because we are using the whole XML, the root element is the document root, and the child elements are the ones just down one level from the root (all "**Level 1**" elements):

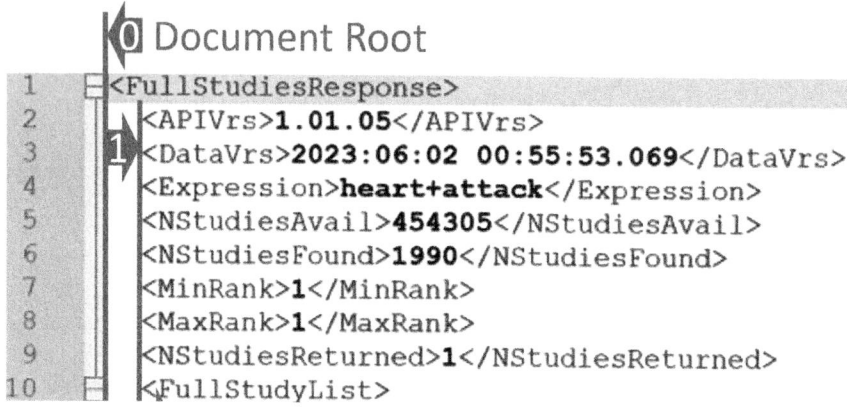

Figure 11.15: XML first level of hierarchy

Notice that for each child element, we also got a `<ChildElement>_OuterXML` field. Each of these fields contains the XML portion, from the opening to the closing tag for that element.

> **Important note**
>
> The most important thing to understand in this case is that for each `<ChildElement>_OuterXML` field, the corresponding `<Child Element>` becomes the root element of that XML portion, with which we can apply the same logic to extract the child elements of each one and use their `_OuterXML` to further drill down into the hierarchy of the elements.

Also, with the **XML Parse** tool, we can access directly any element tag within the file. Since we identified that the data is being held in the **Field** tag, let's extract the contents of the field elements, but first, let's do some cleanup:

1. Drop a **Select** tool following the **XML Parse** tool:

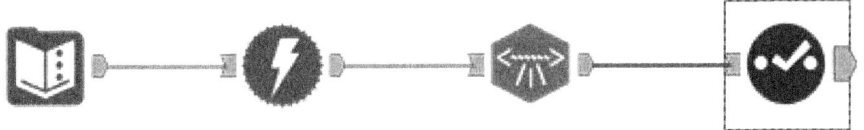

Figure 11.16: Adding a Select tool

2. From the **Select** tool configuration, click on **Options→ Select→ Deselect All**.

3. Once all fields have been deselected, click on the following:

    APIVrs, **DataVrs**, **Expression**, **NStudiesAvail**, **NStudiesFound**, **MinRank**, **MaxRank**, **NStudiesReturned**, **FullStudyList_OuterXML**, and ***Unknown** to enable them.

	Field	Type	Size	Rename	Des
☐	url	String ▾	109		
☐	DownloadHeaders	V_String ▾	214...		
☐	FullStudiesResponse	V_String ▾	28		
☑	APIVrs	V_String ▾	7		
☐	APIVrs_OuterXML	V_String ▾	24		
☑	DataVrs	V_String ▾	23		
☐	DataVrs_OuterXML	V_String ▾	42		
☑	Expression	V_String ▾	12		
☐	Expression_OuterXML	V_String ▾	37		
☑	NStudiesAvail	V_String ▾	6		
☐	NStudiesAvail_OuterXML	V_String ▾	37		
☑	NStudiesFound	V_String ▾	4		
☐	NStudiesFound_OuterXML	V_String ▾	35		
☑	MinRank	V_String ▾	1		
☐	MinRank_OuterXML	V_String ▾	20		
☑	MaxRank	V_String ▾	1		
☐	MaxRank_OuterXML	V_String ▾	20		
☑	NStudiesReturned	V_String ▾	1		
☐	NStudiesReturned_OuterXML	V_String ▾	38		
☐	FullStudyList	V_String ▾	8		
☑	FullStudyList_OuterXML	V_String ▾	52191		
☐	FullStudiesResponse_OuterXML	V_String ▾	52515		
☑	*Unknown	Unknown ▾	0		Dyna

Options ▾ | ↑ ↓   TIP: To reorder multiple rows: select, right-click and drag.

Figure 11.17: Removing unnecessary fields with the Select tool

Doing this operation allows us to keep only the fields we need (the description elements of the response, and the outer XML of the field we need to parse now):

APIVrs	DataVrs	Expression	NStudiesAvail	NStudiesFound
1.01.05	2023:06:02 00:55:53.069	heart+attack	454305	1990

MinRank	MaxRank	NStudiesReturned	FullStudyList_OuterXML
1	1	1	<FullStudyList>

Figure 11.18: Results after removing unnecessary fields

Now that we've cleaned up our data, we are going to access the field elements directly.

1. Drop a new **XML Parse** tool:

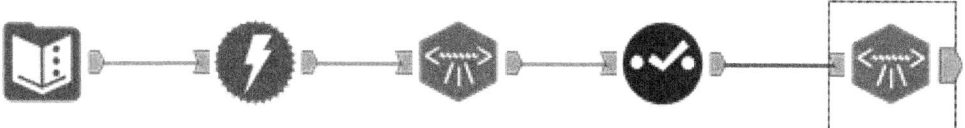

Figure 11.19: Adding a second XML Parse tool

2. From the recently added tool configuration, select `FullStudyList_OuterXML` from the **Field with XML Data** dropdown.

3. Deselect the **Include in Output** checkbox.

4. Select **Specific Child Name** from the **XML Element to Parse** option, and enter `Field` in the textbox.

5. Make sure none of the three options at the bottom is selected:

Field with XML Data

FullStudyList_OuterXML ⌄   ☐ Include in Output

XML Element to Parse

○ Root

○ Auto Detect Child

● Specific Child Name

Field

☐ Return Child Values

☐ Return Outer XML

☐ Ignore XML Errors and Continue

Figure 11.20: XML Parse tool configuration

6. Run the workflow and review the results:

Record	APIVrs	DataVrs	Expression	NStudiesAvail	NStudiesFound	MinRank	MaxRank	NStudiesReturned	Field	Name
1	1.01.05	2023:06:02 00:55:53.069	heart+attack	454305	1990	1	1	1	NCT00929994	NCTId
2	1.01.05	2023:06:02 00:55:53.069	heart+attack	454305	1990	1	1	1	Brooks - 001	OrgStudyId
3	1.01.05	2023:06:02 00:55:53.069	heart+attack	454305	1990	1	1	1	Toronto Rehabilitation Institute	OrgFullName
4	1.01.05	2023:06:02 00:55:53.069	heart+attack	454305	1990	1	1	1	OTHER	OrgClass
5	1.01.05	2023:06:02 00:55:53.069	heart+attack	454305	1990	1	1	1	Effects of Cardiac Rehabilitation for Individuals W...	BriefTitle
6	1.01.05	2023:06:02 00:55:53.069	heart+attack	454305	1990	1	1	1	Effects of Cardiac Rehabilitation for Individuals W...	OfficialTitle
7	1.01.05	2023:06:02 00:55:53.069	heart+attack	454305	1990	1	1	1	April 2019	StatusVerifiedDate
8	1.01.05	2023:06:02 00:55:53.069	heart+attack	454305	1990	1	1	1	Completed	OverallStatus
9	1.01.05	2023:06:02 00:55:53.069	heart+attack	454305	1990	1	1	1	No	HasExpandedAccess

Figure 11.21: Results after parsing the outer XML

Alteryx extracted all the values, generating two new columns/fields:

- `Field`: Corresponding to the element being extracted. Every record value represents one value of that element within the XML:

```
<FullStudyList>
  <FullStudy Rank="1">
    <Struct Name="Study">
      <Struct Name="ProtocolSection">
        <Struct Name="IdentificationModule">
          <Field Name="NCTId">NCT00929994</Field>
          <Struct Name="OrgStudyIdInfo">
            <Field Name="OrgStudyId">Brooks - 001</Field>
          </Struct>
```

Figure 11.22: Location of parsed content within the XML

- `Name`: Represents the attribute/s (descriptors within the targeted tag) present in the XML. Since each targeted element (`Field`) has only one attribute (in this case, `Name`), only this one column is created:

```
<FullStudyList>
  <FullStudy Rank="1">
    <Struct Name="Study">
      <Struct Name="ProtocolSection">
        <Struct Name="IdentificationModule">
          <Field Name="NCTId">NCT00929994</Field>
          <Struct Name="OrgStudyIdInfo">
            <Field Name="OrgStudyId">Brooks - 001</Field>
          </Struct>
```

Figure 11.23: Location of the tag attribute in the XML

How it works...

XML parsing is all about understanding the structure of the content to be interpreted.

The best way to approach such a case is to review the contents of the data to identify where what we need to extract is located and then configure the Alteryx tool according to our findings.

Many times, we will be presented with the need to carry out extractions in multiple steps, as we go "down" in the hierarchy of the XML content. For this, it is essential to extract the `OuterXML` element from the elements that contain the data to be extracted.

As a final piece of advice, extracting data from XML tends to generate a huge number of fields/columns, so cleaning up our dataset as we go along will help simplify our task.

Parsing JSON

JSON is a lightweight, language-independent data interchange format that provides a simple and efficient way to represent structured data. Its ease of use, widespread support, and ability to handle different data types (unlike XML, which can only represent data in string format) have made it a popular choice for data exchange in various applications and systems.

One of the key advantages of JSON is its simplicity and readability, both for humans and machines. Its syntax is straightforward and easy to understand, which makes it widely adopted and supported by various programming languages and platforms. JSON also offers a compact data representation, making it efficient for data transmission and storage.

JSON represents data in a key-value pair format, where data is organized into objects and arrays. An object is enclosed in curly braces ({ }) and consists of a collection of key-value pairs. Each key is a string and is followed by a colon (:). The corresponding value can be of various types, including strings, numbers, Booleans, null objects, or arrays.

Arrays in JSON are versatile and commonly used for representing lists, sets, ordered sequences, or any scenario where multiple values need to be grouped while preserving their order:

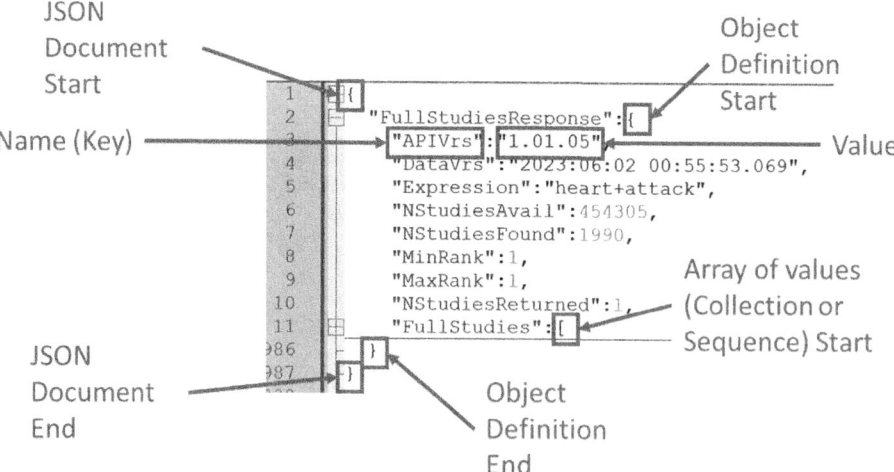

Figure 11.24: JSON representation of data

Getting ready

For this recipe, we prepared a test set to follow along that you can download from here: `https://github.com/PacktPublishing/Alteryx-Designer-Cookbook`.

Within the `DATA` folder, you can find a file with the response contents returned by the API in case you can't access the internet while following this recipe.

How to do it...

We'll be using the same API we used in the previous recipe but telling it that we want our response in JSON formal:

1. Start by dropping a **Text Input** tool onto the canvas.

2. Create a column called URL, and paste the following text into the first row of data:

   ```
   https://clinicaltrials.gov/api/query/full_studies?expr=heart+at-
   tack&fields=NCTId,Condition,BriefTitle&fmt=json
   ```

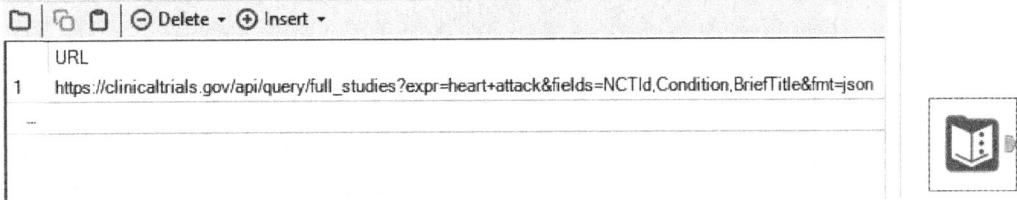

Figure 11.25: Setting the URL to connect to

3. Add a **Download** tool to the workflow:

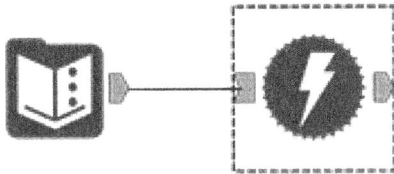

Figure 11.26: Adding a Download tool

4. From the **Download** tool configuration options, select **URL** from the **Field** dropdown.

5. Make sure the **Encode URL Text** option is checked.

6. For the **Output** field, make sure **String** is the active option and **Unicode UTF-8** is selected for the **Data Encoded As** dropdown:

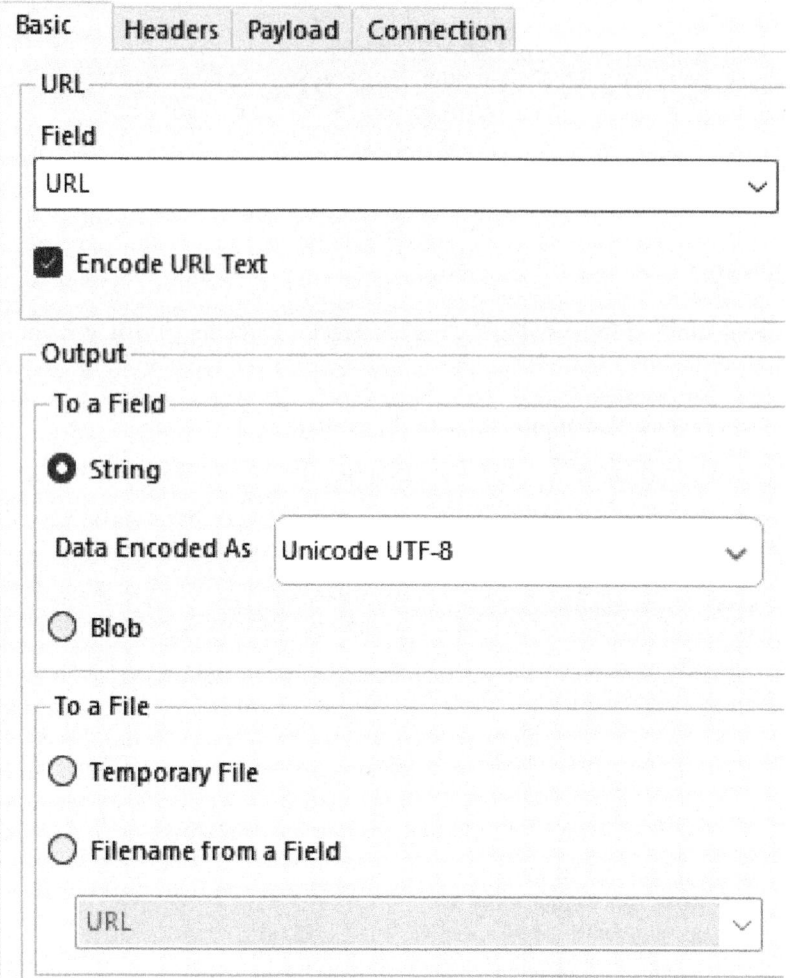

Figure 11.27: Basic setting to perform a request

7. Run the workflow.

    In the **Results** pane, check for the DownloadHeaders field value. It should read HTTP/1.1
    200 OK. This means the API successfully responded (you may notice that you can receive
    different HTTP messages, such as 302 Moved Temporarily, and still get correct results).

8. Double-click on the DownloadData field (double-clicking on a field activates the **Cell Viewer**
    functionality, which allows us to explore a little more of the field's content). You'll see a JSON
    structured response received from the API:

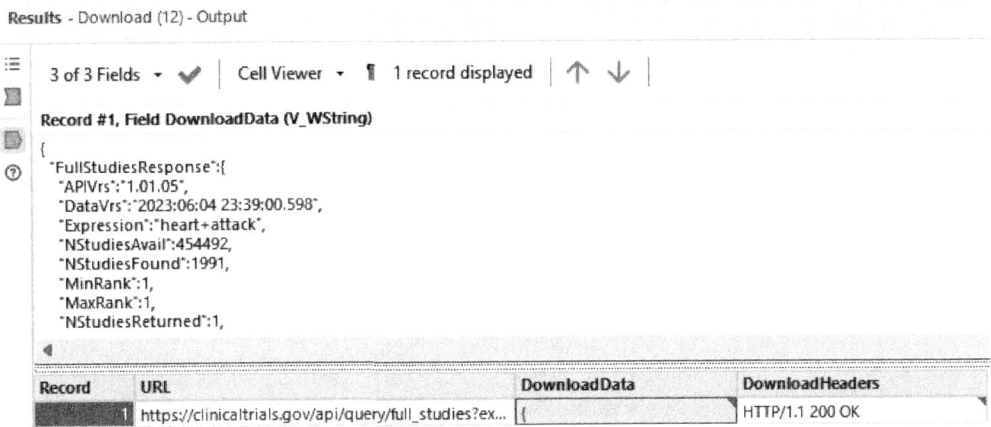

Figure 11.28: JSON response

Now, it's time to parse the contents of the `DownloadData` field.

9. Drop a **JSON Parse** tool (from the **Developer** category):

Figure 11.29: Adding a JSON Parse tool

10. Select **DownloadData** from the **JSON Field** dropdown, uncheck **Include in Output**, and make sure **Output values into single string fields** is selected:

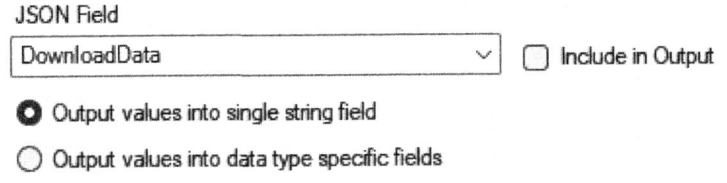

Figure 11.30: JSON Parse tool configuration

11. Run the workflow again, and view the **Results** pane. Two new fields were generated: `JSON_Name` and `JSON_ValueString`.

Unlike what we saw with the XML format, in this case, the hierarchy in the data is represented by the values of the `JSON_Name` field using a dot notation:

Record	URL	: DownloadHeaders	JSON_Name	JSON_ValueString
1	https://clinicaltrials.gov/api/query/full_studies?ex...	HTTP/1.1 200 OK	FullStudiesResponse.APIVrs	1.01.05
2	https://clinicaltrials.gov/api/query/full_studies?ex...	HTTP/1.1 200 OK	FullStudiesResponse.DataVrs	2023:06:04 23:39:00.598
3	https://clinicaltrials.gov/api/query/full_studies?ex...	HTTP/1.1 200 OK	FullStudiesResponse.Expression	heart+attack
4	https://clinicaltrials.gov/api/query/full_studies?ex...	HTTP/1.1 200 OK	FullStudiesResponse.NStudiesAvail	454492
5	https://clinicaltrials.gov/api/query/full_studies?ex...	HTTP/1.1 200 OK	FullStudiesResponse.NStudiesFound	1991
6	https://clinicaltrials.gov/api/query/full_studies?ex...	HTTP/1.1 200 OK	FullStudiesResponse.MinRank	1
7	https://clinicaltrials.gov/api/query/full_studies?ex...	HTTP/1.1 200 OK	FullStudiesResponse.MaxRank	1
8	https://clinicaltrials.gov/api/query/full_studies?ex...	HTTP/1.1 200 OK	FullStudiesResponse.NStudiesReturned	1
9	https://clinicaltrials.gov/api/query/full_studies?ex...	HTTP/1.1 200 OK	FullStudiesResponse.FullStudies.0.Rank	1
10	https://clinicaltrials.gov/api/query/full_studies?ex...	HTTP/1.1 200 OK	FullStudiesResponse.FullStudies.0.Study.Protocol...	NCT00929994
11	https://clinicaltrials.gov/api/query/full_studies?ex...	HTTP/1.1 200 OK	FullStudiesResponse.FullStudies.0.Study.Protocol...	Brooks - 001
12	https://clinicaltrials.gov/api/query/full_studies?ex...	HTTP/1.1 200 OK	FullStudiesResponse.FullStudies.0.Study.Protocol...	Toronto Rehabilitation Institute
13	https://clinicaltrials.gov/api/query/full_studies?ex...	HTTP/1.1 200 OK	FullStudiesResponse.FullStudies.0.Study.Protocol...	OTHER
14	https://clinicaltrials.gov/api/query/full_studies?ex...	HTTP/1.1 200 OK	FullStudiesResponse.FullStudies.0.Study.Protocol...	Effects of Cardiac Rehabilitation for Individuals W...
15	https://clinicaltrials.gov/api/query/full_studies?ex...	HTTP/1.1 200 OK	FullStudiesResponse.FullStudies.0.Study.Protocol...	Effects of Cardiac Rehabilitation for Individuals W...
16	https://clinicaltrials.gov/api/query/full_studies?ex...	HTTP/1.1 200 OK	FullStudiesResponse.FullStudies.0.Study.Protocol...	April 2019

Figure 11.31: Results after parsing the JSON

Also, record numbers are present in this hierarchy with a zero-index notation (meaning that record #1 is represented with a 0):

Record ID

FullStudiesResponse.FullStudies.0.Rank	1
FullStudiesResponse.FullStudies.0.Study.ProtocolSection.IdentificationModule.NCTId	NCT00929994
FullStudiesResponse.FullStudies.0.Study.ProtocolSection.IdentificationModule.OrgStudyIdInfo.OrgStudyId	Brooks - 001
FullStudiesResponse.FullStudies.0.Study.ProtocolSection.IdentificationModule.Organization.OrgFullName	Toronto Rehabilitation Ir
FullStudiesResponse.FullStudies.0.Study.ProtocolSection.IdentificationModule.Organization.OrgClass	OTHER
FullStudiesResponse.FullStudies.0.Study.ProtocolSection.IdentificationModule.BriefTitle	Effects of Cardiac Rehabi

Figure 11.32: Identifying the record number

So, we need to parse the JSON_Name field to get our column names.

We saw in the results that the record number of this JSON is after the second separator (.), so it's in the third part of the string.

12. Drop a **Text To Columns** tool onto the canvas:

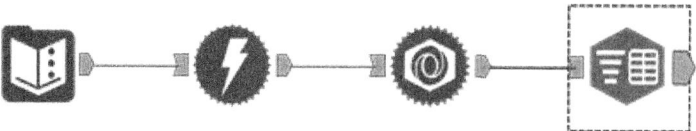

Figure 11.33: Adding a Text to Columns tool

13. From the tool configuration panel, select JSON_Name from the **Column to split** dropdown, and enter a period (.) as the **Delimiter** type.

14. Make sure **Split to columns** is selected, and use 4 for the **Number of columns** option (this is where we found our record number #1).

15. **Leave extra in last column** must be the selected option for **Extra characters**, and for **Output root name**, you can use anything (this will be the prefix of the newly created fields, followed by 1, 2, 3, and 4 since we selected 4 columns):

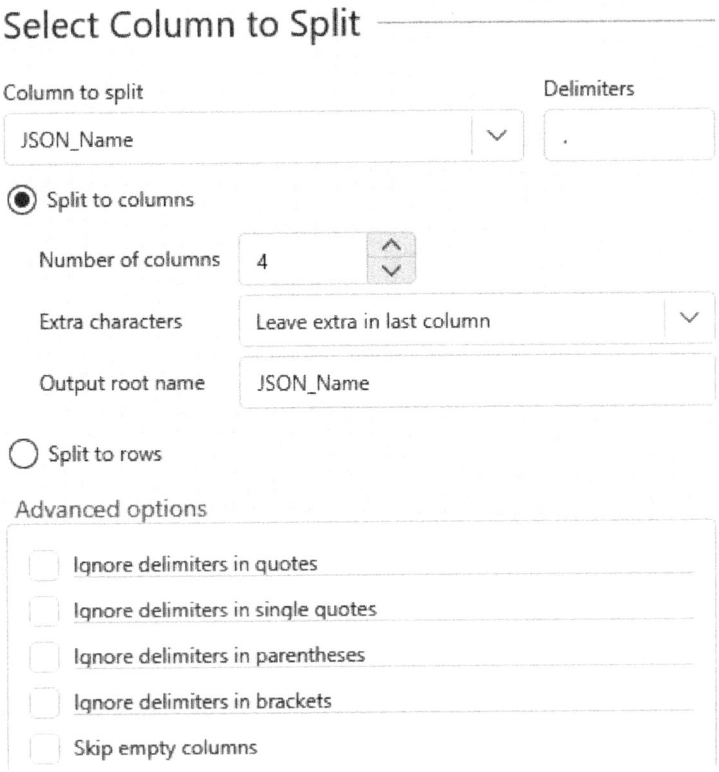

Select Column to Split

Column to split

| JSON_Name | ∨ |

Delimiters

.

◉ Split to columns

Number of columns   4   ⌃⌄

Extra characters | Leave extra in last column | ∨ |

Output root name | JSON_Name |

◯ Split to rows

Advanced options

☐ Ignore delimiters in quotes

☐ Ignore delimiters in single quotes

☐ Ignore delimiters in parentheses

☐ Ignore delimiters in brackets

☐ Skip empty columns

Figure 11.34: Text to Columns tool configuration

16. Run the workflow and check the **Results** pane:

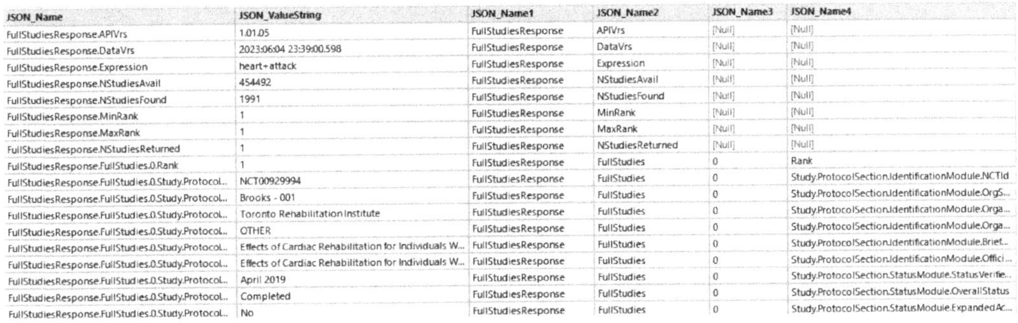

JSON_Name	JSON_ValueString	JSON_Name1	JSON_Name2	JSON_Name3	JSON_Name4
FullStudiesResponse.APIVrs	1.01.05	FullStudiesResponse	APIVrs	[Null]	[Null]
FullStudiesResponse.DataVrs	2023:06:04 23:39:00.598	FullStudiesResponse	DataVrs	[Null]	[Null]
FullStudiesResponse.Expression	heart+attack	FullStudiesResponse	Expression	[Null]	[Null]
FullStudiesResponse.NStudiesAvail	454492	FullStudiesResponse	NStudiesAvail	[Null]	[Null]
FullStudiesResponse.NStudiesFound	1991	FullStudiesResponse	NStudiesFound	[Null]	[Null]
FullStudiesResponse.MinRank	1	FullStudiesResponse	MinRank	[Null]	[Null]
FullStudiesResponse.MaxRank	1	FullStudiesResponse	MaxRank	[Null]	[Null]
FullStudiesResponse.NStudiesReturned	1	FullStudiesResponse	NStudiesReturned	[Null]	[Null]
FullStudiesResponse.FullStudies.0.Rank	1	FullStudiesResponse	FullStudies	0	Rank
FullStudiesResponse.FullStudies.0.Study.Protocol...	NCT00929994	FullStudiesResponse	FullStudies	0	Study.ProtocolSection.IdentificationModule.NCTid
FullStudiesResponse.FullStudies.0.Study.Protocol...	Brooks - 001	FullStudiesResponse	FullStudies	0	Study.ProtocolSection.IdentificationModule.OrgS...
FullStudiesResponse.FullStudies.0.Study.Protocol...	Toronto Rehabilitation Institute	FullStudiesResponse	FullStudies	0	Study.ProtocolSection.IdentificationModule.Orga...
FullStudiesResponse.FullStudies.0.Study.Protocol...	OTHER	FullStudiesResponse	FullStudies	0	Study.ProtocolSection.IdentificationModule.Orga...
FullStudiesResponse.FullStudies.0.Study.Protocol...	Effects of Cardiac Rehabilitation for Individuals W...	FullStudiesResponse	FullStudies	0	Study.ProtocolSection.IdentificationModule.Brief...
FullStudiesResponse.FullStudies.0.Study.Protocol...	Effects of Cardiac Rehabilitation for Individuals W...	FullStudiesResponse	FullStudies	0	Study.ProtocolSection.IdentificationModule.Offici...
FullStudiesResponse.FullStudies.0.Study.Protocol...	April 2019	FullStudiesResponse	FullStudies	0	Study.ProtocolSection.StatusModule.StatusVerifie...
FullStudiesResponse.FullStudies.0.Study.Protocol...	Completed	FullStudiesResponse	FullStudies	0	Study.ProtocolSection.StatusModule.OverallStatus
FullStudiesResponse.FullStudies.0.Study.Protocol...	No	FullStudiesResponse	FullStudies	0	Study.ProtocolSection.StatusModule.ExpandedAc...

Figure 11.35: New fields added after splitting into columns

You'll notice that now, we have four new columns (JSON_Name from 1 to 4). Each column contains the value between the separator (period) we configured, except for the fourth column, which contains everything that was after the third separator (because we instructed Alteryx to **Leave extra in last column**).

17. Drop a **Select** tool onto the canvas. We are going to rename the generated fields to something more meaningful:

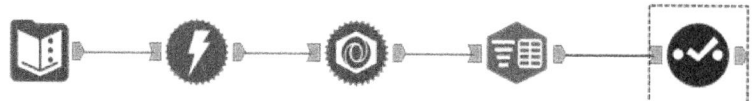

Figure 11.36: Adding a Select tool

18. Rename the JSON_Name1 field to Root, JSON_Name2 to Query_Attributes, and JSON_Name3 to RecordId. We'll leave JSON_Name4 as it is because we need to further parse it:

Options ▾ | ↑ ↓   TIP: To reorder multiple rows: select, right-click and drag

		Field	Type		Size	Rename	Description
▶	✓	URL	String	▾	110		
	✓	DownloadHeaders	V_String	▾	214...		
	✓	JSON_Name	V_WString	▾	107...		
	✓	JSON_ValueString	V_WString	▾	107...		
	✓	JSON_Name1	V_WString	▾	107...	Root	TextToCol..
	✓	JSON_Name2	V_WString	▾	107...	Query_Attributes	TextToCol..
	✓	JSON_Name3	V_WString	▾	107...	RecordId	TextToCol..
	✓	JSON_Name4	V_WString	▾	107...		TextToCol..
	✓	*Unknown	Unknown	▾	0		Dynamic or.

Figure 11.37: Renaming using the Select tool

Let's analyze what we need from the JSON_Name4 field. The last part of the whole value is the field name, so we'll use the *Reversing strings* recipe from *Chapter 5* to get the field names from it:

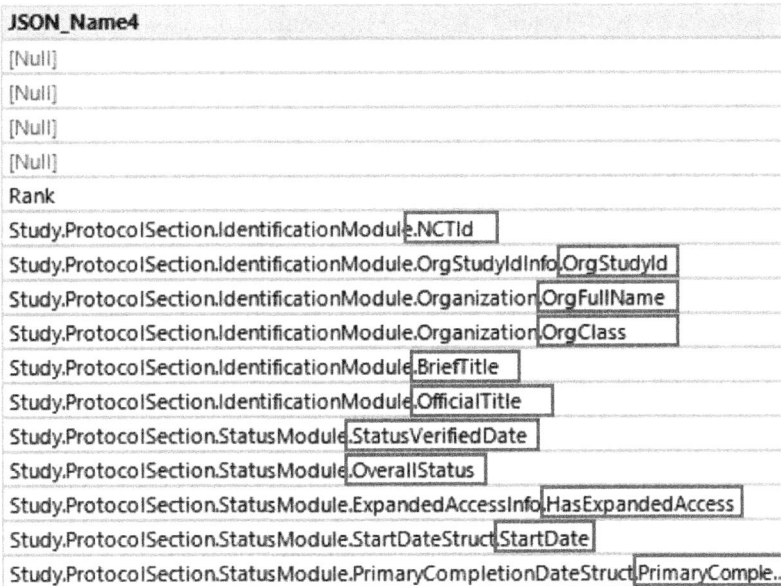

Figure 11.38: JSON inspection to get field names

19. Drop a **Formula** tool following the **Select** tool:

Figure 11.39: Adding a Formula tool

20. Within the **Formula** tool, create a new field called Reversed, and use this formula as the expression:

```
ReverseString([JSON_Name4])
```

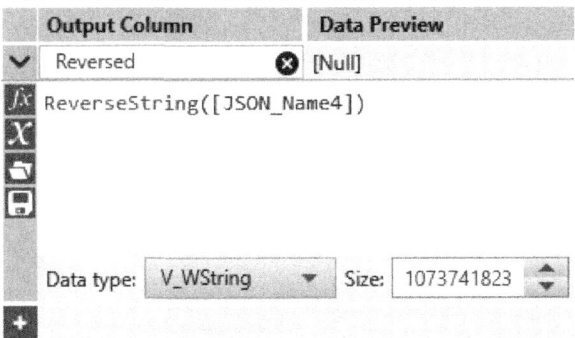

Figure 11.40: Formula tool expression to reverse the contents of the field

21. Drop another **Text To Columns** tool after the **Formula** tool:

Reversed =
ReverseString
([JSON_Name4])

Figure 11.41: Adding a second Text to Columns tool

22. Configure the **Text To Columns** tool as follows:

- From the **Column to split** dropdown, select **Reversed**.
- Change the **Delimiters** type to a period (.).
- Make sure **Split to columns** is selected, and enter 2 for the **Number of columns** option.
- Leave the extra characters in the last column.

23. Use Reversed as the **Output root name** value:

Select Column to Split

Column to split   Delimiters

| Reversed | ⌄ | . |

◉ Split to columns

Number of columns   2   ⌃⌄

Extra characters   Leave extra in last column   ⌄

Output root name   Reversed

◯ Split to rows

Advanced options

☐ Ignore delimiters in quotes

☐ Ignore delimiters in single quotes

☐ Ignore delimiters in parentheses

☐ Ignore delimiters in brackets

☐ Skip empty columns

Figure 11.42: Text to Columns configuration on the Reversed field

24. Add a new **Formula** tool to the workflow:

Figure 11.43: Adding a new Formula tool

25. This time, create a new column called `FieldName` and use this expression:

```
ReverseString([Reversed1])
```

Output Column	Data Preview
FieldName ❌	[Null]

```
ReverseString([Reversed1])
```

Data type: V_WString ▼ Size: 1073741823 ▲▼

Figure 11.44: Formula tool expression to return the Reversed field to its original content

This should give us the field names, but if you run the workflow and scroll down, you'll see that there are some 0s as values for `FieldName`:

Reversed	Reversed1	Reversed2	FieldName
emaNrotaroballoC.0.rotaroballoC.tsiLrotaroballo…	emaNrotaroballoC	0.rotaroballoC.tsiLrotaroballoC.eludoMsrotarobal…	CollaboratorName
ssalCrotaroballoC.0.rotaroballoC.tsiLrotaroballoC…	ssalCrotaroballoC	0.rotaroballoC.tsiLrotaroballoC.eludoMsrotarobal…	CollaboratorClass
CMDsaHthgisrevO.eludoMthgisrevO.noitceSlocot…	CMDsaHthgisrevO	eludoMthgisrevO.noitceSlocotorP.ydutS	OversightHasDMC
yrammuSfeirB.eludoMnoitpircseD.noitceSlocotor…	yrammuSfeirB	eludoMnoitpircseD.noitceSlocotorP.ydutS	BriefSummary
noitpircseDdeliateD.eludoMnoitpircseD.noitœSlo…	noitpircseDdeliateD	eludoMnoitpircseD.noitceSlocotorP.ydutS	DetailedDescription
0.noitidnoC.tsiLnoitidnoC.eludoMsnoitidnoC.noit…	0	noitidnoC.tsiLnoitidnoC.eludoMsnoitidnoC.noitœ…	0
0.drowyeK.tsiLdrowyeK.eludoMsnoitidnoC.noitce…	0	drowyeK.tsiLdrowyeK.eludoMsnoitidnoC.noitceSl…	0
epyTydutS.eludoMngiseD.noitceSlocotorP.ydutS	epyTydutS	eludoMngiseD.noitceSlocotorP.ydutS	StudyType
yrtsigeRtneitaP.eludoMngiseD.noitceSlocotorPy…	yrtsigeRtneitaP	eludoMngiseD.noitceSlocotorP.ydutS	PatientRegistry

Figure 11.45: Previewing the results

The cause is the object hierarchy within the file, so we are going to change (replace) those 0s in the `Reversed` field, before splitting them into columns.

26. Let's go back and click on the **Formula** tool that generated the `Reversed` field:

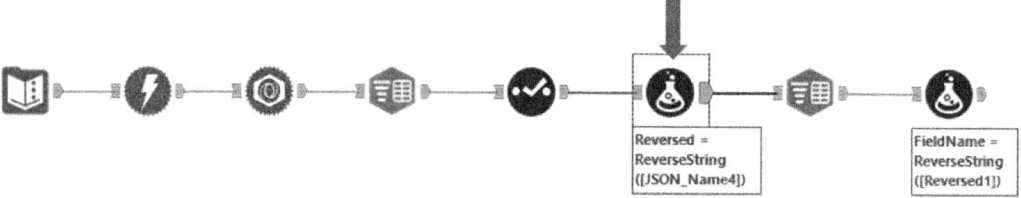

Figure 11.46: Formula tool to be edited

27. In this tool configuration, click on the white + symbol with a blue background:

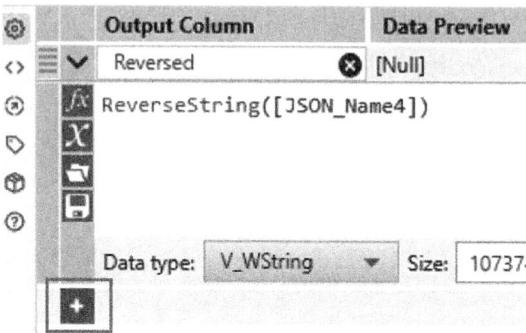

Figure 11.47: The + sign allows you to add a new expression to an existing Formula tool

28. From the **Fields** list, select `Reversed` and enter this expression:

```
IF StartsWith([Reversed],"0.")
THEN ReplaceFirst([Reversed],"0.",'')
ELSE [Reversed]
ENDIF
```

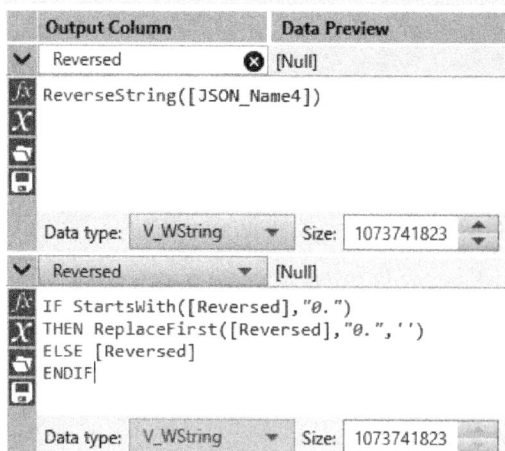

Figure 11.48: The new formula will be applied to the Reversed field

29. Run the workflow and scroll down to where the 0s were. You'll see that now, we have the field name there:

Reversed	Reversed1	Reversed2	FieldName
ssalCrosnopSdaeL.rosnopSdaeL.eludoMsrotaroba...	ssalCrosnopSdaeL	rosnopSdaeL.eludoMsrotaroballoCrosnopS.noitc...	LeadSponsorClass
emaNrotaroballoC.0.rotaroballoC.tsiLrotaroballo...	emaNrotaroballoC	0.rotaroballoC.tsiLrotaroballoC.eludoMsrotarobal...	CollaboratorName
ssalCrotaroballoC.0.rotaroballoC.tsiLrotaroballoC....	ssalCrotaroballoC	0.rotaroballoC.tsiLrotaroballoC.eludoMsrotarobal...	CollaboratorClass
CMDsaHthgisrevO.eludoMthgisrevO.noitceSlocot...	CMDsaHthgisrevO	eludoMthgisrevO.noitceSlocotorP.ydutS	OversightHasDMC
yrammuSfeirB.eludoMnoitpircseD.noitceSlocotor...	yrammuSfeirB	eludoMnoitpircseD.noitceSlocotorP.ydutS	BriefSummary
noitpircseDdeliateD.eludoMnoitpircseD.noitceSlo...	noitpircseDdeliateD	eludoMnoitpircseD.noitceSlocotorP.ydutS	DetailedDescription
noitidnoC.tsiLnoitidnoC.eludoMsnoitidnoC.noitce...	noitidnoC	tsiLnoitidnoC.eludoMsnoitidnoC.noitceSlocotorP...	Condition
drowyeK.tsiLdrowyeK.eludoMsnoitidnoC.noitceSl...	drowyeK	tsiLdrowyeK.eludoMsnoitidnoC.noitceSlocotorPy...	Keyword
epyTydutS.eludoMngiseD.noitceSlocotorP.ydutS	epyTydutS	eludoMngiseD.noitceSlocotorP.ydutS	StudyType

Figure 11.49: Results after fixing the Reversed field

Our dataset now requires a little cleanup.

30. Add a **Select** tool at the end of the workflow:

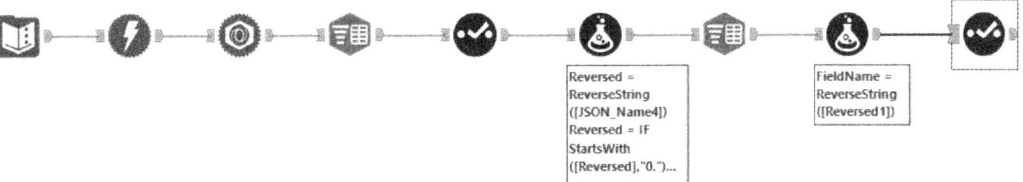

Figure 11.50: Adding a Select tool to clean up the dataset

31. Within the **Select** tool configuration, uncheck the following fields:

- `DownloadHeaders`
- `JSON_Name`
- `JSON_Name4`
- `Reversed`
- `Reversed1`
- `Reversed2`

32. Once done, move the `JSON_ValueString` field to the bottom so that your **Select** tool looks like this:

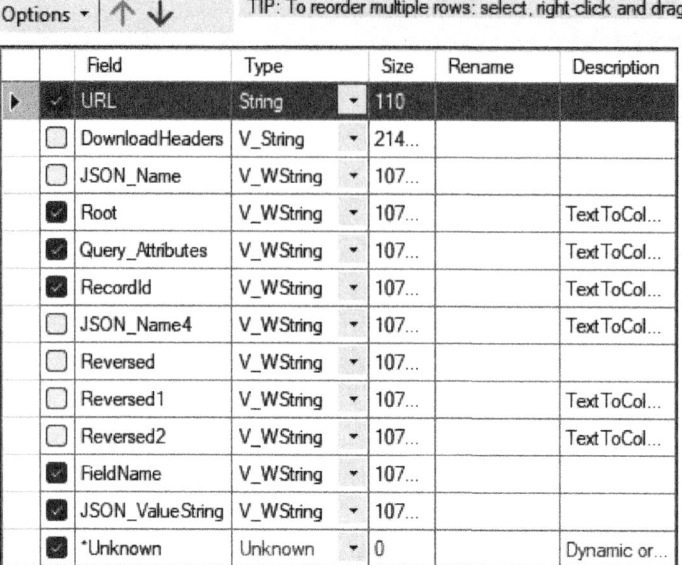

Figure 11.51: Select tool configuration

At this point, we can perform additional actions—for example, filtering all values where `RecordId=0` (those are the attributes of the downloaded JSON) and use them as headers for the whole content:

URL	Root	Query_Attributes	RecordId	FieldName	JSON_ValueString
https://clinicaltrials.gov/api/query/full_studies?ex...	FullStudiesResponse	APIVrs	[Null]	[Null]	1.01.05
https://clinicaltrials.gov/api/query/full_studies?ex...	FullStudiesResponse	DataVrs	[Null]	[Null]	2023:06:04 23:39:00.598
https://clinicaltrials.gov/api/query/full_studies?ex...	FullStudiesResponse	Expression	[Null]	[Null]	heart+attack
https://clinicaltrials.gov/api/query/full_studies?ex...	FullStudiesResponse	NStudiesAvail	[Null]	[Null]	454492
https://clinicaltrials.gov/api/query/full_studies?ex...	FullStudiesResponse	NStudiesFound	[Null]	[Null]	1991
https://clinicaltrials.gov/api/query/full_studies?ex...	FullStudiesResponse	MinRank	[Null]	[Null]	1
https://clinicaltrials.gov/api/query/full_studies?ex...	FullStudiesResponse	MaxRank	[Null]	[Null]	1
https://clinicaltrials.gov/api/query/full_studies?ex...	FullStudiesResponse	NStudiesReturned	[Null]	[Null]	1
https://clinicaltrials.gov/api/query/full_studies?ex...	FullStudiesResponse	FullStudies	0	Rank	1
https://clinicaltrials.gov/api/query/full_studies?ex...	FullStudiesResponse	FullStudies	0	NCTId	NCT00929994
https://clinicaltrials.gov/api/query/full_studies?ex...	FullStudiesResponse	FullStudies	0	OrgStudyId	Brooks - 001

Figure 11.52: Final results

I kept the URL field (which has the same value for each record) in case we need to transpose the gathered fields. If you decide to filter the headers, you can use `RecordId` for this task.

Getting paged results from APIs (Iterative Macros)

Working with paginated results adds an extra complication to our work. We must repeat certain operations while there are still results to be received. Although there are no loop-type structures in Alteryx (`while`, `until`, and so on), we do have a way to solve it. To do this, we will use **Iterative Macros**.

An Iterative Macro is a type of macro that runs a specified number of times or until a defined condition is met for all records. Every execution of the macro is identified by a zero-index (when its value is zero, it means it's the first iteration) internal variable called [Engine.IterationNumber].

In basic terms, the process of an Iterative Macro goes like this:

- It ingests all incoming data

- It processes the records

- It evaluates if a condition is met and splits the records

- For those records that met the condition, it outputs them as results

- For those that have not met the condition, it feeds them again to the selected **Macro Input** tool and starts over (now with the remaining records):

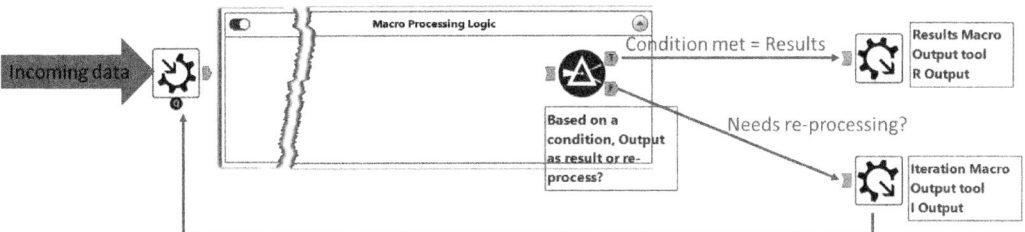

Figure 11.53: The basic process of an Iterative Macro

This process is repeated until there are no records that don't meet the condition or the **Maximum Number of Iterations** limit is reached.

You can tell Alteryx Designer the type of macro you want from within the **Workflow** configuration panel:

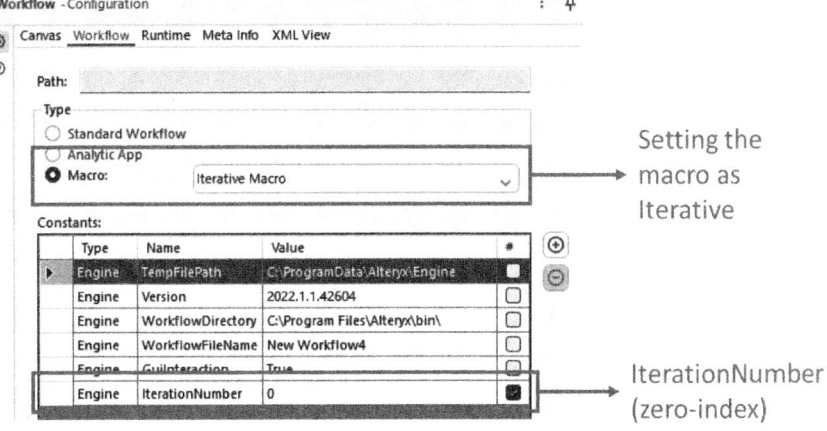

Figure 11.54: Setting a macro as Iterative within the Workflow configuration panel

From the **Interface Designer**, you can select which **Macro Input** tool will receive the records in each iteration, from which **Macro Output** tool those records will come, and the maximum number of iterations the macro will run.

If the condition is not met in the running iterations, you can choose what to do with the remaining records: **Error**, **Warn (and output left over records)**, or just **Output left over records**).

Also, it's important to identify whether your dataset's schema will change after iterations; otherwise, your macro will error:

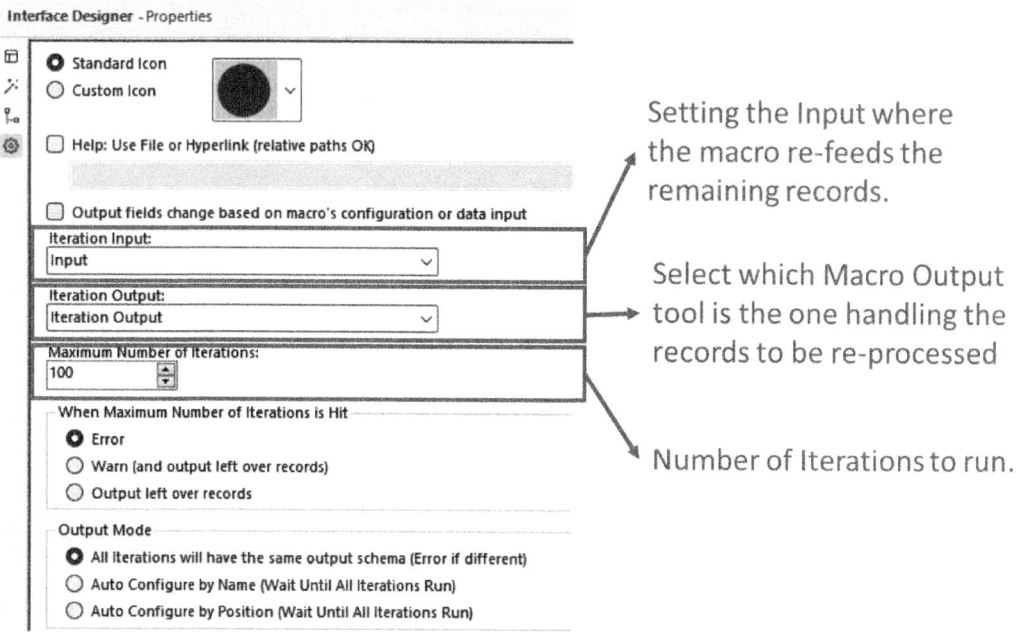

Figure 11.55: Interface Designer options for an Iterative Macro

Iterative Macros can be scary at first, but once the main concept of operation is understood, they are a very useful tool.

Getting ready

In this recipe, we are going to gather user posts from the Alteryx Community. To do it, you'll need your user ID from the community.

If you are still not registered in the Alteryx Community, I'd highly recommend doing it, not only because you'll be able to follow this recipe but because you'll find a huge number of resources to keep improving your Alteryx skills.

To get the one that corresponds to you, log in to the Alteryx Community at `https://community.alteryx.com/` and go to your profile. You'll see the URL in your browser (`https://community.alteryx.com/t5/user/viewprofilepage/user-id/XXXX`, where XXXX is your user ID).

Once you have it, you can use the following URL, replacing `<your userid>` with the real user ID: `https://community.alteryx.com/restapi/vc/users/id/<your userid>/posts?page_size=1000&page=`

As with all of the recipes in this book, we prepared a test set in case you want to use it to follow along. You can download it from here: `https://github.com/PacktPublishing/Alteryx-Designer-Cookbook`.

How to do it...

As I mentioned previously, we are going to get all the posts made by a user within the Alteryx community.

The software used to support the community provides a REST API to get its contents. For posts, the URL is this: `https://community.alteryx.com/restapi/vc/users/id/<your userid>/posts`

It has some additional parameters, as follows:

- `Page_size`: Tells the API how many posts we'll download per request.
- `Page`: Each page is a group of `page_size` number of posts. The maximum number of pages is given by the total posts by the user/`page_size` number.

For this recipe, we'll use a `page_size` number of 500 posts per call, so the complete URL is this: `https://community.alteryx.com/restapi/vc/users/id/<your userid>/posts?page_size=500&page=`

> **Important note**
> v2 of the API uses the permissions granted to the user within the community. Therefore, anonymous users cannot perform REST calls that post messages or access private boards or categories, and since we're going to use an anonymous user call, we'll only retrieve public content.
>
> More info about the API is available at `https://developer.khoros.com/`.

To start, we'll need an Iterative Macro. This macro will connect to the API and get individual pages of posts until all posts from the specified user are retrieved (or the **Maximum Number of Iterations** limit is reached). Once we have the macro built, we'll create a new workflow to use it and parse the results.

The best way to build macros is to start with a plain workflow. This will help us get the logic right, test it, and then add the specifics on the macro we want:

1. Drop a **Text Input** tool onto the canvas.

2. Create a column called `Endpoint` and use this as the value for the first row:

    ```
    https://community.alteryx.com/restapi/vc/users/id/xxxx/posts
    ```

3. Create a second column, called `page_size`, and use `500` as its value.

4. Create a third column called `page` and use `1` as its value:

	Endpoint	page_size	page
1	https://community.alteryx.com/restapi/vc/users/id/xxxx/posts	500	1
...			

Figure 11.56: Setting the initial input data

> **Important note**
>
> Notice that we called the columns *EXACTLY* as the API calls its parameters. This is crucial if you want to build payloads within the **Download** tool in Alteryx (unless you use a **Select** tool to rename them before using the **Download** tool).

Now, we need to adjust the `Endpoint` column to use your `userID` value instead of `xxxx`.

5. Drop a **Formula** tool onto the canvas:

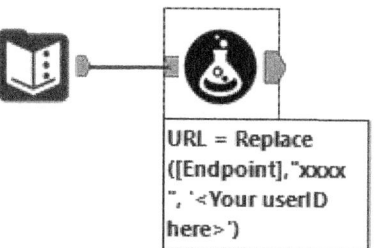

Figure 11.57: Adding a Formula tool

6. From the **Output Column** dropdown, select + **Add Column** and name the new column URL. We are creating a new column because Alteryx sets the field sizes based on their contents when reading a **Text Input** tool, and we need to have the ability to grow the field size based on the userID value's length we want to use.

7. Use this expression in the URL formula:

```
Replace([Endpoint],"xxxx", '<Your userID here>')
```

8. Replace the `<Your userID here>` text with the userID value you want to query:

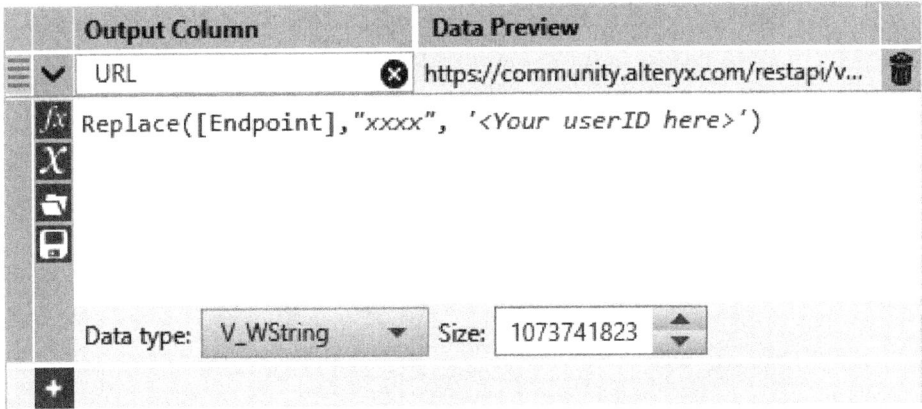

Figure 11.58: Formula tool configuration

9. Drop a **Download** tool following the **Text Input** tool:

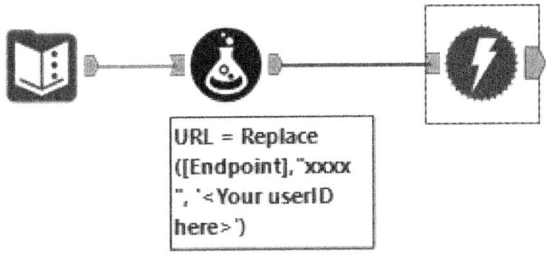

Figure 11.59: Adding a Download tool

10. From the **Basic** tab in the **Download** tool configuration, select the recently created field URL column from the **Field** dropdown.

11. Make sure **Encode URL Text** is checked:

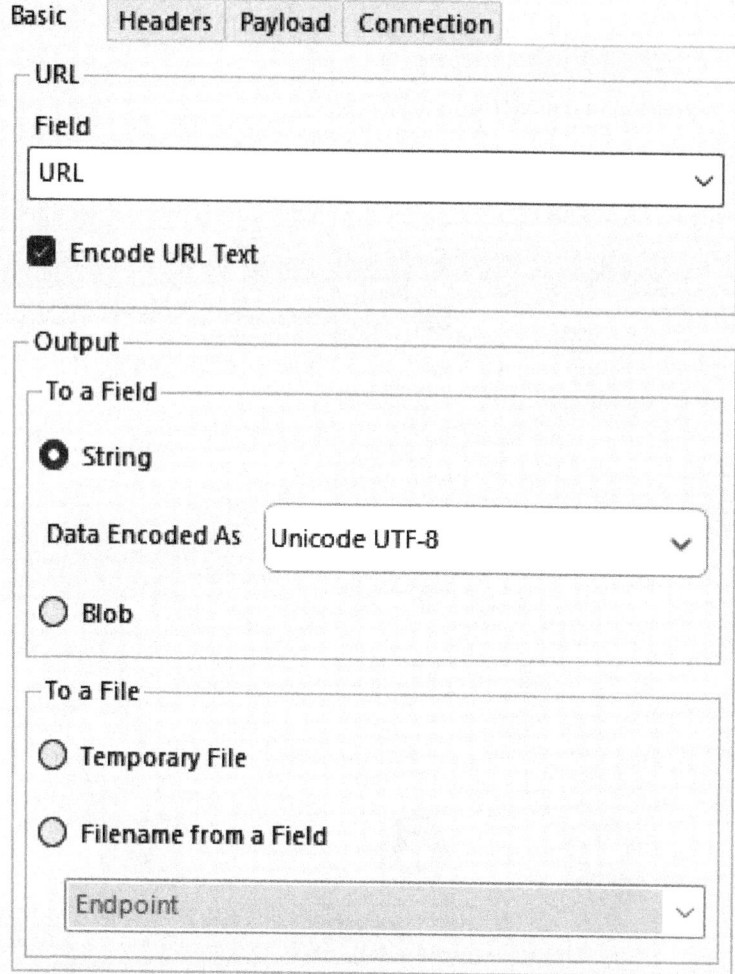

Figure 11.60: Download tool basic configuration

12. From the **Payload** tab, make sure **GET (or FTP)** is the selected **HTTP Action** type.

13. Check **Compose Query String/Body** to enable it, and from the **And values from these fields** list, select **page_size** and **page**:

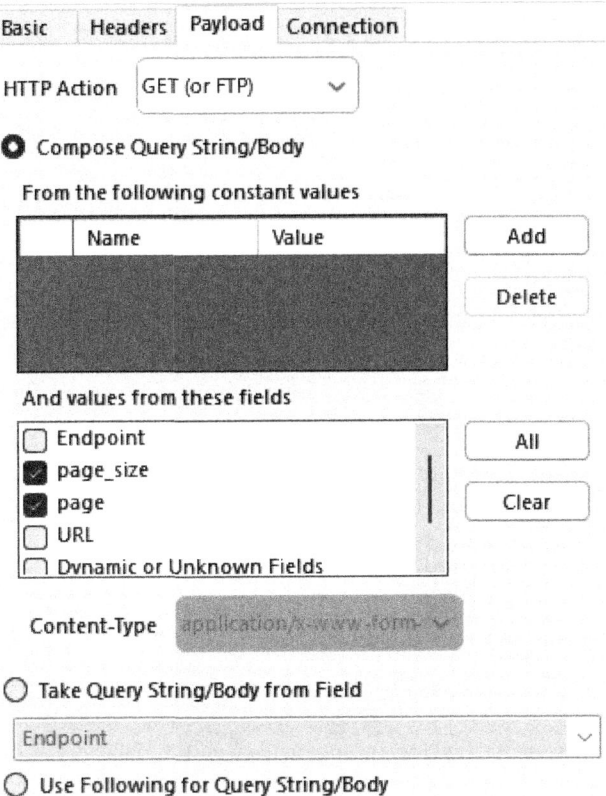

Figure 11.61: Download tool payload construction settings

This will tell Alteryx Designer to create the complete request URL using the selected parameters. (That's why the original columns were created with the exact name of the parameters. If your data comes from a different source, make sure you rename the fields so you can use them here.) It'll create the URL in the following form:

```
[URL] + ? + First Parameter Name + = + First Parameter Value + &
+ Second Parameter Name + = + Second Parameter Value
```

In our case, this results in the following output:

```
https://community.alteryx.com/restapi/vc/users/id/<The userID
you used>/posts?page_size=500&page=1
```

Notice that the URL field is not checked in the **Fields** list. This is because we selected it in the **Basic** configuration tab.

At this point, we can run the workflow.

We'll see that `DownloadData` and `DownloadHeaders` fields were added, and the result was `HTTP/1.1 200 OK`, which means the call was successful:

Figure 11.62: Results after running the workflow

Now that we've received our response (even though it's only the first page), we can see within the results (`DownloadData`) that we have the total record count:

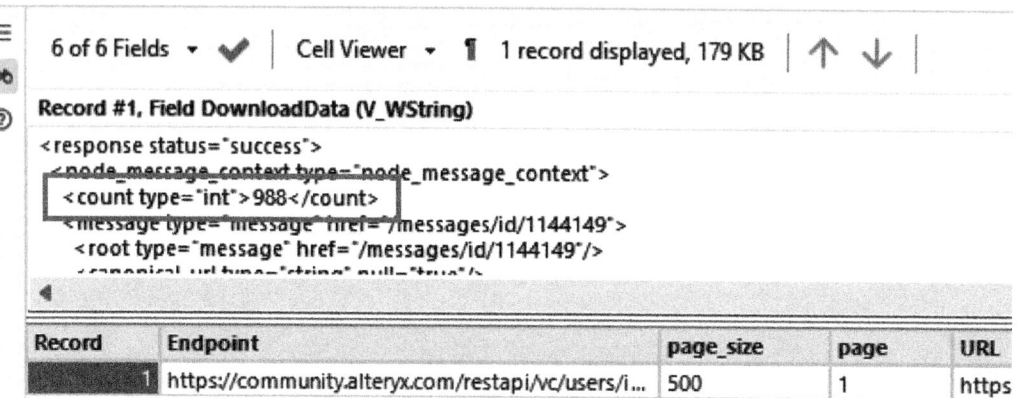

Figure 11.63: Response in XML contents

We made a unique call to the API. We need to instruct our tool to keep executing itself until there are no more records to retrieve. This can be done using a statement such as *"If there are any remaining records, call to the next page; otherwise, output the results and stop iterating."*

To determine whether there are any remaining records, we need to identify an attribute from the response that can be evaluated and tell us those are records.

If we explore the received XML, we'll notice that every message is a child node of the `node_message_context` tag:

```
  1 ⊟<response status="success">
  2   └─⊟<node_message_context type="node_message_context">
  3      ├─⊞<count type="int">
  4      ├─⊞<message type="message" href="/messages/id/1144149">
 48      ├─⊞<message type="message" href="/messages/id/1135805">
 82      ├─⊞<message type="message" href="/messages/id/1134500">
L16      ├─⊞<message type="message" href="/messages/id/1134478">
L50      ├─⊞<message type="message" href="/messages/id/1134469">
L84      ├─⊞<message type="message" href="/messages/id/1134460">
```

Figure 11.64: Exploring the XML received

Also, all attributes for a particular message are children of the `message` tag:

```
 1 ⊟<response status="success">
 2  └⊟<node_message_context type="node_message_context">
 3    ├⊞<count type="int">
 4    └⊟<message type="message" href="/messages/id/1144149">
 5       ├─<root type="message" href="/messages/id/1144149" />
 6       ├─<canonical_url type="string" null="true" />
 7       ├⊞<post_time type="date_time">
 8       ├─<seo_title type="string" null="true" />
 9       ├─<seo_description type="string" null="true" />
10       ├⊞<labels>
20       ├⊞<kudos>
23       ├⊞<last_edit_time type="date_time">
24       ├⊞<message_rating type="float">
25       ├⊞<last_edit_author type="user" href="/users/id/1536">
28       ├⊞<author type="user" href="/users/id/1536">
31       ├⊞<deleted type="boolean">
32       ├─<board type="board" href="/boards/id/product-ideas" />
33       ├─<thread type="thread" href="/threads/id/1144149" />
34       ├─<parent type="message" null="true" />
35       ├─<teaser type="string" />
36       ├⊞<views>
39       ├⊞<subject type="string">
40       ├⊞<message_status type="message_status" href="/message_statuses/id/5">
44       ├⊞<board_id type="int">
45       ├⊞<id type="int">
46       └⊞<read_only type="boolean">
48    ├⊞<message type="message" href="/messages/id/1135805">
82    ├⊞<message type="message" href="/messages/id/1134500">
```

Figure 11.65: Attributes for each message tag

So, with this in mind, if the response XML contains, for example, `post_time` (or `subject`, or any specific attribute related to a message), we can assume that the response contents have posts.

Now, the next set of tools is the core of the Iterative Macro.

14. Drop a **Formula** tool onto the canvas:

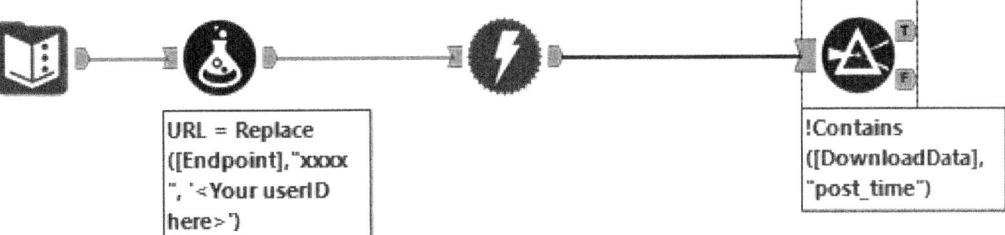

Figure 11.66: Adding a Formula tool

15. From the tool configuration, select **Basic Filter**.

16. Select the `DownloadData` field, use the **Does not contain** condition, and type `post_time` in the value:

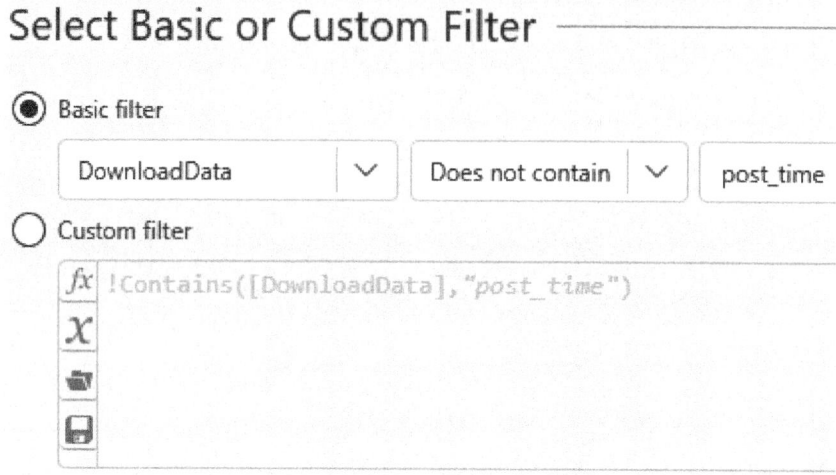

Figure 11.67: Setting a basic filter

This filter will behave as a stop light for our dataset, as follows:

- If the `post_time` string is not present within the response received from the API (the response is not retrieving posts), it'll output the response to the T output anchor

- If the `post_time` string is found, this means the content contains posts, and it'll send the records through the F output anchor

At this point, we have the basic logic for retrieving posts. Now, we need to make it dynamic and iterative so that we can retrieve all posts and not only the first 500.

17. Start by connecting a **Macro Output** tool to each of the output anchors of the **Filter** tool:

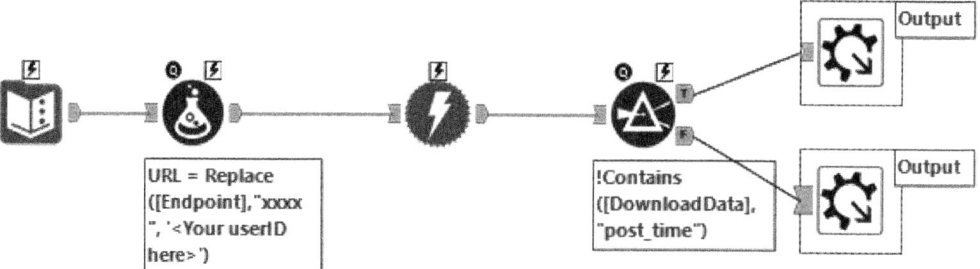

Figure 11.68: Adding Macro Output tools

18. Select the **Macro Output** tool connected to the T anchor of the **Filter** tool, rename it RESULTS, and use R for the **Anchor Abbreviation** value:

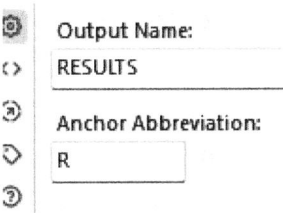

Figure 11.69: Renaming the first Macro Output tool

19. Click on the **Macro Output** tool connected to the F output anchor of the **Filter** tool, rename it ITERATION, and use I for the **Anchor Abbreviation** value:

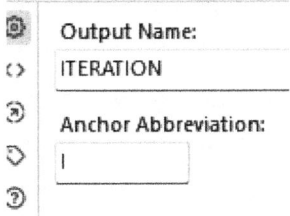

Figure 11.70: Renaming the second (iteration) Macro Output tool

20. Right-click on the **Text Input** tool and select **Convert To Macro Input**:

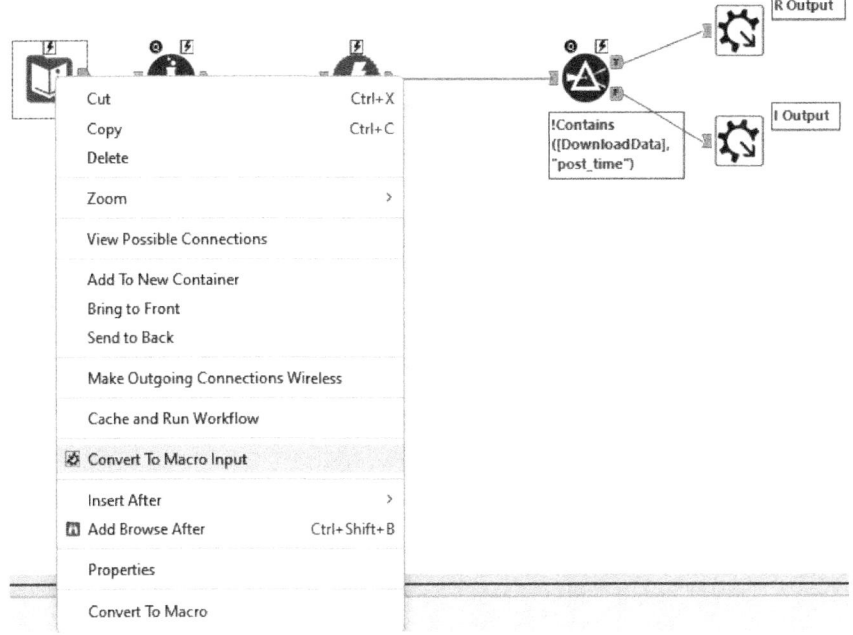

Figure 11.71: Convert to Macro Input menu option

You'll see that the tool has been converted:

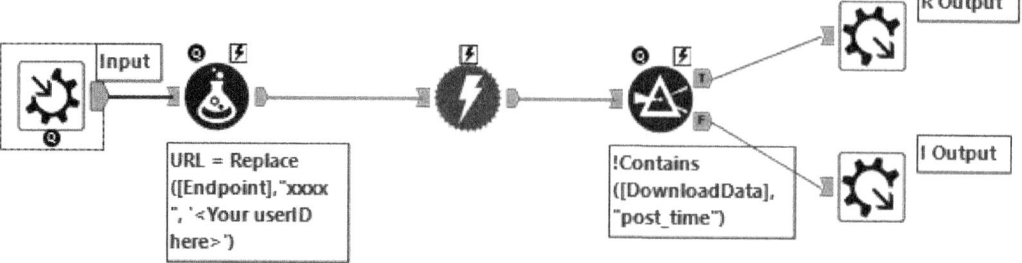

Figure 11.72: Text Input tool converted to Macro Input tool

So far, it looks like any other macro we created with Alteryx Designer.

21. Click on any blank part of the canvas to access the **Workflow** configuration panel:

○ Standard Workflow
○ Analytic App
● Macro:

Standard Macro ⌄

Constants:

	Type	Name	Value	#	
▶	Engine	TempFilePath	C:\ProgramData\Alteryx\Engine	☐	
	Engine	Version	2022.1.1.42604	☐	
	Engine	WorkflowDirectory	C:\Exercises\ch11\Recipe3\WORKFLOWS	☐	
	Engine	WorkflowFileName	Starting Workflow.yxmd	☐	
	Engine	GuiInteraction	True	☐	

Figure 11.73: Workflow configuration options

22. In the **Type** section, make sure **Macro** is the active option, and from the dropdown, select **Iterative Macro**:

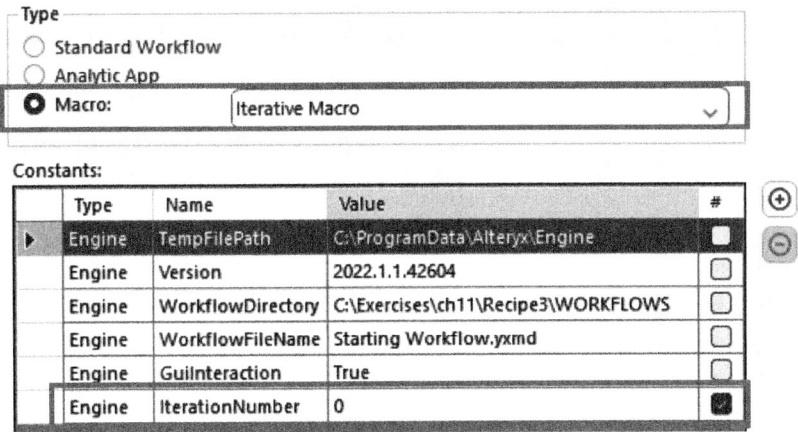

Figure 11.74: Selecting Iterative Macro as the Macro type

Notice that an `IterationNumber` constant was added to the available constants for the workflow.

23. Open the **Interface Designer** (from the **View** menu or with the *Ctrl* + *Alt* + *D* shortcut). Click on the gear icon to the left of the panel to access the macro configuration.

Here, you'll see the options to handle the iterations:

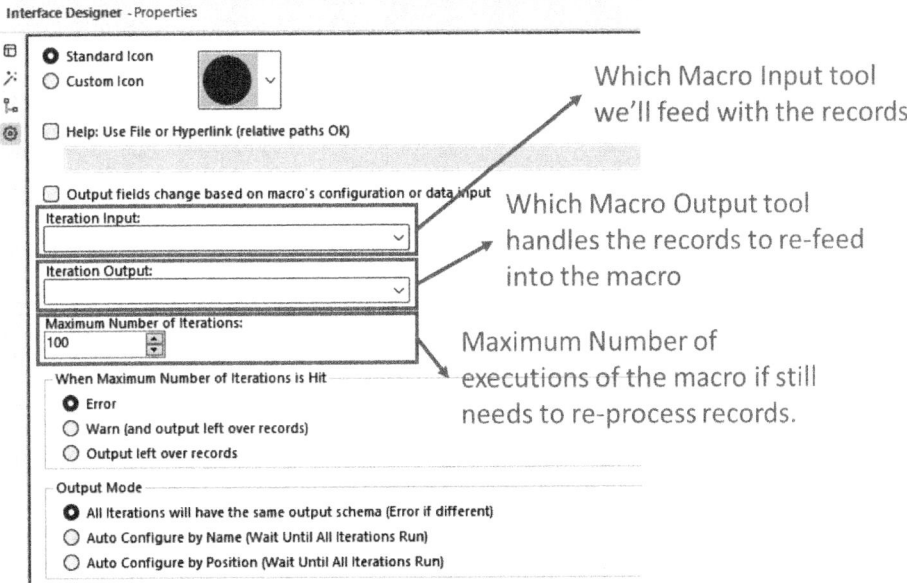

Figure 11.75: Interface Designer options for Iterative Macros

24. From the **Iteration Input** dropdown, select **Input2** (it should be the only tool listed here).

25. From the **Iteration Output** dropdown, select **ITERATION**.

26. Leave the **Maximum Number of Iterations** limit at 100.

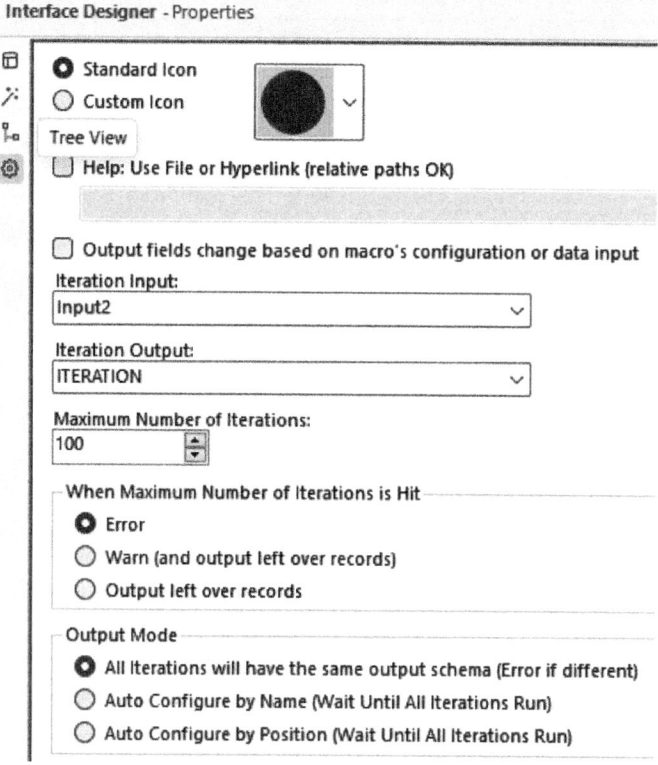

Figure 11.76: Our macro configuration in the Interface Designer

---

Important note

It's highly recommended that you evaluate if the recordset structure will vary between iterations (fields added, removed, and so on), and if so, check the **Output fields change** option right above the **Iteration Input** dropdown; otherwise, your macro will error due to that field change.

If we run the workflow now and explore the outputs we have, we'll notice that in both cases, the data has a couple of added fields. So, we have two options here:

- Check the **Output fields change** option based on the macro's configuration or data input so that Alteryx Designer won't error

- Remove the added fields for the iterations

I always recommend doing the latter because it optimizes the data being processed; for iterations, we don't need the added fields, since we need to re-enter the original data into the process.

27. So, drag a **Select** tool and drop it over the connection between the **F** output anchor of the filter tool and the **Macro Output** tool (remember that you also can click on the connection and double-click the tool you want to insert in the toolbar):

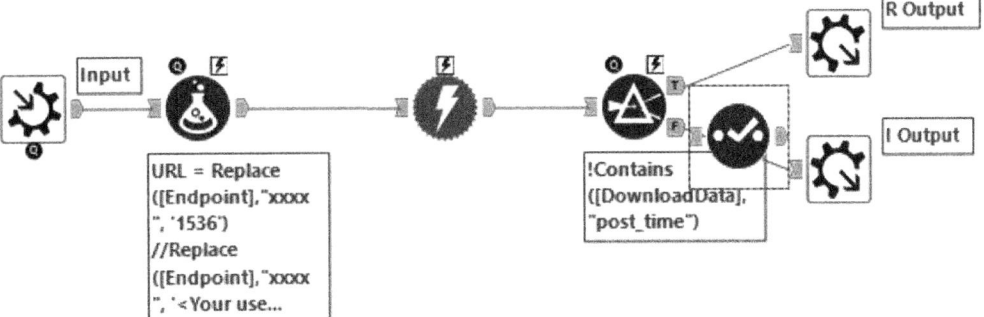

Figure 11.77: Inserting a Select tool

28. From the recently inserted **Select** tool configuration, de-select the following fields:

- URL (It's being created every time the macro executes)

- DownloadData

- DownloadHeaders

	Field	Type		Size	Ren
☑	Endpoint	String	▼	59	
☑	page_size	Int 16	▼	2	
☑	page	Byte	▼	1	
☐	URL	V_WString	▼	107...	
☐	DownloadData	V_WString	▼	107...	
☐	DownloadHeaders	V_String	▼	214...	
☑	*Unknown	Unknown	▼	0	

Options ▾ | ↑ ↓   TIP: To reorder multiple rows:

Figure 11.78: Select tool with unneeded fields deselected

Doing this ensures that the **Iteration output** option will send the same fields that the input is expecting and make sure the macro doesn't process fields we don't need.

We also need to pay attention to the **Filter** tool. This tool splits the output, so, if the first iteration contains posts, it'll route the records through the **F** output anchor. In other words, the **T** output (the expected results output) won't have any records.

If we want to output the received data, we need to union the **T** and **F** outputs so that we can stream those records through the RESULTS **Macro Output** tool.

29. Drop a **Union** tool over the **T** output connection:

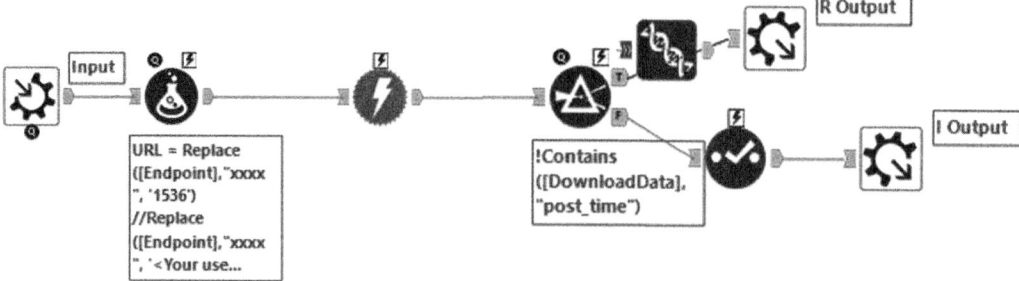

Figure 11.79: Inserting a Union tool to output results

30. Once the **Union** tool is inserted between the **Filter** tool and the **Macro Output** tool, connect the **F** output anchor from the **Filter** tool to the **Union** tool:

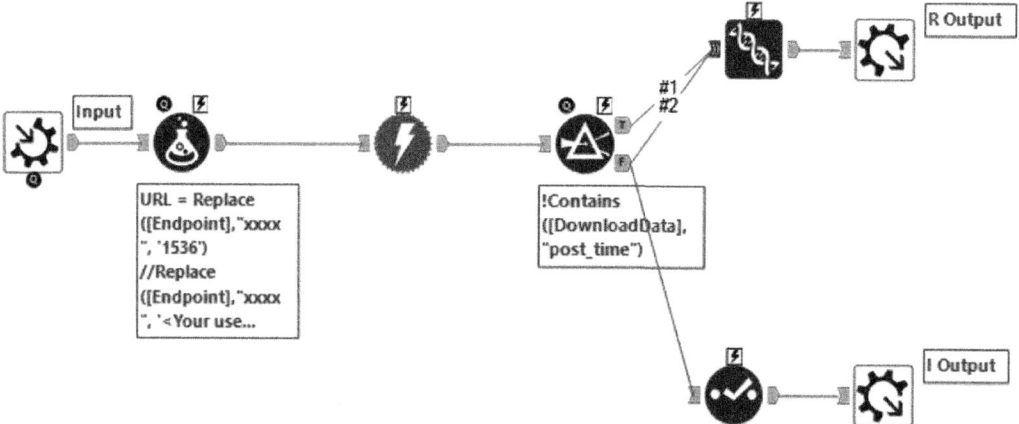

Figure 11.80: Union tool connections

Finally, the last touch to the tool. We need to update the page field for each iteration that the macro runs.

31. Drop a new **Formula** tool between the existing one and the **Download** tool (or use the existing one if you like):

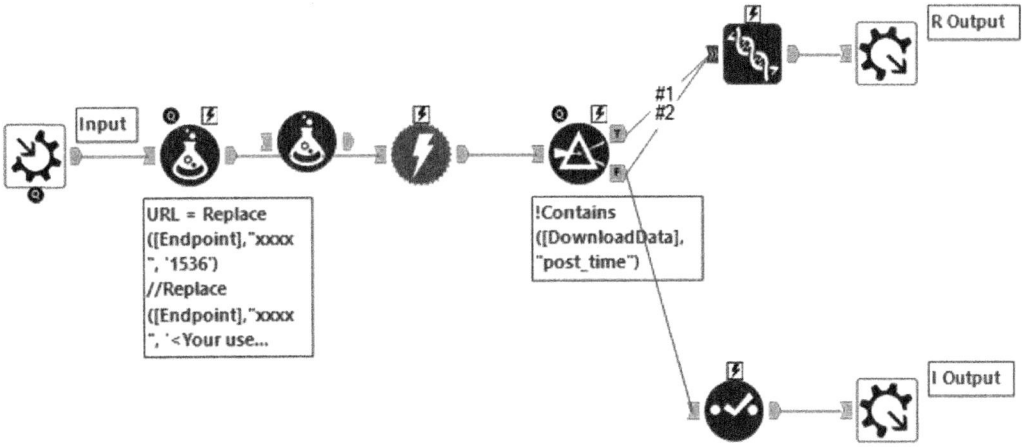

Figure 11.81: Inserting a new Formula tool

32. From the **Output Column** dropdown, select the **page** field:

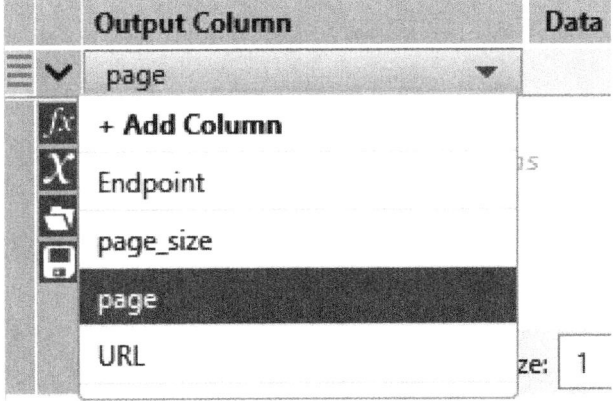

Figure 11.82: Formula tool field selection

33. Use the following as the expression for the formula:

```
[Engine.IterationNumber] +1
```

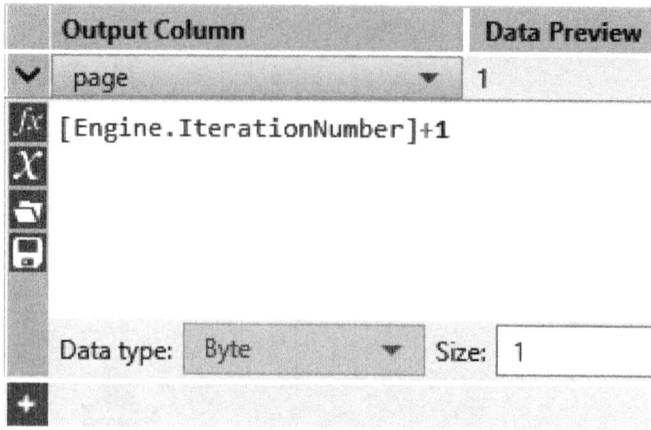

Figure 11.83: Formula tool expression

Now, we can save the macro. You can select to save it wherever you want, but consider that if the macro needs to be redistributed (as part of the workflow or to be used in other workflows), it'll be better to save it in a shared repository.

34. Save your macro and name it GetUserPosts.yxmc. Leave it open in Alteryx Designer.

35. Create a new workflow.

36. Go to the macro and copy the **Macro Input** tool:

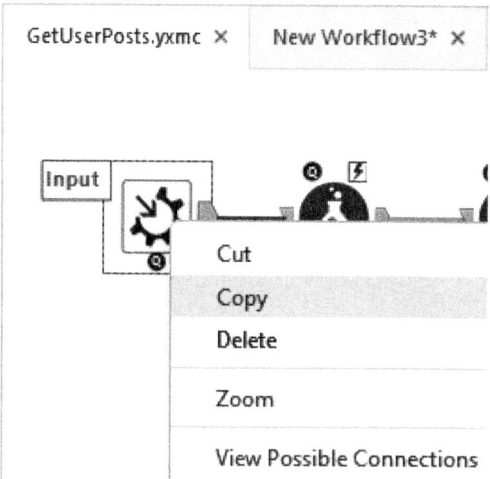

Figure 11.84: Copying the Macro Input tool

37. Return to the new workflow and paste it.

38. Once you see the tool in the workflow, right-click on it and select **Convert From Macro Input**:

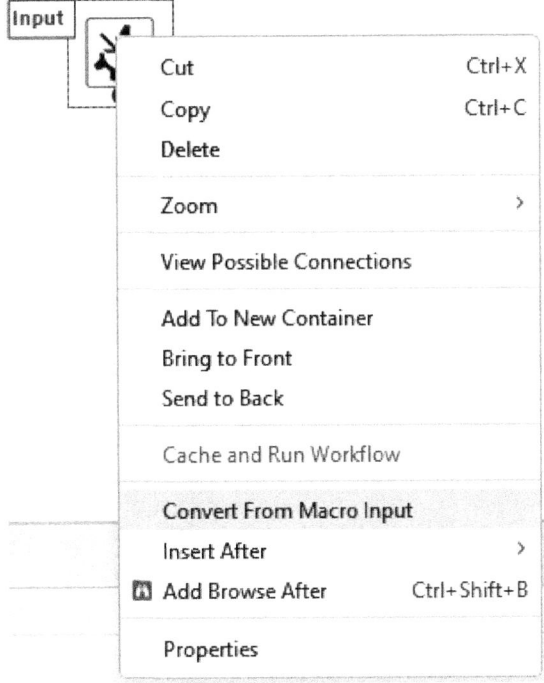

Figure 11.85: Convert From Macro Input option

This procedure will convert the pasted tool into a **Text Input** tool, with the same data we have in the **Macro Input** tool:

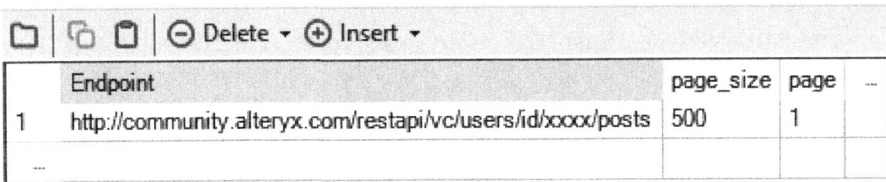

Figure 11.86: Macro Input converted persists the data it had

39. Right-click on any blank part of the canvas. Select **Insert** and scroll down to the **Macro** option:

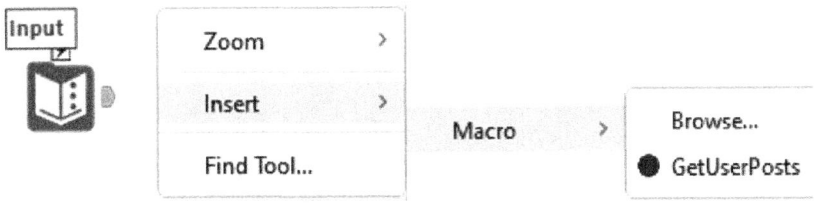

Figure 11.87: Inserting the created macro

From the options, if you kept the macro open, you can select `GetUserPosts` from the list of open macros; otherwise, click on **Browse...** and find the macro where you saved it.

You can run the workflow now and check the results:

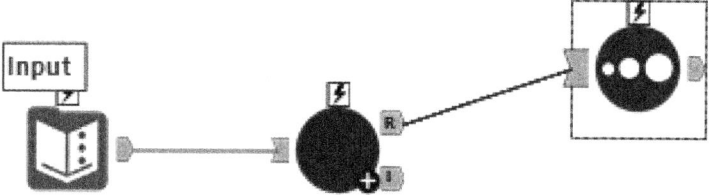

Record	Endpoint	page_size	page	URL	DownloadData
1	http://community.alteryx.com/restapi/vc/users/id...	500	1	http://community.alteryx.com/restapi/vc/users/id...	<response status="success">
2	http://community.alteryx.com/restapi/vc/users/id...	500	2	http://community.alteryx.com/restapi/vc/users/id...	<response status="success">
3	http://community.alteryx.com/restapi/vc/users/id...	500	3	http://community.alteryx.com/restapi/vc/users/id...	<response status="success">

Figure 11.88: Results after running the workflow

You'll notice that you received N records (depending on the number of posts `userID` has in the community), with one additional record (the last one) that corresponds to the last call to the API.

To parse the results, we are going to drop the last record.

The easiest way is to sort the records by page in descending order and skip the first record.

40. Drop a **Sort** tool and connect it to the **R** output of the `GetUserPosts` macro:

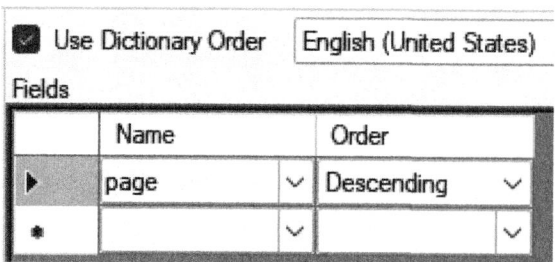

Figure 11.89: Adding a Sort tool

41. From the **Sort** tool configuration panel, select **page** from the **Name** dropdown and **Descending** from the **Order** one:

	Name		Order	
☑ Use Dictionary Order	English (United States)			
Fields				
▶	page	⌄	Descending	⌄
＊		⌄		⌄

Figure 11.90: Configuring the Sort tool

42. Connect a **Sample** tool to the **Sort** tool:

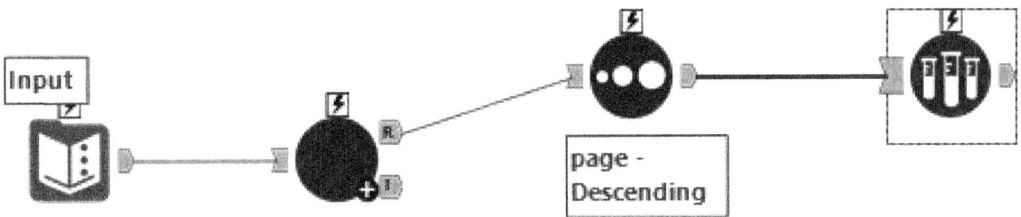

Figure 11.91: Adding a Sample tool

43. In the **Sample** tool configuration, select **Skip 1st N rows** as the sampling type and set **N** to 1. Leave the **Group by column** options all deselected:

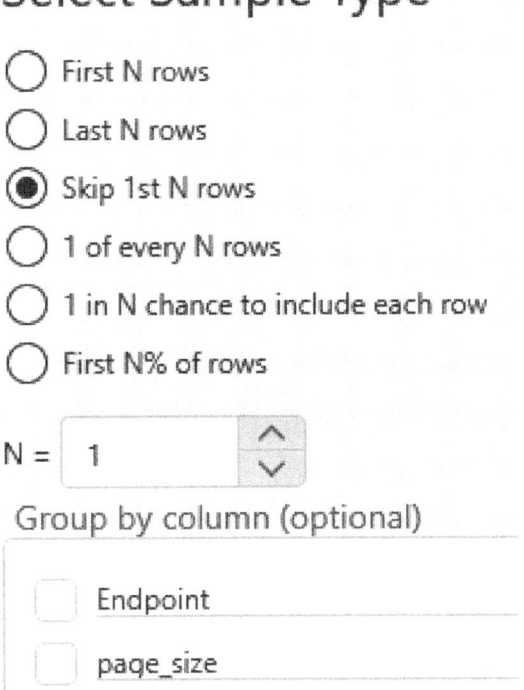

Figure 11.92: Sample tool configuration

Now, we need to re-sort the pages to the original order.

44. Copy the **Sort** tool and paste it after the **Sample** tool (or drag and drop a new one from the toolbar).

45. Change the sort order to **Ascending** by **page**:

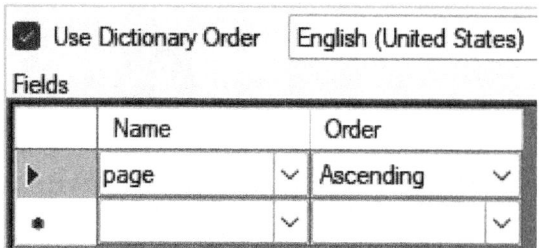

Figure 11.93: Second Sort tool configuration

Now, we need to parse the received responses.

46. Drop an **XML Parse** tool after the last **Sort** tool:

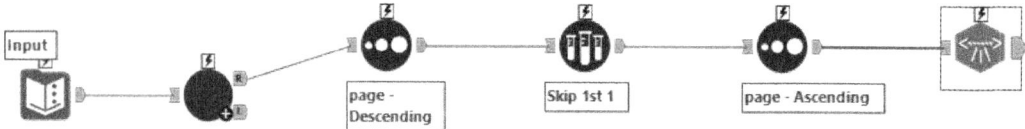

Figure 11.94: Adding an XML Parse tool

47. From the **XML Parse** tool configuration, select `DownloadData` from the **Field with XML Data** dropdown.

48. From the **XML Element to Parse** options, select **Specific Child Name**, and enter `message` as the tag to use.

49. Finally, make sure **Return Child Values** is the only option selected:

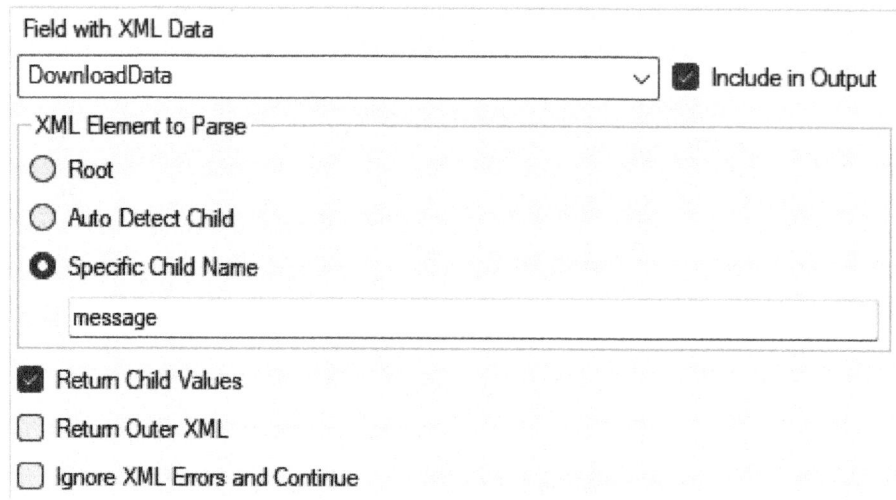

Figure 11.95: XML Parse tool configuration

Run the workflow, and you'll have the results retrieved and parsed:

type	href	root	root_type	root_href	canonical_url	canonical_url_type	canonical_url_null	post_time
1 message	/messages/id/1152665		message	/messages/id/1151959		string	true	2023-06-21T23:14:11+00:00
2 message	/messages/id/1152626		message	/messages/id/1151941		string	true	2023-06-21T21:52:56+00:00
3 message	/messages/id/1152485		message	/messages/id/1151941		string	true	2023-06-21T16:54:28+00:00
4 message	/messages/id/1152464		message	/messages/id/1151941		string	true	2023-06-21T16:40:04+00:00
5 message	/messages/id/1152439		message	/messages/id/1152345		string	true	2023-06-21T16:10:21+00:00
6 message	/messages/id/1144149		message	/messages/id/1144149		string	true	2023-06-06T15:36:25+00:00
7 message	/messages/id/1135805		message	/messages/id/1135273		string	true	2023-05-19T19:08:48+00:00
8 message	/messages/id/1134500		message	/messages/id/1134409		string	true	2023-05-17T19:57:59+00:00
9 message	/messages/id/1134478		message	/messages/id/1134409		string	true	2023-05-17T19:30:37+00:00
10 message	/messages/id/1134469		message	/messages/id/1134466		string	true	2023-05-17T19:27:17+00:00
11 message	/messages/id/1134460		message	/messages/id/1134409		string	true	2023-05-17T19:16:45+00:00
12 message	/messages/id/1134435		message	/messages/id/1134409		string	true	2023-05-17T18:52:55+00:00
13 message	/messages/id/1126914		message	/messages/id/1126770		string	true	2023-05-15T18:38:47+00:00

Figure 11.96: Final results

From this point, you can refine the final results by keeping the needed fields, removing those you don't, setting the proper data types, and more until you get a clean output dataset depending on your needs.

There's more…

At this point, our macro only retrieves a particular user's posts—the one you embedded with the **Formula** tool in the macro:

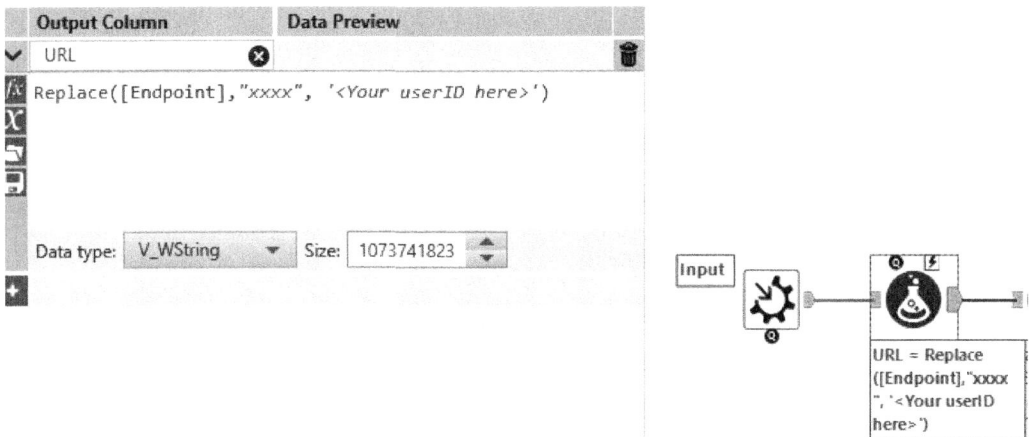

Figure 11.97: Formula tool showing that the user ID is hardcoded

We can make a little adjustment to our macro to make it work with any user ID:

1. Go to the macro and drop a **Text Box** tool onto the canvas, above the **Formula** tool:

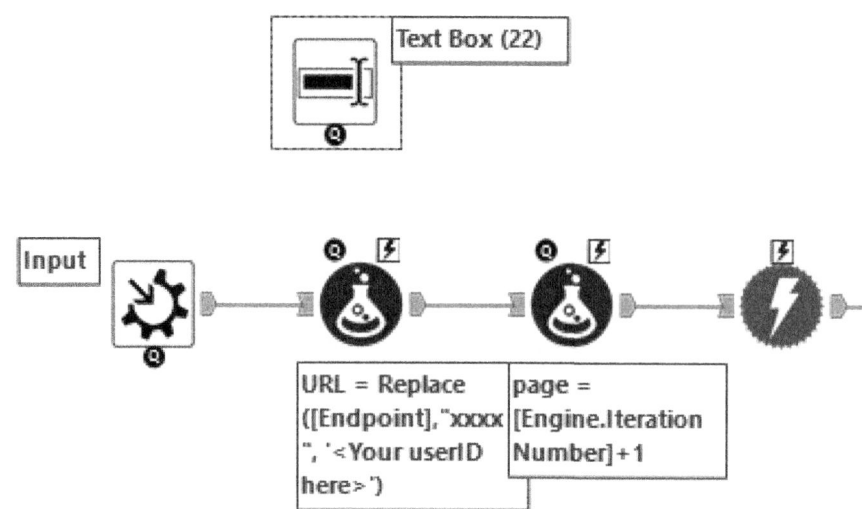

Figure 11.98: Adding a Text Box tool

2. Click on the **Text Box** tool and change the statement to be displayed to the following:

```
Enter the userID:
```

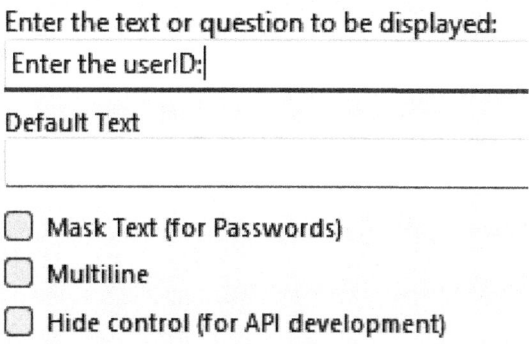

Figure 11.99: Text Box tool options

3. Connect the **Q** connector below the inserted **Text Box** with the **Q** connector above the **Formula** tool:

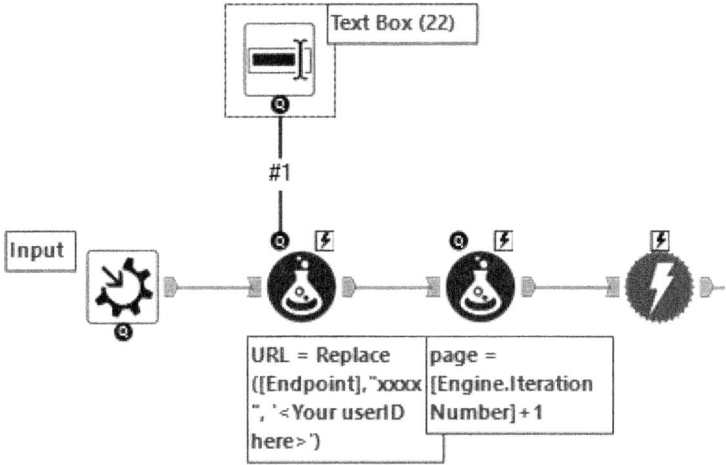

Figure 11.100: Connecting the Text Box to the Formula tool

4. Click on the **Formula** tool and replace the existing expression with this one:

```
Replace([Endpoint],"xxxx", [#1])
```

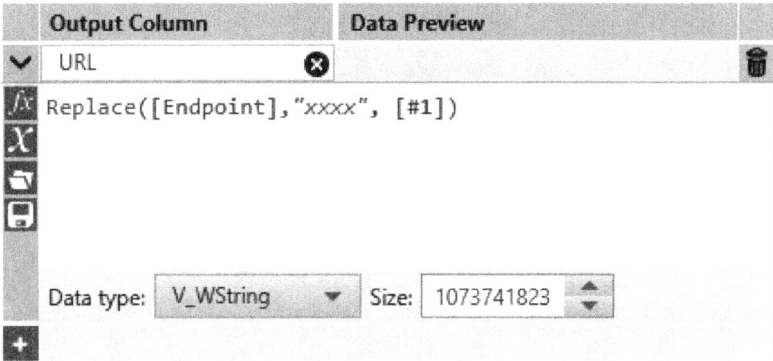

Figure 11.101: Using the value from the Text box tool ([#1]) to replace xxxx

5. Save the macro, and return to the workflow that uses it.

You'll see an alert that Alteryx Designer refreshed the macro since you changed it (if don't see it, the most probable cause is that the macro was not saved):

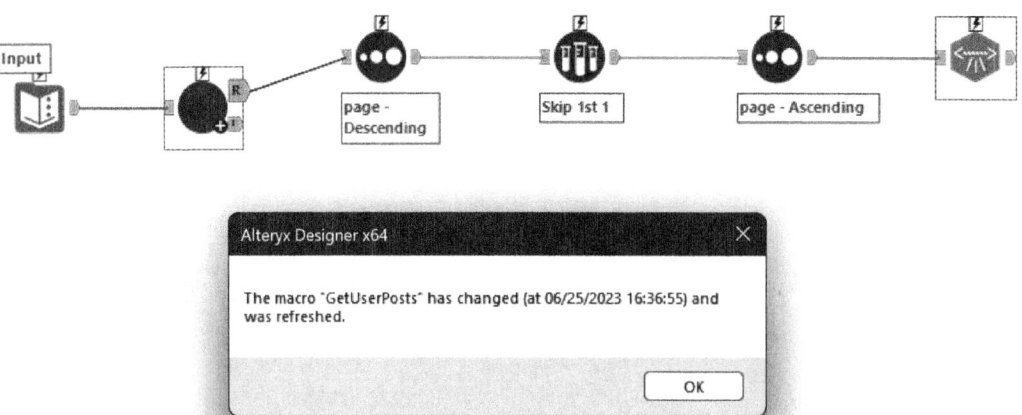

Figure 11.102: Notification on the macro refresh due to changes made to it

This simple change will take whatever code you enter in the macro UI and replace the xxxx string in the **Endpoint** column with it:

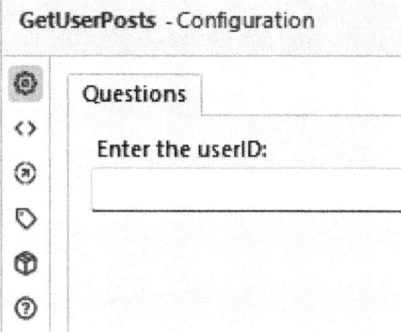

Figure 11.103: Modified macro UI

12
Developer Tools

The **Developer** tool category offers a vast set of tools to leverage workflow operations, interact with external tools, and manage binary sources such as images, raw data fields, and even programming languages, such as Python, R, or Spark.

In this set of tools, we'll find the **Run Command** tool, which allows the generation of batch files and external program execution (such as running any application from the operating system command line) but remaining within an Alteryx workflow; the **Python** tool, which gives us an entire programming environment; and the **Blob** tools (**Convert**, **Input**, and **Output**) for managing binary data, including entire files.

In this chapter, we'll be focusing on these mentioned tools, but the functionality offered by this tool category is worth investigating once you finish this chapter. This chapter will cover the following topics:

- Executing external programs/batches/scripts from inside a workflow
- Basic Python usage—performing **optical character recognition** (**OCR**) from images
- Using **binary large objects** (**blobs**) to read and write raw/binary fields

Executing external programs/batches/scripts from inside a workflow

Even when there are some operations that Alteryx won't do for you, it offers tools to perform them. One of these tasks, which is very frequent when working with files, is to create folders and copy or move existing files.

In this recipe, we'll use the **Run Command** tool to execute external commands, also called shells, from within Alteryx. Doing this leverages our potential to build, call, or execute external applications from within a workflow.

Getting ready

We have a test set for you to follow along with here: `https://github.com/PacktPublishing/Alteryx-Designer-Cookbook/tree/main/ch12/Recipe1`.

You can try this recipe with your own data without any prerequisites, so feel free to do so.

To use the bonus feature of zipping files, you need to have **7-Zip** installed on your computer. You can download **7-Zip** from here: `https://www.7-zip.org/`.

We are going to use a dynamic batch file, which we'll be updating from within our workflow in Alteryx. The code for this batch file starts as follows:

```
@echo off
set Origin= %1
set Destination= %2
rem ***************************
rem Checks if Origin exist
rem ***************************
if exist %Origin% (
        echo Origin %Origin% exist.
        ) else (
        echo Origin %Origin% doesn't exist.
        rem Since Origin doesn't exist, we error.
        goto Error
        )
rem ***************************
rem Checks if Destination exists
rem ***************************
if exist %Destination% (
        echo Destination %Destination% exists.
        ) else (
        echo Destination %Destination% doesn't exist. Creating it...
        rem Destination doesn't exist, so we create it
        md %Destination%
        )
rem ***************************
rem Move the files
rem ***************************
if %ERRORLEVEL% EQU 0 (
move /y %Origin%\*.* %Destination%
pause
rem exit
) else (
goto Error)
```

```
:Error
            rem Exit with an error state
            echo Error processing batch.
            pause
            rem exit 3
```

If you're familiar with batch files (if you're not, you can learn a lot from this website: `https://www.tutorialspoint.com/batch_script/index.htm`), you'll see that this one is a pretty simple one that takes two parameters (`%1` and `%2`) and assigns their values to two variables (`Origin` and `Destination`). Then, it checks whether both exist; if `Origin` doesn't exist, it outputs an error, and if `Destination` doesn't exist, it creates it.

Finally, it moves everything within `Origin` to `Destination`. Pretty simple, yet powerful.

> **Important note**
>
> As a general recommendation, start with a fully functional batch file (written and tested from the command line). This will save you a lot of troubleshooting later. Also, use the `pause` command instead of `exit` when developing and testing (notice that I have them commented in the script, and added a `pause` command before), so you can see what's going on; otherwise, the `cmd` window will close after executing the batch.

Once you're sure the batch file works from the command line, you can start customizing it in Alteryx.

How to do it...

We are going to create a macro (because it allows us to reuse it in every workflow) that will allow us to move all the files within a folder to a new one, and if the selected folder doesn't exist, it'll create it:

1. Start with a blank workflow and drop a **Folder Browse** tool onto the canvas.

2. Select the tool and change its label to `Select Origin Folder::`

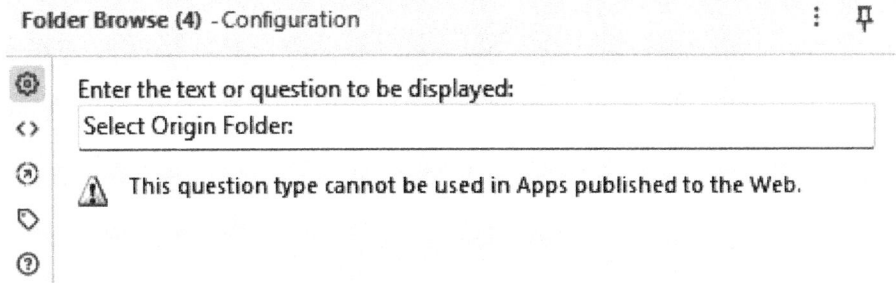

Figure 12.1: Editing the Folder Browse label

3. Drop a second **Folder Browse** tool and again change the label. In this case, use `Select Destination Folder:`.

4. Drop a **Macro Input** tool into the workflow, placing it a little under the existing **Folder Browse** tools:

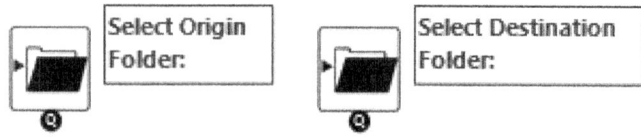

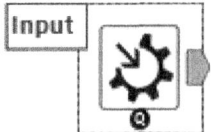

Figure 12.2: Adding a Macro Input tool

5. Click on the **Macro Input** tool to access its configuration.

6. Make sure **Text Input** is selected and click on the **Edit Data...** button. A new window will pop up, and you'll see it's like the **Text Input** interface.

7. Name the first column x and add a row with any value (in this case, 1). This will be replaced later with whatever we connect to the macro, so don't worry:

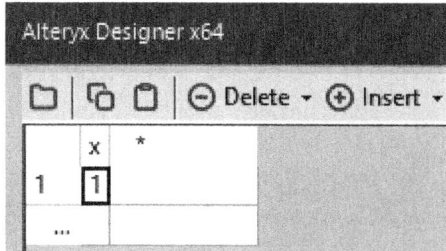

Figure 12.3: Creating dummy data

8. Click **OK** so that Alteryx saves the configuration and changes the **Input Name** value to `Incoming Data` and the **Anchor Abbreviation** value to D:

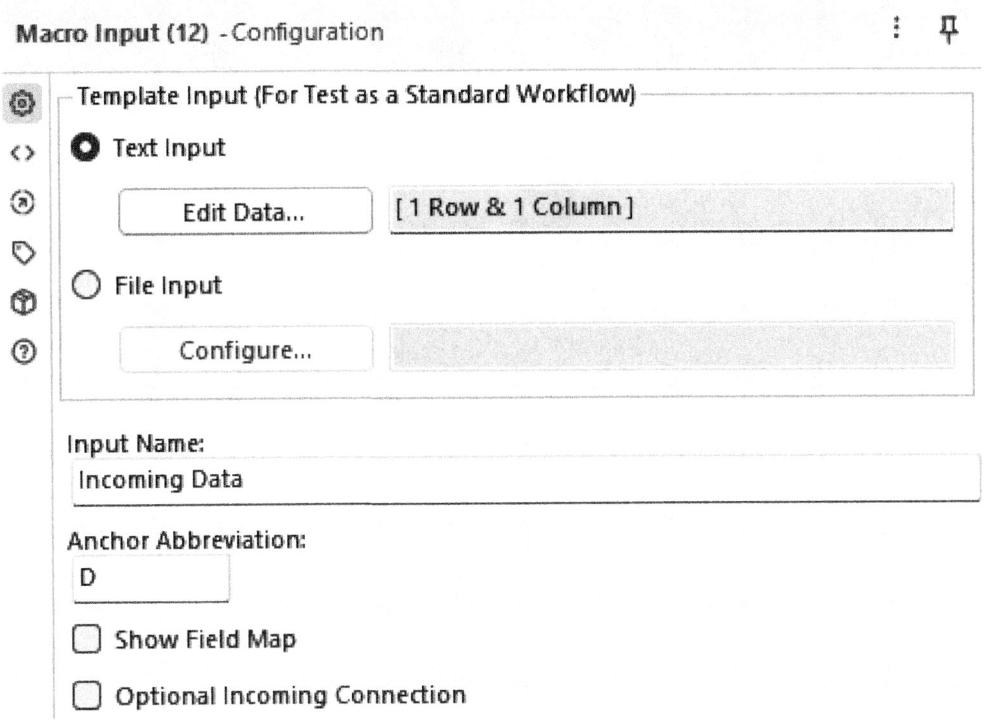

Macro Input (12) - Configuration

Template Input (For Test as a Standard Workflow)

● Text Input

[Edit Data...]   [1 Row & 1 Column]

○ File Input

[Configure...]

Input Name:
Incoming Data

Anchor Abbreviation:
D

☐ Show Field Map

☐ Optional Incoming Connection

Figure 12.4: Macro Input configuration

We have a breakpoint here; let me elaborate a bit on this.

We want this tool to move the existing files from one folder to another so that we can write where the existing files were. To do so, we need to be sure that the moving operation completes before trying to output the records downstream. We can use a **Block Until Done** tool here to ensure that everything works as needed (remember that **Block Until Done** executes sequentially the processes that follow its outputs in order—#1 first, then once output #1 is completed, it executes #2, and so on).

9. Drop a **Block Until Done** tool following the **Macro Input** tool. This step will allow us to create the moving files process following the labeled 1 output and the output of the passed records following the labeled 2 output.

   Also, since we don't know how many records will be passed to the tool, and we only need one record to create the batch file, we'll add a **Sample** tool to the 1 output anchor of the **Block Until Done** tool.

10. Drop a **Sample** tool and connect it to the 1 output anchor:

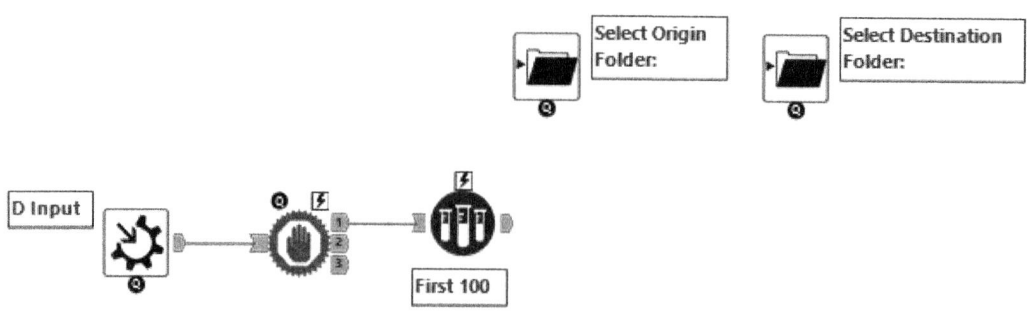

Figure 12.5: Adding a Sample tool

11. Within the **Sample** tool configuration, make sure the **First N rows** option is selected, and change **N** from 100 to 1:

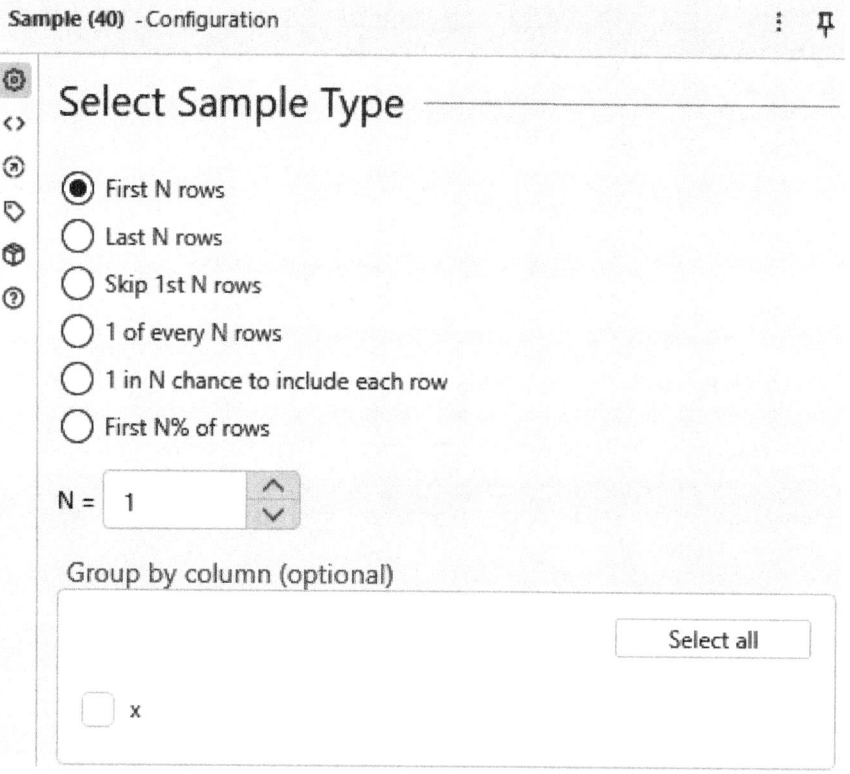

Figure 12.6: Sample tool configuration

12. Drop a **Formula** tool following the **Sample** tool:

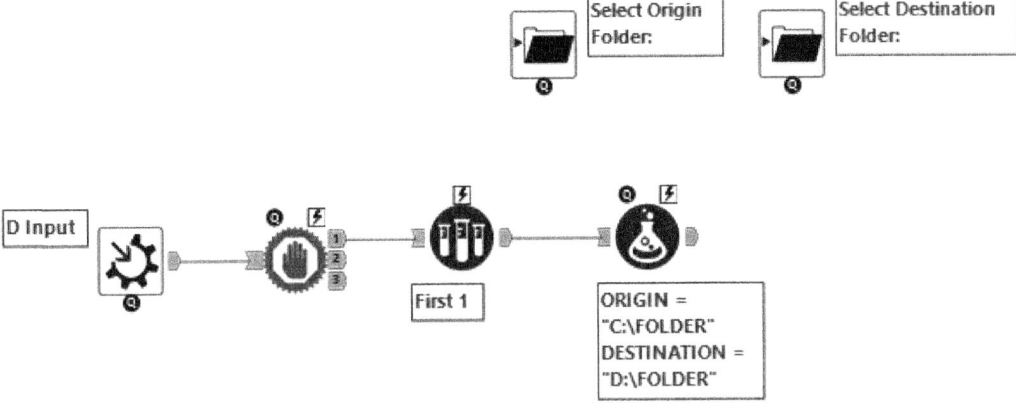

Figure 12.7: Adding a Formula tool

13. Add a new column called `ORIGIN` with a `"C:\FOLDER"` expression.

14. Add a second column called `DESTINATION` with a `"D:\FOLDER"` expression.

    After creating the new fields, the **Formula** tool should look like this:

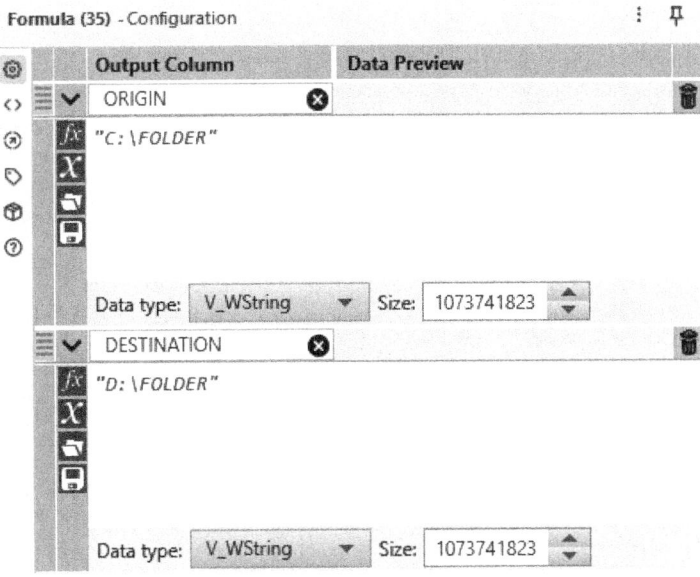

Figure 12.8: Creating new fields for origin and destination

15. Now, click and drag from the black **Q** connector of the first **Folder Browse** tool and connect it to the lightning connector you have on top of the **Formula** tool. An **Action** tool must appear between both tools.

16. Click on it to access its configuration:

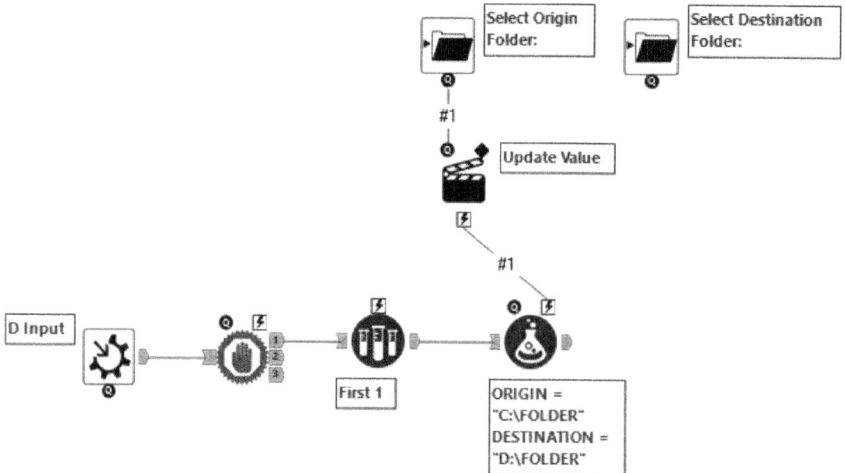

Figure 12.9: Connecting the Interface tool to the Formula tool

17. Make sure that **Update Value** is selected from the **Select an action type** dropdown.

18. Expand the values below the Formula and FormulaFields objects so that you can select a value for ORIGIN.

19. Click on @expression - value=""C:\FOLDER"" below FormulaField[@field='ORIGIN'].

20. Click **Replace a specific string** in the lower part of the **Configuration** panel and remove all the quotes, leaving C:\FOLDER, as shown in the following screenshot:

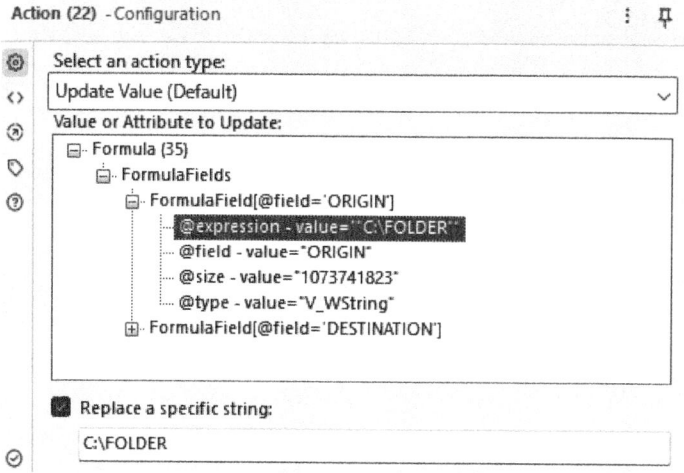

Figure 12.10: Action tool configuration

21. Drag a new connection from the **Q** connector of the other **Folder Browse** tool and drop it to the lightning connector on top of the **Formula** tool. Now, you'll have two connections there:

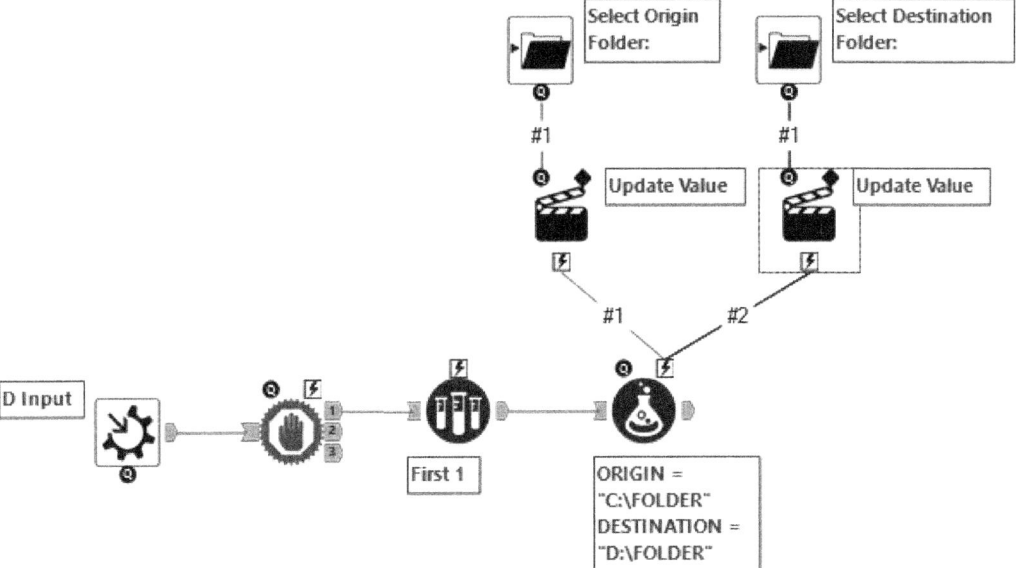

Figure 12.11: Connecting the other Action tool to the Formula tool

For this **Action** tool, we'll repeat the previous steps, but for the DESTINATION field.

22. Make sure that **Update Value** is selected from the **Select an action type** dropdown.

23. Expand the values below the Formula and FormulaFields objects so that you can select a value for DESTINATION.

24. Click on @expression - value=""D:\FOLDER"" below FormulaField[@ field='DESTINATION'].

25. Click **Replace a specific string** in the lower part of the configuration panel and remove all the quotes, leaving D:\FOLDER, as shown in the following screenshot:

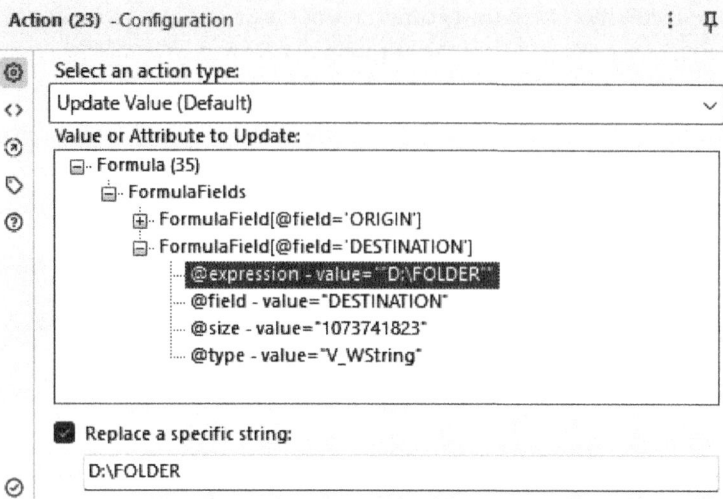

Figure 12.12: Second Action tool configuration

26. Drop another **Formula** tool following the existing **Formula** tool (you can use the same existing one, but I prefer to use another one for maintainability and ease of debugging). We are going to use it to build the batch script (by modifying the one that we wrote and tested outside Alteryx Designer) and make it work with the selected ORIGIN and DESTINATION folders selected by the user:

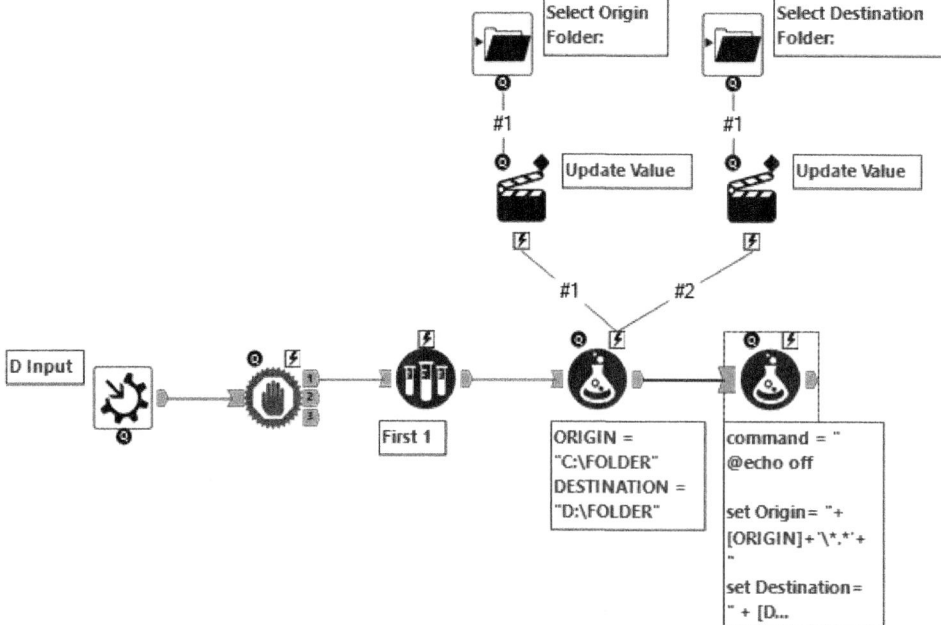

Figure 12.13: Adding a Formula tool to handle a dynamic batch script

27. Select **+ Add Column** and name it command. Paste the following text into the expression editor:

```
"
@echo off
set Origin= "+ [ORIGIN]+'\*.*'+
"
set Destination= " + [DESTINATION] + "\" +
"
if exist %Origin% (
    rem Origin %Origin% exists.
    ) else (
    echo Origin %Origin% doesn't exist.
    rem Since Origin doesn't exist, we error.
    goto Error
    )
rem Checks if Destination exists
if exist %Destination% (
    echo Destination %Destination% exists.
    ) else (
    echo Destination %Destination% doesn't exist. Creating it...
    rem Destination doesn't exist, so we create it
    md %Destination%
    )
if %ERRORLEVEL% EQU 0 (
rem Here we move the files."+
'
move /y "' + [ORIGIN]+'\*.*' + '" "'+ [DESTINATION] + '\"
>"'+[Engine.TempFilePath]+'log.csv"
' +
"
exit
) else (
goto Error)
:Error
    rem Exit with an error state
    echo Error processing batch.
    exit 3
pause"
```

As you can see, we made some modifications to the original script so that it executes with the values grabbed from the user input:

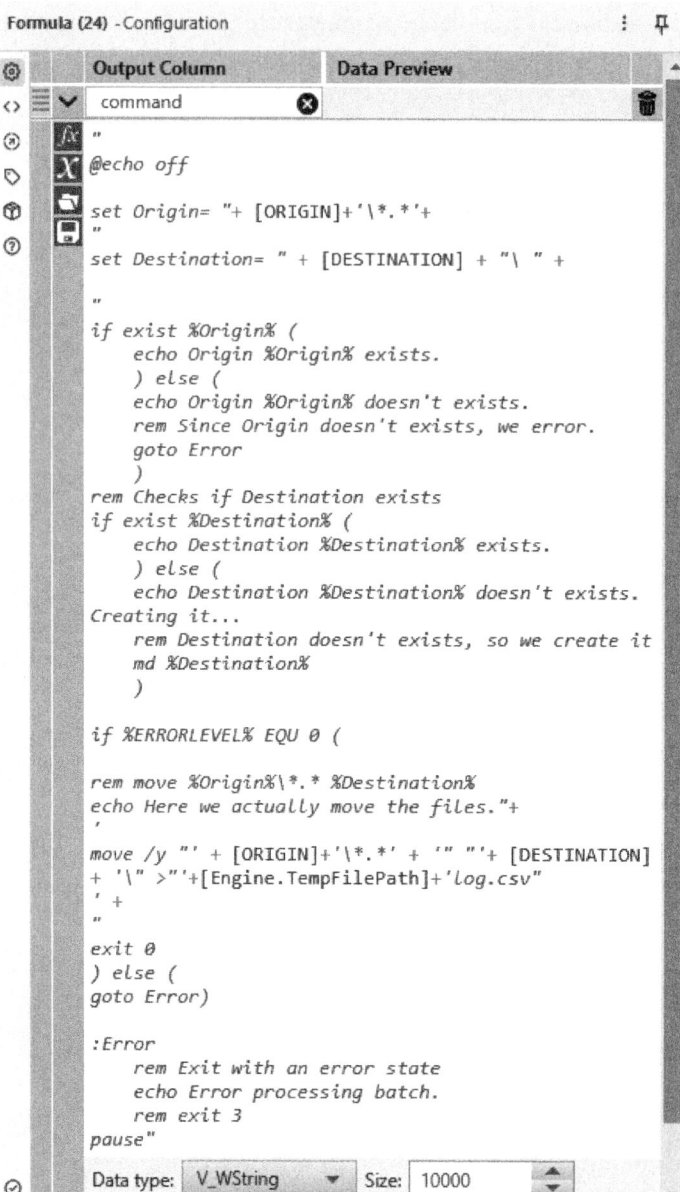

Figure 12.14: Formula tool with the new command field

Notice that we changed the field size too. This is because we are going to save the contents in a format that has size limits.

28. Drop a **Select** tool following the **Formula** tool:

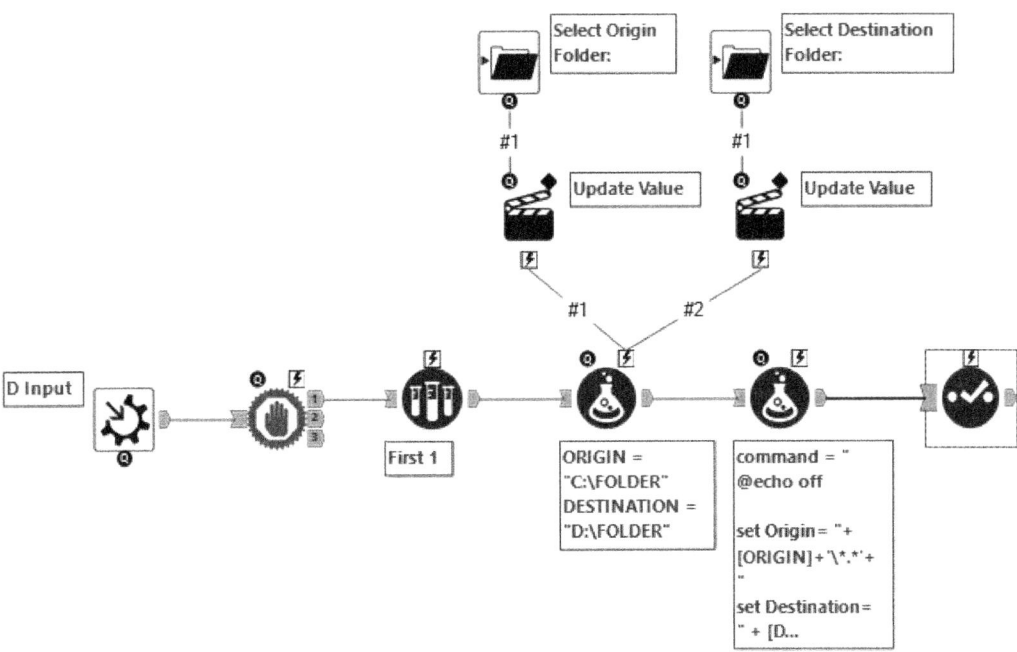

Figure 12.15: Adding a Select tool to the workflow

29. In the **Select** tool configuration, deselect all except the command field:

	Field	Type		Size	Rename	Description
☐	x	Byte	▼	1		
☐	ORIGIN	V_WString	▼	107...		
☐	DESTINATION	V_WString	▼	107...		
☑	command	V_WString	▼	10000		
☐	*Unknown	Unknown	▼	0		Dynamic or ...

Select (25) - Configuration

Options ▼ ↑ ↓   TIP: To reorder multiple rows: select, right-click and dr

Figure 12.16: Select tool configuration

30. Drop a **Run Command** tool following the **Select** tool. Notice that the tool may show an error indicator; just ignore it at this moment:

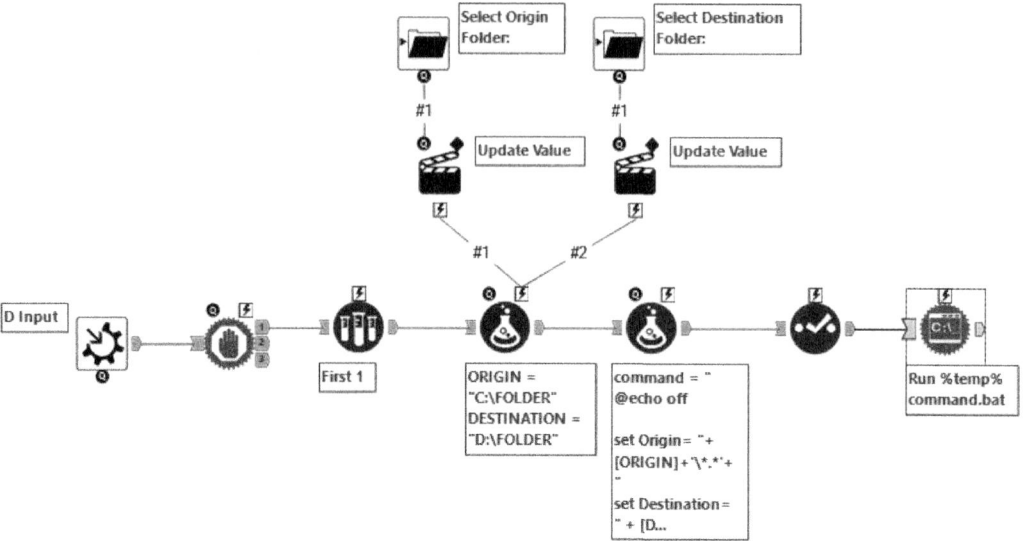

Figure 12.17: Placing the Run Command tool into the workflow

Now, we are going to configure the **Run Command** tool.

31. Click on the **Output…** button so that the **Write to File** window shows up.

32. Use `%temp%command.bat` as the filename (`%temp%` is a special variable that refers to the temp directory used by the workflow).

33. For the **File Format** parameter, select **Flat ASCII (*.flat)**. This will allow us to write a plain text file:

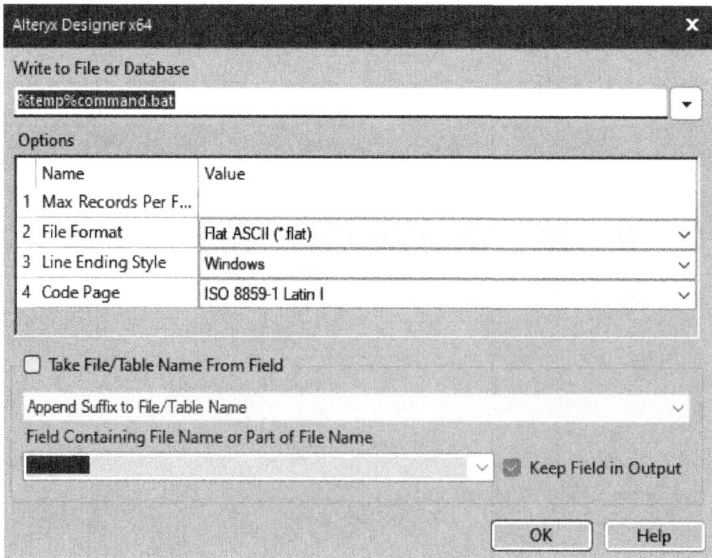

Figure 12.18: Run Command tool write output configuration

This will cause Alteryx Designer to save a file in its `temp` folder that we can run later.

34. In the **Command:** textbox, enter the same `%temp%command.bat` expression we used for the saved file.

35. Also, leave the **Command Arguments** and **Working Directory** fields empty, and **Run Minimized** and **Run Silent** unchecked. (At least for now. I recommend using them once we distribute the macro.)

36. For the last step, click on the **Input...** button and write `%temp%log.csv` for the file to read (and output downstream). Also, use `\0` for the **Delimiters** field and make sure **First Row Contains Field Names** is unchecked:

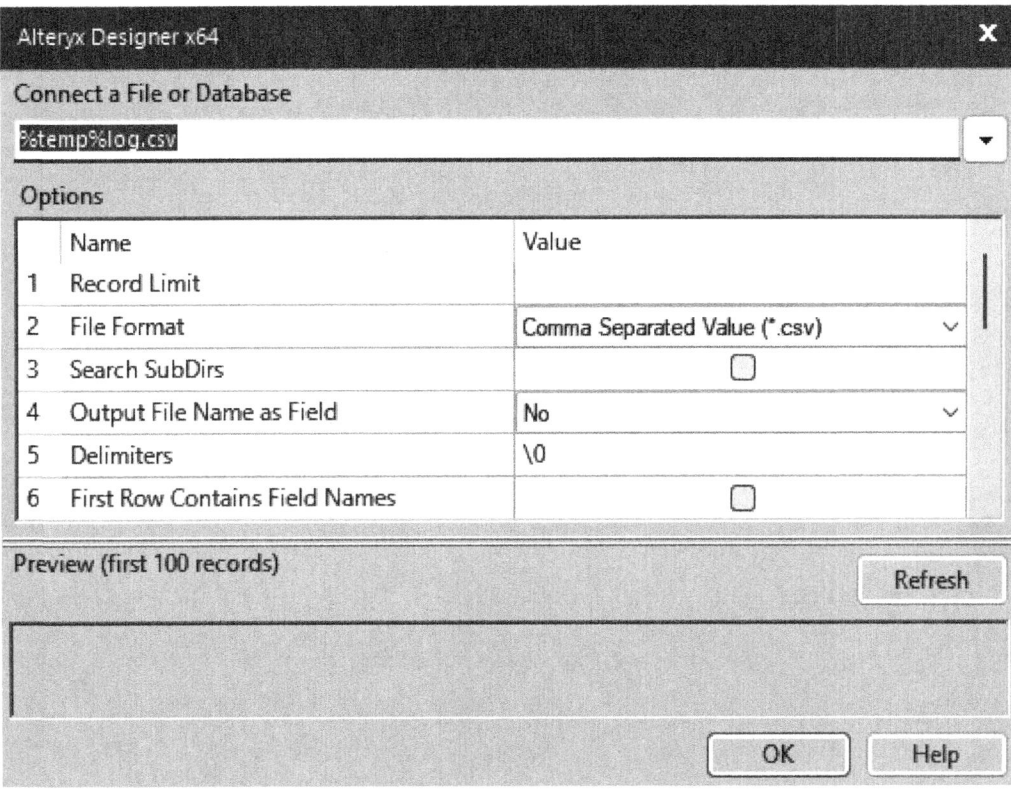

Figure 12.19: Run Command tool read results configuration

The **Run Command** tool configuration should look like this:

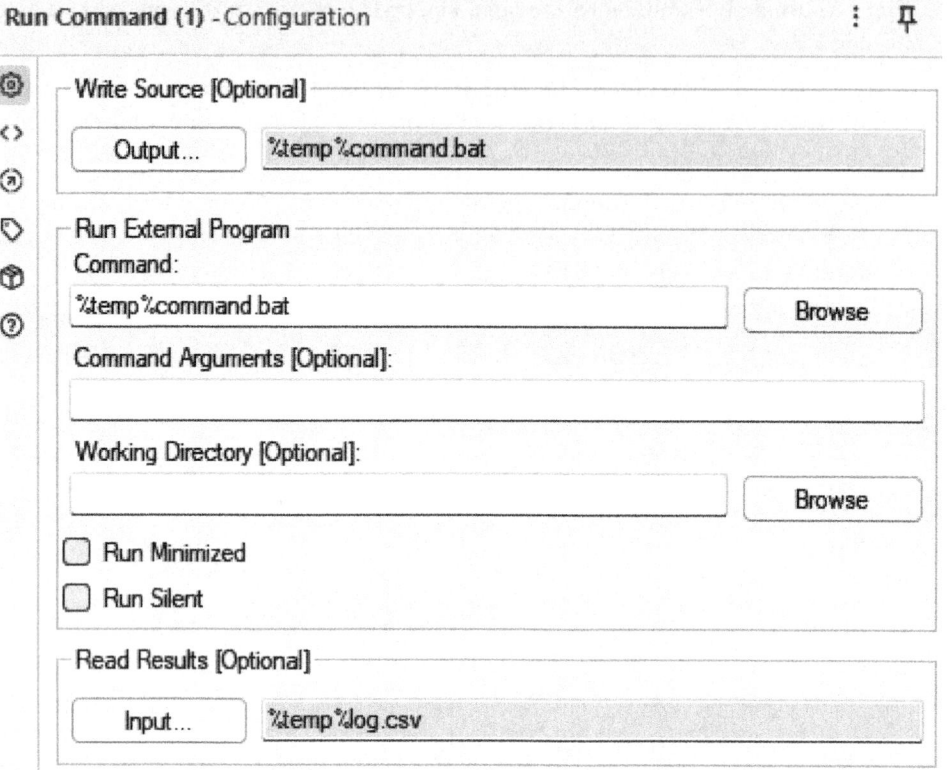

Figure 12.20: Run Command configuration

This referenced log.csv file is created within the script (command field) in this line:

```
move /y "' + [ORIGIN]+'\*.*' + '" "'+ [DESTINATION] + '\"
>"'+[Engine.TempFilePath]+'log.csv"
```

You can see that there is a > character followed by the [Engine.TempFilePath]+log.csv expression. The > character allows you to save the results of the script to a file—in this case, log.csv located in the temp directory. Using it will allow us to create a results dataset based on the batch execution and output it to the user.

But since the log created by the batch execution will be like the following, we first need a little workaround to give the resulting field a name; otherwise, we won't be able to filter the results:

```
C:\FOLDER\SUBFOLDER\fileName1.extension
C:\FOLDER\SUBFOLDER\fileName2.extension
C:\FOLDER\SUBFOLDER\fileName3.extension
        3 file(s) moved.
```

37. Drop a **Text Input** tool onto the canvas, below the **Run Command** tool:

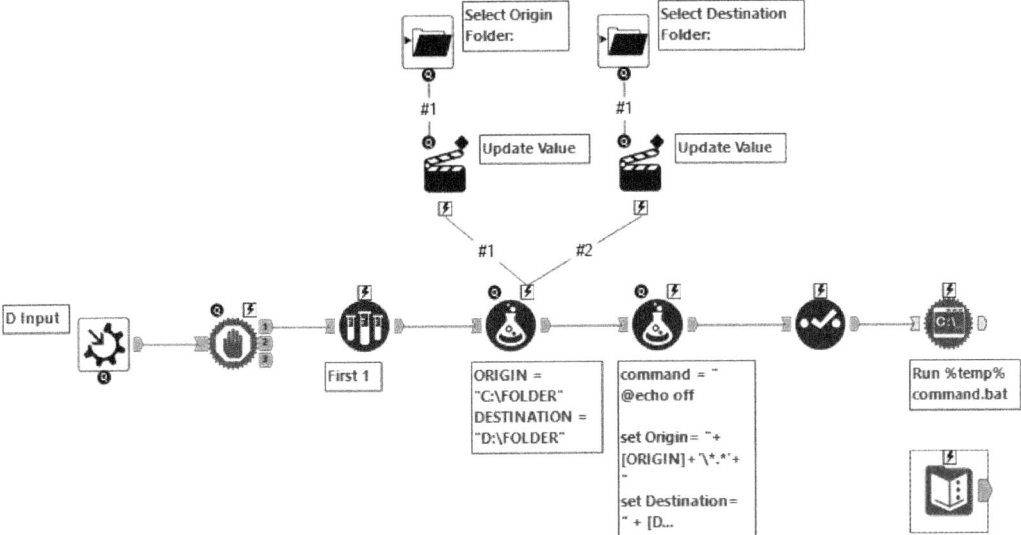

Figure 12.21: Adding a Text Input tool

38. In the **Text Input** tool, create a `Name` column and add a row with a `Results` value:

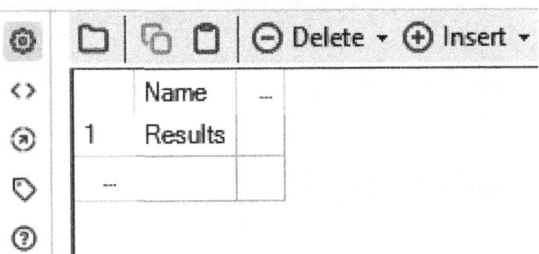

39. Now, drop a **Dynamic Rename** tool and connect the **Run Command** output anchor to the L input and the **Text Input** tool to the R input:

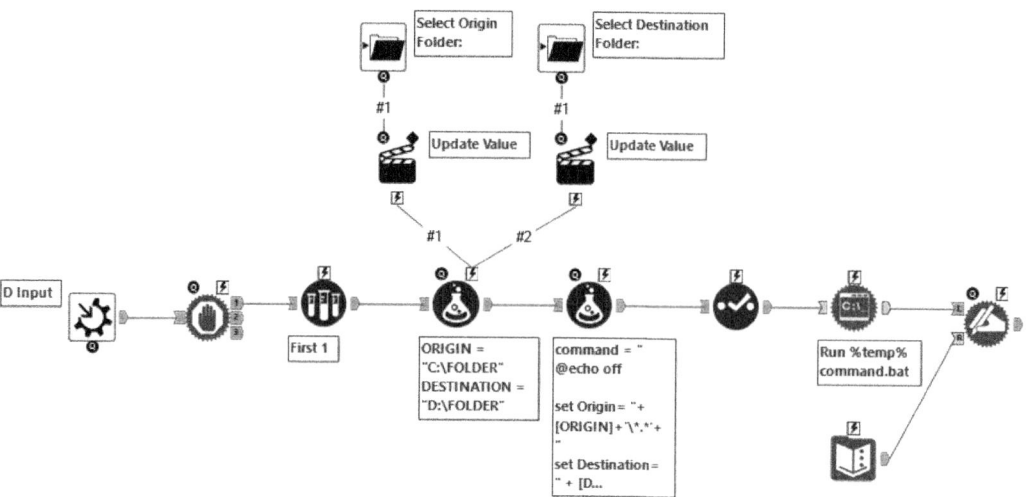

Figure 12.23: Adding and connecting a Dynamic Rename tool

40. Click on the **Dynamic Rename** tool to access its configuration panel.

41. Select **Take Field Names from Right Input Rows** from the **Rename Mode** dropdown.

42. From the **Old Field Name from Column** dropdown, select -Use positional rename-.

43. From the **New Field Name from Column** dropdown, select Name:

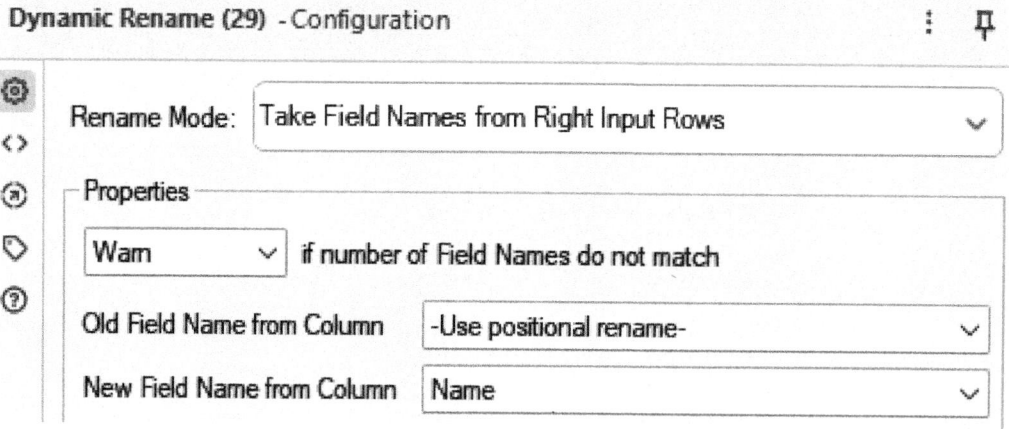

Figure 12.24: Dynamic Rename tool configuration

This will assure us that every time we use or run the workflow, the field returned by the log. csv file will be called Results (as we indicated in the first row of the **Input Data** tool).

44. Add a **Filter** tool after the **Dynamic Rename** tool:

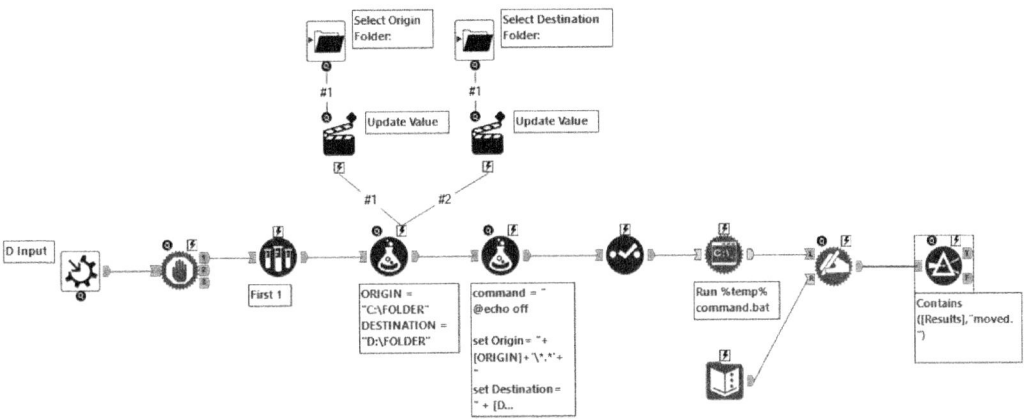

Figure 12.25: Adding a Filter tool

45. Select **Custom filter** and use this expression in the formula editor:

```
Contains([Results],"moved.")
```

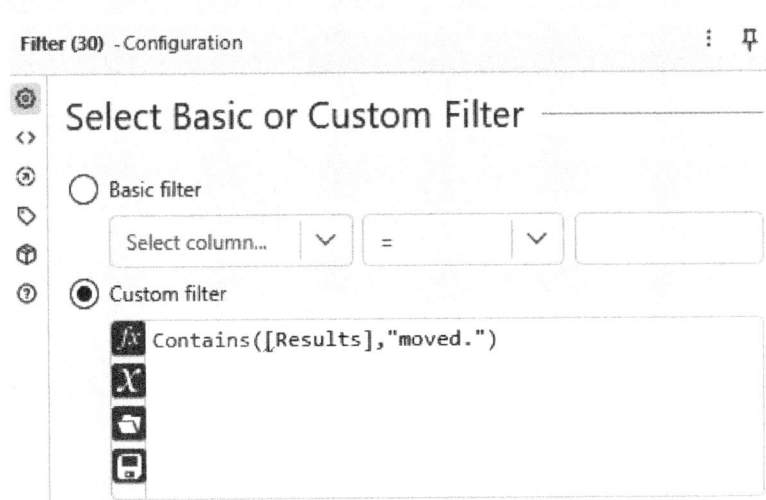

Figure 12.26: Filter tool configuration

This will only output the last record on the log (the one that indicates the number of files affected). If you want to list the files affected and not the number of files, place an exclamation mark before the Contains function:

```
!Contains([Results],"moved.")
```

If you want the whole log, remove the **Filter** tool.

Note that you may also receive an error such as the following:

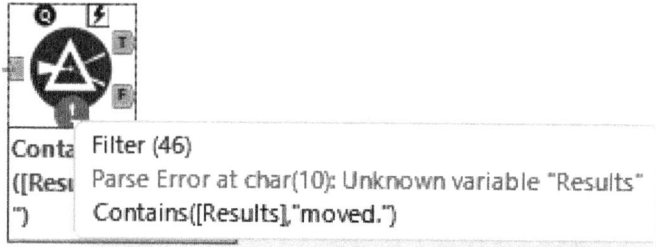

Figure 12.27: Error because the workflow hasn't run yet

This is caused because the workflow still has no metadata loaded yet, and the [Results] field will be created when the workflow runs, so don't pay attention to it right now.

46. Now, to output the log results, drop a **Macro Output** tool following the **Filter** tool (or the **Dynamic Rename** tool if you decided not to filter the results):

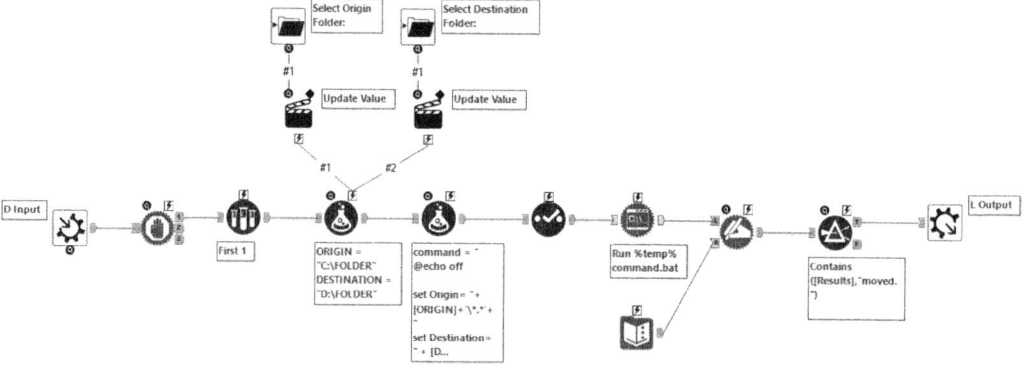

Figure 12.28: Adding a Macro Output tool to output the log

47. Change its name to Batch execution Log and use L as the anchor abbreviation:

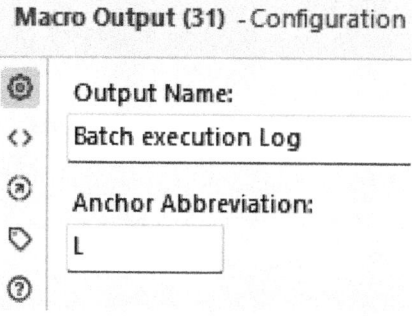

Figure 12.29: Macro Output configuration

Now that we've completed the moving files part of our logic, let's move on to handling the incoming data connected to the tool (the data that we need to process).

48. Drop a **Select** tool onto the canvas, connected to the output labeled 2 on the **Block Until Done** tool:

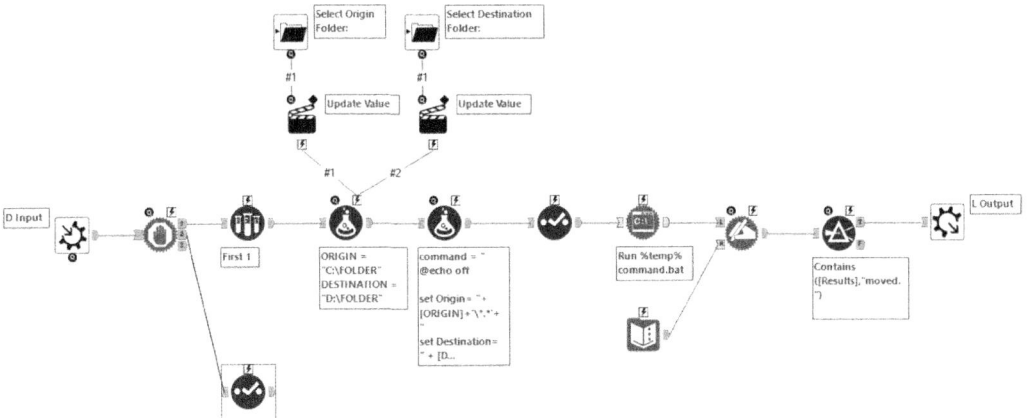

Figure 12.30: Adding a Select tool

49. Within the **Select** tool configuration, deselect everything and leave only the *Unknown field selected:

Select (48) - Configuration   ⋮   📌

Options ▾ | ↑ ↓   TIP: To reorder multiple rows: select, right-click and dr

		Field	Type		Size	Rename	Description
🖉	☐	x	Byte	▾	1		
	☐	ORIGIN	V_WString	▾	107...		
	☐	DESTINATION	V_WString	▾	107...		
	☐	command	V_WString	▾	10000		
	☑	*Unknown	Unknown	▾	0		Dynamic or ...

Figure 12.31: Select tool configuration

You may see an error such as this one:

Figure 12.32: Error until the workflow runs

Leave it for now, because when the workflow runs, the *Unknown fields will be replaced by the fields of the incoming data.

50. Once done, drop another **Macro Output** tool following the **Select** tool:

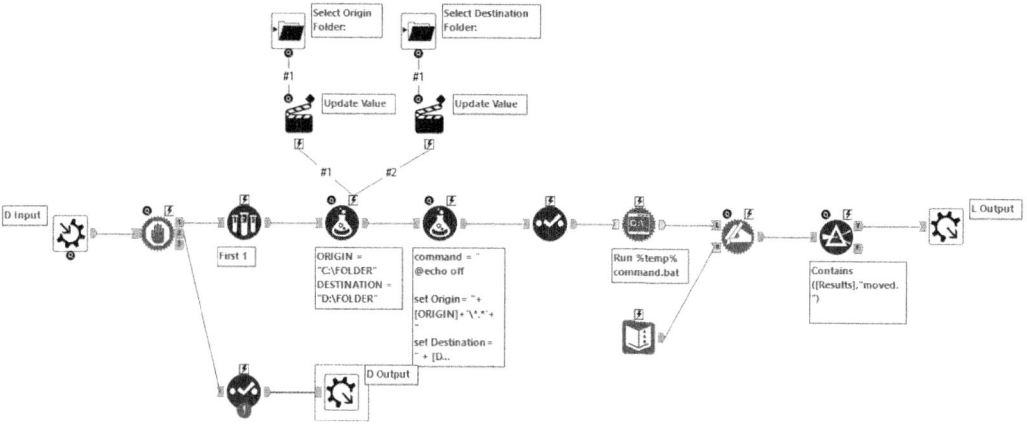

Figure 12.33: Adding a second Macro Output tool to output the data

51. Change the **Output Name** value to Outgoing Data and the **Anchor Abbreviation** value to D:

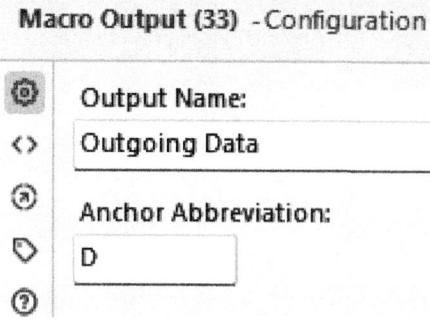

Figure 12.34: Macro Output configuration

Now, save your macro into your macro repository (remember that if you want this tool to be available to others, you need to save it within a shared repository; otherwise it'll only be available to you).

In this case, name the macro `MoveFiles` (make sure the extension is `.yxmc`) when prompted.

Keep the macro opened so that it'll be easy to insert it later.

Now, we'll use and see our new tool in action.

52. Create a new workflow.

53. Drop an **Input Data** tool onto the canvas and connect it to your desired dataset (we'll use `..\DATA\Customers.csv`).

54. Right-click on any blank part of the canvas, select **Insert | Macro**, and click on the **MoveFiles** macro to insert it:

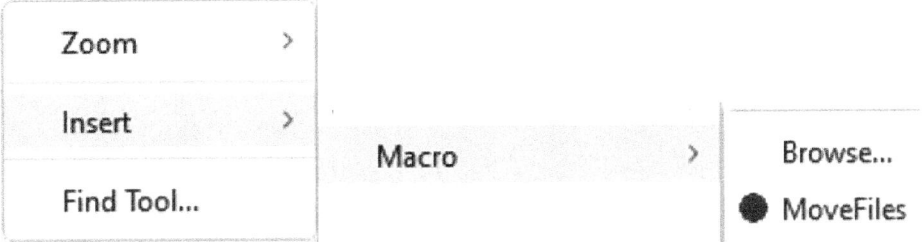

Figure 12.35: Right-click menu for inserting macros onto the canvas

55. Make sure you select a non-empty folder as the origin folder and select the destination folder you want to use to move the existing files:

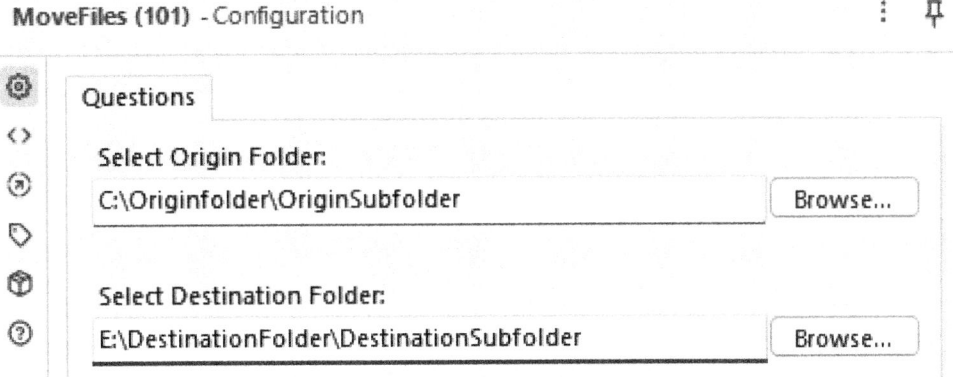

Figure 12.36: Configuring the macro

56. Add a **Browse** tool to the L output of the new tool.

57. Drop an **Output Data** tool and connect it to the D output anchor of the macro:

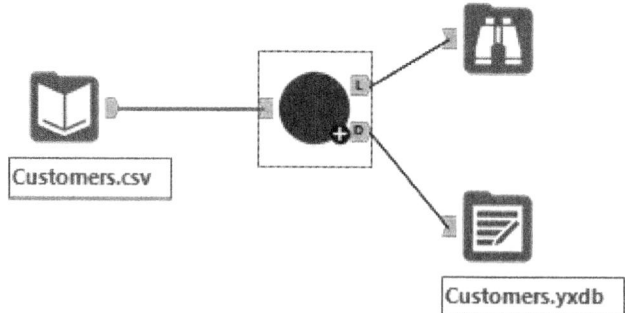

Figure 12.37: Final workflow

Run the workflow, and you'll see that all contents from the origin folder were moved to the destination, and the new file was written:

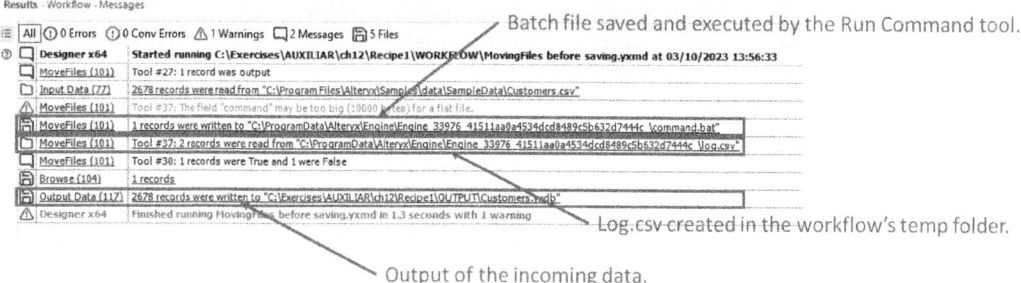

Figure 12.38: Results pane after running the workflow

How it works...

The **Run Command** tool executes a series of sequential tasks on every run:

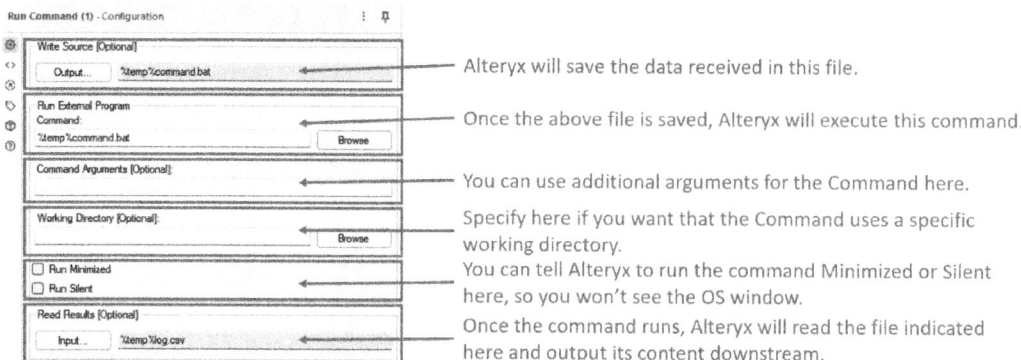

Figure 12.39: Run Command tool options

We created a working script outside Alteryx and then adjusted it to work with the necessary replacements to match the user's input gathered from the **Interface** tools (**Folder Browse** tools, in this case).

There's more...

This same mechanism can be used from the **Events** options of a workflow:

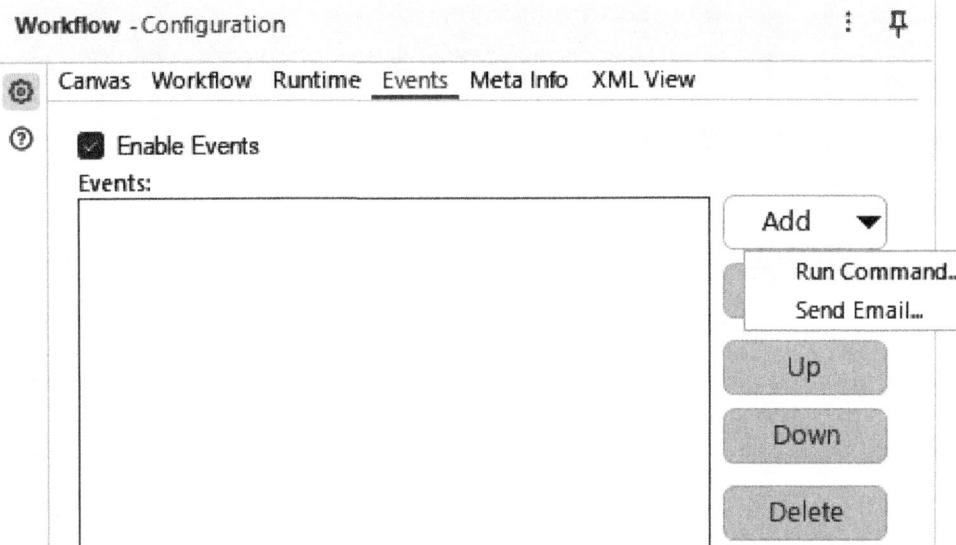

Figure 12.40: Events pane in the Workflow options pane

This option will allow you to select when to run the external command, as follows:

- **Before Run**: Will always execute the shell before running the workflow.

- **After Run**: Once the workflow runs, the command will be executed.

- **After Run With Errors**: If the workflow errors, the selected command will be executed. Very useful when you have external programs that may fix the causes that make the workflow error.

- **After Run Without Errors**: The selected command will run after the workflow execution ends without errors. Very useful when you need the assets produced by the workflow to execute an external application.

- **Disabled**: The command execution is disabled and will never run. When we use external applications to debug a workflow, using this option allows us to disable the debugger when in production, without losing the command configuration in case we need it later:

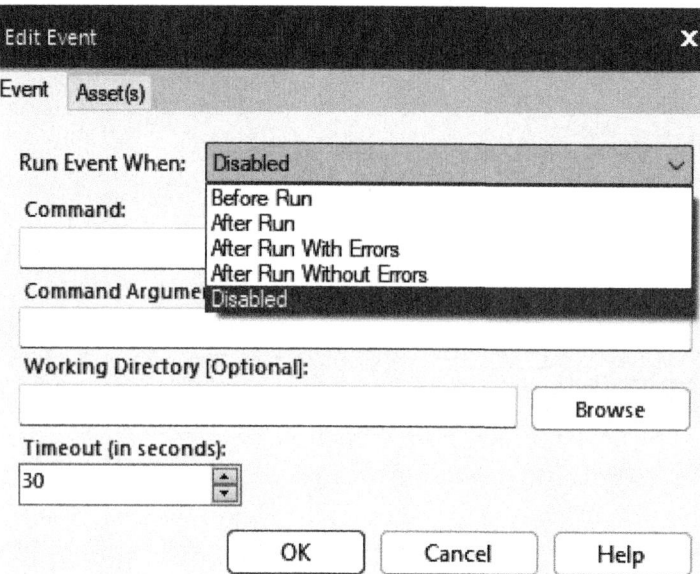

Figure 12.41: Event options

If we want to disable any **Event** execution, we can uncheck the **Enable Events** option at the top of the panel:

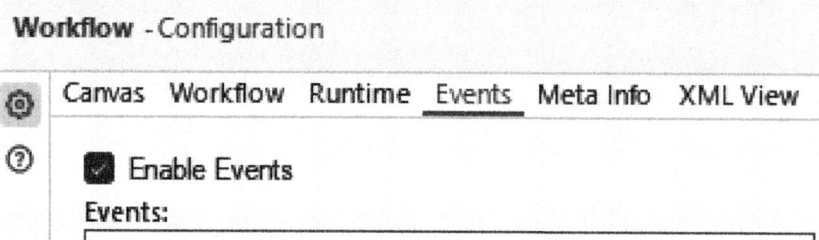

Figure 12.42: Enable Events option

See also

Using the same logic process, we can zip the files and create a zipped backup:

1. Make sure you have **7-Zip** installed and accessible.

2. Replace the following line with the move command:

```
move /y "' + [ORIGIN]+'\*.*' + '" "'+ [DESTINATION] + '\"
>"'+[Engine.TempFilePath]+'log.csv"
```

3. Change it to this:

```
7z a "' + [DESTINATION] + '\backup_'+ToString(DateTimeFormat(Dat
eTimeStart(),"%Y-%m-%d_%H-%M-%S"))+'.zip" "' +[ORIGIN]+'\*.*' +
'" '+ ' >"'+[Engine.TempFilePath]+'log.csv"
```

Also, by changing the filter expression that evaluates `Contains([Results],"moved.")` for `Contains([Results],"Add new data to archive: ")`, you'll get a resulting log of the processed files.

Basic Python usage – performing optical character recognition (OCR) from images

More often than I'd like, I run into situations where users require some special kind of functionality that can only be achieved through some kind of programming.

Python has become the most popular programming language in recent times, and there are endless resources on the web, not only to learn it but also ready-to-use solutions. Working with Python in an Alteryx workflow is very easy using the **Python** tool that Alteryx provides. This tool creates a new instance of a Jupyter notebook so that we can program inside it.

A common use case I found is that some data must be read from images. In this recipe, we are going to see how we can easily make Python scripts work within Alteryx, starting from an existing one that we found on the web.

Getting ready

We have a test set with all the assets we'll use throughout this recipe here: `https://github.com/PacktPublishing/Alteryx-Designer-Cookbook/tree/main/ch12/Recipe2`.

The use case, as mentioned, is to acquire text from images, so my first step (as I'm not a programmer) is to get into a web search for something useful to use.

Searching the web for `python + images to text`, I found this article: `https://towardsdatascience.com/extract-text-from-image-using-python-8e8cfbbce743`.

In it, you can see that there is an explanation and a script that may solve our text extraction problem.

As listed in the article, we need a couple of things in place before starting.

First and foremost is the **Tesseract** engine, an open source text recognition (OCR) engine, available under the Apache 2.0 license.

You can download it from the University of Mannheim's GitHub page: `https://github.com/UB-Mannheim/tesseract/wiki`.

If you decide to install **Tesseract** in a different path than the default, take note of that path because we'll need it later.

Once you have the engine installed, there are two Python packages we need to make this script work:

- `pytesseract`
- `pillow`

We'll install them from within Alteryx Designer.

> **Important note**
>
> When working with Python and needing to install packages, you must have administrator privileges to the computer and execute Alteryx Designer as an administrator (**Running Elevated**).
>
> To check whether Alteryx Designer is running in administrator mode, you can click on **Help** | **About** and check the **About** windows that pop up for the mode Alteryx is using to run.

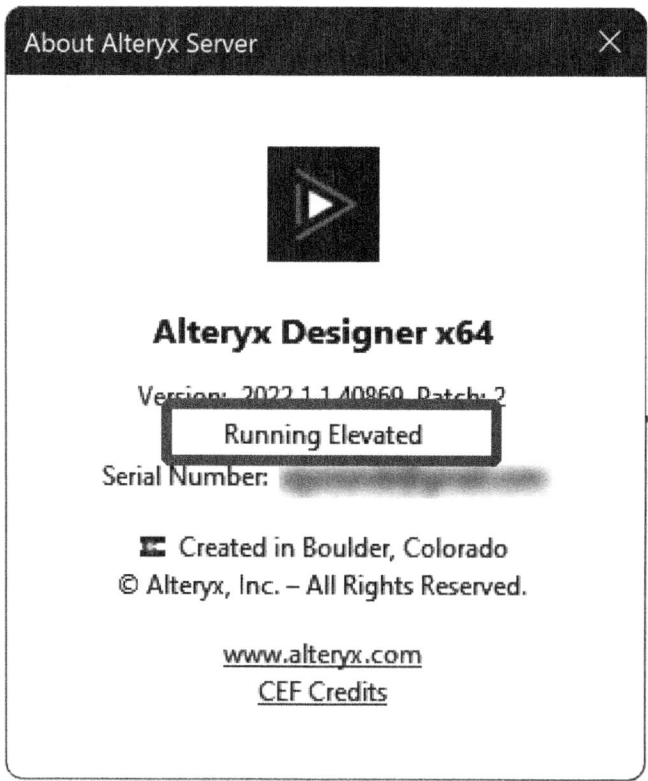

Figure 12.43: About Alteryx window

How to do it...

Somewhere close to the middle of the article, you'll find that the author provided the code to extract text from an image:

Now we have everything we need and can easily extract text from image using Python:

```
1    from PIL import Image
2    from pytesseract import pytesseract
3
4    #Define path to tessaract.exe
5    path_to_tesseract = r'C:\Program Files\Tesseract-OCR\tesseract.exe'
6
7    #Define path to image
8    path_to_image = 'images/sampletext1-ocr.png'
9
10   #Point tessaract_cmd to tessaract.exe
11   pytesseract.tesseract_cmd = path_to_tesseract
12
13   #Open image with PIL
14   img = Image.open(path_to_image)
15
16   #Extract text from image
17   text = pytesseract.image_to_string(img)
18
19   print(text)
```

textfromimage1.py hosted with 💜 by GitHub   view raw

Figure 12.44: Code in the web article

1. Select the code and copy and paste it into a text editor for later use.
2. Create a new workflow and drop a **Python** tool onto the canvas.
3. Paste the code you copied below the line that reads `from ayx import Alteryx`:

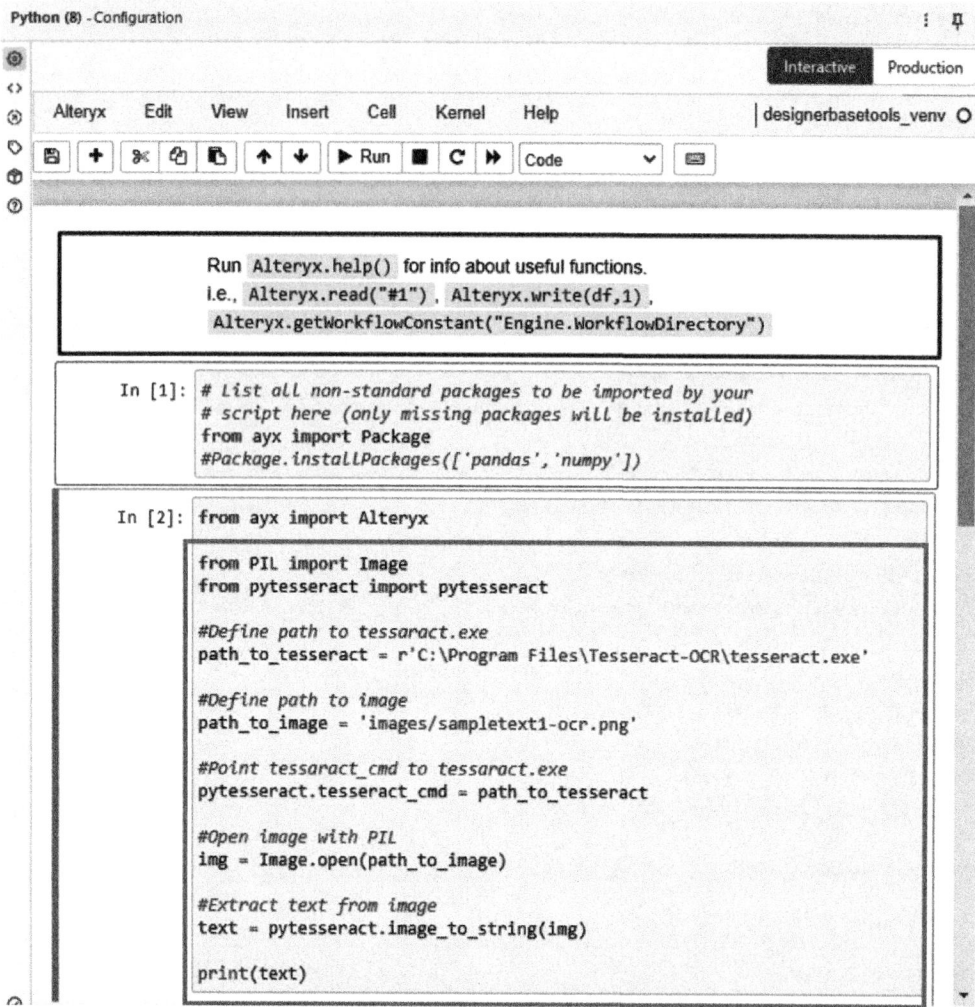

Figure 12.45: Code pasted into the Python tool notebook

Now, we need to make some adjustments to the script so that we can run it within Alteryx and test it.

The first two lines of code tell Python to import some libraries:

```
from PIL import Image
from pytesseract import pytesseract
```

These libraries are not part of the standard libraries installed with Alteryx, so we need to install them ourselves.

If you pay attention to the first cell within the notebook, you'll see there is a commented line at the end that says the following:

```
#Package.installPackages(['pandas','numpy'])
```

This line refers to a method that Alteryx Designer offers to install additional packages into the virtual environment it uses to run the scripts.

In our case, we'll modify this line to install the required packages mentioned in the article we are using as a reference:

- `pytesseract`

- `pillow`

4. Modify the mentioned line so that it reads as follows:

```
Package.installPackages(['pytesseract','pillow'])
```

Once you've done that, you have two options to install the packages. One is to run the workflow as we always do, or you can run the single code cell containing the command you want to execute.

Since the script is not ready yet, I'd recommend using the second method.

5. Save the code we have so far by clicking the **Save** icon on the toolbar of the Jupyter notebook:

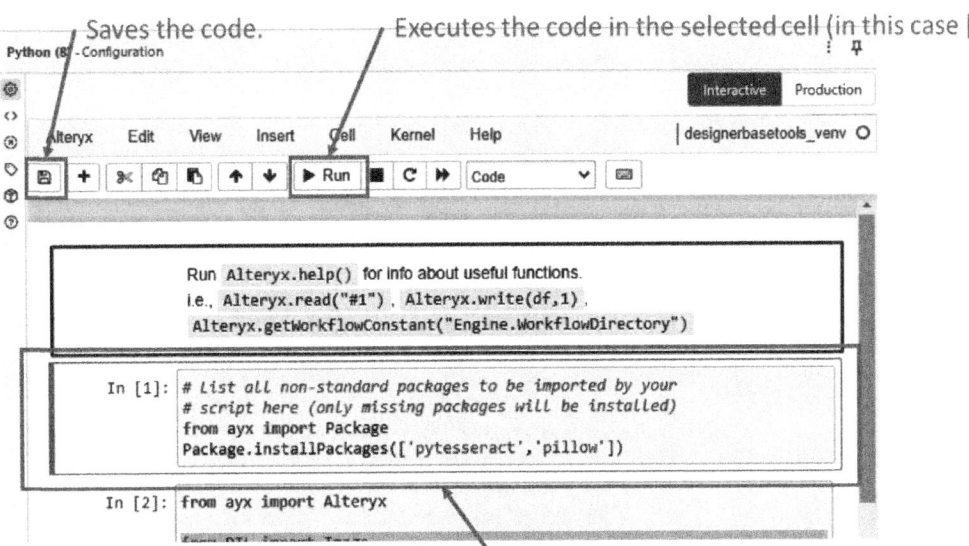

Figure 12.46: Python notebook options

6. Click the **Run** button.

Once you run the selected cell, you'll see some messages indicating the status of the code execution. In this case, `pytesseract` was installed, and since the `pillow` package was already installed, you'll get a `Requirement already satisfied` message:

```
In [1]: # List all non-standard packages to be imported by your
        # script here (only missing packages will be installed)
        from ayx import Package
        Package.installPackages(['pytesseract','pillow'])
```

```
Collecting pytesseract
  Using cached pytesseract-0.3.10-py3-none-any.whl (14 kB)
Requirement already satisfied: pillow in c:\program files\alteryx\bin\m
iniconda3\envs\designerbasetools_venv\lib\site-packages (8.4.0)
Requirement already satisfied: packaging>=21.3 in c:\program files\alte
ryx\bin\miniconda3\envs\designerbasetools_venv\lib\site-packages (from
pytesseract) (21.3)
Requirement already satisfied: pyparsing!=3.0.5,>=2.0.2 in c:\program f
iles\alteryx\bin\miniconda3\envs\designerbasetools_venv\lib\site-packag
es (from packaging>=21.3->pytesseract) (2.4.0)
Installing collected packages: pytesseract
  WARNING: The script pytesseract.exe is installed in 'c:\program files
\alteryx\bin\miniconda3\envs\designerbasetools_venv\Scripts' which is n
ot on PATH.
  Consider adding this directory to PATH or, if you prefer to suppress
this warning, use --no-warn-script-location.
Successfully installed pytesseract-0.3.10
```

Figure 12.47: Results of running the cell [1]

Once you've installed the required packages, you can comment this line of code by adding a # character in front of it.

Now, let's move to the code itself.

Even though the code provided by the author is well commented and explains every line, I'll try to explain a little more about each line:

- The first three lines of code tell the Python interpreter to import and make available the required libraries for the code to work:

```
In [2]: from ayx import Alteryx

        from PIL import Image
        from pytesseract import pytesseract
```

Figure 12.48: Importing the libraries

- The following line creates a variable called `path_to_tesseract` with a `C:\Program files\Tesseract-OCR\tesseract.exe` value and tells the Python interpreter to treat that value as a raw (literal) string by adding `r` in front of it (the backslash character is used to escape characters in Python).

If you decided to install **Tesseract** in a path different from the default, you'll need to replace this value with the path you chose to install it:

```
#Define path to tessaract.exe
path_to_tesseract = r'C:\Program Files\Tesseract-OCR\tesseract.exe'
```

Figure 12.49: Defining a path for the engine

- The next line creates another variable called `path_to_image` with an `images/sampletext1-ocr.png` value. Note that it uses forward slashes, so it doesn't need to have `r` in front. Forward slashes are the way that Python handles paths, and a lot of debugging is caused by not using them and taking backslashes directly as Windows uses them:

```
#Define path to image
path_to_image = 'images/sampletext1-ocr.png'
```

Figure 12.50: Defining a path for the picture

- The next line assigns the path we entered to `pytesseract_tesseract_cmd` so that the library can use it:

```
#Point tessaract_cmd to tessaract.exe
pytesseract.tesseract_cmd = path_to_tesseract
```

Figure 12.51: Binding the path value to the engine

- The next line declares an object called `img` that contains the result of opening an image—in this case, the image contained in the `path_to_image` variable:

```
#Open image with PIL
img = Image.open(path_to_image)
```

Figure 12.52: Using the .open method to open a picture

- In the next line, the `img` object is passed to the `image_to_string` function of the `pytesseract` library and saved in an object called `text`:

```
#Extract text from image
text = pytesseract.image_to_string(img)
```

Figure 12.53: Calling the engine to perform text recognition

- Finally, the contents of text are output via a print statement:

```
print(text)
```

Figure 12.54: Printing the resulting text

Now that we know what every line does, let's make the changes to make them work for our use case.

7. Make sure path_to_tesseract points to where you installed **Tesseract** (in our case, we installed it in the default directory) so that it reads C:\Program Files\Tesseract-OCR\tesseract.exe.

8. Change the value for path_to_image so that it reads as follows:

```
path_to_image = Alteryx.getWorkflowConstant("Engine.
WorkflowDirectory")+r'..\DATA\Sample-4.jpg'
```

9. Click on the **Save** icon in the code editor.

Here, we are using a method provided by Alteryx Designer to access workflow constants within Python, and since they return with Windows backslashes, we adapted the remaining part of the path accordingly.

Finally, we need to change the way our script outputs the result because we want the text extracted from the images to pass downstream via an output connector, and the print() command will show us the text in the **Results** pane, like this:

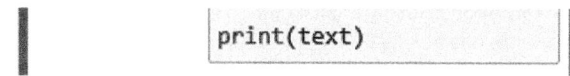

Results - Python (8) - Messages

All	① 0 Errors	① 0 Conv Errors	⚠ 0 Warnings	▭ 41 Messages	🖬 0 Files
Python (8)	C:\Exercises\AUXILIAR\ch12\Recipe2\WORKFLOW\..\DATA\Sample-4.jpg
Python (8)	5. Images to Text
Python (8)	
Python (8)	Convert your Images or scanned photos to Text by using this fabulous
Python (8)	automation script. This script uses the Pytesseract module which is an AI
Python (8)	algorithm that can extract the text from images. Pillow on the other hand
Python (8)	will help you to optimize and enhance your Photos before Pytesseract does
Python (8)	its job.
Python (8)	
Python (8)	Extracting from OCR Images
Python (8)	

Figure 12.55: Results of the print(text) command in the Results pane

The Alteryx package provides an `Alteryx.write()` method to accomplish what we need, but it is very important to know that Alteryx only allows you to output a DataFrame via this method, so we need to convert the OCR resulting text into a DataFrame. A DataFrame is a particular data structure provided by the `pandas` Python library.

So, to be able to create a DataFrame, we need to import the `pandas` library, which is already installed in Alteryx.

10. Comment the `print(text)` command by adding a # character in front of it, and add the three lines of code below it, to finish our script:

```
#print(text)
import pandas as pd
results=pd.DataFrame(text.split('\n'))
Alteryx.write(results,1)
```

Also, notice that we use the `split('\n')` method on the obtained text to break it on a newline character (`'\n'`).

The final script should look like this:

```
from ayx import Alteryx
from PIL import Image
from pytesseract import pytesseract
#Define path to tessaract.exe
path_to_tesseract = r'C:\Program Files\Tesseract-OCR\tesseract.exe'
#Define path to image
#path_to_image = 'images/sampletext1-ocr.png'
path_to_image = Alteryx.getWorkflowConstant("Engine.WorkflowDirectory")+r'..\DATA\Sample-4.jpg'
print(path_to_image)
#Point tessaract_cmd to tessaract.exe
pytesseract.tesseract_cmd = path_to_tesseract
#Open image with PIL
img = Image.open(path_to_image)
#Extract text from image
text = pytesseract.image_to_string(img)
#print(text)
import pandas as pd
results=pd.DataFrame(text.split('\n'))
Alteryx.write(results,1)
```

11. Save the code in the editor (by clicking on the **Save** icon) and run the workflow.

You'll notice that the #1 output anchor of the **Python** tool outputs the text extracted from the image:

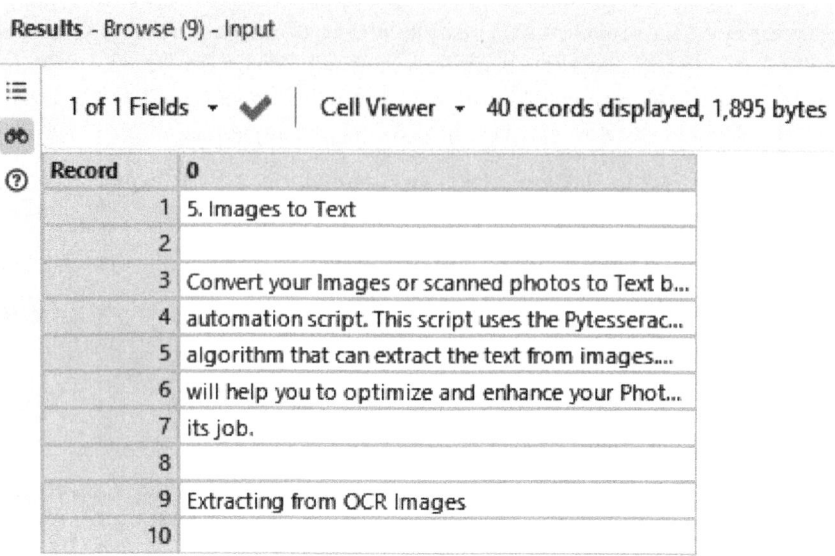

Figure 12.56: Workflow results after outputting the text through an output anchor

How it works...

Alteryx Designer has a very deep integration with Python, allowing even people who are not developers to take advantage of this programming language's benefits and making the possibilities of a workflow almost endless.

The idea behind this recipe is, of course, not to teach you Python (you will find some very good books on this subject online but to help you leverage your workflows, even when you don't know much about Python, by taking existing scripts and making them work within your workflow.

Using binary large objects (blobs) to read and write raw/binary fields

Sometimes, we find it necessary to work with binary data (for example, when our records have raw data such as attachments, images, and so on).

To achieve this, Alteryx provides us with a series of tools to manage blobs, which allow us to read binary files (in this case, images) as raw type fields in databases and/or save them exactly as we read them in a field.

In our previous recipe, we took a Python script from the web and made it work on Alteryx, giving our workflow functionality we wouldn't have had otherwise.

In this recipe, we are going to use an improved version of that script, and we are going to feed it with images saved in binary format.

Getting ready

We prepared a test set that you can download from here: `https://github.com/PacktPublishing/Alteryx-Designer-Cookbook/tree/main/ch12/Recipe3`.

As mentioned before, we tweaked our Python script to work by receiving the binary content from an Alteryx **Blob** tool, instead of reading the files directly from the disk. The resulting script looks like this:

```python
from ayx import Alteryx
import pandas as pd
from PIL import Image
from pytesseract import pytesseract
import io
#Define path to tessaract.exe
path_to_tesseract = r'C:\Program Files\Tesseract-OCR\tesseract.exe'
#Point tessaract_cmd to tessaract.exe
pytesseract.tesseract_cmd = path_to_tesseract
# Define the function so we can call it with each received image.
def do_ocr(row):
    img=Image.open(io.BytesIO(row['Blob']))
    file_name=row['FileName']
    text = pytesseract.image_to_string(img)
    return text
# Read from Alteryx connection
data=Alteryx.read("#1")
# Add a field to the received data, with the results from the OCR
data['Text']=data.apply(lambda row:do_ocr(row),axis=1)
#Ouput the data + the OCR results
Alteryx.write(data,1)
```

How to do it...

Let's start by going over the modifications we made to our script:

```python
from ayx import Alteryx
import pandas as pd
from PIL import Image
from pytesseract import pytesseract
import io
```

Figure 12.57: Importing the libraries

1. The first lines import all the libraries we'll use. As you can see, we added one (`io`). This library will help us with reading and interpreting the binary data we receive:

```
#Define path to tessaract.exe
path_to_tesseract = r'C:\Program Files\Tesseract-OCR\tesseract.exe'

#Point tessaract_cmd to tessaract.exe
pytesseract.tesseract_cmd = path_to_tesseract
```

Figure 12.58: Defining and binding the engine location

2. We are going to use the same library (tesseract) we used before to perform the OCR, so we need to tell the script where to find it, and that's what these lines of code do:

```
# Define the function so we can call it with each received image.
def do_ocr(row):
    img=Image.open(io.BytesIO(row['Blob']))
    file_name=row['FileName']
    text = pytesseract.image_to_string(img)
    return text
```

Figure 12.59: New function defined to handle the process

3. The basic functionality of reading an image and performing OCR has been moved to a function (do_ocr()). This function receives the data that arrives through the Alteryx connector (#1) as a parameter. It is responsible for opening the image (binary data (blob)), and with that data, it performs OCR and saves the result in a variable called text. Then, the function returns the text extracted from the image:

```
# Read from Alteryx connection
data=Alteryx.read("#1")
```

Figure 12.60: Reading the data that comes from the previous tool in the workflow

4. Next, we read the data arriving from the previous tool in the stream and save it in a DataFrame called data:

```
# Add a field to the received data, with the results from the OCR
data['Text']=data.apply(lambda row:do_ocr(row),axis=1)
```

Figure 12.61: Creating a new column on the DataFrame and filling it with the function's results

The preceding line of code adds a new column, called Text, to the DataFrame that we previously read and assigns the result returned by the do_ocr() function as its value, calling the function with the entire row of data received (row).

5. The last line outputs the results through the #1 output connector of the Python tool:

```
#Ouput the data + the OCR results
Alteryx.write(data,1)
```

Figure 12.62: Writing the results through the #1 output anchor

Now that we understand what the script does, let's put it to wor:.

1. On a new workflow, drop a **Directory** tool and point it to ..\DATA:

Figure 12.63: Adding a Directory tool

If you have different types of files in that folder, you can specify which one you want to read by changing the value of the **File Specification** wildcards (such as *.jpg, *.png, and so on). I'll leave it as *.* because I only have the files I want to process within that folder (I recommend you always configure your Alteryx solutions this way too):

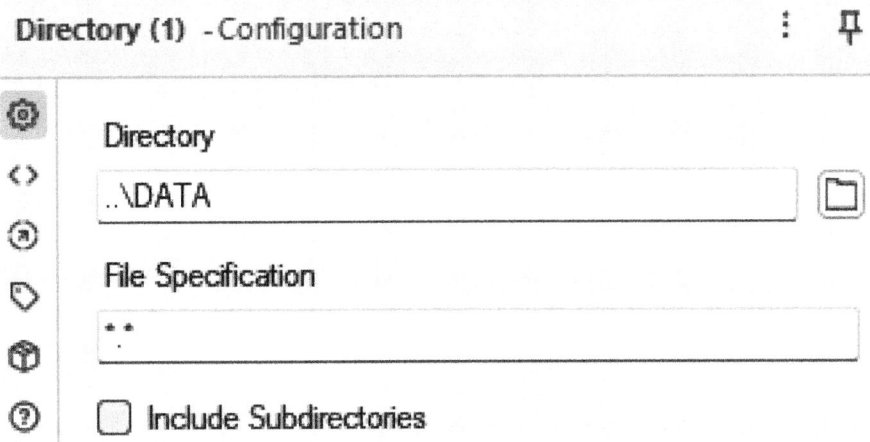

Figure 12.64: Directory tool configuration

2. Drop a **Blob Input** tool (from the **Developer** category) following the **Directory** tool:

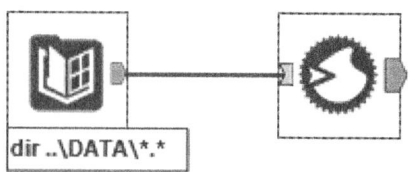

Figure 12.65: Adding a Blob Input tool

3. Point the **File Name** value to any of your images in the disk (I do this to avoid possible future errors in the tool when Alteryx refreshes its metadata). Actually, you can use anything here, since we are going to replace it with whatever comes from the **Directory** tool.

4. For the **Modify File Name Using Optional Input** section, select **Replacing Entire Path With Field** from the **Modify File Name By** dropdown.

5. Select **FullPath** from the **Using This Field** dropdown.

6. Leave the other options as they are:

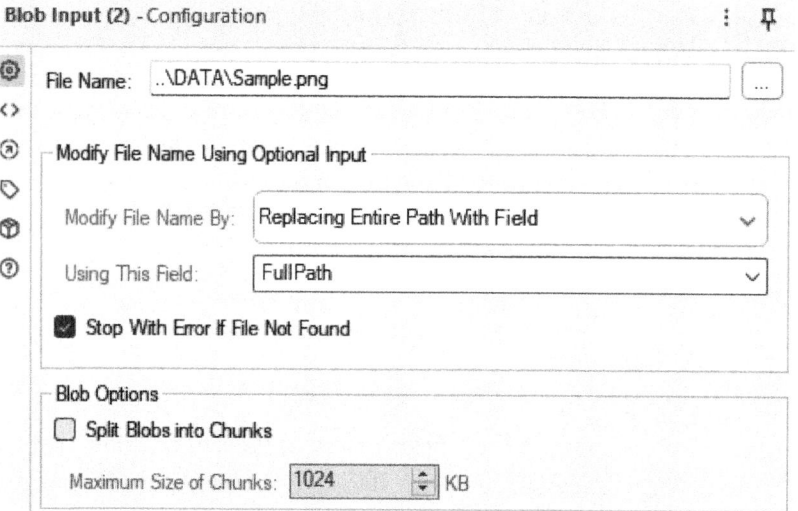

Figure 12.66: Blob Input tool configuration

7. Drop a **Select** tool following the **Blob Input** tool:

Figure 12.67: Adding a Select tool

8. Deselect all fields (**Options | Select | Deselect All**):

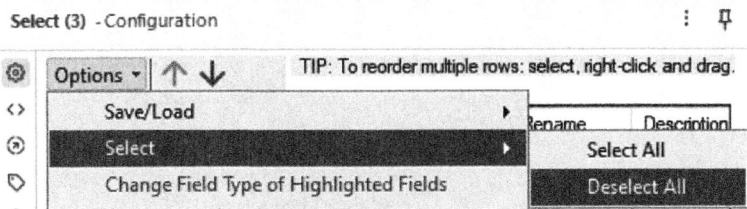

Figure 12.68: Deselecting all fields

9. Then, select only the `FullPath` and `Blob` fields:

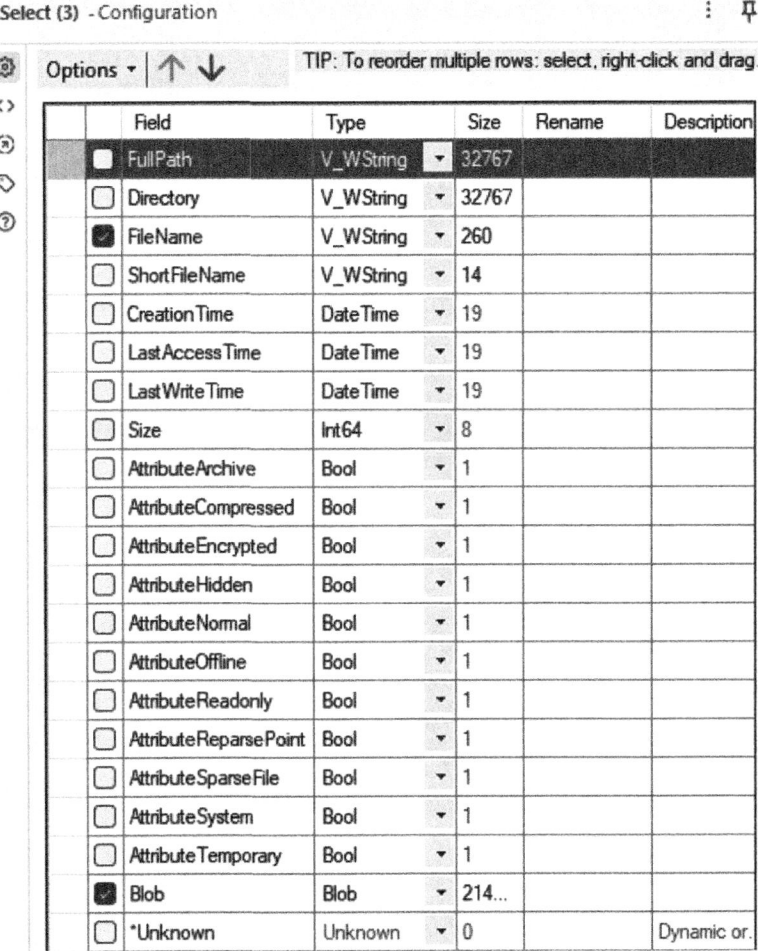

Figure 12.69: Select tool configuration, keeping only what we'll use

10. Drop a **Python** tool following the **Select** tool:

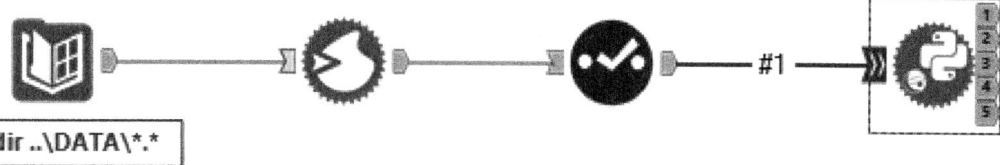

Figure 12.70: Adding a Python tool

You may encounter an error when inserting the **Python** tool, such as the one in the following screenshot. That is caused by the tool not having any metadata yet. After the first run, it'll disappear:

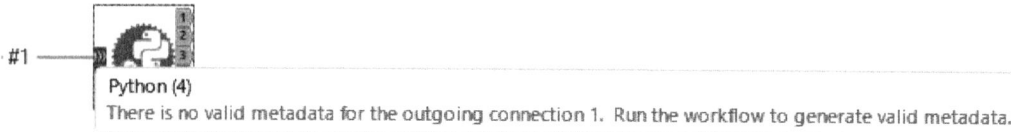

Figure 12.71: Error when there's no metadata (until the workflow runs)

11. Copy and paste the following code, below the last line in cell *2* (the one that reads from ayx import Alteryx):

```python
import pandas as pd
from PIL import Image
from pytesseract import pytesseract
import io
#Define path to tessaract.exe
path_to_tesseract = r'C:\Program Files\Tesseract-OCR\tesseract.
exe'
#Point tessaract_cmd to tessaract.exe
pytesseract.tesseract_cmd = path_to_tesseract
# Define the function so we can call it with each received
image.
def do_ocr(row):
    img=Image.open(io.BytesIO(row['Blob']))
    file_name=row['FileName']
    text = pytesseract.image_to_string(img)
    return text
# Read from Alteryx connection
```

```
data=Alteryx.read("#1")
# Add a field to the received data, with the results from the
OCR
data['Text']=data.apply(lambda row:do_ocr(row),axis=1)
#Ouput the data + the OCR results
Alteryx.write(data,1)
```

12. Add a **Browse** tool to the output anchor labeled #1 in the **Python** tool:

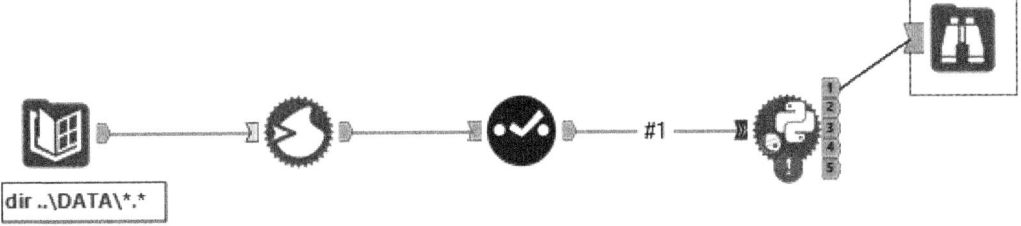

dir ..\DATA*.*

Figure 12.72: Adding a Browse tool

13. Run the workflow, and you can see that OCR was performed on each picture:

Results - Browse (5) - Input

3 of 3 Fields ▾ ✔ | Cell Viewer ▾ 3 records displayed, 980 KB | ↑ ↓ |

Record	FileName	Blob	Text
1	Sample-1.png	669401 Bytes	5. Images to Text
2	Sample-2.png	170743 Bytes	DateTime Functions
3	Sample.jpg	172084 Bytes	Automatic PDF to CSV Converter

Figure 12.73: Browsing the workflow results

The Text field contains all the text extracted from the image stored in the Blob field.

14. Double-click on any of the Text fields generated to see its content in the **Cell Viewer**:

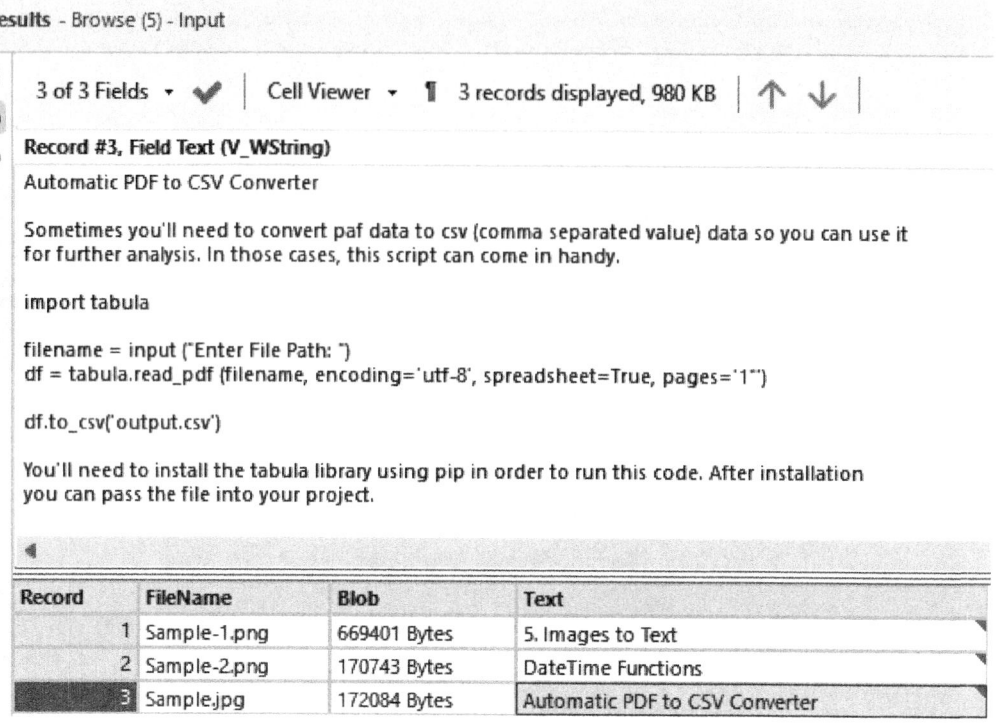

Figure 12.74: Using the Cell Viewer to expand what you can view

There's more...

There are some additional benefits of using **blob** tools.

If you add a **Blob Convert** tool to the #1 output anchor of the **Python** tool, you can render the contents of a `Blob` field, so let's try it:

1. Drag a **Blob Convert** tool and drop it over the line that connects the `1` output anchor of the **Python** tool and the existing **Browse** tool (this will cause the new tool to insert itself between the others):

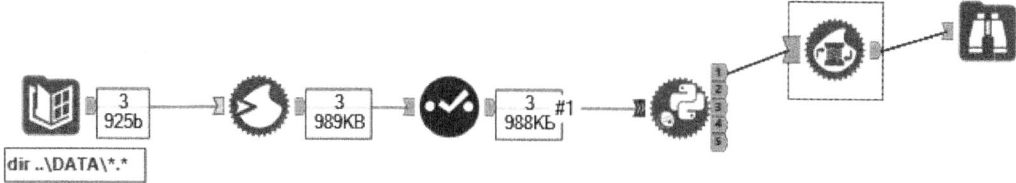

Figure 12.75: Adding a Blob Convert tool

2. In the **Blob Convert** configuration, click **Convert From a Blob Field**.

3. Make sure `Blob` is the selected field in the **Blob Field** dropdown.

4. Select **Convert PNG, GIF or JPG Blob to Report Snippet**:

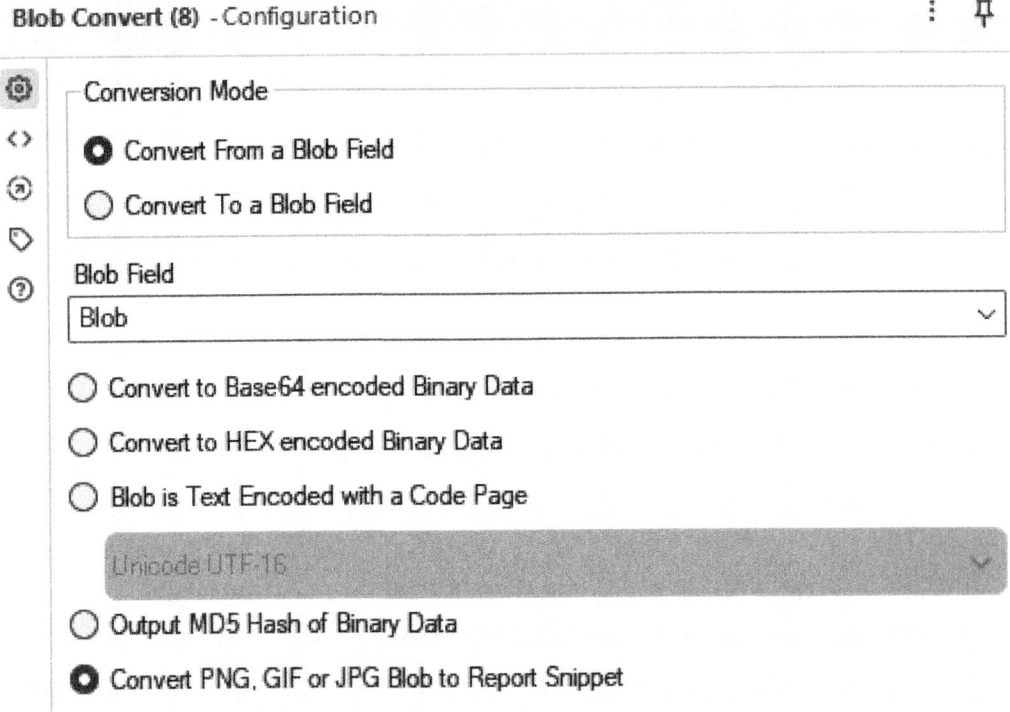

Figure 12.76: Blob Convert tool configuration

5. Run the workflow and click on the **Browse** tool. You will find the rendered pictures in the **Browse** panel:

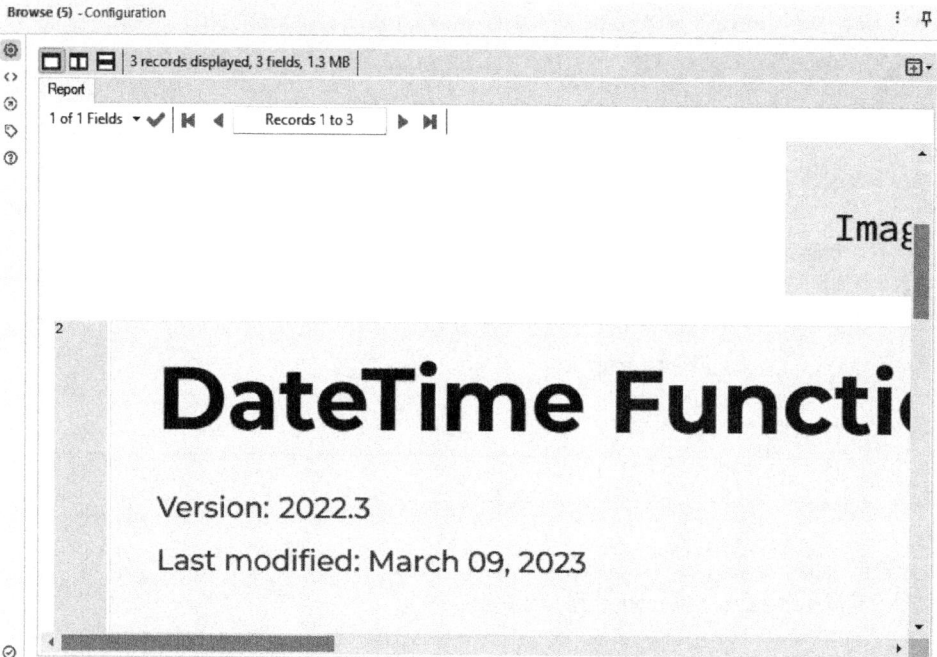

Figure 12.77: Browsing the converted data (pictures)

Finally, you can also save the blobs to the hard disk by using the **Blob Output** tool.

6. Add a **Blob Output** tool to the canvas, connected to the 1 output anchor of the **Python** tool:

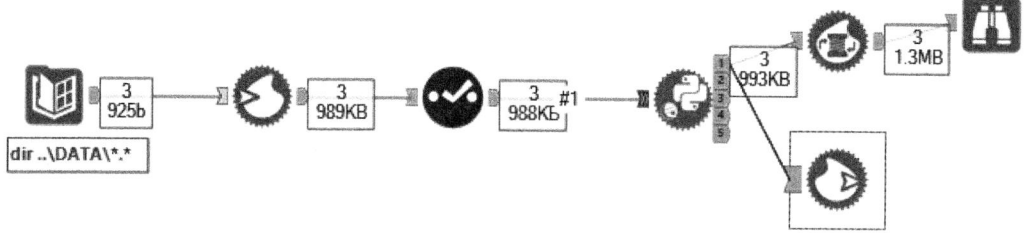

Figure 12.78: Adding a Blob Output tool

7. Click on it to access its configuration.

8. In the **File Name** field, use any folder you want in your hard drive where the pictures will be saved. Note that the folder must exist; otherwise, you'll get an error.

    In this case, I used the SCANNED subfolder within the DATA folder.

    I added a partial filename (scanned_) because with the next settings, we'll make the filename dynamic, based on the original filename of each picture.

9. Select **Appending Field To File Name** from the **Modify File Name By** dropdown.

10. Select FileName from the **Using This Field** dropdown.

11. And as the **Blob Field** value, make sure Blob is selected:

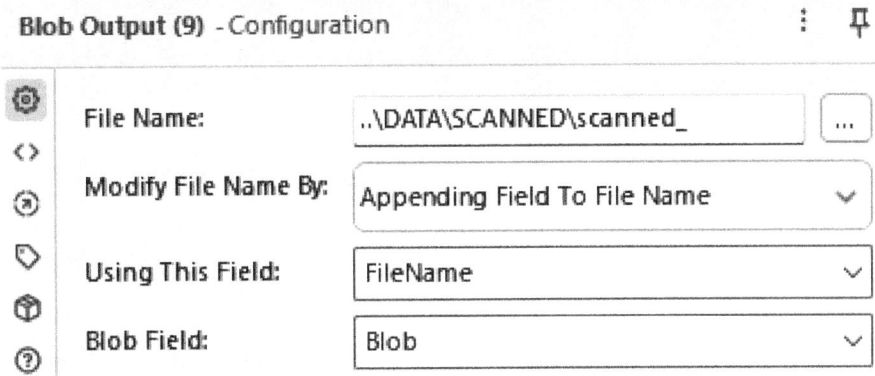

Figure 12.79: Blob Output tool configuration

12. Run the workflow one last time, and you'll notice that there are copies of the processed images, all with the scanned_ prefix in front of them:

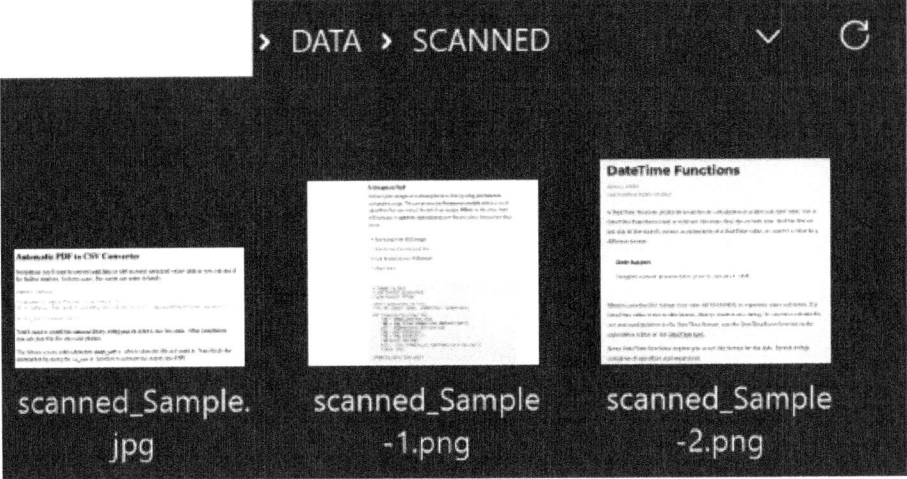

Figure 12.80: Blob Output tool results in the hard drive

13

Reporting with Alteryx

Generating effective and, at the same time, attractive reports is an important task to stand out as analysts. Not only is the quality of the data and the analysis performed important, but how we present it is what will make us stand out.

Knowing our audience and planning how we will present data and insights to them is vital to completing the analysis cycle; ultimately, the report is the result of all our hard work.

Alteryx has a super-powerful set of tools to achieve high-quality reports, although its many options can seem daunting at first. In this chapter, we will review some techniques that we will use frequently when we have to make reports, such as the following:

- Loading images for reports dynamically
- Using and rendering HTML in your reports
- Arranging your report snippets
- Preventing the Render tool from overwriting an existing version of a report
- Overlaying content in your reports
- Using the Render tool to format your Excel files

Technical requirements

While we don't have any special technical requirements for this chapter, we must understand how reporting works in Alteryx.

Alteryx manages its reporting functionalities based on the concept of snippets – that is, small pieces of content that, when combined horizontally or vertically, generate a report.

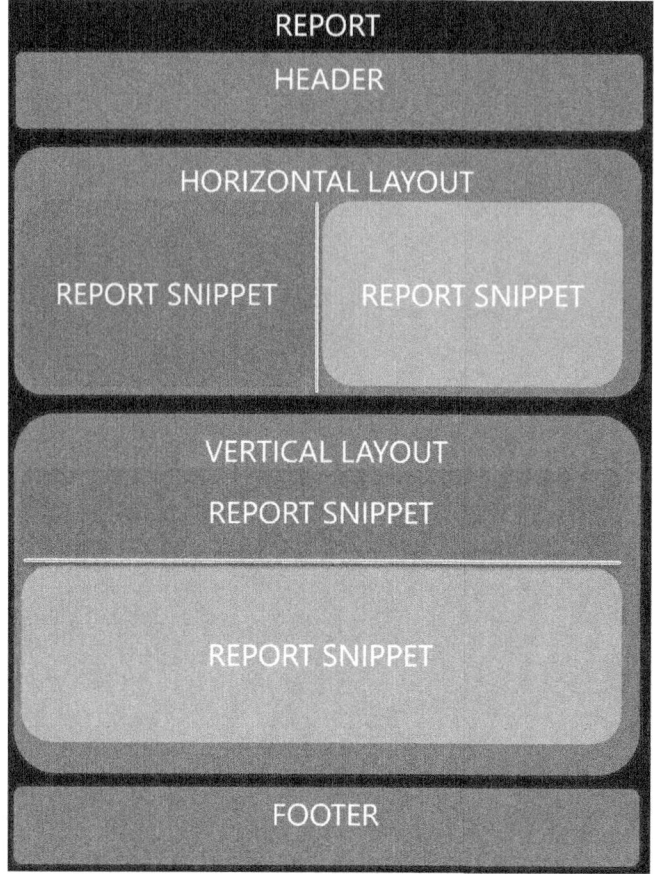

Figure 13.1: The anatomy of an Alteryx report

Both the header and the footer have specialized tools to configure them (the Report Header and Report Footer tool), while for the other snippets, we have tools that allow us to present data, such as the following:

- Maps
- Tables
- Text
- Charts

So, we can display data in any way we want.

Additionally, to make sense of all the pieces of content, Alteryx offers an additional tool to combine snippets, the Layout tool.

We can create very complete and complex reports using these tools, according to what they were created for.

As a first step in generating a report, I always sketch it out on whatever piece of paper I have to hand.

This helps me a lot to identify the snippets that I can use/need to compose the type of report I want, as well as the best way to organize them:

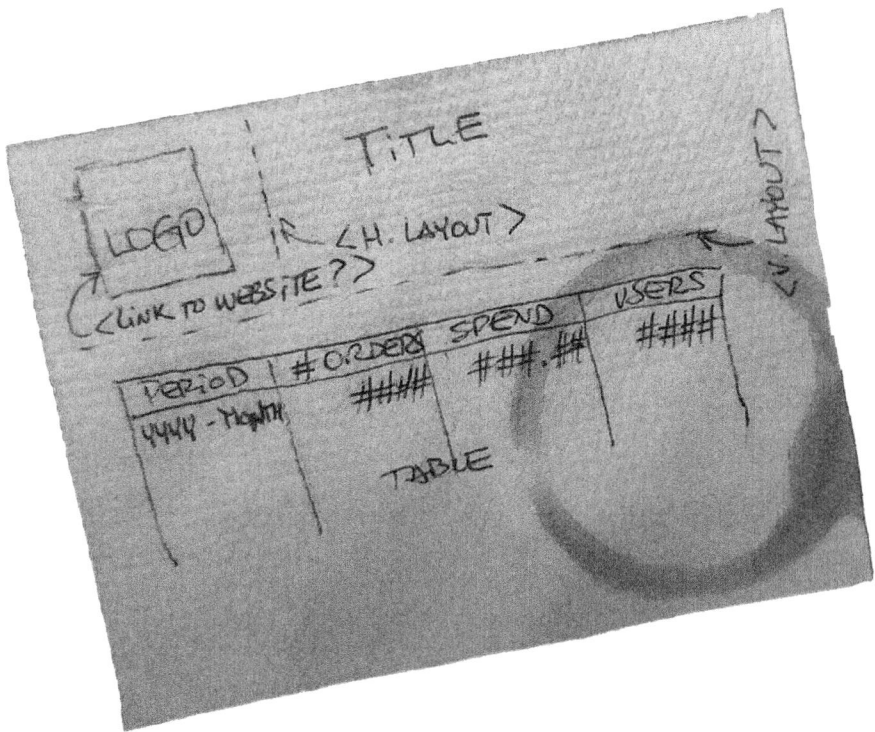

Figure 13.2: Sketching reports always helps

Loading images for reports dynamically

Including images in our reports can enhance their visual appeal and, simultaneously, help our audience to better understand what we are trying to convey. When you're processing batch reports – say, for different clients – you've probably come across the need to incorporate the logos of those companies into a corresponding report. Doing this manually would be time-consuming, so we will use Alteryx's capabilities to automatically achieve these customized reports in this recipe.

In the previous chapter, we learned how to read binary fields and/or files using **Blobs**. In the case of images, Alteryx has a specialized tool that allows us to read JPG, PNG, and GIF files from the hard drive, or a shared directory on the network.

Getting ready

We have a test set ready for you to follow along with this recipe here: `https://github.com/PacktPublishing/Alteryx-Designer-Cookbook`.

We will start with a dataset, which represents transactions made through a marketplace and corresponds to various restaurants.

Order	Restaurant_Id	Restaurant	Total	User	Date
2416351	30261	Life of Fi Bistro	13.96	6393230	2022-01-03 07:31:14
2416355	30261	Life of Fi Bistro	86.11	6389974	2022-01-03 07:36:08
2416383	30261	Life of Fi Bistro	35.46	7548140	2022-01-03 07:55:00
2416388	30261	Life of Fi Bistro	16.7	8809585	2022-01-03 08:01:33
2416410	30261	Life of Fi Bistro	14.86	9825409	2022-01-03 08:24:35

Figure 13.3: A dataset containing restaurant transactions

We need to generate a report for each restaurant with the monthly number of orders registered, the number of users who placed orders, and the total paid. We have been asked that the report include each restaurant's logo as part of its header.

> **Important note**
>
> One of the best recommendations that I can give you is to always organize all the assets of a model/project within a directory structure, ensuring that they can not only be easily accessed and automatically read but also that their distribution is transparent to users.

How to do it...

First, we will prepare and load the logos:

1. Drop an **Input Data** tool onto the canvas and point it to `..\DATA\restaurant_transactions.yxdb`.

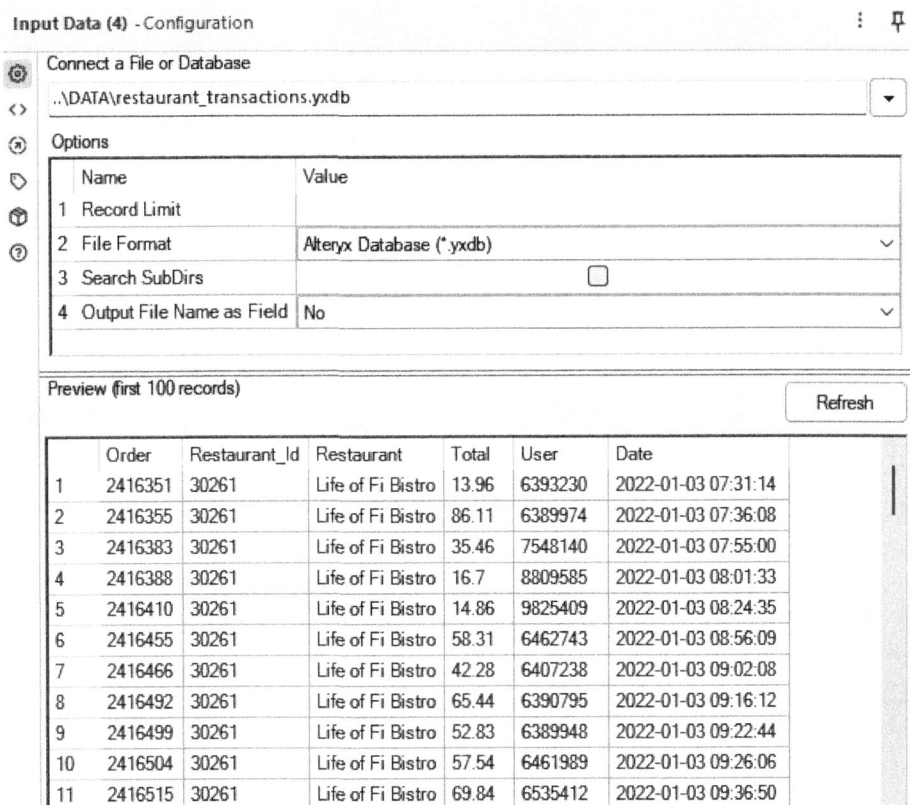

Figure 13.4: The Input Data tool configuration

As you may have noticed, we have the data at a transaction level, so we'll need to summarize it to get the monthly values. Also, we do not have information about the logos of each restaurant, which will force us to create a personalized dictionary to reference each one.

So, we'll extract the values from the Date field for the specified period.

2.   Drop a **Formula** tool after the **Input Data** tool.

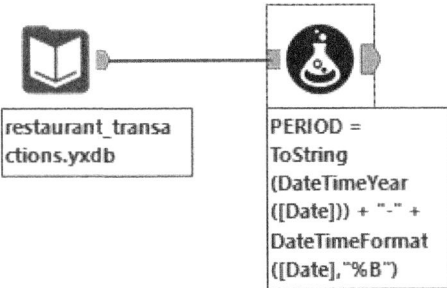

Figure 13.5: Adding the Formula tool

3. Create a new column called PERIOD, and use this expression:

    ```
    ToString(DateTimeYear([Date])) + "-" +
    DateTimeFormat([Date],"%B")
    ```

This will create a string variable containing the year (ToString(DateTimeYear([Date]))), followed by a dash (+ "-" +) and the month of our Date value, but formatted as the month name (DateTimeFormat([Date],"%B")), as you can see in the **Data Preview** field.

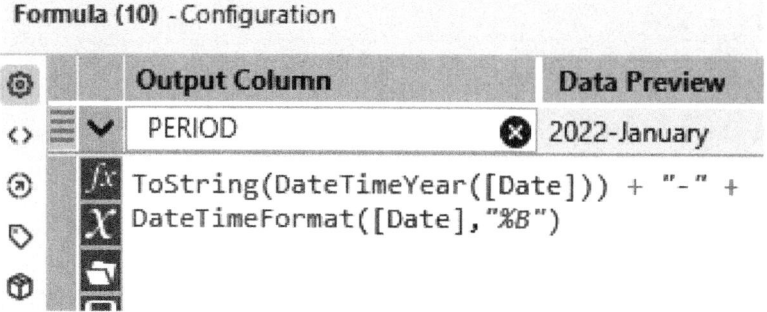

Figure 13.6: The Formula tool configuration

Now that we have the period, it's time to load our logos. To do this, we will restrict the list to the different restaurant names we have (obtaining a record for each restaurant).

4. Drop a **Summarize** tool after the **Formula** tool.

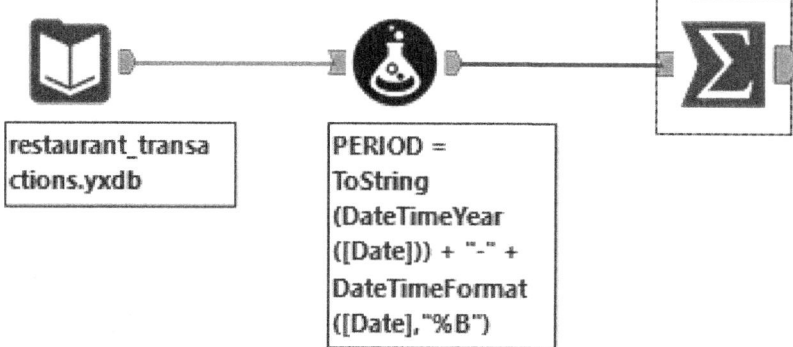

Figure 13.7: Adding the Summarize tool

5. In the **Summarize** tool configuration, select Restaurant_Id and Restaurant, click on **Add**, and select **Group By**.

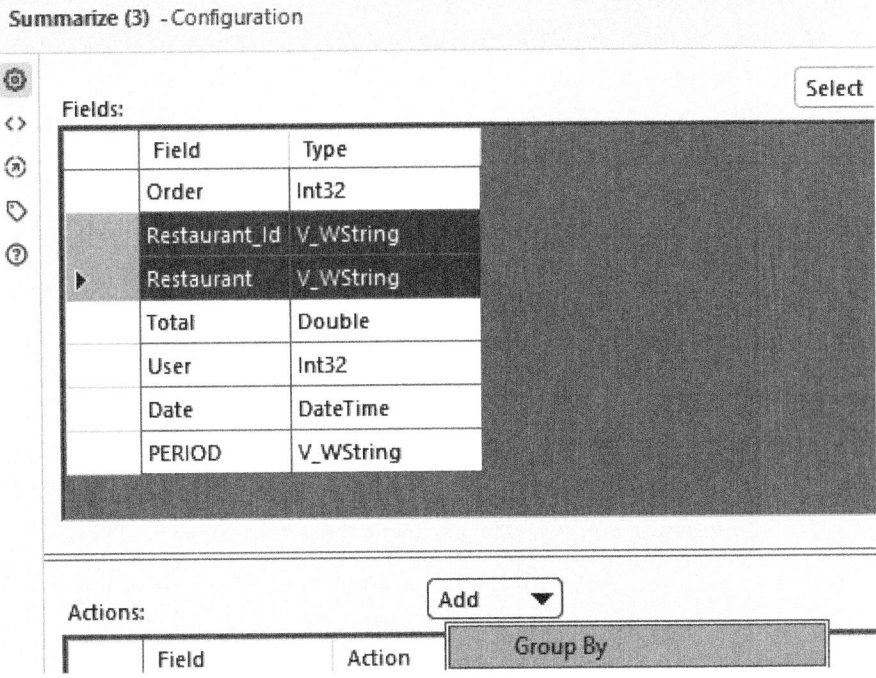

Figure 13.8: The Summarize tool configuration

Here is where having well-organized assets usually saves us a lot of preparation time, since we can generate the corresponding paths through a formula. Also, we have renamed the JPG files corresponding to each logo, which share the name of the restaurant to which they belong. Doing this prevents us from keeping and maintaining an external dictionary to relate logos to restaurants.

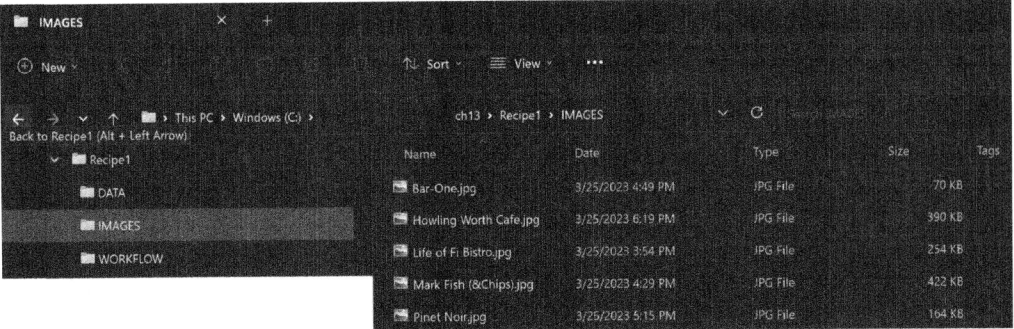

Figure 13.9: Organized assets will simplify your workflow development

Before creating the path for the images, I would like to show you a resource that I use a lot when I find that, in a workflow, I am going to have some manual data that may vary or need to be modified later.

Using Alteryx's **workflow constants**, we can define a value that will then be referenced throughout a workflow and, when this value needs to be changed, just do it once in its definition and Alteryx will use that new value in future executions.

To create a new workflow constant, follow these steps:

1. Click on any blank part of the canvas to access the workflow configuration options.

2. Click on the **Workflow** tab, where we will find a list of constants for that particular workflow. By default, we have certain constants (identified with Type = Engine) and the possibility of defining our own (identified as Type = User).

3. To create a new constant, click the + icon on the right of the **Constants** pane.

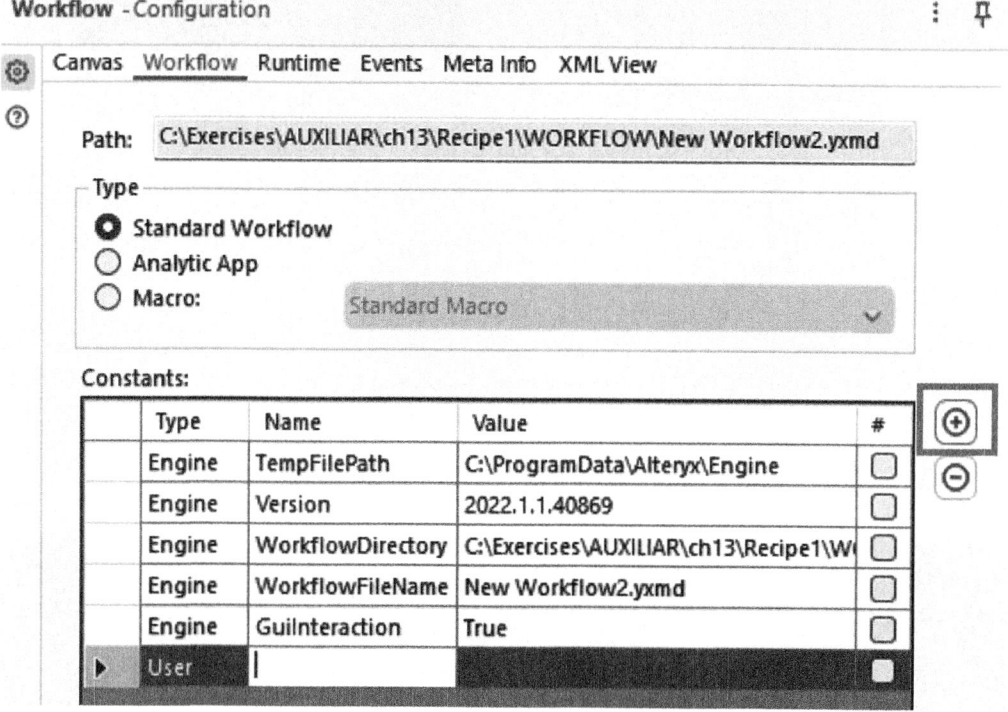

Figure 13.10: Adding a Workflow constant

A new row will be added with the **Type** User value in it, and you need to fill in the name and value for the variable (in this case, **Name** = logo_path and **Value** = . . \images\).

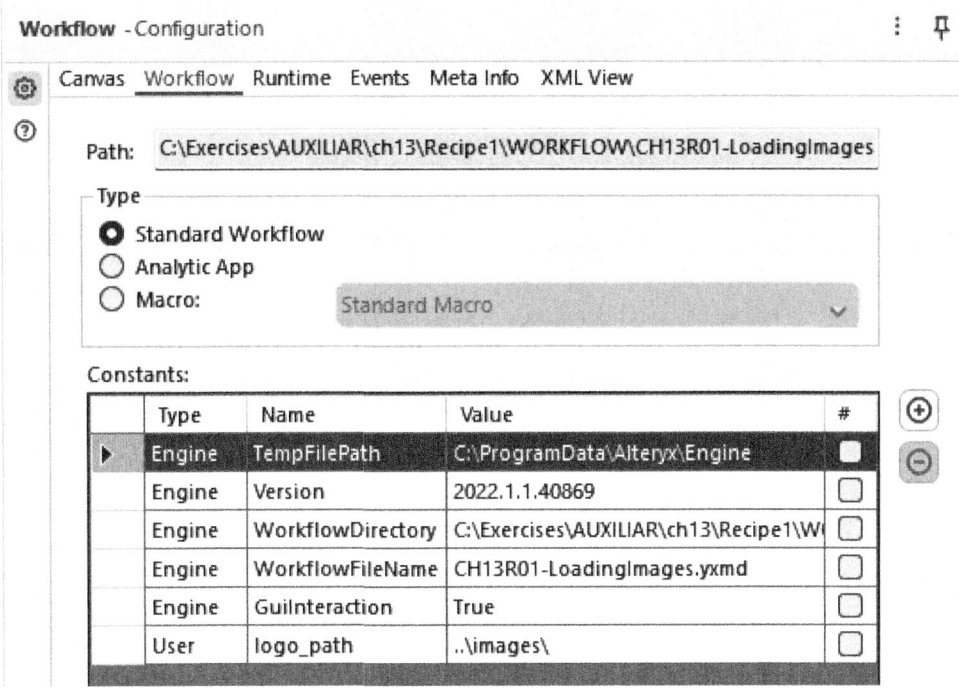

Figure 13.11: Workflow constant added

Note that each workflow has its constants, and they are not shared between workflows. If you need the same variables between workflows, either create and update them in both workflows manually, or use an external dictionary to load and/or update those values.

Now, we have everything we need to create a reference to each restaurant's logo image.

4. Drop a **Formula** tool following the **Summarize** tool.

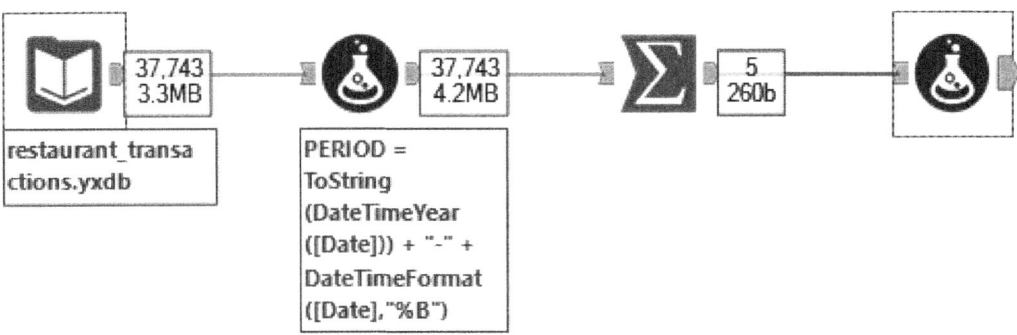

Figure 13.12: Adding another Formula tool

5. For **Output Column**, select **+ Add Column**, and name the new column image.

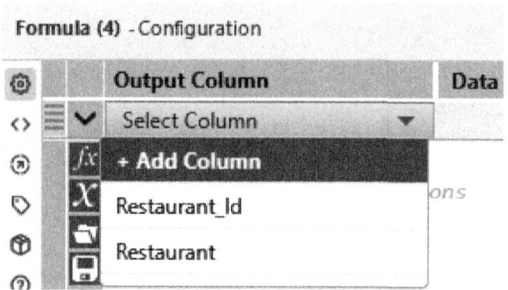

Figure 13.13: Creating a new column inside the Formula tool

6.   For the expression, use the following formula:

```
[User.logo_path]+[Restaurant]+".jpg"
```

As you can see, we use the value from the recently created workflow constant, `logo_path` (`..\images\`), and since we renamed the picture files to match exactly the `Restaurant` field values, adding those names to the path and the `.jpg` file gives us a complete path to each file for each restaurant.

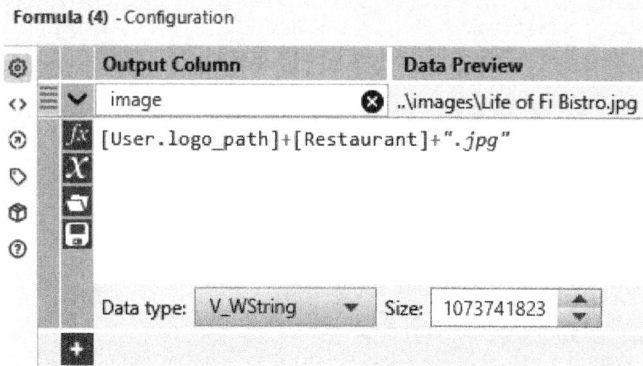

Figure 13.14: The Formula tool configuration

7.   Run the workflow, and you'll see how the paths for the images were added to the restaurant info we had.

	Restaurant_Id	Restaurant	image
1	30261	Life of Fi Bistro	..\images\Life of Fi Bistro.jpg
2	30405	Howling Worth Cafe	..\images\Howling Worth Cafe.jpg
3	30412	Bar-One	..\images\Bar-One.jpg
4	40742	Mark Fish (&Chips)	..\images\Mark Fish (&Chips).jpg
5	41961	Pinet Noir	..\images\Pinet Noir.jpg

Figure 13.15: The results so far

Now, we will use these paths to load the images into our workflow.

8. Add an **Image** tool to the canvas, and select it to access its settings.

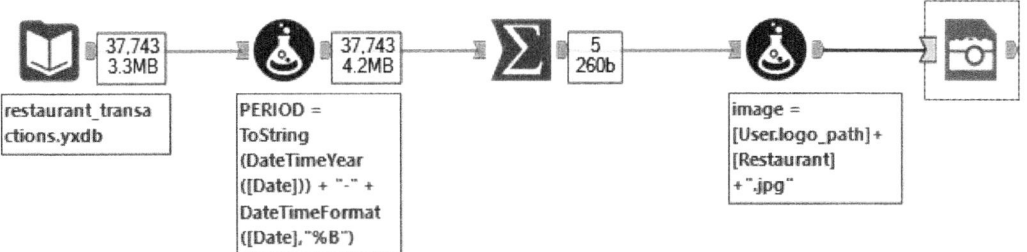

Figure 13.16: Adding the Image tool

9. Click on **Modify filename for each record** to enable it (the default will be deselected). That will enable the following drop-down menus.

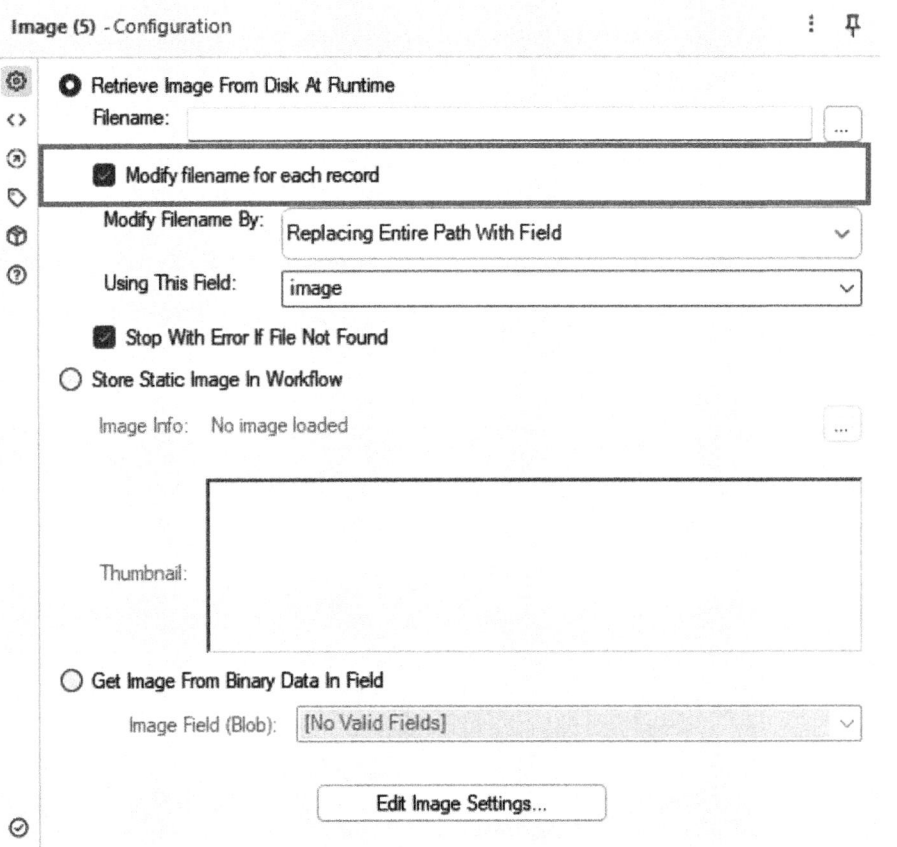

Figure 13.17: Enabling the image dynamic loading

10. For **Modify Filename By**, select **Replacing Entire Path With Field**.

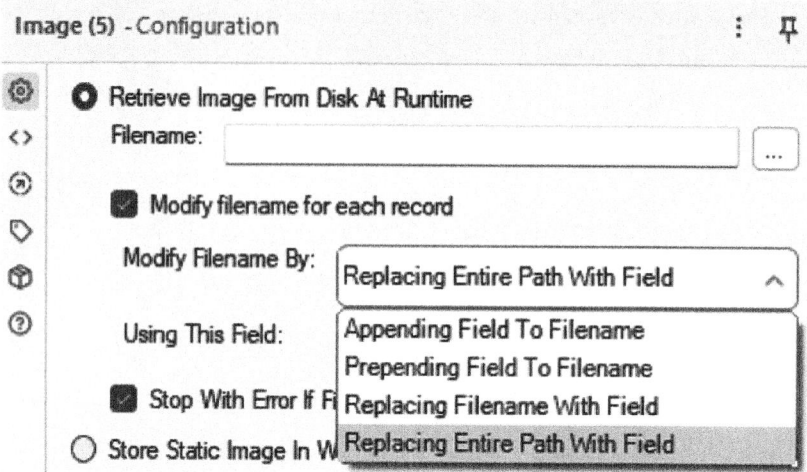

Figure 13.18: Replacing the image path method selection

11. For the **Using This Field** dropdown, select **image**.

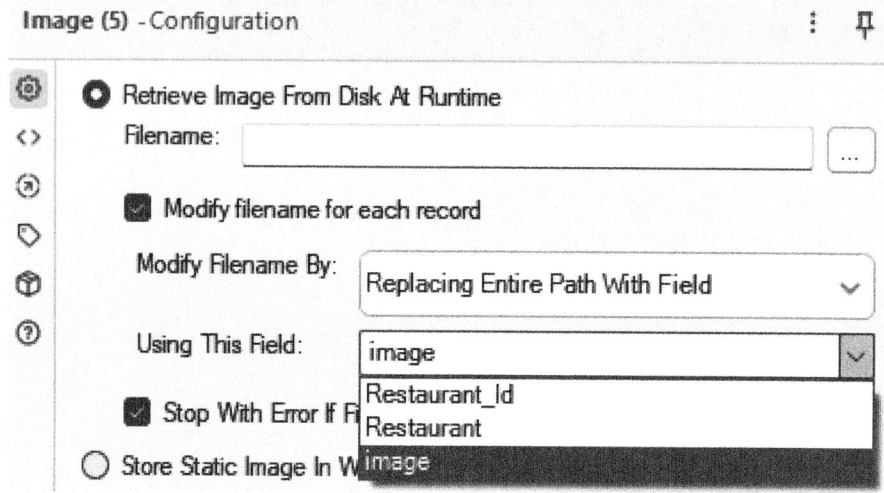

Figure 13.19: Telling Alteryx to use the image field to dynamically load images

These settings will make Alteryx use, for each record, the path stored in the image field; look for that file and load it.

Also, as **Stop With Error If File Not Found** is checked (the default setting), if any of the referenced files within the image field are not present, the workflow will error. (If you want, you can deselect this option.)

12. Drop a **Browse** tool after the **Image** tool to be able to see the loaded images.

13. Run the workflow, and click on the **Browse** tool. You'll notice that the images were loaded full-size in the dataset. Alteryx allows us to determine whether we want to load the pictures with a fixed width.

14. Click on the **Edit Image Settings…** button at the bottom of the **Image** tool configuration options.

Figure 13.20: The Edit Image Settings… button

A new window will pop up, offering two options (both with the default value of **No**).

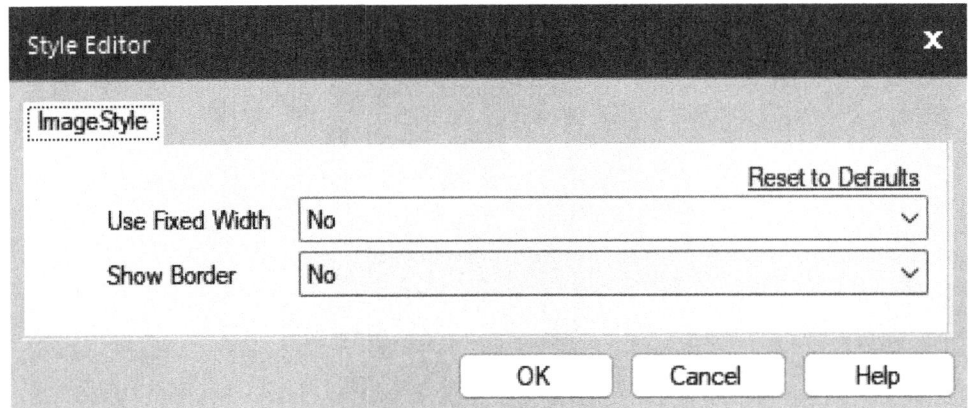

Figure 13.21: The image Style Editor options

15. Select **Yes** from the **Use Fixed Width** dropdown, and a field to set the width value will appear. Set it to **200**.

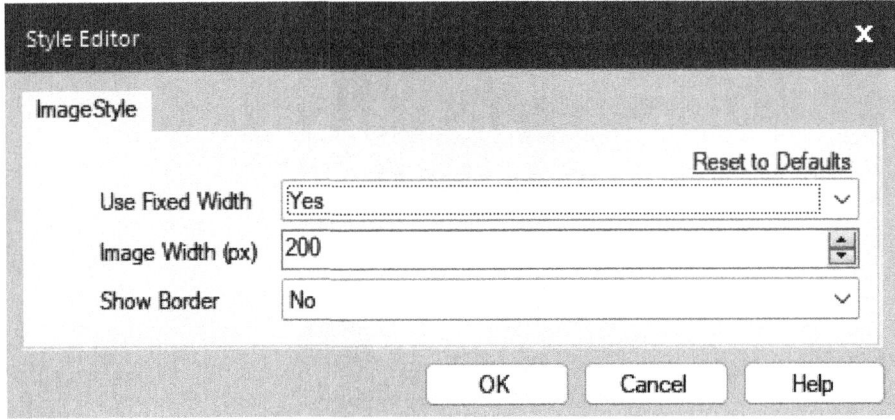

Figure 13.22: Changing the image width

16. Run the workflow again, and you'll see all images ready to be part of the report, with the same width (200 px).

Figure 13.23: The loaded images

Also, if you look at the data, you'll notice that each image was loaded into a new field. (By default, Alteryx calls it Image, but since we already have an image field, it is automatically renamed Image2.)

Table | Report

4 of 4 Fields ▾ ✔ | Cell Viewer ▾ | ↑ ↓ |

Record	Restaurant_Id	Restaurant	image	Image2
1	30261	Life of Fi Bistro	..\images\Life of Fi Bistro.jpg	Image - View Browse Tool Report Tab
2	30405	Howling Worth Cafe	..\images\Howling Worth Cafe.jpg	Image - View Browse Tool Report Tab
3	30412	Bar-One	..\images\Bar-One.jpg	Image - View Browse Tool Report Tab
4	40742	Mark Fish (&Chips)	..\images\Mark Fish (&Chips).jpg	Image - View Browse Tool Report Tab
5	41961	Pinet Noir	..\images\Pinet Noir.jpg	Image - View Browse Tool Report Tab

Figure 13.24: Images loaded after running the workflow

Save your workflow because we will use it throughout this chapter.

Arranging your report snippets

In the previous recipe, we incorporated image snippets from the hard drive into our workflow to use them in our reports.

We will begin loading the workflow we built in the previous recipe. This workflow dynamically generates the paths and loads the images corresponding to the logos of the restaurants, for which we must generate the reports.

In this recipe, we will incorporate additional snippets to complete the header of each report (which will include the name and code of each restaurant, to the right of the logo), and we will add a table with certain monthly values corresponding to the activity of each restaurant.

Getting ready

We will start with the workflow we built in the previous recipe. If you don't have it, you can download the complete version from here: https://github.com/PacktPublishing/Alteryx-Designer-Cookbook.

How to do it...

To start, we will load the workflow we created in the previous recipe:

1. From the **File** menu, click **Open** and select the workflow you saved in the previous recipe (*Loading images for reports dynamically*).

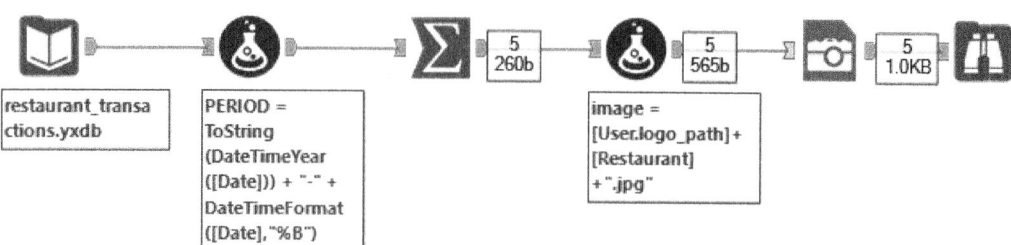

Figure 13.25: The previous recipe workflow

If we review the previous recipe, the **Summarize** tool was included to obtain the list of unique values for `Restaurant_Id` and `Restaurant`, from which we will build the path for each logo.

	Restaurant_Id	Restaurant
1	30261	Life of Fi Bistro
2	30405	Howling Worth Cafe
3	30412	Bar-One
4	40742	Mark Fish (&Chips)
5	41961	Pinet Noir

Figure 13.26: Unique values for Restaurant_Id and Restaurant

Using these values, we'll build the report title, using `Restaurant` and `Restaurant_Id` between parenthesis values.

2. Drop a **Report Text** tool below the **Summarize** tool, creating a second data stream from the same origin.

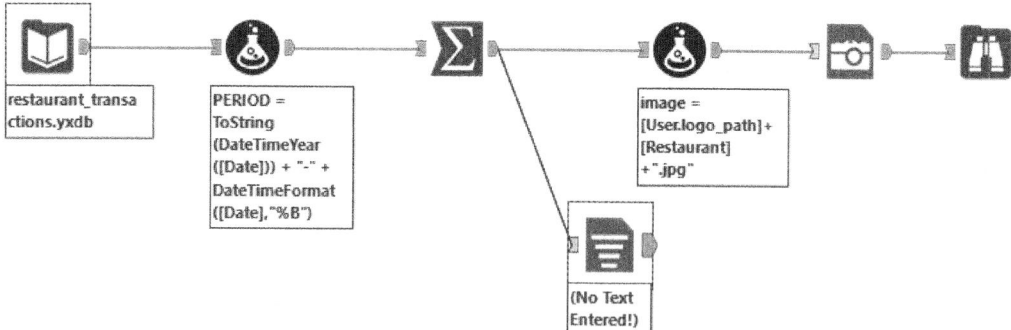

Figure 13.27: Adding the Report Text tool

3. In the **Report Text** tool configuration, make sure that **Create a new field for this text** is selected in **Text Mode**.

4. Replace the default `Text` field name with `Title`.

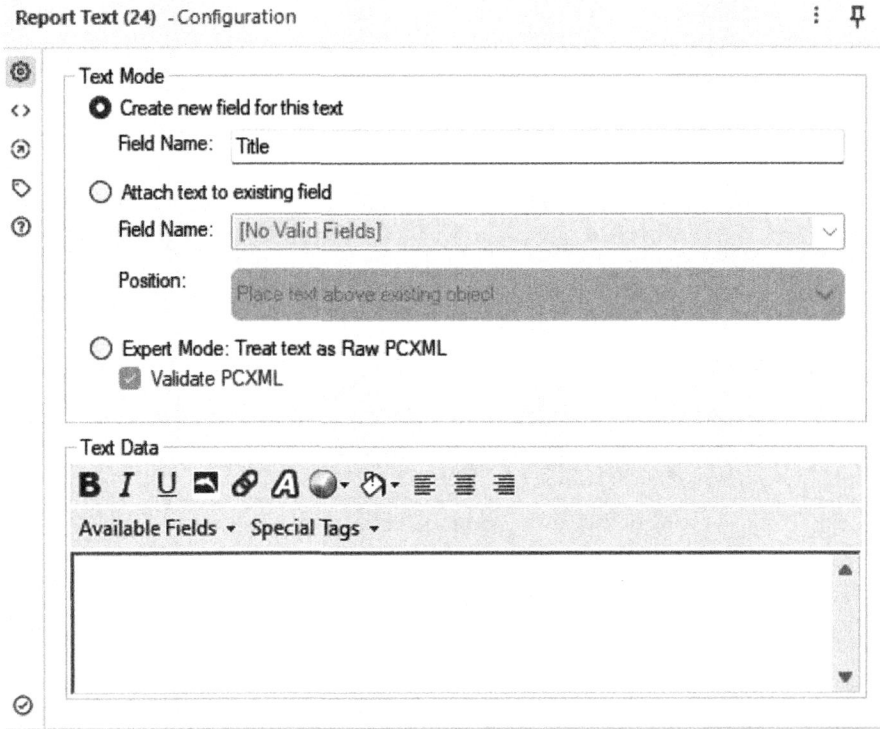

Figure 13.28: Renaming the Text field

Important note

Force yourself to give each piece of a report a meaningful name so that, when composing a report, you can easily identify the snippets. Otherwise, you will waste a lot of time trying to figure out where a field with a generic (or default) name comes from and what values it contains.

In the **Text Data** editor, there are a lot of options to format exactly how you want your title to appear in a report. However, we first need to tell the editor which fields we want.

5.   From the **Available Fields** dropdown, select Restaurant.

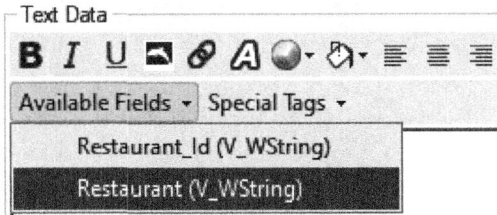

Figure 13.29: The Report Text editor

Note that the field was added with : A following the field name inside the brackets. This indicates that the field is a `String` type:

`[Restaurant:A]`

In the case of numbers, the digit following the colon indicates the number of decimal places to show. So, for a numeric field with the value `123.45678`, `[Field_name:0]` will show `123`, `[field_name:1]` will produce `123.4`, and so on.

Once we have added `Restaurant`, we need to add `Restaurant_Id`, but this time within parenthesis, so open parenthesis, click on **Available Fields**, select `Restaurant_Id`, and then close parenthesis.

You will get something like this:

Figure 13.30: The inserted fields

We'll use a simple format to show what you can do, but you are more than welcome to format the title as you want, using the **Text Data** editor options.

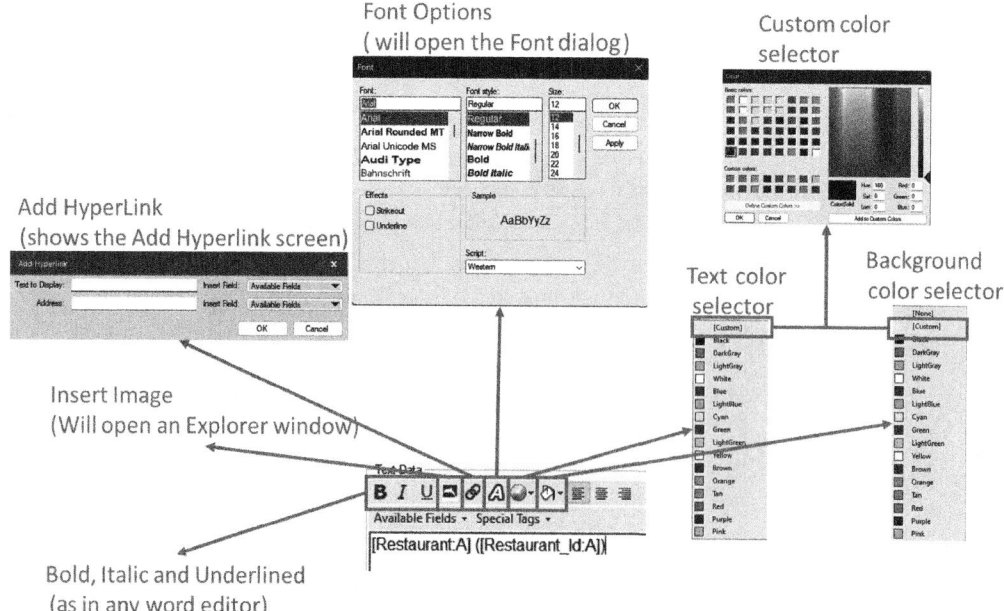

Figure 13.31: All the Text Data editor options

6. Select [Restaurant:A], and then click on **Bold**.

7. Click on **Font options**, and select **16** as the size so that you get something like this:

Figure 13.32: Formatting the restaurant name

8. Now, select ([Restaurant_Id:A]), click on **Font Options**, and select **14** from the **Size** pane.

Figure 13.33: Formatting the Restaurant_Id field

9. Add a **Browse** tool after the **Report Text** tool.

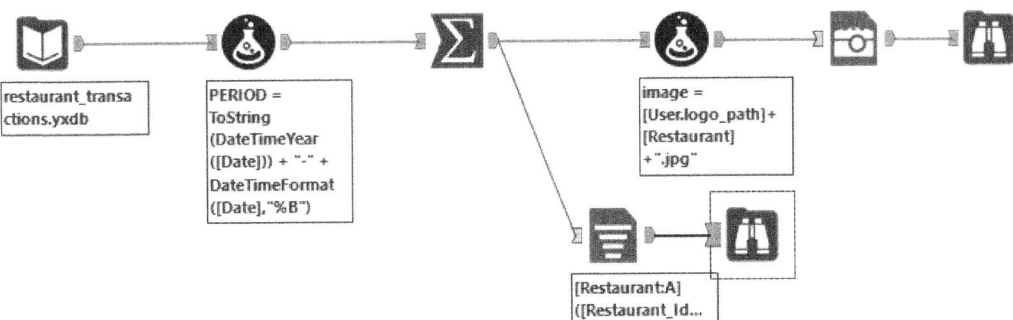

Figure 13.34: Adding a Browse tool to preview the results

10. Run the workflow.

    You'll see all the titles in the **Browse** pane.

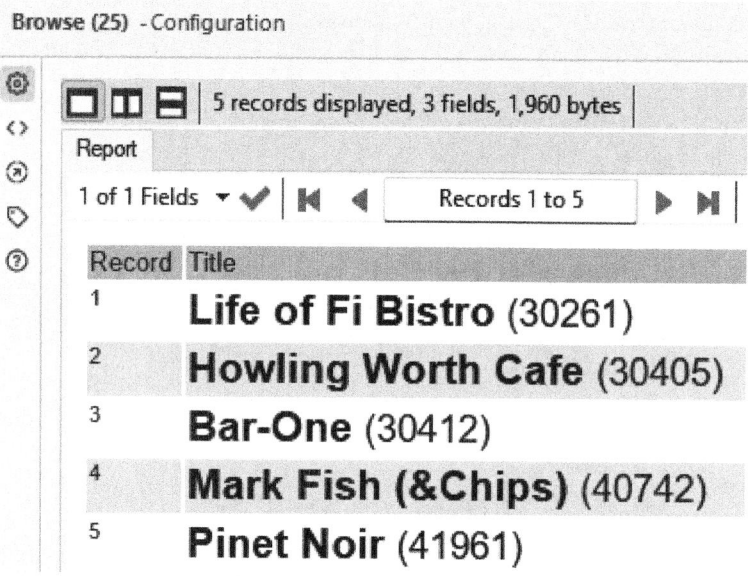

Figure 13.35: Generated report text (visible through the Browse tool pane)

Now, it's time to combine the images and the titles to create the report header.

Since the image and titles come from two different data streams, we need to join them. We will use the `Restaurant_Id` field to perform the join.

11. Drop a **Join** tool onto the canvas, and connect the **Image** tool output anchor to the **L** input and the **Report Text** output anchor to the **R** input of the **Join** tool.

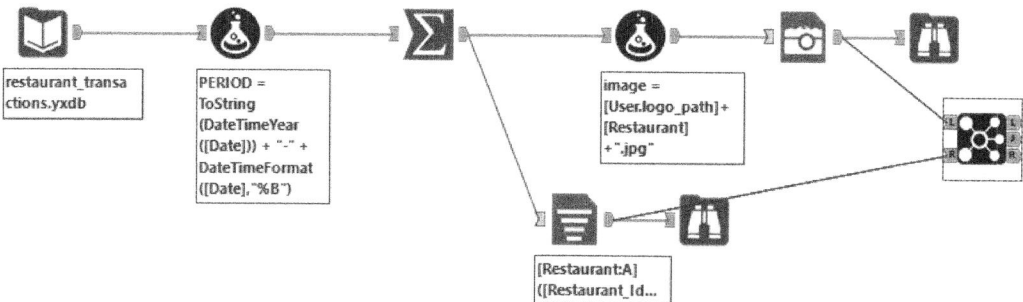

Figure 13.36: Joining images and text

12. In the **Join** tool configuration, select `Restaurant_Id` from the **Left** field selector. (The **Right** field selector will be automatically filled by Alteryx. If not, select `Restaurant_Id` for the right one too.)

13. Deselect `Restaurant_Id` and `Restaurant` from the **Right** input so that we don't have duplicated fields in our dataset (or use **Options | Deselect Duplicate Fields**).

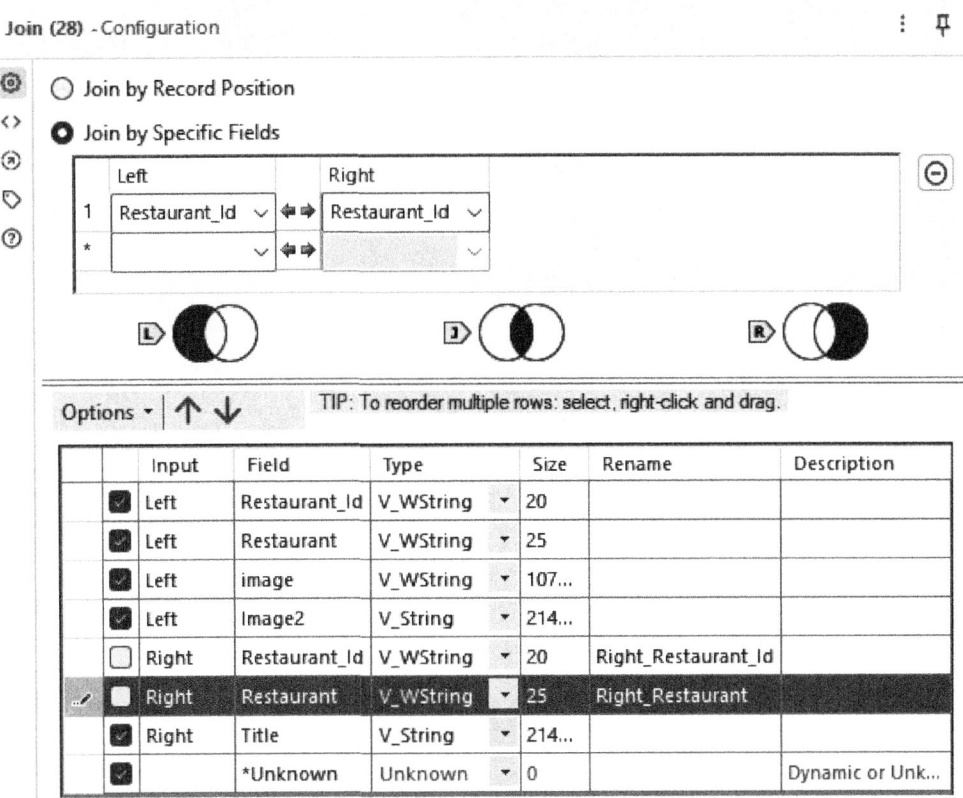

Figure 13.37: The Join tool configuration

14. Run the workflow.

Note that the `Title` and `Image2` fields are in the dataset but as separate fields (each snippet is a field). Also, if you try to see the rendered results of the image and title, they're not there. You need to add a **Browse** tool to be able to see them rendered.

Results - Join (28) - Out - Join

5 of 5 Fields ▾ ✔ | Cell Viewer ▾ 5 records displayed | ↑ ↓ |

Record	Restaurant_Id	Restaurant	image	Image2	Title
1	30261	Life of Fi Bistro	.\images\Life of Fi Bistro.jpg	Image - View Browse Tool Report Tab	Text - View Browse Tool Report Tab
2	30405	Howling Worth Cafe	.\images\Howling Worth Cafe.jpg	Image - View Browse Tool Report Tab	Text - View Browse Tool Report Tab
3	30412	Bar-One	.\images\Bar-One.jpg	Image - View Browse Tool Report Tab	Text - View Browse Tool Report Tab
4	40742	Mark Fish (&Chips)	.\images\Mark Fish (&Chips).jpg	Image - View Browse Tool Report Tab	Text - View Browse Tool Report Tab
5	41961	Pinet Noir	.\images\Pinet Noir.jpg	Image - View Browse Tool Report Tab	Text - View Browse Tool Report Tab

Figure 13.38: The results after running the workflow

Now, we can combine both fields using a **Layout** tool to get both snippets as a unit.

15. Drop a **Layout** tool and connect it to the J output anchor of the **Join** tool.

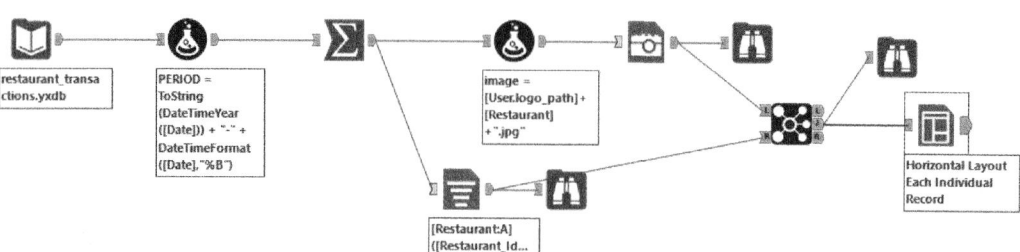

Figure 13.39: Adding the Layout tool

The default options of the tool will suffice to get what we need. (There'll be more about the other options in the *How it works...* section.)

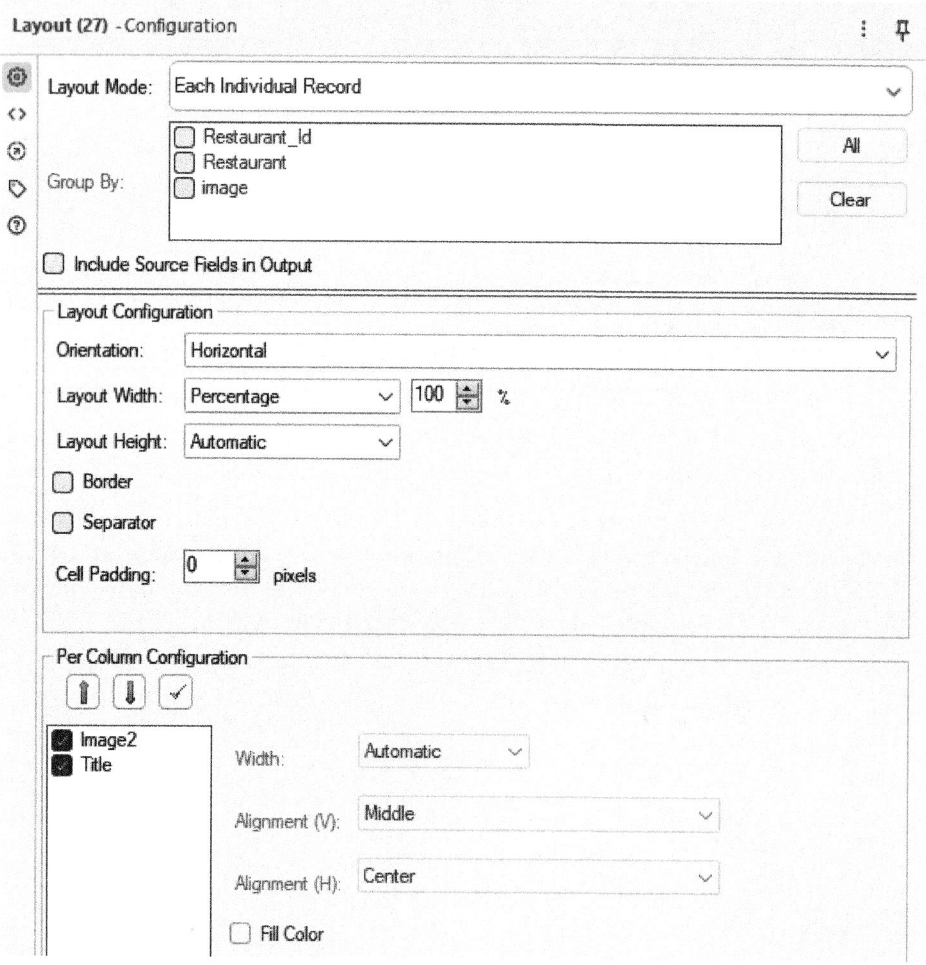

Figure 13.40: The Layout tool configuration

16. Add a **Browse** tool to the **Layout** tool and run the workflow.

Note that the header is complete.

Figure 13.41: The rendered preview of the Layout tool

Also, both original snippets (Image2 and Title) were merged into a new one, called Layout.

Results - Browse (29) - Input

Record	Restaurant_Id	Restaurant	image	Layout
1	30261	Life of Fi Bistro	..\images\Life of Fi Bistro.jpg	Layout - View Browse Tool Report Tab
2	30405	Howling Worth Cafe	..\images\Howling Worth Cafe.jpg	Layout - View Browse Tool Report Tab
3	30412	Bar-One	..\images\Bar-One.jpg	Layout - View Browse Tool Report Tab
4	40742	Mark Fish (&Chips)	..\images\Mark Fish (&Chips).jpg	Layout - View Browse Tool Report Tab
5	41961	Pinet Noir	..\images\Pinet Noir.jpg	Layout - View Browse Tool Report Tab

Figure 13.42: The Layout field in the results

17. Insert a **Select** tool between the **Layout** tool and **Browse**.

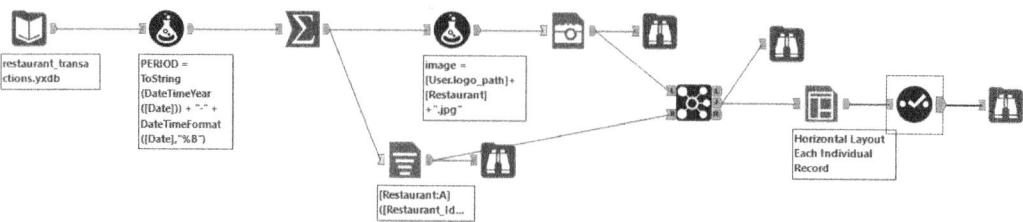

Figure 13.43: Adding a Select tool

18. In the **Select** tool configuration, rename the Layout field Header. It might appear as an extra and unnecessary step at this point, but believe me, renaming report snippets as you go along the workflow will help you a lot.

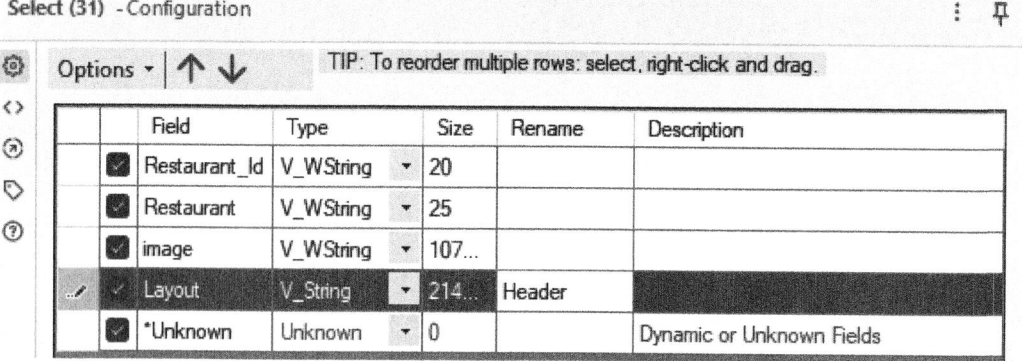

Figure 13.44: Renaming the field in the Select tool

How it works...

The **Layout** tool combines report snippets horizontally or vertically, providing many options to get them exactly as you want.

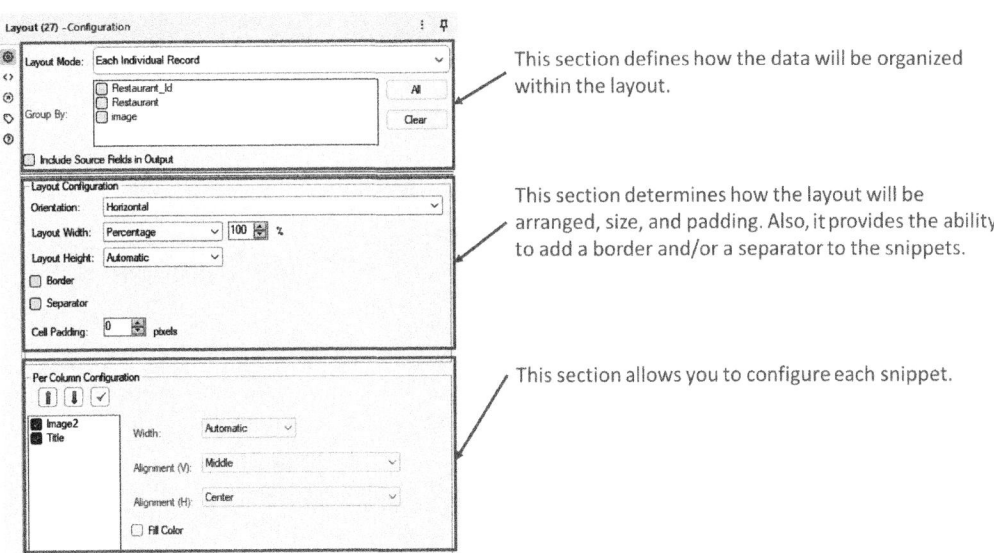

This section defines how the data will be organized within the layout.

This section determines how the layout will be arranged, size, and padding. Also, it provides the ability to add a border and/or a separator to the snippets.

This section allows you to configure each snippet.

Figure 13.45: The Layout tool options

The **Layout Mode** section contains record grouping configuration options.

Let's say we have this dataset:

	RecordId	Value	Group
1	1	AAAAA	Group1
2	2	BBBBB	Group1
3	3	CCCCC	Group2
4	4	DDDDD	Group2
5	5	EEEEE	Group3

Figure 13.46: Testing data

Then, we create a report text for each record, called `Title`, based on the fields we have, like this:

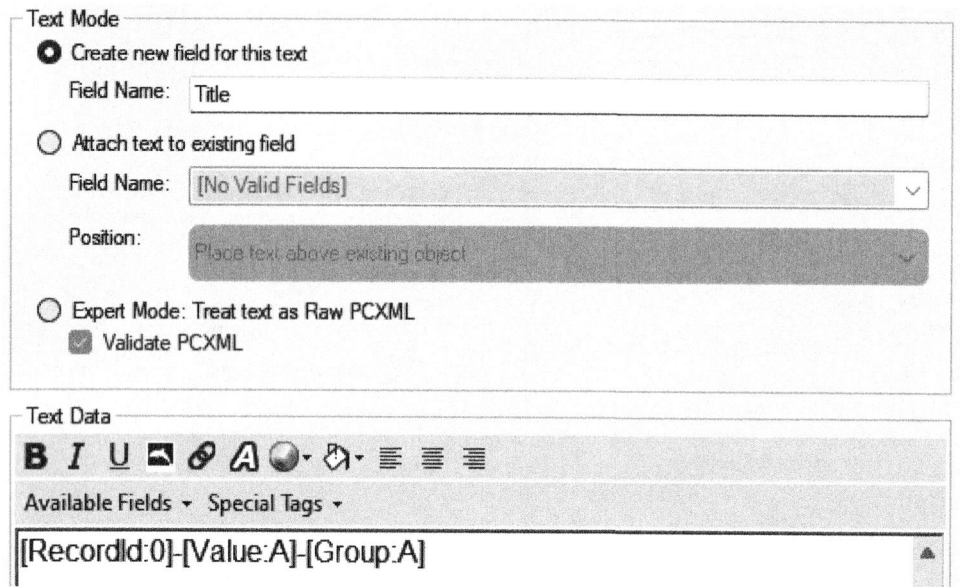

Figure 13.47: Fields added to the Report Text tool

So, our dataset becomes the following:

RecordId	Value	Group	Title
1	AAAAA	Group1	Text - View Browse Tool Report Tab
2	BBBBB	Group1	Text - View Browse Tool Report Tab
3	CCCCC	Group2	Text - View Browse Tool Report Tab
4	DDDDD	Group2	Text - View Browse Tool Report Tab
5	EEEEE	Group3	Text - View Browse Tool Report Tab

Figure 13.48: Results after running the workflow

Let's review the results of selecting each option within the **Layout Mode** dropdown:

Layout Mode: Each Individual Record

Each Individual Record
Each Group Of Records
All Records Combined

Group By:

Figure 13.49: The layout grouping options

- **Each Individual Record**: This will create a layout value for each record in the dataset. Also, it'll enable the **Per Column Configuration** options, which will allow you to select what fields will be included in the output snippet and set their attributes, such as width, vertical alignment, horizontal alignment (in this case, note that since it's a report text snippet, its horizontal alignment is set and determined within the **Text** tool configuration), and whether they have a fill color.

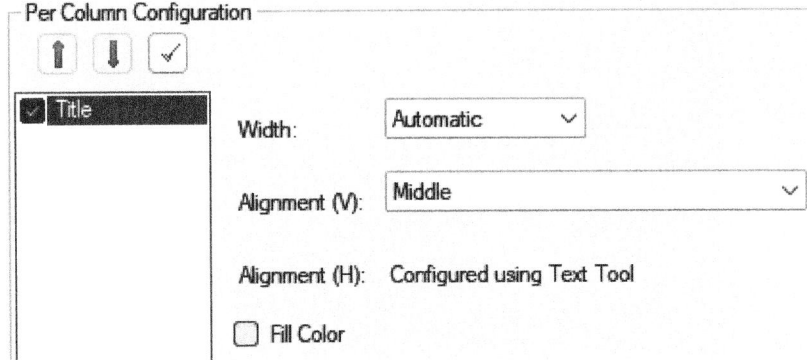

Figure 13.50: The Per Column Configuration options (select the field to enable them)

So, our output will be one snippet per record:

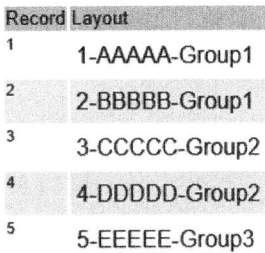

Figure 13.51: The rendered text

- **Each Group Of Records**: First, we'll enable the **Group By** section, allowing us to select which fields we'll use as each group identifier.

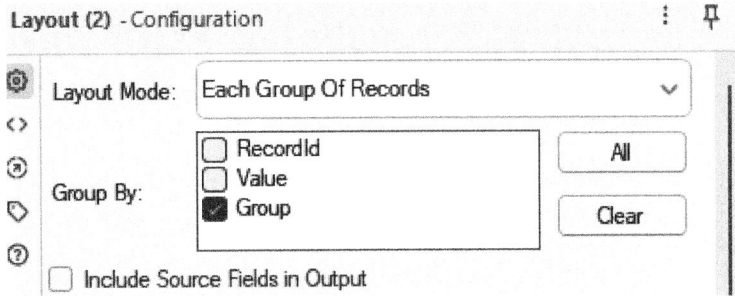

Figure 13.52: Selecting a grouping option enables the Group By fields

Also, the column selection options in the **Per Column Configuration** pane change, and unlike when we do it for **Each Individual Record**, this option will only allow us to select one data field (or snippet).

Per Column Configuration

Data Field:	Title ⌄
Width:	Automatic ⌄
Alignment (V):	Middle ⌄
Alignment (H):	Configured using Text Tool
☐ Fill Color	

Figure 13.53: The Per Column Configuration options (with grouping selected)

In this example, we'll get three records because we grouped by **Group**, and there are three groups in our dataset.

Record	Layout	
1	1-AAAAA-Group1	2-BBBBB-Group1
2	3-CCCCC-Group2	4-DDDDD-Group2
3	5-EEEEE-Group3	

Figure 13.54: The results when grouping

- **All Records Combined**: This will generate a unique record with a unique field, with all the snippets combined.

Record	Layout				
1	1- AAAAA- Group1	2- BBBBB- Group1	3- CCCCC- Group2	4- DDDDD- Group2	5- EEEEE- Group3

Figure 13.55: The results of selecting All Records Combined

For the **Layout Configuration** options, we can instruct Alteryx to arrange snippets horizontally or vertically.

If we choose **Vertical**, we can also define whether we want Alteryx to add section breaks, which can be very useful, depending on the format of rendering you decide to use in your report:

- For XLSX, the section name is used as the worksheet name

- For PDF, the section name is used as bookmarks, which act as links to that part of the PDF file

- For DOC, DOCX, and RTF, section names are used for bookmarks

- For PPTX, PNG, and HTML files, section names are not used

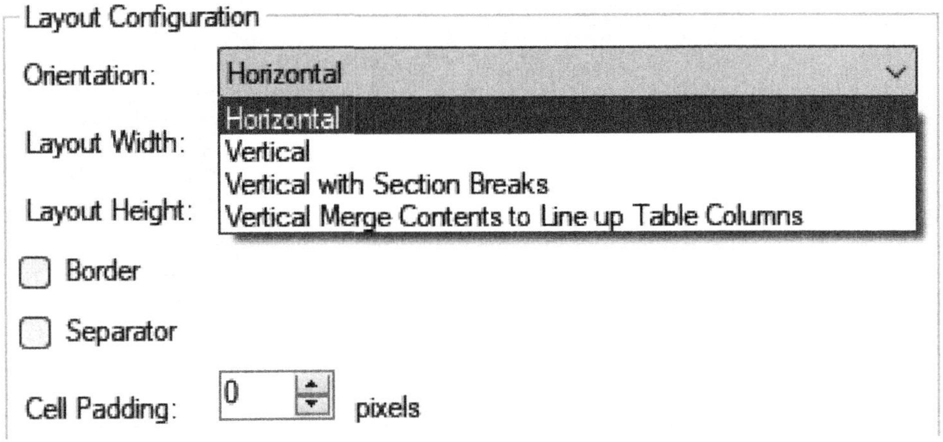

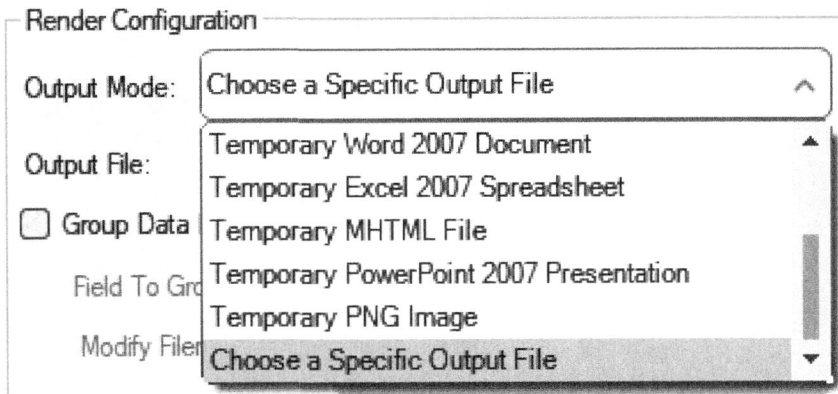

Figure 13.56: The layout Orientation options

Rendering your reports

So far, we have seen how to create report snippets and combine them in a layout. Once all of our pieces are defined and combined, we need to compose the report itself. This is achieved using the **Render** tool, which will allow us to translate those layouts and snippets into complete documents in various formats.

Figure 13.57: Choosing a specific file type for report rendering

The **Output Mode** dropdown shows the format options available. These options are available:

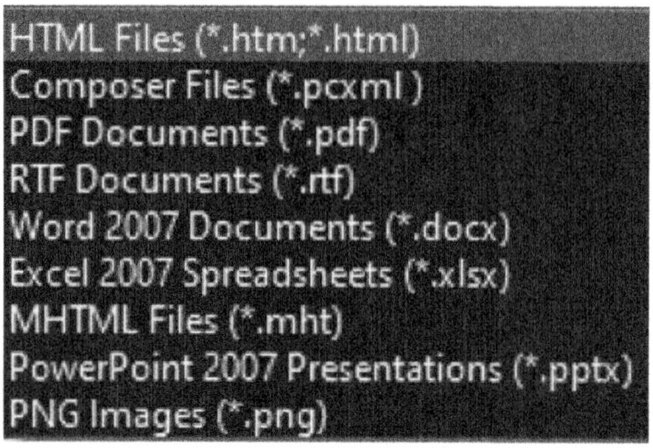

Figure 13.58: File types generated by the Render tool (.zip is not listed)

The supported formats are as follows:

- HTML files (`*.html`).

- Composer files (`*.pcxml`).

- PDF documents (`*.pdf`): PDF output is limited to 8,191 pages. If you generate a large number of PDF files, you might experience degraded performance. We recommend a record limit of 500 per PDF output. For large PDF files, we recommend a smaller record limit.

- RTF documents (`*.rtf`).

- Word documents (`*.docx`).

- Excel documents (`*.xlsx`).

- MHTML files (`*.mht`).

- PowerPoint presentations (`*.pptx`).

- PNG images (`*.png`): PNG output is limited to a size of 10,000 x 10,000 pixels or 100 million pixels.

> **Important note**
>
> Note that the ZIP option does not appear in Alteryx dialogs, but adding this extension to the name of the report to be generated will save the report in the HTML format and all dependent files in the resulting ZIP file.

In the **Output Mode** drop-down menu, we will see that Alteryx presents each possible format individually and with a temporary option.

This is used to generate the output files in the folder referenced in the [`Engine.TempFilePath`] workflow constant (available through the **Workflow Configuration** pane).

If you want to generate your report in a specific folder, you will need to select **Choose a Specific Output File** from the **Output Mode** drop-down menu.

An important point here is that the final format of the report will be determined by the extension that you select for the file to be generated.

Getting ready

We'll continue working with the previous recipe's workflow, so if you don't have it, you can download it from https://github.com/PacktPublishing/Alteryx-Designer-Cookbook; otherwise, open it.

How to do it...

As mentioned, we'll start with an existing workflow from the previous recipe.

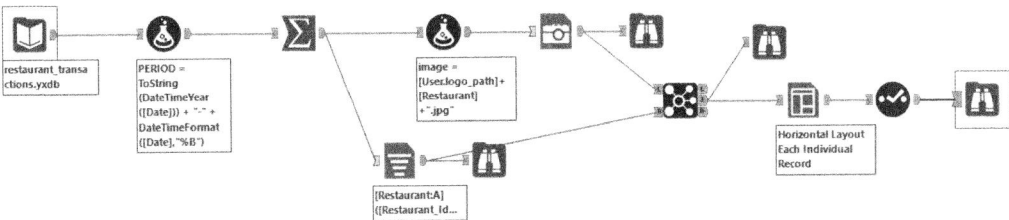

Figure 13.59: Starting a workflow for this recipe

So far, we have a layout field, called `Header`, composed of the `Restaurant` logo and a title based on the `Restaurant` name and `Restaurant_Id`.

Restaurant_Id	Restaurant	image	Header
30261	Life of Fi Bistro	.\images\Life of Fi Bistro.jpg	Layout - View Browse Tool Report Tab
30405	Howling Worth Cafe	.\images\Howling Worth Cafe.jpg	Layout - View Browse Tool Report Tab
30412	Bar-One	.\images\Bar-One.jpg	Layout - View Browse Tool Report Tab
40742	Mark Fish (&Chips)	.\images\Mark Fish (&Chips).jpg	Layout - View Browse Tool Report Tab
41961	Pinet Noir	.\images\Pinet Noir.jpg	Layout - View Browse Tool Report Tab

Figure 13.60: The Layout field already generated

To complete this report, we'll create a table that will contain all the transactions for each restaurant, grouped by month.

If we look again at our input data, we can see that each record represents an individual order for a restaurant.

	Order	Restaurant_Id	Restaurant	Total	User	Date
1	2416351	30261	Life of Fi Bistro	13.96	6393230	2022-01-03 07:31:14
2	2416355	30261	Life of Fi Bistro	86.11	6389974	2022-01-03 07:36:08
3	2416383	30261	Life of Fi Bistro	35.46	7548140	2022-01-03 07:55:00
4	2416388	30261	Life of Fi Bistro	16.7	8809585	2022-01-03 08:01:33
5	2416410	30261	Life of Fi Bistro	14.86	9825409	2022-01-03 08:24:35
6	2416455	30261	Life of Fi Bistro	58.31	6462743	2022-01-03 08:56:09
7	2416466	30261	Life of Fi Bistro	42.28	6407238	2022-01-03 09:02:08
8	2416492	30261	Life of Fi Bistro	65.44	6390795	2022-01-03 09:16:12
9	2416499	30261	Life of Fi Bistro	52.83	6389948	2022-01-03 09:22:44
10	2416504	30261	Life of Fi Bistro	57.54	6461989	2022-01-03 09:26:06
11	2416515	30261	Life of Fi Bistro	69.84	6535412	2022-01-03 09:36:50
12	2416544	30261	Life of Fi Bistro	30.2	7232940	2022-01-03 09:58:27

Figure 13.61: Data as output from the Input Data tool

Also, the `Date` field values are at the second level of granularity, so that's why we created the `PERIOD` field using the **Formula** tool, so now, we can have the year and month of each transaction in our dataset.

Order	Restaurant_Id	Restaurant	Total	User	Date	PERIOD
2416351	30261	Life of Fi Bistro	13.96	6393230	2022-01-03 07:31:14	2022-January
2416355	30261	Life of Fi Bistro	86.11	6389974	2022-01-03 07:36:08	2022-January
2416383	30261	Life of Fi Bistro	35.46	7548140	2022-01-03 07:55:00	2022-January
2416388	30261	Life of Fi Bistro	16.7	8809585	2022-01-03 08:01:33	2022-January
2416410	30261	Life of Fi Bistro	14.86	9825409	2022-01-03 08:24:35	2022-January
2416455	30261	Life of Fi Bistro	58.31	6462743	2022-01-03 08:56:09	2022-January
2416466	30261	Life of Fi Bistro	42.28	6407238	2022-01-03 09:02:08	2022-January
2416492	30261	Life of Fi Bistro	65.44	6390795	2022-01-03 09:16:12	2022-January
2416499	30261	Life of Fi Bistro	52.83	6389948	2022-01-03 09:22:44	2022-January

Figure 13.62: Data after creating the PERIOD field

Now, we'll get the monthly values for each restaurant:

1. Drop a **Summarize** tool below and a little to the right of the **Formula** tool.

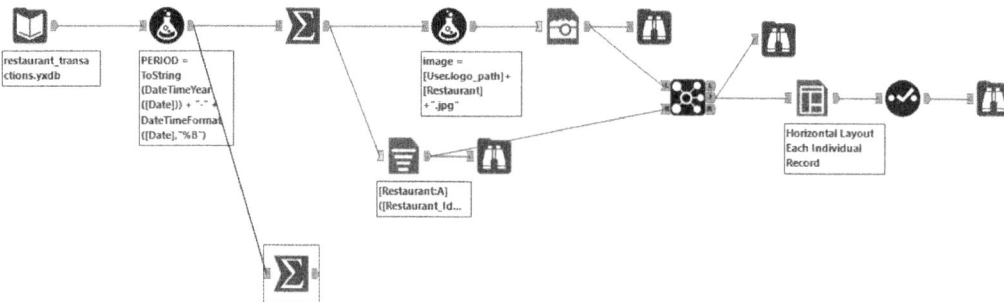

Figure 13.63: Adding the Summarize tool

2. Connect both tools, and click on the **Summarize** tool to access its configuration.

3. Click on `Restaurant_Id`, *Ctrl* + click on `Restaurant`, and *Ctrl* + click on `PERIOD` so that three fields are highlighted.

Fields:

	Field	Type
	Order	Int32
	Restaurant_Id	V_WString
	Restaurant	V_WString
	Total	Double
	User	Int32
	Date	DateTime
▶	PERIOD	V_WString

Figure 13.64: Multiple field selection (Ctrl + click) to group by

4. Click on **Add** and then on **Group By**.

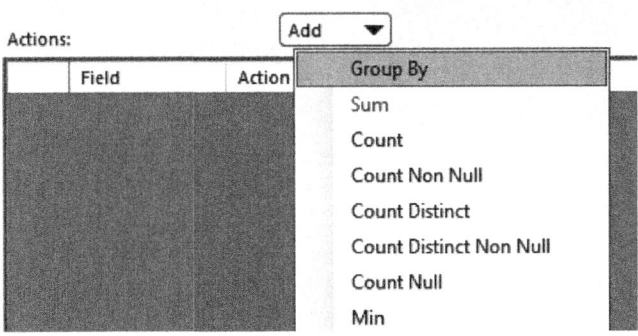

Figure 13.65: Selecting an action on the selected fields

The three fields will be added to the **Actions** pane with the selected action (**Group By**). This means that the calculations we'll configure later will be performed for each combination of values within these three fields.

5.   For the calculations, click on **Order**, *Ctrl* + click on **User**, click on **Add**, and then on **Count Distinct**. This will give us the total number of different orders and users that we have for each period, in each of the restaurants.

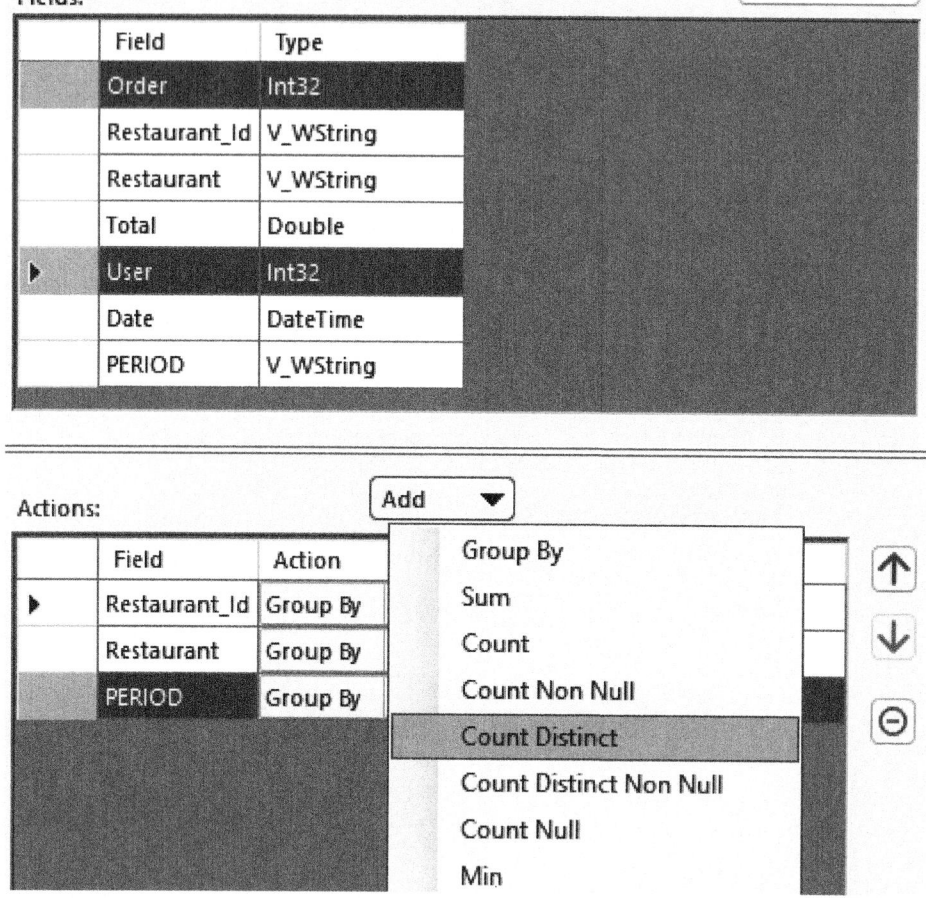

Figure 13.66: Selecting Count Distinct as the action for the User and Order fields

6. Finally, click on `Total`, then on **Add**, and select **Sum** so that we get the total sum per period, per restaurant.

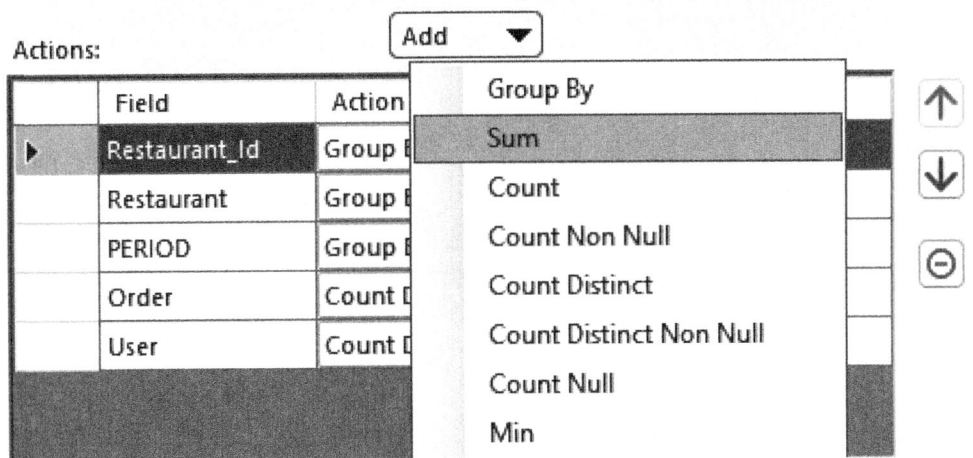

Figure 13.67: Selecting Sum as the aggregation method for Total

Your **Summarize** tool will look like this:

Fields: Select ▼

	Field	Type
	Order	Int32
	Restaurant_Id	V_WString
	Restaurant	V_WString
▶	Total	Double
	User	Int32
	Date	DateTime
	PERIOD	V_WString

Actions: Add ▼

	Field	Action		Output Field Name
	Restaurant_Id	Group By	∨	Restaurant_Id
	Restaurant	Group By	∨	Restaurant
	PERIOD	Group By	∨	PERIOD
▶	Order	Count Distinct	∨	CountDistinct_Order
	User	Count Distinct	∨	CountDistinct_User
	Total	Sum	∨	Sum_Total

Figure 13.68: The Summarize tool configuration

7. Now, click on the output field name for Order, and replace the CountDistinct_Order field name with Total_Orders.

8. Do the same for CountDistinct_User, and name it Total_Users. Change Sum_Total to Total_Spend.

    Additionally, we need to select some value to sort on PERIOD. Since it's a string, the default sorting order will be alphabetical, but we need to sort by dates.

9. Click on **Date**, click on **Add**, and select **Max**. This will bring up the maximum value for each period, enough to sort them correctly.

    Once you're done, your **Summarize** tool will look like this:

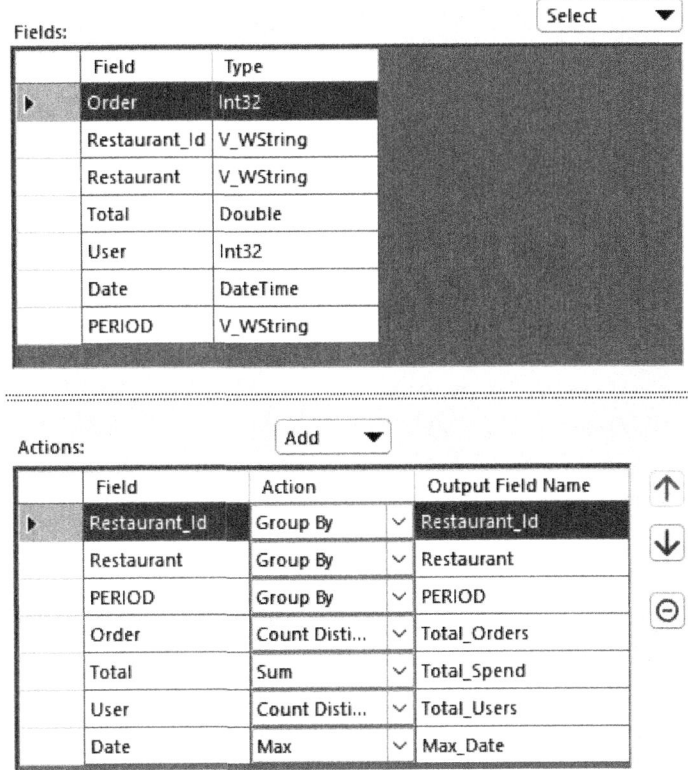

Figure 13.69: The Summarize tool final configuration (after all the renames)

10. Run the workflow and review the results.

Restaurant_Id	Restaurant	PERIOD	Total_Orders	Total_Spend	Total_Users	Max_Date
30261	Life of Fi Bistro	2022-October	234	10940.28	149	2022-10-31 15:37:08
30261	Life of Fi Bistro	2022-September	258	11296.21	164	2022-09-30 14:07:37
30261	Life of Fi Bistro	2023-February	205	8018.16	144	2023-02-28 14:03:33
30261	Life of Fi Bistro	2023-January	205	9255.41	132	2023-01-31 11:30:46
30261	Life of Fi Bistro	2023-March	217	8692.95	143	2023-03-30 14:37:59
30405	Howling Worth Cafe	2022-April	140	3748.59	108	2022-04-30 21:17:25
30405	Howling Worth Cafe	2022-August	138	3098.2	115	2022-08-31 21:51:17
30405	Howling Worth Cafe	2022-December	160	4850.24	129	2022-12-31 15:56:17

Figure 13.70: The results after running the Summarize tool

We have our measures (`Total_Orders`, `Total_Users`, and `Total_Spend`) per month (`PERIOD`) for each restaurant (`Restaurant_Id` and `Restaurant`), but the periods are still unsorted.

11. Drop a **Sort** tool after the **Summarize** tool.

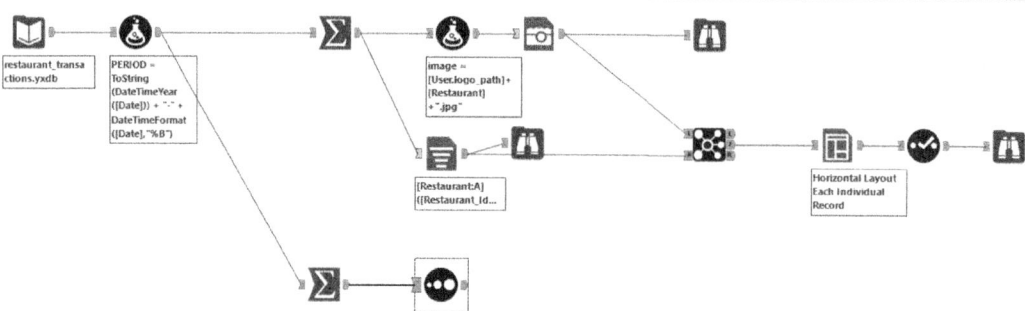

Figure 13.71: Adding a Sort tool

12. From the **Sort** tool configuration options, select `Restaurant_Id` from the **Name** dropdown and leave the **Order** value in **Ascending**.

13. Select `Max_Date` in the **Sort** tool's second sorting criteria, and select the order you want to use for the periods. I used **Ascending**, so the oldest will be on top.

Use Dictionary Order	English (United States)	

Fields

	Name	Order	
	Restaurant_Id ⌄	Ascending	⌄
▶	Max_Date ⌄	Ascending	⌄
✱	⌄		⌄

Figure 13.72: The Sort tool configuration

Now, we will put these values in a table so that we can combine them later with the existing `Header`, building a report for each restaurant.

14. Drop a **Table** tool next to the **Sort** tool, and since we need the **Browse** tool to see the table's output, add it now.

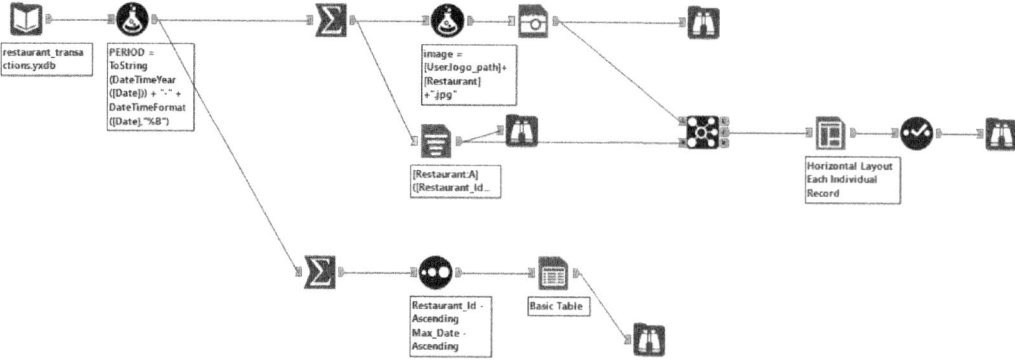

Figure 13.73: The Table tool added to the workflow

15. In the configuration options for the table, make sure **Basic** is selected for **Table Mode**.

16. For the **Group By** fields, select Restaurant_Id and Restaurant.

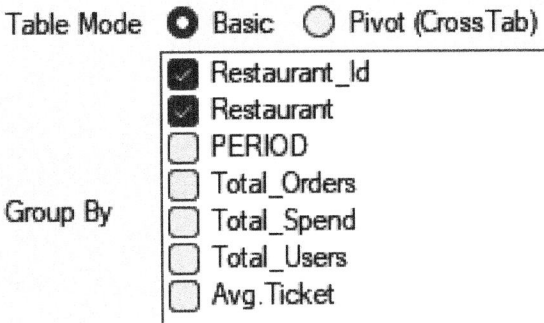

Figure 13.74: The Table tool grouping options

17. Leave the table configuration as it is for now, and focus on the **Per Column Configuration** section. This panel shows the fields that will appear in the generated table.

18. Because we are creating a report for each restaurant, it'll be redundant to have the name and ID of each one in the table rows, so deselect Restaurant_Id and Restaurant from the list.

Figure 13.75: The Table tool fields list

19. Drop a **Browse** tool after the **Table** tool, and run the workflow.

Note that the results show a table for each restaurant, with the selected fields but no formats for the values.

Record	Table			
1	**PERIOD**	**Total_Orders**	**Total_Users**	**Total_Spend**
	2022-April	304	178	13,006
	2022-August	244	144	9,895
	2022-December	232	144	8,449
	2022-February	273	169	8,851
	2022-January	391	231	15,523
	2022-July	320	191	12,183
	2022-June	307	182	13,501
	2022-March	329	173	12,773
	2022-May	267	167	11,754
	2022-November	215	133	8,312
	2022-October	234	149	10,940
	2022-September	258	164	11,296
	2023-February	205	144	8,018
	2023-January	205	132	9,255
	2023-March	217	143	8,693
2	**PERIOD**	**Total_Orders**	**Total_Users**	**Total_Spend**
	2022-April	140	108	3,749
	2022-August	138	115	3,098
	2022-December	160	129	4,850
	2022-February	179	146	5,181
	2022-January	296	238	8,565
	2022-July	177	144	5,199
	2022-June	254	208	6,905

Figure 13.76: The generated tool preview (using the Browse tool)

20. Click on the **Table** tool to access its configuration.

21. Click on the `Total_Orders` field, and note that the options on the right are enabled.

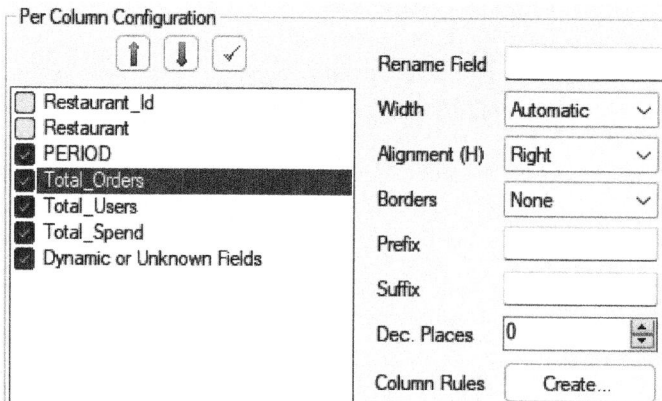

Figure 13.77: The Per Column Configuration options

Here, you can set some options for each field in your table.

22. In the **Rename Field** textbox, enter Total Orders.

23. Click on Total_Users, and rename it Total Users.

Since both fields are integers, we will not set any decimal places. Note that this renaming can also be achieved using the **Select** tool, but we'll rename the field using the **Table** tool, as it only renames the output names for the resulting table.

24. Click on Total_Spend, rename it Total Spend, enter $ for the prefix, and select **2** in the **Dec. Places** Numeric UpDown control.

25. Run the workflow again, and see how the changes were applied.

Record	Table			
1	PERIOD	Total Orders	Total Users	Total Spend
	2022-April	304	178	$13,005.59
	2022-August	244	144	$9,894.94
	2022-December	232	144	$8,448.82
	2022-February	273	169	$8,850.98
	2022-January	391	231	$15,522.65
	2022-July	320	191	$12,182.98
	2022-June	307	182	$13,501.01
	2022-March	329	173	$12,773.32
	2022-May	267	167	$11,754.32
	2022-November	215	133	$8,312.12
	2022-October	234	149	$10,940.28
	2022-September	258	164	$11,296.21
	2023-February	205	144	$8,018.16
	2023-January	205	132	$9,255.41
	2023-March	217	143	$8,692.95
2	PERIOD	Total Orders	Total Users	Total Spend
	2022-April	140	108	$3,748.59
	2022-August	138	115	$3,098.20
	2022-December	160	129	$4,850.24
	2022-February	179	146	$5,181.26
	2022-January	296	238	$8,565.22
	2022-July	177	144	$5,198.53
	2022-June	254	208	$6,904.87

Figure 13.78: The resulting table after the per column configurations

Seeing the results so far, an idea came to me that may offer another interesting measure to each restaurant report. How useful would it be to add the average ticket for each period? After validating that it may be very useful for our users, we decided to add it.

26. Go to the **Preparation** category on the toolbox, and drag a **Formula** tool to the line that connects the **Sort** and **Table** tools. When you see the line turn blue, drop the tool, and Alteryx Designer will insert it into the workflow.

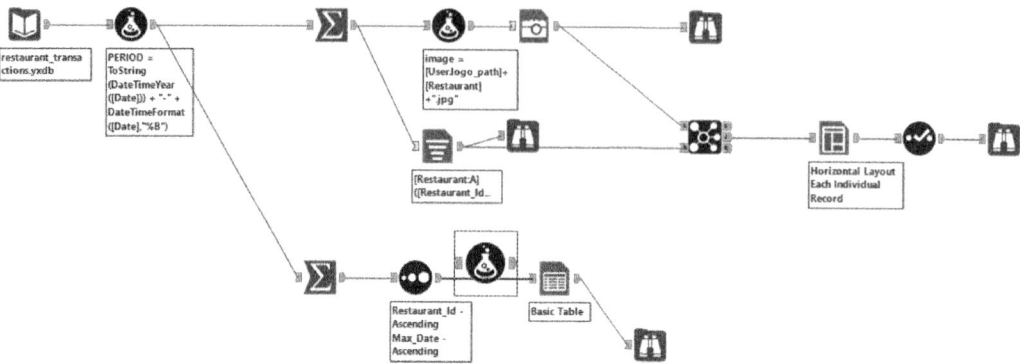

Figure 13.79: Inserting a Formula tool in the workflow

27. Click on the **Formula** tool and create a new column, called `Avg.Ticket`, and use the following expression as the formula:

```
[Total_Spend]/[Total_Orders]
```

28. Change the data type to **Double**.

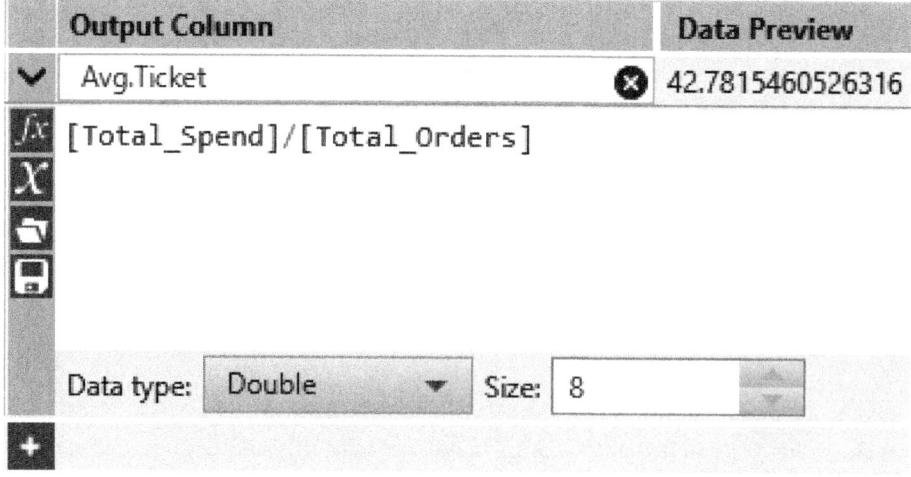

Figure 13.80: The inserted Formula tool configuration

If you return to the **Table** tool, you'll see that the new field is available in the fields selected for the report.

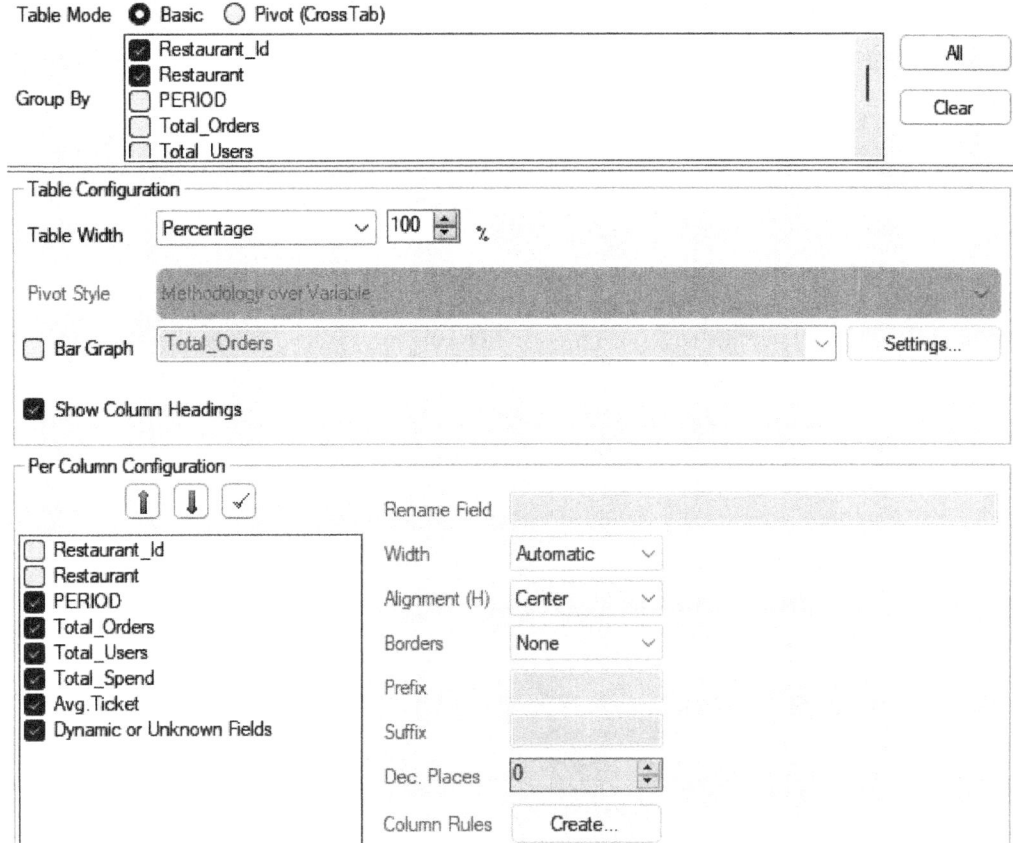

Figure 13.81: A new field added to the field list

29. Click on the Avg.Ticket field to enable its options.

30. Rename it Average Ticket, set the Prefix to $, and set **2** as the **Dec. Places** option.

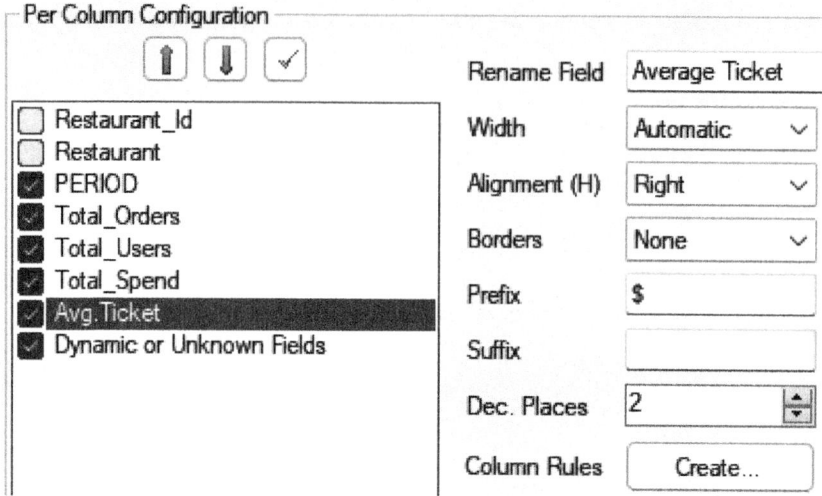

Figure 13.82: Setting the options for Avg.Ticket

31. Run the workflow again, and you'll see that the new field was added.

Record	Table
1	

PERIOD	Total Orders	Total Users	Total Spend	Average Ticket
2022-January	391	231	$15,522.65	$39.70
2022-February	273	169	$8,850.98	$32.42
2022-March	329	173	$12,773.32	$38.82
2022-April	304	178	$13,005.59	$42.78
2022-May	267	167	$11,754.32	$44.02
2022-June	307	182	$13,501.01	$43.98
2022-July	320	191	$12,182.98	$38.07
2022-August	244	144	$9,894.94	$40.55
2022-September	258	164	$11,296.21	$43.78
2022-October	234	149	$10,940.28	$46.75
2022-November	215	133	$8,312.12	$38.66
2022-December	232	144	$8,448.82	$36.42
2023-January	205	132	$9,255.41	$45.15
2023-February	205	144	$8,018.16	$39.11
2023-March	217	143	$8,692.95	$40.06

Record	
2	

PERIOD	Total Orders	Total Users	Total Spend	Average Ticket
2022-January	296	238	$8,565.22	$28.94
2022-February	179	146	$5,181.26	$28.95
2022-March	175	147	$4,596.13	$26.26
2022-April	140	108	$3,748.59	$26.78
2022-May	226	186	$5,956.77	$26.36
2022-June	254	208	$6,904.87	$27.18

Figure 13.83: The table rendered, with the Avg.Ticket field added and formatted

So far, we've concentrated on getting our data table right. We could improve its look a lot (a task I recommend doing once the report has been collated), but for now, we will arrange all the snippets (`Header` and `Table`) in a report. Again, the **Layout** tool can help us arrange `Header` and `Table` vertically, but first, just give `Table` a meaningful name.

32. Drop a **Select** tool after the **Table** tool.

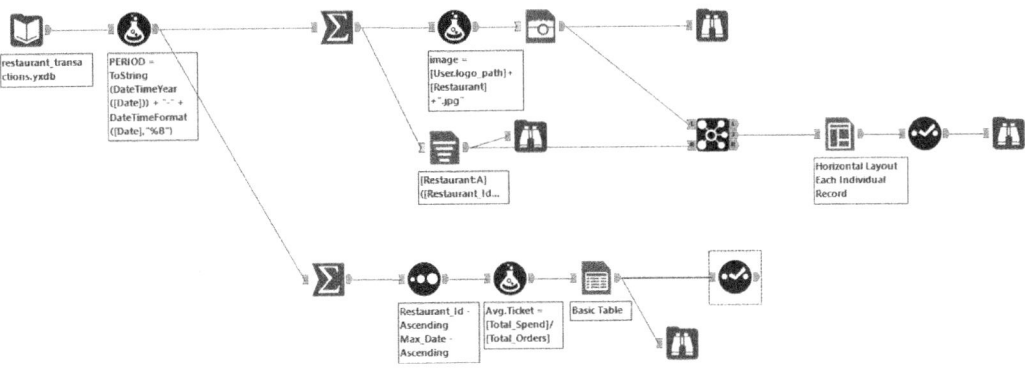

Figure 13.84: Adding the Select tool

33. Rename the `Table` field `Orders Table`.

	Field	Type		Size	Rename	Description
▶	Restaurant_Id	V_WString	▾	20		
	Restaurant	V_WString	▾	25		
	Table	V_String	▾	214...	Orders Table	
	*Unknown	Unknown	▾	0		Dynamic or Unknown

TIP: To reorder multiple rows: select, right-click and drag.

Options ▾ | ↑ ↓

Figure 13.85: Renaming the Table field

Now, we need to join `Header` and `Orders Table` so that we have both on each restaurant record.

34. Drop a **Join** tool, and connect the Header's last **Select** tool to the **L** input anchor, and the Orders Table section's **Select** tool to the **R** input, as shown here.

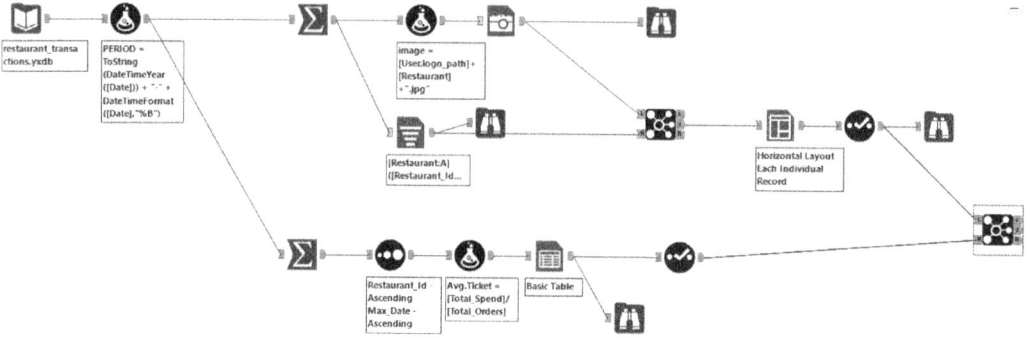

Figure 13.86: Adding a Join tool to combine Header and Order Table

Disregard any error message you may find with the **Join** tool at this moment (Now, we'll configure the fields and make the message disappear.)

35. In the **Join** configuration options, make sure **Join by Specific Fields** is selected.

36. Select Restaurant_Id from the **Left** dropdown. Alteryx Designer will auto-select Restaurant_Id for the **Right** dropdown. If this doesn't happen, the fields were probably renamed in a previous step, or there's a typo in the name. Review this, or select the field name that corresponds to Restaurant_Id on the **R** input manually.

37. Do the same for the Restaurant field.

38. Deselect any duplicated fields (in this case, Restaurant_Id and Restaurant from any of the incoming anchors; we deselected the ones coming from the **Right** dropdown).

Your **Join** tool configuration should look like this:

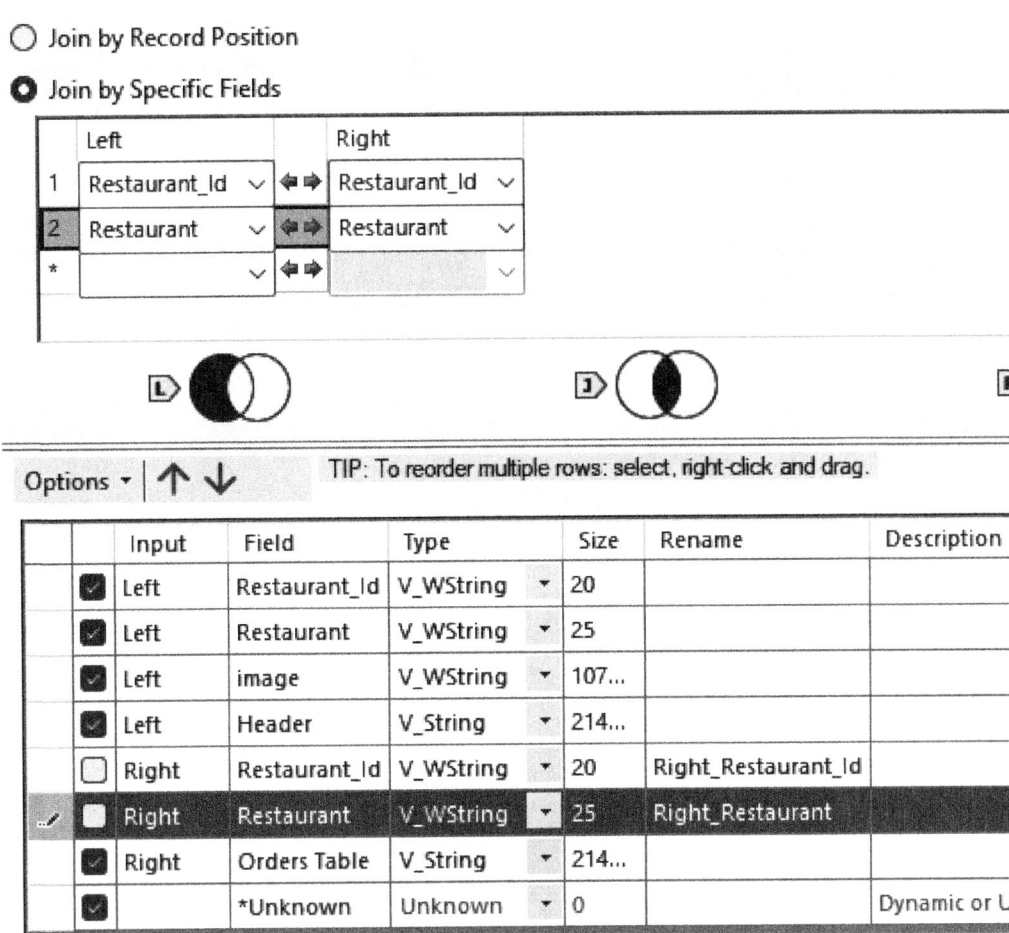

Figure 13.87: Configuring the Join tool on Restaurant_Id and Restaurant

39. Run the workflow to ensure that each record corresponds to a restaurant, both report snippets (Header and Orders Table) are present, and no records are missing due to a non-matching ID or name.

Restaurant_Id	Restaurant	image	Header	Orders Table
30261	Life of Fi Bistro	..\images\Life of Fi Bistro.jpg	Layout - View Browse Tool Report Tab	Table - View Browse Tool Report Tab
30405	Howling Worth Cafe	..\images\Howling Worth Cafe.jpg	Layout - View Browse Tool Report Tab	Table - View Browse Tool Report Tab
30412	Bar-One	..\images\Bar-One.jpg	Layout - View Browse Tool Report Tab	Table - View Browse Tool Report Tab
40742	Mark Fish (&Chips)	..\images\Mark Fish (&Chips).jpg	Layout - View Browse Tool Report Tab	Table - View Browse Tool Report Tab
41961	Pinet Noir	..\images\Pinet Noir.jpg	Layout - View Browse Tool Report Tab	Table - View Browse Tool Report Tab

Figure 13.88: The results after joining data streams

At this point, we have two options for proceeding:

- Use a vertical layout to compose the report page(s), combining Header on top and the table below

- Since we have Header and a single snippet (in this case, it's a table, but it could be a layout composed of several snippets combined), we can use the **Render** tool directly

> **Important note**
>
> As we'll see in the next recipe, this second method doesn't work for the HTML format, since headers and footers are not rendered in that format.

Let's see both options so that you know the pros and cons of each and can choose which one to use, depending on what you need.

40. To go with the **Layout** option, drop a **Layout** tool connected to the **J** output anchor of the **Join** tool.

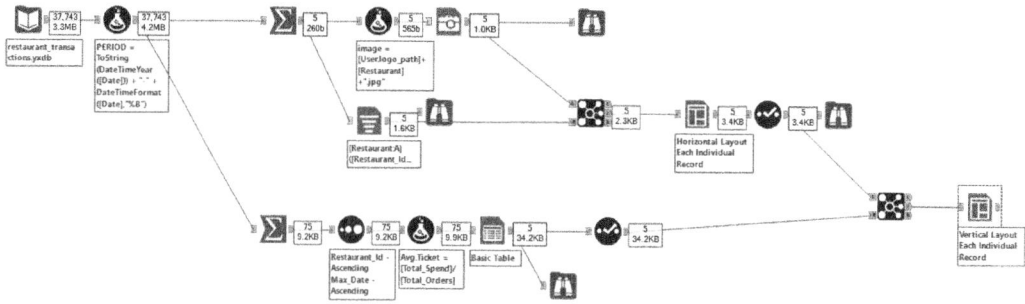

Figure 13.89: Adding a Layout tool to combine Header and Table

41. From the **Layout** tool configuration, make sure **Each Individual Record** is selected in **Layout Mode**.

42. For **Orientation**, select **Vertical** from the dropdown. Leave the other options as default.

43. Make sure Header is above Orders Table in **Per column Configuration**. If it's not, click on it, and arrange it using the green arrows above the field box to put it on top.

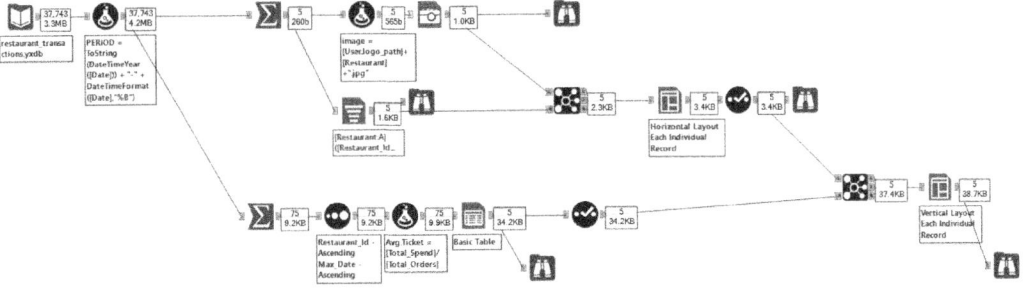

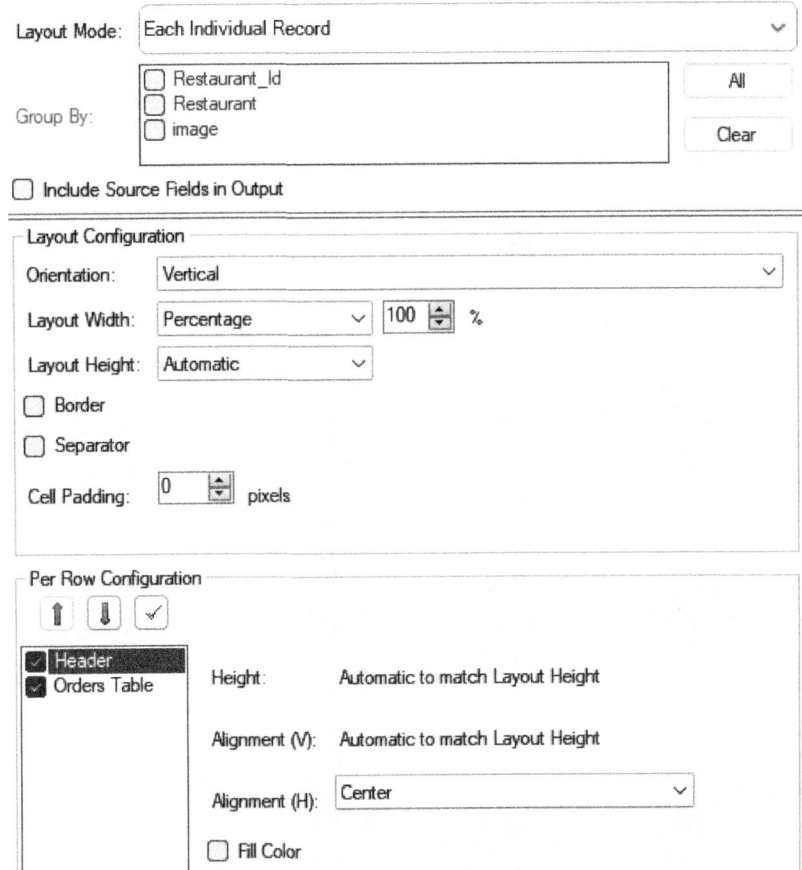

Figure 13.90: Configuring the layout on a vertical orientation

Note that when you click on any field to adjust its options, since we set **Layout Height** to **Automatic**, we are not allowed to configure the snippet's height and vertical alignment.

44. Drop a **Browse** tool after the **Layout** tool, and run the workflow.

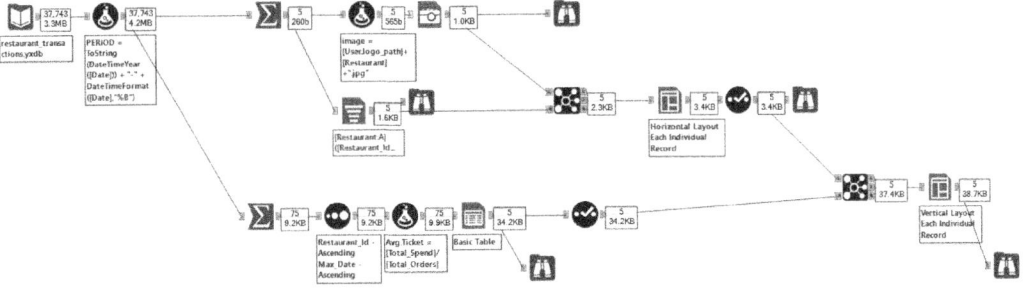

Figure 13.91: To preview report snippets, add a Browse tool

45. If you click on the added **Browse** tool, you'll see in the **Browse** panel that the content is aligned vertically, and all the restaurants are still in the same generated dataset.

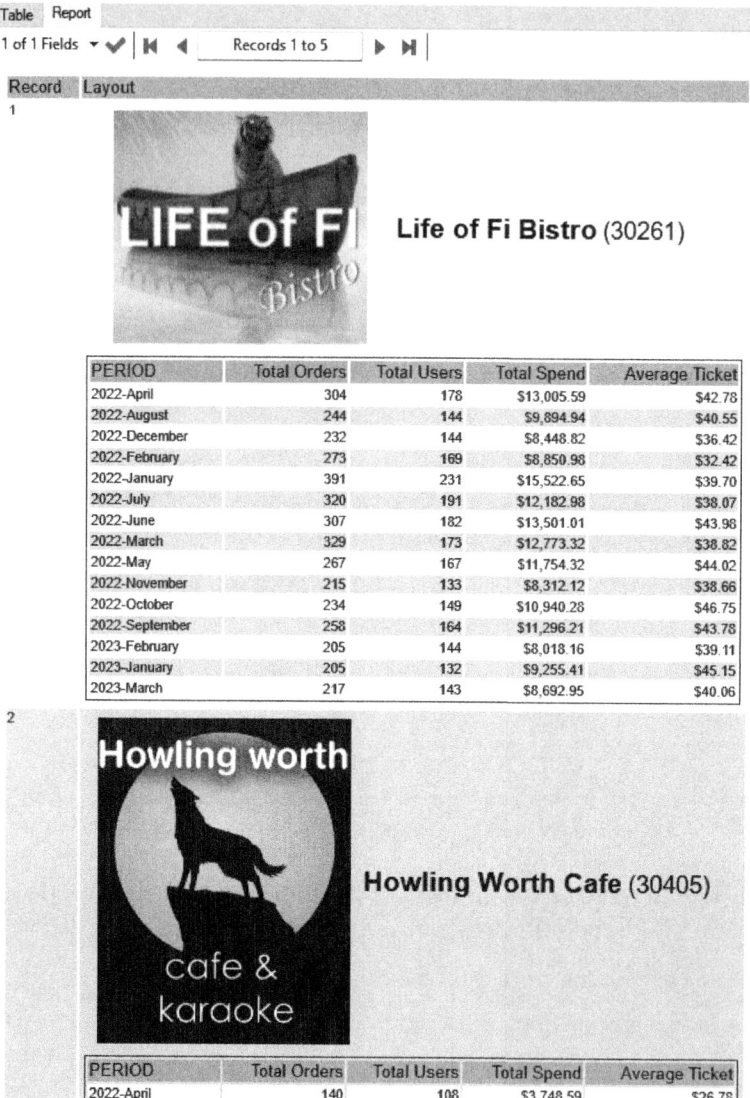

Figure 13.92: A rendered preview of Header and Table

Now that we have arranged the snippets, we'll tell Alteryx Designer to generate a report file for each restaurant in a folder.

To do it, we'll start creating a folder called REPORT within the recipe folder structure, where we'll save all the generated files.

Figure 13.93: The project folder structure

46. Return to Alteryx Designer, and drop a **Render** tool onto the canvas after the **Layout** tool.

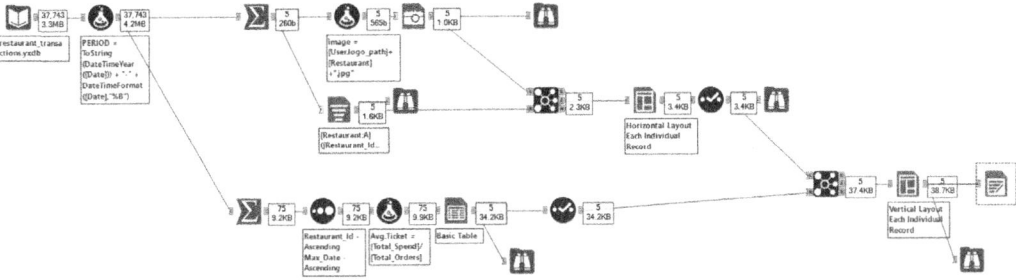

Figure 13.94: Adding a Render tool

47. From the **Render** tool configuration, select **Choose a Specific Output File** (otherwise, the grouping options won't be available).

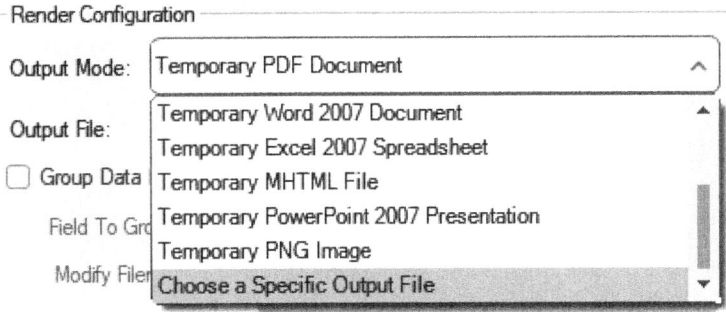

Figure 13.95: Selecting a specific output file

Once you select a specific output file, the **Output File** field will be enabled. Point the generated files to the following path:

```
..\REPORT\_Report.pdf
```

48. Click on **Group Data Into Separate Reports** to enable the options.

49. From the **Field To Group On** dropdown, select **Restaurant**.

50. From the **Modify Filename By** dropdown, select **Prepending Group To Filename** (so that we'll get [Restaurant]_Report.pdf as the filenames).

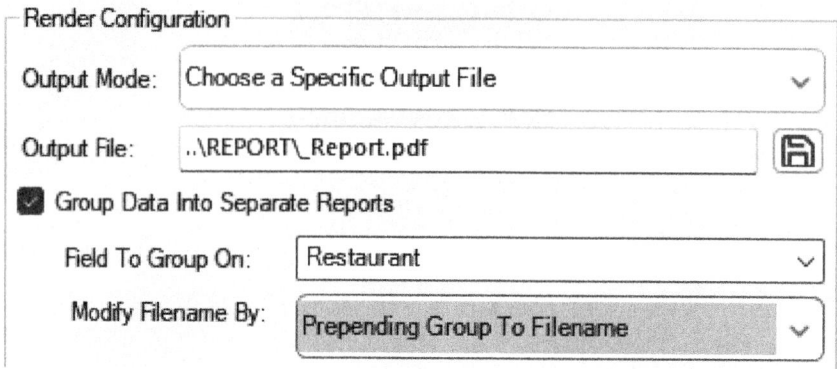

Figure 13.96: Grouping and renaming output files

51. Run the workflow and review the **Results** pane. Note that Alteryx generated one file per restaurant, prepending the restaurant name (the contents of the Restaurant field saved under a filename) in the REPORT folder. (Your absolute path may vary, depending on where you created the recipe's root folder.)

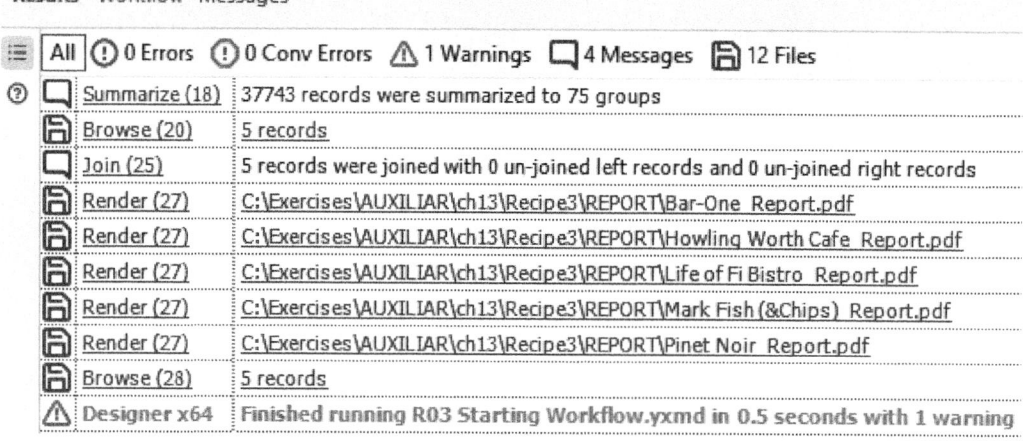

Figure 13.97: The execution log for the current workflow

From there, you can click on any filename to open the report, or you can right-click and access the **Open Folder** option, which takes you directly to the REPORT folder on your disk.

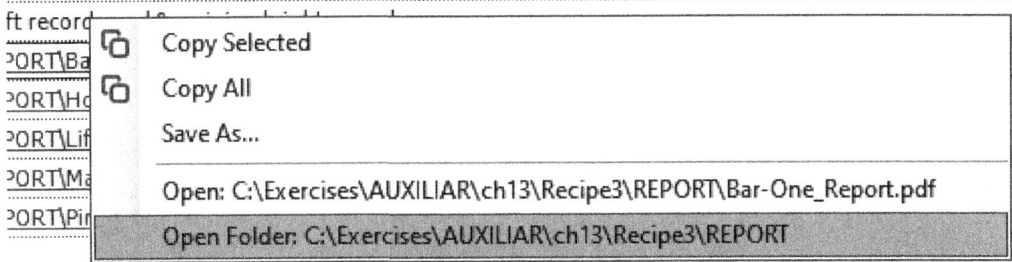

Figure 13.98: The REPORT folder shortcuts

As mentioned previously, you can use the **Render** tool options directly to configure the same (or very similar) outcome.

52. Drop a new **Render** tool onto the canvas, and connect it to the **J** output anchor of the **Join** tool.

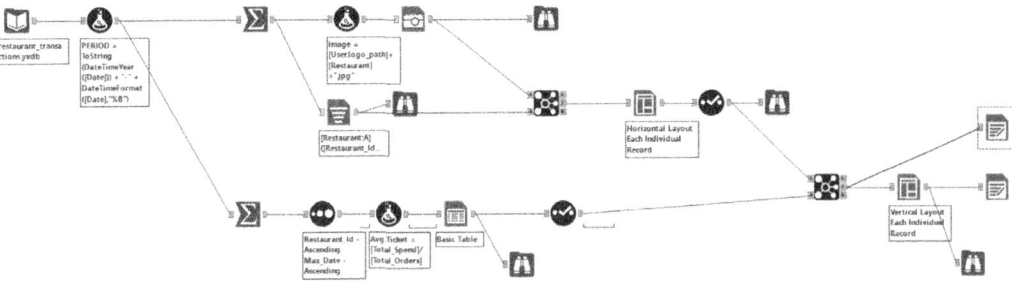

Figure 13.99: Adding a second Render tool to try out the Header field without using the Layout tool

Disregard any arising error messages for now.

53. In the new **Render** tool, select **Choose a Specific Output File** for **Output Mode**.

54. This time, I'll reverse the pieces of the filename so that we can identify each report later. I'll point the output file to `..\REPORT\Report_.pdf` and select **Appending Group To Filename** under **Modify Filename By**.

This way, we know that reports starting with Report_ followed by the restaurant name are generated by this tool/method.

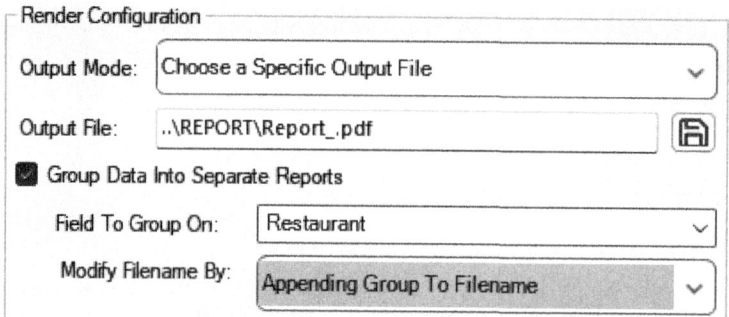

Figure 13.100: The Render tool filename configuration

Here is where we'll take advantage of some additional settings.

55. From the **Data Field** dropdown, select **Orders Table**.

56. Click on the **Header** checkbox to enable it, and select **Header** from the dropdown.

57. Also, check the **Show header and footer on first page** option; otherwise, we won't see the header on the first page. (This is a very useful setting when composing multi-page reports and we need a cover page, or just the first page not showing any header.)

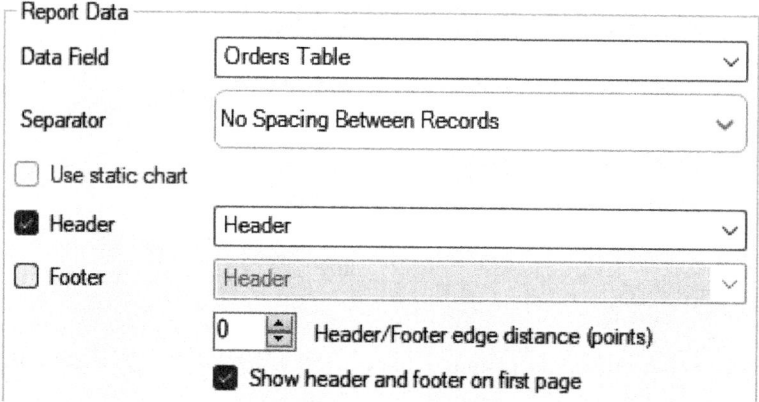

Figure 13.101: Selecting the Header field for the report header

If you check the results, you'll see that a warning message appears for each report generated by this method.

The size of a header will be larger than the top margin. The top margin will be adjusted.

Figure 13.102: A warning caused by the size of the composed header

This is caused by the size of the header we built (it's bigger than the default `0.5 inch` value), and Alteryx will adjust it automatically. However, if you want to remove the warnings, you can set up the margins manually, using the options available in the **Report Style** pane.

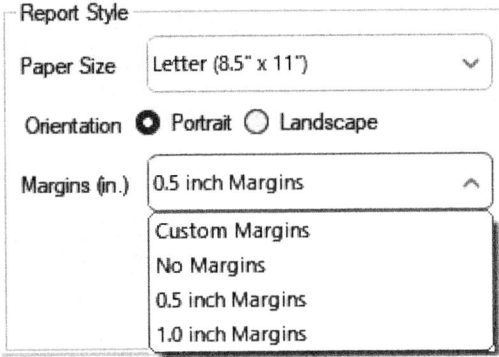

Figure 13.103: The margin options for reports

> **Important note**
>
> Once you finish building your report workflow, remember to enable **Disable All Browse Tools** from the workflow configuration options, under the **Runtime** tab.

Canvas Workflow Runtime Events Meta Info XML View

Memory Limit
- ⦿ Use Global Default
- ◯ Use Specific Amount: 16352 ⬍ Megabytes

Temporary files
- ⦿ Use Global Default
- ◯ Use Specific Folder:
  C:\ProgramData\Alteryx\Engine   [...]

Conversion Errors
- ☑ Limit Conversion Errors
  - Maximum Errors per Location: 10 ⬍
  - ☐ Stop Processing When Limit is Reached

Predictive Tools Code Page   ⓘ

Western European (CP 1252)   ⌄

Record Limit for All Inputs: No Limit

- ☐ Cancel Running Workflow on Error
- ☑ Disable All Browse Tools
- ☐ Show All Macro Messages
- ☐ Disable All Tools that Write Output
- ☐ Enable Performance Profiling

Figure 13.104: Disable All Browse Tools under the Runtime tab

Using HTML and JavaScript in your reports

In the previous recipe, we automatically generated a report in the PDF format for each existing restaurant in our dataset.

Alteryx allows us to do this, and it is a widely used use case – for example, to provide web access to each client's respective report, or to integrate them into a web portal.

In this recipe, we will reuse a large part of what has been built so far in this chapter, and with some simple modifications, we will generate a report in HTML, adding to each period a link that will navigate to the details of transactions carried out in that period, plus the capacity to navigate back to the summary report, using a **Go Back** button. (For this, we will use the JavaScript embedded in the report.) We also will generate detailed HTML files for each restaurant, for each period.

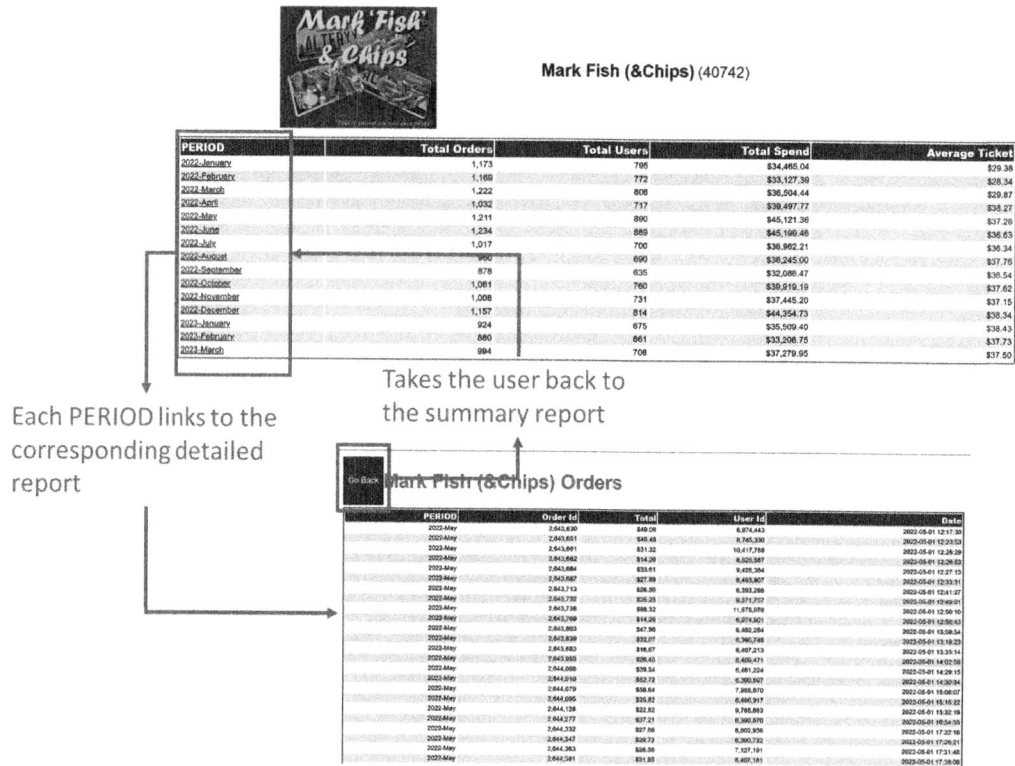

Figure 13.105: The HTML report navigation options

Alteryx has a special way of achieving this, and it is through a reserved tag called `<htmlpassthrough>`, and its corresponding closing tag (`</htmlpassthrough>`).

This tag tells Alteryx that everything between the tags should be considered HTML and should not be altered or parsed. (Alteryx formats certain characters internally, so they can be seen later in a report.)

The way to use them correctly is as follows:

```
<htmlpassthrough>
<![CDATA[
<Put here your HTML>
]]>
</htmlpassthrough>
```

> **Important note**
> This method only works for HTML reports, and you must select **Expert Mode**. (The **Validate PCXML** setting is optional but always recommended.)

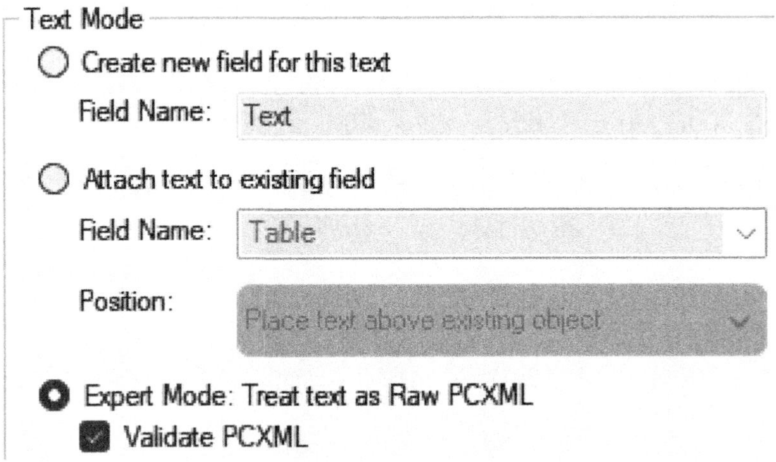

Figure 13.106: Expert Mode selection

Getting ready

We will use the previous recipe's resulting workflow as the starting point for this recipe. If you didn't complete it, you can download the assets from here: `https://github.com/PacktPublishing/Alteryx-Designer-Cookbook`.

Before we start, we will clean up the workflow of the previous recipe a bit so that we can work properly. This type of process is highly recommended for all the workflows you develop.

If you don't have the workflow open, please open it. The previous recipe's resulting workflow was as follows:

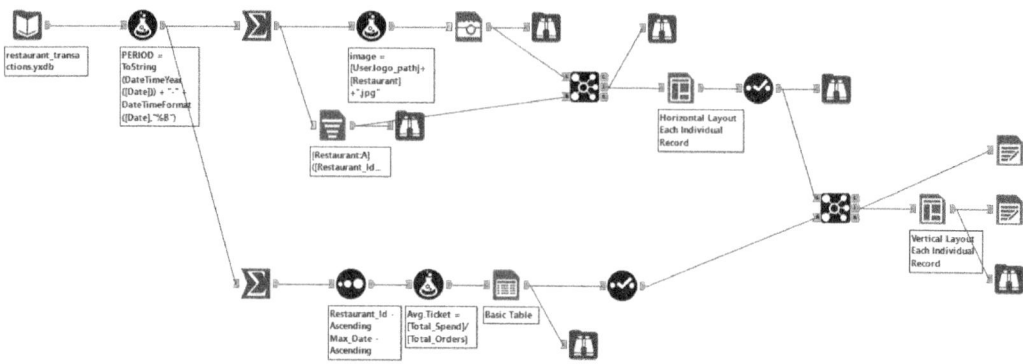

Figure 13.107: The previous recipe workflow

1. Click and drag around the table generation section of the workflow, as you can see in the following diagram. This will select all the existing tools within the blue area.

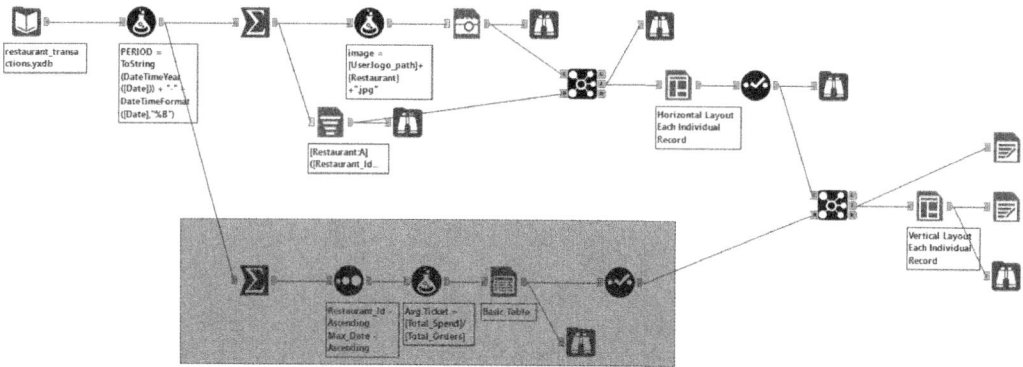

Figure 13.108: Selecting a group of tools

You can confirm that the tools were selected because they show a blue dashed square around them.

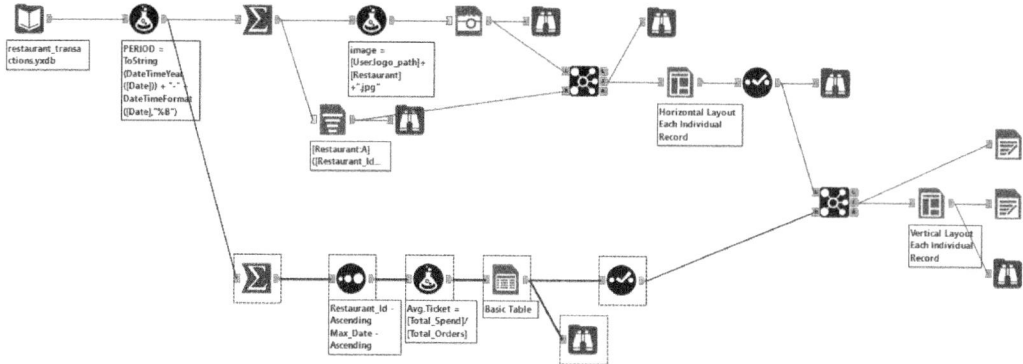

Figure 13.109: The selected tools show a blue border around them

2. Right-click on any of the selected tools, and select the **Add To New Container** option from the menu.

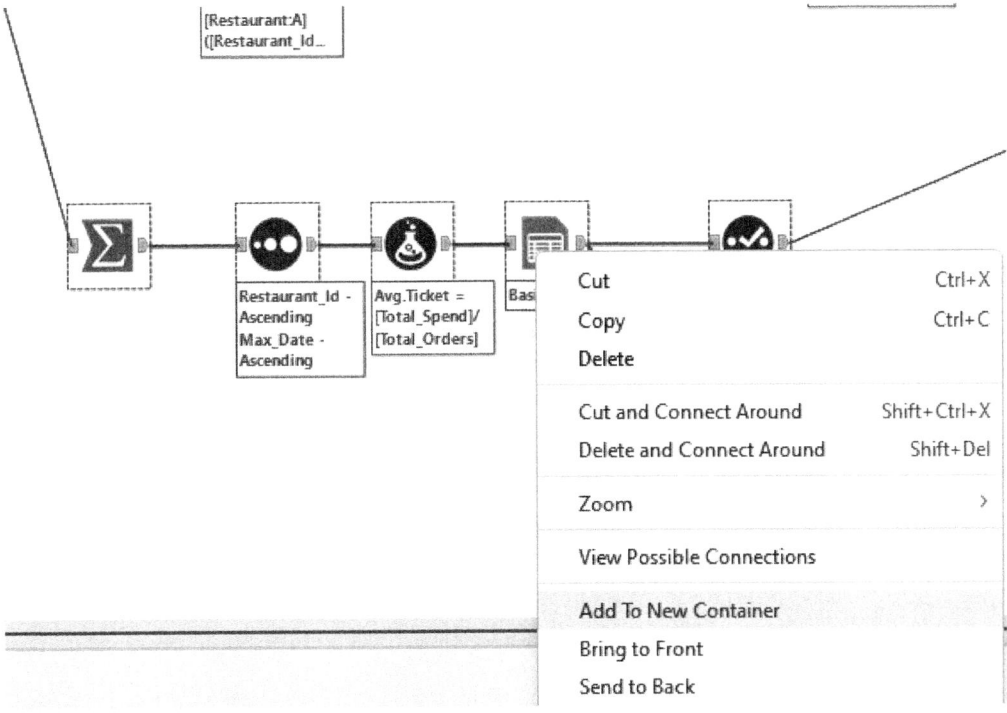

Figure 13.110: Right-click to wrap the selected tools into a new container

A new **Tool Container** tool will wrap all the selected tools. If you double-click on its title (**Container 50** in this example), you'll be able to change the title to something meaningful. (You can do the same by clicking on the title and renaming the container from its configuration panel.)

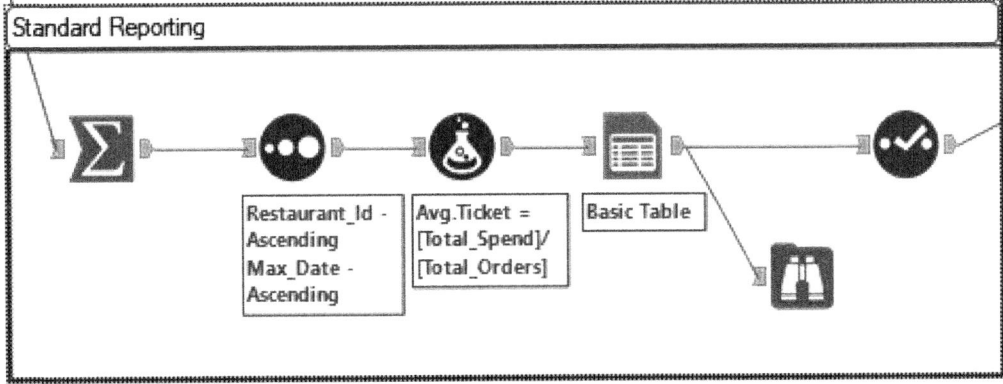

Figure 13.111: Renaming a Tool Container tool from its header

3. Rename it `Standard Reporting`.

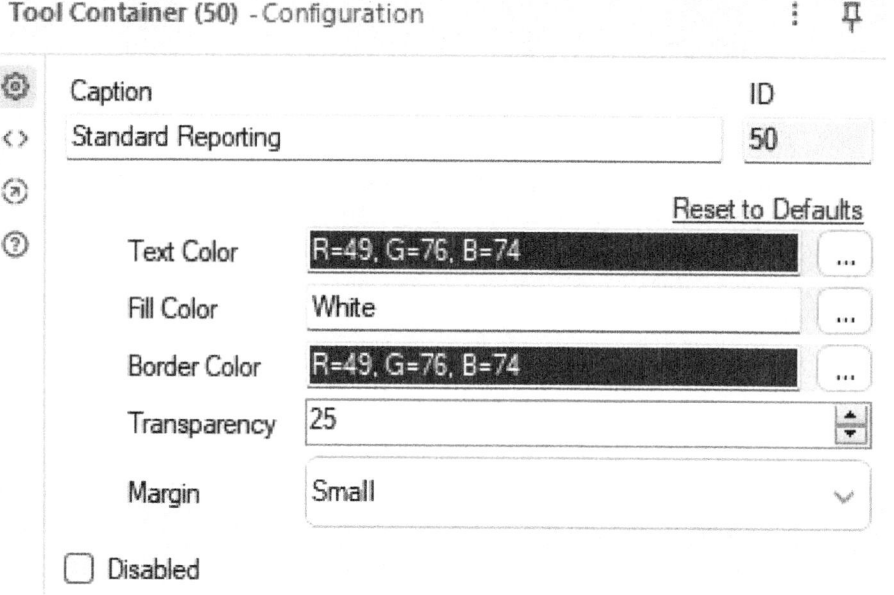

Figure 13.112: The Tool Container tool configuration options

4. Once you have done that, click on any part of the canvas so that the UI refreshes it.

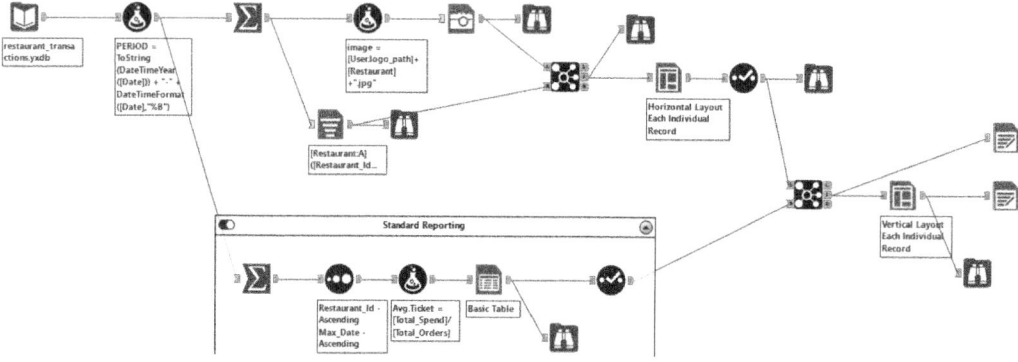

Figure 13.113: The Tool Container tool added and refreshed

5. Repeat the marquee selection around the two existing **Render** tools.
6. Add them to a new container.

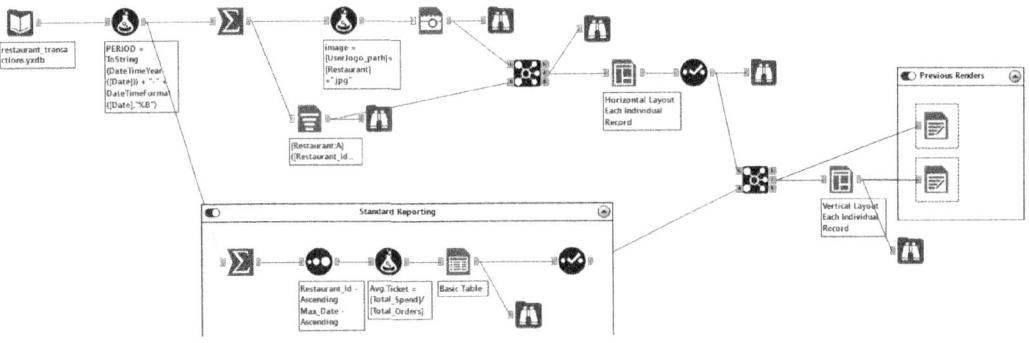

Figure 13.114: The Tool Container tool around the existing Render tools

7. Rename the added container `Previous Renders`.

8. This time, check **Disabled** too so that none of the tools within the disabled container will execute.

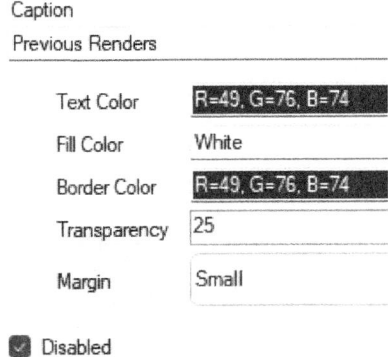

Figure 13.115: The Tool Container tool configuration

Now, your workflow looks like this:

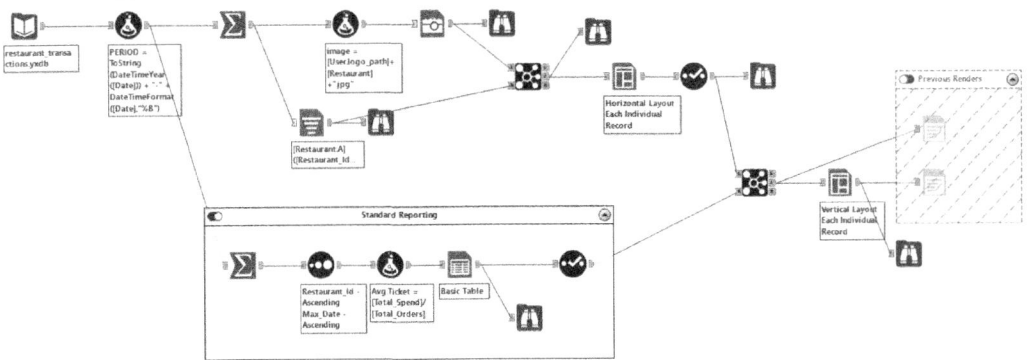

Figure 13.116: The resulting workflow

9.   Go to the **File** menu and hit **Save As**. Name your file `WORKFLOW\HTML Report.yxmd` within this recipe's folder.

While we could remove what's in the tool containers because we're going to create that logic again, since we have it, we won't do that at the moment (just in case we need something from them). Once the new workflow logic is finished with and we can confirm that we don't need it, we will proceed to eliminate the disabled containers.

Now, we are ready to start.

How to do it...

Let's start by modifying what we already built. As we saw in the introduction to this recipe, this report consists of several HTML pages, each one containing the details of each transaction carried out in the corresponding period.

We will name each page according to the following convention:

`DETAILS\Restaurant_Id_PERIOD.html`

They will all be stored in a subfolder of `REPORT` (which is itself a folder within the structure of this recipe) called `DETAILS`:

1.   If you don't have this folder structure, go to an Explorer window and create it. It needs to be there when Alteryx renders the files.

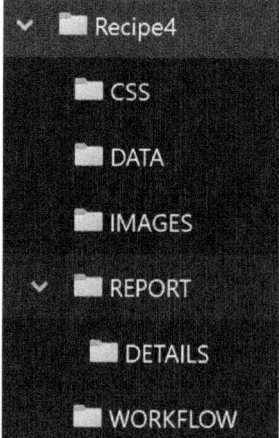

Figure 13.117: The folder structure

2.   From the **Preparation** category, drag a **Formula** tool, and drop it over the connection between the existing **Formula** tool and **Table** tool, as shown in the following diagram.

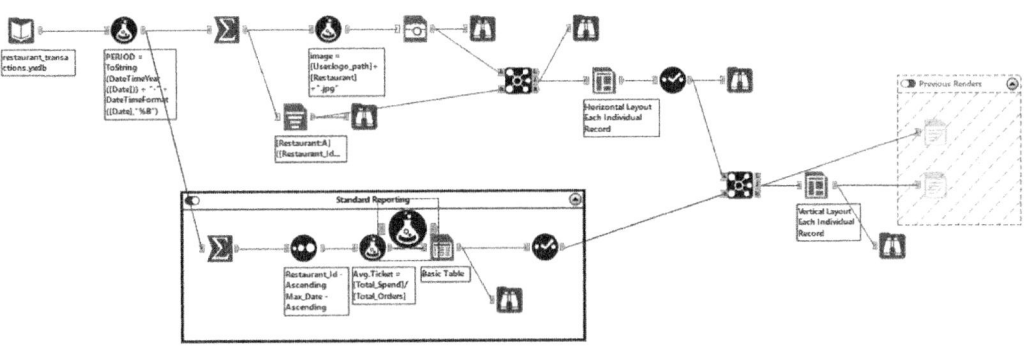

Figure 13.118: Inserting the Formula tool

> **Tip**
>
> The preceding operation can also be done by clicking on the tool that will precede the one to be inserted (in this case, the existing **Formula** tool), and then double-clicking on the tool to be inserted in the top bar of Alteryx Designer (with the existing **Formula** tool selected, click on **Preparation**, then find the **Formula** tool, and double-click it). This will insert the tool after the one we selected first.

3. We will modify the PERIOD field values, so from the **Formula** tool's **Output Column** dropdown, select **PERIOD**, and in the expression editor, enter the following text (quotation marks included):

```
"[a href=DETAILS\"+[Restaurant_Id]+"_"+[PERIOD]+".html]" +
[PERIOD] + "[/a]"
```

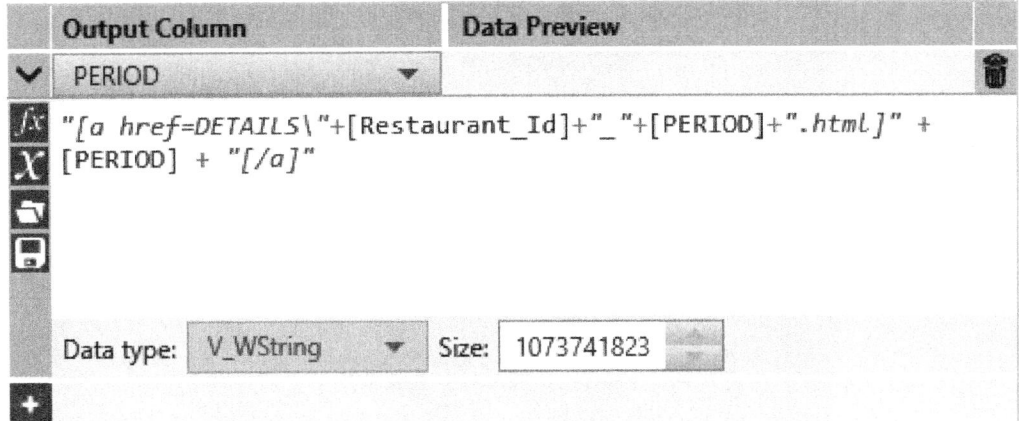

Figure 13.119: The Formula tool configuration

As you can see, I'm using squared brackets for the HTML tags. Don't worry – we'll replace them later.

4. Run the workflow, and check the **Browse** tool; you'll see that the PERIOD field has now been changed by our formula but doesn't show links (yet).

Record	Table				
1	**PERIOD**	**Total Orders**	**Total Users**	**Total Spend**	**Average Ticket**
	[a href=DETAILS\30261_2022-January.html]2022-January[/a]	391	231	$15,522.65	$39.70
	[a href=DETAILS\30261_2022-February.html]2022-February[/a]	273	169	$8,850.98	$32.42
	[a href=DETAILS\30261_2022-March.html]2022-March[/a]	329	173	$12,773.32	$38.82
	[a href=DETAILS\30261_2022-April.html]2022-April[/a]	304	178	$13,005.59	$42.78
	[a href=DETAILS\30261_2022-May.html]2022-May[/a]	267	167	$11,754.32	$44.02
	[a href=DETAILS\30261_2022-June.html]2022-June[/a]	307	182	$13,501.01	$43.98
	[a href=DETAILS\30261_2022-July.html]2022-July[/a]	320	191	$12,182.98	$38.07
	[a href=DETAILS\30261_2022-August.html]2022-August[/a]	244	144	$9,894.94	$40.55
	[a href=DETAILS\30261_2022-September.html]2022-September[/a]	258	164	$11,296.21	$43.78
	[a href=DETAILS\30261_2022-October.html]2022-October[/a]	234	149	$10,940.28	$46.75
	[a href=DETAILS\30261_2022-November.html]2022-November[/a]	215	133	$8,312.12	$38.66
	[a href=DETAILS\30261_2022-December.html]2022-December[/a]	232	144	$8,448.82	$36.42
	[a href=DETAILS\30261_2023-January.html]2023-January[/a]	205	132	$9,255.41	$45.15
	[a href=DETAILS\30261_2023-February.html]2023-February[/a]	205	144	$8,018.16	$39.11
	[a href=DETAILS\30261_2023-March.html]2023-March[/a]	217	143	$8,692.95	$40.06
2	**PERIOD**	**Total Orders**	**Total Users**	**Total Spend**	**Average Ticket**
	[a href=DETAILS\30405_2022-January.html]2022-January[/a]	296	238	$8,565.22	$28.94
	[a href=DETAILS\30405_2022-February.html]2022-February[/a]	179	146	$5,181.26	$28.95
	[a href=DETAILS\30405_2022-March.html]2022-March[/a]	175	147	$4,596.13	$26.26
	[a href=DETAILS\30405_2022-April.html]2022-April[/a]	140	108	$3,748.59	$26.78
	[a href=DETAILS\30405_2022-May.html]2022-May[/a]	226	186	$5,956.77	$26.36
	[a href=DETAILS\30405_2022-June.html]2022-June[/a]	254	208	$6,904.87	$27.18
	[a href=DETAILS\30405_2022-July.html]2022-July[/a]	177	144	$5,198.53	$29.37
	[a href=DETAILS\30405_2022-August.html]2022-August[/a]	138	115	$3,098.20	$22.45
	[a href=DETAILS\30405_2022-September.html]2022-September[/a]	155	126	$4,166.46	$26.88

Figure 13.120: A preview of the rendered table

To get our links in the PERIOD field, we need to replace the opening square bracket with <, and the closing one with >, so that the PERIOD field renders the links correctly.

In this example, I'll do this replacement using a **Text Input** tool, and I'll use a **Find Replace** tool to perform all the substitutions.

5. Drop a **Text Input** tool onto the canvas.

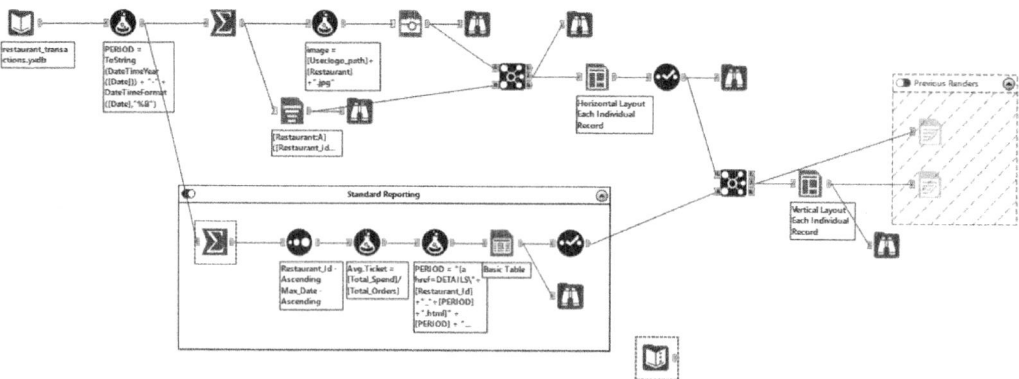

Figure 13.121: Inserting a Text Input tool to create a replacement dictionary

6. Create two columns. (Click on the column header to create each column.) Name the first one Find and the second one Replace.

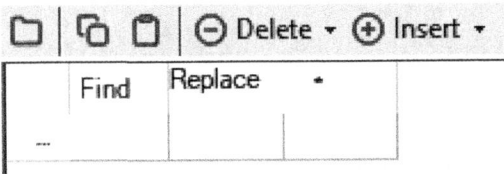

Figure 13.122: The field headers

7. For the first row, enter [in the Find column, and for Replace, type < html-passthrough><![CDATA[<.

8. For the second row, type] in the Find column and >]]></htmlpassthrough> in Replace.

	Find	Replace	---
1	[	<htmlpassthrough><![CDATA[<	
2	]	>]]></htmlpassthrough>	
•			

Figure 13.123: The field contents

Since this method will alter the underlying code that the **Table** tool generates, we also need to replace the quotation marks' appearance.

9. In a third row, for the Find field, enter ", and for the Replace field, enter ".

The **Text Input** tool should look like this:

	Find	Replace	---
1	[	<htmlpassthrough><![CDATA[<	
2	]	>]]></htmlpassthrough>	
3	&quot;	"	

Figure 13.124: The quotes need to be replaced too

10. Drop a **Find Replace** tool from the **Join** category, and connect the output anchor from the **Select** tool to the **F** input anchor, and the **Text Input** output anchor to the **R** input, as shown here:

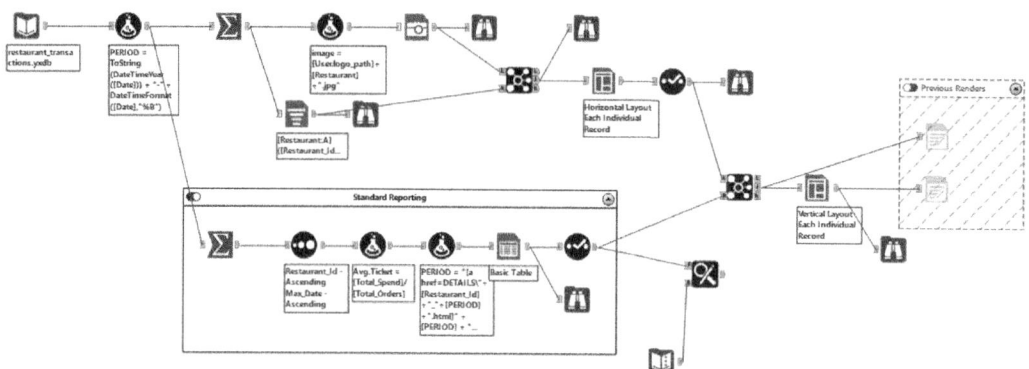

Figure 13.125: Adding the Find Replace tool

11. Click on the **Find Replace** tool to access its configuration.

12. Make sure **Any Part of Field** is selected.

13. From the **Find Within Field** dropdown, select **Orders Table**.

14. From the **Find Value** drop-down, select **Find**.

15. In the **Replace** section, make sure **Replace Find Text With Value** is selected, and pick **Replace** from the dropdown.

16. Also, check the **Replace Multiple Found Items (Find Any Part of Field only)** option if it's not enabled.

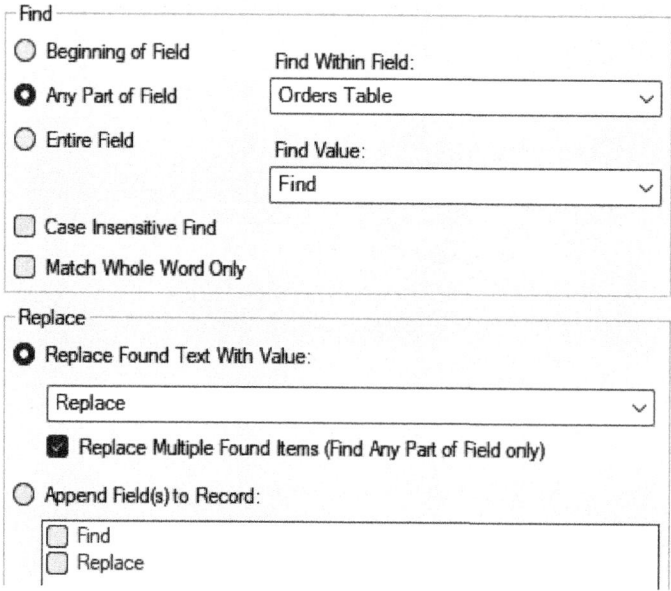

Figure 13.126: The Find Replace tool configuration

17. Add a **Browse** tool after the **Find Replace** tool to see the rendered results.

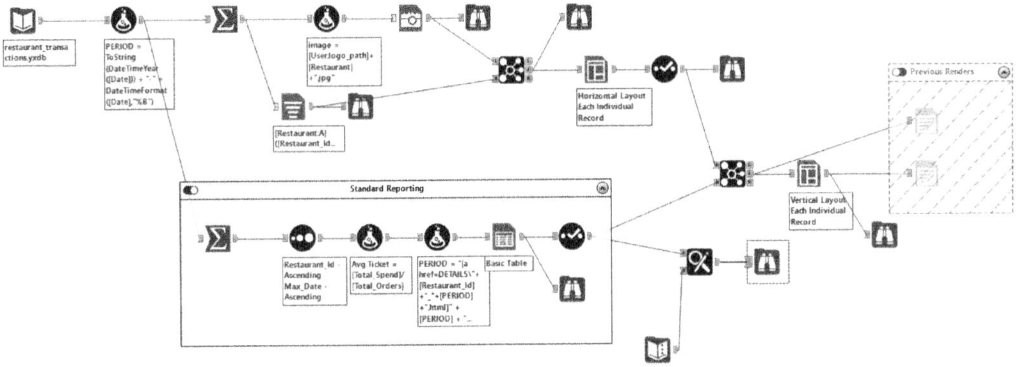

Figure 13.127: Adding a Browse tool to preview the rendered snippets

18. Run the workflow, and in the **Browse** pane, you'll see that we now have the links added to the PERIOD values.

PERIOD	Total Orders	Total Users	Total Spend	Average Ticket
2022-January	296	238	$8,565.22	$28.94
2022-February	179	146	$5,181.26	$28.95
2022-March	175	147	$4,596.13	$26.26
2022-April	140	108	$3,748.59	$26.78
2022-May	226	186	$5,956.77	$26.36
2022-June	254	208	$6,904.87	$27.18
2022-July	177	144	$5,198.53	$29.37
2022-August	138	115	$3,098.20	$22.45
2022-September	155	126	$4,166.46	$26.88
2022-October	144	121	$3,633.73	$25.23
2022-November	137	114	$3,893.52	$28.42
2022-December	160	129	$4,850.24	$30.31
2023-January	146	124	$4,227.84	$28.96
2023-February	96	81	$2,900.56	$30.21
2023-March	105	80	$2,937.53	$27.98
PERIOD	Total Orders	Total Users	Total Spend	Average Ticket

Figure 13.128: The resulting table with HTML links

Let's create the details pages now.

19. Drop a **Formula** tool onto the canvas, right below the **Tool Container** tool.

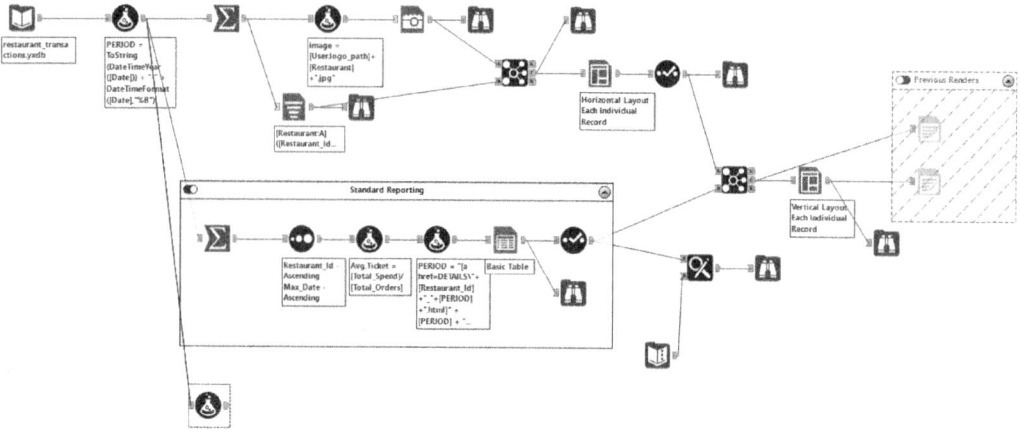

Figure 13.129: Adding a Formula tool to start building the details pages

20. From this **Formula** tool, we'll create a new column called `filename`, with this expression:

```
[Restaurant_Id]+"_"+[PERIOD]
```

This field will be the name for each generated detailed HTML page.

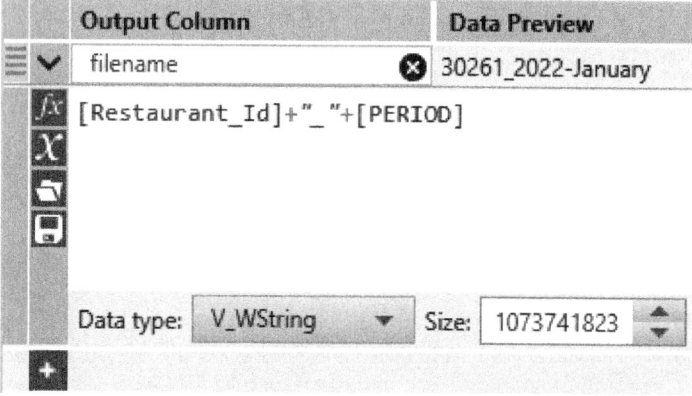

Figure 13.130: The Formula tool configuration

21. Drop a **Table** tool after the **Formula** tool.

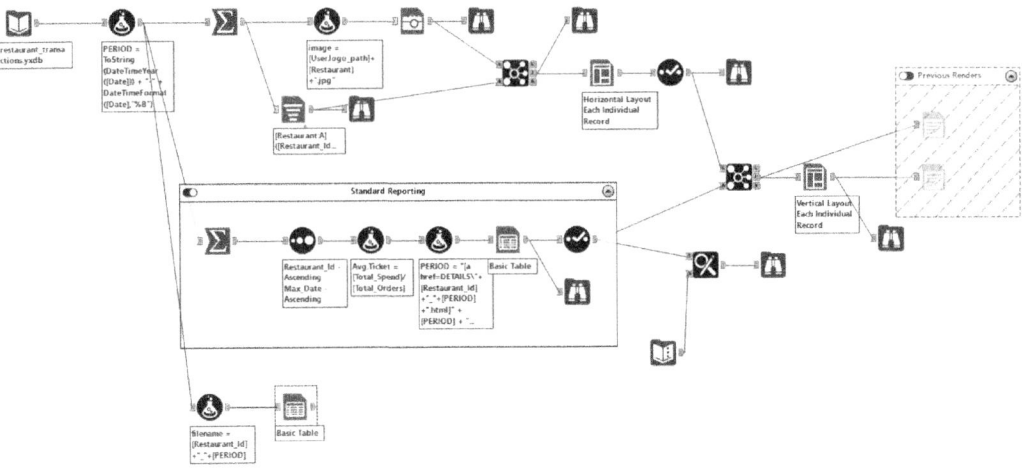

Figure 13.131: Adding the Table tool

22. In the **Table** tool configuration, make sure **Basic** is selected.

23. Select `Restaurant_Id`, `Restaurant`, and `filename` from the **Group By** list.

24. Make sure **Show Column Headings** is checked.

25. In **Per Column Configuration**, deselect `Restaurant_Id`, `Restaurant`, and `filename`.

26. Reorder the selected fields using the green arrows above, until you get the following:

- `PERIOD`
- `Order`
- `Total`
- `User`
- `Date`

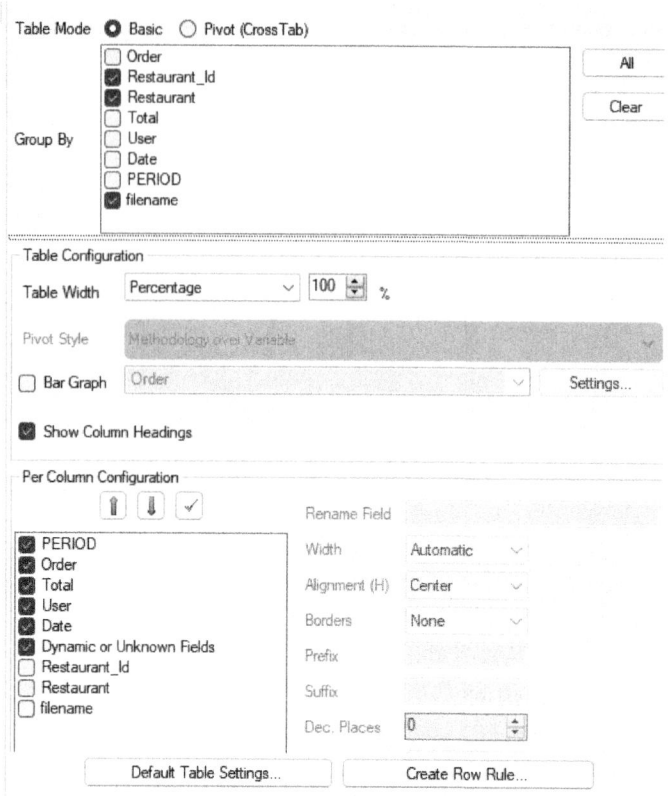

Figure 13.132: The Table tool configuration

27. Drop a **Report Text** tool after the **Table** tool.

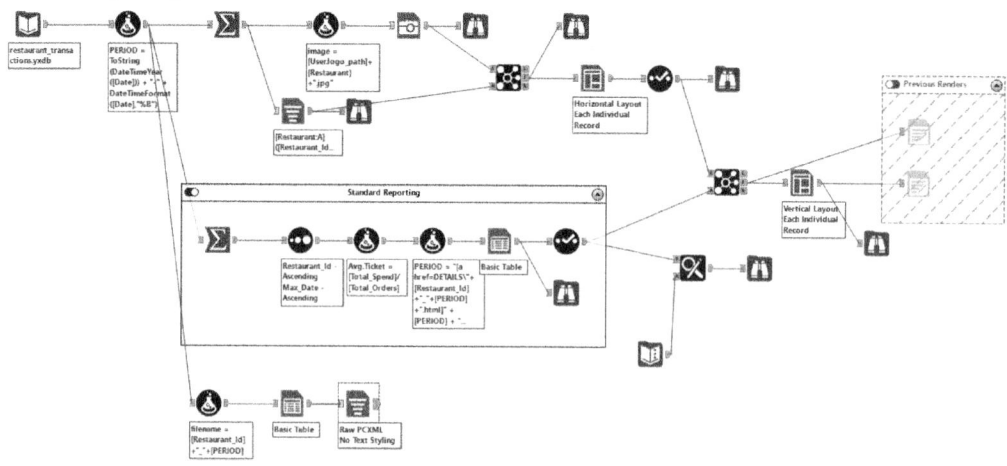

Figure 13.133: Adding a Report Text tool

28. For its configuration, click on **Expert Mode**, and make sure **Validate PCXML** is checked.

29. Enter the following text in the **Text Data** field:

```
<htmlpassthrough>
<![CDATA[
<link rel="stylesheet" href="..\..\CSS\Report.css">
<div class="same_line">
<button onclick="history.back()">Go Back</button>
<h1>[Restaurant:A] Orders</h1>
</div>
]]>
</htmlpassthrough>
```

30. Your **Report Text** tool code must look like this:

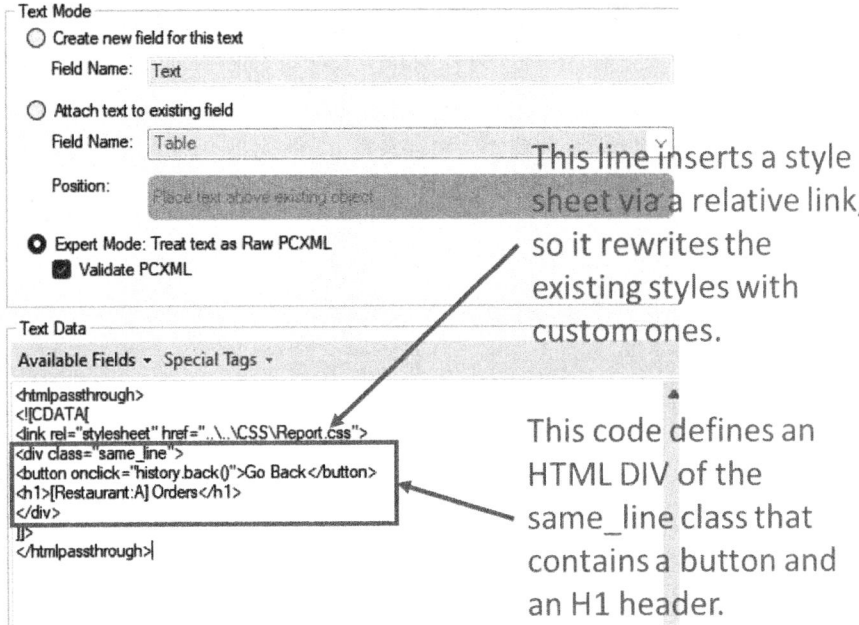

This line inserts a style sheet via a relative link, so it rewrites the existing styles with custom ones.

This code defines an HTML DIV of the same_line class that contains a button and an H1 header.

Figure 13.134: The Report Text tool code

The CSS used for this example is included in the download link, and you can find it in the CSS folder:

```
h1 {
    color: #FF0000;
}
thead tr td {
    background-color: #336699;
```

```
    font-family: "Arial black" !important;
    color: #FFFFFF;
}
.same_line {
  display: flex;
}
button {
    background-color: #336699;
    color: #FFFFFF;
}
```

As you can see, it's very simple code that involves rewriting some standard tags, such as `h1`, table headers, and buttons, and creating a class, `.same_line`, to display its contents as flex.

Of course, feel free to include whatever you want when rewriting your CSS, or change the attributes to change the report's appearance.

Now, we need to organize `Text` and `Table` (note that **Expert Mode** doesn't allow you to attach the generated `Text` to an existing field), so we'll use **Layout** in vertical mode.

31. Drop a **Layout** tool next to the **Report Text** tool.

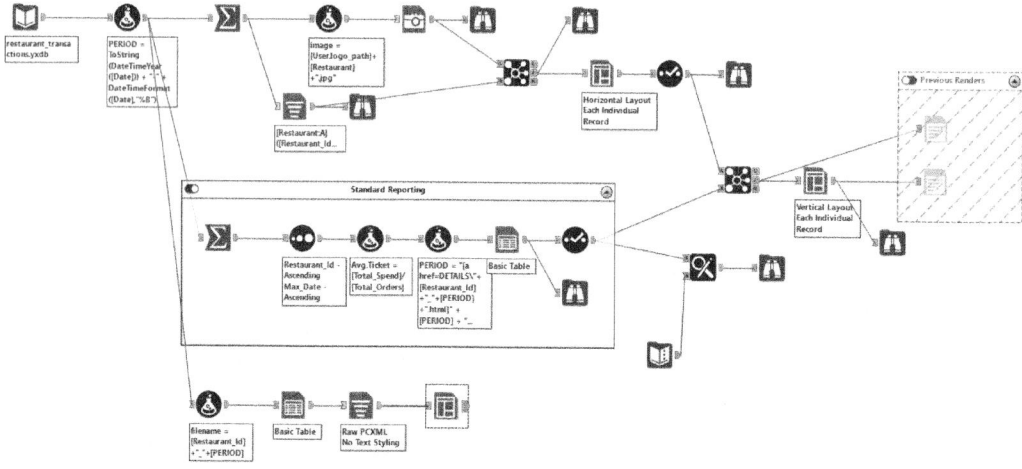

Figure 13.135: Adding the Layout tool

32. Select **Vertical** from the **Orientation** dropdown, and reorder the fields that so `Text` appears above `Table`.

Layout Mode:	Each Individual Record	⌄

Group By:	☐ Restaurant_Id ☐ Restaurant ☐ filename	All
		Clear

☐ Include Source Fields in Output

Layout Configuration

Orientation:	Vertical	⌄
Layout Width:	Percentage ⌄	100 ⇅ %
Layout Height:	Automatic ⌄	

☐ Border

☐ Separator

Cell Padding: 0 ⇅ pixels

Per Row Configuration

☑ Text
☑ Table

Height:	Automatic ⌄
Alignment (V):	Middle ⌄
Alignment (H):	Center ⌄

☐ Fill Color

Figure 13.136: The Layout tool configuration

33. Drop a **Render** tool after the **Layout** tool.

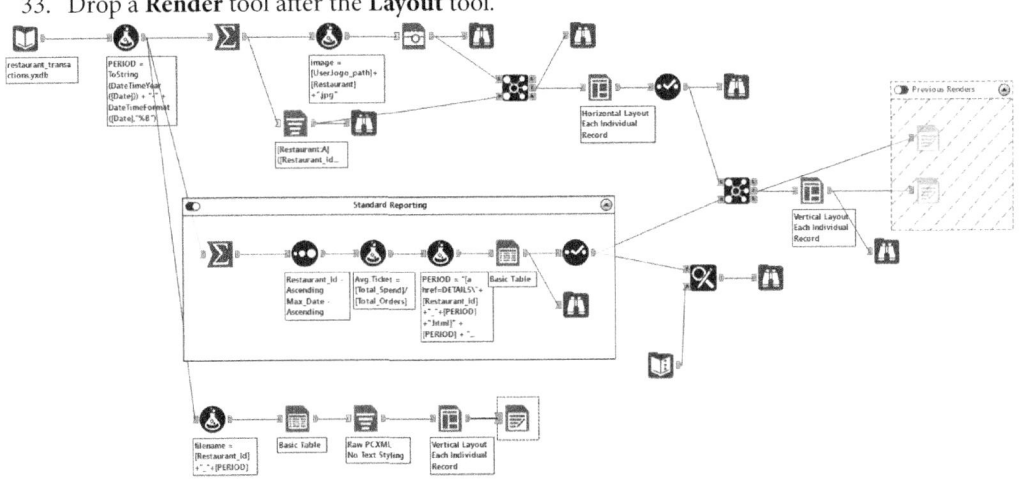

Figure 13.137: Adding the Render tool to the details page

34. From the **Output Mode** dropdown, select **Choose a Specific Output File**.

35. For the output file, use `. . \REPORT\DETAILS\Details.html`.

36. Enable the **Group Data Into Separate Reports** option.

37. Select **filename** from the **Fields To Group On** dropdown. (This will generate an HTML file for each value within the `filename` field.)

38. Select **Replacing Filename With Group** so that each generated file will be called `filename` (with the `.html` extension).

39. For **Data Field**, **Layout** should be the only option, so leave it as is.

40. Leave the remaining options as their default values.

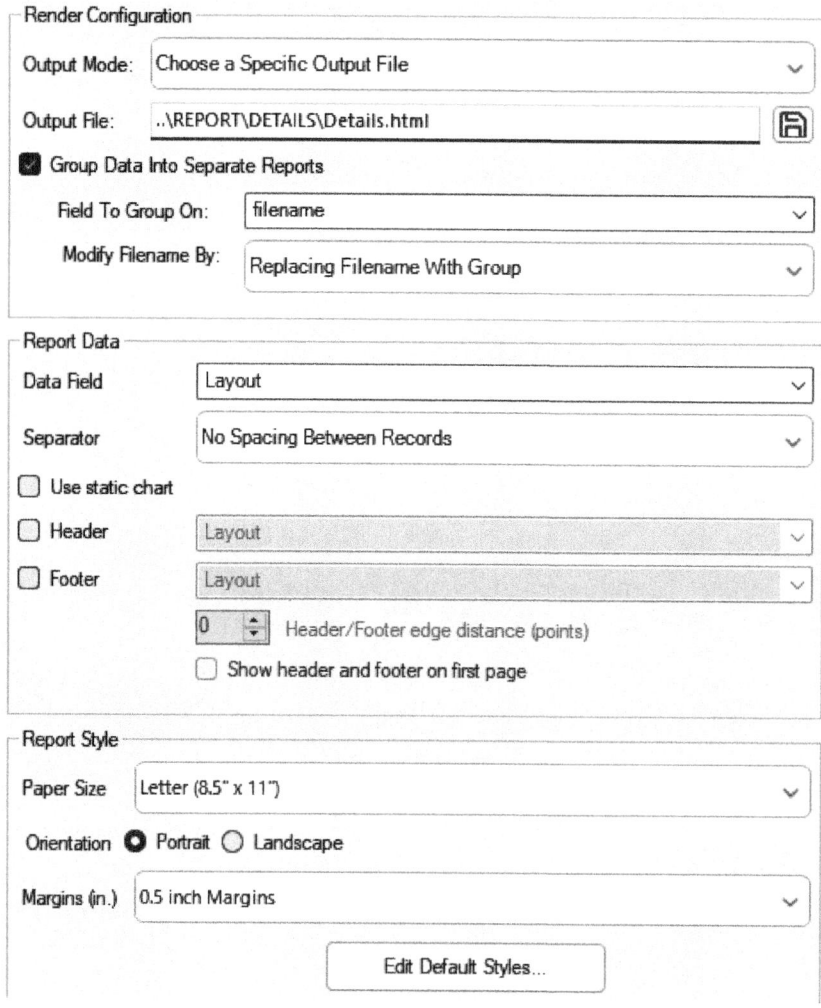

Figure 13.138: The Render tool configuration for the details page

41. Run the workflow. You'll see that the HTML files are created in `<Home directory for your recipe>\REPORT\DETAILS\` and each file has the `Restaurant_Id_PERIOD.HTML` convention we configured.

Results - Workflow - Messages

≡	**All** ⊘ 4 Errors ⊘ 0 Conv Errors ⚠ 1 Warnings ▭ 7 Messages ⊟ 83 Files	
⊘	🖫 Browse (18)	5 records
	▭ Find Replace (57)	5 records were found and 0 records were not found.
	🖫 Browse (58)	5 records
	🖫 Render (65)	C:\Exercises\AUXILIAR\ch13\Recipe4\REPORT\DETAILS\30261_2022-April.html
	🖫 Render (65)	C:\Exercises\AUXILIAR\ch13\Recipe4\REPORT\DETAILS\30261_2022-August.html
	🖫 Render (65)	C:\Exercises\AUXILIAR\ch13\Recipe4\REPORT\DETAILS\30261_2022-December.html
	🖫 Render (65)	C:\Exercises\AUXILIAR\ch13\Recipe4\REPORT\DETAILS\30261_2022-February.html

Figure 13.139: The Render tool generated all the pages

If you click on any of the file links, you'll open the file in your default browser.

Go Back **Life of Fi Bistro Orders**

PERIOD	Order	Total
2022-August	2,832,968	48
2022-August	2,832,983	16
2022-August	2,832,997	23
2022-August	2,833,037	40
2022-August	2,833,063	43

Figure 13.140: A preview of the details page with embedded JavaScript

Now, let's go and generate the summary page for each restaurant.

If you've paid attention to what we have done so far, you'll notice that we still have the **Join** tool connected to the original **Select** tool, and not to the results of the **Find Replace** tool we added.

42. Select and delete the existing connection between the **Select** tool and the **R** input anchor of the **Join** tool.

> **Tip**
>
> Sometimes, it can be difficult to click on the connection lines. A trick that I use to never miss this kind of selection is to marquee-select any part of the line. It's then impossible to miss it!

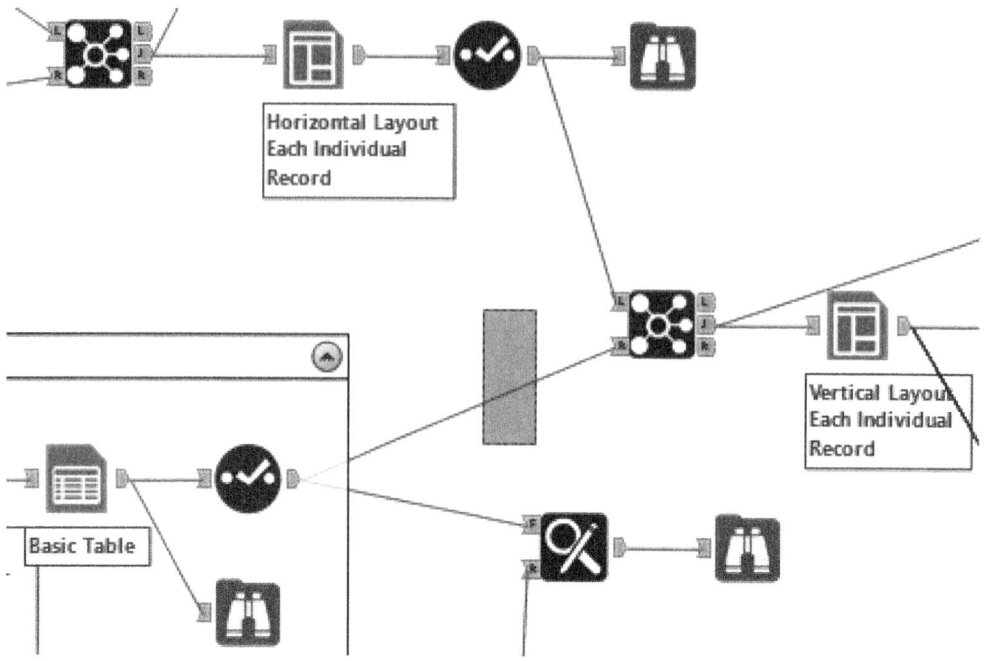

Figure 13.141: The best way to select a connection

43. Once the connection is selected, hit *Delete*.

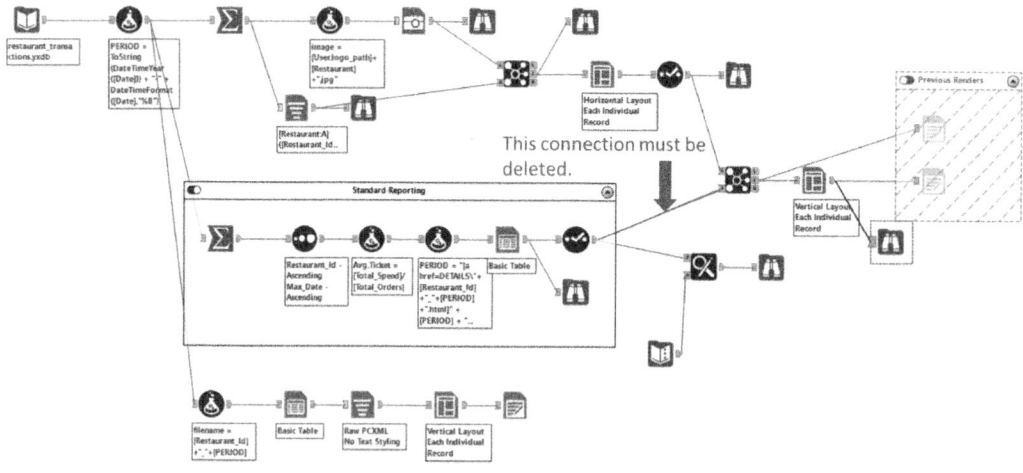

Figure 13.142: The connection to be deleted

44. Now, connect the **Find Replace** tool output anchor to the **R** input of the **Join** tool so that the **Join** tool receives the correct data.

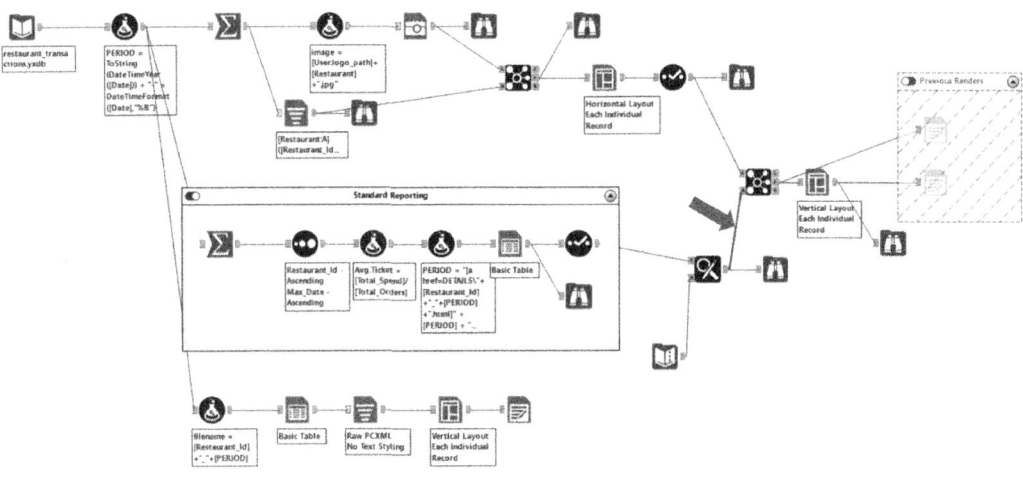

Figure 13.143: A new connection to replace the deleted one

45. Run the workflow, and note that in the right-most **Browse** tool, we already have the summary page with the links.

Record	Layout
1	

Life of Fi Bistro (30261)

PERIOD	Total Orders	Total Users	Total Spend	Average
2022-January	391	231	$15,522.65	
2022-February	273	169	$8,850.98	
2022-March	329	173	$12,773.32	
2022-April	304	178	$13,005.59	
2022-May	267	167	$11,754.32	
2022-June	307	182	$13,501.01	
2022-July	320	191	$12,182.98	
2022-August	244	144	$9,894.94	
2022-September	258	164	$11,296.21	
2022-October	234	149	$10,940.28	
2022-November	215	133	$8,312.12	
2022-December	232	144	$8,448.82	
2023-January	205	132	$9,255.41	
2023-February	205	144	$8,018.16	
2023-March	217	143	$8,692.95	

Figure 13.144: A preview of the summary report with its links

Now, let's move on to rendering the HTML for the summary pages.

46. Drop a **Report Text** tool, and connect it to the **J** output of the **Join** tool.

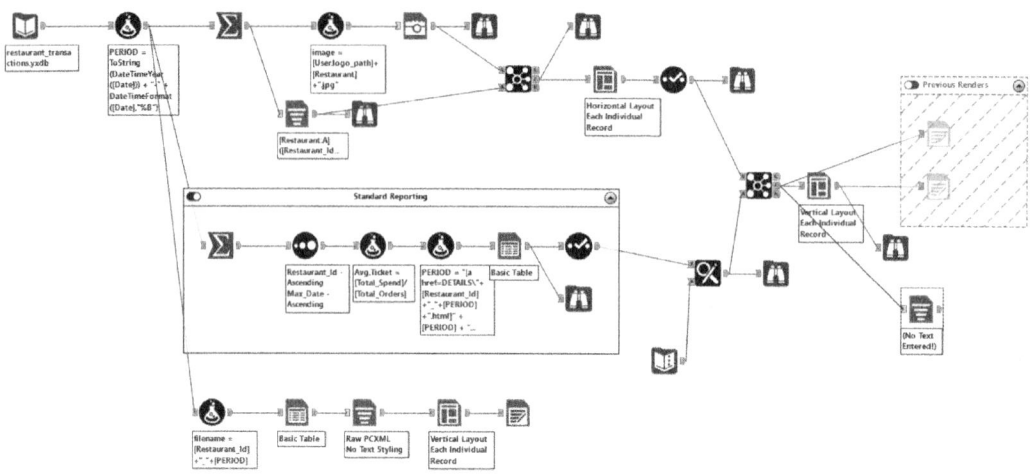

Figure 13.145: Adding the Report Text tool

47. Select **Expert Mode** from the **Text Mode** section, and introduce this code to the text data:

```
<htmlpassthrough>
<![CDATA[
<link rel="stylesheet" href="..\CSS\Report.css">
]]>
</htmlpassthrough>
```

Note that the relative path to the CSS file has changed. This is because the generated files will be inside the REPORT folder (one step higher in the folder hierarchy than the detail files).

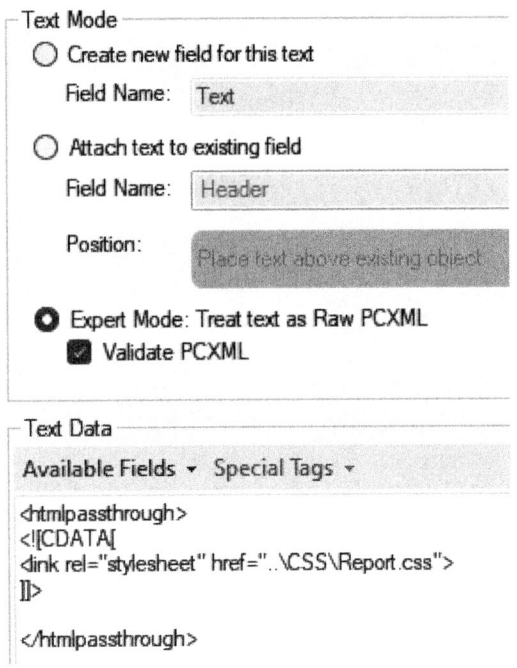

Figure 13.146: The Report Text tool configuration

48. Now, drop a **Layout** tool after the **Report Text** tool.

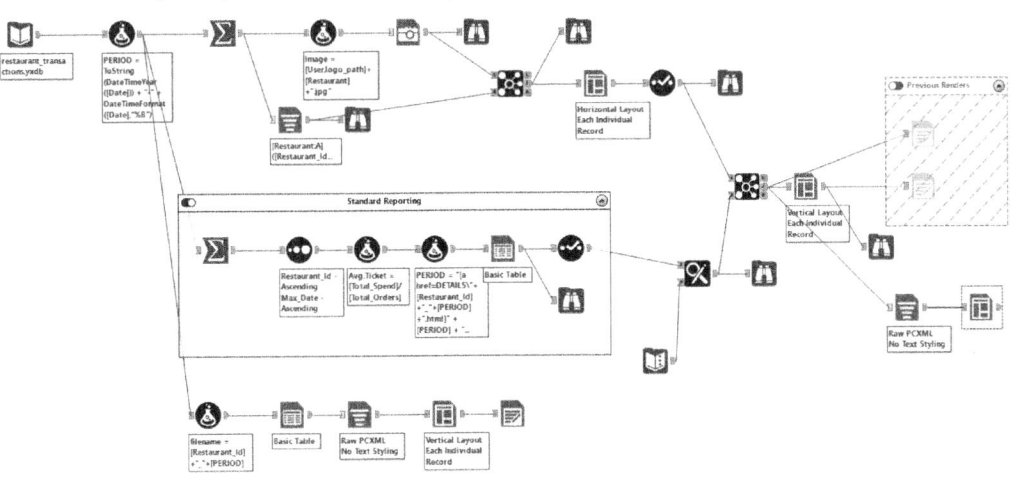

Figure 13.147: Adding the Layout tool

49. Make sure that **Each Individual Record** is selected in the **Layout Mode** dropdown.

50. Select **Vertical** from the **Orientation** dropdown.

51. If necessary, reorder the fields so that you get the following:

- Text

- Header

- Orders Table

You can see these in the following figure:

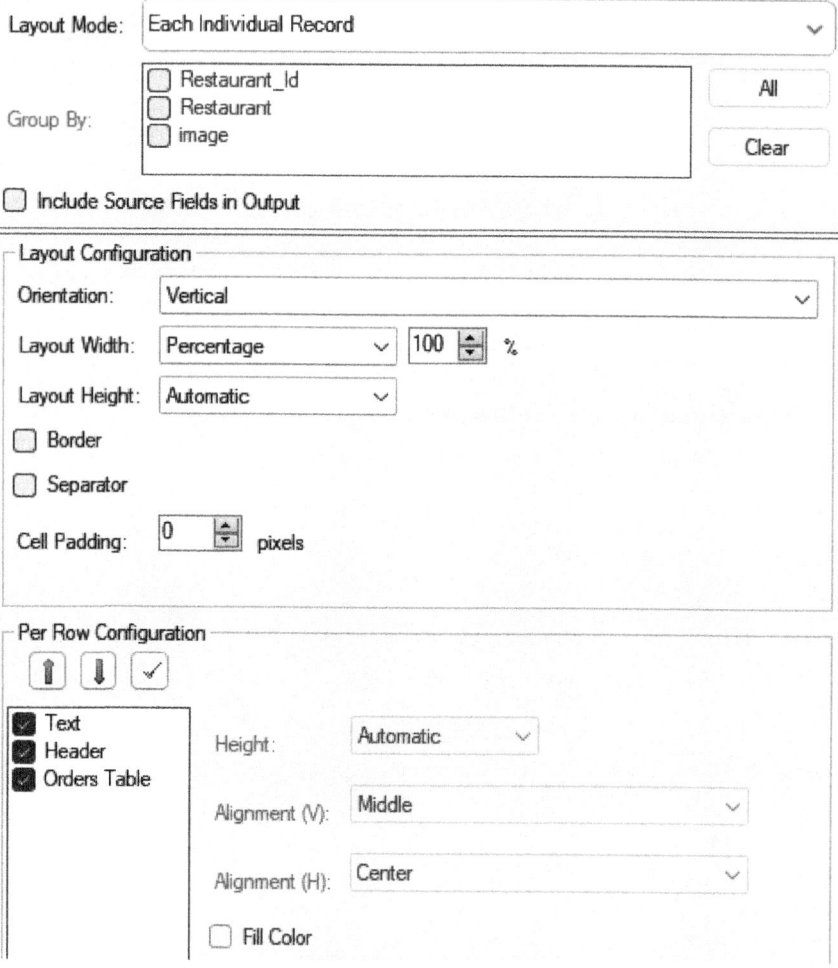

Figure 13.148: The Layout tool configuration

52. Drop a **Render** tool and connect it to the **Layout** tool.

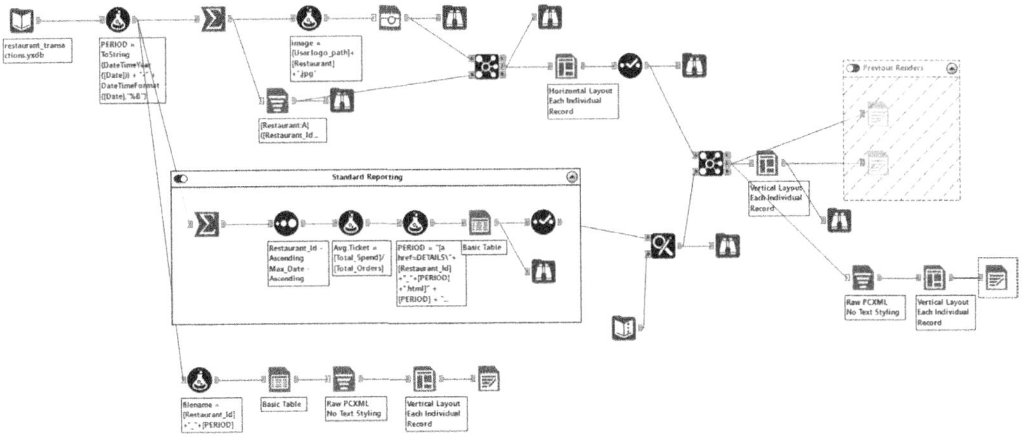

Figure 13.149: Adding the Render tool for the summary pages

53. In its configuration, select **Choose a Specific Output File** from the **Output Mode** dropdown.

54. Enter `..\REPORT\_Summary.html` for the output file.

55. Click **Group Data Into Separate Reports** to enable the options.

56. From the **Field To Group On** dropdown, select **Restaurant**.

57. For the **Modify Filename By**, select **Prepending Group To Filename** (so that we'll get `Restaurant_Summary.html`).

58. **Layout** should be selected in the **Data Field** dropdown, since it's the only report snippet.

59. Leave the remaining options untouched.

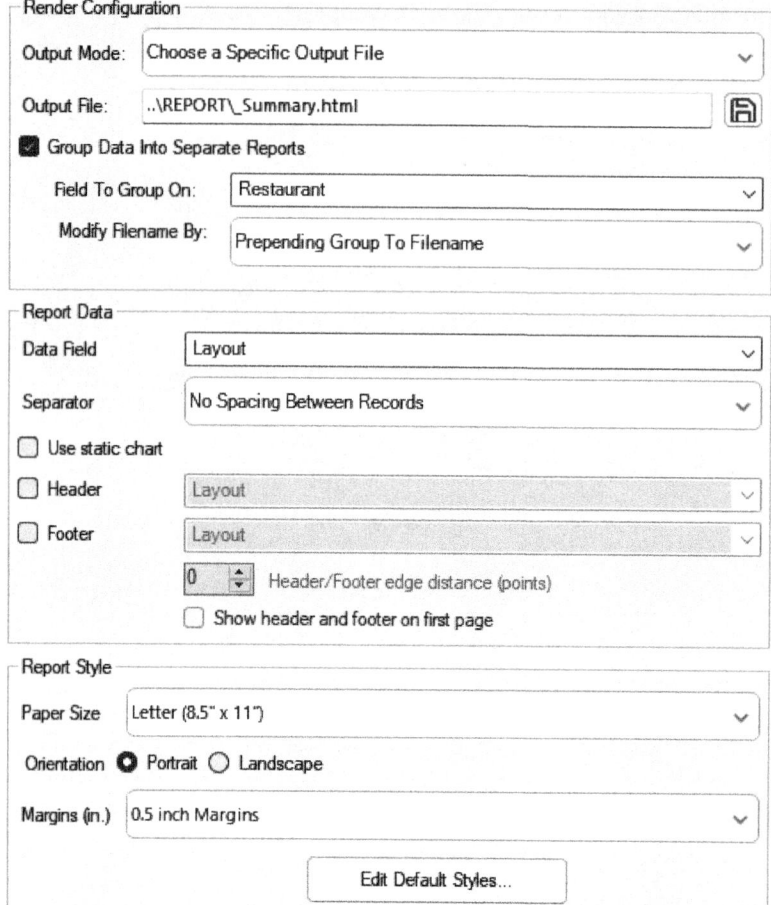

Figure 13.150: The Render tool configuration

60. Run the workflow.

61. Go to an Explorer window and open the REPORT folder. (You can right-click on the generated _Summary HTML files, and then select **Open Folder**.)

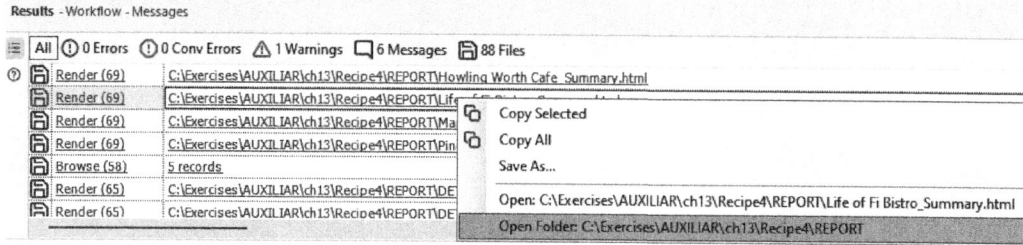

Figure 13.151: A shortcut to access the generated summary pages

You'll see all the generated summary pages and their corresponding folder, containing all the assets. (Since our example is a simple report, only the logo file is there.)

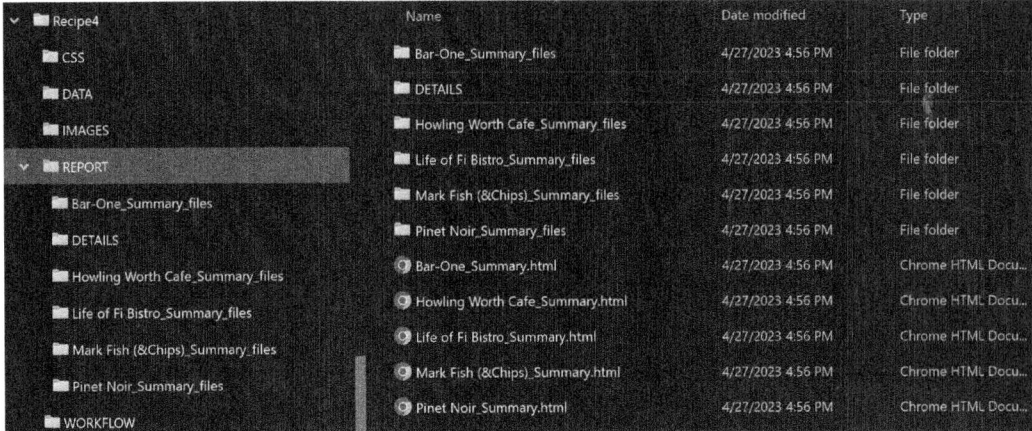

Figure 13.152: Seeing what's been generated in the output folder

62. Double-click on any HTML file, which will open in your default browser. Note the styles from the CSS applied to it.

Howling Worth Cafe (30405)

PERIOD	Total Orders	Total Users	Total Spend	Average Ticket
2022-January	296	238	$8,565.22	$28.94
2022-February	179	146	$5,181.26	$28.95
2022-March	175	147	$4,596.13	$26.26
2022-April	140	108	$3,748.59	$26.78
2022-May	226	186	$5,956.77	$26.36
2022-June	254	208	$6,904.87	$27.18
2022-July	177	144	$5,198.53	$29.37
2022-August	138	115	$3,098.20	$22.45
2022-September	155	126	$4,166.46	$26.88
2022-October	144	121	$3,633.73	$25.23
2022-November	137	114	$3,893.52	$28.42
2022-December	160	129	$4,850.24	$30.31
2023-January	146	124	$4,227.84	$28.96
2023-February	96	81	$2,900.56	$30.21
2023-March	105	80	$2,937.53	$27.98

Figure 13.153: The resulting summary page

Now, if you click on any PERIOD link, the page corresponding to all orders at that restaurant for the selected period will open. Also, as you can see in the following screenshot, these pages use the linked CSS styles, and there is a JavaScript button inserted too, which will allow you to go back to the summary page.

PERIOD	Order	Total	User	Date
2022-January	2,411,325	32	8,535,894	2022-01-01 13:07:16
2022-January	2,411,408	33	6,393,525	2022-01-01 13:24:34
2022-January	2,411,504	17	9,453,736	2022-01-01 13:54:37
2022-January	2,411,574	30	8,014,158	2022-01-01 14:10:18
2022-January	2,411,689	17	6,554,273	2022-01-01 14:41:38
2022-January	2,411,984	31	8,760,339	2022-01-01 16:30:41

Figure 13.154: The resulting details page

There's more...

Just change the output folder from a local folder to one in your web server, and you'll be able to access the reports through it.

14

Outputting Data

So far we have spent a lot of time and effort reading, cleaning, preparing, and processing our data, but doing this is not enough. We need to save and store processed data properly. Not doing it properly can lead to a series of problems that negatively affect your analysis, productivity, and decision-making.

First, saving the processed data allows it to be accessed efficiently and reused for future tasks and analysis. Once the data has been cleaned, analyzed, and transformed, there is no need to duplicate those efforts every time the data is needed again. Saving processed datasets in a structured format means they can simply be retrieved and used immediately for downstream applications. This saves a lot of time and resources compared to reprocessing raw data over and over again.

Additionally, properly saving processed data helps ensure that it maintains its integrity and accuracy over long periods of time. Raw data often needs significant preprocessing before it can generate information. If interim data from cleaning, analysis, and manipulation tasks is not saved, subsequent analyses may not be able to reproduce consistent results.

Finally, proper data retention also allows for auditing and reprocessing when necessary. Data pipelines and processing logic can contain errors that go unnoticed for some time. By retaining the processed results, organizations can rerun parts of that pipeline if they suspect errors, saving many resources in the process.

Whether we need to save the data in files or databases, transfer them to applications such as Tableau or Power BI, or upload them to a cloud repository, Alteryx offers a wide range of possibilities to do so in a very simple and easy way.

In this chapter, we'll explore some options to use Alteryx wisely when saving data:

- Using the Render tool to conditionally format your Excel files
- Creating your own metadata to track the status of a process run
- Using Events to back up your data before saving
- Using Pre and Post SQL statements

Technical requirements

In the *Using Pre and Post SQL statements* recipe, you'll need access to a database environment (we'll use SQL Server for the demonstration). In the *Getting ready* section of the recipe, you'll find all you need to prepare yourself.

Using the Render tool to conditionally format your Excel files

No matter the number and variety of reporting tools that we may have at our disposal, we will likely have to deliver reports in Excel more often than we would like.

We know that we can easily generate Excel files with the **Output Data** tool, but these will not have any formatting unless you follow recipe #4 from *Chapter 1*. However, this method could be an additional demand on our development effort, especially when we have to use various conditional formats in our final report.

This is where this recipe will be extremely useful, allowing us to generate Excel files with conditional formats generated directly with Alteryx.

We are going to build an Excel worksheet, where we have the header we already built plus a table (similar to what we built), that incorporates some useful techniques to conditionally format its contents, as you can see in the following figure.

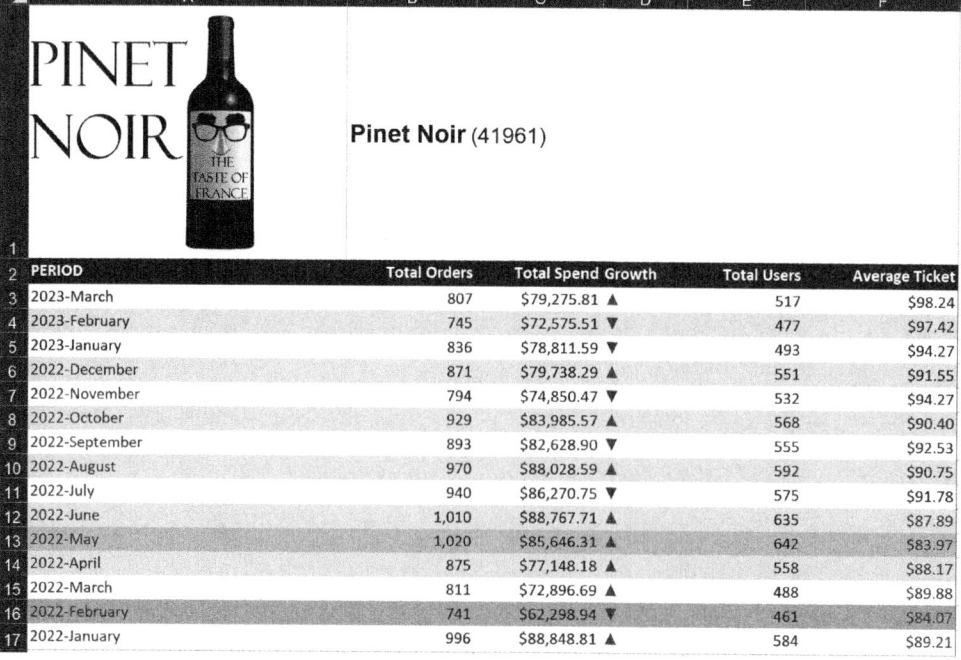

Figure 14.1: The Excel report we'll build

We will add a growth comparison of each period against the previous period, which will be shown with a symbol and color according to the result.

Also, we will add the logic to show all those periods in which each restaurant had an average ticket below the threshold determined for each one (which comes from another data source) and show them in red.

Finally, we will add an identifier that will highlight the period with the highest (in light green) and lowest (in light red) volume of users in each restaurant.

Getting ready

Again, for this recipe, we'll be reusing parts of the previous recipe's workflow. If you never completed it, you can download it from here: `https://github.com/PacktPublishing/Alteryx-Designer-Cookbook`.

If you're starting with the downloaded version of the workflow, we did the initial cleanup for you. If you're using what you accomplished in the previous recipe, we need to get rid of some functionality that won't apply to this recipe:

1. Get rid of the tools that are in the selected area:

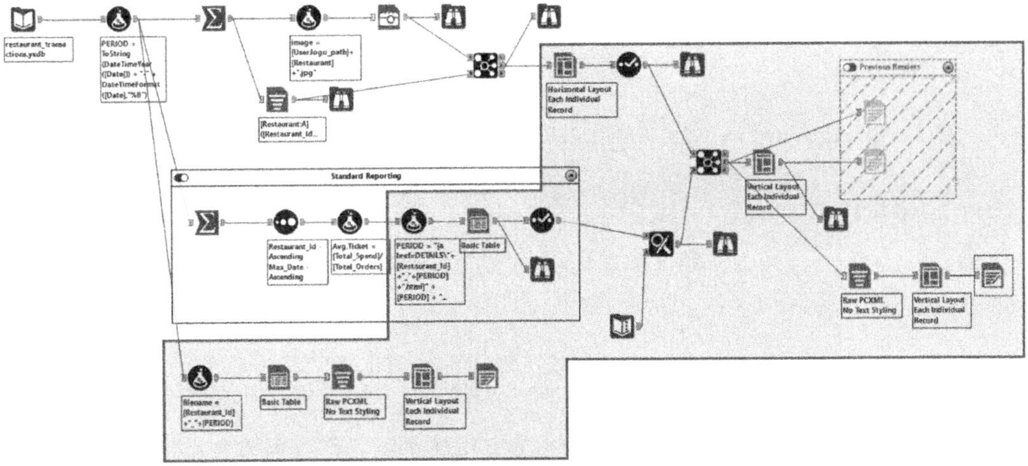

Figure 14.2: Select and delete the tools in the marked area

Your workflow will look like this one (we used the **Tool Container** tool to add a container around the top group of tools to identify the portion of the workflow that builds the report header):

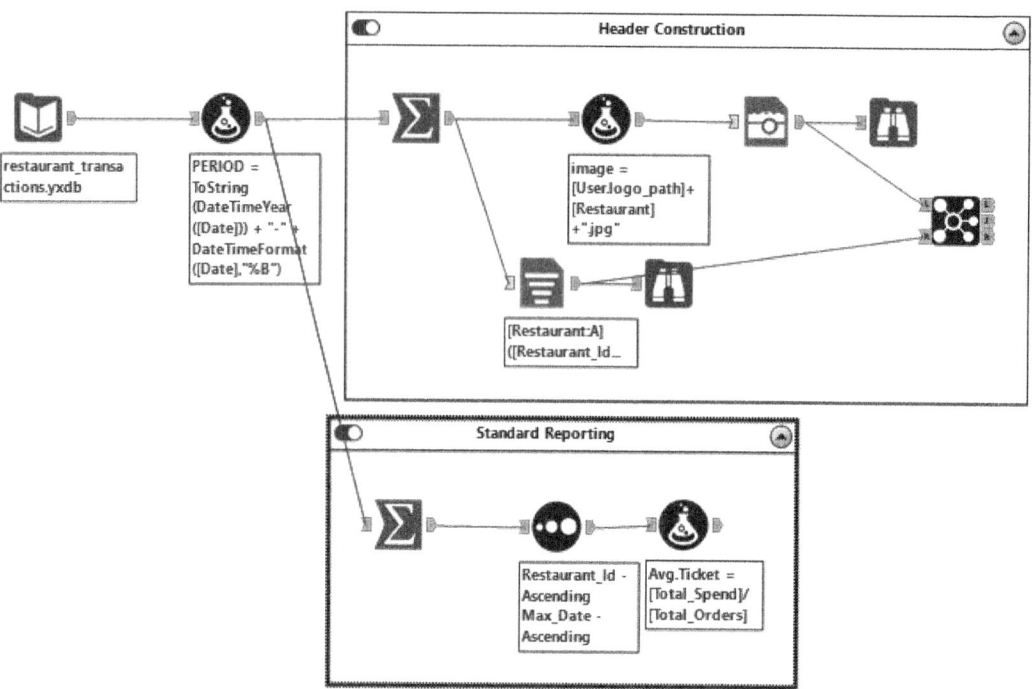

Figure 14.3: Starting workflow for this recipe

2. Save it into the current recipe folder in the WORKFLOW directory.

How to do it...

So far, we know that the top part of the workflow composes the report header, and the lower part summarizes the data to build the data table.

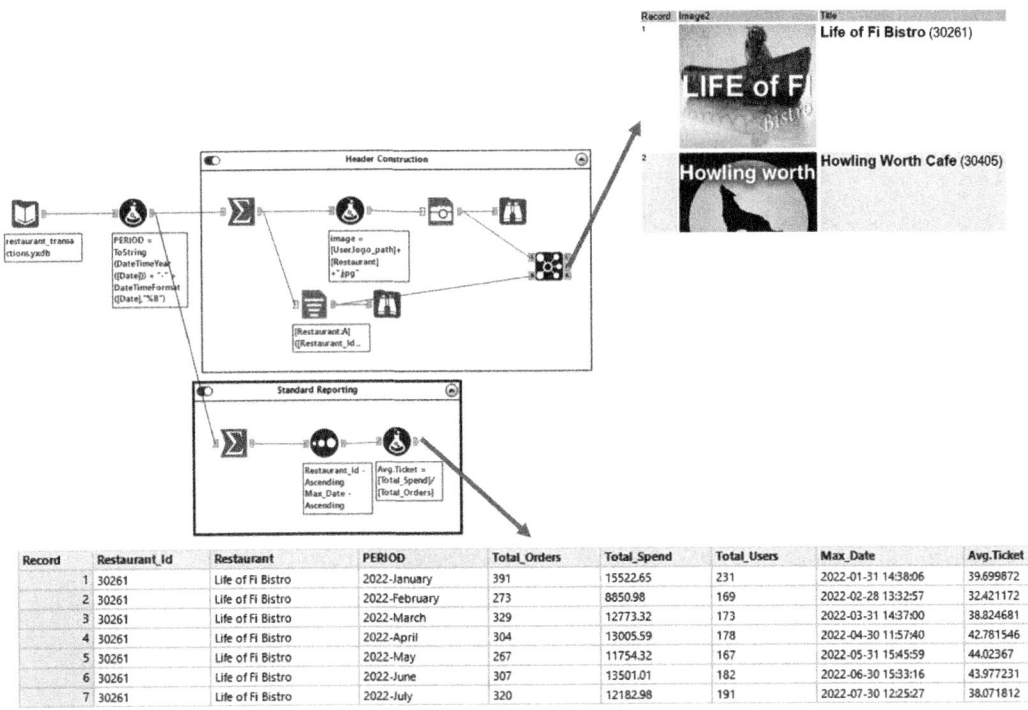

Record	Restaurant_Id	Restaurant	PERIOD	Total_Orders	Total_Spend	Total_Users	Max_Date	Avg.Ticket
1	30261	Life of Fi Bistro	2022-January	391	15522.65	231	2022-01-31 14:38:06	39.699872
2	30261	Life of Fi Bistro	2022-February	273	8850.98	169	2022-02-28 13:32:57	32.421172
3	30261	Life of Fi Bistro	2022-March	329	12773.32	173	2022-03-31 14:37:00	38.824681
4	30261	Life of Fi Bistro	2022-April	304	13005.59	178	2022-04-30 11:57:40	42.781546
5	30261	Life of Fi Bistro	2022-May	267	11754.32	167	2022-05-31 15:45:59	44.02367
6	30261	Life of Fi Bistro	2022-June	307	13501.01	182	2022-06-30 15:33:16	43.977231
7	30261	Life of Fi Bistro	2022-July	320	12182.98	191	2022-07-30 12:25:27	38.071812

Figure 14.4: What we have so far

For our new report, we'll need to perform some additional operations on the data, so we'll start with that:

1. First, click on the existing **Sort** tool to access its configuration options. You'll see that it's configured to sort on `Restaurant_Id` and `Max_Date`, both in **Ascending** order.

2. Click on the **Order** criteria for the `Max_Date` field, and change it to **Descending** to sort from the newest period to the oldest.

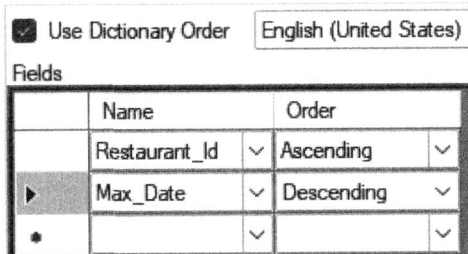

Figure 14.5: Changing the Sort order

3. Drop a **Summarize** tool connected to the existing one within the **Standard Reporting** Tool Container.

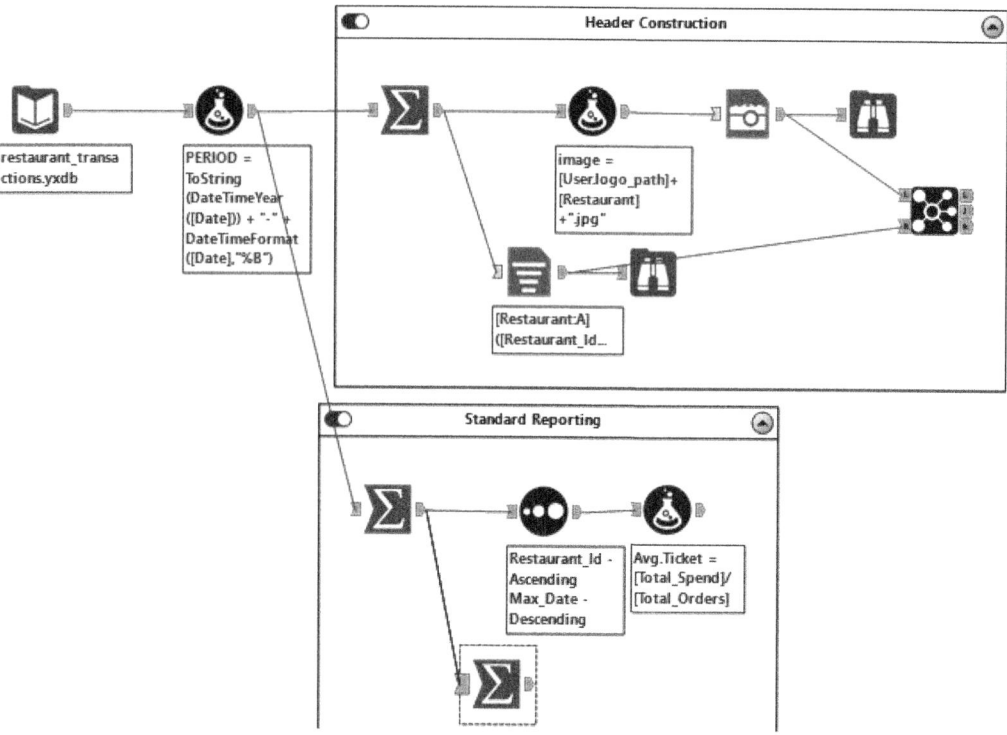

Figure 14.6: Adding the Summarize tool

We are going to use it to get, from the already summarized list by PERIOD, the maximum and minimum values of Total_Users per Restaurant, which we'll use later.

4.   Click on Restaurant_Id, then press *Ctrl* + click on Restaurant, then on **Add,** and select Group By.

5.   Click on Total_Users, click on **Add**, and then on Min.

6.   With Total_Users still selected, click again on **Add**, and then on Max.

Your **Summarize** tool configuration should look like this one:

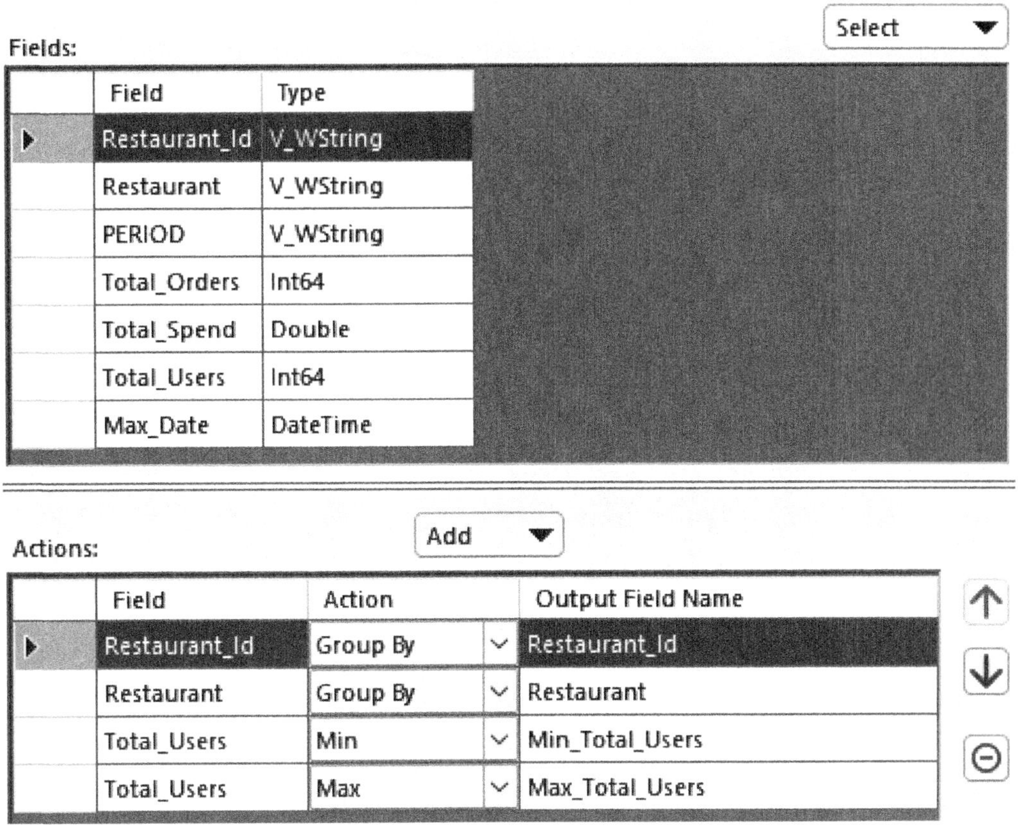

Fields:

Select ▼

	Field	Type
▶	Restaurant_Id	V_WString
	Restaurant	V_WString
	PERIOD	V_WString
	Total_Orders	Int64
	Total_Spend	Double
	Total_Users	Int64
	Max_Date	DateTime

Actions:

Add ▼

	Field	Action		Output Field Name
▶	Restaurant_Id	Group By	∨	Restaurant_Id
	Restaurant	Group By	∨	Restaurant
	Total_Users	Min	∨	Min_Total_Users
	Total_Users	Max	∨	Max_Total_Users

↑ ↓ ⊖

Figure 14.7: Summarize tool configuration

Now, we're going to add the `Max_Total_Users` and `Min_Total_Users` fields to the existing records. We can use a **Join** tool, but for this type of case, I prefer a **Find Replace** tool (it is faster and less resource-consuming).

1. So, drop a **Find Replace** tool inside the **Standard Reporting** Tool Container, and connect the **Formula** tool output anchor to the **F** input and the **Summarize** output to the **R** anchor.

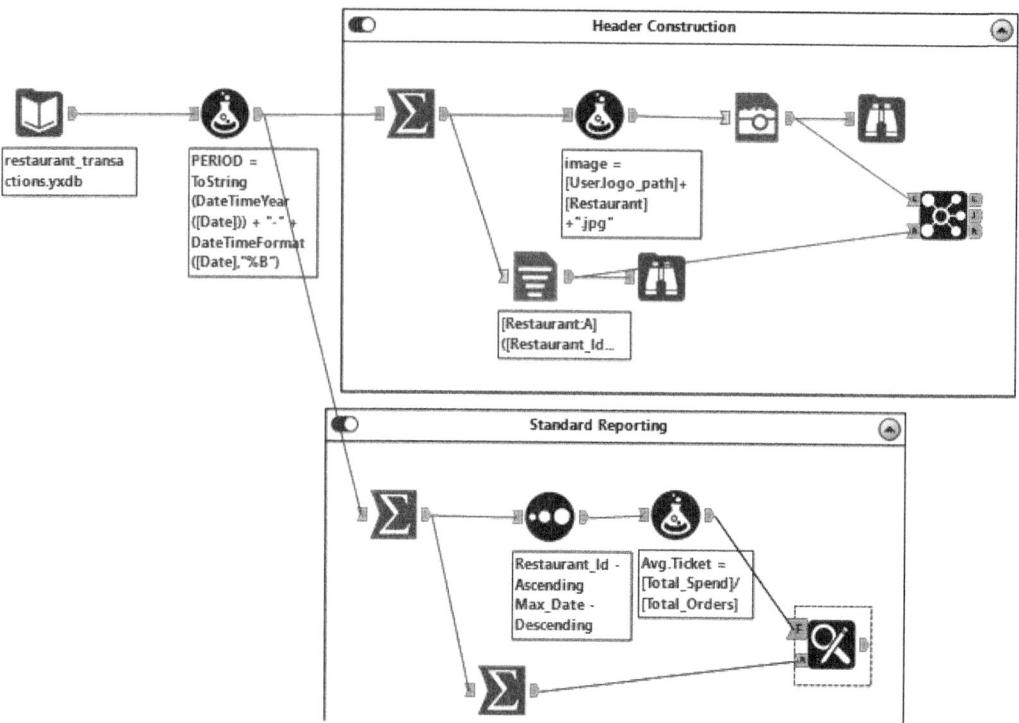

Figure 14.8: Adding the Find Replace tool

2. From its configuration pane, click on **Entire Field** and **Match Whole Word Only** (this will mimic the behavior of a **Join** tool).

3. From the **Find Within Field** dropdown, select `Restaurant_Id`.

4. From the **Find Value** dropdown, select `Restaurant_Id` too.

5. Click on **Append Field(s) to Record** so you enable the field selector, and from there, select `Min_Total_Users` and `Max_Total_Users`.

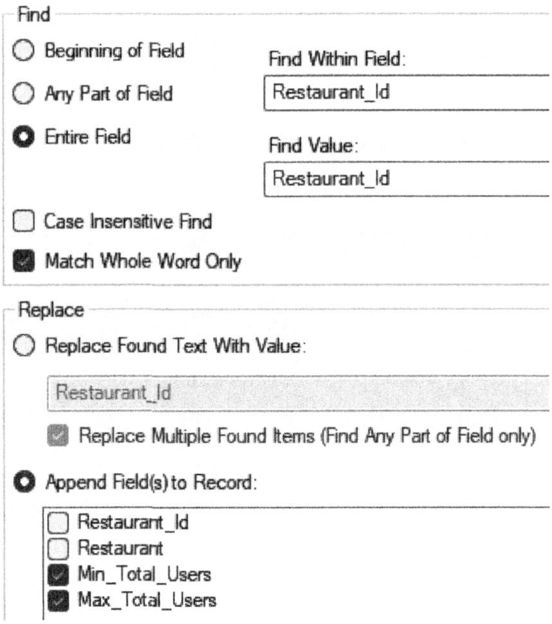

Find

- ○ Beginning of Field
- ○ Any Part of Field
- ● Entire Field

Find Within Field:

Restaurant_Id

Find Value:

Restaurant_Id

- ☐ Case Insensitive Find
- ☑ Match Whole Word Only

Replace

○ Replace Found Text With Value:

Restaurant_Id

☑ Replace Multiple Found Items (Find Any Part of Field only)

● Append Field(s) to Record:

- ☐ Restaurant_Id
- ☐ Restaurant
- ☑ Min_Total_Users
- ☑ Max_Total_Users

Figure 14.9: The Find Replace tool configuration

Now, we have the maximum and minimum number of users in a period for each restaurant.

Restaurant_Id	Restaurant	PERIOD	Total_Orders	Total_Spend	Total_Users	Max_Date	Avg.Ticket	Min_Total_Users	Max_Total_Users
30261	Life of Fi Bistro	2022-March	329	12773.32	173	2022-03-31 14:37:00	38.824681	132	231
30261	Life of Fi Bistro	2022-February	273	8850.98	169	2022-02-28 13:32:57	32.421172	132	231
30261	Life of Fi Bistro	2022-January	391	15522.65	231	2022-01-31 14:38:06	39.699872	132	231
30405	Howling Worth Cafe	2023-March	105	2937.53	80	2023-03-30 14:42:44	27.976476	80	238
30405	Howling Worth Cafe	2023-February	96	2900.56	81	2023-02-28 21:09:08	30.214167	80	238
30405	Howling Worth Cafe	2023-January	146	4227.84	124	2023-01-31 20:07:04	28.957808	80	238

Figure 14.10: Resulting dataset

At this point, we need to incorporate the given threshold for each restaurant. In our case, it comes from an Excel file with a simple structure, as you can see in the following figure:

	A	B	C
1	Restaurant	Restaurant_Id	Avg. Ticket Threshold
2	Life of Fi Bistro	30261	40
3	Howling Worth Cafe	30405	28
4	Bar-One	30412	31
5	Mark Fish (&Chips)	40742	37
6	Pinet Noir	41961	90
7			

Figure 14.11: Threshold per restaurant data

Those thresholds will indicate whether to show the results in red or in black (when the monthly Avg. Ticket value is below the threshold, we'll show its value in red; otherwise, we'll show it in black).

6.   Drop an **Input Data** tool onto the canvas:

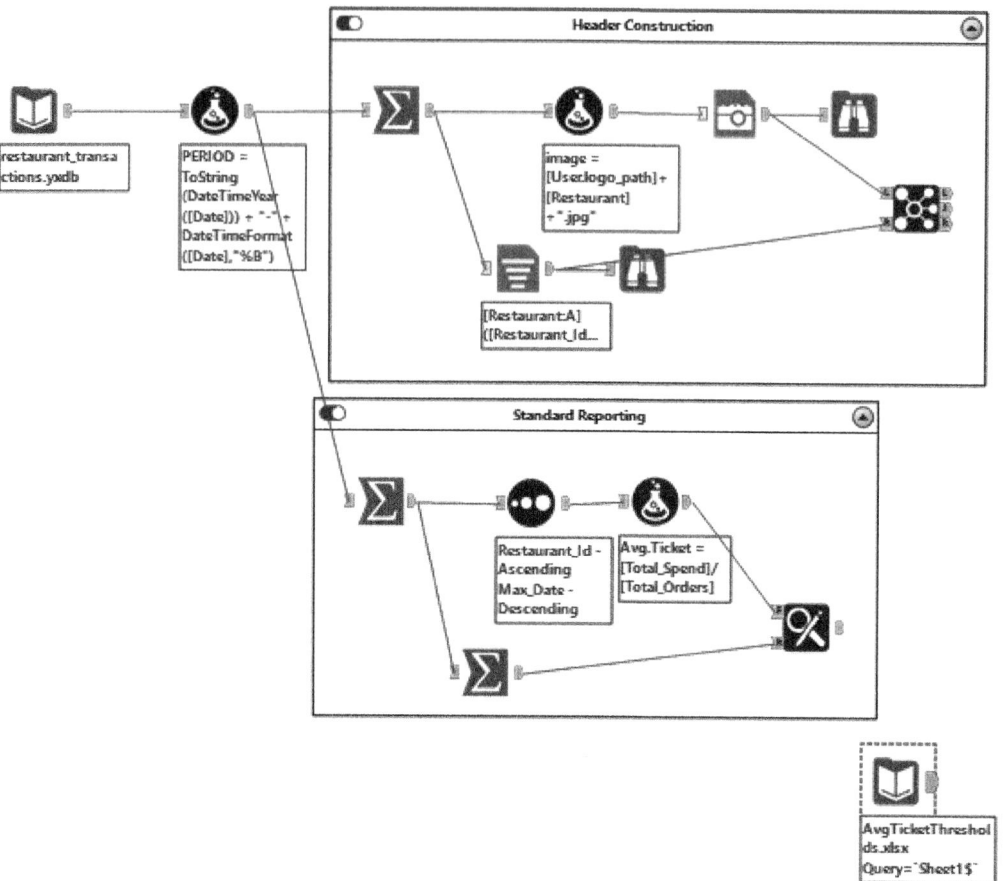

Figure 14.12: Adding the Input Data tool

7.   Point it to `..\DATA\AvgTicketThresholds.xlsx` and select `Sheet1$` (the only one available) as the data source.

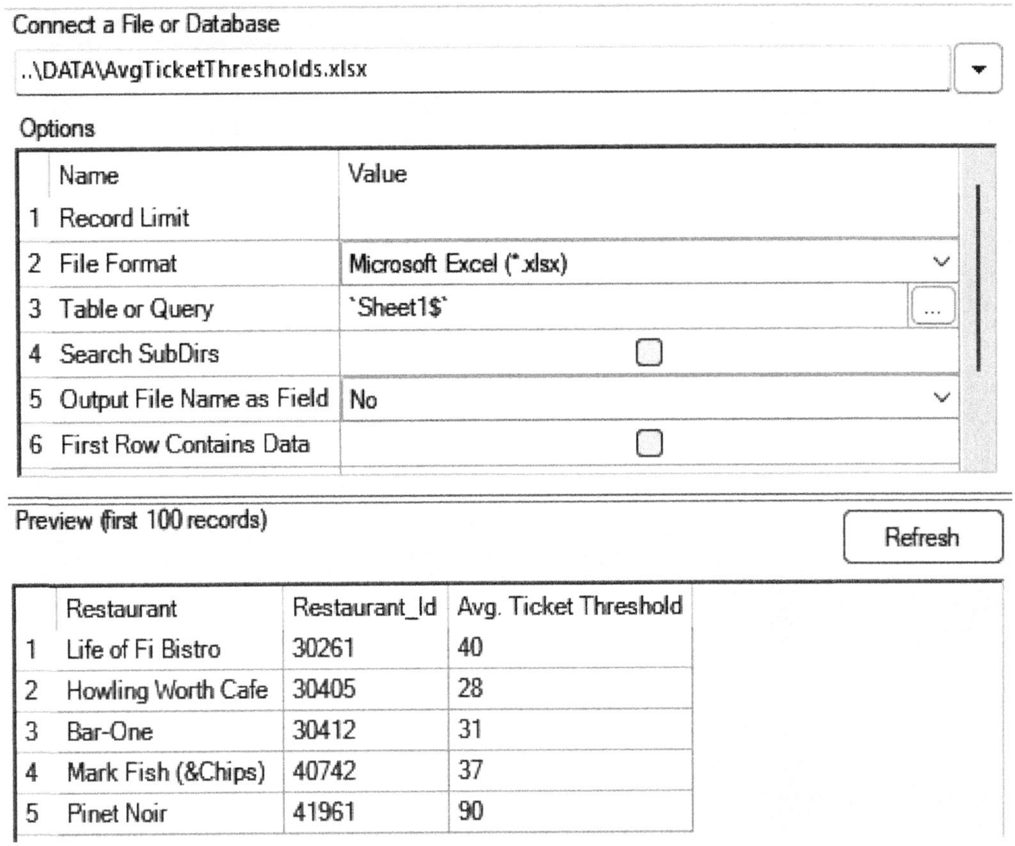

Connect a File or Database

..\DATA\AvgTicketThresholds.xlsx

Options

	Name	Value
1	Record Limit	
2	File Format	Microsoft Excel (*.xlsx)
3	Table or Query	`Sheet1$`
4	Search SubDirs	☐
5	Output File Name as Field	No
6	First Row Contains Data	☐

Preview (first 100 records)   Refresh

	Restaurant	Restaurant_Id	Avg. Ticket Threshold
1	Life of Fi Bistro	30261	40
2	Howling Worth Cafe	30405	28
3	Bar-One	30412	31
4	Mark Fish (&Chips)	40742	37
5	Pinet Noir	41961	90

Figure 14.13: Input Data tool configuration

8. Drop another **Find Replace** tool and connect the previous one's output to the **F** input and the output from the **Input Data** tool to the **R** input, as shown here:

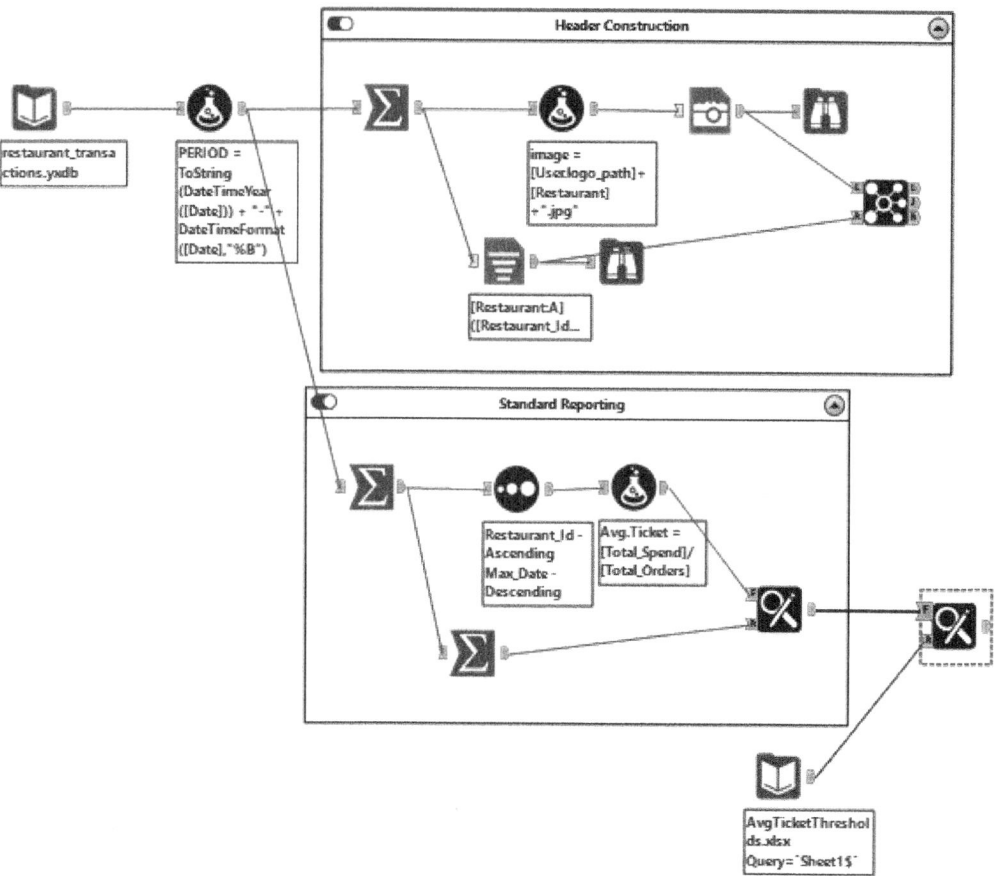

Figure 14.14: Adding the second Find Replace tool

9. In the newly added **Find Replace** tool, select **Entire Field** as the matching mode; for both of the **Find** dropdowns, select Restaurant_Id, and check the **Match Whole Word Only** option.

10. Click on **Append Field(s) to Record** to enable it, and select Avg. Ticket Threshold.

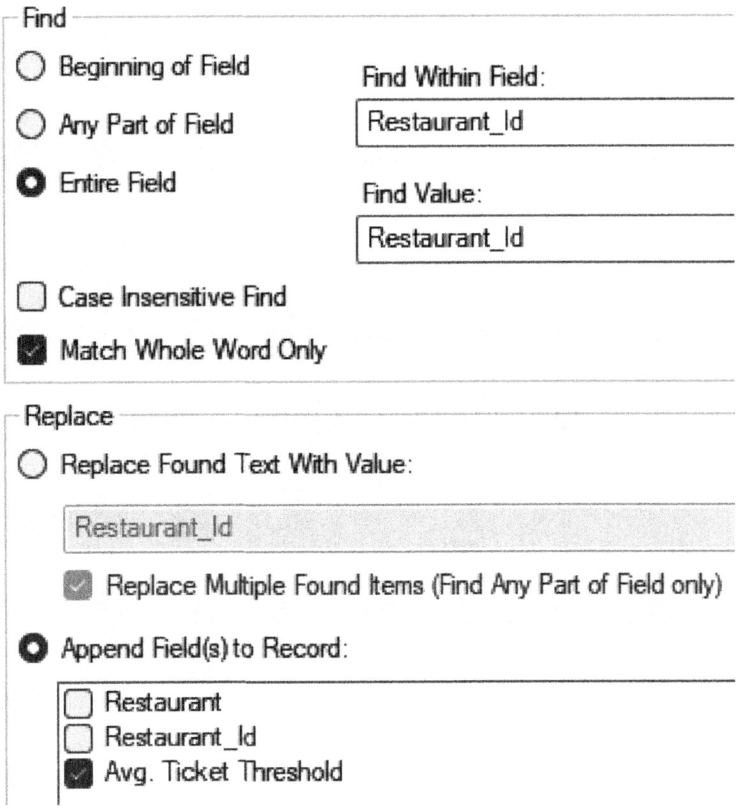

Figure 14.15: Second Find Replace tool configuration

At this point, we have almost all the data we need. The only part we don't have is the comparison from one period with the previous one to determine whether we had growth, a decrease, or the same `Total_Spend`, so let's get into it.

11. Drop a **Multi-Row Formula** tool onto the canvas following the second **Find Replace** tool.

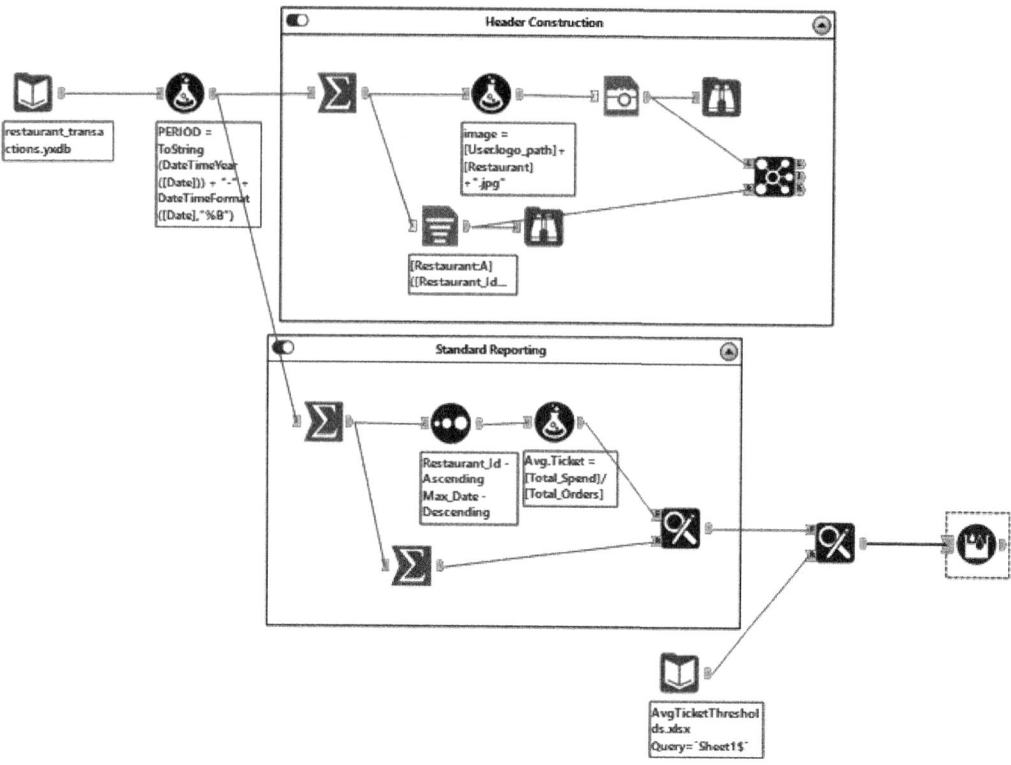

Figure 14.16: Adding the Multi-Row Formula tool

12. From its configuration pane, make sure **Create New Field** is selected.

13. Name the new field `Growth`, and set **Type** to **String** with a **Size** value of `1` (we'll use `G` to indicate growth, `D` for decrease, `E` for equal spend between periods, and `S` for the starting period).

14. For the **Group By** fields, select `Restaurant_Id` and `Restaurant`.

15. For **Expression**, use the following code:

```
IF !IsEmpty([Row+1:Restaurant]) THEN
    IF [Total_Spend]>[Row+1:Total_Spend]
            THEN "G"
            ELSEIF [Total_Spend]=[Row+1:Total_Spend]
            THEN "E"
    ELSE "D"
    ENDIF
ELSE "S"
ENDIF
```

The **Multi-Row Formula** tool settings should look like this:

Figure 14.17: Multi-Row Formula tool configuration

> **Important note**
>
> The wrapping IF statement was added to control what to do when there are no Row+1 values for each group.
>
> As you can see in the following figure, every time we reach the cut on each group (change of Restaurant in our example), the Row+1 value for the field will be Empty, and we can control what to do with that because Empty is not a valid value for that field.
>
> Don't use numeric fields for this because Alteryx Designer sets the Row+1 value to 0, and 0 can be a valid value within a dataset.

	Restaurant_Id	Restaurant	PERIOD	Total_Orders	Total_Spend	Total_Users	Max_Date	Avg.Ticket	next_value
1	30261	Life of Fi Bistro	2023-March	217	8692.95	143	2023-03-30 14:37:59	40.059677	Life of Fi Bistro
2	30261	Life of Fi Bistro	2023-February	205	8018.16	144	2023-02-28 14:03:33	39.112976	Life of Fi Bistro
3	30261	Life of Fi Bistro	2023-January	205	9255.41	132	2023-01-31 11:30:46	45.148341	Life of Fi Bistro
4	30261	Life of Fi Bistro	2022-December	232	8448.82	144	2022-12-31 09:28:52	36.417328	Life of Fi Bistro
5	30261	Life of Fi Bistro	2022-November	215	8312.12	133	2022-11-30 15:11:09	38.661023	Life of Fi Bistro
6	30261	Life of Fi Bistro	2022-October	234	10940.28	149	2022-10-31 15:37:08	46.753333	Life of Fi Bistro
7	30261	Life of Fi Bistro	2022-September	258	11296.21	164	2022-09-30 14:07:37	43.78376	Life of Fi Bistro
8	30261	Life of Fi Bistro	2022-August	244	9894.94	144	2022-08-31 15:38:30	40.553033	Life of Fi Bistro
9	30261	Life of Fi Bistro	2022-July	320	12182.98	191	2022-07-30 12:25:27	38.071812	Life of Fi Bistro
10	30261	Life of Fi Bistro	2022-June	307	13501.01	182	2022-06-30 15:33:16	43.977231	Life of Fi Bistro
11	30261	Life of Fi Bistro	2022-May	267	11754.32	167	2022-05-31 15:45:59	44.02367	Life of Fi Bistro
12	30261	Life of Fi Bistro	2022-April	304	13005.59	178	2022-04-30 11:57:40	42.781546	Life of Fi Bistro
13	30261	Life of Fi Bistro	2022-March	329	12773.32	173	2022-03-31 14:37:00	38.824681	Life of Fi Bistro
14	30261	Life of Fi Bistro	2022-February	273	8850.98	169	2022-02-28 13:32:57	32.421172	Life of Fi Bistro
15	30261	Life of Fi Bistro	2022-January	391	15522.65	231	2022-01-31 14:38:06	39.699872	
16	30405	Howling Worth Cafe	2023-March	105	2937.53	80	2023-03-30 14:42:44	27.976476	Howling Worth Cafe
17	30405	Howling Worth Cafe	2023-February	96	2900.56	81	2023-02-28 21:09:08	30.214167	Howling Worth Cafe
18	30405	Howling Worth Cafe	2023-January	146	4227.84	124	2023-01-31 20:07:04	28.957808	Howling Worth Cafe
19	30405	Howling Worth Cafe	2022-December	160	4850.24	129	2022-12-31 15:56:17	30.314	Howling Worth Cafe
20	30405	Howling Worth Cafe	2022-November	137	3893.52	114	2022-11-30 18:05:25	28.419854	Howling Worth Cafe
21	30405	Howling Worth Cafe	2022-October	144	3633.73	121	2022-10-31 21:03:47	25.234236	Howling Worth Cafe
22	30405	Howling Worth Cafe	2022-September	155	4166.46	126	2022-09-30 21:58:10	26.880387	Howling Worth Cafe
23	30405	Howling Worth Cafe	2022-August	138	3098.2	115	2022-08-31 21:51:17	22.450725	Howling Worth Cafe
24	30405	Howling Worth Cafe	2022-July	177	5198.53	144	2022-07-31 20:11:01	29.370226	Howling Worth Cafe
25	30405	Howling Worth Cafe	2022-June	254	6904.87	208	2022-06-30 13:31:28	27.184528	Howling Worth Cafe
26	30405	Howling Worth Cafe	2022-May	226	5956.77	186	2022-05-31 21:56:40	26.357389	Howling Worth Cafe
27	30405	Howling Worth Cafe	2022-April	140	3748.59	108	2022-04-30 21:17:25	26.775643	Howling Worth Cafe
28	30405	Howling Worth Cafe	2022-March	175	4596.13	147	2022-03-31 20:55:58	26.2636	Howling Worth Cafe
29	30405	Howling Worth Cafe	2022-February	179	5181.26	146	2022-02-28 21:10:32	28.945587	Howling Worth Cafe
30	30405	Howling Worth Cafe	2022-January	296	8565.22	238	2022-01-31 21:53:47	28.936554	
31	30412	Bar-One	2023-March	106	3416.61	85	2023-03-30 20:51:37	32.23217	Bar-One
32	30412	Bar-One	2023-February	70	2456.85	63	2023-02-28 20:08:20	35.097857	Bar-One

Figure 14.18: Checking the Row+1 values (Empty)

Now, let's build the table.

1. Drop a **Report Table** tool onto the canvas, following the **Multi-Row Formula** tool.

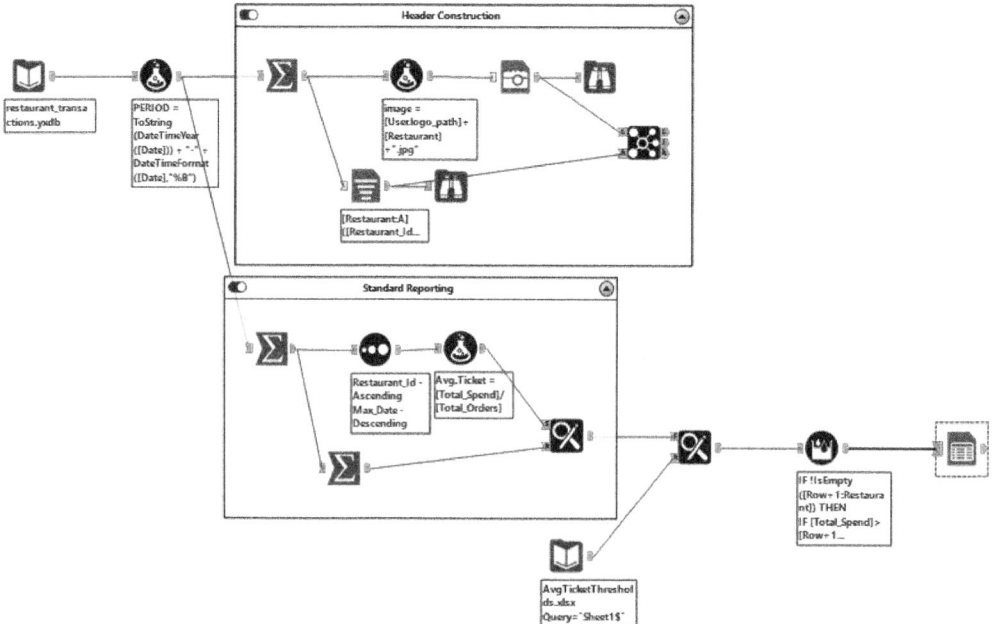

Figure 14.19: Adding a Report Table tool

We are going to configure the table as follows.

2. From the **Group By** list, select `Restaurant_Id` and `Restaurant`.

3. In the **Per Column Configuration** pane, deselect the following:

    *   `Restaurant_Id`

    *   `Restaurant`

    *   `Max_Date`

    *   `Min_Total_Users`

    *   `Max_Total_Users`

    *   `Avg. Ticket Threshold`

    *   `Dynamic or Unknown Fields`

At this point, your **Report Table** tool configuration should look like this:

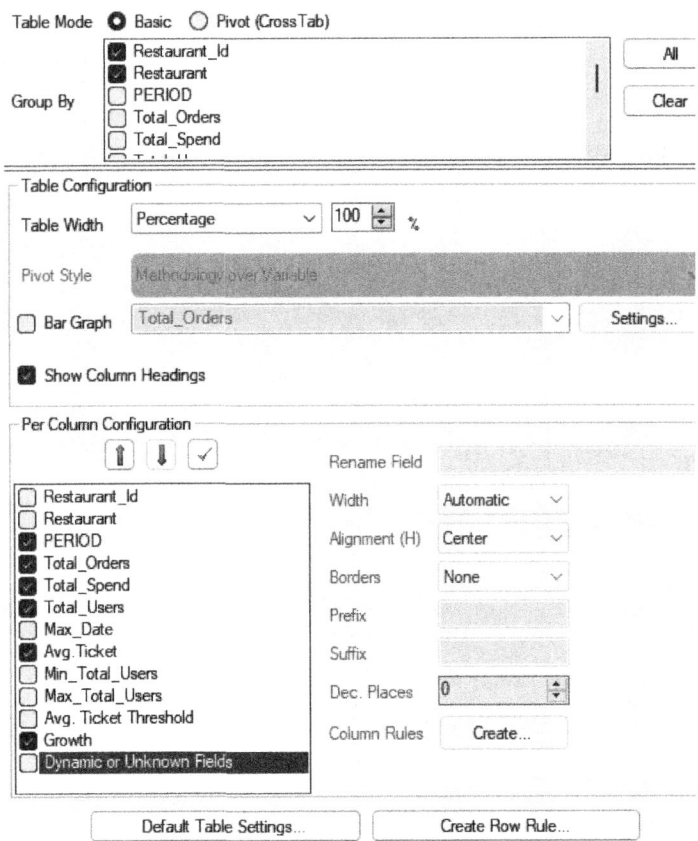

Figure 14.20: Report Table tool configuration

If we add a **Browse** tool following the **Report Table** tool and run the workflow, we'll get the following:

Record	Table				

Record 1

PERIOD	Total_Orders	Total_Spend	Total_Users	Avg.Ticket	Growth
2023-March	217	8,693	143	40	G
2023-February	205	8,018	144	39	D
2023-January	205	9,255	132	45	G
2022-December	232	8,449	144	36	G
2022-November	215	8,312	133	39	D
2022-October	234	10,940	149	47	D
2022-September	258	11,296	164	44	G
2022-August	244	9,895	144	41	D
2022-July	320	12,183	191	38	D
2022-June	307	13,501	182	44	G
2022-May	267	11,754	167	44	D
2022-April	304	13,006	178	43	G
2022-March	329	12,773	173	39	G
2022-February	273	8,851	169	32	D
2022-January	391	15,523	231	40	S

Record 2

PERIOD	Total_Orders	Total_Spend	Total_Users	Avg.Ticket	Growth
2023-March	105	2,938	80	28	G
2023-February	96	2,901	81	30	D
2023-January	146	4,228	124	29	D
2022-December	160	4,850	129	30	G
2022-November	137	3,894	114	28	G
2022-October	144	3,634	121	25	D
2022-September	155	4,166	126	27	G
2022-August	138	3,098	115	22	D
2022-July	177	5,199	144	29	D

Figure 14.21: Preview of the resulting table

As you can see, now it's time to format our table.

We have three types of configuration to perform:

- Table configuration
- Per-column configurations
- Per-row configurations

Let's start with the whole table settings.

4. Return to the **Report Table** tool configuration and look for the **Default Table Settings…** button at the bottom of the panel.

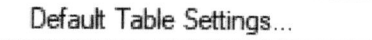

Figure 14.22: Default Table Settings… button

5. Click on it and the **Style Editor** window will pop up.

The **Data** tab allows us to set how the data will be shown in the table.

6. Change **Data Font** to **Calibri**.

7. Change **Font Size** to **11**.

8. Leave the others on their default values.

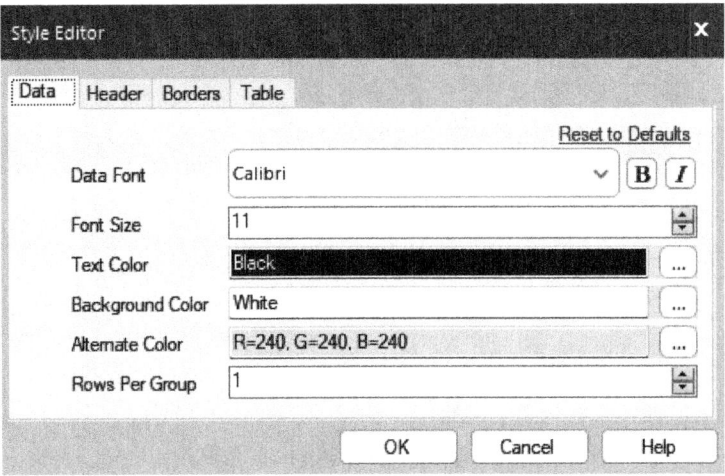

Figure 14.23: Style Editor – Data tab

9.   Click on the **Header** tab to set up how the table header must look.

10. Change **Header Font** to **Calibri**, and click on the **Bold** button.

11. Change **Font Size** to **11**.

12. Click on the ellipsis button to the right of the **Text Color** setting to access the **Color** picker. Select *white* from there.

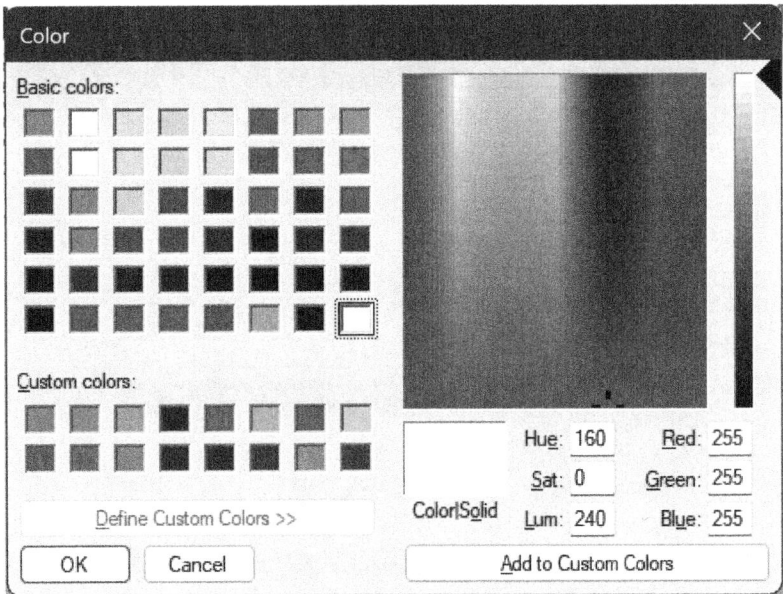

Figure 14.24: Color picker

13. Click on the ellipsis of the **Background Color** setting and select the color you want to use for the table headers (to get the same blue as the example, you can enter the RGB values in the **Color** picker):

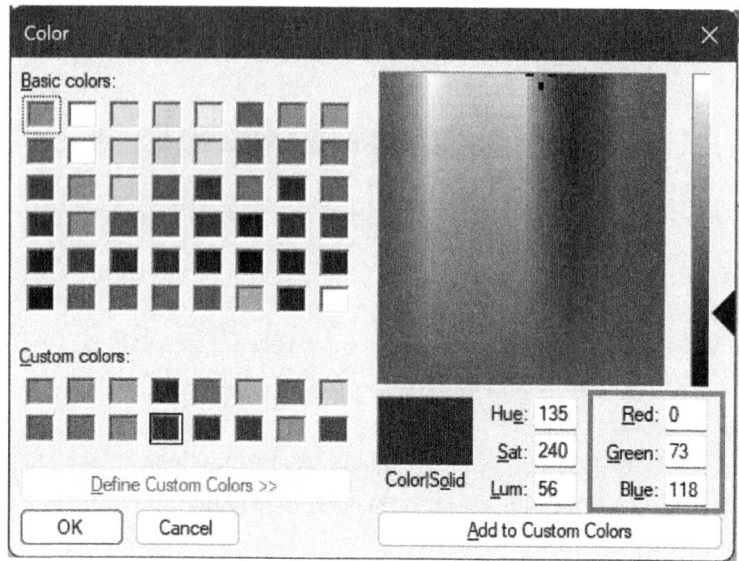

Figure 14.25: Setting RGB values in the Color picker

Once you finish, the **Header** tab will look like this:

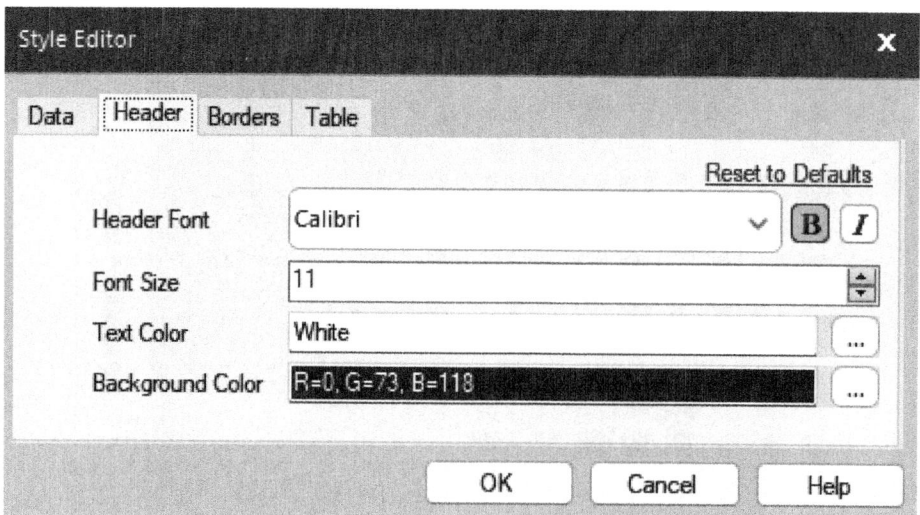

Figure 14.26: Style Editor – Header tab

14. Click on the **Borders** tab.

We are not changing anything here, but it's helpful to know that, from here, you can change the settings for the internal borders of the table.

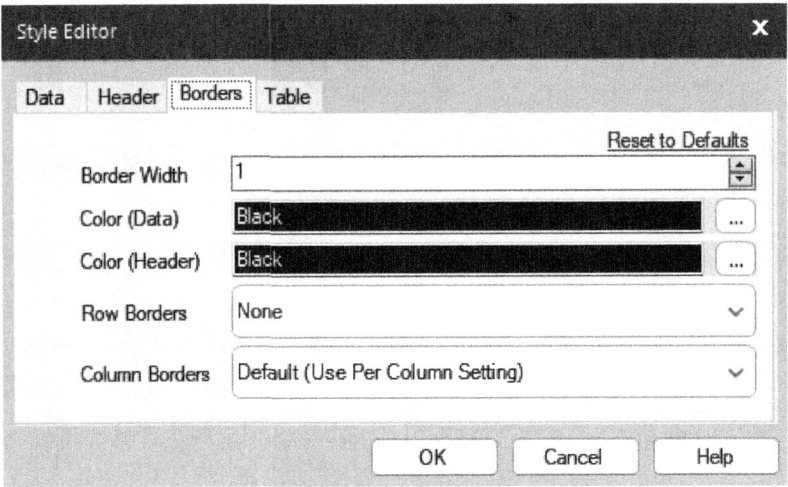

Figure 14.27: Style Editor – Borders tab

15. Click on the **Table** tab. This option will allow us to set the outside borders for the table and the padding options.

16. Click on the ellipsis button and set the same color as you used for the table headers.

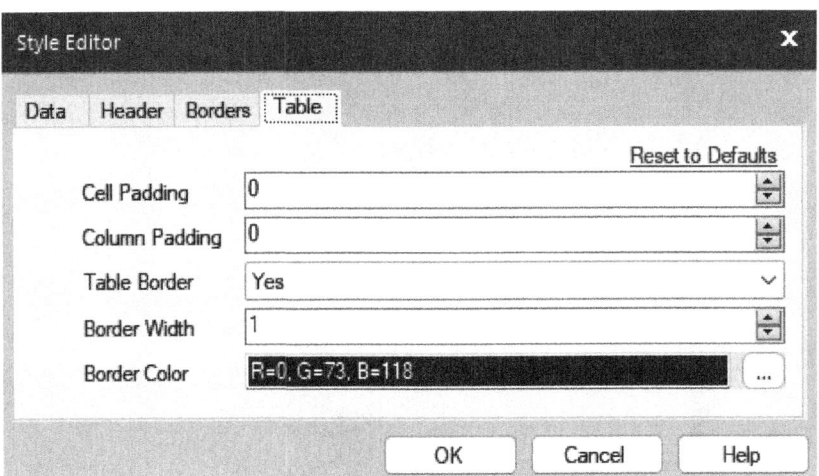

Figure 14.28: Style Editor – Table tab

17. Hit **OK** to apply the changes and run the workflow.

You'll see how the new settings were applied to the table.

Record	Table					
1	**PERIOD**	**Total_Orders**	**Total_Spend**	**Total_Users**	**Avg.Ticket**	**Growth**
	2023-March	217	8,693	143	40	G
	2023-February	205	8,018	144	39	D
	2023-January	205	9,255	132	45	G
	2022-December	232	8,449	144	36	G
	2022-November	215	8,312	133	39	D
	2022-October	234	10,940	149	47	D
	2022-September	258	11,296	164	44	G
	2022-August	244	9,895	144	41	D
	2022-July	320	12,183	191	38	D
	2022-June	307	13,501	182	44	G
	2022-May	267	11,754	167	44	D
	2022-April	304	13,006	178	43	G
	2022-March	329	12,773	173	39	G
	2022-February	273	8,851	169	32	D
	2022-January	391	15,523	231	40	S
2	**PERIOD**	**Total_Orders**	**Total_Spend**	**Total_Users**	**Avg.Ticket**	**Growth**
	2023-March	105	2,938	80	28	G
	2023-February	96	2,901	81	30	D
	2023-January	146	4,228	124	29	D
	2022-December	160	4,850	129	30	G
	2022-November	137	3,894	114	28	G
	2022-October	144	3,634	121	25	D
	2022-September	155	4,166	126	27	G

Figure 14.29: Table after applying default table settings

Now, we'll take care of the column rules.

18. On the **Table** configuration panel, click on the PERIOD field in the **Per Column Configuration** section. You'll notice that the field's options are now enabled.

19. For the PERIOD field, we'll dim the black color of the data for those periods corresponding to 2022, so we need to check whether or not every value contains 2022.

20. Click on the **Create…** button next to **Column Rules**.

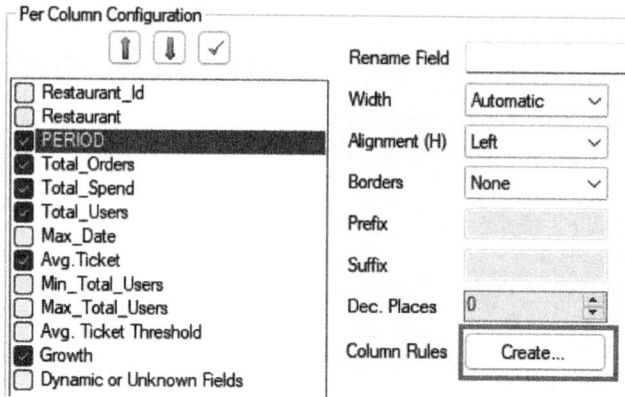

Figure 14.30: Create… button for Column Rules

The **Column Styling Rules** editor will pop up.

21. Change **Rule Name** to 2022 Identification.

22. Click to select **Formula** in the **Apply** section, and type the following expression:

    Contains ([PERIOD], "2022")

    When the result of the expression is true, Alteryx will replace the existing attributes of the field with the ones we selected from the list at the bottom of the pane.

23. Click on **Text Color** and, from the **Color** picker, select some gray tone (as you can see in the following field configuration, we used 107 for the **R**, **G**, and **B** values).

    So your column rule for the PERIOD field ends up looking like this:

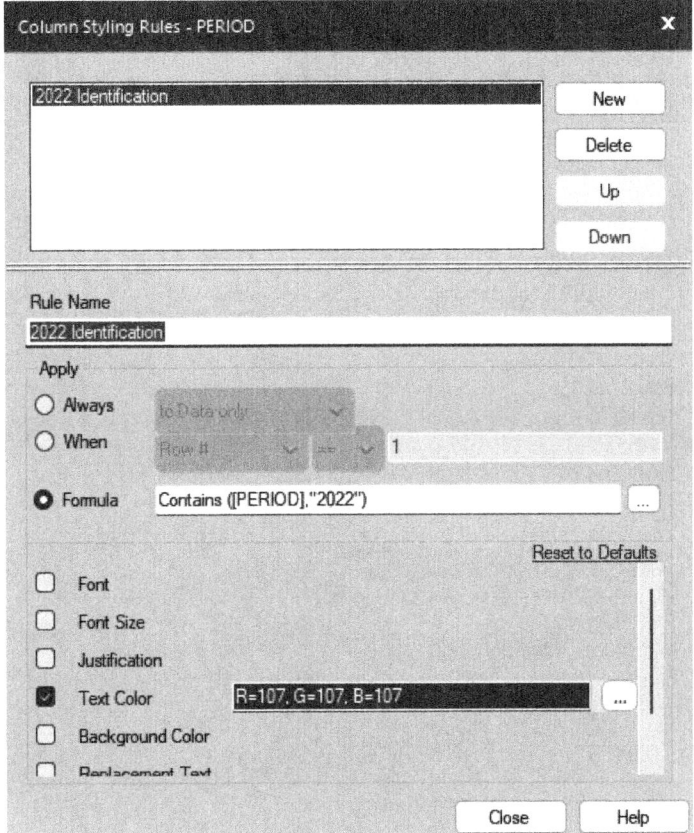

Figure 14.31: Column rule to identify 2022 periods

24. Run the workflow again, and notice how all the period values corresponding to 2022 are dimmed compared to the 2023 ones.

Record	Table					
1	**PERIOD**	**Total_Orders**	**Total_Spend**	**Total_Users**	**Avg.Ticket**	**Growth**
	2023-March	217	8,693	143	40	G
	2023-February	205	8,018	144	39	D
	2023-January	205	9,255	132	45	G
	2022-December	232	8,449	144	36	G
	2022-November	215	8,312	133	39	D
	2022-October	234	10,940	149	47	D
	2022-September	258	11,296	164	44	G
	2022-August	244	9,895	144	41	D

Figure 14.32: Results of applying the PERIOD column rule (2022 periods are dimmed)

25. Click on the **Report Table** tool to access its configuration. Note that the PERIOD field now is displayed in bold (this indicates that it has column rules associated with it).

26. Click on Avg. Ticket and rename it to Average Ticket.

27. Set $ as its **Prefix** value.

28. Set **Dec. Places** to **2**.

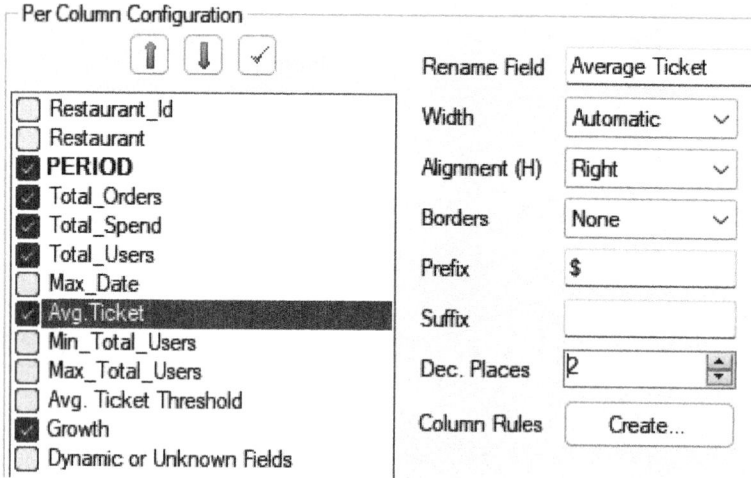

Figure 14.33: Avg. Ticket settings

29. Finally, click on the **Create…** button to set column rules for this field.

    This field's rule will check whether the Avg. Ticket value for each PERIOD is below the threshold defined for the restaurant. If it is, we'll show its value in red in the report.

30. Rename the rule to Avg. Ticket Below Threshold.

31. Select **Formula** from the **Apply** options.

32. Use this expression as the formula:

    ```
    [Avg.Ticket]<[Avg. Ticket Threshold]
    ```

33. Click on **Text Color** to enable it, and select a red tone (we used **R**=195, **G**=0, and **B**=47 in our example).

    Your Avg. Ticket rule will look like this:

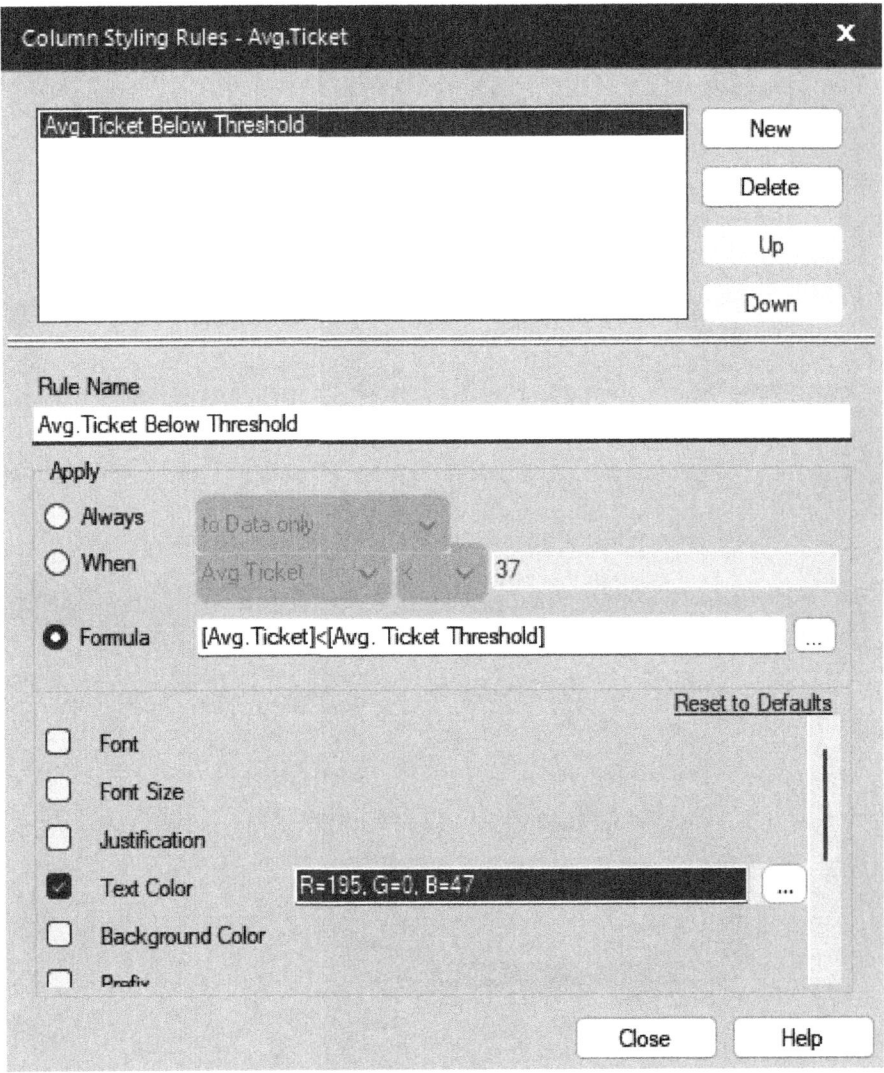

Figure 14.34: Column rule settings for Avg.Ticket

34. Click on **Close** and run the workflow again.

If you see the resulting values in the **Browse** tool, you'll see that all the `Average Ticket` amounts below the defined threshold are in red, and the others remain untouched.

Record						
1	Table					

PERIOD	Total_Orders	Total_Spend	Total_Users	Average Ticket	Growth
2023-March	217	8,693	143	$40.06	G
2023-February	205	8,018	144	$39.11	D
2023-January	205	9,255	132	$45.15	G
2022-December	232	8,449	144	$36.42	G
2022-November	215	8,312	133	$38.66	D
2022-October	234	10,940	149	$46.75	D
2022-September	258	11,296	164	$43.78	G
2022-August	244	9,895	144	$40.55	D
2022-July	320	12,183	191	$38.07	D
2022-June	307	13,501	182	$43.98	G
2022-May	267	11,754	167	$44.02	D
2022-April	304	13,006	178	$42.78	G
2022-March	329	12,773	173	$38.82	G
2022-February	273	8,851	169	$32.42	D
2022-January	391	15,523	231	$39.70	S

2					

PERIOD	Total_Orders	Total_Spend	Total_Users	Average Ticket	Growth
2023-March	105	2,938	80	$27.98	G
2023-February	96	2,901	81	$30.21	D
2023-January	146	4,228	124	$28.96	D
2022-December	160	4,850	129	$30.31	G
2022-November	137	3,894	114	$28.42	G
2022-October	144	3,634	121	$25.23	D

Figure 14.35: Column rule applied to Avg.Ticket (in red, all those below the threshold)

Now, back to the table configuration options.

35. Click on the `Growth` field.

36. The first thing to do is move it just below `Total_Spend`. Using the *green arrows*, place it right after `Total_Spend`.

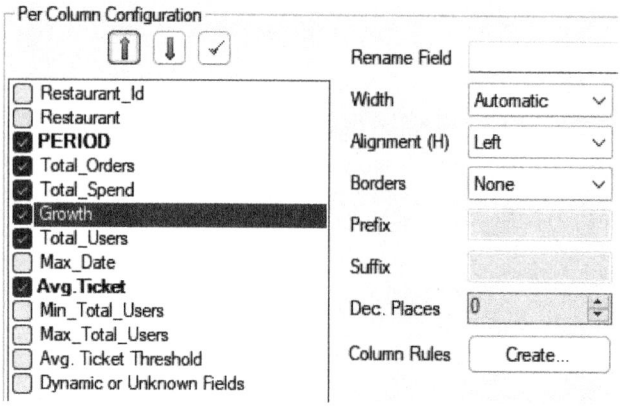

Figure 14.36: Placing the Growth field

For this field, we'll have three rules:

- When Growth=G, we'll show an up arrow (▲, Unicode=25B2, or *Alt* + 30 on the numeric pad) in green

- When Growth=D, we'll show a down-pointing arrow (▼, Unicode=25BC, or *Alt* + 31 on the numeric pad) in red

- When Growth is either E or S, we'll show a dash (■, Unicode=25AC, or *Alt* + 22 on the numeric pad) in yellow

37. Click on the **Create…** button to start building the rules.

38. Rename the rule Growth Symbol.

39. Click on **When** to set the **Apply** condition.

40. From the **Fields** dropdown, select **Growth**, select == from the **Condition** dropdown, and enter G for the value to compare to.

41. Click on **Text Color** to enable it and select any green you like (we used 0, 150, and 166 in the example).

42. Click on **Replacement Text** to enable it and its text field, and while pressing the *Alt* key, type 30 on your numeric pad.

If you don't have a numeric pad on your computer, you can go to https://jrgraphix. net/r/Unicode/25A0-25FF, copy the characters from there, and then paste them into **Replacement Text**.

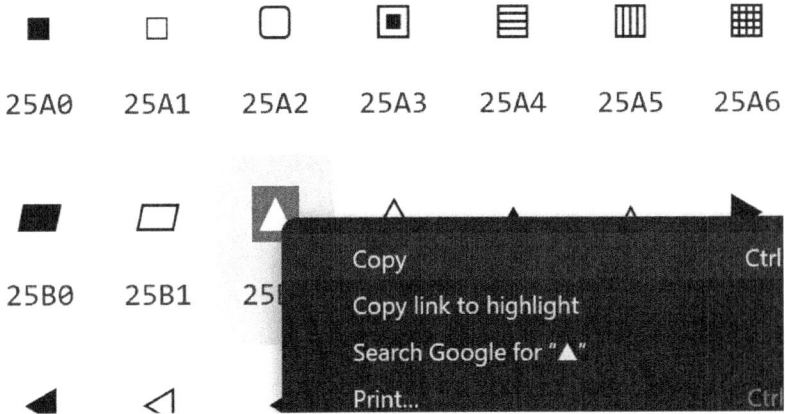

Figure 14.37: jrgraphix.net provides access to useful symbols

Also, you can use **Character Map** to find these characters using **Go to Unicode** and insert the code for each one, then copy and paste them as needed.

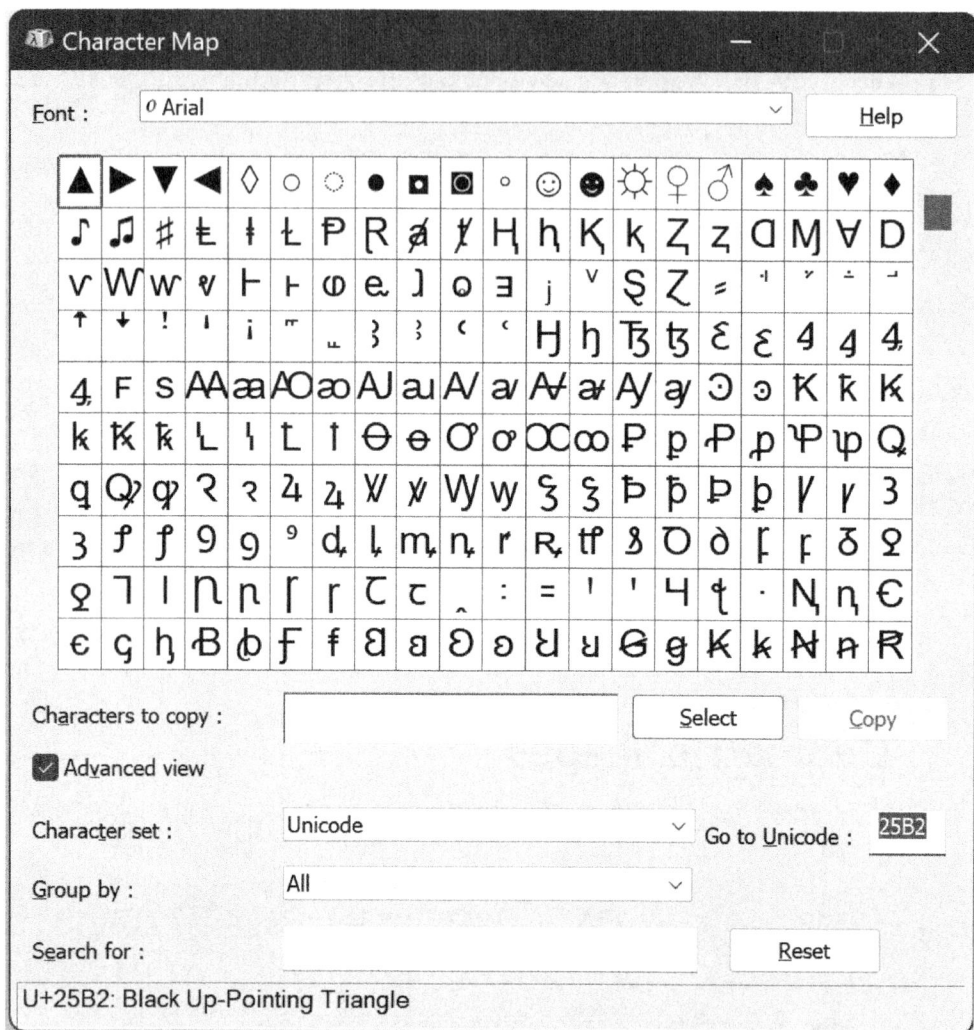

Figure 14.38: Windows Character Map (search by Unicode)

Your first rule should look like this:

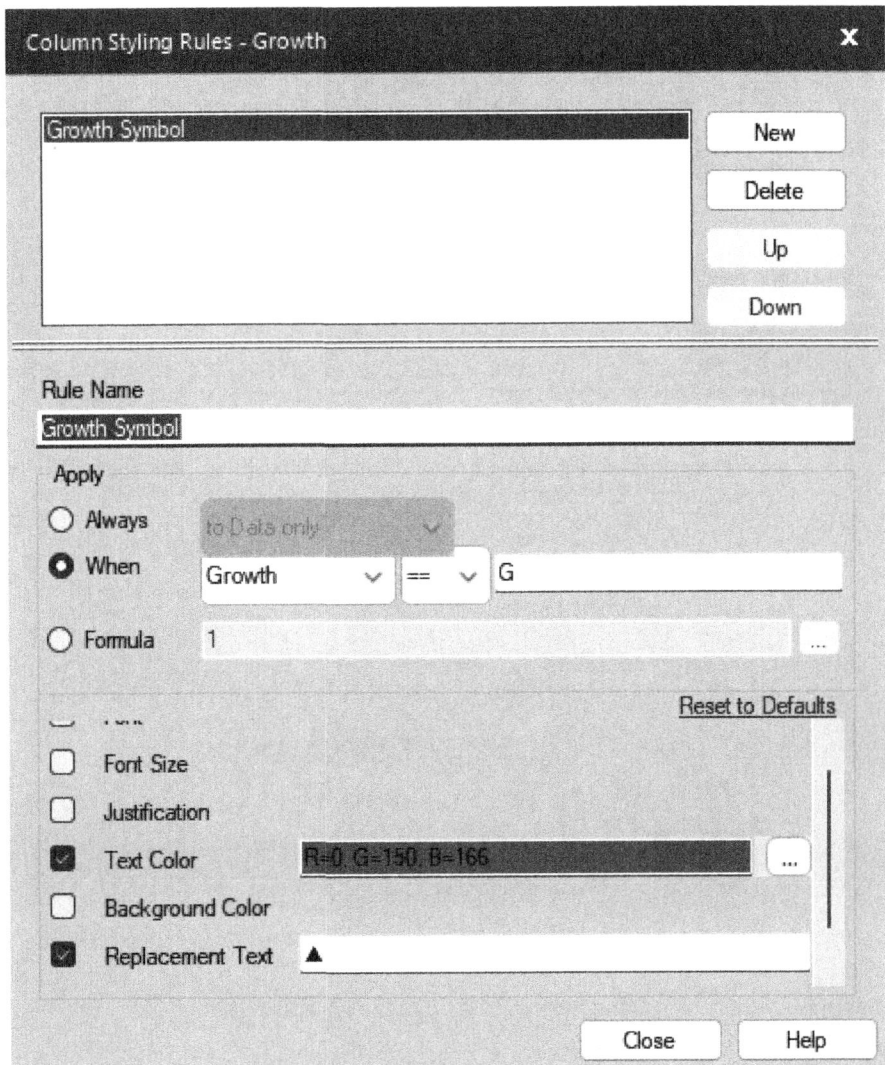

Figure 14.39: Rule to apply when there is growth versus the previous period spend

43. Click on the **New** button on the top right of the screen to add a second rule.

44. Rename the rule Decrease Symbol.

45. For **Apply**, select **When** and **Growth** == D.

46. Select **Text Color** and get a red tone (we used 195, 0, and 47 in the example).

47. Click on **Replacement Text**, and now, using the same method as you used to add the arrow in the previous rule, select the down-pointing arrow.

So, your second rule looks like this:

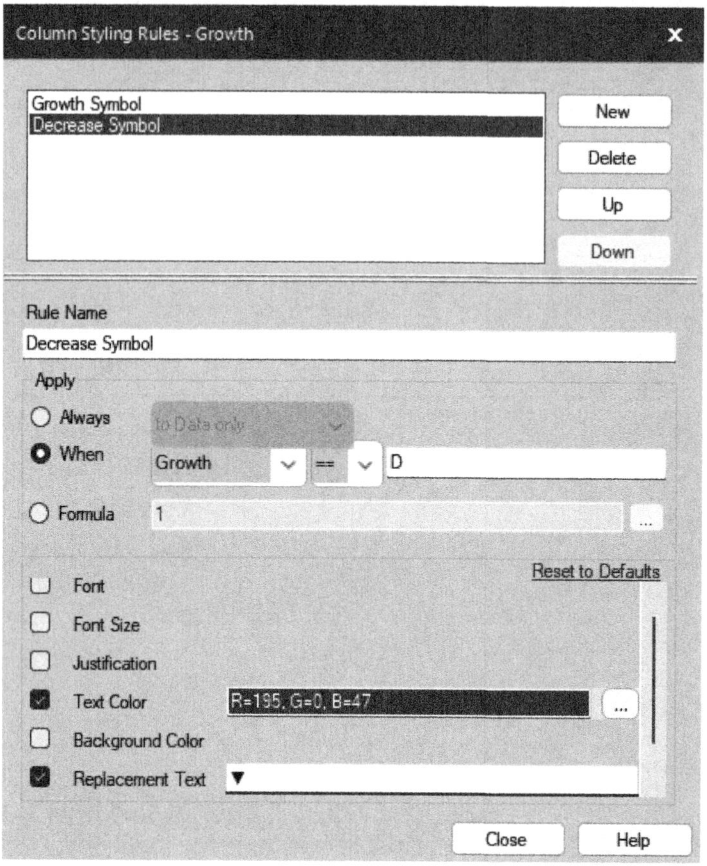

Figure 14.40: Rule to apply when there is a decrease versus the previous period spend

48. Click again on the **New** button to create the third rule for this field.

49. We'll rename it `Equal and 1st. Symbol`.

    Since we need to evaluate two conditions to apply the same rule, we'll use **Formula** as the **Apply** method.

50. Click on **Formula** and use this expression for it:

    ```
    [Growth] IN ("S","E")
    ```

51. Click **Text Color** and select any yellow you like (we used 250, 241, and 133 in our example).

52. Click on **Replacement Text** and paste the dash character in the textbox, using your chosen method to get the special characters.

The completed rules for the Growth field will look like this:

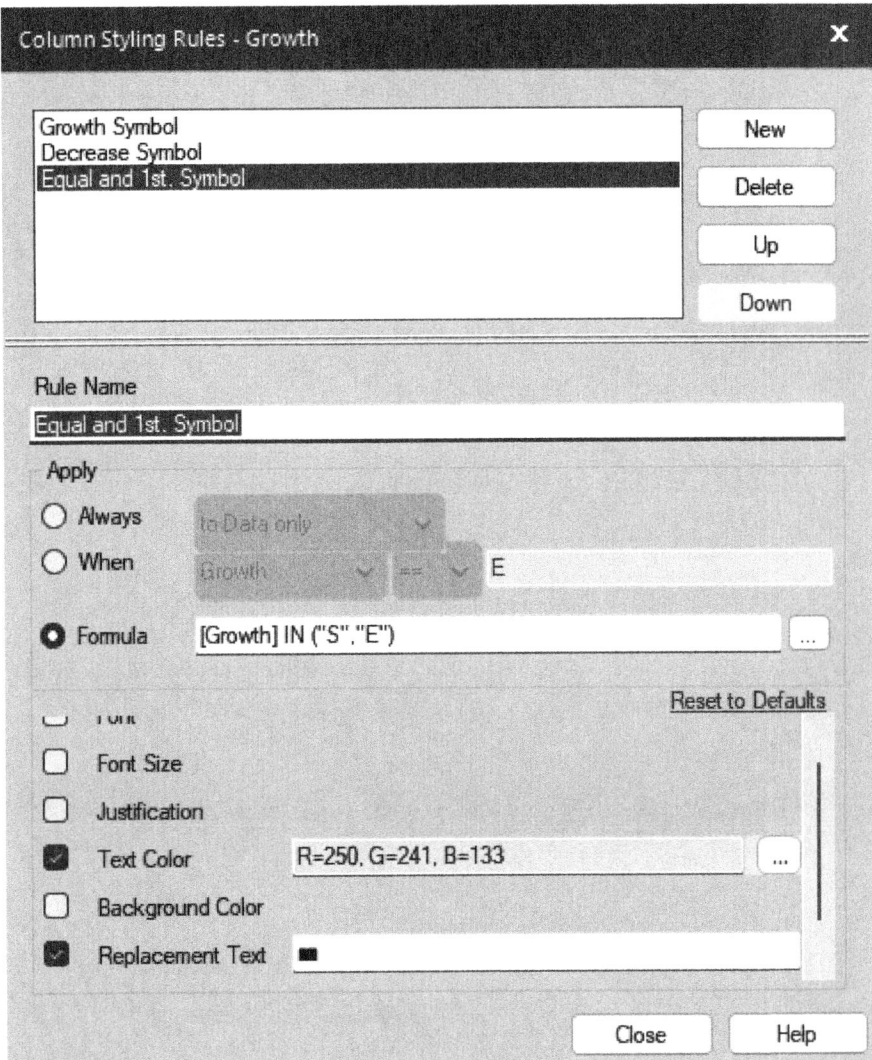

Figure 14.41: Rule configuration for the first period and when there is no change in spend

53. Click on **Close** and run the workflow.

Record	Table					
1	**PERIOD**	**Total_Orders**	**Total_Spend**	**Growth**	**Total_Users**	**Average Ticket**
	2023-March	217	8,693	▲	143	$40.06
	2023-February	205	8,018	▼	144	$39.11
	2023-January	205	9,255	▲	132	$45.15
	2022-December	232	8,449	▲	144	$36.42
	2022-November	215	8,312	▼	133	$38.66
	2022-October	234	10,940	▼	149	$46.75
	2022-September	258	11,296	▲	164	$43.78
	2022-August	244	9,895	▼	144	$40.55
	2022-July	320	12,183	▼	191	$38.07
	2022-June	307	13,501	▲	182	$43.98
	2022-May	267	11,754	▼	167	$44.02
	2022-April	304	13,006	▲	178	$42.78
	2022-March	329	12,773	▲	173	$38.82
	2022-February	273	8,851	▼	169	$32.42
	2022-January	391	15,523	—	231	$39.70
2	**PERIOD**	**Total_Orders**	**Total_Spend**	**Growth**	**Total_Users**	**Average Ticket**
	2023-March	105	2,938	▲	80	$27.98
	2023-February	96	2,901	▼	81	$30.21
	2023-January	146	4,228	▼	124	$28.96
	2022-December	160	4,850	▲	129	$30.31
	2022-November	137	3,894	▲	114	$28.42

Figure 14.42: Resulting table after applying the rules

We have the Growth field completely formatted and showing the symbols we need.

Back on the **Table** tool configuration, we are going to fix the remaining header labels.

54. Click on the Total_Orders field, and rename it Total Orders.

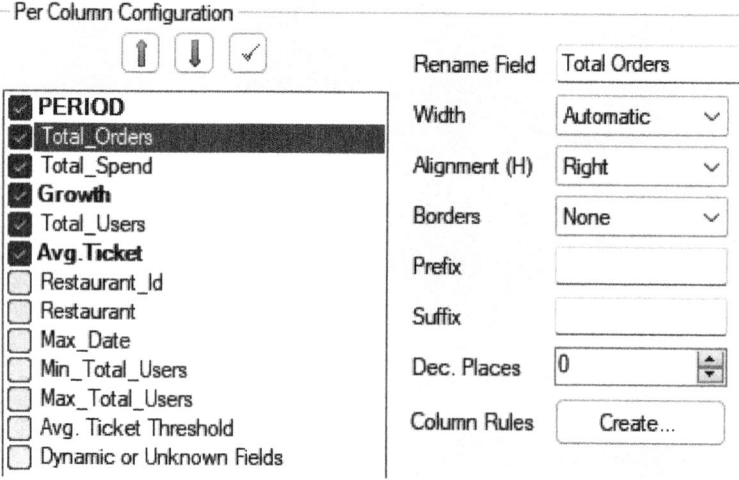

Figure 14.43: Total_Orders field settings

55. Click on `Total_Spend`, rename it `Total Spend`, set **Prefix** to $, and set **Dec. Places** to **2**.

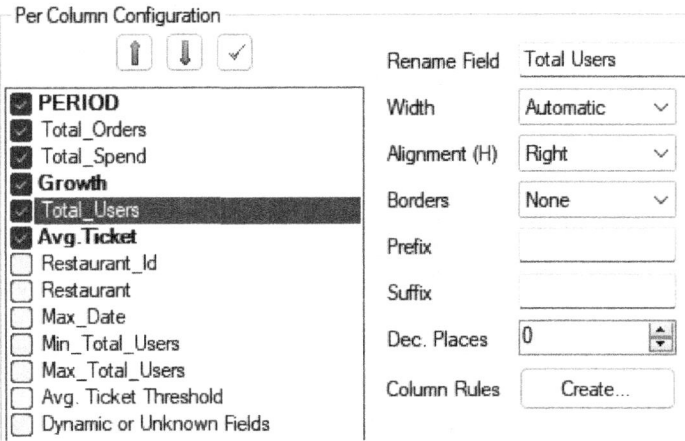

Figure 14.44: Total_Spend field settings

56. Click on `Total_Users` and rename it `Total Users`.

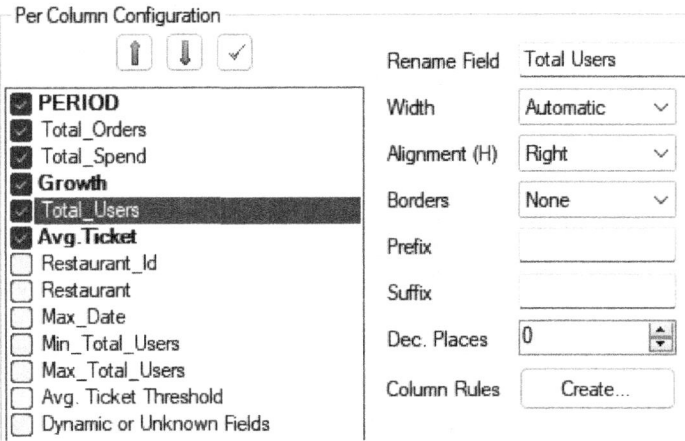

Figure 14.45: Total_Users field settings

Now, for the final step in our table, we need to identify and conditionally format the periods with the maximum and minimum user volume per restaurant accordingly. Since this will highlight the entire row when the condition is met, we'll create a row rule.

57. Click on the **Create Row Rule…** button at the bottom right of the **Table** configuration pane.

Figure 14.46: Create Row Rule... button

The **Row Styling Rules** window will show up. As you can see, it's very similar to **Column Styling Rules**, with a little additional setting that deserves an explanation.

There is a hierarchy in Alteryx for applying the rules.

This is how it is explained in the Alteryx documentation:

To use rules effectively, you should understand which rules come 1st, and which ones override other ones. When 2 rules intend to change different styles (one changes a font, and the other changes the font size, for example), it doesn't matter which one executes 1st. But when 2 rules both intend to change the same style, only 1 of them wins. Rules are executed in this order (later rules override earlier rules):

- *Default Table Settings have the lowest priority.*

- *Per-Column Configurations*

- *Row Rule with Only Basic (Non-Formula) Styles*

- *Column Rule with Only Basic Styles*

- *Row Rule with Only Basic Styles with the Override Check Box Selected*

- *Row Rule With Formula Styles*

- *Column Rule with Formula Styles*

- *Row Rule with Formula Styles with the Override Check Box Selected*

Here is another way to look at this:

- *Formula styles always take precedence over non-formula (basic) styles.*

- *Column rules usually take precedence over row rules, unless the row rule explicitly has its "override column rules" check box checked.*

- *Rules take precedence over the per-column and default table settings.*

- *Multiple rules of a given type (row or column, basic, or formula) execute in the order they are listed in the rule editor.*

That's why we have the **This Rule should override conflicting Per-Column Rules** setting in the **Apply** section.

58. So, for the first row rule, rename it Min Users.

59. Select **Formula** as the **Apply** method for the formatting, with the following expression:

    ```
    [Total_Users] = [Min_Total_Users]
    ```

60. In the formatting section, select a light tone of red (we used 255, 196, and 210 in ours).

    So, your first row rule looks like this:

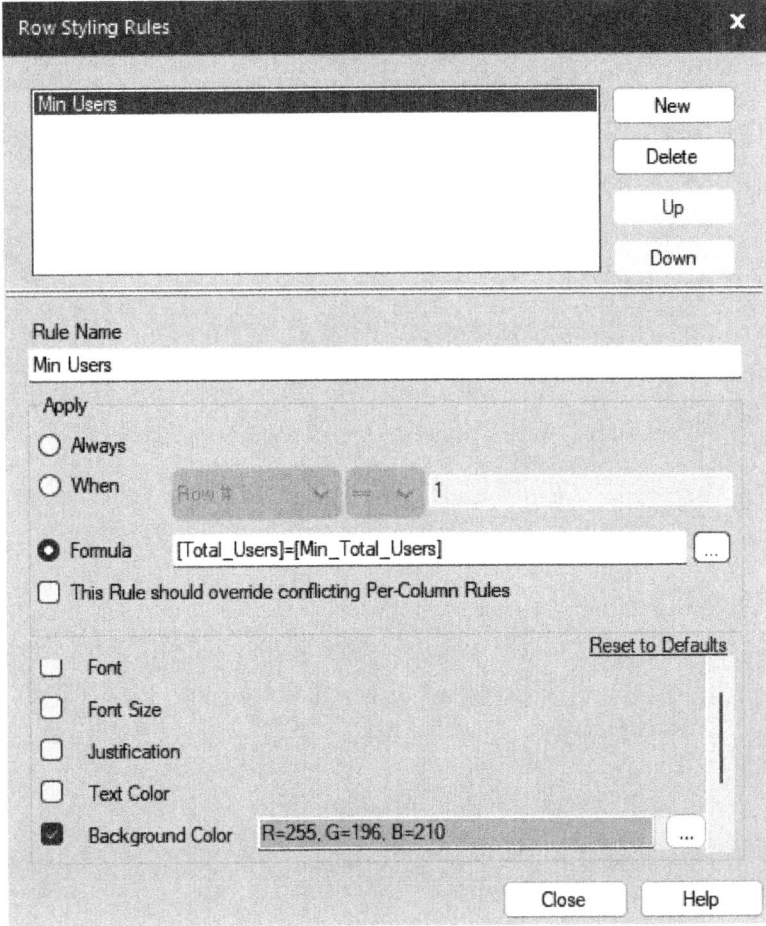

Figure 14.47: Row rule to highlight the period with fewer users

61. Click on the **New** button.

62. Rename the new rule Max Users.

63. Select **Formula** as the **Apply** method too, but use this expression:

    ```
    [Total_Users]=[Max_Total_Users]
    ```

64. Click on **Background Color** to enable it and select some light green (we used 201, 228, and 228 in our example).

So, the second row rule looks like this:

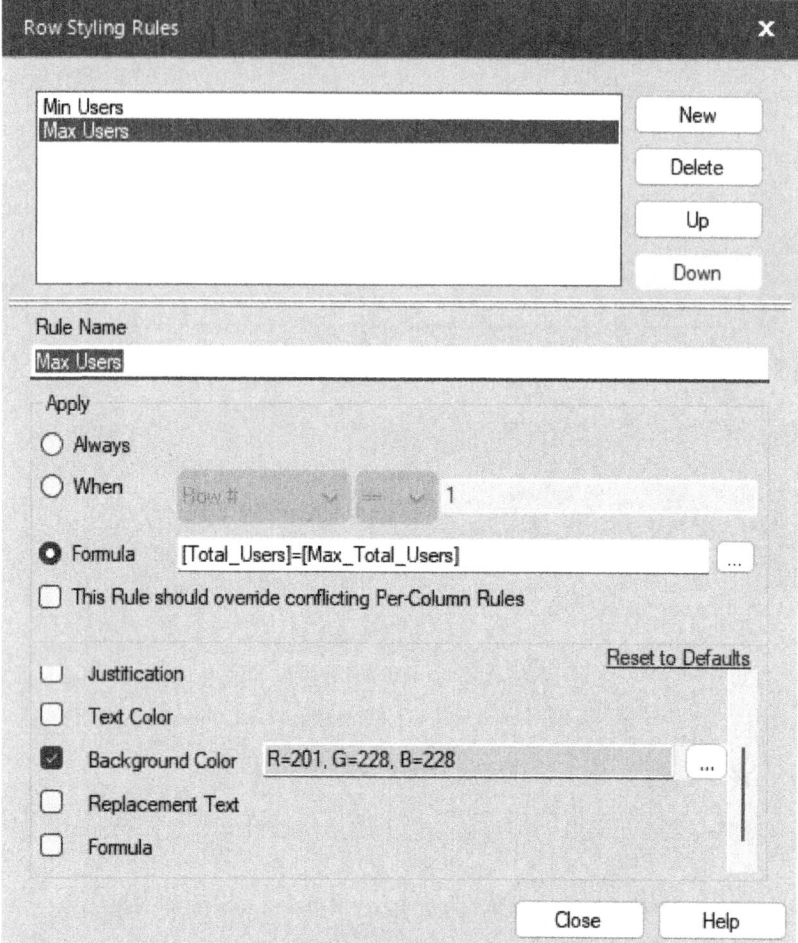

Figure 14.48: Row rule to highlight the period with the most users

65. Click on **Close** and run the workflow. You'll see that the table looks exactly as we wanted.

Record	Table

PERIOD	Total Orders	Total Spend	Growth	Total Users	Average Ticket
2023-March	217	$8,692.95	▲	143	$40.06
2023-February	205	$8,018.16	▼	144	$39.11
2023-January	205	$9,255.41	▲	132	$45.15
2022-December	232	$8,448.82	▲	144	$36.42
2022-November	215	$8,312.12	▼	133	$38.66
2022-October	234	$10,940.28	▼	149	$46.75
2022-September	258	$11,296.21	▲	164	$43.78
2022-August	244	$9,894.94	▼	144	$40.55
2022-July	320	$12,182.98	▼	191	$38.07
2022-June	307	$13,501.01	▲	182	$43.98
2022-May	267	$11,754.32	▼	167	$44.02
2022-April	304	$13,005.59	▲	178	$42.78
2022-March	329	$12,773.32	▲	173	$38.82
2022-February	273	$8,850.98	▼	169	$32.42
2022-January	391	$15,522.65		231	$39.70

Record 2

PERIOD	Total Orders	Total Spend	Growth	Total Users	Average Ticket
2023-March	105	$2,937.53	▲	80	$27.98
2023-February	96	$2,900.56	▼	81	$30.21
2023-January	146	$4,227.84	▼	124	$28.96
2022-December	160	$4,850.24	▲	129	$30.31
2022-November	137	$3,893.52	▲	114	$28.42
2022-October	144	$3,633.73	▼	121	$25.23

Figure 14.49: Resulting table after applying all the rules

Now it's time to add the header to the report and render the Excel files.

66. Drop a **Layout** tool and connect the **J** output anchor from the **Join** tool in the **Header Construction** Tool Container to its input anchor.

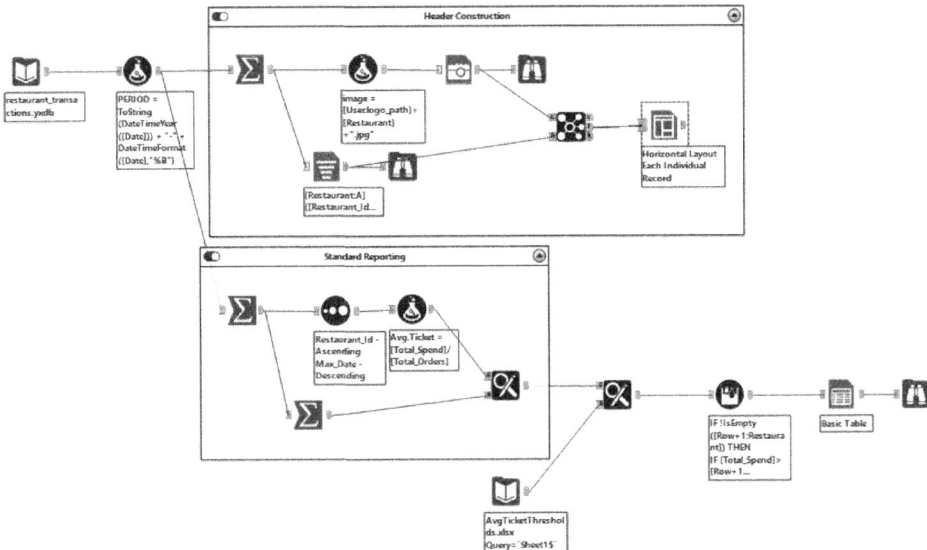

Figure 14.50: Adding a Layout tool to compose the header

67. From the **Layout** tool configuration, just make sure that Image2 is on top of Title. Leave all other options as their default values.

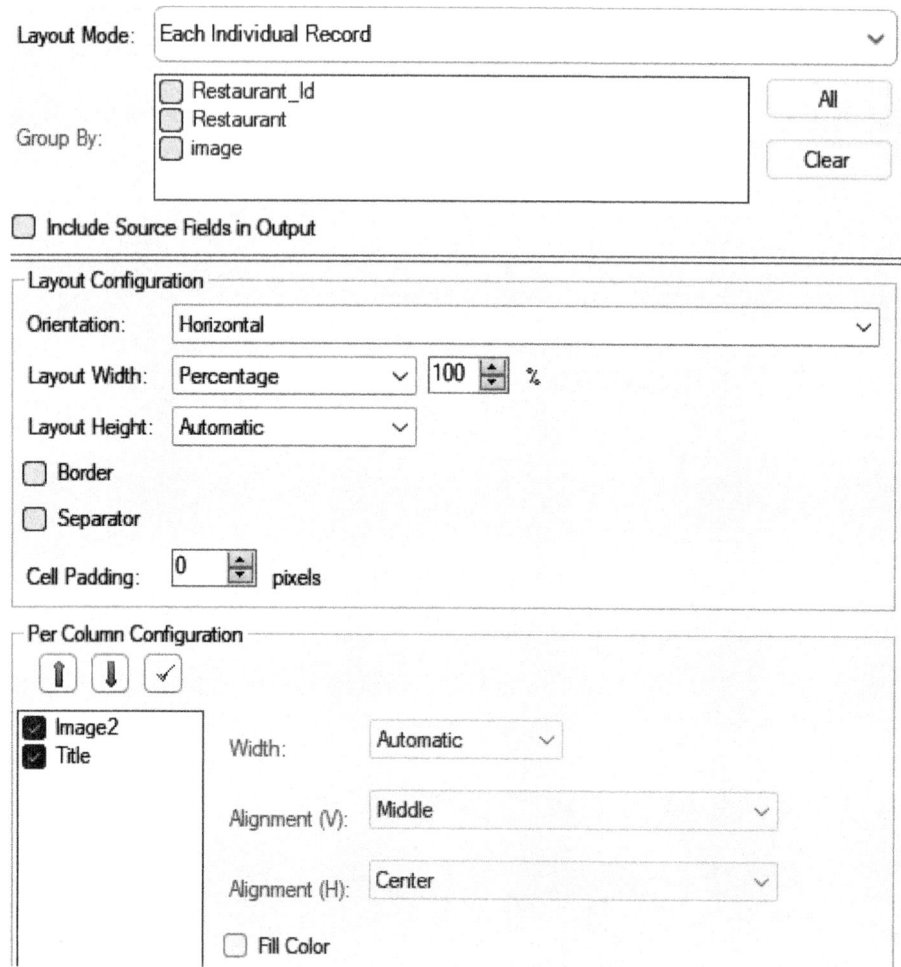

Figure 14.51: Layout tool configuration

68. Drop a **Select** tool following the recently added **Layout** tool.

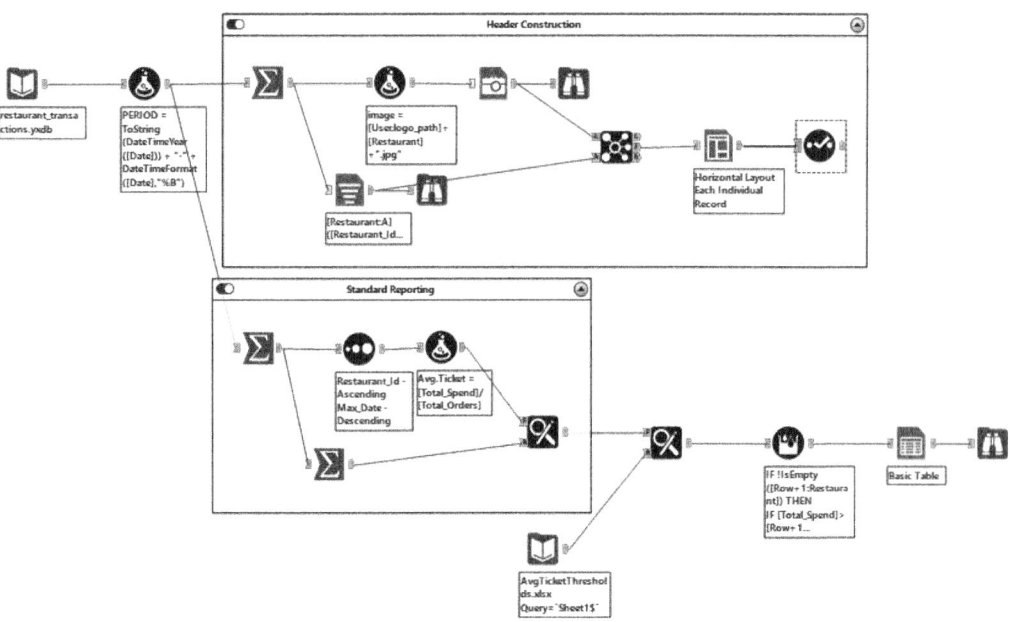

Figure 14.52: Adding a Select tool

69. From its configuration, rename the Layout field to Header.

		Field	Type		Size	Rename	Descript
▶	☑	Restaurant_Id	V_WString	▾	20		
	☑	Restaurant	V_WString	▾	25		
	☑	image	V_WString	▾	107...		
	☑	Layout	V_String	▾	214...	Header	
	☑	*Unknown	Unknown	▾	0		Dynamic

Options ▾ | ↑ ↓   TIP: To reorder multiple rows: select, right-clic

Figure 14.53: Renaming the Layout field to Header with the Select tool

70. Drop a **Find Replace** tool onto the canvas.

71. Connect the **Select** tool output to the **F** input and the **Table** tool output to the **R** input, as shown here:

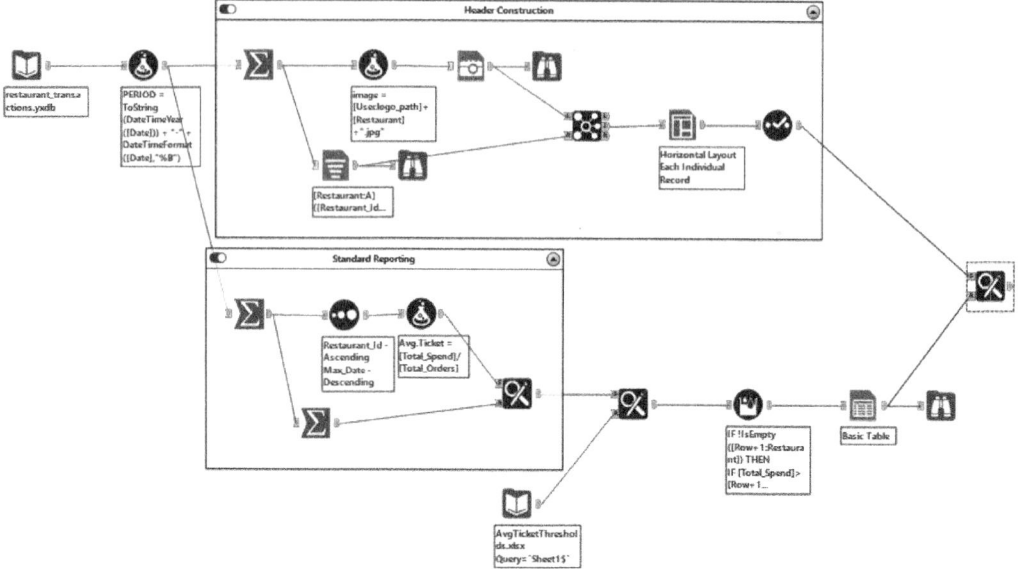

Figure 14.54: Adding a Find Replace tool

72. Click on the **Find Replace** tool to configure it.

73. In the **Find** section, select **Entire Field**.

74. In both the **Find Within Field** and **Find Value** dropdowns, select Restaurant_Id.

75. Click on **Match Whole Word Only** to enable it.

76. In the **Replace** section, click on **Append Field(s) to Record** and only select Table.

    Your **Find Replace** tool configuration will look like this:

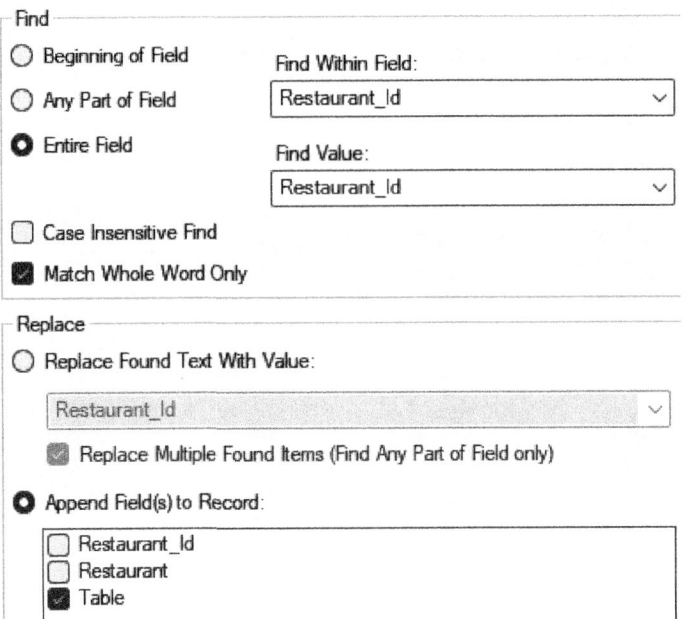

Figure 14.55: Find Replace tool configuration

77. Drop a new **Layout** tool following the **Find Replace** tool.

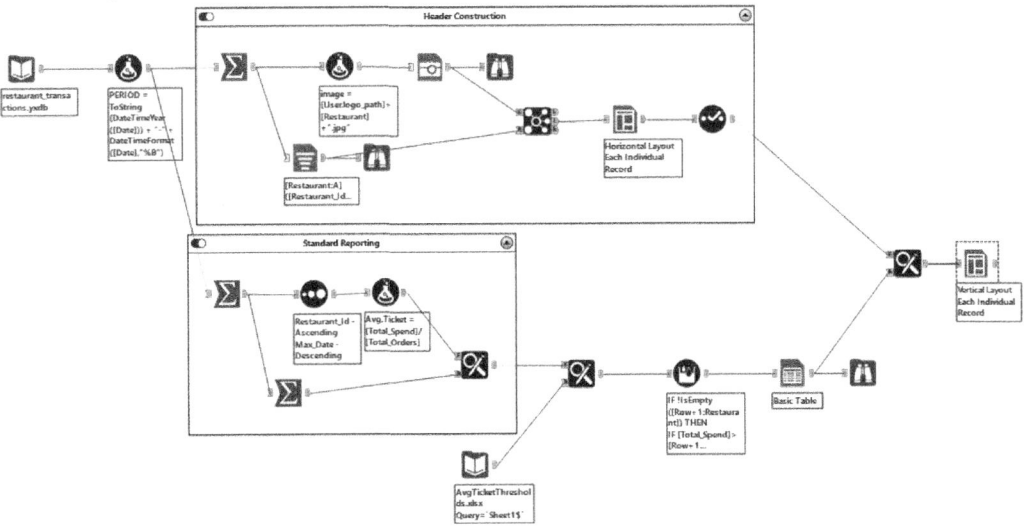

Figure 14.56: Adding a Layout tool to build the resulting report

78. Under **Layout Configuration**, select **Vertical** from the **Orientation** dropdown.

79. Make sure Header appears on top of Table in **Per Row Configuration**.

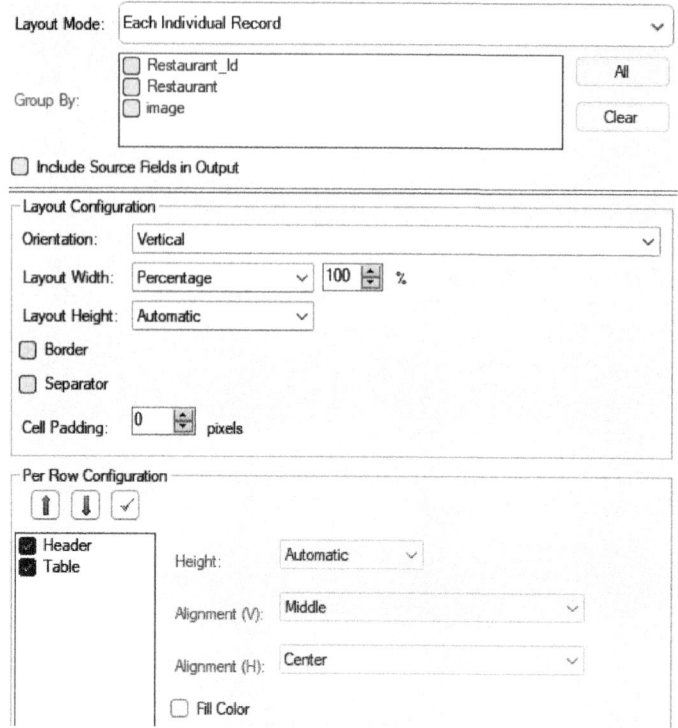

Figure 14.57: Layout tool configuration

80. Finally, drop a **Render** tool after the **Layout** tool.

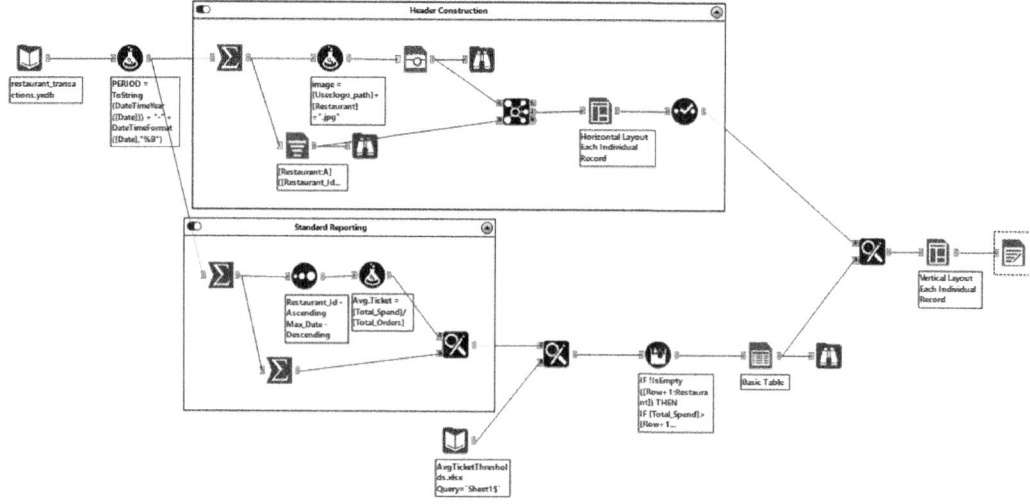

Figure 14.58: Adding the Render tool that'll generate the Excel files

Configure the **Render** tool as follows to create the Excel reports.

81. From the **Output Mode** dropdown, select **Choose a Specific Output File**.

82. For **Output File** use `..\REPORT\EXCEL\_Summary.xlsx`.

83. Click on the **Group Data Into Separate Reports** checkbox to enable it.

84. In **Field To Group On**, select `Restaurant`.

85. From the **Modify Filename By** dropdown, select **Prepending Group To Filename**.

86. Make sure **Layout** is the value selected in the **Data Field** dropdown.

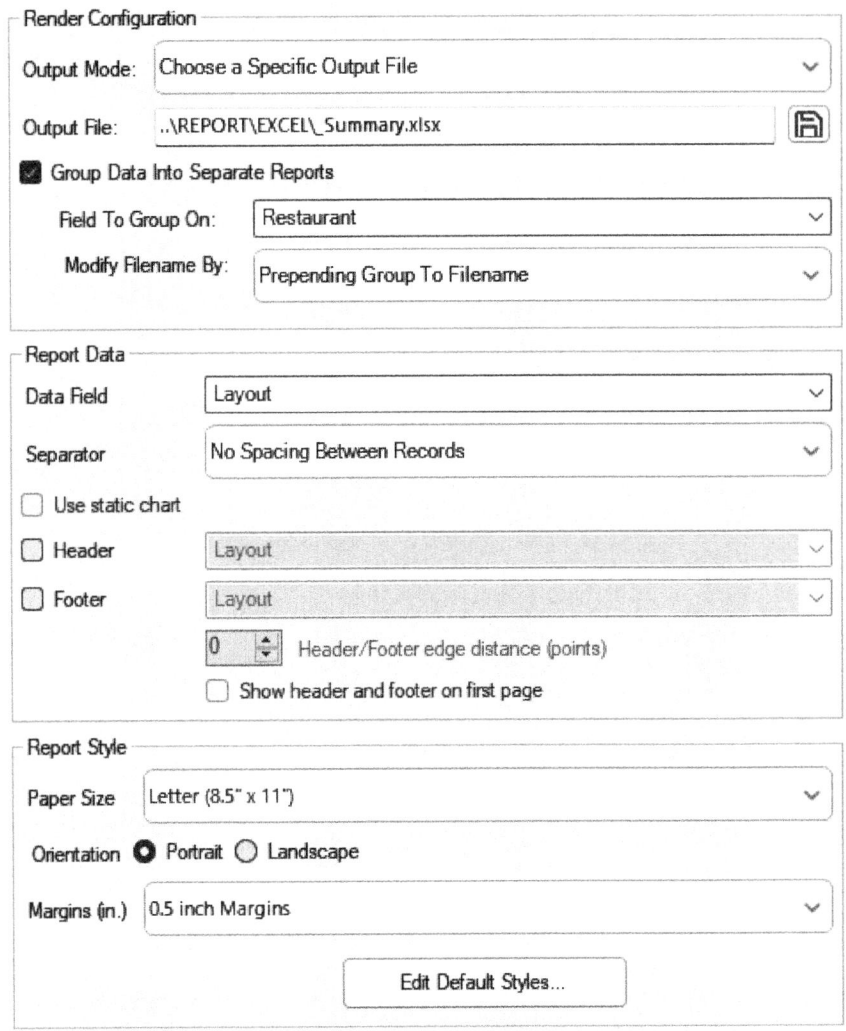

Figure 14.59: Render tool configuration

87. Run the workflow and check your Excel folder; all reports should be there.

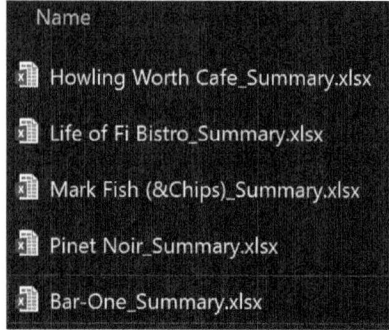

Figure 14.60: Resulting files in the output folder

88. Open any (or all) to see the final output you got from Alteryx.

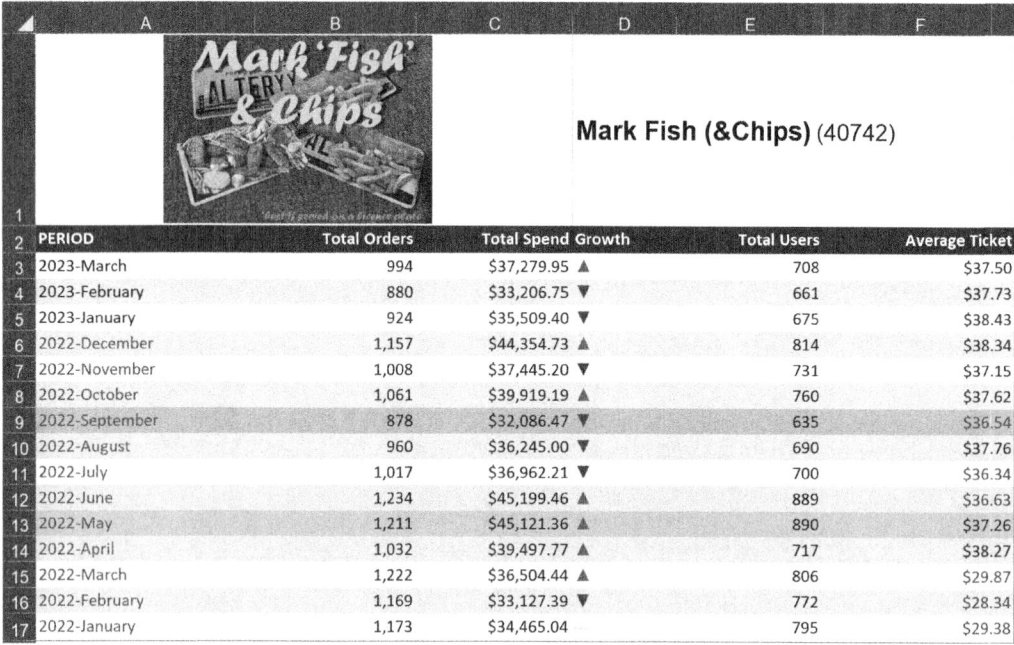

Figure 14.61: Final version of the generated report

Creating your own execution metadata

When you deploy a solution based on a workflow (or workflows), it becomes very important to keep track of the executions. Alteryx Designer allows us, through the **Email** tool (or through **Events**), to access the execution log of a workflow through internal variables. The only drawback I find in this functionality is that we do not have direct access to the execution log until the workflow finishes executing, making it impossible to read and parse it at runtime in the same workflow.

Therefore, to carry out basic monitoring of the execution of our workflows, we will generate certain indicators that will later be saved in a proprietary log and will allow us to easily determine how our workflow is behaving on every execution.

These indicators are the following:

- Workflow name
- Number of records read
- Number of records saved
- Execution date and time
- Read data source name
- Workflow execution time

Getting ready

You can download a test set for this recipe from here: `https://github.com/PacktPublishing/Alteryx-Designer-Cookbook`.

Even though this method works great with a database, we are going to use an Excel file to store our logs, so we don't need to provision anything for it to work.

Also, I want to point out that there are two main parts of the workflow where we are going to get pieces of information.

At the beginning, after each input data source is read, we'll get the following:

- Data source name
- Number of records read

At the end of the workflow, just before we save the workflow's output, we'll get the following:

- Workflow name and full path
- Number of records being written
- Workflow execution start date and time
- Workflow execution duration (in seconds)

We'll then join the values and write our log, which will look like this:

WORKFLOW	FileName	STARTED_DATE_TIME	EXECUTION_TIME	Records_IN	Records_OUT
C:\Exercises\ch14\Recipe1\WORKFLOW\Create your own metadata.yxmd	C:\DATASETS\CitiBikes\CityBike_2013.yxdb	9/16/2023 9:21	28	5614888	367
C:\Exercises\ch14\Recipe1\WORKFLOW\Create your own metadata.yxmd	C:\DATASETS\CitiBikes\CityBike_2013.yxdb	9/16/2023 9:23	13	5614888	366
C:\Exercises\ch14\Recipe1\WORKFLOW\Create your own metadata.yxmd	C:\DATASETS\CitiBikes\CityBike_2013.yxdb	9/16/2023 9:59	2	1000000	366
C:\Exercises\ch14\Recipe1\WORKFLOW\Create your own metadata.yxmd	C:\DATASETS\CitiBikes\CityBike_2013.yxdb	9/16/2023 10:01	14	1000000	366
C:\Exercises\ch14\Recipe1\WORKFLOW\Create your own metadata.yxmd	C:\DATASETS\CitiBikes\CityBike_2013.yxdb	9/16/2023 10:02	14	1000000	366
C:\Exercises\ch14\Recipe1\WORKFLOW\Create your own metadata.yxmd	C:\DATASETS\CitiBikes\CityBike_2013.yxdb	9/16/2023 10:05	13	1000000	366

Figure 14.62: Final results for the log

How to do it...

Let's start with a simple workflow that reads a data source (bike trip information), performs some aggregations (counts the number of trips between each station), and writes an output:

1. Start by dropping an **Input Data** tool onto the canvas and point it to `..\DATA\Bike_Rides.yxdb`.

2. In the **Options** panel, select **Full Path** in the **Output File Name as Field** option.

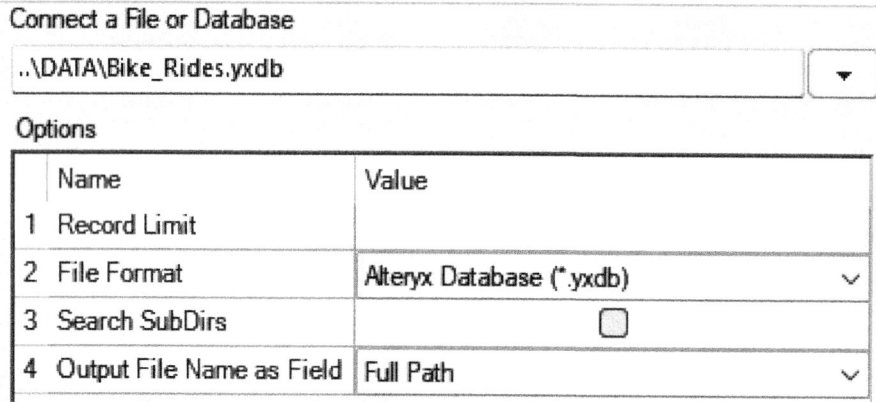

Figure 14.63: Input Data tool configuration

3. Drop a **Summarize** tool following the **Input Data** tool.

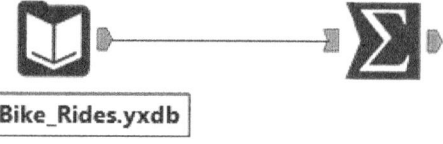

Figure 14.64: Adding the Summarize tool

4. From the **Summarize** tool's configuration panel, click on START_STATION_NAME and *Ctrl* + click on END_STATION_NAME so both are highlighted.

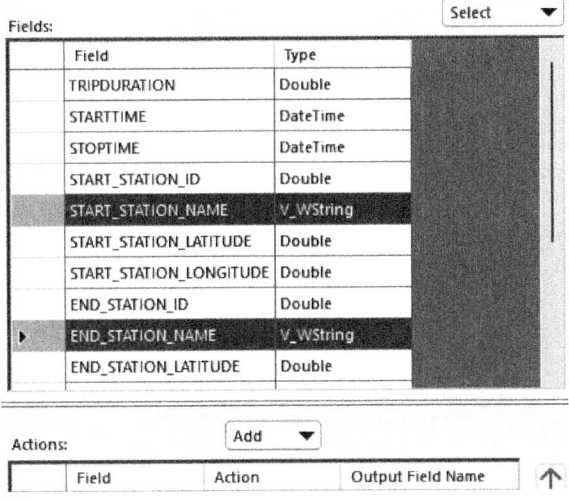

Figure 14.65: Selecting multiple fields (Ctrl + click)

5. Click on **Add** and select **Group By**.

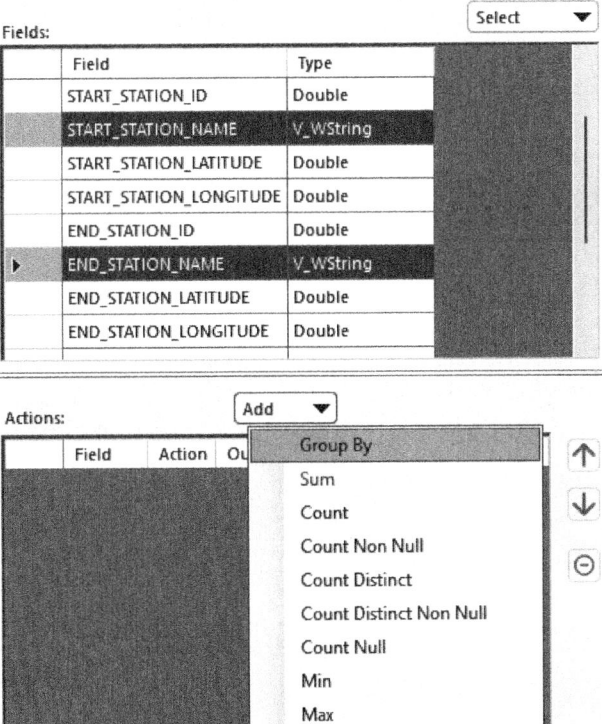

Figure 14.66: Selecting Group By as the action

6. Once the **Action** panel reflects both fields and the **Group By** action, click on BIKEID in the **Fields** pane to select it.

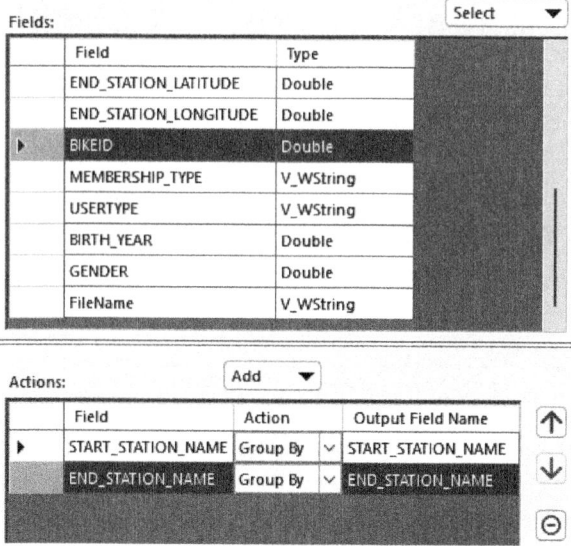

Figure 14.67: Summarize Group By fields

7. Click on **Add** and select **Count** as the aggregation action.

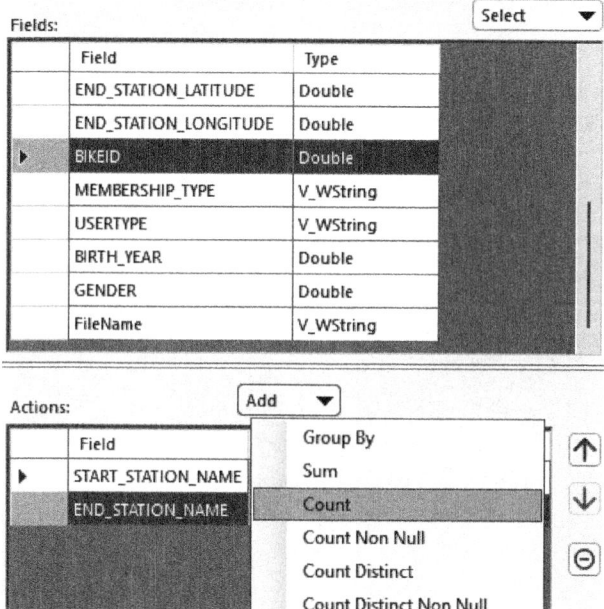

Figure 14.68: Selecting Count as the aggregation action for the BIKEID field

8. Drop an **Output Data** tool following the **Summarize** tool.

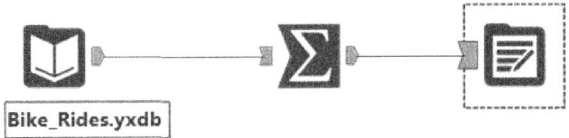

Figure 14.69: Adding the Output Data tool

9. From its configuration options, point to `..\OUTPUT\Output.yxdb` for the output file to be written. Leave the other options untouched.

Write to File or Database

..\OUTPUT\Output.yxdb ▼

Options

	Name	Value
1	Max Records Per File	
2	File Format	Alteryx Database (*.yxdb) ⌄
3	No Spatial Index	☐
4	Save Source & Description	☑
5	AMP Only: Compatible with 18.1 and Earlier	☐

Figure 14.70: Output Data tool configuration

Now, that we have our workflow, let's start getting some metrics from it.

The first one will be the number of records read from the input.

10. Drop a **Count Records** tool (from the **Transform** category) onto the canvas connected to the **Input Data** tool output anchor, as shown here:

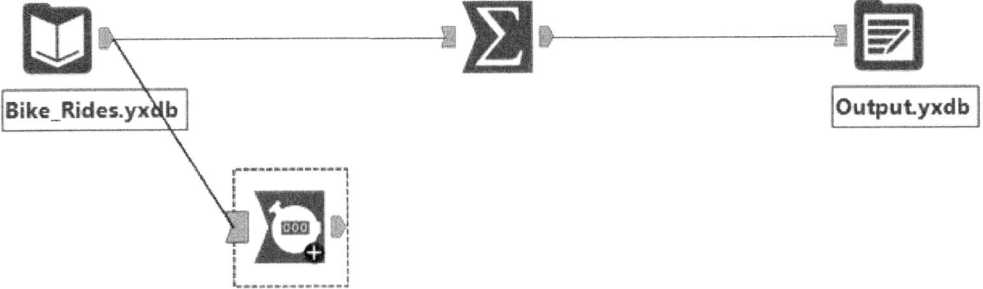

Figure 14.71: Adding the Count Records tool

If you run the workflow now, you'll notice that the **Count Records** tool always outputs a field called `Count`. To better identify our data at a later point, we'll rename this field.

11. Drop a **Select** tool following the **Count Records** tool.

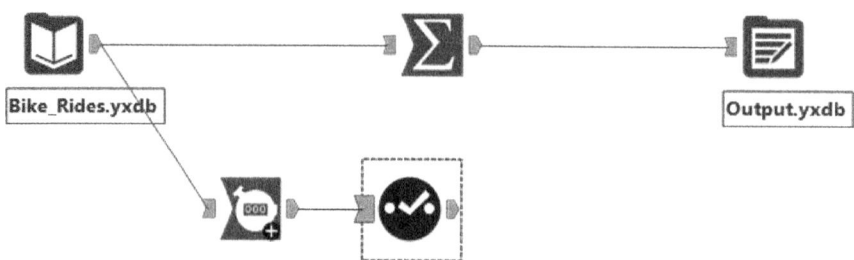

Figure 14.72: Using a Select tool to rename fields

12. Rename the Count field from its configuration panel to Records_IN, and deselect the *Unknown field.

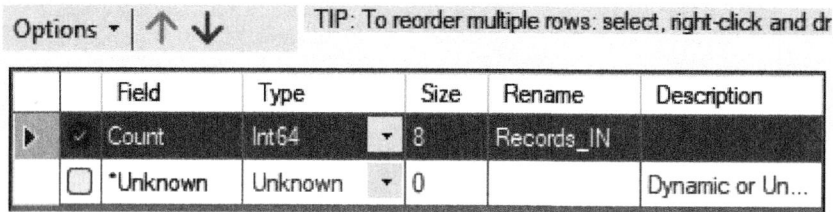

Figure 14.73: Select tool configuration

At this same point, we are going to extract two additional values: the data source being read and the workflow name.

13. Drop a **Sample** tool and connect it to the **Input Data** tool output anchor.

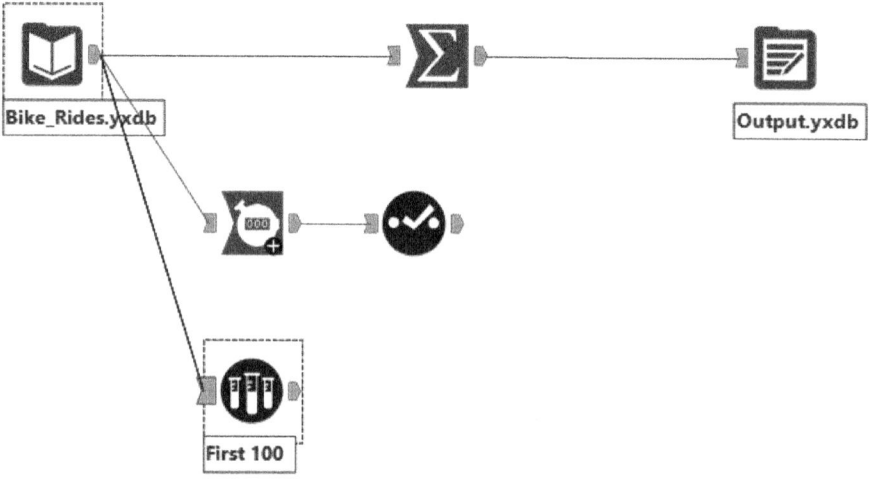

Figure 14.74: Adding a Sample tool to the workflow

14. Leave the **First N rows** option selected, and set **N** = to **1** (we need just one record to get the values).

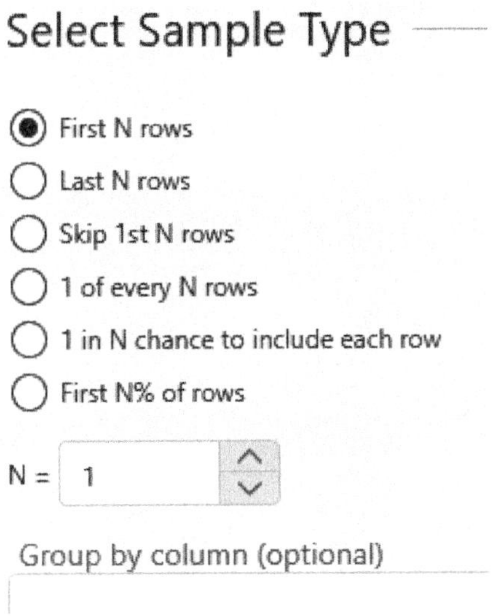

Select Sample Type ───

- ◉ First N rows
- ○ Last N rows
- ○ Skip 1st N rows
- ○ 1 of every N rows
- ○ 1 in N chance to include each row
- ○ First N% of rows

N = [1]

Group by column (optional) ───

Figure 14.75: Sample tool configuration

15. After the **Sample** tool, connect a **Select** tool.

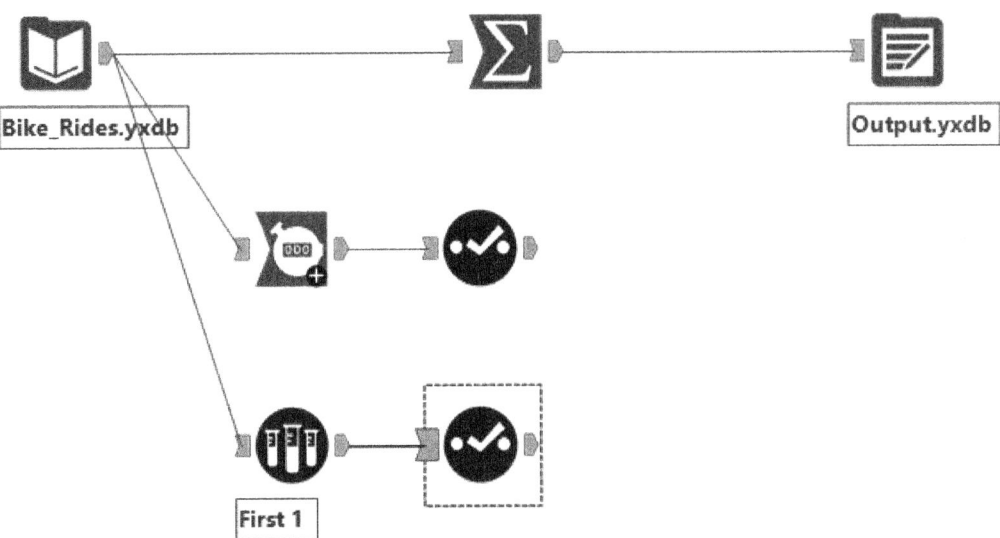

Figure 14.76: Select tool added

16. Within the **Select** tool configuration options, deselect everything (including the *Unknown field) except the FileName field.

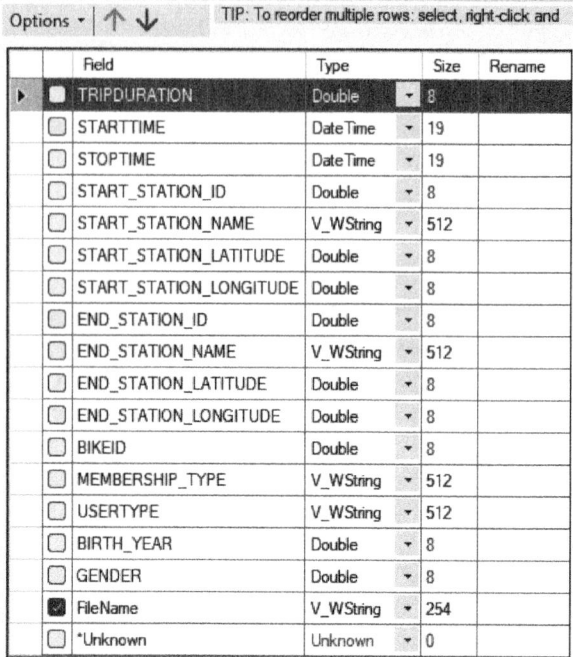

Figure 14.77: Select tool configuration to keep only the FileName field

17. Drop a **Formula** tool connected to the output anchor of the **Select** tool.

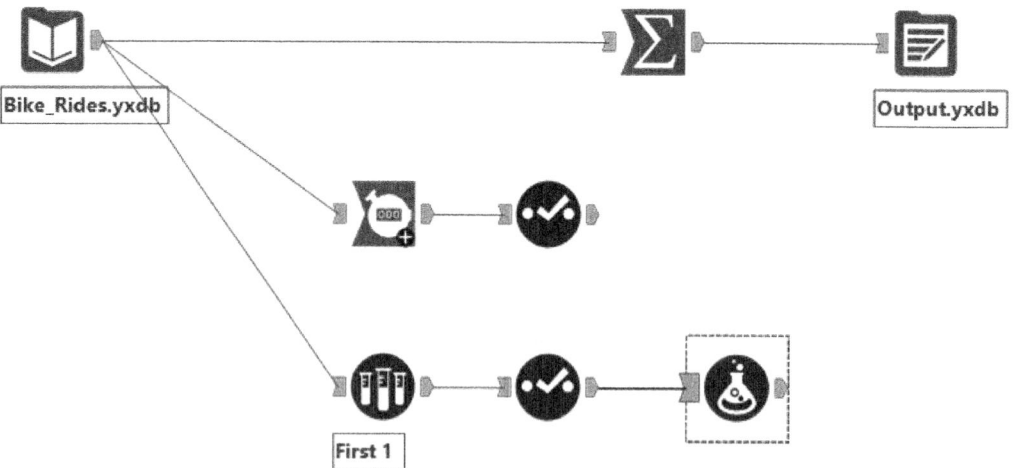

Figure 14.78: Adding a Formula tool

18. From the **Formula** tool configuration, create a new column with the default **Data** type (**V_WString**) and call it WORKFLOW.

Use the following formula for the expression:

```
FileAddPaths([Engine.WorkflowDirectory],[Engine.
WorkflowFileName])
```

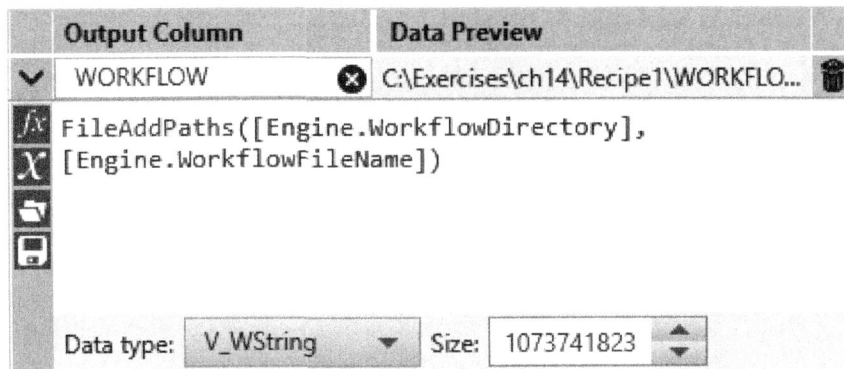

Figure 14.79: Formula tool configuration

So far, we have the workflow name, the input filename, and the records read from the input source, but in two different streams. We'll put them together.

19. Drop a **Join Multiple** tool onto the canvas and connect the output anchor points from the **Formula** and **Select** tools to its input anchor.

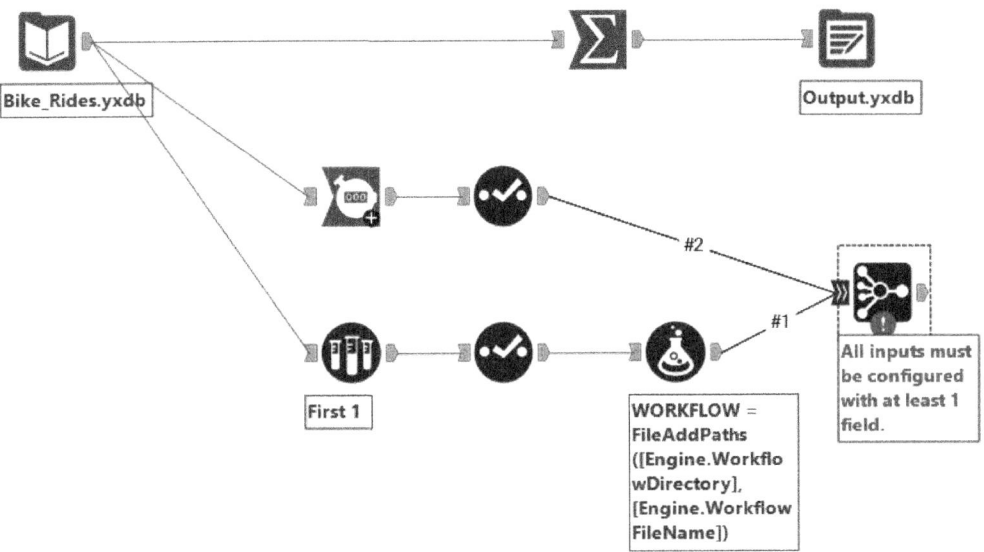

Figure 14.80: Join Multiple tool added to the workflow

You may notice that Alteryx Designer throws an error message at the **Join Multiple** tool. This is because no fields were selected (yet), so leave it as it is for now because our next step will fix it.

20. In the configuration options of the **Join Multiple** tool, select **Join by Record Position**.

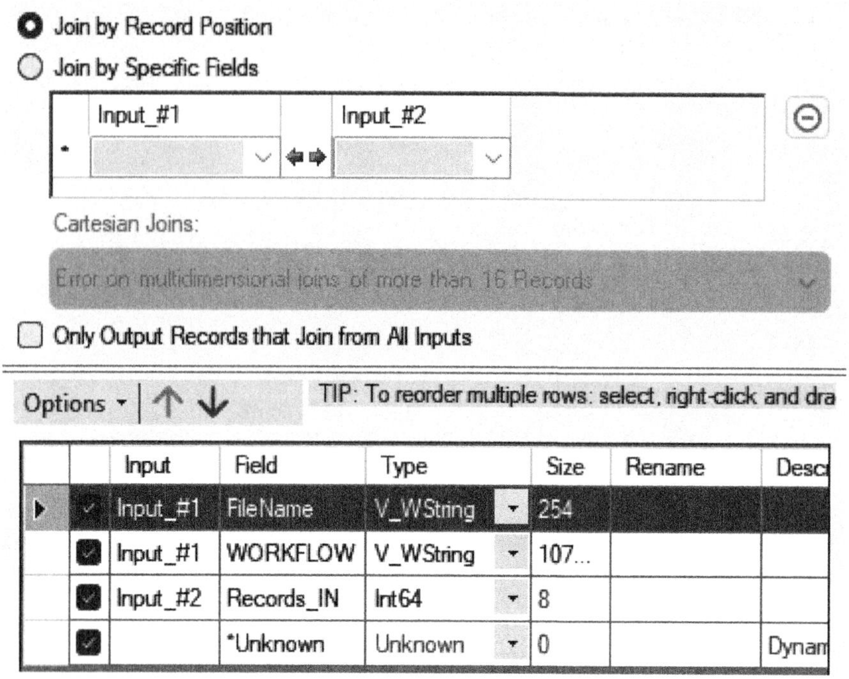

Figure 14.81: Join Multiple tool configuration

Doing so will ensure that both records are combined into only one, including all the columns, as you can verify by running the workflow.

Record	Records_IN	FileName	WORKFLOW
1	200456	C:\Exercises\ch14\Recipe1\DATA\Bike_Rides.yxdb	C:\Exercises\ch14\Recipe1\WORKFLOW\Base_Wo...

Figure 14.82: Results after joining by record position

Now, we need to focus on the metrics after we process our raw data.

21. Drop a **Count Records** tool and connect it to the output anchor of the **Summarize** tool (in our example, it's the final step of our logic and represents the last operation before saving our data).

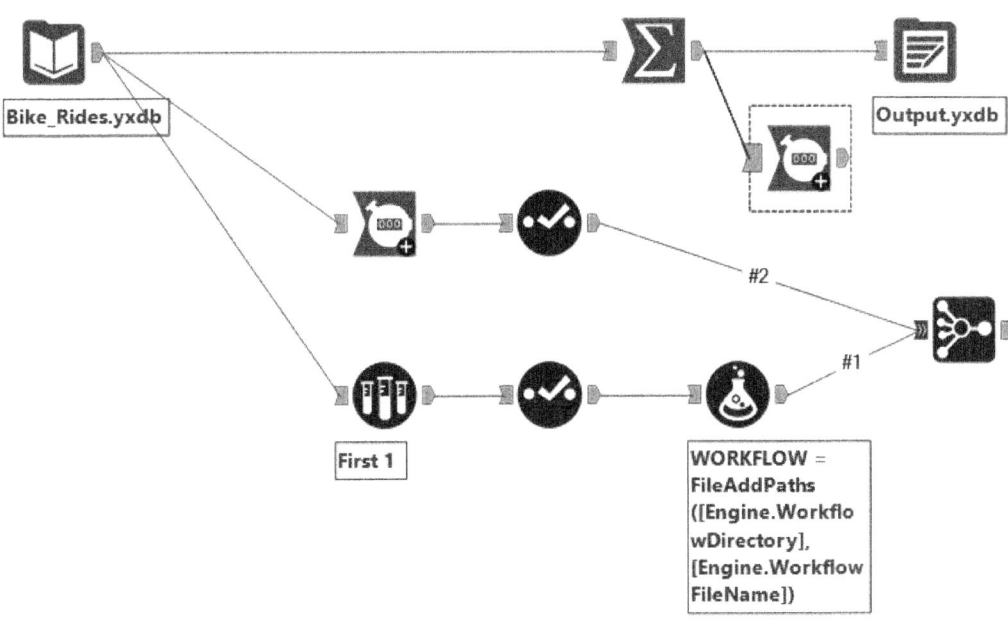

Figure 14.83: Adding a second Count Records tool (after the record processing)

As we did with the **Count Records** tool after reading the input file, we are going to rename the Count field generated by the tool.

22. Drop a **Select** tool following the **Count Records** tool.

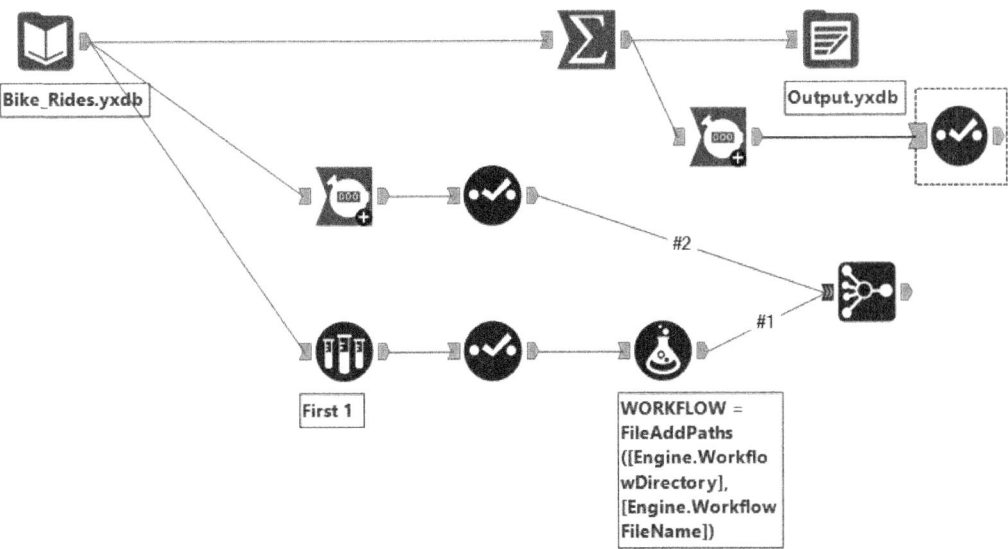

Figure 14.84: Adding a Select tool to rename fields

23. In the **Select** tool configuration panel, deselect the *Unknown field and rename the Count field Records_OUT.

Now, we may need to reorder the tools in the canvas.

24. Select the tools that are connected to the **Input Data** tool.

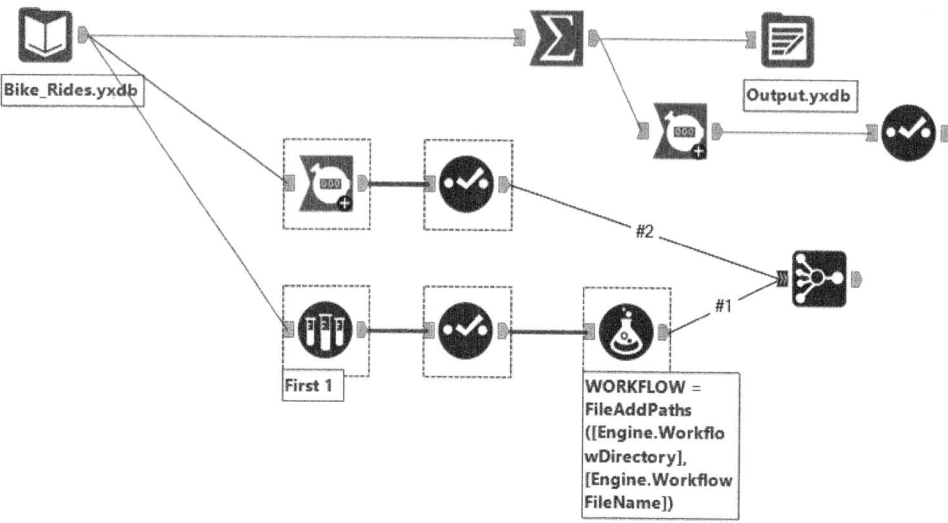

Figure 14.85: Selecting multiple tools (Marquee select)

25. Right-click with the mouse pointer over any of the selected tools, and select **Add To New Container**.

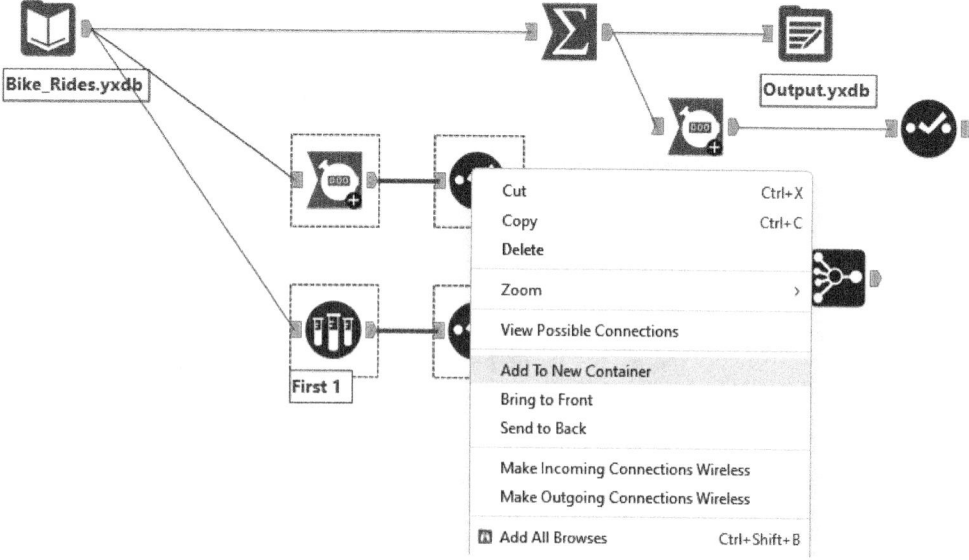

Figure 14.86: Adding the selected tools to a Tool Container

26. A Tool Container will appear on the canvas around all the selected tools.

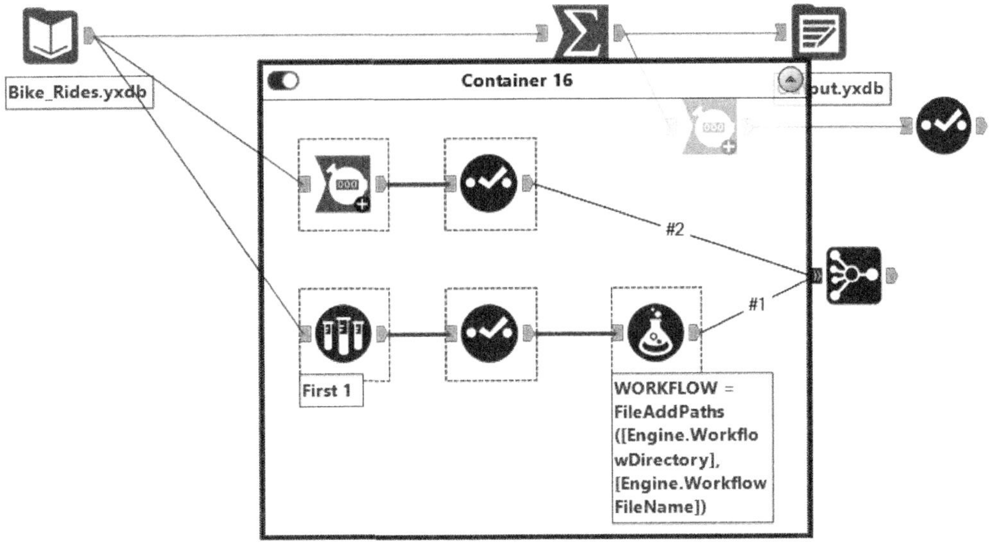

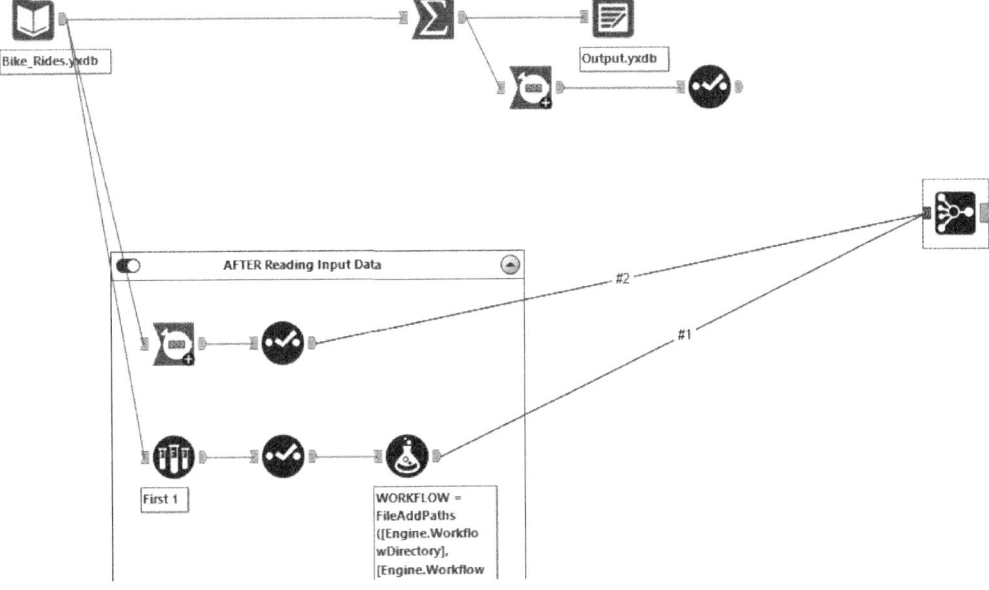

Figure 14.87: Tool Container added

27. Move the Tool Container to make some space above it, and rename it `AFTER Reading Input Data`.

28. Move the **Join Multiple** tool so it appears to the right of the last **Select** tool.

Figure 14.88: Spread the tools so you can work comfortably

Now, we'll get the date and time of the workflow execution and its duration.

29. Drop a **Formula** tool connected to the **Summarize** tool.

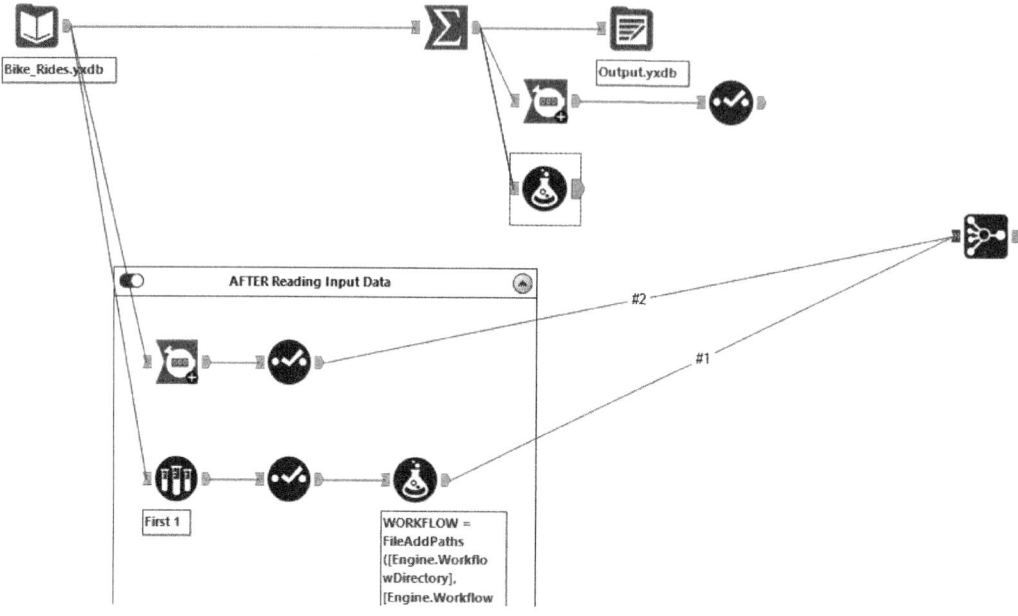

Figure 14.89: Adding a Formula tool after the record processing (just before saving the results)

30. From its configuration, create a new field called STARTED_DATE_TIME of the **DateTime** data type.

31. Use the DateTimeStart() expression (it'll assign the date and time the workflow started running).

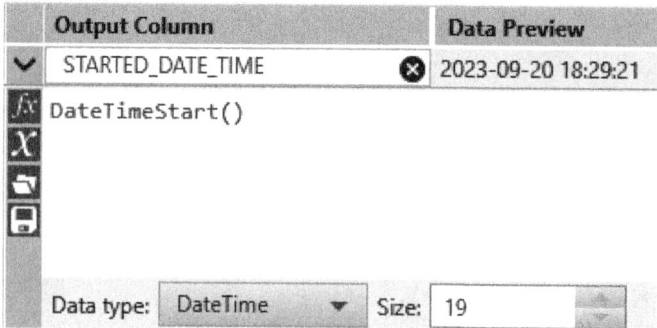

Figure 14.90: Formula tool configuration

32. Drop another **Formula** tool following the last one (or use the same, but I prefer to add one).

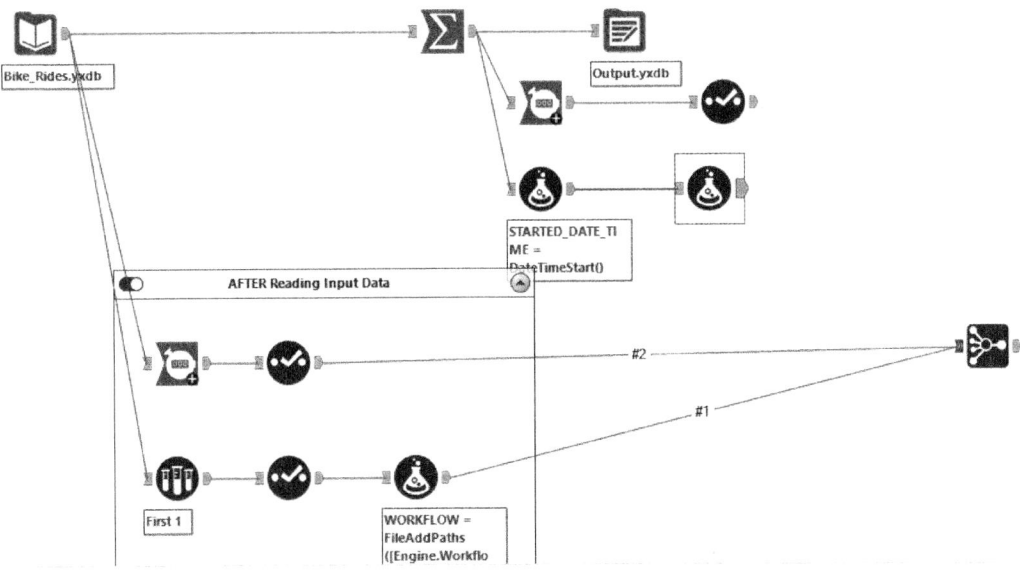

Figure 14.91: Adding another Formula tool

33. We'll create a new column here called `EXECUTION_TIME` of the **Int64** data type, using the following expression:

```
DateTimeDiff(DateTimeNow(),[STARTED_DATE_TIME],'seconds')
```

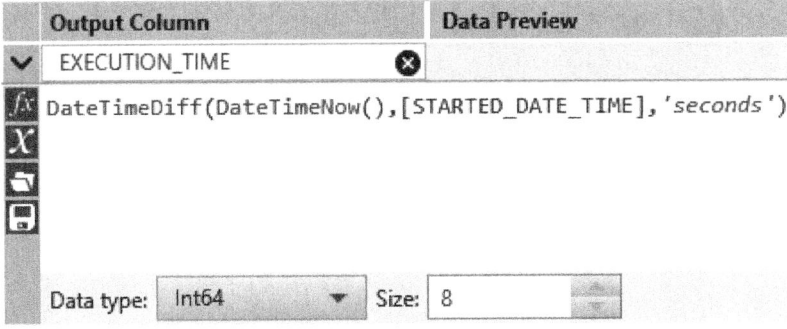

Figure 14.92: Formula tool configuration

> **Note**
>
> We use the `Int64` data type because Alteryx will always return the integer part of the result, without decimals.
>
> Also, we can use `Double` as well, since both use 8 bytes.
>
> As of version 23.X, Alteryx Designer will start supporting time units up to attoseconds (one quintillionth (10^{-18}) of a second).

This column will store the elapsed time (in seconds) since the start of the workflow and the processing of each record.

To get the elapsed time for the workflow, we need to grab the last one (we also can grab the MAX, but it may consume more resources to process).

34. Drop a **Summarize** tool following the **Formula** tool.

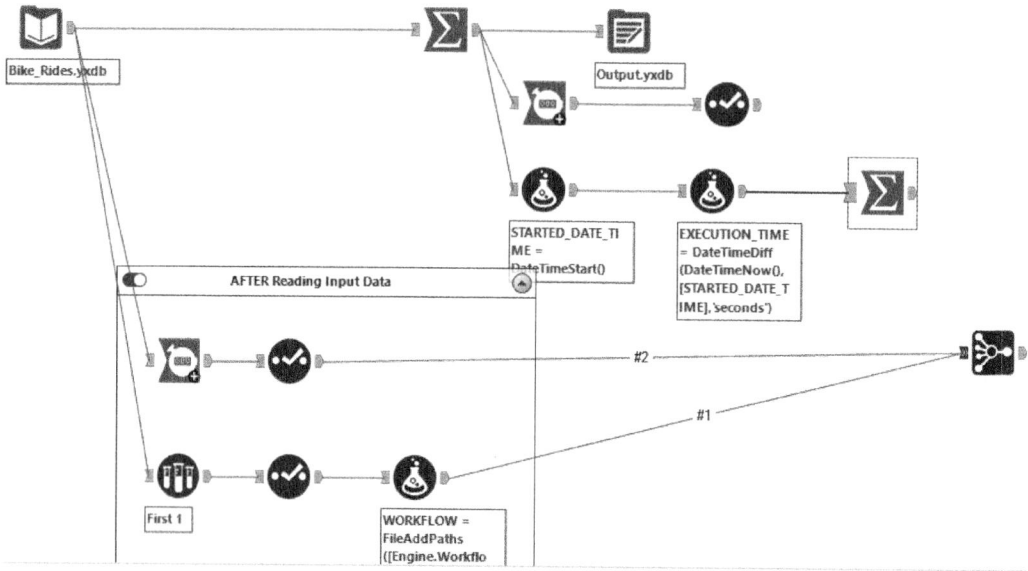

Figure 14.93: Adding a Summarize tool to get the last execution time

35. Configure the **Summarize** tool so it groups by STARTED_DATE_TIME and retrieves the **Last** EXECUTION_TIME.

36. Rename **Output Field Name** from Last_EXECUTION_TIME to EXECUTION_TIME.

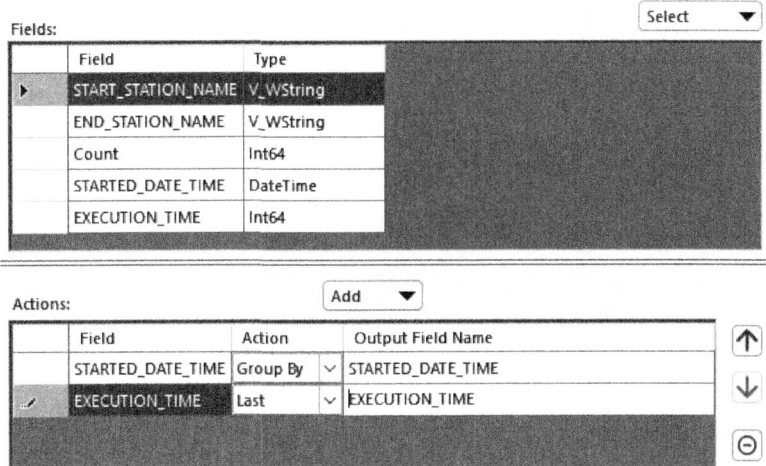

Figure 14.94: Summarize tool configuration

> **Important note**
>
> If you're using AMP to execute your workflow, you may notice significant differences in the elapsed time.

Now that we have all the metrics from the post-processing, we'll join them with the previous ones to save the log.

37. Connect the **Select** tool and the last added **Summarize** tool output anchors to the **Join Multiple** input anchor.

38. Select the tools that gather the metrics after the **Summarize** tool, as shown in the following figure:

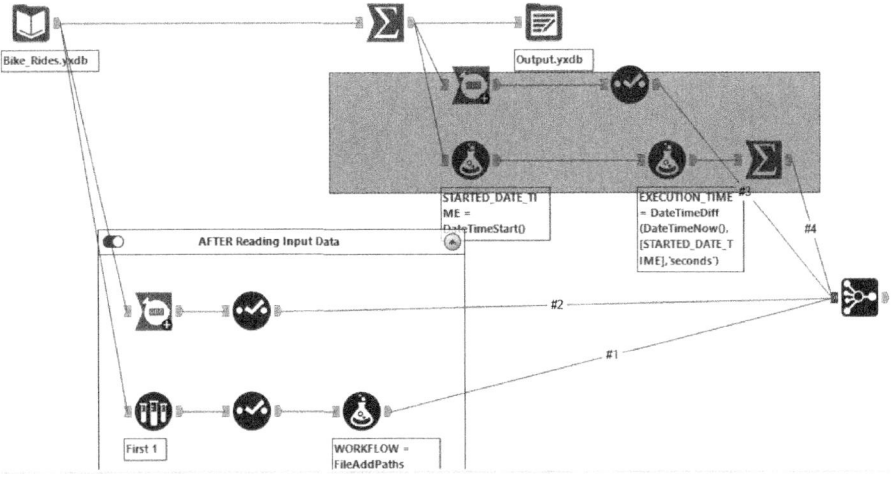

Figure 14.95: Selecting the tools to add a new container

39. Right-click over any of the selected tools and select **Add To New Container**. Rename the container BEFORE writing output.

40. Reorganize your canvas so you can see all the tools.

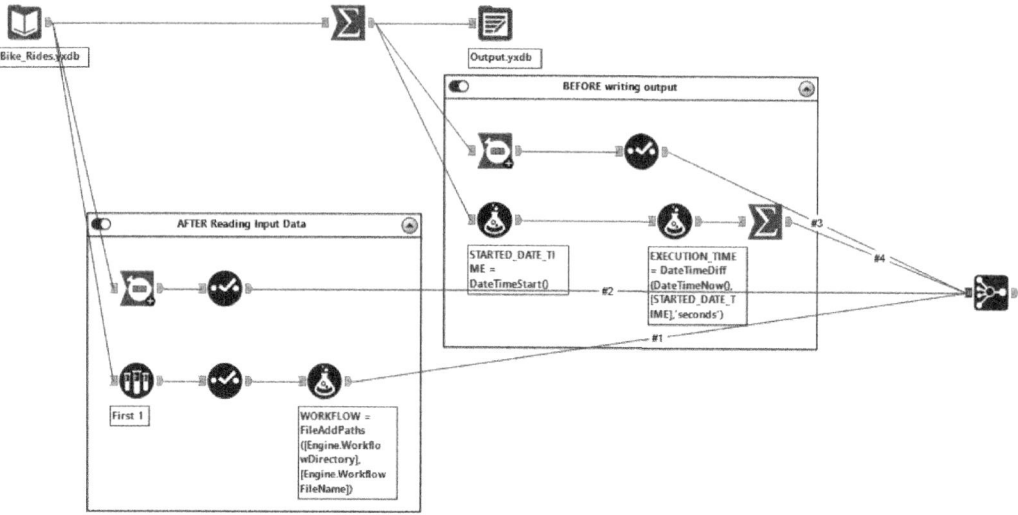

Figure 14.96: The tools added to a new container

41. Now, drop a **Block Until Done** tool following the **Join Multiple** tool.

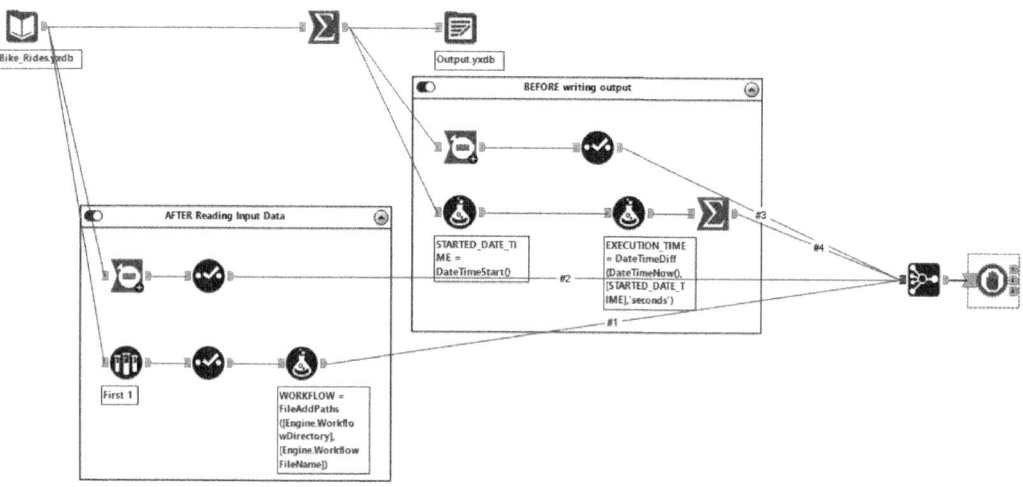

Figure 14.97: Adding the Block Until Done tool after the Join Multiple tool

42. To finalize our workflow, connect an **Output Data** tool to the **Block Until Done** output anchor labeled **1**.

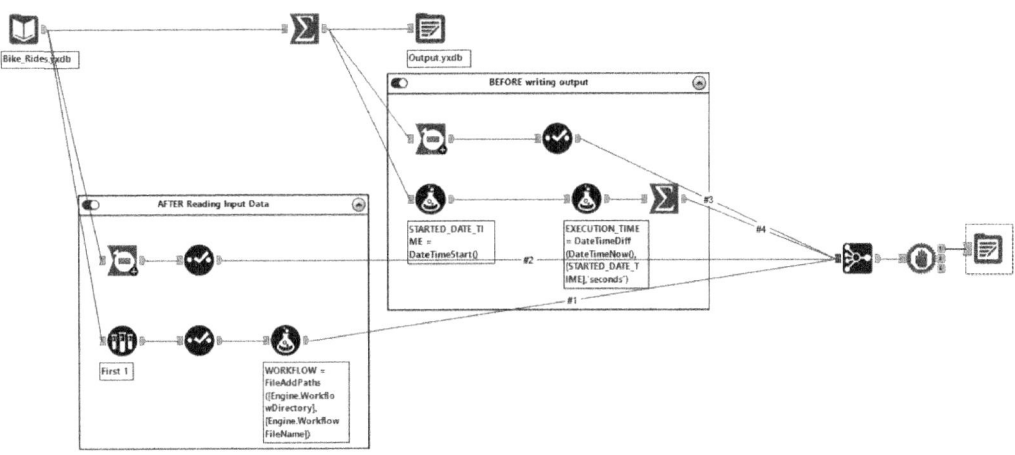

Figure 14.98: Adding the Output Data tool for the log

43. Point the **Write to File or Database** value to `..\LOG\Executions_Log.xlsx|||Log` and, from the **Output Options** dropdown, select **Append To Existing Sheet**, so every workflow execution is added to the log.

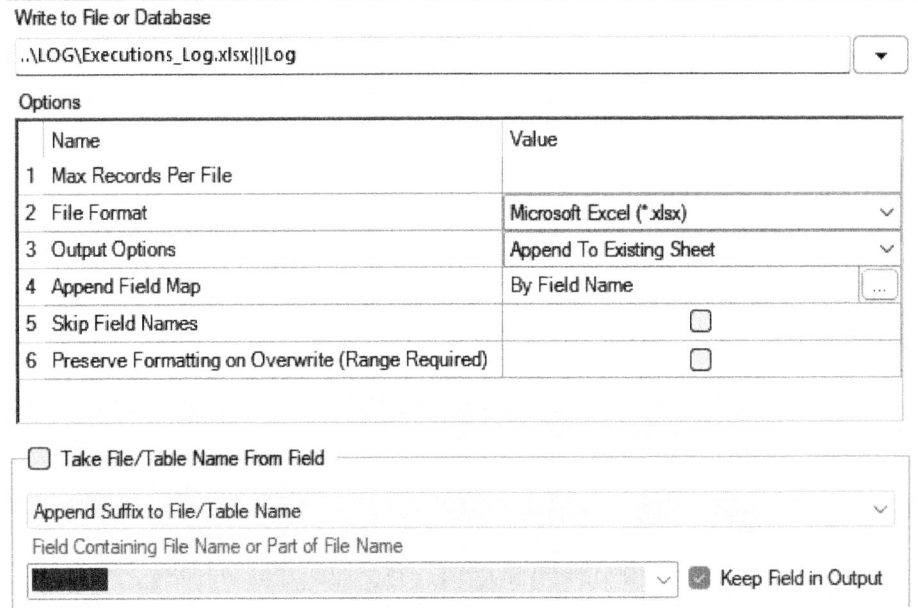

Figure 14.99: The Output Data tool configuration

44. Run the workflow and check the `LOG` subfolder. There you'll find the Excel file that contains the execution log.

WORKFLOW	FileName	STARTED_DATE_TIME	EXECUTION_TIME	Records_IN	Records_OUT
C:\Exercises\ch14\Recipe1\WORKFLOW\Create your own metadata.yxmd	C:\DATASETS\CitiBikes\CityBike_2013.yxdb	9/16/2023 9:21	28	5614888	367
C:\Exercises\ch14\Recipe1\WORKFLOW\Create your own metadata.yxmd	C:\DATASETS\CitiBikes\CityBike_2013.yxdb	9/16/2023 9:23	13	5614888	366
C:\Exercises\ch14\Recipe1\WORKFLOW\Create your own metadata.yxmd	C:\DATASETS\CitiBikes\CityBike_2013.yxdb	9/16/2023 9:59	2	1000000	366
C:\Exercises\ch14\Recipe1\WORKFLOW\Create your own metadata.yxmd	C:\DATASETS\CitiBikes\CityBike_2013.yxdb	9/16/2023 10:01	14	1000000	366
C:\Exercises\ch14\Recipe1\WORKFLOW\Create your own metadata.yxmd	C:\DATASETS\CitiBikes\CityBike_2013.yxdb	9/16/2023 10:02	14	1000000	366
C:\Exercises\ch14\Recipe1\WORKFLOW\Create your own metadata.yxmd	C:\DATASETS\CitiBikes\CityBike_2013.yxdb	9/16/2023 10:05	13	1000000	366
C:\Exercises\ch14\Recipe1\WORKFLOW\Create your own metadata.yxmd	C:\DATASETS\CitiBikes\CityBike_2013.yxdb	9/16/2023 10:11	13	100000	330
C:\Exercises\ch14\Recipe1\WORKFLOW\Create your own metadata.yxmd	C:\DATASETS\CitiBikes\CityBike_2013.yxdb	9/16/2023 10:16	12	100000	330
C:\Exercises\ch14\Recipe1\WORKFLOW\Create your own metadata.yxmd	C:\DATASETS\CitiBikes\CityBike_2013.yxdb	9/16/2023 10:18	12	100000	330
C:\Exercises\ch14\Recipe1\WORKFLOW\Create your own metadata.yxmd	C:\DATASETS\CitiBikes\CityBike_2013.yxdb	9/16/2023 20:33	13	100000	330

Figure 14.100: Log generated after several runs

Using Events to back up your files

Events in Alteryx Designer is a very handy functionality that allows us to execute external commands or send notifications via email, based on certain workflow execution conditions.

The conditions for when you can run an event (external command, script, etc.) or send emails are as follows:

- Before running the workflow

- After running the workflow

- After executing the workflow when there were errors

- After executing the workflow when there were no errors in its execution

These conditions are shown in the following figure:

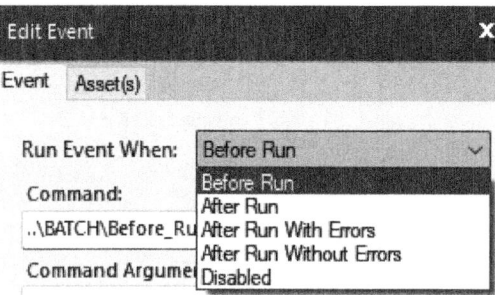

Figure 14.101: Conditions available to run events

In this recipe, we will see how to use workflow events to make a backup of our files before executing a workflow.

Getting ready

We prepared a test example for you to follow along with this recipe. You can download it here: https://github.com/PacktPublishing/Alteryx-Designer-Cookbook.

As we did in the first recipe in *Chapter 12, Executing External Programs from a Workflow*, we will use batch files to perform some operations.

Even when the provided script is fully functional for its purpose (copying files from one directory to another), if you want to use this method for different kinds of additional operations, it's important that you know the basics of batch files. You can find a very thorough and complete tutorial here: `https://www.tutorialspoint.com/batch_script/index.htm`.

Also, as part of our best practices, we will use a directory structure to organize our project assets for easy access and reference. This structure contains the following folder hierarchy:

Figure 14.102: Recipe folder structure

For this recipe, we are assuming that our workflow writes all its outputs within the `..\OUTPUT` folder.

How to do it...

We are going to start reviewing the batch file, which will be responsible for copying files from the source to the destination, in addition to adding the date on which the copy was made. Also, we'll use the date in the YYYYMMDD format to make it easier to sort by date later.

This batch file could be even simpler than the one we present here, containing a single line with the command to execute and its corresponding parameters. We have made it a little more complex so that the same batch file can be used to receive both the origin and destination of the copies to be made as parameters in such a way as to be valid for any workflow. Follow these steps:

1. Use the following code in a text editor of your choice, and save it as `do_backup.bat` within the BATCH subfolder:

```
@echo off
set origin=%1%
set destination=%2%
set backup_date=%date:~10,4%%date:~4,2%%date:~7,2%
xcopy /y %origin% %destination%\%backup_date%\ >log.txt
```

We are going to create a very simple workflow to demonstrate the use of **Events**, so in Alteryx Designer, create a new workflow.

2. Drop an **Input Data** tool onto the canvas and point it to `..\DATA\Customers.csv`.

3. Add a **Formula** tool to the workflow and use it to create a new column of the **DateTime** data type called `SAVED_DATE_TIME`.

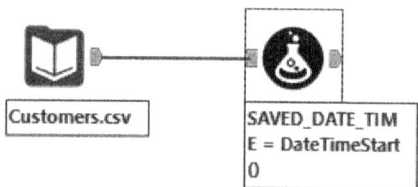

Figure 14.103: Adding the Formula tool

4. Use the following expression to assign a value to the new field:

    ```
    DateTimeStart()
    ```

		Output Column		Data Preview
⟨⟩	✔	SAVED_DATE_TIME	⊗	2023-09-14 15:16:03
	fx	DateTimeStart()		

Data type: DateTime ▼   Size: 19

Figure 14.104: Formula tool configuration

This will allow us to check (within the resulting saved file) when the data was saved and compare it with the backup (which must have an earlier value for that field).

5. Drop an **Output Data** tool following the **Formula** tool.

Figure 14.105: Output Data tool added to the workflow

We'll use this **Output Data** tool to save our results (the file we'll be backing up on the workflow's next run).

6. From the tool's configuration options, select `..\OUTPUT\Output.yxdb` as the **Write to File or Database** option.

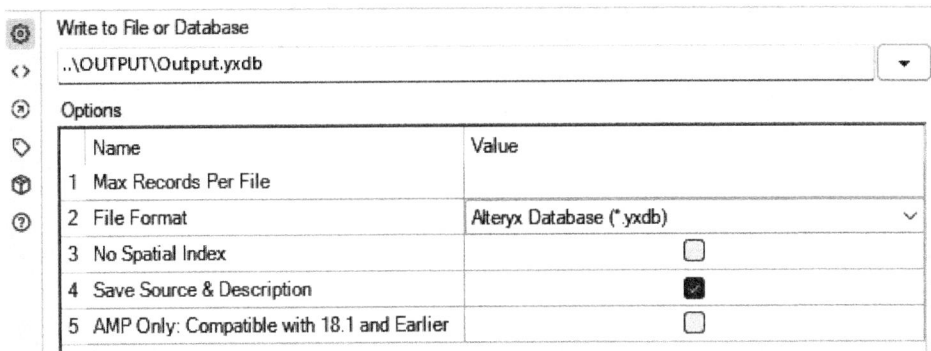

Figure 14.106: Output Data tool configuration

7. Leave the remaining options as they are.

    If you run the workflow now, you'll see that a file (`..\DATA\Customers.csv`) is being read, a column is added (`SAVED_DATE_TIME`), and a resulting file (`..\OUTPUT\Output.yxdb`) is written over any existing version of the same file at the same location.

    Now, we'll use our batch script to make a copy of the existing file within the `..\OUTPUT` folder into the `..\BACKUP` folder.

8. Click on any blank part of the canvas to access the workflow configuration options.

9. Click on the **Events** tab and make sure **Enable Events** is selected.

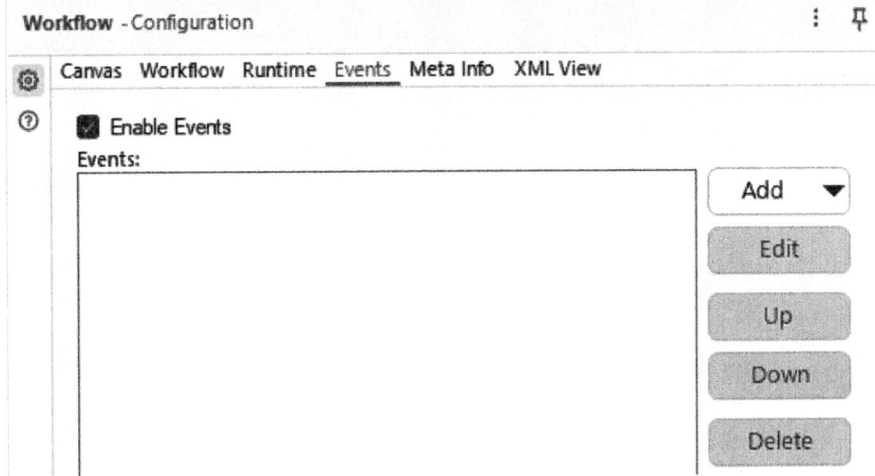

Figure 14.107: Events options panel (in Workflow configuration)

10. Click on **Add** and select **Run Command…** from the dropdown.

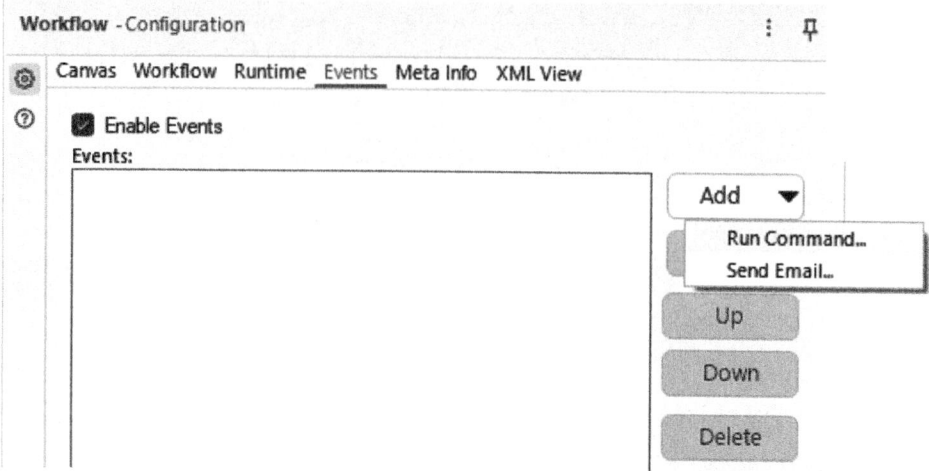

Figure 14.108: Option to execute based on the selected condition

A new window will pop up with all the options to manage the **Run Command** event.

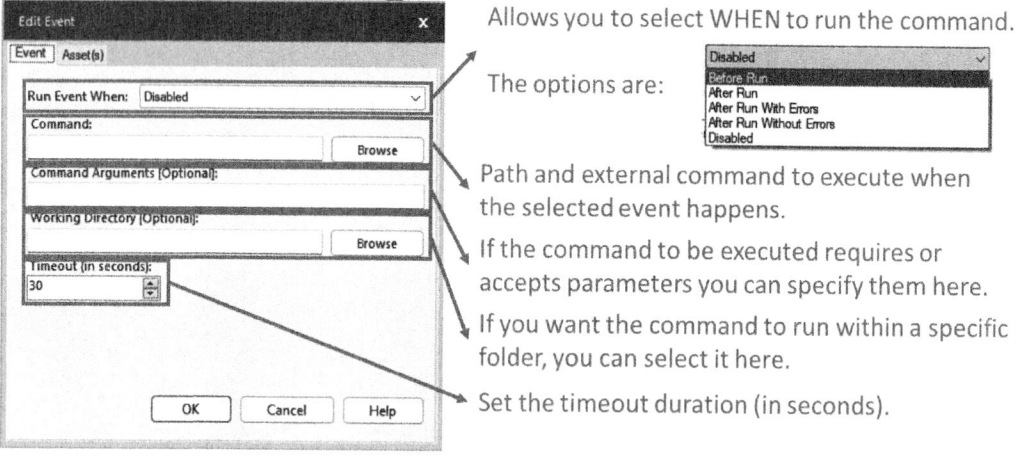

Figure 14.109: Event configuration panel options

11. Select **Before Run** from the **Run Event When** dropdown.

12. For **Command**, enter `..\BATCH\do_backup.bat`.

13. In **Command Arguments**, enter the following:

```
..\OUTPUT\*.*  ..\BACKUP
```

These are going to be the values that %1% and %2% will have when the batch file is executed (batch files take the arguments in order from how they were stated, so the origin must always be first and then the destination).

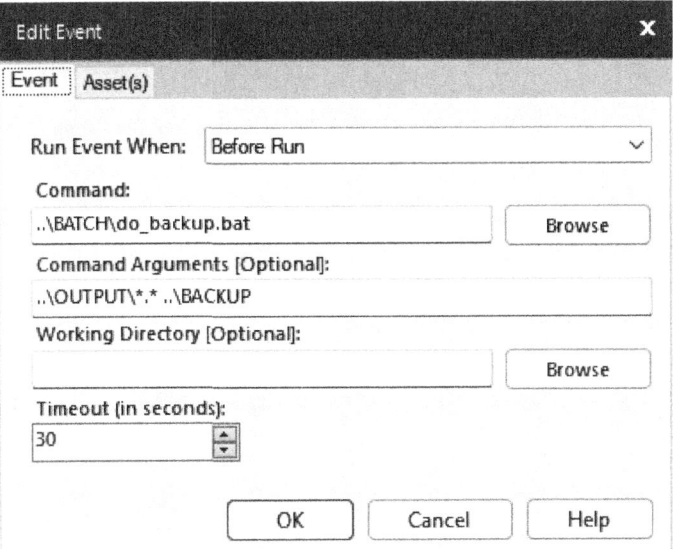

Figure 14.110: Event configuration

14. Hit **OK** and run the workflow.

Go to the disk and locate your main folder for this recipe. Look within the ..\BACKUP subfolder and you'll see that it contains a new folder with the date you ran the workflow, and inside it, there should be a copy of the Output.yxdb file.

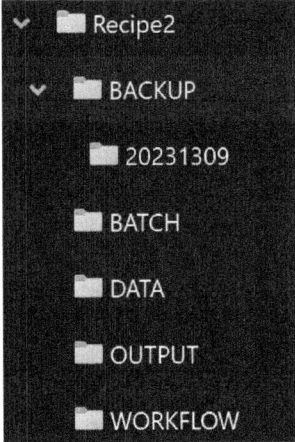

Figure 14.111: Folder created when the event runs

How it works...

We'll start with a little description of the batch file.

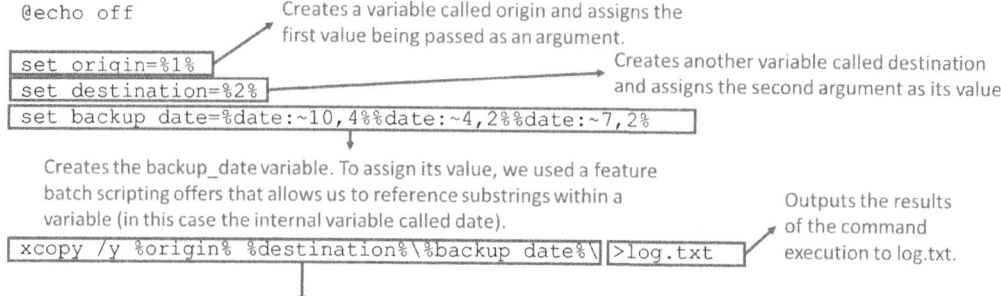

Figure 14.112: The batch file used explained

> **Note**
>
> The date command stores its value in a zero index array so it can be accessed by the position and number of characters.

If we run the date command in Command Prompt, we'll get this information:

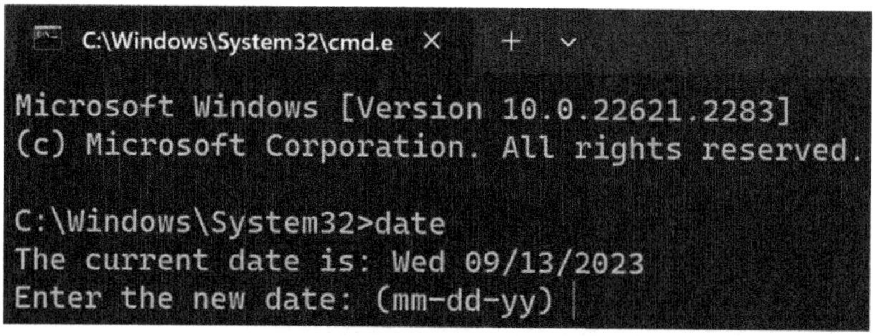

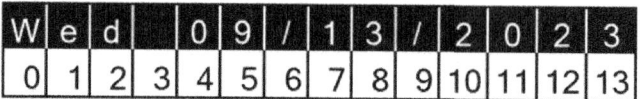

Figure 14.113: Execution of the date command

As you can see, the value for the date command is Wed 09/13/2023, and it's stored like this:

W	e	d		0	9	/	1	3	/	2	0	2	3
0	1	2	3	4	5	6	7	8	9	10	11	12	13

Figure 14.114: How the date command stores the date

With the combination of `%` symbols to reference the command results and the `:~` notation, we can access individual parts of the value – in our case, we have `%date:~10,4%%date:~4,2%%date:~7,2%`. Let's look at this in more detail.

With `%date:~10,4%`, we start at position **10** and extract 4 characters (the year):

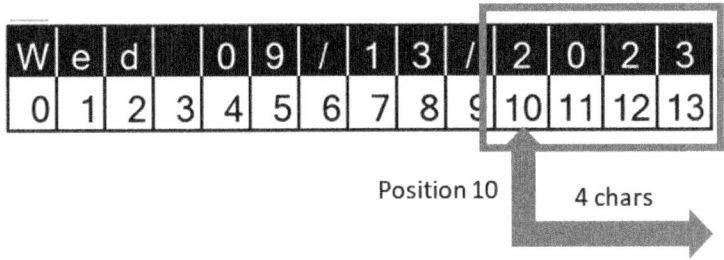

Figure 14.115: Portion of the vector containing the year

With `%date:~4,2%`, for the month, we extract 2 characters starting at position **4**:

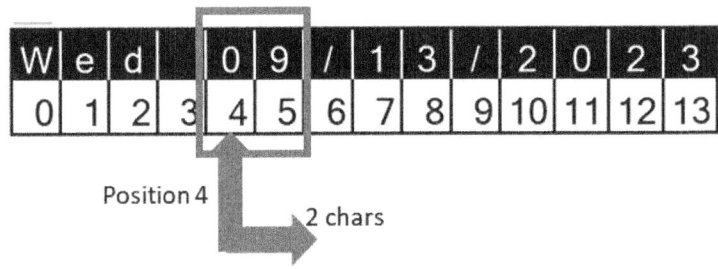

Figure 14.116: Portion that contains the month

With `%date:~7,2%`, starting at position **7** and considering 2 characters, we have the day:

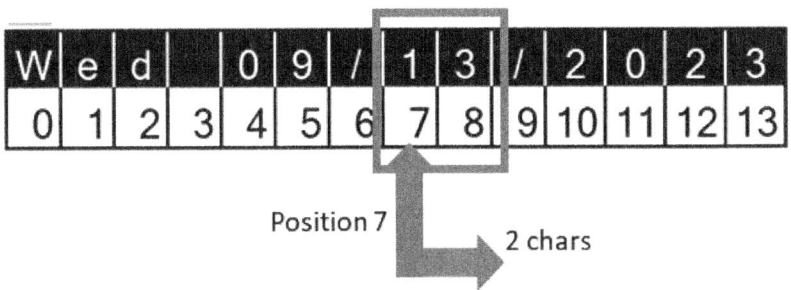

Figure 14.117: Portion of the vector with the date

The concatenation is done automatically by the scripting engine, just by putting the different values one after another, as we did in the declaration of the `backup_date` variable (`set backup_date=%date:~10,4%%date:~4,2%%date:~7,2%`).

As for the event management within Alteryx Designer, since we selected **Before Run** as the condition, the backup will be performed before executing the workflow; then, the workflow will execute and the new resulting file will overwrite the existing one, but we already have it copied within the `. . \` BACKUP folder.

Finally, since we used the > symbol to write the results of the batch script execution into a file (`log. txt`), we can use it in our workflow to make further decisions (such as if 0 files were copied, we can abort overwriting the output files).

Just drop an **Input Data** tool and point it to `log.txt` to access its contents.

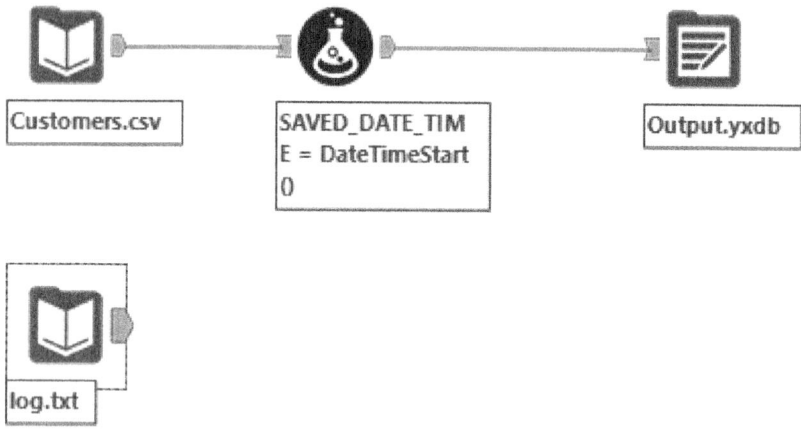

Figure 14.118: Reading the log generated by the event

From this point on, you can make your own decision on how to proceed further in your workflow(s).

There's more...

By now, you have probably thought of a thousand use cases for this recipe. Changing what the batch file does will allow you to solve all of them.

But one particular use case I want to mention is the one where you can run another workflow after another workflow using this recipe.

To be able to do it, you'll need an Alteryx server, the Engine API, or a **Desktop Automation** license.

Select when you want to run the second workflow and use the following to instruct Alteryx Designer to "chain" your workflows:

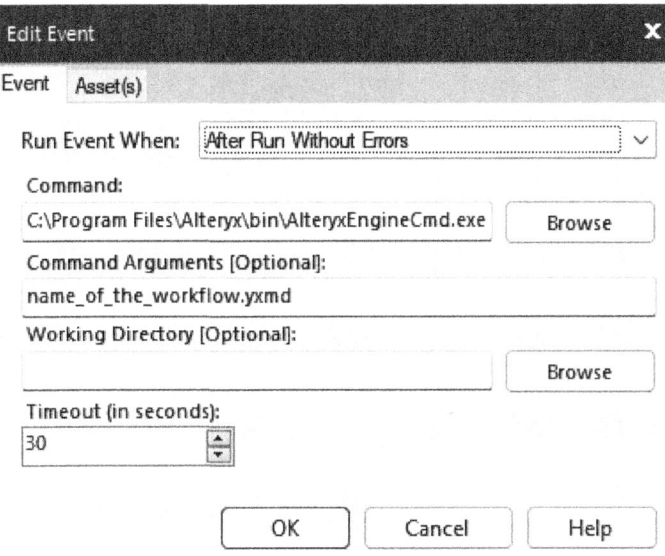

Figure 14.119: Event to chain workflows

If your Alteryx Designer is installed in a different folder, replace C:\Program Files\Alteryx\ with your installation path, keeping the \bin\AlteryxEngineCmd.exe part untouched.

See also (follow-up steps)

More on running another workflow using the Run command can be found here: https://community.alteryx.com/t5/Alteryx-Designer-Desktop-Knowledge-Base/How-to-run-a-workflow-from-an-event/ta-p/532171.

Another very nice and useful knowledge base article in **Alteryx Mission Control**, about scheduling workflows using the Event Run command, can be found here: https://knowledge.alteryx.com/index/s/article/Scheduling-Workflows-Using-Event-Run-Command-1583460630153.

Using Pre and Post SQL commands

When we use databases to obtain data and/or save it, using the **PRE** and **POST** SQL options opens up a huge range of options for us, both for those who are not SQL programmers and for those who must provide access mechanisms to databases in a secure, governed way.

Common uses of this functionality include creating temporary tables and dropping or updating a table before running a query. With this, you also have the ability to run stored procedures (using the EXEC command) before and after the actual query as well.

One thing to highlight about this facility is that the stored procedures are executed entirely in the database engine.

On the other hand, when distributing database connections to our end users, it can be very useful to use custom queries in **stored procedures**, since they will surely go through certification processes before going to production, unlike custom queries, which, when executed, can throw errors and even break the database(s).

In this recipe, we will see a mechanism widely used when having to process a subset of our data (obtained through a query), using a temporary table and deleting it at the end of our process.

> **Note on the order of execution of the SQL statements**
>
> The Pre-SQL statement would run first, then the table or query (the standard read/write operation you perform with Alteryx), and finally, the Post-SQL statement.

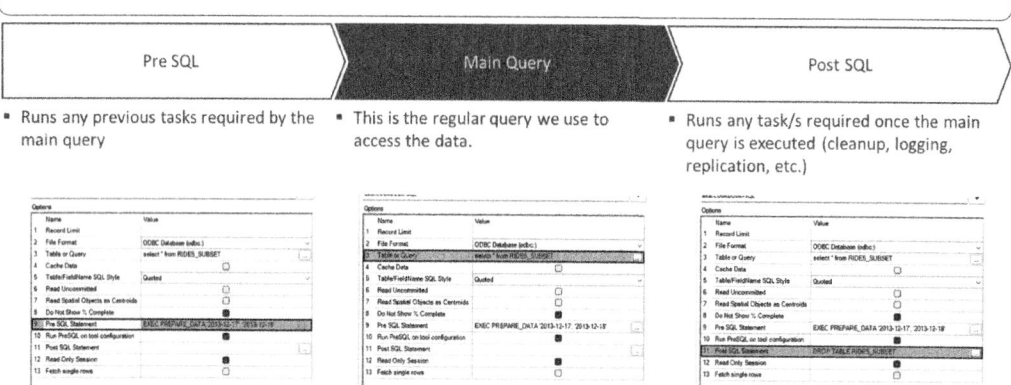

Figure 14.120: How Alteryx runs the queries and where they appear in the tool

> **Important note**
>
> One very important thing to note is that Alteryx will not output the results from the Pre/Post SQL statements into the workflow.

Getting ready

We prepared a test set for this recipe that you can download here: https://github.com/PacktPublishing/Alteryx-Designer-Cookbook.

Note that you'll need access to a database to follow along with this recipe. We'll use SQL Server for the example, but we won't focus on the SQL part, mostly because what I want to showcase is the process and how things are done within Alteryx Designer.

If you don't have access to a SQL Server environment, you can download the Express version for free using this link: `https://www.microsoft.com/en-us/download/details.aspx?id=101064`.

If you are having problems setting up the environment for this recipe, contact somebody from your IT department; they'll be able to help you for sure.

If you want to deep dive into SQL, you can check these books within the Packt collection: *The MySQL Workshop* by Thomas Pettit and *SQL Server Query Tuning and Optimization* by Benjamin Nevarez.

We are going to start setting the environment in SQL Server, so we'll use **Management Studio** for it. If you don't have it installed, you can download it from here: `https://learn.microsoft.com/en-us/sql/ssms/download-sql-server-management-studio-ssms?view=sql-server-ver16`.

Follow these steps:

1. Log in to your SQL Server instance with your credentials.

2. Create a new database called COOKBOOK.

3. From the **File** menu, select **Open**, then **File...**.

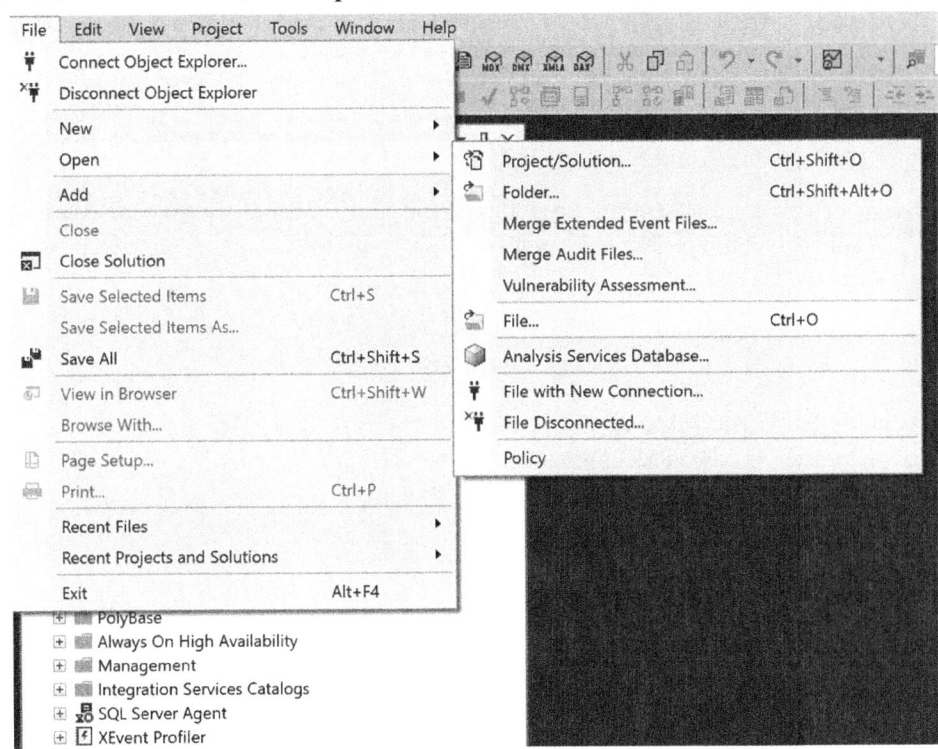

Figure 14.121: Opening a .sql file in Management Studio

4. Locate and select the COOKBOOK_Database.sql file that comes with the sample set of this recipe, within the SQL CODE folder (you may need to unzip it first).

The script will be open in a **New Query** window.

5. Once it opens, click on **Execute**.

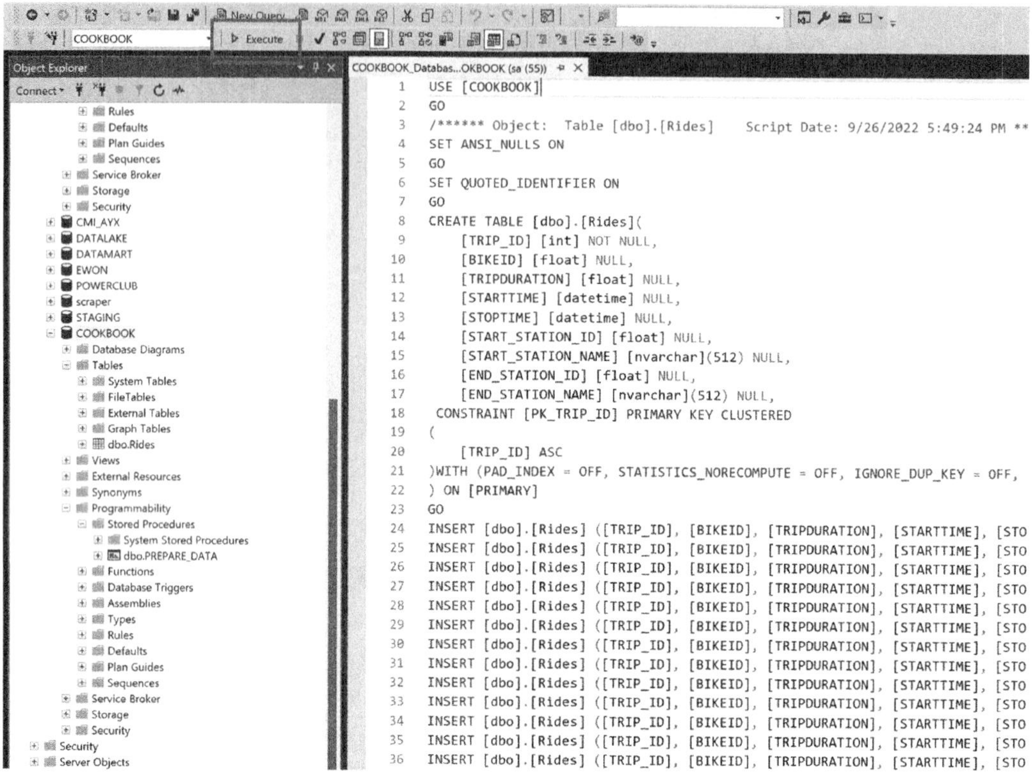

Figure 14.122: The .sql file opened in a New Query window

Wait until the script finishes running, and you'll find a Rides table in your database and a stored procedure called PREPARE_DATA.

The Rides table contains information about ~400K rides made on rented bikes. For this recipe, we'll evaluate a subset between a date range, which we'll specify when calling the PREPARE_DATA stored procedure.

The operations we are going to execute within a simple **Input Data** tool are shown here:

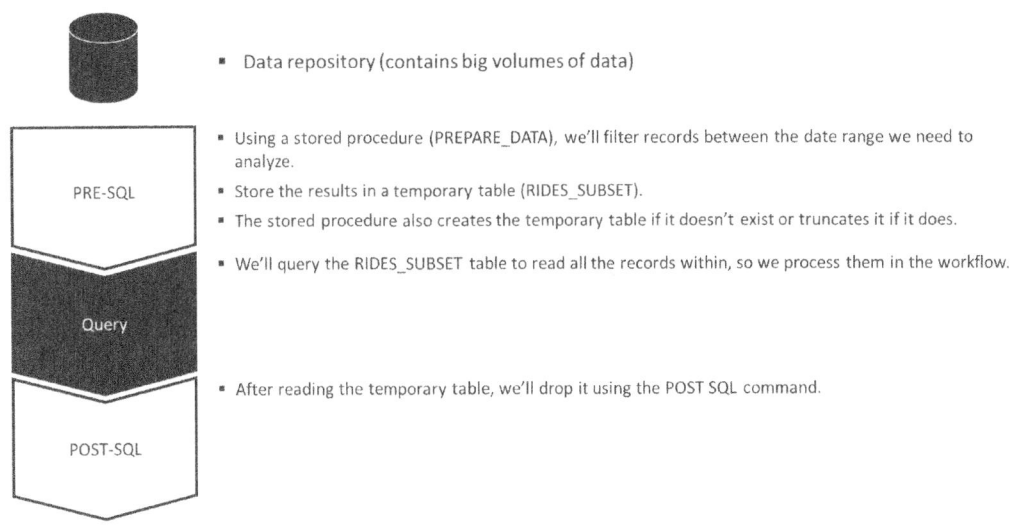

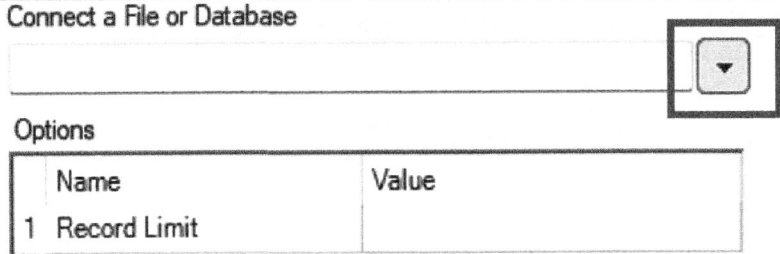

Figure 14.123: Process of query execution

How to do it...

Now that our environment is ready to be accessed, we need to create a workflow in Alteryx:

1. Drop an **Input Data** tool onto the canvas.

2. Click on **Connect a File or Database**.

Figure 14.124: Opening a connection

A new window will appear showing all the **Data connections** options.

3. Click on **Data sources** and then select **Quick connect** in the **Microsoft SQL Server** options.

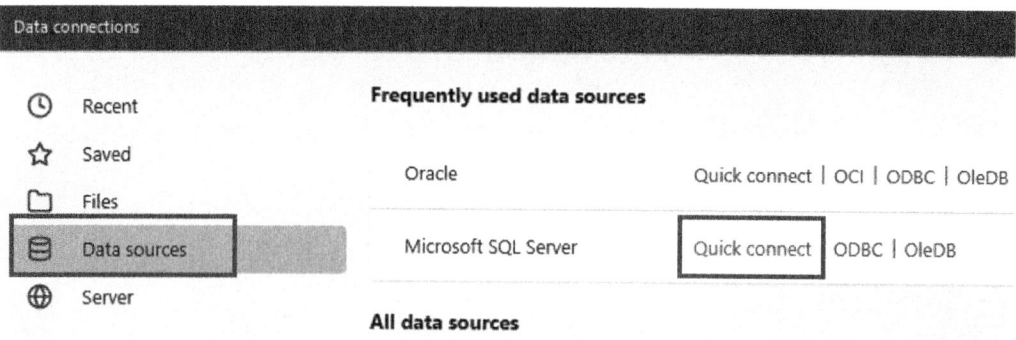

Figure 14.125: SQL Server options to connect

The **SQL Server Database Connection** window will appear.

4. Fill in the configuration data as needed so you can connect to your database:

    *   **Connection Name**: Call it Cookbook-SQL.

    *   **Host**: Use YOUR_SERVER_NAME\YOUR_SQL_INSTANCE.

    *   **Authentication Type**: This information will depend on how you access your database. For most company environments, an Active Directory account is the one that manages your access. If this is the case with your environment, select **Windows Authentication**.

If you installed SQL Server on your machine, or there is a user and password for the server in the credentials provided, select **SQL Authentication** and use your provided **User Name** and **Password** in the corresponding fields. You can use the **Test** button to make sure you have access and the credentials are correct.

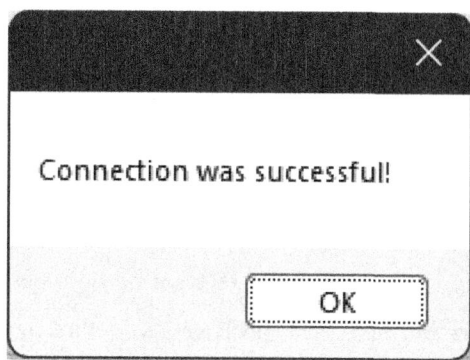

Figure 14.126: Message when the connection succeeds

5.   For **Default Database**, select COOKBOOK (if you connected correctly, it'll show in the dropdown).

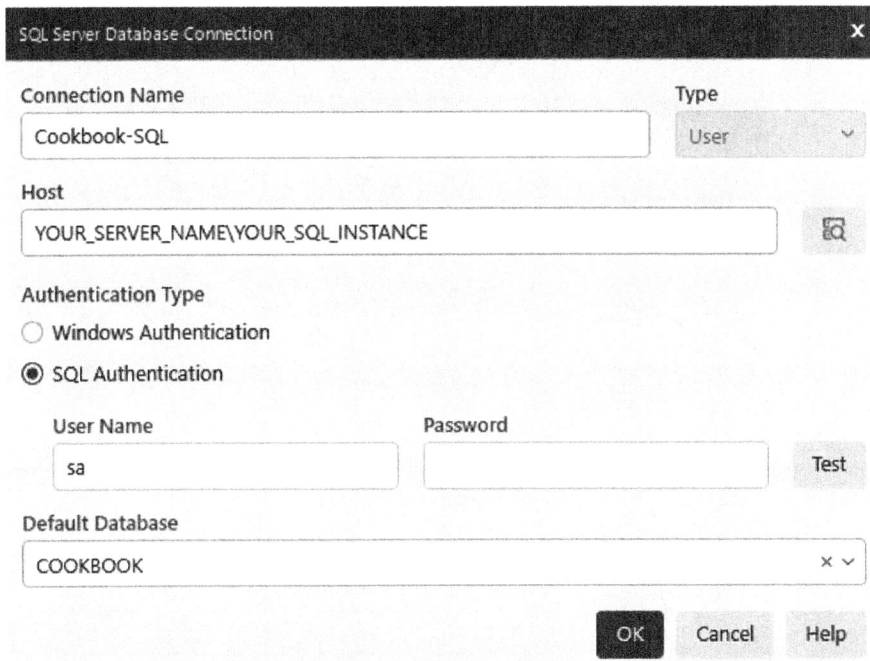

Figure 14.127: SQL Server quick connection configuration

6.   Click on **OK** and the **Choose Table or Specify Query** window will pop up.

7.   Click on the **SQL Editor** tab if it's not your active selection.

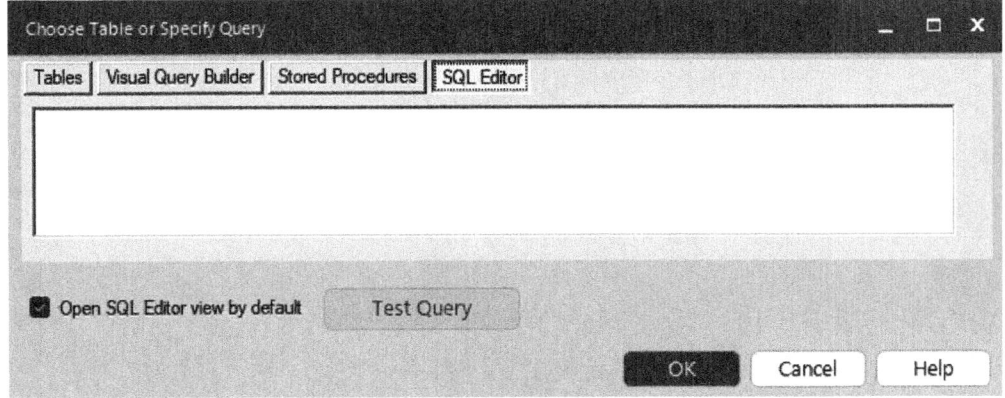

Figure 14.128: SQL Editor tab

8. When you have selected **SQL Editor**, use the following code inside, which you will see in the following screenshot:

```
SELECT * FROM RIDES_SUBSET
```

Figure 14.129: SQL statement in SQL Editor

This is going to be our main query and will be the one shown for option 3, **Table or Query**, in the **Input Data** tool configuration.

Options

	Name	Value
1	Record Limit	
2	File Format	ODBC Database (odbc:)
3	Table or Query	SELECT * FROM RIDES_SUBSET
4	Cache Data	
5	Table/FieldName SQL Style	Quoted
6	Read Uncommitted	

Figure 14.130: SQL statement in the Input Data tool configuration

But at this point, the `RIDES_SUBSET` table doesn't even exist in our environment.

Here, when using the **Pre SQL Statement** option, we'll call the `PREPARE_DATA` stored procedure to create and populate it with the records that fall within the date range we want to extract.

9. Click on the ellipsis in **Pre SQL Statement** (option 9).

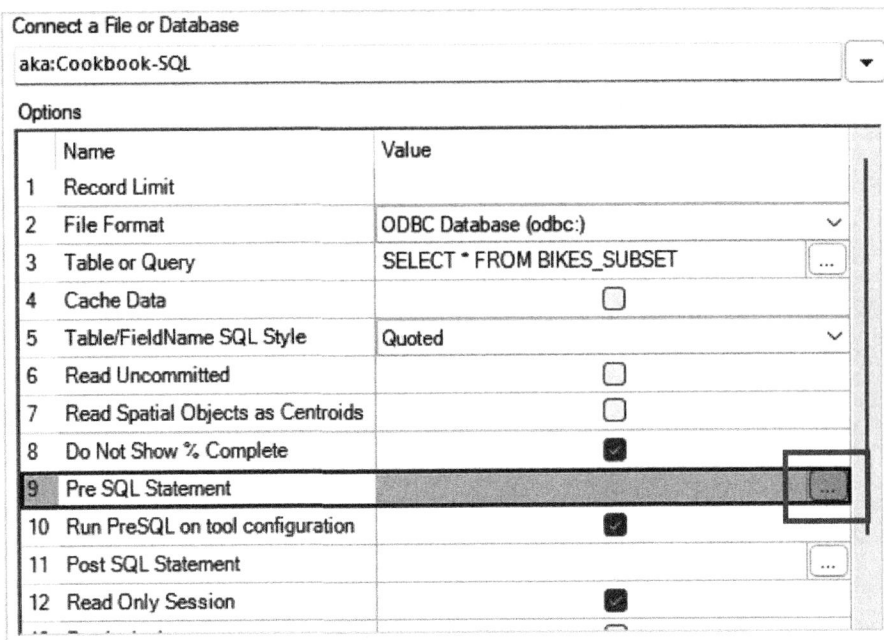

Figure 14.131: The Pre SQL Statement option

The **Configure Pre SQL Statements and Stored Procedures** window will show.

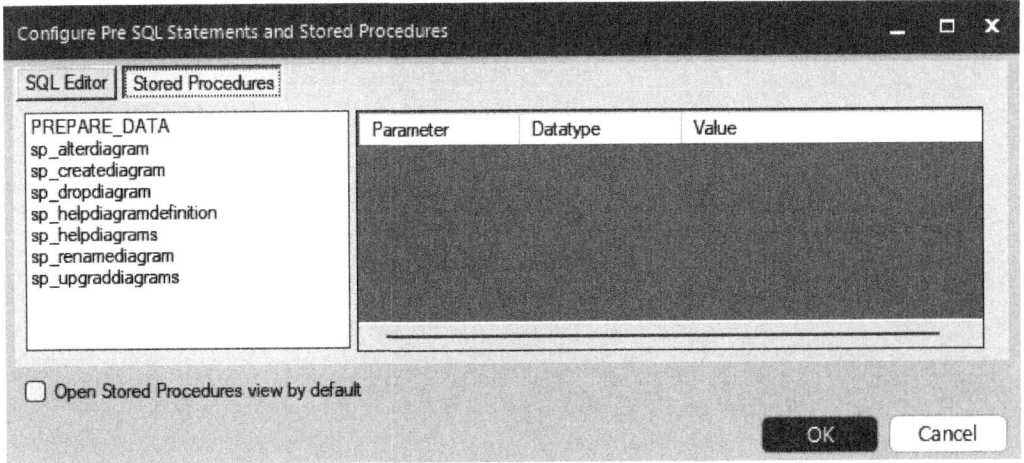

Figure 14.132: The Stored Procedures tab

10. Click on the PREPARE_DATE stored procedure, and in the right panel, Alteryx Designer will show you the parameters that this procedure uses.

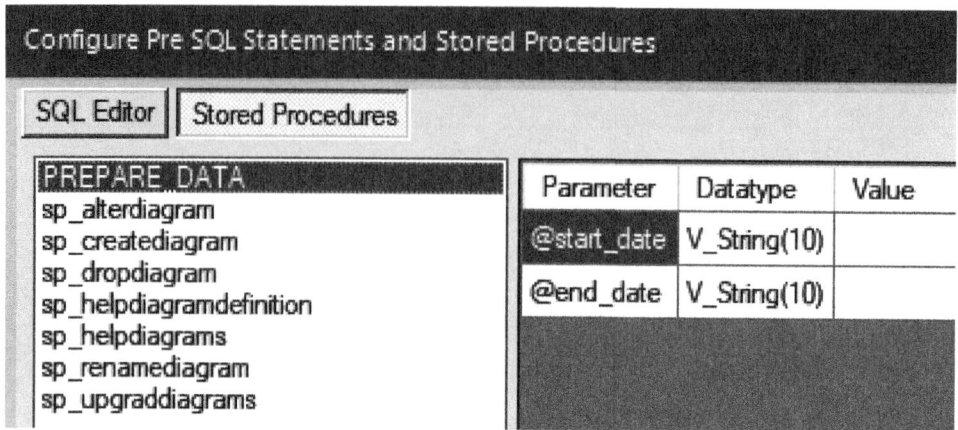

Figure 14.133: Selected Stored Procedure parameters

In our case, we have @start_date and @end_date.

11. Fill the **Value** field for @start_date with '2013-12-17' and for @end_date with
'2013-12-18' so your configuration looks like the following figure:

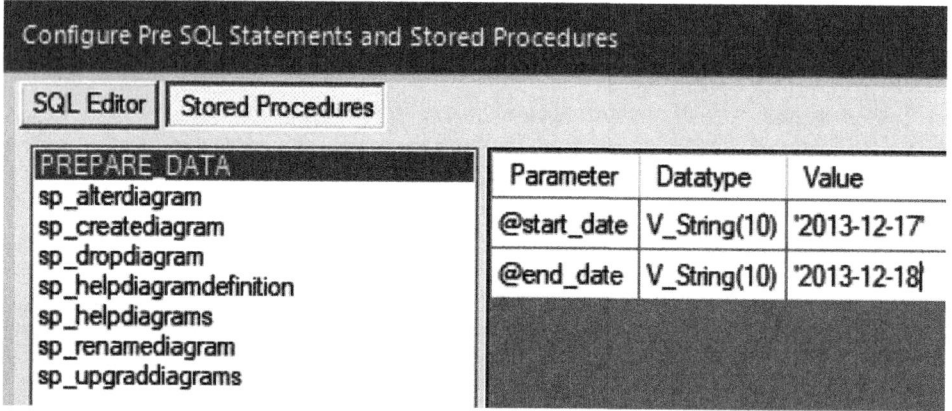

Figure 14.134: Parameters filled for the stored procedure

12. Click on **OK** and, in the **Input Data** tool configuration panel, you'll see that Alteryx Designer
completed the information with a SQL statement, as also shown in the following figure:

```
EXEC PREPARE_DATA ''2013-12-17,'2013-12-18'
```

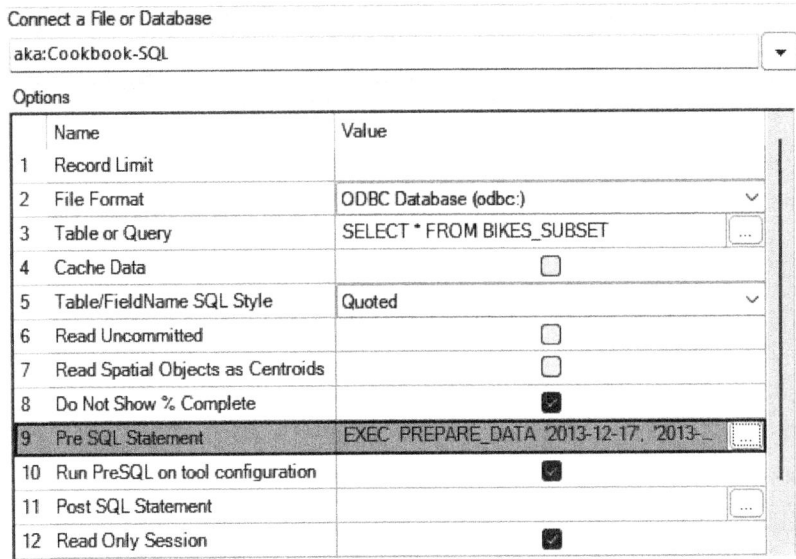

Figure 14.135: Pre SQL Statement configured in the Input Data tool

Since BIKES_SUBSET is a temporary table containing only the data of the days we used as parameters, we need to delete it after Alteryx Designer reads all the records.

13. To tell Alteryx Designer to delete the contents of the temporary table (or even drop the table completely), click on the ellipsis in **Post SQL Statement** (option 11).

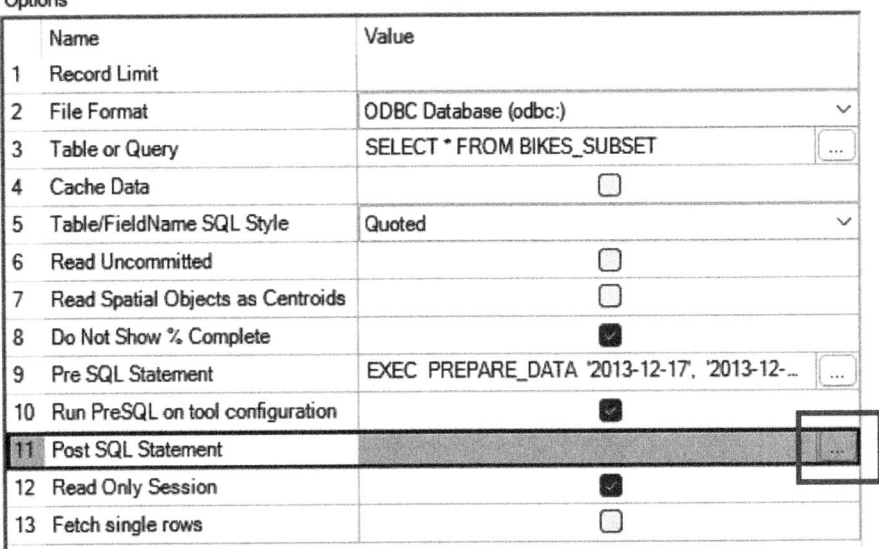

Figure 14.136: The Post SQL Statement option

14. Click on **SQL Editor** and use the following code inside:

```
DROP TABLE BIKES_SUBSET
```

You can also use the TRUNCATE command (this command will delete the contents of the table but will keep the table definition), but I prefer dropping the whole table since the provided stored procedure creates the temporary table when needed, so feel free to use either DROP or TRUNCATE for **Post SQL Statement**. In fact, use both to see how they behave.

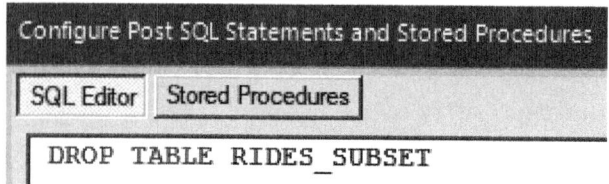

Figure 14.137: Post SQL Statement configured

At this point, you've completed the configuration needed to perform what we're looking for.

15. Drop a **Browse** tool following the **Input Data** tool and run the workflow.

Results - Workflow - Messages

≔	**All**	① 0 Errors	① 0 Conv Errors	⚠ 0 Warnings	☐ 5 Messages	☐ 1 Files
⑦	☐ **Designer x64**	**Started running C:\Exercises\ch14\Recipe3\WORKFLOW\Pre-and-Post-SQL.yxmd**
	☐ Input Data (10)	Alias translated to odbc:DRIVER={ODBC Driver 17 for SQL Server};UID=sa;PWD=__EncPwd
	☐ Input Data (10)	ODBC Driver version: 03.80
	☐ Input Data (10)	Executing PreSQL: "EXEC PREPARE_DATA '2013-12-17', '2013-12-18';"
	☐ Input Data (10)	Executing PostSQL: "TRUNCATE TABLE RIDES_SUBSET;"
	☐ Input Data (10)	579 records were read from aka:Cookbook-SQL (SELECT * FROM RIDES_SUBSET)
	☐ Browse (11)	579 records
	☐ **Designer x64**	**Finished running Pre-and-Post-SQL.yxmd in 0.5 seconds**

Figure 14.138: Execution log of the workflow

16. Inspect the **Results** pane, and you'll notice that the data returned corresponds to the range you selected.

Record	TRIP_ID	BIKEID	TRIPDURATION	STARTTIME	STOPTIME	START_STATION_ID	START_STATION_NAME
9 of 9 Fields	1	21134	1008	2013-12-17 21:51:48	2013-12-17 22:08:36	503	E 20 St & Park Ave
2	2	18657	472	2013-12-17 21:52:27	2013-12-17 22:00:19	435	W 21 St & 6 Ave
3	3	15375	245	2013-12-17 21:52:37	2013-12-17 21:56:42	401	Allen St & Rivington St

Figure 14.139: Workflow results

Also, you can check the following within **Management Studio**:

- If you used the DROP Post SQL statement, the table no longer exists
- If you used the TRUNCATE Post SQL statement, the table exists, but it is empty

Index

Packtpub.com

Subscribe to our online digital library for full access to over 7,000 books and videos, as well as industry leading tools to help you plan your personal development and advance your career. For more information, please visit our website.

Why subscribe?

- Spend less time learning and more time coding with practical eBooks and Videos from over 4,000 industry professionals

- Improve your learning with Skill Plans built especially for you

- Get a free eBook or video every month

- Fully searchable for easy access to vital information

- Copy and paste, print, and bookmark content

Did you know that Packt offers eBook versions of every book published, with PDF and ePub files available? You can upgrade to the eBook version at packtpub.com and as a print book customer, you are entitled to a discount on the eBook copy. Get in touch with us at customercare@packtpub.com for more details.

At www.packtpub.com, you can also read a collection of free technical articles, sign up for a range of free newsletters, and receive exclusive discounts and offers on Packt books and eBooks.

Other Books You May Enjoy

If you enjoyed this book, you may be interested in these other books by Packt:

Data Engineering with Alteryx

Paul Houghton

ISBN: 9781803236483

- Build a working pipeline to integrate an external data source
- Develop monitoring processes for the pipeline example
- Understand and apply DataOps principles to an Alteryx data pipeline
- Gain skills for data engineering with the Alteryx software stack
- Work with spatial analytics and machine learning techniques in an Alteryx workflow Explore Alteryx workflow deployment strategies using metadata validation and continuous integration
- Organize content on Alteryx Server and secure user access
-

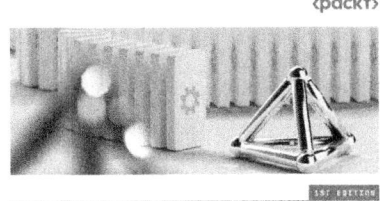

Business Intelligence Career Master Plan

Eduardo Chavez, Danny Moncada

ISBN: 9781801077958

- Understand BI roles, roadmap, and technology stack
- Accelerate your career and land your first job in the BI industry
- Build the taxonomy of various data sources for your organization
- Use the AdventureWorks database and PowerBI to build a robust data model
- Create compelling data stories using data visualization
- Automate, templatize, standardize, and monitor systems for productivity

Packt is searching for authors like you

If you're interested in becoming an author for Packt, please visit `authors.packtpub.com` and apply today. We have worked with thousands of developers and tech professionals, just like you, to help them share their insight with the global tech community. You can make a general application, apply for a specific hot topic that we are recruiting an author for, or submit your own idea.

Share Your Thoughts

Now you've finished *Alteryx Designer Cookbook*, we'd love to hear your thoughts! Scan the QR code below to go straight to the Amazon review page for this book and share your feedback or leave a review on the site that you purchased it from.

`https://packt.link/r/1-804-61508-0`

Your review is important to us and the tech community and will help us make sure we're delivering excellent quality content.

Download a free PDF copy of this book

Thanks for purchasing this book!

Do you like to read on the go but are unable to carry your print books everywhere?

Is your eBook purchase not compatible with the device of your choice?

Don't worry, now with every Packt book you get a DRM-free PDF version of that book at no cost.

Read anywhere, any place, on any device. Search, copy, and paste code from your favorite technical books directly into your application.

The perks don't stop there, you can get exclusive access to discounts, newsletters, and great free content in your inbox daily

Follow these simple steps to get the benefits:

1. Scan the QR code or visit the link below

https://packt.link/free-ebook/9781804615089

2. Submit your proof of purchase

3. That's it! We'll send your free PDF and other benefits to your email directly

Printed in Great Britain
by Amazon

43285011R00410